Methods for Applied Macroeconomic Research

Methods for Applied Macroeconomic Research

Fabio Canova

Princeton University Press
Princeton and Oxford

Published by Princeton University Press,
41 William Street, Princeton, New Jersey 08540

In the United Kingdom: Princeton University Press,
3 Market Place, Woodstock, Oxfordshire OX20 1SY

Library of Congress Cataloguing-in-Publication Data

ISBN-13: 978-0-691-11504-7 (alk. paper)
ISBN-10: 0-691-11504-4 (alk. paper)

Library of Congress Control Number: 2006935302

British Library Cataloguing-in-Publication Data

A catalogue record for this book is available from the British Library

This book has been composed in Times and typeset by T&T Productions Ltd, London
Printed on acid-free paper ∞
press.princeton.edu

Printed in the United States of America

10 9 8 7 6

To Luca and Jane,
who are gone.

To Evi and Amaranta,
who are here to stay.

Chevaliers felons et merchants, qui tramez complots malfaisants...

Claude Debussy: *Monsieur Croche*

Sabio é o que se contenta com o espectáculo do mundo.

José Saramago: *O ano da morte de Ricardo Reis*

Sentí il suo corpo piegarsi, salire e scendere sempre piú rapidamente... finché a un certo momento ebbe l'impressione di staccarsi da terra e di volare.

Renzo Biasion: *Σαγαπο*

El desembre ha congelat
m'ha glaçat la fava
al matí quan m'he llevat
no me la trobava.

Manuel Vasquez-Montalban: *Erec y Enide*

At the heart they were kind people but they had drunk so many toasts to science, enlightenment and progress that they had become inveterate drunkards.

Nikolai Gogol: *Dead Souls*

Contents

Preface **xi**

1 Preliminaries **1**
- 1.1 Stochastic Processes 2
- 1.2 Convergence Concepts 3
- 1.3 Time Series Concepts 8
- 1.4 Laws of Large Numbers 14
- 1.5 Central Limit Theorems 16
- 1.6 Elements of Spectral Analysis 18

2 DSGE Models, Solutions, and Approximations **26**
- 2.1 A Few Useful Models 27
- 2.2 Approximation Methods 45

3 Extracting and Measuring Cyclical Information **70**
- 3.1 Statistical Decompositions 72
- 3.2 Hybrid Decompositions 83
- 3.3 Economic Decompositions 100
- 3.4 Time Aggregation and Cycles 104
- 3.5 Collecting Cyclical Information 105

4 VAR Models **111**
- 4.1 The Wold Theorem 112
- 4.2 Specification 118
- 4.3 Moments and Parameter Estimation of a VAR(q) 126
- 4.4 Reporting VAR Results 130
- 4.5 Identification 141
- 4.6 Problems 151
- 4.7 Validating DSGE Models with VARs 159

5 GMM and Simulation Estimators **165**
- 5.1 Generalized Method of Moments and Other Standard Estimators 166
- 5.2 IV Estimation in a Linear Model 169
- 5.3 GMM Estimation: An Overview 176
- 5.4 GMM Estimation of DSGE Models 191
- 5.5 Simulation Estimators 197

6 Likelihood Methods **212**
6.1 The Kalman Filter 214
6.2 The Prediction Error Decomposition of Likelihood 221
6.3 Numerical Tips 228
6.4 ML Estimation of DSGE Models 230
6.5 Two Examples 240

7 Calibration **248**
7.1 A Definition 249
7.2 The Uncontroversial Parts 250
7.3 Choosing Parameters and Stochastic Processes 252
7.4 Model Evaluation 259
7.5 The Sensitivity of the Measurement 279
7.6 Savings, Investments, and Tax Cuts: An Example 282

8 Dynamic Macro Panels **288**
8.1 From Economic Theory to Dynamic Panels 289
8.2 Panels with Homogeneous Dynamics 291
8.3 Dynamic Heterogeneity 304
8.4 To Pool or Not to Pool? 315
8.5 Is Money Superneutral? 321

9 Introduction to Bayesian Methods **325**
9.1 Preliminaries 326
9.2 Decision Theory 335
9.3 Inference 336
9.4 Hierarchical and Empirical Bayes Models 345
9.5 Posterior Simulators 353
9.6 Robustness 370
9.7 Estimating Returns to Scale in Spain 370

10 Bayesian VARs **373**
10.1 The Likelihood Function of an m-Variable VAR(q) 374
10.2 Priors for VARs 376
10.3 Structural BVARs 390
10.4 Time-Varying-Coefficient BVARs 397
10.5 Panel VAR Models 404

11 Bayesian Time Series and DSGE Models **418**
11.1 Factor Models 419
11.2 Stochastic Volatility Models 427
11.3 Markov Switching Models 433
11.4 Bayesian DSGE Models 440

Appendix A Statistical Distributions **463**

References **469**

Index **487**

Preface

There has been a tremendous improvement over the last twenty years in the mathematical, statistical, probabilistic, and computational tools available to applied macroeconomists. This extended set of tools has changed the way researchers have approached the problem of estimating parameters, validating theories, or simply identifying regularities in the data. The rational expectation and the calibration revolutions have also forced researchers to try to build a more solid bridge between theoretical and applied work, a bridge that was often missing in much of the applied exercises conducted in the 1970s and the 1980s.

This book attempts to bring together dynamic general equilibrium theory, data analysis, and advanced econometric and computational methods to provide a comprehensive set of techniques that can be used to address questions of interest to academics, business and central bank economists in the fields of macroeconomics, business cycle analysis, growth, monetary, financial, and international economics. The point of view taken is one of an applied economist facing time series data (at times a panel of them, coming from different countries), who is interested in verifying the prediction of dynamic theories, in advising model builders and theorists on how to respecify existing constructions to obtain a better match between the model and the data and in drawing policy conclusions from the exercises. The book illustrates a number of techniques which can be used to address the questions of interest, agnostically evaluates their usefulness in bringing out information relevant to the users, provides examples where the methods work and others where they do not, and points out problems when approaches developed for microeconomic data are used in time series frameworks.

Unavoidably, a modern treatment of such a complex topic requires a quantitative perspective, a solid dynamic theory background, and the development of both empirical and numerical methods. A quantitative perspective is needed to give empirical content to theories; empirical methods must provide an effective link between economic theory and the data; numerical techniques help us to solve complicated dynamic stochastic general equilibrium (DSGE) models and to implement advanced econometric estimators, both in the classical and Bayesian tradition. In some cases empirical methods are intimately linked with the numerical procedure chosen to solve the model. In others, they are only constrained by the restrictions economic theory imposes on the data.

Given this background, the structure of this book is quite different from the typical graduate textbooks in both macroeconomics and in econometrics. Rather than listing a series of estimators and their properties for different data-generating processes, this book starts from a class of DSGE models, finds an approximate representation for the decision rules, and describes methods to estimate/choose their parameters, to examine their fit to the data and to conduct interesting policy exercises. The first three chapters of the book are introductory and review the material used extensively in later chapters. In particular, chapter 1 presents basic time series and probability concepts and a list of useful laws of large numbers and central limit theorems, which are employed in chapters 4–8. It also gives a brief overview of the basic elements of spectral analysis, which is used heavily in chapters 3, 5, and 7. Chapter 2 presents a number of macroeconomic models currently used in the profession and discusses the numerical methods needed to solve them. Most of the examples and exercises of this book are based on simplified or extended versions of these models. Chapter 3 discusses procedures for obtaining interesting information about secular and cyclical fluctuations in the data.

In the remaining chapters we present various methodologies to confront models to the data and discuss how they can be used to address interesting economic questions. Given our empirical perspective, formal results are often stated without proofs and emphasis is given to their use in particular macroeconomic applications. Chapter 4 describes minimalist vector autoregressive (VAR) approaches, where only a limited amount of economic theory is used to structure the data. Chapter 5 presents limited information methodologies such as generalized methods of moments (GMM), simulated method of moments (SMM), and general simulation approaches. Chapter 6 examines full-information maximum likelihood, and in chapter 7 calibration techniques are discussed. In chapter 8, we then branch into dynamic macro panel methods, which can be used to effectively study cross-country issues, and conclude the book with an extensive description of Bayesian methods and their use for VAR and panel VAR models, for advanced time series specifications, and for DSGE models (chapters 9–11).

The approach of this book differs, for example, from that of Hamilton (1994) or Hayashi (2002), both of which are primarily directed to econometricians and are not directly concerned with the question of validating DSGE models. The emphasis also differs from more macroeconomically oriented books like Sargent and Liungqvist (2004) or computationally oriented books like Judd (1998) or Miranda and Fackler (2002) in that empirical methods play a larger role and the connection between theory, numerical, and empirical tools is explicitly spelled out.

The book is largely self-contained but presumes a basic knowledge of modern macroeconomic theory (say, one or two quarters of a PhD course in macroeconomics), of standard econometrics (say, a quarter of a PhD course in econometrics) and assumes that the reader has or will acquire in the process some programming skills (e.g., RATS, Matlab, Gauss). The book is designed for a year-long sequence starting from the second semester of a first-year econometric or applied macroeconomics course and continuing with the first semester of a second-year macroeconometric course. Roughly, the first five chapters and the seventh could be used in the first part, chapter 6 and the last four chapters in the second part. This is the setup I have used in teaching this material over a number of years and it seems the natural division between what I consider basic and advanced material.

PhD students at Brown University, the University of Rochester, Universitat Pompeu Fabra, Università di Napoli, Universidade do Porto, the University of Southampton, the London Business School, Bocconi University, and Università Milano-Bicocca; participants in various editions of the Barcelona Summer School in Macroeconomics (BSSM), of the European Economic Association (EEA) Summer school in Macroeconomics, of the Center for Financial Studies (CFS) Summer school in Macroeconomics, of the ZEI Summer School, of the course for Central Bankers in Genzersee (Switzerland); and attendants of various intensive and short courses at the European Central Bank, the Bank of England, the Bank of Italy, the Bank of Canada, the Bank of Hungary, the Riksbank, the Bundesbank, the Bank of Argentina, the Swiss National Bank, the European Commission, and the European Business Cycle Network (EABCN) have passed through several versions of this book and played around with some of the codes which implement the procedures discussed in the book with some practical examples. Some suffered; some enthusiastically embraced the philosophy of this book; some were critical; some made useful comments and helped in debugging the codes; all were encouraging. My thanks go to them all. I have learned a lot through the process of writing this book and teaching its material, probably as much as students have learned from the lectures and practical sessions.

Three people taught me to approach empirical problems in a sensible but rigorous way, combining economic theory with advanced statistical tools and numerical methods, and to be suspicious and critical of analyses which leave out one of the main ingredients of the cake. Christopher Sims and Tom Sargent were of crucial importance in making me understand that the gray area at the crossroads between theory and econometrics is a difficult but exciting place to be and their uncompromising intellectual curiosity, their stern intuition, and their deep understanding of economic and policy issues have been an extraordinary lever behind this book. Adrian Pagan shaped my (somewhat cynical) view of what should and can be done with the data and the models. I always like to argue with him because his unconventional views help bring out often forgotten methodological and practical aspects. And on most issues of interest to applied macroeconomists he was more often right than wrong. This book would not have been possible without their fundamental inputs. As mentors, there was no one comparable to them. I also have an intellectual debit with Ed Prescott. It was his brusk refusal to follow the traditional econometric track that made me understand the need to create a different and more solid link between theory, econometric and statistical techniques, and the data. Several colleagues, in particular Albert Marcet, Morten Ravn, Jordi Gali, Lucrezia Reichlin, Harald Uhlig, Carlo Favero, Marco Maffezzoli, and Luca Sala, contributed to form and develop some of the ideas presented in the book. Thanks also go to Tom Doan,

Chris Sims, Kirdan Lees, and Adrian Pagan, who spotted mistakes and imprecise terminology in earlier versions of the manuscript; and special thanks go to Marco del Negro, who patiently combed through the text and spent a considerable amount of his precious time providing useful and insightful comments.

Writing a textbook is difficult. Writing an advanced textbook, which brings together material from different fields, is even more formidable. Many times I ran out of steam, got bored, and was ready to give up and do something else. Yet, when I found a new example or an application where the ideas of this book could be used, I regained the excitement of those first days when the project was still fresh. I also thank my (restricted and extended) family for the patience with which they have endured during the long process that led to the completion of this book. Dynamic macroeconomics is in part about intertemporal substitution. Patience is probably built on the same principle.

Methods for Applied Macroeconomic Research

1

Preliminaries

This chapter is introductory and intended for readers who are unfamiliar with time series concepts, with the properties of stochastic processes, with basic asymptotic theory results, and with the principles of spectral analysis. Those who feel comfortable with these topics can skip directly to chapter 2.

Since the material is vast and complex, an effort is made to present it at the simplest possible level, emphasizing a selected number of topics and only those aspects which are useful for the central topic of this book: comparing the properties of dynamic stochastic general equilibrium (DSGE) models to the data. This means that intuition rather than mathematical rigor is stressed. More specialized books, such as those by Brockwell and Davis (1991), Davidson (1994), Priestley (1981), or White (1984), provide a comprehensive and in-depth treatment of these topics.

When trying to provide background material, there is always the risk of going too far back to the basics, of trying to reinvent the wheel. To avoid this, we assume that the reader is familiar with simple concepts of calculus such as limits, continuity, and uniform continuity of functions of real numbers, and that she is familiar with distributions functions, measures, and probability spaces.

The chapter is divided into six sections. The first defines what a stochastic process is. The second examines the limiting behavior of stochastic processes introducing four concepts of convergence and characterizing their relationships. Section 1.3 deals with time series concepts. Section 1.4 deals with laws of large numbers. These laws are useful to ensure that functions of stochastic processes converge to appropriate limits. We examine three situations: a case where the elements of a stochastic process are dependent and identically distributed; one where they are dependent and heterogeneously distributed; and one where they are martingale differences. Section 1.5 describes three central limit theorems corresponding to the three situations analyzed in section 1.4. Central limit theorems are useful for deriving the limiting distribution of functions of stochastic processes and are the basis for (classical) tests of hypotheses and for some model evaluation criteria.

Section 1.6 presents elements of spectral analysis. Spectral analysis is useful for breaking down economic time series into components (trends, cycles, etc.), for building measures of persistence in response to shocks, for computing the asymptotic covariance matrix of certain estimators, and for defining measures of distance between a model and the data. It may be challenging at first. However, once it is realized that most of the functions typically performed in everyday life employ spectral methods (frequency modulation in a stereo, frequency band reception in a cellular phone, etc.), the reader should feel more comfortable with it. Spectral analysis offers an alternative way to look at time series, translating serially dependent time observations into contemporaneously independent frequency observations. This change of coordinates allows us to analyze the primitive cycles which compose time series and to discuss their length, amplitude, and persistence.

Whenever not explicitly stated, the machinery presented in this chapter applies to both scalar and vector stochastic processes. The objects of interest in this book are defined on a probability space $(\mathbb{K}, \mathcal{F}, P)$, where $\mathbb{K}$ is the space of possible state of nature $\varkappa$, $\mathcal{F}$ is the collection of Borel sets of $\mathbb{R}^m_\infty = \mathbb{R}^m \times \mathbb{R}^m \times \cdots$, and P is a probability function for $\varkappa$ that determines the joint distribution of the vector of stochastic processes of interest. The notation $\{y_t(\varkappa)\}_{t=-\infty}^{\infty}$ indicates the sequence $\{\dots, y_0(\varkappa), y_1(\varkappa), \dots, y_t(\varkappa), \dots\}$, where, for each t, the random variable $y_t(\varkappa)$ is a measurable function[1] of the state of nature $\varkappa$, i.e., $y_t(\varkappa) : \mathbb{K} \to \mathbb{R}^m$, where $\mathbb{R}$ is the real line. We assume that at each t $\{y_\tau(\varkappa)\}_{\tau=-\infty}^{t}$ belongs to $\mathcal{F}_t$, so that any function $h(y_\tau)$ will be "adapted" to $\mathcal{F}_t$. To simplify the notation, at times we write $\{y_t(\varkappa)\}$ or y_t. A normal random variable with zero mean and variance Σ_y is denoted by $y_t \sim \mathbb{N}(0, \Sigma_y)$ and a random variable uniformly distributed over the interval $[a_1, a_2]$ is denoted by $y_t \sim \mathbb{U}[a_1, a_2]$. Finally, "i.i.d." indicates identically and independently distributed random variables and a white noise is an i.i.d. process with zero mean and constant variance.

1.1 Stochastic Processes

Definition 1.1 (stochastic process). A stochastic process $\{y_t(\varkappa)\}_{t=1}^{\infty}$ is a probability measure defined on sets of sequences of real vectors (the "paths" of the process).

The definition implies, among other things, that the set $\mathbb{X} = \{y : y_t(\varkappa) \leqslant \varrho\}$, for arbitrary $\varrho \in \mathbb{R}$ and t fixed, has well-defined probabilities. In other words, choosing different $\varrho \in \mathbb{R}$ for a given t, and performing countable unions, finite intersections, and complementing the above set of paths, we generate a set of events with proper probabilities. Note that y_t is unrestricted for all $\tau \leqslant t$: the realization need not exceed ϱ only at t. Observable time series are realizations of a stochastic process $\{y_t(\varkappa)\}$, given $\varkappa$[2]. Two simple stochastic processes are the following.

Example 1.1. (i) $\{y_t(\varkappa)\} = e_1 \cos(t \times e_2)$, where e_1 and e_2 are random variables, $e_1 > 0$ and $e_2 \sim \mathbb{U}[0, 2\pi)$, $t > 0$. Here y_t is periodic: e_1 controls the amplitude and e_2 the periodicity of y_t.

---

[1] A function of h is $\mathcal{F}$-measurable if, for every real number ϱ, the set $[\varkappa : h(\varkappa) < \varrho]$ belongs to $\mathcal{F}$.

[2] A stochastic process could also be defined as a sequence of random variables which are jointly measurable (see, for example, Davidson 1994, p. 177).

(ii) $\{y_t(\varkappa)\}$ is such that $P[y_t = \pm 1] = 0.5$ for all t. Such a process has no memory and flips between -1 and 1 as t changes.

Example 1.2. It is easy to generate complex stochastic processes from primitive ones. For example, if $e_{1t} \sim \mathbb{N}(0, 1)$, $e_{2t} \sim \mathbb{U}(0, 1]$, and e_{1t} and e_{2t} are independent of each other, $y_t = e_{2t} e^{e_{1t}/(1+e_{1t})}$ is a stochastic process. Similarly, $y_t = \sum_{t=1}^{T} e_t$, $e_t \sim$ i.i.d. (0, 1) is a stochastic process.

1.2 Convergence Concepts

In a classical framework the properties of estimators are obtained by using sequences of estimators indexed by the sample size, and by showing that these sequences approach the true (unknown) parameter value as the sample size grows to infinity. Since estimators are continuous functions of the data, we need to ensure that the data possess a proper limit and that continuous functions of the data inherit these properties. To show that the former is the case, one can rely on a variety of convergence concepts. The first two deal with convergence of the sequence, the next with its moments, and the last with its distribution.

1.2.1 Almost Sure Convergence

The concept of almost sure (a.s.) convergence extends the idea of convergence to a limit employed in the case of a sequence of real numbers.

As we have seen, the elements of the sequence $y_t(\varkappa)$ are functions of the state of nature. However, once $\varkappa = \bar{\varkappa}$ is drawn, $\{y_1(\bar{\varkappa}), \dots, y_t(\bar{\varkappa}), \dots\}$ looks like a sequence of real numbers. Hence, given $\varkappa = \bar{\varkappa}$, convergence can be similarly defined.

Definition 1.2 (a.s. convergence). $y_t(\varkappa)$ converges almost surely to $y(\varkappa) < \infty$, denoted by $\{y_t(\varkappa)\} \stackrel{\text{a.s.}}{\longrightarrow} y(\varkappa)$, if $\lim_{T\to\infty} P[\|y_t(\varkappa) - y(\varkappa)\| \leqslant \varepsilon, \forall t > T] = 1$, for $\varkappa \in \mathbb{K}_1 \subseteq \mathbb{K}$, and every $\varepsilon > 0$.

According to definition 1.2 $\{y_t(\varkappa)\}$ converges a.s. if the probability of obtaining a path for y_t which converges to $y(\varkappa)$ after some T is 1. The probability is taken over $\varkappa$. The definition implies that failure to converge is possible, but it will almost never happen. When $\mathbb{K}$ is infinite dimensional, a.s. convergence is called convergence almost everywhere; sometimes a.s. convergence is termed convergence with probability 1 or strong consistency criteria.

Next, we describe the limiting behavior of functions of a.s. convergent sequences.

Result 1.1. Let $\{y_t(\varkappa)\} \stackrel{\text{a.s.}}{\longrightarrow} y(\varkappa)$. Let h be an $n \times 1$ vector of functions, continuous at $y(\varkappa)$. Then $h(y_t(\varkappa)) \stackrel{\text{a.s.}}{\longrightarrow} h(y(\varkappa))$.

Result 1.1 is a simple extension of the standard fact that continuous functions of convergent sequences are convergent.

Example 1.3. Given $\varkappa$, let $\{y_t(\varkappa)\} = 1 - 1/t$ and $h(y_t(\varkappa)) = (1/T)\sum_t y_t(\varkappa)$. Then $h(y_t(\varkappa))$ is continuous at $\lim_{t\to\infty} y_t(\varkappa) = 1$ and $h(y_t(\varkappa)) \xrightarrow{\text{a.s.}} 1$.

Exercise 1.1. Suppose $\{y_t(\varkappa)\} = 1/t$ with probability $1 - 1/t$ and $\{y_t(\varkappa)\} = t$ with probability $1/t$. Does $\{y_t(\varkappa)\}$ converge a.s. to 1? Suppose $h(y_t) = (1/T) \times \sum_t (y_t(x) - (1/T)\sum_t y_t(x))^2$. What is its a.s. limit?

In some applications we will be interested in examining situations where a.s. convergence does not hold. This can be the case when the observations have a probability density function that changes over time or when matrices appearing in the formula for estimators do not converge to fixed limits. However, even though $h(y_{1t}(\varkappa))$ does not converge to $h(y(\varkappa))$, it may be the case that the distance between $h(y_{1t}(\varkappa))$ and $h(y_{2t}(\varkappa))$ becomes arbitrarily small as $t \to \infty$, where $\{y_{2t}(\varkappa)\}$ is another sequence of random variables. To obtain convergence in this situation we need to strengthen the conditions by requiring uniform continuity of h (for example, assuming continuity on a compact set).

Result 1.2. Let h be continuous on a compact set $\mathbb{R}_2 \in \mathbb{R}^m$. Suppose that $\{y_{1t}(\varkappa)\} - \{y_{2t}(\varkappa)\} \xrightarrow{\text{a.s.}} 0$ and there exists an $\epsilon > 0$ such that, for all $t > T$, y_{2t} is in the interior of $\mathbb{R}_2$, uniformly in t. Then $h(y_{1t}(\varkappa)) - h(y_{2t}(\varkappa)) \xrightarrow{\text{a.s.}} 0$.

One application of result 1.2 is the following: suppose $\{y_{1t}(\varkappa)\}$ is some actual time series and $\{y_{2t}(\varkappa)\}$ is its counterpart simulated from a model where the parameters of the model and $\varkappa$ are given, and let h be some continuous statistics, e.g., the mean or the variance. Then, result 1.2 tells us that if simulated and actual paths are close enough as $t \to \infty$, statistics generated from these paths will also be close.

1.2.2 Convergence in Probability

Convergence in probability is a weaker concept than a.s. convergence.

Definition 1.3 (convergence in probability). If there exists a $y(\varkappa) < \infty$ such that, for every $\epsilon > 0$, $P[\varkappa : \|y_t(\varkappa) - y(\varkappa)\| < \epsilon] \to 1$ for $t \to \infty$, then $\{y_t(\varkappa)\} \xrightarrow{\text{P}} y(\varkappa)$.

$\xrightarrow{\text{P}}$ is weaker than $\xrightarrow{\text{a.s.}}$ because in the former we only need the joint distribution of $(y_t(\varkappa), y(\varkappa))$ not the joint distribution of $(y_t(\varkappa), y_\tau(\varkappa), y(\varkappa))$, $\forall \tau > T$. $\xrightarrow{\text{P}}$ implies that it is less likely that one element of the $\{y_t(\varkappa)\}$ sequence is more than an ϵ away from $y(\varkappa)$ as $t \to \infty$. $\xrightarrow{\text{a.s.}}$ implies that after T the path of $\{y_t(\varkappa)\}$ is not far from $y(\varkappa)$ as $T \to \infty$. Hence, it is easy to build examples where $\xrightarrow{\text{P}}$ does not imply $\xrightarrow{\text{a.s.}}$.

Example 1.4. Let y_t and y_τ be independent $\forall t, \tau$, let y_t be either 0 or 1 and let

$$P[y_t = 0] = \begin{cases} \frac{1}{2}, & t = 1, 2, \\ \frac{2}{3}, & t = 3, 4, \\ \frac{3}{4}, & t = 5, \ldots, 8, \\ \frac{4}{5}, & t = 9, \ldots, 16. \end{cases}$$

Then $P[y_t = 0] = 1 - 1/(j+1)$ for $t = 2^{j-1}+1, \ldots, 2^j$, $j > 1$, so that $y_t \xrightarrow{\text{P}} 0$. This is because the probability that y_t is in one of these classes is $1/j$ and, as $t \to \infty$, the number of classes goes to infinity. However, y_t does not converge a.s. to 0 since the probability that a convergent path is drawn is 0; i.e., the probability of getting a 1 for any $t = 2^{j-1}+1, \ldots, 2^j$, $j > 1$, is small but, since the streak $2^{j-1}+1, \ldots, 2^j$ is large, the probability of getting a 1 is $1 - [1 - 1/(j+1)]^{2^{(j-1)}}$, which converges to 1 as j goes to infinity. In general, $y_t \xrightarrow{\text{P}} 0$ is too slow to ensure that $y_t \xrightarrow{\text{a.s.}} 0$.

Although convergence in probability does not imply a.s. convergence, the following result shows how the latter can be obtained from the former.

Result 1.3. If $y_t(\varkappa) \xrightarrow{\text{P}} y(\varkappa)$, there exists a subsequence $y_{t_j}(\varkappa)$ such that $y_{t_j}(\varkappa) \xrightarrow{\text{a.s.}} y(\varkappa)$ (see, for example, Lukacs 1975, p. 48).

Intuitively, since convergence in probability allows a more erratic behavior in the converging sequence than a.s. convergence, one can obtain the latter by disregarding the erratic elements. The concept of convergence in probability is useful to show "weak" consistency of certain estimators.

Example 1.5. (i) Let y_t be a sequence of i.i.d. random variables with $E(y_t) < \infty$. Then $(1/T)\sum_{t=1}^{T} y_t \xrightarrow{\text{a.s.}} E(y_t)$ (Kolmogorov strong law of large numbers).

(ii) Let y_t be a sequence of uncorrelated random variables, $E(y_t) < \infty$, $\text{var}(y_t) = \sigma_y^2 < \infty$, $\text{cov}(y_t, y_{t-\tau}) = 0, \forall \tau \neq 0$. Then $(1/T)\sum_{t=1}^{T} y_t \xrightarrow{\text{P}} E(y_t)$ (Chebyshev weak law of large numbers).

In example 1.5 strong consistency requires i.i.d. random variables, while for weak consistency we just need a set of uncorrelated random variables with identical means and variances. Note also that weak consistency requires restrictions on the second moments of the sequence which are not needed in the former case.

The analogs of results 1.1 and 1.2 for convergence in probability can be easily obtained.

Result 1.4. Let $\{y_t(\varkappa)\}$ be such that $\{y_t(\varkappa)\} \xrightarrow{\text{P}} y(\varkappa)$. Then $h(y_t(\varkappa)) \xrightarrow{\text{P}} h(y(\varkappa))$ for any continuous function h (see White 1984, p. 23).

Result 1.5. Let h be continuous on a compact $\mathbb{R}_2 \subset \mathbb{R}^m$. Let $\{y_{1t}(\varkappa)\}$ and $\{y_{2t}(\varkappa)\}$ be such that $\{y_{1t}(\varkappa)\} - \{y_{2t}(\varkappa)\} \xrightarrow{\text{P}} 0$ and, for large t, y_{2t} is in the interior of $\mathbb{R}_2$, uniformly in t. Then $h(y_{1t}(\varkappa)) - h(y_{2t}(\varkappa)) \xrightarrow{\text{P}} 0$ (see White 1984, p. 25).

Sometimes y_t may converge to a limit which does not belong to the space of the random variables which make up the sequence; e.g., the sequence $y_t = \sum_j e_j$, where each e_j is i.i.d., has a limit which is not in the space of i.i.d. variables. In other cases, the limit point may be unknown. For all these cases, we can redefine a.s. convergence and convergence in probability by using the concept of Cauchy sequences.

Definition 1.4 (convergence a.s. and in probability). $\{y_t(\varkappa)\}$ converges a.s. if and only if, for every $\epsilon > 0$, $\lim_{T\to\infty} P[\|y_t(\varkappa) - y_\tau(\varkappa)\| > \epsilon$ for some $\tau > t > T(\varkappa, \epsilon)] \to 0$ and converges in probability if and only if, for every $\epsilon > 0$, $\lim_{t,\tau\to\infty} P[\|y_t(\varkappa) - y_\tau(\varkappa)\| > \epsilon] \to 0$.

1.2.3 Convergence in L^q-Norm

While a.s. convergence and convergence in probability concern the path of y_t, L^q-convergence refers to the qth moment of y_t. L^q-convergence is typically analyzed when $q = 2$ (convergence in mean square), when $q = 1$ (absolute convergence), and when $q = \infty$ (minmax convergence).

Definition 1.5 (convergence in the norm). $\{y_t(\varkappa)\}$ converges in the L^q-norm (or in the qth mean), denoted by $y_t(\varkappa) \xrightarrow{\text{q.m.}} y(\varkappa)$, if there exists a $y(\varkappa) < \infty$ such that $\lim_{t\to\infty} E[|y_t(\varkappa) - y(\varkappa)|^q] = 0$ for some $q > 0$.

Obviously, if the qth moment does not exist, convergence in L^q does not apply (i.e., if y_t is a Cauchy random variable, L^q-convergence is meaningless for all q), while convergence in probability applies even when moments do not exist. Intuitively, the difference between the two types of convergence lies in the fact that the latter allows the distance between y_t and y to get large faster than the probability gets smaller, while this is not possible with L^q-convergence. Consequently, L^q-convergence is stronger than convergence in probability.

Exercise 1.2. Let y_t converge to 0 in L^q. Show that y_t converges to 0 in probability. (Hint: use Chebyshev's inequality.)

The following result provides conditions ensuring that convergence in probability implies L^q-convergence.

Result 1.6. If $y_t(\varkappa) \xrightarrow{\text{P}} y(\varkappa)$ and $\sup_t\{\lim_{\Delta\to\infty} E(|y_t|^q \mathcal{I}_{[|y_t|\geq\Delta]})\} = 0$, where $\mathcal{I}$ is an indicator function, then $y_t(\varkappa) \xrightarrow{\text{q.m.}} y(\varkappa)$ (Davidson 1994, p. 287).

Hence, convergence in probability plus the restriction that $|y_t|^q$ is uniformly integrable, ensures convergence in the L^q-norm. In general, there is no relationship between L^q and a.s. convergence. The following shows that the two concepts are distinct.

Example 1.6. Let $y(\varkappa) = t$ if $\varkappa \in [0, 1/t)$ and $y(\varkappa) = 0$ if $\varkappa \in (1/t, 1]$. Then the set $\{\varkappa : \lim_{t\to\infty} y_t(\varkappa) \neq 0\}$ includes only the element $\{0\}$ so $y_t \xrightarrow{\text{a.s.}} 0$. However, $E|y_t|^q = 0 \times (1 - 1/t) + t^q \times (1/t)$. Since y_t is not uniformly integrable it fails to converge in the q mean for any $q > 1$ (for $q = 1$, $E|y_t| = 1, \forall t$). Hence, the limiting expectation of y_t differs from its a.s. limit.

Exercise 1.3. Let

$$y_t = \begin{cases} 1, & \text{with probability } 1 - 1/t^2, \\ t, & \text{with probability } 1/t^2. \end{cases}$$

Show that the first and second moments of y_t are finite. Show that $y_t \xrightarrow{\text{P}} 1$ but that y_t does not converge in quadratic mean to 1.

The next result shows that convergence in the $L^{q'}$-norm obtains when we know that convergence in the L^q-norm occurs, $q > q'$. The result makes use of Jensen's inequality, which we state next. Let h be a convex function on $\mathbb{R}_1 \subset \mathbb{R}^m$ and let y be a random variable such that $P[y \in \mathbb{R}_1] = 1$. Then $h(E(y)) \leqslant E(h(y))$. If h is concave on $\mathbb{R}_1$, $h(E(y)) \geqslant E(h(y))$.

Example 1.7. For $h(y) = y^{-2}$, $Eh(y) = E(y^{-2}) \leqslant 1/E(y^2) = h(E(y))$.

Result 1.7. Let $q' < q$. If $y_t(\varkappa) \xrightarrow{\text{q.m.}} y(\varkappa)$, then $y_t(\varkappa) \xrightarrow{\text{q.'m.}} y(\varkappa)$.

Example 1.8. Let $\mathbb{K} = \{\varkappa_1, \varkappa_2\}$ and $P(\varkappa_1) = P(\varkappa_2) = 0.5$. Let $y_t(\varkappa_1) = (-1)^t$, $y_t(\varkappa_2) = (-1)^{t+1}$ and let $y(\varkappa_1) = y(\varkappa_2) = 0$. Clearly, y_t converges in the L^q-norm. To confirm this, note, for example, that $\lim_{t\to\infty} E[|y_t(\varkappa) - y(\varkappa)|^2] = 1$. Since y_t converges in mean square, it must converge in absolute mean. In fact, $\lim_{t\to\infty} E[|y_t(\varkappa) - y(\varkappa)|] = 1$.

1.2.4 Convergence in Distribution

Definition 1.6 (convergence in distribution). Let $\{y_t(\varkappa)\}$ be an $m \times 1$ vector with joint distribution $\mathcal{D}_t$. If $\mathcal{D}_t(z) \to \mathcal{D}(z)$ as $t \to \infty$, for every point of continuity z, where $\mathcal{D}$ is the distribution function of a random variable $y(\varkappa)$, then $y_t(\varkappa) \xrightarrow{\text{D}} y(\varkappa)$.

Convergence in distribution is the weakest convergence concept and does not imply, in general, anything about the convergence of a sequence of random variables. Moreover, while the previous three convergence concepts require $\{y_t(\varkappa)\}$ and the limit $y(\varkappa)$ to be defined on the same probability space, convergence in distribution is meaningful even when this is not the case.

It is useful to characterize the relationship between convergence in distribution and convergence in probability.

Result 1.8. Suppose $y_t(\varkappa) \xrightarrow{\text{P}} y(\varkappa) < \infty$, $y(\varkappa)$ constant. Then $y_t(\varkappa) \xrightarrow{\text{D}} \mathcal{D}_y$, where $\mathcal{D}_y$ is the distribution of a random variable z such that $P[z = y(\varkappa)] = 1$. Conversely, if $y_t(\varkappa) \xrightarrow{\text{D}} \mathcal{D}_y$, then $y_t \xrightarrow{\text{P}} y$ (see Rao 1973, p. 120).

Note that the first part of result 1.8 could have been obtained directly from result 1.4, had we assumed that $\mathcal{D}_y$ is a continuous function of y.

The next two results are handy when demonstrating the limiting properties of a class of estimators in dynamic models. Note that $y_{1t}(\varkappa)$ is $O_p(t^j)$ if there exists an $O(1)$ nonstochastic sequence y_{2t} such that $(1/t^j)y_{1t}(\varkappa) - y_{2t} \xrightarrow{\text{P}} 0$ and that y_{2t} is $O(1)$ if for some $0 < \Delta < \infty$, there exists a T such that $|y_{2t}| < \Delta$ for all $t \geqslant T$.

Result 1.9. If $y_{1t} \xrightarrow{\text{P}} \varrho$, $y_{2t} \xrightarrow{\text{D}} y$, then $y_{1t}y_{2t} \xrightarrow{\text{D}} \varrho y$, $y_{1t} + y_{2t} \xrightarrow{\text{D}} \varrho + y$, where ϱ is a constant (Davidson 1994, p. 355). If y_{1t} and y_{2t} are sequences of random vectors, $y_{1t} - y_{2t} \xrightarrow{\text{P}} 0$ and $y_{2t} \xrightarrow{\text{D}} y$ imply that $y_{1t} \xrightarrow{\text{D}} y$ (Rao 1973, p. 123).

Result 1.9 is useful when the distribution of y_{1t} cannot be determined directly. In fact, if we can find a y_{2t} with known asymptotic distribution which converges in probability to y_{1t}, then the distribution of y_{1t} can automatically be obtained. We will use this result in chapter 5 when discussing two-step estimators.

The limiting behavior of continuous functions of sequences which converge in distribution is easy to characterize. In fact, we have the following result.

Result 1.10. Let $y_t \xrightarrow{\text{D}} y$. If h is continuous, $h(y_t) \xrightarrow{\text{D}} h(y)$ (Davidson 1994, p. 355).

1.3 Time Series Concepts

Most of the analysis conducted in this book assumes that observable time series are stationary and have memory which dies out sufficiently fast over time. In some cases we will use alternative and weaker hypotheses which allow for selected forms of nonstationarity and/or for more general memory requirements. This section provides definitions of these concepts and compare various alternatives.

We need two preliminary definitions.

Definition 1.7 (lag operator). The lag operator is defined by $\ell y_t = y_{t-1}$ and $\ell^{-1} y_t = y_{t+1}$. The matrix lag operator $A(\ell)$ is defined by $A(\ell) = A_0 + A_1\ell + A_2\ell^2 + \cdots$, where A_j, $j = 1, 2, \ldots$, are $m \times m$ matrices.

Definition 1.8 (autocovariance function). The autocovariance function of $\{y_t(\varkappa)\}$ is $\text{ACF}_t(\tau) \equiv E[y_t(\varkappa) - E(y_t(\varkappa))][y_{t-\tau}(\varkappa) - E(y_{t-\tau}(\varkappa))]'$ and its autocorrelation function is

$$\text{ACRF}_t(\tau) \equiv \text{corr}(y_t, y_{t-\tau}) = \frac{\text{ACF}_t(\tau)}{\sqrt{\text{var}(y_t(\varkappa))\,\text{var}(y_{t-\tau}(\varkappa))}}. \tag{1.1}$$

In general, both the autocovariance and the autocorrelation functions depend on time and on the gap between y_t and $y_{t-\tau}$.

Definition 1.9 (stationarity 1). $\{y_t(\varkappa)\}_{t=-\infty}^{\infty}$ is stationary if, for any set of paths $\mathbb{X} = \{y_t(\varkappa) : y_t(\varkappa) \leqslant \varrho,\ \varrho \in \mathbb{R},\ \varkappa \in \mathbb{K}\}$, $P(\mathbb{X}) = P(\ell^\tau \mathbb{X})$, $\forall\tau$, where $\ell^\tau \mathbb{X} = \{y_{t-\tau}(\varkappa) : y_{t-\tau}(\varkappa) \leqslant \varrho\}$.

A process is stationary if shifting a path over time does not change the probability distribution of that path. In this case, the joint distribution of $\{y_{t_1}, \ldots, y_{t_j}\}$ is the same as the joint distribution of $\{y_{t_1+\tau}, \ldots, y_{t_j+\tau}\}$, $\forall\tau$. A weaker concept is the following.

Definition 1.10 (stationarity 2). $\{y_t(\varkappa)\}_{t=-\infty}^{\infty}$ is covariance (weakly) stationary if $E(y_t)$ is constant; $E|y_t|^2 < \infty$; $\text{ACF}_t(\tau)$ is independent of t.

Definition 1.10 is weaker than 1.9 since it concerns the first two moments of y_t rather than its joint distribution. Clearly, a stationary process is weakly stationary, while the converse is true only when the y_t are normal random variables. In fact, when y_t is normal, the first two moments characterize the entire distribution and the joint distribution of a $\{y_t\}_{t=1}^{\infty}$ path is normal.

Example 1.9. Let $y_t = e_1 \cos(\omega t) + e_2 \sin(\omega t)$, where e_1, e_2 are uncorrelated with mean zero, unit variance, and $\omega \in [0, 2\pi]$. Clearly, the mean of y_t is constant and $E|y_t|^2 < \infty$. Also, $\text{cov}(y_t, y_{t+\tau}) = \cos(\omega t)\cos(\omega(t+\tau)) + \sin(\omega t) \times \sin(\omega(t+\tau)) = \cos(\omega\tau)$. Hence, y_t is covariance stationary.

Exercise 1.4. Suppose $y_t = e_t$ if t is odd and $y_t = e_t + 1$ if t is even, where $e_t \sim$ i.i.d. $(0, 1)$. Show that y_t is not covariance stationary. Show that $y_t = \bar{y} + y_{t-1} + e_t$, where $e_t \sim$ i.i.d. $(0, \sigma_e^2)$ and $\bar{y}$ is a constant, is not a stationary process, but that $\Delta y_t = y_t - y_{t-1}$ is stationary.

When $\{y_t\}$ is stationary, its autocovariance function has the following three properties: (i) $\text{ACF}(0) \geqslant 0$, (ii) $|\text{ACF}(\tau)| \leqslant \text{ACF}(0)$, (iii) $\text{ACF}(-\tau) = \text{ACF}(\tau)$ for all τ. Furthermore, if y_{1t} and y_{2t} are two stationary uncorrelated processes, $y_{1t} + y_{2t}$ is stationary and the autocovariance function of $y_{1t} + y_{2t}$ is $\text{ACF}_{y_1}(\tau) + \text{ACF}_{y_2}(\tau)$.

Example 1.10. Consider the process $y_t = \bar{y} + at + De_t$, where $|D| < 1$ and $e_t \sim$ i.i.d. $(0, \sigma^2)$. Clearly, y_t is not covariance stationary since $E(y_t) = \bar{y} + at$, which depends on time. Taking first difference we have $\Delta y_t = a + D\Delta e_t$. Here $E(\Delta y_t) = a$, $E(\Delta y_t - a)^2 = 2D^2\sigma^2 > 0$, $E(\Delta y_t - a)(\Delta y_{t-1} - a) = -D^2\sigma^2 < E(\Delta y_t - a)^2$, and $E(\Delta y_t - a)(\Delta y_{t+1} - a) = -D^2\sigma^2$.

Exercise 1.5. Suppose $y_{1t} = \bar{y} + at + e_t$, where $e_t \sim$ i.i.d. $(0, \sigma_e^2)$ and $\bar{y}, a$ are constants. Define $y_{2t} = (1/(2J+1)) \sum_{j=-J}^{J} y_{1t+j}$. Compute the mean and the autocovariance function of y_{2t}. Is y_{2t} stationary? Is it covariance stationary?

Definition 1.11 (autocovariance generating function). The autocovariance generating function of a stationary $\{y_t(\varkappa)\}_{t=-\infty}^{\infty}$ is $\text{CGF}(z) = \sum_{\tau=-\infty}^{\infty} \text{ACF}(\tau) z^{\tau}$, provided that the sum converges for all z satisfying $\varrho^{-1} < |z| < \varrho$, $\varrho > 1$.

Example 1.11. Consider the process $y_t = e_t - De_{t-1} = (1 - D\ell)e_t$, $|D| < 1$, $e_t \sim$ i.i.d. $(0, \sigma_e^2)$. Here, $\text{cov}(y_t, y_{t-j}) = \text{cov}(y_t, y_{t+j}) = 0$, $\forall j \geqslant 2$, $\text{cov}(y_t, y_t) = (1 + D^2)\sigma_e^2$, $\text{cov}(y_t, y_{t-1}) = -D\sigma_e^2$, $\text{cov}(y_t, y_{t+1}) = -D^{-1}\sigma_e^2$. Hence,

$$\begin{aligned}\text{CGF}_y(z) &= -D\sigma_e^2 z^{-1} + (1 + D^2)\sigma_e^2 z^0 - D\sigma_e^2 z^1 \\ &= \sigma_e^2(-Dz^{-1} + (1 + D^2) - Dz) = \sigma_e^2(1 - Dz)(1 - Dz^{-1}). \qquad (1.2)\end{aligned}$$

Example 1.11 can be generalized to more complex processes. In fact, if $y_t = D(\ell)e_t$, $\text{CGF}_y(z) = D(z)\Sigma_e D(z^{-1})'$, and this holds for both univariate and multivariate y_t. One interesting special case occurs when $z = \mathrm{e}^{-\mathrm{i}\omega} = \cos(\omega) - \mathrm{i}\sin(\omega)$, $\omega \in (0, 2\pi)$, $\mathrm{i} = \sqrt{-1}$, in which case

$$\mathcal{S}(\omega) \equiv \frac{\text{CGF}_y(\mathrm{e}^{-\mathrm{i}\omega})}{2\pi} = \frac{1}{2\pi} \sum_{\tau=-\infty}^{\infty} \text{ACF}(\tau)\mathrm{e}^{-\mathrm{i}\omega\tau} \qquad (1.3)$$

is the spectral density of y_t.

Exercise 1.6. Consider $y_t = (1 + 0.5\ell + 0.8\ell^2)e_t$, and $(1 - 0.25\ell)y_t = e_t$, where $e_t \sim$ i.i.d. $(0, \sigma_e^2)$. Are these processes covariance stationary? If so, show the autocovariance and the autocovariance generating functions.

Exercise 1.7. Let $\{y_{1t}(\varkappa)\}$ be a stationary process and let h be an $n \times 1$ vector of continuous functions. Show that $y_{2t} = h(y_{1t})$ is also stationary.

Stationarity is a weaker requirement than i.i.d., where no dependence between elements of a sequence is allowed, but it is stronger that the identically (not necessarily independently) distributed assumption.

Example 1.12. Let $y_t \sim$ i.i.d. $(0, 1)$, $\forall t$. Since $y_{t-\tau} \sim$ i.i.d. $(0, 1)$, $\forall \tau$, any finite subsequence $y_{t_1+\tau}, \ldots, y_{t_j+\tau}$ will have the same distribution and therefore y_t is stationary. It is easy to see that a stationary series is not necessarily i.i.d. For instance, let $y_t = e_t - De_{t-1}$. If $|D| < 1$, y_t is stationary but not i.i.d.

Exercise 1.8. Give an example of a process which is identically (but not necessarily independently) distributed but nonstationary.

In this book, processes which are stationary will sometimes be indicated with the notation $I(0)$, while processes which are stationary after d differences will be denoted by $I(d)$.

A property of stationary sequences which ensures that the sample average converges to the population average is ergodicity (see section 1.4). Ergodicity is typically defined in terms of invariant events.

Definition 1.12 (ergodicity 1). Suppose $y_t(\varkappa) = y_1(\ell^{t-1}\varkappa)$, $\forall t$. Then $\{y_t(\varkappa)\}$ is ergodic if and only if, for any set of paths $\mathbb{X} = \{y_t(\varkappa) : y_t(\varkappa) \leqslant \varrho,\ \varrho \in \mathbb{R}\}$, with $P(\ell^\tau \mathbb{X}) = P(\mathbb{X})$, $\forall \tau$, $P(\mathbb{X}) = 0$, or $P(\mathbb{X}) = 1$.

Note that the ergodicity definition applies only to stationary sequences and that not all stationary sequences are ergodic. In fact, only those for which the set of paths $\mathbb{X}$ is itself invariant to shifts qualify for the definition. Intuitively, if a process is stationary, its path converges to some limit. If it is stationary and ergodic, all paths (indexed by $\varkappa$) will converge to the same limit. Hence, one path is sufficient to infer the moments of its distribution.

Example 1.13. Consider a path on a unit circle. Let $\mathbb{X} = (y_0, \ldots, y_t)$, where each element of the sequence satisfies $y_j(\varkappa) = y_{j-1}(\ell\varkappa)$. Let $P(\mathbb{X})$ be the length of the interval $[y_0, y_t]$. Let $\ell^\tau \mathbb{X} = \{y_{0-\tau}, \ldots, y_{t-\tau}\}$ displace $\mathbb{X}$ by half a circle. Since $P(\ell^\tau \mathbb{X}) = P(\mathbb{X})$, y_t is stationary. However, $P(\ell^\tau \mathbb{X}) \neq 1$ or 0 so y_t is not ergodic.

Example 1.14. Consider the process $y_t = e_t - 2e_{t-1}$, where $e_t \sim$ i.i.d. $(0, \sigma_e^2)$. It is easy to verify that $E(y_t) = 0$, $\text{var}(y_t) = 5\sigma_e^2 < \infty$ and $\text{cov}(y_t, y_{t-\tau})$ does not depend on t. Therefore, the process is covariance stationary. To verify that it is ergodic, consider the sample mean $(1/T)\sum_t y_t$, which is easily shown to converge to 0 as $T \to \infty$. The sample variance is $(1/T)\sum_t y_t^2 = (1/T)\sum_t (e_t - 2e_{t-1})^2 = (5/T)\sum_t e_t^2$, which converges to $\text{var}(y_t)$ as $T \to \infty$.

Example 1.15. Let $y_t = e_1 + e_{2t}$, where $e_{2t} \sim$ i.i.d. $(0, 1)$ and $e_1 \sim$ i.i.d. $(1, 1)$. Clearly, y_t is stationary and $E(y_t) = 1$. However, $(1/T)\sum_t y_t = e_1 + (1/T) \times \sum_t e_{2t}$ and $\lim_{T\to\infty}(1/T)\sum_t y_t = e_1 + \lim_{T\to\infty}(1/T)\sum_t e_{2t} = e_1$, because $(1/T)\sum_t e_{2t} \xrightarrow{\text{a.s.}} 0$. Since the time average of y_t (equal to e_1) is different from the population average of y_t (equal to 1), y_t is not ergodic.

What is wrong with example 1.15? Intuitively, y_t is not ergodic because it has "too much" memory (e_1 appears in y_t for every t). In fact, for ergodicity to hold, the process must "forget" its past reasonably fast. The laws of large numbers of section 1.4 give conditions ensuring that the memory of the process is not too strong.

Exercise 1.9. Suppose $y_t = 0.6y_{t-1} + 0.2y_{t-2} + e_t$, where $e_t \sim$ i.i.d. $(0, 1)$. Is y_t stationary? Is it ergodic? Find the effect of a unitary change in e_t on y_{t+3}. Repeat the exercise for $y_t = 0.4y_{t-1} + 0.8y_{t-2} + e_t$.

Exercise 1.10. Consider the bivariate process:

$$y_{1t} = 0.3y_{1t-1} + 0.8y_{2t-1} + e_{1t},$$

$$y_{2t} = 0.3y_{1t-1} + 0.4y_{2t-1} + e_{2t},$$

where $E(e_{1t}e_{1\tau}) = 1$ for $\tau = t$ and 0 otherwise, $E(e_{2t}e_{2\tau}) = 2$ for $\tau = t$ and 0 otherwise, and $E(e_{1t}e_{2\tau}) = 0$ for all τ, t. Is the system covariance stationary? Is it ergodic? Calculate $\partial y_{1t+\tau}/\partial e_{2t}$ for $\tau = 2, 3$. What is the limit of this derivative as $\tau \to \infty$?

Exercise 1.11. Suppose that at t time 0, $\{y_t\}_{t=1}^{\infty}$ is given by

$$y_t = \begin{cases} 1 & \text{with probability } \frac{1}{2}, \\ 0 & \text{with probability } \frac{1}{2}. \end{cases}$$

Show that y_t is stationary but not ergodic. Show that a single path (i.e., a path composed of only 1s and 0s) is ergodic.

Exercise 1.12. Let $y_t = \cos(\frac{1}{2}\pi t) + e_t$, where $e_t \sim$ i.i.d. $(0, \sigma_e^2)$. Show that y_t is neither stationary nor ergodic. Show that the sequence $\{y_t, y_{t+4}, y_{t+8}, \ldots\}$ is stationary and ergodic.

Exercise 1.12 shows an important result: if a process is nonergodic, it may be possible to find a subsequence which is ergodic.

Exercise 1.13. Show that if $\{y_{1t}(\varkappa)\}$ is ergodic, $y_{2t} = h(y_{1t})$ is ergodic if h is continuous.

A concept which bears some resemblance to ergodicity is that of mixing.

Definition 1.13 (mixing 1). Let $\mathbb{B}_1$ and $\mathbb{B}_2$ be two Borel algebras[3] and $B_1 \in \mathbb{B}_1$ and $B_2 \in \mathbb{B}_2$ two events. Then ϕ-mixing and α-mixing are defined as follows:

$$\left.\begin{aligned} \phi(\mathbb{B}_1, \mathbb{B}_2) &\equiv \sup_{\{B_1 \in \mathbb{B}_1, B_2 \in \mathbb{B}_2 : P(B_1) > 0\}} |P(B_2 \mid B_1) - P(B_2)|, \\ \alpha(\mathbb{B}_1, \mathbb{B}_2) &\equiv \sup_{\{B_1 \in \mathbb{B}_1, B_2 \in \mathbb{A}_2\}} |P(B_2 \cap B_1) - P(B_2)P(B_1)|. \end{aligned}\right\} \tag{1.4}$$

Intuitively, ϕ-mixing and α-mixing measure the dependence of events. We say that events in $\mathbb{B}_1$ and $\mathbb{B}_2$ are independent if both ϕ and α are zero. The function ϕ provides a measure of relative dependence while α measures absolute dependence.

For a stochastic process α-mixing and ϕ-mixing are defined as follows. Let $\mathbb{B}^t_{-\infty}$ be the Borel algebra generated by values of y_t from the infinite past up to t and $\mathbb{B}^{\infty}_{t+\tau}$ be the Borel algebra generated by values of y_t from $t + \tau$ to infinity. Intuitively, $\mathbb{B}^t_{-\infty}$ contains information up to t and $\mathbb{B}^{\infty}_{t+\tau}$ information from $t + \tau$ on.

Definition 1.14 (mixing 2). For a stochastic process $\{y_t(\varkappa)\}$, the mixing coefficients ϕ and α are defined as $\phi(\tau) = \sup_t \phi(\mathbb{B}^t_{-\infty}, \mathbb{B}^{\infty}_{t+\tau})$ and $\alpha(\tau) = \sup_t \alpha(\mathbb{B}^j_{-\infty}, \mathbb{B}^{\infty}_{t+\tau})$.

$\phi(\tau)$ and $\alpha(\tau)$, called respectively uniform and strong mixing, measure how much dependence there is between elements of $\{y_t\}$ separated by τ periods. If $\phi(\tau) = \alpha(\tau) = 0$, y_t and $y_{t+\tau}$ are independent. If $\phi(\tau) = \alpha(\tau) = 0$ as $\tau \to \infty$, they are asymptotically independent. Note that, because $\phi(\tau) \geqslant \alpha(\tau)$, ϕ-mixing implies α-mixing.

Example 1.16. Let y_t be such that $\text{cov}(y_t y_{t-\tau_1}) = 0$ for some τ_1. Then $\phi(\tau) = \alpha(\tau) = 0, \forall \tau \geqslant \tau_1$. Let $y_t = A y_{t-1} + e_t$, $|A| \leqslant 1$, $e_t \sim$ i.i.d. $(0, \sigma_e^2)$. Then $\alpha(\tau) = 0$ as $\tau \to \infty$.

Exercise 1.14. Show that, if $y_t = A y_{t-1} + e_t$, $|A| \leqslant 1$, $e_t \sim$ i.i.d. $(0, \sigma_e^2)$, $\phi(\tau)$ does not go to zero as $\tau \to \infty$.

Mixing is a somewhat stronger memory requirement than ergodicity. Rosenblatt (1978) shows the following result.

Result 1.11. Let y_t be stationary. If $\alpha(\tau) \to 0$ as $\tau \to \infty$, y_t is ergodic.

Exercise 1.15. Use result 1.11 and the fact that $\phi(\tau) \geqslant \alpha(\tau)$ to show that, if $\phi(\tau) \to 0$ as $\tau \to \infty$, a ϕ-mixing process is ergodic.

Both ergodicity and mixing are hard to verify in practice. A concept which bears some relationship to both and is easier to check is the following.

Definition 1.15 (asymptotic uncorrelatedness). $y_t(\varkappa)$ has asymptotic uncorrelated elements if there exist constants $0 \leqslant \varrho_\tau \leqslant 1$, $\tau \geqslant 0$, such that $\sum_{\tau=0}^{\infty} \varrho_\tau < \infty$ and $\text{cov}(y_t, y_{t-\tau}) \leqslant \varrho_\tau \sqrt{\text{var}(y_t)\,\text{var}(y_{t-\tau})}$, $\forall \tau > 0$, where $\text{var}(y_t) < \infty$, $\forall t$.

---

[3] A Borel algebra is the smallest collection of subsets of the event space which allows us to express the probability of an event in terms of the sets of the algebra.

Intuitively, if we can find an upper bound to the correlation of y_t and $y_{t-\tau}, \forall\tau$, and if the accumulation over τ of this bound is finite, the process has a memory that asymptotically dies out.

Example 1.17. Let $y_t = Ay_{t-1} + e_t, e_t \sim$ i.i.d. $(0, \sigma_e^2)$. Here $\text{corr}(y_t, y_{t-\tau}) = A^\tau$ and if $0 \leqslant A < 1, \sum_t A^\tau < \infty$, so that y_t has asymptotically uncorrelated elements.

Note that in definition 1.15 only $\tau > 0$ matters. From example 1.17 it is clear that when $\text{var}(y_t)$ is constant and the covariance of y_t with $y_{t-\tau}$ only depends on τ, asymptotic uncorrelatedness is the same as covariance stationarity.

Exercise 1.16. Show that for $\sum_{\tau=0}^{\infty} \varrho_\tau < \infty$ it is necessary that $\varrho_\tau \to 0$ as $\tau \to \infty$ and sufficient that $\rho_\tau < \tau^{-1-b}$ for some $b > 0$, τ sufficiently large.

Exercise 1.17. Suppose that y_t is such that the correlation between y_t and $y_{t-\tau}$ goes to zero as $\tau \to \infty$. Is this sufficient to ensure that y_t is ergodic?

Instead of assuming stationarity and ergodicity or mixing, one can assume that y_t satisfies an alternative set of conditions. These conditions considerably broaden the set of time series a researcher can work with.

Definition 1.16 (martingale). $\{y_t\}$ is a martingale with respect to the information set $\mathcal{F}_t$ if $y_t \in \mathcal{F}_t, \forall t > 0$, and $E_t[y_{t+\tau}] \equiv E[y_{t+\tau} \mid \mathcal{F}_t] = y_t$ for all t, τ.

Definition 1.17 (martingale difference). $\{y_t\}$ is a martingale difference with respect to the information set $\mathcal{F}_t$ if $y_t \in \mathcal{F}_t$, $\forall t > 0$, and $E_t[y_{t+\tau}] \equiv E[y_{t+\tau} \mid F_t] = 0$, $\forall t, \tau$.

Example 1.18. Let y_t be i.i.d. with $E(y_t) = 0$. Let $\mathcal{F}_t = \{\dots, y_{t-1}, y_t\}$ and let $\mathcal{F}_{t-1} \subseteq \mathcal{F}_t$. Then y_t is a martingale difference sequence.

Martingale difference is a much weaker requirement than stationarity and ergodicity since it only involves restrictions on the first conditional moment. It is therefore easy to build examples of processes which are martingale differences but are not stationary.

Example 1.19. Suppose that y_t is i.i.d. with mean zero and variance t^2. Then y_t is a martingale difference, nonstationary process.

Exercise 1.18. Let y_{1t} be a stochastic process and let $y_{2t} = E[y_{1t} \mid \mathcal{F}_t]$ be its conditional expectation. Show that y_{2t} is a martingale.

Using the identity $y_t = y_t - E(y_t \mid \mathcal{F}_{t-1}) + E(y_t \mid \mathcal{F}_{t-1}) - E(y_t \mid \mathcal{F}_{t-2}) + E(y_t \mid \mathcal{F}_{t-2}) \cdots$, one can write $y_t = \sum_{j=0}^{\tau-1} \text{Rev}_{t-j}(t) + E(y_t \mid \mathcal{F}_{t-\tau})$ for $\tau = 1, 2, \dots$, where $\text{Rev}_{t-j}(t) \equiv E[y_t \mid \mathcal{F}_{t-j}] - E[y_t \mid \mathcal{F}_{t-j-1}]$ is the one-step-ahead revision in y_t, made with new information accrued from $t-j-1$ to $t-j$. $\text{Rev}_{t-j}(t)$ plays an important role in deriving the properties of functions of stationary processes, and will be extensively used in chapters 4 and 10.

Exercise 1.19. Show that $\text{Rev}_{t-j}(t)$ is a martingale difference.

1.4 Laws of Large Numbers

Laws of large numbers provide conditions to ensure that quantities like $(1/T) \times \sum_t x_t' x_t$ or $(1/T)\sum_t z_t' x_t$, which appear in the formulas of OLS or IV estimators stochastically converge to well-defined limits. Since different conditions apply to different kinds of economic data, we consider here situations which are typically encountered in macro-time series contexts. Given the results of section 1.2, we will describe only strong laws of large numbers since weak laws of large numbers hold as a consequence.

Laws of large numbers typically come in the following form: given restrictions on the dependence and the heterogeneity of the observations and/or some restrictions on moments,

$$\frac{1}{T}\sum y_t - E(y_t) \xrightarrow{\text{a.s.}} 0. \tag{1.5}$$

We will consider three cases: (i) y_t has dependent and identically distributed elements; (ii) y_t has dependent and heterogeneously distributed elements; (iii) y_t has martingale difference elements. To better understand the applicability of each case note that in all cases observations are serially correlated. In the first case we restrict the distribution of the observations to be the same for every t; in the second we allow some carefully selected form of heterogeneity (for example, structural breaks in the mean or in the variance or conditional heteroskedasticity); in the third we do not restrict the distribution of the process, but impose conditions on its moments.

1.4.1 Dependent and Identically Distributed Observations

To state a law of large numbers (LLN) for stationary processes, we need conditions on the memory of the sequence. Typically, one assumes ergodicity since this implies average asymptotic independence of the elements of the $\{y_t(\varkappa)\}$ sequence.

The LLN is then as follows. Let $\{y_t(\varkappa)\}$ be stationary and ergodic with $E|y_t| < \infty, \forall t$. Then $(1/T)\sum_t y_t \xrightarrow{\text{a.s.}} E(y_t)$ (see Stout 1974, p. 181).

To use this law when dealing with econometric estimators, recall that, for any measurable function h such that $y_{2t} = h(y_{1t})$, y_{2t} is stationary and ergodic if y_{1t} is stationary and ergodic.

Exercise 1.20 (strong consistency of OLS and IV estimators). Let $y_t = x_t\alpha_0 + e_t$; let $x = [x_1, \ldots, x_T]'$, $z = [z_1, \ldots, z_T]'$, $e = [e_1, \ldots, e_T]'$, and assume

(i) $x'e/T \xrightarrow{\text{a.s.}} 0$, $x'x/T \xrightarrow{\text{a.s.}} \Sigma_{xx}$, Σ_{xx} finite, $|\Sigma_{xx}| \neq 0$;

(ii) $z'e/T \xrightarrow{\text{a.s.}} 0$, $z'x/T \xrightarrow{\text{a.s.}} \Sigma_{zx}$, Σ_{zx} finite, $|\Sigma_{zx}| \neq 0$;

(ii′) $z'e/T \xrightarrow{\text{a.s.}} 0$, $z'x/T - \Sigma_{zx,T} \xrightarrow{\text{a.s.}} 0$, where $\Sigma_{zx,T}$ is an $O(1)$ random matrix which depends on T and has uniformly continuous column rank.

Show that $\alpha_{\text{OLS}} = (x'x)^{-1}(x'y)$ and $\alpha_{\text{IV}} = (z'x)^{-1}(z'y)$ exist a.s. for T large and that $\alpha_{\text{OLS}} \xrightarrow{\text{a.s.}} \alpha_0$ under (i) and that $\alpha_{\text{IV}} \xrightarrow{\text{a.s.}} \alpha_0$ under (ii). Show that under (ii′) α_{IV} exists a.s. for T large, and $\alpha_{\text{IV}} \xrightarrow{\text{a.s.}} \alpha_0$. (Hint: if A_n is a sequence of $k_1 \times k$

matrices, then A_n has uniformly full column rank if there exists a sequence of $k \times k$ submatrices A_n^* which is uniformly nonsingular.)

1.4.2 Dependent and Heterogeneously Distributed Observations

To derive an LLN for dependent and heterogeneously distributed processes, we drop the ergodicity assumption and we substitute it with a mixing requirement. In addition, we need to define the *size* of the mixing conditions.

Definition 1.18. Let $1 \leqslant a \leqslant \infty$. Then $\phi(\tau) = O(\tau^{-b})$ for $b > a/(2a-1)$ implies that $\phi(\tau)$ is of size $a/(2a-1)$. If $a > 1$ and $\alpha(\tau) = O(\tau^{-b})$ for $b > a/(a-1)$, $\alpha(\tau)$ is of size $a/(a-1)$.

With definition 1.18 one can make precise statements on the memory of the process. In fact, a regulates the memory of a process. As $a \to \infty$, the dependence increases while as $a \to 1$, the sequence exhibits less and less serial dependence.

The LLN is the following. Let $\{y_t(\varkappa)\}$ be a sequence with $\phi(\tau)$ of size $a/(2a-1)$ or $\alpha(\tau)$ of size $a/(a-1)$, $a > 1$, and $E(y_t) < \infty, \forall t$. If, for some $0 < b \leqslant a$, $\sum_{t=1}^{\infty}(E|y_t - E(y_t)|^{a+b}/t^{a+b})^{1/a} < \infty$, then $(1/T)\sum_t y_t - E(y_t) \xrightarrow{\text{a.s.}} 0$ (see McLeish 1974, theorem 2.10).

In this law, the elements of y_t are allowed to have time-varying distributions (e.g., $E(y_t)$ may depend on t) but the condition $((E|y_t - E(y_t)|^{a+b})/t^{a+b})^{1/a} < \infty$ restricts the moments of the process. Note that, for $a = 1$ and $b = 1$, the above collapses to Kolmogorov law of large numbers.

The moment condition can be weakened somewhat if we are willing to impose a bound on the $(a+b)$th moment.

Result 1.12. Let $\{y_t(\varkappa)\}$ be a sequence with $\phi(\tau)$ of size $a/(2a-1)$ or with $\alpha(\tau)$ of size $a/(a-1)$, $a > 1$, such that $E|y_t|^{a+b}$ is bounded for all t. Then $(1/T)\sum_t y_t - E(y_t) \xrightarrow{\text{a.s.}} 0$.

The next result mirrors the one obtained for stationary ergodic processes.

Result 1.13. Let h be a measurable function and $y_{2\tau} = h(y_{1t}, \ldots, y_{1t+\tau})$, τ finite. If y_{1t} is mixing such that $\phi(\tau)$ $(\alpha(\tau))$ is $O(\tau^{-b})$ for some $b > 0$, $y_{2\tau}$ is mixing such that $\phi(\tau)$ $(\alpha(\tau))$ is $O(\tau^{-b})$.

From the above result it immediately follows that, if $\{z_t, x_t, e_t\}$ is a vector of mixing processes, $\{x_t'x_t\}$, $\{x_t'e_t\}$, $\{z_t'x_t\}$, and $\{z_t'e_t\}$ are also mixing processes of the same size.

The following result is useful when observations are heterogeneous.

Result 1.14. Let $\{y_t(\varkappa)\}$ be such that $\sum_{t=1}^{\infty} E|y_t| < \infty$. Then $\sum_{t=1}^{\infty} y_t$ converges a.s. and $E(\sum_{t=1}^{\infty} y_t) = \sum_{t=1}^{\infty} E(y_t) < \infty$ (see White 1984, p. 48).

The LLN for processes with asymptotically uncorrelated elements is the following. Let $\{y_t(\varkappa)\}$ be a process with asymptotically uncorrelated elements, mean $E(y_t)$, and variance $\sigma_t^2 < \Delta < \infty$. Then $(1/T)\sum_t y_t - E(y_t) \xrightarrow{\text{a.s.}} 0$.

Compared with result 1.12, we have relaxed the dependence restriction from mixing to asymptotic uncorrelation at the cost of altering the restriction on moments of order $a + b$ ($a \geqslant 1$, $b \leqslant a$) to second moments. Note that, since functions of asymptotically uncorrelated processes are not asymptotically uncorrelated, to prove consistency of econometric estimators when the regressors have asymptotic uncorrelated increments, we need to make assumptions on quantities like $\{x_t'x_t\}$, $\{x_t'e_t\}$, etc., directly.

1.4.3 Martingale Difference Process

The LLN for this type of process is the following. Let $\{y_t(\varkappa)\}$ be a martingale difference. If, for some $a \geqslant 1$, $\sum_{t=1}^{\infty} E|y_t|^{2a}/t^{1+a} < \infty$, then $(1/T)\sum_t y_t \xrightarrow{\text{a.s.}} 0$.

The martingale LLN requires restrictions on the moments of the process which are slightly stronger than those assumed in the case of independent y_t. The analogue of result 1.12 for martingale differences is the following.

Result 1.15. Let $\{y_t(\varkappa)\}$ be a martingale difference such that $E|y_t|^{2a} < \Delta < \infty$, for some $a \geqslant 1$ and all t. Then $(1/T)\sum_t y_t \xrightarrow{\text{a.s.}} 0$.

Exercise 1.21. Suppose $\{y_{1t}(\varkappa)\}$ is a martingale difference. Show that $y_{2t} = y_{1t}z_t$ is a martingale difference for any $z_t \in \mathcal{F}_t$.

Exercise 1.22. Let $y_t = x_t\alpha_0 + e_t$ and assume that e_t is a martingale difference and $E(x_t'x_t)$ is positive and finite. Show that α_{OLS} exists and $\alpha_{\text{OLS}} \xrightarrow{\text{a.s.}} \alpha_0$.

1.5 Central Limit Theorems

There are also several central limit theorems (CLTs) available in the literature. Clearly, their applicability depends on the type of data a researcher has available. In this section we list CLTs for the three cases we have described in section 1.4. Loeve (1977) or White (1984) provide theorems for other relevant cases.

1.5.1 Dependent and Identically Distributed Observations

A central limit theorem for dependent and identically distributed observations can be obtained by using two conditions. First, we need a restriction on the variance of the process. Second, we need to impose $E(y_t \mid \mathcal{F}_{t-\tau}) \to 0$ for $\tau \to \infty$ (referred to as linear regularity in chapter 4) or $E[y_t \mid \mathcal{F}_{t-\tau}] \xrightarrow{\text{q.m.}} 0$ as $\tau \to \infty$. The second condition is obviously stronger than the first one. Restrictions on the variance of the process are needed since when y_t is a dependent and identically distributed process its variance is the sum of the variances of the forecast revisions made at each t, and this may not converge to a finite limit. We ask the reader to show this in the next two exercises.

Exercise 1.23. Let $\text{var}(y_t) = \sigma_y^2 < \infty$. Show that $\text{cov}(\text{Rev}_{t-j}(t), \text{Rev}_{t-j'}(t)) = 0$, $j < j'$, where $\text{Rev}_{t-j}(t)$ was defined just before exercise 1.19. Note that this implies that $\sigma_y^2 = \text{var}(\sum_{j=0}^{\infty} \text{Rev}_{t-j}(t)) = \sum_{j=0}^{\infty} \text{var}(\text{Rev}_{t-j}(t))$.

Exercise 1.24. Let $\bar{\sigma}_T^2 = T \times E((T^{-1}\sum_{t=1}^{T} y_t)^2)$. Show that $\bar{\sigma}_T^2 = \sigma_y^2 + 2\sigma_y^2 \sum_{\tau=1}^{T-1} \rho_\tau(1 - \tau/T)$, where $\rho_\tau = E(y_t y_{t-\tau})/\sigma_y^2$. Give conditions on y_t that make ρ_τ independent of t. Show that $\bar{\sigma}_T^2$ goes to ∞ as $T \to \infty$.

A sufficient condition ensuring that $\bar{\sigma}_T^2$ converges is that

$$\sum_{j=0}^{\infty} (\text{var Rev}_{t-j}(t))^{1/2} < \infty. \tag{1.6}$$

A CLT is then as follows. Let (i) $\{y_t(\varkappa)\}$ be stationary and ergodic process, $y_t \in \mathcal{F}_t, \forall t > 0$; (ii) $E(y_t^2) = \sigma_y^2 < \infty$; (iii) $E(y_t \mid F_{t-\tau}) \xrightarrow{\text{q.m.}} 0$ as $\tau \to \infty$; (iv) $\sum_{j=0}^{\infty} (\text{var Rev}_{t-j}(t))^{1/2} < \infty$. Then, as $T \to \infty$, $0 \neq \bar{\sigma}_T^2 \to \bar{\sigma}_y^2 < \infty$ and

$$\sqrt{T}\frac{(1/T)\sum_t y_t}{\bar{\sigma}_T} \xrightarrow{\text{D}} \mathbb{N}(0, 1)$$

(see Gordin 1969).

Example 1.20. An interesting pathological case obtains when $\bar{\sigma}_T^2 = 0$. Consider, for example, $y_t = e_t - e_{t-1}$, $e_t \sim$ i.i.d. $(0, \sigma_e^2)$. Then $\bar{\sigma}_T^2 = 2\sigma_e^2 - 2\sigma_e^2 = 0$. Hence, $(1/T)\sum_t y_t = (1/T)(y_t - y_0)$ and $\sqrt{T}((1/T)\sum_t y_t) \xrightarrow{\text{P}} 0$.

Exercise 1.25. Assume that (i) $E[x_{tji}e_{tj} \mid \mathcal{F}_{t-1}] = 0, \forall t, i = 1, \ldots, j = 1, \ldots;$ (ii) $E[x_{tji}e_{tj}]^2 < \infty$; (iii) $\Sigma_T \equiv \text{var}(T^{-1/2}x'e) \to \text{var}(x'e) \equiv \Sigma$ as $T \to \infty$ is nonsingular and positive definite; (iv) $\sum_j (\text{var Rev}_{t-j}(t))^{-1/2} < \infty$; (v) (x_t, e_t) are stationary ergodic sequences; (vi) $E|x_{tji}|^2 < \infty$; (vii) $\Sigma_{xx} \equiv E(x_t' x_t)$ is positive definite. Show that $(\Sigma_{xx}^{-1}\Sigma(\Sigma_{xx}^{-1})')^{-1/2}\sqrt{T}(\alpha_{\text{OLS}} - \alpha_0) \overset{\text{D}}{\sim} \mathbb{N}(0, I)$, where α_{OLS} is the OLS estimator of α_0 in the model $y_t = x_t\alpha_0 + e_t$ and T is the number of observations.

1.5.2 Dependent Heterogeneously Distributed Observations

The CLT in this case is the following. Let $\{y_t(\varkappa)\}$ be a sequence of mixing random variables such that either $\phi(\tau)$ or $\alpha(\tau)$ is of size $a/a - 1$, $a > 1$, with $E(y_t) = 0$ and $E|y_t|^{2a} < \Delta < \infty, \forall t$. Define $y_{b,T} = (1/\sqrt{T})\sum_{t=b+1}^{b+T} y_t$ and assume there exists a $0 \neq \bar{\sigma}^2 < \infty$, such that $E(y_{b,T}^2) \to \bar{\sigma}^2$ for $T \to \infty$, uniformly in b. Then

$$\sqrt{T}\frac{(1/T)\sum_t y_t}{\bar{\sigma}_T} \xrightarrow{\text{D}} \mathbb{N}(0, 1)$$

as $T \to \infty$, where $\bar{\sigma}_T^2 \equiv E(y_{0,T}^2)$ (see White and Domowitz 1984).

As in the previous CLT, we need the condition that the variance of y_t is consistently estimated. Note also that the assumption of mixing substitutes the assumptions of stationarity and ergodicity and that we need uniform convergence of $E(y_{b,T}^2)$ to $\bar{\sigma}^2$ in b. This is equivalent to imposing that y_t is asymptotically covariance stationary, that is, that heterogeneity in y_t dies out as T increases (see White 1984, p. 128).

1.5.3 Martingale Difference Observations

The CLT in this case is as follows. Let $\{y_t(\varkappa)\}$ be a martingale difference process with $\sigma_t^2 \equiv E(y_t^2) < \infty$, $\sigma_t^2 \neq 0$, $\mathcal{F}_{t-1} \subset \mathcal{F}_t$, $y_t \in \mathcal{F}_t$; let $\mathcal{D}_t$ be the distribution function of y_t and let $\bar{\sigma}_T^2 = (1/T)\sum_{t=1}^T \sigma_t^2$. If, for every $\epsilon > 0$,

$$\lim_{T\to\infty} \frac{1}{\bar{\sigma}_T^2}\frac{1}{T}\sum_{t=1}^{T}\int_{y^2>\epsilon T\bar{\sigma}_T^2} y^2 \, \mathrm{d}\mathcal{D}_t(y) = 0 \quad \text{and} \quad \frac{1}{\bar{\sigma}_T^2}\left(\frac{1}{T}\sum_{t=1}^{T} y_t^2\right) - 1 \xrightarrow{\text{P}} 0,$$

then, as $T \to \infty$,

$$\sqrt{T}\frac{(1/T)\sum_t y_t}{\bar{\sigma}_T} \xrightarrow{\text{D}} \mathbb{N}(0,1)$$

(see McLeish 1974).

The last condition is somewhat mysterious: it requires that the average contribution of the extreme tails of the distribution to the variance of y_t is zero in the limit. If this condition holds, then y_t satisfies a uniform asymptotic negligibility condition. In other words, none of the elements of $\{y_t(\varkappa)\}$ can have a variance which dominates the variance of $(1/T)\sum_t y_t$. We illustrate this condition in the next example.

Example 1.21. Suppose that $\sigma_t^2 = \rho^t$, $0 < \rho < 1$. Then $T\bar{\sigma}_T^2 \equiv \sum_{t=1}^T \sigma_t^2 = \sum_{t=1}^T \rho^t = \rho/(1-\rho)$ as $T \to \infty$. Then $\max_{1\leqslant t\leqslant T} \sigma_t^2/T\bar{\sigma}_T^2 = \rho/(\rho/(1-\rho)) = 1-\rho \neq 0$, $\forall T$. Hence, the asymptotic negligibility condition is violated. Now let $\sigma_t^2 = \sigma^2$, $\bar{\sigma}_T^2 = \sigma^2$. Then $\max_{1\leqslant t\leqslant T} \sigma_t^2/T\bar{\sigma}_T^2 = (1/T)(\sigma^2/\sigma^2) \to 0$ as $T \to \infty$ and the asymptotic negligibility condition holds.

The martingale difference assumption allows us to weaken several of the conditions needed to prove a central limit theorem relative to the case of stationary processes, and it will be the assumption used in several parts of this book.

A result, which will become useful in later chapters, concerns the asymptotic distribution of functions of converging stochastic processes.

Result 1.16. Suppose the $m \times 1$ vector $\{y_t(\varkappa)\}$ is asymptotically normally distributed with mean $\bar{y}$ and variance $a_t^2\Sigma_y$, where Σ_y is a symmetric, nonnegative definite matrix and $a_t \to 0$ as $t \to \infty$. Let $h(y) = (h_1(y), \dots, h_n(y))'$ be such that each $h_j(y)$ is continuously differentiable in the neighborhood of $\bar{y}$ and let $\Sigma_h = (\partial h(\bar{y})/\partial y')\Sigma_y(\partial h(\bar{y})/\partial y')'$ have nonzero diagonal elements, where $\partial h(\bar{y})/\partial y'$ is an $n \times m$ matrix. Then $h(y_t) \xrightarrow{\text{D}} \mathbb{N}(h(\bar{y}), a_t^2\Sigma_h)$.

Example 1.22. Suppose y_t is i.i.d. with mean $\bar{y}$ and variance σ_y^2, $\bar{y} \neq 0$, $0 < \sigma_y^2 < \infty$. Then by the CLT $(1/T)\sum_t y_t \xrightarrow{\text{D}} N(\bar{y}, \sigma_y^2/T)$ and by result 1.16 $((1/T)\sum_t y_t)^{-1} \xrightarrow{\text{D}} N(\bar{y}^{-1}, \sigma_y^2/T\bar{y}^4)$.

1.6 Elements of Spectral Analysis

A central object in the analysis of time series is the spectral density (or spectrum).

Definition 1.19 (spectral density). The spectral density of a stationary $\{y_t(\varkappa)\}$ process at frequency $\omega \in [0, 2\pi]$ is $\mathcal{S}_y(\omega) = (1/2\pi)\sum_{\tau=-\infty}^{\infty} \text{ACF}_y(\tau)\text{e}^{-\text{i}\omega\tau}$.

We have already mentioned that the spectral density is a reparametrization of the covariance generating function and is obtained by setting $z = \text{e}^{-\text{i}\omega} = \cos(\omega) - \text{i}\sin(\omega)$, where $\text{i} = \sqrt{-1}$. Definition 1.19 also shows that the spectral density is the Fourier transform of the autocovariance of y_t. Hence, the spectral density simply repackages the autocovariances of $\{y_t(\varkappa)\}$ by using sine and cosine functions as weights but can be more useful than the autocovariance function since, for ω appropriately chosen, its elements are uncorrelated.

In fact, if we evaluate the spectral density at Fourier frequencies, i.e., at $\omega_j = 2\pi j/T$, $j = 1, \dots, T-1$, for any two $\omega_1 \neq \omega_2$ such frequencies, $\mathcal{S}(\omega_1)$ is uncorrelated with $\mathcal{S}(\omega_2)$. Note that Fourier frequencies change with T, making recursive evaluation of the spectral density cumbersome.

Example 1.23. There are two elements of the spectral density which are of interest: $\mathcal{S}(\omega = 0)$ and $\sum_j \mathcal{S}(\omega_j)$. It is easily verified that

$$\mathcal{S}(\omega = 0) = \frac{1}{2\pi}\sum_{\tau} \text{ACF}(\tau) = \frac{1}{2\pi}\left(\text{ACF}(0) + 2\sum_{\tau=1}^{\infty}\text{ACF}(\tau)\right), \tag{1.7}$$

that is, the spectral density at frequency zero is the (unweighted) sum of all the elements of the autocovariance function. When $\omega_j = 2\pi j/T$,

$$\sum_j \mathcal{S}(\omega_j) = \frac{1}{2\pi}\sum_j\sum_{\tau} \text{ACF}_y(\tau)\text{e}^{-\text{i}(2\pi j/T)\tau}. \tag{1.8}$$

Since $\sum_{j=1}^{T-1} \text{e}^{-\text{i}(2\pi j/T)\tau} = 0$ for $\tau \neq 0$, $\sum_j \mathcal{S}(\omega_j) = \text{var}(y_t)$, that is, the variance of the process is the area below the spectral density.

To understand how the spectral density transforms the autocovariance function, select, for example, $\omega = \pi/2$. Note that $\cos(\pi/2) = 1$, $\cos(3\pi/2) = -1$, $\cos(\pi) = \cos(2\pi) = 0$, and that $\sin(\pi/2) = \sin(3\pi/2) = 0$, $\sin(0) = 1$, and $\sin(\pi) = -1$, and that these values repeat themselves since the sine and cosine functions are periodic.

Exercise 1.26. Calculate $\mathcal{S}(\omega = \pi)$. Which autocovariances enter at frequency π?

For a Fourier frequency, the corresponding period of oscillation is $2\pi/\omega_j = T/j$.

Example 1.24. Suppose you have quarterly data. Then, at the Fourier frequency $\pi/2$, the period is equal to 4. That is, at frequency $\pi/2$ you have fluctuations with an annual periodicity. Similarly, at the frequency π, the period is 2 so that semiannual cycles are present at π.

Exercise 1.27. Business cycles are typically thought to occur with a periodicity between two and eight years. Assuming that you have quarterly data, find the Fourier frequencies characterizing business cycle fluctuations. Repeat the exercise for annual and monthly data.

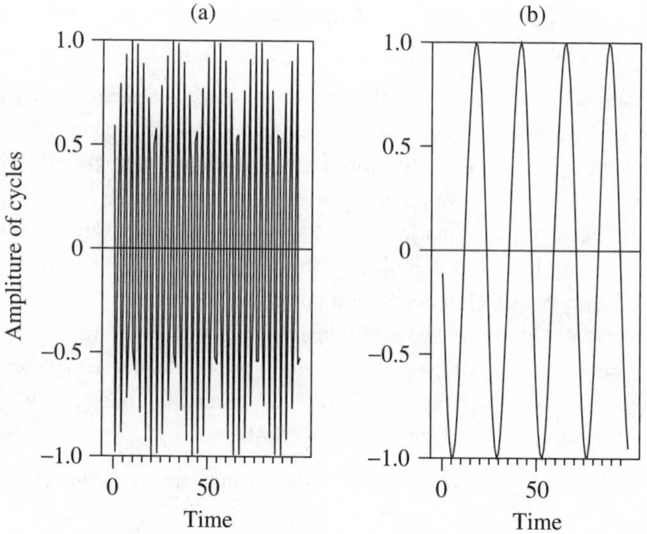

Figure 1.1. (a) Short and (b) long cycles.

Given the formula to calculate the period of oscillation, we can immediately see that low frequencies are associated with cycles of long periods of oscillation, that is, with infrequent shifts from a peak to a through, and high frequencies with cycles of short periods of oscillation, that is, with frequent shifts from a peak to a through (see figure 1.1). Hence, trends (i.e., cycles with an infinite periodicity) are located in the lowest frequencies of the spectrum and irregular fluctuations in the highest frequencies. Since the spectral density is periodic mod(2π) and symmetric around $\omega = 0$, it is sufficient to examine $\mathcal{S}(\omega)$ over the interval $[0, \pi]$.

Exercise 1.28. Show that $\mathcal{S}(\omega_j) = \mathcal{S}(-\omega_j)$.

Example 1.25. Suppose $\{y_t(\varkappa)\}$ is i.i.d. $(0, \sigma_y^2)$. Then $\text{ACF}_y(\tau) = \sigma_y^2$ for $\tau = 0$ and zero otherwise and $\mathcal{S}_y(\omega_j) = \sigma^2/2\pi, \forall\omega_j$. That is, the spectral density of an i.i.d. process is constant for all $\omega_j \in [0, \pi]$.

Exercise 1.29. Consider a stationary AR(1) process $\{y_t(\varkappa)\}$ with autoregressive coefficient equal to $0 \leqslant A < 1$. Calculate the autocovariance function of y_t. Show that the spectral density is monotonically increasing as $\omega_j \to 0$.

Exercise 1.30. Consider a stationary MA(1) process $\{y_t(\varkappa)\}$ with MA coefficient equal to D. Calculate the autocovariance function and the spectral density of y_t. Show their shape when $D > 0$ and $D < 0$.

Economic time series have a typical bell-shaped spectral density (see figure 1.2) with a large portion of the variance concentrated in the lower part of the spectrum. Given the result of exercise 1.29, it is therefore reasonable to posit that most economic time series can be represented with relatively simple AR processes.

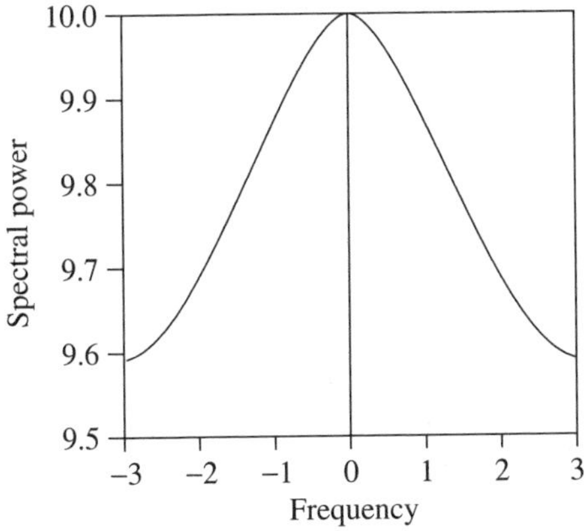

Figure 1.2. Spectral density.

The definitions we have given are valid for univariate processes but can be easily extended to vectors of stochastic processes.

Definition 1.20 (spectral density matrix). The spectral density of an $m \times 1$ vector of stationary processes $\{y_t(\varkappa)\}$ is $\mathcal{S}_y(\omega) = (1/2\pi)\sum_\tau \mathrm{ACF}_y(\tau)\mathrm{e}^{-\mathrm{i}\omega\tau}$, where

$$\mathcal{S}_y(\omega) = \begin{bmatrix} \mathcal{S}_{y_1y_1}(\omega) & \mathcal{S}_{y_1y_2}(\omega) & \cdots & \mathcal{S}_{y_1y_m}(\omega) \\ \mathcal{S}_{y_2y_1}(\omega) & \mathcal{S}_{y_2y_2}(\omega) & \cdots & \mathcal{S}_{y_2y_m}(\omega) \\ \cdots & \cdots & \cdots & \cdots \\ \mathcal{S}_{y_my_1}(\omega) & \mathcal{S}_{y_my_2}(\omega) & \cdots & \mathcal{S}_{y_my_m}(\omega) \end{bmatrix}.$$

The elements on the diagonal of the spectral density matrix are real while the off-diagonal elements are typically complex. A measure of the strength of the relationship between two series at frequency ω is given by the coherence.

Definition 1.21. Consider a bivariate stationary process $\{y_{1t}(\varkappa), y_{2t}(\varkappa)\}$. The coherence between $\{y_{1t}(\varkappa)\}$ and $\{y_{2t}(\varkappa)\}$ at frequency ω is

$$\mathrm{Co}(\omega) = \frac{|\mathcal{S}_{y_1,y_2}(\omega)|}{\sqrt{\mathcal{S}_{y_1,y_1}(\omega)\mathcal{S}_{y_2,y_2}(\omega)}}. \tag{1.9}$$

The coherence is the frequency domain version of the correlation coefficient. Note that $\mathrm{Co}(\omega)$ is a real-valued function, where $|y|$ indicates the real part (or the modulus) of the complex number y.

Example 1.26. Suppose $y_t = D(\ell)e_t$, where $e_t \sim$ i.i.d. $(0, \sigma_e^2)$. It can be immediately verified that the coherence between e_t and y_t is 1 at all frequencies. Suppose, on the other hand, that $\mathrm{Co}(\omega)$ monotonically declines to 0 as ω moves from 0 to π. Then y_t and e_t have similar low-frequency but different high-frequency components.

Exercise 1.31. Suppose that $e_t \sim$ i.i.d. $(0, \sigma_e^2)$ and let $y_t = Ay_{t-1} + e_t$. Calculate $\mathrm{Co}_{y_t,e_t}(\omega)$.

Interesting transformations of y_t can be obtained with the use of filters.

Definition 1.22. A filter is a linear transformation of a stochastic process, i.e., if $y_t = \mathcal{B}(\ell)e_t$, $e_t \sim$ i.i.d. $(0, \sigma_e^2)$, then $\mathcal{B}(\ell)$ is a filter.

A moving average (MA) process is therefore a filter since a white noise is linearly transformed into another process. In general, stochastic processes can be thought of as filtered versions of some white noise process. To study the spectral properties of filtered processes, let $\text{CGF}_e(z)$ be the covariance generating function of e_t. Then the covariance generating function of y_t is $\text{CGF}_y(z) = \mathcal{B}(z)\mathcal{B}(z^{-1})\,\text{CGF}_e(z) = |\mathcal{B}(z)|^2\,\text{CGF}_e(z)$, where $|\mathcal{B}(z)|$ is the modulus of $\mathcal{B}(z)$.

Example 1.27. Suppose that $e_t \sim$ i.i.d. $(0, \sigma_e^2)$ so that its spectrum is $\mathcal{S}_e(\omega) = \sigma^2/2\pi, \forall\omega$. Consider now the process $y_t = D(\ell)e_t$, where $D(\ell) = D_0 + D_1\ell + D_2\ell^2 + \cdots$. It is usual to interpret $D(\ell)$ as the response function of y_t to a unitary change in e_t. Then $\mathcal{S}_y(\omega) = |D(\mathrm{e}^{-\mathrm{i}\omega})|^2\mathcal{S}_e(\omega)$, where $|D(\mathrm{e}^{-\mathrm{i}\omega})|^2 = D(\mathrm{e}^{-\mathrm{i}\omega})D(\mathrm{e}^{\mathrm{i}\omega})$ and $D(\mathrm{e}^{-\mathrm{i}\omega}) = \sum_\tau D_\tau \mathrm{e}^{-\mathrm{i}\omega\tau}$ measures how a unitary change in e_t affects y_t at frequency ω.

Example 1.28. Suppose that $y_t = \bar{y} + at + D(\ell)e_t$, where $e_t \sim$ i.i.d. $(0, \sigma_e^2)$. Since y_t displays a (linear) trend is not stationary and $\mathcal{S}(\omega)$ does not exist. Differencing the process we have $y_t - y_{t-1} = a + D(\ell)(e_t - e_{t-1})$ so that $y_t - y_{t-1}$ is stationary if $e_t - e_{t-1}$ is a stationary and all the roots of $D(\ell)$ are greater than one in absolute value. If these conditions are met, the spectrum of Δy_t is well-defined and equals $\mathcal{S}_{\Delta y}(\omega) = |D(\mathrm{e}^{-\mathrm{i}\omega})|^2\mathcal{S}_{\Delta e}(\omega)$.

The quantity $\mathcal{B}(\mathrm{e}^{-\mathrm{i}\omega})$ is called the transfer function of the filter. Various functions of this quantity are of interest. For example, $|\mathcal{B}(\mathrm{e}^{-\mathrm{i}\omega})|^2$, the square modulus of the transfer function, measures the change in variance of e_t induced by the filter. Furthermore, since $\mathcal{B}(\mathrm{e}^{-\mathrm{i}\omega})$ is complex, two alternative representations of the transfer function exist. The first decomposes it into its real and complex parts, i.e., $\mathcal{B}(\mathrm{e}^{-\mathrm{i}\omega}) = \mathcal{B}^\dagger(\omega) + \mathrm{i}\mathcal{B}^\ddagger(\omega)$, where both $\mathcal{B}^\dagger$ and $\mathcal{B}^\ddagger$ are real. Then the phase shift, $\text{Ph}(\omega) = \tan^{-1}[-\mathcal{B}^\ddagger(\omega)/\mathcal{B}^\dagger(\omega)]$, measures how much the lead–lag relationships in e_t are altered by the filter. The second can be obtained by using the polar representation $\mathcal{B}(\mathrm{e}^{-\mathrm{i}\omega}) = \text{Ga}(\omega)\mathrm{e}^{-\mathrm{i}\text{Ph}(\omega)}$, where $\text{Ga}(\omega)$ is the gain. Here $\text{Ga}(\omega) = |\mathcal{B}(\mathrm{e}^{-\mathrm{i}\omega})|$ measures the change in the amplitude of cycles induced by the filter.

Filtering is an operation frequently performed in everyday life (e.g., tuning a radio on a station filters out all other signals (waves)). Several types of filter are used in modern macroeconomics. Figure 1.3 presents three general types of filter: a low pass, a high pass, and a band pass. A low pass filter leaves the low frequencies of the spectrum unchanged but wipes out high frequencies. A high pass filter does exactly the opposite. A band pass filter can be thought of as a combination of a low pass and a high pass filter: it wipes out very high and very low frequencies and leaves unchanged frequencies in middle range.

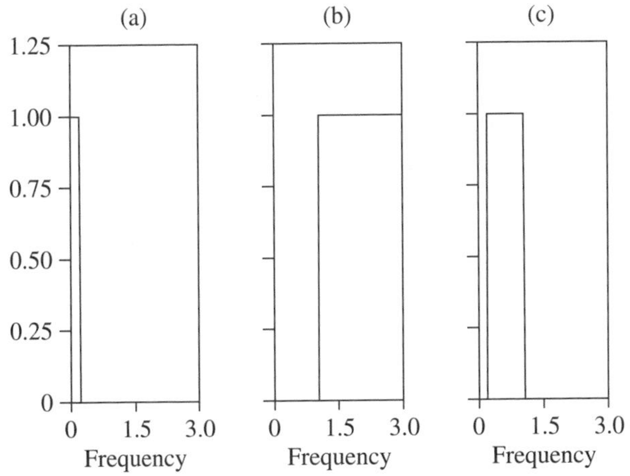

Figure 1.3. Filters: (a) low pass; (b) high pass; (c) band pass.

Low pass, high pass, and band pass filters are nonrealizable, in the sense that, with samples of finite length, it is impossible to construct objects that look like those of figure 1.3. In fact, by using the inverse Fourier transform, one can show that these three filters (denoted, respectively, by $\mathcal{B}(\ell)^{\text{lp}}$, $\mathcal{B}(\ell)^{\text{hp}}$, $\mathcal{B}(\ell)^{\text{bp}}$) have the following time representations.

- Low pass: $\mathcal{B}_0^{\text{lp}} = \omega_1/\pi$; $\mathcal{B}_j^{\text{lp}} = \sin(j\omega_1)/j\pi$, $\forall j > 0$, for some $\omega_1 \in (0, \pi)$.
- High pass: $\mathcal{B}_0^{\text{hp}} = 1 - \mathcal{B}_0^{\text{lp}}$; $\mathcal{B}_j^{\text{hp}} = -\mathcal{B}_j^{\text{lp}}$, $\forall j > 0$.
- Band pass: $\mathcal{B}_j^{\text{bp}} = \mathcal{B}_j^{\text{lp}}(\omega_2) - \mathcal{B}_j^{\text{lp}}(\omega_1)$, $\forall j > 0$, $\omega_2 > \omega_1$.

When j is finite the box-like spectral shape of these filters can only be approximated with a bell-shaped function. This means that relative to the ideal, realizable filters generate a loss of power at the edges of the band (a phenomenon called leakage) and an increase in the importance of the frequencies in the middle of the band (a phenomenon called compression). Approximations to these ideal filters are discussed in chapter 3.

Definition 1.23. The periodogram of a stationary $y_t(\varkappa)$ is $\text{Pe}_y(\omega) = \sum_\tau \widehat{\text{ACF}}(\tau) \times e^{-i\omega\tau}$, where $\widehat{\text{ACF}}_y = (1/T)\sum_t [y_t - (1/T)\sum_t y_t][y_{t-\tau} - (1/T)\sum_t y_{t-\tau}]'$.

Perhaps surprisingly, the periodogram is an inconsistent estimator of the spectrum (see, for example, Priestley 1981, p. 433). Intuitively, this occurs because it consistently captures the power of y_t over a band of frequencies but not in each single one of them. To obtain consistent estimates it is necessary to "smooth" periodogram estimates with a filter. Such a smoothing filter is typically called a "kernel."

Definition 1.24. For any $\epsilon > 0$, a filter $\mathcal{B}(\omega)$ is a kernel (denoted by $\mathcal{K}_T(\omega)$) if $\mathcal{K}_T(\omega) \to 0$ uniformly as $T \to \infty$, for $|\omega| > \epsilon$.

Kernels can be applied to both autocovariance and periodogram estimates. When applied to the periodogram, a kernel produces an estimate of the spectrum at frequency ω by using a weighted average of the values of the periodogram in a neighborhood of ω. Note that this neighborhood is shrinking as $T \to \infty$, since the bias in autocovariance function (ACF) estimates asymptotically disappears. Hence, in the limit, $\mathcal{K}_T(\omega)$ looks like a δ-function, i.e., it puts all its mass at one point.

There are several types of kernel. Those used in this book are the following.

(1) Box-car (truncated):

$$\mathcal{K}_{\mathrm{TR}}(\omega) = \begin{cases} 1 & \text{if } |\omega| \leqslant J(T), \\ 0 & \text{otherwise.} \end{cases}$$

(2) Bartlett:

$$\mathcal{K}_{\mathrm{BT}}(\omega) = \begin{cases} 1 - \dfrac{|\omega|}{J(T)} & \text{if } |\omega| \leqslant J(T), \\ 0 & \text{otherwise.} \end{cases}$$

(3) Parzen:

$$\mathcal{K}_{\mathrm{PR}}(\omega) = \begin{cases} 1 - 6\left(\dfrac{\omega}{J(T)}\right)^2 + 6\left(\dfrac{|\omega|}{J(T)}\right)^3 & 0 \leqslant |\omega| \leqslant J(T)/2, \\ 2\left(1 - \dfrac{|\omega|}{J(T)}\right)^3 & J(T)/2 \leqslant |\omega| \leqslant J(T), \\ 0 & \text{otherwise.} \end{cases}$$

(4) Quadratic spectral:

$$\mathcal{K}_{\mathrm{QS}}(\omega) = \frac{25}{12\pi^2\omega^2}\left(\frac{\sin(6\pi\omega/5)}{6\pi\omega/5} - \cos(6\pi\omega/5)\right).$$

Here $J(T)$ is a truncation point, typically chosen to be a function of the sample size T. Note that the quadratic spectral kernel has no truncation point. However, it is useful to define the first time that $\mathcal{K}_{\mathrm{QS}}$ crosses zero (call it $J^*(T)$) and this point plays the same role as $J(T)$ in the other three kernels.

The Bartlett kernel and the quadratic spectral kernel are the most popular ones. The Bartlett kernel has the shape of a tent with width $2J(T)$. To ensure consistency of the spectral estimates, it is standard to select $J(T)$ so that $J(T)/T \to 0$ as $T \to \infty$. In figure 1.4 we have set $J(T) = 20$. The quadratic spectral kernel has the form of a wave with infinite loops, but after the first crossing, the side loops are small.

Exercise 1.32. Show that $\widehat{\mathrm{Co}(\omega)} = |\hat{\mathcal{S}}_{y_1,y_2}(\omega)|/\sqrt{\hat{\mathcal{S}}_{y_1,y_1}(\omega)\hat{\mathcal{S}}_{y_2,y_2}(\omega)}$ is consistent, where $\hat{\mathcal{S}}_{y_i,y_{i'}}(\omega) = (1/2\pi)\sum_{\tau=-T+1}^{T-1}\widehat{\mathrm{ACF}}_{y_i,y_{i'}}(\tau)\,\mathcal{K}_T(\omega)\,\mathrm{e}^{-\mathrm{i}\omega\tau}$, $\mathcal{K}_T(\omega)$ is a kernel, and $i, i' = 1, 2$.

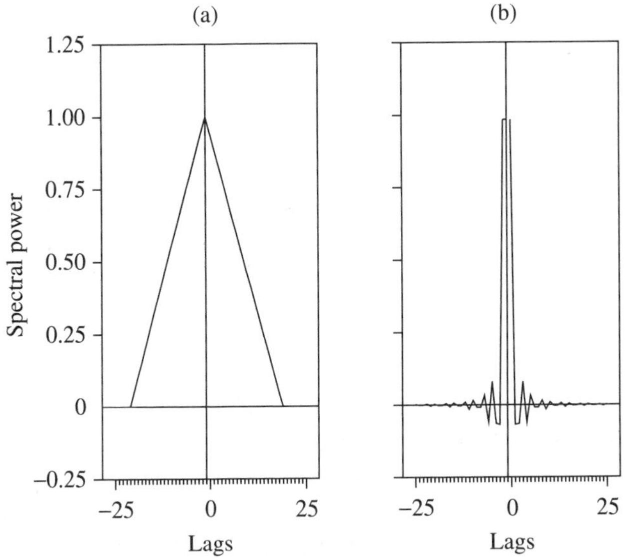

Figure 1.4. (a) Bartlett and (b) quadratic spectral kernels.

While for the most part of this book we will consider stationary processes, we will deal at times with processes which are only locally stationary (e.g., processes with time-varying coefficients). For these processes, the spectral density is not defined. However, it is possible to define a "local" spectral density and practically all the properties we have described also apply to this alternative construction. For details, see Priestley (1981, chapter 11).

Exercise 1.33. Compute the spectral density of consumption, investment, output, hours, real wage, consumer prices, M1, and the nominal interest rate by using quarterly U.S. data and compute their pairwise coherence with output. Are there any interesting features at business cycle frequencies you would like to emphasize? Repeat the exercise using euro area data. Are there important differences with the United States? (Hint: be careful with potential nonstationarities in the data.)

2

DSGE Models, Solutions, and Approximations

This chapter describes some standard dynamic stochastic general equilibrium (DSGE) models and some issues concerning their specification and solution. Such models will be used in examples and exercises throughout the book. It aims to familiarize the reader with such objects rather than providing a fully fledged introduction to DSGE modeling. Since the models we consider do not have a closed-form solution, except in very special circumstances, we also present several methods for obtaining approximate solutions to the optimization problems.

There is a variety of models currently used in macroeconomics. The majority is based on two simple setups: a competitive structure, where allocations are, in general, Pareto optimal; and a monopolistic competitive structure, where one type of agent can set the price of the goods she supplies and allocations are suboptimal. Typically, an expression for the variables of interest in terms of the exogenous forces and the states is found in two ways. When competitive allocations are Pareto optimal, the principle of dynamic programming is typically used and iterations on the Bellman equation are employed to compute the value function and the policy rules, whenever they are known to exist and to be unique. As we will see, calculating the value function is a complicated enterprise except with simple but often economically unpalatable specifications. For general preference and technological specifications, quadratic approximations of the utility function, and discretizations of the dynamic programming problem, are generally employed.

When the equilibrium allocations are distorted, one must alter the dynamic programming formulation and in that case the Bellman equation does not have a hedge over a more standard stochastic Lagrangian multipliers methodology, where one uses the first-order conditions, the constraints, and the transversality condition to obtain a solution. Solutions are also hard to find with the Lagrangian approach since the problem is nonlinear and involves expectations of future variables. Euler equation methods, which approximate the first-order conditions, the expectational equations, or the policy function can be used in these frameworks. Many methods exist in the literature. Here we restrict attention to the three widely used approaches: discretization of the state and shock space; log-linear and second-order approximations; and parametrizing expectations. For a thorough discussion of the various methodologies, see Cooley (1995, chapters 2 and 3) or Marimon and Scott (1999).

The next two sections illustrate features of various models and the mechanics of different solution methods with the aid of examples and exercises. A comparison between various approaches concludes the chapter.

2.1 A Few Useful Models

It is impossible to provide a thorough description of the models currently used in macroeconomics. We therefore focus attention on two prototype structures: one involving only real variables and one also considering nominal ones. In each case, we analyze models with both representative and heterogeneous agents and consider both optimal and distorted setups.

2.1.1 A Basic Real Business Cycle (RBC) Model

Much of the current macroeconomic literature uses versions of the one-sector growth model to jointly explain the cyclical and the long-run properties of the data. In the basic setup we consider there is a large number of identical households that live forever and are endowed with one unit of time, which they can allocate to leisure or to work, and K_0 units of productive capital, which depreciates at the rate $0 < \delta < 1$ every period. The social planner chooses $\{c_t, N_t, K_{t+1}\}_{t=0}^{\infty}$ to maximize

$$E_0 \sum_t \beta^t u(c_t, c_{t-1}, N_t), \tag{2.1}$$

where c_t is consumption, N_t is total hours, K_t is capital, and $E_0 \equiv E[\cdot \mid \mathcal{F}_0]$ is the expectation operator, conditional on the information set $\mathcal{F}_0$, $0 < \beta < 1$. The instantaneous utility function is bounded, twice continuously differentiable, strictly increasing, and strictly concave in all arguments. It depends on c_t and c_{t-1} to account for possible habit formation in consumption. The maximization of (2.1) is subject to the sequence of constraints

$$c_t + K_{t+1} \leqslant (1 - T^y) f(K_t, N_t, \zeta_t) + T_t + (1 - \delta)K_t, \quad 0 \leqslant N_t \leqslant 1, \tag{2.2}$$

where $f(\cdot)$ is a production technology, twice continuously differentiable, strictly increasing, and strictly concave in K_t and N_t; ζ_t is a technological disturbance; T^y is a (constant) income tax rate; and T_t are lump sum transfers.

There is a government which finances a stochastic flow of current expenditure with income taxes and lump sum transfers: expenditure is unproductive and does not yield utility for the agents. We assume a period-by-period balanced budget of the form

$$G_t = T^y f(K_t, N_t, \zeta_t) - T_t. \tag{2.3}$$

The economy is closed by the resource constraint, which provides a national account identity:

$$c_t + K_{t+1} - (1 - \delta)K_t + G_t = f(K_t, N_t, \zeta_t). \tag{2.4}$$

Note that in (2.3) we have assumed that the government balances the budget at each t. This is not restrictive since households in this economy are Ricardian; that is, the addition of government debt does not change optimal allocations. This is because, if debt is held in equilibrium, it must bear the same rate of return as capital, so that $(1 + r_t^{\mathrm{B}}) = E_t[f_k(1 - T^y) + (1 - \delta)]$, where $f_k = \partial f / \partial K$. In other words, debt is a redundant asset and can be priced by arbitrage, once (δ, T^y, f_k) are known. An example where debt matters is considered later on.

Exercise 2.1. Decentralize the RBC model so that there is a representative household and a representative firm. Assume that the household makes the investment decision while the firm hires capital and labor from the household. Is it true that decentralized allocations are the same as those obtained in the social planner's problem? What conditions need to be satisfied? Repeat the exercise assuming that the firm makes the investment decision.

Exercise 2.2. Set $c_{t-1} = 0$ in (2.1) and assume $T^y = 0, \forall t$.

(i) Define the variables characterizing the state of the economy (the states) and the choice variables (the controls) at each t.

(ii) Verify that the problem in (2.1)–(2.4) can be equivalently written as

$$\mathbb{V}(K, \zeta, G) = \max_{\{K^+, N\}} u\{[f(K, N, \zeta) + (1 - \delta)K - G - K^+], N\} \\ + \beta E[\mathbb{V}(K^+, \zeta^+, G^+) \mid K, \zeta, G], \quad (2.5)$$

where the value function $\mathbb{V}$ is the utility value of the optimal plan, given (K_t, ζ_t, G_t), $E(\mathbb{V} \mid \cdot)$ is the expectation of $\mathbb{V}$ conditional on the available information, the superscript "+" indicates future values, and $0 < N_t < 1$.

(iii) Assume that $u(c_t, c_{t-1}, N_t) = \ln c_t + \ln(1 - N_t)$ and that $\mathrm{GDP}_t \equiv f(K_t, N_t, \zeta_t) = \zeta_t K_t^{1-\eta} N_t^{\eta}$. Find values for $(K_t/\mathrm{GDP}_t, c_t/\mathrm{GDP}_t, N_t)$ when ζ_t, G_t are set to their unconditional values (we call this the steady state of the economy).

Note that (2.5) defines the so-called Bellman equation, a recursive functional equation giving the maximum value of the problem for each value of the states and the shocks, given that the next period value of the function is optimally chosen.

There are a few conditions that need to be satisfied for a model to be fitted into a Bellman equation format. First, preferences and technologies must define a convex optimization problem. Second, the utility function must be time separable in the contemporaneous control and state variables. Third, the objective function and the constraints have to be such that current decisions affect current and future utilities but not past ones. While these conditions are typically satisfied, there are situations where the Bellman equation (and its associated optimality principle) may fail to characterize particular economic problems. One is the time inconsistency problem analyzed by Kydland and Prescott (1977), a version of which is described in the next example.

Example 2.1. Suppose a representative household maximizes $E_0 \sum_t \beta^t(\ln c_t + \gamma \ln B_{t+1}/p_t)$ subject to $c_t + B_{t+1}/p_t \leqslant w_t + B_t/p_t + T_t \equiv \text{We}_t$, by choosing sequences for c_t and B_{t+1}, given T_t, p_t, where B_{t+1} are government backed nominal assets, p_t the price level, w_t labor income, T_t lump sum taxes (transfers), and We_t the wealth at t. The government budget constraint is $g_t = B_{t+1}/p_t - B_t/p_t + T_t$, where g_t is random. We assume that the government chooses B_{t+1} to maximize the household's welfare. The household problem is recursive. In fact, the Bellman equation is $\mathbb{V}(\text{We}) = \max_{\{c,B^+\}}(\ln c + \gamma \ln B^+/p) + \beta E \mathbb{V}(\text{We}^+)$ and the constraint is $\text{We} = c + B/p$. The first-order conditions for the problem can be summarized via $1/(c_t p_t) = E_t[\beta/(c_{t+1}p_{t+1}) + \gamma/B_{t+1}]$. Therefore, solving forward and using the resource constraint, we have

$$\frac{1}{p_t} = (w_t - g_t)E_t \sum_{j=0}^{\infty} \beta^j \frac{\gamma}{B_{t+j+1}}. \tag{2.6}$$

The government takes (2.6) as given and maximizes utility subject to the resource constraint. Substituting (2.6) into the utility function we have

$$\max_{B_t} E_0 \sum_t \beta^t \left(\ln c_t + \gamma \ln \left\{ B_t \left[\gamma(w_t - g_t) \sum_{j=0}^{\infty} \frac{\beta^j}{B_{t+j+1}} \right] \right\} \right). \tag{2.7}$$

Clearly, in (2.7) future values of B_t affect current utility. Therefore, the government problem cannot be cast into a Bellman equation.

A solution to (2.5) is typically hard to find since $\mathbb{V}$ is unknown and there is no analytic expression for it. Had the solution been known, we could have used (2.5) to define a function h mapping every (K, G, ζ) into (K^+, N) that gives the maximum.

Since $\mathbb{V}$ is unknown, methods to prove its existence and uniqueness and to describe its properties have been developed (see, for example, Stokey and Lucas 1989). These methods implicitly provide a way of computing a solution to (2.5), which we summarize next.

Algorithm 2.1.

(1) Choose a differentiable and concave function $\mathbb{V}^0(K, \zeta, G)$.

(2) Compute $\mathbb{V}^1(K, \zeta, G) = \max_{\{K^+,N\}} u\{[f(K, \zeta, N) + (1 - \delta)K - G - K^+], N\} + \beta E[\mathbb{V}^0(K^+, \zeta^+, G^+) \mid K, \zeta, G]$.

(3) Set $\mathbb{V}^0 = \mathbb{V}^1$ and iterate on (2) until $|\mathbb{V}^{l+1} - \mathbb{V}^l| < \iota$, ι small.

(4) When $|\mathbb{V}^{l+1} - \mathbb{V}^l| < \iota$, compute $K^+ = h_1(K, \zeta, G)$ and $N = h_2(K, \zeta, G)$.

Hence, $\mathbb{V}$ can be obtained as the limit of $\mathbb{V}^l$ for $l \to \infty$. Under regularity conditions, this limit exists, it is unique, and the sequence of iterations defined by algorithm 2.1 achieves it.

For simple problems algorithm 2.1 is fast and accurate. For more complicated ones, where the combined number of states and shocks is large, it may be computationally demanding. Moreover, unless $\mathbb{V}^0$ is appropriately chosen, the iteration process may be time-consuming. In a few simple cases, the solution to the Bellman equation has a known form and the simpler method of undetermined coefficients can be used. We analyze one of these cases in the next example.

Example 2.2. Assume, in the basic RBC model, that $u(c_t, c_{t-1}, N_t) = \ln c_t + \vartheta_n \ln(1 - N_t)$, $\delta = 1$, the production function is $\mathrm{GDP}_{t+1} = \zeta_{t+1} K_t^{1-\eta} N_t^{\eta}$, the resource constraint is $\mathrm{GDP}_t = K_t + c_t$, $\ln \zeta_t$ is an AR(1) process with persistence ρ, and set $G_t = T^y = T_t = 0$. The states of the problem are GDP_t and ζ_t while the controls are c_t, K_t, N_t. We guess that the value function has the form $\mathbb{V}(K, \zeta) = \mathbb{V}_0 + \mathbb{V}_1 \ln \mathrm{GDP}_t + \mathbb{V}_2 \ln \zeta_t$. Since the Bellman equation maps logarithmic functions into logarithmic ones, the limit, if it exists, will also have a logarithmic form. To find $\mathbb{V}_0$, $\mathbb{V}_1$, $\mathbb{V}_2$, we proceed as follows. First, we substitute the constraint into the utility function and use the guess to eliminate future GDP. That is,

$$\begin{aligned}\mathbb{V}_0 + \mathbb{V}_1 \ln \mathrm{GDP}_t + \mathbb{V}_2 \ln \zeta_t = \ln(\mathrm{GDP}_t - K_t) + \vartheta_N \ln(1 - N_t) + \beta \mathbb{V}_0 \\ + \beta \mathbb{V}_1 (1 - \eta) \ln K_t + \beta \mathbb{V}_1 \eta \ln N_t \\ + \beta(\mathbb{V}_2 + \mathbb{V}_1) E_t \ln \zeta_{t+1}. \qquad (2.8)\end{aligned}$$

Maximizing (2.8) with respect to (K_t, N_t) we have $N_t = \beta \mathbb{V}_1 \eta / (\vartheta_N + \beta \mathbb{V}_1 \eta)$ and $K_t = [\beta(1-\eta)\mathbb{V}_1 / (1 + \beta(1-\eta)\mathbb{V}_1)] \, \mathrm{GDP}_t$. Substituting into (2.8) and using the fact that $E_t \ln \zeta_{t+1} = \rho \ln \zeta_t$, we obtain

$$\begin{aligned}&\mathbb{V}_0 + \mathbb{V}_1 \ln \mathrm{GDP}_t + \mathbb{V}_2 \ln \zeta_t \\ &\quad = \text{const.} + (1 + (1-\eta)\beta \mathbb{V}_1) \ln \mathrm{GDP}_t + \beta\rho(\mathbb{V}_2 + \mathbb{V}_1) \ln \zeta_t. \qquad (2.9)\end{aligned}$$

Matching coefficients on the two sides of the equation we have $1 + (1-\eta)\beta \mathbb{V}_1 = \mathbb{V}_1$ or $\mathbb{V}_1 = 1/(1-(1-\eta)\beta)$ and $\beta\rho(\mathbb{V}_2 + \mathbb{V}_1) = \mathbb{V}_2$ or $\mathbb{V}_2 = \rho\beta/(1-(1-\eta)\beta)^2$. Using the solution for $\mathbb{V}_1$ into the expressions for K_t, N_t we have that $K_t = (1-\eta)\beta \, \mathrm{GDP}_t$ and $N_t = \beta\eta / [\vartheta_N(1 - \beta(1-\eta)) + \beta\eta]$. From the resource constraint one has that $c_t = (1 - (1-\eta)\beta) \, \mathrm{GDP}_t$. Hence, with this preference specification, the optimal labor supply decision is very simple: keep hours constant, no matter what the state and the shocks are.

Exercise 2.3. Assume, in the basic RBC model, that $u(c_t, c_{t-1}, N_t) = \ln c_t$, $\delta = 1$, the production function has the form $\mathrm{GDP}_t = \zeta_t K_t^{1-\eta} N_t^{\eta}$, the resource constraint is $c_t + K_{t+1} + G_t = \mathrm{GDP}_t$, $G_t = T_t$, and that both (ζ_t, G_t) are i.i.d. Guess that the value function is $\mathbb{V}(K, \zeta, G) = \mathbb{V}_0 + \mathbb{V}_1 \ln K_t + \mathbb{V}_2 \ln \zeta_t + \mathbb{V}_3 \ln G_t$. Determine $\mathbb{V}_1$, $\mathbb{V}_2$, $\mathbb{V}_3$. Show the optimal policy for K^+.

Two other cases where a solution to the Bellman equation can be found analytically are analyzed in the next exercise.

Exercise 2.4. (i) Suppose that, in the basic RBC model, $u(c_t, c_{t-1}, N_t) = a_0 + a_1 c_t - a_2 c_t^2$ and that $G_t = T_t = T^y = 0, \forall t$. Show that the value function is of the form $\mathbb{V}(K, \zeta) = [K, \zeta]'\mathbb{V}_2[K, \zeta] + \mathbb{V}_0$. Find the values of $\mathbb{V}_0$ and $\mathbb{V}_2$. (Hint: use the fact that $E(e_t'\mathbb{V}_2 e_t) = \text{tr}(\mathbb{V}_2)E(e_t'e_t) = \text{tr}(\mathbb{V}_2)\sigma_e^2$, where σ_e^2 is the covariance matrix of e_t and $\text{tr}(\mathbb{V}_2)$ is the trace of $\mathbb{V}_2$.) Show that the decision rule for c and K^+ is linear in K and ζ.

(ii) Suppose $u(c_t, c_{t-1}, N_t) = c_t^{1-\varphi}/(1-\varphi)$, $K_t = 1, \forall t$, and assume that ζ_t can take three values. Let ζ_t evolve according to $P(\zeta_t = i \mid \zeta_{t-1} = i') = p_{ii'} > 0$. Assume that there are claims to the output in the form of stocks S_t, with price p_t^{s} and dividend sd_t. Write down the Bellman equation. Let $\beta = 0.9$, $p_{ii} = 0.8$, $i = 1, \dots, 3$, $p_{i,i+1} = 0.2$, and $p_{ii'} = 0$, $i' \neq i, i+1$. Calculate the first two iterations of the value function. Can you guess what the limit is?

We can relax some of the assumptions we have made (e.g., we can use a more general law of motion for the shocks), but, except for these simple cases, even the most basic stochastic RBC model does not have a closed-form solution. As we will see later, existence of a closed-form solution is not necessary to estimate the structural parameters of the model (here β, δ, η), and the parameters of the process for ζ_t and G_t and to examine its fit to the data. However, a solution is needed when one wishes to simulate the model, compare its dynamics with those of the data, and/or perform policy analyses.

There is an alternative to the Bellman equation approach to solve simple optimization problems. It involves substituting all the constraints in the utility function and maximizing the resulting expression unconstrained or, if this is not possible, using a stochastic Lagrange multiplier approach. We illustrate the former approach next with an example.

Example 2.3. Suppose a representative household obtains utility from the services of durable and nondurable goods according to $E_0 \sum_t \beta^t (\text{cs}_t - \upsilon_t)'(\text{cs}_t - \upsilon_t)$, where $0 < \beta < 1$, υ_t is a preference shock and consumption services cs_t satisfy $\text{cs}_t = b_1 \text{cd}_{t-1} + b_2 c_t$, where cd_{t-1} is the stock of durable goods, accumulated according to $\text{cd}_t = b_3 \text{cd}_{t-1} + b_4 c_t$, where $0 < b_1, b_3 < 1$, and $0 < b_2, b_4 \leqslant 1$ are parameters. Output is produced with the technology $f(K_{t-1}, \zeta_t) = (1-\eta)K_{t-1} + \zeta_t$, where $0 < \eta \leqslant 1$ and ζ_t is a productivity disturbance, and divided between consumption and investment goods according to $b_5 c_t + b_6 \text{inv}_t = \text{GDP}_t$. Physical capital accumulates according to $K_t = b_7 K_{t-1} + b_8 \text{inv}_t$, where $0 < b_7 < 1, 0 < b_8 \leqslant 1$.

Using the definition of $(\text{cs}_t, \text{cd}_t, K_t)$ and the resource constraint we have

$$\text{cs}_t + \text{cd}_t = (b_1 + b_3)\text{cd}_{t-1} + \frac{b_2 + b_4}{b_5}\left((1-\eta)K_{t-1} + \zeta_t - \frac{b_6}{b_8}(K_t - b_7 K_{t-1})\right). \quad (2.10)$$

Letting $b_9 = b_1 + b_3$, $b_{10} = (b_2 + b_4)/b_5$, $b_{11} = b_{10}b_6/b_8$, $b_{12} = b_{11}b_7$, and using (2.10) in the utility function, the problem can be reformulated as

$$\max_{\{\text{cd}_t, K_t\}} E_0 \sum_t \beta^t \{\mathcal{C}_1[\text{cd}_t, K_t]' + \mathcal{C}_2[\text{cd}_{t-1}, k_{t-1}, \zeta_t, \upsilon_t]'\}' \times \{\mathcal{C}_1[\text{cd}_t, K_t]' + \mathcal{C}_2[\text{cd}_{t-1}, k_{t-1}, \zeta_t, \upsilon_t]'\},$$

where $\mathcal{C}_1 = [-1, -b_{11}]$, $\mathcal{C}_2 = [b_9, b_{12} + b_{10}(1-\eta), b_{10}, -1]$. If $\mathcal{C}_1'\mathcal{C}_1$ is invertible, and the shocks (ζ_t, υ_t) are known at each t, the first-order condition of the model imply $[\text{cd}_t, K_t]' = (\mathcal{C}_1'\mathcal{C}_1)^{-1}(\mathcal{C}_1'\mathcal{C}_2)[\text{cd}_{t-1}, K_{t-1}, \zeta_t, \upsilon_t]'$. Given $(\text{cd}_t, K_t, \zeta_t, \upsilon_t)$, values for cs_t and c_t can be found from (2.10) and from the consumption services constraint.

Economic models with quadratic objective functions and linear constraints can also be cast into a standard optimal control problem format. Such a format allows one to compute the solution with simple and fast algorithms.

Exercise 2.5. Take the model of example 2.3 but let $\upsilon_t = 0$. Cast it into an optimal linear regulator problem of the form $\max_{\{y_{1t}\}} E_0 \sum_t \beta^t (y_{2t}\mathcal{Q}_2 y_{2t}' + y_{1t}\mathcal{Q}_1 y_{1t}' + 2y_{2t}\mathcal{Q}_3 y_{1t}')$ subject to $y_{2t+1} = \mathcal{Q}_4 y_{2t} + \mathcal{Q}_5 y_{1t} + \mathcal{Q}_6 y_{3t+1}$, where y_{3t} is a vector of (serially correlated) shocks, y_{2t} a vector of states, and y_{1t} a vector of controls. Show the form of $\mathcal{Q}_i$, $i = 1, \dots, 6$.

A stochastic Lagrange multiplier approach works even when the Bellman equation cannot be used but requires a somewhat stronger set of assumptions to be applicable. Basically, we need the objective function to be strictly concave, differentiable, and its derivatives to have finite expectations; the constraints to be convex, differentiable, and their derivatives to have finite expectations; the choice variables to be observable at time t; the utility function to be bounded in expectations and to converge to a limit as $T \to \infty$; and the sequence of multipliers λ_t to be such that at the optimum the Kuhn–Tucker conditions hold with probability 1 (see Sims (2002) for a formal statement of these requirements).

It is straightforward to check that these conditions are satisfied for the simple RBC model we have considered so far. Then, letting $f_N = \partial f/\partial N$, $U_{c,t} = \partial u(c_t, c_{t-1}, N_t)/\partial c_t$, $U_{N,t} = \partial u(c_t, c_{t-1}, N_t)/\partial N_t$, the Euler equation for capital accumulation is

$$E_t \beta \frac{U_{c,t+1}}{U_{c,t}} [(1 - T^y) f_k + (1 - \delta)] - 1 = 0, \tag{2.11}$$

while the intratemporal marginal condition between consumption and labor is

$$\frac{U_{c,t}}{U_{N,t}} = -\frac{1}{(1 - T^y) f_N}. \tag{2.12}$$

Equations (2.11) and (2.12), the budget constraint, and the transversality conditions,

$\lim_{t\to\infty} \sup \beta^t (U_{c,t} - \lambda_t g_{c,t})(c_t - \hat{c}_t) \leqslant 0$, $\lim_{t\to\infty} \sup \beta^t (U_{N,t} - \lambda_t g_{N,t}) \times (N_t - \hat{N}_t) \leqslant 0$, where $g_{j,t}$ is the derivative of the constraints with respect to $j = c, N$, $\hat{j}_t$ is the optimal choice, and j_t any other choice, then need to be solved for (K_{t+1}, N_t, c_t), given (G_t, ζ_t, K_t). This is not easy. Since the system of equations is nonlinear and involves expectations of future variables, no analytical solution exists in general.

Exercise 2.6. Solve the problem of example 2.3 by using a Lagrange multiplier approach. Show that the conditions you need for the solution are the same as in example 2.3.

Versions of the basic RBC model with additional shocks, alternative inputs in the production function, or different market structures have been extensively examined in the macroeconomic literature. We consider some of these extensions in the next four exercises.

Exercise 2.7 (utility producing government expenditure). Consider a basic RBC model and suppose that government expenditure provides utility to the representative household, that private and public consumption are substitutes in the utility function, and that there is no habit in consumption, e.g., $U(c_t, c_{t-1}, G_t, N_t) = (c_t + \vartheta_{\mathrm{G}} G_t)^{\vartheta}(1 - N_t)^{1-\vartheta}$.

(i) Using steady-state relationships describe how private and public consumption are related. Is there some form of crowding out?

(ii) In a cross section of steady states, is it true that countries which have a higher level of government expenditure will also have lower levels of leisure, i.e., is it true that the income effect of distortionary taxation is higher when G is higher?

Exercise 2.8 (noncompetitive labor markets). Assume that, in a basic RBC model, there are one-period labor contracts. The contracts set the real wage on the basis of the expected marginal product of labor. Once shocks are realized, and given the contractual real wage, the firm chooses hours worked to maximize its profits. Write down the contractual wage equation and the optimal decision rule by firms. Compare it with a traditional Phillips curve relationship where $\ln N_t - E_{t-1}(\ln N_t) \propto \ln p_t - E_{t-1}(\ln p_t)$.

Exercise 2.9 (capacity utilization). Assume that $G_t = T_t = T^y = 0$, that the production function depends on capital (K_t) and its utilization (ku_t), and that it is of the form $f(K_t, \mathrm{ku}_t, N_t, \zeta_t) = \zeta_t (K_t \mathrm{ku}_t)^{1-\eta} N_t^{\eta}$. This production function allows firms to respond to shocks by varying utilization even when the stock of capital is fixed. Assume that capital depreciates in proportion to its use. In particular, assume that $\delta(\mathrm{ku}_t) = \delta_0 + \delta_1 \mathrm{ku}_t^{\delta_2}$, where δ_0, δ_1, and δ_2 are parameters.

(i) Write down the optimality conditions of the firm's problem and the Bellman equation.

(ii) Show that, if capital depreciates instantaneously, the solution of this problem is identical to the one of the standard RBC model examined in exercise 2.2.

Exercise 2.10 (production externalities). In a basic RBC model assume that output is produced with firm-specific inputs and the aggregate capital stock, i.e., $f(K_{it}, N_{it}, \zeta_t, K_t) = K_t^{\aleph} K_{it}^{1-\eta} N_{it}^{\eta} \zeta_t$, $\aleph > 0$, and $K_t = \int K_{it}\, \mathrm{d}i$.

(i) Derive the first-order conditions and discuss how to find optimal allocations.

(ii) Can the Bellman equation be used for this problem? What assumptions are violated?

Although it is common to proxy for technological disturbances with Solow residuals, such an approach is often criticized in the literature. The main reason is that such a proxy tends to overstate the variability of these shocks and may capture not only technology but also other sources of disturbances. The example below provides a case where this can occur.

Example 2.4. Suppose that output is produced with part-time hours (N^{PT}) and full-time hours (N^{FT}) according to the technology $\mathrm{GDP}_t = \zeta_t K_t^{1-\eta} (N_t^{\mathrm{FT}})^{\eta} + \zeta_t K_t^{1-\eta} (N_t^{\mathrm{PT}})^{\eta}$. Typically, Solow accounting proceeds by assuming that part-time and full-time hours are perfect substitutes and by using total hours in the production function, i.e., $\mathrm{GDP}_t = \zeta_t K_t^{1-\eta} (N_t^{\mathrm{FT}} + N^{\mathrm{PT}})^{\eta}$. An estimate of ζ_t is obtained via $\widehat{\ln \zeta_t} = \ln \mathrm{GDP}_t - (1-\eta) \ln K_t - \eta \ln(N_t^{\mathrm{FT}} + N_t^{\mathrm{PT}})$, where η is the share of labor income. It is easy to see that $\widehat{\ln \zeta_t} = \ln \zeta_t + \ln[(N_t^{\mathrm{FT}})^{\eta} + (N^{\mathrm{PT}})^{\eta}] - \eta \ln(N_t^{\mathrm{FT}} + N^{\mathrm{PT}})$, so that the variance of $\widehat{\ln \zeta_t}$ overestimates the variance of $\ln \zeta_t$. This is a general problem: whenever a variable is omitted from an estimated equation, the variance of the estimated residuals is at least as large as the variance of the true one. Note also that, if $N_t^{\mathrm{FT}} > N_t^{\mathrm{PT}}$ and if N_t^{FT} is less elastic than N_t^{PT} to shocks (e.g., if there are differential costs in adjusting full- and part-time hours), $\ln[(N_t^{\mathrm{FT}})^{\eta} + (N^{\mathrm{PT}})^{\eta}] - \eta \ln(N_t^{\mathrm{FT}} + N^{\mathrm{PT}}) > 0$. In this situation any (preference) shock which alters the relative composition of N^{FT} and N^{PT} could induce procyclical labor productivity movements, even if $\zeta_t = 0$, $\forall t$.

Several examples in this book are concerned with the apparently puzzling correlation between hours (employment) and labor productivity. Since with competitive markets labor productivity is equal to the real wage, we will interchangeably use the two, unless otherwise stated. What is puzzling is that the contemporaneous correlation between hours and labor productivity is roughly zero in the data while it is high and positive in an RBC model. We will study later how demand shocks can affect the magnitude of this correlation. In the next example we examine how the presence of government capital alters this correlation when an alternative source of technological disturbances is considered.

Example 2.5 (Finn). Suppose $u(c_t, c_{t-1}, N_t) = [c_t^{\vartheta}(1-N_t)^{1-\vartheta}]^{1-\varphi}/(1-\varphi)$, the budget constraint is $(1 - T^y) w_t N_t + [r_t - T^K(r_t - \delta)] K_t^{\mathrm{P}} + T_t + (1 + r_t^{\mathrm{B}}) B_t = c_t + \mathrm{inv}_t^{\mathrm{P}} + B_{t+1}$, and private capital evolves according to $K_{t+1}^{\mathrm{P}} = (1-\delta) K_t^{\mathrm{P}} + \mathrm{inv}_t^{\mathrm{P}}$, where T^K (T^y) are capital (income) taxes, r^{B} is the net rate on real bonds, and r_t the net return on private capital. Suppose also that the government budget constraint is $T^y w_t N_t + T^K(r_t - \delta)K_t^{\mathrm{P}} + B_{t+1} = \mathrm{inv}_t^{\mathrm{G}} + T_t + (1 + r_t^{\mathrm{B}})B_t$, and government investments increase government capital according to $\mathrm{inv}_t^{\mathrm{G}} = K_{t+1}^{\mathrm{G}} - (1-\delta)K_t^{\mathrm{G}}$. The production function is $\mathrm{GDP}_t = \zeta_t N^\eta (K^{\mathrm{P}})^{1-\eta}(K^{\mathrm{G}})^{\aleph}$ and $\aleph \geqslant 0$. Output is used for private consumption and investment.

This model does not have an analytic solution but some intuition on how hours and labor productivity move can be obtained by analyzing the effects of random variations in government investment. Suppose that $\mathrm{inv}_t^{\mathrm{G}}$ is higher than expected. Then, less income is available for private use and, at the same time, more public capital is available in the economy. Which will be the dominant factor depends on the size of the investment increase relative to $\aleph$. If it is small, there will be a positive instantaneous wealth effect so that hours, investment, and output decline while consumption and labor productivity increases. If it is large, a negative wealth effect will result, so hours and output will increase and consumption and labor productivity decrease. In both cases, despite the RBC structure, the contemporaneous correlation between hours and labor productivity will be negative.

2.1.2 Heterogeneous Agent Models

Although representative agent models constitute the backbone of current dynamic macroeconomics, the literature has started examining setups where some heterogeneities in either preferences, the income process, or the type of constraints that agent face are allowed for. The presence of heterogeneities does not change the structure of the problem: it is only required that the sum of individual variables match aggregate ones and that the planner problem is appropriately defined. The solution still requires casting the problem into a Bellman equation or setting up a stochastic Lagrange multiplier structure.

We consider a few of these models here. Since the scope is purely illustrative we restrict attention to situations where there are only two types of agent. The generalization to a larger but finite number of types of agent is straightforward.

Example 2.6 (a two-country model with full capital mobility). Consider two countries and one representative household in each country. The household in country i chooses sequences for consumption, hours, capital, and contingent claim holdings to maximize $E_0 \sum_{t=0}^{\infty} \beta^t [c_{it}^{\vartheta}(1 - N_{it})^{1-\vartheta}]^{1-\varphi}/(1-\varphi)$ subject to the following constraint,

$$c_{it} + \sum_j B_{jt+1} p_{jt}^{\mathrm{B}} \leqslant B_{jt} + w_{it} N_{it} + r_{it} K_{it} - \left(K_{it+1} - (1-\delta)K_{it} - \frac{b}{2}\left(\frac{K_{it+1}}{K_{it}} - 1\right)^2 K_{it} \right), \tag{2.13}$$

where $w_{it} N_{it}$ is labor income, $r_{it} K_{it}$ is capital income, B_{jt} is a set of Arrow–Debreu one-period contingent claims and p_{jt}^{B} is its price, b is an adjustment cost parameter, and δ is the depreciation rate of capital. Since financial markets are complete, the household can insure itself against all forms of idiosyncratic risk.

We assume that factors of production are immobile. The domestic household rents capital and labor to domestic firms which produce a homogeneous intermediate good by using a constant returns-to-scale technology. Domestic markets for factors of production are competitive and intermediate firms maximize profits. Intermediate goods are sold to domestic and foreign final-good-producing firms. The resource constraints are

$$\text{inty}^1_{1t} + \text{inty}^1_{2t} = \zeta_{1t} K_{1t}^{1-\eta} N_{1t}^{\eta}, \tag{2.14}$$

$$\text{inty}^2_{1t} + \text{inty}^2_{2t} = \zeta_{2t} K_{2t}^{1-\eta} N_{2t}^{\eta}, \tag{2.15}$$

where inty^1_{2t} are exports of goods from country 1 and inty^2_{1t} imports from country 2.

Final goods are an aggregate of the goods produced by intermediate firms of the two countries. They are assembled with a constant returns-to-scale technology $\text{GDP}_{it} = [a_i(\text{inty}^1_{it})^{1-a_3} + (1-a_i)(\text{inty}^2_{it})^{1-a_3}]^{1/(1-a_3)}$, where $a_3 \geqslant -1$ while a_1 and $(1-a_2)$ measure the domestic content of domestic spending. The resource constraint in the final goods market is $\text{GDP}_{it} = c_{it} + \text{inv}_{it}$. The two countries differ in the realizations of technology shocks. We assume $\ln(\zeta_{it})$ is an AR(1) with persistence $|\rho_\zeta| < 1$ and variance σ^2_ζ.

To map this setup into a Bellman equation assume that there is a social planner who attributes the weights $\mathbb{W}_1$ and $\mathbb{W}_2$ to the utilities of the households of the two countries. Let the planner's objective function be $u^{\text{SP}}(c_{1t}, c_{2t}, N_{1t}, N_{2t}) = \sum_{i=1}^{2} \mathbb{W}_i E_0 \sum_{t=0}^{\infty} \beta^t [c_{it}^{\vartheta}(1-N_{it})^{1-\vartheta}]^{1-\varphi}/(1-\varphi)$; let $y_{2t} = [K_{1t}, K_{2t}, B_{1t}]$, $y_{3t} = [\zeta_{1t}, \zeta_{2t}]$, and $y_{1t} = [\text{inty}^1_{it}, \text{inty}^2_{it}, c_{it}, N_{it}, K_{it+1}, B_{1t+1},\ i = 1, 2]$. Then the Bellman equation is given by $\mathbb{V}(y_2, y_3) = \max_{\{y_1\}} u^{\text{SP}}(c_1, c_2, N_1, N_2) + E\beta\mathbb{V}(y_2^+, y_3^+ \mid y_2, y_3)$ and the constraints are given by (2.14) and (2.15), the law of motion of the shocks and the resource constraint $c_{1t} + c_{2t} + K_{1t+1} + K_{2t+1} = \text{GDP}_{1t} + \text{GDP}_{2t} - \frac{1}{2}b(K_{1t+1}/K_{1t} - 1)^2 K_{1t} - \frac{1}{2}b(K_{2t+1}/K_{2t} - 1)^2 K_{2t}$.

Clearly, the value function has the same format as in (2.5). Since the functional form for utility is the same in both countries, the utility function of the social planner will also have the same functional form. Some information about the properties of the model can be obtained by examining the first-order conditions and the properties of the final good production function. In fact, we have

$$c_{it} + \text{inv}_{it} = p_{1t}\text{inty}^1_{it} + p_{2t}\text{inty}^2_{it}, \tag{2.16}$$

$$\text{ToT}_t = \frac{p_{2t}}{p_{1t}}, \tag{2.17}$$

$$\text{nx}_t = \text{inty}^1_{2t} - \text{ToT}_t\text{inty}^2_{1t}. \tag{2.18}$$

Equation (2.16) implies that output of the final good is allocated to the inputs according to their prices, $p_{2t} = \partial\,\text{GDP}_{1t}/\partial\,\text{inty}^2_{1t}$, $p_{1t} = \partial\,\text{GDP}_{1t}/\partial\,\text{inty}^1_{1t}$; (2.17) gives an expression for the terms of trade and (2.18) defines the trade balance.

Exercise 2.11. (i) Show that the demand functions for the two goods in country 1 are

$$\begin{aligned}\text{inty}_{1t}^{1} &= a_1^{1/a_3}[a_1^{1/a_3} + (1-a_1)^{1/a_3}\,\text{ToT}_t^{-(1-a_3)/a_3}]^{-a_3/(1-a_3)}\,\text{GDP}_{1t},\\ \text{inty}_{1t}^{2} &= (1-a_1)^{1/a_3}\,\text{ToT}_t^{-1/a_3}\\ &\qquad\times [a_1^{1/a_3} + (1-a_1)^{1/a_3}\,\text{ToT}_t^{-(1-a_3)/a_3}]^{-a_3/(1-a_3)}\,\text{GDP}_{1t}.\end{aligned}$$

(ii) Describe how the terms of trade relate to the variability of final goods demands.

(iii) Noting that $\text{ToT}_t = (1-a_1)(\text{inty}_{1t}^2)^{-a_3}/(a_1(\text{inty}_{1t}^1)^{-a_3})$, show that when the elasticity of substitution between domestic and foreign good $1/a_3$ is high, any excess of demand in either of the two goods induces small changes in the terms of trade and large changes in the quantities used.

Exercise 2.12. Consider the same two-country model of example 2.6 but now assume that financial markets are incomplete. That is, households are forced to trade only a one-period bond which is assumed to be in zero net supply (i.e., $B_{1t} + B_{2t} = 0$). How would you solve this problem? What does the assumption of incompleteness imply? Would it make a difference if the household of country 1 has limited borrowing capabilities, e.g., $B_{1t} \leqslant K_{1t}$?

Interesting insights can be added to a basic RBC model when some agents are not optimizers.

Example 2.7. Suppose that the economy is populated by standard RBC households (their fraction in the total population is Ψ) which maximize $E_0 \sum_t \beta^t u(c_t, c_{t-1}, N_t)$ subject to the constraint $c_t + \text{inv}_t + B_{t+1} = w_t N_t + r_t K_t + (1+r_t^{\text{B}})B_t + \text{prf}_t + T_t$, where prf_t are the firm's profits, T_t are government transfers, and B_t are real bonds. Suppose that capital accumulates according to $K_{t+1} = (1-\delta)K_t + \text{inv}_t$. The remaining $1-\Psi$ households are myopic and consume all their income every period, that is, $c_t^{\text{RT}} = w_t N_t + T_t^{\text{RT}}$ and supply all their work time inelastically at each t.

Rule-of-thumb households play the role of an insensitive buffer in this economy. Therefore, total hours, aggregate output, and aggregate consumption will be much less sensitive to shocks than in an economy where all households are optimizers. For example, government expenditure shocks crowd out consumption less and under some efficiency wage specification, they can even make it increase.

Exercise 2.13 (Kiyotaki and Moore). Consider a model with two goods, land La, which is in fixed supply, and fruit which is not storable, and a continuum of two types of agent: farmers of measure 1 and gatherers of measure Ψ. Utilities are of the form $E_t \sum_t \beta_j^t c_{j,t}$, where $c_{j,t}$ is the consumption of fruit of type j, $j =$ farmers, gatherers, and where $\beta_{\text{farmers}} < \beta_{\text{gatherers}}$. Let p_t^{L} be the price of land in terms of fruit and r_t the rate of exchange of a unit of fruit today for tomorrow. There are technologies to produce fruit from land. Farmers use $f(\text{La}_t)_{\text{farmer}} = (b_1 + b_2)\text{La}_{t-1}$, where b_1 is the tradable part and b_2 the bruised one (nontradable); gatherers use

$f(\mathrm{La}_t)_{\text{gatherer}}$, where f_{gatherer} displays decreasing returns-to-scale and all output is tradable. The budget constraint for the two agents is $p_t^{\mathrm{L}}(\mathrm{La}_{jt} - \mathrm{La}_{jt-1}) + r_t B_{jt-1} + c_{jt}^{\dagger} = f(\mathrm{La}_t)_j + B_{jt}$, where $c_{jt}^{\dagger} = c_{jt} + b_2\mathrm{La}_{t-1}$ for farmers and $c_{jt}^{\dagger} = c_{jt}$ for gatherers, B_{jt} are loans, and $p_t^{\mathrm{L}}(\mathrm{La}_{jt} - \mathrm{La}_{jt-1})$ is the value of new land acquisitions. The farmers' technology is idiosyncratic so that only farmer i has the skill to produce fruit from it. The gatherers' technology does not require specific skills. Note that, if no labor is used, fruit output is zero.

(i) Show that in equilibrium $r_t = r = 1/\beta_{\text{gatherers}}$ and that for farmers to be able to borrow a collateral is required. Show that the maximum amount of borrowing is $B_t \leqslant p_{t+1}^{\mathrm{L}}\mathrm{La}_t/r$.

(ii) Show that, if there is no aggregate uncertainty, farmers borrow from gatherers up to their maximum, invest in land, and consume $b_2\mathrm{La}_{t-1}$. That is, for farmers $\mathrm{La}_t = (1/(p_t^{\mathrm{L}} - r^{-1}p_{t+1}^{\mathrm{L}}))(b_1 + p_t^{\mathrm{L}})\mathrm{La}_{t-1} - rB_{t-1}$, where $p_t^{\mathrm{L}} - r^{-1}p_{t+1}^{\mathrm{L}}$ is the user cost of land (the down payment needed to purchase land) and $B_t = r^{-1} \times p_{t+1}^{\mathrm{L}}\mathrm{La}_t$. Argue that, if p_t^{L} increases, La_t and B_t will increase provided $b_1 + p_t^{\mathrm{L}} > rB_{t-1}/\mathrm{La}_{t-1}$. Hence, the higher the land price, the higher the net worth of farmers and the more they will borrow.

2.1.3 *Monetary Models*

The next set of models explicitly includes monetary factors. Finding a role for money in a general equilibrium model is difficult: with a full set of Arrow–Debreu claims, money is a redundant asset. Therefore, frictions of some sort need to be introduced for money to play some role. This means that the allocations produced by the competitive equilibrium are no longer optimal and that the Bellman equation formulation needs to be modified to take this into account (see, for example, Cooley 1995, pp. 50–60). We focus attention on two popular specifications — a competitive model with transactional frictions and a monopolistic competitive framework where either sticky prices or sticky wages or both are exogenously imposed — and examine what they have to say about two questions of interest to macroeconomists: do monetary shocks generate liquidity effects? That is, do monetary shocks imply negative comovements between short-term interest rates and (a narrow measure of) money? Do expansionary monetary shocks imply expansionary and persistent output effects?

Example 2.8 (Cooley and Hansen). The representative household maximizes $E_0 \times \sum_t \beta^t u(c_{1t}, c_{2t}, N_t)$, where c_{1t} is consumption of a cash good, c_{2t} is consumption of a credit good, and N_t is the number of hours worked. The budget constraint is $c_{1t} + c_{2t} + \mathrm{inv}_t + M_{t+1}/p_t \leqslant w_t N_t + r_t k_t + M_t/p_t + T_t/p_t$, where $T_t = M_{t+1} - M_t$ and p_t is the price level. There is a cash-in-advance constraint that forces households to buy c_{1t} with cash. We require $p_t c_{1t} \leqslant M_t + T_t$ and assume that the monetary authority sets $\ln M_{t+1}^s = \ln M_t^s + \ln M_t^{\mathrm{g}}$, where $\ln M_t^{\mathrm{g}}$ is an AR(1) process with mean $\bar{M}$, persistence ρ_M, and variance σ_M^2. The household chooses sequences for the two consumption goods, for hours, for investment, and for real balances to satisfy the budget constraint. We assume that shocks are realized at the beginning of each t so that the household knows the value of the shocks when taking decisions. The resource constraint is $c_{1t} + c_{2t} + \text{inv}_t = f(K_t, N_t, \zeta_t)$, where $\ln \zeta_t$ is an AR(1) process with persistence ρ_ζ and variance σ_ζ^2. Since the expected rate of return on money is lower than the expected return on capital, the cash-in-advance constraint will be binding and agents hold just the exact amount of money needed to purchase c_{1t}.

When $\bar{M} > 0$, money (and prices) grow over time. To map this setup into a stationary problem define $M_t^* = M_t / M_t^s$ and $p_t^* = p_t / M_{t+1}^s$. The value function is

$$\begin{aligned} V(K, k, M^*, \zeta, M^g) &\\ = \max \Bigg[U\Bigg(&\frac{M^* + M^g - 1}{p^* M^g}; wN + [r + (1-\delta)]k - k^+ - \frac{(M^*)^+}{p^*}; N\Bigg)\Bigg] \\ &+ \beta E V[K^+, k^+, (M^*)^+, \zeta^+, (M^g)^+], \end{aligned} \tag{2.19}$$

where $K^+ = (1-\delta)K + \text{INV}$, $k^+ = (1-\delta)k + \text{inv}$, $c_1 = (M^* + M^g - 1)/(M^g p^*)$, and K represents the aggregate capital stock. The problem is completed by the consistency conditions $k^+ = h_1(K, \zeta, M^g)$, $N = h_2(K, \zeta, M^g)$, $p^* = h_3(K, \zeta, M^g)$, where h_j are functions mapping aggregate shocks and states into optimal per capita decision variables and the aggregate price level.

Not much can be done with this model without taking some approximation. However, we can show that monetary disturbances have perverse output effects and produce expected inflation but not liquidity effects. Suppose $c_{2t} = 0, \forall t$. Then an unexpected increase in M_t^g makes agents substitute away from c_{1t} (which is now more expensive) toward credit goods—leisure and investment—which are cheaper. Hence, consumption and hours fall while investment increases. With a standard Cobb–Douglas production function output then declines. Also, since positive monetary shocks increase inflation, the nominal interest rate will increase, because both the real rate and expected inflation have temporarily increased. Hence, a surprise increase in M_t^g does not produce a liquidity effect or output expansions.

There are several ways to correct for the lack of positive correlation between money and output. For example, introducing one-period labor contracts (as we have done in exercise 2.8) does change the response of output to monetary shocks. The next exercise provides a way to generate the right output and interest rate effects by introducing a loan market, forcing the household to take decisions before shocks are realized and the firm to borrow to finance its wage bill.

Exercise 2.14 (working capital). Consider the same economy of example 2.8 with $c_{2t} = 0, \forall t$, but assume that the household deposits part of its money balances at the beginning of each t in banks. Assume that deposit decisions are taken before shocks occur and that the representative firm faces a working capital constraint, i.e., it has to pay for the factors of production before the receipts from the sale of the goods are received. The representative household maximizes utility by choice of consumption, labor, capital, and deposits, i.e., $\max_{\{c_t, N_t, K_{t+1}, \text{dep}_t\}} E_0 \sum_t \beta^t \times [c_t^{\vartheta}(1-N_t)^{1-\vartheta}]^{1-\varphi}/(1-\varphi)$. There are three constraints. First, goods must be purchased with money, i.e., $c_t p_t \leqslant M_t - \text{dep}_t + w_t N_t$. Second, there is a budget constraint $M_{t+1} = \text{prf}_{1t} + \text{prf}_{2t} + r_t p_t K_t + M_t - \text{dep}_t + w_t N_t - c_t p_t - \text{inv}_t p_t$, where $\text{prf}_{1t}(\text{prf}_{2t})$ represent the share of firm's (bank's) profits and r_t is the real return to capital. Third, capital accumulation is subject to an adjustment cost $b \geqslant 0$, i.e., $\text{inv}_t = K_{t+1} - (1-\delta)K_t - \frac{1}{2}b(K_{t+1}/K_t - 1)^2 K_t$. The representative firm rents capital and labor and borrows cash from the representative banks to pay for the wage bill. The problem is $\max_{\{K_t, N_t\}} \text{prf}_{1t} = p_t \zeta_t K_t^{1-\eta} N_t^{\eta} - p_t r_t K_t - (1+i_t) w_t N_t$, where i_t is the nominal interest rate. The representative bank takes deposits and lends them together with new money to firms. Profits, prf_{2t}, are distributed pro rata to the household. The monetary authority sets its instrument according to

$$M_t^{a_0} = i_t^{a_1} \text{GDP}_t^{a_2} \pi_t^{a_3} M_t^{\text{g}}, \tag{2.20}$$

where a_i are parameters and $\text{GDP}_t = \zeta_t K_t^{1-\eta} N_t^{\eta}$. For example, if $a_0 = 0$, $a_1 = 1$, the monetary authority sets the nominal interest rate as a function of output and inflation and stands ready to provide money when the economy needs it. Let $(\ln \zeta_t, \ln M_t^{\text{g}})$ be AR(1) processes with persistence ρ_ζ, ρ_M and variances σ_ζ^2, σ_M^2.

(i) Set $b = 0$. Show that the labor demand and the labor supply are $-U_{N,t} = (w_t/p_t) E_t \beta U_{c,t+1} p_t / p_{t+1}$ and $w_t i_t / p_t = f_{N,t}$. Argue that labor supply changes in anticipation of inflation while labor demand is directly affected by interest rate changes so that output will be positively related to money shocks.

(ii) Show that the optimal saving decision satisfies $E_{t-1} U_{c,t}/p_t = E_{t-1} i_t \beta \times U_{c,t+1}/p_{t+1}$. How does this compare with the saving decisions of the basic cash-in-advance (CIA) model of example 2.8?

(iii) Show that the money demand can be written as $p_t \text{GDP}_t / M_t = 1/(1 + \eta / i_t)$. Conclude that velocity $p_t \text{GDP}_t / M_t$ and the nominal rate are positively related and that a liquidity effect is generated in response to monetary disturbances.

Exercise 2.15 (Dunlop–Tarshis puzzle). Suppose the representative household maximizes $E_0 \sum_{t=0}^{\infty} \beta^t [\ln c_t + \vartheta_{\text{m}} \ln M_{t+1}/p_t + \vartheta_N \ln(1 - N_t)]$ subject to $c_t + M_{t+1}/p_t + K_{t+1} = w_t N_t + r_t K_t + (M_t + T_t)/p_t$. Let $\pi_{t+1} = p_{t+1}/p_t$ be the inflation rate. The representative firm rents capital from the household and produces using $\text{GDP}_t = \zeta_t K_t^{1-\eta} N_t^{\eta}$, where $\ln \zeta_t$ is a technological disturbance and capital depreciates in one period. Let the quantity of money evolve according to $\ln M_{t+1}^s = \ln M_t^s + \ln M_t^{\text{g}}$ and assume that at each t the government takes away G_t units of output.

(i) Assume $G_t = G$, $\forall t$. Write down the first-order conditions for the optimization problem of the household and the firm and find the competitive equilibrium for $(c_t, K_{t+1}, N_t, w_t, r_t, M_{t+1}/p_t)$.

(ii) Show that, in equilibrium, hours worked are independent of the shocks, that output and hours are uncorrelated, and that real wages are perfectly correlated with output.

(iii) Show that monetary disturbances are neutral. Are they also superneutral, i.e., do changes in the growth rate of money have real effects?

(iv) Suppose there are labor contracts where the nominal wage rate is fixed one period in advance according to $w_t = E_{t-1}M_t + \ln(\eta) - \ln(\vartheta_{\mathrm{m}}(\eta\beta)/(1-\beta)) - E_{t-1}\ln N_t$. Show that monetary disturbances produce a contemporaneous negative correlation between real wages and output.

(v) Now assume that G_t is stochastic and set $\ln M_t^{\mathrm{g}} = 0, \forall t$. What is the effect of government expenditure shocks on the correlation between real wages and output? Give some intuition for why adding labor contracts or government expenditure could reduce the correlation between real wages and output found in (ii).

The final type of model we consider adds nominal rigidities to a structure where monopolistic competitive firms produce intermediate goods which they sell to competitive final goods producers.

Example 2.9 (sticky prices). Suppose the representative household maximizes $E_0\sum_t \beta^t[c_t^{\vartheta}(1-N_t)^{1-\vartheta}]^{1-\varphi}/(1-\varphi)+(1/(1-\varphi_{\mathrm{m}}))(M_{t+1}/p_t)^{1-\varphi_{\mathrm{m}}}$ by choices of c_t, N_t, K_{t+1}, M_{t+1} subject to the budget constraint $p_t(c_t + \mathrm{inv}_t) + B_{t+1} + M_{t+1} \leqslant r_t p_t K_t + M_t + (1+i_t)B_t + w_t N_t + \mathrm{prf}_t$ and the capital accumulation equation $\mathrm{inv}_t = K_{t+1} - (1-\delta)K_t - \frac{1}{2}b(K_{t+1}/K_t - 1)^2 K_t$, where b is an adjustment cost parameter. Here $\mathrm{prf}_t = \int \mathrm{prf}_{it}\, di$ are profits obtained from owning intermediate firms. There are two types of firm: monopolistic competitive, intermediate-good-producing firms and perfectly competitive, final-good-producing firms. Final goods firms take the continuum of intermediate goods and bundle it up for final consumption. The production function for final goods is $\mathrm{GDP}_t = (\int_0^1 \mathrm{inty}_{it}^{1/(1+\varsigma_p)}\, di)^{1+\varsigma_p}$, where $\varsigma_p > 0$. Profit maximization implies that the demand for each input i is $\mathrm{inty}_{it}/\mathrm{GDP}_t = (p_{it}/p_t)^{-(1+\varsigma_p)/\varsigma_p}$, where p_{it} is the price of intermediate good i and p_t the price of the final good, $p_t = (\int_0^1 p_{it}^{-1/\varsigma_p}\, di)^{-\varsigma_p}$.

Intermediate firms minimize costs and choose prices to maximize profits. Price decisions cannot be taken every period: only $(1-\zeta_{\mathrm{p}})$ of the firms are allowed to change prices at t. Their costs-minimization problem is $\min_{\{K_{it},N_{it}\}}(r_t K_{it} + w_t N_{it})$ subject to $\mathrm{inty}_{it} = \zeta_t K_{it}^{1-\eta} N_{it}^{\eta}$ and their profit-maximization problem is $\max_{\{p_{it+j}\}} E_t \sum_j \beta^j (U_{c,t+j}/p_{t+j})\zeta_{\mathrm{p}}^j \mathrm{prf}_{it+j}$, where $\beta^j U_{c,t+1}/p_{t+1}$ is the value of a unit of profit, prf_{it}, to shareholders next period, subject to the demand function from final goods firms. Here $\mathrm{prf}_{t+j} = (p_{it+j} - \mathrm{mc}_{it+j})\mathrm{inty}_{it+j}$ and mc_{it} are nominal marginal costs.

We assume that the monetary authority uses a rule of the form (2.20). Since only a fraction of the firms can change prices at each t, aggregate prices evolve according to $p_t = (\zeta_{\mathrm{p}} p_{t-1}^{-1/\varsigma_p} + (1-\zeta_{\mathrm{p}})\tilde{p}_t^{-1/\varsigma_p})^{-\varsigma_p}$, where $\tilde{p}_t$ is the common solution (all firms allowed to change prices are identical) to the following optimality condition (dropping the subscript i):

$$0 = E_t \sum_j \beta^j \zeta_{\mathrm{p}}^j \frac{U_{c,t+j}}{p_{t+j}} \left(\frac{\pi^j p_t}{1+\varsigma_p} - \mathrm{mc}_{t+j} \right) \mathrm{inty}_{t+j}, \tag{2.21}$$

where π is the steady-state inflation rate. Hence, intermediate firms choose prices so that the discounted marginal revenues equals the discounted marginal costs in expected terms. Note that, if $\zeta_{\mathrm{p}} \to 0$ and no capital is present, (2.21) reduces to the standard condition that the real wage equals the marginal product of labor. Expression (2.21) is the basis for the so-called New Keynesian Phillips curve (see, for example, Woodford 2003, chapter 3), an expression relating current inflation to expected future inflation and to current marginal costs. To explicitly obtain such a relationship, (2.21) needs to be log-linearized around the steady state.

To see what expression (2.21) involves, consider the case in which utility is logarithmic in consumption, linear in leisure, and the marginal utility of real balances is negligible, i.e., $U(c_t, N_t, M_{t+1}/p_t) = \ln c_t + (1 - N_t)$, output is produced with labor, prices are set every two periods, and, in each period, half of the firms change their price. Optimal price setting is

$$\frac{\tilde{p}_t}{p_t} = (1+\varsigma_p) E_t \left(\frac{U_{c,t} c_t w_t + \beta U_{c,t+1} c_{t+1} w_{t+1} \pi_{t+1}^{(1+\varsigma_p)/\varsigma_p}}{U_{c,t} c_t + \beta U_{c,t+1} c_{t+1} \pi_{t+1}^{1/\varsigma_p}} \right), \tag{2.22}$$

where $\tilde{p}_t$ is the optimal price, p_t the aggregate price level, w_t the wage rate, and $\pi_t = p_{t+1}/p_t$ the inflation rate. Ideally, firms would like to charge a price which is a constant markup $(1+\varsigma_p)$ over marginal (labor) costs. However, because individual prices are set for two periods, firms cannot do this and when prices are allowed to be changed, they are set as a constant markup over current and expected future marginal costs. Note that, if there are no shocks, $\pi_{t+1} = 1$, $w_{t+1} = w_t$, $c_{t+1} = c_t$, and $\tilde{p}_t/p_t = (1+\varsigma_p) w_t$.

Exercise 2.16. (i) Cast the household problem of example 2.9 into a Bellman equation format. Define states, controls, and the value function.

(ii) Show that, if prices are set one period in advance, the solution to (2.21) is

$$p_{it} = (1+\varsigma_p) E_{t-1} \frac{E_t (U_{c,t+j}/p_{t+j}) p_t^{(1+\varsigma_p)/\varsigma_p} \mathrm{inty}_{it}}{E_{t-1}(U_{c,t+j}/p_{t+j}) p_t^{(1+\varsigma_p)/\varsigma_p} \mathrm{inty}_{it}} \mathrm{mc}_{it}.$$

Give conditions that ensure that intermediate firms set prices as a constant markup over marginal costs.

(iii) Intuitively explain why monetary expansions are likely to produce positive output effects. What conditions need to be satisfied for monetary expansions to produce a liquidity effect?

Extensions of the model that also allow for sticky wages are straightforward. We ask the reader to study a model with both sticky prices and sticky wages in the next exercise.

Exercise 2.17 (sticky wages). Assume that households are monopolistic competitive in the labor market so that they can choose the wage at which to work. Suppose capital is in fixed supply and that the period utility function is $u_1(c_t)+u_2(1-N_t)+(M_{t+1}/p_t)^{1-\varphi_\mathrm{m}}/(1-\varphi_\mathrm{m})$. Suppose that households set nominal wages in a staggered way and that a fraction $1-\zeta_\mathrm{w}$ can do this every period. When the household is allowed to reset the wage, she maximizes the discounted sum of utilities subject to the budget constraint.

(i) Show that utility maximization leads to

$$E_t \sum_{j=0}^{\infty} \beta^j \zeta_\mathrm{w}^j \left(\frac{\pi^j w_t}{(1+\varsigma_\mathrm{w}) p_{t+j}} U_{1,t+j} + U_{2,t+j} \right) N_{t+j} = 0, \tag{2.23}$$

where β is the discount factor and $\varsigma_\mathrm{w} > 0$ is a parameter in the labor aggregator $N_t = [\int N_t(i)^{1/(1+\varsigma_\mathrm{w})}\, \mathrm{d}i]^{1+\varsigma_\mathrm{w}}$, $i \in [0,1]$. (Note: whenever the wage rate cannot be changed $w_{t+j} = \pi^j w_t$, where π is the steady-state inflation.)

(ii) Show that, if $\zeta_\mathrm{w} = 0$, (2.23) reduces to $w_t/p_t = -U_{2,t}/U_{1,t}$.

(iii) Calculate the equilibrium output, the real rate, and the real wage when prices and wages are flexible.

Exercise 2.18 (Taylor contracts). Consider a sticky wage model with no capital. Here labor demand is $N_t = \mathrm{GDP}_t$, real marginal costs are $\mathrm{mc}_t = w_t = 1$, where w_t is the real wage and $\mathrm{GDP}_t = c_t$. Suppose consumption and real balances are not substitutable in utility so that the money demand function is $M_{t+1}/p_t = c_t$. Suppose $\ln M_{t+1}^s = \ln M_t^s + \ln M_t^\mathrm{g}$, where $\ln M^\mathrm{g}$ is i.i.d. with mean $\bar{M} > 0$ and assume two-period staggered labor contracts.

(i) Show that $w_t = [0.5(\tilde{w}_t/p_t)^{-1/\varsigma_\mathrm{w}} + (w_{t-1}/p_t)^{-1/\varsigma_\mathrm{w}}]^{-\varsigma_\mathrm{w}}$, where $\tilde{w}_t$ is the nominal wage reset at t.

(ii) Show that $\pi_t \equiv p_t/p_{t-1} = [(\tilde{w}_{t-1}/p_{t-1})^{-1/\varsigma_\mathrm{w}}/(2 - \tilde{w}_t/p_t^{-1/\varsigma_\mathrm{w}})]^{-\varsigma_\mathrm{w}}$ and that $N_{it} = N_t[(\tilde{w}_t/p_t)/w_t]^{-(1+\varsigma_\mathrm{w})/\varsigma_\mathrm{w}}$ if the wage was set at t and $N_{it} = N_t[(\tilde{w}_{t-1}/p_{t-1})/(w_t\pi_t)]^{-(1+\varsigma_\mathrm{w})/\varsigma_\mathrm{w}}$ if the wage was set at $t-1$.

(iii) Show that if utility is linear in N_t, monetary shocks have no persistence.

While expansionary monetary shocks in models with nominal rigidities produce expansionary output effects, their size is typically small and their persistence minimal, unless nominal rigidities are extreme. The next example shows a way to make output effects of monetary shocks sizeable.

Example 2.10 (Benhabib and Farmer). Consider an economy where utility is $E_0 \sum_t \beta^t [c^{1-\varphi_c}/(1-\varphi_c) - (1/(1-\varphi_n))(n_t^{1-\varphi_n}/N_t^{\varphi_N-\varphi_n})]$, where n_t is individual employment, N_t is aggregate employment, and ϕ_c, ϕ_n, ϕ_N are parameters. Suppose output is produced with labor and real balances, i.e., $\mathrm{GDP}_t = (a_1 N_t^\eta + a_2(M_t/p_t)^\eta)^{1/\eta}$, where η is a parameter. The consumers' budget constraint is $M_t/p_t = M_{t-1}/p_t + f[N_t, (M_{t-1}+M_t^\mathrm{g})/p_t] - c_t$ and assume that M_t^g is i.i.d. with mean $\bar{M} \geqslant 0$. Equilibrium in the labor market implies $-U_N/U_c = f_N(N_t, M_t/p_t)$

and the demand for money is $E_t(f_{M,t+1}U_{c,t+1}/\pi_{t+1}) = E_t(i_{t+1}U_{c,t+1}/\pi_{t+1})$, where $1 + i_t$ is the gross nominal rate on a one-period bond, π_t the inflation rate, and $f_M = \partial f/\partial(M/p)$. These two standard conditions are somewhat special in this model. Decentralizing in a competitive equilibrium and log-linearizing the labor market condition, we have $\varphi_c \ln c_t + \varphi_n n_t - (\varphi_N + \varphi_n) \ln N_t = \ln w_t - \ln p_t$. Since agents are all identical, the aggregate labor supply will be a downward-sloping function of the real wage and given by $\varphi_c \ln c_t - \varphi_N \ln N_t = \ln w_t - \ln p_t$. Hence, a small shift in labor demand increases consumption (which is equal to output in equilibrium) and makes real wages fall and employment increase. As a consequence, a demand shock can generate procyclical consumption and employment paths. Note also that, since money enters the production function, an increase in money could shift labor demand as in the working-capital model. However, contrary to that case, labor market effects can be large because of the slope of the aggregate labor supply curve, and this occurs even when money is relatively unimportant as a productive factor.

We will see in exercise 2.34 that there are other more conventional ways to increase output persistence following monetary shocks while maintaining low price stickiness.

Sticky price models applied to an international context produce two interesting implications for exchange rate determination and for international risk sharing.

Example 2.11 (Obstfeld and Rogoff). Consider a structure like the one of example 2.9 where prices are chosen one period in advance, there are two countries, purchasing power parity holds, and international financial markets are incomplete, in the sense that only a real bond, denominated in the composite consumption good, is traded. In this economy the domestic nominal interest rate is priced by arbitrage and satisfies $1 + i_{1t} = E_t(p_{1t+1}/p_{1t})(1 + r_t^{\mathrm{B}})$, where r_t^{B} is the real rate on internationally traded bonds and uncovered interest parity holds, i.e., $1 + i_{1t} = E_t(\mathrm{ner}_{t+1}/\mathrm{ner}_t)(1+i_{2t})$, where $\mathrm{ner}_t = p_{1t}/p_{2t}$ and p_{jt} is the consumption-based money price index in country j, $j = 1, 2$. Furthermore, the Euler equations imply the international risk-sharing condition $E_t[(c_{1t+1}/c_{1t})^{-\varphi} - (c_{2t+1}/c_{2t})^{-\varphi}] = 0$. Hence, while consumption growth need not be a random walk, the difference in scaled consumption growth is a martingale difference.

The money demand in country j is $M_{jt+1}/p_{jt} = \vartheta_{\mathrm{m}} c_{jt}[(1 + i_{jt})/i_{jt}]^{1/\varphi_{\mathrm{m}}}$, $j = 1, 2$. Using uncovered interest parity and log-linearizing, $\hat{M}_{1t} - \hat{M}_{2t} \propto (1/\varphi_{\mathrm{m}})(\hat{c}_{2t} - \hat{c}_{1t}) + [\beta/(1-\beta)\varphi_{\mathrm{m}}]\,\widehat{\mathrm{ner}}_t$, where the hat indicates deviations from the steady state. Hence, whenever $\hat{M}_{1t} - \hat{M}_{2t} \neq 0$ or $\hat{c}_{2t} - \hat{c}_{1t} \neq 0$, the nominal exchange rate jumps to a new equilibrium.

Variations or refinements of the price (wage) technology exist in the literature (see Rotemberg 1984; Dotsey et al. 1999). Since these refinements are tangential to the scope of this chapter, we invite the interested reader to consult the original sources for details and extensions.

2.2 Approximation Methods

As mentioned, finding a solution to the Bellman equation is, in general, complicated. The Bellman equation is a functional relationship and a fixed point needs to be found in the space of functions. When the regularity conditions for existence and uniqueness are satisfied, calculation of this fixed point requires iterations which involve the computation of expectations and the maximization of the value function.

We have also seen in example 2.2 and exercise 2.3 that, when the utility function is quadratic (logarithmic) and time separable and the constraints are linear, the form of the value function and of the decision rules is known. In these two situations, if the solution is known to be unique, the method of undetermined coefficients can be used to find the unknown parameters. Quadratic utility functions are not very appealing, however, as they imply implausible behavior for consumption and asset returns. Log-utility functions are easy to manipulate but they are also restrictive regarding the attitude of agents toward risk. Based on a large body of empirical research, the macroeconomic literature typically uses a general power specification for preferences. With this choice one has either to iterate on the Bellman equation or resort to approximations to find a solution.

We have also mentioned that solving general nonlinear expectational equations, such as those emerging from the first-order conditions of a stochastic Lagrangian multiplier problem, is complicated. Therefore, approximations also need to be employed in this case.

This section considers a few approximation methods currently used in the literature. The first approximates the objective function quadratically around the steady state. In the second, the approximation is calculated forcing the states and the exogenous variables to take only a finite number of possible values. This method can be applied to both the value function and to the first-order conditions. The other two approaches directly approximate the optimal conditions of the problem. In one case a log-linear (or a second-order) approximation around the steady state is calculated. In the other, the expectational equations are approximated by nonlinear functions and a solution is obtained by finding the parameters of these functions.

2.2.1 Quadratic Approximations

Quadratic approximations are easy to compute but work under two restrictive conditions. The first is that there exists a point — typically, the steady state — around which the approximation can be taken. Although this requirement may appear innocuous, it should be noted that some models do not possess a steady or a stationary state and in others the steady state may be multiple. The second is that local dynamics are well-approximated by linear difference equations. Consequently, such approximations are inappropriate when problems involve large perturbations away from the approximation point (e.g., policy shifts), dynamic paths are nonlinear, or transitional issues are considered. Moreover, they are likely to give incorrect answers for problems with inequality (e.g., borrowing or irreversibility) constraints, since the nonstochastic steady state ignores them.

Quadratic approximations of the objective function are used in situations where the social planner decisions generate competitive equilibrium allocations. When this is not the case the method requires some adaptation to take into account the fact that aggregate variables are distinct from individual ones (see, for example, Hansen and Sargent 2005; Cooley 1995, chapter 2), but the same principle works in both cases.

Quadratic approximations can be applied to both value function and Lagrangian multiplier problems. We will discuss applications to the first type of problem only since the extension to the second type of problem is straightforward. Let the Bellman equation be

$$\mathbb{V}(y_2, y_3) = \max_{\{y_1\}} \tilde{u}(y_1, y_2, y_3) + \beta E \mathbb{V}(y_2^+, y_3^+ \mid y_2, y_3), \tag{2.24}$$

where y_2 is an $m_2 \times 1$ vector of the states, y_3 is an $m_3 \times 1$ vector of exogenous variables, and y_1 is an $m_1 \times 1$ vector of the controls. Suppose that the constrains are $y_2^+ = h(y_3, y_1, y_2)$ and the law of motion of the exogenous variables is $y_3^+ = \rho_3 y_3 + \epsilon^+$, where h is continuous and ϵ a vector of martingale difference disturbances. Using the constraints into (2.24) we have

$$\mathbb{V}(y_2, y_3) = \max_{\{y_2^+\}} u(y_2, y_3, y_2^+) + \beta E \mathbb{V}(y_2^+, y_3^+ \mid y_2, y_3). \tag{2.25}$$

Let $\bar{u}(y_2, y_3, y_2^+)$ be the quadratic approximation of $u(y_2, y_3, y_2^+)$ around $(\bar{y}_2, \bar{y}_3, \bar{y}_2)$. If $\mathbb{V}^0$ is quadratic, then (2.25) maps quadratic functions into quadratic functions and the limit value of $V(y_2, y_3)$ will also be quadratic. Hence, under some regularity conditions, the solution to the functional equation is quadratic and the decision rule for y_2^+ linear. When the solution to (2.25) is known to be unique, an approximation to it can be found either by iterating on (2.25) starting from a quadratic $\mathbb{V}^0$ or by guessing that $\mathbb{V}(y_2, y_3) = \mathbb{V}_0 + \mathbb{V}_1[y_2, y_3] + [y_2, y_3]\mathbb{V}_2[y_2, y_3]'$, and finding $\mathbb{V}_0, \mathbb{V}_1, \mathbb{V}_2$.

It is important to stress that certainty equivalence is required when computing the solution to a quadratic approximation. This principle allows us to eliminate the expectation operator from (2.25) and reinsert it in front of all future unknown variables once a solution is found. This operation is possible because the covariance matrix of the shocks does not enter the decision rule. That is, certainty equivalence implies that we can set the covariance matrix of the shocks to zero and replace random variables with their unconditional mean.

Exercise 2.19. Consider the basic RBC model with no habit persistence in consumption and utility given by $u(c_t, c_{t-1}, N_t) = c_t^{1-\varphi}/(1-\varphi)$, no government sector, and no taxes and consider the recursive formulation provided by the Bellman equation.

(i) Compute the steady states and a quadratic approximation to the utility function.

(ii) Compute the value function assuming that the initial V^0 is quadratic and calculate the optimal decision rule for capital, labor, and consumption.

While exercise 2.19 takes a brute force approach to iterations, one should remember that approximate quadratic value function problems fit into the class of optimal linear regulator problems. Therefore, an approximate solution to the functional equation (2.25) can also be found by using methods developed in the control literature. One example of an optimal linear regulator problem was encountered in exercise 2.5. Recall that, in that case, we want to maximize $E_t \sum_t \beta^t([y_{2t}, y_{3t}]'\mathcal{Q}_2[y_{2t}, y_{3t}] + y_{1t}'\mathcal{Q}_1 y_{1t} + 2[y_{2t}, y_{3t}]'\mathcal{Q}_3' y_1)$ with respect to y_{1t}, y_{20} given, subject to $y_{2t+1} = \mathcal{Q}_4' y_{2t} + \mathcal{Q}_5' y_{1t} + \mathcal{Q}_6' y_{3t+1}$. The Bellman equation is

$$\mathbb{V}(y_2, y_3) = \max_{\{y_1\}}[y_2, y_3]'\mathcal{Q}_2[y_2, y_3] + y_1'\mathcal{Q}_1 y_1 + 2[y_2, y_3]'\mathcal{Q}_3' y_1 + \beta E\mathbb{V}(y_2^+, y_3^+ \mid y_2, y_3). \quad (2.26)$$

Hansen and Sargent (2005) show that, starting from arbitrary initial conditions, iterations on (2.26) yield at the jth step the quadratic value function $\mathbb{V}^j = y_2'\mathbb{V}_2^j y_2 + \mathbb{V}_0^j$, where

$$\mathbb{V}_2^{j+1} = \mathcal{Q}_2 + \beta\mathcal{Q}_4\mathbb{V}_2^j\mathcal{Q}_4' - (\beta\mathcal{Q}_4\mathbb{V}_2^j\mathcal{Q}_5' + \mathcal{Q}_3')(\mathcal{Q}_1 + \beta\mathcal{Q}_5\mathbb{V}_2^j\mathcal{Q}_5')^{-1}(\beta\mathcal{Q}_5\mathbb{V}_2^j\mathcal{Q}_4' + \mathcal{Q}_3) \quad (2.27)$$

and $\mathbb{V}_0^{j+1} = \beta\mathbb{V}_0^j + \beta\,\mathrm{tr}(\mathbb{V}_2^j\mathcal{Q}_6'\mathcal{Q}_6)$. Equation (2.27) is the so-called matrix Riccati equation which depends on the parameters of the model (i.e., the matrices $\mathcal{Q}_i$), but it does not involve $\mathbb{V}_0^j$. Equation (2.27) can be used to find the limit value $\mathbb{V}_2$ which, in turn, allows us to compute the limit of $\mathbb{V}_0$ and of the value function. The decision rule which attains the maximum at iteration j is $y_{1t}^j = -(\mathcal{Q}_1 + \beta\mathcal{Q}_5\mathbb{V}_2^j\mathcal{Q}_5')^{-1} \times (\beta\mathcal{Q}_5\mathbb{V}_2^j\mathcal{Q}_4' + \mathcal{Q}_3)y_{2t}$ and can be calculated given $\mathbb{V}_2^j$, y_{2t}, and the parameters of the model.

While it is common to iterate on (2.27) to find the limits of $\mathbb{V}_0^j, \mathbb{V}_2^j$, the reader should be aware that algorithms which produce this limit in one step are available (see, for example, Hansen et al. 1996).

Exercise 2.20. Consider the two-country model analyzed in example 2.6.

(i) Take a quadratic approximation to the objective function of the social planner around the steady state and map the problem into a linear regulator framework.

(ii) Use the matrix Riccati equation to find a solution to the maximization problem.

Example 2.12. Consider the setup of exercise 2.7, where the utility function is $u(c_t, G_t, N_t) = \ln(c_t + \vartheta_G G_t) + \vartheta_N(1 - N_t)$ and where G_t is an AR(1) process with persistence ρ_G and variance σ_G^2 and is financed with lump sum taxes. The resource constraint is $c_t + K_{t+1} + G_t = K_t^{1-\eta}N_t^{\eta}\zeta_t + (1-\delta)K_t$, where $\ln\zeta_t$ is an AR(1) disturbance with persistence ρ_ζ and variance σ_ζ^2. Setting $\vartheta_G = 0.7$, $\eta = 0.64$, $\delta = 0.025$, $\beta = 0.99$, $\vartheta_N = 2.8$, we have that $(K/\mathrm{GDP})^{ss} = 10.25$, $(c/\mathrm{GDP})^{ss} = 0.745$, $(\mathrm{inv}/\mathrm{GDP})^{ss} = 0.225$, $(G/\mathrm{GDP})^{ss} = 0.03$, and $N^{ss} = 0.235$. Approximating the utility function quadratically and the constraint linearly, we can use the matrix Riccati equation to find a solution. Convergence was achieved at iteration 243 and the increment in the value function at the last iteration was 9.41×10^{-6}. The value function is proportional to $[y_2, y_3]\mathbb{V}_2[y_2, y_3]'$, where $y_2 = K$, $y_3 = (G, \zeta)$, and

$$\mathbb{V}_2 = \begin{bmatrix} 1.76 \times 10^{-9} & 3.08 \times 10^{-7} & 7.38 \times 10^{-9} \\ -1.54 \times 10^{-8} & -0.081 & -9.38 \times 10^{-8} \\ -2.14 \times 10^{-6} & -3.75 \times 10^{-4} & -8.98 \times 10^{-6} \end{bmatrix}.$$

The decision rule for $y_1 = (c, N)'$ is

$$y_{1t} = \begin{bmatrix} -9.06 \times 10^{-10} & -0.70 & -2.87 \times 10^{-9} \\ -9.32 \times 10^{-10} & -1.56 \times 10^{-7} & -2.95 \times 10^{-9} \end{bmatrix} y_{2t}.$$

The alternative to brute force or Riccati iterations is the method of undetermined coefficients. Although the approach is easy conceptually, it may be mechanically cumbersome, even for small problems. If we knew the functional form of the value function (and/or of the decision rule), we could posit a specific parametric representation and use the first-order conditions to solve for the unknown parameters, as we did in exercise 2.3. We highlight a few steps of the approach in the next example and let the reader fill in the details.

Example 2.13. Suppose that the representative household chooses sequences for $(c_t, M_{t+1}/p_t)$ to maximize $E_0 \sum_t \beta^t [c_t^{\vartheta} + (M_{t+1}/p_t)^{1-\vartheta}]$, where c_t is consumption and $M_{t+1}^{\dagger} = M_{t+1}/p_t$ are real balances. The budget constraint is $c_t + M_{t+1}/p_t = (1 - T^y)w_t + M_t/p_t$, where T^y is an income tax. We assume that w_t and M_t are exogenous and stochastic. The government budget constraint is $G_t = T^y w_t + (M_{t+1} - M_t)/p_t$, which, together with the consumer budget constraint, implies $c_t + G_t = w_t$. Substituting the constraints in the utility function we have $E_0 \sum_t \beta^t \{[(1 - T^y)w_t + M_t^{\dagger}/\pi_t + M_{t+1}^{\dagger}]^{\vartheta} + (M_{t+1}^{\dagger})^{1-\vartheta}\}$, where π_t is the inflation rate. The states of the problem are $y_{2t} = (M_t^{\dagger}, \pi_t)$ and the shocks are $y_{3t} = (w_t, M_t^{g})$. The Bellman equation is $\mathbb{V}(y_2, y_3) = \max_{\{c, M^{\dagger}\}}[u(c, M^{\dagger}) + \beta E \mathbb{V}(y_2^+, y_3^+ \mid y_2, y_3)]$. Let $(c^{ss}, M^{\dagger ss}, w^{ss}, \pi^{ss})$ be the steady-state value of consumption, real balances, income, and inflation. For $\pi^{ss} = 1$, $w^{ss} = 1$, consumption and real balances in the steady state are $c^{ss} = (1 - T^y)$ and $(M^{\dagger})^{ss} = \{[(1-\beta)\vartheta(1 - T^y)^{\vartheta-1}]/(1-\vartheta)\}^{-1/\vartheta}$. A quadratic approximation to the utility function is $\mathfrak{B}_0 + \mathfrak{B}_1 x_t + x_t' \mathfrak{B}_2 x_t$, where $x_t = (w_t, M_t^{\dagger}, \pi_t, M_{t+1}^{\dagger})$,

$$\mathfrak{B}_0 = (c^{ss})^{\vartheta} + [(M^{\dagger})^{ss}]^{1-\vartheta},$$

$$\mathfrak{B}_1 = \left[\vartheta (c^{ss})^{\vartheta-1}(1 - T^y); \frac{\vartheta (c^{ss})^{\vartheta-1}}{\pi^{ss}}; \vartheta (c^{ss})^{\vartheta-1}\left(-\frac{(M^{\dagger})^{ss}}{(\pi^{ss})^2}\right); \right.$$
$$\left. -\vartheta (c^{ss})^{\vartheta-1} + (1+\vartheta)((M^{\dagger})^{ss})^{-\vartheta}\right],$$

and the matrix $\mathfrak{B}_2$ is

$$\begin{bmatrix} \kappa(1-T^y)^2 & \kappa(1-T^y)/\pi^{ss} & \kappa(1-T^y)[-(M^\dagger)^{ss}/(\pi^{ss})^2] & -\kappa(1-T^y) \\ \kappa(1-T^y)/\pi^{ss} & \kappa/(\pi^{ss})^2 & [-(M^\dagger)^{ss}/(\pi^{ss})^2][\kappa/\pi^{ss}+\vartheta(c^{ss})^{\vartheta-1}] & -\kappa/\pi^{ss} \\ \kappa(1-T^y)[-(M^\dagger)^{ss}/(\pi^{ss})^2] & [-(M^\dagger)^{ss}/(\pi^{ss})^2][\kappa/\pi^{ss}+\vartheta(c^{ss})^{\vartheta-1}] & \kappa\left(-\dfrac{(M^\dagger)^{ss}}{(\pi^{ss})^2}\right)\left[-\dfrac{2c^{ss}}{(\vartheta-1)\pi^{ss}}-\left(-\dfrac{(M^\dagger)^{ss}}{(\pi^{ss})^2}\right)\right] & -\kappa\left[-\dfrac{(M^\dagger)^{ss}}{(\pi^{ss})^2}\right] \\ -\kappa(1-T^y) & -\kappa/\pi^{ss} & -\kappa[-(M^\dagger)^{ss}/(\pi^{ss})^2] & \kappa+\vartheta(1+\vartheta)[(M^\dagger)^{ss}]^{-\vartheta-1} \end{bmatrix},$$

where $\kappa = \vartheta(\vartheta-1)(c^{ss})^{\vartheta-2}$. One could then guess a quadratic form for the value function and solve for the unknown coefficients. Alternatively, if only the decision rule is needed, one could directly guess a linear policy function (in deviation from steady states) of the form $M^\dagger_{t+1} = \mathcal{Q}_0 + \mathcal{Q}_1 M^\dagger_t + \mathcal{Q}_2\pi_t + \mathcal{Q}_3 w_t + \mathcal{Q}_4 M^g_t$ and solve for $\mathcal{Q}_i$ by using the linear version of the first-order conditions.

Exercise 2.21. Find the approximate first-order conditions of the problem of example 2.13. Show the form of $\mathcal{Q}_j$, $j = 0, 1, 2, 3$. (Hint: use the certainty equivalence principle.)

When the number of states is large, analytic calculation of first- and second-order derivatives of the utility function may take quite some time. As an alternative, numerical derivatives, which are much faster to calculate and only require the solution of the model at a pivotal point, could be used. Hence, in example 2.13, to approximate $\partial u/\partial c$, one could use $\{[(1-T^y)w^{ss}+\iota]^\vartheta - [(1-T^y)w^{ss}-\iota]^\vartheta\}/2\iota$, for ι small.

Exercise 2.22 (Ramsey). Suppose that the representative household maximizes $E_0\sum_t \beta^t[\upsilon_t c_t^{1-\varphi_c}/(1-\varphi_c) - N_t^{1-\varphi_n}/(1-\varphi_n)]$, where υ_t is a preference shock and φ_c, φ_n are parameters. The consumer budget constraint is $E_0\sum_t \beta^t p^0_t \times [(1-T^y_t)\,\mathrm{GDP}_t + s^{0b}_t - c_t] = 0$, where s^{0b}_t is a stream of coupon payments promised by the government at time 0 and p^0_t is the Arrow–Debreu price. The resource constraint is $c_t + G_t = \mathrm{GDP}_t = \zeta_t N^\eta_t$. The government budget constraint is $E_0\sum_t \beta^t p^0_t[(G_t + s^{0b}_t) - T^y_t \mathrm{GDP}_t] = 0$. Given a process for G_t and the present value of coupon payments $E_0\sum_t \beta^t p^0_t s^{0b}_t$, a feasible tax process must satisfy the government budget constraint. Assume that $(\upsilon_t, \zeta_t, s^{0b}_t, G_t)$ are random variables with AR(1) representation. The representative household chooses sequences for consumption and hours and the government selects the tax process preferred by the household. The government commits at time 0 to follow the optimal tax system, once and for all.

(i) Take a quadratic approximation to the problem, calculate the first-order conditions of the household problem, and show how to calculate p_t^0.

(ii) Show the allocations for c_t, N_t and the optimal tax policy T_t^y. Is it true that the optimal tax rate implies tax smoothing (random walk taxes), regardless of the process for G_t?

2.2.2 *Discretization*

As an alternative to quadratic approximations, one could solve the value function problem by discretizing the state space and the space over which the exogenous processes take values. This is the method popularized, for example, by Merha and Prescott (1985). The idea is that the states are forced to lie in the set $Y_2 = \{y_{21}, \dots, y_{2n_1}\}$ and the exogenous processes in the set $Y_3 = \{y_{31}, \dots, y_{3n_2}\}$. Then the space of possible (y_{2t}, y_{3t}) combination has $n_1 \times n_2$ points. For simplicity, assume that the process for the exogenous variables is first-order Markov with transition $P(y_{3t+1} = y_{3j'} \mid y_{3t} = y_{3j}) = p_{j'j}$. The value function associated with each pair of states and exogenous processes is $\mathbb{V}(y_{2i}, y_{3j})$, which is of dimension $n_1 \times n_2$. Because of the Markov structure of the shocks, and the assumptions made, we have transformed an infinite-dimensional problem into the problem of mapping $n_1 \times n_2$ matrices into $n_1 \times n_2$ matrices. Therefore, iterations on the Bellman equation are easier to compute. The value function can be written as $(\mathcal{T}\mathbb{V}_{ij})(y_2, y_3) = \max_n u(y_1, y_{2i}, y_{3j}) + \beta \sum_{l=1}^{n_2} \mathbb{V}_{n,l} p_{l,j}$, where y_{1n} is such that $h(y_{1n}, y_{2i}, y_{3j}) = y_{2n}, n = 1, \dots, n_1$. An illustration of the approach is given in the next example.

Example 2.14. Consider an RBC model where a random stream of government expenditure is financed by distorting income taxes, labor supply is inelastic, and production uses only capital. The social planner chooses $\{c_t, K_{t+1}\}$ to maximize $E_0 \sum_t \beta^t c_t^{1-\varphi}/(1-\varphi)$, given G_t and K_t, subject to $c_t + K_{t+1} - (1-\delta)K_t + G_t = (1-T^y)K_t^{1-\eta}$, where G_t is an AR(1) with persistence ρ_{G}, variance σ_{G}^2, and $(\varphi, \beta, T^y, \eta, \delta)$ are parameters. Given K_0, the Bellman equation is

$$\mathbb{V}(K, G) = \max_{\{K^+\}} [(1-T^y)K^{1-\eta} + (1-\delta)K - G - K^+]^{1-\varphi}/(1-\varphi) \\ + \beta E[\mathbb{V}(K^+, G^+ \mid K, G)].$$

Suppose that the capital stock and government expenditure can take only two values, and let the transition for G_t be $p_{j',j}$. Then the discretization algorithm works as follows.

Algorithm 2.2.

(1) Choose values for $(\delta, \eta, \varphi, T^y, \beta)$ and specify the elements of $p_{j',j}$.

(2) Choose an initial 2×2 matrix $\mathbb{V}(K, G)$, e.g., $\mathbb{V}^0 = 0$.

(3) For each $i, j = 1, 2$, calculate

$$(\mathcal{T}\mathbb{V}_{i,j})(K, G) = \max \left\{ \frac{[(1-T^y)K_i^{1-\eta} + (1-\delta)K_i - K_i - G_j]^{1-\varphi}}{1-\varphi} + \beta[\mathbb{V}_{i,j}p_{j,j} + \mathbb{V}_{i,j'}p_{j,j'}], \frac{[(1-T^y)K_i^{1-\eta} + (1-\delta)K_i - K_{i'} - G_j]^{1-\varphi}}{1-\varphi} + \beta[\mathbb{V}_{i',j}p_{j,j} + \mathbb{V}_{i',j'}p_{j,j'}] \right\}.$$

(4) Iterate on (3) until, for example, $\max_{i,i'} |\mathcal{T}^l\mathbb{V}_{i,j} - \mathcal{T}^{l-1}\mathbb{V}_{i,j}| \leqslant \iota$, ι small, $l = 2, 3, \dots$.

Suppose $T^y = 0.1$, $\delta = 0.1$, $\beta = 0.9$, $\varphi = 2$, $\eta = 0.66$; choose $G_1 = 1.1$, $G_2 = 0.9$, $K_1 = 5.3$, $K_2 = 6.4$, $p_{11} = 0.8$, $p_{22} = 0.7$, $\mathbb{V}^0 = 0$. Then

$$(\mathcal{T}\mathbb{V}_{11}) = \max_{1,2} \left\{ \frac{[(1-T^y)K_1^{1-\eta} + (1-\delta)K_1 - K_1 - G_1]^{1-\varphi}}{1-\varphi}, \frac{[(1-T^y)K_1^{1-\eta} + (1-\delta)K_1 - K_2 - G_1]^{1-\varphi}}{1-\varphi} \right\}$$

$$= \max_{1,2}\{14.38, 0.85\} = 14.38.$$

Repeating for the other entries,

$$\mathcal{T}\mathbb{V} = \begin{bmatrix} 14.38 & 1.03 \\ 12.60 & -0.81 \end{bmatrix}, \quad \mathcal{T}^2\mathbb{V} = \begin{bmatrix} 24.92 & 3.91 \\ 21.53 & 1.10 \end{bmatrix}, \quad \lim_{l\to\infty} \mathcal{T}^l\mathbb{V} = \begin{bmatrix} 71.63 & 31.54 \\ 56.27 & 1.10 \end{bmatrix}.$$

Implicitly the solution defines the decision rule; for example, from $(\mathcal{T}\mathbb{V}_{11})$ we have that $K_t = K_1$.

Clearly, the quality of the approximation depends on the fineness of the grid. It is therefore a good idea to start from coarse grids and after convergence is achieved check whether finer grids produce different results.

The discretization approach is well-suited for problems of modest dimension (i.e., when the size of the state variables and of the exogenous processes is small) since constructing a grid which systematically and effectively covers high-dimensional spaces is difficult. For example, when we have one state, two shocks, and 100 grid points, 1 000 000 evaluations are required in each step. Nevertheless, even with this large number of evaluations, it is easy to leave large portions of the space unexplored. Therefore, one has to be careful when using such an approach.

Exercise 2.23 (search). Suppose a worker has the choice of accepting or rejecting a wage offer. If she has worked at $t-1$, the offer is $w_t = b_0 + b_1 w_{t-1} + e_t$, where e_t is an i.i.d. shock; if she was not working at $t-1$, the offer w_t^* is drawn from some stationary distribution. Having observed w_t, the worker decides whether to work or not (i.e., whether $N_t = 0$ or $N_t = 1$). The worker cannot save so $c_t = w_t$

if $N_t = 1$ and $c_t = \bar{c}$ if $N_t = 0$, where $\bar{c}$ measures unemployment compensations. The worker maximizes discounted utility, where $u(c) = c_t^{1-\varphi}/(1-\varphi)$ and φ is a parameter.

(i) Write down the maximization problem and the first-order conditions.

(ii) Define states and controls and the Bellman equation. Suppose $e_t = 0, b_0 = 0, b_1 = 1, \beta = 0.96$, and $w_t^* \sim \mathbb{U}(0,1)$. Calculate the optimal value function and the decision rules.

(iii) Assume that the worker now also has the option of retiring so that $x_t = 0$ or $x_t = 1$. Suppose $x_t = x_{t-1}$ if $x_{t-1} = 0$ and that $c_t = w_t$ if $N_t = 1, x_t = 1$; $c_t = \bar{c}$ if $N_t = 0, x_t = 1$ and $c_t = \bar{\bar{c}}$ if $N_t = 0, x_t = 0$, where $\bar{\bar{c}}$ is the retirement pay. Write down the Bellman equation and calculate the optimal decision rules.

(iv) Suppose that the worker now has the option to migrate. For each location $i = 1, 2$ the wage is $w_t^i = b_0 + b_1 w_{t-1}^l + e_t^i$ if she has worked at $t-1$ in location i, and $w_t^i \sim \mathbb{U}(0, i)$ otherwise. Consumption is $c_t = w_t$ if $i_t = i_{t-1}$ and $c_t = \bar{c} - \varrho$ if $i_t \neq i_{t-1}$, where $\varrho = 0.1$ is a migration cost. Write down the Bellman equation and calculate the optimal decision rules.

Exercise 2.24 (Lucas tree model). Consider an economy where an infinitely lived representative household has a random stream of perishable endowments sd_t and decides how much to consume and save, where savings can take the form of either stocks or bonds, and let $u(c_t, c_{t-1}, N_t) = \ln c_t$.

(i) Write down the maximization problem and the first-order conditions. Write down the Bellman equation specifying the states and the controls.

(ii) Assume that the endowment process can take only two values $\mathrm{sd}_1 = 6$, $\mathrm{sd}_2 = 1$ with transition $\left[\begin{smallmatrix} 0.7 & 0.3 \\ 0.2 & 0.8 \end{smallmatrix}\right]$. Find the 2×1 vector of value functions.

(iii) Find the policy function for consumption, stock, and bond holdings and the pricing functions for stocks and bonds.

One can also employ a discretization approach to directly solve the optimality conditions of the problem. Hence, the methodology is applicable to problems where the value function may not exist.

Example 2.15. For general preferences, the Euler equation of exercise 2.24 is

$$p_t^{\mathrm{s}}(\mathrm{sd}_t) U_{c,t} = \beta E[U_{c,t+1}(p_{t+1}^s(\mathrm{sd}_{t+1}) + \mathrm{sd}_{t+1})], \tag{2.28}$$

where we have made explicit the dependence of p_t^{s} on sd_t. If we assume that $\mathrm{sd}_t = [\mathrm{sd}_h, \mathrm{sd}_L]$, use the equilibrium condition $c_t = \mathrm{sd}_t$, and let $U_i^1 \equiv p^s(\mathrm{sd}_i) U_{\mathrm{sd}_i}$ and $U_i^2 = \beta \sum_{i'=1}^{2} p_{ii'} U_{\mathrm{sd}_i} \mathrm{sd}_i$, (2.28) can be written as $U_i^1 = U_i^2 + \beta \sum_{i'} p_{ii'} U_{i'}^1$ or $U^1 = (1-\beta P)^{-1} U^2$, where P is the matrix with typical element $\{p_{ii'}\}$. Therefore, share prices satisfy $p^s(\mathrm{sd}_i) = \sum_{i'} (I + \beta P + \beta^2 P^2 + \cdots)_{ii'} U_{i'}^2 / U_{\mathrm{sd}_i}$, where the sum is over the (i, i') elements of the matrix.

Exercise 2.25. Consider the intertemporal condition (2.11), the intratemporal condition (2.12) of a standard RBC economy. Assume $T^y = 0$ and that (K_t, ζ_t) can take two values. Describe how to find the optimal consumption/leisure choice when $U(c_t, c_{t-1}, N_t) = \ln c_t + \vartheta_N(1 - N_t)$.

2.2.3 Loglinear Approximations

Log-linearizations have been extensively used in recent years following the work of Blanchard and Kahn (1980), King et al. (1988a,b), and Campbell (1994). Uhlig (1999) has systematized the methodology and provided software useful for solving a variety of problems. King and Watson (1998) and Klein (2000) provided algorithms for singular systems and Sims (2001) a method for solving linear systems where the distinction between states and controls is unclear.

Loglinear approximations are similar, in spirit, to quadratic approximations and the solutions are computed by using similar methodologies. The former may work better when the problem displays some mild nonlinearities. The major difference between the two approaches is that quadratic approximations are typically performed on the objective function while log-linear approximations are calculated by using the optimality conditions of the problem. Therefore, the latter can be used in situations where, because of distortions, the competitive equilibrium is suboptimal.

The basic principles of log-linearization are simple. We need a point around which the log-linearization takes place. This could be the steady state or, in models with friction, the frictionless solution. Let $y = (y_1, y_2, y_3)$. The optimality conditions of the problem can be divided into two blocks, the first containing expectational equations and the second nonexpectational equations:

$$1 = E_t[h(y_{t+1}, y_t)], \tag{2.29}$$

$$1 = f(y_t, y_{t-1}), \tag{2.30}$$

where $f(0,0) = 1$ and $h(0,0) = 1$. Taking a first-order Taylor expansion around $(\bar{y}, \bar{y}) = (0,0)$, we have

$$0 \approx E_t[h_{t+1} y_{t+1} + h_t y_t], \tag{2.31}$$

$$0 \approx f_t y_t + f_{t-1} y_{t-1}, \tag{2.32}$$

where $f_j = \partial \ln f / \partial y_j'$ and $h_j = \partial \ln h / \partial y_j'$. Equations (2.31) and (2.32) form a system of linear expectational equations.

Although log-linearization only requires the first derivatives of f and h, Uhlig (1999) suggests a set of approximations to calculate (2.31), (2.32) directly without differentiation. The tricks involve replacing Y_t with $\bar{Y} e^{\hat{y}_t}$, where $\hat{y}_t$ is small, and using the following three rules (here a_0 is a constant and b_{1t}, b_{2t} small numbers).

(i) $e^{b_{1t} + a_0 b_{2t}} \approx 1 + b_{1t} + a_0 b_{2t}$.

(ii) $b_{1t} b_{2t} \approx 0$.

(iii) $E_t[a_0 e^{b_{1t+1}}] \propto E_t[a_0 b_{1t+1}]$.

Example 2.16. To illustrate these rules, consider the resource constraint $C_t + G_t + \text{Inv}_t = \text{GDP}_t$. Set $\bar{C}e^{\hat{c}_t} + \bar{G}e^{\hat{g}_t} + \overline{\text{Inv}}\, e^{\widehat{\text{inv}}_t} = \overline{\text{GDP}}\, e^{\widehat{\text{gdp}}_t}$ and use rule (i) to get $\bar{C}(1+\hat{c}_t) + \bar{G}(1+\hat{g}_t) + \overline{\text{Inv}}\,(1+\widehat{\text{inv}}_t) - \overline{\text{GDP}}\,(1+\widehat{\text{gdp}}_t) = 0$. Then, using $\bar{C} + \bar{G} + \overline{\text{Inv}} = \overline{\text{GDP}}$, we get $\bar{C}\hat{c}_t + \bar{G}\hat{g}_t + \overline{\text{Inv}}\,\widehat{\text{inv}}_t - \overline{\text{GDP}}\,\widehat{\text{gdp}}_t = 0$ or $(\bar{C}/\overline{\text{GDP}})\hat{c}_t + (\bar{G}/\overline{\text{GDP}})\hat{g}_t + (\overline{\text{Inv}}/\overline{\text{GDP}})\,\widehat{\text{inv}}_t - \widehat{\text{gdp}}_t = 0$.

Exercise 2.26. Suppose y_t and y_{t+1} are conditionally jointly lognormal and homoskedastic. Replace (2.29) with $0 = \ln\{E_t[e^{\bar{h}(y_{t+1}, y_t)}]\}$, where $\bar{h} = \ln(h)$. Using $\ln h(0,0) \approx 0.5 \operatorname{var}_t[\bar{h}_{t+1} y_{t+1} + \bar{h}_t y_t]$, show that the log-linear approximation is $0 \approx E_t[\bar{h}_{t+1} y_{t+1} + \bar{h}_t y_t]$. What is the difference between this approximation and the one in (2.31)?

Exercise 2.27. Suppose that the private production is $\text{GDP}_t = (K_t/\text{Pop}_t)^{\aleph_1/(1-\eta)} \times (N_t/\text{Pop}_t)^{\aleph_2/\eta} K_t^{1-\eta} N_t^{\eta} \zeta_t$, where (K/Pop_t) and (N_t/Pop_t) are the average endowment of capital and hours in the economy. Suppose the utility function is $E_t \times \sum_t \beta^t [\ln(c_t/\text{Pop}_t) - (1/(1-\varphi_N))(N_t/\text{Pop}_t)^{1-\varphi_N}]$. Assume that $(\ln \zeta_t, \ln \text{Pop}_t)$ are AR(1) processes with persistence equal to ρ_ζ and 1.

(i) Show that the optimality conditions of the problem are

$$\frac{c_t}{\text{Pop}_t}\left(\frac{N_t}{\text{Pop}_t}\right)^{-\varphi_N} = \eta \frac{\text{GDP}_t}{\text{Pop}_t}, \tag{2.33}$$

$$\frac{\text{Pop}_t}{c_t} = E_t \beta \frac{\text{Pop}_{t+1}}{c_{t+1}}\left[(1-\delta) + (1-\eta)\frac{\text{GDP}_{t+1}}{K_{t+1}}\right]. \tag{2.34}$$

(ii) Find expressions for the log-linearized production function, the labor market equilibrium, the Euler equation, and the budget constraint.

(iii) Write the log-linearized expectational equation in terms of an Euler equation error. Find conditions under which there are more stable roots than state variables (in which case sunspot equilibria may be obtained).

There are several economic models which do not fit the setup of (2.29), (2.30). For example, Rotemberg and Woodford (1997) describe a model where consumption at time t depends on the expectation of variables dated at $t+2$ and on. This model can be accommodated in the setup of (2.29), (2.30) by using dummy variables, as the next example shows. In general, restructuring of the timing convention of the variables, or enlarging the vector of states, suffices to fit these problems into (2.29), (2.30).

Example 2.17. Suppose that (2.29) is $1 = E_t[h(y_{2t+2}, y_{2t})]$. We can transform this second-order expectational equation into a 2×1 vector of first-order expectational equations by using a dummy variable y_{2t}^*. In fact, the above is equivalent to $1 = E_t[h(y_{2t+1}^*, y_{2t})]$ and $y_{2t+1} = y_{2t}^*$ as long as $[y_{2t}, y_{2t}^*]$ are used as state variables for the problem.

Exercise 2.28. Consider a model with optimizers and rule-of-thumb households like the one of example 2.7 and assume that optimizing households display habit in consumption. In particular, assume that their utility function is $(c_t - \gamma c_{t-1})^{\vartheta} \times (1 - N_t)^{1-\vartheta}$. Derive the first-order conditions of the model and map them into (2.29), (2.30).

Example 2.18. Log-linearizing around the steady state the equilibrium conditions of the model of exercise 2.13, and assuming an unexpected change in the productivity of farmers' technology (represented by Δ) lasting one period, we have $(1 + 1/\varrho)\widehat{\mathrm{La}}_t = \Delta + (r/(r-1))\hat{p}^{\mathrm{L}}_t$ for $\tau = 0$ and $(1 + 1/\varrho)\widehat{\mathrm{La}}_{t+\tau} = \widehat{\mathrm{La}}_{t+\tau-1}$ for $\tau \geqslant 1$, where ϱ is the elasticity of the supply of land with respect to the user costs in the steady state and $\hat{p}^{\mathrm{L}}_t = ((r-1)/(r\varrho))\{1/[1 - \varrho/(r(1+\varrho))]\}\widehat{\mathrm{La}}_t$, where the hat indicates percentage deviations from the steady state. Solving these two expressions we have $\hat{p}^{\mathrm{L}}_t = \Delta/\varrho$ and $\widehat{\mathrm{La}}_t = [1/(1+1/\varrho)][1 + r/((r-1)\varrho)]\Delta$. Three interesting conclusions follow. First, if $\varrho = 0$, temporary shocks have permanent effects on farmers' land and on its price. Second, since $[1/(1 + 1/\varrho)][1 + r/((r-1)\varrho)] > 1$, the effect on land ownership is larger than the shock. Finally, in the static case $(\widehat{\mathrm{La}}_t)^* = \Delta < \widehat{\mathrm{La}}_t$ and $(\hat{p}^{\mathrm{L}}_t)^* = [(r-1)/(r\varrho)]\Delta < \hat{p}^{\mathrm{L}}_t$. This is because Δ affects the net worth of farmers: a positive Δ reduces the value of the obligations and implies a larger use of capital by the farmers, therefore magnifying the effect of the shock on land ownership.

Exercise 2.29. Show that the log-linearized first-order conditions of the sticky price model of example 2.9 when $K_t = 1, \forall t$, and when monopolistic firms use $\beta u_{c,t+1}/u_{c,t}$ as discount factor are

$$\left.\begin{aligned}
0 &= \hat{w}_t + \frac{N^{\mathrm{ss}}}{1-N^{\mathrm{ss}}}\hat{N}_t - \hat{c}_t,\\
\left(\frac{1}{1+i^{\mathrm{ss}}}\right)\hat{\imath}_{t+1} &= [1 - \vartheta(1-\varphi)](\hat{c}_{t+1} - \hat{c}_t)\\
&\quad - (1-\vartheta)(1-\varphi)(\hat{N}_{t+1} - \hat{N}_t)\frac{N^{\mathrm{ss}}}{1-N^{\mathrm{ss}}} - \hat{\pi}_{t+1},\\
\left(\widehat{\frac{M_{t+1}}{p_t}}\right) &= \frac{\vartheta(1-\varphi)-1}{\varphi_{\mathrm{m}}}\hat{c}_t + \frac{N^{\mathrm{ss}}}{1-N^{\mathrm{ss}}}\frac{(1-\vartheta)(1-\varphi)}{\varphi_{\mathrm{m}}}\hat{N}_t\\
&\quad - \frac{1}{\varphi_{\mathrm{m}}(1+i^{\mathrm{ss}})}\hat{\imath}_t,\\
\beta E_t\hat{\pi}_{t+1} &= \hat{\pi}_t - \frac{(1-\zeta_{\mathrm{p}})(1-\zeta_{\mathrm{p}}\beta)}{\zeta_{\mathrm{p}}}\widehat{\mathrm{mc}}_t,
\end{aligned}\right\} \tag{2.35}$$

where mc_t are the real marginal costs, ζ_{p} is the probability of not changing prices, w_t is the real wage, φ is the risk-aversion parameter, ϑ is the share of consumption in utility, φ_{m} is the exponent on real balances in utility, the superscript "ss" refers to the steady state, and a hat denotes percentage deviation from the steady state.

As with quadratic approximations, the solution of the system of equations (2.31), (2.32) can be obtained in two ways when the solution is known to exist and to be unique: using the method of the undetermined coefficients or finding the saddle-point solution (Vaughan's method). The method of undetermined coefficients is analogous to the one described in exercise 2.19. Vaughan's method works with the state-space representation of the system. Both methods require the computation of eigenvalues and eigenvectors. For a thorough discussion of the methods, the reader should consult, for example, the chapter of Uhlig in Marimon and Scott (1999) or Klein (2000). Here we briefly describe the building blocks of the procedure and highlight the important steps with some examples.

Rather than using (2.31) and (2.32), we employ a slightly more general setup which directly allows for structures like those considered in example 2.17 and exercise 2.28, without any need to enlarge the state space.

Let y_{1t} be of dimension $m_1 \times 1$, y_{2t} of dimension $m_2 \times 1$, and y_{3t} of dimension $m_3 \times 1$, and suppose the log-linearized optimality conditions and the law of motion of the exogenous variables can be written as

$$0 = \mathcal{Q}_1 y_{2t} + \mathcal{Q}_2 y_{2t-1} + \mathcal{Q}_3 y_{1t} + \mathcal{Q}_4 y_{3t}, \tag{2.36}$$

$$\begin{aligned} 0 = E_t(&\mathcal{Q}_5 y_{2t+1} + \mathcal{Q}_6 y_{2t} + \mathcal{Q}_7 y_{2t-1} + \mathcal{Q}_8 y_{1t+1} \\ &+ \mathcal{Q}_9 y_{1t} + \mathcal{Q}_{10} y_{3t+1} + \mathcal{Q}_{11} y_{3t}), \end{aligned} \tag{2.37}$$

$$0 = y_{3t+1} - \rho y_{3t} - \epsilon_t, \tag{2.38}$$

where $\mathcal{Q}_3$ is an $m_4 \times m_1$ matrix of rank $m_1 \leqslant m_4$, and ρ has only stable eigenvalues. Assume that a solution is given by

$$y_{2t} = \mathcal{A}_{22} y_{2t-1} + \mathcal{A}_{23} y_{3t}, \tag{2.39}$$

$$y_{1t} = \mathcal{A}_{12} y_{2t-1} + \mathcal{A}_{13} y_{3t}. \tag{2.40}$$

Letting $\mathcal{Z}_1 = \mathcal{Q}_8 \mathcal{Q}_3^{+} \mathcal{Q}_2 - \mathcal{Q}_6 + \mathcal{Q}_9 \mathcal{Q}_3^{+} \mathcal{Q}_1$, Uhlig (1999) shows the following.

(a) $\mathcal{A}_{22}$ satisfies the (matrix) quadratic equations:

$$\left.\begin{aligned} 0 &= \mathcal{Q}_3^{0} \mathcal{Q}_1 \mathcal{A}_{22} + \mathcal{Q}_3^{0} \mathcal{Q}_2, \\ 0 &= (\mathcal{Q}_5 - \mathcal{Q}_8 \mathcal{Q}_3^{+} \mathcal{Q}_1)\mathcal{A}_{22}^2 - \mathcal{Z}_1 \mathcal{A}_{22} - \mathcal{Q}_9 \mathcal{Q}_3^{+} \mathcal{Q}_2 + \mathcal{Q}_7. \end{aligned}\right\} \tag{2.41}$$

The equilibrium is stable if all eigenvalues of $\mathcal{A}_{22}$ are less than 1 in absolute value.

(b) $\mathcal{A}_{12}$ is given by $\mathcal{A}_{12} = -\mathcal{Q}_3^{+}(\mathcal{Q}_1 \mathcal{A}_{22} + \mathcal{Q}_2)$.

(c) Given $\mathcal{Z}_2 = (\mathcal{Q}_5 \mathcal{A}_{22} + \mathcal{Q}_8 \mathcal{A}_{12})$ and $\mathcal{Z}_3 = \mathcal{Q}_{10}\rho + \mathcal{Q}_{11}$, $\mathcal{A}_{13}$ and $\mathcal{A}_{23}$ satisfy

$$\begin{bmatrix} I_{m_3} \otimes \mathcal{Q}_1 & I_{m_3} \otimes \mathcal{Q}_3 \\ \rho' \otimes \mathcal{Q}_5 + I_{m_3} \otimes (\mathcal{Z}_2 + \mathcal{Q}_6) & \rho' \otimes \mathcal{Q}_8 + I_{m_3} \otimes \mathcal{Q}_9 \end{bmatrix} \begin{bmatrix} \operatorname{vec}(\mathcal{A}_{23}) \\ \operatorname{vec}(\mathcal{A}_{13}) \end{bmatrix} = - \begin{bmatrix} \operatorname{vec}(\mathcal{Q}_4) \\ \operatorname{vec}(\mathcal{Z}_3) \end{bmatrix},$$

where $\operatorname{vec}(\cdot)$ is columnwise vectorization, $\mathcal{Q}_3^{\mathrm{G}}$ is a pseudo-inverse of $\mathcal{Q}_3$ and satisfies $\mathcal{Q}_3^{\mathrm{G}} \mathcal{Q}_3 \mathcal{Q}_3^{\mathrm{G}} = \mathcal{Q}_3^{\mathrm{G}}$ and $\mathcal{Q}_3 \mathcal{Q}_3^{\mathrm{G}} \mathcal{Q}_3 = \mathcal{Q}_3$. $\mathcal{Q}_3^{0}$ is an $(m_4 - m_1) \times m_4$ matrix whose rows are a basis for the space of $\mathcal{Q}_3'$ and I_{m_3} is the identity matrix of dimension m_3.

Example 2.19. Consider an RBC model with an intermediate monopolistic competitive sector. Let the profits in firm i be $\text{prf}_{it} = (p_{it} - \text{mc}_{it})\text{inty}_t$ and let $\text{mk}_{it} = (p_{it} - \text{mc}_{it})$ be the markup. If the utility function is of the form $u(c_t, c_{t-1}, N_t) = c_t^{1-\varphi}/(1-\varphi) + \vartheta_N(1-N_t)$, the dynamics depend on the markup only via the steady states. For this model the log-linearized conditions are

$$0 = -\text{Inv}^{\text{ss}}\,\widehat{\text{inv}}_t - C^{\text{ss}}\hat{c}_t + \text{GDP}^{\text{ss}}\,\widehat{\text{gdp}}_t, \tag{2.42}$$

$$0 = -\text{Inv}^{\text{ss}}\,\widehat{\text{inv}}_t - K^{\text{ss}}\hat{k}_{t+1} + (1-\delta)K^{\text{ss}}\hat{k}_t, \tag{2.43}$$

$$0 = (1-\eta)\hat{k}_t - \widehat{\text{gdp}}_t + \eta\hat{N}_t + \zeta_t, \tag{2.44}$$

$$0 = -\varphi\hat{c}_t + \widehat{\text{gdp}}_t - \hat{N}_t, \tag{2.45}$$

$$0 = \text{mk}^{\text{ss}}(1-\eta)(\text{GDP}^{\text{ss}}/K^{\text{ss}})[\hat{k}_t + \widehat{\text{gdp}}_t] - r^{\text{ss}}\hat{r}_t, \tag{2.46}$$

$$0 = E_t[-\varphi\hat{c}_{t+1} + \hat{r}_{t+1} + \varphi\hat{c}_t], \tag{2.47}$$

$$0 = \hat{\zeta}_{t+1} - \rho_\zeta\hat{\zeta}_t - \hat{\epsilon}_{1t+1}, \tag{2.48}$$

where $(\text{Inv}^{\text{ss}}/\text{GDP}^{\text{ss}})$ and $(C^{\text{ss}}/\text{GDP}^{\text{ss}})$ are the steady-state investment and consumption to output ratios, r^{ss} is the steady-state real rate, and mk^{ss} the steady-state markup. Letting $y_{1t} = (\hat{c}_t, \widehat{\text{gdp}}_t, \hat{N}_t, \hat{r}_t, \widehat{\text{inv}}_t)$, $y_{2t} = \hat{k}_t$, $y_{3t} = \hat{\zeta}_t$, we have $\mathcal{Q}_5 = \mathcal{Q}_6 = \mathcal{Q}_7 = \mathcal{Q}_{10} = \mathcal{Q}_{11} = [0]$,

$$\mathcal{Q}_2 = \begin{bmatrix} 0 \\ (1-\delta)K^{\text{ss}} \\ 1-\eta \\ 0 \\ -D^{\text{ss}} \end{bmatrix}, \quad \mathcal{Q}_3 = \begin{bmatrix} -C^{\text{ss}} & \text{GDP}^{\text{ss}} & 0 & 0 & -\text{Inv}^{\text{ss}} \\ 0 & 0 & 0 & 0 & \text{Inv}^{\text{ss}} \\ 0 & -1 & \eta & 0 & 0 \\ -\varphi & 1 & -1 & 0 & 0 \\ 0 & D^{\text{ss}} & 0 & -r^{\text{ss}} & 0 \end{bmatrix},$$

$$\mathcal{Q}_1 = \begin{bmatrix} 0 \\ -K^{\text{ss}} \\ 0 \\ 0 \\ 0 \end{bmatrix}, \quad \mathcal{Q}_4 = \begin{bmatrix} 0 \\ 0 \\ 1 \\ 0 \\ 0 \end{bmatrix},$$

$$\mathcal{Q}_8 = [-\varphi, 0, 0, 1, 0], \quad \mathcal{Q}_9 = [\varphi, 0, 0, 0, 0], \quad \rho = [\rho_\zeta],$$

where $D^{\text{ss}} = \text{mk}^{\text{ss}}(1-\eta)(\text{GDP}^{\text{ss}}/K^{\text{ss}})$.

It is important to stress that the method of undetermined coefficients properly works only when the state space is chosen to be of minimal size; that is, no redundant state variables are included. If this is not the case, $\mathcal{A}_{22}$ may have zero eigenvalues and this will produce "bubble" solutions.

Computationally, the major difficulty is to find a solution to the matrix equation (2.41). The toolkit of Uhlig (1999) recasts the problem into a generalized eigenvalue–eigenvector problem. Klein (2000) and Sims (2001) calculate a solution by using the generalized Shur decomposition. When applied to some of the problems of this chapter, the two approaches yield similar solutions. In general, the Shur (QZ) decomposition is useful when generalized eigenvalues may not be distinct. However, the QZ decomposition is not necessarily unique.

Exercise 2.30. Suppose that the representative household maximizes $E_0 \sum_t \beta^t \times (c_t^{1-\varphi_c}/(1-\varphi_c) + (M_{t+1}/p_t)^{1-\varphi_m}/(1-\varphi_m))$, where φ_c and φ_m are parameters, subject to the resource constraint $c_t + K_{t+1} + M_{t+1}/p_t = \zeta_t K_t^{1-\eta} N_t^{\eta} + (1-\delta) \times K_t + M_t/p_t$, where $\ln \zeta_t$ is an AR(1) process with persistence ρ_ζ and standard error σ_ζ. Let $M_{t+1}^{\dagger} = M_{t+1}/p_t$ be real balances, π_t the inflation rate, r_t the rental rate of capital, and assume $\ln M_{t+1}^s = \ln M_t^s + \ln M_t^g$, where $\ln M_t^g$ has mean $\bar{M} \geqslant 0$ and standard error σ_M.

(i) Verify that the first-order conditions of the problem are

$$\left.\begin{aligned} r_t &= (1-\eta)\zeta_t K_t^{-\eta} N_t^{\eta} + (1-\delta), \\ 1 &= E_t[\beta(c_{t+1}/c_t)^{-\varphi_c} r_{t+1}], \\ (M_{t+1}^{\dagger})^{-\vartheta_m} c_t^{-\varphi_c} &= 1 + E_t[\beta(c_{t+1}/c_t)^{-\varphi_c} \pi_{t+1}]. \end{aligned}\right\} \tag{2.49}$$

(ii) Log-linearize (2.49), the resource constraint, and the law of motion of the shocks and cast these equations into the form of equations (2.36)–(2.38).

(iii) Guess that a solution for $[K_{t+1}, c_t, r_t, M_{t+1}^{\dagger}]$ is linear in $(K_t, M_t^{\dagger}, \zeta_t, M_t^g)$. Determine the coefficients of the relationship. Is the selected state space minimal?

Exercise 2.31. Suppose that the representative household maximizes $E_0 \sum_{t=0}^{\infty} \beta^t \times u(c_t, 1-N_t)$ subject to $c_t + M_{t+1}/p_t + K_{t+1} \leqslant (1-\delta)K_t + (\mathrm{GDP}_t - G_t) + M_t/p_t + T_t$, $M_t/p_t \geqslant c_t$, where $\mathrm{GDP}_t = \zeta_t K_t^{1-\eta} N_t^{\eta}$ and assume that the monetary authority sets $\Delta \ln M_{t+1}^s = \ln M_t^g + a i_t$, where a is a parameter and i_t the nominal interest rate. The government budget constraint is $G_t + (M_{t+1} - M_t)/p_t = T_t$. Let $[\ln G_t, \ln \zeta_t, \ln M_t^g]$ be a vector of random disturbances.

(i) Assume a binding CIA constraint, $c_t = M_{t+1}/p_t$. Derive the optimality conditions and the equation determining the nominal interest rate.

(ii) Compute a log-linear approximation of the first-order conditions and of the budget constraint, of the production function, of the CIA constraint, of the equilibrium pricing equation for nominal bonds, and of the government budget constraint around the steady states.

(iii) Show that the system is recursive and can be solved for $(N_t, K_t, M_{t+1}/p_t, i_t)$ first, while $(\mathrm{GDP}_t, c_t, \lambda_t, T_t)$ can be solved in a second stage as a function of $(N_t, K_t, M_{t+1}/p_t, i_t)$, where λ_t is the Lagrangian multiplier on the private budget constraint.

(iv) Write down the system of difference equations for $(N_t, K_t, M_t/p_t, i_t)$. Guess a linear solution (in deviation from steady states) in K_t and $[\ln G_t, \ln \zeta_t, \ln M_t^g]$ and find the coefficients of the solution.

(v) Assume prices are set one period in advance as a function of the states and of past shocks, i.e., $p_t = a_0 + a_1 K_t + a_{21} \ln G_{t-1} + a_{22} \ln \zeta_{t-1} + a_{23} \ln M_{t-1}^g$.

What is the state vector in this case? Use the method of undetermined coefficients to find a solution.

The next example shows the log-linearized decision rules of a version of the sticky price, sticky wage model described in exercise 2.17.

Example 2.20. Assume that capital is in fixed supply and the utility function is $E_0 \sum_t \beta^t[(c_t^{\vartheta}(1-N_t)^{1-\vartheta})^{1-\varphi}/(1-\varphi) + (\vartheta_{\mathrm{m}}/(1-\varphi_{\mathrm{m}}))(M_{t+1}/p_t)^{1-\varphi_{\mathrm{m}}}]$. Set $N^{\mathrm{ss}} = 0.33, \eta = 0.66, \pi^{\mathrm{ss}} = 1.005, \beta = 0.99, c^{\mathrm{ss}}/\mathrm{GDP}^{\mathrm{ss}} = 0.8$, where $c^{\mathrm{ss}}/\mathrm{GDP}^{\mathrm{ss}}$ is the share of consumption in GDP, N^{ss} is the number of hours worked, and π^{ss} is the gross inflation in the steady states, η is exponent of labor in the production function, β is the discount factor. These choices imply, for example, that in the steady state the gross real interest rate is 1.01, output is 0.46, real balances 0.37, and the real (fully flexible) wage 0.88. We select the degree of price and wage rigidity to be the same and set $\zeta_{\mathrm{p}} = \zeta_{\mathrm{w}} = 0.75$. Given the quarterly frequency of the model, this choice implies that on average firms (households) change their price (wage) every three quarters. Also, we choose the elasticity of money demand $\vartheta_{\mathrm{m}} = 7$. In the monetary policy rule we set $a_2 = -1.0, a_1 = 0.5, a_3 = 0.1, a_0 = 0$. Finally, ζ_t and M_t^{g} are AR(1) processes with persistence 0.95. The log-linearized decision rules for the real wage, output, nominal interest rate, real balances, and inflation, in terms of lagged real wages and the two shocks, are

$$\begin{bmatrix} \hat{w}_t \\ \hat{y}_t \\ \hat{i}_t \\ \hat{M}_t^{\dagger} \\ \hat{\Pi}_t \end{bmatrix} = \begin{bmatrix} 0.0012 \\ 0.5571 \\ 0.0416 \\ 0.1386 \\ 0.1050 \end{bmatrix} \begin{bmatrix} \hat{w}_{t-1} \end{bmatrix} + \begin{bmatrix} 0.5823 & -0.0005 \\ 0.2756 & 0.0008 \\ 0.0128 & 0.9595 \\ 0.0427 & -0.1351 \\ -0.7812 & 0.0025 \end{bmatrix} \begin{bmatrix} \hat{\zeta}_t \\ \hat{M}_t^{\mathrm{g}} \end{bmatrix}.$$

Two features of this approximate solution are worth commenting upon. First, there is little feedback from the state to the endogenous variables, except for output. This implies that the propagation properties of the model are limited. Second, monetary disturbances have little contemporaneous impact on all variables, except interest rates and real balances. These two observations imply that monetary disturbances have negligible real effects. This is confirmed by standard statistics. For example, technology shocks explain about 99% of the variance of output at the four years' horizon and monetary shocks the rest. This model also misses the sign of a few important contemporaneous correlations. For example, using linearly detrended U.S. data, the correlation between output and inflation is 0.35. For the model, the correlation is −0.89.

Exercise 2.32 (delivery lag). Suppose that the representative household maximizes $E_0 \sum_t \beta^t[\ln c_t - \vartheta_N N_t]$ subject to $c_t + \mathrm{inv}_t \leqslant \zeta_t K_t^{1-\eta} N_t^{\eta}$ and assume one-period delivery lag, i.e., $K_{t+1} = (1-\delta)K_t + \mathrm{inv}_{t-1}$. Show that the Euler equation is $\beta E_t[c_{t+1}^{-1}(1-\eta)\,\mathrm{GDP}_{t+1} K_{t+1}^{-1}] + (1-\delta)c_t^{-1} - \beta^{-1} c_{t-1}^{-1} = 0$. Log-linearize the system and find a solution by using K_t and $c_t^* = c_{t-1}$ as states.

Vaughan's method, popularized by Blanchard and Kahn (1980) and King et al. (1988a,b), takes a slightly different approach. First, using the state-space representation for the (log-)linearized version of the model, it eliminates the expectation operator either assuming certainty equivalence or substituting expectations with actual values of the variables plus an expectational error. Second, it uses the law of motion of the exogenous variables, the linearized solution for the state variables, and the costate (the Lagrangian multiplier) to create a system of first-order difference equations (if the model delivers higher-order dynamics, the dummy variable trick described in example 2.17 can be used to get the system in the required form). Third, it computes an eigenvalue–eigenvector decomposition on the matrix governing the dynamics of the system and divides the roots into explosive and stable ones. Then, the restrictions implied by the stability condition are used to derive the law of motion for the control (and the expectational error, if needed).

Suppose that the log-linearized system is $\Upsilon_t = \mathcal{A} E_t \Upsilon_{t+1}$, where $\Upsilon_t = [y_{1t}, y_{2t}, y_{3t}, y_{4t}]$, y_{2t} and y_{1t} are, as usual, the states and the controls, y_{4t} are the costates, and y_{3t} are the shocks and partition $\Upsilon_t = [\Upsilon_{1t}, \Upsilon_{2t}]$. Let $\mathcal{A} = \mathcal{P}\mathcal{V}\mathcal{P}^{-1}$ be the eigenvalue–eigenvector decomposition of $\mathcal{A}$. Since the matrix $\mathcal{A}$ is symplectic, the eigenvalues come in reciprocal pairs when distinct. Let $\mathcal{V} = \operatorname{diag}(\mathcal{V}_1, \mathcal{V}_1^{-1})$, where $\mathcal{V}_1$ is a matrix with eigenvalues greater than 1 in modulus and

$$\mathcal{P}^{-1} = \begin{bmatrix} \mathcal{P}_{11}^{-1} & \mathcal{P}_{12}^{-1} \\ \mathcal{P}_{21}^{-1} & \mathcal{P}_{22}^{-1} \end{bmatrix}.$$

Multiplying both sides by $\mathcal{A}^{-1}$, using certainty equivalence, and iterating forward, we have

$$\begin{bmatrix} \Upsilon_{1t+j} \\ \Upsilon_{2t+j} \end{bmatrix} = \mathcal{P}^{-1} \begin{bmatrix} \mathcal{V}_1^{-j} & 0 \\ 0 & \mathcal{V}_1^{j} \end{bmatrix} \begin{bmatrix} \mathcal{P}_{11}\Upsilon_{1t} + \mathcal{P}_{12}\Upsilon_{2t} \\ \mathcal{P}_{21}\Upsilon_{1t} + \mathcal{P}_{22}\Upsilon_{2t} \end{bmatrix}. \tag{2.50}$$

We want to solve (2.50) under the condition that Υ_{2t+j} goes to zero as $j \to \infty$, starting from some Υ_{20}. Since the components of $\mathcal{V}_1$ exceed unity, this is possible only if the terms multiplying $\mathcal{V}_1$ are zero. This implies $\Upsilon_{2t} = -\mathcal{P}_{22}^{-1}\mathcal{P}_{21}\Upsilon_{1t} \equiv \mathcal{Q}\Upsilon_{1t}$ so that (2.50) is

$$\begin{bmatrix} \mathcal{Q}\Upsilon_{1t+j} \\ \Upsilon_{2t+j} \end{bmatrix} = \begin{bmatrix} \mathcal{Q}\mathcal{P}_{11}^{-1}\mathcal{V}_1^{-j}(\mathcal{P}_{11}\Upsilon_{1t} + \mathcal{P}_{12}\Upsilon_{2t}) \\ \mathcal{P}_{21}^{-1}\mathcal{V}_1^{-j}(\mathcal{P}_{11}\Upsilon_{1t} + \mathcal{P}_{12}\Upsilon_{2t}) \end{bmatrix}, \tag{2.51}$$

which also implies $\mathcal{Q} = \mathcal{P}_{21}^{-1}\mathcal{P}_{11}$. Note that, for quadratic problems, the limit value of $\mathcal{Q}$ is the same as the limit of the Riccati equation (2.27).

Example 2.21. The basic RBC model with labor–leisure choice, no habit, $G_t = T_t = T^y = 0$, production function $f(K_t, N_t, \zeta_t) = \zeta_t K_t^{1-\eta} N_t^{\eta}$, and utility function $u(c_t, c_{t-1}, N_t) = \ln c_t + \vartheta_N(1 - N_t)$ when log-linearized, delivers the representation $\Upsilon_t = \mathcal{A}_0^{-1}\mathcal{A}_1 E_t \Upsilon_{t+1}$, where $\Upsilon_t = [\hat{c}_t, \hat{K}_t, \hat{N}_t, \hat{\zeta}_t]$ (since there is a one-to-one relationship between c_t, N_t, and λ_t, we can solve λ_t out of the system), where the hat indicates percentage deviations from steady states and

$$\mathcal{A}_0 = \begin{bmatrix} 1 & \eta - 1 & 1-\eta & -1 \\ -1 & 0 & 0 & 0 \\ -\left(\dfrac{c}{K}\right)^{\mathrm{ss}} & (1-\eta)\left(\dfrac{N^{\mathrm{ss}}}{K^{\mathrm{ss}}}\right)^{\eta} + (1-\delta) & \eta\left(\dfrac{N^{\mathrm{ss}}}{K^{\mathrm{ss}}}\right)^{\eta} & \left(\dfrac{N^{\mathrm{ss}}}{K^{\mathrm{ss}}}\right)^{\eta} \\ 0 & 0 & 0 & \rho \end{bmatrix},$$

$$\mathcal{A}_1 = \begin{bmatrix} 0 & 0 & 0 & 0 \\ -1 & -\beta\eta(1-\eta)\left(\dfrac{N^{\mathrm{ss}}}{K^{\mathrm{ss}}}\right)^{\eta} & \beta\eta(1-\eta)\left(\dfrac{N^{\mathrm{ss}}}{K^{\mathrm{ss}}}\right)^{\eta} & \beta(1-\eta)\left(\dfrac{N^{\mathrm{ss}}}{K^{\mathrm{ss}}}\right)^{\eta} \\ 0 & 1 & 0 & 0 \\ 0 & 0 & 0 & 1 \end{bmatrix}.$$

Let $\mathcal{A}_0^{-1}\mathcal{A}_1 = \mathcal{P}\mathcal{V}\mathcal{P}^{-1}$, where $\mathcal{P}$ is a matrix whose columns are the eigenvectors of $\mathcal{A}_0^{-1}\mathcal{A}_1$ and $\mathcal{V}$ contains, on the diagonal, the eigenvalues. Then

$$\mathcal{P}^{-1}\Upsilon_t \equiv \Upsilon_t^{\dagger} = \mathcal{V}E_t\Upsilon_{t+1}^{\dagger} \equiv \mathcal{V}E_t\mathcal{P}^{-1}\Upsilon_{t+1}. \tag{2.52}$$

Since $\mathcal{V}$ is diagonal, there are four independent equations which can be solved forward, i.e.,

$$\Upsilon_{it}^{\dagger} = v_i E_t \Upsilon_{i,t+\tau}^{\dagger}, \quad i = 1, \dots, 4. \tag{2.53}$$

Since one of the conditions describes the law of motion of the technology shocks, one of the eigenvalues is ρ_{ζ}^{-1} (the inverse of the persistence of technology shocks). One other condition describes the intratemporal efficiency condition (see equation (2.12)): since this is a static relationship, the eigenvalue corresponding to this equation is zero. The other two conditions, the Euler equation for capital accumulation (equation (2.11)) and the resource constraint (equation (2.4)), produce two eigenvalues: one above and one below 1. The stable solution is associated with the $v_i > 1$ since $\Upsilon_{it}^{\dagger} \to \infty$ for $v_i < 1$. Hence, for (2.53) to hold for each t in the stable case, it must be that $\Upsilon_{it}^{\dagger} = 0$ for all $v_i < 1$.

Assuming $\beta = 0.99$, $\eta = 0.64$, $\delta = 0.025$, $\vartheta_N = 3$, the resulting steady states are $c^{\mathrm{ss}} = 0.79$, $K^{\mathrm{ss}} = 10.9$, $N^{\mathrm{ss}} = 0.29$, $\mathrm{GDP}^{\mathrm{ss}} = 1.06$, and

$$\Upsilon_t^{\dagger} = \begin{bmatrix} 1.062 & 0 & 0 & 0 \\ 0 & 1.05 & 0 & 0 \\ 0 & 0 & 0.93 & 0 \\ 0 & 0 & 0 & 0 \end{bmatrix} E_t \begin{bmatrix} -2.18 & -0.048 & 0.048 & 24.26 \\ 0 & 0 & 0 & 23.01 \\ -2.50 & 1.36 & 0.056 & 1.10 \\ -2.62 & 0.94 & -0.94 & 2.62 \end{bmatrix} \Upsilon_{t+1}^{\dagger}.$$

The second row has $v_2 = \rho_{\zeta}^{-1}$, the last row the intertemporal condition. The remaining two rows generate a saddle path. Setting the third and fourth rows to zero ($v_3, v_4 < 1$), we have $\hat{c}_t = 0.54\hat{N}_t + 0.02\hat{K}_t + 0.44\hat{\zeta}_t$ and $\hat{N}_t = -2.78\hat{c}_t + \hat{K}_t + 2.78\hat{\zeta}_t$. The third rows of $\mathcal{A}_0$ and $\mathcal{A}_1$ provide the law of motion for capital: $\hat{K}_{t+1} = -0.07\hat{c}_t + 1.01\hat{K}_t + 0.06\hat{N}_t + 0.10\hat{\zeta}_t$.

Exercise 2.33. Suppose the representative household chooses consumption, hours, and nominal money balances to maximize $E_0 \sum_{t=0}^{\infty} u(c_t, 1 - N_t)$ subject to the following three constraints:

$$\left.\begin{aligned} \text{GDP}_t &= \zeta_t N_t^{\eta} = G_t + c_t, \\ c_t &= M_t / p_t, \\ M_{t+1} &= (M_t - p_t c_t) + p_t(y_t - G_t) + M_t(\bar{M} + M_t^{\mathrm{g}}), \end{aligned}\right\} \tag{2.54}$$

where ζ_t is a technology shock, G_t government expenditure, c_t consumption, M_t nominal balances, and p_t prices. Here G_t, ζ_t, and M_t^{g} are exogenous. Note that the third constraint describes the accumulation of money: $\bar{M}$ is a constant and M_t^{g} is a mean zero random variable.

(i) Derive and log-linearize the first-order conditions of the problem. What are the states?

(ii) Solve the linear system assuming that the growth rate of the exogenous variables $(\zeta_t, G_t, M_t^{\mathrm{g}})$ is an AR(1) process with common parameter ρ. Calculate the equilibrium expressions for inflation, output growth, and real balances.

(iii) Suppose you want to price the term structure of nominal bonds. Such bonds cost 1 unit of money at time t and give $1 + i_{t+\tau}$ units of money at time $t + \tau$, $\tau = 1, 2, \dots$. Write the equilibrium conditions to price these bonds. Calculate the log-linear expression of the slope for the term structure between a bond with maturity $\tau \to \infty$ and a one-period bond.

(iv) Calculate the equilibrium pricing formula and the rate of return for stocks which cost p_t^{s} units of consumption at t, and pay dividends $p_t^{\mathrm{s}} \mathrm{sd}_t$ which can be used for consumption only at $t + 1$. (Hint: the value of dividends at $t + 1$ is $p_t^{\mathrm{s}} \mathrm{sd}_t / p_{t+1}$.) Calculate a log-linear expression for the equity premium (the difference between the nominal return on stocks and the nominal return on a one-period bond).

(v) Simulate the responses of the slope of term structure and of the equity premium to a unitary shock in the technology (ζ_t), in government expenditure (G_t), and in money growth (M_t^{g}). Is the pattern of responses economically sensible?

Exercise 2.34 (Pappa). Consider the sticky price model analyzed in exercise 2.9 with the capital utilization setup but without adjustment costs to capital. Log-linearize the model and compute output responses to monetary shocks (still assume the monetary rule (2.20)). How does the specification compare in terms of persistence and amplitude of real responses to the standard one, without capacity utilization, but with capital adjustment costs?

2.2.4 *Second-Order Approximations*

First-order (linear) approximations are fairly easy to construct, useful for a variety of purposes, and accurate enough for fitting DSGE models to the data. However, first-order approximations are insufficient, when evaluating welfare across policies that do not affect the deterministic steady state of the model, when analyzing asset pricing problems, or when risk considerations become important. In some cases it may be enough to assume that nonlinearities, although important, are small in some sense (see, for example, Woodford 2003). In general, one may want to have methods to solve a second-order system and produce locally accurate approximations to the dynamics of the model, without having to explicitly consider global (nonlinear) approximations.

Suppose the model has the form

$$E_t[\mathfrak{J}(y_{t+1}, y_t, \sigma\epsilon_{t+1})] = 0, \tag{2.55}$$

where $\mathfrak{J}$ is an $n \times 1$ vector of functions, y_t is an $n \times 1$ vector of endogenous variables, and ϵ_t is an $n_1 \times 1$ vector of shocks. Clearly, some components of (2.55) may be deterministic and others may be static. So far we have been concerned with the first-order expansions of (2.55), i.e., with the following system of equations:

$$E_t[\mathfrak{J}_1\,\mathrm{d}y_{t+1} + \mathfrak{J}_2\,\mathrm{d}y_t + \mathfrak{J}_3\sigma\,\mathrm{d}\epsilon_{t+1}] = 0, \tag{2.56}$$

where $\mathrm{d}x_t$ is the deviation of x_t from some pivotal point, $x_t = (y_t, \epsilon_t)$. As we have seen, solutions to (2.56) are found positing a functional relationship $y_{t+1} = \mathfrak{J}^*(y_t, \sigma\epsilon_t, \sigma)$, linearly expanding it around the steady state $\mathfrak{J}^*(y^{\mathrm{ss}}, 0, 0)$, substituting the linear expression in (2.56), and matching coefficients.

Here we are concerned with approximations of the form

$$\begin{aligned} E_t[&\mathfrak{J}_1\,\mathrm{d}y_{t+1} + \mathfrak{J}_2\,\mathrm{d}y_t + \mathfrak{J}_3\sigma\,\mathrm{d}\epsilon_{t+1} \\ &+ 0.5(\mathfrak{J}_{11}\,\mathrm{d}y_{t+1}\,\mathrm{d}y_{t+1} + \mathfrak{J}_{12}\,\mathrm{d}y_{t+1}\,\mathrm{d}y_t + \mathfrak{J}_{13}\,\mathrm{d}y_{t+1}\sigma\,\mathrm{d}\epsilon_{t+1} \\ &\quad + \mathfrak{J}_{22}\,\mathrm{d}y_t\,\mathrm{d}y_t + \mathfrak{J}_{23}\,\mathrm{d}y_t\sigma\,\mathrm{d}\epsilon_t + \mathfrak{J}_{33}\sigma^2\,\mathrm{d}\epsilon_{t+1}\,\mathrm{d}\epsilon_{t+1})] = 0, \end{aligned} \tag{2.57}$$

which are obtained from a second-order Taylor expansion of (2.55). These differ from standard linearizations with lognormal errors since second-order terms in $\mathrm{d}y_t$, $\mathrm{d}y_{t+1}$ appear in the expression.

Since the second-order terms enter linearly in the specification, solutions to (2.57) can also be obtained with the method of undetermined coefficients, assuming there exists a solution of the form $y_{t+1} = \mathfrak{J}^*(y_t, \sigma\epsilon_t, \sigma)$, taking a second-order expansion of this guess around the steady states $\mathfrak{J}^*(y^{\mathrm{ss}}, 0, 0)$, substituting the second-order expansion for y_{t+1} into (2.57), and matching coefficients. As shown by Schmitt-Grohe and Uribe (2004), the problem can be sequentially solved, finding first the first-order terms and then the second-order ones.

Clearly, we need regularity conditions for the solution to exist and to have good properties. Kim et al. (2004) provide a set of necessary conditions. We first need the solution to imply that y_{t+1} remains in the stable manifold defined by $\mathfrak{H}(y_{t+1}, \sigma) = 0$ and satisfies $\{\mathfrak{H}(y_t, \sigma) = 0$, $\mathfrak{H}(y_{t+1}, \sigma) = 0$ a.s., and $\mathfrak{J}^1(y_{t+1}, y_t, \sigma\epsilon_{t+1}) = 0$ a.s. imply $E_t\mathfrak{J}^2(y_{t+1}, y_t, \sigma\epsilon_{t+1}) = 0\}$, where $\mathfrak{J} = (\mathfrak{J}^1, \mathfrak{J}^2)$. Second, we need $\mathfrak{H}(y_{t+1}, \sigma)$ to be continuous and twice differentiable in both its arguments. Third, we need the smallest unstable root of the first-order system to exceed the square of its largest stable root. This last condition is automatically satisfied if the dividing line is represented by a root of 1.0.

Under these conditions, Kim et al. argue that the second-order approximate solution to the dynamics of the model is accurate, in the sense that the error in the approximation converges in probability to zero at a more rapid rate than $\|\mathrm{d}y_t, \sigma\|^2$, when $\|\mathrm{d}y_t, \sigma\|^2 \to 0$. This claim does not depend on the a.s. boundedness of the process for ϵ_t, which is violated when its distribution has unbounded support, or on the stationarity of the model. However, for nonstationary systems the n-step-ahead accuracy deteriorates quicker than in the stationary case.

Example 2.22. We consider a version of the two-country model analyzed in example 2.6, where the population is the same in the two countries, the social planner equally weights the utility of the household of the two countries, there is no intermediate good sector, capital adjustment costs are zero, and output is produced with capital only. The planner's objective function is $E_0 \sum_t \beta^t (c_{1t}^{1-\varphi} + c_{2t}^{1-\varphi})/(1-\varphi)$, the resource constraint is $c_{1t} + c_{2t} + k_{1t+1} + k_{2t+1} - (1-\delta)(k_{1t} + k_{2t}) = \zeta_{1t} k_{1t}^{1-\eta} + \zeta_{2t} k_{2t}^{1-\eta}$, and $\ln \zeta_{it}$, $i = 1, 2$, is assumed to be i.i.d. with mean zero and variance σ_ζ^2. Given the symmetry of the two countries, it must be the case that in equilibrium $c_{1t} = c_{2t}$ and that the Euler equations for capital accumulations in the two countries are identical. Letting $\varphi = 2$, $\delta = 0.1$, $1 - \eta = 0.3$, $\beta = 0.95$, the steady state is $(k_i, \zeta_i, c_i) = (2.62, 1.00, 1.07)$, $i = 1, 2$, and a first-order expansion of the policy function is

$$k_{it+1} = \begin{bmatrix} 0.444 & 0.444 & 0.216 & 0.216 \end{bmatrix} \begin{bmatrix} k_{1t} \\ k_{2t} \\ \zeta_{1t} \\ \zeta_{2t} \end{bmatrix}, \quad i = 1, 2. \tag{2.58}$$

A second-order expansion of the policy function in country $i = 1, 2$ is

$$\begin{aligned} k_{it+1} &= \begin{bmatrix} 0.444 & 0.444 & 0.216 & 0.216 \end{bmatrix} \begin{bmatrix} k_{1t} \\ k_{2t} \\ \zeta_{1t} \\ \zeta_{2t} \end{bmatrix} - 0.83\sigma^2 \\ &\quad + 0.5 \begin{bmatrix} k_{1t} & k_{2t} & \zeta_{1t} & \zeta_{2t} \end{bmatrix} \begin{bmatrix} 0.22 & -0.18 & -0.02 & -0.08 \\ -0.18 & 0.22 & -0.08 & -0.02 \\ -0.02 & -0.08 & 0.17 & -0.04 \\ -0.08 & -0.02 & -0.04 & 0.17 \end{bmatrix} \begin{bmatrix} k_{1t} \\ k_{2t} \\ \zeta_{1t} \\ \zeta_{2t} \end{bmatrix}. \end{aligned} \tag{2.59}$$

Hence, apart from the quadratic terms in the states, (2.58) and (2.59) differ because the variance of the technology shock enters (2.59). In particular, when technology shocks are highly volatile, more consumption and less capital will be chosen with the second-order approximation. Clearly, the variance of the shocks is irrelevant for the decision rules obtained with the first-order approximation.

Exercise 2.35. Consider the sticky price model whose log-linear approximation is described in exercise 2.29. Assuming that $\vartheta = 0.5$, $\varphi = 2$, $\varphi_{\mathrm{m}} = 0.5$, $\zeta_{\mathrm{p}} = 0.75$, $\beta = 0.99$, compare first- and second-order expansions of the solution for c_t, N_t, i_t, π_t, assuming that there are only monetary shocks, which are i.i.d. with variance σ_M^2, that monetary policy is conducted by using a rule of the form $i_t = \pi_t^{a_3} M_t^{\mathrm{g}}$, and that w_t is equal to the marginal product of labor.

2.2.5 *Parametrizing Expectations*

The method of parametrizing expectations was suggested by Marcet (1992) and further developed by Marcet and Lorenzoni (1999). With this approach, the approximation is globally valid as opposed to valid only around a particular point as it is the case with quadratic, log-linear, or second-order approximations. Therefore, with such a method we can undertake experiments which are, for example, far away from the steady state, unusual from the historical point of view, or involve switches of steady states. The approach has two advantages. First, it can be used when inequality constraints are present. Second, it has a built-in mechanism that allows us to check whether a candidate solution satisfies the optimality conditions of the problem. Therefore, the accuracy of the approximation can be implicitly examined.

The essence of the method is simple. First, one approximates the expectational equations of the problem with a vector of functions $\hbar$, i.e., $\hbar(\alpha, y_{2t}, y_{3t}) \approx E_t[h(y_{2t+1}, y_{2t}, y_{3t+1}, y_{3t})]$, where y_{2t} and y_{3t} are known at t and α is a vector of (nuisance) parameters. Polynomial, trigonometric, logistic, or other simple functions which are known to have good approximation properties can be used. Second, one estimates α by minimizing the distance between $E_t[h(y_{2t+1}(\alpha), y_{2t}(\alpha), y_{3t+1}, y_{3t})]$ and $\hbar(\alpha, y_{2t}(\alpha), y_{3t})$, where $\{y_{2t}(\alpha)\}_{t=1}^T$ are simulated time series for the states obtained with the approximate solution. Let $Q(\alpha, \alpha^*) = |E_t[h(y_{2t+1}(\alpha), y_{2t}(\alpha), y_{3t+1}, y_{3t})] - \hbar(\alpha^*, y_{2t}, y_{3t})|^q$ some $q \geqslant 1$, where α^* is the distance minimizer. The method then looks for an $\tilde{\alpha}$ such that $Q(\tilde{\alpha}, \tilde{\alpha}) = 0$.

Example 2.23. Consider a basic RBC model with inelastic labor supply, where utility is given by $u(c_t) = c_t^{1-\varphi}/(1-\varphi)$ and φ is a parameter, the budget constraint is $c_t + K_{t+1} + G_t = (1 - T^y)\zeta_t K_t^{1-\eta} + (1-\delta)K_t + T_t$, and $(\ln \zeta_t, \ln G_t)$ are AR processes with persistence $(\rho_\zeta, \rho_{\mathrm{G}})$ and unit variance. The expectational (Euler) equation is

$$c_t^{-\varphi} = \beta E_t\{c_{t+1}^{-\varphi}[(1 - T^y)\zeta_{t+1}(1-\eta)K_{t+1}^{-\eta} + (1-\delta)]\}, \tag{2.60}$$

where β is the rate of time preferences. We wish to approximate the expression on the right-hand side of (2.60) with a function $\hbar(K_t, \zeta_t, G_t, \alpha)$, where α is a set of parameters. Then the parametrizing expectation algorithm works as follows.

Algorithm 2.3.

(1) Select $(\varphi, T^y, \delta, \rho_\zeta, \rho_{\mathrm{G}}, \eta, \beta)$. Generate (ζ_t, G_t), $t = 1, \ldots, T$, choose an initial α^0.

(2) Given a choice for $\hbar$ calculate $c_t(\alpha^0)$ from (2.60) with $\hbar(\alpha^0, k_t, \zeta_t, G_t)$, in place of $\beta E_t[c_{t+1}^{-\varphi}((1-T^y)\zeta_{t+1}(1-\eta)K_{t+1}^{-\eta}+(1-\delta))]$ and $K_{t+1}(\alpha^0)$ from the resource constraint. Do this for every t. This produces a time series for $c_t(\alpha^0)$ and $K_{t+1}(\alpha^0)$.

(3) Run a nonlinear regression using simulated $c_t(\alpha^0)$, $K_{t+1}(\alpha^0)$ of $\hbar(\alpha, K_t(\alpha^0), \zeta_t, G_t)$ on $\beta c_{t+1}(\alpha^0)^{-\varphi}[(1-T^y)\zeta_{t+1}(1-\eta)K_{t+1}(\alpha^0)^{-\eta}+(1-\delta)]$. Call the resulting nonlinear estimator α^{0*} and with this α^{0*} construct $Q(\alpha^0, \alpha^{0,*})$.

(4) Set $\alpha^1 = (1-\varrho)\alpha^0 + \varrho Q(\alpha^0, \alpha^{0*})$, where $\varrho \in (0, 1]$.

(5) Repeat steps (2)–(4) until $Q(\alpha^{*L-1}, \alpha^{*L}) \leqslant \iota$ or $|\alpha^{\mathrm{L}} - \alpha^{L-1}| \leqslant \iota$, or both, ι small.

(6) Use another $\hbar$ function and repeat steps (2)–(5).

When convergence is achieved, $\hbar(\alpha^*, K_t, \zeta_t, G_t)$ is the required approximating function. Since the method does not specify how to choose $\hbar$, one typically starts with a simple function (a first-order polynomial or a trigonometric function) and then checks the robustness of the solution by using more complex functions (e.g., a higher-order polynomial).

For the model of this example, setting $\varphi = 2$, $T^y = 0.15$, $\delta = 0.1$, $\rho_{\mathrm{G}} = \rho_\zeta = 0.95$, $\eta = 0.66$, $\beta = 0.99$, $q = 2$, and choosing $\hbar = \exp(\ln\alpha_1 + \alpha_2 \ln K_t + \alpha_3 \ln\zeta_t + \alpha_4 \ln G_t)$, 100 iterations of the above algorithm led to the following optimal approximating values, $\alpha_1 = -0.0780$, $\alpha_2 = 0.0008$, $\alpha_3 = 0.0306$, $\alpha_4 = 0.007$, and with these values $Q(\alpha^{*L-1}, \alpha^{*L}) = 0.000\,008$.

Next we show how to apply the method when inequality constraints are presented.

Example 2.24. Consider a small open economy which finances current account deficits issuing one-period nominal bonds. Assume that there is a borrowing constraint $\bar{B}$ so that $B_t - \bar{B} < 0$. The Euler equation for debt accumulation is

$$c_t^{-\varphi} - \beta E_t[c_{t+1}^{-\varphi}(1+r_t) - \lambda_{t+1}] = 0, \tag{2.61}$$

where r_t is the exogenous world real rate, λ_t the Lagrangian multiplier on the borrowing constraint, and the Kuhn–Tucker condition is $\lambda_t(B_t - \bar{B}) = 0$. To find a solution use $0 = c_t^{-\varphi} - \beta\hbar(\alpha, r_t, \lambda_t, c_t)$ and $\lambda_t(B_t - \bar{B}) = 0$ and calculate c_t and B_t, assuming $\lambda_t = 0$, for some $\alpha = \alpha^0$. If $B_t > \bar{B}$, set $B_t = \bar{B}$, find λ from the first equation and c_t from the budget constraint. Do this for every t; find α^{0*}; generate α^1 and repeat until convergence. In essence, λ_t is treated as an additional variable, to be solved for in the model.

Exercise 2.36. Suppose in the model of example 2.23 that $u(c_t, c_{t-1}, N_t) = (c_t - \gamma c_{t-1})^{1-\varphi}/(1-\varphi)$, $T_t = T^y = 0$. Provide a parametrized expectation algorithm to solve this model. (Hint: there are two state variables in the Euler equation.)

Exercise 2.37 (CIA with taxes). Consider a model where a representative household maximizes a separable utility function of the form $E_0\sum_{t=0}^{\infty}\beta^t[\vartheta_c \ln(c_{1t}) + (1-\vartheta_c)\ln(c_{2t}) - \vartheta_N(1-N_t)]$ by choices of consumption of cash and credit goods, leisure, nominal money balances, and investments, $0 < \beta < 1$. Suppose that the household is endowed with K_0 units of capital and one unit of time. The household receives income from capital and labor which is used to finance consumption purchases, investments, and holdings of money and government bonds. c_{1t} is the cash good and needs to be purchased with money; c_{2t} is the credit good. Output is produced with capital and labor by a single competitive firm with constant returns-to-scale technology and $1-\eta$ is the share of capital. In addition, the government finances a stochastic flow of expenditure by issuing currency, taxing labor income with a marginal tax rate T_t^y, and issuing nominal bonds, which pay an interest rate i_t. Assume that money supply evolves according to $\ln M_{t+1}^s = \ln M_t^s + \ln M_t^g$. Suppose agents start at time t with holdings of money M_t and bonds B_t. Assume that all the uncertainty is resolved at the beginning of each t.

(i) Write down the optimization problem mentioning the states and the constraints and calculate the first-order conditions. (Hint: you will need to make the economy stationary.)

(ii) Solve the model by parametrizing the expectations and using a first-order polynomial.

(iii) Describe the effects of an i.i.d. shock in T_t^y on real variables, prices, and interest rates, when B_t adjusts to satisfy the government budget constraint. Would your answer change if you kept B_t fixed and instead let G_t change to satisfy the government budget constraint?

As mentioned, the method of parametrizing expectations has a built-in mechanism to check the accuracy of the approximation. In fact, whenever the approximation is appropriate, the simulated time series must satisfy the Euler equation. As we will describe in more detail in chapter 5, this implies that, if $\tilde{\alpha}$ solves $Q(\tilde{\alpha},\tilde{\alpha}) = 0$, then $Q(\tilde{\alpha},\tilde{\alpha}) \otimes \mathfrak{h}(z_t) = 0$, where z_t is any variable in the information set at time t and $\mathfrak{h}$ is a $q \times 1$ vector of continuous differential functions. Under regularity conditions, when T is large, $T \times [(1/T)\sum_t Q_t \otimes \mathfrak{h}(z_t)]' W_t [(1/T)\sum_t Q_t \otimes \mathfrak{h}(z_t)]$, where Q_t is the sample counterpart of Q, v is equal to the dimension of the Euler conditions times the dimension of $\mathfrak{h}$, and $W_T \xrightarrow{\text{P}} W$ is a weighting matrix. For example 2.23, the first-order approximation is accurate since $\mathfrak{S}$ has a p-value of 0.36, when two lags of consumption are used as z_t.

While useful for a variety of problems, the parametrizing expectations approach has two important drawbacks. First, the iterations defined by algorithm 2.3 may lead nowhere since the fixed point problem does not define a contraction operator. In other words, there is no guarantee that the distance between the actual and approximating function will get smaller as the number of iterations grows. Second, the method relies on the sufficiency of the Euler equation. Hence, if the utility function is not strictly concave, the solution that the algorithm delivers may be inappropriate.

2.2.6 A Comparison of Methods

There exists a literature comparing various approximation approaches. For example, the special issue of the *Journal of Business and Economic Statistics* of July 1991 shows how various methods perform in approximating the decision rules of a particular version of the one-sector growth model for which an analytic solution is available. Some additional evidence is in Ruge-Murcia (2002) and Fernandez-Villaverde and Rubio-Ramirez (2003a,b). In general, little is known about the properties of various methods in specific applications. Experience suggests that even for models possessing simple structures (i.e., models without habit, adjustment costs of investment, etc.), simulated series may display somewhat different dynamics depending on the approximation used. For more complicated models no evidence is available. Therefore, caution should be employed in interpreting the results obtained by approximating models with any of the methods described in this chapter.

Exercise 2.38 (growth with corruption). Consider a representative household who maximizes $E_0 \sum_t \beta^t c_t^{1-\varphi}/(1-\varphi)$ by choices of consumption c_t, capital K_{t+1}, and bribes br_t subject to

$$c_t + K_{t+1} = (1 - T_t^y) N_t w_t + r_t K_t - \mathrm{br}_t + (1-\delta) K_t, \tag{2.62}$$

$$T_t^y = T_t^{\mathrm{e}}(1 - a \ln \mathrm{br}_t) + T_0^y, \tag{2.63}$$

where w_t is the real wage, T_t^y is the income tax rate, T_t^{e} is an exogenously given tax rate, T_0^y is a constant, and (φ, a, δ) are parameters. The technology is owned by the firm and given by $f(K_t, N_t, \zeta_t, K_t^{\mathrm{G}}) = \zeta_t K_t^{1-\eta} N_t^{\eta} (K_t^{\mathrm{G}})^{\aleph}$, where $\aleph \geqslant 0$, K_t is the capital stock, and N_t hours worked. Government capital K_t^{G} evolves according to $K_{t+1}^{\mathrm{G}} = (1-\delta) K_t^{\mathrm{G}} + N_t w_t T_t^y$. The resource constraint is $c_t + K_{t+1} + K_{t+1}^{\mathrm{G}} + \mathrm{br}_t = f(K_t, N_t, \zeta_t) + (1-\delta)(K_t + K_t^{\mathrm{G}})$ and $(\zeta_t, T_t^{\mathrm{e}})$ are independent AR(1) processes, with persistence (ρ_ζ, ρ_e) and variances $(\sigma_\zeta^2, \sigma_e^2)$.

(i) Define a competitive equilibrium and compute the first-order conditions.

(ii) Assume $\varphi = 2$, $a = 0.03$, $\beta = 0.96$, $\delta = 0.10$, $\rho_e = \rho_\zeta = 0.95$, and set $\sigma_\zeta^2 = \sigma_e^2 = 1$. Take a quadratic approximation of the utility and find the decision rules for the variables of interest.

(iii) Assume that $(\zeta_t, T_t^{\mathrm{e}})$ and the capital stock can take only two values (say, high and low). Solve the model by discretizing the state and shock spaces. (Hint: use the fact that shocks are independent and the values of the AR parameter to construct the transition matrix for the shocks.)

(iv) Solve the model by using a first-order log-linear approximation method.

(v) Use the parametrized expectations method with a first-order power function to find a global solution.

(vi) Compare the time series properties of consumption, investment and bribes in (ii)–(v).

Exercise 2.39 (transmission with borrowing constraints). Consider an economy where preferences are described by $u(c_t, c_{t-1}, N_t) = (c_t^{\vartheta}(1-N_t)^{1-\vartheta})^{1-\varphi}/(1-\varphi)$, which accumulates capital according to $K_{t+1} = (1 - \delta)K_t + \text{inv}_t$, where δ is the depreciation rate. Assume that the production function is of the form $\text{GDP}_t = \zeta_t K_t^{\eta_k} N_t^{\eta_N} \text{La}_t^{\eta_L}$, where La_t is land. Suppose individual agents have the ability to borrow and trade land and that their budget constraint is $c_t + K_{t+1} + B_{t+1} + p_t^{\text{L}}\text{La}_{t+1} \leqslant \text{GDP}_t + (1 - \delta)K_t + (1 + r_t^{\text{B}})B_t + p_t^{\text{L}}\text{La}_t$, where B_t are bond holdings, and suppose that there is a borrowing constraint of the form $p_t^{\text{L}}\text{La}_t - B_{t+1} \geqslant 0$, where p_t^{L} is the price of land in terms of consumption goods.

(i) Show that, in the steady state, the borrowing constraint is binding if $(1 + r^{\text{B}}) < \text{GDP}^{\text{ss}}/K^{\text{ss}} + (1 - \delta)$. Give conditions which ensure that the constraint is always binding.

(ii) Describe the dynamics of output following a technology shock when the borrowing constraint (a) never binds, (b) always binds, (c) binds at some t. (Hint: use an approximation method which allows the comparison across cases.)

(iii) Is it true that the presence of (collateralized) borrowing constraints amplifies and stretches over time the real effects of technology shocks?

3
Extracting and Measuring Cyclical Information

Most of the models considered in chapter 2 are designed to explain or replicate cyclical features of the actual data. Unfortunately, most economic time series display trends or marked growth patterns so that it is not immediately obvious what the cyclical properties of the data are. This chapter is concerned with the process of obtaining cyclical information from the actual data and with the problem of meaningfully summarizing it.

Cyclical information can be obtained in many ways. For example, Burns and Mitchell (1946) and the traditional cycle-dating literature look at turning points of a reference series to extract this information. Following Lucas (1977), in macroeconomics it is, however, more common to obtain cyclical information by first eliminating the permanent component (the "trend") from the data, typically thought to be unrelated to those features that business cycle models are interested in explaining, and then computing second moments for the residuals (the "cycle" or, better, the "growth cycle"). In practice, since trends and cycles are unobservable, assumptions are needed to split observable series into components. Many assumptions can be made and it is impossible to formally choose among alternatives with a finite amount of data. This means that standard criteria, such as lack of empirical relevance or statistical optimality, cannot be used.

The picture is further complicated by the fact that the literature has used the terms "detrending" and "filtering" for the process of extracting growth cycles interchangeably, even though the two concepts are distinct. Detrending should be intended as the process of making economic series (covariance) stationary. Detrending is necessary if one wants to compute functions of second moments of the data, which may not exist if a time series is, for example, a random walk, or to estimate the parameters of the model with several of the procedures described in this book; but detrending is unnecessary for other purposes, such as dating turning points, measuring amplitudes or the response to behavioral shocks. That is, certain cyclical information can be directly obtained from the raw data without any detrending.

The term "filtering" has a much broader applicability. As we have seen in chapter 1, filters are operators which carve out particular frequencies of the spectrum. One can build filters to eliminate very low frequency movements, to emphasize the variability in a particular frequency range, to smooth out high frequency movements, or to mitigate the effect of measurement errors. Filtering is unnecessary when comparing the cyclical behavior of the data to those of the models. However, since variability at frequencies corresponding to cycles of 6 to 24–32 quarters is considered to be of crucial economic importance—because business cycles reported, for example, by the NBER and the CEPR have periodicity which is, approximately, in this range—filtering may facilitate the comparison.

An important source of confusion emerges when time series econometricians and applied macroeconomists attempt to communicate the results of their studies since the former attempt to isolate "periodic" components in growth cycles, that is, components which are representable with sine and cosine functions and that show up as peaks in the spectral density in a particular frequency band. The latter, on the other hand, often interpret the presence of serial correlation in the growth cycle as indicating the existence of business cycles (see, for example, Long and Plosser 1983). Therefore, while they are satisfied when the growth cycle produced by their model is, for example, an AR(1) process, time series econometricians often use the argument that AR(1) processes have no peaks at business cycle frequencies and therefore there is no business cycle to speak of.

A final problem arises because some economic models feature shocks which have both transitory (short-run) and permanent (long-run) effects, in which case decompositions which assume that the two phenomena are separate are wrong; or because the effects they describe are not necessarily linked to statistical permanent/growth cycle decompositions. Monetary disturbances are a classic example of shocks having transitory effects on real variables (meaning, not specifically located at any frequencies or of a particular periodicity) and a permanent effect on nominal ones (meaning, in this case, full, pass-through in the long run). Because the link between economic theory and empirical practice is embryonic, and because there is little consensus on the type of economic model one should use to guide the decomposition (which shocks are permanent, which are transitory, which dominate, etc.), it is also hard to use economic theory to guide the decomposition.

Since traditional procedures displayed both conceptual and practical problems, new approaches have appeared over the last twenty years. We describe a subset of these methods, characterize their properties, discuss their relative merits, and highlight possible distortions that may appear when using them in comparing the output of a DSGE model and the data. We consider both univariate and multivariate methods and categorize decompositions into three somewhat arbitrary classes: statistical methods, economic methods, and hybrid methods. In the first class we include procedures which have a statistical or a probabilistic justification. They use time series assumptions on the observables or on the trend to measure the cycle. In the second class, extraction procedures are dictated by economic theory. Here, the cycles we obtain have relevance only to the extent that the model is a valid approximation to the data-generating process (DGP). In the third class we include procedures which are statistical in nature but have an economic justification of some sort.

Throughout this chapter we denote the logarithm of the observables by y_t, their growth rate by $\Delta y_t = (1 - \ell)y_t$, the trend (permanent component) by y_t^x, and the cycle by y_t^{c}.

3.1 Statistical Decompositions

3.1.1 Traditional Methods

Traditionally, the trend of a series was taken to be deterministic and the cyclical component was measured as the residual of a regression of y_t on polynomials in time. That is, $y_t = y^x + y_t^{\mathrm{c}}$, $y_t^x = a_0 + \sum_{j=1}^{J} a_j t^j$, and $\mathrm{corr}(y_t^x, y_t^{\mathrm{c}}) = 0$ so that $\hat{y}_t^{\mathrm{c}} = y_t - \hat{a}_0 - \sum_j \hat{a}_j t^j$ and $\hat{a}_j$, $j = 0, 1, 2, \dots$, are estimates of a_j. While the trend in such a setup can be easily estimated with least squares methods, the specification is unsatisfactory in two senses. First, since the trend is deterministic, it can be perfectly predicted arbitrarily far into the future. Second, the growth rate of y_t cannot accelerate or decelerate, contradicting the evidence of a number of macroeconomic time series in many countries since World War II. This latter problem can be partially eliminated if we allow for structural breaks at preselected dates.

Example 3.1. Suppose $y_t = y^x + y_t^{\mathrm{c}}$, $y_t^x = \sum_{j=0}^{J} a_{1j} t^j$ for $t < t_1$ and $y_t^x = \sum_{j=0}^{J} a_{2j} t^j$ for $t \geqslant t_1$, $a_{1j} \neq a_{2j}$, some $j \geqslant 0$, and let $\mathrm{corr}(y_t^x, y_t^{\mathrm{c}}) = 0, \forall t$. Then $\hat{y}_t^{\mathrm{c}} = y_t - \sum_j \hat{a}_{1j} t^j$ for $t < t_1$ and $\hat{y}_t^{\mathrm{c}} = y_t - \sum_j \hat{a}_{2j} t^j$ for $t \geqslant t_1$. Multiple breaks at known dates can be similarly modeled.

The traditional alternative to linear/segmented trend specifications is to assume that the growth rate of y_t captures the cyclical properties of the data. Here $\Delta y_t = y_t^{\mathrm{c}}$ and therefore $y_t^x = y_{t-1}$. This approach is also simple but has several disadvantages. First, the time plot of y_t^{c} does not visually conform to the idea one has of cyclical fluctuations. Second, y_t^{c} does not necessarily have zero mean. Third, somewhat counterintuitively, the variance of y_t^x may be very large.

Exercise 3.1. Let $\Delta y_t = y_t^{\mathrm{c}}$. Show that $E(y_t^{\mathrm{c}} y_{t-\tau}^{\mathrm{c}}) = 2\mathrm{ACF}_y(\tau) - \mathrm{ACF}_y(\tau - 1) - \mathrm{ACF}_y(\tau + 1)$, $\tau > 0$, where $\mathrm{ACF}_y(\tau) = \mathrm{cov}(y_t, y_{t-\tau})$. What can you say about the autocorrelation properties of y_t^{c} if $y_t = \rho y_{t-1} + e_t$, $e_t \sim$ i.i.d. $(0, 1)$, $0 < \rho < 1$?

3.1.2 Beveridge–Nelson (BN) Decomposition

Beveridge and Nelson (1981) also assume that y_t is integrated of order one but define the trend as the conditional mean of the predictive distribution for future y_t. Then, the cyclical component is the forecastable momentum in y_t at each t. Let y_t be represented as

$$\Delta y_t = \bar{y} + D(\ell) e_t, \quad e_t \sim \text{i.i.d. } (0, \sigma_e^2), \tag{3.1}$$

where $D(\ell) = 1 + D_1 \ell + D_2 \ell^2 + \cdots$, $\bar{y}$ is a constant, and the roots of $D(\ell)$ lie on or outside the complex unit circle. Let $y_t(\tau) \equiv E(y_{t+\tau} \mid y_t, y_{t-1}, \dots, y_0) =$

$y_t + E[\Delta y_{t+1} + \cdots + \Delta y_{t+\tau} \mid \Delta y_t, \ldots, \Delta y_0] \equiv y_t + \sum_{j=1}^{\tau} \widehat{\Delta y_t}(j)$ be the forecast of $y_{t+\tau}$ based on time t information. Using (3.1), $\widehat{\Delta y_t}(j) = \bar{y} + D_j e_t + D_{j+1} e_{t-1} + \cdots$ so that $y_t(\tau) = y_t + \tau\bar{y} + (\sum_{j=1}^{\tau} D_j)e_t + (\sum_{j=2}^{\tau+1} D_j)e_{t-1} + \cdots$. Let $y_t^x(\tau)$ be the time t forecast of $y_{t+\tau}$, adjusted for its mean rate of change, i.e., $y_t^x(\tau) \equiv y_t(\tau) - \tau\bar{y}$. For τ large, $y_t(\tau)$ is approximately constant and $y_t^x(\tau)$ is the value the series would have taken if it were on its long-run path. Hence,

$$\begin{aligned} y_t^x &= \lim_{\tau\to\infty}\left[y_t + \left(\sum_{j=1}^{\tau} D_j\right)e_t + \left(\sum_{j=2}^{\tau} D_j\right)e_{t-1} + \cdots\right] \\ &= y_{t-1}^x + \bar{y} + \left(\sum_{j=0}^{\infty} D_j\right)e_t, \end{aligned} \tag{3.2}$$

where the second equality comes from the definition of Δy_t and the fact that $y_t^x - y_{t-1}^x = y_t - y_{t-1} + (\sum_{j=1}^{\infty} D_j)e_t - \sum_{j=1}^{\infty} D_j e_{t-j}$. Hence, the trend is a random walk, since $(\sum_{j=1}^{\infty} D_j)e_t$ is a white noise, and the cyclical component is $y_t^{\mathrm{c}} = y_t - y_t^x = -\sum_{j=0}^{\infty}(\sum_{i=j+1}^{\infty} D_i)e_{t-j}$.

One advantage of the BN decomposition over traditional approaches is that it produces a decomposition without any assumptions on the structure of the components or on their correlation. In fact, since it uses a forecast-based definition of the trend, it does not need additional identifying restrictions to become operative.

Example 3.2 (Pagan and Harding). Suppose $\Delta y_t - \bar{y} = \rho(\Delta y_{t-1} - \bar{y}) + e_t$, $\rho < 1$, $e_t \sim$ i.i.d. $(0, \sigma_e^2)$. Then $y_t^x = y_t + [\rho/(1-\rho)](\Delta y_t - \bar{y})$ and $y_t^{\mathrm{c}} = -[\rho/(1-\rho)](\Delta y_t - \bar{y})$. Since ρ is a constant, the properties of y_t^{c} and Δy_t are similar. Hence, for simple AR(1) processes, the BN and the growth rate decompositions give cycles with similar correlation properties.

Several interesting features of the BN decomposition should be noted. First, since the two components are driven by the same shock, trend and cycle are perfectly correlated. Second, since estimates of D_j and forecasts $\widehat{\Delta y_t}(j)$ are typically obtained from ARIMA models, the standard identification problems of ARIMA specifications plague this method. Third, since long-run forecasts of Δy_t are based on past values of y_t only, trend estimates may be very imprecise and estimates of $\mathrm{var}(\Delta y_t^{\mathrm{c}})/\mathrm{var}(\Delta y_t^x)$ arbitrarily small. Finally, since innovations in y_t^x are $e_t^x \equiv (\sum_{j=0}^{\infty} D_j)e_t$, the variability of the innovations in the trend may be larger than the variability of the innovations in the series.

Example 3.3. Suppose $y_t = y_{t-1} + \bar{y} + e_t + D_1 e_{t-1}$ with $0 < |D_1| < 1$ and $e_t \sim$ i.i.d. $(0, \sigma_e^2)$. Note that if D_1 is positive, Δy_t is positively correlated. Then $\Delta y_t^x = \bar{y} + (1 + D_1)e_t = \bar{y} + e_t^x$ and $y_t^{\mathrm{c}} = -D_1 e_t$. Here $\mathrm{var}(e_t^x) > \mathrm{var}(e_t)$ and y_t^{c} is a white noise. In general, if $D_j > 0, \forall j \geqslant 1$, $\mathrm{var}(e_t^x) > \mathrm{var}(e_t)$. Note that, if $D_1 = 0$, $\Delta y_t^x = e_t$ and $y_t^{\mathrm{c}} = 0$. Hence, the presence of AR components is necessary to have serially correlated cycles and the decomposition correctly recognizes that, if they are missing, the cycle is either a white noise or nonexistent.

Exercise 3.2 (Coddington and Winters). Show that, if $\Delta y_t = \bar{y} + (D_2(\ell)/D_1(\ell))e_t$, $e_t \sim$ i.i.d. $(0, \sigma_e^2)$, the BN trend satisfies

$$y_t^x = y_{t-1}^x + \bar{y} + \frac{1 - \sum_{j=1}^{d_2} D_{2j}}{1 - \sum_{j=1}^{d_1} D_{1j}} e_t,$$

where d_1 and d_2 are the lengths of the polynomials $D_1(\ell)$ and $D_2(\ell)$. Suggest a way to recursively estimate y_t^x.

Exercise 3.3. Suppose $y_t = (1 - A)y_{t-1} + Ay_{t-2} + e_t$, $e_t \sim$ i.i.d. $(0, \sigma_e^2)$. Find y_t^x and y_t^c.

Extending the BN decomposition to multivariate frameworks is straightforward (see, for example, Evans and Reichlin 1994). Let $y_t = [\Delta y_{1t}, y_{2t}]$ be an $(m \times 1)$ vector of stationary processes, where y_{1t} are $I(1)$ variables and y_{2t} are (covariance) stationary; assume $y_t = \bar{y} + D(\ell)e_t$, where $e_t \sim$ i.i.d. $(0, \Sigma_e)$ and (i) $D_0 = I$; (ii) the roots of $\det(D(\ell))$ are on or outside the complex unit circle; (iii) $D_1(1) \neq 0$, where $D_1(\ell)$ is the matrix formed with the first m_1 rows of $D(\ell)$. Condition (i) is a simple normalization; condition (ii) ensures that $D(\ell)$ is invertible so that e_t are the innovations in y_t; condition (iii) ensures the existence of at least one stochastic trend. Note that for $m_1 = m$ there are m stochastic trends and that $m_1 \neq 0$ is necessary for the decomposition to be meaningful. Then the multivariate Beveridge and Nelson decomposition is

$$\begin{pmatrix} \Delta y_{1t} \\ \Delta y_{2t} \end{pmatrix} = \begin{pmatrix} \bar{y}_1 \\ 0 \end{pmatrix} + \begin{pmatrix} D_1(1) \\ 0 \end{pmatrix} e_t + \begin{pmatrix} (1-\ell)D_1^{\dagger}(\ell) \\ (1-\ell)D_2^{\dagger}(\ell) \end{pmatrix} e_t, \tag{3.3}$$

where $D_1^{\dagger}(\ell) \equiv [D_1(\ell) - D_1(1)]/(1-\ell)$, $D_2^{\dagger}(\ell) \equiv D_2(\ell)/(1-\ell)$, $\operatorname{rank}[D_1(1)] \leqslant m_1$ and $y_t^x = y_{t-1}^x + [\bar{y}_1 + D_1(1)e_t, 0]'$ is the trend (permanent component) of y_t.

Example 3.4. It is easy to verify that equation (3.3) is consistent with a BN univariate decomposition. Let the first component of y_{1t} be y_{1t}^1. Then $y_{1t}^{x1} = \lim_{\tau\to\infty}(E_t y_{1t+\tau}^1 - \tau\bar{y}^1)$, where $\bar{y}^1$ is the first element of $\bar{y}$. Hence, $\Delta y_{1t}^{x1} = \bar{y}^1 + D_1^1(1)e_t$, where D_1^1 is the first row of D_1 and $\Delta y_{1t}^{c1} = (1-\ell)D_1^{1\dagger}(\ell)e_t$, where $D_1^{1\dagger}(\ell) = [D_1^1(\ell) - D_1^1(1)]/(1-\ell)$ and $y_{1t}^{c1} = \sum_j(\sum_{i=j+1} D_{1i}^1)e_{t-j}$.

Exercise 3.4. Consider a system with output, prices, interest rates and money, and U.S. quarterly data. Suggest a way to estimate the two components of a multivariate BN decomposition. (Hint: specify a VAR of the form $A(\ell)y_t = \bar{y} + e_t$ and find out which variables are in y_{1t} and which in y_{2t}.)

Three properties of multivariate BN decompositions should be noted. First, $\operatorname{var}(\Delta y_t^x) = D_1(1)\Sigma_e D_1(1)' = \mathcal{S}_{\Delta y_1}(0)$. That is, the variance of the (difference in the) permanent component is equal to the spectral density of Δy_{1t} at frequency $\omega = 0$. Hence, the spectral density of $\Delta y_{1t}^{\mathrm{c}}$ at $\omega = 0$ is zero. Second, permanent and transitory components can be obtained without identifying meaningful economic shocks. Third, the variance of the (difference in the) cycle depends on the variables used to forecast y_t. In fact, $\mathrm{var}(\Delta y_{1t}^{\mathrm{c}}) = \mathrm{var}(\Delta y_{1t}) + \mathrm{var}(\Delta y_{1t}^{x}) + \mathrm{cov}(\Delta y_{1t}, \Delta y_{1t}^{x})$, which, after a few manipulations, implies $\mathrm{var}(\Delta y_{1t}^{\mathrm{c}}) / \mathrm{var}(\Delta y_{1t}^{x}) \geqslant \mathrm{var}(\Delta y_{1t}) / \mathrm{var}(\Delta y_{1t}^{x}) + 1 - 2\sqrt{\mathrm{var}(\Delta y_{1t} \mid \mathcal{F}_{t-1}) / \mathrm{var}(\Delta y_{1t}^{x})}$, where $\mathcal{F}_{t-1}$ is the information set available at t. Since $\mathrm{var}(\Delta y_{1t} \mid \mathcal{F}_{t-1}^{1}) \leqslant \mathrm{var}(\Delta y_{1t} \mid \mathcal{F}_{t-1}^{2})$ if $\mathcal{F}_{t-1}^{2} \subset \mathcal{F}_{t-1}^{1}$, it is possible to increase the variability of the (difference in the) cycle relative to the variability of the (difference in the) trend by enlarging the set of variables included in y_t (adding irrelevant variables does not help). Hence, the magnitude of $\mathrm{var}(\Delta y_{1t}^{\mathrm{c}}) - \mathrm{var}(\Delta y_{1t}^{x})$ in univariate and multivariate decompositions could be dramatically different.

Example 3.5. Let y_t be a 2×1 vector and let the first element be $\Delta y_{1t} = e_{1t} + D_{11}e_{1t-1} + D_{21}e_{2t-1}$. Here $\mathrm{var}(\Delta y_{1t}^{\mathrm{c}}) - \mathrm{var}(\Delta y_{1t}^{x}) = (D_{11}^2 - 1 - 2D_{11})\sigma_{e_1}^2 + D_{21}^2\sigma_{e_2}^2 \geqslant (D_{11}^2 - 1 - 2D_{11})\sigma_{e_1}^2 = \mathrm{var}(\Delta y_t^{\mathrm{c}}) - \mathrm{var}(\Delta y_t^{x})$ obtained from a univariate model. Note that, if D_{21} is large enough or if $\sigma_{e_2}^2 \gg \sigma_{e_1}^2$, $\mathrm{var}(\Delta y_{1t}^{\mathrm{c}}) - \mathrm{var}(\Delta y_{1t}^{x})$ could be positive even if $\mathrm{var}(\Delta y_t^{\mathrm{c}}) - \mathrm{var}(\Delta y_t^{x})$ is negative. Clearly, complicated patterns may arise when y_t is a large-scale VAR.

Exercise 3.5. Show that, if Δy_t is positively correlated at all lags, $\mathrm{var}(\Delta y_t) < \mathrm{var}(\Delta y_t^{x})$, $\mathrm{cov}(\Delta y_t^{\mathrm{c}}, \Delta y_t^{x}) < 0$, and $\mathrm{cov}(\Delta y_t, y_t^{\mathrm{c}}) = -\sum_{\tau=1}^{\infty} \mathrm{ACF}_{\Delta y_t}(\tau) < 0$.

As in the univariate case, the properties of estimated multivariate BN decompositions depend on a number of auxiliary assumptions, e.g., the lag length of the model, the number of cointegrating relationships, etc. It is therefore important to carefully monitor the sensitivity of the results and the quality of the estimates to alterations in these assumptions.

Exercise 3.6. Consider a bivariate VAR(1) where both variables are $I(1)$. Show how to compute a multivariate BN decomposition in this case. Repeat the exercise when one variable is $I(2)$ and one is $I(1)$.

3.1.3 Unobservable Component (UC) Decompositions

Unobservable component decompositions are popular in the time series literature since the cycle estimates obtained enjoy certain optimality properties. UC specifications are generally preferred to ARIMA representations for obtaining cyclical components for two reasons. First, there is no guarantee that an ARIMA model identified with standard methods will have those features that a series is postulated to exhibit (e.g., a cycle of the BN type requires the identification of an AR component). Second, the ARIMA(0, 1, 1) model favored by applied researchers fails to forecast certain long-run components.

Two basic features characterize UC decompositions. First, a researcher specifies flexible structures for the trend, the cycle, and other features of the data. These structures in turns imply an ARIMA representation for the observables which is more complicated than the one typically selected by standard methods. Second, given the assumed structure, the data are allowed to select the characteristics of the various components and diagnostic testing can be employed to examine what is left unexplained.

For most of the discussion, we assume two unobservable components, i.e.,

$$y_t = y_t^x + y_t^c. \tag{3.4}$$

Extensions to series containing, for example, seasonals or irregulars are immediate and left as an exercise to the reader. Assume that y_t^x can be represented as

$$y_t^x = \bar{y} + y_{t-1}^x + e_t^x, \quad e_t^x \sim \text{i.i.d. } (0, \sigma_x^2), \tag{3.5}$$

and that (y_t^c, e_t^x) is a jointly covariance stationary process. Note that, if $\sigma_x^2 = 0$, $\forall t$, y_t^x is a linear trend. While for the rest of this subsection we restrict attention to (3.5), more general trend specifications are possible. For example, "cyclical" trend movements are obtained by setting $y_t^x = \bar{y} + y_{t-1}^x + y_{t-1}^c + e_t^x$, $e_t^x \sim \text{i.i.d. } (0, \sigma_x^2)$. This specification, which implies that trend and cycle are correlated, was shown to fit U.S. data better than (3.5) plus a simple cycle specification where y_t^c is uncorrelated with e_t^x (see Harvey 1985). Trends with a higher order of integration are obtained if $\bar{y}$ drifts itself as a random walk.

Exercise 3.7 (Harvey and Jeager). Suppose

$$y_t^x = y_{t-1}^x + \bar{y}_{t-1} + e_t^x, \quad e_t^x \sim \text{i.i.d. } (0, \sigma_x^2), \tag{3.6}$$

$$\bar{y}_t = \bar{y}_{t-1} + v_t, \quad v_t \sim \text{i.i.d. } (0, \sigma_v^2). \tag{3.7}$$

Show that, if $\sigma_v^2 > 0$ and $\sigma_x^2 = 0$, y_t^x is an $I(2)$ process. Under what conditions is y_t^x "smooth," i.e., $\Delta^2 y_t^x$ are small? Verify that, if $\sigma_v^2 = 0$, (3.6), (3.7) collapse to (3.5) and that, if $\sigma_v^2 = \sigma_x^2 = 0$, the trend is deterministic.

To complete the specification we need to postulate a process for y_t^c and the relationship between y_t^c and e_t^x. There are three possibilities. In the first case we assume

$$y_t^c = D^c(\ell)e_t^c, \quad e_t^c \sim \text{i.i.d. } (0, \sigma_c^2), \tag{3.8}$$

where $D^c(\ell) = 1 + D_1^c\ell + \cdots$ and e_t^c is orthogonal to $e_{t-\tau}^x$, $\forall\tau$. Then (3.1), (3.5), and (3.8) imply that

$$D(\ell)e_t = e_t^x + (1-\ell)D(\ell)^c e_t^c, \tag{3.9}$$

so that $|D(1)|^2\sigma_e^2 = \sigma_x^2$ and the coefficients of $D(\ell)^c$ can then be found by using $D(\ell)D(\ell^{-1})\sigma_e^2 - \sigma_x^2 = (1-\ell)(1-\ell^{-1})D(\ell)^c D(\ell^{-1})^c\sigma_c^2$, provided that the roots of $D^c(\ell)$ are on or outside the complex unit circle. Note that, as in the BN decomposition, $\text{var}(\Delta y_t^x) = \mathcal{S}_{\Delta y}(0)$ so that the spectral density of Δy_t^c has zero power at the zero frequency. Hence, (3.9) places restrictions on y_t as we show next.

Exercise 3.8. Show that when the model is composed of (3.1), (3.5), and (3.8) $\mathcal{S}_{\Delta y_t}(\omega)$ has a global minimum at $\omega = 0$. Conclude that y_t cannot be represented as an ARIMA$(1, 1, 0)$ with a high autoregressive root.

Since the restrictions imposed by (3.9) may not be appropriate for all y_t, we want to have other cyclical structures to describe models of the form (3.1). A second possibility is

$$y_t^{\mathrm{c}} = D^{\mathrm{c}x}(\ell)e_t^x, \tag{3.10}$$

where $D^{\mathrm{c}x}(\ell) = 1 + D_1^{\mathrm{c}x}\ell + \cdots$. In (3.10) innovations to the trend and to the cycle are perfectly correlated. Note that, while the orthogonality of e_t^{c} and e_t^x restricts the ARIMA processes suitable to represent y_t, perfect correlation of the two innovations place no testable constraints on the ARIMA model for y_t. In particular, it is no longer true that an ARIMA$(1, 1, 0)$ is an unlikely representation for y_t. A third representation for y_t^{c} is

$$y_t^{\mathrm{c}} = D^{\mathrm{c}}(\ell)e_t^{\mathrm{c}} + D^{\mathrm{c}x}(\ell)e_t^x. \tag{3.11}$$

This specification is observationally equivalent to the "cyclical" trend model discussed above.

While it is usual to specify an AR process for y_t^{c}, one could also choose trigonometric functions. Such representations are useful if one is interested in emphasizing a particular frequency where the cycle may have most of its power. For example, one could set

$$y_t^{\mathrm{c}} = \frac{(1 - \rho_y \cos \omega\ell)e_t^{1\mathrm{c}} + (\rho_y \sin \omega\ell)e_t^{2\mathrm{c}}}{1 - 2\rho_y \cos \omega\ell + \rho_y^2\ell^2}, \tag{3.12}$$

where $e_t^{i\mathrm{c}} \sim$ i.i.d. $(0, \sigma_{e_i}^2)$, $i = 1, 2$, $0 \leqslant \rho_y \leqslant 1$, and $0 \leqslant \omega \leqslant \pi$.

Exercise 3.9. Show that y_t^{c} in (3.12) is an ARMA$(2, 1)$ process. Show that it reduces to an AR(2) if $\sigma_{e_1}^2 = 0$. Note that, for $0 < \omega < \pi$, the roots of the AR(2) polynomial are complex with modulus ρ_y. Finally, show that, for $\omega = 0$ or $\omega = \pi$, y_t^{c} is an AR(1) process.

Since cycles at frequency ω_i specified via (3.12) are orthogonal to cycles at frequency $\omega_{i'}$ when ω_i and $\omega_{i'}$ are Fourier frequencies, cycles of multiple length can be accounted for by taking a linear combination of (3.12) at any two frequencies.

Example 3.6. Suppose we are convinced that the average periodicity of cycles in the data has changed over time from, say, eight to six years. If quarterly data are available, then

$$y_t^{\mathrm{c}} = y_t^{c_1} + y_t^{c_2} = \frac{(1 - \rho_y \cos \omega_1\ell)e_t^{1\mathrm{c}} + (\rho_y \sin \omega_1\ell)e_t^{2\mathrm{c}}}{1 - 2\rho_y \cos \omega_1\ell + \rho_y^2\ell^2} + \frac{(1 - \rho_y \cos \omega_2\ell)e_t^{1\mathrm{c}} + (\rho_y \sin \omega_2\ell)e_t^{2\mathrm{c}}}{1 - 2\rho_y \cos \omega_2\ell + \rho_y^2\ell^2},$$

where $\omega_1 = 2\pi/32$ and $\omega_2 = 2\pi/24$.

Given (3.5) and a model for y_t^c, we can immediately show that y_t has an ARIMA format.

Example 3.7. Consider the trend specification (3.5), the trigonometric cycle specification (3.12), and assume that $y_t = y_t^x + y_t^c + e_t$, where $e_t \sim$ i.i.d. $(0, \sigma_e^2)$. Then $\Delta y_t = \bar{y} + e_t^x + \Delta y_t^c + \Delta e_t$. Therefore, if y_t^c is an ARMA(2, 1) process, Δy_t is a restricted ARMA(2, 3) process. The restrictions ensure (i) that, if it exists, a cycle can be found and (ii) the local identifiability of the various components (if $\rho_y > 0$, there are no common factors in the AR and MA parts).

Two methods are typically employed to obtain estimates of y_t^x in UC models: linear minimum mean square (LMMS) and the Kalman filter. The Kalman filter will be discussed in chapter 6. Let $\mathcal{F}_{-\infty}^{\infty} = \{\dots, y_{-1}, y_0, y_1, \dots\}$. To obtain LMMS estimates we use the Wiener–Kolmogorov prediction formulas (see, for example, Whittle 1980). Then $y_t^x = \mathcal{B}^x(\ell) y_t$, where $\mathcal{B}^x(\ell)$ is two-sided and, for a model composed of (3.1), (3.5), and (3.11), given by $\mathcal{B}^x(\ell) = \sigma_x^2[1 + (1 - \ell^{-1}) D^{cx}(\ell^{-1})][D(\ell)D(\ell^{-1})\sigma_y^2]^{-1}$. Since only $\mathcal{F}_0^{\tau} = \{y_0, y_1, \dots, y_\tau\}$ is available, define $y_t^x(\tau) \equiv E[y_t^x \mid \mathcal{F}_0^{\tau}]$. Then $y_t^x(\tau) = \sum_j \mathcal{B}_j^x E[y_{t-j} \mid \mathcal{F}_0^{\tau}]$ and estimates of the trend are obtained by substituting unknown values of y_t with forecasts or backcasts constructed from $\mathcal{F}_0^{\tau}$. Clearly, $\mathcal{B}^x(\ell)$ depends on the model for y_t^c but differences across specifications arise only from the way future data are used to construct $y_t^x(\tau)$.

Exercise 3.10. Show that estimates of $y_t^x(\tau)$ for all $\tau < t$ are the same regardless of whether (3.8), (3.10), or (3.11) are used.

One implication of exercise 3.10 is that to obtain $y_t^c(t)$, it is sufficient to construct an ARIMA model for y_t, forecast in the distant future, and set $y_t^c(t) = y_t - y_t^x(t)$, where $y_t^x(t)$ is the (forecast) estimate of the trend based on $\mathcal{F}_0^t$, adjusted for deterministic increases. Hence, $y_t^x(t)$ is similar to the permanent component obtained with the BN decomposition. However, as Morley et al. (2003) have shown, this does not mean that the two cyclical components have similar (time series) properties.

Multivariate versions of UC decompositions were initially suggested by Stock and Watson (1989, 1991) and used by several other researchers. Multivariate UC decompositions typically impose the restriction that a y_t vector is driven in the long run by a reduced number of permanent components; the transitory components, on the other hand, are allowed to be series specific. The multivariate UC setup is very close to the one employed in factor models (which we discuss in chapter 11). In factor models there is an unobservable factor which captures that part of the dynamics which is common to the series. Here the unobservable factor only captures the long-run patterns in the data.

For an $m \times 1$ vector of integrated series, a multivariate UC decomposition is

$$\Delta y_t = \bar{y} + \mathbb{Q}(\ell)\Delta y_t^x + y_t^c, \tag{3.13}$$

$$A^c(\ell) y_t^c = e_t^c, \tag{3.14}$$

$$A^x(\ell)\Delta y_t^x = \bar{y}^x + e_t^x, \tag{3.15}$$

where y_t and y_t^c are $m \times 1$ vectors and y_t^x is an $m_1 \times 1$ vector, $m_1 < m$; while $A^c(\ell)$ and $A^x(\ell)$ are one-sided polynomial matrices in the lag operator.

There are two main identifying assumptions implicit in (3.13)–(3.15). First, the long-run movements in y_t are driven by $m_1 < m$ processes. Second, $(y_{1t}^c, \dots, y_{mt}^c)$ and $(\Delta y_{1t}^x, \dots, \Delta y_{m_1 t}^x)$ are uncorrelated at all leads and lags. Since it is impossible to separately identify $A^x(\ell)$ and $\mathbb{Q}(\ell)$, one typically sets $\mathbb{Q}(\ell) = \mathbb{Q}$ and assumes that at least one $\Delta y_{i't}^x$ enters each Δy_{it}. Note that when $A^x(\ell) \neq 1$, $y_t^x(t)$ is an $m_1 \times 1$ vector of coincident indicators, while $y_t^c(t)$ captures idiosyncratic movements.

Since the system (3.13)–(3.15) has a state-space format, the unknown parameters $(A^c(\ell), A^x(\ell), \bar{y}^x, \bar{y}, \mathbb{Q}, \Sigma_c, \Sigma_x)$ and the unobservable components can be estimated by likelihood methods, recursively, with the Kalman filter. We defer the presentation of the Kalman filter recursions and of the prediction error decomposition of the likelihood to chapter 6.

3.1.4 Regime Shifting Decomposition

Although Hamilton's (1989) method was devised to model recurrently segmented trends rather than to extract cycles, it naturally produces cyclical components which can be used as a benchmark to compare the properties of simulated DSGE models.

The idea of the approach is simple. Instead of choosing either a deterministic or a continuously changing stochastic specification, the trend is assumed to be regime specific, with the regime varying randomly over time. Within a regime, trend movements are deterministic. Two features of the approach need to be emphasized: (i) the model for y_t is nonlinear in the conditional mean; (ii) shifts in the trend are driven by nonnormal errors.

For simplicity, we consider here only two regimes. Extensions to multiple regimes are straightforward and left as an exercise to the reader. Let Δy_t be stationary, let y_t^x and y_t^c be mutually independent, and let $y_t^x = a_0 + a_1 \varkappa_t + y_{t-1}^x$, where $\varkappa_t \in (1, 0)$ is an unobservable two-state Markov chain indicator with

$$P(\varkappa_t = i \mid \varkappa_{t-1} = i') = \begin{bmatrix} p_1 & 1 - p_1 \\ 1 - p_2 & p_2 \end{bmatrix}, \quad p_1, p_2 < 1.$$

Because $\varkappa_t$ has a first-order Markov structure, we can rewrite it as

$$\varkappa_t = (1 - p_2) + (p_1 + p_2 - 1)\varkappa_{t-1} + e_t^x, \tag{3.16}$$

where e_t^x can take four values $[1 - p_1, -p_1, -(1 - p_2), p_2]$ with probabilities $[p_1, 1 - p_1, p_2, 1 - p_2]$.

Exercise 3.11. Show that $\varkappa_t$ is covariance stationary. Is the process ergodic?

The residuals e_t^x in (3.16) have two properties which we summarize next.

Exercise 3.12. Show that $E(e_t^x \mid \varkappa_{t-1} = i,\ i = 0, 1) = 0$, $\text{var}(e_t^x \mid \varkappa_{t-1} = 1) = p_1(1 - p_1)$, and $\text{var}(e_t^x \mid \varkappa_{t-1} = 0) = p_2(1 - p_2)$.

Exercise 3.12 shows that e_t^x are uncorrelated with previous realizations of the state but not independent. Note that, if e_t^x were normal, uncorrelation implies independence. Therefore, the particular structure present in e_t^x implies separation between the two concepts.

Since e_t^x is dependent, $\varkappa_t$ will also be dependent. Solving (3.16) backwards and taking expectations at time zero, we have $E_0\varkappa_t = [(1 - p_2)/(2 - p_1 - p_2)] \times (1 - (p_1 + p_2 - 1)^t) + (p_1 + p_2 - 1)^t E_0\varkappa_0$ and, taking limits, $\lim_{t\to\infty} E_0\varkappa_t = (1 - p_2)/(2 - p_1 - p_2) \equiv \tilde{p}$. Let $P[\varkappa_0 = 1 \mid \mathcal{F}_0] = p^0$.

Exercise 3.13. Show that $\text{var}_0\, \varkappa_t = [(1 - p_2)/(2 - p_1 - p_2)^2][1 - (p_1 + p_2 - 1)^t]^2 + (p_1 + p_2 - 1)^{2t} E(\varkappa_0 - E\varkappa_0)^2$. Compute $\lim_{t\to\infty} \text{var}_0\, \varkappa_t$ and show that it is not statistically independent of $\varkappa_{t-j}$.

Exercise 3.13 shows that the moment structure of $\varkappa_t$ is nonlinear. This is important for forecasting y_t^x. In fact, the model for y_t^x can be rewritten as

$$[1 - (p_1 + p_2 - 1)\ell]\Delta y_t^x = a_1(1 - p_2) + a_0(2 - p_1 - p_2) + a_1 e_t^x. \qquad (3.17)$$

Hence, although y_t^x looks like an ARIMA(1, 1, 0) structure, forecasts of $y_{t+\tau}^x$, $\tau \geqslant 1$, based on a such a model are suboptimal since the nonlinear structure in e_t^x is ignored. In fact, the optimal trend forecasts are

$$E_t \Delta y_{t+\tau}^x = a_0 + a_1 E_t \varkappa_{t+\tau} = a_0 + a_1\{\tilde{p} + (p_1 + p_2 - 1)^t [P(\varkappa_t = 1 \mid \mathcal{F}_t) - \tilde{p}]\}, \qquad (3.18)$$

where $\mathcal{F}_t$ represents the information set at time t. Equation (3.18) is optimal since it incorporates the information that y_t^x changes only occasionally due to the discrete shifts in e_t^x.

Exercise 3.14. Let $\bar{\varkappa}_t \equiv \sum_{j=1}^t \varkappa_j$, i.e., $\bar{\varkappa}_t$ is the cumulative number of 1s. Show that $y_t^x = y_0^x + a_1\bar{\varkappa}_t + a_0 t$, $E_0[y_t^x \mid y_0^x, p^0] = y_0^x + a_1[\sum_{j=1}^t (p_1 + p_2 - 1)^j \times (p^0 - \tilde{p}) + \tilde{p}t] + a_0 t$, and $\lim_{t\to\infty} E_0[y_t^x - y_{t-1}^x \mid y_0^x, p^0] = a_0 + a_1\tilde{p}$.

Exercise 3.14 indicates that the growth rate of y_t^x is asymptotically independent of the information at time 0. Intuitively, as $t \to \infty$, y_t will be in the growth state $a_0 + a_1$ with probability $\tilde{p}$ and in the growth state a_0 with probability $(1 - \tilde{p})$. Note also that information concerning the initial state has permanent effects on y_t^x. In fact, $p^0 - \tilde{p} \neq 0$ produces permanent changes in y_t^x.

To complete the specification, a process for y_t^c needs to be selected.

Example 3.8. Suppose that $y_t^c \sim$ i.i.d. $\mathbb{N}(0, \sigma_c^2)$. Then y_t has the representation $[1 - (p_1 + p_2 - 1)\ell]\Delta y_t = a_1(1 - p_2) + a_0(2 - p_1 - p_2) + e_t - D_1 e_{t-1}$ with $e_t -$

$D_1 e_{t-1} = a_1 e_t^x + y_t^c - (p_1 + p_2 - 1) y_{t-1}^c$, where D_1 and σ_e^2 satisfy $(1 - D_1^2)\sigma_e^2 = [1 - (p_1 + p_2 - 1)^2]\sigma_c^2 + \sigma_x^2 a_1^2$ and $D_1^2 \sigma_e^2 = (p_1 + p_2 - 1)^2 \sigma_c^2$.

Exercise 3.15. Suppose that $\Delta y_t^c = A^c(\ell)\Delta y_{t-1}^c + e_t^c$, where $e_t^c \sim$ i.i.d. $\mathbb{N}(0, \sigma_c^2)$, $\forall \tau > 1$, and $A^c(\ell)$ is of order q_c. Show the implied model for y_t.

Given (3.16) and a model for y_t^c (for example, the one of exercise 3.15), our task is to estimate the unknown parameters and to obtain an estimate of $\varkappa_t$. First, we consider a recursive algorithm to estimate $\varkappa_t$. That is, given $P(\varkappa_{t-1} = \bar{\varkappa}_{t-1}, \varkappa_{t-2} = \bar{\varkappa}_{t-2}, \dots, \varkappa_{t-\tau} = \bar{\varkappa}_{t-\tau} \mid y_{t-1}, y_{t-2}, \dots)$, we want $P(\varkappa_t = \bar{\varkappa}_t, \varkappa_{t-1} = \bar{\varkappa}_{t-1}, \dots, \varkappa_{t-\tau+1} = \bar{\varkappa}_{t-\tau+1} \mid y_t, y_{t-1}, \dots)$. The algorithm consists of five steps.

Algorithm 3.1.

(1) Compute $P(\varkappa = \bar{\varkappa}_t, \dots, \varkappa_{t-\tau} = \bar{\varkappa}_{t-\tau} \mid \Delta y_{t-1}, \Delta y_{t-2}, \dots) = P(\varkappa = \bar{\varkappa}_t \mid \varkappa_{t-1} = \bar{\varkappa}_{t-1}) P(\varkappa_{t-1} = \bar{\varkappa}_{t-1}, \dots, \varkappa_{t-\tau} = \bar{\varkappa}_{t-\tau} \mid \Delta y_{t-1}, \Delta y_{t-2}, \dots)$, where $P(\varkappa_t = \bar{\varkappa}_t \mid \varkappa_{t-1} = \bar{\varkappa}_{t-1})$ is the transition matrix of $\varkappa_t$.

(2) Compute the joint probability of Δy_t and $\{\varkappa_j\}_{j=t-\tau}^t$, i.e., $f(\Delta y_t, \varkappa_t = \bar{\varkappa}_t, \dots, \varkappa_{t-\tau} = \bar{\varkappa}_{t-\tau} \mid \Delta y_{t-1}, \Delta y_{t-2}, \dots) = f(\Delta y_t \mid \varkappa = \bar{\varkappa}_t, \dots, \Delta y_{t-1}, \Delta y_{t-2}, \dots) P(\varkappa = \bar{\varkappa}_t, \dots, \varkappa_{t-\tau} = \bar{\varkappa}_{t-\tau} \mid \Delta y_{t-1}, \Delta y_{t-2}, \dots)$, where $f(\Delta y_t \mid \varkappa_t = \bar{\varkappa}_t, \dots, \Delta y_{t-1}, \Delta y_{t-2}, \dots) = (1/\sqrt{2\pi}\sigma_c) \times \mathrm{e}^{(-(\Delta y_t(\varkappa) - a_0 - a_1 \varkappa_t)(1 - A^c(\ell))^2)/2\sigma_c^2}$.

(3) Compute $f(\Delta y_t \mid \Delta y_{t-1}, \Delta y_{t-2}, \dots) = \sum_{\varkappa_t=0}^1 \cdots \sum_{\varkappa_{t-\tau}=0}^1 f(\Delta y_t, \varkappa = \bar{\varkappa}_t, \dots, \varkappa_{t-\tau} = \bar{\varkappa}_{t-\tau} \mid \Delta y_{t-1}, \Delta y_{t-2}, \dots)$. This is the predictive density of Δy_t based on $t - 1$ information.

(4) Apply Bayes theorem to obtain $P(\varkappa_t = \bar{\varkappa}_t, \dots \mid \Delta y_t, \Delta y_{t-1}, \Delta y_{t-2}, \dots) = f(\Delta y_t, \varkappa_t = \bar{\varkappa}_t, \dots, \varkappa_{t-\tau} = \bar{\varkappa}_{t-\tau} \mid \Delta y_{t-1}, \Delta y_{t-2}, \dots) / f(\Delta y_t \mid \Delta y_{t-1}, \Delta y_{t-2}, \dots)$.

(5) Obtain $P(\varkappa_t = \bar{\varkappa}_t, \dots, \varkappa_{t-\tau+1} = \bar{\varkappa}_{t-\tau+1} \mid \Delta y_t, \Delta y_{t-1}, \Delta y_{t-2}, \dots) = \sum_{\varkappa_{\tau-r}=0}^1 P(\varkappa_t = \bar{\varkappa}_t, \dots, \varkappa_{t-\tau} = \bar{\varkappa}_{t-\tau} \mid \Delta y_t, \Delta y_{t-1}, \Delta y_{t-2}, \dots)$.

To start the algorithm, one needs $P(\varkappa_0 = \bar{\varkappa}_0, \varkappa_{-1} = \bar{\varkappa}_{-1}, \dots, \varkappa_{-\tau+1} = \bar{\varkappa}_{-\tau+1} \mid y_0, y_{-1}, \dots)$. When this is unknown, one can use $P(\varkappa_0 = \bar{\varkappa}_0, \varkappa_{-1} = \bar{\varkappa}_{-1}, \dots, \varkappa_{-\tau+1} = \bar{\varkappa}_{-\tau+1})$, the unconditional probability of the $\tau - 1$ histories of $\varkappa_0$, which is obtained by setting $P(\varkappa_{-\tau+1} = 1) = \tilde{p}$, $P(\varkappa_{-\tau+1} = 0) = 1 - \tilde{p}$ and recursively constructing $P(\varkappa_{-\tau+j})$, $j = 2, 3, \dots$, using step (1) of the algorithm. Alternatively, one could treat $P(\varkappa_{-\tau+1} = 1)$ as a parameter to be estimated.

Extensions of the basic setup are considered in the next exercise.

Exercise 3.16. (i) Suppose there are n states. Write down the algorithm to estimate $\varkappa_t$ with information up to $t - 1$.

(ii) Let $A^c(\ell) = A^c(\ell, \varkappa_t)$. Write down the algorithm to estimate $\varkappa_t$.

(iii) Let $\sigma_c^2 = \sigma_c^2(\varkappa_t)$. Write down the algorithm to estimate $\varkappa_t$.

Example 3.9. One interesting extension is obtained when the probability of switching states depends on observable variables. For example, set $P(\varkappa_t = i \mid \varkappa_{t-1} = i, x_{t-1}\alpha_i) = \mathrm{e}^{x'_{t-1}\alpha_i}/(1 + \mathrm{e}^{x'_{t-1}\alpha_i})$ and $P(\varkappa = i \mid \varkappa_{t-1} = i', x_{t-1}\alpha_{i'}) = 1 - P(\varkappa = i \mid \varkappa_{t-1} = i, x_{t-1}\alpha_i)$, where $x_{t-1} = (1, y_{1,t-1}, \dots, y_{q,t-1})$, $\alpha_i = (\alpha_{i0}, \alpha_{i1}, \dots, \alpha_{iq})$ and let $f(\Delta y_t \mid \varkappa, \theta) = (1/\sqrt{2\pi}\sigma_c)\mathrm{e}^{(-(\Delta y_t(\varkappa) - \overline{\Delta y}(\varkappa))^2)/2\sigma_c^2}$. Then Δy_t has potentially a switching mean and the probability of switching is time dependent. Hence, there may be duration dependence in the fluctuations of Δy_t.

Next, we consider how to estimate the parameters. Since in step (2) of algorithm 3.1 we constructed the likelihood of the tth observation, parameters' estimates can be obtained once algorithm 3.1 has been run for all t, summing the log of these likelihoods. In fact, $\ln f(\Delta y_t, \Delta y_{t-1}, \dots, \Delta y_1 \mid \Delta y_0, \dots, \Delta y_{-\tau+1}) = \sum_{t=1}^{T} \ln f(\Delta y_t \mid \Delta y_{t-1}, \dots, \Delta y_1, \dots, \Delta y_{-\tau+1})$ can be numerically maximized with respect to $(\alpha_0, \alpha_1, p_1, p_2, A_j)$ (and $P(\varkappa_{-\tau+1} = 1)$ if needed).

From step (4) of the algorithm, we can also infer $\varkappa_t$ given current and past values of y_t, integrating out $\varkappa_{t-j}$, $j \geqslant 1$, i.e., $P(\varkappa_t = \bar{\varkappa}_t \mid \Delta y_t, \Delta y_{t-1}, \dots) = \sum_{\varkappa_{t-1}=0}^{1}, \dots, \sum_{\varkappa_{t-\tau}=0}^{1} P(\varkappa = \bar{\varkappa}_t, \varkappa_{t-1} = \bar{\varkappa}_{t-1}, \dots \mid \Delta y_t, \Delta y_{t-1}, \dots)$. This could be useful, for example, to decide whether at some date the economy was in a recession.

Example 3.10. Step (4) of algorithm 3.1 can also be used to evaluate the *ex post* probability that $\varkappa_{t-j} = \bar{\varkappa}_{t-j}$ (given time t information). For example, we could calculate the probability that in 1975:1 we were in the low growth state, given information up to, say, 2003:4. This involves computing $P(\varkappa_{\bar{t}} = \bar{\varkappa}_{\bar{t}} \mid \Delta y_t, \Delta y_{t-1}, \dots)$ for some $t - \tau \leqslant \bar{t} \leqslant t$.

The above framework is easy to manipulate but it unrealistically assumes that the cyclical component has a unit root. Eliminating this unit root brings realism to the specification but substantially complicates the calculations since the algorithm has to keep track of the entire past history of $\varkappa_t$. To illustrate the point suppose $y_t = y_t^x + y_t^c$ and

$$y_t^x = y_{t-1}^x + a_0 + a_1\varkappa_t, \tag{3.19}$$

$$(1 - A^c(\ell))y_t^c = e_t^c, \quad e_t^c \sim \text{i.i.d. } \mathbb{N}(0, \sigma_c^2), \tag{3.20}$$

where $\varkappa_t$ is a two-state Markov chain. Then $\Delta y_t = a_0 + a_1\varkappa_t + \Delta y_t^c$ and solving backward $y_t^c = (\sum_{i=1}^{t} \Delta y_i - a_0 t - a_1 \sum_{i=1}^{t} \varkappa_i) + y_0^c$ and

$$\begin{aligned} e_t^c = {} & (1 - A_1^c\ell - A_2^c\ell^2, \dots, -A_{q_c}^c\ell^{q_c})\Bigl(\sum_{i=1}^{t} \Delta y_i - a_0 t\Bigr) \\ & + (1 - A_1^c - A_2^c, \dots, -A_{q_c}^c)y_0^c - a_1(1 - A_1^c - A_2^c - \dots - A_{q_c}^c)\sum_i \varkappa_i \\ & + a_1 \sum_{j=1}^{q_c}\Bigl(\sum_{i=j}^{q_c} A_i^c\Bigr)\varkappa_{t-j+1}. \end{aligned}$$

If $A^c(\ell)$ has a unit root $(1 - A^c(1)) = 0$ and $e_t^c = (1 - A_1^c\ell - A_2^c\ell^2 - \cdots) \times (\sum_i \Delta y_i - a_0 t) + a_1 \sum_j (\sum_i A_i^c)\varkappa_{t-j+1}$, which is the same expression obtained when y_t^c is an ARIMA$(q_c, 1, 0)$. If it is not the case, the entire history of $\varkappa_t$ becomes a state variable. To solve this computation problem, Lam (1990) uses the sum of $\varkappa_t$ as a state variable. Note that, since y_0^c affects the likelihood, it is treated as a parameter to be estimated.

Exercise 3.17. Modify algorithm 3.1 to allow $(\sum_{i=1}^t \varkappa_i)$ to be a new state variable.

Note that the distribution of $\sum_{i=1}^t \varkappa_i$ is $P(\sum_i \varkappa_i = \bar{\bar{\varkappa}}_i \mid \Delta y_t, \ldots, \Delta y_1) = \sum_{\varkappa_t=0}^1 \cdots \sum_{\varkappa_{t-\tau}=0}^1 P(\varkappa_t = \bar{\varkappa}_t, \ldots, \varkappa_{t-\tau} = \bar{\varkappa}_{t-\tau}, \sum_i \varkappa_i = \bar{\bar{\varkappa}}_i \mid \Delta y_t, \ldots, \Delta y_1)$. An estimate of y_t^c is $\hat{y}_t^c = \sum_{i=1}^t \Delta y_i - a_0 t + y_0^c - a_1 \sum_{j=0}^t \bar{\bar{\varkappa}} P(\sum_i \varkappa_i = \bar{\bar{\varkappa}} \mid \Delta y_t, \Delta y_{t-1}, \ldots, \Delta y_1)$ and, given y_0^c, an estimate of the Markov trend is $\hat{y}_t^x = y_t - \hat{y}_t^c$.

3.2 Hybrid Decompositions

3.2.1 *The Hodrick and Prescott (HP) Filter*

The HP filter has been and still is one of the preferred methods to extract cyclical components from economic time series. Two basic features characterize HP decompositions. First, trend and cycle are assumed to be uncorrelated. Second, the trend is assumed to be a "smooth" process, that is, it is allowed to change over time as long as the changes are not abrupt. Hodrick and Prescott make the "smoothness" concept operational by penalizing variations in the second difference of the trend. Under these conditions y_t^x can be identified and estimated by using the following program,

$$\min_{y_t^x} \left\{ \sum_{t=0}^{x} (y_t - y_t^x)^2 + \lambda \sum_{t=0}^{T} [(y_{t+1}^x - y_t^x) - (y_t^x - y_{t-1}^x)]^2 \right\}, \tag{3.21}$$

where λ is a parameter. As λ increases, the trend y_t^x becomes smoother and for $\lambda \to \infty$, it becomes linear. A program like (3.21) can be formally derived as follows. Let the cyclical component and the second difference of the trend be white noises. Then weighted least squares minimization leads to

$$\min_{\{y_t^x\}} \left\{ \sum_{t=0}^{T} \frac{(y_t - y_t^x)^2}{\sigma_{y^c}^2} + \frac{1}{\sigma_{\Delta^2 y^x}^2} \left(\sum_{t=0}^{T} (y_{t+1}^x - 2y_t^x + y_{t-1}^x)^2 \right) \right\},$$

which produces $\lambda = \sigma_{y^c}^2 / \sigma_{\Delta^2 y^x}^2$, where $\sigma_{\Delta^2 y^x}^2$ is the variance of the innovations in the second difference of the trend and $\sigma_{y^c}^2$ is the variance of the innovations in the cycle. When $\lambda = \sigma_{y^c}^2 / \sigma_{\Delta^2 y^x}^2$, Wabha (1980) shows that (3.21) defines the best curve in a cloud of points, in the sense of making the mean square of the fitting error as small as possible.

Interestingly, the trend produced by (3.21) is identical to the one produced by a UC decomposition where the drift in the trend is itself a random walk and the cyclical component is a white noise (see Harvey and Jeager 1993). In particular, if we set $\lambda = \sigma_c^2/\sigma_v^2$, restrict $\sigma_x^2 = 0$ in the setup of exercise 3.7, and let $T \to \infty$, (3.21) is the optimal signal extraction method to recover y_t^x (see, for example, Gomez 1997). Clearly, if y_t is not simply trend plus noise or when the cyclical component is not i.i.d., the filter is no longer optimal. Hence, rather than estimating λ, the literature selects it *a priori* so as to carve out particular frequencies of the spectrum. For example, the value $\lambda = 1600$, typically used for quarterly data, implies that the standard error of the cycle is 40 times larger than the standard error of the second difference of the trend and this, in turns, implies that cycles longer than six to seven years are attributed to the trend. The choice of λ is not necessarily innocuous and implicit estimates of λ obtained by using BN or UC decompositions are only in the range $[2, 8]$.

Exercise 3.18. Show that the solution to (3.21) is $y^x = (\mathbb{F}^{\mathrm{HP}})^{-1}y$, where $y = [y_1, y_2, \dots, y_T]'$, $y_t^x = [y_1^x, y_2^x, \dots, y_T^x]'$. Write down the $T \times T$ matrix $\mathbb{F}^{\mathrm{HP}}$.

For quarterly data $\mathbb{F}^{\mathrm{HP}}$ has a particular form: only $t-2, t-1, t, t+1, t+2$ observations at each t matter in constructing y_t^x and the weights on leads and lags of y_t depend on λ but are symmetric. Therefore, the HP trend extractor is a two-sided, symmetric moving average filter. Once y_t^x is available, an estimate of the cyclical component is $y_t^{\mathrm{c}} = y_t - y_t^x$.

The filter defined by exercise 3.18 is time dependent. Furthermore, its two-sided nature creates beginning- and end-of-sample problems. In fact, the elements of $\mathbb{F}^{\mathrm{HP}}$ for the initial two and the final two observations differ from those of observations in the middle of the sample. This creates distortions when one is interested in the properties of y_t around the end of the sample. One unsatisfactory solution is to throw away these observations when constructing interesting statistics. Alternatively, one could dump the effects of these observations by appropriately weighting them in the computation of the autocovariance function of the filtered data. The preferred solution is to use a version of (3.21) where t runs from $-\infty$ to $+\infty$. This modified problem defines a set of linear, time-invariant weights which, away from the beginning and the end, are close to those obtained in exercise 3.18.

The modified minimization problem produces an estimate of the cycle of the form $y_t^{\mathrm{c}} = \mathcal{B}(\ell)^{\mathrm{c}} y_t$, where $\mathcal{B}^{\mathrm{c}}(\ell) \equiv \mathcal{B}(\ell)(1-\ell)^4 y_t$ and $\mathcal{B}(\ell)$ is (see, for example, Cogley and Nason 1995a)

$$\mathcal{B}(\ell) = \frac{|\lambda_1|^2}{\ell^2}[1-2\,\mathrm{Re}(\lambda_1)\ell+|\lambda_1|^2\ell^2]^{-1}[1-2\,\mathrm{Re}(\lambda_1)\ell^{-1}+|\lambda_1|^2\ell^{-2}]^{-1}. \quad (3.22)$$

λ_1^{-1} is the stable root of $[\lambda^{-1}\ell^2 + (1-\ell)^4]$, $\mathrm{Re}(\lambda_1)$ is the real part of λ_1, and $|\lambda_1|^2$ is its squared modulus. Note that, when $\lambda = 1600$, $\mathrm{Re}(\lambda_1) = 0.89$, $|\lambda_1|^2 \simeq 0.8$, and the cyclical weights $\mathcal{B}_j^{\mathrm{c}}$, $j = -\infty, \dots, 0, \dots, \infty$, can be written as (see Miller

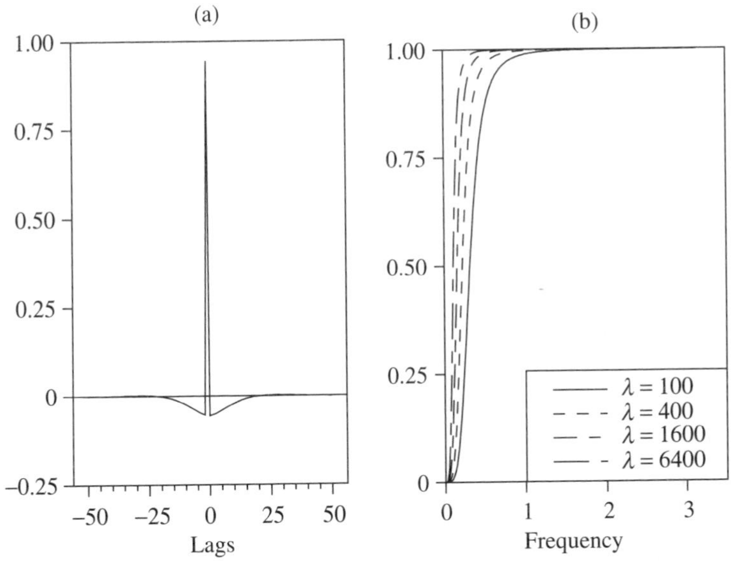

Figure 3.1. (a) Cyclical weights and (b) gain function, HP filter.

1976)

$$\mathcal{B}_j^{\mathrm{c}} = \begin{cases} -(0.8941)^j[0.0561\cos(0.1116j) + 0.0558\sin(0.1116j)], & j \neq 0, \\ 1 - [0.0561\cos(0) + 0.0558\sin(0)], & j = 0. \end{cases} \tag{3.23}$$

The cyclical filter can also be written as (see King and Rebelo 1993)

$$\mathcal{B}^{\mathrm{c}}(\ell) = \frac{(1-\ell)^2(1-\ell^{-1})^2}{1/\lambda + (1-\ell)^2(1-\ell^{-1})^2}. \tag{3.24}$$

Figure 3.1 plots $\mathcal{B}_j^{\mathrm{c}}$ obtained by using (3.23) and its gain function for $\lambda = 100, 400, 1600, 6400$. The weights have a sharp bell-shaped appearance, with the first-time crossing of the zero line at lag 2 and again around lag 20. Furthermore, for stationary y_t, increasing λ, adds to y_t^{c} cycles with longer and longer periodicity. Alternatively, since the area under the spectrum is the variance of y_t, increasing λ increases the importance of y_t^{c} relative to y_t^x.

To study the properties of the cyclical HP filter, it is worth distinguishing whether y_t is covariance stationary or integrated (and of what order). When y_t is stationary and $\lambda = 1600$, the gain of $\mathcal{B}^{\mathrm{c}}(\ell)$ is $\mathrm{Ga}^0(\omega) \simeq 16\sin^4(\frac{1}{2}\omega)/(\frac{1}{1600}+16\sin^4(\frac{1}{2}\omega)) = 4(1-\cos(\omega))^2/(\frac{1}{1600} + 4(1-\cos(\omega))^2)$, which has the form depicted in the top left panel of figure 3.2. We can immediately see that $\mathrm{Ga}^0(\omega = 0) = 0$, so that the power of y_t at frequency zero goes to the trend. Furthermore, $\mathrm{Ga}^0(\omega) \to 1$ for $\omega \to \pi$. Hence, the cyclical HP filter operates like a high pass filter, damping fluctuations with mean periodicity greater than 24 quarters per cycle ($\omega = 0.26$),

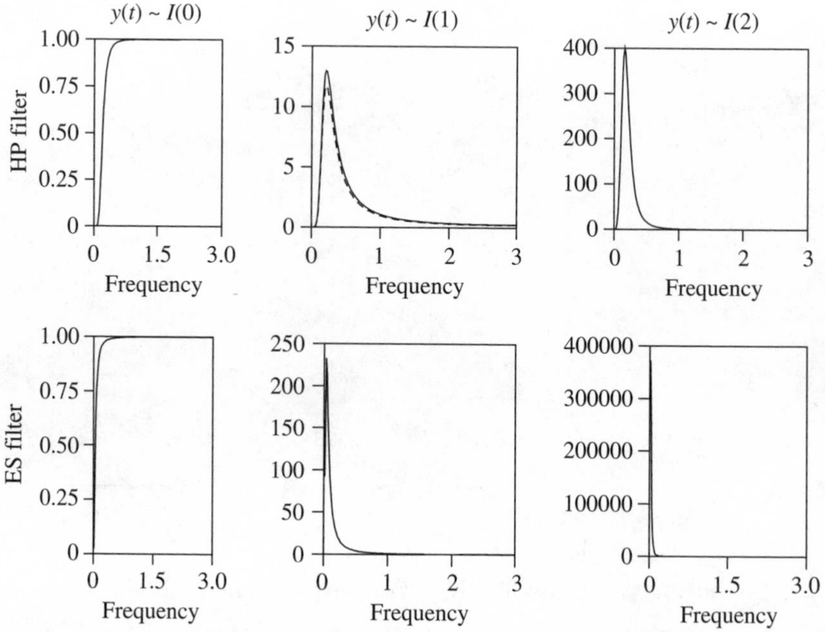

Figure 3.2. Gain functions: HP and ES filters.

and passing short cycles without changes. Because of this last feature, the cyclical HP filter leaves "undesirable" high frequency variability in y_t^{c}.

When y_t is integrated, the cyclical HP filter has different properties. In fact, one can think of $\mathcal{B}^{\mathrm{c}}(\ell)$ as a two-step filter: in the first step it renders y_t stationary; in the second it smooths the resulting stationary series with asymmetric moving average weights.

Example 3.11. When y_t is integrated of order 1, the first-step filter is $(1-\ell)$ and the second is $\mathcal{B}(\ell)(1-\ell)^3$. When $\lambda = 1600$, the gain function of the latter is $\mathrm{Ga}^1(\omega) \simeq [2(1-\cos(\omega))]^{-1}\mathrm{Ga}^0(\omega)$, which has a peak at $\omega^* = \arccos(1 - \sqrt{\frac{0.75}{1600}}) = 0.21$ (roughly 7.6 years cycles) (see top central panel of figure 3.2). Hence, $\mathrm{Ga}^1(\omega = 0) = 0$, but when applied to quarterly data, $\mathcal{B}(\ell)(1-\ell)^3$ damps long- and short-run growth cycles and strongly amplifies growth cycles at business cycle frequencies. For example, the variance of the cycles with average duration of 7.6 years is multiplied by 13 and the variance for cycles with periodicity between 3.2 and 13 years by a factor of 4.

Exercise 3.19. Suppose that y_t is $I(2)$. What is the gain of $\mathcal{B}(\ell)(1-\ell)^2$? (Call it $\mathrm{Ga}^2(\omega)$.)

A plot of $\mathrm{Ga}^2(\omega)$ is in the top right panel of figure 3.2. Here, $\mathrm{Ga}^2(\omega = 0) = 0$ but the cyclical peak is very large. In fact, the variability of cycles corresponding to about 14 years is increased by 400 times. To summarize, the cyclical HP filter may induce spurious periodicity in integrated series. In particular, it may produce "periodic" cycles in series which have no power at business cycle frequencies (Yule–Slutsky effect).

Example 3.12. While macroeconomists agree that aggregate time series display persistent fluctuations, it is an open question whether they are integrated or not. Therefore, one may be tempted to dismiss the above arguments suggesting that a largest root of around 0.95 is more probable than a root of 1.0. Unfortunately, for roots of the order of 0.95, the problem still remains. In fact, in this case the cyclical HP filter is $\mathcal{B}(\ell)(1-\ell)^3(1-\ell)/(1-0.95\ell)$. The upper central panel of figure 3.2 plots the gain of this filter (dashed line). It is easy to see that the shape of the gain function and the magnitude of the amplification produced at business cycle frequencies is similar to the $I(1)$ case.

Exercise 3.20. Suppose that $y_t = a_0 + a_1 t + a_2 t^2 + e_t$. Show that the HP filter eliminates linear and quadratic trends. (Hint: you can do this (i) analytically, (ii) by applying the HP filter to a simulated process and explaining what is going on, or (iii) by figuring out the spectral power of deterministic trends.)

Exercise 3.21. Consider the process $y_t = 10 + 0.4t + e_t$, where $e_t = 0.8e_{t-1} + v_t$ and $v_t \sim$ i.i.d. $(0, 1)$. Generate y_t, $t = 1, \dots, 200$, and filter it with the HP filter. Repeat the exercise by using $y_t = \rho_y y_{t-1} + 10 + e_t$, where $\rho_y = 0.8, 0.9, 1.0$ and $y_0 = 10$. Compare the autocovariance functions of y_t^{c} in the two cases. Is there any pattern in the results? Why?

Because $\mathcal{B}^{\mathrm{c}}(\ell)$ contains a term of the form $(1-\ell)^4$, y_t^{c} will have, in general, a noninvertible MA representation (see chapter 4 for a definition of invertibility). For example, if y_t is stationary, y_t^{c} has four MA unit roots while, if y_t is $I(1)$, y_t^{c} has three MA unit roots. Noninvertibility implies that no finite AR representation for y_t^{c} exists. In other words, y_t^{c} will display strong serial correlation, regardless of whether y_t is serially correlated or not.

Example 3.13. We have simulated data by using $y_t = 10 + 0.4t + e_t$, where $e_t = \rho_e e_{t-1} + v_t$, $v_t \sim$ i.i.d. $(0, 1)$, and $\rho_e = 0.4, 0.7, 1.0$. Figure 3.3 reports the ACFs of the HP filtered cyclical component. Clearly, the higher is ρ_e the stronger is the persistence in the y_t^{c} and the longer it takes for the ACF to settle down at zero.

The cyclical HP filter may not only induce artificial persistence or spurious periodicity; it may also create comovements that look like business cycle fluctuations in series which have no cycle. We show one extreme version of this phenomenon in the next exercise.

Exercise 3.22. Let $y_{1t} = y_{1t-1} + e_{1t}$, $y_{2t} = y_{2t-1} + e_{2t}$, and $(e_{1t}, e_{2t})' \sim (0, \Sigma_e)$.
(i) Show that the spectral density matrix of $(\Delta y_{1t}, \Delta y_{2t})$ is $\mathcal{S}(\omega) \propto \Sigma_e$.
(ii) Show that the spectral density matrix of $[y_{1t}^{\mathrm{c}}, y_{2t}^{\mathrm{c}}]'$ is $\mathcal{S}(\omega)\mathrm{Ga}^1(\omega)$, where $\mathrm{Ga}^1(\omega)$ is the gain of $\mathcal{B}(\ell)(1-\ell)^3$.

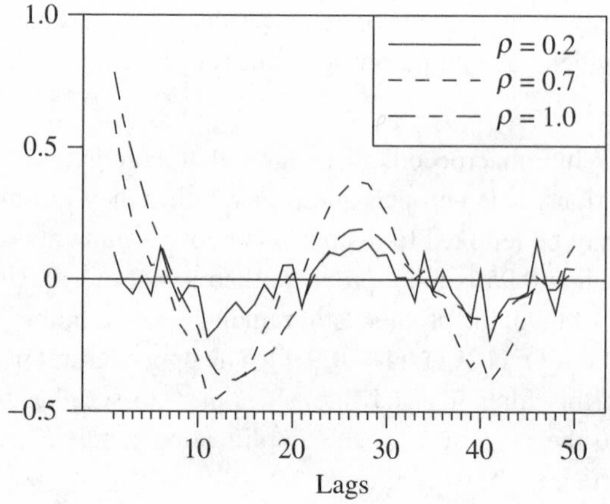

Figure 3.3. ACF of the cyclical component.

(iii) Let $\sigma_1 = \sigma_2 = 1$ and let $\sigma_{12} = 0.9, 0.5, 0.0$. Simulate y_{1t}, y_{2t} and plot $\mathcal{S}_{y^c}(\omega)$ in the three cases. Argue that when $\sigma_{12} \neq 0$, y^c_{1t} and y^c_{2t} display cycles of roughly the same periodicity as NBER cycles and that y^c_{1t} and y^c_{2t} have strong comovements.

Exercise 3.23. Using quarterly U.S. data for consumption and output, plot the spectral density matrix of $[\Delta c_t, \Delta \mathrm{GDP}_t]'$. Plot the spectral density matrix of the HP detrended version of consumption and output. Describe the features of the plots and contrast them.

In general, the use of the HP filter should be carefully monitored: uncritical use may produce a misleading impression of the ability of a model to reproduce the data. In particular, models which have little propagation mechanism and minor fluctuations, may acquire strong propagation and significant cyclical components once filtered with the HP filter (for examples, see Soderlin (1994) and Cogley and Nason (1995a)). Furthermore, as exercise 3.22 shows, even though the model and the data are only contemporaneously linked, application of the HP filter may make the similarities strong precisely at business cycle frequencies.

Example 3.14. We have simulated 200 data points from a basic RBC model with no taxes, utility given by $U(c_t, c_{t-1}, N_t) = c_t^{1-\varphi}/(1-\varphi) + \ln(1-N_t)$, assuming $\beta = 0.99$, $\varphi_c = 2.0$, $\delta = 0.025$, $\eta = 0.64$, and steady-state hours equal to 0.3. We log-linearize the model and assume an AR(1) parameter equal to 0.9 and a variance equal to 0.0066 for the logarithm of the technology shock and an AR(1) parameter equal to 0.8 and a variance equal to 0.0146 for the logarithm of government expenditure shock. Table 3.1 reports the mean of the cross-correlation function of GDP_{t-j} with capital (K_t), real wage (W_t), and labor productivity (np_t) for $j = 0, 1$ and the mean standard deviations of the latter three variables calculated over 100 simulations, before and after HP filtering. Since the data generated by the model is

Table 3.1. Simulated statistics.

	Raw data			HP filtered data		
Statistic	K_t	W_t	np_t	K_t	W_t	np_t
Correlation of GDP_t with	0.49	0.65	0.09	0.84	0.95	−0.20
Correlation of GDP_{t-1} with	0.43	0.57	0.05	0.60	0.67	−0.38
Standard deviation	1.00	1.25	1.12	1.50	0.87	0.50

stationary, the filtered statistics should be interpreted as describing the medium-to-high frequency properties of the simulated data. Clearly, both the relative ranking of variabilities and the size of the cross-correlations are significantly different in the raw and filtered data.

Since the smoothing parameter is chosen *a priori*, one may wonder how to translate $\lambda = 1600$ into a value for monthly or annual data. For example, researchers have used $\lambda = 400, 100, 10$ to compute y_t^{c} with annual data. Ravn and Uhlig (2002) show that insistence on the requirement that cycles of the same periodicity should be extracted, regardless of the frequency of the data, leads to select $\lambda = 129\,600$ for monthly data and $\lambda = 6.25$ for annual data when end-of-period data are used. While it is possible to derive these values analytically, we illustrate the logic for these choices by means of an example.

Example 3.15. We generated 12 000 (monthly) data points from an AR(1) process with $\rho = 0.98$ and the variance of the innovations equal to 1.0 and sampled it at quarterly and annual frequencies (using either end-of-period values or time averages) for a total of 4000 and 1000 observations. We then applied the HP filter to monthly, quarterly, and annual data where for quarterly data $\lambda = 1600$, for monthly data $\lambda_j = 3^j\lambda$, and for annual data $\lambda_j = 0.25^j\lambda$, $j = 3, 4, 5$. The variability of the quarterly HP filtered cycles are 2.20 (end-of-period sampling) and 2.09 (averaging monthly data). The variability of the monthly series are 1.95 for $j = 3$, 2.21 for $j = 4$, and 2.48 for $j = 5$. The variability of the annual series are 2.42 for $j = 3$, 2.09 for $j = 4$, and 1.64 for $j = 5$ (end-of-period sampling) and 2.15 for $j = 3$, 1.74 for $j = 4$, and 1.33 for $j = 5$ (time-averaged data). Hence, with end-of-period data, $j = 4$ is the most appropriate. For averaged data, $j = 4$ or $j = 5$ should be used.

Exercise 3.24. Let $\mathcal{B}^{\text{c}}(\omega, \lambda)$ be the cyclical HP filter for the quarterly data and let $\mathcal{B}^{\text{c}}(\omega/\tau, \lambda_\tau)$ be the cyclical HP filter for the sampling frequency ω/τ, where τ measures the frequency of the observations relative to quarterly data, i.e., $\tau = 0.25$ for annual data and $\tau = 3$ for monthly data. Let $\lambda_\tau = \tau^j\lambda$. Calculate the gain function for monthly and annual data when $j = 3.8, 3.9, 4.0, 4.1, 4.2$. For which value of j is the gain function closer to the one for quarterly data?

As we have seen, the HP filter is a mechanical device which defines the cycles it extracts via the selection of λ. In cross-country comparisons the use of a single λ may be problematic since the mean length of domestic cycles in not necessarily the same. For example, if a country has cycles with an average length of nine years, mechanical application of the HP filter will move these cycles to the trend. The fact that quarterly HP filtered GDP data for Japan, Italy, or Spain display very improbable expansions around the time of the first oil shock, when $\lambda = 1600$ is used, has prompted researchers to look for alternative ways to introduce smoothness in the trend. Marcet and Ravn (2001) suggested that for cross-country comparisons one could either fix the amount of variability assigned to the trend or restrict the relative variability of the trend to the cycle. Roughly speaking, this latter choice amounts to making λ endogenous (as opposed to exogenous) when splitting the spectrum of y_t into components. The problem (3.21) in the latter case can be written as

$$\min_{y_t^x} \sum_{t=1}^{T} (y_t - y_t^x)^2, \tag{3.25}$$

$$\mathcal{V}_1 \geqslant \frac{\sum_{t=1}^{T-2}[(y_{t+1}^x - y_t^x) - (y_t^x - y_{t-1}^x)]^2}{\sum_{t=1}^{T}(y_t - y_t^x)^2}, \tag{3.26}$$

where $\mathcal{V}_1 \geqslant 0$ is a constant, to be determined by the researcher, which measures the variability of the acceleration in the trend relative to the variability of the cyclical component. Expressions (3.25), (3.26), and (3.21) are equivalent, as the next exercise shows.

Exercise 3.25. (i) Show that if $\mathcal{V}_1 = 0$, y_t^x is a linear trend and if $\mathcal{V}_1 \to \infty$, $y_t^x = y_t$.

(ii) Let $\bar{\lambda}$ be the (exogenous) value of λ. Show that the Lagrangian multiplier on (3.26) is $\bar{\lambda} = \lambda/(1 - \lambda\mathcal{V}_1)$. Compute λ when $\bar{\lambda} = 1600$ and the ratio of variabilities is $1, \frac{1}{2}, \frac{1}{4}, \frac{1}{8}, \frac{1}{16}$.

(iii) Show that a solution for $\mathcal{V}_1$ can be found by iterating on $\mathcal{V}_1(\lambda) = \sum_{t=2}^{T-1}[y_{t+1}^x(\lambda) - 2y_t^x(\lambda) + y_{t-1}^x(\lambda)]^2 / \sum_{t=2}^{T-1}[y_t - y_t^x(\lambda)]^2$.

Intuitively, exercise 3.25(ii) indicates that, if we want to make useful international comparisons (say, using the United States as a benchmark), we should choose a λ that satisfies $\bar{\lambda} = \lambda(1 - \mathcal{V}_1\lambda)^{-1}$, where $\bar{\lambda} = 1600$ and $\mathcal{V}_1$ is the relative variability of the two components in the United States. Keeping $\mathcal{V}_1$ fixed is more appealing, since it is a parameter with some economic interpretation. In international comparisons it may not be clear which benchmark country one should use. Therefore, one could substitute (3.26) with

$$\mathcal{V}_2 \geqslant \frac{1}{T-2} \sum_{t=2}^{T-1} [(y_{t+1}^x - y_t^x) - (y_t^x - y_{t-1}^x)]^2. \tag{3.27}$$

Note that if $\mathcal{V}_2$ is the same across countries, the acceleration in the trend is common. Therefore, (3.27) imposes some form of balanced growth across countries. The main difference between (3.26) and (3.27) is that the former allows countries with more volatile cyclical components to also have more volatile trends, while this is not possible in the latter.

Endogenously selecting the frequencies belonging to the cycle in international comparisons can be useful in certain contexts but care should be exercised since uncritical application of this idea may lead to absurd conclusions if the mechanism generating the data differs across countries.

Exercise 3.26. Consider the following processes: (i) $(1 - 0.99\ell)y_t = e_t$; (ii) $(1 - 1.34\ell + 0.7\ell^2)y_t = e_t$; (iii) $y_t = (1 - 0.99\ell)e_t$. Calculate the implied value of λ in the three cases when $\mathcal{V}_1 = 0.5$ and $\bar{\lambda} = 1600$ and show the resulting business cycle frequencies.

3.2.2 *Exponential Smoothing (ES) Filter*

The exponential smoothing filter, used, for example, in Lucas (1980), is obtained from the program:

$$\min_{y_t^x} \left\{ \sum_{t=0}^{T} (y_t - y_t^x)^2 + \lambda \sum_{t=0}^{T} (y_t^x - y_{t-1}^x)^2 \right\}. \tag{3.28}$$

The ES filter therefore differs from the HP filter in the penalty function: here we penalize changes in the trend, while in the HP we penalize the acceleration of the trend.

The first-order conditions of the problem are $0 = -2(y_t - y_t^x) + 2\lambda(y_t^x - y_{t-1}^x) - 2\lambda(y_{t+1}^x - y_t^x)$. Therefore, as in the HP filter, the trend component is $y_t^x = (\mathbb{F}^{\text{ES}})^{-1} y_t$ and the cyclical component is $y_t^c = y_t - y_t^x = (1 - (\mathbb{F}^{\text{ES}})^{-1})y_t$.

Exercise 3.27. Write down the form of $\mathbb{F}^{\text{ES}}$ and compare it with $\mathbb{F}^{\text{HP}}$.

Note that, if t runs from $-\infty$ to ∞, the solution of the minimization problem can be written as $y_t^x = [\lambda(1-\ell)(1-\ell^{-1}) + 1]^{-1} y_t$.

Example 3.16. The ES filter removes a linear trend from y_t. To show this let $\mathbb{F}^{\text{ES}} y_t^x = y_t$ and $\mathbb{F}^{\text{ES}} \tilde{y}_t^x = \tilde{y}_t$, where $\tilde{y}_t = y_t + a_0 + a_1 t$. Combining the two expressions we have $\mathbb{F}^{\text{ES}}(y_t^x - \tilde{y}_t^x) = y_t - \tilde{y}_t = -a_0 - a_1 t$ or $\mathbb{F}^{\text{ES}}(y_t^c - \tilde{y}_t^c) + (\mathbb{F}^{\text{ES}} - 1)(-a_0 - a_1 t) = 0$. Hence, for $y_t^c = \tilde{y}_t^c$, we need $(\mathbb{F}^{\text{ES}} - 1)(-a_0 - a_1 t) = 0$. The result follows since $(\mathbb{F}^{\text{ES}} - 1)$ is symmetric.

Exercise 3.28. Using the same logic of example 3.16, examine whether the ES filter is able to remove a quadratic trend from the data.

Given the form of the trend remover ES filter, one can show that $y_t^c = (1 - \mathcal{B}^x(\ell))y_t = \{(1-\ell)(1-\ell^{-1})/[1/\lambda + (1-\ell)(1-\ell^{-1})]\}y_t$. Hence, application of the ES filter induces stationarity in y_t^c for y_t integrated up to order 2. Conversely, if y_t is integrated of order less than 2, y_t^c will display a unit root in the moving average and therefore strong (and possibly artificial) persistence.

The next exercise shows the effect of applying the ES filter to various types of data.

Exercise 3.29. (i) Show that, when y_t is stationary, the gain function of the cyclical ES filter is $2(1-\cos(\omega))/[1/\lambda + 2(1-\cos(\omega))]$. Show that y_t^{c} has zero power at $\omega = 0$, has the same power as y_t at $\omega \to \pi$, and that the larger λ is, the smoother is y_t^x (the more variable is y_t^{c}).

(ii) Show that the gain function of the ES filter is $1/[1/\lambda + 2(1-\cos(\omega))]$ when y_t is $I(2)$. Describe the effect of this filter at $\omega = 0, \pi$ and at business cycle frequencies.

The broad similarities of ES and HP filters can be appreciated in figure 3.2, where we plot the gain function of the two filters when $\lambda = 1600$. It is clear that the ES filter picks up trends with longer periodicity, but generally speaking, the two filters are very similar.

Exercise 3.30. Let $y_t = \rho_y y_{t-1} + e_t$, $e_t \sim$ i.i.d. $(0, 1)$, and $\rho_y = 0.5, 0.9, 1.0$. Simulate 2000 data points with $y_0 = 10$ and pass the last 1500 through the HP and ES filters. Plot the cyclical components, compute their variability, and their auto- and cross-correlation.

Both the HP and the ES trend extractors are special cases of a general class of low pass filter that engineers call Butterworth (BW) filters. Such filters have a squared gain function of the form $|\mathrm{Ga}(\omega)|^2 = 1/\{1 + [\sin(\omega/2)/\sin(\bar{\omega}/2)]^{2\kappa}\}$, where κ is a parameter and $\bar{\omega}$ is the frequency where the frequency response of the filter is equal to 0.5. For BW filters, the trend estimate is $y_t^x = \{1/[1 - \lambda(1-\ell)^{\kappa}(1-\ell^{-1})^{\kappa}]\}y_t$, where $\lambda = 1/2^{2\kappa}\sin^{2\kappa}(\bar{\omega}/2)$.

Example 3.17. It is easy to show that if $\kappa = 2$ and $\bar{\omega}$ solves $\lambda = (16\sin^4(\bar{\omega}/2))^{-1}$, $|\mathrm{Ga}(\omega)|^2$ is the squared gain function of the HP trend extractor filter while, if $\kappa = 1$ and $\bar{\omega}$ solves $\lambda = (4\sin^2(\bar{\omega}/2))^{-1}$, $|\mathrm{Ga}(\omega)|^2$ is the squared gain function of the ES trend extractor filter.

Relative to HP and ES filters, general BW filters have a free parameter κ, which can be used to tailor the gain function to particular needs. In fact, a higher κ moves $|\mathrm{Ga}(\omega)|^2$ to the right (i.e., $\bar{\omega}$ increases). Hence, for a fixed λ, it controls which cycles are included in y_t^{c}. Designing a low pass BW filter is easy. We need two parameters a_1, a_2, and two frequencies ω_1, ω_2 such that $1 - a_1 < \mathrm{Ga}^{\mathrm{BW}}(\omega) \leqslant 1$ for $\omega \in (0, \omega_1)$ and $0 < \mathrm{Ga}^{\mathrm{BW}}(\omega) \leqslant a_2$ for $\omega \in (\omega_2, \pi)$. Given a_1, a_2, ω_1, ω_2, one finds $\bar{\omega}$ and κ solving $1 + [\sin(\omega_1/2)/\sin(\bar{\omega}/2)]^{2\kappa} = (1-a_1)^{-1}$ and $1 + [\sin(\omega_2/2)/\sin(\bar{\omega}/2)]^{2\kappa} = (a_2)^{-1}$, rounding off κ to the closest integer.

3.2.3 *Moving Average (MA) Filters*

MA filters have a long history as smoothing devices and their use goes back, at least, to the work of Burns and Mitchell (1946). MA filters are defined by a polynomial

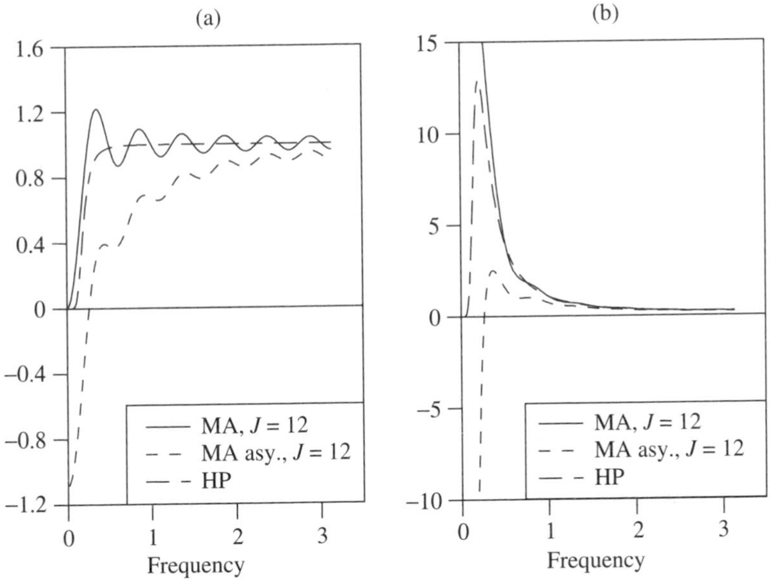

Figure 3.4. Gain functions: symmetric and asymmetric MA and HP filters. (a) $y(t) \sim I(0)$; (b) $y(t) \sim I(1)$.

in the lag operator $\mathcal{B}(\ell)$, which is either one- or two-sided (that is, it operates on J lags or on J leads and J lags of y_t). An MA filter is symmetric if $\mathcal{B}_j = \mathcal{B}_{-j}, \forall j$.

The frequency response function of a symmetric MA filter is $\mathcal{B}(\omega) = \mathcal{B}_0 + 2\sum_j \mathcal{B}_j \cos(\omega j)$, where we have used the trigonometric identity $2\cos(\omega) = e^{i\omega} + e^{-i\omega}$. Symmetric filters are typically preferred since they have zero phase shift. This is a desirable property to have since the timing of the cycles in the original and filtered series is the same.

Example 3.18. A simple symmetric two-sided (truncated) moving average filter is $\mathcal{B}_j = 1/(2J+1)$, $0 \leqslant j \leqslant |J|$, and $\mathcal{B}_j = 0$, $j > |J|$. If we set $y_t^c = (1 - \mathcal{B}(\ell))y_t \equiv \mathcal{B}^c(\ell)y_t$, the cyclical weights are $\mathcal{B}_0^c = 1 - 1/(2J+1)$ and $\mathcal{B}_j^c = \mathcal{B}_{-j}^c = -1/(2J+1)$, $j = 1, 2, \dots, J$. It is easy to recognize that $\mathcal{B}_j$ are the weights used in the box-car kernel in chapter 1. The Bartlett and the quadratic spectral kernels are also two-sided symmetric filters.

Since $\mathcal{B}(\omega = 0) = \sum_{j=-\infty}^{\infty} \mathcal{B}_j$, the condition $\lim_{j\to\infty} \sum_{j=-J}^{J} \mathcal{B}_j = 1$ is necessary and sufficient for an MA filter to have unitary gain at the zero frequency. If this is the case, $\mathcal{B}^c(\omega = 0) = 1 - \mathcal{B}(\omega = 0) = 0$, and y_t^c has zero power at the zero frequency.

Example 3.19. The effect of asymmetric filters can be appreciated in figure 3.4, where we present the gain of the filter of example 3.18, of the HP filter, and of an asymmetric filter with right-hand side weights equal to those of the filter of example 3.18 and left-hand side weights equal to $1/(2j+1)$, $j < J = 12$. In general, MA filters have unit gain only for $\omega \approx \pi$ and leave a lot of high frequency variability in the trend. Relative to a symmetric MA filter, an asymmetric one has gain different from zero at $\omega = 0$ and leaves much more cyclical variability in the trend.

Exercise 3.31 (Baxter and King). (i) Show that a symmetric MA filter with $\lim_{J\to\infty} \sum_{-J}^{J} \mathcal{B}_j = 1$ is sufficient to extract the quadratic trend from $y_t = e_t + a_0 + a_1 t + a_2 t^2$, where e_t is arbitrarily serially correlated, stationary process.

(ii) Show that, if $\lim_{J\to\infty} \sum_{-J}^{J} \mathcal{B}_j = 1$, the cyclical filter can be decomposed as $\mathcal{B}^{\mathrm{c}}(\ell) = (1-\ell)(1-\ell^{-1})\mathcal{B}^{\mathrm{c}\dagger}(\ell)$, where $\mathcal{B}^{\mathrm{c}\dagger}$ is a symmetric MA filter with $J-1$ leads and lags. That is, y_t^{c} will be stationary when y_t is integrated of order up to two.

Exercise 3.32. Is the ES trend extractor a symmetric MA filter? Does it satisfy $\lim_{J\to\infty} \sum_{j=-J}^{J} \mathcal{B}_j = 1$?

Example 3.20. One type of MA filter that is extensively used in the seasonal adjustment literature is the so-called Henderson filter. The filter is symmetric and operates on J leads and J lags of y_t. The weights $\mathcal{B}_j$ are found by solving $\min_j \sum_{j=-J}^{J} [(1-\ell)^3 \mathcal{B}_j]^2$ subject to $\sum_{j=-J}^{J} \mathcal{B}_j = 1$, $\sum_{j=-J}^{J} j\mathcal{B}_j = 0$, and $\sum_{j=-J}^{J} j^2 \mathcal{B}_j = 0$. Intuitively, the objective function of the problem measures the degree of smoothness of the curve described by the weights. The constraints imply that polynomials of degree up to the second are required to be part of the weights. When $J = 6$, $\mathcal{B}_0 = 0.2401$ and $\mathcal{B}_j = (0.2143, 0.1474, 0.0655, 0, -0.279, -0.19)$. These bell-shaped weights define a filter whose gain function resembles the one of the HP trend extractor filter and is smoother than the one constructed by using a tent-like filter.

3.2.4 Band Pass (BP) Filters

Band pass filters have become popular in applied macroeconomics following the work of Canova (1998), Baxter and King (1999), and Christiano and Fitzgerald (2003). One reason for preferring BP filters is that the majority of the other filters have high pass characteristics and therefore leave or exaggerate the amount of variability present at high frequencies. As we have seen in chapter 1, band pass filters are combinations of MA filters designed to eliminate both high and low frequency movements in the data. Furthermore, BP filters are appealing because they make the notion of business cycle operational by selecting fluctuations in a prespecified range.

The output of high, low, and band pass filters can be represented in the time domain with an infinite two-sided symmetric moving average of y_t. In chapter 1 we saw that the coefficients of a low pass filter are $\mathcal{B}_0^{\mathrm{lp}} = \omega_1/\pi$, $\mathcal{B}_j^{\mathrm{lp}} = \sin(j\omega_1)/(j\pi)$, $j = \pm 1, \pm 2, \dots$, where ω_1 is the upper frequency of the band; the coefficients of a high pass filter are $\mathcal{B}_0^{\mathrm{hp}} = 1 - \mathcal{B}_0^{\mathrm{lp}}$, $\mathcal{B}_j^{\mathrm{hp}} = -\mathcal{B}_j^{\mathrm{lp}}$; and the coefficients of a band pass filter are $\mathcal{B}_j^{\mathrm{bp}} = \mathcal{B}_j^{\mathrm{lp}}(\omega_2) - \mathcal{B}_j^{\mathrm{lp}}(\omega_1)$ for $\omega_1 < \omega_2$. Unfortunately, with a finite amount of data, these filters are not implementable. Therefore, one needs to approximate them with finite MA filters. Let $\mathcal{B}$ be an ideal filter, $\mathcal{B}^{\mathrm{A}}$ a generic approximate filter, and $\mathcal{B}^{\mathrm{A}}_J$ an approximate filter with J leads and lags. One such approximating filter can be found as follows.

Exercise 3.33 (Koopman). Show that, if one chooses the symmetric approximate filter $\mathcal{B}^{\mathrm{A}}_J$ to minimize $\int_{\pi}^{\pi} |\mathcal{B}^{\mathrm{A}}(\omega) - \mathcal{B}(\omega)|^2 \,\mathrm{d}\omega$, the solution is $\mathcal{B}^{\mathrm{A}}_j = \mathcal{B}_j$ for $|j| \leqslant J$ and $\mathcal{B}^{\mathrm{A}}_j = 0$ otherwise.

Intuitively, such a truncation is optimal since the weights for $|j| > J$ are small.

To ensure that the approximating BP filter has unit root removal properties we impose $\mathcal{B}^{\mathrm{A}}(\omega = 0) = 0$. The next exercise shows how to modify $\mathcal{B}^{\mathrm{A}}_J$ to account for this restriction.

Exercise 3.34 (Baxter and King). Show that, for a low pass filter, imposing $\mathcal{B}^{\mathrm{A}}(\omega = 0) = 1$ implies that the constrained approximate weights are $\mathcal{B}^{\mathrm{A}}_j + 1 - \sum_{j=-J}^{J} \mathcal{B}^{\mathrm{A}}_j/(2J + 1)$. Calculate the constrained approximate weights for an approximate BP filter.

Clearly, the quality of the approximation depends on the truncation point J (see chapter 5 for a similar problem). One way to quantify the biases introduced by the truncation is as follows.

Exercise 3.35. (i) Plot the gain function of the optimal and the approximate band pass filter obtained when $J = 4, 8, 12, 24$. Examine both the leakage and the compression that the approximate filter has relative to the optimal one at business cycle frequencies.

(ii) Simulate $y_t = 0.9y_{t-1} + e_t$, where $e_t \sim$ i.i.d. $\mathbb{N}(0, 1)$. Apply the approximate band pass filter weights for $J = 4, 8, 12, 24$. Calculate sample statistics of the filtered data for each J.

(iii) Simulate the model $(1 - \ell)y_t = e_t - 0.7e_{t-1}$. Repeat the steps in (ii).

Roughly speaking, J must be sufficiently large for the approximation to be reasonable. However, the larger J is, the shorter is the time series available for y_t^{c} (we are losing J observations at the beginning and at the end of the sample), and therefore the less useful the approximation is to measure the current state of the cycle. Simulation studies have shown that, if one is to extract cycles with periodicity between 6 and 24–32 quarters, a constrained band pass filter with $J \approx 12$ has little leakage and minor compression relative to other filters. Furthermore, it produces cyclical components which are similar (but less volatile) to those extracted with the HP filter for observations in the middle of the sample.

The modified approximate band pass filter has the same problems as other high pass filters when applied to $I(1)$ series. In fact, for symmetric MA filters with zero gain at $\omega = 0$, we can write $\mathcal{B}^{\mathrm{A}}(\ell) = -(1 - \ell)(1 - \ell^{-1})\mathcal{B}^{\mathrm{A}\dagger}(\ell)$, where $\mathcal{B}^{\mathrm{A}\dagger}_{|j|} = \sum_{i=|j|+1}^{J} (i - |j|)\mathcal{B}^{\mathrm{A}}_i$.

The next exercise shows that, if the data are stationary up to a quadratic trend, then no distortion in y_t^c results. Distortions, however, obtain if y_t is integrated.

Exercise 3.36 (Murray). Show that, if $y_t = a + b_1 t + b_2 t^2 + e_t$, then $y_t^c = \mathcal{B}^A(\ell)e_t$. Show that, if $(1-\ell)y_t = e_t$, then $y_t^c = -(1-\ell^{-1})B^{A\dagger}(\ell)e_t$. Plot the gain functions of $\mathcal{B}^A(\ell)$ and $-(1-\ell^{-1})\mathcal{B}^{A\dagger}(\ell)$ and describe their differences.

Example 3.21. If y_t is integrated, the BP filter may also generate spurious periodicity in filtered data. To show this we have generated 1000 samples of 500 data points from $\Delta y_t = e_t, e_t \sim \text{i.i.d.}\ (0, 1)$, and constructed y_t^c by using the $-(1-\ell^{-1})\mathcal{B}^{A\dagger}(\ell)$ filter. We then computed the mean value of the ACF of y_t^c for $J = 4, 8, 12$. The ACF of Δy_t is zero for all $\tau \geqslant 1$ while $\text{ACF}_{y^c}(\tau)$ is different from zero, at least for $\tau < 10$. Hence, an integrated process produces autocorrelated y_t^c if passed with the above filter. Interestingly, the persistence of y_t^c increases with J. For example, the mean of $\text{ACF}_{y^c}(\tau)$ fails to converge to zero for $J = 12$ for at least $\tau \leqslant 15$.

Exercise 3.37 (Murray). Let $y_t = y_t^x + y_t^c$ and let

$$y_t^x = 0.82 + y_{t-1}^x + e_t^x, \quad e_t^x \sim \text{i.i.d. } \mathbb{N}(0, (1.24)^2), \tag{3.29}$$

$$(1 - 1.34\ell + 0.71\ell^2)y_t^c = e_t^c, \quad e_t^c \sim \text{i.i.d. } \mathbb{N}(0, (0.75)^2). \tag{3.30}$$

(i) Calculate the autocovariance function of the cyclical component.

(ii) Simulate 2000 data points for y_t, filter them with an approximate BP filter using $J = 8, 16, 24, 40$. Calculate the autocovariance function of the estimated y_t^c.

(iii) Simulate 2000 data points for y_t setting $\text{var}(e_t^x) = 0$. Pass the simulated time series through an approximate BP filter using $J = 8, 16, 24, 40$. Calculate the autocovariance function of the estimated cyclical component. When is the autocovariance function in (ii) and (iii) closer to the one you have calculated in (i)?

(iv) Repeat (i), (ii), and (iii) 1000 times and store the values of the first five elements of the ACF. Calculate the number of times that the ACF in (i) lies within the 68% band you have computed for each step.

The approximate BP filter of exercise 3.33 equally penalizes deviations from the ideal filter at all frequencies. This may not be the best approximating distance. Intuitively, we would like the approximate filter to reproduce as closely as possible the ideal filter at those frequencies where the spectrum of y_t is large while we are less concerned about deviations when the spectrum of y_t is small. Christiano and Fitzgerald (CF) (2003) construct an approximation to the ideal filter which has these features by using projection techniques. The filter they obtain is nonstationary, asymmetric, and depends on the time series properties of y_t. The nonstationarity comes from the fact that there is a different projection problem for each t. Asymmetry is produced since all observations are used at each t to construct the filtered series. The dependence on the properties of y_t comes from the fact that the power of $\mathcal{S}_y(\omega)$ at different ω depends on the features of y_t. Contrary to the approximating filter of exercise 3.33, the approximating filter of Christiano and Fitzgerald does not truncate the optimal weights, except for some special DGP. Note that the CF filter could be made stationary and symmetric if these features are deemed necessary.

The CF filter can be obtained as follows. Suppose that we want to minimize $\int_{-\pi}^{\pi}[|\mathcal{B}^{\mathrm{A},t-1,T-t}(\omega)-\mathcal{B}(\omega)|/(1-\mathrm{e}^{-\mathrm{i}\omega})]\mathcal{S}_{\Delta y}(\omega)\,\mathrm{d}\omega$ by choice of $\mathcal{B}_j^{\mathrm{A},t-1,T-t}$, $j = T-t,\dots,t-1$. CF show that the solution to this problem can be represented as a $(T+1)$ system of linear equations of the form $\mathbb{F}_0^{\mathrm{CF}} = \mathbb{F}_1^{\mathrm{CF}}\mathcal{B}^{\mathrm{A},t-1,T-t}$, where $\mathbb{F}_0^{\mathrm{CF}}$, $\mathbb{F}_1^{\mathrm{CF}}$ depend on the properties of $\mathcal{S}_{\Delta y}$ and $\mathcal{B}(\omega)$.

Example 3.22. There are a few cases for which the solution to the problem is of interest. The first is when y_t is a random walk. Here, the approximate band pass filtered version of y_t is

$$\begin{aligned} y_t^{\mathrm{c}} = \mathcal{B}_{T-t}^{\mathrm{A}} y_T + \mathcal{B}_{T-t-1}^{\mathrm{A}} y_{T-1} + \cdots + \mathcal{B}_1^{\mathrm{A}} y_{t+1} \\ + \mathcal{B}_0^{\mathrm{A}} y_t + \mathcal{B}_1^{\mathrm{A}} y_{t-1} + \cdots + \mathcal{B}_{t-2}^{\mathrm{A}} y_2 + \mathcal{B}_{t-1}^{\mathrm{A}} y_1 \end{aligned}$$

for $t = 2,3,\dots,T-1$, where $\mathcal{B}_0^{\mathrm{A}} = (2\pi/\omega_1 - 2\pi/\omega_2)/\pi$, $\mathcal{B}_j^{\mathrm{A}} = [\sin(2j\pi/\omega_1) - \sin(2j\pi/\omega_2)]/j\pi$, $j \neq t-1, T-t$, $\mathcal{B}_{T-t}^{\mathrm{A}} = -0.5\mathcal{B}_0^{\mathrm{A}} - \sum_{j=1}^{T-t-1}\mathcal{B}_j^{\mathrm{A}}$, while $\mathcal{B}_{t-1}^{\mathrm{A}}$ solves $0 = \mathcal{B}_0^{\mathrm{A}} + \mathcal{B}_1^{\mathrm{A}} + \cdots + \mathcal{B}_{T-1-t}^{\mathrm{A}} + \mathcal{B}_{T-t}^{\mathrm{A}} + \mathcal{B}_1^{\mathrm{A}} + \cdots + \mathcal{B}_{t-2}^{\mathrm{A}} + \mathcal{B}_{t-1}^{\mathrm{A}}$, and $\omega_2(\omega_1)$ is the upper (lower) frequency of the band. For $t = 1$ the expression is $y_1^{\mathrm{c}} = 0.5\mathcal{B}_0^{\mathrm{A}} y_1 + \mathcal{B}_1^{\mathrm{A}} y_2 + \cdots + \mathcal{B}_{T-2}^{\mathrm{A}} y_{T-1} + \mathcal{B}_{T-1}^{\mathrm{A}} y_T$ and for $t = T$ it is $y_T^{\mathrm{c}} = 0.5\mathcal{B}_0^{\mathrm{A}} y_T + \mathcal{B}_1^{\mathrm{A}} y_{T-1} + \cdots + \mathcal{B}_{T-2}^{\mathrm{A}} y_2 + \mathcal{B}_{T-1}^{\mathrm{A}} y_1$. From the above, it is clear that the filter uses all the observations for each t, that the weights change with t and become asymmetric if t is away from the middle of the sample. A second interesting case obtains if y_t is i.i.d. in which case the weights $\mathcal{S}_y(\omega) = \sigma_y^2/2\pi$ are independent of ω. Then $\mathcal{B}_j^{\mathrm{A},t-1,T-t} = \mathcal{B}_j$ for $j = T-t,\dots,t-1$ and zero otherwise, which produces the solution of exercise 3.33 if the filter is required to be symmetric and $\mathcal{B}_j$ is truncated for $j > J$.

We present the gain functions of the approximate asymmetric and approximate symmetric truncated CF filters, both obtained when y_t is a random walk, of the ideal filter and of the approximate BK filter produced in exercise 3.33 in figure 3.5. The two truncated symmetric filters are similar but the CF filter gives more weights to the lower frequencies of the band (since a random walk has more power in those frequencies) and has smaller side loops. The asymmetric filter, on the other hand, is very close to the ideal one.

Exercise 3.38. Describe how to make the approximate CF filter symmetric.

The approximate CF filter is general and solves beginning- and end-of-sample problems. This generality comes at a costs: one has to *a priori* choose the shape of $\mathcal{S}_{\Delta y}(\omega)$ (in particular, if y_t is stationary or integrated and what are its serial correlation properties) and the filter induces phase shifts in the autocovariance function of y_t. By way of examples, Christiano and Fitzgerald suggest that phase shifts are small in practice and can be safety neglected in the analysis. Also, they indicate that the approximation obtained arbitrarily assuming that y_t is a random walk works well for a variety of macroeconomic time series.

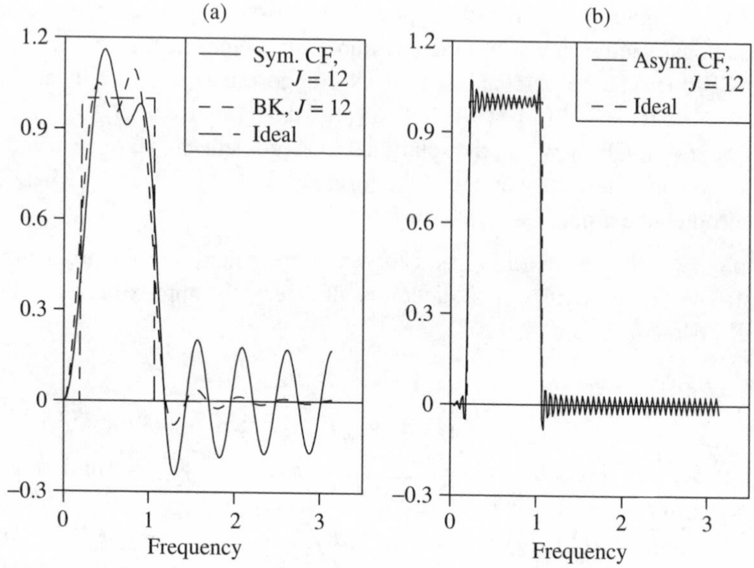

Figure 3.5. Gains functions of ideal and approximate BP filters. (a) Symmetric BK and CF; (b) asymmetric CF.

As with other MA filters, the approximate CF filter also faces problems when y_t is integrated. In fact, it increases the variability at business cycle frequencies if a term $(1 - \ell)$ is used to make y_t stationary.

What kind of statistics should one use to compare the quality of the approximation to the ideal BP filter? The following exercise suggests two possible alternatives.

Exercise 3.39. Suppose the optimal band pass filtered series is y_t^{c} and the approximate band pass filtered series is y_t^{Ac}. Let $y_t^{\mathrm{c}} = y_t^{\mathrm{Ac}} + e_t$, where by optimality of the projection problem $E(e_t \mid \mathcal{F}_t) = 0$, and $\mathcal{F}_t$ is the information set at time t. Show that $\mathrm{var}(y_t^{\mathrm{c}} - y_t^{\mathrm{Ac}} \mid \mathcal{F}_t) = \mathrm{var}(y_t^{\mathrm{c}})(1 - \mathrm{corr}(y_t^{\mathrm{Ac}}, y_t^{\mathrm{c}}))$. Conclude that $\mathrm{corr}(y_t^{\mathrm{Ac}}, y_t^{\mathrm{c}})$ and $\mathrm{var}(y_t^{\mathrm{Ac}})/\mathrm{var}(y_t^{\mathrm{c}})$ can be used to evaluate the closeness of the approximation.

Exercise 3.40. Consider the DGP used in exercise 3.37. Simulate data for the two components, compute y_t 1000 times, and calculate $\mathrm{ACF}(\tau)$ of y_t^{c} for $\tau = 1, \dots, 6$. For each draw, estimate y_t^{c} by using the fixed-weight approximate BP filter, the nonstationary, asymmetric CF filter, and the simulated y_t, and compute $\mathrm{ACF}(\tau)$ of y_t^{c} for $\tau = 1, \dots, 6$. Using the true and the simulated distribution of $\mathrm{ACF}(\tau)$ for each filter, examine which approach better approximates the cyclical component of the data.

While it has become common to use the time domain representation of the filter and therefore worry about the effects of truncation, one can directly implement BP filters in the frequency domain (see Canova 1998). The advantage of this approach is that no approximation is needed and no loss of data is involved. However, two major drawbacks need to be mentioned. First, the definition of the cyclical component depends on the sample size. This is because Fourier frequencies are function of T. Hence, when new information arrives, the measurement of y_t^c for all t needs to be changed. The time domain version of the truncated BP filter does not have this problem since the filter weights are independent of t. Second, since the spectrum of y_t is undefined at $\omega = 0$ when the series is nonstationary, a stationary transformation is required before the spectrum is computed. Hence, one should decide whether a deterministic or a stochastic trend should first be removed.

Recently, Corbae and Ouliaris (2001) suggested a way to band pass the data in the frequency domain which does not suffer from the latter problem. Their implementation is useful since it also solves the problem of the spurious periodicity induced by band pass filters when y_t is integrated. Suppose $\Delta y_t = D(\ell)e_t$, where $\sum_j D_j^2 < \infty$ and $e_t \sim$ i.i.d. $(0, \sigma^2)$ has finite fourth moments. For $\omega \neq 0$, Corbae, Ouliaris, and Phillips (COP) (Corbae et al. 2002) show that

$$\mathcal{S}_y(\omega) = \frac{1}{1-e^{i\omega}} D(\omega)\mathcal{S}_e(\omega) - \frac{1}{\sqrt{T}} \frac{e^{i\omega}}{1-e^{i\omega}}(y_T - y_0), \tag{3.31}$$

where the last term is the bias induced by the unit root at $\omega = 0$. From (3.31) one can see that $\mathcal{S}_y(\omega_1)$ is not independent of $\mathcal{S}_y(\omega_2)$ for $\omega_1 \neq \omega_2$ and both Fourier frequencies. Since $(y_T - y_0)$ is independent of ω, COP also show that the leakage from frequency zero creates biases in y_t^c that do not disappear if y_t is first detrended in the time domain.

Expression (3.31) suggests a simple way to eliminate this bias. The last term looks like a deterministic trend (in the frequency domain) with a random coefficient $(y_T - y_0)$. Hence, to construct an ideal BP filter in the frequency domain when y_t is integrated, one could use the following algorithm.

Algorithm 3.2.

(1) Compute $\mathcal{S}_y(\omega)$ for $\omega \neq 0$.

(2) Run a (cross-frequency) regression of $\mathcal{S}_y(\omega)$ on $(1/\sqrt{T})(e^{i\omega}/(1-e^{i\omega}))$ for $\omega \in (0, \pi]$ and let $\widehat{(y_T - y_0)}$ be the resulting estimator of $(y_T - y_0)$.

(3) Construct $\mathcal{S}_y^*(\omega) = \mathcal{S}_y(\omega) - \widehat{(y_T - y_0)}(1/\sqrt{T})(e^{i\omega}/(1-e^{i\omega}))$. Apply the ideal band pass filter to $\mathcal{S}_y^*(\omega)$.

Two features of algorithm 3.2 should be mentioned. First $\widehat{y_T - y_0}$ is a $\sqrt{T}$-consistent estimator of $(y_T - y_0)$ and when y_t is stationary $\widehat{y_T - y_0} = 0$. Second, no data are lost because of the filter and no parameters are chosen by the investigator (the approximate BP filter requires, at least, a truncation point J).

Exercise 3.41. Suppose you are willing to lose two observations, y_T and y_0. Show how to modify algorithm 3.2 to obtain an ideal BP filter. Intuitively describe why this modified filter may have better finite sample properties than the one produced by algorithm 3.2.

3.3 Economic Decompositions

The decompositions of this group are diverse, but have one feature in common: they all use an economic model to guide the extraction of the cyclical component. They should be more appropriately called permanent–transitory decompositions since they define the trend as the component of the series driven by permanent shocks. All decompositions use structural VARs (which we discuss in chapter 4) even though the "level" of identification is minimal. In fact, instead of trying to obtain behavioral disturbances, they simply look for shocks with permanent or transitory features.

3.3.1 Blanchard and Quah (BQ) Decomposition

The most prominent decomposition of this class was suggested by Blanchard and Quah (1989), who use a version of Fisher's (1977) partial equilibrium model with overlapping labor contracts consisting of four equations:

$$\text{GDP}_t = M_t - P_t + a\zeta_t, \tag{3.32}$$

$$\text{GDP}_t = N_t + \zeta_t, \tag{3.33}$$

$$P_t = W_t - \zeta_t, \tag{3.34}$$

$$W_t = W|\{E_{t-1}N_t = N^{\text{fe}}\}, \tag{3.35}$$

where $M_t = M_{t-1} + \epsilon_{3t}, \epsilon_{3t} \sim \text{i.i.d. } (0, \sigma_M^2)$, $\zeta_t = \zeta_{t-1} + \epsilon_{1t}, \epsilon_{1t} \sim \text{i.i.d. } (0, \sigma_\zeta^2)$, and where GDP_t is output, N_t is employment, N^{fe} is full employment, M_t is money, P_t are prices, ζ_t is a productivity disturbance (all these variables are measured in logarithms), and W_t is the real wage. The first equation is an aggregate demand equation, the second a short-run production function, and the third and the fourth describe price- and wage-setting behavior. Here money supply and productivity are exogenous and integrated processes. Also, contrary to the models of chapter 2, these equations are postulated and not derived from micro-principles.

Letting $\text{UN}_t = N_t - N^{\text{fe}}$, the solution to the model implies a bivariate representation for $(\text{GDP}_t, \text{UN}_t)$ of the form

$$\text{GDP}_t = \text{GDP}_{t-1} + \epsilon_{3t} - \epsilon_{3t-1} + a(\epsilon_{1t} - \epsilon_{1t-1}) + \epsilon_{1t}, \tag{3.36}$$

$$\text{UN}_t = -\epsilon_{3t} - a\epsilon_{1t}. \tag{3.37}$$

The model therefore places restrictions on the data. In particular, (3.36), (3.37) imply that fluctuations in UN_t are stationary while GDP_t is integrated. Furthermore, its permanent component is $\text{GDP}_t^x \equiv \text{GDP}_{t-1} + a(\epsilon_{1t} - \epsilon_{1t-1}) + \epsilon_{1t}$ and its transitory component is $\text{GDP}_t^c \equiv \epsilon_{3t} - \epsilon_{3t-1}$. In other words, while demand shocks drive the cycle in GDP_t, both supply and demand shocks drive the cycle in UN_t. To extract the transitory component of GDP we need the following steps.

Algorithm 3.3.

(1) Check that GDP_t is integrated and UN_t is stationary (possibly after some transformation).

(2) Identify two shocks, one which has a permanent effect on GDP_t and one which has a transitory effect on both GDP_t and UN_t.

(3) Compute $\mathrm{GDP}^{\mathrm{c}}_t = \mathrm{GDP}_t - \mathrm{GDP}^x_t$ and $\mathrm{UN}^{\mathrm{c}}_t \equiv \mathrm{UN}_t$.

In step (2) one could generically specify a bivariate VAR for the data (if the model is believed to provide only qualitative restrictions) or condition on the exact structure provided by (3.36) and (3.37) to derive the shocks. Details on how to identify the shocks in (2) are in chapter 4.

It is important to stress that decompositions like (3.36), (3.37) are conditional on the economic model. Hence, it is possible to produce different cyclical components by using the same model but introducing different features or frictions.

Exercise 3.42 (Lippi and Reichlin). Suppose the productivity shock has the structure $\zeta_t = \zeta_{t-1} + \mathbb{Q}(\ell)\epsilon_{1t}$, where $\sum_j \mathbb{Q}_j = 1$ and $\epsilon_{1t} \sim$ i.i.d. $(0, \sigma^2)$. Show that a solution for $\Delta\mathrm{GDP}_t$ and UN_t can be written as

$$\begin{bmatrix} \Delta\mathrm{GDP}_t \\ \mathrm{UN}_t \end{bmatrix} = \begin{bmatrix} -1 & -a \\ 1-\ell & (1-\ell)a + \mathbb{Q}(\ell) \end{bmatrix} \begin{bmatrix} \epsilon_{1t} \\ \epsilon_{3t} \end{bmatrix}.$$

Argue that trend and cycle may not be identifiable from the data for $y_t = [\Delta\mathrm{GDP}_t, \mathrm{UN}_t]$. (Hint: the data have a representation $y_t = \bar{y} + D(\ell)e_t$, where the roots of $D(\ell)$ are on or inside the complex unit circle, see also section 4.6.)

Exercise 3.43 (Gali). Suppose a representative household maximizes $E_0 \sum_t \beta^t \times \{\ln C_t + \vartheta_M \ln(M_t/P_t) - [\vartheta_n/(1-\varphi_n)]N_t^{1-\varphi_n} - [\vartheta_{\mathrm{ef}}/(1-\varphi_{\mathrm{ef}})]\mathrm{ef}_t^{1-\varphi_{\mathrm{ef}}}\}$, where $C_t = (\int_0^1 C_{it}^{1/(1+\varsigma_p)}\,\mathrm{d}i)^{1+\varsigma_p}$, $\varsigma_p > 0$, $p_t = (\int_0^1 p_{it}^{-1/\varsigma_p}\,\mathrm{d}i)^{-\varsigma_p}$ is the aggregate price index, M_t/P_t are real balances, N_t is the number of hours worked, and ef_t is effort. The budget constraint is $\int_0^1 p_{it}C_{it}\,\mathrm{d}i + M_t = w_{Nt}N_t + w_{et}\mathrm{ef}_t + M_{t-1} + T_t + \mathrm{Prf}_t$, where T_t are monetary transfers and Prf_t profits distributed by firms. A continuum of firms produces a differentiated good: $\mathrm{inty}_{it} = \zeta_t(N_{it}^{\eta_2}\mathrm{ef}_{it}^{1-\eta_2})^{\eta_1}$, where $N_{it}^{\eta_2}\mathrm{ef}^{1-\eta_2}$ is the quantity of effective input, ζ_t an aggregate technology shock, $\ln\Delta\zeta_t = \epsilon_{1t}$, where $\epsilon_{1t} \sim$ i.i.d. $(0, \sigma_\zeta^2)$. Firms set prices one period in advance, taking p_t as given but not knowing the current realization of the shocks. Once shocks are realized, firms optimally choose employment and effort. So long as marginal costs are below the predetermined price, firms will then meet demand and choose an output level, equal to $(p_{it}/p_t)^{-(1+\varsigma_p)/\varsigma_p}C_t$. Optimal price setting implies $E_{t-1}\{(1/C_t)[(\eta_1\eta_2)p_{it}\mathrm{inty}_{it} - (\varsigma_p+1)w_{Nt}N_{it}]\} = 0$. Assume $\ln\Delta M_t = \epsilon_{3t} + a_{\mathrm{M}}\epsilon_{1t}$, where $\epsilon_{3t} \sim$ i.i.d. $(0, \sigma_M^2)$ and a_{M} is a parameter.

(i) Letting lowercase letters denote natural logarithms, show that, in equilibrium, output growth ($\Delta\mathrm{gdp}_t$), log employment (n_t), and labor productivity growth ($\Delta\mathrm{np}_t$) satisfy

$$\Delta\mathrm{gdp}_t = \Delta\epsilon_{3t} + a_{\mathrm{M}}\epsilon_{1t} + (1-a_{\mathrm{M}})\epsilon_{1t-1}, \tag{3.38}$$

$$n_t = \frac{1}{\eta_s}\epsilon_{3t} - \frac{1-a_{\mathrm{M}}}{\eta_s}\epsilon_{1t}, \tag{3.39}$$

$$\Delta \text{np}_t = \left(1 - \frac{1}{\eta_s}\right)\Delta\epsilon_{3t} + \left(\frac{1 - a_{\text{M}}}{\eta_s} + a_{\text{M}}\right)\epsilon_{1t} + (1 - a_{\text{M}})\left(1 - \frac{1}{\eta_s}\right)\epsilon_{1t-1}, \tag{3.40}$$

where $\text{np}_t = \text{gdp}_t - n_t$ and $\eta_s = \eta_1(\eta_2 + (1 - \eta_2)(1 + \varphi_n)/(1 + \varphi_{\text{ef}}))$.

(ii) Describe a trend-cycle decomposition by using $(\Delta\text{gdp}, n_t)$. How does this decomposition differ from the one computed by using $(\Delta\text{np}_t, n_t)$?

BQ and multivariate BN decompositions share important similarities. However, while here trend and cycle are driven by orthogonal shocks, in the BN decomposition they are driven by the same combination of shocks. Hence, the disturbances in a BQ decomposition have some vague economic interpretation, while this is not the case for those of a multivariate BN decomposition.

Example 3.23. We have taken a bivariate system with GDP growth and the unemployment rate and used U.S. data for the period 1950:1–2003:3. Both series are demeaned and a linear trend is eliminated from the unemployment rate. The cyclical component of output is computed by using "structural" shocks (BQ decomposition) or "reduced-form" shocks (BN decomposition). The estimated cyclical components are quite different. For example, while both of them have similar AR(1) coefficients (0.93 for BN and 0.90 for BQ), their contemporaneous correlation is only 0.21. This occurs because the BQ cyclical component is much more volatile (the standard error is 2.79 as opposed to 0.02) and the swings induced by temporary shocks have a mean length of about 10 quarters, while the mean length of BN cycles is about 5 quarters.

3.3.2 King, Plosser, Stock, and Watson (KPSW) Decomposition

King, Plosser, Stock, and Watson (1991) start from an RBC model where the log of total factor productivity (TFP) is driven by a unit root. This assumption and the structure of the model imply that all endogenous variables except hours will be trending and that the trend will be common, in the sense that the long-run movements will be driven by changes in TFP. Hence, if y_t has the representation $\Delta y_t = \bar{y} + D(\ell)e_t$, and the underlying economic model has the form $\Delta y_t = \bar{\bar{y}} + \mathcal{D}(\ell)\epsilon_t$ the presence of (common) trends implies that $D(1)e_t = \mathcal{D}(1)\epsilon_t$, where

$$\mathcal{D}(1) = \begin{bmatrix} 1 & 0 & 0 & \cdots \\ \cdots & \cdots & \cdots & \cdots \\ 1 & 0 & 0 & \cdots \end{bmatrix}. \tag{3.41}$$

Therefore, $D(1)e_t = [1, \dots, 1]'\epsilon_t^x$, where ϵ_t^x is the innovation which has balanced growth effects on y_t (see chapter 4 for a thorough description of this scheme).

Exercise 3.44. Suppose that there exists a structural model of the form $\Delta y_t = \mathcal{A}(\ell)\Delta y_{t-1} + \mathcal{A}_0\epsilon_t$, where $E(\epsilon_{it}\epsilon'_{i't}) = 0, \forall i, i'$. Show how to compute y_t^{c}.

Exercise 3.45. Consider a system with $(\Delta\text{GDP}, c/\text{GDP}, \text{inv}/\text{GDP})$ and suppose that ϵ_{1t} has long-run effects only on GDP. Show that, if the RBC model is correct c/GDP, inv/GDP are stationary. How would you identify a permanent and two transitory shocks?

BQ and KPSW procedures are similar. However, in the latter, more information is used to estimate the trend, including cointegration restrictions and a larger number of variables. Also, the KPSW approach is easily generalized to large systems while the BQ decomposition is primarily designed for bivariate models.

The KPSW decomposition is also similar to the BN decomposition. The major difference is the "behavioral" content of identified shocks: here the trend is driven by one of the identified shocks of the system, while in the BN decomposition Δy_t^x is driven by a combination of all reduced-form shocks.

Example 3.24. General equilibrium models that extensively exploit BQ and KPSW decompositions to identify permanent "behavioral" shocks are somewhat difficult to construct since multiple permanent shocks may not be separately identifiable. One exception is the two-country RBC model of Ahmed et al. (1993). Here output is produced via $\text{GDP}_{it} = K_{it}^{1-\eta}(\zeta_t^{b_1} N_{it})^{\eta}, i = 1, 2$, where $\Delta \ln \zeta_t = \bar{\zeta} + \epsilon_{1t}$ is the common world technology shock and b_1 measures the (asymmetric) impact of the shock in the two countries (i.e., $b_1 = 1$ if $i = 1$ and $b_1 < 1$ if $i = 2$). Labor supply is exogenously given (in the long run) by $\Delta \ln N_{it} = \bar{N} + \epsilon_{2t}^i$. Governments consume an exogenously given amount $g_{it} \equiv G_{it}/\text{GDP}_{it} = g_{it-1} + \epsilon_{3t}^i + b_2\epsilon_{3t}^{i'}$, where b_2 captures the comovements of the shocks in the two countries. The representative agent in country i maximizes $E_t \sum_t \beta^t [\upsilon_{it} \ln C_{it} + \upsilon_{i't} \ln C_{i't} + V(N_{it})]$, where $\upsilon_{i't}/\upsilon_{it}$ measures the extent of home bias in consumption. We assume that $\ln \upsilon_{it}$ are random walks with disturbances ϵ_{4t}^i, $i = 1, 2$. Finally, the growth rate of relative money supplies evolves according to $\Delta \ln M_{1t} - \Delta \ln M_{2t} = b_4 + b_6\epsilon_{1t} + b_5\epsilon_{2t}^1 + b_7\epsilon_{2t}^2 + b_8(1 - b_2)(\epsilon_{3t}^2 - \epsilon_{3t}^1) + b_9(\epsilon_{4t}^2 - \epsilon_{4t}^1) + b_{10}(1 - b_5^1)(\epsilon_{5t}^1 - \epsilon_{5t}^2)$, where ϵ_{5t}^i are money demand shocks.

Let $p_t = p_{1t}^{b_3} p_{2t}^{1-b_3}$ and let the relative price of foreign goods in terms of domestic price be $\text{ToT}_t = p_{2t}/p_{1t}$. The model delivers an expression for the evolution of private output ($\text{GDP}_{it}^{\text{p}}$) which can be added to those determining aggregate domestic labor supply, total output in the two countries, relative money supplies, and the terms of trade to produce a system of the form $\Delta y_t - \bar{y} = \mathcal{D}_0\epsilon_t$, where $\Delta y_t = [\Delta \ln N_{1t}, \Delta \ln \text{GDP}_{1t}, \Delta \ln \text{GDP}_{2t}, \Delta \ln \text{GDP}_{1t}^{\text{p}} - \Delta \ln \text{GDP}_{2t}^{\text{p}}, \Delta \ln \text{ToT}_t, \Delta \ln M_{1t} - \Delta \ln M_{2t}]$, $\epsilon_t = [\epsilon_{2t}^1, \epsilon_{1t}, \epsilon_{2t}^2, (1-b_2)(\epsilon_{3t}^2 - \epsilon_{3t}^1), \epsilon_{4t}^2 - \epsilon_{4t}^1, b_{10}(\epsilon_{5t}^1 - \epsilon_{5t}^2)]$,

$$\mathcal{D}_0 = \begin{bmatrix} 1 & 0 & 0 & 0 & 0 & 0 \\ 1 & 1 & 0 & 0 & 0 & 0 \\ 0 & b_1 & 1 & 0 & 0 & 0 \\ 1 & 1-b_1 & -1 & 1 & 0 & 0 \\ b_3 & b_3(1-b_1) & -b_3 & b_3 & b_3 & 0 \\ b_5 & b_6 & b_7 & b_8 & b_9 & 1 \end{bmatrix},$$

$\bar{y} = \{\bar{N}_1, \bar{\zeta}+\bar{N}_1, b_1\bar{\zeta}+\bar{N}_2, (\bar{N}_1-\bar{N}_2)+(1-b_1)\bar{\zeta}, b_3[(\bar{N}_1-\bar{N}_2)+(1-b_1)\bar{\zeta}], b_4\}'$. Given the (restricted) lower triangular structure of $\mathcal{D}_0$, it is possible to obtain six long-run shocks. Methods to identify them are described in chapter 4. Note that, because there is no cointegrating relationship, all shocks have permanent effects on y_t. Hence, the permanent–transitory decomposition produced by this model is trivial ($\Delta y_t^{\mathrm{c}} = 0$ for all t). Clearly, if a general system $\Delta y_t = D(\ell)e_t$ is estimated, $\Delta y_t^{\mathrm{c}} \neq 0$. Note that a BN decomposition for this latter system is $\Delta y_t = D(1)e_t + \{[D(\ell) - D(1)]/(1-\ell)\}\Delta e_t$, where e_t are reduced-form shocks.

3.4 Time Aggregation and Cycles

A problem not fully appreciated in the literature occurs when data are time aggregated. In fact, time series showing important high frequency periodicities may display significant power at business cycle frequencies, when the data are time aggregated. Time aggregation is essentially a two-step filter. In the first step, the variable under consideration is passed through a one-sided filter $\mathcal{B}(\ell) = 1 + \ell + \ell^2 + \cdots + \ell^{n-1}$ if averages over n periods are taken, or $\mathcal{B}(\ell) = \ell^k$, $k = \{0, 1, \dots, n-1\}$, if systematic sampling takes place. In the second step, one typically samples $\mathcal{B}(\ell)y_t$ every nth observation to obtain nonoverlapping aggregates.

In terms of spectra, a time aggregated series is related to its original counterpart via the folding operator $\mathfrak{F}(\mathcal{S}(\omega)) = \sum_{j=-I}^{I} \mathcal{S}(\omega + 2\pi j/n)$, where $\mathfrak{F}(\mathcal{S}(\omega))$ is defined over $\omega = [-\pi/n, \pi/n]$ and I is the largest integer such that $(\omega+2\pi j/n) \in [-\omega, \omega]$. The folding operator reflects the aliasing problem where harmonics of the various frequencies cannot be distinguished from one another in the data. In essence, aliasing implies that frequencies outside $[-\pi/n, \pi/n]$ in the original process are folded back inside the $[-\pi/n, \pi/n]$ range in the time aggregated one. Then $\mathcal{S}_{y^{\mathrm{TA}}}(\omega) = \mathfrak{F}(|\mathcal{B}(\ell)|^2\mathcal{S}(\omega))$.

Example 3.25. Using the folding operator, it is easy to show that a monthly series which shows no power at business cycle frequencies (meaning that no peaks in the spectral density at the frequency range corresponding to cycles from 18 to 96 months is visible) has power at these frequencies when quarterly aggregates are constructed. Consider, for example, the process depicted in figure 3.6(a), which has most of its power in the area around $\omega = 2.2$ (which corresponds to cycles of slightly less than three months). If we aggregate this series quarterly, the area between $\omega = 1.05$ and $\omega = 3.14$ will be folded over the range $\omega \in [0.0, 1.04]$. Hence, the spectrum of the quarterly series has a peak around $\omega = 0.20$, which corresponds to cycles of roughly 30 quarters (see the dashed lines).

Time series which have these features are not unusual. For example, in figure 3.6(b) we plot the spectrum of the U.S. industrial production growth series by using monthly and quarterly data. Clearly, the same phenomenon occurs.

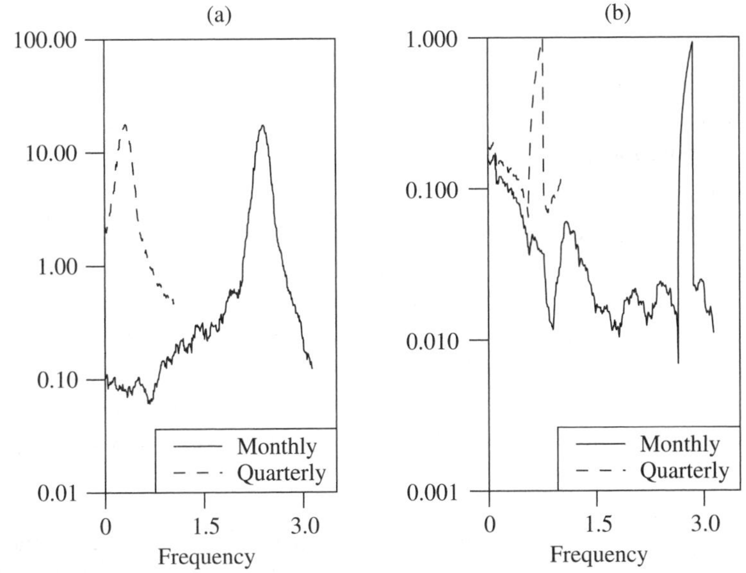

Figure 3.6. Monthly and quarterly spectra: (a) simulated data and (b) IP growth.

Exercise 3.46. Using monthly, quarterly, and annual data for stock returns in the G7 countries, examine whether time aggregation generates spurious business cycle peaks.

3.5 Collecting Cyclical Information

Once the components of a time series are obtained, statistics summarizing their features can be computed and reported. Typically, two complementary scopes should be balanced. First, statistics should contain sufficient information to allow policy makers and practitioners to assess the state of the economy. Second, they should summarize the characteristics of the cycle efficiently to allow academics to distinguish between different theoretical models of propagation.

While the growth literature concentrates on great ratios (consumption to output, investment in physical and human capital to output, saving ratios, etc.), the business cycle literature typically focuses attention on the autocovariance function of y_t^c. Hence, in general, variability, auto- and cross-correlations are presented. When a detailed description of the variability and of the correlations at various frequencies is of interest, spectral densities or bivariate coherence measures are reported. All these statistics can be analytically computed from the ACF of y_t if the form of the cyclical filter $\mathcal{B}^c(\ell)$ is known.

Example 3.26. Let $\mathcal{B}^c(\ell)$ be a cyclical filter and let $\mathrm{ACF}_y(\tau)$ be the autocovariance function of y_t. The autocovariance function of the cyclical component of y_t^c is $\mathrm{ACF}_{y^c}(\tau) = \mathrm{ACF}_y(0)\sum_{i=-\infty}^{\infty}\mathcal{B}_i^c\mathcal{B}_{i-\tau}^c + \sum_{\tau'=1}^{\infty}\mathrm{ACF}_y(\tau') \times$

$\sum_{i=-\infty}^{\infty} \mathcal{B}_i^{\mathrm{c}} \mathcal{B}_{i+\tau'-\tau}^{\mathrm{c}} + \sum_{\tau'=1}^{\infty} [\mathrm{ACF}_y(\tau')]' \sum_{i=-\infty}^{\infty} \mathcal{B}_i^{\mathrm{c}} \mathcal{B}_{i-\tau'-\tau}^{\mathrm{c}}$. The actual computation of $\mathrm{ACF}_c(\tau)$ requires truncation of the infinite sums, for example, letting i go from $\underline{i}$ to $\bar{i}$ and letting τ' go from 1 to $\bar{\tau}'$. For some cyclical filters (e.g., the growth filter), no truncation is needed. In general, a researcher needs to take a stand on the truncation points and, for comparability, it is important to clearly state what $\bar{\tau}'$, $\underline{i}$, and $\bar{i}$ are.

Apart from differences in truncation points, different studies may report different cyclical statistics because the $\mathcal{B}^{\mathrm{c}}(\ell)$ used is different. As we have seen, $\mathcal{B}^{\mathrm{c}}(\ell)$ are different because (a) some decompositions use univariate information while others use multivariate information (hence, estimates of y_t^{c} may have different precision); (b) some decompositions impose orthogonality between the components while others do not (hence, estimates of y_t^{c} have different spectra); (c) some decompositions produce estimated long-run components with both business cycle as well as high frequency variability (so that the average periodicity of estimated cycles is different); and (d) the weights used in different cyclical filters differ—they could be tent-like or wave-like, they could be symmetric or asymmetric, they could be truncated or exact, etc. Hence, it is by mere accident that alternative methods produce cyclical components with similar ACFs. While there is a tendency to sweep these differences under the rug or treat them as unimportant, major discrepancies may result.

Example 3.27. We repeat the exercise of Canova (1998) and pass output (GDP), consumption (C), investment (Inv), and real wage (W) through a number of filters. In table 3.2 we report the results produced by using the HP filter with $\lambda = 1600$ and $\lambda = 4$, the BN filter, a frequency domain BP filter, and the KPSW filter by using U.S. data from 1955:1 to 1986:4.

A few features deserve attention. First, not only does the variability of each series change with the method, so does the relative ranking of variabilities. Particularly striking is the alteration of the relative variability in the real wage. Second, the magnitude of correlations differs significantly (see, for example, the consumption–output correlations). Third, the two HP filters deliver different statistics and the HP4 results mimic those of the BN filter. Finally, the average periodicity of the GDP cycles produced is substantially different.

These difference are also present in other statistics. For example, Canova (1999) shows that the dating of cyclical turning points is not robust and that, apart from the BP filter, most methods generate several false alarms relative to the standard NBER classification.

While somewhat disturbing, the results of example 3.27 should not be a deterrent to conscientious researchers and do not support the claim that "there are no business cycle facts" to compare models with. On the contrary, observed differences stress the need to properly define a criterion to assess the empirical relevance of various decompositions. If it were possible to know with reasonable precision what assumptions characterize observables and unobservables—for example, whether the series

Table 3.2. Summary statistics.

Method	Variability GDP	Relative variability C	Relative variability W	Contemporaneous correlations (GDP, C)	Contemporaneous correlations (GDP, Inv)	Contemporaneous correlations (GDP, W)	Periodicity (quarters)
HP1600	1.76	0.49	0.70	0.75	0.91	0.81	24
HP4	0.55	0.48	0.65	0.31	0.65	0.49	7
BN	0.43	0.75	2.18	0.42	0.45	0.52	5
BP	1.14	0.44	1.16	0.69	0.85	0.81	28
KPSW	4.15	0.71	1.68	0.83	0.30	0.89	6

is integrated or the trend deterministic, whether the trend is cyclical or not, whether relevant cycles have constant median periodicity or not—one could select among methods on the basis of some statistical optimality criteria (e.g., minimization of the mean square error (MSE)). Given that this is not possible, the literature has arbitrarily concentrated on an economic criterion: interesting periodicities are those within 6 and 24–32 quarters. However, even with this focus, care should be exercised for three reasons. First, within the class of methods which extract cycles with these periodicities, differences may emerge if variables have most of their spectral power concentrated in a neighborhood of the trend/cycle cut-off point (see Canova (1998) for an example involving the hours and productivity correlation). Second, especially in international comparisons, results may differ if a series has different cyclical periodicity across countries. Third, filters which allow us to single out these frequencies may produce spurious correlations.

Exercise 3.47. Simulate data for the output gap, inflation, and the nominal interest rate from a basic sticky price model (e.g., the one whose solution is given in exercise 2.29, after you proxy marginal costs with the output gap and use the identity that consumption is equal to the output gap) driven by three shocks: a monetary policy, a cost push, and an Euler equation shock. Choose the parameters appropriately and compute the spectral density of simulated data and for actual euro data. How do they compare? Repeat the exercise by using HP and band pass filtered versions of the actual data.

These arguments bring us to an important aspect of the comparison between the actual data and the data produced by DSGE models. It is often stressed that, for comparability, the same filtering approach should be used to compute the ACF of y_t^c for both kinds of data. Rarely, however, does this principle take into account the (known) properties of simulated data. For example, in several of the models of chapter 2, the simulated series inherit the properties of the driving forces (they are persistent if shocks are, integrated if shocks are, etc.). If the purpose of filtering is the removal of the trend, no transformation (or a growth transformation) should then be applied to simulated data. On the other hand, if the purpose of filtering is to bring out cycles with a certain periodicity, one should remember that approximate BP or HP filters may produce distortions in highly persistent series like the one typically produced by DSGE models. Hence, it is not very difficult to build examples where simulated and actual filtered data look similar at business cycle frequencies even though the model and the data are substantially at odds with each other.

Example 3.28. Consider two AR(1) processes: $y_{1t} = 1.0 + 0.8y_{1t-1} + e_t$ and $y_{2t} = 1.0 - 0.55y_{2t-1} + e_t$, where $e_t \sim \mathbb{N}(0, 1)$. The spectra of the two series are specular but, since the shock driving the two series is the same, their variability at business cycle frequencies will be similar. In fact, BP filtered variabilities are 1.32 in both cases. Clearly, the two DGPs have very different features.

Hence, it is not clear that comparability is a relevant criterion and, for some purposes, it may be more reasonable to filter actual data but not simulated data or filter the two types of data with different filters, especially if the model is not assumed to be the correct process generating the actual data.

All in all, mechanical application of filters is dangerous. If one insists on trying to compare actual and simulated data by using second moments, one should carefully look into the properties of the data and be aware of the features of the cycle-extracting filter used.

The alternative is to shift attention away from the second moments of the growth cycle and, as in Pagan and Harding (2002, 2005), use statistics which can be obtained directly from the observable series (see also Hess and Iwata 1997; King and Plosser 1994).

The approach is closely related to the methodology of Burns and Mitchell (1946) and requires the identification of turning points in a "reference" variable (say, GDP or an aggregate of important macroeconomic series), the measurement of durations, amplitudes and cumulative changes of the cycles and of their phases, and the documentation of asymmetries over various phases. All these statistics can be computed from the (log) level of y_t by using a version of the so-called Bry and Boschen (1971) algorithm, which we describe next.

Algorithm 3.4.

(1) Smooth y_t with a series of filters (to eliminate outliers, high frequency variations, irregulars, or uninteresting fluctuations). Call y_t^{sm} the smoothed series.

(2) Use a dating rule to determine a potential set of turning points. One simple rule is $\Delta^2 y_t^{\text{sm}} > 0$ (< 0), $\Delta y_t^{\text{sm}} > 0$ (< 0), $\Delta y_{t+1}^{\text{sm}} < 0$ (> 0), $\Delta^2 y_{t+1}^{\text{sm}} < 0$ (> 0).

(3) Use a censoring rule to ensure that peaks and troughs alternate and that the duration and the amplitude of phases is meaningful.

Hence, to obtain turning points and business cycle phases, one needs to make some choices. While there are differences in the literature, the consensus is that

Table 3.3. U.S. business cycle statistics.

Variable	Duration (quarters) PT	TP	Amplitude (percentage) PT	TP	Excess change (percentage) PT	TP	Concordance (percentage)
GDP	3	18.7	−2.5	20.7	−0.1	1.1	
C	2.9	38	−2.0	39	0.2	0.1	0.89
Inv	5.2	11.1	−23.3	34.7	1.7	2.7	0.78

a two-quarter rule like the one used in step (2) or slight variations of it (see, for example, Lahiri and Moore 1991) suffices to date turning points. As for censoring rules, it is usual to impose a minimum duration of each phase of 2 or 3 quarters, so that complete cycles should be at least 5–7 quarters long, and/or some minimum amplitude restriction, for example, peak-to-trough drops of less than 1% should be excluded. Note also that the first step could be dispensed with if the censoring rule in (3) is strong enough.

Once turning points are identified, one could compute average durations (AD), i.e., average length of time spent between peaks or between peaks and troughs; average amplitudes (AA), i.e., the average size of the drop between peaks and troughs or of the gain between troughs and peaks; average cumulative changes over phases $(\text{CM} = 0.5 * (\text{AD} * \text{AA}))$; and excess average cumulative changes $((\text{CM} - \text{CM}^{\text{A}} + 0.5 * \text{AA})/\text{AD})$, where CM^{A} is the actual average cumulative change. Finally, one can compute a concordance index $\text{CI}_{i,i'} = n^{-1}[\sum \mathcal{I}_{i't}\mathcal{I}_{it} - (1 - \mathcal{I}_{i't})(1 - \mathcal{I}_{it})]$, which can be used to assess the strength of the comovements of variables i and i' over business cycle phases. Here n is the number of complete cycles, $\mathcal{I}_{it} = 1$ in expansions, and $\mathcal{I}_{it} = 0$ in contractions. Note that $\text{CI}_{i,i'} = 1$ if the two series are in the same phase at all times and zero if the series are perfectly negatively correlated.

Example 3.29. Applying the dating rule described in algorithm 3.4 with a minimum duration of the cycle of 5 quarters, to U.S. output, U.S. consumption, and U.S. investment for the period 1947:1–2003:1, the statistics contained in table 3.3 are obtained. Expansion phases are under the heading TP and recession phases under the heading PT.

On average, expansions in consumption are much longer and much stronger than those in GDP. Also, investment displays a much stronger change in expansions than GDP but shorter average duration and relatively long contraction phases. In general, asymmetries over cyclical phases are present in all three series.

Exercise 3.48. Repeat the calculations performed in example 3.29 by using the dating rule $\Delta y_t^{\text{sm}} > 0, \Delta y_{t+1}^{\text{sm}} < 0$ to find peaks and $\Delta y_t^{\text{sm}} < 0, \Delta y_{t+1}^{\text{sm}} > 0$ to find troughs, and by requiring a minimum duration of 7 quarters for the full cycle.

Exercise 3.49. Using euro area data for output, consumption, and investment for the period 1970:1–2004:4, calculate the same four statistics presented in example 3.29 and compare them to those of the United States. Is there any interesting pattern that makes the euro area different?

There are two appealing features of the approach. First, cyclical statistics can be obtained without extracting cyclical components. Second, they can be computed even when no cycle exists, in the sense that all shocks have permanent effects or that y_t does not have any power at business cycle frequencies. This latter feature is important in comparing DSGE models and the data. In fact, barring a few cases, the models described in chapter 2 produce (approximate) VAR(1) solutions. Hence, the data produced by the model do not display peaks in the spectral density at cyclical frequencies, and therefore are ill-suited to be compared with the data by using decompositions which look for important periodicities or simply emphasize business cycle frequencies. A couple of drawbacks should also be mentioned. First, statistics may be sensitive to dating and censoring rules. Since the rules of algorithm 3.4 are arbitrary, one should carefully monitor the sensitivity of turning-point dates to the choices made. Second, it is not clear how to adapt dating and censoring rules when international comparisons need to be made.

Finally, one should remember that both second moments and turning-point statistics provide reduced-form information. That is, they are uninformative about comovements in response to economically interesting shocks and silent about the sources of cyclical fluctuations. This kind of conditional information is exactly what structural VARs, considered in the next chapter, deliver.

4
VAR Models

This chapter describes a set of techniques which stand apart from those considered in the next three chapters, in the sense that economic theory is only minimally used in the inferential process. VAR models, pioneered by Chris Sims about 25 years ago, have acquired a permanent place in the toolkit of applied macroeconomists, both to summarize the information contained in the data and to conduct certain types of policy experiments. VAR models are well-suited to the first purpose: the Wold theorem ensures that any vector of time series has a VAR representation under mild regularity conditions and this makes them the natural starting point for empirical analyses. We discuss the Wold theorem, and the issues connected with nonuniqueness, nonfundamentalness, and nonorthogonality of the innovation vector in the first section. The Wold theorem is generic but imposes important restrictions; for example, the lag length of the VAR model should go to infinity for the approximation to be "good." Section 4.2 deals with specification issues and describes methods to verify some of the restrictions imposed by the Wold theorem and to test other related implications. Section 4.3 presents alternative formulations of a VAR(q). These are useful when computing moments or spectral densities, and for deriving estimators for the parameters and for the covariance matrix of the shocks. Section 4.4 presents statistics commonly used to summarize the informational content of VARs and methods to compute their standard errors. We discuss generalized impulse response functions, which are useful in dealing with time-varying coefficients VAR models analyzed in chapter 10. Section 4.5 discusses identification, i.e., the process of transforming the information content of reduced-form dynamics into behavioral ones. Up to this point, economic theory has played no role. However, to give an economic interpretation to the estimated relationships, economic theory needs to be used. Contrary to the approaches of the next three chapters, only a minimalist set of restrictions, loosely related to the classes of models presented in chapter 2, are employed to obtain behavioral relationships. We describe identification methods which rely on conventional short-run restrictions, on long-run restrictions, and on sign restrictions. In the latter two cases, the link between theory and the data is explicitly made. Section 4.6 describes problems which may distort the interpretation of structural VAR results. Time aggregation, omission of variables and shocks, nonfundamentalness, and lack of finite-order representation should always be in the back of the mind of applied researchers when conducting policy analyses with VARs. In section 4.7 we propose a method to validate a class of DSGE models using structural VARs. Log-linearized DSGE models have a restricted VAR representation. When a researcher has confidence in the theory, a set of quantitative restrictions can be considered, in which case the methods described in chapters 5–7 could be used. When theory only provides qualitative implications or when its exact details are doubtful, one can still validate a model conditioning on its qualitative implications. Since DSGE models provide a wealth of robust sign restrictions, one can take the ideas of section 4.5 one step further, use sign restrictions to identify behavioral disturbances, and evaluate the model by examining the qualitative (and quantitative) features of the dynamic responses to identified shocks. In this sense, VAR identified with sign restrictions offers a natural setting to validate incompletely specified (and possibly false) DSGE models.

4.1 The Wold Theorem

The use of VAR models can be justified in many ways. Here we employ the Wold representation theorem as a major building block (see Hansen and Sargent (2005) for an alternative approach). While the theory of Hilbert spaces is needed to make the arguments sound, we keep the presentation simple and invite the reader to consult Rozanov (1967) or Brockwell and Davis (1991) for precise statements.

The Wold theorem decomposes any $m \times 1$ vector stochastic process $y_t^\dagger$ into two orthogonal components: one linearly predictable and one linearly unpredictable (linearly regular). To show what the theorem involves let $\mathcal{F}_t$ be the time t information set, $\mathcal{F}_t = \mathcal{F}_{t-1} \oplus \mathcal{E}_t$, where $\mathcal{F}_{t-1}$ contains time $t-1$ information, and let $\mathcal{E}_t$ be the news at t. Here $\mathcal{E}_t$ is orthogonal to $\mathcal{F}_{t-1}$ (written $\mathcal{E}_t \perp \mathcal{F}_{t-1}$) and $\oplus$ indicates direct sum, that is, $\mathcal{F}_t = \{y_{t-1}^\dagger + e_t,\ y_{t-1}^\dagger \in \mathcal{F}_{t-1},\ e_t \in \mathcal{E}_t\}$. Intuitively, orthogonality implies that news cannot be predicted with $t-1$ information. Consequently, current news is orthogonal to past news.

Exercise 4.1. Show that $\mathcal{E}_t \perp \mathcal{F}_{t-1}$ implies $\mathcal{E}_t \perp \mathcal{E}_{t-1}$. Conclude that $\mathcal{E}_{t-j}$ is orthogonal to $\mathcal{E}_{t-j'}$, $j' < j$.

Since the decomposition of $\mathcal{F}_t$ can be repeated for each t, iterating backwards we have

$$\mathcal{F}_t = \mathcal{F}_{t-1} \oplus \mathcal{E}_t = \cdots = \mathcal{F}_{-\infty} \oplus \sum_{j=0}^{\infty} \mathcal{E}_{t-j}, \tag{4.1}$$

where $\mathcal{F}_{-\infty} = \bigcap_j \mathcal{F}_{t-j}$ contains what was known at the beginning of history. Since $y_t^\dagger$ is known at time t (this condition is sometimes referred to as adaptability of $y_t^\dagger$ to $\mathcal{F}_t$), we can write $y_t^\dagger \equiv E[y_t^\dagger \mid \mathcal{F}_t]$, where $E[\cdot \mid \mathcal{F}_t]$ is the conditional expectation operator. Orthogonality of the news with past information then implies

$$y_t^\dagger = E\left[y_t^\dagger \,\middle|\, \mathcal{F}_{-\infty} \oplus \sum_j \mathcal{E}_{t-j}\right] = E[y_t^\dagger \mid \mathcal{F}_{-\infty}] + \sum_{j=0}^{\infty} E[y_t^\dagger \mid \mathcal{E}_{t-j}]. \tag{4.2}$$

We make two assumptions. First, we consider linear representations, that is, we substitute expectations with linear projections. Then (4.2) becomes

$$y_t^\dagger = a_t y_{-\infty} + \sum_{j=0}^{\infty} D_{jt} e_{t-j}, \tag{4.3}$$

where $e_{t-j} \in \mathcal{E}_{t-j}$ and $y_{-\infty} \in \mathcal{F}_{-\infty}$. The sequence $\{e_t\}_{t=0}^{\infty}$, defined by $e_t \equiv y_t^\dagger - E[y_t^\dagger \mid \mathcal{F}_{t-1}]$, $\forall t$, is a white noise process (i.e., $E(e_t) = 0$ and $E(e_t e'_{t-j}) = 0$ if $j \neq 0$). Second, we assume a time-invariant representation, i.e., $a_t = a$, $D_{jt} = D_j$, $\forall t$, and

$$y_t^\dagger = a y_{-\infty} + \sum_{j=0}^{\infty} D_j e_{t-j}. \tag{4.4}$$

Exercise 4.2. Show that, if $y_t^\dagger$ is covariance stationary, $a_t = a$, $D_{jt} = D_j$, and $E(e_t e'_t)$ is constant.

The term $a y_{-\infty}$ on the right-hand side of (4.4) is the linearly deterministic component of $y_t^\dagger$ and can be perfectly predicted, given the infinite past. The term $\sum_j D_j e_{t-j}$ is the linearly regular component, that is, the component produced by the news at each t. We say that $y_t^\dagger$ is deterministic if and only if $y_t^\dagger \in \mathcal{F}_{-\infty}$ and regular if and only if $\mathcal{F}_{-\infty} = \{0\}$.

Three important points need to be highlighted. First, for (4.2) to hold, no assumptions about $y_t^\dagger$ are required. Second, both linearity and stationary are unnecessary. For example, if stationarity is not assumed, there will still be a linearly regular and a linearly deterministic component even though each will have time-varying coefficients (see (4.3)). Third, if we insist on requiring covariance stationary, preliminary transformations of $y_t^\dagger$ may be needed to produce the representation (4.4).

The Wold theorem is a powerful tool but is too generic to guide empirical analyses. To impose more structure, we assume that the data are a mean zero process, possibly after deseasonalization (with deterministic periodic functions), removal of constants, etc., and let $y_t = y^\dagger - a y_{-\infty}$. Using the lag operator we write $\sum_{j=0}^{\infty} D_j e_{t-j} = \sum_j D_j \ell^j e_t = D(\ell) e_t$ so that $y_t = D(\ell) e_t$ is the MA representation for y_t, where D_j is an $m \times m$ matrix of rank m for each j. Were the rank less than m, it would be possible to perfectly predict linear combinations of the elements of y_t. Cases where this happens in the long run will be dealt with later on.

MA representations are not unique: in fact, for any nonsingular matrix in the lag operator $\mathcal{H}(\ell)$ of rank m for each ℓ, satisfying $\mathcal{H}(\ell)\mathcal{H}(\ell^{-1})' = I$, such that $\mathcal{H}(z)$ has no singularities for $|z| \leqslant 1$, where $\mathcal{H}(\ell^{-1})'$ is the transpose (and possibly complex conjugate) of $\mathcal{H}(\ell)$, we have $y_t = \tilde{D}(\ell)\tilde{e}_t$ with $\tilde{D}(\ell) = D(\ell)\mathcal{H}(\ell)$, $\tilde{e}_t = \mathcal{H}(\ell^{-1})' e_t$.

Exercise 4.3. Show that $E(\tilde{e}_t \tilde{e}'_{t-j}) = E(e_t e'_{t-j})$, $j \neq 0$. Conclude that, if e_t is covariance stationary, the two representations produce equivalent autocovariance functions for y_t.

Example 4.1. Consider $y_{1t} = e_t - 0.5e_{t-1}$ and $y_{2t} = \tilde{e}_t - 2\tilde{e}_{t-1}$. It is easy to verify that the roots of $D(z)$ are $z_1 = 2$ in the first case and $z_2 = 0.5 = 1/z_1$ in the second. This implies that the two processes span the same information space as long as the variance of innovations is appropriately adjusted. In fact, using the covariance generating function we have $\mathrm{CGF}_{y_1}(z) = (1 - 0.5z)(1 - 0.5z^{-1})\sigma_1^2$ and $\mathrm{CGF}_{y_2}(z) = (1-2z)(1-2z^{-1})\sigma_2^2 = (1-0.5z)(1-0.5z^{-1})(4\sigma_2^2)$. Hence, if $\sigma_1^2 = 4\sigma_2^2$, the CGF of the two processes is the same.

Exercise 4.4. Let $y_{1t} = e_t - 4e_{t-1}, e_t \sim$ i.i.d. $(0, \sigma^2)$. Set $y_{2t} = (1-0.25\ell)^{-1}y_{1t}$. Show that the CGF$(z)$ of y_{2t} is a constant for all z. Show that $y_{2t} = \tilde{e}_t - 0.25\tilde{e}_{t-1}$, where $\tilde{e}_t \sim$ i.i.d. $(0, 16\sigma^2)$ is equivalent to y_{1t} in terms of the CGF.

Objects like $\mathcal{H}(\ell)$ are called Blaschke matrices and are of the form $\mathcal{H}(\ell) = \prod_{i=1}^{m} \varrho_i \mathcal{H}^\dagger(d_i, \ell)$, where d_i are the roots of $D(z)$, $|d_i| < 1$, $\varrho_i \varrho_i' = I$, and, for each i, $\mathcal{H}^\dagger(d_i, \ell)$ is given by

$$\mathcal{H}^\dagger(d_i, \ell) = \begin{bmatrix} 1 & 0 & \cdots & 0 \\ \cdots & \cdots & \cdots & \cdots \\ 0 & \dfrac{\ell - d_i^{-1}}{1 - \bar{d}_i \ell} & \cdots & 0 \\ 0 & 0 & \cdots & 1 \end{bmatrix} \tag{4.5}$$

and $\bar{d}_i$ is the complex conjugate of d_i.

Exercise 4.5. Suppose

$$\begin{pmatrix} y_{1t} \\ y_{2t} \end{pmatrix} = \begin{pmatrix} 1 + 4\ell & 0 \\ 0 & 1 + 10\ell \end{pmatrix} \begin{pmatrix} e_{1t} \\ e_{2t} \end{pmatrix}.$$

Find the Blaschke factors of $D(\ell)$. Construct two alternative moving average representations for y_t.

Among the class of equivalent MA representations, it is usual to choose the "fundamental" one. The following two definitions are equivalent.

Definition 4.1 (fundamentalness). (1) An MA representation is fundamental if $\det(D_0 E(e_t e_t') D_0') > \det(D_j E(e_{t-j} e_{t-j}') D_j'), \forall j \neq 0$. (2) An MA representation is fundamental if the roots of $D(z)$ are all greater than 1 in modulus.

The roots of $D(z)$ are related to the eigenvalues of the companion matrix of the system (see section 4.3). Fundamental representations, also termed Wold representations, could also be identified, loosely speaking, by the requirement that the space spanned by linear combinations of the y_t and of the e_t has the same information. In this sense Wold representations are invertible: knowing y_t is the same as knowing e_t.

As shown in the next example, construction of a fundamental representation requires "flipping" all roots that are less than 1 in absolute value.

Example 4.2. Suppose $y_t = \left[\begin{smallmatrix} 1.0 & 0 \\ 0.2 & 0.9 \end{smallmatrix}\right] e_t + \left[\begin{smallmatrix} 2.0 & 0 \\ 0 & 0.7 \end{smallmatrix}\right] e_{t-1}$, where $e_t \sim$ i.i.d. $(0, I)$. Here $\det(D_0) = 0.9 < \det(D_1) = 1.4$ so the representation is not fundamental. To find a fundamental one, we compute the roots of $D_0 + D_1 z = 0$; their absolute values are 0.5 and 1.26 (these are the diagonal elements of $-D_1^{-1} D_0$). The problematic root is 0.5, which we flip to $1.0/0.5 = 2.0$. The fundamental MA is then $y_t = \left[\begin{smallmatrix} 1.0 & 0 \\ 0.2 & 0.9 \end{smallmatrix}\right] e_t + \left[\begin{smallmatrix} 0.5 & 0 \\ 0 & 0.7 \end{smallmatrix}\right] e_{t-1}$.

Exercise 4.6. Determine which of the following polynomials produces fundamental representations when applied to a white noise innovation process: (i) $D(\ell) = 1 + 2\ell + 3\ell^2 + 4\ell^3$; (ii) $D(\ell) = I + \left[\begin{smallmatrix} 0.8 & -0.7 \\ 0.7 & 0.8 \end{smallmatrix}\right] \ell$; (iii) $D(\ell) = \left[\begin{smallmatrix} 1 & 1 \\ 3 & 4 \end{smallmatrix}\right] + \left[\begin{smallmatrix} 3 & 2 \\ 4 & 1 \end{smallmatrix}\right] \ell + \left[\begin{smallmatrix} 4 & 3 \\ 2 & 1 \end{smallmatrix}\right] \ell^2$.

Exercise 4.7. Consider $y_t = e_t + \left[\begin{smallmatrix} 1.0 & 0 \\ 0 & 0.8 \end{smallmatrix}\right] e_{t-1}$, where $\operatorname{var}(e_t) = \left[\begin{smallmatrix} 2.0 & 1.0 \\ 1.0 & 1.0 \end{smallmatrix}\right]$, and $y_{2t} = e_t + \left[\begin{smallmatrix} 0.9091 & 0.1909 \\ 0 & 0.8 \end{smallmatrix}\right] e_{t-1}$, where $\operatorname{var}(e_t) = \left[\begin{smallmatrix} 2.21 & 1.0 \\ 1.0 & 1.0 \end{smallmatrix}\right]$. Show that y_{1t} and y_{2t} have the same ACF for y_t. Which representation is fundamental?

Exercise 4.8. Let

$$\begin{pmatrix} y_{1t} \\ y_{2t} \end{pmatrix} = \begin{pmatrix} 1 + 4\ell & 1 + 0.5\ell \\ 0 & 1 + 5\ell \end{pmatrix} \begin{pmatrix} e_{1t} \\ e_{2t} \end{pmatrix},$$

where $e_t = (e_{1t}, e_{2t})$ has mean zero and unitary variance. Is the space spanned by linear combinations of the y_t and e_t the same? If the MA is not fundamental, find a fundamental one.

While it is usual to use Wold representations in applied work, one should be aware that there are economic models that do not generate a fundamental format for the endogenous variables y_t. Two are presented in the next examples.

Example 4.3. Consider an RBC model where the representative household maximizes $E_0 \sum_t \beta^t (\ln(c_t) - \vartheta_N N_t)$ subject to $c_t + \text{inv}_t \leqslant K_t^{1-\eta} N_t^{\eta} \zeta_t$, $K_{t+1} = (1-\delta) K_t + \text{inv}_t$, $c_t \geqslant 0$, $\text{inv}_t \geqslant 0$, $0 \leqslant N_t \leqslant 1$, where $0 < \beta < 1$ and δ, ϑ_n are parameters, and $\ln \zeta_t = \ln \zeta_{t-1} + 0.1\epsilon_{1t} + 0.2\epsilon_{1t-1} + 0.4\epsilon_{1t-2} + 0.2\epsilon_{1t-3} + 0.1\epsilon_{1t-4}$. Such a diffusion of technological innovations is appropriate when, for example, only the most advanced sectors employ the new technology (say, a new computer chip) and it takes some time for the innovation to spread to the economy. If $\epsilon_{1t} = 1$, $\epsilon_{1t+\tau} = 0$, $\forall \tau \neq 0$, $\ln \zeta_t$ looks like in figure 4.1. Clearly, a process with this shape does not satisfy the restrictions given in definition 4.1.

Example 4.4. Consider a model where fiscal shocks drive economic fluctuations. Typically, fiscal policy changes take time to have effects: between the programming, the legislation, and the implementation of, say, a change in income tax rates, several quarters may elapse. If agents are rational, they may react to tax changes before the policy is implemented and, conversely, no variations may be visible when the changes actually take place. Since the information contained in tax changes may have a different timing than the information contained, say, in the income process, fiscal shocks may produce non-Wold representations.

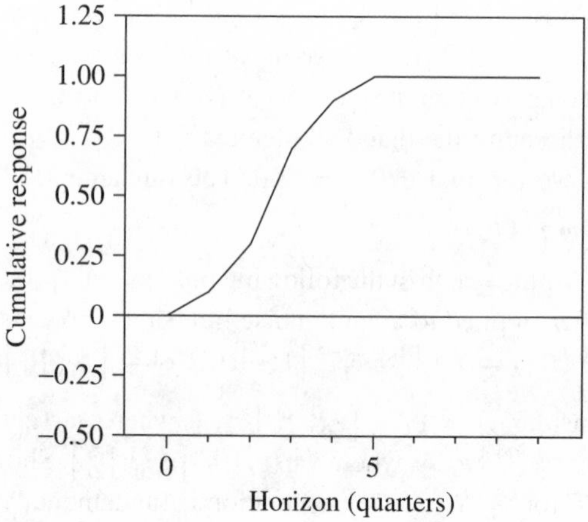

Figure 4.1. Nonfundamental technological progress.

As we will see, neglecting the possibility that economic theory generates nonfundamental MAs may induce researchers to wrongly infer the nature of the economic relationships. When this is a possibility one could use Blaschke factors to flip the MA representations provided by standard packages, as, for example, in Lippi and Reichlin (1994). In what follows, we will consider only fundamental structures and take $y_t = D(\ell)e_t$ to be such a representation.

The "innovation" vector e_t plays an important role in VAR analyses. Since $E(e_t \mid \mathcal{F}_{t-1}) = 0$ and $E(e_t e_t' \mid \mathcal{F}_{t-1}) = \Sigma_e$, e_t is serially uncorrelated but contemporaneously correlated. This means that we cannot attach a "name" to the disturbances. To do so we need an orthogonal representation for the innovations. Let $\Sigma_e = \mathcal{P}\mathcal{V}\mathcal{P}' = \tilde{\mathcal{P}}\tilde{\mathcal{P}}'$, where $\mathcal{V}$ is a diagonal matrix and $\tilde{\mathcal{P}} = \mathcal{P}\mathcal{V}^{0.5}$. Then $y_t = D(\ell)e_t$ is equivalent to

$$y_t = \tilde{D}(\ell)\tilde{e}_t \tag{4.6}$$

for $\tilde{D}(\ell) = D(\ell)\tilde{\mathcal{P}}$ and $\tilde{e}_t = \tilde{\mathcal{P}}^{-1}e_t$. There are many ways of generating (4.6). One is a Choleski factorization, i.e., $\mathcal{V} = I$ and $\mathcal{P}$ is a lower triangular matrix. Another is obtained when $\mathcal{P}$ contains the eigenvectors and $\mathcal{V}$ the eigenvalues of Σ_e.

Example 4.5. If e_t is a 2×1 vector with correlated entries, orthogonal innovations are $\tilde{e}_{1t} = e_{1t} - be_{2t}$ and $\tilde{e}_{2t} = e_{2t}$, where $b = \text{cov}(e_{1t}e_{2t})/\text{var}(e_{2t})$, $\text{var}(\tilde{e}_{1t}) = \sigma_1^2 - b^2\sigma_2^2$, and $\text{var}(\tilde{e}_{2t}) = \sigma_2^2$.

It is important to stress that orthogonalization devices are void of economic content: they only transform the MA representation into a form which is more useful when tracing out the effect of a particular shock. To attach economic interpretations to the representation, these orthogonalizations ought to be linked to economic theory. Note also that, while with the Choleski decomposition $\mathcal{P}$ has zero restrictions placed on the upper triangular part, no such restrictions are present when an eigenvalue–eigenvector decomposition is performed.

As already mentioned, when the polynomial $D(z)$ has all its roots greater than 1 in modulus (and this condition holds if, for example, $\sum_{j=0}^{\infty} D_j^2 < \infty$ (see Rozanov 1967)), the MA representation is invertible and we can express e_t as a linear combination of current and past y_t, i.e., $[A_0 - A(\ell)\ell]y_t = e_t$, where $[A_0 - A(\ell)\ell] = (D(\ell))^{-1}$. Moving lagged y_t onto the right-hand side and normalizing $A_0 = I$, a vector autoregressive (VAR) representation is obtained:

$$y_t = A(\ell)y_{t-1} + e_t. \tag{4.7}$$

In general, $A(\ell)$ will be of infinite length for any reasonable specification of $D(\ell)$.

There is an important relationship, which we highlight next, between the concept of invertibility and that of stability.

Definition 4.2 (stability). A VAR(q) is stable if $\det(I_m - A_1 z - \cdots - A_q z^q) \neq 0, \forall |z| \leqslant 1$.

Definition 4.2 implies that all eigenvalues of $A(\ell)$ have modulus less than or equal to 1 (or that the matrix $A(\ell)$ has no roots inside or on the complex unit circle). Hence, if y_t has an invertible MA representation, it also has a stable VAR structure. Therefore, one could start from stable processes to motivate VAR analyses (as is done, for example, in Lutkepohl (1991)). Our derivation shows the primitive restrictions needed to obtain stable VARs.

Example 4.6. Suppose $y_t = \begin{bmatrix} 0.5 & 0.1 \\ 0.0 & 0.2 \end{bmatrix} y_{t-1} + e_t$. Here $\det(I_2 - Az) = (1 - 0.5z) \times (1 - 0.2z) = 0$ and $|z_1| = 2 > 1$, $|z_2| = 5 > 1$. Hence, the system is stable.

Exercise 4.9. Check if $y_t = \begin{bmatrix} 0.6 & 0.4 \\ 0.5 & 0.2 \end{bmatrix} y_{t-1} + \begin{bmatrix} 0.1 & 0.3 \\ 0.2 & 0.6 \end{bmatrix} y_{t-2} + e_t$ is stable or not.

To summarize, any vector of time series can be represented with a constant coefficients VAR(∞) under linearity, stationarity, and invertibility. Hence, one can interchangeably think of y_t or the VAR for y_t. Also, with a finite stretch of data, only, a VAR(q), q finite, can be used. For a VAR(q) to approximate any y_t sufficiently well, we need D_j to converge to zero rapidly as j increases. Otherwise the approximation will be poor. What kind of processes are more likely to satisfy this condition? We give a hint in the next exercise.

Exercise 4.10. Consider $y_t = e_t + 0.9e_{t-1}$ and $y_t = e_t + 0.3e_{t-1}$. Compute the AR representations. What lag length is needed to approximate the two processes? What if $y_t = e_t + e_{t-1}$?

Two concepts which are of some use in applied work are those of Granger noncausality and Sims (econometric) exogeneity. It is important to stress that they refer to the ability of one variable to predict another one and do not imply any sort of economic causality (e.g., the central bank changes interest rates, the exchange rate will move). Let (y_{1t}, y_{2t}) be a partition of a covariance stationary y_t with fundamental innovations e_{1t} and e_{2t}, let Σ_e be diagonal, and let $D_{i,i'}(\ell)$ be the (i, i')th block of $D(\ell)$.

Definition 4.3 (Granger causality). y_{2t} fails to Granger cause y_{1t} if and only if $D_{12}(\ell) = 0$.

Definition 4.4 (Sims exogeneity). $y_{2t} = \mathbb{Q}(\ell)y_{1t} + \epsilon_{2t}$ with $E_t[\epsilon_{2t}y_{1t-\tau}] = 0$, $\forall \tau \geqslant 0$, $\mathbb{Q}(\ell) = \mathbb{Q}_0 + \mathbb{Q}_1\ell + \cdots$ if and only if y_{2t} fails to Granger cause y_{1t} and $D_{21}(\ell) \neq 0$.

Exercise 4.11. Show what Granger noncausality of y_{2t} for y_{1t} implies in a trivariate VAR.

We next examine cases where the data deviates from the setup considered so far.

Exercise 4.12. (i) Suppose that $y_t = D(\ell)e_t$, where $D(\ell) = (1-\ell)D^{\dagger}(\ell)$. Derive a VAR for y_t. Show that, if $D^{\dagger}(\ell) = 1$, there is no convergent VAR representation for y_t.

(ii) Suppose that $y_t^{\dagger} = a_0 + a_1 t + D(\ell)e_t$ if $t \leqslant \bar{T}$ and $y_t^{\dagger} = a_0 + a_2 t + D(\ell)e_t$ if $t > \bar{T}$. How would you derive a VAR representation for y_t in this case?

(iii) Suppose that $y_t = D(\ell)e_t$ and $\text{var}(e_t) \propto y_{t-1}^2$. Find a VAR for y_t.

(iv) Suppose that $y_t = D(\ell)e_t$, $\text{var}(e_t) = b\,\text{var}(e_{t-1}) + \sigma^2$. Find a VAR for y_t.

4.2 Specification

In section 4.1 we showed that a constant coefficients VAR is a good approximation to any vector of time series. Here we examine how to verify whether the restrictions needed for the approximation to be appropriate hold. The model we consider is (4.7), where $A(\ell) = A_1\ell + \cdots + A_q\ell^q$, y_t is an $m \times 1$ vector, and $e_t \sim$ i.i.d. $(0, \Sigma_e)$. VARs with econometrically exogenous variables can be obtained via restrictions on $A(\ell)$ as indicated in definition 4.4. We let $\mathbb{A}_1' = (A_1', \dots, A_q')'$ be an $(mq \times m)$ matrix and set $\alpha = \text{vec}(\mathbb{A}_1)$, where $\text{vec}(\mathbb{A}_1)$ stacks the columns of $\mathbb{A}_1$ (so α is an $m^2q \times 1$ vector).

4.2.1 Lag Length 1

There are several methods for selecting the lag length of a VAR. The simplest is based on a likelihood ratio (LR) test. Here the model with a smaller number of lags is treated as a restricted version of a larger-dimensional model. Since the two models are nested, under the null hypothesis that the restricted model is correct, differences in the likelihoods should be small. Let $R(\alpha) = 0$ be a set of restrictions and $\mathcal{L}(\alpha, \Sigma_e)$ the likelihood function. Then

$$\text{LR} = 2[\ln \mathcal{L}(\alpha^{\text{un}}, \Sigma_e^{\text{un}}) - \ln \mathcal{L}(\alpha^{\text{re}}, \Sigma_e^{\text{re}})] \tag{4.8}$$

$$= (R(\alpha^{\text{un}}))' \left[\frac{\partial R}{\partial \alpha^{\text{un}}} (\Sigma_e^{\text{re}} \otimes (X'X)^{-1}) \left(\frac{\partial R}{\partial \alpha^{\text{un}}} \right)' \right]^{-1} (R(\alpha^{\text{un}})) \tag{4.9}$$

$$= T(\ln |\Sigma_e^{\text{re}}| - \ln |\Sigma_e^{\text{un}}|) \xrightarrow{\text{D}} \chi^2(\nu), \tag{4.10}$$

where $X_t = (y'_{t-1}, \dots, y'_{t-q})'$, $X' = (X_0, \dots, X_{T-1})$ is an $mq \times T$ matrix, ν is the number of restrictions, and "un" and "re" indicate unrestricted and restricted estimators. Expressions (4.8)–(4.10) are equivalent formulations of the likelihood ratio test. The first is the standard one. Equation (4.9) is obtained by maximizing the likelihood function with respect to α, subject to $R(\alpha) = 0$. Equation (4.10) is convenient for computing actual test values and comparing LR results with those of other testing procedures. The exact forms of α^{un}, α^{re}, Σ_u^{un}, and Σ_u^{re} are in section 4.3.

Exercise 4.13. Derive (4.9) by using a Lagrangian multiplier approach.

Four important features of LR tests need to be highlighted. First, an LR test is valid when y_t is stationary and ergodic. Second, it can be computed without explicit distributional assumptions on the y_t. What is required is that e_t is a sequence of independent white noises with bounded fourth moments under the null and that T is sufficiently large, in which case α^{un}, Σ_e^{un}, α^{re}, Σ_e^{re} are pseudo-maximum likelihood estimators. Third, an LR test is biased against the null in small samples. Hence, it is common to use $\text{LR}^{\text{c}} = (T - qm)(\ln|\Sigma^{\text{re}}| - \ln|\Sigma^{\text{un}}|)$, where qm is the number of estimated parameters in each equation of the unrestricted system. Finally, one should remember that the distribution of the LR test is only asymptotically valid. That is, significance levels only approximate probabilities of type I errors.

In practice, an estimate of q is obtained sequentially, as the next algorithm shows.

Algorithm 4.1.

(1) Choose an upper bound $\bar{q}$.

(2) Test a VAR$(\bar{q} - 1)$ against VAR$(\bar{q})$ by using an LR test. If the null hypothesis is not rejected, go to (3).

(3) Test a VAR$(\bar{q} - 2)$ against VAR$(\bar{q} - 1)$ by using an LR test. Continue testing until rejection occurs.

Clearly, $\bar{q}$ depends on the frequency of the data. Typical choices are $\bar{q} = 3$ for annual data, $\bar{q} = 8$ for quarterly data, and $\bar{q} = 18$ for monthly data. Alternatively, one could choose $q = T^{1/3}$. Note that with a sequential approach each null hypothesis is tested conditionally on all the previous ones being true and that the chosen q crucially depends on the significance level. Furthermore, when a sequential procedure is used it is important to distinguish between the significance level of individual tests and the significance level of the procedure as a whole; in fact, rejection of a VAR$(\bar{q} - j)$ implies that all VAR$(\bar{q} - j')$ will also be rejected, $\forall j' > j$.

Example 4.7. Choose as a significance level 0.05, set $\bar{q} = 6$, and assume that the following sequence of tests is asymptotically independent (as shown, for example, by Paulsen and Tjostheim (1985)). A likelihood ratio test for $q = 5$ versus $q = 6$ has significance level $1 - 0.95 = 0.05$. Conditional on choosing $q = 5$, a test for $q = 4$ versus $q = 5$ has a significance level $1 - (0.95)^2 = 0.17$ and the (asymptotic) significance level at the jth stage is $1 - (1 - 0.05)^j$. If we expect the model to have

Table 4.1. Penalties of Akaike, Hannan and Quinn, and Schwarz criteria.

	$T = 40,\ m = 4$			$T = 80,\ m = 4$		
Criterion	$q = 2$	$q = 4$	$q = 6$	$q = 2$	$q = 4$	$q = 6$
AIC	0.4	3.2	4.8	0.8	1.6	2.4
HQC	0.52	4.17	6.26	1.18	2.36	3.54
SIC	2.95	5.9	8.85	1.75	3.5	5.25
	$T = 120,\ m = 4$			$T = 160,\ m = 4$		
Criterion	$q = 2$	$q = 4$	$q = 6$	$q = 2$	$q = 4$	$q = 6$
AIC	0.53	1.06	1.6	0.32	0.64	0.96
HQC	0.83	1.67	2.50	0.53	1.06	1.6
SIC	1.27	2.55	3.83	0.84	1.69	2.52

three or four lags, we better adjust the significance level so that, at the second or third stage of the testing, the significance is around 0.05.

Exercise 4.14. An LR test chooses the same lag length for each equation. Is it possible to have different lag lengths in different equations? How would you do this in a bivariate VAR?

While popular, LR tests are unsatisfactory lag-selection approaches when the VAR is used for forecasting. This is because LR tests look at the in-sample fit of models (see equation (4.10)). When forecasting, one would like to have lag-selection methods which minimize the (out-of-sample) forecast error. Let $y_{t+\tau} - y_t(\tau)$ be the τ-steps-ahead forecast error constructed using time t information and let $\Sigma_y(\tau) = E[y_{t+\tau} - y_t(\tau)][y_{t+\tau} - y_t(\tau)]'$ be its mean square error (MSE). When $\tau = 1$, $\Sigma_y(1) \approx [(T + mq)/T]\Sigma_e$, where Σ_e is the variance covariance matrix of the innovations (see, for example, Lutkepohl 1991, p. 88). The next three information criteria choose lag lengths by using transformations of $\Sigma_y(1)$.

Akaike information criterion (AIC): $\min_q \text{AIC}(q) = \ln|\Sigma_y(1)|(q) + \dfrac{2qm^2}{T}$.

Hannan–Quinn criterion (HQC): $\min_q \text{HQC}(q) = \ln|\Sigma_y(1)|(q) + \dfrac{2qm^2}{T}\ln(\ln T)$.

Schwarz criterion (SIC): $\min_q \text{SIC}(q) = \ln|\Sigma_y(1)|(q) + \dfrac{2qm^2}{T}\ln T$.

All criteria add a penalty to the one-step-ahead MSE which depends on the sample size T, the number of variables m, and the number of lags q. While for large T penalty differences are unimportant, this is not the case when T is small, as shown in table 4.1. In general, for $T \geqslant 20$, SIC and HQC will always choose smaller models than AIC.

Table 4.2. Lag length of a VAR.

Hypothesis	LR	Modified LR	AIC	HQC	SIC
$q = 6$ vs. $q = 7$	2.9314×10^{-5}	0.0447	−7.5560	−6.3350	−4.4828
$q = 5$ vs. $q = 6$	3.6400×10^{-4}	0.1171	−7.4139	−6.3942	−4.8514
$q = 4$ vs. $q = 5$	0.0509	0.5833	−7.4940	−6.6758	−5.4378
$q = 3$ vs. $q = 4$	0.0182	0.4374	−7.5225	−6.9056	−5.9726
$q = 2$ vs. $q = 3$	0.0919	0.6770	−7.6350	−7.2196	−6.5914
$q = 1$ vs. $q = 2$	3.0242×10^{-7}	6.8182×10^{-3}	−7.2266	−7.0126	−6.6893

The three criteria have different asymptotic properties. AIC is inconsistent (in fact, it overestimates the true order with positive probability) while HQC and SIC are consistent and when $m > 1$ they are both strongly consistent (i.e., they will choose the correct model a.s.). Intuitively, AIC is inconsistent because the penalty function used does not simultaneously go to infinity as $T \to \infty$ and to zero when scaled by T. Consistency, however, is not the only yardstick one wants to use since consistent methods may have poor small-sample properties. Kilian and Ivanov (2005) extensively study the small-sample properties of these three criteria by using a variety of data-generating processes and data frequencies and found that HQC is best for quarterly and monthly data, both when y_t is covariance stationary and when it is a near-unit-root process.

Example 4.8. Consider a quarterly VAR for the euro area for the sample 1980:1–1999:4 ($T = 80$); restrict $m = 4$ and use output, prices, interest rates, and money (M3) as variables. A constant is eliminated previous to the search. We set $\bar{q} = 7$. Table 4.2 reports the sequential p-values of basic and modified LR tests (first two columns) and the values of AIC, HQC, and SIC (the other three columns). Different tests select somewhat different lag lengths. The LR tests select seven lags but the p-values are nonmonotonic and it matters what $\bar{q}$ is. For example, if $\bar{q} = 6$, the modified LR test selects two lags. Nonmonotonicity also appears for the other three criteria. SIC, which uses the harshest penalty, has a minimum at 1; HQC and AIC have minima at 2. Based on these outcomes, we tentatively select a VAR(2).

4.2.2 Lag Length 2

The Wold theorem implies, among other things, that VAR residuals must be white noise. An LR test can therefore be interpreted as a diagnostic to check whether residuals satisfy this property. Similarly, AIC, HQC, and SIC can be seen as trading-off the white noise assumption on the residuals with the best possible out-of-sample forecasting performance.

Another class of lag-selection tests directly examines the properties of VAR residuals. Let $\mathrm{ACRF}_{i,i'}(\tau)$ denote the cross-correlation of e_{it} and $e_{i't}$ at lag $\tau = \dots, -1, 0, 1, \dots$. Then, $\mathrm{ACRF}_{i,i'}(\tau) = \mathrm{ACF}_{i,i'}(\tau)/\sqrt{\mathrm{ACF}_{i,i}(0)\,\mathrm{ACF}_{i',i'}(0)} \xrightarrow{\mathrm{D}} \mathbb{N}(0, 1/T)$ for each τ under the null of white noise (see, for example, Lutkepohl 1991, p. 141).

Exercise 4.15. Design a test for the joint hypothesis that $\mathrm{ACRF}_e(\tau) = 0, \forall i, i'$, τ fixed.

Care must be exercised in implementing white noise tests sequentially—say, starting from an upper $\bar{q}$, checking if the residuals are white noise and, if they are, decrease $\bar{q}$ by one value at a time until the null hypothesis is rejected. Since serial correlation is present in incorrectly specified VARs, one must choose a $\bar{q}$ for which the null hypothesis is satisfied.

Exercise 4.16. Provide a test statistic for the null that $\mathrm{ACRF}_e(\tau)^{i,i'} = 0, \forall \tau$, which is robust to the presence of heteroskedasticity in VAR residuals.

In implementing white noise tests, one should also remember that since VAR residuals are estimated, the asymptotic covariance matrix of the ACRF must include parameter uncertainty. Contrary to what one might expect, the covariance matrix of the estimated residuals is smaller than the one based on the true ones (see, for example, Lutkepohl 1991, p. 142–48). Hence, $1/T$ is conservative, in the sense that the null hypothesis will be rejected less often than indicated by the significance level.

Portmanteau or Q-tests for the whiteness of the residuals can also be used to choose the lag length of a VAR. Both Portmanteau and Q-tests are designed to verify the null that $\mathrm{ACRF}_e^\tau = (\mathrm{ACRF}_e(1), \dots, \mathrm{ACRF}_e(\tau)) = 0$ (the alternative is $\mathrm{ACRF}_e^\tau \neq 0$). The Portmanteau statistic is

$$\mathrm{PS}(\tau) = T \sum_{i=1}^{\tau} \mathrm{tr}(\mathrm{ACF}(i)'(\mathrm{ACF}(0)^{-1})'\mathrm{ACF}(i)\,\mathrm{ACF}(0)^{-1}) \xrightarrow{\mathrm{D}} \chi^2(m^2(\tau - q)) \tag{4.11}$$

for $\tau > q$ under the null. The Q-statistic is

$$\mathrm{QS}(\tau) = T(T+2) \sum_{i=1}^{\tau} \frac{1}{T-i}\,\mathrm{tr}(\mathrm{ACF}(i)'(\mathrm{ACF}(0)^{-1})'\mathrm{ACF}(i)\,\mathrm{ACF}(0)^{-1}). \tag{4.12}$$

For large T, it has the same asymptotic distribution as $\mathrm{PS}(\tau)$.

Exercise 4.17. Use U.S. quarterly data from 1960:1 to 2004:4 to optimally select the lag length of a VAR with output, prices, nominal interest rate, and money. Use modified LR, AIC, HQC, SIC, and white noise tests. Does it make a difference if the sample is 1970–2004 or 1980–2004? How do you interpret differences across tests and/or samples?

4.2.3 Nonlinearities and Nonnormalities

So far we have focused our attention on linear specifications. Since time aggregation washes most of the nonlinearities out, the focus is hardly restrictive, at least for quarterly data. However, with monthly data nonlinearities could be important, especially if financial variables are used. Furthermore, time variations in the coefficients (see chapter 10), outliers, or structural breaks may also generate (in a reduced-form sense) nonlinearities and nonnormalities in the residuals of a constant coefficients VAR. Hence, one wants methods to detect departures from linearity and nonnormality if they exist.

In deriving the MA representation we have used the linearity assumption. Since omitted nonlinear terms will end up in the error term, the same ideas employed in testing for white noise residuals can be used to check if nonlinear effects are present.

Two ways of formally testing for nonlinearities are the following. (i) Run a regression of estimated VAR residuals on nonlinear functions of the lagged dependent variables and examine the significance of estimated coefficients, adjusting standard errors for the fact that e_t is proxied by estimated residuals. (ii) Directly insert high-order terms in the VAR and examine their significance. Graphical techniques, for example, a scatter plot of estimated residuals against nonlinear functions of the regressors, could also be used as diagnostics.

There is also an indirect approach to check for nonlinearities which builds on the idea that whenever nonlinear terms are important, the moments of the residuals have a special structure. In particular, their distribution will be nonnormal, even in large samples.

Testing for nonnormalities is simple: a normal white noise process with unit variance has zero skewness (third moment) and kurtosis (the fourth moment) equal to 3. Hence, an asymptotic test for the presence of nonnormalities is as follows. Let $\hat{e}_t = y_t - \sum_j \hat{A}_j y_{t-j}$, $\Sigma_e = [1/(T-1)]\sum_t \hat{e}_t\hat{e}_t'$, $\tilde{e}_t = \tilde{\mathcal{P}}^{-1}\hat{e}_t$, and $\tilde{\mathcal{P}}\tilde{\mathcal{P}}' = \Sigma_e$, where $\hat{A}_j$ is an estimator of A_j. Define $\mathfrak{S}_{1i} = (1/T)\sum_t \tilde{e}_{it}^3$, $\mathfrak{S}_{2i} = (1/T)\sum_t \tilde{e}_{it}^4$, $i = 1, \dots, m$, $\mathfrak{S}_j = (\mathfrak{S}_{j1}, \dots, \mathfrak{S}_{jm})'$, $j = 1, 2$, and let 3_m be an $m \times 1$ vector with 3 in each entry. Then

$$\sqrt{T}\begin{bmatrix} \mathfrak{S}_1 \\ \mathfrak{S}_2 - 3_m \end{bmatrix} \xrightarrow{\mathrm{D}} \mathbb{N}\left(0, \begin{bmatrix} 6 \times I_m & 0 \\ 0 & 24 \times I_m \end{bmatrix}\right).$$

4.2.4 Stationarity

Covariance stationarity is crucial in order to derive a VAR representation with constant coefficients. However, a time-varying MA representation for a nonstationary y_t always exists if the other assumptions used in the Wold theorem hold. If $\sum_j D_{jt}^2 < \infty$ for all t, a nonstationary VAR representation can be derived. Hence, VAR models with time-varying coefficients, which we examine in chapter 10, are the natural alternative to covariance stationary structures.

While covariance stationarity is unnecessary, it is a convenient property to have when estimating VAR models. Also, although models with smooth changes in the coefficients may be the natural extensions of covariance stationary models, the literature has focused on a more extreme form of nonstationarity: unit root processes. Unit root models are less natural for two reasons: they imply drastically different dynamic properties, and classical statistics has difficulties in testing this null hypothesis in the presence of a near-unit-root alternative (see, for example, Watson 1995). Despite these problems, contrasting stationary versus unit root behavior has become a rule, the conventional wisdom being that macroeconomic time series are near-unit-root processes, i.e., they are in the gray area where the tests have low power. Hence, a randomly perturbed series reverts to the original state very slowly.

Unit root tests are somewhat tangential to the scope of the book. Favero (2001) provides an excellent review of this literature. Hence, we limit our attention to the implications that nonstationarity (or near nonstationarity) has for the specification of the VAR, for the estimation of the parameters, and for the identification of structural shocks.

If a test has detected one or more unit roots, how should one proceed in specifying a VAR? Suppose we are confident in the testing results and that all variables are either stationary or integrated, but no cointegration is detected. Then one would difference unit-root variables until covariance stationarity is obtained and estimate the VAR by using transformed variables. For example, if all variables are $I(1)$, a VAR in growth rates is appropriate.

Specification is also simple when there are some cointegrating relationships. For example, both prices and money may display unit root behavior but real balances may be stationary. Here, one typically transforms the VAR into a vector error correction model (VECM) and either imposes the cointegrating relationships (using the theoretical or the estimated restrictions) or jointly estimates short-run and long-run coefficients from the data. VECMs are preferable to differenced VARs because the latter throws away information about the long-run properties of the data. Plugging in estimates of the long-run relationships is justified by the fact that they are superconsistent, i.e., they asymptotically converge at the rate T (estimates of short-run relationships converge at the rate $\sqrt{T}$). Since a VECM is a reparametrization of the VAR in levels, the latter is appropriate if all variables are cointegrated, even though some (or all) of its components are not covariance stationary.

Despite more than two decades of work in the area, unit root tests still have poor small-sample properties. Furthermore, barring exceptional circumstances, neither explosive nor unit root behavior has been observed in long stretches of OECD macroeconomic data. Both reasons may cast doubt on the nonstationarities detected and the usefulness of such tests.

When doubts about the tests exist, one can indirectly check the reasonableness of the stationarity assumption by studying estimated residuals. In fact, if y_t is nonstationary and no cointegration emerges, the estimated residuals are likely to display nonstationary path. Hence, a plot of the VAR residuals may indicate if a problem exists. Practical experience suggests that VAR residuals show breaks and outliers but they rarely display unit root type behavior. Hence, a level VAR could be appropriate even when y_t looks nonstationary. It is also important to remember that the properties of y_t are important in testing hypotheses about the coefficients since classical distribution theory is different when unit roots are present. However, they are irrelevant for estimation. Consistent estimates of VAR coefficients, in fact, obtain with classical methods even when unit roots are present (see Sims et al. 1990).

Another argument against the use of specification tests for stationarity comes from a Bayesian perspective. In Bayesian analysis the posterior distribution of the quantities of interest is all that matters. While Bayesian and classical analyses have many common aspects, they differ dramatically when unit roots are present. In particular, while the classical asymptotic distribution of the coefficients' estimates depends on whether unit roots are present or not, the posterior distribution has the same shape with or without unit roots. Therefore, if one takes a Bayesian perspective to testing, no adjustment for nonstationarity is required.

Finally, one should remember that pretesting has consequences for the distribution of estimates, since incorrect choices produce inconsistent estimates of the quantities of interest. To minimize pretesting problems, we recommend starting by assuming covariance stationarity and deviate from it only if the data overwhelmingly suggest the opposite.

4.2.5 Breaks

While exact unit root behavior is unlikely to be relevant in macroeconomics, changes in the intercept, in the dynamics, or in the covariance matrix of a vector of time series are quite common. A time series with breaks is neither stationary nor covariance stationary. To avoid problems, applied researchers typically focus attention on subsamples which are (assumed to be) homogeneous. However, this is not always possible: the break may occur at the end of the sample (e.g., creation of the euro), there may be several of them, or they may be linked to expansions and contractions and it may be unwise to throw away runs with these characteristics.

While structural breaks with dramatic changes in dynamics may sometimes occur (e.g., breakdown or unification of a country), it is more often the case that time series display slowly evolving features with no abrupt changes at one specific point — a pattern which would be more consistent with time-varying-coefficient specifications. Nevertheless, it may be useful to have tools to test for structural breaks if visual inspection suggests that such a pattern may be present. If the break date is known, Chow tests can be used. Let Σ_e^{re} be the covariance matrix of the VAR residuals with no breaks and let $\Sigma_e^{\text{un}} = \Sigma_e^{\text{un}}(1, \bar{t}) + \Sigma_e^{\text{un}}(\bar{t}+1, T)$ be the covariance matrix when a break is allowed at $\bar{t}$. Then $\text{CS}(\bar{t}) = [(|\Sigma_e^{\text{re}}| - |\Sigma_e^{\text{un}}|)/\nu]/(|\Sigma_e^{\text{un}}|/(T-2\nu)) \sim F(\nu, T-2\nu)$, where ν is the number of regressors in the model. When $\bar{t}$ is unknown, but suspected to occur within an interval, one could run Chow tests for all $\bar{t} \in [t_1, t_2]$, take $\max_{\bar{t}} \mathrm{CT}(\bar{t})$ and compare it with a modified F-distribution (critical values are in Stock and Watson (2002, p. 111)).

An alternative testing approach is obtained by noting that, if no break occurs, the τ-steps-ahead forecast error $e_t(\tau) \equiv y_{t+\tau} - y_t(\tau)$ should have properties similar to those of the sample residuals. Then, under the null of no breaks at forecasting horizon τ, $e_t(\tau) \xrightarrow{\text{D}} \mathbb{N}(0, \Sigma_e(\tau))$.

Exercise 4.18. Show that a statistic to check for the null of no breaks over τ forecasting horizons is $e_t \Sigma_e^{-1} e_t \xrightarrow{\text{D}} \chi^2(\tau)$, T large, where $e_t = (e_t(1), \dots, e_t(\tau))$ and Σ is a $\tau \times \tau$ matrix. (The alternative here is that the DGP for y_t differs before and after t.)

As usual these tests may be biased in small samples. A small-sample version of the forecasting test is obtained by using $\Sigma_e^{\text{c}}(\tau) = \Sigma_e(\tau) + (1/T)E[(\partial y_t(\tau)/\partial\alpha') \times \Sigma_\alpha(\partial y_t(\tau)/\partial\alpha')']$ in place of $\Sigma_e(\tau)$.

4.3 Moments and Parameter Estimation of a VAR(q)

There are two alternative representations of a VAR(q) which are easier to manipulate than (4.7) and are of use when deriving estimators of the unknown parameters.

4.3.1 Companion Form Representation

The companion form representation transforms a VAR(q) model in a larger scale VAR(1) model and is useful when one needs to compute moments or derive parameter estimates.

Let

$$\mathbb{Y}_t = \begin{bmatrix} y_t \\ y_{t-1} \\ \cdots \\ y_{t-q+1} \end{bmatrix}, \quad \mathbb{E}_t = \begin{bmatrix} e_t \\ 0 \\ \cdots \\ 0 \end{bmatrix} 0, \quad \mathbb{A} = \begin{bmatrix} A_1 & A_2 & \cdots & A_q \\ I_m & 0 & \cdots & 0 \\ \cdots & \cdots & \cdots & \cdots \\ 0 & \cdots & I_m & 0 \end{bmatrix}.$$

Then (4.7) is

$$\mathbb{Y}_t = \mathbb{A}\mathbb{Y}_{t-1} + \mathbb{E}_t, \quad \mathbb{E}_t \sim (0, \Sigma_E), \tag{4.13}$$

where $\mathbb{Y}_t$, $\mathbb{E}_t$ are $mq \times 1$ vectors and $\mathbb{A}$ is an $mq \times mq$ matrix.

Example 4.9. Consider a bivariate VAR(2) model. Here $\mathbb{Y}_t = [y_t, y_{t-1}]'$ and $\mathbb{E}_t = [e_t, 0]'$ are 4×1 vectors, and $\mathbb{A} = \left[\begin{smallmatrix} A_1 & A_2 \\ I_2 & 0 \end{smallmatrix}\right]$ is a 4×4 matrix.

Moments of y_t can be immediately calculated from (4.13).

Example 4.10. The unconditional mean of y_t can be obtained by using $E(\mathbb{Y}_t) = [(I - \mathbb{A}\ell)^{-1}]E(\mathbb{E}_t) = 0$ and a selection matrix which picks the first m elements out of $E(\mathbb{Y}_t)$. To calculate the unconditional variance, note that, because of covariance stationarity, $E[(\mathbb{Y}_t - E(\mathbb{Y}_t))(\mathbb{Y}_t - E(\mathbb{Y}_t))'] = \mathbb{A}E_t[(\mathbb{Y}_{t-1} - E(\mathbb{Y}_{t-1})) \times (\mathbb{Y}_{t-1} - E(\mathbb{Y}_{t-1}))']\mathbb{A}' + \Sigma_E$, or

$$\Sigma_Y = \mathbb{A}\Sigma_Y\mathbb{A}' + \Sigma_E. \tag{4.14}$$

To solve (4.14) for Σ_Y we will make use of the following result.

Result 4.1. If T, V, R are conformable matrices, $\text{vec}(TVR) = (R' \otimes T)\text{vec}(V)$.

Then $\text{vec}(\Sigma_Y) = [I_{(mq)^2} - (\mathbb{A} \otimes \mathbb{A})]^{-1}\text{vec}(\Sigma_E)$, where $I(mq)^2$ is an $(mq)^2 \times (mq)^2$ identity matrix.

Unconditional covariances and correlations can also be easily computed. In fact,

$$\begin{aligned}\text{ACF}_Y(\tau) &\equiv E[(\mathbb{Y}_t - E(\mathbb{Y}_t))(\mathbb{Y}_{t-\tau} - E(\mathbb{Y}_{t-\tau}))'] \\ &= \mathbb{A}E_t[(\mathbb{Y}_{t-1} - E(\mathbb{Y}_{t-1}))(\mathbb{Y}_{t-\tau} - E(\mathbb{Y}_{t-\tau}))'] \\ &\quad + E[\mathbb{E}_t(\mathbb{Y}_{t-\tau} - E(\mathbb{Y}_{t-\tau}))'] \\ &= \mathbb{A}\text{ACF}_Y(\tau-1) = \mathbb{A}^\tau \Sigma_Y, \quad \tau = 1, 2, \ldots. \end{aligned} \tag{4.15}$$

The companion form could also be used to obtain the spectral density matrix of y_t. Let $\text{ACF}_E(\tau) = \text{cov}(\mathbb{E}_t, \mathbb{E}_{t-\tau})$. Then the spectral density of $\mathbb{E}_t$ is $\mathcal{S}_E(\omega) = (1/2\pi)\sum_{\tau=-\infty}^{\infty} \mathrm{e}^{-\mathrm{i}\omega\tau}\text{ACF}_E(\tau)$ and $\text{vec}[\mathcal{S}_Y(\omega)] = [I(\omega) - \mathbb{A}(\omega)\mathbb{A}(-\omega)'] \times \text{vec}[\mathcal{S}_E(\omega)]$, where $I(\omega) = \sum_j \mathrm{e}^{-\mathrm{i}\omega j} I$, $\mathbb{A}(\omega) = \sum_j \mathrm{e}^{-\mathrm{i}\omega j}\mathbb{A}^j$, and $\mathbb{A}(-\omega)'$ is the complex conjugate of $\mathbb{A}(\omega)$.

Exercise 4.19. Suppose a VAR(2) has been fitted to unemployment and inflation data and $\hat{A}_1 = \left[\begin{smallmatrix} 0.95 & 0.23 \\ 0.21 & 0.88 \end{smallmatrix}\right]$, $\hat{A}_2 = \left[\begin{smallmatrix} -0.05 & 0.13 \\ -0.11 & 0.03 \end{smallmatrix}\right]$, and $\hat{\Sigma}_e = \left[\begin{smallmatrix} 0.05 & 0.01 \\ 0.01 & 0.06 \end{smallmatrix}\right]$ have been obtained. Calculate the spectral density matrix of y_t. What is the value of $\mathcal{S}_Y(\omega = 0)$?

A companion form representation also has computational advantages when deriving estimators of the unknown parameters. We first consider estimators obtained when no constraints (lag elimination, exogeneity restrictions, etc.) are imposed on the VAR; when $y_{-q+1}, \ldots, y_0$ are fixed and e_t are normally distributed with covariance matrix Σ_e.

Given the VAR structure, $(y_t \mid y_{t-1}, \ldots, y_0, \ldots, y_{-q+1}) \sim \mathbb{N}(\mathbb{A}_1\mathbb{Y}_{t-1}, \Sigma_e)$, where $\mathbb{A}_1$ is an $m \times mq$ matrix containing the first m rows of $\mathbb{A}$. The density of y_t is $f(y_t \mid y_{t-1}, \ldots, \mathbb{A}_1, \Sigma_e) = (2\pi)^{-0.5m}|\Sigma_e^{-1}|^{0.5}\exp[-0.5(y_t - \mathbb{A}_1\mathbb{Y}_{t-1})' \times \Sigma_e^{-1}(y_t - \mathbb{A}_1\mathbb{Y}_{t-1})]$. Since the joint density of $f(y_t, y_{t-1}, \ldots \mid y_0, \ldots, \mathbb{A}_1, \Sigma_e)$ is $\prod_{t=1}^T f(y_t \mid y_{t-1}, \ldots, y_0, \ldots, \mathbb{A}_1, \Sigma_e)$, the log likelihood is

$$\begin{aligned}\mathcal{L}(\mathbb{A}_1, \Sigma_e \mid y_t) &= -\tfrac{1}{2}T(m\ln(2\pi) - \ln|\Sigma_e^{-1}|) \\ &\quad - \tfrac{1}{2}\sum_t (y_t - \mathbb{A}_1\mathbb{Y}_{t-1})'\Sigma_e^{-1}(y_t - \mathbb{A}_1\mathbb{Y}_{t-1}).\end{aligned} \tag{4.16}$$

Taking the first-order conditions with respect to $\text{vec}(\mathbb{A}_1)$ leads to

$$\mathbb{A}'_{1,\text{ML}} = \left(\sum_{t=1}^T \mathbb{Y}_{t-1}\mathbb{Y}'_{t-1}\right)^{-1}\left(\sum_{t=1}^T \mathbb{Y}_{t-1}y'_t\right) = \mathbb{A}'_{1,\text{OLS}}. \tag{4.17}$$

Hence, when no restrictions are imposed and the initial conditions are taken to be fixed, maximum likelihood (ML) and OLS estimators of $\mathbb{A}_1$ coincide. Note that an estimator of the jth row of $\mathbb{A}_1$ (a $1 \times mq$ vector) is $\mathbb{A}'_{1j} = [\sum_t \mathbb{Y}_{t-1}\mathbb{Y}'_{t-1}]^{-1} \times [\sum_t \mathbb{Y}_{t-1}y_{jt}]$.

Exercise 4.20. Provide conditions for $\mathbb{A}_{1,\mathrm{ML}}$ to be consistent. Is it efficient?

Exercise 4.21. Show that, if there are no restrictions on the VAR, OLS estimation of the parameters, equation by equation, is consistent and efficient.

The result of exercise 4.21 is important: as long as all variables appear with the same lags in every equation, single-equation OLS estimation is sufficient. Intuitively, an unrestricted VAR is a seemingly unrelated regression (SUR) model and for such models single-equation and system-wide methods are equally efficient (see, for example, Hamilton 1994, p. 315).

Using $\mathbb{A}_{1,\mathrm{ML}}$ in the log likelihood we obtain $\ln \mathcal{L}(\Sigma_e \mid y_t) = -\frac{1}{2}Tm\ln(2\pi) - \frac{1}{2}T\ln|\Sigma_e^{-1}| - \frac{1}{2}\sum_{t=1}^{T} e'_{t,\mathrm{ML}}\Sigma_e^{-1}e_{t,\mathrm{ML}}$, where $e_{t,\mathrm{ML}} = (y_t - \mathbb{A}_{1,\mathrm{ML}}\mathbb{Y}_{t-1})$. Taking the first-order conditions with respect to $\mathrm{vech}(\Sigma_e)$, where $\mathrm{vech}(\Sigma_e)$ vectorizes the symmetric matrix Σ_e, and, using the fact that $\partial(b'\mathcal{Q}b)/\partial\mathcal{Q} = bb'$ and $\partial\ln|\mathcal{Q}|/\partial\mathcal{Q} = (\mathcal{Q}')^{-1}$, we have $\frac{1}{2}T\Sigma'_e - \frac{1}{2}\sum_{t=1}^{T} e_{t,\mathrm{ML}}e'_{t,\mathrm{ML}} = 0$ or

$$\Sigma'_{\mathrm{ML}} = \frac{1}{T}\sum_{t=1}^{T} e_{t,\mathrm{ML}}e'_{t,\mathrm{ML}} \tag{4.18}$$

and the ML estimate of the (i, i') element of Σ_e is $\sigma_{i,i'} = (1/T)\sum_{t=1}^{T} e_{it,\mathrm{ML}}e'_{i't,\mathrm{ML}}$.

Exercise 4.22. Show that Σ_{ML} is biased but consistent.

4.3.2 Simultaneous Equations Format

Two other useful representations of a VAR(q) are obtained by using the format of a simultaneous equations system. The first is obtained as follows. Set $x_t = [y_{t-1}, y_{t-2}, \dots]$, $\boldsymbol{X} = [x_1, \dots, x_T]'$ (a $T \times mq$ matrix), $\boldsymbol{Y} = [y_1, \dots, y_T]'$ (a $T \times m$ matrix), and let $\boldsymbol{A} = [A'_1, \dots, A'_q]' = \mathbb{A}'_1$ be an $mq \times m$ matrix:

$$\boldsymbol{Y} = \boldsymbol{X}\boldsymbol{A} + \boldsymbol{E}. \tag{4.19}$$

The second transformation is obtained from (4.19). The equation for variable i is $\boldsymbol{Y}_i = \boldsymbol{X}\boldsymbol{A}_i + \boldsymbol{E}_i$. Stacking the columns of $\boldsymbol{Y}_i$, $\boldsymbol{E}_i$ into $mT \times 1$ vectors, we have

$$y = (I_m \otimes X)\alpha + e \equiv \mathcal{X}\alpha + e. \tag{4.20}$$

Note that in (4.19) all variables are grouped together for each t; in (4.20) all time periods for one variable are grouped together. As shown in chapter 10, (4.20) is useful for decomposing the likelihood function of a VAR(q) into the product of a normal density of α, conditional on the OLS estimates of the VAR parameters, and a Wishart density for Σ_e^{-1}.

Using these representations we can immediately compute the moments of y_t.

Example 4.11. Using (4.20) we can verify that $E(y) = E(I \otimes X)\alpha$ is the mean of y_t and that $\Sigma_Y = E\{[(I_m \otimes X) - E(I_m \otimes X)]\alpha + e\}^2$ is the unconditional MSE.

Exercise 4.23. Using (4.20), assuming that $\Sigma_{xx} = p\lim X'X/T$ exists and is nonsingular and that $(1/\sqrt{T})\mathrm{vec}(X'e) \xrightarrow{\mathrm{D}} \mathbb{N}(0, \Sigma_{xx} \otimes \Sigma_e)$, show that

(i) $p\lim_{T\to\infty} \alpha_{\mathrm{OLS}} = \alpha$;

(ii) $\sqrt{T}(\alpha_{\mathrm{OLS}} - \alpha) \xrightarrow{\mathrm{D}} \mathbb{N}(0, \Sigma_{xx}^{-1} \otimes \Sigma_e)$;

(iii) $\Sigma_{e,\mathrm{OLS}} = (y - X\alpha_{\mathrm{OLS}})(y - X\alpha_{\mathrm{OLS}})'/(T - mq)$ is such that $p\lim \sqrt{T} \times (\Sigma_{e,\mathrm{OLS}} - ee'/T) = 0$.

Estimators of the VAR parameters can also be obtained via the Yule–Walker equations. From (4.7) we can immediately see that $E[(y_t - E(y_t))(y_{t-\tau} - E(y_{t-\tau}))] = A(\ell)E[(y_{t-1} - E(y_{t-1}))(y_{t-\tau} - E(y_{t-\tau}))] + E[e_t(y_{t-\tau} - E(y_{t-\tau}))]$ for all $\tau \geqslant 0$. Hence, letting $\mathrm{ACF}_y(\tau) = E[(y_t - E(y_t))(y_{t-\tau} - E(y_{t-\tau}))]$ we have

$$\mathrm{ACF}_y(\tau) = A_1\mathrm{ACF}_y(\tau - 1) + A_2\mathrm{ACF}_y(\tau - 2) + \cdots + A_q\mathrm{ACF}_y(\tau - q) \quad (4.21)$$

or, more compactly, $\mathrm{ACF}_y = \mathbb{A}_1\mathrm{ACF}_y^*$, where $\mathrm{ACF}_y = [\mathrm{ACF}_y(1), \dots, \mathrm{ACF}_y(q)]$ and

$$\mathrm{ACF}_y^* = \begin{bmatrix} \mathrm{ACF}_y(0) & \cdots & \mathrm{ACF}_y(q-1) \\ \cdots & \cdots & \cdots \\ \mathrm{ACF}_y(-q+1) & \cdots & \mathrm{ACF}_y(0) \end{bmatrix}.$$

Then an estimate of $\mathbb{A}_1$ is $\mathbb{A}_{1,\mathrm{YW}} = \mathrm{ACF}_y(\mathrm{ACF}_y^*)^{-1}$.

Example 4.12. If $q = 1$, (4.21) reduces to $\mathrm{ACF}_y(\tau) = A_1\mathrm{ACF}_y(\tau - 1)$. Given estimates of A_1 and Σ_e, we have that $\mathrm{ACF}_y(0) \equiv \Sigma_y = A_1\Sigma_y A_1' + \Sigma_e$ so that $\mathrm{vec}(\Sigma_y) = (I - A_1 \otimes A_1)\mathrm{vec}(\Sigma_e)$ and $\mathrm{ACF}_y(1) = A_1\mathrm{ACF}_y(0)$, $\mathrm{ACF}_y(2) = A_1\mathrm{ACF}_y(1)$, etc.

Exercise 4.24. Show that $\mathbb{A}_{1,\mathrm{YW}} = \mathbb{A}_{1,\mathrm{ML}}$. Conclude that Yule–Walker and ML estimators have the same asymptotic properties.

Exercise 4.25. Show how to modify the Yule–Walker estimator when $E(y_t)$ is unknown. Show that the resulting estimator is asymptotically equivalent to $\mathbb{A}_{1,\mathrm{YW}}$.

It is interesting to study what happens when a VAR is estimated under some restrictions (exogeneity, cointegration, lag elimination, etc.). Suppose restrictions are of the form $\alpha = R\theta + r$, where R is an $mk \times k_1$ matrix of rank k_1, r is an $mk \times 1$ vector, and θ is a $k_1 \times 1$ vector.

Example 4.13. (i) Suppose that $A_q = 0$. Here $k_1 = m^2(q - 1)$, $r = 0$, and $R = [I_{k_1}, 0]$. (ii) Suppose that y_{2t} is exogenous for y_{1t} in a bivariate VAR(2). Here $R = \mathrm{blockdiag}[R_1, R_2]$, where R_i, $i = 1, 2$, is upper triangular.

Using (4.20) we have $y = (I_m \otimes X)\alpha + e = (I_m \otimes X)(R\theta + r) + e$ or $y - (I_m \otimes X)r = (I_m \otimes X)R\theta + e$. Since $\partial \ln \mathcal{L}/\partial\alpha = R\partial \ln \mathcal{L}/\partial\theta$,

$$\theta_{\mathrm{ML}} = [R'(\Sigma_e^{-1} \otimes X'X)R]^{-1}R'(\Sigma_e^{-1} \otimes X)[y - (I_m \otimes X)r], \quad (4.22)$$

$$\alpha_{\mathrm{ML}} = R\theta_{\mathrm{ML}} + r, \quad (4.23)$$

$$\Sigma_e = \frac{1}{T}\sum_t e_{\mathrm{ML}}e_{\mathrm{ML}}', \quad e_{\mathrm{ML}} = y - (I_m \otimes X)\alpha_{\mathrm{ML}}. \quad (4.24)$$

Exercise 4.26. Verify that, when a VAR is estimated under some restrictions,

(i) ML estimates are different from OLS estimates,

(ii) ML estimates are consistent and efficient if the restrictions are true but inconsistent if the restrictions are false,

(iii) OLS estimates are consistent when stationarity is incorrectly assumed but t-tests are incorrect,

(iv) OLS estimates are inconsistent if lag restrictions are incorrect.

4.4 Reporting VAR Results

It is rare to report estimated VAR coefficients. Since the number of parameters is large, presenting all of them is cumbersome. Furthermore, they are poorly estimated: except for the first own lag, they are all insignificant. It is therefore usual to report functions of the VAR coefficients which summarize information better, have some economic meaning, and, hopefully, are more precisely estimated. Among the many possible functions, three are typically used: impulse responses, variance, and historical decompositions. Impulse responses trace out the MA of the system, i.e., they describe how $y_{it+\tau}$ responds to a shock in $e_{i't}$; the variance decomposition measures the contribution of $e_{i't}$ to the variability of the forecast error in $y_{it+\tau}$; the historical decomposition describes the contribution of shock $e_{i't}$ to the deviations of $y_{it+\tau}$ from its baseline forecasted path, $\tau = 1, 2, \dots$.

4.4.1 Impulse Responses

There are three ways to calculate impulse responses and these roughly correspond to recursive, nonrecursive (companion form), and forecast revision approaches. In the recursive approach, the impulse response matrix at horizon τ is $D_\tau = \sum_{j=1}^{\max[\tau,q]} D_{\tau-j} A_j$, where $D_0 = I, A_j = 0, \forall\tau \geqslant q$. Clearly, a consistent $\hat{D}_j$ is obtained if a consistent $\hat{A}_j$ is used in place of A_j.

Example 4.14. Consider a VAR(2) with $y_t = A_0 + A_1 y_{t-1} + A_2 y_{t-2} + e_t$. Then the response matrices are $D_0 = I, D_1 = D_0 A_1, D_2 = D_1 A_1 + D_0 A_2, \dots, D_\tau = D_{\tau-1} A_1 + D_{\tau-2} A_2$.

Calculation of meaningful impulse responses requires orthogonal disturbances. Let $\tilde{\mathcal{P}}$ be a square matrix such that $\tilde{\mathcal{P}}\tilde{\mathcal{P}}' = \Sigma_e$. Then the impulse response matrix to orthogonal shocks $\tilde{e}_t = \tilde{\mathcal{P}}^{-1} e_t$ at horizon τ is $\tilde{D}_\tau = D_\tau \tilde{\mathcal{P}}$.

Exercise 4.27. Show the first four elements of the MA representation of a bivariate VAR(3) with orthogonal shocks.

When the VAR is in a companion form, we can compute impulse responses in a different way. Using (4.13) and repeatedly substituting for $\mathbb{Y}_{t-\tau}$, $\tau = 1, 2, \dots$, we have

$$\mathbb{Y}_t = \mathbb{A}^t \mathbb{Y}_0 + \sum_{\tau=0}^{t-1} \mathbb{A}^\tau \mathbb{E}_{t-\tau}, \tag{4.25}$$

$$= \mathbb{A}^t \mathbb{Y}_0 + \sum_{\tau=0}^{t-1} \tilde{\mathbb{A}}^\tau \tilde{\mathbb{E}}_{t-\tau}, \tag{4.26}$$

where $\tilde{\mathbb{A}}^\tau = \mathbb{A}^\tau \tilde{\mathbb{P}}$, $\tilde{\mathbb{E}}_{t-\tau} = \tilde{\mathbb{P}}^{-1}\mathbb{E}_{t-\tau}$, $\tilde{\mathbb{P}}\tilde{\mathbb{P}}' = \Sigma_E$. Equation (4.25) is used with non-orthogonal residuals, (4.26) with orthogonal ones. The first m rows of $\mathbb{A}^\tau$ provide the responses to the shocks.

Exercise 4.28. Show the first four elements of $\mathbb{A}^\tau$ for a bivariate VAR(2).

Finally, one can compute impulse responses by using forecast revisions of future y_t. We will use the companion form representation to illustrate this approach but the argument is valid for any representation. Let $\mathbb{Y}_t(\tau) \equiv \mathbb{A}^\tau \mathbb{Y}_t$ and $\mathbb{Y}_{t-1}(\tau+1) \equiv \mathbb{A}^{\tau+1}\mathbb{Y}_{t-1}$ be the forecast of $\mathbb{Y}_{t+\tau}$ obtained in information at time t and $t-1$, $\tau = 1, 2, \dots$. Then, the one-step-ahead forecast revision of $\mathbb{Y}_{t+\tau}$ is

$$\text{Rev}_t(\tau) = \mathbb{Y}_t(\tau) - \mathbb{Y}_{t-1}(\tau+1) = \mathbb{A}^\tau[\mathbb{Y}_t - \mathbb{A}\mathbb{Y}_{t-1}] = \mathbb{A}^\tau \mathbb{E}_t. \tag{4.27}$$

Example 4.15. Suppose we shock the i'th component of e_t once at time t, i.e., $e_{i't} = 1$, $e_{i'\tau} = 0$, $\tau > t$, $e_{it} = 0$, $\forall i \neq i'$, $\forall t$. Then $\text{Rev}_{t,i'}(1) = \mathbb{A}_{i',\cdot}$, $\text{Rev}_{t,i'}(2) = \mathbb{A}^2_{i',\cdot}$, and $\text{Rev}_{t,i'}(\tau) = \mathbb{A}^\tau_{i',\cdot}$, where $\mathbb{A}_{i',\cdot}$ is the i'th column of $\mathbb{A}$. Therefore, the response of $y_{i,t+\tau}$ to a shock in $e_{i't}$ can be read off the τ-steps-ahead forecast revisions.

Cumulative multipliers are sometimes required. For example, in examining the effects of fiscal disturbances on output one may want to measure the cumulative displacement produced by a shock up to horizon τ. Alternatively, in examining the relationship between money growth and inflation, one may want to know whether an increase in the former translates into an increase of the same amount in the latter in the long run. In the first case one computes $\sum_{j=0}^{\tau} D_j$, in the second $\lim_{\tau\to\infty} \sum_{j=0}^{\tau} D_j$.

4.4.2 Variance Decomposition

To derive the variance decomposition we use (4.7). The τ-steps-ahead forecast error is $e_t(\tau) \equiv y_{t+\tau} - y_t(\tau) = \sum_{j=0}^{\tau-1} \tilde{D}_j \tilde{e}_{t+\tau-j}$, where $D_0 = I$ and $\tilde{e}_t = \tilde{\mathcal{P}}^{-1} e_t = \tilde{\mathcal{P}}_1^{-1} e_{1t} + \cdots + \tilde{\mathcal{P}}_m^{-1} e_{mt}$ are orthogonal disturbances, P_j is the jth column of P, and e_t are reduced-form residuals. Since $\text{var}(\tilde{e}_t) = I$ the MSE of the forecast is

$$\text{MSE}(\tau) = E[y_{t+\tau} - y_t(\tau)]^2 = \Sigma_e + D_1 \Sigma_e D_1' + \cdots + D_{\tau-1}\Sigma_e D_{\tau-1}'$$

$$= \sum_{i=1}^{m} (\tilde{\mathcal{P}}_i \tilde{\mathcal{P}}_i' + \tilde{D}_1 \tilde{\mathcal{P}}_i \tilde{\mathcal{P}}_i' \tilde{D}_1' + \cdots + \tilde{D}_{\tau-1} \tilde{\mathcal{P}}_i \tilde{\mathcal{P}}_i' \tilde{D}_{\tau-1}'). \tag{4.28}$$

Hence, the percentage of the variance in $y_{i,t+\tau}$ due to $e_{i',t}$ is

$$\text{VD}_{i,i'}(\tau) = \frac{(\tilde{\mathcal{P}}_{i'} \tilde{\mathcal{P}}_{i'}' + \tilde{D}_{1i} \tilde{\mathcal{P}}_{i'} \tilde{\mathcal{P}}_{i'}' \tilde{D}_{1i}' + \cdots + \tilde{D}_{\tau-1,i} \tilde{\mathcal{P}}_{i'} \tilde{\mathcal{P}}_{i'}' \tilde{D}_{\tau-1,i}')}{\text{MSE}(\tau)}. \tag{4.29}$$

A compact way to rewrite (4.29) is $\text{VD}(\tau) = \Sigma_{D_\tau}^{-1} \sum_{j=0}^{\tau-1} D_j \odot D_j$, where $\Sigma_{D_\tau} = \text{diag}[\Sigma_{D_{\tau,11}}, \dots, \Sigma_{D_{\tau,mm}}] = \sum_{j=0}^{\tau-1} D_j D_j'$, $D_j \odot D_j$ is a matrix with $D_j(i,i') * D_j(i,i')$ in the i, i' position and $\odot$ is called the Hadamard product (see, for example, Mittnik and Zadrozky 1993).

4.4.3 Historical Decomposition

Let $e_{i,t}(\tau) = y_{i,t+\tau} - y_{i,t}(\tau)$ be the τ-steps-ahead forecast error in the ith variable of the VAR. The historical decomposition of $e_{i,t}(\tau)$ can be calculated by using

$$e_{i,t}(\tau) = \sum_{i'=1}^{m} \tilde{D}_{i,i'}(\ell)\tilde{e}_{i't+\tau}. \tag{4.30}$$

Example 4.16. Consider a bivariate VAR(1). At horizon τ we have $y_{t+\tau} = Ay_{t+\tau-1} + e_{t+\tau} = A^\tau y_t + \sum_{j=0}^{\tau-1} A^j e_{t+\tau-j}$, so that $e_t(\tau) = \sum_{j=0}^{\tau-1} A^j e_{t+\tau-j} = A(\ell)e_{t+\tau}$. Hence, deviations from the baseline forecasts of the first variable from t to $t+\tau$ due to, say, supply shocks are $\tilde{A}_{11}(\ell)\tilde{e}_{1,t+\tau}$ and to, say, demand shocks are $\tilde{A}_{12}(\ell)\tilde{e}_{2,t+\tau}$.

From (4.29) and (4.30) we can see straightaway that the ingredients needed to compute impulse responses, variance, and historical decompositions are the same. Therefore, these statistics simply package the same information in a different way.

Exercise 4.29. Using the estimate provided in exercise 4.19, compute the variance and the historical decomposition for the two variables at horizons 1, 2, and 3.

4.4.4 Distribution of Impulse Responses

To assess the statistical significance of the dynamics induced by certain shocks, we need standard errors. As we have shown, impulse responses, variance, and historical decompositions are complicated functions of the estimated VAR coefficients and of the covariance matrix of the shocks. Therefore, even when the distribution of the latter is known, it is not easy to find their distribution. In this subsection we describe three approaches to computing standard errors: one based on asymptotic theory and two based on resampling methods. All procedures are easy to implement when orthogonal shocks are generated by Choleski factorizations, i.e., if $\tilde{P}$ is lower triangular, and need minor modifications when the system is not contemporaneously recursive (but just identified). In the other cases, resampling methods have a slight computational hedge.

Since impulse responses, variance, and historical decompositions all use the same information, we only discuss how to compute standard errors for impulse responses. The reader will be asked to derive the corresponding expressions for the other two statistics.

4.4.4.1 The δ-Method

The method pioneered by Lutkepohl (1991) and Mittnik and Zadrozky (1993) uses asymptotic approximations and works as follows. Suppose that $\alpha \xrightarrow{\text{D}} \mathbb{N}(0, \Sigma_\alpha)$.

Then any differentiable function $f(\alpha)$ will asymptotically have the distribution $\mathbb{N}(0, (\partial f/\partial\alpha)\Sigma_\alpha(\partial f/\partial\alpha)')$, provided that $\partial f/\partial\alpha \neq 0$. Since impulse responses are differentiable functions of the VAR parameters and of the covariance matrix, their asymptotic distribution can be easily obtained.

Let $\mathbb{S} = [I, 0, \dots, 0]$ be an $m \times mq$ selection matrix so that $y_t = \mathbb{S}\mathbb{Y}_t$ and $\mathbb{E}_t = \mathbb{S}'e_t$, consider the revision of the forecast at step τ and let

$$\text{rev}_t(\tau) = \mathbb{S}\,\text{Rev}_t(\tau) = \mathbb{S}[\mathbb{Y}_t(\tau) - \mathbb{Y}_{t-1}(\tau+1)] = \mathbb{S}[\mathbb{A}^\tau\mathbb{S}'e_t] \equiv \psi_\tau e_t. \quad (4.31)$$

We want the asymptotic distribution of the $m \times m$ matrix ψ_τ. Taking total differentials

$$\mathrm{d}\psi_\tau = \mathbb{S}[I(\mathrm{d}\mathbb{A})\mathbb{A}^{\tau-1} + \mathbb{A}(\mathrm{d}\mathbb{A})\mathbb{A}^{\tau-2} + \cdots + \mathbb{A}^{\tau-1}(\mathrm{d}\mathbb{A})I]\mathbb{S}'. \quad (4.32)$$

Since $\text{var}(\mathbb{Y}_{t+\tau}) = \mathbb{A}^\tau\,\text{var}(\mathbb{E}_{t+k})(\mathbb{A}^\tau)'$, using result 4.1 and the fact that

$$\mathrm{d}Z = \begin{bmatrix} \mathrm{d}Z_1 \\ 0 \end{bmatrix} = \mathbb{S}'\,\mathrm{d}Z_1,$$

we have that $\text{vec}(\mathbb{S}\mathbb{A}^j(\mathrm{d}\mathbb{A})\mathbb{A}^{\tau-(j+1)}\mathbb{S}') = \text{vec}(\mathbb{S}\mathbb{A}^j(\mathbb{S}'\,\mathrm{d}\mathbb{A}_1)\mathbb{A}^{\tau-(j+1)}\mathbb{S}') = [\mathbb{S}(\mathbb{A}^{\tau-(j+1)})' \otimes \mathbb{S}\mathbb{A}^j\mathbb{S}']\text{vec}(\mathrm{d}\mathbb{A}_1) = [\mathbb{S}(\mathbb{A}^{\tau-(j+1)})' \otimes \psi_j]\text{vec}(\mathrm{d}\mathbb{A}_1)$. Hence,

$$\frac{\text{vec}(\mathrm{d}\psi_\tau)}{\text{vec}(\mathrm{d}\mathbb{A}_1)} = \sum_{j=0}^{\tau-1}[\mathbb{S}(\mathbb{A}')^{\tau-(j+1)} \otimes \psi_j] \equiv \frac{\partial\,\text{vec}(\psi_\tau)}{\partial\,\text{vec}(\mathbb{A}_1)}. \quad (4.33)$$

Given (4.33), we can immediately find the distribution of ψ_τ. In fact, if $\mathbb{A}_1 \sim \mathbb{N}(0, \Sigma_{\mathbb{A}_1})$, ψ_τ is normal with zero mean and variance $[\partial\,\text{vec}(\psi_\tau)/\partial\,\text{vec}(\mathbb{A}_1)]\Sigma_{\mathbb{A}_1} \times [\partial\,\text{vec}(\psi_\tau)/\partial\,\text{vec}(\mathbb{A}_1)]'$.

The above formulas, which use the companion form, may be computationally cumbersome when either m or q is large. In these cases, the following recursive formula may be useful:

$$\frac{\partial D_\tau}{\partial\alpha} = \sum_{j=1}^{\max[\tau,q]}\left[(D'_{\tau-j} \otimes I_m)\frac{\partial A_j}{\partial\alpha} + (I_m \otimes A_j)\frac{\partial D_{\tau-j}}{\partial\alpha}\right]. \quad (4.34)$$

Exercise 4.30. Derive the distribution of $\text{VD}_{i,i'}(\tau)$ for orthogonal shocks.

Standard error bands computed with the δ-method have three problems. First, they tend to have poor properties in experimental designs featuring small-scale VARs and samples of 100–120 observations. Second, the asymptotic coverage is also poor when near-unit-roots or near singularities are present. Third, since estimated VAR coefficients have large asymptotic standard errors, impulse responses have large standard errors as well, resulting, in many cases, in insignificant responses at all horizons. For these reasons, methods which employ the small-sample properties of the VAR coefficients might be preferred.

Exercise 4.31. Derive the asymptotic distribution of the τth term of a historical decomposition.

4.4.4.2 *Bootstrap Methods*

Bootstrapping is a method for estimating the sampling distribution of an estimator by resampling with replacement from the original sample. Bootstrap standard errors, first employed in VARs by Runkle (1987), are easy to compute. Using equation (4.7) one proceeds as follows.

Algorithm 4.2.

(1) Obtain $A(\ell)_{\text{OLS}}$ and $e_{t,\text{OLS}} = y_t - A(\ell)_{\text{OLS}} y_{t-1}$.

(2) Obtain $e^l_{t,\text{OLS}}$ via bootstrap and construct $y^l_t = A(\ell)_{\text{OLS}} y^l_{t-1} + e^l_{t,\text{OLS}}$, $l = 1, 2, \dots, L$.

(3) Estimate $A(\ell)^l_{\text{OLS}}$ by using data constructed in (2). Compute D^l_j, $(\tilde{D}^l_j)$, $j = 1, \dots, \tau$.

(4) Report percentiles of the distribution of D_j, $(\tilde{D}_j)$ (i.e., 16–84% or 2.5–97.5%), or the simulated mean and the standard deviation of D_j, $(\tilde{D}_j)$, $j = 1, \dots, \tau$.

Algorithm 4.2 is easily modified to produce confidence bands for other statistics.

Example 4.17. To compute standard error bands for the variance decomposition, insert the calculation of $\text{VD}_{i,i'}(\tau)^l$ as suggested in (4.29) after step (3). $\text{VD}_{i,i'}(\tau)^l$ is the percentage of the variance of the forecast error of $y_{i,t+\tau}$ explained by $e_{i',t}$ at horizon τ in replication l. Then in (4) order $\text{VD}_{i,i'}(\tau)^l$ and report percentiles or the first two moments.

A few remarks are in order. First, bootstrapping is appropriate when e_t is a white noise with constant variance. Therefore, the approach yields poor standard error band estimates when the lag length of the VAR is misspecified or when heteroskedasticity is present. Since conditional heteroskedasticity is less likely to emerge with low frequency data, one possible way to avoid this problem is to time aggregate the data before a VAR is run and standard errors are computed.

Second, estimates of the VAR coefficients are typically biased downward in small samples. For example, in a VAR(1) with the largest root around 0.95, a downward bias of about 30% is to be expected even when $T = 80$–100. A biased $A(\ell)$ is problematic because the bootstrap samples $\{y^e_t\}^T_{t=1}$ are also biased. Hence, the resulting distribution is likely to be centered around an incorrect estimate of the true VAR coefficients.

Third, the bootstrap distribution of $D_j(\tilde{D}_j)$ is not scale invariant. In particular, units matter. This implies that standard error bands may not include point estimates of the impulse responses. This is evident in figure 4.2, where we report point estimates of the responses and a 68% bootstrap error band for (a) the log output or (b) linearly detrended level of output following an orthogonal price shock in a bivariate VAR(4) system. Clearly, the size and the shape of the band depend on the units and, in (b), there are horizons where the point estimate is outside the computed band.

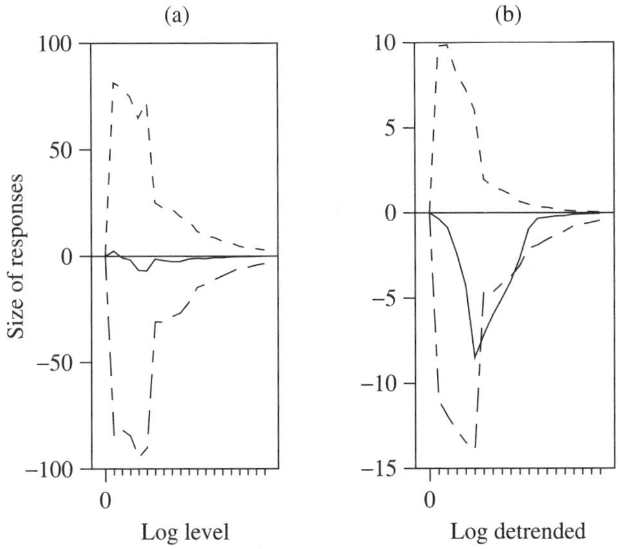

Figure 4.2. Bootstrap responses.

Finally, while it is common to report the mean and construct confidence bands by using numerical standard deviations (computed across replications) and a normal approximation, this approach is unsatisfactory since it assumes symmetric distributions. Since simulated distributions of impulse responses tend to be highly skewed when $T \leqslant 100$, we recommend the use of simulated distribution percentiles in constructing confidence intervals (i.e., extract the relevant band directly from the ordered replications at each horizon as we have done in figure 4.2). The reason why the distribution of impulse responses is nonnormal can be easily seen from example 4.14. For example, $D_2 = A_1^2 + A_2$. Hence, if A_1 and A_2 are normal, D_2 is more likely to have a gamma distribution.

To eliminate the bias and the lack of scale invariance, Kilian (1998) suggested a bootstrap-after-the-bootstrap procedure. The approach can be summarized as follows.

Algorithm 4.3.

(1) Given $A(\ell)_{\text{OLS}}$, obtain $e^l_{t,\text{OLS}}$ and construct $y^l_t = A(\ell)_{\text{OLS}} y^l_{t-1} + e^l_{t,\text{OLS}}$, $l = 1, 2, \dots, L$.

(2) Estimate $A(\ell)^l_{\text{OLS}}$ for each l. If the bias is approximately constant in a neighborhood of $A(\ell)_{\text{OLS}}$, $\text{Bias}(\ell) = E[A(\ell)_{\text{OLS}} - A(\ell)] \approx E[A(\ell)^l_{\text{OLS}} - A(\ell)_{\text{OLS}}]$.

(3) Calculate the largest root of the system. If it is greater than or equal to 1, set $\tilde{A}(\ell) = A(\ell)_{\text{OLS}}$; here the bias is irrelevant since estimates are superconsistent. Otherwise set $\tilde{A}(\ell) = A(\ell)_{\text{OLS}} - \text{Bias}(\ell)_{\text{OLS}}$, where $\text{Bias}(\ell)_{\text{OLS}} = (1/L)\sum_{l=1}^{L}[A(\ell)^l_{\text{OLS}} - A(\ell)_{\text{OLS}}]$.

(4) Repeat (1)–(3) of algorithm 4.2 L_1 times by using $\tilde{A}(\ell)$ in place of $A(\ell)_{\mathrm{OLS}}$.

Kilian shows that the procedure of eliminating the bias, assuming that it is constant in a neighborhood of $A(\ell)_{\mathrm{OLS}}$, has an asymptotic justification and that the bias correction becomes negligible asymptotically. He also shows that such an approach has better small-sample coverage properties than a simple bootstrap. However, when the bias is not constant in the neighborhood of $A(\ell)_{\mathrm{OLS}}$, the properties of the bands produced from algorithm 4.3 may still be poor.

4.4.4.3 *Monte Carlo Methods*

Monte Carlo methods will be described in detail in chapter 9 of this book. Here we describe a simple approach which allows the computation of standard error bands using the simultaneous equation representation of an unrestricted VAR(q).

As mentioned, the likelihood function of a VAR(q), $\mathcal{L}(\alpha, \Sigma_e \mid y_t)$, can be decomposed into a normal portion for α, conditional on α_{OLS} and Σ_e, and a Wishart portion for Σ_e^{-1}. Assuming that no prior information for α, Σ_e is available, i.e., $g(\alpha, \Sigma_e) \propto |\Sigma_e|^{-(m+1)/2}$, the posterior distribution, which is proportional to the product of the likelihood and the prior, will have the same format as the likelihood. Furthermore, the posterior for (α, Σ_e) will be proportional to the product of the posterior of $(\alpha \mid \Sigma_e, y_t)$ and that of $(\Sigma_e \mid y_t)$. As detailed in chapter 10, the posterior for Σ_e^{-1} has a Wishart form with $T - mq$ degrees of freedom. The posterior of $(\alpha \mid \Sigma_e, y_t)$ is normal centered at α_{OLS} with variance equal to $\mathrm{var}(\alpha_{\mathrm{OLS}})$. Hence, standard error bands for impulse responses can be constructed as follows.

Algorithm 4.4.

(1) Draw e_t^{-1} i.i.d. from $\mathbb{N}(0, (Y - XA_{\mathrm{OLS}})'(Y - XA_{\mathrm{OLS}}))$ $T - mq$ times. Compute $\Sigma_e^l = ((1/(T - mq))\sum_{t=1}^{T-mq}(e_t^{-1} - (1/(T - mq))\sum_{t=1}^{T-mq} e_t^{-1})^2)^{-1}$.

(2) Draw $\alpha^l = \alpha_{\mathrm{OLS}} + \epsilon_t^l$, where $\epsilon_t^l \sim$ i.i.d. $\mathbb{N}(0, \Sigma_e^l)$. Compute $D_j^l(\tilde{D}_j^l)$, $j = 1, \dots, \tau$.

(3) Repeat (1) and (2) L times and report percentiles.

Three features of algorithm 4.4 are important. First, the posterior distribution is exact and conditional on the OLS estimator, which summarizes the information contained in the data. Therefore, the existence of a bias in A_{OLS} is not an issue. Second, given the exact small-sample nature of the posterior distribution, standard error bands are likely to be skewed and, possibly, leptokurtic. Therefore, bands extracted from percentiles are preferable to one or two approximate normal standard error bands around the mean. Third, algorithm 4.4 is appropriate only for just identified systems. When the VAR system is overidentified, the technique described in section 10.3 should be used.

Exercise 4.32. Show how to use algorithm 4.4 to compute confidence bands for variance and historical decompositions.

All three approaches we have described produce standard error band estimates which are correlated. This is because, at each step, responses are correlated (see, for example, the recursive computation of impulse responses). Hence, plots connecting the points at each horizon are likely to misrepresent the true uncertainty. Sims and Zha (1999) propose a transformation which eliminates this correlation. Their approach relies on the following result.

Result 4.2. If $\tilde{D}_1, \dots, \tilde{D}_\tau$ are normally distributed with covariance matrix $\Sigma_{\tilde{D}}$, the best coordinate system is given by the projection on the principal components of $\Sigma_{\tilde{D}}$.

Intuitively, we need to orthogonalize the covariance matrix of the impulse responses to break down the correlation of its elements. To implement such an orthogonalization when Monte Carlo methods are used, steps (1)–(3) of algorithm 4.4 remain unchanged, but we need to add the following two steps.

(4) Let the $\tau \times \tau$ covariance matrix of $\tilde{D}$ be decomposed as $\mathcal{P}_{\tilde{D}} \mathcal{V}_{\tilde{D}} \mathcal{P}'_{\tilde{D}} = \Sigma_{\tilde{D}}$, where $\mathcal{V}_{\tilde{D}} = \operatorname{diag}\{v_j\}$, $\mathcal{P}_{\tilde{D}} = \operatorname{col}\{pp_{\cdot,j}\}$, $j = 1, \dots, \tau$, $\mathcal{P}_{\tilde{D}} \mathcal{P}'_{\tilde{D}} = I$.

(5) For each (i, i') report $\tilde{D}^*_{i,i'} \pm \sum_{j=1}^{\tau} \varrho_j pp_{\cdot,j}$, where $\tilde{D}^*_{i,i'}$ is the mean of $\tilde{D}_{i,i'}$ and $v_j = \varrho_j \varrho_j$.

In practice, it is often sufficient to use the largest eigenvalue of $\Sigma_{\tilde{D}}$ to have a good idea of the existing uncertainty. Then standard error bands are $\tilde{D}^*_{i,i'} \pm pp_{\cdot,j} \sqrt{v_{\sup}}$ (symmetric) and $[\tilde{D}^*_{i,i'} - \varrho_{\sup,16}; \tilde{D}^*_{i,i'} + \varrho_{\sup,84}]$ (asymmetric), where $\varrho_{\sup,r}$ is the rth percentile of ϱ_j computed by using the largest eigenvalue of $\Sigma_{\tilde{D}}$ and $v_{\sup} = \sup_j v_j$.

Exercise 4.33. Show how to apply the Sims and Zha approach to orthogonalize standard error bands computed with the δ-method.

Given that the asymptotic approach has poor small-sample properties, which of the two resampling methods should one prefer? *A priori* the choice is difficult and it may be a matter of taste. However, one should remember that, while the Monte Carlo approach is generally applicable, the bootstrap method requires homoskedasticity and, unless the Kilian method is used, bands may have little meaning. In controlled experiments, Sims and Zha (1999) have shown that the MC approach outperforms the bootstrap approach but not uniformly so.

4.4.5 Generalized Impulse Responses

In this subsection we discuss the computation of impulse responses for nonlinear structures. Since VARs with time-varying coefficients fit well into this class, it is worthwhile studying how impulse responses for these models can be constructed. The discussion is basic; details are in Gallant et al. (1993) and Koop et al. (1996).

In linear models impulse responses do not depend on the sign or the size of shocks nor on their history. This simplifies the computations but prevents researchers from studying interesting economic questions such as: Do shocks which occur in a recession produce different dynamics than those which occur in an expansion? Are large shocks different to small ones? In nonlinear models, responses do depend on the sign, the size, and the history of the shocks up to the point where they are computed. Let $\mathcal{F}_{t-1}$ be the history of y up to $t-1$. In general, $y_{t+\tau}$ depends on $\mathcal{F}_{t-1}$, the parameters α of the model, and the innovations e_{t+j}, $j=0,\dots,\tau$. For the purpose of this section we let $\mathrm{Rev}(\tau,\mathcal{F}_{t-1},\alpha,e^*)\equiv E(y_{t+\tau}\mid\alpha,\ \mathcal{F}_{t-1},\ e_t=e^*,\ e_{t+j}=0,\ j\geqslant 1)-E(y_{t+\tau}\mid\alpha,\ \mathcal{F}_{t-1},\ e_{t+j}=0,\ j\geqslant 0)$.

Example 4.18. Consider $y_t=Ay_{t-1}+e_t$, let $\tau=2$ and assume $|A|<1$. Then $E(y_{t+2}\mid A,\ \mathcal{F}_{t-1},\ e_{t+j}=0,\ j\geqslant 0)=A^3y_{t-1}$ and $E(y_{t+2}\mid A,\ \mathcal{F}_{t-1},\ e_t=e^*,\ e_{t+j}=0,\ j\geqslant 1)=A^3y_{t-1}+A^2e^*$ and $\mathrm{Rev}(\tau,\mathcal{F}_{t-1},A,e^*)=A^2e^*$, which depends on A, but is independent of the history of y_t, the size of the shocks (hence set $e^*=1$ or $e^*=\sigma_e$), and is symmetric in the sign of the shocks (hence set $e^*>0$).

Exercise 4.34. Consider the model $\Delta y_t=A\Delta y_{t-1}+e_t$, $|A|<1$. Calculate the impulse response function for a generic τ. Show that it is independent of the history and that the size of e^* scales the whole impulse response function. Consider an ARIMA$(d_1,1,d_2)$: $D_1(\ell)\Delta y_t=D_2(\ell)e_t$. Show that $\mathrm{Rev}(\tau,\mathcal{F}_{t-1},D_2(\ell),D_1(\ell),e^*)$ is history and size independent.

Example 4.19. Consider the model $\Delta y_t=A_1\Delta y_{t-1}+A_2\Delta y_{t-1}\mathcal{I}_{[\Delta y_{t-1}\geqslant 0]}+e_t$, where $\mathcal{I}_{[\Delta y_{t-1}\geqslant 0]}=1$ if $\Delta y_{t-1}\geqslant 0$ and zero otherwise. Let $0<A=A_1+A_2<1$. Then, for $e_t=e^*$, $\mathrm{Rev}(\tau,\Delta y_{t-1},A,e^*)=[(1-A^{\tau+1})/(1-A)]e^*$ if $\Delta y_{t-1}\geqslant 0$ and $\mathrm{Rev}(\tau,\Delta y_{t-1},A,e^*)=[(1-A_1^{\tau+1})/(1-A_1)]e^*$ if $\Delta y_{t-1}<0$. Here $\mathrm{Rev}(\tau,\Delta y_{t-1},A,e^*)$ depends on the estimates of A_1 and A_2, the history of Δy_{t-1}, but not on the sign or the size of e^*.

Exercise 4.35. Consider the logistic map $\tilde{y}_t=a\tilde{y}_{t-1}(1-\tilde{y}_{t-1})+v_t$, where $0\leqslant a\leqslant 4$. This model can be transformed into a nonlinear AR(1) model: $y_t=A_1y_{t-1}-A_2y_{t-1}^2+e_t$ when $A_2\neq 0$, $-2\leqslant A_1\leqslant 2$, $A_1=2-a$, $e_t=[(2-A_1)/A_2]v_t$, $y_t=(A_1-1)/A_2+[(2-A_1)/A_2]\tilde{y}_t$. Simulate the impulse response function. Do the sign and the size of e^* matter?

In impulse responses computed from linear models $e_{t+j}=0,\forall j\geqslant 1$. This may be inappropriate in nonlinear models since it may violate bounds for e_t. In exercise 4.35 a bound occurs because the logistic map is unstable if y_{t-1} passes a threshold. Furthermore, the bound depends on the realizations of $v_{t-\tau}$ and therefore varies over time. Also, when parameters are estimated, we either need to condition on a particular estimate (e.g., α_{OLS}) or integrate α out to compute forecast revisions. Generalized impulse (GI) responses are designed so that we can condition on the size and on the sign of the shocks, the history of y_t and, if required, on a particular estimate of α. Moreover, they allow future shocks to be different from zero.

Definition 4.5. Generalized impulse responses conditional on a shock e_t, a history $\mathcal{F}_{t-1}$, and a vector α are $\mathrm{GI}_y(\tau, \mathcal{F}_{t-1}, \alpha, e_t) \equiv E(y_{t+\tau} \mid \alpha, e_t, \mathcal{F}_{t-1}) - E(y_{t+\tau} \mid \alpha, \mathcal{F}_{t-1})$.

Responses produced by definition 4.5 have three important properties. First, $E(\mathrm{GI}_y) = 0$. Second, $E(\mathrm{GI}_y \mid \mathcal{F}_{t-1}) = 0$. Third, $E(\mathrm{GI}_y \mid e_t) = E(y_{t+\tau} \mid e_t) - E(y_{t+\tau})$.

Example 4.20. Three interesting cases where definition 4.5 is useful are the following.

(i) (Impulse responses in recession.) GI conditional on a history $\mathcal{F}_{t-1}$ in a region: $\mathrm{GI}_y(\tau, \mathcal{F}_{t-1} \in \mathcal{F}_1, \alpha, e_t) = E(y_{t+\tau} \mid \alpha, e_t, \mathcal{F}_{t-1} \in \mathcal{F}_1) - E(y_{t+\tau} \mid \alpha, \mathcal{F}_{t-1} \in \mathcal{F}_1)$.

(ii) (Impulse responses on average.) GI conditional only on α: $\mathrm{GI}_y(\tau, \alpha, e_t) = E(y_{t+\tau} \mid \alpha, e_t) - E(y_{t+\tau} \mid \alpha)$.

(iii) (Impulse responses if oil prices go above 70 dollars a barrel.) GI conditional on a shock in a region: $\mathrm{GI}_y(\tau, \mathcal{F}_{t-1}, \alpha, e_t) = E(y_{t+\tau} \mid \alpha, e_t \in \mathcal{E}_1, \mathcal{F}_{t-1}) - E(y_{t+\tau} \mid \alpha, \mathcal{F}_{t-1})$.

Definition 4.5 conditions on a particular value of α. In some situations we may want to treat parameters as random variables. This is important in applications where symmetric shocks may have asymmetric impact on y_t depending on the value of α. Alternatively, we may want to average α out of GI. As an alternative to definition 4.5 one could use the following.

Definition 4.6. Generalized impulse responses, conditional on a shock e_t and a history $\mathcal{F}_{t-1}$, are $\mathrm{GI}_y(\tau, \mathcal{F}_{t-1}, e_t) = E(y_{t+\tau} \mid \mathcal{F}_{t-1}, e_t) - E(y_{t+\tau} \mid \mathcal{F}_{t-1})$.

Exercise 4.36. Extend definitions 4.5 and 4.6 to condition on the size and the sign of e_t.

In practice, GIs are computed numerically by using Monte Carlo methods. We show how to do this conditional on a history and a set of parameters in the next algorithm.

Algorithm 4.5.

(1) Fix $y_{t-1} = \hat{y}_{t-1}, \ldots, y_{t-\tau} = \hat{y}_{t-\tau}, \alpha = \hat{\alpha}$.

(2) Draw e^l_{t+j}, $j = 0, 1, \ldots$, i.i.d. from $\mathbb{N}(0, \Sigma_e)$, $l = 1, \ldots, L$, and compute $\mathrm{GI}^l = (y^l_{t+\tau} \mid \hat{y}_{t-1}, \ldots, \hat{y}_{t-\tau}, \hat{\alpha}, e_t, e^l_{t+j}, j > 1) - (y^l_{t+\tau} \mid \hat{y}_{t-1}, \ldots, \hat{y}_{t-\tau}, \hat{\alpha}, e_t = 0, e^l_{t+j}, j > 1)$.

(3) Compute $\mathrm{GI} = (1/L) \sum_{l=1}^{L} \mathrm{GI}^l$, $E(\mathrm{GI}^l - \mathrm{GI})^2$ and/or the percentiles of the distribution.

Note that in algorithm 4.5 the history $(y_{t-1}, \dots, y_{t-\tau})$ could be a recession or expansion and $\hat{\alpha}$ an OLS or a posterior estimator. In practice, when the model is multivariate we need to orthogonalize the shocks so as to be able to measure the effect of a shock. When e_t is normal, $E(e_t \mid e_{i't} = e_{i'}^*) = E(e_t e_{i't})\sigma_{i'}^{-2} e_{i'}^*$, where $\sigma_i^2 = E(e_{i't})^2$ and this can be inserted in step (2) of algorithm 4.5. For a linear VAR, $\mathrm{GI}(\tau, \mathcal{F}_{t-1}, e_{it}) = (A_\tau E(e_t, e_{i't})/\sigma_i) e_{i'}^*/\sigma_i$ and the generalized impulse of variable i equals $\mathbb{S}_i \mathrm{GI}(\tau, \mathcal{F}_{t-1}, e_{it})$, where $\mathbb{S}_i$ is a selection vector with 1 in the ith position and 0 everywhere else. Here the term $e_{i'}^*/\sigma_i$ is a scale factor and the first term measures the effect of a one-standard-error shock in the i'th variable. Note that $(A_\tau E(e_t, e_{i't})/\sigma_i)$ is the effect obtained when the variables are assumed to have a Wold causal chain. Hence, meaningful interpretations are possible only if the orthogonalization is derived from relevant economic restrictions.

Exercise 4.37. Describe a Monte Carlo method to compute GIs without conditioning on a particular history or a particular α.

Example 4.21. Consider the model $\Delta y_t = A_1 \Delta y_{t-1} + A_2 \Delta y_{t-1} \mathcal{I}_{[\Delta y_{t-1} \geqslant 0]} + e_t$, where $\mathcal{I}_{[\Delta y_{t-1} \geqslant 0]}$ is an indicator function. Then:

- GI responses allowing for randomness in future e_t can be computed by fixing y_{t-1}, A_1, A_2 and drawing e_{t+j}^l, $j \geqslant 0$, $l = 1, \dots, L$.
- GI responses allowing for randomness in history can be computed by fixing e_{t+j}, $j \geqslant 0$, A_1, A_2, and drawing y_{t-1}^l.
- GI responses allowing for randomness in the parameters can be computed by fixing y_{t-1}, e_{t+j}, $j \geqslant 0$, and drawing A_1^l, A_2^l from some distribution (e.g., the asymptotic one).
- GI responses allowing for randomness in the size of e_t can be computed by fixing y_{t-1}, A_1, A_2, e_{t+j}, $j \geqslant 1$, and keeping those e_t^l that satisfy $e_t^l \geqslant e^*$ or $e_t^l < e^*$. If the process is multivariate, apply the above to, for example, e_{1t}, after averaging over draws of $(e_{2t}, \dots, e_{mt})$.

Exercise 4.38. Consider a bivariate model with inflation π and unemployment UN, $y_t = A_1 y_{t-1} + A_2 y_{t-1} \mathcal{I}_{[\pi \geqslant 0]} + e_t$, where $\mathcal{I}_{[\pi > 0]}$ is an indicator function. Calculate the GI at steps one and two for an orthogonal shock in π when $\pi \geqslant 0$ and $\pi < 0$. Does the size of the shock matter?

Exercise 4.39. Consider a switching bivariate AR(1) model with money and output:

$$\Delta y_t = \begin{cases} \alpha_{01} + \alpha_{11} \Delta y_{t-1} + e_{1t} & \text{if } \Delta y_{t-1} \leqslant \Delta \bar{y},\ e_{1t} \sim \text{i.i.d. } \mathbb{N}(0, \sigma_1^2), \\ \alpha_{02} + \alpha_{12} \Delta y_{t-1} + e_{2t} & \text{if } \Delta y_{t-1} > \Delta \bar{y},\ e_{2t} \sim \text{i.i.d. } \mathbb{N}(0, \sigma_2^2). \end{cases}$$

Fix the size of the shock and the parameters and compute the GI as a function of history. Fix the size of shocks and the history and compute the GI as a function of the parameters.

4.5 Identification

So far in this chapter, economic theory has played no role. Projection methods are used to derive the Wold theorem; statistical and numerical analyses are used to estimate the parameters and the distributions of interesting functions of the parameters. Since VARs are reduced-form models, it is impossible to economically interpret the dynamics induced by their disturbances unless theory comes into play. As seen in chapter 2, Markovian DSGE models when approximated linearly or log-linearly around the steady state typically deliver VAR(1) solutions for the vector of endogenous variables of the model. The parameters of this VAR are complicated functions of the underlying preference, technology, and policy parameters and the resulting set of extensive cross-equation restrictions could be used to recover the mapping between reduced-form VAR coefficients and DSGE parameters if one is willing to take the model seriously as the process generating the data. When doubts about the quality of the model exist, or one is not willing to subscribe to all the details of the DSGE specification, it is still possible to conduct useful inference as long as a subset of the model restrictions are credible or uncontroversial. Typical restrictions employed in the literature include constraints on the short-run or the long-run impact of certain shocks on VAR variables or informational delays (e.g., output is not contemporaneously observed by central banks when deciding interest rates). As we will argue later on, these restrictions are rarely produced by DSGE models. Restrictions involving lag responses or the dynamics of the variables are generally ignored, being perceived as nonrobust or controversial.

Selecting meaningful identifying restrictions is always a difficult task. When one uses DSGE models to make the link between the theory and the data explicit, two complications typically emerge: only a subset of the endogenous variables produced by the DSGE model is used in the VAR; and the number of shocks in the DSGE and in the VAR differ. As we will see later, both complications may create problems in recovering behavioral disturbances and the dynamics they induce because the VAR representation of the DSGE model may require an infinite number of lags and/or may not be recoverable from the empirical VAR. For the moment we sidestep these complications and assume that the number of variables and shocks is the same in the DSGE and in the VAR and that the innovations of the two systems span the same space.

Under these conditions, one can conduct economically meaningful analyses employing an unrestricted VAR(q), q relatively large, where all variables appear with the same lags in each equation; estimating the parameters of the VAR by OLS; imposing a minimal set of restrictions, possibly consistent with a variety of behavioral theories to identify structural shocks, and constructing impulse responses, historical decomposition, etc., to identified shocks. In this sense, VARs are at the antipodes of the maximum likelihood or generalized method of moments approaches: most of the theoretical restrictions are disregarded; there is no interest in direct estimation of DSGE parameters; and only an economic interpretation of the shocks is sought.

We first examine the mapping between a class of theoretical models and a VAR when zero-type (or constant-type) restrictions are used. Later, we discuss how to recover the mapping when sign restrictions are employed.

4.5.1 Stationary VARs

Let the reduced-form VAR be

$$y_t = A(\ell)y_{t-1} + e_t, \quad e_t \sim \text{i.i.d. } (0, \Sigma_e). \tag{4.35}$$

We assume that there exists a class of economic models whose solution is of the form

$$y_t = \mathcal{A}(\ell)y_{t-1} + \mathcal{A}_0\epsilon_t, \quad \epsilon_t \sim \text{i.i.d. } (0, \Sigma_\epsilon = \text{diag}\{\sigma^2_{\epsilon_i}\}). \tag{4.36}$$

Equation (4.36) is generic but it is easy to show that the class of models producing it is nonempty. For example, many of the log-linearized models of chapter 2 produce solutions like (4.36) with $\mathcal{A}(\ell) = \mathcal{A}(\theta)$ and $\mathcal{A}_0 = \mathcal{A}_0(\theta)$, where θ are the parameters of preferences, technologies, and policies. Matching contemporaneous coefficients in (4.35) and (4.36) implies $e_t = \mathcal{A}_0\epsilon_t$, or

$$\mathcal{A}_0\Sigma_\epsilon\mathcal{A}_0' = \Sigma_e. \tag{4.37}$$

Definition 4.7. The dynamics in response to shocks in (4.36) are identifiable from the VAR in (4.35) if the mapping (4.37) has at least one solution.

To identify shocks and trace out the dynamics of the endogenous variables, we can proceed in two steps. First, we can estimate $A(\ell)$ and Σ_e from (4.35) by using the techniques described in section 4.3. Second, given identification restrictions, we estimate Σ_ϵ and the free parameters of $\mathcal{A}_0$ from (4.37). Given these estimates we can recover the model's dynamics $\mathcal{A}(\ell) = A(\ell)\mathcal{A}_0$. This two-step approach resembles the indirect least squares (ILS) technique used in a system of (static) structural equations (see Hamilton 1994, p. 244). However, here restrictions are imposed only on the covariance matrix of VAR residuals and not on the lags of the VAR. This is convenient: had we imposed restrictions on the lags of the VAR, joint estimation of $A(\ell)$, Σ_e, Σ_ϵ, and of free elements of $\mathcal{A}_0$ would be required.

As in systems of simultaneous equations, there are necessary and sufficient conditions that need to be satisfied for economic shocks to be identifiable from (4.37). An "order" condition can be calculated as follows. On the left-hand side of (4.37) there are m^2 free parameters, while, given the symmetry of Σ_e, the right-hand side has only $m(m+1)/2$ free parameters. Hence, (4.37) will have a solution if at least $m(m-1)/2$ restrictions are imposed. When there are exactly $m(m-1)/2$ restrictions, economic shocks are identified; with more restrictions, they are overidentified.

Example 4.22. Consider a trivariate model with hours, productivity, and interest rates. Suppose that $\mathcal{A}_0$ is lower triangular, that is, that shocks to hours enter contemporaneously in the productivity and interest rate equations and that productivity shocks enter contemporaneously in the interest rate equation. This could be the case if interest rate shocks take time to produce effects and if hours are predetermined with respect to productivity. If shocks are independent, $\mathcal{A}_0$ has $m(m-1)/2 = 3$ zero restrictions. Hence, the order condition is satisfied.

Example 4.23. Consider a VAR with output, prices, nominal interest rates, and money, and let $y_t = [\mathrm{GDP}_t, p_t, i_t, M_t]$. Suppose that a class of models suggests that output contemporaneously reacts only to its own shocks, that prices respond contemporaneously to output and money shocks, and that interest rates respond contemporaneously only to money shocks, while money contemporaneously responds to all shocks. Then

$$\mathcal{A}_0 = \begin{bmatrix} 1 & 0 & 0 & 0 \\ a^0_{12} & 1 & 0 & a^0_{22} \\ 0 & 0 & 1 & a^0_{31} \\ a^0_{41} & a^0_{42} & a^0_{43} & 1 \end{bmatrix}.$$

Since there are six (zero) restrictions, ϵ_t shocks are identifiable from the VAR residuals.

Exercise 4.40. Suppose we have extraneous information which allows us to pin down some of the parameters of $\mathcal{A}_0$. For example, suppose that, in a trivariate system with output, hours, and taxes, we can obtain estimates of the elasticity of hours with respect to taxes. How many restrictions do you need to identify the shocks? Does it make a difference if zero or constant restrictions are used?

Exercise 4.41. Specify and estimate a bivariate VAR by using euro area GDP growth and M3 growth. Using the restriction that output growth is not contemporaneously affected by money growth shocks, trace out impulse responses and evaluate the claim that money shocks have no medium- to long-run effect on output. Repeat the exercise assuming that the contemporaneous effect of money growth on GDP growth is in the interval $[-0.5, 1.5]$ (do this in increments of 0.1 each). What can you say about the medium- to long-run effect of money shocks on output?

There is one additional (rank) condition one should typically check: $\mathrm{rank}(\Sigma_e) = \mathrm{rank}(\mathcal{A}_0 \Sigma_\epsilon \mathcal{A}_0')$ (see Hamilton (1994) for a formal derivation). Intuitively, this restriction rules out that any column of $\mathcal{A}_0$ can be expressed as linear combination of the others. While the rank condition is typically important in large-scale simultaneous equation systems (SES), it is almost automatically satisfied in small-scale VARs under the conditions we impose in this section, when restrictions based on economic theory are used. When other types of restriction are employed, the condition should always be checked.

Rank and order conditions are only valid for "local identification." That is, there may be different economic shocks or different classes of economic model which are consistent with one set of VAR residuals even when $m(m-1)/2$ restrictions are imposed.

Example 4.24. Suppose $\Sigma_\epsilon = I$ and $\mathcal{A}_0^1 = \left[\begin{smallmatrix} 1 & 0 \\ 4 & 5 \end{smallmatrix}\right]$. It is immediate to verify that the likelihood obtained with these two matrices and any positive definite Σ_e is equivalent to the one obtained with the same Σ_ϵ and Σ_e and $\mathcal{A}_0^2 = \left[\begin{smallmatrix} 5 & 0 \\ 0.8 & 0.6 \end{smallmatrix}\right]$. Clearly, the two decompositions have different economic interpretations. Depending on the initial conditions, the maximum can be reached at $\mathcal{A}_0^2$ or $\mathcal{A}_0^1$.

A priori, one cannot rule out situations like the one described in example 4.24. If the class of economic models are locally distinct, economic considerations can be used to select among the two observationally equivalent theoretical models.

To estimate the free parameters in (4.37), one typically has two options. The first is to write down the likelihood function of the free parameters in (4.37), that is,

$$\ln \mathcal{L}(\mathcal{A}_0, \Sigma_\epsilon \mid \Sigma_e) = -0.5T\{2\ln|\mathcal{A}_0| + \ln|\Sigma_\epsilon| + \mathrm{tr}(\Sigma_\epsilon^{-1}\mathcal{A}_0^{-1}\Sigma_e(\mathcal{A}_0^{-1})')\}. \tag{4.38}$$

Maximizing (4.38) with respect to Σ_ϵ and concentrating it out, we obtain $2\ln|\mathcal{A}_0| + \sum_{i=1}^m \ln(\mathcal{A}_0^{-1}\Sigma_e\mathcal{A}_0^{-1\prime})_{ii}$, which can be maximized with respect to the free entries of $\mathcal{A}_0$. Since this concentrated likelihood is nonstandard, maximization is typically difficult. Therefore, it is advisable to obtain some estimates of the free entries of $\mathcal{A}_0$ with a simple method (e.g., a simplex algorithm) and then use these as initial conditions in other algorithms (see chapter 6) to find a global maximum.

A likelihood approach is general and works with both just identified and overidentified systems. For a just identified system, one could also use an instrumental variable (IV) approach. We describe in an example how this works.

Example 4.25. Consider a bivariate model with inflation and unemployment. Suppose that theory tells us that (4.36) is

$$\begin{bmatrix} \pi_t \\ \mathrm{UN}_t \end{bmatrix} = \begin{bmatrix} \mathcal{A}_{11}(\ell) & \mathcal{A}_{12}(\ell) \\ \mathcal{A}_{21}(\ell) & \mathcal{A}_{22}(\ell) \end{bmatrix} \begin{bmatrix} \pi_{t-1} \\ \mathrm{UN}_{t-1} \end{bmatrix} + \begin{bmatrix} 1 & 0 \\ \alpha_{01} & 1 \end{bmatrix} \begin{bmatrix} \epsilon_{1t} \\ \epsilon_{2t} \end{bmatrix}. \tag{4.39}$$

Since $\epsilon_{1t} = e_{1t}$ is predetermined with respect to ϵ_{2t}, it can be used as an instrument to estimate α_{01}. Therefore, choosing $z_t = [e_{1t}, e_{1t-1}, \ldots, e_{2t-1}, \ldots]$ as a vector of instruments, applying the IV techniques described in chapter 5, joint estimates of the α and $\mathcal{A}(\ell)$ can be obtained directly, without any need to first estimate $A(\ell)$ and Σ_e.

4.5.2 Nonstationary VARs

The identification process in nonstationary VAR models is similar but additional identification restrictions are available. Furthermore, the presence of cointegration relationships may change the nature of the order condition.

Let the MA representations of the VAR and of the class of economic models be

$$\Delta y_t = D(\ell)e_t = D(1)e_t + D^*(\ell)\Delta e_t, \tag{4.40}$$
$$\Delta y_t = \mathcal{D}(\ell)\mathcal{A}_0\epsilon_t = \mathcal{D}(1)\mathcal{A}_0\epsilon_t + \mathcal{D}^*(\ell)\mathcal{A}_0\Delta\epsilon_t, \tag{4.41}$$

where $D^*(\ell) \equiv [D(\ell) - D(1)]/(1-\ell)$, $\mathcal{D}^*(\ell) \equiv [\mathcal{D}(\ell) - \mathcal{D}(1)]/(1-\ell)$, $\Delta = (1-\ell)$, $\mathcal{D}(\ell) = \mathcal{A}(\ell)^{-1}$, and $D(\ell) = A(\ell)^{-1}$.

In (4.40), (4.41) we have rewritten the system in two ways: the first is a standard MA; the second exploits the multivariate BN decomposition (see chapter 3). Matching coefficients we have $\mathcal{D}(\ell)\mathcal{A}_0\epsilon_t = D(\ell)e_t$. Separating permanent and transitory components and using only contemporaneous restrictions in the latter case, we have

$$\mathcal{D}(1)\mathcal{A}_0\epsilon_t = D(1)e_t, \tag{4.42}$$

$$\mathcal{A}_0\Delta\epsilon_t = \Delta e_t. \tag{4.43}$$

When y_t is stationary, $\mathcal{D}(1) = D(1) = 0$, (4.42) is vacuous and only (4.43) is available. However, if y_t is integrated, the restrictions linking the permanent components of the VAR and of the economic model could also be used for identification. When y_t is a bivariate process, (4.42) is the basis, for example, for the Blanchard and Quah decomposition discussed in chapter 3. To obtain estimates of economic shocks, we need the same order and rank restrictions we have outlined in section 4.5.1. However, the $m(m-1)/2$ constraints could be placed either on (4.42) or (4.43) or on both. In this latter case, iterative approaches are needed to estimate the free parameters of $\mathcal{A}_0$ and the structural shocks ϵ_t.

Example 4.26. In a bivariate VAR, imposing (4.42) is simple since only one restriction is needed. Suppose that $\mathcal{D}_{12}(1) = 0$ (i.e., ϵ_{2t} has no long-run effect on y_{1t}). If $\Sigma_\epsilon = I$, the three elements of $\mathcal{D}(1)\mathcal{A}_0\Sigma_\epsilon\mathcal{A}_0'\mathcal{D}(1)'$ can be obtained from the Choleski factor of $D(1)\Sigma_e D(1)'$.

Exercise 4.42. Consider the model of example 4.23 and assume that all variables are integrated. Suppose we impose the same six restrictions via the long-run multipliers $\mathcal{D}(1)\mathcal{A}_0$. Describe how to undertake maximum likelihood estimation of the free parameters.

Exercise 4.43 (Gali). Consider a class of models of the form

$$\text{GDP}_t = \alpha_0 + \epsilon_t^{\text{S}} - \alpha_1(i_t - E_t\Delta p_{t+1}) + \epsilon_t^{\text{IS}}, \tag{4.44}$$

$$M_t - p_t = \alpha_2\text{GDP}_t - \alpha_3 i_t + \epsilon_t^{\text{MD}}, \tag{4.45}$$

$$\Delta M_t = \epsilon_t^{\text{MS}}, \tag{4.46}$$

$$\Delta p_t = \Delta p_{t-1} + \alpha_4(\text{GDP}_t - \epsilon_t^{\text{S}}), \tag{4.47}$$

where ϵ_t^{S} is a supply shock, ϵ_t^{IS} is an IS shock, ϵ_t^{MS} is a money supply shock, ϵ_t^{MD} is a money demand shock, GDP_t is output, p_t prices, i_t the nominal interest rate, and M_t money. Such an ISLM structure can be obtained as special case of a sticky price model, when there is no capital and when all prices are chosen one period in advance. Identify these shocks from a VAR with $(\Delta\text{GDP}_t, \Delta i_t, i_t - \Delta p_t, \Delta M_t - \Delta p_t)$ by using euro area data and the following restrictions: (i) only supply shocks have long-run effects on output; (ii) money demand and money supply shocks have no contemporaneous effects on ΔGDP; (iii) money demand shocks have no contemporaneous effects on the real interest rate. Trace out the effects of a money supply shock on interest rates and output.

The free parameters of the mapping (4.42) can also be obtained with an instrumental variables procedure.

Example 4.27. Suppose an economic model has a bivariate VAR(1) representation $\mathcal{A}(\ell)y_t = \epsilon_t$, and suppose its MA representation is $y_t = \mathcal{D}(\ell)\epsilon_t$. Since $\mathcal{D}(\ell) = \mathcal{A}(\ell)^{-1}$, in the long run it must be the case that $\mathcal{D}(1) = \mathcal{A}(1)^{-1}$. Since the system is bivariate, there is only one lag in the structural model, if we assume that the second shock has no long-run effect on the first variable, we have

$$\begin{bmatrix} \mathcal{D}_{11}(1) & 0 \\ \mathcal{D}_{21}(1) & \mathcal{D}_{22}(1) \end{bmatrix} \begin{bmatrix} 1-\mathcal{A}_{11}^1 & -\mathcal{A}_{12}^0-\mathcal{A}_{12}^1 \\ -\mathcal{A}_{12}^0-\mathcal{A}_{12}^1 & 1-\mathcal{A}_{22}^1 \end{bmatrix} = \begin{bmatrix} 1 & 0 \\ 0 & 1 \end{bmatrix}, \tag{4.48}$$

which implies that $\mathcal{A}_{12}^0 = -\mathcal{A}_{12}^1$ if $\mathcal{D}_{11}(1) \neq 0$. Then the first equation of the system is $y_{1t} = \mathcal{A}_{11}^1 y_{1t-1} + \mathcal{A}_{12}^0(y_{2t} - y_{2t-1}) + \epsilon_{1t}$: its parameters can be estimated by using y_{1t-1} and y_{2t-1} as instruments for y_{1t-1} and Δy_{2t} and an estimate $\hat{\epsilon}_{1t}$ can be obtained. The second equation is $y_{2t} = \mathcal{A}_{21}^0 y_{1t} + \mathcal{A}_{21}^1 y_{1t-1} + \mathcal{A}_{22}^1 y_{2t-1} + \epsilon_{2t}$, its parameters can be estimated by using $y_{1t-1}, y_{2t-1}, \hat{\epsilon}_{1t}$ as instruments for y_{1t-1}, y_{2t-1}, y_{1t}. Then (4.48) can be solved for $\mathcal{D}_{11}(1)$, $\mathcal{D}_{21}(1)$, $\mathcal{D}_{22}(1)$, given estimates of $\mathcal{A}$ obtained from these IV regressions.

When some of the variables of the system are cointegrated, the number of permanent economic shocks is lower than m. Therefore, if long-run restrictions are used, one only needs $(m-m_1)(m-m_1-1)/2$ constraints to identify all m shocks, where m_1 is the number of common trends (the rank of $\mathcal{D}(1)$ is $m-m_1$).

Example 4.28. As we have seen in exercise 3.45, an RBC model driven by integrated technology shocks implies that all variables but hours are integrated and that C_t/GDP_t and $\text{Inv}_t/\text{GDP}_t$ are stationary. Consider a trivariate VAR with $\Delta\text{gdp}_t, c_t - \text{gdp}_t, \text{inv}_t - \text{gdp}_t$, where lowercase letters indicate logarithms of the variables. Since the system has two cointegrating vectors, there is one permanent shock and two transitory shocks and $(1,1,1)'\epsilon_t = D(1)e_t$ identifies the permanent shock. If all economic shocks are orthogonal, we need one extra restriction to separate the two transitory disturbances; for example, we could assume a Choleski structure. Clearly, saying that there is one permanent and two transitory shocks does not tell us anything about their behavioral content. Nevertheless, the profession has associated, somewhat arbitrarily, permanent shocks with supply disturbances and transitory shocks with demand disturbances.

4.5.3 Alternative Identification Schemes

The identification of economically sensible shocks is a highly controversial enterprise because researchers using different identifying assumptions may reach different conclusions about interesting economic questions (e.g., the proportion of the

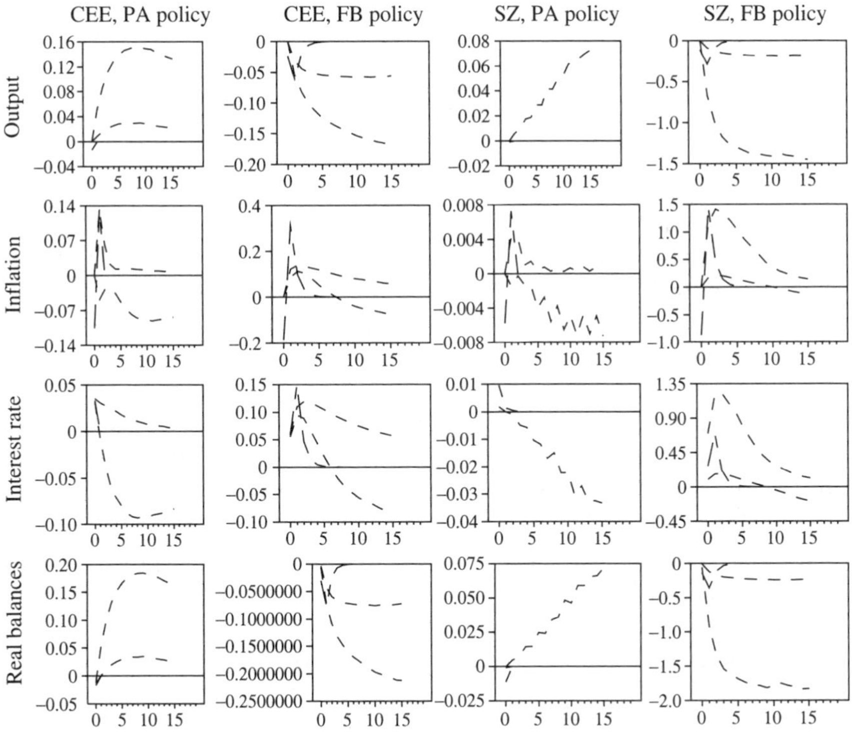

Figure 4.3. Responses to monetary shocks, working-capital model.

variance of the forecast error of output due to certain shocks). However, an embarrassing uniformity has emerged over time as identifying restrictions have become largely conventional and unrelated to the class of DSGE models that researchers use to interpret the results of their analysis. Criticisms of the nature of identification process have repeatedly appeared in the literature. For example, Cooley and LeRoy (1985) criticize Choleski decompositions because contemporaneous recursive structures are hard to obtain in general equilibrium models. Faust and Leeper (1997) argue that long-run restrictions are unsatisfactory as they may exclude models which generate perfectly reasonable short-run dynamics but fail to satisfy long-run constraints by infinitesimal amounts, and allow others with little economic content. Cooley and Dwyer (1998) indicate that long-run restrictions may also incompletely disentangle permanent and transitory disturbances. Canova and Pina (2005) show that standard DSGE models almost never provide the zero restrictions employed to identify monetary disturbances and that misspecification of the features of the model economy can be substantial.

Figure 4.3 shows the extent of the latter problem when a working-capital model—similar to the one presented in chapter 2, with either a partial accommodative (PA) rule ($i_t = 0.8M_t/p_t + \epsilon_t$) or a feedback (FB) rule ($i_t = 0.5\pi_t + 0.1y_t + \epsilon_t$)

for monetary policy — is used to generate data and monetary shocks are identified in the VAR for simulated data either with a Choleski scheme as in Christiano, Eichenbaum, and Evans (CEE) (Christiano et al. 1999), with variables in the order ($GDP_t, \pi_t, i_t, M_t/p_t$), or via an overidentified structure as in Sims and Zha (SZ) (Sims and Zha 1999), where i_t responds only to M_t/p_t. The straight line represents the response produced by the model and the dashed lines represent a 68% Monte Carlo error band produced by the VAR. Note that a Choleski system correctly recognizes the policy inputs when an FB rule is used, while the overidentified model correctly characterizes the policy rule in the partial accommodative case. Misspecification is pervasive, even when one correctly selects the inputs of the monetary policy rule. For example, a Choleski scheme fails to capture the persistent response of real balances to interest rate increases, produces perverse output responses (first box, first column), and an inflation puzzle (second row, first and third boxes).

The patterns presented in figure 4.3 are not obtained because the model is unrealistic or the parametrization "crazy." As shown in Canova and Pina (2005), a sticky price, sticky wage model, parametrized in a standard way, produces similar outcomes. The problem is that a large class of DSGE structures do not display the zero restrictions imposed by the two identification schemes (in particular, that output and inflation have a Wold causal structure and do not respond instantaneously to policy shocks). Therefore, misspecification results even when the policy rule is correctly identified.

To produce a more solid bridge between DSGE models and VARs, a new set of identification approaches has emerged. Although justified by different arguments, the procedures of Faust (1998), Canova and De Nicolò (2002), and Uhlig (2005) have one feature in common: they do not use zero-type restrictions. Instead, they achieve identification by restricting the sign (and/or shape) of structural responses. Restrictions of this type are routinely used by applied researchers informally: for example, monetary shocks which do not generate a liquidity effect (e.g., negative comovements in interest rate and money) are typically discarded and the zero restrictions reshuffled in the hope of producing the required outcome. One advantage of these approaches is to make these restrictions explicit.

Sign restrictions are enticing. While (log-)linearized versions of DSGE models seldom deliver the whole set of zero restrictions needed to recover all economic shocks, they contain a large number of sign restrictions usable for identification purposes.

Example 4.29 (technology shocks). All the flexible price models examined in chapter 2 have the feature that positive technology disturbances increase output, consumption, and investment either instantaneously or with a short lag, while prices and nominal interest rates decline as the aggregate supply curve shifts to the right. Hence, this class of models suggests that technology disturbances can be identified by assuming that in response to positive shocks real variables increase and prices decrease, either contemporaneously or with a lag.

Example 4.30 (monetary shocks). Several of the models of chapter 2 have the feature that policy-driven increases in the nominal interest rate reduce real balances instantaneously and induce a fall in inflation. Hence, contemporaneous (and lagged) comovements of real balances, inflation, and nominal interest rates can be used to identify monetary disturbances.

The restrictions of examples 4.29 and 4.30 could be imposed on two or more variables, and at one or more horizons. In other words, we can "weakly" or "strongly" identify the shocks. To maintain comparability with other structural VARs, weak forms of identification should be preferred. However, there is another trade-off one should consider. Restrictions which are too weak may be unable to distinguish shocks with somewhat similar features, i.e., labor supply and technology shocks, and restrictions which are too strong (or false) may fail to produce any meaningful economic shock.

It is relatively complicated to impose sign restrictions on the coefficients of the VAR, as this requires maximum likelihood estimation of the full system under inequality constraints. However, it is relatively easy to do it *ex post* on impulse responses or on their correlation. For example, as in Canova and De Nicolò (2002), one could estimate $A(\ell)$ and Σ_e from the data by using OLS and orthogonalize the VAR residuals by using, for example, an eigenvalue–eigenvector decomposition, $\Sigma_e = \mathcal{P}\mathcal{V}\mathcal{P}' = \tilde{\mathcal{P}}\tilde{\mathcal{P}}'$, where $\mathcal{P}$ is a matrix of eigenvectors and $\mathcal{V}$ is a diagonal matrix of eigenvalues. This decomposition does not have any economic content, but produces uncorrelated shocks without employing zero restrictions. For each of the orthogonalized shocks one can check whether the identifying restrictions are satisfied. If a shock is found, the process terminates. If more than one shock satisfies the restrictions, one may want to increase the number of restrictions (either across variables or across leads and lags) until one candidate remains. Alternatively, one could average responses across shocks satisfying the identification restrictions. In practice, contemporaneous and/or one-lag restrictions suffice to select shocks with the required characteristics.

If no shock satisfies the restrictions, the nonuniqueness of the MA representation can be used to provide alternative economic shocks. In fact, for any $\mathcal{H}$ with $\mathcal{H}\mathcal{H}' = I$, $\Sigma_e = \tilde{\mathcal{P}}\tilde{\mathcal{P}}' = \tilde{\mathcal{P}}\mathcal{H}\mathcal{H}'\tilde{\mathcal{P}}'$. Hence, one can construct a new decomposition by using $\tilde{\mathcal{P}}\mathcal{H}$ and examine whether the shocks produce the required pattern.

While the approach is straightforward, a few interesting practical questions remain. The first one is the choice of $\mathcal{H}$. The second is how to systematically explore the space of MA representations, which is infinite dimensional, if this is of interest. The third is what to do if different $\mathcal{H}$ produce different economic shocks satisfying the restrictions imposed. Regarding the first question, it is convenient to choose $\mathcal{H} = \mathcal{H}_{i,i'}(\omega)$, $\omega \in (0, 2\pi)$, where $\mathcal{H}_{i,i'}$ are matrices rotating columns i and i' of $\mathcal{P}$ by an angle ω, and search the space of $\mathcal{H}$ by varying ω, i, and i'.

Example 4.31. Consider a bivariate VAR with unemployment and inflation and suppose that a basic decomposition has not found a shock which produced contemporaneously negative comovements in inflation and unemployment. Set

$$\mathcal{H}(\omega) = \begin{bmatrix} \cos(\omega) & -\sin(\omega) \\ \sin(\omega) & \cos(\omega) \end{bmatrix}.$$

Then we can trace out all possible MA representations for the bivariate system by varying $\omega \in (0, 2\pi)$. Note that

$$\begin{aligned} I &= \mathcal{H}(\omega)\mathcal{H}(\omega)' = \mathcal{H}(\omega)'\mathcal{H}(\omega) \\ &= \begin{bmatrix} \cos^2(\omega) + \sin^2(\omega) & -\cos(\omega)\sin(\omega) + \cos(\omega)\sin(\omega) \\ -\cos(\omega)\sin(\omega) + \cos(\omega)\sin(\omega) & \cos^2(\omega) + \sin^2(\omega) \end{bmatrix}. \end{aligned}$$

In larger-scale systems, rotation matrices are more complex.

Exercise 4.44. Consider a four-variable VAR. How many matrices rotating two or pairs of two columns exist? How would you explore the space of rotations simultaneously by flipping the first and the second columns together with the third and the fourth?

When m is of medium size, $\mathcal{H}(\omega)$ has the following form

$$\mathcal{H}_{i,i'}(\omega) = \begin{pmatrix} 1 & 0 & 0 & \cdots & 0 & 0 \\ 0 & 1 & 0 & \cdots & 0 & 0 \\ \cdots & \cdots & \cdots & \cdots & \cdots & \cdots \\ 0 & 0 & \cos(\omega) & \cdots & -\sin(\omega) & 0 \\ \vdots & \vdots & \vdots & 1 & \vdots & \vdots \\ 0 & 0 & \sin(\omega) & \cdots & \cos(\omega) & 0 \\ \cdots & \cdots & \cdots & \cdots & \cdots & \cdots \\ 0 & 0 & 0 & 0 & 0 & 1 \end{pmatrix}.$$

Let $\mathcal{Z}(\mathcal{H}_{i,i'}(\omega))$ be the space of orthonormal rotation matrices where, given ω, each i, i' element has probability $2/m(m-1)$. Then the following algorithm could be used to explore the space of identifications.

Algorithm 4.6.

(1) Draw ω^l from $(0, 2\pi)$. Draw $\mathcal{H}_{i,i'}(\omega^l)$ from $\mathcal{Z}(\mathcal{H}_{i,i'}(\omega^l))$.

(2) Use $\mathcal{H}_{i,i'}(\omega^l)$ to compute ϵ_t and $\mathcal{A}(\ell)$. Check whether, in response to ϵ_{it}, $i = 1, \ldots, m$, restrictions are satisfied. If they are, keep the draw; if they are not, drop the draw.

(3) Repeat (1) and (2) until L draws satisfying the restrictions are found. Report percentile response bands.

By continuity, it is usual to find an interval (ω_1, ω_2) which produces a shock with the required characteristics. Since within this interval the dynamics produced by structural shocks are similar, one can average statistics for the shocks in the interval, choose the shock corresponding to the median point of the interval or keep all of them, as we have done in algorithm 4.6. At times one may find disjoint intervals where one or more shocks satisfy the restrictions. In this case, it is a good idea to graphically inspect the outcome since responses may not be economically meaningful (for example, a shock may imply an unreasonable contemporaneous output response). When visual inspection fails, increasing the number of restrictions is typically sufficient to eliminate economically "unreasonable" intervals.

Exercise 4.45. Provide a Monte Carlo algorithm to construct standard error bands for structural impulse responses identified with sign restrictions which takes into account parameter uncertainty.

Example 4.32. Figure 4.4 presents the responses of industrial output, prices, and M1 in the United States in response to a monetary policy shock. In the right column are the 68% Monte Carlo response bands obtained by requiring that a nominal interest rate increase must be accompanied by a liquidity effect — a contemporaneous decline in M1. In the left column are the 68% Monte Carlo response bands obtained with the Choleski system where the interest rate is assumed to contemporaneously react to industrial output and prices but not to money. Clearly, the standard identification has unpleasant outcomes: point estimates of money, output, and prices are all positive after the shock even though the increase is not significant. With sign restrictions, output and prices significantly decline after a contractionary shock and they do so for about five months. Note that in both systems no measure of commodity prices is used.

It should be stressed that if multiple shocks are of interest, the same $\mathcal{H}_{i,i'}(\omega)$ should be used to obtain them. That is to say, shocks with different characteristics must be *simultaneously* identified with the same rotation matrix. Finally, while we have used the same notation to indicate Blaschke and rotation factors, since they both belong to the class of orthonormal matrices, it should be clear that they are distinct. In particular, rotation matrices do not flip the roots of an MA polynomial.

4.6 Problems

While popular among applied researchers, VARs are not free of problems and care should be used when performing economic analyses and interpreting the results.

First, one should be aware of time aggregation problems. Recall that time aggregation may induce important periodicities in time series (see section 3.4). Furthermore, as Sims (1971), Hansen and Sargent (1991), Marcet (1991), and others have shown, time aggregation may make inference difficult. While this is not a problem specific to VARs, it acquires particular importance when trying to give VAR dynamics an

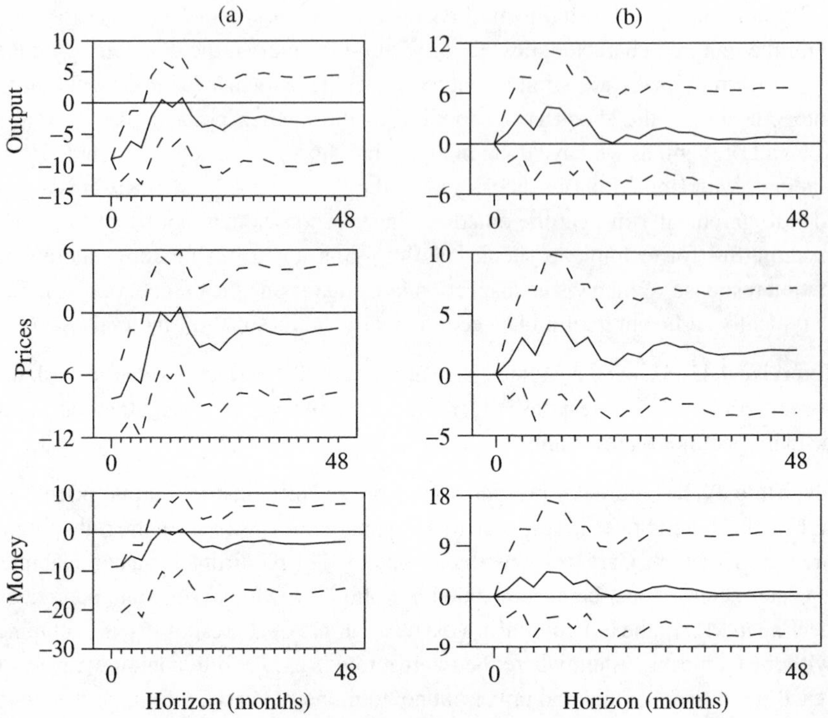

Figure 4.4. Responses to a U.S. policy shock, 1964:1–2001:10: (a) sign restrictions; (b) Choleski restrictions.

economic interpretation. In fact, if agents take decisions every τ periods but an econometrician observes data only every $j\tau$, $j > 1$, the statistical model she uses (with data sampled at every $j\tau$) may have little to do with the one produced by agents' decisions. For example, the MA traced out by the econometrician is not necessarily the MA of the model sampled every j periods, but a complex function of all MA coefficients from that point on to infinity.

Example 4.33. Marcet (1991) showed that, if agents' decisions are taken in continuous time, continuous and discrete time MA representations are related via $D_j = [\int_0^\infty d_{u+j} v_u' \, du][\int_0^\infty v_u v_u' \, du]^{-1}$, where d is the moving average in continuous time and $v_j = d_j - b \times (d_j \mid D)$ is the forecast error in predicting d_j using the information contained in the discrete time MA coefficients, b is a constant, and $j = 1, 2, \ldots, \tau$. Since D_j is a weighted average of d from j up to ∞, a hump-shaped monthly response can be easily transformed into a smoothly declining quarterly response (see figure 4.5).

One important special case obtains when agents' decisions generate a VAR(1) for the endogenous variables. In that case, the MA coefficients of, say, a quarterly model are the same as the quarterly sampled version of MA coefficients of a monthly

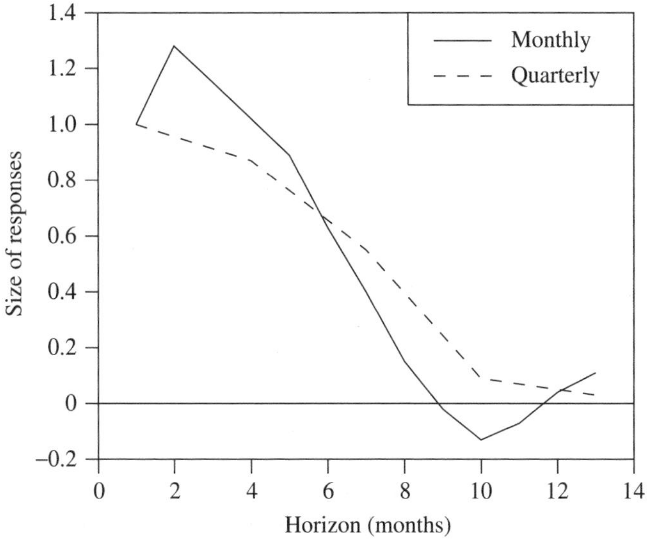

Figure 4.5. Quarterly and monthly MA representations.

model. While log-linear or quadratic approximate solutions to many DSGE models do deliver VAR(1) models, one should be aware that models with, for example, habit in consumption or quadratic costs of adjustment to investments, and models with unobservable variables, produce more complicated dynamics and therefore may face important aggregation problems.

Exercise 4.46. Consider an RBC model perturbed by technology and government expenditure disturbances. Suppose that $g_t = T_t$, where T_t are lump-sum taxes and that the utility function depends on current and lagged leisure, i.e., $U(c_t, N_t, N_{t-1}) = \ln c_t - (N_t - \gamma N_{t-1})^{\varphi_n}$.

(i) Calculate the log-linearized decision rules after you have appropriately parametrized the model at quarterly and annual frequencies. Compare the MA coefficients of the annual model with the annual sampling of the MA coefficients of the quarterly model.

(ii) Simulate consumption and output for the two specifications. Sample at annual frequencies the quarterly data and compare the two autocovariance functions.

(iii) Set $\gamma = 0$ and assume that both capital and its utilization enter in the production function as in exercise 2.9. Repeat steps (i) and (ii) and comment on the results.

Exercise 4.46 suggests that one way to detect possible aggregation problems is to run VARs with data at different frequencies and compare their ACFs or their MA representations. If the sample size is the same and differences are detected, aggregation could be a problem.

A second important problem has to do with the dimensionality of the VAR. Small-scale VAR models are typically preferred by applied researchers since parameter estimates are more precise (and impulse response bands are tighter) and because identification of behavioral shocks is easier. However, small-scale VARs are prone to several types of misspecification. For example, there may be important omitted variables; shocks may be confounded or misaggregated; and a finite-order VAR representation for the economic model may not exist. As Braun and Mittnik (1993), Cooley and Dwyer (1998), Canova and Pina (2005), and Chari et al. (2005) have shown, important biases may result. To illustrate the effects of omitting variables, we make use of the following result.

Result 4.3. In a bivariate VAR(q), $\left[\begin{smallmatrix} A_{11}(\ell) & A_{12}(\ell) \\ A_{21}(\ell) & A_{22}(\ell) \end{smallmatrix}\right]\left[\begin{smallmatrix} y_{1t} \\ y_{2t} \end{smallmatrix}\right] = \left[\begin{smallmatrix} e_{1t} \\ e_{2t} \end{smallmatrix}\right]$, the univariate representation for y_{1t} is $[A_{11}(\ell) - A_{12}(\ell)A_{22}(\ell)^{-1}A_{21}(\ell)]y_{1t} = e_{1t} - A_{12}(\ell) \times A_{22}(\ell)^{-1}e_{2t} \equiv \upsilon_t$.

Example 4.34. Suppose the true DGP has $m = 4$ variables but an investigator incorrectly estimates a bivariate VAR (there are three of these models). Using result 4.3 we can immediately see that the system with, for example, variables 1 and 3 has errors of the form

$$\begin{bmatrix} \upsilon_{1t} \\ \upsilon_{2t} \end{bmatrix} \equiv \begin{bmatrix} e_{1t} \\ e_{3t} \end{bmatrix} - \mathbb{Q}_1(\ell)\mathbb{Q}_2^{-1}(\ell) \begin{bmatrix} e_{2t} \\ e_{4t} \end{bmatrix},$$

where

$$\mathbb{Q}_1(\ell) = \begin{bmatrix} A_{12}(\ell) & A_{14}(\ell) \\ A_{32}(\ell) & A_{34}(\ell) \end{bmatrix} \quad \text{and} \quad \mathbb{Q}_2(\ell) = \begin{bmatrix} A_{22}(\ell) & A_{24}(\ell) \\ A_{42}(\ell) & A_{44}(\ell) \end{bmatrix}.$$

From this one can verify that:

- if the true system is a VAR(1), a model with $m_1 < m$ variables is a VAR(∞);
- if e_t are contemporaneously and serially uncorrelated, υ_t are typically contemporaneously and serially correlated;
- two small-scale VARs, both with $m_1 < m$ variables, have different innovations;
- υ_t is a linear combination of current, past, and future e_t. The timing of innovations is preserved if the m_1 included variables are Granger causally prior to the $m - m_1$ omitted ones (i.e., if $\mathbb{Q}_1(\ell) = 0$).

Example 4.35. Suppose an economic model has a bivariate VAR(1) representation $y_t = \mathcal{A}_1 y_{t-1} + \mathcal{A}_0 \epsilon_t$. Then the model for the first variable is $y_{1t} = \alpha_{11}^1 y_{1t-1} + \alpha_{12}^1\alpha_{21}^1 y_{1t-2} + \alpha_{12}^1\alpha_{22}^1 y_{2t-2} + \alpha_{11}^0\epsilon_{1t} + \alpha_{12}^1\alpha_{21}^0\epsilon_{1t-1} + \alpha_{12}^0\epsilon_{2t} + \alpha_{12}^1\alpha_{22}^0\epsilon_{2t-1}$. It is easy to verify that no MA component exists if $\alpha_{12}^1 = 0$ or $\alpha_{21}^0 = \alpha_{22}^0 = 0$, that the correct AR length obtains if $\alpha_{12}^1 = 0$ or $\alpha_{21}^1 = \alpha_{22}^1 = 0$ and $\alpha_{21}^0 = \alpha_{22}^0 = 0$, and that only ϵ_1 shocks will matter for y_{1t} if $\alpha_{12}^0 = 0$ and either $\alpha_{12}^1 = 0$ or $\alpha_{22}^0 = 0$.

There are several implications one can draw from examples 4.34 and 4.35. First, if relevant variables are omitted a long lag length is needed to whiten the residuals. While long lags do not always indicate misspecification (for example, if y_t is nearly nonstationary, long lags are necessary to approximate its autocovariance function), care should be exercised in drawing inference in such models. Second, two researchers estimating small-scale models with different variables may obtain different innovations, even if the same identification restrictions are used. Finally, innovation accounting exercises when variables are omitted may misrepresent the timing of the responses to behavioral shocks.

Exercise 4.47 (Giordani). Consider a sticky price model composed of an output gap ($\text{gdpgap}_t = \text{gdp}_t - \text{gdp}^{\text{P}}_t$) equation, a potential output (gdp^{P}_t) equation, a backward looking Phillips curve (normalized on π_t), and a Taylor rule of the type

$$\text{gdpgap}_{t+1} = a_1 \,\text{gdpgap}_t - a_2(i_t - \pi_t) + \epsilon^{\text{AD}}_{t+1}, \tag{4.49}$$

$$\text{gdp}^{\text{P}}_{t+1} = a_3 \,\text{gdp}^{\text{P}}_t + \epsilon^{\text{P}}_{t+1}, \tag{4.50}$$

$$\pi_{t+1} = \pi_t + a_4 \,\text{gdpgdp}_t + \epsilon^{\text{CP}}_{t+1}, \tag{4.51}$$

$$i_t = a_5 \pi_t + a_6 \,\text{gdpgap}_t + \epsilon^{\text{MP}}_{t+1}. \tag{4.52}$$

The last equation has an error term (monetary policy shock) since the central bank may not always follow the optimal solution to its minimization problem. Let $\text{var}(\epsilon^i_{t+1}) = \sigma^2_i$, $i = \text{AD, P, CP, MP}$, and assume that the four shocks are uncorrelated with each other.

(i) Argue that contractionary monetary policy shocks have one-period lagged (negative) effects on output and two-period lagged (negative) effects on inflation. Show that monetary policy actions do not Granger cause gdp^{P}_t for all t.

(ii) Derive a VAR for $[\text{gdp}_t, \text{gdp}^{\text{P}}_t, \pi_t, i_t]$. Write down the matrix of impact coefficients.

(iii) Derive a representation for a three-variable system $[\text{gdp}_t, \pi_t, i_t]$. Label the three associated shocks $e_t = [e^{\text{AD}}_t, e^{\text{CP}}_t, e^{\text{MP}}_t]$ and their covariance matrix Σ_e. Show the matrix of impact coefficients in this case.

(iv) Show that $\text{var}(e^{\text{AD}}_t) > \text{var}(\epsilon^{\text{AD}}_t)$, $\text{var}(e^{\text{MP}}_t) > 0$ even when $\epsilon^{\text{MP}}_t = 0$, $\forall t$, and that $\text{corr}(e^{\text{MP}}_t, \epsilon^{\text{P}}_t) < 0$. Show that, in a trivariate system, contractionary monetary policy shocks produce positive inflation responses (compare this with what you have in (i)).

(v) Intuitively explain why the omission of potential output from the VAR causes problems.

It is worthwhile to look at omitted variable problems from another perspective. Suppose the MA for a partition with $m_1 < m$ variables of the true model is

$$y_t = D(\ell)\epsilon_t, \tag{4.53}$$

where ϵ_t is an $m \times 1$ vector, so that $D(\ell)$ is an $m_1 \times m$ matrix, $\forall \ell$. Suppose a researcher specifies a VAR with $m_1 < m$ variables and obtains an MA of the form

$$y_t = \tilde{D}(\ell)e_t, \tag{4.54}$$

where e_t is an $m_1 \times 1$, and $\tilde{D}(\ell)$ is an $m_1 \times m_1$ matrix, $\forall \ell$. Matching (4.53) and (4.54) one obtains $\tilde{D}(\ell)e_t = D(\ell)\epsilon_t$ or letting $D^{\ddagger}(\ell)$ be an $m_1 \times m$ matrix

$$D^{\ddagger}(\ell)\epsilon_t = e_t. \tag{4.55}$$

As shown by Faust and Leeper (1997), (4.55) teaches us an important lesson. Assume that there are m^{a} shocks of one type and m^{b} shocks of another, $m^{\mathrm{a}} + m^{\mathrm{b}} = m$, and that $m_1 = 2$. Then e_{it}, $i = 1, 2$, recovers a linear combination of shocks of type $i' = \mathrm{a}, \mathrm{b}$ only if $D^{\ddagger}(\ell)$ is block diagonal. It correctly recovers current shocks if $D^{\ddagger}(\ell) = D^{\ddagger}, \forall \ell$, and $D^{\ddagger}$ is block diagonal. In all other cases, estimated behavioral innovations mix different types of true innovation.

These problems have nothing to do with estimation or identification. Misspecification occurs because a VAR(q) is transformed into a VAR(∞) whenever a variable is omitted and this occurs even when the MA representation of the small-scale model is known.

Example 4.36. Suppose the true structural model has $m = 4$ shocks, that there are two supply and two demand shocks, and that an investigator estimates a bivariate VAR. When would the two estimated structural shocks correctly aggregate shocks of the same type? Using (4.55) we have

$$\begin{bmatrix} D^{\ddagger}_{11}(\ell) & D^{\ddagger}_{12}(\ell) & D^{\ddagger}_{13}(\ell) & D^{\ddagger}_{14}(\ell) \\ D^{\ddagger}_{21}(\ell) & D^{\ddagger}_{22}(\ell) & D^{\ddagger}_{23}(\ell) & D^{\ddagger}_{24}(\ell) \end{bmatrix} \begin{bmatrix} \epsilon_{1t} \\ \epsilon_{2t} \\ \epsilon_{3t} \\ \epsilon_{4t} \end{bmatrix} = \begin{bmatrix} e_{1t} \\ e_{2t} \end{bmatrix}.$$

Hence, e_{1t} will recover only type 1 shocks if $D^{\ddagger}_{13}(\ell) = D^{\ddagger}_{14}(\ell) = 0$ and e_{2t} will recover type 2 shocks if $D^{\ddagger}_{21}(\ell) = D^{\ddagger}_{22}(\ell) = 0$. Furthermore, e_{1t} recovers current type 1 shocks if $D^{\ddagger}_{13}(\ell) = D^{\ddagger}_{14}(\ell) = 0$ and $D^{\ddagger}_{1i}(\ell) = D^{\ddagger}_{1i}, \forall \ell, i = 1, 2$.

The conditions required for correct aggregation are therefore somewhat strong. As shown in the next example, they are not satisfied in at least one type of DSGE model. It is likely that such a problem also appears in other models macroeconomists currently use.

Example 4.37. We simulate data from a version of the working capital economy of exercise 2.14 with a permanent (technology) disturbance and temporary labor supply, monetary and government expenditure shocks. Monetary policy is characterized by a Taylor rule. Using output and hours data we estimate a bivariate VAR and extract a permanent and a transitory shock, where the latter is identified by the requirement that it has no long-run effects on output. Table 4.3 presents the estimated

Table 4.3. Regressions on simulated data, t-statistics in parentheses.

	Technology shocks			Monetary shocks			
	0	−1	−2	0	−1	−2	p-value
Estimated	1.20	0.10	0.04	0.62	−0.01	−0.11	
Permanent shocks	(80.75)	(6.71)	(3.05)	(45.73)	(−0.81)	(−8.22)	0.000
Estimated	−0.80	0.007	0.08	0.92	−0.48	−0.20	
Transitory shocks	(−15.27)	(0.13)	(1.59)	(19.16)	(−10.03)	(−4.11)	0.000

coefficients of a distributed lag regression of estimated shocks on the two theoretical ones. The t-statistics are in parentheses. The last column presents the p-value of an F-test excluding monetary disturbances from the first equation and technological disturbances from the second. Estimated supply shocks mix both current and lagged monetary and technology disturbances, while for estimated demand shocks, current and lagged monetary disturbances matter but only current technology disturbances are important. This pattern is independent of the sample size.

Exercise 4.48 (Cooley and Dwyer). Simulate data from a model where a representative agent maximizes $E_0 \sum_t \beta^t [a \ln c_{1t} + (1-a) \ln c_{2t} - \vartheta_N N_t]$ subject to $p_t c_{1t} \leqslant M_t + (1+i_t)B_t + T_t - B_{t-1}$ and $c_{1t} + c_{2t} + \text{inv}_t + M_{t+1}/p_t + B_{t+1}/p_t \leqslant w_t N_t + r_t K_t + M_t/p_t + (1+i_t)B_t/p_t + T_t/p_t$, where $K_{t+1} = (1-\delta)K_t + \text{inv}_t$, $y_t = \zeta_t K_t^{1-\eta} N_t^{\eta}$, $\ln \zeta_t = \rho_\zeta \ln \zeta_{t-1} + \epsilon_{1t}$, $\ln M_{t+1}^s = \ln M_t^s + \ln M_t^g$, M_t^g is a constant, and $\rho_\zeta = 0.99$ (you are free to choose the other parameters, but explain your choices). Consider a bivariate system with output and hours and verify that standard unit root tests fail to reject the null for output but reject the null for hours. Using the restriction that demand shocks have no long-run effects on output, plot output and hours responses in the theory and in the VAR. Is there any feature of the theoretical economy which is distorted?

In section 4.5 we have seen that in the just identified case, a two-step estimation approach is equivalent to a direct two-stage least squares (2SLS) approach on the solution of the economic system. Since economic shocks depend on the identification restrictions, we may have situations where a 2SLS approach produces "good' estimators, in the sense that they are highly correlated with the structural shocks they instrument for, and situations where they are bad. Cooley and Dwyer (1998) present an example where, by changing the identifying restrictions, the correlation of the instruments with the economic shocks goes from high to very low, therefore resulting in instrumental variables failures (see chapter 5). Hence, if such a problem is suspected, a maximum likelihood approach should be preferred.

Chari et al. (2005) have recently pointed out that certain economic models may not possess a finite-order VAR representation. Such a problem also occurs when some variables are solved out of the solution of the model (see examples 4.34 and 4.35).

Chapter 6 gives sufficient conditions which ensure that finite-order VARs approximate the solutions of a DSGE model well. When these conditions are not satisfied, the economic inference one conducts with a finite-order identified VAR may have little to do with the dynamics of the model the VAR is trying to approximate. We show the extent of the problem in the next example.

Example 4.38. Consider the simplest version of the Blanchard–Quah model used in section 3.3.1. The model has implications for four variables (GDP, inflation, employment, and real wages) but the solution is typically collapsed to two equations — one for GDP growth, the other for unemployment — of the form

$$\Delta\text{GDP}_t = \epsilon_{3t} - \epsilon_{3t-1} + a(\epsilon_{1t} - \epsilon_{1t-1}) + \epsilon_{1t}, \tag{4.56}$$

$$\text{UN}_t = -\epsilon_{3t} - a\epsilon_{1t}. \tag{4.57}$$

It is easy to show that a finite-order VAR may not be able to approximate the theoretical dynamics of this model. To see this, we set $a = 0.1$ and plot in figure 4.6 the theoretical responses of output and unemployment to the two shocks and the responses obtained by using a VAR(1) and a VAR(4), where the econometrician uses the correct (but truncated) VAR coefficients. While there is some improvement in moving from a VAR(1) to a VAR(4), the true theoretical responses are very poorly approximated even with a VAR(4). Since a VAR(q), $q > 4$, has responses which are indistinguishable from those of a VAR(4) — matrices on longer VAR lags are all zero — no finite-order VAR can capture (4.56) and (4.57).

Finally, it is worth stressing again that there are several economic models which generate non-Wold decompositions (see, for example, Leeper 1991; Quah 1990; Hansen and Sargent 1991). Hence, examining these models with standard VARs is meaningless. When a researcher suspects that this is a problem, Blaschke factors should be used to construct nonfundamental Wold representations before the mapping between economic and reduced-form VAR is examined. Results do depend on the representations used. For example, Lippi and Reichlin (1993) present a non-Wold version of Blanchard and Quah's (1989) model which gives opposite conclusions regarding the relative importance of demand and supply shocks in generating business cycle fluctuations.

Exercise 4.49 (Quah). Consider a three-equation permanent income model

$$\left.\begin{aligned} c_t &= r\text{We}_t, \\ \text{We}_t &= \text{sa}_t + \left[(1+r)^{-1}\sum_j (1+r)^{-j} E_t\,\text{GDP}_{t+j}\right], \\ \text{sa}_{t+1} &= (1+r)\text{sa}_t + \text{GDP}_t - c_t, \end{aligned}\right\} \tag{4.58}$$

where c_t is consumption, We_t is wealth, r is the (constant) real rate, sa_t are savings, and $\Delta\text{GDP}_t = D(\ell)\epsilon_t$ is the labor income. Show that a bivariate representation for

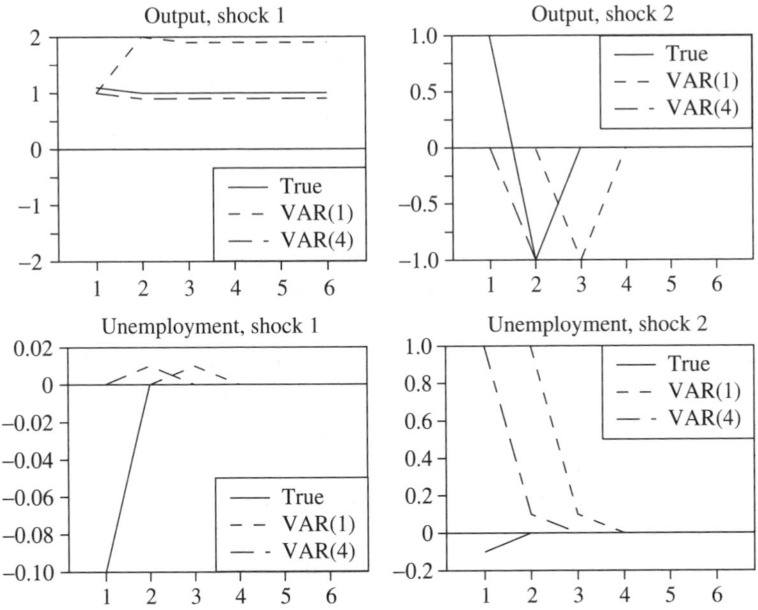

Figure 4.6. Responses in the Blanchard–Quah model.

consumption and output growth is

$$\begin{bmatrix} \Delta \mathrm{GDP}_t \\ \Delta c_t \end{bmatrix} = \begin{bmatrix} A_1(\ell) & (1-\ell)A_0(\ell) \\ A_1(\beta) & (1-\beta)A_0(\beta) \end{bmatrix} \begin{bmatrix} e_{1t} \\ e_{0t} \end{bmatrix},$$

where $\beta = (1+r)^{-1}$, e_{1t} is a permanent shock, and e_{0t} is a transitory shock. Find $A_1(\ell)$ and $A_0(\ell)$. Show that, if $\Delta \mathrm{GDP}_t = \epsilon_t$, the representation collapses to

$$\begin{bmatrix} \Delta \mathrm{GDP}_t \\ \Delta c_t \end{bmatrix} = \begin{bmatrix} 1 & (1-\ell) \\ 1 & (1-\beta) \end{bmatrix} \begin{bmatrix} e_{1t} \\ e_{0t} \end{bmatrix},$$

which is nonfundamental. Show that

$$\begin{bmatrix} \Delta \mathrm{GDP}_t \\ \Delta c_t \end{bmatrix} = b(\beta)^{-1} \begin{bmatrix} (2-\beta)\{1 - [(1-\beta)/(2-\beta)]\ell\} & (1-\beta\ell) \\ 1 + (1-\beta)^2 & 0 \end{bmatrix} \begin{bmatrix} \tilde{e}_{1t} \\ \tilde{e}_{0t} \end{bmatrix},$$

$\mathrm{var}(\tilde{e}_{0t}) = \mathrm{var}(\tilde{e}_{1t}) = 1$ is the fundamental MA.

4.7 Validating DSGE Models with VARs

VARs are extensively used to summarize those conditional and unconditional moments that "good" models should be able to replicate. Generally, informal comparisons are performed. At times, the model's statistics are compared with 68 or 95% bands for the statistics of the data (see, for example, Christiano et al. 2005) and conclusions about the quality of the model rest on whether the model's statistics are inside or outside these bands for a number of variables. If parameter uncertainty is allowed for, comparison of posterior distributions of these statistics is possible (see chapters 7 and 11).

While this is a simple and intuitive approach, there are other ways of testing DSGE theories via VARs. For example, in Canova et al. (1994), theoretical cointegration restrictions coming from an RBC model driven by permanent technology shocks are imposed on a VAR and tested by using standard tools. Their point of view can be generalized and the applicability of their idea extended if qualitative implications, which are more robust than quantitative ones, are used to restrict the data and if restrictions are used for identification rather than for estimation.

DSGE models are misspecified in the sense that they are, in general, too simple to capture the complex probabilistic nature of the data. Hence, it may be fruitless to compare their outcomes with the data: if one looks hard enough and data are abundant, statistically or economically large deviations can always be found. Both academic economists and policy makers use DSGE models to tell stories about how the economy responds to unexpected movements in the exogenous variables. Hence, there may be substantial consensus in expecting output to decline after an unexpected interest rate increase but considerable uncertainty about the size of the impact and the timing of the output responses. The techniques described in chapters 5 and 6 have a hard time dealing with this uncertainty. For example, estimation and testing with maximum likelihood (ML) requires the whole model to be the correct DGP (up to uncorrelated measurement errors), at least under the null. Generalized methods of moments and simulation estimators can be tailored to focus only on those aspects where misspecification could be smaller (e.g., the Euler equation or the great ratios). However, estimation and validation still require that these aspects of the model are quantitatively correct under the null. When one feels comfortable only with the qualitative implications of a class of models and is not willing to (quantitatively) entertain a part or the whole of it as a null hypothesis, the approach described in section 4.5.3 can be used to design a simple limited information criterion to evaluate the fit of any model or the relative merit of two competitor models.

The method we propose here agrees with the minimalist identification philosophy underlying VARs. In fact, one can use some of the least controversial qualitative implications of the theory to identify economic shocks in the data. Once shocks in data and the model are forced to have qualitatively similar features, the dynamic discrepancy between the two in the dimensions of interest can be easily examined. We summarize the main features of the approach in the next algorithm.

Algorithm 4.7.

(1) Find qualitative, robust implications of a class of models.

(2) Use (a subset of) these implications to identify shocks in the actual data. Stop validation if data do not conform to the qualitative robust restrictions of the model.

(3) If theoretical restrictions have a data counterpart, *qualitatively* evaluate the model (use, for example, sign and shape of responses to shocks, the pattern of peak/trough responses, etc.).

(4) Validate *qualitatively* across models if more than one candidate is available.

(5) If results in (3) and (4) are satisfactory, and policy analyses need to be performed, compare the model and the data *quantitatively*.

(6) Repeat (2)–(5) by using another subset of robust implications of the model(s), if needed.

(7) If mismatch between theory and data is relevant, alter the model while maintaining the restrictions in (1) and repeat (3) and/or (5) to evaluate improvements. Otherwise, proceed to policy analyses.

A few comments on algorithm 4.7 are in order. In (1) we require theoretical restrictions to be robust, that is, independent of parametrization and/or of the functional forms of primitives. The idea is to avoid restrictions which emerge only in special cases of the theory. In the second step we force certain shocks in the data and the model to be qualitatively similar. In steps (2)–(7) evaluation is conducted at different levels: first, we examine whether the restrictions are satisfied in the data; second, we evaluate qualitative dynamic features of the model; finally, quantitative properties are considered. Qualitative evaluation should be a prerequisite to a quantitative one: many models can be discarded by using the former alone. Also, to make the evaluation meaningful economic measures of discrepancy, as opposed to statistical ones, should be used.

The algorithm is simple and computationally affordable, particularly in comparison with ML or the methods we discuss in chapter 11; the results are easily reproducible; the method can be used when models are very simplified descriptions of the actual data; and can be employed to evaluate one or more dimensions of the model. In this sense, it provides a flexible, limited-information criterion which can be made more or less demanding, depending on the desires of the investigator. We illustrate the use of algorithm 4.7 in an example.

Example 4.39. We consider a working capital (WK) and a sticky price (SP) model to study the welfare costs of different monetary rules. We concentrate on the first step of the exercise, i.e., on examining which model is more appropriate to answer the policy question.

Canova (2002a) shows that these two models produce a number of robust sign restrictions in response to technology and monetary policy shocks. For example, in response to a policy disturbance the WK economy generates negative comovements of inflation and output, of inflation and real balances, and of inflation and the slope of the term structure and positive comovements of output and real balances. In the SP economy, the correlation between inflation and output is positive contemporaneously and for lags of output and negative for leads of output. The one between inflation and real balances is negative everywhere, the one between output and real balances is positive for lags of real balances and negative contemporaneously and for leads of real balances. Finally, the correlation of the slope of the term structure with inflation is negative everywhere. One could use some or all of these restrictions to characterize monetary shocks. Here we select restrictions on the contemporaneous cross-correlation of output, inflation, and the slope of the term structure for the WK model and on the cross-correlation of output, inflation, and real balances in the SP model. We impose these restrictions on a VAR composed of output, inflation, real balances, the slope of the term structure, and labor productivity by using U.S., U.K., and euro data from 1980:1 to 1998:4.

We find that WK sign restrictions fail to recover monetary shocks in the United Kingdom, while SP sign restrictions do not produce monetary shocks in the euro land. That is to say, out of 10 000 draws for ω and $\mathcal{H}_{i,i'}(\omega)$ we are able to find less than 0.1% of the cases where the restrictions are satisfied. Since no combination of reduced-form residuals produces cross-correlations for output, inflation, and the slope (or real balances) with the required sign, both models are at odds with the dynamic comovements in response to monetary shocks in at least one data set. One may stop here and try to respecify the models, or proceed with the data sets where restrictions hold and evaluate, for example, the dynamic responses of other VAR variables to identified monetary shocks.

There are at least two reasons why a comparison based on real balances (or the slope) and labor productivity may be informative on the quality of the model's approximation to the data. First, we would like to know if identified monetary shocks produce liquidity effects, a feature present in both models and a simple "test" often used to decide whether a particular identification scheme is meaningful or not (see, for example, Gordon and Leeper 1994).

Second, it is common to use the dynamics of labor productivity to discriminate between flexible price real business cycle and sticky price demand-driven explanations of economic fluctuations (see Gali 1999). Since the dynamics of labor productivity in response to contractionary monetary shocks are similar in the two models (hours declines more than output, hence, labor productivity increases), it is interesting to check whether the qualitative data conform to these predictions.

Figure 4.7 plots the responses of these two variables for each data set (straight lines) together with the responses obtained in the two models (dashed lines), scaled so that the variance of the monetary policy innovation is the same. Two conclusions can be drawn. First, the WK identification scheme cannot account for the sign or the shape of the responses of labor productivity in the United States and euro area and generates monetary disturbances in the euro area which lack liquidity effects. Second, with the SP identification scheme monetary shocks generate instantaneous responses of the slope of the term structure which have the wrong sign in the United States and lack persistence with U.K. data.

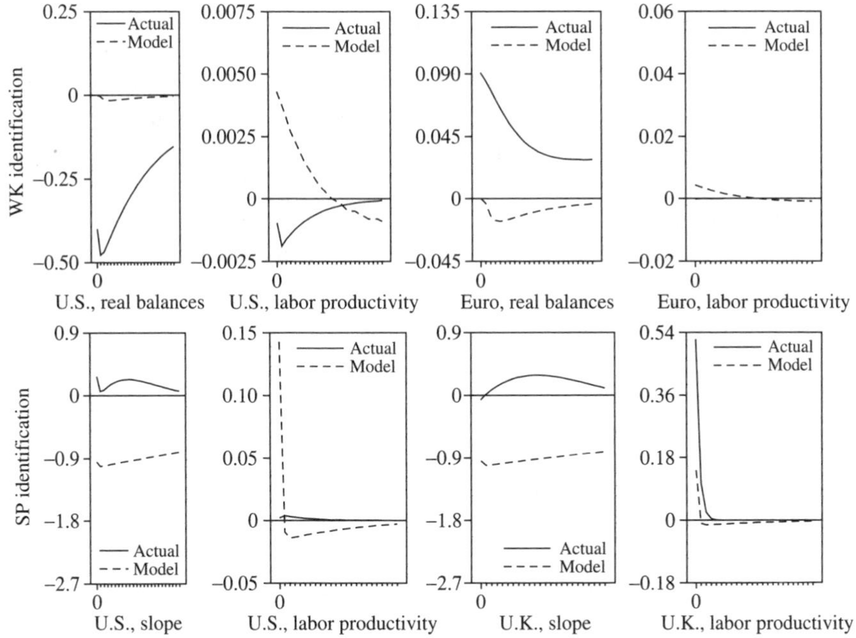

Figure 4.7. Responses to monetary shocks.

Given that the two theories produce dynamics which are qualitatively at odds with the data, it is not surprising to find that quantitative predictions are also unsatisfactory. For example, the percentage of output variance accounted for by monetary shocks in the United States at the 24-step horizon is between 11 and 43% with the WK scheme and between 3 and 34% with the SP scheme. In comparison, and regardless of the parametrization used, monetary disturbances account for 1% of output variance in both models. Hence, both models lack internal propagation.

Given the mismatch of the models and the data, one should probably go back to the drawing board before answering any policy question. Canova (2002a) shows that adding capacity utilization and/or labor hoarding is not enough to enhance the qualitative match of the models. Whether other frictions change this outcome is an open question.

Exercise 4.50 (Dedola and Neri). Take a standard RBC model with habit persistence in consumption and highly persistent but stationary technology shocks. Examine whether robust sign restrictions for the correlation of output, hours, and labor productivity exist when the extent of habit (γ), the power of utility parameter (φ), the share of hours in production (η), the depreciation rate (δ), and the persistence of technology shocks (ρ_ζ) are varied within reasonable ranges. Using a VAR with labor productivity, real wages, hours, investment, consumption, and output, examine whether the model fits the data, when robust sign restrictions are used to identify technology shocks in the data.

Exercise 4.51 (Pappa). In a simple sticky price model with monopolistic competitive firms anything that moves aggregate demand (e.g., government shocks) induces a shift in the labor demand curve and therefore induces positive comovements of hours and real wages. In a simple flexible-price RBC model, on the other hand, government expenditure shocks shift both the aggregate supply and the aggregate demand curve. For many parametrizations movements in the former are larger than movements in the latter and therefore negative comovements of hours and real wages are generated. Using a VAR with labor productivity, hours, real wages, investment, consumption, and output, verify whether an RBC style model fits the data better than a sticky price, monopolistic competitive model.

5

GMM and Simulation Estimators

A class of statistical and economic models features orthogonality conditions of the form

$$E[g(y_t, \theta) - \varrho] \equiv g_\infty(\theta) = 0, \tag{5.1}$$

where y_t is an $m \times 1$ vector of data observed at t, θ is a $k \times 1$ vector of parameters, g is an $n \times 1$ vector of functions, and ϱ is a constant vector. Typically, E is the conditional expectation operator, i.e., $E[\cdot] \equiv E[\cdot \mid \mathcal{F}_t]$, where $\mathcal{F}_t$ is the information set at t. Sometimes, it represents unconditional expectations, i.e., $E[\cdot] \equiv E(E[\cdot \mid \mathcal{F}_t])$.

Orthogonality conditions like (5.1) can be obtained from the first-order conditions of an intertemporal optimization problem, in which case θ contains preferences and technology parameters and y_t are the endogenous and the exogenous variables of the model; however, they also emerge from steady-state relationships or appear among the identifying restrictions in (time series) regression models.

Whenever the model (5.1) is thought to represent the true data-generating process (DGP), one can estimate θ by using a variety of techniques. For example, noting that $E[g(y_t, \theta)] = g(y_t, \theta) - e_t$, where e_t is an expectational error, one could estimate θ by using nonlinear least squares (NLLS). Alternatively, one could use maximum likelihood (ML) once (a) the distributional properties of y_t are specified, and (b) an explicit closed-form solution, expressing the endogenous variables as a function of parameters and exogenous variables, is found. Clearly, in nonlinear models (b) is hard to obtain. Moreover, if n is large, both NLLS and ML may be computationally burdensome. Finally, distributional assumptions may be hard to justify when y_t includes endogenous variables.

The techniques we present in this chapter are designed to estimate θ and to test the validity of (5.1) without requiring either distributional assumptions or an explicit solution for the endogenous variables. The methodology can be applied to both linear and nonlinear specifications; it can be used for univariate ($n = 1$) and multivariate setups; and it requires mild regularity conditions to produce estimators with "good" properties. One restriction we impose, at least in the initial framework, is that y_t only contains observable variables. Later, we relax it and allow some of the components of y_t to be unobservable.

The approaches we discuss in this chapter are of the limited-information type. That is, estimation and testing are limited to conditions like (5.1). Therefore, although the model may produce additional equations, its degree of approximation to the data is examined only through (5.1). In the context of DSGE models this is not so restrictive: optimality conditions and constraints will, in fact, imply restrictions like (5.1).

5.1 Generalized Method of Moments and Other Standard Estimators

Definition 5.1. Let $g_\infty(\theta)$ be the population mean of $g(y_t, \theta) - \varrho$, let $g_T(\theta) = (1/T)\sum_{t=1}^{T}[g(y_t, \theta) - \varrho]$ be its sample mean, and let W_T be a symmetric, positive definite $n \times n$ matrix. Then a generalized method of moments (GMM) estimator θ_T solves

$$\underset{\theta}{\operatorname{argmin}}[g_T(\theta_T) - g_\infty(\theta)]' W_T [g_T(\theta_T) - g_\infty(\theta)]. \tag{5.2}$$

A GMM estimator makes the sample version of orthogonality conditions "close" to their population counterpart and the matrix W_T describes what "close" means. GMM is therefore similar to a number of other estimators. For example, minimum distance estimators (see Malinvaud 1980) also solve a problem like (5.2) but $g_T(\theta) - g_\infty(\theta)$ is not necessarily the difference between sample and population orthogonality conditions. Extreme estimators, i.e., estimators maximizing a criterion function (see Amemiya 1985) are also obtained from a problem similar to (5.2).

Definition 5.1 includes several subcases of interest. For example, in many setups $g_\infty(\theta) = 0$, in which case a GMM estimator sets the sample version of orthogonality conditions to zero. In other problems, expectations are conditional on time t information. Hence, if $E_t[g_{1t}(\theta)] = 0$, where g_1 is a scalar function, we also have $g_\infty(\theta) = E[z_t g_{1t}(\theta)] = 0$ for any $z_t \in \mathcal{F}_t$, in which case the solution to (5.2) produces a generalized instrumental variable (GIV) estimator. When z_t is a constant, conditional and unconditional expectations are the same, so that GMM and GIV coincide.

We next present examples of economic models which deliver orthogonality conditions like (5.1) as part of the optimality conditions of the problem.

Example 5.1. Suppose a social planner maximizes $E_0 \sum_t \beta^t u(c_t, (1 - N_t))$ by choices of $\{c_t, N_t, K_{t+1}\}_{t=0}^{\infty}$ subject to $c_t + K_{t+1} \leqslant f(K_t, N_t) - G_t + (1-\delta)K_t$, where N_t is the number of hours worked, K_t is the capital stock, and G_t is a random government expenditure disturbance. The first-order conditions of the problem imply an Euler equation of the form

$$E_t\left[\beta \frac{U_{c,t+1}}{U_{c,t}}[f_K + (1 - \delta)] - 1\right] = 0, \tag{5.3}$$

where $f_K = \partial f / \partial K$, $U_{c,t} = \partial u / \partial c_t$. Equation (5.3) fits (5.1) for $g(y_t, \theta) = \beta(U_{c,t+1}/U_{c,t})[f_K + (1 - \delta)]$ and $\varrho = 1$.

Example 5.2. In the model of exercise 2.18, the wage-setting equation of monopolistic competitive workers was given by

$$E_t \sum_{j=0}^{\infty} \beta^j \zeta_{\mathrm{w}}^j \left[\frac{\pi^j w_t}{(1+\varsigma_{\mathrm{w}}) p_{t+j}} U_{c,t+j} + U_{n,t+j} \right] N_{t+j} = 0, \tag{5.4}$$

where β is the discount factor, $U_{c,t+j}$ ($U_{n,t+j}$) is the marginal utility of consumption (labor) at $t+j$, p_t is the price level, π the steady-state inflation rate, w_t the wage rate, ς_{w} is a parameter in the labor aggregator, $N_t = (\int N_t(i)^{1/(1+\varsigma_{\mathrm{w}})}\,\mathrm{d}i)^{1+\varsigma_{\mathrm{w}}}$, $i \in [0,1]$, and $1-\zeta_{\mathrm{w}}$ is the fraction of workers allowed to change the wage each t. Then (5.4) fits (5.1) for $g(y_t, \theta) = \sum_{j=0}^{\infty} \beta^j \zeta_{\mathrm{w}}^j [(\pi^j w_t/(1+\varsigma_{\mathrm{w}}) p_{t+j}) U_{c,t+j} + U_{n,t+j}] N_{t+j}$ and $\varrho = 0$.

Exercise 5.1. Suppose that agents maximize $E_0 \sum_t \beta^t u(c_t - \gamma c_{t-1})$ by choosing $\{c_t, \mathrm{sa}_{t+1}\}_{t=0}^{\infty}$, subject to the constraint $c_t + \mathrm{sa}_{t+1} \leqslant w_t + (1+r)\mathrm{sa}_t$, where w_t is an exogenous labor income, sa_{t+1} are savings maturing at $t+1$, and $r_t = r$ for all t. Show the orthogonality conditions of this problem. When is consumption a martingale process?

Note that, by solving the budget constraint in exercise 5.1 and assuming that $\lim_{j\to\infty} \mathrm{sa}_{t+j} = 0$, we have that $c_t + \sum_j (1+r)^{-j} c_{t+j} \leqslant w_t + \sum_j (1+r)^{-j} \times w_{t+j} + \mathrm{sa}_t$. When $\gamma = 0$ and $U(c_t) = \ln c_t$, the optimal saving decision implies the life-cycle consumption function $c_t = (1-\beta)[w_t + \mathrm{sa}_t + E_t \sum_j (1+r)^{-j} w_{t+j}]$, which is also an orthogonality condition.

Exercise 5.2. A class of asset pricing models generates conditions like

$$E_{t-1} r_{it} = \mathrm{rp}_{0,t-1} + \sum_{j=1}^{J} \alpha_{ij} \mathrm{rp}_{j,t-1}, \quad i = 0, 1, \dots, m, \tag{5.5}$$

where r_{it} is the rate of return on asset i from $t-1$ to t, rp_{jt-1} are market-wide expected risk premiums (conditional expected excess returns), and α_{ij} is the conditional beta of asset i relative to the jth "risk factor." Here rp_{jt-1} are latent variables.

Let $\tilde{r}_{it} = r_{it} - r_{0t}$, where r_{0t} is the return on an arbitrarily chosen asset. Show that (5.5) implies $E_{t-1}(\tilde{r}_t) = \mathrm{rp}_{t-1}\theta$, where θ is a $J \times m$ matrix with $\theta_{ij} = \alpha_{ij} - \alpha_{0j}$. Show that, for any partition $\tilde{r} = (\tilde{r}_1, \tilde{r}_2)$, $E_{t-1}\tilde{r}_{2t}$ must be proportional to $E_{t-1}\tilde{r}_{1t}$. Set up orthogonality conditions to estimate this proportionality factor.

Conditions like (5.1) are also common in consumption-based capital asset pricing models.

Example 5.3. Suppose a representative agent maximizes $E_0 \sum_t \beta^t U(c_t)$ by choosing $\{c_t, B_{t+1}, S_{t+1}\}_{t=0}^{\infty}$, subject to $c_t + B_{t+1} + p_t^{\mathrm{s}} S_{t+1} \leqslant w_t + (1+r_t)B_t + (p_t^{\mathrm{s}} + \mathrm{sd}_t)S_t$, where B_t are one-period bond holdings, S_t are stock holdings, sd_t

are the dividends paid at t, r_t^{B} is the return on bonds, and p_t^{s} is the price of stocks at t. Optimality implies

$$E_t\left[\beta\frac{U_{c,t+1}}{U_{c,t}}\frac{p_{t+1}^s+\mathrm{sd}_{t+1}}{p_t^{\mathrm{s}}}-1\right]=0, \tag{5.6}$$

$$E_t\left[\beta\frac{U_{c,t+1}}{U_{c,t}}(1+r_{t+1}^{\mathrm{B}})-1\right]=0, \tag{5.7}$$

where the first condition holds for stocks and the second for bonds. Equations (5.6) and (5.7) fit (5.1) by setting $g_1(y_t,\theta)=\beta[(U_{c,t+1}/U_{c,t})(p_{t+1}^s+\mathrm{sd}_{t+1})/p_t^{\mathrm{s}}]$ and $g_2(y_t,\theta)=\beta[(1+r_{t+1}^{\mathrm{B}})U_{c,t+1}/U_{c,t}]$, and $\varrho_1=\varrho_2=1$.

In summary, rational expectations models displaying some intertemporal link will generate at least one equation where a conditional expectation of some function of the variables is set to zero. Therefore, structures like (5.1) are pervasive in modern macroeconomics. For future reference, note that in example 5.1 we have one orthogonality condition and at least two parameters to estimate, (β,δ). In contrast, in example 5.3 we have two orthogonality conditions and, if utility is logarithmic, only one parameter to be estimated (β). Hence, while in the first case we need to generate artificial orthogonality conditions by using instruments, in the second we need to weight the information in (5.6) and (5.7) to estimate β.

Many econometric and time series estimators can also be derived from orthogonality conditions like (5.1). Next, we consider a few examples.

Example 5.4. Let $f(y_t,\theta)$ be the density of y_t. Let $E(y_t^i(\theta))=\int y_t^i f(y_t,\theta)\,\mathrm{d}y_t$ and $\hat{y}_T^i=(1/T)\sum_{t=1}^T y_t^i$ be, respectively, the ith population and sample moment of y_t. A method of moments estimator θ_{MM} solves $E(y_t^i(\theta))=\hat{y}_T^i$, $i=1,\dots,k$. Hence, $g_i(y_t,\theta)=[y_t^i-E(y_t^i(\theta))]$ and $\varrho=0$.

Note that the estimator of example 5.4 requires k moments but it does not specify which ones a researcher should use. Since different moments produce different estimators, a method of moments estimator is not necessarily efficient. As we will see, a GMM estimator eliminates this source of inefficiency.

Example 5.5. Let $y_t=x_t\theta+e_t$ with $E_t(x_t'e_t)=0$, where y_t is a scalar and x_t a $1\times k$ vector. Premultiplying by x_t' and taking conditional expectations, we have $E_t(x_t'y_t)=E_t(x_t'x_t)\theta+E_t(x_t'e_t)$. Let $y=(y_1,\dots,y_t)'$ and $x=(x_1,\dots,x_t)'$. Then $\theta_{\mathrm{OLS}}=(x'x)^{-1}x'y$, is a GMM estimator for $g(x_t,\theta)\equiv x_t'y_t-x_t'x_t\theta=x_t'e_t$.

Exercise 5.3. Suppose in example 5.5 that $E_t(x_t'e_t)\neq 0$. Let z_t be a set of instruments, correlated with x_t and satisfying $E_t(z_t'e_t)=0$. Show the orthogonality conditions in this case. Show the g function that θ_{IV} solves.

When g is linear in θ, a solution to the minimization problem is easy to find. When g is nonlinear, an estimator is found with an iterative procedure.

Example 5.6. Suppose $y_t = \mathfrak{H}(x_t, \theta) + e_t$. Assume $E_t[\mathfrak{H}(x_t, \theta)' e_t] \neq 0$ and that there exists a set of z_t correlated with x_t such that $E_t[z_t' e_t] = 0$. Then $E_t[z_t' e_t] = E_t[z_t'(y_t - \mathfrak{H}(x_t, \theta))] = E_t[g(y_t, z_t, x_t, \theta)] = 0$. Hence, θ_{NLIV} is a GMM estimator for $g(y_t, z_t, x_t, \theta) = z_t'(y_t - \mathfrak{H}(x_t, \theta))$.

Exercise 5.4. Consider an NLLS estimator of the model of example 5.6 when $E_t(\mathfrak{H}(x_t, \theta)' e_t) = 0$. Show the orthogonality conditions that the NLLS solves.

Perhaps surprisingly, a maximum likelihood estimator also solves orthogonality conditions. Let $\{y_t\}_{t=0}^T$ be a stochastic process with density $f(y_t, \theta)$. Let $\mathcal{L}_T(\theta) = \sum_{t=1}^T \ln f(y_t, \theta)$ be the log likelihood function for a sample with T observations. If $\mathcal{L}_T(\theta)$ is strictly concave and differentiable, $\partial \mathcal{L}_T(\theta)/\partial\theta' = 0$ is sufficient for the maximum. Hence, if $g(y_t, \theta) = (1/T)\partial \mathcal{L}_T(\theta)/\partial\theta' = (1/T) \times \sum_{t=1}^T \partial \ln f(y_t, \theta)/\partial\theta'$ and $E[\partial \ln f(y_t, \theta)/\partial\theta'] = 0$, θ_{ML} is a GMM estimator. Note that when $\mathcal{L}(\theta)$ is not globally concave, θ_T may be different from the θ_{ML} obtained by evaluating the likelihood directly, since the former may only locate a local maximum of the likelihood.

Exercise 5.5. Consider an $m \times 1$ VAR(q): $y_t = A(\ell) y_{t-1} + e_t$, with $e_t \sim$ i.i.d. $(0, \Sigma_e)$ and $E_t(e_t e_{t-\tau}') = 0, \forall \tau \neq 0$. Show that $E_t(y_t y_{t-1}') = \mathbb{A} E_t(y_{t-1} y_{t-1}')$, where $\mathbb{A}$ is the companion of the matrix $A(\ell)$. Show the g function when $\theta = \text{vec}[\mathbb{A}_1]$ and $\mathbb{A}_1$ are the first m rows of $\mathbb{A}$.

While the class of GMM estimators is dense, there are less popular estimators that do not fit this framework. An example is given below.

Example 5.7 (robust estimators). Consider the model of example 5.5, but suppose that you want to neglect outliers. One way to do this is to minimize the sum of squares of e_t in a prescribed set, i.e., $\min(\sum_t e_t^2) \times \mathcal{I}_{[\underline{e}, \bar{e}]}$, where $\mathcal{I}$. is an indicator function. The resulting trimmed estimator is generated from a g function with jumpy derivatives and violates one of the conditions given in section 5.3.

5.2 IV Estimation in a Linear Model

To understand the intuition behind GMM estimation it is useful to start with the problem of estimating regression parameters by using instrumental variables. The intuition gained in this case carries over to more complicated nonlinear setups. Let $y = x\theta_0 + e$, $e \sim (0, \sigma^2 I)$, where y is a $(T \times 1)$ vector, x is a $(T \times k)$ stochastic matrix of rank k, θ_0 is a $(k \times 1)$ vector, and e is a $(T \times 1)$ vector of disturbances. Let z be a $(T \times n)$ matrix of instruments satisfying either $E[z_t' e_t] = 0$ or the stronger conditions $E(e_t \mid z_t) = 0, \forall t$, where z_t is the tth row of z (x_t could be an element of z_t). Let $z'e = (1/T)\sum_t z_t' e_t(\theta)$, where $e_t(\theta) = y_t - x_t\theta$, and let $z'x \equiv (1/T)\sum_t z_t' x_t$, $z'y \equiv (1/T)\sum_t z_t' y_t$. Finally, let $W_T \xrightarrow{\text{a.s.}} W$ be an $n \times n$ positive definite, symmetric matrix and define

$$Q_T(\theta) = [e(\theta)' z] W_T [z' e(\theta)]. \tag{5.8}$$

Let $\theta_{\text{IV}} = \text{argmin}[Q_T(\theta)]$. Taking the first-order condition of (5.8) with respect to θ and using the definition of $e(\theta)$, we have $x'zW_Tz'y = x'zW_Tz'x\theta$. We consider two cases $n = k$ and $n > k$. We neglect the third one, $n < k$, since in this case θ is underidentified, i.e., there is insufficient information to estimate θ. This is because the $(k \times k)$ matrix $x'zW_Tz'x$ will have rank $n < k$.

When $n = k$, the number of instruments is the same as the number of parameters and $x'z$ is a square matrix. Hence,

$$\theta_{\text{IV}} = (z'x)^{-1}z'y = \theta_0 + (z'x)^{-1}z'e, \tag{5.9}$$

as long as $(z'x)$ is nonsingular. To show that θ_{IV} is consistent note that, since $E(z'e) = 0, \forall t$, by the strong law of large numbers, we have that $z'e(\theta_0) \xrightarrow{\text{a.s.}} 0$. Also, since $W_T > 0$, $Q_T(\theta) \geqslant 0$. Hence, if $\theta_{\text{IV}} = \text{argmin}[Q_T(\theta)]$, $z'e(\theta_0) \xrightarrow{\text{a.s.}} 0$ and $z'x$ is bounded; it must be that $\theta_{\text{IV}} \xrightarrow{\text{a.s.}} \theta_0$. Clearly, the argument breaks down if for some z_t, $E[z_t'e(\theta_0)] \neq 0$, i.e., the instruments are invalid, or when $E[z_t'x_t] \approx 0$, i.e., the instruments are weak. Note that in this case θ_{IV} does not depend on W_T.

When $n > k$, θ is overidentified, i.e., there is more information (orthogonality conditions) than necessary to estimate θ. In this case, the choice of W_T matters. In fact, $x'zW_T$ is a $(k \times n)$ matrix so that $x'zW_Tz'e(\theta_{\text{IV}}) = 0$ does not necessarily imply that $z'e(\theta_{\text{IV}}) = 0$ but only that k linear combinations of the n orthogonality conditions $z'e(\theta)$ are set to zero with weights given by $x'zW_T$. The solution for θ_{IV} is

$$\theta_{\text{IV}} = (x'zW_Tz'x)^{-1}x'zW_Tz'y. \tag{5.10}$$

Exercise 5.6. Give sufficient conditions to ensure that $\theta_{\text{IV}} \xrightarrow{\text{a.s.}} \theta_0$ in (5.10).

To characterize the asymptotic distribution of θ_{IV} when $n \geqslant k$, use the model and (5.10) to obtain

$$\sqrt{T}(\theta_{\text{IV}} - \theta_0) = (x'zW_Tz'x)^{-1}x'zW_T\sqrt{T}z'e. \tag{5.11}$$

We make three assumptions: (i) $\lim_{T\to\infty} z'z = \Sigma_{zz}, |\Sigma_{zz}| \neq 0$; (ii) $\lim_{T\to\infty} x'z = \Sigma_{xz}$, rank $|\Sigma_{xz}| = k$; (iii) $\lim_{T\to\infty} \sqrt{T}z'e \xrightarrow{\text{D}} \mathbb{N}(0, \sigma^2\Sigma_{zz})$. The first condition requires that each instrument provides unique information; the second that at least k instruments correlate with the x; the third that the scaled sample orthogonality conditions evaluated at θ_0 converge to a normal distribution.

Exercise 5.7. Using the above three conditions, show that (5.11) implies

$$\sqrt{T}(\theta_{\text{IV}} - \theta_0) \xrightarrow{\text{D}} \mathbb{N}(0, \Sigma_\theta), \tag{5.12}$$

where $\Sigma_\theta = (\Sigma_{xz}W\Sigma_{zx})^{-1}\Sigma_{xz}W\sigma^2\Sigma_{zz}W'\Sigma_{zx}((\Sigma_{xz}W\Sigma_{zx})^{-1})'$ and $\Sigma_{zx} \equiv \Sigma_{xz}'$. Show that, when $k = n$, the expression simplifies to $\Sigma_\theta = (\Sigma_{xz}^{-1}\sigma^2\Sigma_{zz}\Sigma_{zx}^{-1})$.

Exercise 5.8. Suppose that rank $|\Sigma_{xz}| < k$. What does this tell you about your instruments? Would an IV approach work? Would the distribution in (5.12) be normal?

To summarize, θ_{IV} minimizes a quadratic form in $z'e(\theta)$. The estimator is consistent because $E[z'e(\theta)] = 0$ and asymptotically normal because all quantities converge to nonstochastic matrices. These same principles underlie GMM estimation and the analysis of its asymptotic properties.

Since both θ_{IV} and Σ_θ depend on W, it is natural to ask which W will lead to the most efficient θ_{IV}, i.e., the one which minimizes Σ_θ. Once such a W is found, W_T could be any sequence of matrices converging a.s. to W.

Exercise 5.9. Show that a solution to $\min_W \Sigma_\theta(W)$ is $W^\dagger = \sigma^{-2}\Sigma_{zz}^{-1}$ and that $\Sigma_\theta^\dagger \equiv \Sigma_\theta(W^\dagger) = \Sigma_{zx}^{-1}\sigma^2\Sigma_{zz}\Sigma_{xz}^{-1}$.

The optimal weighting matrix is therefore proportional to the asymptotic covariance matrix of the instruments. To gain intuition into this choice, note that different instruments contain different information about θ (because they have different variabilities). The optimal weighting matrix gives less weight to instruments which are very volatile.

When $n > k$, one can choose which conditions to use. If the first k restrictions are employed, the estimator (say, θ_{IV}^1) would be numerically different but has the same asymptotic properties of θ_{IV}^2 obtained by using, say, the last k conditions. The optimal weighting matrix combines the information contained in all conditions and maximizes efficiency.

Exercise 5.10. Consider the money demand function $M_t/p_t = \mathrm{GDP}_t\theta + e_t$, where θ is the inverse of the constant velocity and e_t appears because GDP_t could be measured with error or because variables such as the nominal interest rate are omitted. Since current GDP could be correlated with e_t, consider two sets of instruments $z_t^1 = [\mathrm{GDP}_{t-1}]$ and $z_t^2 = [\mathrm{GDP}_{t-1}, \mathrm{GDP}_{t-2}]$. Show that θ_{IV}^2 obtained by using z_t^2 is at least as efficient as θ_{IV}^1 obtained by using z_t^1. Give some intuition as to why it is the case. Provide conditions under which the asymptotic covariance matrix of the two estimators is identical.

When $W^\dagger$ is used, θ_{IV} becomes

$$\theta_{\mathrm{IV}}^\dagger = (\hat{x}'\hat{x})^{-1}\hat{x}'y, \tag{5.13}$$

where $\hat{x} = z(z'z)^{-1}z'x$. Consistent estimators of σ^2 and Σ_θ can be constructed by using $\hat{\sigma}^2 = (y - x\theta_{\mathrm{IV}}^\dagger)'(y - x\theta_{\mathrm{IV}}^\dagger)/T$ and the sample matrices $(1/T)\sum_t z_t'x_t$ and $(1/T)\sum_t z_t'z_t$. In general, we need an iterative approach to compute $W^\dagger$ since it depends on $\theta_{\mathrm{IV}}^\dagger$ via $\hat{\sigma}^{-2}$ and $\theta_{\mathrm{IV}}^\dagger$ depends on $W^\dagger$ via $(z'z)^{-1}$. Hence, we need to start with a suboptimal W_T, e.g., $W_T = I$ or $W_T \propto (1/T)\sum_t z_t'z_t$, and obtain a θ_{IV}^1, which is consistent although inefficient. Given θ_{IV}^1, we construct $W_T^\dagger$ and obtain θ_{IV}^2. Under regularity conditions, θ_{IV}^2 is equivalent to $\theta_{\mathrm{IV}}^\dagger$.

Exercise 5.11. Show that $\theta_{\mathrm{2SLS}} = [(x'z)(z'z)^{-1}(z'x)]^{-1}[(x'z)(z'z)^{-1}(z'y)]$ is identical to the optimal estimator in (5.13). Write down the orthogonality conditions and the g function in this case.

Extending these concepts to an $m \times 1$ vector of equations is straightforward and left as an exercise for the reader.

Exercise 5.12. Consider the model $\boldsymbol{Y} = (I \otimes \boldsymbol{X})\theta + e$, where $e \sim$ i.i.d. $(0, \Sigma_e)$, $\boldsymbol{Y}$ is an $N \times 1$ vector, $\boldsymbol{X}$ is a $1 \times k$ vector, and θ is an $Nk \times 1$ vector. Suppose we have available a $1 \times m$ vector $\boldsymbol{Z}$ and that we want to minimize $[(I \otimes \boldsymbol{Z})'e]W[(I \otimes \boldsymbol{Z})'e]'$. Show that $\theta_{\text{3SLS}} = ([(\boldsymbol{Z}'\boldsymbol{X}) \otimes I][\Sigma_e^{-1} \otimes (\boldsymbol{Z}'\boldsymbol{Z})^{-1}][I \otimes (\boldsymbol{Z}'\boldsymbol{X})])^{-1}[(\boldsymbol{Z}'\boldsymbol{X}) \otimes I] \times [\Sigma_e^{-1} \otimes (\boldsymbol{Z}'\boldsymbol{Z})^{-1}][(I \otimes \boldsymbol{Z})\boldsymbol{Y}]$ is the optimal GMM estimator obtained from the $mN \times 1$ vector of orthogonality conditions $E[(I \otimes \boldsymbol{Z})'e] = 0$. Show the form of the optimal W and of $\text{var}(\theta_{\text{3SLS}})$.

Example 5.8. As we saw in chapter 4, a VAR is a particular simultaneous equation system with the same regressors in every equation. Here the orthogonality conditions are $E[(I \otimes \boldsymbol{X})'e] = 0$ and $\theta_{\text{3SLS}} = \theta_{\text{SUR}}$.

Exercise 5.13. Consider the linear model

$$y = x\theta_1 + e, \quad e \sim (0, \sigma_e^2), \tag{5.14}$$

$$x = z\theta_2 + v, \quad v \sim (0, \sigma_v^2), \tag{5.15}$$

where y, x, e, v are $T \times 1$ vectors, z is a $T \times n$ matrix, θ_2 is an $n \times 1$ vector, and θ_1 is a scalar. Suppose that $E_t(v \mid z) = 0$, let $\theta_{1,\text{OLS}} = (x'x)^{-1}(x'y)$ and $\theta_{1,\text{IV}} = (\hat{x}'\hat{x})^{-1}(\hat{x}y)$.

(i) Show that $p\lim \theta_{1,\text{OLS}} = \theta_1 + \text{cov}(x, e)/\text{var}(x)$ and $p\lim \theta_{1,\text{IV}} = \theta_1 + \text{cov}(\hat{x}, e)/\text{var}(\hat{x})$. Argue that, unless $E_t(e \mid z) = 0$ and $E_t(x \mid z) \neq 0$, $p\lim \theta_{1,\text{IV}}$ may not exist.

(ii) Show that $\text{RI} = (\text{cov}(\hat{x}, e)/\text{cov}(x, e))/R_{xz}^2$, where R_{xz}^2 is the regression R^2 in (5.15), is the inconsistency of $\theta_{1,\text{IV}}$ relative to $\theta_{1,\text{OLS}}$.

(iii) Let $n = 1$. Show that, if z is weakly correlated with x, $RI \to \infty$ even if $E_t(e \mid z) = 0$.

For an instrumental variable approach to work well, instruments should be relevant and strong, in the sense that the correlation between z and x should be large. Weak instruments not only cause trouble in small samples, as shown in exercise 5.13. In fact, the asymptotic distribution of IV estimators may be different from normal if such a correlation is sufficiently small. One way to measure the size of this correlation is via the concentration statistics $\mathcal{S}_c = \theta_2' z' z \theta_2 / \sigma_v^2$, where θ_2 and σ_v^2 are the quantities appearing in (5.15). One intuitive interpretation of $\mathcal{S}_c$ is in terms of the F-statistics for testing $\theta_2 = 0$ in (5.15). In fact, $n \times F \sim \chi^2(n, \mathcal{S}_c)$ and $E(F) - 1 = \mathcal{S}_c/n$. Hence, large values of $\mathcal{S}_c/n$ shift the χ^2 distribution out, while small values make it nonnormal. Furthermore, when $\mathcal{S}_c/n = 0$, $p\lim \theta_{1,\text{IV}} = p\lim \theta_{1,\text{OLS}}$, while when $\mathcal{S}_c/n$ is small $p\lim \theta_{1,\text{IV}}$ is close to $p\lim \theta_{1,\text{OLS}}$.

One way to detect the presence of weak instruments is to examine whether the relative bias of IV (measured by the ratio $E(\theta_{1,\text{IV}} - \theta_1)/p\lim(\theta_{1,\text{OLS}} - \theta_1)$) exceeds some reference value (say, 10%). This is equivalent to testing whether $\mathcal{S}_c/n$ exceeds some threshold. For example, when θ_1 is a scalar and $n = 3, 5, 10$, the thresholds are 3.71, 5.82, 7.41, respectively (see, for example, Stock and Yogo 2001). Given these thresholds, the instruments are weak if the F-statistics do not exceed 9.08 ($n = 3$), 10.83 ($n = 5$), 11.49 ($n = 10$). When θ_1 is a vector, $\mathcal{S}_c/n$ is an $n \times n$ matrix and instruments are relevant and strong if the smallest eigenvalue of this matrix is large, a condition which also needs to be satisfied in more complicated frameworks (see section 5.5).

So far we have assumed that e_t are conditional homoskedastic. In some applications it is more reasonable to assume that $E_t[z_t'e_te_t'z_t]$ cannot be factored into the product of σ^2 and of Σ_{zz}. Most of the arguments made go through if $E_t[z_t'e_te_t'z_t] = \Sigma_{ez}$. However, to prove consistency and asymptotic normality we need to strengthen the assumptions to include the condition that $E(z'xx'z)$ exists and is finite (see Hayashi 2002, p. 212).

Exercise 5.14. Suppose $\lim_{T\to\infty} \sqrt{T}z'e \xrightarrow{\text{D}} \mathbb{N}(0, \Sigma_{ez})$. Derive the distribution of the optimal IV estimator. Provide an estimate for $W_T^\dagger$ and show the form of $\Sigma_\theta^\dagger$.

Example 5.9. A widely used statistical model with conditional heteroskedasticity is a linear regression model with GARCH errors. Here $y_t = x_t\theta_0 + e_t$ and $\text{var}(e_t) \equiv \sigma_t^2 = b_1\sigma_{t-1}^2 + e_t^2 + b_2e_{t-1}^2$. Since σ_t^2 depends on x_t, instruments correlated with the level of the regressors will make $E(z_t'e_t)(z_t'e_t)' \equiv \Sigma_t$ potentially time varying and serially correlated.

Exercise 5.15. Suppose that the true money demand function is $\ln M_t = \ln \text{CPI}_t + \ln \text{GDP}_t$ but an investigator erroneously used GDP deflator (GDPD) in place of CPI for measuring prices. In that case she estimates $\ln M_t = \theta_1 \ln \text{GDPD}_t + \theta_2 \ln \text{GDP}_t + e_t$, where e_t captures the differences between $\ln \text{CPI}_t$ and $\ln \text{GDPD}_t$. Guessing that some misspecification occurs, she estimates $\theta = (\theta_1, \theta_2)$ by using one lag of $\ln \text{GDPD}_t$ and $\ln \text{GDP}_t$ as instruments. Show the conditions under which the orthogonality conditions will display conditional heteroskedasticity. Are there conditions that make the orthogonality conditions serially uncorrelated?

In some applications, the condition that $E_t(g(y_t, \theta)) = 0$ is hard to maintain. For example, e_t may be serially correlated in which case $E(g_tg_{t-j}) \neq 0$, $j = 1, \dots$. The asymptotic distribution and the consistency proof are unchanged by this alteration. However, as in regression models with serially correlated errors, the asymptotic covariance matrix needs to be modified. We defer the presentation of such covariance matrices to a later section.

Example 5.10. Consider the problem of a representative agent who chooses how much to consume and save and at what maturities to lock her savings in. Assume that there are only one- and τ-period government bonds, issued in fixed supply every period, paying $(1+r_{jt})$ at time t, $j = 1, \tau$. The Euler equations are

$$E_t\left[\beta\frac{U_{c,t+1}}{U_{c,t}} - \frac{1}{1+r_{1t}}\right] = 0, \tag{5.16}$$

$$E_t\left[\beta^{\tau}\frac{U_{c,t+\tau}}{U_{c,t}} - \frac{1}{1+r_{\tau t}}\right] = 0. \tag{5.17}$$

These two conditions imply that the expected (at t) forward rate for $\tau-1$ periods must satisfy the no-arbitrage condition $E_t\beta^{\tau-1}[U_{c,t+\tau}/U_{c,t+1} - (1+r_{1t})/(1+r_{\tau t})] = 0$. Log-linearizing around the steady state, assuming a separable log utility and letting $y_{t+\tau} \equiv -\hat{c}_{t+\tau} + \hat{c}_{t+1}$, $x_t = (r_1/(1+r_1))\hat{r}_{1t} - (r_\tau/(1+r_\tau))\hat{r}_{\tau t}$, where the hat represents percentage deviations from the state, $y_{t+\tau} = \theta x_t + e_{t+\tau}$ and $\theta_0 = 1$. Here $E_t[e_{t+\tau}] = 0$; however, unless the sampling interval of the data equals the forward rate interval, $e_{t+\tau}$ will be serially correlated. For example, if data are monthly and τ is 12, e_t will display moving average terms of order 11.

Exercise 5.16. Suppose analysts are asked each quarter to produce output forecasts $\tau > 1$ periods ahead and suppose an investigator is asked to evaluate whether forecasts are rational or not. Let $y_{t+\tau}$ be realized output at $t+\tau$ and $y_t(\tau)$ be the forecast at t of $y_{t+\tau}$.

(i) Show that rationality implies orthogonality conditions with moving average terms of order up to τ.

(ii) Explain why GLS estimates obtained from $y_{t+\tau} = \theta_1 + \theta_2 y_t(\tau) + e_{t+\tau}$ are inconsistent.

(iii) Show that the asymptotic covariance matrix for $\theta = (\theta_1, \theta_2)$ is $[(1/T) \times \sum_t z_t' x_t]^{-1}[(1/T)\sum_t z_t' \Sigma z_t][(1/T)\sum_t x_t' z_t]$, where z_t are instruments, $\Sigma = \{\sigma_{ij}\}$ and $\sigma_{ij} = \sigma^2 \mathrm{ACF}(|i-j|)$ for $|i-j| < \tau$ and zero otherwise and $\mathrm{ACF}(|i-j|)$ is the $(i-j)$th element of the autocovariance function of $e_{t+\tau}$.

Exercise 5.17. In the context of example 5.10, consider the question of pricing a "crop insurance." Let $p_{t,\tau}(c_t, \theta)$ be the price at t in terms of consumption goods of a claim to consumption at $t+\tau$ if the crop c_t falls below θ. It is easy to verify that $p_{t,\tau}(c_t,\theta) = \beta^t \int_0^\theta (U_{c,t+\tau}/U_{c,t}) P_{t,t+\tau}\, \mathrm{d}c_{t+\tau}$, where $P_{t,t+\tau}$ is the probability of going from c_t to $c_{t+\tau}$. Show the pricing formula for a crop insurance of maturity up to 2. Conclude that the Euler equation for pricing crop insurance up to maturity τ has errors with up to $\tau - 1$ MA components.

Before testing hypotheses on θ, one may want to check whether the orthogonality conditions are correctly specified. For a simple regression setup, many tests for adequacy exist, e.g., tests for serial correlation, for heteroskedasticity, etc. In general setups, including those implied by DSGE models, the assumption that e_t are serially uncorrelated or homoskedastic cannot be made. Hence, we need a procedure to check model adequacy without focusing on these statistical features.

When $n = k$, $z'e(\theta) = 0$ by construction, so no test is possible. When $n > k$, only k linear combinations of $z'e(\theta)$ are set to zero so that $z'e(\theta_{\mathrm{IV}})$ may differ from zero.

Table 5.1. GMM estimates of a New Keynesian Phillips curve.

	Reduced form				Structural				
Country	α_1		α_2		β		ζ_p		J-test p-value
U.S.–Gap	0.99	(16.83)	−0.04	(−0.31)	0.90	(10.35)	0.700	(5.08)	$\chi^2(5) = 0.15$
U.S.–ULC	0.86	(10.85)	0.001	(1.75)	0.93	(7.74)	0.991	(150.2)	$\chi^2(9) = 0.54$
U.K.–Gap	0.66	(7.18)	0.528	(1.30)	0.92	(4.96)	0.684	(1.37)	NA
U.K.–ULC	0.41	(3.81)	0.004	(4.05)	0.85	(4.07)	0.994	(166.1)	$\chi^2(1) = 0.25$
GE–Gap	0.76	(10.02)	−0.01	(−0.22)	0.97	(7.48)	1.014	(0.03)	NA
GE–ULC	0.49	(3.34)	0.03	(1.85)	0.91	(4.45)	0.958	(7.18)	$\chi^2(1) = 0.83$

However, if the population conditions are true, one should expect $z'e(\theta_{\text{IV}}) \approx 0$. Hence, if $E[z'e(\theta_0)] = 0$, a specification test is $T \times [e(\theta_{\text{IV}}^{\dagger})'z] \times [\sigma^2 \Sigma_{zz}]^{-1} \times [z'e(\theta_{\text{IV}}^{\dagger})] \xrightarrow{\text{D}} \chi^2(n-k)$. (This is typically called a J-test.) Intuitively, since k conditions are used to obtain $\theta_{\text{IV}}^{\dagger}$, $n-k$ conditions are left free for testing. Hence, the number of degrees of freedom of the test equals the number of overidentifying restrictions. Note that consistent estimators can be used in place of the true σ^2 and Σ_{zz} without changing the distribution of the tests.

Tests of hypotheses on θ can be conducted in standard ways. We defer the discussion of general testing to a later section.

Example 5.11. In exercise 2.29 we asked the reader to verify that a log-linearized version of a New Keynesian Phillips curve in a model with no capital is

$$\pi_t = \beta E_t \pi_{t+1} + \frac{(1-\zeta_p)(1-\zeta_p\beta)}{\zeta_p}\text{mc}_t, \tag{5.18}$$

where $\text{mc}_t = N_t w_t/\text{GDP}_t$ are real marginal costs, ζ_p is the probability of not changing the prices, and π_t is the inflation rate. Clearly, (5.18) can be written as $E_t[g(y_t, \theta)] \equiv E_t\{\beta\pi_{t+1} - \pi_t + [(1-\zeta_p)(1-\zeta_p\beta)/\zeta_p]\text{mc}_t\} = 0$, which is an orthogonality condition. Also, since $E_t[g(y_t,\theta)] = g(y_t,\theta) + e_t$, where e_t is an expectational error, $E_t[g(y_t,\theta)z_t] = 0$ for any $z_t \in \mathcal{F}_t$. In earlier works, the marginal cost was proxied by the output gap and the parameters of the reduced-form regression $\pi_{t+1} = \alpha_1\pi_t + \alpha_2\text{gdpgap}_t + e_{t+1}$, where gdpgap_t is the difference between output and its potential, were estimated by using $z_t = (\pi_t, \text{gap}_t)$ as instruments. By using U.S. data, Gali and Gertler (1999) found α_2 to be negative and significant, contrary to the theory. However, when marginal costs were proxied by the labor share, estimates of α_2 were positive and significant.

We estimate (5.18) by using CPI inflation data for the United States, the United Kingdom, and Germany for the sample 1980:1–2000:4. Marginal costs are proxied with the output gap (computed by using a HP filter) or with unit labor costs (ULC). The first two columns of table 5.1 show that Gali and Gertler's conclusions roughly hold, even though the coefficient on unit labor costs in the United States is only marginally significant (t-tests are in parentheses). Columns 3 and 4 report IV estimates of ζ_{p} and β. Instruments include a constant, and up to nine lags of π_t and of the output gap (or of unit labor costs). In each case we report estimates which are most favorable to the theory. In many cases estimates obtained from just identified or overidentified specifications, where the optimal weighting matrix is used, are similar. Three main results stand out from the table. First, when the output gap is used, estimates of ζ_{p} are reasonable for the United States and the United Kingdom (they imply, on average, slightly less than three quarters between price changes) but not for Germany. Second, when unit labor costs are used estimates of ζ_{p} are close to 1, except for Germany, while estimates of β are smaller, indicating that the two parameters may not be separately identifiable. Third, despite the poor structural estimates, the model's orthogonality conditions are not rejected, probably because some instruments are poor. In fact, the concentration statistics for the four cases in the last column never exceed the critical threshold for instrument relevance.

5.3 GMM Estimation: An Overview

The machinery described in section 5.2 can be applied with slight variations to setups where the orthogonality conditions are nonlinear in θ.

Assume that g satisfies $E(E_t[g(y_t, \theta_0)]) = E[g(y_t, \theta_0)]$. Let $g_T(\theta) = (1/T) \times \sum_{t=1}^{T} g(y_t, \theta)$ and $h_T(\theta) = g_T(\theta) - g_\infty(\theta)$. The θ_T which minimizes $Q_T(\theta) = h_T(\theta)' W_T h_T(\theta)$ solves

$$H_T(\theta_T)' W_T h_T(\theta_T) = 0, \tag{5.19}$$

where $H_T(\theta_T)$ is an $n \times k$ matrix of rank k, $[H_T(\theta_T)]_{ij} = \partial h_{T_i}(\theta_T)/\partial\theta_j$, where $h_{T_i}(\theta_T)$ is the ith element of $h_T(\theta_T)$. When $n = k$ and $H_T(\theta_T)$ and W_T are nonsingular, θ_T solves $h_T(\theta_T) = 0$. When $k < n$, θ_T depends on W_T. To derive the asymptotic distribution of θ_T, we need a closed-form solution for θ_T, which, in general, is unavailable. Using the mean value theorem we can write (5.19) as

$$(\theta_T - \theta_0) = -[H_T(\bar\theta)' W_T H_T(\bar\theta)]^{-1} H_T(\bar\theta)' W_T h_T(\theta_0), \tag{5.20}$$

where $\bar\theta \in [\theta_0, \theta_T]$. To show that θ_T is consistent, the expression on the right-hand side of (5.20) must go to zero a.s. or in probability. To prove asymptotic normality we need to make assumptions on h_T so that $\lim_{T\to\infty} \sqrt{T} h_T(\theta_0) \xrightarrow{\text{D}} \mathbb{N}(0, \Sigma_h)$ and make sure that the other quantities in the right-hand side of (5.20) have finite, nonrandom limiting value. Then the asymptotic covariance matrix of θ_T is a multiple of Σ_h.

As in section 5.2, the optimal W_T minimizes the asymptotic covariance matrix of θ_T. Here the computation of $W_T^\dagger$ is also complicated by the fact that θ_T depends on $W_T^\dagger$ and $W_T^\dagger$ can be computed only if θ_T is known. With a large T, a two-step GMM is as efficient as fully iterative GMM if the first-step estimate converges to the true parameter at the rate $\sqrt{T}$ ($\sqrt{T}$-consistency). In small samples, iterative estimators may be more accurate.

To perform tests on θ_T we need a consistent estimate of the asymptotic covariance matrix. While $W_T \xrightarrow{\text{a.s.}} W$ by construction, and consistent estimators of H_T can easily be obtained, care is needed to get a consistent estimator of Σ_h which is positive semi-definite.

As in linear models, when θ is overidentified $h_T(\theta_T) \neq 0$, but if θ_T is "correct" $h_T(\theta_T) \approx 0$. Hence, if $h(\theta_0) = 0$, $T \times h_T(\theta_T)'\Sigma_h^{-1}h_T(\theta_T) \xrightarrow{\text{D}} \chi^2(n-k)$. General hypotheses can be tested by using Wald, Lagrange, or distance tests. In the next subsections we make these arguments more precise.

5.3.1 Asymptotics of GMM Estimators

The discussion here is sketchy and brief. For a more thorough presentation the reader should refer to Gallant (1987) or Newey and McFadden (1994). The conditions are general and need to be specialized when applied to orthogonality conditions derived from stationary DSGE models. Throughout this subsection we assume that there exists a θ_0 such that $h_T(\theta_0) \xrightarrow{\text{a.s.}} 0$ as $T \to \infty$ and that $\sqrt{T}h_T(\theta_0) \xrightarrow{\text{D}} \mathbb{N}(0, \Sigma_h)$. The first condition implies strong ergodicity of h_T; the second asymptotic normality of the difference between sample and population g functions.

To prove consistency we need three assumptions. First, that θ is in a closed and bounded set Θ. Second, that $h_T(\theta)$ is continuous and converges uniformly to $h(\theta)$ on Θ, a.s. Third, that θ_0 is the unique solution of $h(\theta) = 0$. Under these conditions $Q_T(\theta)$ converges uniformly on Θ to some $Q(\theta) = h'(\theta)Wh(\theta)$, which has a unique minimum at θ_0. Since we assumed that $h_T(\theta_0) \xrightarrow{\text{a.s.}} 0$, we have that $h(\theta_0) = 0$. Then, if θ_0 is the unique solution of $h(\theta) = 0$ on Θ, $Q(\theta)$ has a unique minimum and $\lim_{T\to\infty} \theta_T \xrightarrow{\text{a.s.}} \theta_0$.

Uniform convergence of $h_T(\theta)$ is hard to verify in practice. As an alternative, one typically assumes that $E[\sup_\theta \|h(y_t, \theta)\|] < \infty$—a condition that is easier to check. This, together with continuity of g in θ, measurability of g in y_t (i.e., g must be continuous in y_t for each θ), and the uniform law of large numbers, can be used to show that $h_T(\theta)$ converges uniformly to $h(\theta)$. Compactness of Θ is also hard to obtain in practice (it requires knowing the upper and lower bounds of the parameter space). The alternative assumption typically made—that the objective function is concave together with pointwise convergence of $h_T(\theta)$ to $h(\theta)$ (see Newey and McFadden 1994, p. 2133)—is not very appealing since in general $h_T(\theta)$ may not be concave. Another alternative (see Gallant 1987) is to impose restrictions on the tails of the distribution of h_T and to show that, for large T, they imply that θ will lie in a closed and bounded set for all $t \geqslant T$.

To specialize this theorem to the setup generated by DSGE models, we need to ensure $h_T(\theta_0) \xrightarrow{\text{a.s.}} 0$ and that $\sqrt{T}h_T(\theta_0) \xrightarrow{\text{D}} \mathbb{N}(0, \Sigma_h)$. If y_t is stationary and ergodic and if g is continuous, then g_t is also stationary and ergodic. Furthermore, the sum of stationary and ergodic processes is also stationary and ergodic, so that $h_T(\theta_0) \xrightarrow{\text{a.s.}} 0$ (see chapter 1). If y_t is stationary and g_t is a martingale difference, the martingale central limit theorem ensures that $\sqrt{T}g_T(\theta_0) \xrightarrow{\text{D}} \mathbb{N}(0, \text{var}[g(y_t, \theta_0)])$ and, if

$g_\infty \equiv 0$, $\sqrt{T}h_T(\theta_0) \xrightarrow{\text{D}} \mathbb{N}(0, \Sigma_h)$. Recall that the martingale difference assumption is weaker than independence: it requires only first moment independence.

Exercise 5.18. Let $y_t = x_t\theta + e_t$, where (y_t, x_t) are jointly stationary and ergodic sequences, $E(x_t'e_t) = 0$, $E(x_t'x_t) = \Sigma_{xx} < \infty$, $|\Sigma_{xx}| \neq 0$. Show $\theta_{\text{OLS}} \xrightarrow{\text{a.s.}} \theta_0$. How does the proof differ from the case where observations are i.i.d.?

In certain applications the assumption of identically (homogeneously) distributed time series is implausible. (Can you give an example when this is the case?) In this case, one substitutes the stationarity–ergodicity assumptions for y_t with some mixing requirement.

Exercise 5.19. State conditions for $\theta_{2\text{SLS}} = [x'z(z'z)^{-1}z'x]^{-1}(x'z)(z'z)^{-1}z'y$ to be consistent in the model $y_t = x_t\theta + e_t$, where x_t is a $(1 \times k)$ vector, z_t is a $(1 \times n)$, $k < n$, and when y_t, x_t, z_t satisfy α-mixing conditions.

To show asymptotic normality we need a few more assumptions: first, that θ_0 is in the interior of Θ; second, that $H_T(\theta) = \partial h_T(\theta)/\partial\theta'$ is continuous and converges uniformly to $H(\theta)$; third, that $H(\theta)$ is full rank (in addition to the fact that $\theta_T \xrightarrow{\text{a.s.}} \theta_0$). The first assumption makes the Taylor expansion presented below well-behaved. The second ensures that the partial derivatives of h_T carry proper information for θ. For the ith row of $h_T(\theta)$ we have

$$\sqrt{T}h_{i,T}(\theta_T) = \sqrt{T}h_{i,T}(\theta_0) + \frac{\partial h_{iT}(\bar{\theta})}{\partial\theta'}\sqrt{T}(\theta_T - \theta_0), \tag{5.21}$$

where $\bar{\theta} \in [\theta_0, \theta_T]$. Because $\bar{\theta}$ is in the line segment joining θ_0 and θ_T, and because $\theta_T \xrightarrow{\text{a.s.}} \theta_0$ we also have $\bar{\theta} \xrightarrow{\text{a.s.}} \theta_0$. Moreover, given the assumptions, the typical row of $H_T(\theta)$ converges uniformly over Θ to $H(\theta_0)$. Applying the argument to each row we have that $\sqrt{T}h_T(\theta_T) = \sqrt{T}h_T(\theta_0) + H(\theta_0)\sqrt{T}(\theta_T - \theta_0)$. Substituting in (5.19) we have

$$0 = H_T(\theta_T)'W_T\sqrt{T}h_T(\theta_0) + H_T(\theta_T)'W_T H(\theta_0)\sqrt{T}(\theta_T - \theta_0). \tag{5.22}$$

Because $H_T(\theta_T)'W_T \xrightarrow{\text{a.s.}} H(\theta_0)'W$ and $\sqrt{T}h_T(\theta_0) \xrightarrow{\text{D}} \mathbb{N}(0, \Sigma_h)$, we have that $H_T(\theta_T)'W_T\sqrt{T}h_T(\theta_0) \xrightarrow{\text{D}} \mathbb{N}(0, H(\theta)'W\Sigma_h W'H(\theta))$. Furthermore, $H_T(\theta_T)' \times W_T H(\theta_0) \xrightarrow{\text{a.s.}} H(\theta_0)'WH(\theta_0)$. Therefore, $\sqrt{T}(\theta_T - \theta_0) \xrightarrow{\text{D}} \mathbb{N}(0, \Sigma_\theta)$, where $\Sigma_\theta = [H(\theta_0)'WH(\theta_0)]^{-1}H(\theta_0)'W\Sigma_h W'H(\theta_0)([H(\theta_0)'WH(\theta_0)]^{-1})'$, which simplifies to $\Sigma_\theta^\dagger = [H(\theta_0)'\Sigma_h^{-1}H(\theta_0)]^{-1}$ when $W^\dagger = \Sigma_h^{-1}$.

To intuitively understand the proof of asymptotic normality, note that we need to translate knowledge of $h_T(\theta)$ into information about $\theta_T - \theta_0$. For this to happen we need conditions so that the mapping is well-defined. In particular, we need that (i) h_T is differentiable for all y_t and (ii) H_T is such that $H_T(\theta_T)$ and $H_T(\theta_0)$ do not differ too much. While these conditions appear to be generally satisfied, it is easy to build examples where they are not.

Example 5.12. Suppose $P[y_t > \theta] = 0.5, \forall t$, where θ is the median, and let

$$g(y_t, \theta) = \begin{cases} 1 & \text{if } y_t > \theta, \\ -1 & \text{if } y_t < \theta, \\ 0 & \text{if } y_t = \theta. \end{cases}$$

If $g_T(\theta) = \sum_{t=1}^{T} g(y_t, \theta)$, then $E(g(\theta)) = 0$ and $g_T(\theta_T) = 0$. However, the g function has discrete jumps. Since the discontinuity does not get smaller as $T \to \infty$, information about $h_T(\theta)$ cannot be transformed into information about θ.

Continuity and uniform convergence of $H_T(\theta)$ ensure that pathologies like those in example 5.12 do not occur.

The assumptions that there exists a unique zero to $h(\theta) = 0$ and that $H(\theta)$ is full rank require some comments. Both are identifying assumptions. The first globally excludes the presence of multiple zeros in the objective function. The second excludes the possibility that some of the parameters are underidentified. In fact, if the rank of $H(\theta)$ is less than the dimension of the parameter space, at least one of the parameters is underidentified.

Exercise 5.20. Show the asymptotic covariance matrix of the NLLS estimator by using the formula $(H(\theta_0)' \Sigma_h^{-1} H(\theta_0))^{-1}$. Show that, for an ML estimator, $\Sigma_\theta = -H(\theta_0)^{-1}$.

5.3.2 Estimating the Covariance Matrix

We have seen that, when $W^\dagger = \Sigma_h^{-1}$, $\Sigma_\theta^\dagger = [H(\theta_0)' \Sigma_h^{-1} H(\theta_0)]^{-1}$. Estimates of $H(\theta)$ and Σ_h can be obtained by using $(1/T) \sum_t [\partial h_t(\theta_T)/\partial \theta_T']$ and $(1/T) \times \sum_{t=1}^{T} h_t h_t'$. When g_t is not a martingale difference, the central limit theorem for serially correlated processes (see chapter 1) can be used to show that the asymptotic covariance matrix is $\Sigma_\theta^+ = [H(\theta_0)'(\Sigma_h^+)^{-1} H(\theta_0)]^{-1}$ when $W = (\Sigma_h^+)^{-1}$. Here Σ_h^+ is the frequency zero of the spectrum of h_t and can be estimated by using the autocorrelations of h_t, i.e., $\hat{\Sigma}^+ = \sum_{\tau=-\infty}^{\infty} T^{-1} \sum_t h_t h_{t-\tau}'$.

When deviations from the martingale assumption are of known form, one should use this information in constructing an estimate of Σ_h^+. The next exercise examines situations where g_t is linear, covering the cases studied by Hansen and Hodrick (1980), Hansen and Singleton (1982), Cumby et al. (1982), and Hansen and Sargent (1982).

Exercise 5.21. Let $g_t = [e_t \otimes z_t]$, where $\otimes$ is the Kronecker product, e_t is a vector of residuals, and z_t a vector of instruments, and let $g_\infty = 0$.

(i) (Serial correlation up to lag τ and conditional homoskedasticity.) Suppose that $E_t[e_t \mid z_t, e_{t-\tau}, z_{t-1}, e_{t-\tau-1}, \ldots] = 0$. Show that the g_t function satisfies $E_t[g_t \mid g_{t-\tau}, g_{t-\tau-1}, \ldots] = 0$. Let $E[e_t e_{t-\tau} \mid z_t, e_{t-\tau}, z_{t-\tau}, \ldots] = \text{ACF}_e(\tau)$. Show that $\Sigma_h^+ = \sum_{i=-\tau+1}^{\tau-1} \text{ACF}_e(i) \otimes \text{ACF}_z(i)$.

(ii) (Serial correlation up to lag τ and conditional heteroskedasticity.) Let $E_t[e_t \mid z_t, e_{t-\tau}, z_t, e_{t-\tau-1}, \ldots] = 0$ and $E[g_t g'_{t-\tau}] = \text{ACF}_{ez}(\tau)$. Show that $\Sigma_h^+ = \sum_{i=-\tau+1}^{\tau-1} \text{ACF}_{ez}(i)$. Show the form of a typical element of $\text{ACF}_{ez}(i)$.

As we have seen, there are cases when the residuals of the orthogonality conditions display serial correlation of known form. Two were described in section 5.2; one more is considered next.

Exercise 5.22 (Eichenbaum, Hansen, and Singleton). Suppose that a representative agent ranks consumption and leisure streams according to $E \sum_t \beta^t \times (\{[(1+\gamma_1\ell)c_t]^{\vartheta}[(1+\gamma_2\ell)(1-N_t)]^{1-\vartheta}\}^{1-\varphi} - 1)/(1-\varphi)$ subject to the constraint $c_t + \text{sa}_{t+1} = w_t N_t + (1+r_t)\text{sa}_t$, where sa_t are savings and $w_t N_t$ is labor income, γ_1, γ_2 are habit parameters.

Derive the optimal intratemporal consumption/leisure condition and the Euler equation for capital accumulation. Show that, if these relationships are used to estimate the unknown parameters, the g_t function is not a martingale difference. Show exactly the serial correlation structure present. Construct a covariance matrix for the GMM estimator which takes this correlation structure into account.

In general, the presence of adjustment costs, time nonseparability in the utility function, multiperiod forecasts, or time aggregation (see Hansen and Singleton 1988) may produce orthogonality conditions which display serial correlation of known form.

When serial correlation is of unknown form and T is finite, one is forced to estimate Σ_h^+ by truncating the infinite sum, that is, one uses $\Sigma_T^+ = \text{ACF}(0) + \sum_{i=1}^{J(T)}[\text{ACF}(i) + \text{ACF}(i)'] = \sum_{i=-\infty}^{\infty} \mathcal{K}(i, J(T))\,\text{ACF}(i)$, where $J(T)$ is a function of T controlling the number of covariances included and $\mathcal{K}(i, J(T))$ is the box-car kernel (see chapter 1). The truncation clearly biases Σ_T^+, but the bias vanishes reasonably fast as $T \to \infty$ (see Priestley 1981, p. 458). Unfortunately, for arbitrary $J(T)$, Σ_T^+ need not be positive semi-definite. Newey and West (1987) propose to use the Bartlett kernel: $\mathcal{K}(i, J(T)) = 1 - i/(J(T)+1)$ in the computations since it ensures that Σ_T^+ is positive semi-definite. This kernel truncates after $J(T)$ but also reduces the importance of included elements by using weights that decline with i. Since Σ_h^+ gives unitary weights to all ACF elements, this kernel induces an additional source of bias, which typically dominates the one induced by truncation.

In general, the properties of Σ_T^+ depend on the way $J(T)$ is chosen. With the Bartlett kernel, if $J(T) \to \infty$ as $T \to \infty$ and $J(T)/T^{1/3} \to 0$, $\Sigma_T^+ \xrightarrow{\text{P}} \Sigma$. That is, the biases introduced by the Bartlett kernel reduce the convergence rate of Σ_T^+ from $T^{1/2}$ to $T^{1/3}$. This means that, for the typical samples available in macroeconomics, covariance estimates computed with this kernel may be far away from the true Σ_h. Since $W^{\dagger} = \Sigma_h^{-1}$, poor small-sample estimates of Σ_T^+ may result in poor small-sample properties of optimal GMM estimators. Furthermore, if Σ_T^+ has a large bias or a large MSE in finite samples, inference may be severely distorted. For example, t-tests may over reject the null.

Nowadays, it has become common to construct heteroskedasticity and autocorrelation consistent (HAC) covariance matrices. HAC estimates are typically of two types: kernel based (nonparametric) and parametric based. In both cases a number of choices, which may influence the properties of estimates, must be made.

Algorithm 5.1 (kernel-based HAC).

(1) Obtain an estimate of the orthogonality conditions by filtering out some serial correlation.

(2) Given a kernel, choose the bandwidth parameter $J(T)$.

(3) Provide estimates of unknown optimal quantities in (2).

(4) Calculate the spectral density of the orthogonality conditions obtained in (1).

(5) Calculate HAC-consistent estimates of the original orthogonality conditions.

When the orthogonality conditions display autocorrelation of unknown form, it is good practice to eliminate part of this correlation before Σ_T^+ is calculated. The reason is simple. When $h_T(\theta)$ is serially correlated it will have a nonflat spectrum. Kernel estimators average the spectrum of $h_T(\theta)$ over an interval of frequencies. Priestley (1981, p. 458) showed that, if one estimates a function $f(\theta)$ at θ_0, averaging it at a number of points in a neighborhood of θ_0, the estimator is unbiased only if $f(\theta)$ is flat over the neighborhood. Otherwise, the bias depends on the degree of nonconstancy of $f(\theta)$. Hence, if we filter $h_T(\theta)$, so that it has a flatter spectrum in the required interval, a kernel-based estimator will have much better properties. Since the purpose of filtering is not to whiten h_t but only to reduce serial correlation, a researcher regresses h_t on an arbitrary number of lags (typically, one).

We presented a number of kernel estimators in chapter 1. The HAC literature has concentrated on three: the Bartlett kernel, the Parzen kernel (see Gallant 1987), and the quadratic spectral (QS) kernel (see Andrews 1991). In all cases the choice of $J(T)$ is crucial. It can be selected by using a rule of thumb, e.g., $J(T) = T^{1/3}$, or optimally, by requiring that Σ_T^+ is positive definite. It turns out that choosing $J(T)$ is equivalent to selecting $J_2(w_0)$ in $J(T) = J_1(w_0)[J_2(w_0)T]^{1/(2w_0+1)}$, where w_0 is the rate of convergence of the kernel (which is equal to 2 for Parzen and QS kernels and 1 for the Bartlett kernel). Since Σ_T^+ is consistent but asymptotically biased, optimization requires choosing $J_2(w_0)$ to minimize the expectations of $\text{vec}(\Sigma_T^+ - \Sigma^+)' \mathcal{W} \, \text{vec}(\Sigma_T^+ - \Sigma^+)$, given a weighting matrix $\mathcal{W}$. Because of this bias, the resulting estimator is not asymptotically efficient. When $\mathcal{W}$ is diagonal and $\mathcal{W}_{ii} = \text{vec}(ww')_{ii}$, the optimal bandwidth parameter is $J_2(w_0) = [w'(\Sigma^{w_0})w/w'\Sigma w]^2$ (see Den Haan and Levin 1996, pp. 9–10), where $\Sigma^{(w_0)} = \sum_\tau |\tau|^{w_0} T^{-1} \sum_t h_t h_{t-\tau}$ is the w_0th derivative of Σ_T^+ and measures its smoothness around frequency 0; $J_1(w_0) = 1.1447$ if $w_0 = 1$ and $J_1(w_0) = 1.3221$ if $w_0 = 2$.

It turns out that among the kernels which generate positive semi-definite estimators, the QS is optimal (Andrews 1991). Two features of this kernel should be emphasized: first, it does not truncate the ACF of h_t; second, since the weights it gives to elements within $\pm J(T)$ are larger than those given by, for example, the Bartlett kernel, the second source of bias is also reduced. This bias reduction is important: Σ_T^+ now converges to Σ^+ faster than with the Bartlett kernel ($T^{2/5}$ versus $T^{1/3}$). Simulation experiments, however, suggest that the small-sample performance of the two kernels is roughly similar and that the choice of $J(T)$ is what matters most.

In step (3) we need estimates of Σ_0^w and Σ (the optimal choice of $J_2(w_0)$ is nonoperative). There are two approaches in the literature: Andrews and Mohanan (1992) estimate AR(1) representations for the filtered orthogonality conditions and use these estimates to obtain an estimate of $J_2(w_0)$. In this case, $\hat{J}_2(w_0) = \sum_i W_i 4\hat{\rho}_i^2\hat{\sigma}_i^4(1-\hat{\rho}_i)^{-6}(1+\hat{\rho})^{-2}/\sum_i W_i\hat{\sigma}_i^4(1-\hat{\rho}_i)^{-4}$ for $w_0 = 1$ and $\hat{J}_2(w_0) = \sum_j w_j 4\hat{\rho}_j^2\hat{\sigma}_j^4(1-\hat{\rho}_j)^{-8}/\sum_j w_j\hat{\sigma}_j^4(1-\hat{\rho}_j)^{-4}$ for $w_0 = 2$, where $\hat{\rho}_j$ ($\hat{\sigma}_j$) is an estimate of the AR(1) coefficient (standard deviation of the error) for the filtered condition j. Newey and West (1994) instead choose an automatic procedure which depends on T and on one (arbitrary) parameter. Here $\hat{\Sigma}_0^w = \sum_{\tau=-J(T)}^{J(T)} |\tau|^{w_0} \times (1/T)\sum_t e_t e'_{t-\tau}$, where e_t are the filtered orthogonality conditions obtained in (1), $J(T) = b_1(0.01T)^{2/9}$ for $w_0 = 1$, $J(T) = b_2(0.01T)^{2/25}$ for $w_0 = 2$, $b_1 = 4$ or 12, and $b_2 = 3$ or 4.

Once an optimal kernel is obtained (call it $\mathcal{K}^\dagger(i, J(T))$), an estimate of the covariance matrix of the filtered error e_t is $\Sigma_e^\dagger = \sum_i \mathcal{K}^\dagger(i, J(T))(1/T)\sum_t e_t e'_{t-i}$ and an estimate of the covariance matrix of the original conditions is $\Sigma_T^\dagger = (I_N - \sum_i A_i)^{-1}\Sigma_e^\dagger[(I_N - \sum_i A_i)^{-1}]'$, where A_i are the ith AR coefficients obtained in step (1).

There are two important features of kernel-based HAC estimates worth mentioning. First, $J(T)$ must grow with the sample size for the resulting estimator to be consistent. This is unfortunate since it forces the bandwidth parameter to grow with T even when the serial correlation of h_t is known to be finite. Second, even optimal kernel estimators converge slowly. Hence, they may have worse small-sample properties than a parametric estimator (which converges at the rate $\sqrt{T}$).

Algorithm 5.2 (parametric HAC).

(1) For each j, specify a VAR for h_{jt} and select the order of the VAR optimally.

(2) Calculate the spectral density of the "prewhiten" orthogonality conditions.

(3) Calculate HAC-consistent estimates of the original orthogonality conditions.

In step (1) one specifies the autoregression $h_{jt} = \sum_i \sum_\tau A_{i\tau} h_{it-\tau} + e_{jt}$ and chooses the lag length by using information criteria (see chapter 4). Note that the same number of lags of each h_{it} enter the autoregression of h_{jt}. Den Haan and Levin (1996) show that starting the search process from $\bar{\tau} = T^{1/3}$ produces consistent estimates. Once white noise residuals are obtained, an estimate of Σ_e is $\Sigma_e^+ = (1/T)\sum_t e_t e'_t$ and $\Sigma_T^+ = (I_N - \sum A_\tau)^{-1}\Sigma_e^+[(I_N - \sum A_\tau)^{-1}]'$.

Note that, in the parametric approach, the question of positive definiteness does not arise since Σ_T^+ is positive definite by construction. Also, because the parametric estimator produces smaller biases than kernel estimators, it has better convergence properties.

Example 5.13. Suppose that h_t has two components. Then prewhitening works as follows. For each $i = 1, 2$ determine the lag length of $A_{i1}(\ell)$ and $A_{i2}(\ell)$ in $h_{it} = A_{i1}(\ell)h_{it-1} + A_{i2}(\ell)h_{i't-1} + e_{it}, i \neq i'$, which could be different for different i. Collect the two equations into a VAR and transform it into a companion form $\mathbb{Y}_t = \mathbb{A}\mathbb{Y}_{t-1} + \mathbb{E}_t$. Then, $\text{var}(\mathbb{E}_t) = \Sigma_E$, $\text{var}(\mathbb{Y}_t) = (I - \mathbb{A})^{-1}\Sigma_E((I - \mathbb{A})^{-1})'$, and $\text{cov}(\mathbb{Y}_t, \mathbb{Y}_{t-\tau}) = \mathbb{A}^\tau \text{var}(\mathbb{Y}_t)$.

5.3.3 Optimizing the Asymptotic Covariance Matrix

There are a number of ways to make GMM estimators efficient. For example, one can choose W to minimize the asymptotic covariance matrix of θ. As in the linear case, if h_t is a martingale difference, it is optimal to set $W^\dagger = [E(h_t h_t')]^{-1}$, with the obvious adjustments if serial correlation is present.

As mentioned, DSGE models typically deliver orthogonality conditions of the form $E[e(y_t, \theta) \mid z_t] = 0$, where z_t is a set of instruments in the agent's information set and e_t are the residuals of an Euler equation. This restriction implies that $E[z_t' e(y_t, \theta)] = 0$ but also that $E[\mathfrak{H}(z_t)' e(y_t, \theta)] = 0$ for any measurable function $\mathfrak{H}$. What is the optimal $\mathfrak{H}$?

Let $g(y_t, \theta) = \mathfrak{H}(z_t)' e(y_t, \theta)$ and assume $g_\infty(\theta) = 0$. Under the conditions of section 5.3.1, $\text{var}[\sqrt{T}(\theta_T - \theta_0)] = (H\Sigma_h^{-1}H')^{-1} = \{E[(\partial e_t/\partial\theta')'\mathfrak{H}(z_t)]^{-1} \times E[\mathfrak{H}(z_t)'\mathfrak{H}(z_t)]E[\mathfrak{H}(z_t)'(\partial e_t/\partial\theta')]\}^{-1}\sigma_e^2$.

The expression in braces is the inverse of the population covariance matrix of the predicted values of a linear regression of $\partial e_t/\partial\theta$ on $\mathfrak{H}(z_t)$. Therefore, to minimize $\text{var}(\theta_T)$, one should select $\mathfrak{H}$ to maximize the correlation between $\mathfrak{H}(z_t)$ and $\partial e_t/\partial\theta$.

Exercise 5.23. Show that it is optimal to set $\mathfrak{H}(z_t) = E[(\partial e_t/\partial\theta)(y_t, \theta_0) \mid z_t]$. (Hint: any other function will produce a covariance matrix $\tilde{\Sigma}_\theta$ such that $\tilde{\Sigma}_\theta - \Sigma_\theta$ is positive semi-definite.)

Intuitively, the result of exercise 5.23 obtains because the best MSE predictor of a sequence of random variables is its conditional expectation. There are a few features of this result that need to be emphasized. First, the optimal $\mathfrak{H}(z_t)$ is nonunique up to a nonsingular linear transformation of the relationship. Second, a consistent θ_T is typically used to calculate the derivative of e. Third, if $e(y_t, \theta_0)$ is independent of z_t, then for every pair of continuous and measurable functions $\mathfrak{H}_1, \mathfrak{H}_2$ such that $E[\mathfrak{H}_1(e(y_t, \theta_0))] = 0$, $\tilde{g} = \mathfrak{H}_2(z_t)'\mathfrak{H}_1(e(y_t, \theta_0))$ is a potential choice of g function.

Exercise 5.24. Find the optimal $(\mathfrak{H}_1, \mathfrak{H}_2)$ pair in the above problem.

Exercise 5.25. Let $y_t^{\theta_0} = \theta_1 + \theta_2 x_t + e_t$. Assume $E[\mathfrak{H}(z_t)' e_t] = 0$, where $\mathfrak{H}(z_t) \equiv E[\partial e_t/\partial\theta' \mid z_t]$.

(i) Show that an NLIV estimator of $\theta = [\theta_0, \theta_1, \theta_2]$ obtained by using z_t differs from an NLLS estimator obtained by using x_t as the instrument. (Hint: NLLS solves $(1/T)\sum_t[\mathfrak{H}(x_t)'e_t] = 0$.)

(ii) Show that the NLLS estimator is also different from an ML estimator.

(iii) Show that the NLLS estimator is inconsistent.

In many applications, the density $f(y \mid \theta)$ of the endogenous variables cannot be calculated. However, it is possible to simulate a $\{y_t\}$ sequence and compute approximations to the moments of $f(y \mid \theta)$ by using some law of large numbers (see section 5.5). Hence, there are cases where ML is not applicable but GMM is. Since θ_{ML} typically has the smallest asymptotic covariance matrix in the class of estimators which are consistent and asymptotically normal, one may want to know whether it is possible to construct a θ_T which is as efficient as θ_{ML}. In other words, among all possible orthogonality conditions, which ones have the most information for the parameters? Gallant and Tauchen (1996) show that such orthogonality conditions are the scores of each observation.

Example 5.14. Let y_t be i.i.d. with known density $f(y_t \mid \theta)$. Let θ_T be the GMM estimator associated with orthogonality conditions of the form $E(g_t(\theta, y_t)) = 0$ and suppose Σ_θ is its asymptotic covariance matrix. Since ML is efficient $\Sigma_\theta \geqslant -T^{-1}E[\partial^2 \ln f(y_t \mid \theta)/\partial\theta\partial\theta']^{-1}$ with equality holding whenever $g_t(\theta) = \partial \ln f(y_t \mid \theta)/\partial\theta$. Hence, the most efficient GMM estimator solves $(1/T) \times \sum_t \partial \ln f(y_t \mid \theta)/\partial\theta' = 0$.

Exercise 5.26. Suppose that y_t is serially correlated. How would you modify the argument of example 5.14 to fit this case?

5.3.4 Sequential GMM Estimation

There are many applied situations where θ can be naturally separated into two blocks, $\theta = (\theta_1, \theta_2)$, and one may consider sequential estimation of the two sets of parameters or estimation of θ_1 conditional on θ_2. Two cases where this may occur are presented next. Another will appear in section 5.4.

Example 5.15. Consider ML estimation of the parameters of $y_t = x_t\theta + e_t$, $e_t \sim$ i.i.d. $(0, \Sigma_e)$. One common procedure is to get a consistent Σ_e, concentrate the likelihood, and then estimate θ. However, unless x_t is strictly exogenous, the standard formula for Σ_θ obtained by using this approach is incorrect — we need to account for the correlation of x_t and e_t.

Example 5.16. Consider the Euler equation for capital accumulation (5.3). Here β, δ, and the marginal product of capital f_K are unknown. Since β is typically hard to estimate, one may want to fix it and use (5.3) to get GMM estimates of the real return to capital $f_K + (1 - \delta)$. Alternatively, one could use extraneous information to get an estimate of f_K, and use (5.3) to estimate δ and β. In both cases, taking first-stage estimates as if they were the true ones may distort asymptotic standard errors.

Using a GMM approach, it is easy to see what kind of adjustments need to be made. Let $g_T(\theta_1, \theta_2) = (1/T)\sum_{t=1}^{T} g(y_t, \theta_1, \theta_2)$ and $g_\infty(\theta_1, \theta_2) = 0$. When θ_2 is known to be equal to θ_{20}, the asymptotic distribution of θ_{1T} is obtained by using the results of section 5.3.1.

Exercise 5.27. Suppose that $\theta_2 = \theta_{20}$ is known and that (i) $g(y_t, \theta_{10}, \theta_{20})$ is a martingale difference process, $g(y_t, \cdot, \cdot)$ is continuous in the second and third arguments, where θ_{10} is a $k_1 \times 1$ vector; (ii) y_t is stationary and ergodic; (iii) $E[g(y_t, \theta_{10}, \theta_{20})g(y_t, \theta_{10}, \theta_{20})'] = \Sigma_1 < \infty$; (iv) $\theta_{1T} \xrightarrow{\text{a.s.}} \theta_{10}$; (v) $\partial g_T/\partial\theta'$ is uniformly continuous and convergent to $E(\partial g/\partial\theta')$, which is full rank. Show that $\sqrt{T}(\theta_{1T} - \theta_{10}) \xrightarrow{\text{D}} \mathbb{N}(0, \Sigma_{\theta_1})$. Show the form of Σ_{θ_1}.

When both θ_{10} and θ_{20} are unknown, let (i)–(iii) of exercise 5.27 be satisfied and assume that (iv) $\theta_{1T} \xrightarrow{\text{a.s.}} \theta_{10}$, $\theta_{2T} \xrightarrow{\text{a.s.}} \theta_{20}$; (v) $E[\partial h(y_t, \theta_{10}, \theta_{20})/\partial\theta_1', \partial h(y_t, \theta_{10}, \theta_{20})/\partial\theta_2'] = [H_{10}, H_{20}]$; $|H_{10}| \neq 0$, where H_{10} and H_{20} are $n \times k_1$ and $n \times k_2$ matrices; (vi) $[\partial h/\partial\theta_1', \partial h/\partial\theta_2']$ are continuous at θ_{10}, θ_{20} and uniformly convergent to $[H_{10}, H_{20}]$; (vii) $\sqrt{T}(\theta_{2T} - \theta_{20}) \xrightarrow{\text{D}} \mathbb{N}(0, \Sigma_2)$.

Exercise 5.28. Show that under (i)–(vii) $\sqrt{T}(\theta_{1T} - \theta_{10}) \xrightarrow{\text{D}} \mathbb{N}(0, (H_{10}')^{-1}\Sigma_1 H_{10}^{-1} + (H_{10}')^{-1} H_{20}' \Sigma_2 H_{20} H_{10}^{-1})$. (Hint: take the Taylor expansion of the objective function around $(\theta_{10}, \theta_{20})$ and make sure all the quantities converge to nonstochastic limits.)

Exercise 5.28 shows how the asymptotic covariance matrix of θ_{1T} needs to be adjusted when θ_2 has been estimated. There is one situation when the adjustment is superfluous: if the marginal distribution of θ_1 does not depend on θ_2, $H_{20} = 0$ and $\sqrt{T}(\theta_{1T} - \theta_{10}) \xrightarrow{\text{D}} \mathbb{N}(0, (H_{10}')^{-1}\Sigma_1 H_{10}^{-1})$. Hence, sequential estimation does not distort the standard errors of θ_{1T}.

One simple case where the machinery of this section is applicable is the following.

Example 5.17. The literature suggests two ways of estimating (ρ, θ) in the model

$$y_t = x_t\theta + e_t, \tag{5.23}$$

$$e_t = \rho e_{t-1} + \epsilon_t, \quad \epsilon_t \sim \text{i.i.d. } (0, \sigma^2). \tag{5.24}$$

(i) Generalized least squares: $\theta_{\text{GLS}} = (x'\Sigma_e^{-1}x)^{-1}(x'\Sigma_e^{-1}y)$, where $\Sigma_e = (\sigma^2/(1-\rho)^2)V$, where V is

$$\begin{bmatrix} 1 & \rho & \cdots & \rho^{T-1} \\ \rho & 1 & \cdots & \rho^{T-2} \\ \vdots & \vdots & \ddots & \vdots \\ \rho^{T-1} & \rho^{T-2} & \cdots & 1 \end{bmatrix}.$$

(ii) Estimate ρ_{OLS} in (5.24) by using $e_{\text{OLS},t} = y_t - x_t\theta_{\text{OLS}}$. Transform (5.23) to $y_t - \rho_{\text{OLS}} y_{t-1} = (x_t - \rho_{\text{OLS}} x_{t-1})\theta + \epsilon_t$, apply OLS to get $\theta_{2\text{step}} = (X'X)'(X'Y)$, where $\text{var}(\theta_{2\text{step}}) = (X'X)^{-1}\sigma^2$, $X_t = x_t - \rho_{\text{OLS}} x_{t-1}$, $Y_t = y_t - \rho_{\text{OLS}} y_{t-1}$, $X = (X_1, \dots, X_T)'$, and $Y = (Y_1, \dots, Y_T)'$.

Clearly, (ii) does not take into account the fact that ρ has been estimated. Properly reading off the marginal asymptotic distribution from the joint one in (i) will account for this. The second approach gives the correct variance for θ only if the asymptotic covariance matrix of θ and ρ is diagonal. Similar problems emerge in mixed calibration–estimation setups discussed later and in chapter 7 and in certain panel data models (see chapter 8).

5.3.5 *Two-Step Estimators*

GMM estimators require iterative procedures and this may make them computationally demanding when h_t is highly nonlinear and the number of parameters is large. As already mentioned one could use a two-step approach to compute an approximation to the full GMM estimator. Under what conditions is a two-step GMM estimator asymptotically equivalent to a fully iterative GMM estimator? It turns out that, if the initial estimator θ_T^1 is a $\sqrt{T}$-consistent estimator and it is bounded in probability, the difference between θ_T^2 and θ_T vanishes asymptotically. While $\sqrt{T}$-consistency is difficult to verify, for boundedness in probability it suffices that $\theta_T^1 \xrightarrow{\text{D}} \theta_0$ (see chapter 1), which, in practice, is easy to check.

In general, one should prefer full iterative GMM to a two-step GMM estimation when the initial estimator has a large covariance matrix and h_t is not well-approximated by a quadratic function. Note also that the sample size needed for consistency of θ_T^2 and θ_T may be very different: θ_T^1 may be in the tail of the asymptotic distribution and, if the objective function is flat, it may take a large T for θ_T^2 to approximate θ_T.

We ask the reader to verify the asymptotic equivalence of θ_T^2 and θ_T in the next exercise.

Exercise 5.29. Suppose the following: y_t is stationary and ergodic; $g(y_t, \theta_0)$ is a martingale difference; $g(y_t, \cdot)$ is continuous in θ; $h_T(\theta_T) = 0$; $E[H_T(\theta_0)] = H$, $|H| \neq 0$; $E[h(y_t, \theta_0)h(y_t, \theta_0)'] = \Sigma_h < \infty$; $H_T = \partial h(y_T, \theta)/\partial\theta'$ exists and is continuous at θ_0 and uniformly convergent to H; $\theta_T \xrightarrow{\text{P}} \theta_0$. Assume that θ_T^1 is a $\sqrt{T}$-consistent estimator of θ_0 such that $\sqrt{T}(\theta_T^1 - \theta_0)$ is bounded in probability and let $\theta_T^2 \equiv \theta_T^1 - [\partial h_T(\bar{\theta}_T)/\partial\theta']^{-1} h_T(\theta_T^1)$, where $\bar{\theta}_T \in [\theta_T^1, \theta_T^2]$. Show that $\sqrt{T}(\theta_T^2 - \theta_0) \xrightarrow{\text{D}} \mathbb{N}(0, (H')^{-1}\Sigma_h H^{-1})$ and $\sqrt{T}(\theta_T^2 - \theta_T) \xrightarrow{\text{P}} 0$, where θ_T is the fully iterative GMM estimator.

5.3.6 *Hypothesis Testing*

We are concerned with the problem of testing whether a vector of (possibly nonlinear) restrictions of the form $R(\theta) = 0$ holds. The discussion in this subsection is general: we specialize the setup in various examples and exercises.

We assume (i) $g_\infty(\theta) = 0$, (ii) $n = k$, and (iii) $\sqrt{T}(\theta_T - \theta_0) \xrightarrow{D} \mathbb{N}(0, \Sigma_\theta)$, $\Sigma_\theta = (H')^{-1}\Sigma_h H^{-1}$. Under the null, $R(\theta_0) = 0$.

5.3.6.1 Wald-Type Test

To derive a Wald-type test note that, even though $R(\theta_T) \neq 0$, it should be small with high probability if $\theta_T \xrightarrow{P} \theta_0$. Assume that $R(\theta)$ is a smooth function with, at least, the first derivative and that $\partial R_i(\bar\theta)/\partial\theta'_j$ is uniformly continuous (and full rank), $\bar\theta \in (\theta_T, \theta_0)$. Taking an exact Taylor expansion of $R(\theta_T)$ around $R(\theta_0)$ we have

$$R(\theta_T) = R(\theta_0) + \mathcal{R}(\bar\theta)(\theta_T - \theta_0), \tag{5.25}$$

where $\mathcal{R}_{ij}(\bar\theta) = \partial R_i(\bar\theta)/\partial\theta'_j$, $i = 1, 2, \ldots$. Using continuity of $\partial R_i(\bar\theta)/\partial\theta'_j$ and consistency of θ_T, we have $\mathcal{R}(\bar\theta) \xrightarrow{P} \mathcal{R}(\theta_0)$, elementwise. Hence, (5.25) implies that $\sqrt{T}R(\theta_T) = \sqrt{T}\mathcal{R}(\theta_0)(\theta_T - \theta_0) \xrightarrow{D} \mathbb{N}(0, \Sigma_R \equiv \mathcal{R}(\theta_0)\Sigma_\theta\mathcal{R}(\theta_0)')$ by the asymptotic normality of $\theta_T - \theta_0$, and to test $R(\theta) = 0$ one can use

$$\text{Wa} = TR(\theta_T)'\Sigma_R^{-1}R(\theta_T) \sim \chi^2(\dim(R)). \tag{5.26}$$

Equation (5.26) is entirely based on the local properties of $R(\theta_T)$ around θ_0. When g_t is the score of each observation, (5.26) is a standard Wald test.

Exercise 5.30. Find a consistent estimator of $\mathcal{R}(\theta_0)$. What happens to (5.26) if $R(\theta_0) \neq 0$?

5.3.6.2 Lagrange-Multiplier-Type Test

In some problems the imposition of restrictions makes estimation and testing easier.

Example 5.18. Suppose you want to estimate the parameters of the following nonlinear model: $(y_t^{\alpha_0} - 1)/\alpha_0 = \alpha_1 + \alpha_2(x_t^{\alpha_0} - 1)/\alpha_0 + e_t$. If $\alpha_0 = 0$, the model reduces to $\ln y_t = \alpha_1 + \alpha_2 \ln x_t + e_t$ while, if $\alpha_0 = 1$, it reduces to $y_t = (\alpha_1 - \alpha_2 + 1) + \alpha_2 x_t + e_t$. In both cases estimates of α_1 and α_2 can be obtained with least squares techniques. Given these estimates, we may want to test whether $\alpha_0 = 0$ or $\alpha_0 = 1$ are sensible restrictions.

In cases like those of example 5.18, it may be useful to design a test which uses the local properties of $h_T(\theta)$ and $R(\theta)$ around θ_R, a restricted estimator. Let θ_R solve $h_T(\theta_R) = 0$ and assume that $\sqrt{T}(\theta_R - \theta_0) \xrightarrow{P} 0$. Expanding $h_T(\theta_T)$ and $R(\theta_T)$ around θ_R, we have

$$h_T(\theta_T) = h_T(\theta_R) + \frac{\partial h_T(\bar\theta)}{\partial\theta'}(\theta_T - \theta_R), \tag{5.27}$$

$$R(\theta_T) = R(\theta_R) + \frac{\partial R(\bar\theta)}{\partial\theta'}(\theta_T - \theta_R), \tag{5.28}$$

where $\bar\theta \in (\theta_T, \theta_R)$. From (5.27) and $\sqrt{T}(\theta_T - \theta_R) = \sqrt{T}(\partial h_T(\bar\theta)/\partial\theta')^{-1} \times (h_T(\theta_T) - h_T(\theta_R)) \xrightarrow{D} \mathbb{N}(0, \Sigma_\theta)$.

Exercise 5.31. Give conditions on $h_T(\theta_T)$ and $\partial h_T(\bar{\theta})/\partial\theta'$ which are sufficient to ensure the above result. Intuitively explain why the distributions of $(\theta_T - \theta_0)$ and $(\theta_T - \theta_R)$ are the same.

Using (5.28), noting that $R(\theta_R) = 0$ by construction, we have that $\sqrt{T}R(\theta_T) = (\partial R(\bar{\theta})/\partial\theta')\sqrt{T}(\theta_T - \theta_R) \xrightarrow{\text{D}} \mathbb{N}(0, \Sigma_R \equiv \mathcal{R}(\theta_0)\Sigma_\theta \mathcal{R}(\theta_0)')$. Therefore, a test for the null hypothesis $R(\theta) = 0$ is

$$\text{LM} = TR(\theta_T)'\Sigma_R^{-1}R(\theta_T) \sim \chi^2(\dim(R)). \tag{5.29}$$

The quadratic forms in (5.26) and (5.29) are similar—(5.26) uses the properties of an unrestricted estimator while (5.29) those of a restricted estimator—and asymptotically equivalent. In general, this is not the case (see, for example, Engle 1983). Here it occurs because restricted and unrestricted estimators have the same asymptotic covariance matrix, which, in turn, is due to the fact that θ_R is a $\sqrt{T}$-consistent estimator of θ_0.

This class of tests based on the local properties of the h_T function around θ_R is called the Lagrange multiplier test. When $g_T = (1/T)\sum \partial \ln f(y_t \mid \theta)/\partial\theta'$ and $E(g(y_t, \theta)) = 0$, θ_R is the maximum likelihood estimator obtained subject to $R(\theta) = 0$. Then, (5.29) tests the hypothesis that the Lagrangian multiplier on the restriction is zero (see Judge et al. 1985, p. 182).

5.3.6.3 Distance Test

Distance tests examine whether two estimators (a restricted and an unrestricted one) are close in some metric. Let θ_R solve $h_T(\theta_R) = 0$ and let θ_T be a $\sqrt{T}$-consistent (unrestricted) estimator. Then $0 = h_T(\theta_R) = h_T(\theta_T) + H(\bar{\theta})(\theta_R - \theta_T)$ with $\bar{\theta} \in (\theta_R, \theta_T)$, where $H_{ij} = \partial h_{Ti}(\bar{\theta})/\partial\theta_j$.

Exercise 5.32. Give sufficient conditions to ensure that $H(\bar{\theta}) \xrightarrow{\text{P}} H$ and $\sqrt{T} \times (\theta_R - \theta_T) \xrightarrow{\text{D}} \mathbb{N}(0, \Sigma_\theta)$.

Under the conditions of exercise 5.32, a test for the null hypothesis $R(\theta) = 0$ is

$$\text{Dt} = T(\theta_R - \theta_T)'\Sigma_\theta^{-1}(\theta_R - \theta_T) \sim \chi^2(k). \tag{5.30}$$

When θ_R is a random vector, the test has a smaller number of degrees of freedom and this occurs even if $(\theta_R - \theta_T)$ is a $k \times 1$ vector.

Example 5.19. A likelihood ratio test is a special case of a distance test. Expanding $\mathcal{L}_T(\theta_R)$ around a $\sqrt{T}$-consistent unrestricted estimator θ_T, we have $\mathcal{L}_T(\theta_R) = \mathcal{L}_T(\theta_T) + (\partial\mathcal{L}_T(\bar{\theta})/\partial\theta')(\theta_R - \theta_T) + 0.5(\theta_R - \theta_T)'(\partial^2\mathcal{L}_T(\bar{\theta})/\partial\theta\partial\theta') \times (\theta_R - \theta_T)$. Since $\sqrt{T}(\theta_T - \theta_0) \xrightarrow{\text{P}} 0$, $\partial\mathcal{L}_T(\bar{\theta})/\partial\theta' \xrightarrow{\text{P}} \partial\mathcal{L}_T(\theta_T)/\partial\theta' = 0$. Hence, $2T(\mathcal{L}_T(\theta_R) - \mathcal{L}_T(\theta_T)) = T(\theta_R - \theta_T)'(\partial\mathcal{L}_T^2(\bar{\theta})/\partial\theta\partial\theta')(\theta_R - \theta_T)$. Then, since $\partial^2\mathcal{L}_T(\bar{\theta})/\partial\theta\partial\theta' \xrightarrow{\text{P}} \partial^2\mathcal{L}_T(\theta_T)/\partial\theta\partial\theta' \equiv \Sigma_\theta = -H^{-1}$, we have that $-2T(\mathcal{L}_T(\theta_R) - \mathcal{L}_T(\theta_T)) \xrightarrow{\text{P}} T(\theta_R - \theta_T)'H^{-1}(\theta_R - \theta_T) \sim \chi^2(k - k')$ and $k - k'$ is the number of restrictions.

5.3.6.4 Hausman Test

Hausman's (1978) test is based on the idea that it is not necessary for the unrestricted estimator to be efficient as long as restricted and unrestricted estimators have a joint limiting distribution. Let θ_R be an efficient estimator under the null, i.e., it minimizes the asymptotic covariance matrix; let θ_T be any consistent, not necessarily efficient, estimator; let $\theta^0 = [\theta_0, \theta_0]'$; and let $\theta^{TR} = [\theta_T, \theta_R]'$ be such that $\sqrt{T} h_T(\theta^{TR}) \xrightarrow{D} \mathbb{N}(0, \Sigma_\theta)$. If the parameter space is compact, the uniform convergence theorem ensures that the asymptotic covariance matrix of $\sqrt{T}(\theta^{TR} - \theta^0)$ has zero off-diagonal elements (so that the two estimators are asymptotically independent). A version of the Hausman test is then

$$\text{Ha} = T(\theta_T - \theta_R)'(\Sigma_T - \Sigma_R)^{-1}(\theta_T - \theta_R) \xrightarrow{D} \chi^2(k), \tag{5.31}$$

where Σ_T and Σ_R are the asymptotic covariance matrices of the two estimators. Note that, if θ_T is also efficient, $\Sigma_T - \Sigma_R$ is singular. In this case, it is still possible to implement the test by choosing a $k' \times k$ matrix $\mathbb{C}$ such that $|\mathbb{C}(\Sigma_T - \Sigma_R)\mathbb{C}'| \neq 0$ and the test becomes

$$\text{Ha} = T((\theta_T - \theta_R)'\mathbb{C}')(\mathbb{C}(\Sigma_T - \Sigma_R)\mathbb{C}')^{-1}(\mathbb{C}(\theta_T - \theta_R)) \xrightarrow{D} \chi^2(k'). \tag{5.32}$$

It is important to stress that while several of the tests we consider have the same asymptotic distribution, they may have dramatically different properties in small samples.

Wald tests are easy to implement in practice, as shown in the next example.

Example 5.20. Let Σ_{ii} be the ith diagonal element of Σ_θ and let $R(\theta) = 0$ be $\theta_i - \bar{\theta}_i = 0$. Then $T(\theta_{iT} - \bar{\theta}_i)'(\Sigma_{ii})^{-1}(\theta_{iT} - \bar{\theta}_i) \xrightarrow{D} \chi^2(1)$. Alternatively, $\sqrt{T}(\theta_{iT} - \bar{\theta}_i)/\sqrt{\Sigma_{ii}} \xrightarrow{D} \mathbb{N}(0, 1)$. Also, if the restriction is $R\theta = \bar{\theta}$, the statistic is $T(R\theta_T - \bar{\theta})'[R\Sigma_\theta R']^{-1}(R\theta_T - \bar{\theta}) \xrightarrow{D} \chi^2(k)$.

Exercise 5.33. Consider example 5.10. Provide three test statistics for the hypothesis that the term structure of interest rates is flat in the steady state (i.e., $r_\tau = r_1$) which are robust to the presence of autocorrelation in the orthogonality conditions.

Example 5.21. One of the assumptions underlying the RBC model of example 5.1 is that the representative agent likes to smooth consumption. This implies that the coefficient of relative risk aversion should be positive. One can test this hypothesis in a number of ways. Assuming $u(c) = c_t^{1-\varphi}/(1-\varphi)$ and using (5.3), we can easily construct both restricted and unrestricted estimators. Hence, the Wald and distance statistics are $\text{Wa} = T\varphi_T^2/\Sigma_{\varphi_T}$ and $\text{Dt} = T(\varphi_T - \varphi_R)^2/\Sigma_{\varphi_T}$, where Σ_{φ_T} is the variance of the unrestricted estimator.

Exercise 5.34. Simulate data for consumption, investment, output, and the real interest rate from a basic RBC model by using $\beta = 0.99$, $\delta = 0.025$, $\eta = 0.66$, and $\varphi = 1$, assuming that the log of technology disturbance is AR(1) with persistence 0.9 and standard deviation 1. Suppose one wants to estimate a model where the utility function displays habit persistence in consumption. Construct restricted, unrestricted, and minimum distance estimators and test the hypothesis that the habit persistence parameter γ is equal to zero. Repeat the exercise 100 times drawing random technology shocks from a normal distribution. What are the properties of the three tests over the 100 replications?

In some cases, one wants to test a subset of the orthogonality conditions. For example, as in exercise 5.10, we may be interested in knowing whether or not income lagged two periods adds explanatory power to our estimates. In that case a Hausman test could be used.

Example 5.22. Continuing with exercise 5.10, let θ_{1T} be the estimator obtained by using z_{1T} and θ_{2T} the estimator obtained by using z_{2T}. Clearly, θ_{2T} is as efficient as θ_{1T} since it uses more orthogonality conditions. If $\text{var}(\theta_{1T} - \theta_{2T}) = \text{var}(\theta_{1T}) - \text{var}(\theta_{2T})$, the Hausman statistic for testing if the second set of orthogonality conditions holds is $(\theta_{1T} - \theta_{2T})[\text{var}(\theta_{1T}) - \text{var}(\theta_{2T})]^{-1}(\theta_{1T} - \theta_{2T}) \xrightarrow{\text{D}} \chi^2(\nu)$, where ν is the lesser of the number of orthogonality conditions tested and the number of conditions minus the number of instruments used for estimation. When $\nu = 1$, $T\sigma^2[y'(z_1(z_1'z_1)^{-1}z_1')y - y'(z_2(z_2'z_2)^{-1}z_2')y]$ can be used as an estimator for $\text{var}(\theta_{1T}) - \text{var}(\theta_{2T})$.

Exercise 5.35. Consider the situation where the representative agent in one country (say, the United States) has the option to purchase one-period bonds denominated in another currency (say, yen) and let ner_t be the dollar–yen nominal exchange rate. In equilibrium,

$$0 = E_t\left[\beta \frac{U_{c,t+1}/p_{t+1}}{U_{c,t}/p_t}\left((1 + i_{1t}) - \frac{\text{ner}_{t+1}}{\text{ner}_t}(1 + i_{2t})\right)\right], \tag{5.33}$$

where i_{jt} is the nominal interest rate on bonds of country j, p_t is the price level, and $U_{c,t+1}/p_{t+1}$ is the marginal utility of money. Log-linearize (5.33), assuming $u(c_t) = \ln c_t$. Using nominal balances, nominal interest rates, and nominal exchange rate data, verify whether (5.33) holds. Test whether agents do not discount the future (i.e., whether $\beta = 1$).

Exercise 5.36 (MacKinley and Richardson). If a portfolio j of assets is mean–variance efficient and if there exists a risk-free asset, it must be the case that $E(\tilde{r}_{it}) = \alpha E(\tilde{r}_{jt})$ (see exercise 5.2), where $\tilde{r}_{it} = r_{it} - r_{0t}$ is the excess return on asset i at time t, $\tilde{r}_{jt} = r_{jt} - r_{0t}$ is the excess return on a portfolio j at time t, $i = 1, 2, \ldots, I$. Derive the orthogonality conditions implied by mean–variance efficiency. Using Euroxx50 stocks data, provide an estimator for α which is robust to heteroskedasticity (produced, for example, if the variance of return i depends on the return on the market portfolio). Test the hypothesis that the efficient frontier holds.

Example 5.23. Continuing with example 5.11 we test three hypotheses. First, fixing $\beta = 1$ does not change estimates: a distance-style test finds no difference between restricted and unrestricted specifications. Second, we test for full stickiness $\zeta_p = 1$; this corresponds to excluding marginal costs from the specification (under this null, inflation is an AR(1) process). An LR test rejects this hypothesis by using the output gap in the United States, the United Kingdom, and the labor share in Germany at the 5% confidence level. Finally, a test of full flexibility $\zeta_p = 0$ is rejected in five of the six specifications.

5.4 GMM Estimation of DSGE Models

The examples considered so far involve the estimation of one equation of a model. At times one may want instead to examine its full implications so that, for example, comparison with ML estimates can be performed. In this case, systemwide methods are necessary. Typically, there is recursivity in the structure of DSGE models. Hence, estimation can be usefully conducted block by block.

Example 5.24. Suppose a social planner maximizes $E_0 \sum_t \beta^t [c_t^{1-\varphi}/(1-\varphi) + \vartheta_N(1-N_t)]$ by choices of consumption (c_t), hours (N_t), and capital (K_{t+1}) subject to $G_t + c_t + K_{t+1} = \zeta_t K_t^{1-\eta} N_t^{\eta} + (1-\delta)K_t$, where $\ln \zeta_t = \bar{\zeta} + \rho_\zeta \ln \zeta_{t-1} + \epsilon_{1t}$, $\epsilon_{1t} \sim (0, \sigma_\zeta^2)$, $\ln G_t = \bar{G} + \rho_G \ln G_{t-1} + \epsilon_{4t}$, $\epsilon_{4t} \sim (0, \sigma_G^2)$, K_0 given. Assume that government expenditure is financed with lump sum taxes or bond creation. The optimality conditions are

$$\vartheta_N c_t^{\varphi} = \eta \zeta_t K_t^{1-\eta} N_t^{\eta-1}, \tag{5.34}$$

$$c_t^{-\varphi} = E_t \beta c_{t+1}^{-\varphi} [(1-\eta)\zeta_{t+1} K_{t+1}^{-\eta} N_{t+1}^{\eta} + (1-\delta)]. \tag{5.35}$$

Furthermore, competition implies that the real wage is $w_t = \eta \zeta_t K_t^{1-\eta} N_t^{\eta-1}$ and the return to capital is $r_t = (1-\eta)\zeta_t K_t^{-\eta} N_t^{\eta} + (1-\delta)$.

The model has eleven parameters: five structural ones $\theta_1 = (\beta, \vartheta_N, \varphi, \eta, \delta)$ and six auxiliary ones $\theta_2 = (\bar{\zeta}, \bar{G}, \rho_\zeta, \rho_G, \sigma_G^2, \sigma_\zeta^2)$. Hence, we need at least eleven orthogonality conditions to estimate $\theta = (\theta_1, \theta_2)$. From the capital accumulation equation, taking unconditional expectations, we have

$$E\left(\delta - 1 + \frac{K_{t+1}}{K_t} - \frac{\text{inv}_t}{K_t}\right) = 0, \tag{5.36}$$

which determines δ if data for capital and investment are available. The Euler equation (5.35) contains four parameters $(\beta, \varphi, \eta, \delta)$. Since δ is identified from (5.36), we need to transform (5.35) to produce at least three orthogonality conditions. Given that any variable belonging to the information set at time t can be used as an instrument, one could use, for example, a constant, lags of the real return to capital and of consumption growth to estimate the other three parameters. For example, one could employ

$$\left.\begin{aligned} E\left\{\beta\left(\frac{c_{t+1}}{c_t}\right)^{-\varphi}[(1-\eta)\zeta_{t+1}K_{t+1}^{-\eta}N_{t+1}^{\eta}+(1-\delta)]-1\right\}&=0,\\ E\left\{\beta\left(\frac{c_{t+1}}{c_t}\right)^{-\varphi}[(1-\eta)\zeta_{t+1}K_{t+1}^{-\eta}N_{t+1}^{\eta}+(1-\delta)]-1\right\}\frac{c_t}{c_{t-1}}&=0,\\ E\left\{\beta\left(\frac{c_{t+1}}{c_t}\right)^{-\varphi}[(1-\eta)\zeta_{t+1}K_{t+1}^{-\eta}N_{t+1}^{\eta}+(1-\delta)]-1\right\}r_{t-1}&=0.\end{aligned}\right\} \tag{5.37}$$

The intratemporal condition (5.34) implies

$$E[c_t^{-\varphi}\eta\zeta_t K_t^{1-\eta}N_t^{\eta-1}-\vartheta_N]=0, \tag{5.38}$$

which also involves three parameters $(\varphi,\eta,\vartheta_N)$. Given (φ,η), (5.38) determines ϑ_N.

The auxiliary parameters can be estimated by using the properties of ϵ_{1t} and ϵ_{4t}, i.e.,

$$E(\ln\zeta_t-\bar{\zeta}+\rho_\zeta\ln\zeta_{t-1})=0, \tag{5.39}$$

$$E[(\ln\zeta_t-\bar{\zeta}+\rho_\zeta\ln\zeta_{t-1})\ln\zeta_{t-1}]=0, \tag{5.40}$$

$$E[(\ln\zeta_t-\bar{\zeta}+\rho_\zeta\ln\zeta_{t-1})^2-\sigma_\zeta^2]=0, \tag{5.41}$$

$$E(\ln G_t-\bar{G}+\rho_{\mathrm{G}}\ln G_{t-1})=0, \tag{5.42}$$

$$E[(\ln G_t-\bar{G}+\rho_{\mathrm{G}}\ln G_{t-1})\ln G_{t-1}]=0, \tag{5.43}$$

$$E[(\ln G_t-\bar{G}+\rho_{\mathrm{G}}\ln G_{t-1})^2-\sigma_{\mathrm{G}}^2]=0. \tag{5.44}$$

While government expenditure is observable, technological disturbances are not. Therefore an additional auxiliary condition is needed. From the production function and given estimates $\hat{\eta}$, we have that $\hat{\zeta}_t=\ln\mathrm{GDP}_t-(1-\hat{\eta})\ln K_t-\hat{\eta}\ln N_t$ and $\hat{\zeta}_t$ can be used in (5.39)–(5.41). To summarize, the last three conditions could be estimated separately while for the first eight joint or recursive estimation is possible — in the latter case, we need to correct standard errors as described in section 5.3.4.

Given existing experimental evidence and the relatively small sample of data, we decided to estimate θ from a just identified system or from a weakly overidentified one without optimal weighting. Overidentified estimates are obtained with additional lags of r_t, c_{t+1}/c_t, of investment, or of the output–labor ratio. Using linearly detrended U.S. quarterly consumption, investment, government expenditure, output, household hours, and capital stock data for the sample 1956:1–1984:1, we estimate θ, fixing φ, which cannot be estimated from this data set. Since estimates of η are low, we also provide estimates conditioning on a larger value of η. Table 5.2 reports the results; standard errors are in parentheses. Estimates of $\bar{G}$ and $\bar{\zeta}$ are omitted to save space, as they are insignificantly different from zero. Four main features emerge from the table. First, structural parameters are, in general, precisely estimated and to fit the data nonstationary government and technology disturbances are

Table 5.2. Estimates of an RBC model.

Parameter	Just identified	Overidentified	Overidentified	Overidentified
η	0.18 (0.000 2)	0.18 (0.000 2)	0.64	0.18 (0.000 2)
φ	1.0	1.0	1.0	2.0
δ	0.0202 (0.000 22)	0.0202 (0.000 21)	0.0201 (0.000 13)	0.0208 (0.000 13)
β	1.007 (0.000 5)	1.007 (0.000 5)	0.991 (0.000 4)	1.012 (0.000 9)
ϑ_N	3.73 (0.013)	3.73 (0.012)	2.93 (0.006)	0.455 (0.001)
ρ_ζ	1.035 (0.026)	1.021 (0.025)	1.035 (0.026)	1.075 (0.034)
ρ_G	1.025 (0.038)	1.042 (0.033)	1.025 (0.038)	1.027 (0.0039)
σ^2_ζ	0.0001 (0.000 01)	0.0001 (0.000 01)	0.0001 (0.000 01)	0.0001 (0.000 01)
σ^2_G	0.0002 (0.000 02)	0.0002 (0.000 02)	0.0002 (0.000 02)	0.0002 (0.000 02)
J-statistic		$\chi^2(6) = 259.69$	$\chi^2(5) = 260.19$	$\chi^2(6) = 257.71$

required. This obtains regardless of whether just identified or overidentified systems are used, suggesting that the model lacks internal propagation. Second, estimates of β are economically unreasonable, except when we set $\eta = 0.64$. Third, the model is strongly rejected in all cases with smaller χ^2 statistic when $\varphi = 2$. Fourth, results are broadly independent of the value φ. In fact, apart from ρ_ζ and ρ_G, estimates change very little for φ in the range $[0, 3]$.

While J-tests or other statistical devices can give a rough idea of the validity of a model, they are insufficient from an economic point of view since, in the case of failure, they provide no indication of how to respecify the model to improve the fit. Useful information on why the model fails can be obtained by comparing features of the data which have some economic content. Although it is popular to examine these economic features informally, neglecting both parameter and sampling uncertainty is problematic. Whenever features of interest are continuous functions of the unknown parameters, an (economic) Wald-type test can be employed to formally evaluate the quality of the model's approximation to the data.

Let the vector of features of interest be $\mathfrak{S}(\theta)$ and the corresponding vector of features in the data be $\mathfrak{S}_T$, where the subscript "T" indicates the sample size. Let $h_T(\theta_T) = \mathfrak{S}(\theta_T) - \mathfrak{S}_T$, where θ_T is a GMM estimate. Then the covariance matrix of $h_T(\theta_T)$ is $\Sigma_h = (\partial h(\theta_0)/\partial\theta')\Sigma_\theta(\partial h(\theta_0)/\partial\theta')' + \Sigma_{\mathfrak{S}}$. Under the null hypothesis that the model reproduces the features of interest in the data $Th(\theta_T)'\Sigma_h^{-1}h(\theta_T) \xrightarrow{\text{D}} \chi^2(\dim(\mathfrak{S}))$. Hence, a large value of this statistic indicates that the model and the data are different in the dimensions of interest. Since it is possible to perform the test for components of the $\mathfrak{S}(\theta)$ vector, the approach can be used sequentially to check which features of the data are matched and which are not.

One important point needs to be emphasized. While statistical tests can be conducted by using the optimality conditions of the model, economic tests require a

Table 5.3. Moments of the data and of the model.

Moment	Data	Model	Moment	Data	Model	Moment	Data	Model
var(GDP)	0.002	0.001	GDP-AR(1)	0.780	0.859			
var(c)	0.001	0.009	c-AR(1)	0.986	0.927	corr(c, GDP)	0.953	0.853
var(inv)	0.005	0.008	inv-AR(1)	0.976	0.991	corr(inv, GDP)	0.911	0.703
var(N)	0.0004	0.0003	N-AR(1)	0.958	0.898	corr(N, GDP)	0.464	0.570

researcher to generate $\mathfrak{S}(\theta_T)$, given some θ_T. In other words, to conduct economic tests, a solution to the model needs to be computed. Therefore, one of the main advantages of GMM over maximum likelihood and similar techniques disappears.

Example 5.25. Continuing with example 5.24, we log-linearize the conditions and solve the model. Using just identified estimates of the parameters we evaluate the quality of the model approximation to the data considering (i) the variance of output, consumption, investment, and hours, (ii) the first-order autocorrelation of these four variables, and (iii) the contemporaneous cross-correlations of consumption, investment, and hours with output. Table 5.3 reports these statistics for the model and the data, linearly detrending both. Since $\mathfrak{S} = T \times h(\theta_T)'\Sigma_h^{-1}h(\theta_T) > 800$, we strongly reject the idea that the RBC model replicates these eleven moments.

Exercise 5.37 (Burnside and Eichenbaum). Let the representative agent's preferences be $U(c, N, \mathrm{ef}) = \ln c_t + \vartheta_N N_{t-1} \ln(1 - b_0 - b_1\mathrm{ef}_t)$, where ef_t is effort, N_{t-1} is the probability of working, ϑ_N is the fraction of people working, b_1 is a parameter, and b_0 is a fixed cost one has to pay to get to work so that $(1-b_0-b_1\mathrm{ef}_t)$ are effective hours of leisure. Here effort can respond to news instantaneously but N_t cannot. Assume that $\mathrm{GDP}_t = \zeta_t K_t^{1-\eta}(b_1\mathrm{ef}_t N_{t-1})^\eta$, that government consumes a random amount G_t taxing income at the rate T^y, and that capital depreciates at the rate δ.

(i) Calculate steady-state values of $(\mathrm{GDP}/K)^{\mathrm{ss}}$, $(c/\mathrm{GDP})^{\mathrm{ss}}$, N^{ss} when $\mathrm{ef}^{\mathrm{ss}} = 1$.

(ii) Show that the first-order conditions of the problem are

$$-\vartheta_N b_1 N_{t-1}(1 - b_0 - b_1\mathrm{ef}_t)^{-1} + \eta c_t^{-1}\frac{y_t}{\mathrm{ef}_t} = 0, \tag{5.45}$$

$$\vartheta_N E_t \ln(1 - b_0 - b_1\mathrm{ef}_{t+1}) + E_t c_{t+1}^{-1}\eta\frac{y_{t+1}}{N_t} = 0, \tag{5.46}$$

$$-c_t^{-1} + E_t\beta c_{t+1}^{-1}\left[(1-\eta)\frac{y_{t+1}}{K_{t+1}} + (1-\delta)\right] = 0, \tag{5.47}$$

$$\zeta_t K_t^{1-\eta}(b_1\mathrm{ef}_t N_{t-1})^\eta + (1-\delta)K_t - K_{t+1} - G_t - c_t = 0. \tag{5.48}$$

(iii) Describe how to estimate $(b_0, b_1, \eta, \beta, \delta, \vartheta_N)$ by using GMM. Which parameters are identifiable? What data would you use? What instruments would you consider? How would you deal with the fact that effort is nonobservable? (Hint: think of a proxy and consider the effects of measurement error.)

(iv) Test the hypothesis that the model fits the first three terms of the autocovariance function of hours and of the cross-covariance of hours and labor productivity (wage) at lags -1, 0, and 1. Repeat the exercise assuming that effort is fixed (i.e., drop it from the choice variables). Can you test the variable-effort model against the fixed-effort model? How?

Exercise 5.38 (Eichenbaum and Fisher). Consider monopolistic competitive firms which cannot reoptimize their price because information is sticky. This is because, at each t, they only observe variables dated at $t - \tau$.

(i) Show that in this case the (log-linearized) Phillips curve is $\pi_t = E_{t-\tau}[\beta\pi_{t+1} + ((1-\beta\zeta_p)(1-\zeta_p)/\zeta_p)\text{mc}_t]$, where β is the discount factor, ζ_p is the share of firms not changing prices, and mc_t are real marginal costs (lowercase variables are deviations from the steady state).

(ii) Using GDP deflator and (real) labor share data for the United States, provide GMM estimates of β and ζ_p, using as instruments a constant, one/three/five lags of GDP deflator and of the (real) labor share for $\tau = 0, 1, 2$ correcting for serial correlation of unknown order. Provide a test of overidentifying restrictions. Which version of the model fits the data better?

(iii) Repeat (ii) jointly estimating the parameters of the log-linearized Phillips curve and those of the log-linearized Euler equation $c_t = E_{t-\tau}[c_{t+1} - (1/\varphi) \times (i_t - \pi_{t+1})]$, where c_t is consumption, i_t is the nominal interest rate, and φ is the coefficient of relative risk aversion, adding lags of consumption growth and of the nominal interest rates to the instrument list. Do results in (ii) change? Why?

5.4.1 Some Applied Tips

A number of studies have examined the small-sample properties of GMM estimators in macro-based or finance-based experimental data (see, for example, Tauchen 1986; Kocherlakota 1990; Mao 1990; Pagan and Yoon 1993; Ferson and Foerster 1994; Hansen et al. 1996; Newey and West 1994; West and Wilcox 1996; Burnside and Eichenbaum 1996; Christiano and Den Haan 1996; Den Haan and Levin 1996; Anderson and Sörenson 1996; Furher et al. 1995; Lindé 2005; Ruge-Murcia 2002). Four issues have been extensively investigated: (i) how inefficient are estimates obtained by using a subset of the available instruments; (ii) how reasonable are two-step GMM estimators in small samples; (iii) how large are the efficiency gains obtained by using an optimal weighting matrix; (iv) the relative performance of parametric and kernel-based HAC estimates.

On the first issue there is agreement. While a large set of moment conditions improves asymptotic efficiency, it also dramatically increases small-sample biases. Hence, GMM estimates obtained with a smaller number of instruments may have lower MSEs in small samples. There are two reasons for this: first, additional instruments may only be weakly correlated with the quantities that they instrument for. Second, when the dimension of the weighting matrix is large, estimates may fail to converge to a nonstochastic matrix in small samples. In general, when the sample is short, one should be careful in taking strongly overidentified estimates at their face value.

For the second issue, the results are mixed and depend on the environment. In general, a fully iterative GMM estimator has good properties for simple problems. However, when the h_T function is highly nonlinear and/or T is relatively small, the small-sample distribution may poorly approximate the asymptotic one. Note that, in some experimental designs, it has been found that fully iterative GMMs are poor even when $T = 300$.

Estimation of the optimal covariance matrix depends on the number of instruments, the sample size, the serial correlation properties of the h_T function, and a number of other choices made by the investigator. In general, estimates of W_T tend to be poor and this, in turn, affects estimated standard errors and overidentifying tests. When problems are suspected, it may be reasonable to use either the identity matrix or proceed with a just identified version of the model. Hansen et al. (1996) explored the properties of θ_T obtained by minimizing $[(1/T) \times \sum_t h(y_t, \theta)]'(W_T(\theta))^{-1}[(1/T)\sum_t h(y_t, \theta)]$. One reason for preferring a weighting matrix which varies with θ is that, under conditional homoskedasticity, θ_T is invariant to how moment conditions are scaled and corresponds to Sargan's IV estimator for a large class of models. It appears that such a choice produces smaller biases in θ_T than a standard selection in some designs, but evidence on this issue is scant. Researchers have also found that poor kernel estimates of Σ^+ produce biases, induce small-sample confidence intervals with very poor coverage properties, and t-tests which over reject the null hypothesis. Den Haan and Levin (1996) have shown that it may be dangerous to entirely rely on automatic bandwidth selection procedures, as they produce incredible outcomes (e.g., $J(T) = 1$ when $T = 128$). Distortions in Σ^+ could also be created because, to ensure semi-positiveness, the bandwidth parameter must be the same for each orthogonality condition.

The experimental evidence also suggests that estimates of the parameters and of the standard errors are biased in small samples. The direction of the bias of the former depends on the design, while estimates of the standard errors are, in general, downward biased. Since this implies that t-statistics have long and fat tails, tests of hypotheses when T is small should be undertaken with caution.

Regarding the reliability of overidentifying tests, the small-sample evidence is mixed since results depend on W_T, on whether a fully iterative or a two-step GMM is used, on whether instruments carry "good" information, etc. Hence, experimenting with various estimates of W and various instruments is necessary to draw conclusions about parameter estimates and the quality of the model.

Burnside and Eichenbaum (1996) find that Wald tests in an RBC model over reject individual moment restrictions but that their "size" increases uniformly as the dimension of the statistics used increases. Also, in this case, difficulties are due to poor estimates of the W matrix. Lindé (2005) finds that GMM estimates of New

Keynesian Phillips curves (obtained from data simulated by a three-equation New Keynesian model) are inaccurate when the forward-looking element is strong and when there is measurement error in marginal costs. He also shows that ML estimates are preferable, both in large and small samples.

Two further practical issues are of interest. The asymptotic distribution of GMM estimates was derived under stationarity and ergodicity. We can extend the GMM framework to allow for linear trends in y_t, as in Ogaki (1993), with minor changes. However, the procedure does not allow for unit roots or other forms of nonstationarity in y_t. Hence, it is usual to transform the data (take growth rates) or filter it before estimation is undertaken. In example 5.24 we eliminated a linear trend, but this did not seem to be enough as estimates of the persistence of the shocks imply processes in the nonstationary region. The alternative is to employ a band pass or a HP filter. As we saw in chapter 3, filtering is not innocuous. For example, Christiano and Den Haan (1996) find that HP filtering induces large and persistent serial correlation in the residuals of the orthogonality conditions and this creates problems in the estimation of the spectral density at frequency zero. Clearly, problems are more severe when filtered data are very persistent, as is the case with the HP or the band pass filters. If filtering is required, experimentation with different approaches may help us to select the most reasonable one.

Second, how large should T be for asymptotic theory to apply? Experimental evidence on simple specifications suggests that, with $T = 300$, GMM estimators obtained with good W estimates and good instruments approximate the true values in distribution. However, $T = 300$ is a large number: 40 years of time-homogeneous quarterly data make $T = 160$. Experimental evidence also suggests that convergence is slow. Hence, caution should be exercised with any available macroeconomic data.

In conclusion, the small-sample distribution may deviate from the asymptotic one when the weighting matrix is poorly estimated — and this is more of a problem when the orthogonality conditions are highly serially correlated — the instruments are poorly correlated with the functions they want to instrument for and too many moment conditions are used relative to the sample size. Hence, when T is small and h_T serially correlated, we recommend a parametric HAC approach or to avoid, when possible, the estimation of W. For testing purposes, the number of instruments should be chosen to be a function of the sample size.

5.5 Simulation Estimators

Simulation estimators have become popular over the last ten years for at least two reasons: they are cheap and easy to compute, and they can be used in situations where GMMs cannot be employed. Two examples where a GMM is inapplicable follow.

Example 5.26. Suppose in example 5.24 that data on the capital stock are unavailable. Since equations like (5.37) contain unobservable variables, sample counterparts of theoretical conditions cannot be computed, so GMM cannot be employed to estimate the parameters. One could use the competitive rental rate (approximated by the nominal interest rate minus inflation) to proxy for $f_K + (1 - \delta)$ and still estimate (β, φ) with GMM. However, rejection of the orthogonality conditions is hard to interpret, as it may be due to the proxy employed.

Example 5.27. Suppose in example 5.24 that the agent's preferences are subject to an unobservable shock, υ_t with known distribution. If $u(c_t, N_t, \upsilon_t) = (c_t^{1-\varphi}/(1-\varphi))\upsilon_t + \vartheta_N(1 - N_t)$, then $0 = g_\infty(\theta) \equiv E_t[g(y_t, \theta)]$ and

$$g(y_t, \theta) = \beta \frac{c_{t+1}^{-\varphi} \upsilon_{t+1}}{c_t^{-\varphi} \upsilon_t}[f_K + (1 - \delta)] - 1. \tag{5.49}$$

Equation (5.49) does not have a sample counterpart, even if K_t is available, because υ_t is unobservable. As we will see, if we can draw $\{\upsilon_t^l\}$, $l = 1, \dots, L$, we can use $(1/L)\sum_l \{\beta(c_{t+1}^{-\varphi}\upsilon_{t+1}^l / c_t^{-\varphi}\upsilon_t^l)[f_K + (1-\delta)] - 1\}$ in place of $g(y_t, \theta)$ to estimate the parameters. In fact, under regularity conditions, $\lim_{L\to\infty}(1/L) \times \sum_l \{\beta(c_{t+1}^{-\varphi}\upsilon_{t+1}^l / c_t^{-\varphi}\upsilon_t^l)[f_K + (1-\delta)] - 1\} \xrightarrow{\text{P}} g(y_t, \theta)$.

In general, simulation estimators can be used when h_T contains unobservable variables or shocks. Note that h_T need not be the difference between two orthogonality conditions. In fact, in this section, we let h_T be the difference between generic continuous functions of the parameters in the sample and in the population. Such functions could be orthogonality conditions, moments, VAR coefficients, autocovariances, spectral densities, etc.

5.5.1 The General Problem

Let $x_t(\theta)$ be an $m \times 1$ vector of simulated time series given θ, a $k \times 1$ vector of parameters and let y_t be its actual counterpart. Assume that there exists a θ_0 such that $\{x_t(\theta_0)\}_{t=1}^{T_s}$ and $\{y_t\}_{t=1}^{T}$ share the same distribution. Let f be an $n \times 1$ vector of continuous functions; let $F_T(y) = (1/T)\sum_{t=1}^T f(y_t)$ and $F_{T_s}(x, \theta) = (1/T_s)\sum_{t=1}^{T_s} f(x_t(\theta))$. We would like $F_T(y) \to E[f(y_t)]$ and $F_{T_s}(x, \theta) \to E[f(x_t(\theta))]$, for each θ. If $x_t(\theta)$ and y_t are stationary and ergodic, and f is continuous, convergence obtains a.s. Furthermore, given the assumptions made, $E[f(y_t) - f(x_t(\theta_0))] = 0$. Given an $n \times n$ random matrix $W_{T,T_s} \xrightarrow{\text{P}} W$, $\text{rank}(W_{T,T_s}) \geqslant k$, a simulation estimator θ_{T,T_s} solves

$$\text{argmin}\, Q_{T,T_s} = \underset{\theta}{\text{argmin}}[F_T(y) - F_{T_s}(x(\theta))]' W_{T,T_s}[F_T(y) - F_{T_s}(x(\theta))]. \tag{5.50}$$

The estimator in (5.50) is similar to the one in (5.2). To show the analogy set

$$\begin{aligned} h_T(y_t, x_t, \theta) &= \frac{1}{T}\sum_{t=1}^{T} f(y_t) - \frac{1}{\kappa}\sum_{t=1}^{T\times\kappa} f(x_t(\theta)) \\ &= \frac{1}{T}\sum_{t}^{T}\left[f(y_t) - \frac{1}{\kappa}\sum_{i=[1+(t-1)\kappa]}^{[\kappa t]} f(x_i(\theta))\right], \end{aligned} \tag{5.51}$$

where $\kappa = T_s/T > 1$ and $[\kappa t]$ is the largest integer less than or equal to κt. Then θ_{T,T_s} is a GMM estimator for the h_T function given in (5.51). Note that we can produce a time series for $x_t(\theta)$ of length $T\kappa$ or κ time series all of length T. The approach one uses is irrelevant as long as the random numbers used to calculate $x_t(\theta)$ are kept fixed across replications, since continuity of the objective function may be otherwise violated. Finally, for h_T to be well-behaved, we need T_s/T to stay constant as $T, T_s \to \infty$.

Because of the similarities between θ_{T,T_s} and θ_T, the asymptotic properties of θ_{T,T_s} can be obtained by verifying that the general conditions of section 5.3.1 hold. Let $\Sigma_x = \sum_{-\infty}^{\infty} \mathrm{ACF}_x(\tau)$, $\mathrm{ACF}_x(\tau) = E\{f[x_t(\theta_0)] - E[f(x_t(\theta_0))]\} \times \{f[x_{t-\tau}(\theta_0)] - E[f(x_{t-\tau}(\theta_0))]\}'$, $\mathrm{ACF}_y(\tau) = E\{f(y_t) - E[f(y_t)]\}\{f(y_{t-\tau}) - E[f(y_{t-\tau})]\}'$, and $\Sigma_y = \sum_{-\infty}^{\infty} \mathrm{ACF}_y(\tau)$. If the conditions are satisfied, we have that

$$\sqrt{T}\{F_T(y) - E[f(y_t)]\} \xrightarrow{\mathrm{D}} \mathbb{N}(0, \Sigma_y), \tag{5.52}$$

$$\sqrt{T_s}\{F_{T_s}[x(\theta_0)] - E[f(x(\theta_0))]\} \xrightarrow{\mathrm{D}} \mathbb{N}(0, \Sigma_x), \tag{5.53}$$

and $\operatorname{cov}[F_T(y) - F_{T_s}(x(\theta_0))] = (1 + \kappa^{-1})\Sigma_y \equiv \bar{\Sigma}$, because $E[f(y_t)] = E[f(x_t(\theta_0))]$. Hence, as $T, T_s \to \infty$, T_s/T fixed, $\sqrt{T}(\theta_{T,T_s} - \theta_0) \xrightarrow{\mathrm{D}} \mathbb{N}(0, \Sigma_\theta)$.

Exercise 5.39. (i) Show that it is optimal to set $W^\dagger = \bar{\Sigma}^{-1}$. Write down $\Sigma_\theta(W^\dagger)$.
(ii) Show that it is optimal to let $\kappa \to \infty$. (Hint: as $\tau \to \infty$, $\bar{\Sigma} = \Sigma_y$.)
(iii) Show that a goodness-of-fit test is $T \times Q_{T,T_s}(\theta_{T,T_s}) \xrightarrow{\mathrm{D}} \chi^2(n-k)$.

Exercise 5.40. Give the form of $\bar{\Sigma}$ when (i) h_T is i.i.d., (ii) h_T is a finite MA process, and (iii) h_T is generically serially correlated. Provide parametric and nonparametric HAC estimators of $\bar{\Sigma}$ in case (iii).

As mentioned, the vector of functions f could be anything a researcher is interested in (e.g., moments, autocorrelations, impulse responses). The only requirement is that f is continuous and that parameters are identifiable. Identifiability, as we will see later, could create some headaches.

Example 5.28. Suppose that f includes the relative variability of consumption, investment, and hours to output in the data and in the model of example 5.24. Then (5.50) defines an estimator for at most three parameters ($n = 3 \geqslant k$). By exercise 5.39(ii), if the size of simulated time series is sufficiently large (say, $\kappa \geqslant 10$), the resulting simulation estimator will be as efficient as GMM—simulation error washes out.

Exercise 5.41. Consider the setup of exercise 5.2, where $\mathrm{rp}_{j,t-1}$, $j = 1, 2$, are unobservable but known to come from a multivariate normal distribution with mean $\bar{\mathrm{rp}}$ and variance Σ_{rp}. Describe how to estimate α_{ij} by simulation. Make sure you specify the function f you employ. What happens to your estimates if expected returns are measured with (i.i.d.) errors?

The setup we have discussed so far is appropriate in (close to) linear frameworks. In fact, two complications may arise when $x_t(\theta)$ are series generated from a DSGE model. First, draws must be made from the ergodic distribution of x_t, which is unknown. Second, the simulated x_t depends on θ in a nonlinear way and this implies a nonlinear feedback from the parameters to the $h(y_t, x_t, \theta)$ function. We illustrate these two issues with an example.

Example 5.29 (Duffie and Singleton). Let production be $f(K_t, \zeta_t) = \zeta_t K_t^{1-\eta}$ and let the firm maximize the value of dividends by choices of capital, i.e., $\max_{\{K_t\}_{t=0}^{\infty}} \mathrm{sd}_t = \max_{\{K_t\}_{t=0}^{\infty}} \{\zeta_t K_t^{1-\eta} - r_t K_t\}$, where r_t is the rental rate of capital and ζ_t is a technological disturbance. The representative agent problem is $\max_{\{c_t, K_{t+1}, S_{t+1}\}_{t=0}^{\infty}} E[\sum_t \beta^t (c_t^{1-\varphi}/(1-\varphi))\upsilon_t]$ subject to $c_t + K_{t+1} + p_t^{\mathrm{s}} S_{t+1} = (\mathrm{sd}_t + p_t^{\mathrm{s}})S_t + (r_t + \delta)K_t$, where υ_t is a taste disturbance, p_t^{s} is the price of stocks, and δ is the depreciation rate. Let $e_t = (\zeta_t, \upsilon_t)'$ be a stationary Markov process with transition function $e_t = P(e_{t-1}, \phi)$, where ϕ is a vector of parameters. Let $\theta = (\eta, \beta, \varphi, \delta, \phi)$ and let $y_{2t} = (K_t, e_t)$ be the state vector. In equilibrium, y_{2t+1} will be a function of y_{2t} and of θ_0 and this mapping may be computed analytically or by simulation. The vector of other endogenous variables y_{1t} is also a function of y_{2t} and θ. For example, if $\upsilon_t = 1, \forall t, \delta = \varphi = 1, K_{t+1} = \beta(1-\eta)\zeta_t K_t^{1-\eta}$, $c_t = [1 - \beta(1-\eta)]\zeta_t K_t^{1-\eta}$, $\mathrm{sd}_t = \eta\zeta_t K_t^{1-\eta}$, $p_t^{\mathrm{s}} = [\beta/(1-\beta)]\eta\zeta_t K_t^{1-\eta}$.

Suppose we are not willing to make these assumptions. Then we need to compute y_{2t+1} by simulation, i.e., select a $y_{20} = \bar{y}_2$, $\theta_0 = \bar{\theta}$, draw an i.i.d. sequence for the innovations in e_t from some distribution, and compute $y_{2t+1}(\bar{\theta})$ recursively. Define $f_t = f(y_{2t}, y_{2t-1}, \dots, y_{2t-\tau+1})$ and $f_t(\theta) = f(y_{2t}(\bar{\theta}), y_{2t-1}(\bar{\theta}), \dots, y_{2t-\tau+1}(\bar{\theta}))$. Then $\theta_{T,T_{\mathrm{s}}}$ minimizes the distance between $F_{T_{\mathrm{s}}}(\theta) = (1/T_{\mathrm{s}}) \times \sum_t f_t(\theta)$ and $F_T = (1/T)\sum_t f_t$. The properties of $\theta_{T,T_{\mathrm{s}}}$ are different from those of a standard simulation estimator since $\bar{y}_2$ cannot be drawn from its (stationary) ergodic distribution, which is unknown. Since the simulated process for y_{2t} depends on the initial conditions and $\bar{\theta}$, it is nonstationary. If the mapping between y and θ was linear, we could have lessened the problem generating a long time series and throwing away an initial set of observations. However, when the mapping is nonlinear, the dependence on the initial conditions may not die out. Note also that $f_t(\theta)$ depends on θ because of the standard parametric representation and because the transition law of motion of y_{2t} depends on θ. The latter effect is troublesome since $h_t(y_t, x_t, \theta)$ may fail to be uniformly continuous.

To take care of these two problems, one needs to impose somewhat stronger conditions on the f function, namely geometric ergodicity and uniform Lipschitz continuity.

Definition 5.2 (geometric ergodicity). A time-homogeneous Markov process $\{y_t\}_{t=0}^{\infty}$ is geometrically ergodic if for some $b \in (0, 1]$, some probability measure μ (the ergodic distribution of y_t), and any initial point y_0,

$$b^{-\tau}\|P_{t,t+\tau} - \mu\| \to 0 \quad \text{as } \tau \to \infty, \tag{5.54}$$

where $\| \cdot \| \equiv \sup_{\{\mathfrak{H}:|\mathfrak{H}(y)|\leqslant 1|\}} \int \mathfrak{H}(y)\, d\mu(y)$ is the total variation norm of μ and $P_{t,t+\tau}$ is the τ-step transition probability.

In words, geometric ergodicity holds if y_t converges at the rate b to the stationary distribution. Note that geometric ergodicity implies α-mixing with the mixing coefficient converging geometrically to zero. When y_t can take only a finite number of values, geometric ergodicity holds if the Markov chain is irreducible and aperiodic and if the mapping between states and parameters and next-period states is uniformly convergent. Aperiodicity obtains if the transition matrix does not deterministically alternate between blocks of states. Irreducibility means that each state is accessible from every other state with positive probability. Precise definitions of these two concepts are given in chapter 9.

To limit the feedback from θ to $h_t(y_t, x_t, \theta)$ via the transition matrix we need the following.

Definition 5.3 (uniform Lipschitz condition). A family of functions $\{f_t(\theta)\}$ is Lipschitz, uniformly in probability, if there is a sequence $\{b_t\}_{t=1}^{T}$ such that, for all $\theta_1, \theta_2 \in \Theta$,

$$\|f_t(\theta_1) - f_t(\theta_2)\| \leqslant b_t \|\theta_1 - \theta_2\| \tag{5.55}$$

for all t, where $b^T = (1/T)\sum_{t=1}^{T} b_t$ is bounded in probability.

This condition, together with geometric ergodicity of x_t and a boundedness restriction on the norm of $f_t(\theta)$, implies that the ACF of $f_t(\theta)$ exists and is absolutely summable. In turn, this implies that $h_t(y_t, x_t, \theta)$ satisfies a weak law of large number and this ensures consistency of the simulation estimator for problems like those of example 5.29.

To ensure asymptotic normality, we need that h_t is continuous and differentiable, that $E(\partial h_t/\partial \theta')$ exists and is finite, and that θ_0 is in the interior of Θ. In addition we need that $\partial h(y_t, x_t, \theta)/\partial \theta'$ satisfies the Lipschitz condition uniformly in probability, that is, it is bounded and continuous in θ in expectations. Given these conditions, $\sqrt{T} h_T(\theta_0) \xrightarrow{D} \mathbb{N}(0, \bar{\Sigma} = \Sigma_y(1 + \kappa^{-1}))$, where h_T was defined in equation (5.51).

Exercise 5.42. Show the asymptotic distribution of $\sqrt{T}(\theta_{T,T_s} - \theta_0)$. Show that the asymptotic covariance matrix when W is chosen optimally has the form $\Sigma_\theta(W^\dagger) = (1 + \kappa^{-1})[E(\partial h/\partial \theta')' \bar{\Sigma}^{-1} E(\partial h/\partial \theta')]^{-1}$. Argue that, as $\kappa \to \infty$, $\Sigma_\theta(W^\dagger)$ approaches the covariance matrix of θ_T.

Several simulation estimators are popular in the literature. We examine three of them next.

5.5.2 *Simulated Method of Moments Estimator*

In a simulated method of moments (SMM) setup, θ is chosen to minimize the distance between moments of actual and simulated data. Therefore, f_t measures variances, covariances, and autocorrelations, etc. In the context of example 5.24, one could have selected the eleven unknown parameters by simulation by using the following algorithm.

Algorithm 5.3.

(1) Choose arbitrary values for $\theta = (\beta, \vartheta_N, \varphi, \eta, \delta, \bar{\zeta}, \bar{G}, \rho_\zeta, \rho_{\mathrm{G}}, \sigma_{\mathrm{G}}^2, \sigma_\zeta^2)$ and simulate the model after an (approximate) solution is obtained.

(2) Let $\mathfrak{S} = (\mathfrak{S}_1, \mathfrak{S}_2)$ be the statistic of interest, where $\mathfrak{S}_1$ are the conditions dictated by the model — Euler equation, intratemporal conditions, etc. — and $\mathfrak{S}_2$ are those selected by the investigator — variances, covariances, and autocorrelations. Clearly, $\dim(\mathfrak{S}) \geqslant 11$ and $\mathfrak{S}_1$ could be zero. Compute $\mathfrak{S}(\theta) - \mathfrak{S}_T$. Update estimates of θ by using gradient methods (see chapter 6).

(3) Repeat (1) and (2) until $\|\mathfrak{S}(\theta^l) - \mathfrak{S}_T\| < \iota$, or $\|\theta^l - \theta^{l-1}\| < \iota$, or both, ι small.

SMM is particularly useful when $\mathfrak{S}(\theta)$ are moments of variables with no counterpart in the data. Let $x_t = (x_{1t}, x_{2t})$, and let x_{2t} be unobservable with a known distribution. Then, as in example 5.27, one can draw $\{x_{2t}\}$ sequences and construct $\mathfrak{S}^l(x_{1t}, x_{2t}^l, \theta)$, for each $l = 1, 2, \dots, L$. If the draws are i.i.d., by the law of large numbers $(1/L)\sum_{l=1}^{L} \mathfrak{S}^l(x_{1t}, x_{2t}^l, \theta) \xrightarrow{\mathrm{P}} \mathfrak{S}(x_{1t}, x_{2t}, \theta)$. Hence, we can use $\mathfrak{S}_{lT} = (1/T)\sum_t (1/L)\sum_l \mathfrak{S}^l(x_{1t}, x_{2t}^l, \theta)$, as long as L is large enough.

Example 5.30. We reconsider the New Keynesian Phillips curve of example 5.11. We estimate $\theta = (\beta, \zeta_{\mathrm{p}})$ so as to make the variance and the first two autocorrelations of inflation in the data and in the model as close as possible. Using CPI inflation and the output gap, a grid of 100 values for $\beta = [0.98, 1.02]$, and $\zeta_{\mathrm{p}} = [0.20, 0.98]$, we obtain $\beta = (0.986, 1.009, 1.011)$ and $\zeta_{\mathrm{p}} = (0.155, 0.115, 0.422)$ for the United States, the United Kingdom, and Germany, respectively. The values of the criterion function at θ_{T_1,T_2} are $(23.32, 114.14, 37.89)$, indicating, perhaps unsurprisingly, that the model fails to replicate the variability and the autocorrelation structure of inflation in these countries.

Exercise 5.43. Consider a log-linearized version of the model of example 5.24 and suppose you choose parameters to match the cross-covariance function of hours and productivity. Since three parameters can be obtained from the moments of the government expenditure process, you have eight free parameters. Select three autocovariances of each of the two series and three cross-covariances. Using the same data as in example 5.24, provide SMM estimates of the free parameters and a test for overidentification.

Exercise 5.44. Consider the setup of exercise 5.37 but assume that effort is unobservable. Provide an algorithm to obtain SMM estimates of the free parameters. Which moments would you consider? Which instruments? Are there parameters which are not identifiable?

Exercise 5.45. Simulate data from a log-linearized sticky price, sticky wage model. You are free to select how many shocks you want to include and how much measurement error you want to consider, but make sure your parametrization is appropriate. Use GMM and SMM to get estimates of the structural parameters. Set $T = 100, 200$. Repeat the exercise 100 times drawing shocks from normal distributions. What can you say about the bias in estimating the structural parameters that each produces? Make sure you consider both the optimal and the identity matrix to weight moment conditions and both just identified and overidentified systems.

5.5.3 *Simulated Quasi-Maximum Likelihood/Indirect Inference*

The method of simulated quasi-maximum likelihood (SQML) is useful when a researcher is interested in matching the conditional density of the data. Since a VAR(q) with i.i.d. errors can capture this density well if q and T are large, SQML can be thought of as selecting θ so as to match the VAR representation of actual and simulated data. Let the conditional density of simulated data be $f(x_t(\theta) \mid x_{t-1}(\theta), \dots, x_{t-q}(\theta), \alpha)$, where $\alpha \in R^{k'}$ are "shallow" parameters, $k' \geqslant k$. Note that f may be misspecified in the sense that the true conditional density of $x_t(\alpha)$ may not belong to the set of functions $f(x_t(\theta) \mid x_{t-1}(\theta), \dots, x_{t-p}(\theta), \alpha)$. In principle, one could choose f to approximate as best as possible the true conditional density but in practice computational considerations suggest the selection of f so that it is easy to obtain a quasi-maximum likelihood estimate of α. When f is a VAR with i.i.d. errors, α includes the VAR coefficients on lagged variables and the parameters of the covariance matrix. Hence, while the structural model may be highly nonlinear in θ, the estimated model for $x_t(\theta)$ is linear in α.

Let $\mathcal{L}_{T_s}(\{x_t(\theta)\}, \alpha) \equiv \sum_{t=1}^{T_s} \ln f(x_t(\theta), \dots, x_{t-q}(\theta), \alpha)$ be the quasi-log-likelihood of the model. We let $\alpha_{T_s}(\theta) \equiv \operatorname{argmax} \mathcal{L}_{T_s}(\{x_t(\theta)\}, \alpha)$. Since there is no closed-form expression, the mapping between θ and α needs to be computed by simulation. If T_s is sufficiently large, $\alpha_{T_s}(\theta) \xrightarrow{\text{P}} \alpha(\theta)$. Let $\mathcal{L}_T(\{y_t\}, a) \equiv \sum_{t=1}^{T} \ln f(y_t, \dots, y_{t-p}, a)$ be the quasi-log-likelihood of the actual data and let $a_T \equiv \operatorname{argmax} \mathcal{L}_T(\{y_t\}, a)$. If T is sufficiently large, $a_T \xrightarrow{\text{P}} a$. We set $T_s = \kappa T$, $\kappa \geqslant 1$.

We assume that there exists a θ_0 such that $a = \alpha(\theta_0)$ (this condition is typically referred to as encompassing). This does not mean that the model is a good representation of the data: instead, it simply requires the much weaker condition that there exists a θ_0 which makes the "shallow" parameters in actual and simulated data identical. Then, an SQML estimator θ_{T,T_s} solves

$$\theta_{T,T_s} \equiv \operatorname*{argmax}_{\theta} \mathcal{L}_T(\{y_t\}, \alpha(\theta)). \tag{5.56}$$

In words, we maximize the likelihood function of the actual data once we plug in the shallow parameters obtained from maximizing the likelihood function of the simulated data.

Example 5.31 (consumption function). Suppose a researcher is interested in finding out whether the consumption function generated by an RBC model matches the one in the data. Let the actual data be represented by a bivariate normal VAR(1) in consumption and output. Let α include the four VAR coefficients and the three covariance matrix coefficients and let θ include all the parameters of the RBC model. Then the following algorithm can be used.

Algorithm 5.4.

(1) Choose a θ^1 and simulate $x_t(\theta^1)$, $t = 1, \dots, T_s$.

(2) Fit a VAR(1) to simulated consumption and output data and obtain $\alpha(\theta^1)$.

(3) Use $\alpha(\theta^1)$ in the quasi-log-likelihood function of y_t, i.e., compute VAR residuals by using the actual data and $\alpha(\theta^1)$ and construct the log likelihood by using the prediction error decomposition (see chapter 6).

(4) Update θ^1 by using gradient methods; repeat steps (1)–(3) and continue until $\|\mathcal{L}_T(\{y_t\}, \alpha(\theta^l)) - \mathcal{L}_T(\{y_t\}, \alpha(\theta^{l-1}))\| \leqslant \iota$, or $\|\theta^l - \theta^{l-1}\| < \iota$, or both, ι small.

Note that, if $k' \geqslant k$, the SQML estimator maximizes the quasi-log-likelihood function subject to a set of $k' - k$ (nonlinear) restrictions. If the inequality is strict, there are $k' - k$ overidentifying restrictions which can be used to test the quality of the model. For example, a bivariate VAR(3) without a constant has $(2 \times 3) * 2 + 3$ parameters. If $\dim(\theta) = 5$, there are ten testable restrictions.

At times the distinction between SQML and SMM is blurred as the next example shows.

Example 5.32. In exercise 5.43 estimates are obtained by matching the cross-covariance functions of hours and productivity. If we represent actual and simulated data with a bivariate VAR, we can compute cross-covariance functions by using the companion form, $\mathbb{Y}_t = \mathbb{A}\mathbb{Y}_{t-1} + \mathbb{E}_t$. That is, $\text{var}(\mathbb{Y}_t) = (I - \mathbb{A})^{-1} \Sigma_E ((I - \mathbb{A})^{-1})'$ and $\text{cov}(\mathbb{Y}_t, \mathbb{Y}_{t-\tau}) = \mathbb{A}^\tau \, \text{var}(\mathbb{Y}_t)$.

When the "shallow" parameters are not the coefficients of the VAR representation of the data, SQML is typically termed the indirect inference principle.

Example 5.33 (Canova and Marrinan). It is usual to find that the forward rate (fer) is a biased predictor of the future spot exchange rate (ner). That is, in the regression $\text{ner}_{t+1} = a_0 + a_1 \text{fer}_{t,1} + e_{t+1}$, estimates of a_0 and a_1 are significantly differ from 0 and 1, respectively. One question of interest is whether this bias is consistent with optimizing agents and rational expectations. Suppose we can simulate $\text{ner}^s_{t+1}(\theta)$ and $\text{fer}^s_{t,1}(\theta)$ from a model and run the regression $\text{ner}^s_{t+1}(\theta) = \alpha_0 + \alpha_1 \text{fer}^s_{t,1}(\theta) + e^s_{t+1}$. Then we can ask if there is a range of θ such that $\alpha_0 = a_0$ and $\alpha_1 = a_1$ or, at least, such that the sign of (a_0, a_1) and of (α_0, α_1) is the same.

When indirect inference is employed, it is usual to split $\theta = (\theta_1, \theta_2)$, where θ_2 are nuisance parameters, needed for simulations but uninteresting from an economic viewpoint. Let f_T and $f_{T_s}(\theta)$ be vectors of shallow functions in actual and simulated data. Dridi and Renault (1998) showed the following two results.

Result 5.1. If we choose $W_T \xrightarrow{\text{P}} W$ and if there exists a $\bar{\theta}_2 \in \Theta_2$ such that $\lim_{T,T_s\to\infty}(f_T - f_{T_s}(x_t(\theta_1^0, \bar{\theta}_2))) = 0$, $\theta_{1,T,T_s} \equiv \text{argmin}[f_T - f_{T_s}(x_t(\theta_1, \bar{\theta}_2))]' \times W_T[f_T - f_{T_s}(x_t(\theta_1, \bar{\theta}_2))]$ is consistent for θ_1^0.

Result 5.2. Under the conditions stated in result 5.1, $\sqrt{T}(\theta_{1,T,T_s} - \theta_1^0) \xrightarrow{\text{D}} \mathbb{N}(0, (\partial[f_T - f_{T_s}(x_t(\theta_1, \bar{\theta}_2))]/\partial\theta_1')'\Sigma_0^{-1}(\partial[f_T - f_{T_s}(x_t(\theta_1, \bar{\theta}_2))]/\partial\theta')^{-1})$, where Σ_0 depends on $\text{var}(f_T)$, $\text{var}(f_{T_s})$, $\text{cov}(f_T, f_{T_s})$, $\text{cov}(\theta^l_{1,T,T_s}, \theta^{l'}_{1,T,T_s})$ and l, l' refer to simulations.

Note that, if there are no nuisance parameters, the first condition of result 5.1 collapses to a standard encompassing one that there exists a θ^0 such that $\lim_{T,T_s\to\infty}[f_T - f_{T_s}(x_t(\theta^0))] = 0$. Also, the conditions of results 5.1 and 5.2 are only sufficient. For necessary conditions, see, for example, Gourieroux and Monfort (1995).

Example 5.34 (Merha and Prescott). Consider the equity premium puzzle popularized by Merha and Prescott (1985). Here $f_T = [(1/T)\sum_t R_t^{\text{f}}, (1/T)\sum_t \text{EP}_t]$, the average risk-free rate and the average equity premium; θ_2 includes the mean, the variance, and the persistence of the endowment process; while $\theta_1 = (\beta, \varphi)$ are the discount factor and the risk-aversion coefficient. The literature has tried to (informally) find the range of θ_1 such that $f_{T_s}(x_t(\theta_1, \bar{\theta}_2))$ are as close as possible to f_T, given some estimate $\bar{\theta}_2$. A puzzle is generated because when $T_s = T$, values for θ_1 in a reasonable range make f_T and $f_{T_s}(x_t(\theta_1, \bar{\theta}_2))$ very different.

Exercise 5.46. The expectations theory of the term structure suggests that the return obtained on a long-term bond is a weighted average of the returns on successive short-term ones. Using a version of the model of example 5.24, obtain indirect inference estimates of the structural parameters and of the parameters of the technology process so that the coefficients in the regressions $R_{t,t+4} = a_1 + a_2 R_{t,1} + a_3 R_{t+1,1} + a_4 R_{t+2,2} + e_{1t}$ and $R_{t,t+2} = a_5 + a_6 R_{t,1} + a_7 R_{t+1,1} + e_{2t}$ obtained in the data are the same as those in the model, where $R_{t,t+4}$ are returns on one-year bonds and $R_{t,t+1}(R_{t,t+2})$ are returns on 90 and 180 day T-bills. (Hint: you need to impose more conditions to estimate all the parameters: several are not identifiable from these regressions. Also, do not use a log-linear approximation to solve this problem.) Can the model match the short end of the term structure of interest rates?

Example 5.35. We use an indirect inference principle to estimate the parameters of the New Keynesian Phillips curve of example 5.11 by using U.S. data. Here the functions we wish to match are the regression coefficients in $\pi_{t+1} = a_1\pi_t + a_2\,\text{gdpgap}_t + e_{t+1}$. We present results in table 5.4 for two specifications: one where

Table 5.4. Indirect inference estimates of a New Keynesian Phillips curve.

	Inflation coefficient	Output gap coefficient	β	ζ_{p}	Criterion function
Actual	0.993 (0.05)	−0.04 (0.143)			
Simulated (actual gap)	0.996 (0.006 2)	0.032 (0.001)	0.752	0.481	0.010 12
Simulated (simulated gap)	0.997 (0.000 08)	−0.004 (0.0006)	0.980	0.324	0.023 21

we use the actual output gap in the simulation and one where a process for the output gap is estimated by using an AR(2) and a constant on HP filtered data and then simulated. Standard errors are in parentheses. The model can roughly replicate the magnitude of a_1 found in actual regression. Note that, because a_2 is poorly estimated, we have a hard time producing the correct sign for this coefficient when the actual gap is used. Note also that estimated ζ_{p} are low (roughly, prices change every 1–2 quarters) and that β is unreasonably low when the actual gap is used.

Exercise 5.47 (Bayraktar, Sakellaris, and Vermeulen). Consider the investment decision of a monopolistic competitive firm. Output is produced by using $\zeta_{it} K_{it}^{1-\eta}$, where ζ_{it} is a technology shock, which includes both individual and aggregate components. Suppose the firm chooses capital and borrowing to maximize profits and suppose there are convex costs (equal to $\frac{1}{2}b_1(\text{inv}_t/K_t)^2 K_t$) and fixed costs (equal to $b_2 K_t$) to adjust capital. Suppose that investment is partly reversible so that the selling price of capital (p^{ks}) is lower than the buying price of capital (p^{kb}) and suppose there exists an external finance premium of the form $b_3 B_t / p^{ks} K_t$, where B_t is borrowing and b_1, b_2, b_3 are parameters (if $B_t < 0$, $b_3 = 0$). The choice of the firm is partly discrete (it must select an action between buying capital, selling capital, or doing nothing) and partly continuous (select B_{t+1}). The value function associated with each choice is $\mathbb{V}^j(\zeta, K, B) = \max_{\{K^+, B^+\}} \zeta K^{1-\eta} - C^j(K, \text{inv}) + B^+ - (1+r)(1 + b_3 B / p^{ks} K)B + \beta E \mathbb{V}^*(\zeta^+, K^+, B^+)$, where

$$C^j(K_t, \text{inv}_t) = \begin{cases} p^{kb}\text{inv}_t + \frac{1}{2}b_1(\text{inv}_t/K_t)^2 K_t + b_2 K_t & \text{if inv}_t > 0, \\ p^{ks}\text{inv}_t + \frac{1}{2}b_1(\text{inv}_t/K_t)^2 K_t + b_2 K_t & \text{if inv}_t < 0, \\ 0 & \text{if inv}_t = 0, \end{cases} \tag{5.57}$$

subject to $\text{inv} = K^+ - (1-\delta)K$, where "+" indicates future values. The structural parameters are $\theta = (\beta, \delta, \eta, b_1, b_2, b_3, p^{ks}, p^{kb})$ and $(\rho_\zeta, \sigma_\zeta^2)$. Using quarterly data for aggregate output, investment, capital and total bank borrowing, and the regression $(\text{inv}_t - \overline{\text{inv}}) = a_0, +a_1(\text{GDP}_t - \overline{\text{GDP}}) + a_2(\text{GDP}_t - \overline{\text{GDP}})^2 + a_3(B_t - \bar{B})/(K_t - \bar{K}) + a_4(\zeta_t - \bar{\zeta})(B_t - \bar{B})^2/(K_t - \bar{K}) + e_{it}$, where the bar variables are time averages, find indirect inference estimates of $(b_1, b_2, b_3, p^{ks}, p^{kb})$

assuming $r_t = r$, $\beta = 0.99$, $\delta = 0.025$, $\eta = 0.66$, $\rho_\zeta = 0.95$, $\sigma_\zeta = 1.0$. Compute output and investment moments in the data and in the model. Do they match?

5.5.4 Matching Impulse Responses

It is quite popular nowadays to estimate the parameters of a DSGE model by matching structural impulse responses obtained in the data. Leading examples are Rotemberg and Woodford (1997) and Christiano et al. (2005). Matching impulse responses is a special case of an indirect inference approach when the function f is a vector of impulse responses obtained from certain economically meaningful shocks. Most of the existing applications are concerned with the dynamics induced by monetary disturbances. However, responses to technology shocks are also considered (see, for example, Dedola and Neri 2004).

To make the link explicit we need to define a partial indirect inference estimator. Such an estimator is obtained if a subset of the components of $f_{T_s}(x_t,(\theta))$ is used for estimation. That is, we assume that there exists a θ_1^0 such that $f_T^1 = f_{T_s}^1(x_t(\theta_1^0, \bar{\theta}_2))$ with $f_T^1 \subseteq f_T$. This estimator is semi-parametric, since not all the features of the model are fully specified, and $f_T \neq f_{T_s}(x_t(\theta_0^1, \bar{\theta}_2))$, that is, the model is potentially misspecified in some dimensions. Then θ_{1,T,T_s} minimizes $Q_{T,T_s}^1(\bar{\theta}_2) = [f_T^1 - f_{T_s}^1(x_t(\theta_1, \bar{\theta}_2))]' W_{(1,T_1,T_2)} [f_T^1 - f_{T_s}^1(x_t(\theta_1, \bar{\theta}_2))]$ and $\lim_{T\to\infty} T \times Q_{T,T_s}^1(\bar{\theta}_2) \xrightarrow{\text{D}} \chi^2(\dim(f_T^1) - \dim(\theta_1))$. This asymptotic distribution is valid if $\bar{\theta}_2$ is replaced by a θ_{2,T,T_s} satisfying $\sqrt{T}(\theta_{2,T,T_s} - \bar{\theta}_2) \xrightarrow{\text{P}} 0$.

Simulation estimators obtained by using only a subset of the model implications face generic identification problems. We illustrate their importance next in the context of impulse response matching since it is with this particular application that severe identification problems have been noted. The next two examples show what may go wrong.

Example 5.36. Suppose $x_t = [1/(\lambda_2+\lambda_1)]E_t x_{t+1} + [\lambda_1\lambda_2/(\lambda_1+\lambda_2)]x_{t-1} + v_t$, where $\lambda_2 \geqslant 1 \geqslant \lambda_1 \geqslant 0$. The unique stable rational expectations solution is $x_t = \lambda_1 x_{t-1} + [(\lambda_2+\lambda_1)/\lambda_2]v_t$. Therefore, the normalized responses of x_t to a unitary shock in v_t are $[(\lambda_2+\lambda_1)/\lambda_2, \lambda_1(\lambda_2+\lambda_1)/\lambda_2, \lambda_1^2(\lambda_2+\lambda_1)/\lambda_2, \dots]$, and, by using at least two horizons, one can obtain estimates of λ_1 and λ_2. It is easy to construct a different process whose stable rational expectations solution has the same impulse response. Consider, for example, $y_t = \lambda_1 y_{t-1} + w_t$, $0 \leqslant \lambda_1 < 1$. Clearly, the process is stable and, if $\sigma_{\rm w} = [(\lambda_2+\lambda_1)/\lambda_2]\sigma_v$, x_t and y_t responses to shocks will be indistinguishable.

What is it that makes the two processes in example 5.36 observationally equivalent from the point of view of impulse responses? Since the unstable root λ_2 enters the solution only contemporaneously, and since the variance of the shocks is not estimable from normalized impulse responses—any value simply implies a proportional increase in all the elements of the impulse response function—we can arbitrarily set $\sigma_{\rm w}$ so as to capture the effects of λ_2.

Note that, if x_t is inflation and v_t are marginal costs, example 5.36 implies that it is impossible to distinguish backward-looking, mixed backward-looking, and forward-looking types of Phillips curves by using responses to marginal cost shocks.

Example 5.37. Consider a version of a three-equation New Keynesian model:

$$\text{gdpgap}_t = a_1 E_t \,\text{gdpgap}_{t+1} + a_2(i_t - E_t\pi_{t+1}) + v_{1t}, \tag{5.58}$$

$$\pi_t = a_3 E_t \pi_{t+1} + a_4 \,\text{gdpgap}_t + v_{2t}, \tag{5.59}$$

$$i_t = a_5 E_t \pi_{t+1} + v_{3t}, \tag{5.60}$$

where gdpgap_t is the output gap, π_t the inflation rate, i_t the nominal interest rate, and the first equation is the log-linearized Euler condition, the second a log-linearized forward-looking Phillips curve, and the third characterizes monetary policy. Using the method of undetermined coefficients, the rational expectations solution is

$$\begin{bmatrix} \text{gdpgap}_t \\ \pi_t \\ i_t \end{bmatrix} = \begin{bmatrix} 1 & 0 & a_2 \\ a_4 & 1 & a_2 a_4 \\ 0 & 0 & 1 \end{bmatrix} \begin{bmatrix} v_{1t} \\ v_{2t} \\ v_{3t} \end{bmatrix}. \tag{5.61}$$

Two useful points can be made. First, the parameters a_1, a_3, a_5 disappear from (5.61). Interestingly, they are those characterizing the forward-looking dynamics of the model. Second, different shocks carry different information for the remaining parameters: responses to v_{1t} allow us to recover only a_4; responses to v_{3t} may be used to recover both a_4 and a_2 while responses to v_{2t} have no information for the two parameters. Hence, matching responses to v_{2t} leaves all the parameters of the model underidentified.

Example 5.37 suggests that the objective function obtained by matching impulse responses may be completely flat in some dimensions of the parameter space, implying, for example, that its Hessian has reduced rank. Checking the rank of the Hessian should therefore be a precondition for estimation. Unfortunately, the Hessian at the maximum cannot be computed before estimates are obtained. However, since one typically has a good idea where the maximum may be, to avoid problems like those of example 5.37, one could examine the Hessian at various calibrated parameters. If some zero eigenvalue occurs, the Hessian is of reduced rank and some parameters are underidentified. On the other hand, if the smallest eigenvalues of the Hessian are small relative to the average, the determinant of the Hessian is close to singular, and some parameters will only be weakly identifiable.

Example 5.38. We estimate the parameters of the following model,

$$\text{gdpgap}_t = E_t \,\text{gdpgap}_{t+1} - \frac{1}{\varphi}(i_t - E_t\pi_{t+1}) + e_{1t}, \tag{5.62}$$

$$\pi_t = \beta E_t \pi_{t+1} + \frac{(\varphi + \theta_n)(1-\zeta_\text{p})(1-\beta\zeta_\text{p})}{\zeta_\text{p}} \,\text{gdpgap}_t + e_{2t}, \tag{5.63}$$

$$i_t = a_\text{r} i_{t-1} + a_\text{GDP} \,\text{gdpgap}_{t-1} + a_\pi \pi_{t-1} + e_{3t}, \tag{5.64}$$

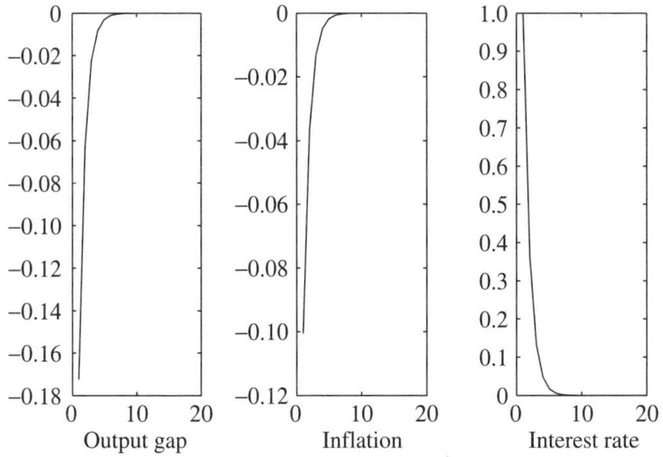

Figure 5.1. Responses to monetary shocks.

by using U.S. quarterly data from 1980:1 to 2000:4 and twenty responses to monetary shocks identified from a trivariate VAR with output gap, inflation, and federal funds rate using a Choleski decomposition with the variables in that order. Here e_{1t} is an AR(1) shock with persistence ρ_1, e_{2t} an AR(1) with persistence ρ_2, and e_{3t} is i.i.d.; φ is the risk-aversion coefficient, θ_n the inverse elasticity of labor supply, ζ_p the Calvo price stickiness parameters, β the discount factor, and a_r, a_{GDP}, a_π are policy parameters. Noting that ρ_1 and ρ_2 are not identified from impulse responses to monetary shocks and fixing $\beta = 0.99$, we obtain the following estimates of the remaining parameters: $\varphi = 9.4395$, $\theta_n = 1.5626$, $\zeta_p = 0.835\,68$, $a_r = 0.528\,33$, $a_\pi = 2.2643$, $a_{GDP} = 0.709\,84$, which appear to be reasonable and in line with theoretical expectations, expect perhaps the risk-aversion coefficient, which is somewhat high. Responses to monetary shocks obtained with estimated parameters show two important features (see figure 5.1). First, despite price stickiness, the largest inflation responses are instantaneous. Second, inflation responses appear to be smaller than output gap responses at all horizons.

Unfortunately, the objective function for this problem is rather flat (see figure 5.2, where we plot it in a neighborhood of the maximum, varying one parameter at a time). The Hessian at the maximum is rank deficient and at least four of its six eigenvalues are small. Inspection of (5.62)–(5.64) indicates that only a combination of ζ_p and θ_n is estimable (and this accounts for the rank deficiency of the Hessian) and, except for a_r and ζ_p, the other parameters are only very weakly identifiable from the responses to monetary shocks. That is to say, the variables of the model provide scarce information to pin down values for these four parameters. Consequently, standard errors are large and neither estimated parameters nor impulse responses are significant at standard confidence levels.

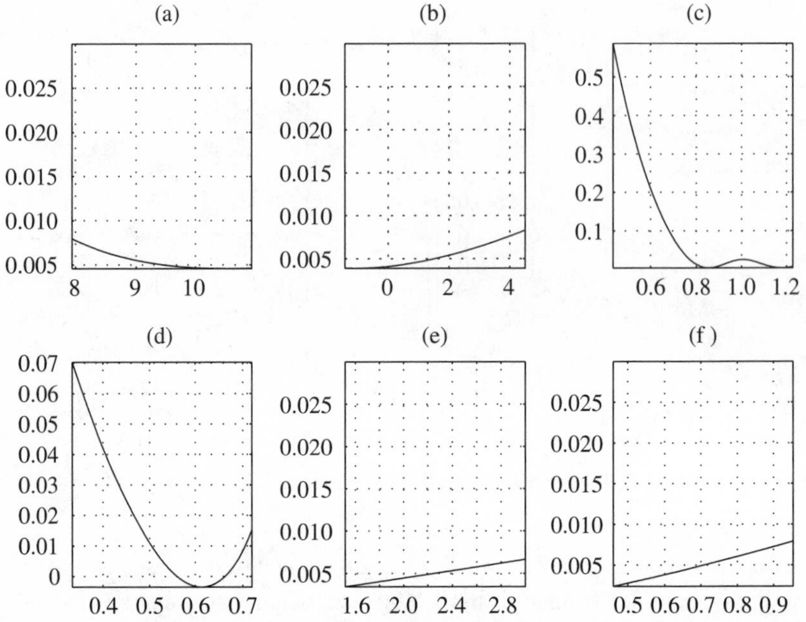

Figure 5.2. Shape of distance function. (a) Risk aversion = 9.4395; (b) inverse labor elasticity = 1.5626; (c) price stickiness = 0.835 68; (d) $a_{\mathrm{r}} = 0.528\,33$; (e) $a_{\pi} = 2.2643$; (f) $a_{\mathrm{GDP}} = 0.709\,84$.

When identification problems occur, one has three options. First, one can calibrate the parameters for which the distance function has no information. Care should be exercised in this case since, as shown by Canova and Sala (2005), severe distortions in the remaining parameter estimates may be produced if the calibrated values differ from the true ones. Second, one can try to add more conditions, for example, jointly match responses to monetary and IS shocks. Adding responses can improve identification since more cross-equation restrictions are considered. In the limit, when all the implications of the model are used, an objective function constructed by using impulse responses will have less information than the likelihood of the model, since the variance of the shocks will never be identifiable. Third, one can try to reparametrize the model or add equations so as to make the distance function more informative. For example, since the elasticity of labor supply is unlikely to be identifiable from output, inflation, and interest rate data, conditions relating this parameter to hours or the real wage may help to make the distance function better behaved.

Inference in models where parameters are (weakly) identified is problematic for two reasons. First, the distribution of estimates is not normal, even in large samples. Therefore, it is difficult to assess the significance of estimates one obtains. Second, since maximization routines have a hard time exploring flat surfaces, one may fail to recover the data-generating process even in large samples, and may confuse models with different frictions or transmission mechanisms (see Canova and Sala (2005) for examples).

Exercise 5.48. Suppose we are interested in matching responses to technology shocks, which we identified in the data by the requirement that in response to such a shock the output gap increases and inflation declines. Using the model of example 5.38, find indirect inference estimates of the parameters that come as close as possible to matching the first ten responses of the output gap, inflation, and interest rates obtained in the data. Check which parameters are identifiable and compare parameter estimates with those presented in example 5.38.

6
Likelihood Methods

Maximum likelihood (ML) techniques have enjoyed a remarkable comeback in the last few years, probably as a consequence of the development of faster computer technology and of the substantial improvement in the specification of structural models. In fact, complex stochastic general equilibrium models have recently been estimated and tested against the data. This represents a shift of attitude relative to the 1980s or the beginning of the 1990s, when GMM and related techniques dominated the scene. While maximum likelihood is a special case of GMM when the scores of the likelihood are used as orthogonality conditions, (full-information) ML differs from GMM in several respects.

In both cases, a researcher starts from a fully specified dynamic stochastic general equilibrium model. However, while with GMM the first-order conditions of the maximization are sufficient for estimation and testing, with maximum likelihood the final form, expressing the endogenous variables of the model as a function of the exogenous variables and the parameters, is needed. As we saw in chapter 2, this is not a small enterprise in general and approximations are often needed, transforming nonlinear specifications into linear ones. The presence of nonlinearities, on the other hand, does not present particular problems for GMM estimation and testing. Moreover, while with GMM one could use only the (limited) information contained in a subset of the equilibrium conditions, e.g., the Euler equations, once the final form is calculated, all the implications of the model must necessarily be taken into account for estimation. Therefore, while with the former one can estimate and test assuming that only some of the equations of the model appropriately characterize the data-generating process, such an assumption is untenable when ML is used. An interesting conundrum arises when misspecification is present. Following White (1982), one can show that a quasi-ML estimator of the parameters, obtained when the distribution of the errors is misspecified, has the same asymptotic properties as the correct ML estimator under regularity conditions. However, the misspecification present in DSGE models is unlikely to be reducible to the distributions of the errors. Hence, the properties of ML in these setups are unknown and care must be used in interpreting estimates and tests.

With both ML and GMM the final scope of the analysis is the evaluation of the quality of the model's approximation to the data and, given estimates, to study the effects of altering interesting economic (policy) parameters. This should be contrasted with the exercises typically performed in VARs. Here the full implications of the model, as opposed to a set of minimal restrictions, are used to obtain estimates of the objects of interest; the analysis is geared toward the estimation of "deep" parameters as opposed to economically meaningful shocks; and model evaluation is often more important than describing the (restricted) structure of the data in response to the disturbances. Which approach one subscribes to depends on how much a researcher trusts the model. With ML one puts a lot of faith in the model as a description of the data — the structure is correct, only the parameters are unknown. With VARs the opposite is true. Therefore, only a limited set of conventional or generic restrictions is considered.

This chapter describes the steps needed to estimate models with ML. We start by describing the use of the Kalman filter for state-space models. State space models are general structures: any multivariate ARMA model and almost all log-linearized DSGE models can be fitted into this framework. The Kalman filter, besides providing minimum MSE forecasts of the endogenous variables and optimal recursive estimates of the unobserved states, is a crucial building block in the prediction error decomposition of the likelihood. In fact, the likelihood function of a state-space model can be conveniently expressed in terms of one-step-ahead forecast errors of the observables, conditional on the initial observations, and of their recursive variance, both of which are obtained with the Kalman filter. Therefore, given some initial parameter values, the Kalman filter can be used to recursively construct the likelihood function; gradient methods can be employed to provide new estimates of the parameters and the two-step procedure can be repeated until the gradient or the parameters do not change across iterations.

In the third section we provide numerical tips on how to update parameter estimates and discuss other numerical issues often encountered in practice. The algorithms are only sketched here. For details the reader should consult Press et al. (1986) or Judge et al. (1985). The last portion of the chapter applies the machinery we have developed to the problem of estimating DSGE models. The (log-)linearized solution of such models naturally comes into a state-space format where the coefficients are highly nonlinear functions of the structural parameters. We discuss a number of peculiarities of DSGE models relative to other time series specifications and describe how to use cross-equation restrictions to identify structural parameters and to test the model. This is the approach popularized by Sargent (1979) and Hansen and Sargent (1979) and exploits the fact that (log-)linearized expectational equations impose restrictions on the VAR of the data. We conclude with a couple of examples illustrating the difficulties encountered in applying ML to the estimation of DSGE models.

6.1 The Kalman Filter

The Kalman filter is one of the most important instruments in the toolkit of applied macroeconomists and we will use it extensively in the rest of this book. The presentation here is basic. Anderson and Moore (1979) or Harvey (1991) have more extensive details.

The Kalman filter is typically employed in state-space models of the form

$$y_t = x'_{1t}\alpha_t + x'_{2t}v_{1t}, \tag{6.1}$$

$$\alpha_t = \mathbb{D}_{0t} + \mathbb{D}_{1t}\alpha_{t-1} + \mathbb{D}_{2t}v_{2t}, \tag{6.2}$$

where x'_{1t} is an $m \times m_1$ matrix, x'_{2t} is an $m \times m_2$ matrix, $\mathbb{D}_{0t}$ is an $m_1 \times 1$ vector, $\mathbb{D}_{1t}$ and $\mathbb{D}_{2t}$ are $m_1 \times m_1$ and $m_1 \times m_3$ matrices, v_{1t} is an $m_2 \times 1$ vector of martingale difference sequences, $v_{1t} \sim \mathbb{N}(0, \Sigma_{v_1})$, and v_{2t} is an $m_3 \times 1$ vector of martingale difference sequences, $v_{2t} \sim \mathbb{N}(0, \Sigma_{v_2})$. We also assume that $E(v_{1t}v'_{2\tau}) = 0$ and $E(v_{1t}\alpha'_0) = 0$ for all t and τ. The first assumption can be dispensed with, as we will see later on. The two together ensure that the states α_t and the disturbances v_{1t} are uncorrelated.

Equation (6.1) is typically referred to as the measurement (observation) equation while (6.2) is the transition (state) equation. In principle, α_t is allowed to vary over time and $x_{1t}, x_{2t}, \mathbb{D}_{0t}, \mathbb{D}_{1t}, \mathbb{D}_{2t}$ could be fixed (i.e., matrices of numbers) or realizations of random variables. For example, x_{1t} could contain lagged y_t and x_{2t} current and/or lagged stochastic volatility terms. Note that m_2 shocks drive the m endogenous variables, $m_2 \leqslant m$.

The framework in (6.1), (6.2) is general: a number of time series and regression models can be cast in such a format. We consider a few special cases next.

Example 6.1. Consider an m-variable VAR $y_t = A(\ell)y_{t-1} + e_t$, where $A(\ell)$ is a polynomial of order q and e_t is a martingale difference process, $e_t \sim \mathbb{N}(0, \Sigma_e)$. The companion form of the VAR is $\mathbb{Y}_t = \mathbb{A}\mathbb{Y}_{t-1} + E_t$, where $\mathbb{A} = [\mathbb{A}_1, \mathbb{A}_2]'$, $\mathbb{A}_1 = (A_1, \dots, A_q)$ contains the first m rows of $\mathbb{A}$, $\mathbb{A}_2$ is a matrix of 1s and 0s, and $E_t = (e_t, 0, \dots, 0)'$, which fits into (6.1), (6.2) setting $\alpha_t = \mathbb{Y}_t = [y'_t, y'_{t-1}, \dots, y'_{t-q}]'$, $x'_{1t} = [I, 0, \dots, 0]$, $\mathbb{D}_{1t} = \mathbb{A}$, $\Sigma_{v_1} = 0$, $v_{2t} = E_t$, $\mathbb{D}_{2t} = I$, $\mathbb{D}_{0t} = 0$. Hence, there is no measurement error; the measurement equation is trivial; states and observables coincide.

Example 6.2. Consider the univariate process, $y_t = A_1y_{t-1} + A_2y_{t-2} + e_t + D_1e_{t-1}$. This process can equivalently be written as

$$y_t = \begin{bmatrix} 1 & 0 \end{bmatrix} \begin{bmatrix} y_t \\ A_2y_{t-1} + D_1e_t \end{bmatrix},$$

$$\begin{bmatrix} y_t \\ A_2y_{t-1} + D_1e_t \end{bmatrix} = \begin{bmatrix} A_1 & 1 \\ A_2 & 0 \end{bmatrix} \begin{bmatrix} y_{t-1} \\ A_2y_{t-2} + D_1e_{t-1} \end{bmatrix} + \begin{bmatrix} 1 \\ D_1 \end{bmatrix} e_t.$$

Hence, an ARMA(2, 1) structure fits (6.1), (6.2) by setting

$$\alpha_t = \begin{bmatrix} y_t \\ A_2 y_{t-1} + D_1 e_t \end{bmatrix}, \quad \mathbb{D}_{1t} = \begin{bmatrix} A_1 & 1 \\ A_2 & 0 \end{bmatrix}, \quad \mathbb{D}_{2t} = \begin{bmatrix} 1 \\ D_1 \end{bmatrix}, \quad \mathbb{D}_{0t} = 0,$$

$$x'_{1t} = \begin{bmatrix} 1 & 0 \end{bmatrix}, \quad \Sigma_{v_1} = 0, \quad \Sigma_{v_2} = \sigma_e^2.$$

Exercise 6.1. Consider a process of the form $y_{1t} = A_1(\ell) y_{1t-1} + D(\ell)e_t + A_2 y_{2t}$, where y_{2t} represents exogenous variables, $A_1(\ell)$ is of order q_1, and $D(\ell)$ is of order q_2. Cast this model into a state-space format and display $\mathbb{D}_{1t}, \mathbb{D}_{2t}, x'_{1t}, x'_{2t}$.

Besides time series models, several structures naturally fit into a state-space framework.

Example 6.3. (i) In many economic problems the *ex ante* real rate of interest is needed but only the *ex post* real rate of interest is computable. Here one could set $\alpha_t \equiv r_t^{\mathrm{e}} = i_t - \pi_t^{\mathrm{e}}$, where π_t^{e} is the expected inflation rate and assume, for example, $\alpha_t = \mathbb{D}_1 \alpha_{t-1} + v_{2t}$. The observed real rate is then $y_t \equiv i_t - \pi_t = \alpha_t + v_{1t}$, where v_{1t} is a measurement error.

(ii) An RBC model driven by unit root technology shocks implies that all endogenous variables except hours have a common trend (see, for example, section 3.4). Here $\alpha_t = \alpha_{t-1} + v_{2t}$ is a one-dimensional process, $x'_{1t} = x'_1$ are the loadings on the trend, and $x'_{2t} = x'_2$ are the loadings on everything else (cycle, irregular, etc.).

Exercise 6.2. When the marginal utility of money is constant and agents do not discount the future, uncovered interest parity implies that interest rate differentials across countries should be related to the expected change in the log of the exchange rate (see exercise 5.35). Cast such a relationship into a state-space format, carefully defining the matrices $x'_{1t}, x'_{2t}, \mathbb{D}_{0t}, \mathbb{D}_{1t}, \mathbb{D}_{2t}$.

Exercise 6.3 (nonlinear state-space model). Consider the model $y_t = \alpha_t + v_{1t}$, $\alpha_{t+1} = \alpha_t \theta + v_{2t}$ and suppose one is interested in θ, which is unobservable, as is α_t. (In a trend-cycle decomposition, θ represents, for example, the persistence of the trend.) Cast the problem in a state-space format; show the state vector and display the matrices of the model.

The Kalman filter can be used to optimally estimate the unobservable state vector α_t and to update estimates when a new observation becomes available. As a byproduct, it also produces recursive forecasts of y_t, consistent with the information available at each t.

Suppose we want to compute $\alpha_{t|t}$, the optimal (MSE) estimator of α_t, by using information up to t, and $\Omega_{t|t}$, the MSE matrix of the forecast errors in the state equation. At this stage we let $x'_{1t} = x'_1, x'_{2t} = x'_2, \mathbb{D}_{1t} = \mathbb{D}_1, \mathbb{D}_{0t} = \mathbb{D}_0, \mathbb{D}_{2t} = \mathbb{D}_2$ be known. We also assume that the sample $\{y_t\}_{t=1}^T$ is available. The Kalman filter algorithm has five steps.

Algorithm 6.1.

(1) Select initial conditions. If all eigenvalues of $\mathbb{D}_1$ are less than 1 in absolute value, set $\alpha_{1|0} = E(\alpha_1)$ and $\Omega_{1|0} = \mathbb{D}_1\Omega_{1|0}\mathbb{D}_1' + \mathbb{D}_2\Sigma_{v_2}\mathbb{D}_2'$ or $\text{vec}(\Omega_{1|0}) = [I - (\mathbb{D}_1 \otimes \mathbb{D}_1')^{-1}]\text{vec}(\mathbb{D}_2\Sigma_{v_2}\mathbb{D}_2')$, in which case the initial conditions are the unconditional mean and variance of the process. When some of the eigenvalues of $\mathbb{D}_1$ are greater than or equal to 1, initial conditions cannot be drawn from the unconditional distribution, which does not exist. In this case, one needs a guess (say, $\alpha_{1|0} = 0$, $\Omega_{1|0} = \kappa * I$, κ large) to start the iterations, alter the recursions (2)–(4) below by using the information filter of Anderson and Moore (1979), or employ the nonstationary Kalman filter of Koopman (1997).

(2) Predict y_t and construct the mean square error of the forecasts by using $t-1$ information:

$$E(y_{t|t-1}) = x_1'\alpha_{t|t-1}, \tag{6.3}$$

$$\begin{aligned} E(y_t - y_{t|t-1})(y_t - y_{t|t-1})' &= E(x_1'(\alpha_t - \alpha_{t|t-1})(\alpha_t - \alpha_{t|t-1})'x_1) + x_2'\Sigma_{v_1}x_2 \\ &= x_1'\Omega_{t|t-1}x_1 + x_2'\Sigma_{v_1}x_2 \equiv \Sigma_{t|t-1}. \end{aligned} \tag{6.4}$$

(3) Update state equation estimates (after observing y_t):

$$\alpha_{t|t} = \alpha_{t|t-1} + \Omega_{t|t-1}x_1\Sigma_{t|t-1}^{-1}(y_t - x_1'\alpha_{t|t-1}), \tag{6.5}$$

$$\Omega_{t|t} = \Omega_{t|t-1} - \Omega_{t|t-1}x_1\Sigma_{t|t-1}^{-1}x_1'\Omega_{t|t-1}, \tag{6.6}$$

where $\Sigma_{t|t-1}^{-1}$ is defined in (6.4).

(4) Predict the variables in the state equation:

$$\alpha_{t+1|t} = \mathbb{D}_1\alpha_{t|t} + \mathbb{D}_0 = \mathbb{D}_1\alpha_{t|t-1} + \mathbb{D}_0 + \mathfrak{K}_t\epsilon_t, \tag{6.7}$$

$$\Omega_{t+1|t} = \mathbb{D}_1\Omega_{t|t}\mathbb{D}_1' + \mathbb{D}_2\Sigma_{v_2}\mathbb{D}_2', \tag{6.8}$$

where $\epsilon_t = y_t - x_1'\alpha_{t|t-1}$ is the one-step-ahead forecast error in predicting y_t and $\mathfrak{K}_t = \mathbb{D}_1\Omega_{t|t-1}x_1\Sigma_{t|t-1}^{-1}$ is the Kalman gain.

(5) Repeat steps (2)–(4) until $t = T$.

In step (3), $\Omega_{t|t-1}x_1 = E(\alpha_t - \alpha_{t|t-1})(y_t - x_1'\alpha_{t|t-1})'$. Hence, updated estimates of α_t are computed by using the least squares projection of $\alpha_t - \alpha_{t|t-1}$ on $y_t - y_{t|t-1}$, multiplied by the prediction error. Similarly, $\Omega_{t|t-1} = E(\alpha_t - \alpha_{t|t-1})(\alpha_t - \alpha_{t|t-1})'$ is updated by using a quadratic form involving the covariance between forecast errors in the two equations and the MSEs of the forecasts. Equations (6.7) and (6.8) provide the inputs for the next step of the recursion.

Example 6.4. Consider extracting a signal α_t, e.g., the long-run trend of output, given that $\alpha_t = \alpha_{t-1}$, and that the trend is linked to output via $y_t = \alpha_t + v_{1t}$, where v_{1t} is a normal martingale difference process with variance $\sigma_{v_1}^2$. Using (6.6) we have that $\Omega_{t|t} = \Omega_{t|t-1} - \Omega_{t|t-1}(\Omega_{t|t-1} + \sigma_{v_1}^2)^{-1}\Omega_{t|t-1} = \Omega_{t|t-1} \times (1 + \Omega_{t|t-1}/\sigma_{v_1}^2)^{-1} = \Omega_{t-1|t-1}(1 + \Omega_{t-1|t-1}/\sigma_{v_1}^2)^{-1}$. Hence, starting from some

$\Omega_0 = \bar{\Omega}_0$, we have $\Omega_{1|1} = \bar{\Omega}_0(1 + \bar{\Omega}_0/\sigma^2_{v_1})^{-1}$, $\Omega_{2|2} = \bar{\Omega}_0(1 + 2\bar{\Omega}_0/\sigma^2_{v_1})^{-1}$, $\dots$, $\Omega_{T|T} = \bar{\Omega}_0(1 + T\bar{\Omega}_0/\sigma^2_{v_1})^{-1}$. From (6.5) and (6.7), $\alpha_{T+1|T+1} = \alpha_{T|T} + (\bar{\Omega}_0/\sigma^2_{v_1})(1+T\bar{\Omega}_0/\sigma^2_{v_1})^{-1}(y_{T+1}-\alpha_{T|T})$. Hence, as $T \to \infty, \alpha_{T+1|T+1} = \alpha_{T|T}$; that is, asymptotically, the contribution of additional observations is negligible.

Exercise 6.4. Consider a vector MA process $y_t = e_t + e_{t-1}$, where $e_t \sim$ i.i.d. $\mathbb{N}(0, I)$. Show that the optimal one-step ahead predictor is $y_{t+1|t} = (t+1)/(t+2)[y_t - y_{t|t-1}]$. Conclude that, as $T \to \infty$, the optimal one-step-ahead predictor is just the last period's forecast error. (Hint: cast the process into a state-space format and apply the Kalman filter.)

Exercise 6.5. Suppose $y_t = A_1 y_{t-1} + A_2 y_{t-2} + e_t$, $e_t \sim$ i.i.d. $\mathbb{N}(0, 1)$. Here $\alpha_t = [y'_t, y'_{t-1}]'$, $v_{2t} = [e_t, 0]$, $\mathbb{D}_{0t} = v_{1t} = 0$, $x'_1 = [1\ 0]$,

$$\mathbb{D}_1 = \begin{bmatrix} A_1 & A_2 \\ 1 & 0 \end{bmatrix}, \quad \Sigma_{v_2} = \begin{bmatrix} \sigma^2_e & 0 \\ 0 & 0 \end{bmatrix}.$$

Show how to start the Kalman filter recursions; compute prediction and updated estimates of α_t for the first two observations.

Exercise 6.6. Suppose $y_{1t} = A_t y_{1t-1} + D_t y_{2t} + v_{1t}$ and $\alpha_t = (A_t, D_t)' = \alpha_{t-1} + v_{2t}$, where y_{2t} are exogenous variables. Show the updating and prediction equations in this case. How would you handle the case of serially correlated v_{2t} disturbances?

At times, it may be useful to construct an estimate of the state vector which, at each t, contains information present in the entire sample. This is the case, in particular, in signal extraction problems; for example, when α_t is a common trend for a vector of y_t, we want estimates at each t to contain all the information available up to T. In this case, the Kalman filter can be applied by starting from the last observation, working backward through the sample, $t = T-1, \dots, 1$, using $\alpha_{T|T}$ and $\Omega_{T|T}$ as initial conditions. That is,

$$\alpha_{t|T} = \alpha_{t|t} + (\Omega_{t|t}\mathbb{D}'_1\Omega^{-1}_{t+1|t})(\alpha_{t+1|T} - \mathbb{D}_1\alpha_{t|t}), \tag{6.9}$$

$$\Omega_{t|T} = \Omega_{t|t} - (\Omega_{t|t}\mathbb{D}'_1\Omega^{-1}_{t+1|t})(\Omega_{t+1|T} - \Omega_{t+1|t})(\Omega_{t|t}\mathbb{D}'_1\Omega^{-1}_{t+1|t})'. \tag{6.10}$$

Equations (6.9) and (6.10) define the recursions of the so-called Kalman smoother.

Example 6.5. Continuing with example 6.4, take $\alpha_{T|T}$ and $\Omega_{T|T}$ as initial conditions. Then $\Omega_{1|t} = \Omega_{T|T}(1+T\Omega_{T|T}/\sigma^2_{v_1})^{-1}$ and $\alpha_{t|T} = \alpha_{t+1|T} + (\bar{\Omega}_{T|T}/\sigma^2_{v_1}) \times (1 + T\bar{\Omega}_{T|T}/\sigma^2_{v_1})^{-1}(y_{t|T} - \alpha_{t+1|T})$. Can you guess what $\alpha_{1|T}$ is?

As a byproduct of the estimation, the Kalman filter allows us to transform the original state space into a system driven by the innovations in the measurement equation. In fact, by using (6.3)–(6.7), we can immediately see that (6.1) and (6.2) are equivalent to

$$y_t = x'_{1t}\alpha_{t|t-1} + \epsilon_t, \tag{6.11}$$

$$\alpha_{t+1|t} = \mathbb{D}_1\alpha_{t|t-1} + \mathbb{D}_0 + \mathfrak{K}_t\epsilon_t, \tag{6.12}$$

where ϵ_t is the forecast error and $E_t(\epsilon_t\epsilon'_t) \equiv \Sigma_{t|t-1}$. Hence, if the Kalman gain $\mathfrak{K}_t$ is available, and given $\alpha_{1|0}$ and $\Sigma_{1|0}$, $\alpha_{t|t-1}$ and ϵ_t can be computed recursively at any t. In turn, the Kalman gain is immediately obtained when $\Omega_{t|t-1}$ is available.

Exercise 6.7. The reparametrization in (6.11), (6.12) is trivial in the case of a constant coefficients VAR(q), since it is always possible to rewrite the measurement equation as $y_t = E[y_t \mid \mathcal{F}_{t-1}] + \epsilon_t$, where $\mathcal{F}_{t-1}$ is the information set at $t-1$. Show how to transform the ARMA(2, 1) model of example 6.2 to fit such a representation.

Hansen and Sargent (2005, p. 190) show that equation (6.6) can also be written as $\Omega_{t|t} = \mathbb{D}_1\Omega_{t-1|t-1}\mathbb{D}'_1 + \mathbb{D}_2\Sigma_{v_2}\mathbb{D}'_2 - \mathbb{D}_1\Omega_{t-1|t-1}x_1\Sigma^{-1}_{t|t-1}x'_1\Omega_{t-1|t-1}\mathbb{D}_1$. One can recognize in this expression a version of the matrix Riccati equation used in chapter 2. Therefore, under regularity conditions, when coefficients are constant, $\lim_{t\to\infty}\Omega_{t|t} = \Omega$. Consequently, $\lim_{t\to\infty}\mathfrak{K}_t = \mathfrak{K}$, and the stationary covariance matrix of the innovations is $\Sigma = \lim_{t\to\infty}\Sigma_{t|t-1} = x'_1\Omega x_1 + x'_2\Sigma_{v_1}x_2$. As we show next, the expressions for Ω, $\mathfrak{K}$, Σ obtained in a constant coefficients model are the same as those asymptotically produced by a recursive least squares estimator.

Example 6.6. Consider estimating the (steady-state) real interest rate α_t by using T observations on the nominal interest rate y_t, de-meaned by using the average inflation rate, where $y_t = \alpha_t + v_{1t}$ and v_{1t} is a martingale difference process with variance $\sigma^2_{v_1}$. An unbiased minimum variance estimator is $\hat{\alpha}_T = (1/T)\sum_{t=1}^{T} y_t$. If y_{T+1} becomes available,

$$\hat{\alpha}_{T+1} = \frac{1}{T+1}\sum_{t=1}^{T+1} y_t = \frac{T}{T+1}\left(\frac{1}{T}\sum_{t=1}^{T} y_t\right) + \frac{1}{T+1}y_{T+1}$$

$$= \frac{T}{T+1}\hat{\alpha}_T + \frac{1}{T+1}y_{T+1},$$

which is a recursive least squares estimator. This estimator weighs previous and current observations by using the number of available observations and does not forget: each observation gets equal weight, regardless of the time elapsed since it was observed. A more informative way to rewrite this expression is $\hat{\alpha}_{T+1} = \hat{\alpha}_T + [1/(T+1)](y_{T+1} - \hat{\alpha}_T)$, where $(y_{T+1} - \hat{\alpha}_T)$ is the innovation in forecasting y_{T+1}. Clearly, $\mathfrak{K}_{T+1} = [1/(T+1)] \to 0$ as $T \to \infty$. Hence, as $T \to \infty$, $\hat{\alpha}_{T+1} = \hat{\alpha}_T$.

The recursions in (6.3)–(6.8) are particularly useful in models with time-varying coefficients, as long as they are conditionally linear in parameters. For example, in the multivariate VAR model,

$$\left.\begin{aligned} y_t &= \alpha_t y_{t-1} + v_{1t}, \\ \alpha_t &= \rho\alpha_{t-1} + v_{2t}, \end{aligned}\right\} \tag{6.13}$$

where the roots of ρ are less than 1 in modulus, recursive estimates of $\alpha_{t|t}$ and the forecast error $\epsilon_t = y_t - \alpha_{t|t-1} y_{t-1}$, consistent with the information available at each t, can be easily obtained. We will use models like (6.13) extensively in chapter 10.

Exercise 6.8. Consider the model $y_t = x_t' \alpha_t + v_{1t}$, where $\alpha_t = (I - \mathbb{D}_1)\alpha_0 + \mathbb{D}_1 \alpha_{t-1} + v_{2t+1}$, α_0 is a constant, v_{1t} is a martingale difference with variance $\sigma_{v_1}^2$, and v_{2t} is a vector of martingale difference with variance Σ_{v_2}. Define $\alpha_t^\dagger = \alpha_t - \alpha_0$. Show the form of the updating equations for $\alpha_t^\dagger$ and Ω_t, assuming $\alpha_1^\dagger \sim \mathbb{N}(\alpha_{1|0}, \Omega_{1|0})$.

A modified version of the Kalman filter can also be used in special nonlinear state-space models, for example, those displaying structures as in exercise 6.3. To compute the Kalman gain in this case it is necessary to linearize the extended state space around the current estimate. For example, the updating equations are

$$\left.\begin{aligned} \alpha_{t|t} &= \alpha_{t|t-1}\theta_{t|t-1} + \mathfrak{K}_{1t}(y_t - \alpha_{t|t-1}), \\ \theta_{t|t} &= \theta_{t|t-1} + \mathfrak{K}_{2t}(y_t - \alpha_{t|t-1}), \end{aligned}\right\} \tag{6.14}$$

where $\mathfrak{K}_{1t}, \mathfrak{K}_{2t}$ are matrices involving linear and quadratic terms in the predictors $\theta_{t|t-1}$ and $\alpha_{t|t-1}$, linear terms in the variance $\sigma_{v_1}^2$ and in past Kalman gains (see Ljung and Söderström (1983, pp. 39–40) for details).

If initial conditions and innovations are normally distributed, the Kalman filter predictor is best in both the class of linear and nonlinear predictors. This is because, under normality, $\alpha_{t+1|t}$ and $\Omega_{t+1|t}$ are the conditional mean and the conditional MSE of α. Moreover, one-step-ahead forecasts of y_t are normal with mean $x_1' \alpha_{t|t-1}$ and variance $\Sigma_{t|t-1}$. When the above two conditions are not satisfied, the Kalman filter only produces the best *linear* predictor for y_t (see, for example, Ljung and Söderström 1983, p. 420). That is, there are nonlinear filters which produce more efficient predictors than those obtained in (6.5) and (6.6). A nonlinear filter for a model with binomial innovations was described in chapter 3.

Example 6.7. A two-state Markov switching model for y_t can be written as $y_t = a_0 + a_1 \varkappa_t + y_{t-1}$, where $\varkappa_t$ has an AR(1) representation of the form

$$\varkappa_t = (1 - p_2) + (p_1 + p_2 - 1)\varkappa_{t-1} + v_{1t}. \tag{6.15}$$

v_{1t} can take four possible values $[1 - p_1, -p_1, -(1 - p_2), p_2]$ with probabilities $[p_1, 1 - p_1, p_2, 1 - p_2]$ and is therefore nonnormal. We can immediately verify that this process can be cast into a state-space format and that the orthogonality assumptions needed for identification are satisfied. Here $\text{corr}(v_{1t}, \varkappa_{t-\tau}) = 0$, $\forall \tau > 0$, but v_{1t} and $\varkappa_{t-\tau}$ are not independent. The model for y_t can be rewritten as

$$\begin{aligned} (1 - (p_1 + p_2 - 1)\ell)\Delta y_t &= a_1(1 - (p_1 + p_2 - 1)\ell)\varkappa_t \\ &= a_1(1 - p_2) + a_0(2 - p_1 - p_2) + v_{1t}. \end{aligned} \tag{6.16}$$

Hence, although y_t looks like an ARIMA(1, 1, 0), Kalman filter estimates of $y_{t+1|t}$ based on such a model are suboptimal since the nonlinear structure present in v_{1t} is ignored. In fact, optimal forecasts are obtained by using

$$\begin{aligned} E_t \Delta y_{t+1} &= a_0 + a_1 E_t \varkappa_{t+1} \\ &= a_0 + a_1 \left[\frac{1-p_2}{2-p_1-p_2} + (p_1+p_2-1)\left(P[\varkappa_t = 1 \mid \mathcal{F}_t] - \frac{1-p_2}{2-p_1-p_2} \right) \right], \end{aligned} \tag{6.17}$$

where $\mathcal{F}_t$ represents the information set at t. The nonlinear filtering algorithm described in chapter 3 uses (6.17) to obtain estimates of $\varkappa_t$.

While we have assumed that errors in the state and the measurement equations are uncorrelated, in some situations this assumption may be unpalatable. For example, in the context of a model like (6.13), one may want to have correlated innovations. Relaxing this assumption requires some ingenuity. The next exercise shows that a system with a serially correlated error in the measurement equation is equivalent to a system with correlation between innovations in the state and the measurement equations.

Exercise 6.9. Suppose $\mathbb{D}_{1t} = \mathbb{D}_1$, $\mathbb{D}_{2t} = \mathbb{D}_2$, $\mathbb{D}_0 = 0$, and that v_{1t} in equation (6.1) is a VAR(1), where all the eigenvalues of the autoregressive matrix ρ_v are less than 1 in absolute value and the vector of shocks v_{3t} is a martingale difference with covariance matrix Σ_{v_1}. Assuming that $E(v_{2t}v'_{1\tau}) = 0, \forall t$, and $\tau \neq t$, show that an equivalent state-space representation is given by (6.2) and $y^\dagger_{t+1} = x^\dagger_{1t+1}\alpha_t + v^\dagger_{1t+1}$, where $y^\dagger_{t+1} = y_{t+1} - \rho_v y_t$, $x^\dagger_{1t+1} = x_{1t+1} - \rho_v x_{1t}$, and $v^\dagger_{1t+1} = (x_{t+1} - \rho x_t)\mathbb{D}_2 v_{2t+1} + x_{2t+1}v_{3t+1}$.

Exercise 6.10. Suppose that α_t is normally distributed with mean $\bar{\alpha}$ and variance $\bar{\Sigma}_\alpha$, that $y_t = x'_1\alpha_t + v_{1t}$, where v_{1t} is orthogonal to α_t, and that $v_{1t} \sim$ i.i.d. $\mathbb{N}(0, \sigma_{v_1})$.

(i) Show that $y_t \sim \mathbb{N}(x'_1\bar{\alpha}, x'_1\bar{\Sigma}_\alpha x_1 + \sigma^2_{v_1})$.

(ii) Using the fact that the posterior of α_t is $g(\alpha_t \mid y_t) = g(\alpha_t)f(y_t \mid \alpha_t)/f(y_t)$, where $f(y_t \mid \alpha)$ is the likelihood, $g(\alpha)$ is the prior, and $f(y_t) = \int f(y_t \mid \alpha) \times g(\alpha)\,d\alpha$, show that $g(\alpha_t \mid y_t) \propto \exp\{-0.5[(\alpha_t - \bar{\alpha})'\bar{\Sigma}^{-1}_\alpha(\alpha_t - \bar{\alpha}) + (y_t - x'_1\alpha_t)' \times \sigma^{-2}_{v_1}(y_t - x'_1\alpha_t)]\} \equiv \exp\{-0.5(\alpha_t - \tilde{\alpha})'\tilde{\Sigma}^{-1}_\alpha(\alpha_t - \tilde{\alpha})\}$, where $\tilde{\alpha} = \bar{\alpha} + \bar{\Sigma}_\alpha \times x_1\sigma^{-2}_{v_1}(y_t - x'_1\bar{\alpha})$ and $\tilde{\Sigma}_\alpha = \bar{\Sigma}_\alpha + \bar{\Sigma}_\alpha x_1\sigma^{-2}_{v_1}x'_1\bar{\Sigma}_\alpha$.

Exercise 6.11. A generalized version of a log-linearized RBC model can be written as $\alpha_t = \mathbb{D}_{1t-1}\alpha_{t-1} + v_{2t}$, $v_{2t} \sim$ i.i.d. $\mathbb{N}(0, \Sigma_t)$, and $y_t = x'_{1t}\alpha_t$, where α_t represents a vector of states and shocks and y_t are the controls. Assume that $\Sigma_t, x_{1t}, \mathbb{D}_{1t-1}$ are known. Find the updating equation for the forecast error variance. Show that $x'_{1t}\Omega_{t|t}x_{1t} = 0$ and that $\Omega_{t+1|t} = \mathbb{D}_{1t}\Omega_{t|t}\mathbb{D}'_{1t} + \Sigma_t$.

Given the recursive nature of Kalman filter estimates, it is easy to compute multistep forecasts of y_t. We leave the derivation of these forecasts as an exercise for the reader.

Exercise 6.12. Consider the model (6.1), (6.2) and the prediction of $y_{t+\tau}$. Show that the τ-steps-ahead forecast error is $x'_{1t+\tau}(\alpha_{t+\tau} - \alpha_{t+\tau,t}) + x'_{2t+\tau}v_{1t+\tau}$ and that the MSE of the forecast is $x'_{1t+\tau}\Omega_{t+\tau|t}x_{1t+\tau} + x'_{2t+\tau}\Sigma_{v_1}x_{2t+\tau}$. Show the form of $\alpha_{t+\tau|t}$ and $\Omega_{t+\tau|t}$.

Example 6.8. Consider an $m \times 1$ VAR(q), $\mathbb{Y}_t = \mathbb{A}\mathbb{Y}_{t-1} + E_t$. As we saw in example 6.1, this is a state-space model for $x'_{1t} = I$, $\alpha_t = \mathbb{Y}_t$, $\mathbb{D}_{1t} = \mathbb{A}$, $\Sigma_{v_1} = 0$, $v_{2t} = E_t$, $\mathbb{D}_{2t} = I$, $\mathbb{D}_{0t} = 0$. The τ-steps-ahead forecast of y_t is $E_t[y_{t+\tau}] = \mathbb{S}\mathbb{A}^{\tau}\mathbb{Y}_t$, where $\mathbb{S}$ is a selection matrix. Hence, the forecast error variance is $[\mathbb{S}(\mathbb{Y}_{t+\tau} - \mathbb{A}^{\tau}\mathbb{Y}_t)][\mathbb{S}(\mathbb{Y}_{t+\tau} - \mathbb{A}^{\tau}\mathbb{Y}_t)']$.

6.2 The Prediction Error Decomposition of Likelihood

Maximum likelihood estimation of nonlinear models is complicated. In models like (6.1), (6.2), which are conditionally linear in the parameters, maximization of the likelihood function may also be computationally demanding when observations are not independent. This section is concerned with the practical question of constructing the likelihood function for models which have a format like (6.1), (6.2), when y_t is serially correlated. It turns out that there is a convenient format, called prediction error decomposition, which can be used to estimate ARMA, structural VARs, and, as we will see, DSGE models.

To understand what the decomposition involves, let $f(y_1, \dots, y_T)$ be the joint density of $\{y_t\}_{t=1}^T$. Given the properties of joint densities, it is possible to decompose $f(y_1, \dots, y_T)$ into the product of a conditional and a marginal, and, repeatedly substituting, we have

$$\begin{aligned} f(y_1, \dots, y_T) &= f(y_T \mid y_{T-1}, \dots, y_1) f(y_{T-1}, \dots, y_1) \\ &= f(y_T \mid y_{T-1}, \dots, y_t) f(y_{T-1} \mid y_{T-2}, \dots, y_1) f(y_{T-2}, \dots, y_1) \\ &\vdots \\ &= \prod_{j=0}^{T-2} f(y_{T-j} \mid y_{T-j-1}, \dots, y_1) f(y_1), \end{aligned} \tag{6.18}$$

and $\ln f(y_1, \dots, y_T) = \sum_j \ln f(y_{T-j}, \mid y_{T-j-1}, \dots, y_1) + \ln f(y_1)$. If $y = [y_1, \dots, y_T] \sim \mathbb{N}(\bar{y}, \Sigma_y)$ and if we let $\phi = (\bar{y}, \Sigma_y)$,

$$\begin{aligned} \mathcal{L}(y \mid \phi) &= \ln f(y_1, \dots, y_T \mid \phi) \\ &= -\tfrac{1}{2}(T \ln 2\pi + \ln |\Sigma_y|) - \tfrac{1}{2}(y - \bar{y})\Sigma_y^{-1}(y - \bar{y})'. \end{aligned} \tag{6.19}$$

Calculation of (6.19) requires the inversion of Σ_y, which is a $T \times T$ matrix, and this may be complicated when T is large. Using the decomposition (6.18), we can write $\mathcal{L}(y_1, \dots, y_T \mid \phi) = \mathcal{L}(y_1, \dots, y_{T-1} \mid \phi)\mathcal{L}(y_T \mid y_{T-1}, \dots, y_1, \phi)$. When $\{y_t\}_{t=1}^T$ is normal, both the conditional and the marginal blocks are normal.

Let $y_{t|t-1}$ be a predictor of y_t using information up to $t-1$. The prediction error is $\epsilon_t = y_t - y_{t|t-1} = y_t - E(y_t \mid y_{t-1}, \dots, y_1) + E(y_t \mid y_{t-1}, \dots, y_1) - y_{t|t-1}$ and its MSE is $E[y_t - E(y_t \mid y_{t-1}, \dots, y_1)]^2 + E[E(y_t \mid y_{t-1}, \dots, y_1) - y_{t|t-1}]^2$. The best predictor of y_t, i.e., the one that makes the MSE of the prediction error as small as possible, is obtained when $E(y_t \mid y_{t-1}, \dots, y_1) = y_{t|t-1}$. Given this choice, the MSE of ϵ_t, denoted by $\sigma^2_{\epsilon_t}$, equals $E[y_t - E(y_t \mid y_{t-1}, \dots, y_1)]^2$.

The conditional density of y_t given $t-1$ information can then be written as

$$\mathcal{L}(y_t \mid y_{t-1}, \dots, y_1, \sigma^2_{\epsilon_t}) = -\frac{\ln(2\pi)}{2} - \ln(\sigma_{\epsilon_t}) - \frac{1}{2}\frac{(y_t - y_{t|t-1})^2}{\sigma^2_{\epsilon_t}}. \tag{6.20}$$

Since (6.20) is valid for any $t > 1$ by using (6.18), we have that

$$\begin{aligned}\mathcal{L}(y \mid \sigma^2_{\epsilon_1}, \dots, \sigma^2_{\epsilon_T}) &= \sum_{t=2}^{T} \mathcal{L}(y_t \mid y_{t-1}, \dots, y_1, \sigma^2_{\epsilon_2}, \dots, \sigma^2_{\epsilon_T}) + \mathcal{L}(y_1 \mid \sigma^2_{\epsilon_1}) \\ &= -\left(\frac{T-1}{2}\ln(2\pi) + \sum_{t=2}^{T} \ln \sigma_{\epsilon_t}\right) - \frac{1}{2}\sum_{t=2}^{T} \frac{(y_t - y_{t|t-1})^2}{\sigma^2_{\epsilon_t}} \\ &\quad - \left(\tfrac{1}{2}\ln(2\pi) + \ln \sigma_{\epsilon_1}\right) - \frac{1}{2}\frac{(y_1 - \bar{y}_1)^2}{\sigma^2_{\epsilon_1}},\end{aligned} \tag{6.21}$$

where $\bar{y}_1$ is the unconditional predictor of y_1. Equation (6.21) is the decomposition we were looking for. Three important features need to be emphasized. First, (6.21) can be computed recursively, since it only involves one-step-ahead prediction errors and their optimal MSEs. This should be contrasted with (6.19), where the entire vector of y_t is used. Second, both the best predictor $y_{t|t-1}$ and the MSE of the forecast $\sigma^2_{\epsilon_t}$ vary with time. Therefore, we have transformed a time-invariant problem into a problem involving quantities that vary over time. Third, if y_1 is a constant, prediction errors are the constant innovations in y_t.

Example 6.9. Consider a univariate AR(1) process $y_t = Ay_{t-1} + e_t, |A| < 1$, where e_t is a normal martingale difference process with variance σ^2_e. Let $\phi = (A, \sigma^2_e)$. Assume that the process has started far in the past but has been observed only from $t = 1$ on. For any t, $y_{t|t-1} \sim \mathbb{N}(Ay_{t-1}, \sigma^2_e)$. Hence, the prediction error $\epsilon_t = y_t - y_{t|t-1} = y_t - Ay_{t-1} = e_t$. Moreover, since the variance of e_t is constant, the variance of the prediction error from time $t = 2$ on is constant and

$$\begin{aligned}\mathcal{L}(\phi) &= \sum_{t=2}^{T} \mathcal{L}(y_t \mid y_{t-1}, \dots, y_1, \phi) + \mathcal{L}(y_1 \mid \phi) \\ &= -\tfrac{1}{2}T\ln(2\pi) - T\ln(\sigma_e) - \frac{1}{2}\sum_{t=2}^{T}\frac{(y_t - Ay_{t-1})^2}{\sigma^2_e} \\ &\quad + \frac{1}{2}\left(\ln(1 - A^2) - \frac{(1 - A^2)y_1^2}{\sigma^2_e}\right).\end{aligned}$$

Hence, $\sigma^2_{\epsilon_t} = \sigma^2_e$ for all $t \geqslant 2$, while $\sigma^2_{\epsilon_1} = \sigma^2_e/(1 - A^2)$.

Exercise 6.13. Consider a univariate version of the model of exercise 6.1 Find $y_{1t|t-1}$ and $\sigma^2_{\epsilon_t}$ in this case. Show the form of the log likelihood function assuming that the first $q = \max[q_1, q_2]$ values of $y_t = [y_{1t}, y_{2t}]$ are fixed.

Taking the initial observations as given is convenient since it eliminates a source of nonlinearities in the maximization. In general, nonlinearities do not allow the computation of an analytical solution to the first-order conditions of the problem and the maximum of the likelihood must be located with numerical techniques. Conditioning on the initial observations makes the maximization problem trivial in many cases. Note also that, as $T \to \infty$, the contribution of the first observation to the likelihood becomes negligible. Therefore, exact and conditional maximum likelihood coincide if the sample is large. Furthermore, when the model has constant coefficients, the errors are normally distributed and the initial observations fixed, maximum likelihood and OLS estimators are identical (see chapter 4 for the case of a constant coefficients VAR). This would not be the case when a model features moving average terms (see example 6.11), since nonlinearities do not wash out, even conditioning on the initial observations.

Example 6.10. Consider finding the ML estimator of the AR process described in example 6.9. Conditioning on y_1, the log likelihood of $(y_2, \dots, y_T)$ is proportional to $\sum_{t=2}^{T}\{-\ln(\sigma_e) - (y_t - Ay_{t-1})^2/2\sigma_e^2\}$. Maximizing this quantity with respect to A (conditional on σ_e^2) is equivalent to minimizing $(y_t - Ay_{t-1})^2$, which produces $A_{\text{ML}} = A_{\text{OLS}}$. Using A_{ML}, the likelihood can be concentrated to obtain $-\frac{1}{2}(T-1)\ln(\sigma_e^2) - (1/2\sigma_e^2)\sum_t \epsilon_t'\epsilon_t$. Maximizing it with respect to σ_e^2 leads to $\sigma^2_{\text{ML}} = [1/(T-1)]\sum_t \epsilon_t'\epsilon_t$. Suppose now that we do not wish to condition on y_1. The likelihood function is proportional to $\sum_{t=2}^{T}\{-\ln(\sigma_e) - (y_t - Ay_{t-1})^2/2\sigma_e^2\} + \{-0.5\ln[\sigma_e^2/(1-A^2)] - y_1^2(1-A^2)/2\sigma_e^2\}$. If $T \to \infty$, the first observation makes a negligible contribution to the likelihood. Therefore, conditional ML estimates of A asymptotically coincide with full ML estimates, provided $|A| < 1$. Consider, finally, the case where A is time varying, e.g., $A_t = \mathbb{D}_1 A_{t-1} + v_{2t}$. Conditional on some A_0, the recursive conditional maximum likelihood estimator of $A_{t|t}$ and the smoothed maximum likelihood estimator $A_{t|T}$ can be obtained with the Kalman filter and the Kalman smoother. As $T \to \infty$, the importance of the initial observation will die out as long as the roots of $\mathbb{D}_1$ are all less than 1 in absolute value.

Exercise 6.14. (i) Suppose that $y_t = x_t'\alpha + e_t$, where e_t is a normal martingale difference with variance $\sigma^2_{e_t}$ and let x_t be fixed regressors. Show how to derive the prediction error decomposition of the likelihood for this model.

(ii) Let x_t be a random variable, normally distributed with mean $\bar{x}$ and variance Σ_x. Show how to compute the prediction error decomposition of the unconditional likelihood.

Multivariate prediction error decompositions present no difficulties. If y_t is an $m \times 1$ vector,

$$\mathcal{L}(y \mid \phi) = -\left(\frac{Tm}{2}\ln(2\pi) + \frac{1}{2}\sum_{t=1}^{T}\ln|\Sigma_{t|t-1}|\right) - \frac{1}{2}\sum_{t=1}^{T}(y_t - y_{t|t-1})\Sigma_{t|t-1}^{-1}(y_t - y_{t|t-1}), \tag{6.22}$$

where $\epsilon_t = y_t - y_{t|t-1} \sim \mathbb{N}(0, \Sigma_{t|t-1})$ and where we assume $y_1 \sim \mathbb{N}(\bar{y}_1, \Sigma_{1|0})$ and $\epsilon_1 = y_1 - \bar{y}_1$.

Exercise 6.15. Consider the setup of exercise 6.11. Show the form of $y_{t|t-1}$ and $\Sigma_{t|t-1}$ and the prediction error decomposition of the likelihood in this case.

The prediction error decomposition is convenient in two respects. First, the building blocks of the decomposition are the forecast errors ϵ_t and their MSEs $\Sigma_{t|t-1}$. Since the Kalman filter produces these quantities recursively, it can be used to build the prediction error decomposition of the likelihood of any model which has a state-space format. Second, since any ARMA process has a state-space format, the prediction error decomposition of the likelihood can be easily obtained for a variety of statistical and economic models.

To maximize the likelihood, conditional on the initial observations, we need to extend algorithm 6.1. Let $\phi = [\text{vec}(x_1'), \text{vec}(x_2'), \text{vec}(\mathbb{D}_1), \text{vec}(\mathbb{D}_0), \text{vec}(\mathbb{D}_2), \Sigma_{v_1}, \Sigma_{v_2}]$. Then we have the following.

Algorithm 6.2.

(1) Choose some initial $\phi = \phi^0$.

(2) Perform steps (1)–(5) of algorithm 6.1.

(3) At each step save $\epsilon_t = y_t - y_{t|t-1}$ and $\Sigma_{t|t-1}$. Construct the log likelihood (6.22).

(4) Update initial estimates of ϕ by using any of the methods described in section 6.3.

(5) Repeat steps (2)–(4) until $|\phi^l - \phi^{l-1}| \leqslant \iota$, or $(\partial\mathcal{L}(\phi)/\partial\phi)|_{\phi=\phi^l} < \iota$, or both, ι small.

Two comments on algorithm 6.2 are in order. First, the initial values of the iterations can be typically obtained by running an OLS regression on the constant coefficients version of the model. If the assumptions underlying the state-space specification are correct this will consistently estimate the average value of the parameters. Second, for large-dimensional problems, maximization routines typically work better if a Choleski factor of $\Sigma_{t|t-1}$ is used in the computations of the likelihood.

The conditional prediction error decomposition is particularly useful for estimating models with MA terms. Such models are difficult to deal with in standard setups but fairly easy to estimate within a state-space framework.

Example 6.11. In testing the efficiency of foreign exchange markets, one runs a monthly regression of the realized three-month change in spot exchange rate at $t+3$ on the forward premium quoted at t for $t+3$. Such a regression has moving average errors of order up to 2 because of overlapping time intervals. Therefore, a model for testing efficiency could be $y_{t+3} = b_0 x_t + \epsilon_{t+3}$ with $\epsilon_{t+3} = e_{t+3} + b_1 e_{t+2} + b_2 e_{t+1}$, where e_t is a normal martingale difference with variance σ_e^2. This model has a state-space format with $\mathbb{D}_0 = 0$, $\mathbb{D}_2 = I$, $x'_{2t} = I$, $v_{1t} = 0$,

$$\alpha_t = \begin{bmatrix} x_t \\ e_{t+3} \\ e_{t+2} \\ e_{t+1} \end{bmatrix}, \quad \mathbb{D}_1 = \begin{bmatrix} 0 & 0 & 0 & 0 \\ 0 & 0 & 0 & 0 \\ 1 & 0 & 0 & 0 \\ 0 & 1 & 0 & 0 \end{bmatrix}, \quad x_{1t} = \begin{bmatrix} b_0 \\ 1 \\ b_1 \\ b_2 \end{bmatrix}, \quad v_{2t} = \begin{bmatrix} x_t \\ e_{t+3} \\ 0 \\ 0 \end{bmatrix}.$$

Suppose we are interested in estimating $[b_0, b_1, b_2]$ and in testing $b_0 = 1$. ML estimates can be obtained by starting the Kalman filter at $\alpha_{1|0} = [x_1, 0, 0, 0]'$ and $\Omega_{1|0} = \mathrm{diag}\{\sigma_x^2, \sigma_e^2, \sigma_e^2, \sigma_e^2\}$, where σ_x^2, is the unconditional variance of the forward premium and σ_e^2 could be either the variance of $\hat{e}_t = y_t - \hat{b}_0 x_{t-3}$ in a training sample (say, from $-\tau$ to 0) or an arbitrarily large number. To start the iterations one needs some initial estimates of (b_0, b_1, b_2). An estimate of b_0 could be obtained in a training sample or, if no such a sample exists, by using the available data but disregarding serial correlation in the error term. Initial estimates of b_1 and b_2 could then be $b_{10} = b_{20} = 0$. Then the sequence of iterations producing $\alpha_{t|t-1}$ and $\Omega_{t|t-1}$ can be used to compute the likelihood function. Note that, for a model like this, the exact likelihood can also be computed (see Pagan 1981). Note also that, since the parameter space has only three dimensions, one could locate the maximum of the likelihood numerically by using successive grids of, say, twenty points in each dimension.

Exercise 6.16. Consider the process $y_t = A_0 + A_1 y_{t-1} + A_2 y_{t-2} + e_t$, where $e_t \sim$ i.i.d. $\mathbb{N}(0, \sigma_e^2)$. Show that the exact log likelihood function is $\mathcal{L}(\phi) \propto -T\ln(\sigma_e) + 0.5\ln\{(1+A_2)^2[(1-A_2)^2 - A_1^2]\} - ((1+A_2)/2\sigma_e^2)[(1-A_2)(y_1-\bar{y})^2 - 2A_1(y_1-\bar{y})(y_2-\bar{y}) + (1-A_2)(y_2-\bar{y})^2] - \sum_{t=3}^{T}(y_t - A_0 - A_1 y_{t-1} + A_2 y_{t-2})^2/2\sigma_e^2$, where $\bar{y} = A_0/(1-A_1-A_2)$. Which terms disappear if a conditional likelihood approach is used? Show that $\sigma_{\mathrm{ML}}^2 = [1/(T-2)]\sum_{t=3}^{T}(y_t - A_{0,\mathrm{ML}} - A_{1,\mathrm{ML}} y_{t-1} - A_{2,\mathrm{ML}} y_{t-2})^2$.

6.2.1 Some Asymptotics of ML Estimators

It is fairly standard to show that, under regularity conditions, ML estimates of the parameters of a state-space model are consistent and asymptotically normal. The conditions needed are of two types. First, we need the state equation to define a covariance stationary process. One simple sufficient condition is that the eigenvalues of $\mathbb{D}_{1t}$ are all less than 1 in absolute value for all t. Second, we need the true parameters not to lie on the boundary of the parameter space. Under these conditions, $\phi_{\mathrm{ML}} \xrightarrow{\mathrm{P}} \phi_0$ and $\sqrt{T}(\phi_{\mathrm{ML}} - \phi_0) \xrightarrow{\mathrm{D}} \mathbb{N}(0, \Sigma_\phi)$, where $\Sigma_\phi = -T^{-1}[E(\partial^2 \mathcal{L}/\partial\phi\partial\phi')|_{\phi=\phi_0}]^{-1}$.

Exercise 6.17. Show that ϕ_{ML} is consistent and asymptotically normal. (Hint: rewrite the state-space model as a VAR(1) (or a VAR(∞) if some variables are unobservable), assume the model is true, and follow the same steps used in chapter 4 to show that estimates of a VAR have the required properties.)

For the case in which the innovations are the errors in the measurement equation, the asymptotic covariance matrix is block diagonal, as is shown next.

Example 6.12. For an AR(1) model it is quite easy to derive Σ_ϕ. In fact, conditional on the initial observations, the log likelihood is $\mathcal{L}(\phi) \propto -\frac{1}{2}(T-1)\ln\sigma_\epsilon^2 - (1/2\sigma_\epsilon^2)\sum_{t=2}^T \epsilon_t^2$, where $\epsilon_t = y_t - Ay_{t-1}$ and the matrix of second derivatives is

$$\begin{bmatrix} -\sigma_\epsilon^{-2}\sum_t y_{t-1}^2 & -\sigma_\epsilon^{-4}\sum_t \epsilon_t y_{t-1} \\ -\sigma_\epsilon^{-4}\sum_t \epsilon_t y_{t-1} & (2\sigma_\epsilon^4)^{-1}(T-1) - \sigma_\epsilon^{-6}\sum_t \epsilon_t^2 \end{bmatrix}.$$

Since the expectation of the off-diagonal elements is zero, the asymptotic covariance matrix is diagonal with $\mathrm{var}(A) = \sigma_\epsilon^2/(T-1)\sum_t y_{t-1}^2$ and $\mathrm{var}(\sigma_e^2) = 2\sigma_\epsilon^4/(T-1)$.

The derivation of the Kalman filter assumes that the innovations in the measurement and in the observation equations are normally distributed. Since the likelihood function is calculated with the Kalman filter estimates, one may wonder what the properties of ML estimates are when the distribution of the driving forces is misspecified.

As mentioned, misspecification of the distribution of the errors does not create consistency problems for Kalman filter estimates. It turns out that this property carries over to ML estimates. In fact, estimates obtained incorrectly assuming a normal distribution (typically called quasi-ML) have nice properties under regularity conditions. Next, we ask the reader to verify that this is the case for a simple problem.

Exercise 6.18. Suppose observations for y_t are drawn from a t-distribution with a small number of degrees of freedom (say, less than five) but that an econometrician estimates the (constant coefficient) state-space model $y_t = \alpha_t + v_{1t}$, $\alpha_t = \alpha_{t-1}$, where v_{1t} is a normal martingale difference with variance $\sigma_{v_1}^2$. Show that the ML estimator of α_t based on the wrong (normal) distribution will be consistent and asymptotically normal. Show the form of the asymptotic covariance matrix.

Intuitively, if the sample size is large and homogeneous, a normal approximation is appropriate. In the context of a constant coefficients state-space model, we could have achieved the same conclusion by noting that recursive OLS is consistent and asymptotically normal if the regressors are stationary, ergodic, and uncorrelated with the errors and that recursive OLS and Kalman filter ML estimates coincide if a conditional likelihood is used.

When the coefficients of the state-space model are time varying, ML estimates obtained with misspecified errors are no longer asymptotically equivalent to those of the correct model and Kalman filter estimates are not best linear MSE estimates of α_t.

We have seen that ML estimates have an asymptotic covariance matrix equal to the information matrix, $-T^{-1}E[(\partial^2 \mathcal{L}(\phi)/\partial\phi\partial\phi')|_{\phi=\phi_0}]^{-1}$. There are many ways to estimate this matrix. One is to evaluate the quantity at the ML estimator, substituting averages for expectations, that is, $\text{var}_1(\phi) = [-\sum_t(\partial^2 \mathcal{L}_t(\phi)/\partial\phi\partial\phi')|_{\phi=\phi_{\text{ML}}}]^{-1}$. An alternative is obtained by noting that an approximation to the second derivatives of the likelihood function can be calculated by taking the derivatives of the scores, i.e., $\text{var}_2(\phi) = -[\sum_t(\partial\mathcal{L}_t(\phi)/\partial\phi)|_{\phi=\phi_{\text{ML}}}\sum_t((\partial\mathcal{L}_t(\phi)/\partial\phi)|_{\phi=\phi_{\text{ML}}})']^{-1}$. Finally, a quasi-ML estimator can be obtained by combining the above two estimators. That is, $\text{var}_3(\phi) = -(\text{var}_1(\phi))(\text{var}_2(\phi))^{-1}(\text{var}_1(\phi))$ (see White 1982).

Exercise 6.19. For the AR(1) model considered in example 6.12, show the form of the three estimators of the asymptotic covariance matrix.

Hypothesis testing on the parameters is fairly standard. Given the asymptotic normality of ML estimates, one could use t-tests to verify simple restrictions on the parameters or likelihood ratio tests when more general hypotheses are involved.

Example 6.13. Continuing with example 6.11, to test $b_0 = 1$ use $(b_{0,\text{ML}}-1)/\sigma_{b_0,\text{ML}}$ and compare it with a t-distribution with $T-1$ degrees of freedoms (or with a normal $(0,1)$, if T is large). Alternatively, one could estimate the model under the restriction $b_0 = 1$, construct the log likelihood function, calculate $2[\mathcal{L}(b_{0,\text{ML}}) - \mathcal{L}(b_0 = 1)]$, and compare it with a $\chi^2(1)$.

As with GMM, it may be at times more convenient to use the estimates of a restricted model. This would be the case, for example, if the model is nonlinear, but it becomes linear under some restrictions, or if it contains MA terms. In this case, one can use the Lagrange multiplier (LM) statistic $(1/T)[\sum_t(\partial\mathcal{L}(\phi)/\partial\phi)|_{\phi=\phi^{\text{re}}}]'\Sigma_\phi^{-1}\times [\sum_t(\partial\mathcal{L}(\phi)/\partial\phi)_{\phi=\phi^{\text{re}}}] \sim \chi^2(\nu)$, where ν is the number of restrictions and ϕ^{re} a restricted estimate.

Example 6.14. For the model of example 6.2, if $D_1 = 0$, conditional ML estimates of $A = [A_1, A_2]'$ solve the normal equations $x'xA = x'y$, where $x_t = [y_{t-1}, y_{t-2}]$, $x = [x_1, \dots, x_t]'$. However, if $D_1 \neq 0$, the normal equations are nonlinear and no analytical solution exists. Therefore, one may impose $D_1 = 0$ for estimation and test whether or not the restriction holds true.

Two nonnested hypotheses can be evaluated by using, for example, the forecasting accuracy test of Diebold and Mariano (1995). Let ϵ_t^i be the prediction errors produced by model $i = 1, 2$ and let $h_t = (\epsilon_t^1)^2 - (\epsilon_t^2)^2$. Then, under the hypothesis of similar predictive accuracy, the statistic $\mathfrak{S} = \bar{h}/\text{se}(h)$, where $\bar{h} = (1/T)\sum_t h_t$, $\text{se}(h) = [(1/T)\sum_t(h_t - \bar{h})^2]^{0.5}$ is asymptotically normally distributed with mean 0 and variance 1. We will use this statistic in section 6.5 when comparing a DSGE model and an unrestricted VAR.

6.3 Numerical Tips

There are many ways to update initial estimates in step (4) of algorithm 6.2. Here we briefly list some of the approaches and highlighting advantages and disadvantages of each.

Grid search

This method is feasible when the dimension of ϕ is small. It involves discretizing the parameter space and selecting the value of ϕ which achieves the maximum on the grid. One advantage of the approach is that no derivatives are needed, which can be useful if differentiation is complicated. When the likelihood is globally concave, the approach will find an approximation to the maximum. However, if multiple peaks are present, it may select a local maximum. For this reason, the grid should be fine enough to avoid pathologies. While care should be exercised in taking them as final estimates, grid estimates are useful as initial conditions for other algorithms.

Simplex method

A k-dimensional simplex is spanned by $k + 1$ vectors which are the vertices of the simplex (e.g., if $k = 2$, two-dimensional simplexes are triangles). This method is typically fast and works as follows. If a maximum is found at some iteration, the method substitutes it with a point on the ray from the maximum through the centroid of the remaining points. Hence, if $\mathcal{L}(\phi_m) = \max_{j=1,\dots,k+1} \mathcal{L}(\phi_j)$, we replace ϕ_m by $\varrho\phi_m + (1-\varrho)\bar{\phi}$, where $\bar{\phi}$ is the centroid, $0 < \varrho < 1$, and repeat the maximization. This approach does not require the calculation of gradients or second derivatives of the likelihood and can be used when other routines fail. The major disadvantage is that no standard errors for the estimates are available.

Gradient methods

All algorithms in this class update initial estimates by taking a step based on the gradient of the likelihood at the initial estimate. They differ in the size and the direction in which the step is taken.

(a) *Method of steepest ascent.* At each iteration l, parameters are updated by using $\phi^l = \phi^{l-1} + (1/2\lambda)\text{gr}(\phi^l)$, where $\text{gr}(\phi^l) = (\partial\mathcal{L}(\phi)/\partial\phi)|_{\phi=\phi^l}$ and λ is the Lagrangian multiplier of the problem $\max_{\phi^l} \mathcal{L}(\phi^l)$ subject to $(\phi^l - \phi^{l-1})' \times (\phi^l - \phi^{l-1}) = \kappa$, and κ is a constant. In words, the method updates current estimates by using the scaled gradient of the likelihood. λ is a smoothness parameter which prevents large jumps in ϕ between iterations (it plays the same role as λ in HP or exponential smoothing filters). Note that, if $\phi^l \approx \phi^{l-1}$, $\text{gr}(\phi^l) \approx \text{gr}(\phi^{l-1})$ and one can use $\phi^l = \phi^{l-1} + \varrho \mathrm{gr}(\phi^{l-1})$, where ϱ is a small positive scalar (e.g., 10^{-5}). This choice is very conservative and avoids jumps in the estimates. However, a lot of iterations are typically needed before convergence is achieved and convergence could only be to local maximum. It is therefore a good idea to start the algorithm from several initial conditions and check whether the same maximum is obtained.

(b) *Newton–Raphson method.* The method is applicable if $(\partial^2 \mathcal{L}(\phi)/\partial\phi\partial\phi')$ exists and if $\mathcal{L}(\phi)$ is concave (i.e., the matrix of second derivatives is positive definite). In this case, taking a second-order expansion of $\mathcal{L}(\phi)$ around ϕ_0, we have

$$\mathcal{L}(\phi) = \mathcal{L}(\phi_0) + \mathrm{gr}(\phi_0)(\phi - \phi_0) - 0.5(\phi - \phi_0)' \frac{\partial^2 \mathcal{L}(\phi)}{\partial\phi\partial\phi'}(\phi - \phi_0). \qquad (6.23)$$

Maximizing (6.23) with respect to ϕ and using ϕ^{l-1} as an estimate of ϕ_0, we have

$$\phi^l = \phi^{l-1} + \left(\frac{\partial^2 \mathcal{L}(\phi)}{\partial\phi\partial\phi'}\bigg|_{\phi=\phi^{l-1}} \right)^{-1} \mathrm{gr}(\phi^{l-1}). \qquad (6.24)$$

If the likelihood is quadratic, (6.24) generates convergence in one step. If it is close to quadratic, iterations on (6.24) will converge quickly and the global maximum will be achieved. However, if the likelihood is far from quadratic, not globally concave, or if ϕ^0 is far away from the maximum, the method may have worse properties than the method of steepest ascent. Note that $(\partial^2 \mathcal{L}(\phi)/\partial\phi\partial\phi')^{-1}$ can be used as an estimate of the covariance matrix of ϕ at each iteration.

One could combine steepest-ascent and Newton–Raphson methods into a hybrid method which shares the good properties of both and which may speed up calculation without producing large jumps in the parameters' estimates. This is done, for example, by choosing $\phi^l = \phi^{l-1} + \varrho[(\partial^2 \mathcal{L}(\phi)/\partial\phi\partial\phi')|_{\phi=\phi^{l-1}}]^{-1}\mathrm{gr}(\phi^{l-1})$, where $\varrho > 0$ is a small scalar.

(c) *Modified Newton–Raphson.* The basic Newton–Raphson method requires the calculation of the matrix $\partial^2 \mathcal{L}(\phi)/\partial\phi\partial\phi'$ and its inversion. When ϕ is of large dimension this may be computationally difficult. The modified Newton–Raphson method uses the fact that $\partial\mathrm{gr}(\phi)/\partial\phi \approx \partial^2 \mathcal{L}(\phi)/\partial\phi\partial\phi'$ and guesses the shape of $\partial^2 \mathcal{L}(\phi)/\partial\phi\partial\phi'$ at the existing estimate by using the derivative of the gradient. Let Σ^l be an estimate of $[\partial^2 \mathcal{L}(\phi)/\partial\phi\partial\phi']^{-1}$ at iteration l. Then the method updates estimates of ϕ by using (6.24), where

$$\Sigma^l = \Sigma^{l-1} - \frac{\Sigma^{l-1}\Delta\mathrm{gr}^l(\Delta\mathrm{gr}^l)'(\Sigma^{l-1})}{(\Delta\mathrm{gr}^l)'\Sigma^{l-1}\Delta\mathrm{gr}^l} - \frac{(\Delta\phi^l)(\Delta\phi^l)'}{(\Delta\mathrm{gr}^l)'(\Delta\phi^l)},$$

$\Delta\phi^l = \phi^l - \phi^{l-1}$, $\Delta\mathrm{gr}(\phi^l) = \mathrm{gr}(\phi^l) - \mathrm{gr}(\phi^{l-1})$. If the likelihood is quadratic and the number of iterations large, $\lim_{l\to\infty}\phi^l = \phi_{\mathrm{ML}}$ and $\lim_{l\to\infty}\Sigma^l = [(\partial^2 \mathcal{L}(\phi)/\partial\phi\partial\phi')|_{\phi=\phi_{\mathrm{ML}}}]^{-1}$. Standard errors can be read off the diagonal elements of Σ^l evaluated at ϕ_{ML}.

(d) *Scoring method.* This method uses the information matrix $E\partial^2\mathcal{L}(\phi)/\partial\phi\partial\phi'$ in place of $\partial^2\mathcal{L}(\phi)/\partial\phi\partial\phi'$ in the calculation, where the expectation is evaluated at $\phi = \phi^{l-1}$. The information matrix approximation is convenient since it has a simpler expression than the Hessian.

(e) *Gauss–Newton scoring method.* The Gauss–Newton method uses a function of $[(\partial e/\partial\phi)|_{\phi=\phi^l}]'[(\partial e/\partial\phi)|_{\phi=\phi^l}]$ as an approximation to $\partial^2\mathcal{L}(\phi)/\partial\phi\partial\phi'$, where ϕ^l is the value of ϕ at iteration l and e_t is the vector of errors in the model. In the case of constant state-space models, the approximation is proportional to the vector of regressors constructed by using the right-hand side variables of both the state and the measurement equations. When the model is linear, Gauss–Newton and scoring approximations are identical.

6.4 ML Estimation of DSGE Models

Maximum likelihood estimation of the parameters of a DSGE model is a straightforward application of the methods we have described so far. As we saw in chapter 2, the log-linearized solution of a DSGE model is of the form

$$y_{2t} = \mathcal{A}_{22}(\theta)y_{2t-1} + \mathcal{A}_{23}(\theta)y_{3t}, \tag{6.25}$$

$$y_{1t} = \mathcal{A}_{12}(\theta)y_{2t-1} + \mathcal{A}_{13}(\theta)y_{3t}, \tag{6.26}$$

where y_{2t} includes the states and the driving forces, y_{1t} all other endogenous variables, and y_{3t} the shocks of the model. Here $\mathcal{A}_{ii'}(\theta)$, $i, i' = 1, 2$, are time-invariant matrices which depend on $\theta = (\theta_1, \dots, \theta_k)$, the structural parameters of preferences, technologies, and government policies. Note also that there are cross-equation restrictions in the sense that some θ_j may appear in more than one entry of these matrices.

Example 6.15. In the working-capital model considered in exercise 2.14, setting $K_t = 1, \forall t$, assuming that the utility is separable in consumption and leisure and logarithmic in both, y_{2t} includes lagged real balances, M_{t-1}/p_{t-1}, and lagged deposits, dep_{t-1}; y_{3t} includes shocks to the technology, ζ_t, and to the monetary rule, M_t^{g}; while y_{1t} includes output, GDP_t, the nominal interest rate, i_t, and the inflation rate, π_t. Setting $N^{\text{ss}} = 0.33$, $\eta = 0.65$, $\pi^{\text{ss}} = 1.005$, $\beta = 0.99$, $(c/\text{GDP})^{\text{ss}} = 0.8$, the persistence of the shocks to 0.95 and the parameters of the policy rule to $a_2 = -1.0$, $a_1 = 0.5$, $a_3 = 0.1$, $a_0 = 0$, the log-linearized solution is

$$\begin{bmatrix} \dfrac{M_t}{p_t} \\ \text{dep}_t \\ \text{GDP}_t \\ i_t \\ \Pi_t \end{bmatrix} = \begin{bmatrix} -0.4960 & 0.3990 \\ -1.0039 & 0.8075 \\ -0.3968 & 0.3192 \\ 0.9713 & -0.7813 \\ 2.0219 & -1.6264 \end{bmatrix} \begin{bmatrix} \dfrac{M_{t-1}}{p_{t-1}} \\ \text{dep}_{t-1} \end{bmatrix} + \begin{bmatrix} 1.3034 & -0.1941 \\ 1.1459 & -1.4786 \\ 1.0427 & -0.1552 \\ -0.3545 & 0.3800 \\ -0.9175 & -1.2089 \end{bmatrix} \begin{bmatrix} \zeta_t \\ M_t^{\text{g}} \end{bmatrix},$$

which has the format of (6.25), (6.26).

Although in example 6.15 we chose a log-linear approximation, DSGE models with quadratic preferences and linear constraints also fit into this structure (see, for example, Hansen and Sargent 2005). In fact, (6.25), (6.26) are very general, do not require certainty equivalence to obtain, and need not be the solution to the model, as is shown next.

Example 6.16 (Watson). Suppose a model delivers the condition $E_t y_{t+1} = \alpha y_t + x_t$, where $x_t = \rho x_{t-1} + e_t^x$, x_0 given. This could be, for example, a New Keynesian Phillips curve, in which case x_t are marginal costs, or an asset price evaluation formula, in which case x_t are dividends. Using the innovation representation we can write $x_t = E_{t-1}x_t + e_t^x$, $y_t = E_{t-1}y_t + e_t^y$, where $E_t x_{t+1} = \rho x_t = \rho(E_{t-1}x_t + e_t^x)$ and $E_t y_{t+1} = \alpha y_t + x_t = \alpha(E_{t-1}y_t + e_t^y) + (E_{t-1}x_t + e_t^x)$. Letting $y_{1t} = [x_t, y_t]'$, $y_{2t} = [E_t x_{t+1}, E_t y_{t+1}]'$, $y_{3t} = [e_t^x, v_t]'$, where $v_t \equiv e_t^y - E(e_t^y \mid e_t^x) = e_t^y - \kappa e_t^x$, $\mathcal{A}_{11}(\theta) = I$,

$$\mathcal{A}_{12}(\theta) = \begin{bmatrix} 1 & 0 \\ \kappa & 1 \end{bmatrix}, \quad \mathcal{A}_{22}(\theta) = \begin{bmatrix} \rho & 0 \\ 1 & \alpha \end{bmatrix}, \quad \mathcal{A}_{21}(\theta) = \begin{bmatrix} \rho & 0 \\ 1 + \alpha\kappa & \alpha \end{bmatrix},$$

the model clearly fits into (6.25), (6.26). Here the parameters to be estimated are $\theta = (\alpha, \rho, \kappa, \sigma_e^2, \sigma_v^2)$.

In general, one has two alternatives to derive a representation which fits into (6.25), (6.26): solve the model, as we did in example 6.15, or use the rational expectations assumption, as we did in example 6.16. The difference is that in the latter case y_{2t} contains nonobservable variables.

Exercise 6.20. Consider a version of a consumption-saving problem where the representative consumer is endowed with utility of the form $u(c) = c^{1-\varphi}/(1-\varphi)$, the economy is small relative to the rest of world and the resource constraint is $c_t + B_{t+1} \leqslant \mathrm{GDP}_t + (1 + r_t)B_t$, where B_t are internationally traded bonds and r_t is the net real interest rate, taken as given by the agents.

Derive a log-linearized version of the Euler equation and map it onto the framework described in example 6.16. Show the entries of the matrices in the state-space representation. How would you include a borrowing constraint $B_t < \bar{B}$ in the setup?

Exercise 6.21. Consider the labor hoarding model studied in exercise 5.37, where agents have preferences over consumption, leisure, and effort and firms distinguish between labor and effort in the production function. Cast the log-linearized Euler conditions into a state-space framework by using an innovation representation.

Clearly, (6.25), (6.26) are in a format estimable with the Kalman filter. In fact, recursive estimates of y_{2t} can be obtained, given some initial y_{20}, if $\mathcal{A}_{ii'}(\theta)$ and $\sigma_{y_3}^2$ are known. Given these recursive estimates, forecast errors can be computed. Hence, for a given θ, we can calculate the likelihood function by using the prediction error decomposition and update estimates with one of the algorithms described in section 6.3. Once the maximum is located, standard errors for the estimated parameters can be read off the Hessian, evaluated at ML estimates, or any approximation to it.

Despite the simplicity of this procedure, there are several issues, specific to DSGE models, one must deal with when using ML to estimate structural parameters. The first has to do with the possible presence of unobservable variables in the vector y_{2t}. If one decides to solve these variables out, care should be exercised when writing down the likelihood of the restricted specification. Marginalizations like these may in fact induce systems where a restricted VAR representation may not exist or where it may have an infinite number of lags.

Example 6.17. Suppose the vector y_{2t} in (6.25) is nonobservable. Solving for y_{3t} from (6.26) and plugging the expression in (6.25), we have $[I - (\mathcal{A}_{22}(\theta) - \mathcal{A}_{23}(\theta)\mathcal{A}_{13}(\theta)^{\mathrm{G}}\mathcal{A}_{12}(\theta))\ell]y_{2t} = \mathcal{A}_{23}(\theta)\mathcal{A}_{13}(\theta)^{\mathrm{G}}y_{1t}$, where $\mathcal{A}_{13}(\theta)^{\mathrm{G}}$ is the generalized inverse of $\mathcal{A}_{13}(\theta)$. Lagging one period and plugging it back into (6.26), we have $y_{1t} = \mathcal{A}_{12}(\theta)[I - (\mathcal{A}_{22}(\theta) - \mathcal{A}_{23}(\theta)\mathcal{A}_{13}(\theta)^{\mathrm{G}}\mathcal{A}_{12}(\theta))\ell]^{-1} \times \mathcal{A}_{23}(\theta)\mathcal{A}_{13}(\theta)^{\mathrm{G}}y_{1t-1} + \mathcal{A}_{13}(\theta)y_{3t}$. Clearly, this equation defines a VAR for y_{1t} provided that $\sum_j [\mathcal{A}_{22}(\theta) - \mathcal{A}_{23}(\theta)\mathcal{A}_{13}(\theta)^{\mathrm{G}}\mathcal{A}_{12}(\theta)]^j$ converges. A sufficient condition for this to occur is that $\mathcal{A}_{13}(\theta)^{\mathrm{G}} = \mathcal{A}_{13}(\theta)^{-1}$ and that the eigenvalues of $\mathcal{A}_{22}(\theta) - \mathcal{A}_{23}(\theta)\mathcal{A}_{13}(\theta)^{-1}\mathcal{A}_{12}(\theta)$ are all less than 1 in modulus. In general, an infinite number of lags is needed to correctly represent the solution for y_{1t}: a finite-order VAR is appropriate only if the largest eigenvalue of $\mathcal{A}_{22}(\theta) - \mathcal{A}_{23}(\theta)\mathcal{A}_{13}(\theta)^{-1}\mathcal{A}_{12}(\theta)$ is sufficiently small in modulus. Since these conditions depend on θ and the nature of the model, they have to be checked for each model considered.

Finally, $y_{1t} = [\mathcal{A}_{12}(\theta)(I - \mathcal{A}_{22}(\theta)\ell)^{-1}\mathcal{A}_{23}(\theta)\ell + \mathcal{A}_{13}(\theta)]y_{3t}$ is the moving average representation, so that $\mathcal{A}_{13}(\theta)$ represents the contemporaneous effect and $\mathcal{A}_{12}(\theta)\mathcal{A}_{22}(\theta)^{j-1}\mathcal{A}_{23}(\theta)$ the effect at lag j of a unitary shock in y_{3t}. Hence, the above two conditions on the eigenvalues of $\mathcal{A}_{22}(\theta) - \mathcal{A}_{23}(\theta)\mathcal{A}_{13}(\theta)^{-1}\mathcal{A}_{12}(\theta)$ are also sufficient to allow us to recover economically meaningful shocks from a finite-order VAR representation for y_{1t}.

Regardless of whether y_{2t} includes observable variables or not, θ_{ML} will be consistent and asymptotically normal if it is identifiable and if the conditions listed in section 6.2.1 are satisfied.

The second problem has to do with the number of series used in the estimation. As is clear from (6.25), (6.26), the covariance matrix of the vector $[y_{1t}, y_{2t}]'$ is singular, a restriction unlikely to hold in the data. In many cases, even solving y_{2t} out, the rank of the $\mathcal{A}_{13}(\theta)$ matrix is less than the dimension of y_{1t}. This singularity clearly appears in the innovation representation (6.11), (6.12). Two options are available to the applied investigator: she can either select as many variables as there are shocks or artificially augment the space of shocks with measurement errors. For example, if the model is driven by a technology and a government expenditure shock, one selects two of the (many) series belonging to (y_{1t}, y_{2t}) to estimate parameters. Kim (2000) and Ireland (2000) use such an approach in estimating versions of sticky price models. While this leaves some arbitrariness in the procedure, some variables may have little information about the θ parameters. Although *a priori* it may be hard to know which equations carry proper information, one could try to select variables so as to maximize the identifiability of the parameters. Alternatively, since some variables may not satisfy the assumptions needed to obtain consistent estimates (e.g., they display structural breaks), one could choose the variables more likely to satisfy these conditions.

Example 6.18. In a log-linearized RBC model driven by technology disturbances, we have that $[GDP_t, N_t, c_t]$ are statically related to the states K_t and the shocks ζ_t via the matrices $\mathcal{A}_{12}(\theta)$ and $\mathcal{A}_{13}(\theta)$. Since the number of shocks is less than the number of endogenous variables, there are linear combinations of the controls which are perfectly predictable. For example, substituting equation (6.25) into (6.26) we have that $\alpha_1 N_t + \alpha_2 GDP_t + \alpha_3 c_t = 0$, where $\alpha_1 = \mathcal{A}_{12}^1 \mathcal{A}_{13}^3 - \mathcal{A}_{13}^1 \mathcal{A}_{12}^3$, $\alpha_2 = \mathcal{A}_{13}^2 \mathcal{A}_{12}^3 - \mathcal{A}_{12}^2 \mathcal{A}_{12}^3$, $\alpha_3 = \mathcal{A}_{13}^2 \mathcal{A}_{12}^1 - \mathcal{A}_{13}^1 \mathcal{A}_{12}^2$, where $\mathcal{A}_{1j}^i$ is the ith element of $\mathcal{A}_{1j}$, $i = 1, 2, 3$, $j = 2, 3$. Similarly, by using the equations for GDP_t, c_t, and the law of motion of the capital stock, we have $\alpha_4 c_t + \alpha_5 c_{t-1} - \alpha_6 \text{GDP}_t - \alpha_7 \text{GDP}_{t-1} = 0$, where $\alpha_4 = \mathcal{A}_1 3^1 + \delta[1 - \delta(K/N)^\eta](\mathcal{A}_{13}^1 \mathcal{A}_{12}^3 - \mathcal{A}_{12}^1 \mathcal{A}_{13}^3)/[1 - \delta(K/N)^\eta]$, $\alpha_5 = (1-\delta)\mathcal{A}_{13}^1$, $\alpha_6 = \mathcal{A}_{13}^3 - \delta(\mathcal{A}_{13}^1 \mathcal{A}_{12}^3 - \mathcal{A}_{12}^1 \mathcal{A}_{13}^3)/[1 - \delta(K/N)^\eta]$, $\alpha_7 = (1-\delta)\mathcal{A}_{13}^3$. Hence, the system is stochastically singular and for any sample size the covariance matrix of the data is postulated to be of reduced rank.

Exercise 6.22. Consider a simple version of a sticky price model driven by technology and monetary shocks, whose log-linearized conditions are presented in exercise 2.29. Show which combination of the controls is perfectly predictable. Which equation needs measurement error to avoid singularities?

Attaching measurement errors to (6.26) is the option taken by Sargent (1979), Altug (1989), or McGrattan et al. (1997). The logic is straightforward: by adding a vector of serially and contemporaneously uncorrelated measurement errors, we complete the probability space of the model (the theoretical covariance matrix of (y_{1t}, y_{2t}) is no longer singular). Since the actual variables typically fail to match their model counterparts (e.g., actual savings are typically different from model-based measures of savings), the addition of measurement errors is justifiable. If this route is taken, a simple diagnostic on the quality of the model is obtained by comparing the size of the estimated standard deviation of the measurement errors and of the economic shocks. Standard deviations for the former that are much larger than for the latter suggest that misspecification is likely to be present.

Example 6.19. In example 6.15, if we wish to complete the probability space of the model, we need to add three measurement errors to the vector of shocks. Alternatively, we could use, for example, real balances and deposits to estimate the parameters of the model. However, it is unlikely that these two series have information to estimate, for example, the share of labor in production function η. Hence, identification of the parameters must be checked when a subset of the variables of the model is used. One possibility, which strikes a balance between these two options, is to eliminate some of the variables and add a smaller set of measurement errors. For example, adding one measurement error to the second set of equations and solving out deposits and real balances, we could estimate the parameters of the model by using a VAR with output, interest rates, and inflation, driven by two structural shocks and one measurement error. For the parametrization used in example 6.15, the conditions for existence of a VAR representation of finite order for these three variables are not satisfied. In fact, while $\mathcal{A}_{13}(\theta)^{-1}$ exists, the eigenvalues of $\mathcal{A}_{22}(\theta) - \mathcal{A}_{23}(\theta)\mathcal{A}_{13}(\theta)^{-1}\mathcal{A}_{12}(\theta)$ are 1.78 and –0.85.

The introduction of a vector of serially and contemporaneously uncorrelated measurement errors does not alter the dynamics of the model. Therefore, the quality of the model's approximation to the data is left unchanged. Ireland (2004), guessing that both dynamic and contemporaneous misspecifications are likely to be present in simple DSGE models, instead adds a VAR(1) vector of measurement errors. The importance of these dynamics for the resulting hybrid model can be used to gauge how far the model is from the data, much in the spirit of Watson (1993), and an analysis of the properties of the estimated VAR may help in respecifying the model (see chapter 7). However, the hybrid model can no longer be considered "structural": the additional dynamics in fact play the same role as distributed lags which were added in the past to specifications derived from static economic theory when confronted with the (dynamics of the) data.

The third issue of interest concerns the quality of the model's approximation to the data. It is clear that to obtain ML estimates of θ and to validate the model, one must assume that it "correctly" represents the process generating the data up to a set of unknown parameters. Some form of misspecification regarding, for example, the distribution of the errors (see White 1982) or the parametrization (see Hansen and Sargent 2005) can be handled by using the quasi-ML approach discussed in section 6.2. However, as we will argue in chapter 7, the misspecification that a DSGE model typically displays is of a different type. Adding contemporaneous uncorrelated measurement errors avoids singularities but it does not necessarily reduce misspecification. Moreover, while with GMM one is free to choose the relationships used to estimate the parameters of interest, this is not the case with ML since joint estimation of all the relationships produced by the model is generally performed. Under these conditions, ML estimates of the parameters are unlikely to be consistent and economic exercises conducted conditional on these estimates may be meaningless. In other words, credible ML estimation of the parameters of a DSGE model requires strong beliefs about the nature of the model.

Fourth, for parameters to be estimable they need to be identifiable. Identification is a generic problem whenever the estimated model is nonlinear in the parameters.

As we saw in chapter 5, limited-information methods may face severe identification problems. Full information ML techniques may also suffer from such problems and the ability to detect them is reduced when a structure like (6.25), (6.26) is used, since the mapping between the likelihood and the θ is only approximate and highly nonlinear. We show a few aspects of the identification problem in the context of log-linearized DSGE models in the next two examples.

Example 6.20. The model of example 5.37 has the solution:

$$\begin{bmatrix} \text{gdpgap}_t \\ \pi_t \\ i_t \end{bmatrix} = \begin{bmatrix} 1 & 0 & a_2 \\ a_4 & 1 & a_2 a_4 \\ 0 & 0 & 1 \end{bmatrix} \begin{bmatrix} v_{1t} \\ v_{2t} \\ v_{3t} \end{bmatrix}. \tag{6.27}$$

Equation (6.27) suggests two considerations. First, if the likelihood function for de-meaned variables is used, the parameters a_1, a_3, a_5 cannot be identified. Second, even if level variables are employed, it may be impossible to recover all the parameters. In fact, the steady states of the three variables are $\text{gdpgap}^{\text{ss}} = 0$, $\pi^{\text{ss}} = 0$, $i^{\text{ss}} = 0$ and therefore have no information for these parameters. In a more complicated model where, for example, a constant is introduced in the last equation, $\text{gdpgap}^{\text{ss}}$, π^{ss}, i^{ss} are different from zero but highly nonlinear in the five parameters of the model and the constant. Since there are only six nonzero coefficients in the solution (three steady states and three MA coefficients) and since only two parameters appear in the three MA coefficients, it is unlikely that all parameters will be identifiable even in this case.

Example 6.21 (Canova and Sala). Suppose a social planner maximizes $\sum_t \beta^t \times c_t^{1-\varphi}/(1-\varphi)$ and the resource constraint is $c_t + K_{t+1} = K_t^{1-\eta}\zeta_t + (1-\delta)K_t$, where c_t is consumption, φ is the risk-aversion coefficient, ζ_t is a first-order autoregressive process with persistence ρ, steady-state value z^{ss}, and unitary variance, K_t is the current capital stock, $1-\eta$ is the share of capital in production, and δ is the depreciation rate of capital. The parameters are $\theta = [\beta, \varphi, \delta, 1-\eta, \rho, z^{\text{ss}}]$. To show the shape of the likelihood function, obtained from the solution of the model in log-deviations from the steady states, when all variables are assumed to be observable, we set $\beta = 0.985$, $\varphi = 2.0$, $\eta = 0.64$, $\delta = 0.025$, $\rho = 0.95$, $z^{\text{ss}} = 1$.

Figure 6.1 plots the likelihood surface, obtained by varying (δ, β) and (φ, ρ) in an economically reasonable neighborhood of the selected values, and the corresponding contour plots. Although there is a unique maximum at the true parameter vector, the likelihood function is somewhat flat either locally around the maximum or globally over the entire parameter range. For example, ρ is very weakly identified in the chosen interval, while there is a ridge of approximately similar height in the depreciation rate δ and the discount factor β, running from $(\delta = 0.005, \beta = 0.975)$ up to $(\delta = 0.03, \beta = 0.99)$, suggesting that only a combination of the two parameters is identifiable. Note that the 1% contour includes the whole range of economically interesting values of δ and β.

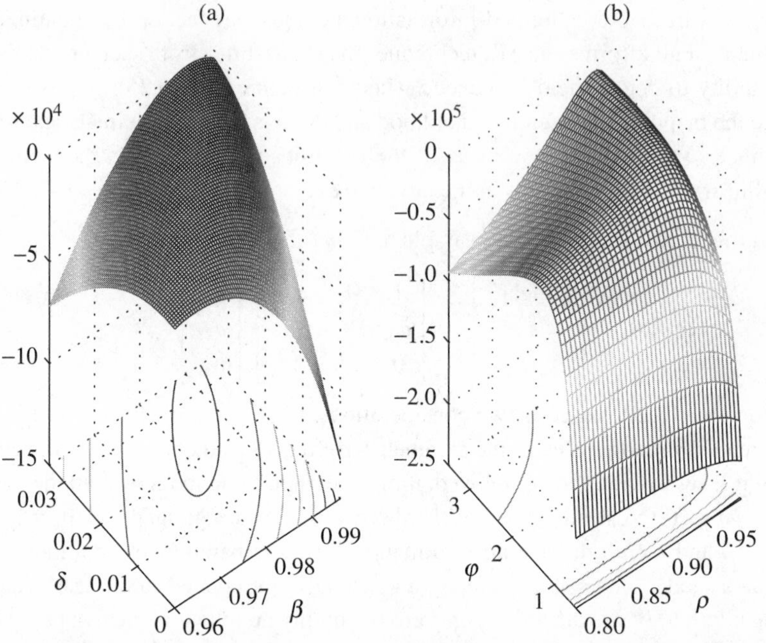

Figure 6.1. Likelihood surface: (a) β, 0.985; δ, 0.025; (b) ρ, 0.95; φ, 2.

While the two examples are illustrative, their message is clear. It is difficult to know *a priori* which parameters are identifiable. Therefore, it is important to check parameter identifiability either prior to estimation, via simulation exercises like those performed in chapter 5, or *ex post*, examining the rank and the relative magnitude of the smallest eigenvalues of the information matrix. Note that calibrating the non-identifiable parameters may induce the same distortions emerging with simulation estimators.

We summarize the problems so far discussed in the context of an example.

Example 6.22 (money demand equation). Consider a representative agent maximizing $E_0 \sum_t \beta^t [(1/(1-\varphi_c))c_t^{1-\varphi_c} + (\vartheta_M/(1-\varphi_M))(M_{t+1}/p_t)^{1-\varphi_M}]$ by choice of (c_t, B_{t+1}, M_{t+1}) subject to $c_t + B_{t+1}/p_t + M_{t+1}/p_t + \frac{1}{2}b_1(M_{t+1} - M_t)^2/p_t + \frac{1}{2}b_2(M_t - M_{t-1})^2/p_t \leqslant w_t + M_t/p_t + (1+i_t)B_t/p_t$, where b_1, b_2 are parameters, w_t is an exogenous labor income, and B_t are nominal one-period bonds. The two optimality conditions are $c_t^{-\varphi_c} = \beta E_t[c_{t+1}^{-\varphi_c}(p_t/p_{t+1})(1+i_{t+1})]$ and $\vartheta_M(M_{t+1}/p_t)^{-\varphi_M} c_t^{\varphi_c} = E_t\{1 - 1/(1+i_{t+1}) + [b_1 + b_2/(1+i_{t+1})]\Delta M_{t+1} - [1/(1+i_{t+1})][b_1 + b_2/(1+i_{t+2})]\Delta M_{t+2}\}$, where $\Delta M_{t+1} = M_{t+1} - M_t$. Log-linearizing the two conditions, solving for $\hat{\imath}_{t+1}$, and using the budget constraint, we have that $\phi_c w_t - \phi_M(M_{t+1} - p_t) = \alpha_1 \Delta M_{t+1} + \alpha_2 \Delta M_{t+2} + \alpha_3 \Delta w_{t+1} + \alpha_4 \Delta w_{t+2} + \alpha_5 \Delta p_{t+1} + \alpha_6 \Delta p_{t+2}$, where α_j are functions of the deep parameters of the model and of the steady states i^{ss}, ΔM^{ss}. If we assume that the central bank chooses i_{t+1} so that $\Delta p_t = 0$, that bonds are in zero net supply, the above equation can be solved for ΔM_t as a function of the current and future labor income $\hat{w}_t$ and real balances $M_{t+1} - p_t$.

The parameters of this model can be estimated in a number of ways. One is GMM. For example, using as instruments lagged values of money growth, real balances, and labor income, one could estimate $(\varphi_M, \varphi_c, b_1, b_2, i^{\text{ss}}, \Delta M^{\text{ss}}, \beta)$ from the two Euler equations. Alternatively, one could use ML. To do so one needs to express the current growth rate of money as a function of current and future consumption and current money holdings. As we will see in example 6.23, this is easier to do if we represent the available data with a VAR.

Since there is only one shock (the exogenous labor income), the system of equations determining the solution is singular. There are three alternatives for dealing with this problem. The one we have used expresses the solution of ΔM_t in terms of current and future labor income and real balances. Then estimates of the parameters can be found by maximizing the likelihood of the resulting equation. The second is to attach to the policy equation an error, $\Delta p_t = \epsilon_{3t}$. This is easily justifiable if inflation targeting is only pursued on average over some period of time. The third is to assume that labor income is measured with error. In the latter two alternatives, the joint likelihood function of the money demand equation and of the consumption Euler equation can be used to find estimates of the parameters. Note also that not all the parameters may be identifiable from the first setup—the forward-looking solution requires elimination of the unstable roots, which may have important information about, for example, the adjustment cost parameters, b_1 and b_2.

Once parameter estimates are obtained, one can proceed to validate the model and/or examine the properties of the implied system. Statistical validation can be conducted in many ways. For example, if interesting economic hypotheses involve restrictions on a subset of the parameters of the model, standard t-tests or likelihood ratio tests using the restricted and the unrestricted versions of the model can be performed. Restricted and unrestricted specifications can also be compared in out-of-sample forecasting races; for example, using the MSEs of the forecasts or the record of turning-point predictions.

Exercise 6.23. Consider two versions of an RBC model, one with capacity utilization and one without. Describe a Monte Carlo procedure to verify which model matches turning points of U.S. output growth better. How would you compare models which are not nested (say, one with capacity utilization and one with adjustment costs to capital)?

The stability of the estimates over subsamples can be examined in a standard way. For example, one can split the sample in two and construct $\mathfrak{S} = (\theta^1 - \theta^2)(\Sigma_{\theta^1} + \Sigma_{\theta^2})^{-1}(\theta^1 - \theta^2)$, where θ^i is the ML estimate obtained in sample $i = 1, 2$ and Σ_{θ^i} its estimated covariance matrix. Recursive tests of this type can also be used to determine when a structural break occurs. That is, for each $1 < \tau < T$, we can construct $\mathfrak{S}_\tau$ by estimating the model over two samples $[1, \tau]$, $[\tau + 1, T]$. Then one would compare $\sup_\tau \mathfrak{S}_\tau$ with a $\chi^2(\dim(\theta))$.

We have seen that the solution of DSGE models can be alternatively written in a state space or restricted VAR(1) format. This latter offers an alternative framework to compare the model with the data. The restrictions that DSGE models impose on VARs are of two types. First, log-linearized DSGE models are typically VAR(1) models. Therefore, the methods described in chapter 4 can be used to examine whether the actual data can be modeled as a VAR(1). Second, it is well-known, at least since Sargent (1979), that rational expectations models impose an extensive set of cross-equation restrictions on the VAR of the data. These restrictions can be used to identify and estimate the free parameters and to test the validity of the model. We discuss how this can be done next.

Example 6.23 (Kurmann). Consider a hybrid Phillips curve, $\pi_t = \alpha_1 E_t \pi_{t+1} + \alpha_2 \pi_{t-1} + \alpha_3 \text{mc}_t + e_t$, which can be obtained from a standard sticky price model once a fraction of the producers fix the price by using a rule of thumb and adding some measurement error e_t. The rule necessary to produce such an expression is that the new price is set to an average of last period's price, updated with last period's inflation rate (as in Gali and Gertler 1999). Assume mc_t is exogenous and let $\mathcal{F}_t$ represent the information set available at each t. For any $z_t \in \mathcal{F}_t$, $E_t[E_t(y_{t+\tau} \mid \mathcal{F}_t) \mid z_t] = E_t(y_{t+\tau} \mid z_t)$, by the law of iterated expectations. Let $\mathbb{Y}_t = \mathbb{A}\mathbb{Y}_{t-1} + E_t$ be the companion form representation of the model, where $\mathbb{Y}_t$ is of dimension $mq \times 1$ (m variables with q lags each). Since $E_t(\text{mc}_{t+\tau} \mid \mathbb{Y}_t) = \mathbb{S}_1 \mathbb{A}^\tau \mathbb{Y}_t$ and $E_t(\pi_{t+\tau} \mid \mathbb{Y}_t) = \mathbb{S}_2 \mathbb{A}^\tau \mathbb{Y}_t$, where $\mathbb{S}_1$ and $\mathbb{S}_2$ are selection matrices, a hybrid Phillips curve implies $\mathbb{S}_2[\mathbb{A} - \alpha_1 \mathbb{A}^2 - \alpha_2 I] = \alpha_3 \mathbb{S}_1 \mathbb{A}$, which produces mq restrictions. If $q = 1$, $\mathbb{Y}_t$ includes a proxy for real marginal costs and inflation and $A_{ii'}$ are the VAR parameters, we have

$$\left.\begin{aligned} A_{12} - \alpha_1 A_{12} A_{11} - \alpha_1 A_{22} A_{12} - \alpha_2 &= \alpha_3 A_{11}, \\ A_{22} - \alpha_1 A_{21} A_{12} - \alpha_1 A_{22}^2 - \alpha_2 &= \alpha_3 A_{21}. \end{aligned}\right\} \tag{6.28}$$

Equations (6.28) require that expectations of real marginal costs and inflation produced by a VAR are consistent with the dynamics of the model. One way to impose these restrictions is to express the coefficients of the inflation equation in the VAR as a function of the remaining $(m - 1)mq$ VAR coefficients and the parameters of the theory. Since the two equations in (6.28) have four unknowns, they force, for example, A_{21} and A_{22} to be a function of A_{11} and A_{12}. The likelihood function for the restricted VAR system can then be constructed by using the prediction error decomposition and tests of the restrictions obtained by comparing the likelihood of restricted and unrestricted VARs.

Exercise 6.24. Consider an endowment economy where agents receive a random income w_t and may either consume or save it. Suppose that stocks S_{t+1} are the only asset, that their price is p_t^{s}, and that the budget constraint is $c_t + p_t^{\text{s}} S_{t+1} =$

$w_t + (p_t^s + \mathrm{sd}_t)S_t$, where sd_t are dividends. Assume that $u(c) = c^{1-\varphi}/(1-\varphi)$ and that agents discount the future at the rate β.

(i) Derive a log-linearized expression for the price of stocks as a function of future dividends, future prices, current and future consumption.

(ii) Assume that $w_t = w, \forall t$, that data on stock prices and stock dividends are available, and that an econometrician specifies the process for the data as a VAR of order 2. Derive the restrictions that the model imposes on the bivariate representation of prices and dividends. (Hint: use the equilibrium conditions to express consumption as a function of dividends.)

(iii) Assume that data on consumption are also available. Does your answer in (ii) change?

Statistical validation is usually insufficient for economic purposes, since it offers scarce indications of the reasons for why the model fails to match the data and provides little information about the properties of the estimated model. Therefore, as we did in chapter 5, one would also like to compare the predictions of the model for a set of economically interesting statistics. For example, given ML estimates, one could compute unconditional moments such as variability, cross-correlations, spectra, or cross-spectra and compare them with those in the data. To learn about the dynamic properties of the estimated model, one could compute impulse responses, variance, and historical decompositions. Informal comparisons are typically performed but there is no reason to do so in an ML context. In fact, under regularity conditions, and since $\sqrt{T}(\theta_{\mathrm{ML}} - \theta_0) \xrightarrow{\mathrm{D}} \mathbb{N}(0, \Sigma_\theta)$, we can compute the asymptotic distribution of any continuous function of θ by using the δ-method, i.e., if $h(\theta)$ is continuously differentiable, $\sqrt{T}(h(\theta_{\mathrm{ML}}) - h(\theta_0)) \xrightarrow{\mathrm{D}} \mathbb{N}(0, \Sigma_h \equiv (\partial h(\theta)/\partial\theta)\Sigma_\theta(\partial h(\theta)/\partial\theta)')$. If an estimate h_T is available in the data, a measure of distance between the model and the data is $(h(\theta_{\mathrm{ML}}) - h_T)(\Sigma_h + \Sigma_{h_T})^{-1}(h(\theta_{\mathrm{ML}}) - h_T)$, which is asymptotically distributed as a $\chi^2(\dim(h))$. Small-sample versions of such tests are also easily designed.

Exercise 6.25. Suppose that $\sqrt{T}(\theta_{\mathrm{ML}} - \theta_0) \xrightarrow{\mathrm{D}} \mathbb{N}(0, \Sigma_\theta)$ and suppose that, for the statistic $h(\theta)$ of interest, both h_T and its standard error are available. Describe how to perform a small-sample test for the fit of a model.

Once the model is found to be adequate in capturing the statistical and the economic features of the data, welfare measures can be calculated and policy exercises performed.

Exercise 6.26 (Blanchard and Quah). The model described in section 3.3.1 produces a solution of the form

$$\left.\begin{aligned} \Delta\mathrm{GDP}_t &= \epsilon_{3t} - \epsilon_{3t-1} + (1+a)\epsilon_{1t} - a\epsilon_{1t-1}, \\ \mathrm{UN}_t &= -\epsilon_{3t} - a\epsilon_{1t}, \end{aligned}\right\} \tag{6.29}$$

where $\Delta\mathrm{GDP}_t = \mathrm{GDP}_t - \mathrm{GDP}_{t-1}$ and $\mathrm{UN}_t = N_t - N^{\mathrm{fe}}$, N^{fe} is the full employment equilibrium, ϵ_{1t} is a technology shock, and ϵ_{3t} a money shock.

(i) Transform (6.29) into a state-space model.

(ii) Using data for output growth and appropriately detrended unemployment provide an ML estimate of a and test three hypotheses, $a = 0$ and $a \pm 1$.

(iii) Provide impulse responses to technology and money shocks by using a_{ML}. Compare them with those obtained with a structural VAR. (Hint: choose an identification approach consistent with (6.29).)

Exercise 6.27 (habit persistence). Consider a basic RBC model driven by technology disturbances and three separate specifications for preferences. The first one assumes intertemporal separability of consumption and leisure, that is, $u(c_t, c_{t-1}, N_t, N_{t-1}) = c_t^{1-\varphi}/(1-\varphi)+\ln(1-N_t)$. The second assumes that there is habit persistence in consumption, that is $u(c_t, c_{t-1}, N_t, N_{t-1}) = (c_t+\gamma_1 c_{t-1})^{1-\varphi}/(1-\varphi) + \ln(1-N_t)$. The third assumes that there is habit persistence in leisure so that $u(c_t, c_{t-1}, N_t, N_{t-1}) = c_t^{1-\varphi}/(1-\varphi) + \ln(1-N_t+\gamma_2(1-N_{t-1}))$. The resource constraint is $c_t + K_{t+1} = \zeta_t K_t^{1-\eta} N_t^{\eta} + (1-\delta)K_t$, where $\ln \zeta_t$ is an AR(1) process. Using U.S. data on consumption, hours, output, and investment, estimate the free parameters of the three models assuming that consumption, investment, and output are measured with error and that each of these errors is a contemporaneously uncorrelated martingale difference process. Test the hypotheses that either $\gamma_1 = 0$ or $\gamma_2 = 0$. Compare the responses of the three models to technology shocks. What is the role of habit persistence in propagating technology disturbances? (Hint: nest the three models in one general specification and test the restrictions.)

6.5 Two Examples

We illustrate the features and the problems that maximum likelihood techniques face when dealing with DSGE models with two examples featuring interesting economic questions.

6.5.1 Does Monetary Policy React to Technology Shocks?

The model we consider is the same as in exercise 3.43. Our task is to estimate its structural parameters, test economic hypotheses concerning the magnitude of production and policy parameters, compare the forecasting performance relative to an unrestricted VAR, and, finally, examine some moment implications of the model and of the data.

For convenience we repeat the basic setup: the representative household maximizes $E_0 \sum_t \beta^t\{\ln c_t + \vartheta_M \ln(M_t/p_t) - [\vartheta_N/(1-\varphi_n)]N_t^{1-\varphi_n} - [\vartheta_{\mathrm{ef}}/(1-\varphi_{\mathrm{ef}})] \times \mathrm{Ef}_t^{1-\varphi_{\mathrm{ef}}}\}$, where $c_t = (\int c_{it}^{1/(\varsigma_p+1)}\,\mathrm{d}i)^{\varsigma_p+1}$ is aggregate consumption, $\varsigma_p > 0$, $p_t = (\int p_{it}^{-1/\varsigma_p}\,\mathrm{d}j)^{-\varsigma_p}$ is the aggregate price index, M_t/p_t are real balances, N_t is the number of hours worked, and Ef_t is effort. The budget constraint is $\int_0^1 p_{it}c_{it}\,\mathrm{d}i + M_t = W_{Nt}N_t + W_{et}\mathrm{Ef}_t + M_{t-1} + T_t + \mathrm{Prf}_t$, where T_t are monetary transfers, Prf_t profits distributed by the firms, and W_{Nt}, W_{et} are the reward to working and to effort. A continuum of firms produces a differentiated good by using $c_{it} = \zeta_t (N_{it}^{\eta_2} \text{Ef}_{it}^{1-\eta_2})^{\eta_1}$, where $N_{it}^{\eta_2} \text{Ef}_{it}^{1-\eta_2}$ is the quantity of effective input and ζ_t an aggregate technology shock, $\Delta\zeta_t = \epsilon_{1t}$, where $\ln \epsilon_{1t} \sim$ i.i.d. $\mathbb{N}(0, \sigma_\zeta^2)$. Firms set prices one period in advance, taking as given the aggregate price level and not knowing the current realization of the shocks. Once shocks are realized, firms optimally choose employment and effort. So long as marginal costs are below the predetermined price, firms will meet the demand for their product and choose an output level equal to $c_{it} = (p_{it}/p_t)^{-1-\varsigma_p^{-1}} c_t$. Optimal price setting implies $E_{t-1}\{(1/c_t)[(\eta_1\eta_2) p_{it} c_{it} - (\varsigma_p + 1) W_{Nt} N_{it}]\} = 0$, which, in the absence of uncertainty, reduces to the standard condition that the price is a (constant) markup over marginal costs. The monetary authority controls the quantity of money and sets $\Delta M_t = \epsilon_{3t} + a_\text{M}\epsilon_{1t}$, where $\ln \epsilon_{3t} \sim$ i.i.d. $\mathbb{N}(0, \sigma_M^2)$ and a_M is a response parameter. Letting lowercase letters denote natural logs, the model implies the following equilibrium conditions for inflation (Δp_t), output growth (Δgdp), employment (n_t), and labor productivity growth (Δnp_t):

$$\Delta p_t = \epsilon_{3t-1} - (1 - a_\text{M})\epsilon_{1t-1}, \tag{6.30}$$

$$\Delta \text{gdp}_t = \Delta\epsilon_{3t} + a_\text{M}\epsilon_{1t} + (1 - a_\text{M})\epsilon_{1t-1}, \tag{6.31}$$

$$n_t = \frac{1}{\eta}\epsilon_{3t} - \frac{1 - a_\text{M}}{\eta}\epsilon_{1t}, \tag{6.32}$$

$$\Delta \text{np}_t = \left(1 - \frac{1}{\eta}\right)\Delta\epsilon_{3t} + \left(\frac{1 - a_\text{M}}{\eta} + a_\text{M}\right)\epsilon_{1t} + (1 - a_\text{M})\left(1 - \frac{1}{\eta}\right)\epsilon_{1t-1}, \tag{6.33}$$

where $\text{np}_t = \text{gdp}_t - n_t$ and $\eta = \eta_1[\eta_2 + (1 - \eta_2)(1 + \varphi_n)/(1 + \varphi_\text{ef})]$.

The model therefore has two shocks (a technology and a monetary one) and implications for at least four variables ($\Delta p_t, \Delta \text{gdp}_t, \Delta \text{np}_t, n_t$). There are eleven free parameters ($\eta_1, \eta_2, \varphi_n, \varphi_\text{ef}, \beta, \sigma_\zeta^2, \sigma_M^2, a_\text{M}, \vartheta_M, \vartheta_n, \vartheta_\text{ef}$), but many of them do not appear in or are not identifiable from (6.30)–(6.33). In fact, it is easy to verify that only a_M and η independently enter the four conditions and therefore, together with σ_ζ^2 and σ_M^2, they are the only ones estimable with likelihood methods.

Since there are only two shocks the covariance matrix produced by the model is singular and we are free to choose which two variables to use to estimate the parameters. In the baseline case we select productivity and hours and repeat estimation also using output and hours, and prices and output. In this latter case, η is also nonidentifiable. As an alternative, we estimate the model by adding serially uncorrelated measurement errors to output and productivity. In this case, we estimate six parameters: the four structural ones and the variances of the two measurement errors.

We examine both the statistical and economic fit of the model. First, we study specifications which restrict a_M and/or η to some prespecified value. A likelihood ratio test is performed in each case and the statistics compared with a χ^2 distribution. For the specification with measurement errors, we also perform a forecasting exercise comparing the one-step-ahead MSE of the model and of a four-variable VAR(1), which has twenty parameters (four constants and sixteen autoregressive coefficients). Since the number of coefficients in the two specifications differs, we also compare the two specifications with a Schwarz criterion (see chapter 4). In this latter case, the VAR model is penalized since it has a larger number of parameters. We also compute tests of forecasting accuracy, as detailed in section 6.2. Conditional on the estimated parameters, we examine the sign of the dynamics of the variables to technology and monetary shocks, and compare elements of the unconditional autocovariance function of the four variables in the model and in the data.

We use CPI, GDP (constant in 1992 prices), and total hours (equal to average weekly hours multiplied by civilian employment) for Canada for the period 1981:2–2002:3 in the estimation. All variables are logged and the first differences of the log are used to compute growth rates, which are then de-meaned. Total hours are detrended by using a constant and a linear trend.

Equations (6.30)–(6.33) have a state-space representation for $\alpha = [\epsilon_{1t}, \epsilon_{1t-1}, \epsilon_{3t}, \epsilon_{3t-1}, v_{1t}, v_{2t}]'$, where v_{it}, $i = 1, 2$, are measurement errors, and

$$x_{1t} = \begin{bmatrix} 0 & a_{\mathrm{M}} - 1 & 0 & 1 & 0 & 0 \\ a_{\mathrm{M}} & 1 - a_{\mathrm{M}} & 1 & -1 & 1 & 0 \\ \dfrac{a_{\mathrm{M}} - 1}{\eta} & 0 & \dfrac{1}{\eta} & 0 & 0 & 0 \\ \dfrac{1 - a_{\mathrm{M}}}{\eta} + a_{\mathrm{M}} & \dfrac{(1 - a_{\mathrm{M}})(\eta - 1)}{\eta} & \dfrac{\eta - 1}{\eta} & -\dfrac{\eta - 1}{\eta} & 0 & 1 \end{bmatrix},$$

$$\mathbb{D}_1 = \begin{bmatrix} 0 & 0 & 0 & 0 & 0 & 0 \\ 1 & 0 & 0 & 0 & 0 & 0 \\ 0 & 0 & 0 & 0 & 0 & 0 \\ 0 & 0 & 1 & 0 & 0 & 0 \\ 0 & 0 & 0 & 0 & 0 & 0 \\ 0 & 0 & 0 & 0 & 0 & 0 \end{bmatrix}, \qquad \mathbb{D}_2 = \begin{bmatrix} 1 & 0 & 0 & 0 \\ 0 & 0 & 0 & 0 \\ 0 & 1 & 0 & 0 \\ 0 & 0 & 0 & 0 \\ 0 & 0 & 1 & 0 \\ 0 & 0 & 0 & 1 \end{bmatrix},$$

with the appropriate adjustments if no measurement error is included. The Kalman filter is initialized by using $\alpha_{1|0} = 0$ and $\Omega_{1|0} = I$. The likelihood function is computed recursively and a simplex method is used to locate the maximum. We use this approach because the likelihood is flat, the maximum is around the boundary of the parameter space, and convergence is hard to achieve. The cost is that no standard errors for the estimates are available. Table 6.1 reports estimates, together with the p-values of various likelihood ratio tests.

Several features of the table deserve comment. First, using bivariate specifications the estimated value of η is less than 1. Since for $\varphi_{\mathrm{ef}} = \varphi_N$, $\eta = \eta_1$, this implies that there is little evidence of short-run increasing returns-to-scale. The lack of increasing returns is formally confirmed by likelihood ratio tests: conditioning on values of $\eta \geqslant 1$ reduces the likelihood. However, when measurement errors are

Table 6.1. ML estimates, sticky price model.

Data set	a_M	η	σ_ζ^2	σ_M^2	$\sigma_{v_1}^2$	$\sigma_{v_2}^2$
$(\Delta np_t, n_t)$	0.553	0.999	1.0×10^{-4}	6.6×10^{-4}		
$(\Delta gdp_t, n_t)$	−7.733	0.744	6.2×10^{-6}	1.0×10^{-4}		
$(\Delta gdp_t, \Delta p_t)$	3.200		1.2×10^{-5}	1.5×10^{-4}		
$(n_t, \Delta np_t, \Delta gdp_t, \Delta p_t)$	−0.904	1.242	5.8×10^{-6}	4.8×10^{-6}	0.023	0.007
Restrictions	$a_M = 0$	$\eta = 1$	$\eta = 1$, $a_M = -1.0$	$\eta = 1.2$		
$(\Delta np_t, n_t)$, p-value	0.03	0.97	0.01	0.00		
$(\Delta gdp_t, n_t)$, p-value	0.00	0.00	0.00	0.00		
$(n_t, \Delta np_t, \Delta gdp_t, \Delta p_t)$, p-value	0.00	0.001	0.00	0.87		
Restrictions	$a_M = 0$	$a_M = 1$	$a_M = -1.0$			
$(\Delta y_t, \Delta p_t)$, p-value	0.00	0.00	0.00			

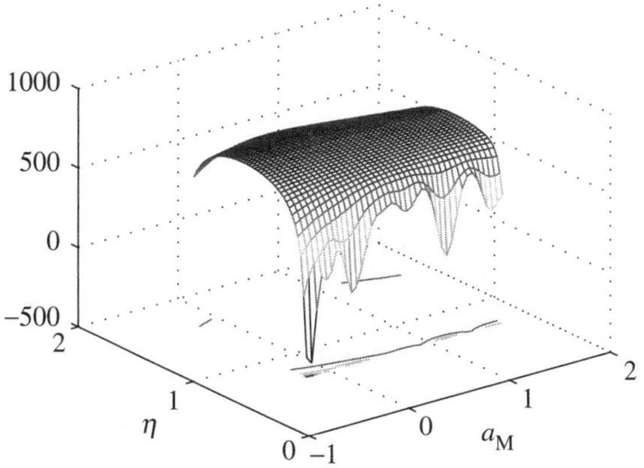

Figure 6.2. Likelihood surface.

included, mild short-run increasing returns-to-scale obtain. Second, the estimated value of a_M depends on the data used: it is positive and moderate when productivity and hours are used, positive and large when output and prices are used, strongly negative when output and hours are used, and moderately negative when the four series are used. Hence, at face value, these estimates imply that monetary policy is countercyclical in two specifications and mildly accommodative in the two others. The reason for this large variety of estimates is that the likelihood function is flat in the a_M dimension. Figure 6.2 illustrates this fact by using the first data set: clearly, $a_M = -0.5, 0, 0.5$ are similarly likely.

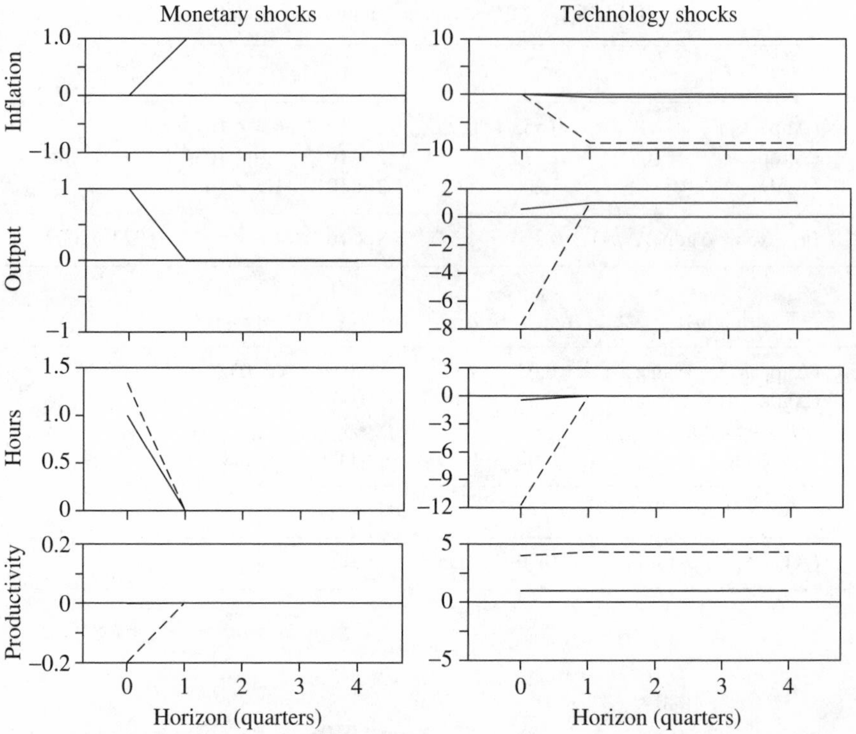

Figure 6.3. Impulse responses (solid lines, DATA 1; dashed lines, DATA 2).

Third, the likelihood function is also relatively flat in the $\sigma_\zeta^2, \sigma_M^2$ space and achieves the maximum around the boundary of the parameter space. Note that, with all bivariate data sets, and somewhat counterintuitively, the variance of monetary shocks is estimated to be larger than the variance of the technology shocks. Fourth, the size of the estimated variance of measurement errors is several orders of magnitude larger than the estimated variance of structural shocks, suggesting that misspecification is likely to be present.

Forecasts produced by the model are poor. In fact, the one-step-ahead MSEs for hours, productivity growth, output growth, and inflation are 30, 12, 7, and 15 times larger than the ones produced by a VAR(1). A test for forecasting accuracy confirms that the forecasts of the model are different from those produced by a VAR(1). The picture mildly improves when a penalty for the larger number of parameters is used: the value of the Schwartz criterion for the model is "only" twice as large as the one of the VAR(1).

Impulse responses to unitary positive technology and money shocks are in figure 6.3. We report responses obtained with the parameters estimated by using productivity and hours data (DATA 1) and output and hours data (DATA 2). Three features are worth discussing. First, estimates of a_M do not affect the responses to

Table 6.2. Cross-covariances.

Moments/data set	$(\Delta \text{np}_t, n_t)$	$(\Delta \text{np}_t, n_t, \Delta p_t, \Delta \text{gdp}_t)$	Actual data
$\text{cov}(\Delta \text{gdp}_t, n_t)$	6.96×10^{-4}	4.00×10^{-6}	1.07×10^{-5}
$\text{cov}(\Delta \text{gdp}_t, \Delta \text{np}_t)$	5.86×10^{-5}	1.56×10^{-6}	1.36×10^{-5}
$\text{cov}(\Delta \text{np}_t, n_t)$	-4.77×10^{-5}	1.80×10^{-6}	-4.95×10^{-5}
$\text{cov}(\Delta \text{gdp}_t, \Delta p_t)$	6.48×10^{-4}	2.67×10^{-6}	2.48×10^{-5}
$\text{cov}(\Delta \text{gdp}_t, \Delta \text{gdp}_{t-1})$	6.91×10^{-4}	3.80×10^{-6}	3.44×10^{-5}
$\text{cov}(\Delta \text{np}_t, \Delta \text{np}_{t-1})$	-1.51×10^{-4}	1.07×10^{-6}	-2.41×10^{-5}

monetary shocks. Second, qualitatively speaking, and excluding the responses of output to technology disturbances, the dynamics induced by the shocks are similar across parametrizations. Third, the shapes of the responses to technology and monetary shocks look similar (up to a sign change) when productivity and hours data are used. Hence, it would be hard to distinguish the two types of shock by looking at the comovements of these two variables only.

Table 6.2 reports cross-covariances in the model and in the data. It is clear that the model estimated with measurement errors fails to capture, both quantitatively and qualitatively, the cross-covariance of the data: estimated cross-covariances are ten times smaller than the data and the signs of the contemporaneous covariance of $(n_t, \Delta \text{np}_t)$, $(\Delta \text{gdp}_t, \Delta p_t)$, and $(\Delta \text{np}_t, \Delta \text{np}_{t-1})$ are wrong. Furthermore, cross-covariances obtained when the model is estimated by using productivity and hours data are still somewhat poor. For example, the estimated cross-covariances of $(\Delta \text{gdp}_t, \Delta \text{gdp}_{t-1})$ and $(\Delta \text{np}_t, \Delta \text{np}_{t-1})$ are ten times larger than in the data and a distance test rejects the hypothesis that the two sets of covariances are indistinguishable. Despite these failures, the model estimated by using hours and productivity captures two important qualitative features of the data: the negative contemporaneous covariance between hours and productivity and the negative lagged covariance of productivity. Finally, neither specification can reproduce the negative covariance between output growth and inflation found in the data.

6.5.2 Does Fiscal Policy Help to Stabilize the Cycle?

The model we consider here is a simple RBC model augmented with government expenditure. The social planner maximizes $E_t \sum_t \beta^t (\ln c_t - \gamma N_t)$ subject to the budget constraint $G_t + c_t + \text{Inv}_t = \zeta_t K_t^{1-\eta} N_t^{\eta}$ and the law of motion of capital $K_{t+1} = (1-\delta)k_t + \text{Inv}_t$. We assume that technology shocks and government expenditure evolve according to $\ln \zeta_t = (1-\rho_\zeta)\ln \zeta + \rho_\zeta \ln \zeta_{t-1} + e_{1t}$ and $\ln G_t = (1-\rho_{\text{G}})\ln G + \rho_{\text{G}} \ln G_{t-1} + a_1 \text{GDP}_{t-1} + a_2 N_t + e_{2t}$, where $e_{1t} \sim$ i.i.d. $\mathbb{N}(0, \sigma_\zeta^2)$ and $e_{2t} \sim$ i.i.d. $\mathbb{N}(0, \sigma_{\text{G}}^2)$.

The parameters of the model are $(\beta, \gamma, \eta, \delta, \zeta, \rho_\zeta, \sigma_\zeta, G, \rho_{\text{G}}, \sigma_{\text{G}}, a_1, a_2)$. As usual β and δ are very difficult to identify from the data and we fix them to $\beta = 0.99$ and

Table 6.3. ML estimates, U.S., 1948–1984.

	γ	$1-\eta$	ρ_ζ	σ_ζ	G	ρ_{G}
Estimate	0.021	0.058	0.999	0.010	67.95	0.496
Standard error	0.0001	0.0001	0.001	0.263	0.0001	0.001

	σ_{G}	a_1	a_2	σ_{1m}	σ_{2m}	σ_{3m}
Estimate	0.487	−3.521	2.650	1.000	0.001	1.001
Standard error	0.157	0.001	0.001	0.873	0.719	0.001

Table 6.4. Diebold and Mariano statistic.

Step	Consumption	Hours	Investment	Output
1	10.3481	6.6850	10.2890	10.5019
2	5.9688	4.4510	5.9342	6.0498
3	4.6164	3.5778	4.5866	4.6739
4	3.8954	3.0688	3.8663	3.9399
5	3.4300	2.7165	3.3986	3.4656
6	3.0974	2.4549	3.0623	3.1260

$\delta = 0.025$. We use U.S. linearly detrended data for consumption, output, (establishment) hours, investment, and federal government expenditure on goods and services and add three measurement errors to the model. Our focus is on the sign and the magnitude of estimates of a_1, a_2. In particular, we are interested in knowing whether government expenditure acts as an output stabilizer or not. ML estimates of the parameters are in table 6.3.

Several features of the estimates are worth discussing. First, while estimates of the parameters of the exogenous processes are reasonable, estimates of some economic parameters are not. For example, the estimated value of γ is unexpectedly low and the estimate of $1-\eta$ is very low. Second, standard errors are typically tight. Hence, most estimates are significant at conventional levels. Third, while estimates of the standard errors of the three measurement errors are larger than the estimates of the standard errors of the driving forces of the model, their difference is not too large. Fourth, the response parameter a_1 is precisely estimated and has the expected sign: over the sample, government expenditure has played an important stabilizing (countercyclical) role. However, a_2 is positive and significant so that government expenditure positively comoves with hours worked.

With these estimates we conduct a simple forecasting exercise comparing the model and a VAR(1). Although the forecasts are systematically below those of a VAR(1) and below the actual data, the forecasting power of the model is reasonable. Moreover, the model appears to capture medium-term patterns better than short-term ones, in particular for hours. Table 6.4 reports the Diebold–Mariano statistic for similarities in the forecasting power of the two models. Here each model is estimated by using data up to 1979 and forecasts are computed for the next five years. Clearly, the performance of the two models is very different at the one-step horizon (with the VAR being significantly better in MSE terms). However, the forecasting performance at longer horizons is qualitatively similar, at least for hours.

Since, as we have mentioned in chapter 5, results may depend on the selected values of (β, δ), we have finally checked whether estimates change when we vary (β, δ) in the ranges $\beta = (0.98, 0.995)$ and $\delta = (0.02, 0.03)$. We do find that results vary with the calibrated parameters. However, estimates of the economic parameters remain unreasonable, regardless of the values of β and δ chosen.

7
Calibration

Calibration is an econometric technique which is somewhat different from those we have discussed in the previous two chapters. Given the many definitions existing in the literature, we start by precisely stating what we mean by calibration in this book. As we will see, the approach involves a series of steps which are intended to provide quantitative answers to a particular economic question. From this perspective, a theoretical model is a tool to undertake "computational experiments" rather than a setup to estimate parameters and/or test hypotheses. As in the previous two chapters, we take the structure of the model seriously. That is, we start from a formal, abstract, tightly parametrized theoretical construction where the general equilibrium interactions are fully specified. However, contrary to what we have done in the previous two chapters, we will not assume that the model is the data-generating process (DGP) for the observables. In fact, one of the basic features of the approach is the idea that theoretical structures used in economic analyses are false in at least two senses: they do not capture all the relevant features of the data, and their probabilistic structure is likely to be misspecified. The reluctance of an investigator to characterize the properties of the discrepancy between the model and the data is also one of the distinctive features of the approach, and this sets it aside from other methodologies, which, for example, assume that the error is a white noise or pay particular attention to its statistical features.

The rest of the chapter describes the steps of the procedure, its relationship with more standard estimation/evaluation techniques, with computable general equilibrium exercises, and with the type of quantitative exercises conducted in other experimental sciences. Since there is no unifying framework to undertake computational experiments, we organize existing practices according to the way they treat the uncertainty present in various parts of the model. As we will see, approaches can be grouped according to the way they treat sampling, model, and other types of uncertainty, and the methodology used to select the parameters drives the way one evaluates the quality of the model's approximation to the data. As an alternative one could characterize methods according to the assumed degree of "falseness" of the model. Different opinions about this feature in fact translate into different loss functions and into different criteria to evaluate the magnitude of the discrepancy between the model and the data.

7.1 A Definition

Since the literature has employed the term calibration to indicate different applied procedures (see, for example, Pagan 1994), confusion may arise when we come to compare outcomes across methods or studies which only apparently use a similar methodology. For example, it has been suggested that one calibrates a model (in the sense of selecting reasonable parameter values) because there are no data to estimate its parameters. This may be the case when one is interested in quantifying, for example, the effect of a new tax or of trade liberalization policies in newly created countries. In other cases, such a procedure is employed because the sample is too short to obtain reasonable estimates of a large-scale and possibly intricate model, or because the data are uninformative about the parameters of interest. In both situations, evaluation of the experimental evidence is problematic. Since all uncertainty is eschewed, back-of-the-envelope calculations, where some interesting parameters are varied within a range, are employed to make the outcomes of the experiments robust of the experiments (see, for example, Pesaran and Smith 1992). Alternatively, one may prefer to calibrate a model (as opposed to estimate it) if the expected misspecification is so large that statistical estimation of its parameters will produce inconsistent and/or unreasonable estimates and formal statistical testing will lead to outright rejection. Finally, some researchers treat calibration as an econometric technique where the parameters are estimated by using "economic," as opposed to "statistical," criteria (see, for example, Canova 1994).

In this chapter, the term calibration is used to indicate a collection of procedures designed to provide an answer to economic questions by using "false" models. The term "false" is used here in a broad sense: a model is "false" if it approximates the DGP of (a subset of) the observable data. The essence of the methodology, as stated, for example, in Kydland and Prescott (1991, 1996), can be summarized as follows.

Algorithm 7.1.

(1) Choose an economic question to be addressed.

(2) Select a model design which bears some relevance to the question asked.

(3) Choose functional forms for the primitives of the model and find a solution for the endogenous variables in terms of the exogenous ones and the parameters.

(4) Select parameters and convenient specifications for the exogenous processes and simulate paths for the endogenous variables.

(5) Evaluate the quality of the model by comparing its outcomes with a set of "stylized facts" of the actual data.

(6) Propose an answer to the question, characterize the uncertainty surrounding the answer, and do policy analyses if required.

The term "stylized facts" is purposely vague. Originally, the literature meant a collection of sample statistics which (i) do not involve estimation of parameters and (ii) are easy to compute. These were typically unconditional moments and, occasionally, conditional moments, histograms, or interesting deterministic (nonlinear) functions of the data. More recently, the coefficients of a vector autoregressive model (VAR), the likelihood function, or structural impulse responses have been taken to be the relevant stylized facts. In step (5) the comparison becomes statistically meaningful only after a measure of distance (a "loss" function) is selected. This is probably the most important step in the approach: answers obtained from a model that is incapable of replicating observed outcomes are likely to be treated with greater care than those produced by a model which has an excellent record in matching certain features of observed data. It is also the most controversial one and it is on this issue that most of the methodological debate takes place.

7.2 The Uncontroversial Parts

The first two steps of the procedure — choose a question of interest and a model to address it — are straightforward. In general, the questions posed display four types of structure:

(i) How much of fact X can be explained with impulses of type Y?

(ii) Is it possible to generate features F by using theory T?

(iii) Can we reduce the discrepancy D of the theory from the data by using feature F?

(iv) How much do endogenous variables change if the process for the exogenous variables is altered?

Two questions which have received considerable attention in the literature concern the contribution of technology and/or monetary disturbances to output variability (see, for example, Kydland and Prescott 1982; Chari et al. 2000) and the ability of a model to quantitatively replicate the excess return of equities over bonds — the so-called equity premium puzzle (see, for example, Merha and Prescott 1985). Recently, the types of friction needed to reduce the discrepancy of certain theories from the data have been investigated in the literature (see, for example, Boldrin et al. 2001; Neiss and Pappa 2005) and studies have examined whether certain policy choices can explain the behavior of real variables in particular historical episodes (e.g., Ohanian 1997; Boldrin et al. 2001; Beaudry and Portier 2002).

As is obvious from this extremely incomplete list, the questions posed are well-specified and the emphasis is on the quantitative implications of the exercise. Occasionally, qualitative implications are also analyzed (e.g., *J*-curves in the trade balance (see Backus et al. 1994) or humps in the responses of certain variables to shocks), but, in general, numerical quantification is the final goal of the analysis.

For the second step — the choice of an economic model — there are essentially no rules: the only requirement being that it has to have some relationship with the question asked. Typically, dynamic general equilibrium models are selected. Both competitive and noncompetitive structures have been used (for the latter, see Danthine and Donaldson 1992; Merz 1995; Rotemberg and Woodford 1997;

Christiano et al. 2005), and models with fundamental or nonfundamental sources of disturbances have also been studied (see, for example, Farmer 1997).

It is important to stress that the question asked determines the type of model used and that rarely does the modeler attempt to capture *all* the features of the data. In other words, one does not expect to have a realistic model to answer interesting questions. However, to give credibility to her answer, a researcher needs a theory that has been tested through use and found to provide reliable answers to a class of questions. A model that has matched reasonably well what happened in previous tax reforms could be a reliable instrument to ask what would happen in a new tax reform. Similarly, a model which captures well features of the real side of the economy could be used to address questions concerning its nominal side.

This observation brings us to an important philosophical aspect of the methodology. In a strict sense, all models are approximations to the DGP and are, as such, false and unrealistic. Literally, this means that it makes no sense to examine the validity of a model by using standard statistical tools which assume it to be true, at least under the null. In a perhaps less extreme vein, this means that it is hard to think of a DSGE model as a null hypothesis to be tested, as, for example, is implicitly assumed with GMM and ML. At best, a DSGE model could be considered an approximation for a subset of the observable data. The problem here has not much to do with limited versus full-information testing — for example, the Euler equation the model delivers is correct but nothing else is — but with degrees of approximations. What is relevant for a calibrator is the extent to which a "false" model gives a coherent explanation of interesting aspects of the data. A calibrator is satisfied with her effort if, through a process of theoretical respecification, the model captures an increasing number of features of the data while maintaining a highly stylized structure. In this sense, the exercises conducted by calibrators belong to the so-called normal science, as described by Kuhn (1970).

Example 7.1. A closed-economy model is probably misspecified to examine, say, the effects of monetary policy disturbances in the EMU: trade with non-EMU countries is about 10–15% of EMU GDP and financial links, especially with the United Kingdom, are large. Nevertheless, such a model can be useful for examining the propagation of monetary shocks if it can, for example, replicate the pattern of real responses to monetary shocks and at the same time, say, the responses of real variables to technology disturbances.

Let y_t be a vector of stochastic processes and $x_t^\dagger = h^\dagger(\{\epsilon_t\}, \theta)$ a model which has something to say about the elements of y_t, where $\{\epsilon_t\} = (\epsilon_1, \dots, \epsilon_t)$ is a sequence of exogenous variables and θ a vector of parameters. Because the model is only an approximation to the DGP of $y_{1t} \subset y_t$, we write

$$y_{1t} = x_t^\dagger + v_t, \tag{7.1}$$

where v_t captures the discrepancy between $h^\dagger(\{\epsilon_t\}, \theta)$ and the DGP of y_{1t}. In general, the properties of v_t are unknown — it need not be a mean zero, serially uncorrelated process as would be the case if $x_t^\dagger = E_t(y_{1t})$, where E_t is the conditional expectation operator. Evaluating the magnitude of v_t without knowing its properties is virtually impossible.

To be able to provide quantitative answers is necessary to find an explicit solution for the endogenous variables in terms of exogenous and predetermined variables and of the parameters. In this sense, calibration is similar to ML and distinct from GMM, where inference can be conducted without explicit model solutions. We have seen in chapter 2 that analytical solutions cannot be obtained, except in very special circumstances. Both local and global approximation procedures generate a $x_t = h(\{\epsilon_t\}, \alpha)$, where α is a function of θ and such that $\|h - h^\dagger\|$ is minimal in some metric. Which of the procedures outlined in chapter 2 one selects depends on the question asked. For example, if the dynamics of the model around the steady state are the focus of the investigation, local approximations are sufficient. On the other hand, in comparing regimes which require drastic changes in the parameters of the control variables, global approximation methods must be preferred.

7.3 Choosing Parameters and Stochastic Processes

With an approximate solution, paths for the endogenous variables can be obtained once the vector θ and the properties of ϵ_t are specified. The selection of the properties of ϵ_t is relatively uncontroversial. One either chooses specifications which are tractable, for example, an AR process with arbitrary persistence and innovations which are transformations of a $\mathbb{N}(0, 1)$ process, or ones that give some realistic connotation to the model, for example, select the Solow residuals of the actual economy, the actual path of government expenditure or of the money supply, with the second alternative being preferred if policy analyses are undertaken. There is more controversy, on the other hand, when it comes to selecting the parameters of the model. Typically, they are chosen so that the model reproduces certain observations. The next example clarifies how this is done and implicitly explains why calibration is at times referred to as "computational experiment."

Example 7.2. Consider the problem of measuring the temperature of the water in various conditions. To conduct this experiment an investigator will have to calibrate the measuring instrument (in this case, a thermometer) to ensure that the outcome is accurate. One way of doing this is to graduate the thermometer to some observations. For example, if the experiment consists in measuring at what temperature the water boils on the top of a mountain, a researcher could, at sea level, set the tick corresponding to the temperature of freezing water to zero and the one corresponding to the temperature of boiling water to 100, interpolate intermediate values with a linear scale and use the graduated thermometer to undertake the measurement.

In a way, the process of selecting the parameters in an economic model is similar. A model is an instrument which needs to be graduated before the measurement of interest is performed. There are at least two ways of doing this graduation: the one suggested in the computable general equilibrium (CGE) tradition summarized, for example, in Shoven and Whalley (1984, 1992) and the one used in modern DSGE models (see, for example, Kydland and Prescott 1982). While similar in spirit, the two methodologies have important differences.

In CGE models, a researcher typically solves a large, nonlinear intersectoral static model, linearizing the system of equations around a hypothetical equilibrium where prices and quantities clear the markets. It is not necessary that this equilibrium exists. However, because the coefficients of the linear equations are functions of equilibrium values, it is necessary to measure it. CGE users need to find a "benchmark data set" and make sure that the linearized model replicates these data. Finding such a data set is complicated and requires ingenuity. Often, the selection process leaves some of the parameters undetermined. In this case, a researcher assigns them arbitrary values or fixes them by using existing estimates (e.g., estimates obtained in countries at similar stages of development) and then performs sensitivity analysis to determine how the outcomes vary when these parameters are changed. Although the procedure to select the free parameters and the way sensitivity analysis is undertaken are arbitrary, the procedure is consistent with the philosophy of CGE models: a researcher is interested in examining deviations from a hypothetical equilibrium not from an economy in real time (see, for example, Kim and Pagan (1994) for a discussion).

In DSGE models, the equilibrium the model needs to reproduce is typically the steady state or, in the case of models with frictions, the Pareto optimal equilibrium. In the former case, parameters are chosen so that the steady state for the endogenous variables replicates time series averages of the actual economy. In the latter case, parameters are selected so that the model without frictions matches certain features of the actual data. Also in this case, the chosen conditions do not pin down all the parameters and different researchers have used different techniques to choose the remaining ones. For example, one can select these parameters *a priori*; pin them down by using available estimates; informally estimate them with a method of moments or formally estimate them by using GMM (see, for example, Christiano and Eichenbaum 1992), SMM (see, for example, Canova and Marrinan 1993), or ML (see, for example, McGrattan 1994) procedures. However, choosing the parameters with one of these last three approaches is inconsistent with the philosophy of the methodology, since the dimensions used to estimate the free parameters can no longer be considered approximations to the DGP.

Formally, let $\theta = (\theta_1, \theta_2, \theta_3)$, let θ_1 be the parameters which appear in the equilibrium conditions, and let θ_2, θ_3 be two sets of free parameters. In CGE models θ_3 are absent while $\theta_1 = \mathfrak{H}_1(y^0, \epsilon^0, \theta_2) \equiv \mathfrak{h}_1(\theta_2)$, where (y^0, ϵ^0) are the hypothetical data and $\mathfrak{H}_1$ is a function defining the final form of the model. Then $y_{1t} = h^{\dagger}(\{\epsilon_t\}, \theta_1, \theta_2) + v_t \equiv \tilde{h}(\{\epsilon_t\}, \theta_2) + v_t$. If $\{\epsilon_t\}$ is deterministic, then the range of y_{it} to variations in θ_2 can be calculated by using the numerical derivatives of $\tilde{h}$, i.e., obtain $(\tilde{h}(\theta_2 + \iota) - \tilde{h}(\theta_2 - \iota))/2\iota$, $\iota > 0$ and small. This can be done informally (trying a few values), conditionally (perturbing one parameter at a time or using a grid), or formally (linearizing $\tilde{h}$ and using asymptotic theory). Also, in DSGE models, given θ_2, $\theta_1 = \mathfrak{H}_1(\bar{y}, \bar{\epsilon}, \theta_2)$, where $\bar{y}, \bar{\epsilon}$ are functions of available data so that $y_{1t} = \tilde{h}(\{\epsilon_t\}, \theta_2, \theta_3) + v_t$. Since θ_3 are free, one typically selects them to minimize some quantity, e.g., $\mathbb{S}[(1/T)\sum_t y_t y'_{t-\tau}] - \mathbb{S}[h(\{\epsilon_t\}, \theta_2, \theta_3)h(\{\epsilon_{t-\tau}\}, \theta_2, \theta_3)]$ for some τ, where $\mathbb{S}$ is a selection matrix, either informally or formally. Then the sensitivity of y_{1t} to variations in θ_2 can be examined as above, conditional on the selected values of θ_3.

Example 7.3 (selecting the parameters of an RBC model). Suppose that the social planner maximizes $E_0 \sum_t \beta^t (c_t^{\vartheta}(1-N_t)^{1-\vartheta})^{1-\varphi}/(1-\varphi)$ by choices of (c_t, K_{t+1}, N_t) subject to

$$G_t + c_t + K_{t+1} = \zeta_t K_t^{1-\eta} N_t^{\eta} + (1-\delta)K_t \equiv \mathrm{GDP}_t + (1-\delta)K_t, \tag{7.2}$$

where $\ln \zeta_t = \bar{\zeta} + \rho_\zeta \ln \zeta_{t-1} + \epsilon_{1t}$, $\epsilon_{1t} \sim (0, \sigma_\zeta^2)$, $\ln G_t = \bar{G} + \rho_{\mathrm{G}} \ln G_{t-1} + \epsilon_{4t}$, $\epsilon_{4t} \sim (0, \sigma_{\mathrm{G}}^2)$, K_0 given, c_t is consumption, N_t is the number of hours worked, and K_t is the capital stock. We assume that G_t is financed with lump sum taxes or bond creation. Letting λ_t be the Lagrangian on (7.2), the first-order conditions are

$$\lambda_t = \vartheta c_t^{\vartheta(1-\varphi)-1}(1-N_t)^{(1-\vartheta)(1-\varphi)}, \tag{7.3}$$

$$\lambda_t \eta \zeta_t k_t^{1-\eta} N_t^{\eta-1} = (1-\vartheta) c_t^{\vartheta(1-\varphi)}(1-N_t)^{(1-\vartheta)(1-\varphi)-1}, \tag{7.4}$$

$$\lambda_t = E_t \beta \lambda_{t+1}[(1-\eta)\zeta_{t+1}K_{t+1}^{-\eta}N_{t+1}^{\eta} + (1-\delta)], \tag{7.5}$$

while the real wage is $w_t = \eta\,\mathrm{GDP}_t/N_t$ and the return to capital $r_t = (1-\delta) + (1-\eta)\,\mathrm{GDP}_t/K_t$. Here K_t is the state, (ζ_t, G_t) the shocks, and there are six control variables $(\lambda_t, c_t, N_t, \mathrm{GDP}_t, w_t, r_t)$. The five first-order conditions, the production function, and the resource constraint (7.2) provide seven equations in seven unknowns (the state plus the controls), so a solution exists. The model has four types of parameter:

(i) technological parameters (η, δ);
(ii) preference parameters $(\beta, \vartheta, \varphi)$;
(iii) steady-state parameters (N^{ss}, $(c/\mathrm{GDP})^{\mathrm{ss}}$, $(K/\mathrm{GDP})^{\mathrm{ss}}$, $(G/\mathrm{GDP})^{\mathrm{ss}}$, w^{ss}, r^{ss}, $\mathrm{GDP}^{\mathrm{ss}}$);
(iv) auxiliary (nuisance) parameters $(\bar{\zeta}, \bar{G}, \rho_{\mathrm{G}}, \rho_\zeta, \sigma_\zeta^2, \sigma_{\mathrm{G}}^2)$.

Letting the superscript "ss" indicate steady-state values, the model implies

$$\frac{1-\vartheta}{\vartheta}\left(\frac{c}{\mathrm{GDP}}\right)^{\mathrm{ss}} = \eta \frac{1-N^{\mathrm{ss}}}{N^{\mathrm{ss}}}, \tag{7.6}$$

$$\beta\left[(1-\eta)\left(\frac{\mathrm{GDP}}{K}\right)^{\mathrm{ss}} + (1-\delta)\right] = 1, \tag{7.7}$$

$$\left(\frac{G}{\mathrm{GDP}}\right)^{\mathrm{ss}} + \left(\frac{c}{\mathrm{GDP}}\right)^{\mathrm{ss}} + \delta\left(\frac{K}{\mathrm{GDP}}\right)^{\mathrm{ss}} = 1, \tag{7.8}$$

$$w^{\mathrm{ss}} = \eta\left(\frac{\mathrm{GDP}}{N}\right)^{\mathrm{ss}}, \tag{7.9}$$

$$r^{ss} = (1-\eta)\left(\frac{\text{GDP}}{K}\right)^{ss} + (1-\delta), \tag{7.10}$$

$$1 = \left[\left(\frac{K}{\text{GDP}}\right)^{ss}\right]^{1-\eta}\left[\left(\frac{N}{\text{GDP}}\right)^{ss}\right]^{\eta}\zeta^{ss}. \tag{7.11}$$

Equations (7.6)–(7.11) are six equations in eleven unknowns. They can therefore be used to determine, for example, (N^{ss}, w^{ss}, r^{ss}, GDP^{ss}, $(c/\text{GDP})^{ss}$, $(K/\text{GDP})^{ss}$) (these are the θ_1 in this example) once $(G/\text{GDP})^{ss}$, β, ϑ, η, and δ are selected (these are the θ_2 in this example). The remaining parameters (φ and the auxiliary parameters) play the role of θ_3. Since they are absent from the steady state, they can be selected as follows. The production function can be used to provide an estimate of ζ_t from which estimates of $\bar{\zeta}$, ρ_ζ, and σ_ζ^2 can be backed out. Data for government expenditure can be used to back out the parameters of the G_t process. For φ, one can appeal to estimates obtained in other studies, noting, for example, that the coefficient of relative risk aversion is $1-\vartheta(1-\varphi)$, arbitrarily fix it, use the Euler equation and the intratemporal condition to get, for example, a GMM estimate, or select it by using simulation estimators (for example, choose φ so that consumption variability in simulated data is the same as in actual data).

Note that, by log-linearizing the seven equilibrium conditions of example 7.3, the solution has the form of a vector autoregression of order 1 or of a state-space system. In fact, letting $y_t = (\hat{\lambda}_t, \hat{k}_t, \hat{c}_t, \hat{N}_t, \widehat{\text{GDP}}_t, \hat{w}_t, \hat{r}_t)$, where hats denote percentage deviations from the steady state, the VAR representation is

$$\mathcal{A}_0 = \begin{bmatrix} 1 & -\dfrac{(1-\eta)(\text{GDP}/K)^{ss}}{(1-\eta)(\text{GDP}/K)^{ss}+(1-\delta)} & 0 & 0 & \dfrac{(1-\eta)(\text{GDP}/K)^{ss}}{(1-\eta)(\text{GDP}/k)^{ss}+(1-\delta)} & 0 & 0 \\ 0 & \dfrac{1}{(\text{GDP}/K)^{ss}} & 0 & 0 & 0 & 0 & 0 \\ & & & 0_{5\times 7} & & & \end{bmatrix},$$

$$\mathcal{A}_1 = \begin{bmatrix} 1 & 0 & 0 & 0 & 0 & 0 & 0 \\ 0 & \dfrac{1-\delta}{(\text{GDP}/K)^{ss}} & -\left(\dfrac{c}{\text{GDP}}\right)^{ss} & 0 & 1 & 0 & 0 \\ 0 & 0 & 1 & \dfrac{1}{1-N^{ss}} & -1 & 0 & 0 \\ -1 & 0 & \vartheta(1-\varphi)-1 & -(1-\vartheta)(1-\varphi)\dfrac{N^{ss}}{1-N^{ss}} & 0 & 0 & 0 \\ 0 & 1-\eta & 0 & \eta & -1 & 0 & 0 \\ 0 & 0 & 0 & 1 & -1 & 1 & 0 \\ 0 & 1 & 0 & 0 & -1 & 0 & 1 \end{bmatrix},$$

$$\mathcal{A}_2 = \begin{bmatrix} 0 & 0 \\ 0 & -\left(\dfrac{G}{\text{GDP}}\right)^{ss} \\ 0 & 0 \\ 0 & 0 \\ -1 & 0 \\ 0 & 0 \\ 0 & 0 \end{bmatrix},$$

where $0_{5\times 7}$ is a 5×7 matrix of zeros, while a state-space representation is obtained by setting $y_{2t} = (\hat{\lambda}_t, \hat{k}_t, \hat{\zeta}_t, \hat{G}_t)$, $y_{3t} = (\epsilon_{1t}, \epsilon_{4t})$, $y_{1t} = (\hat{c}_t, \hat{N}_t, \widehat{\mathrm{GDP}}_t, \hat{w}_t, \hat{r}_t)$:

$$\left.\begin{aligned} \mathcal{A}_0^2 y_{2t+1} &= \mathcal{A}_1^2 y_{2t} + \mathcal{A}_2^2 y_{3t}, \\ \mathcal{A}_0^1 y_{1t+1} &= \mathcal{A}_1^1 y_{2t} + \mathcal{A}_2^1 y_{3t}, \end{aligned}\right\} \tag{7.12}$$

where $\mathcal{A}_0^i, \mathcal{A}_1^i, \mathcal{A}_2^i$, $i = 1, 2$, are obtained by partitioning $\mathcal{A}_0, \mathcal{A}_1, \mathcal{A}_2$ and using the law of motion of the shocks. Note that, if the model is believed to correctly represent the DGP of the data, the techniques of chapters 5 and 6 could be used to estimate its parameters. On the other hand, if the model is thought to provide information about the shocks driving the economy, the techniques of chapter 4 could be used. In all other cases, the techniques described in this chapter become handy.

Exercise 7.1. Consider a sticky price model where the instantaneous utility of the representative household is $U(c, N, M) = \ln c_t + \ln(1 - N_t) + (1/(1 - \varphi_{\mathrm{m}})) \times (M_{t+1}/p_t)^{1-\varphi_{\mathrm{m}}}$, where output is produced via $\mathrm{GDP}_t = N_t\zeta_t$, where ζ_t is a technology shock. Assume Calvo pricing; let $1 - \zeta_{\mathrm{p}}$ be the fraction of agents allowed to change prices at each t and let β be the discount factor. Derive an Euler equation, an intratemporal condition, a money demand function, and a Phillips curve. Log-linearize the conditions around the flexible price equilibrium and describe how to select preferences parameters, relevant steady states, and auxiliary parameters.

Exercise 7.2. Consider adding capacity utilization to the model of example 7.3. That is, assume that the production function depends on both capital K_t and its utilization ku_t and is of the form $\mathrm{GDP}_t = \zeta_t(K_t\mathrm{ku}_t)^{1-\eta}N_t^{\eta}$. Assume also that capital depreciation is related to utilization via the equation $\delta(\mathrm{ku}_t) = \delta_0 + \delta_1\mathrm{ku}_t^{\delta_2}$, where δ_0, δ_1, and δ_2 are parameters. Describe how to select $(\delta_0, \delta_1, \delta_2)$.

Exercise 7.3. Consider the two-country model of example 2.6. Log-linearize the first-order conditions, the budget constraint, and the definitions of the terms of trade (ToT_t) and net export (nx_t). Describe how to choose the parameters of the model.

Because not all parameters can be pinned down by the reference equilibrium, there is a degree of arbitrariness inherent in the procedure. All approaches designed to choose parameters not appearing in the steady state have advantages and disadvantages. For example, employing information present in existing studies has the advantage of allowing a researcher to pin down parameters which cannot be identifiable from the data. However, a selectivity bias is typically present with such an approach (see Canova 1995a): there is a variety of estimates available and different researchers may refer to different studies even when examining the same question. Furthermore, the uncertainty surrounding the predictions of the model is artificially reduced and this may generate an unwarranted confidence in the outcomes of the experiment. In all cases, inference may be spurious and/or distorted. In fact, estimates of θ_3 may be biased and inconsistent unless the selected θ_2 are the true parameters of the DGP or consistent estimates of them. We have already mentioned in chapter 5 that this issue may be important. We next demonstrate the same phenomenon in a more traditional econometric setup.

Table 7.1. Monte Carlo distribution of $\alpha \mid \hat{\rho}$.

	Percentiles		
	25th	50th	75th
$\hat{\rho} = 0$	0.396	0.478	0.599
$\hat{\rho} = 0.4$	0.443	0.492	0.553
$\hat{\rho} = 0.9$	0.479	0.501	0.531

Example 7.4. Suppose there is a linear relationship between x and y and that the disturbance is serially correlated. Letting α be the parameters of the linear relationship and ρ the AR(1) coefficient of the errors, a GLS estimator for (α, ρ) is obtained from $y_t - \rho y_{t-1} = \alpha(x_t - \rho x_{t-1}) + e_t$, where $e_t \sim$ i.i.d. $(0, \sigma_e^2)$. An estimator for α, conditional on ρ, is $(\hat{\alpha} \mid \rho) = [(x_t - \rho x_{t-1})'(x_t - \rho x_{t-1})]^{-1} \times [(x_t - \rho x_{t-1})'(y_t - \rho y_{t-1})]$. If $\hat{\rho}$ is a consistent estimator of ρ, $(\hat{\alpha} \mid \hat{\rho}) \xrightarrow{\text{P}} (\hat{\alpha} \mid \rho)$ as $T \to \infty$. However, if it is not the case, the asymptotic distribution of $(\hat{\alpha} \mid \hat{\rho})$ will be centered around a wrong value. In table 7.1 we verify that biases do occur: we report the mean and the interquartile range of the Monte Carlo distribution of $(\hat{\alpha} \mid \rho)$ obtained by conditioning on $\hat{\rho} = 0.0, 0.4, 0.9$, when $T = 1000$, 1000 replications are used to construct distributions, and the true values are $\alpha = 0.5$ and $\rho = 0.9$.

Exercise 7.4 (Gregory and Smith). Take a simple endowment economy. Assume that $u(c_t) = c_t^{1-\varphi}/(1-\varphi)$ and that output evolves according to $\text{GDP}_{t+1} = \text{gy}_{t+1}\text{GDP}_t$. Assume that gy_{t+1} can take n possible values $(\text{gy}_1, \dots, \text{gy}_n)$ and let $p_{i,i'} \equiv P(\text{gy}_{t+1} = \text{gy}_{i'} \mid \text{gy}_t = \text{gy}_i) = \mu_{i'} + \rho_y(\mathcal{I}_{ii'} - \mu_{i'})$, where $\mu_{i'}$ are unconditional probabilities, $\mathcal{I}_{ii'} = 1$ if $i = i'$ and 0 otherwise, and $\rho_y \in (-(n-1)^{-1}, 1)$. If the current state is $(\text{GDP}_t, \text{gy}_i)$, the price of an asset paying one unit of output next period satisfies $p_t^{\text{s}} U_c(\text{GDP}_t, \text{gy}_i) = \sum_{i'} p_{ii'} \beta [U_c(\text{GDP}_{t+1}, \text{gy}_{i'})]$.

(i) Set $n = 2$, $\text{gy}_1 = 0.9873$, $\text{gy}_2 = 1.0177$, $\mu_1 = 0.2$, $\mu_2 = 0.8$, $\beta = 0.99$, $\rho_y = 0.8$, $\varphi = 2$. Simulate asset price data from the model.

(ii) Set $(n, \text{gy}_i, \mu_i, \beta)$ as in (i) but now select $\rho_y = 0.6$. Choose φ so that the simulated variance of asset prices matches the variance of asset prices produced in (i) (you are free to select the loss function you prefer).

(iii) Repeat (i) 100 times drawing φ from $\mathbb{U}(1, 10)$ (treat these as 100 realizations of the actual data). Repeat (ii) 100 times and show the distributions of $\hat{\varphi}$ that best matches $\text{var}(p_t^{\text{s}})$.

(iv) Repeat (ii) fixing $\varphi = 2$ and choosing ρ_y to minimize $|E_t((p_t^{\text{s}})^{\text{A}} - (p_t^{\text{s}})^{\text{S}})|$, where the superscript "A" ("S") stands for actual (simulated). Is there any pattern worth mentioning?

As pointed out by Kydland and Prescott (1991), choosing parameters by using information obtained from other studies imposes coherence among various branches of the profession. However, for many parameters, available estimates are surprisingly sparse (see, for example, Shoven and Whalley 1992, p. 105) and often obtained with procedures which, although valid in the environment where they were produced, make no sense in DSGE frameworks (see Hansen and Heckman 1996). In summary, any choice is arbitrary and sensitivity analysis is needed to evaluate the robustness of the measurement to changes in the free parameters.

Canova (1994, 1995a) suggested an approach which responds to these criticisms. Instead, of fixing θ_3 to one particular value, he restricts its range to an interval by using theoretical considerations, uses all available information to construct an empirical distribution for θ_{3i}, $i = 1, 2, \ldots$, over this interval (this is treated as the likelihood of a parameter, given existing estimates), and draws θ_3 from the joint "empirical" distribution. Moreover, since the distinction between θ_2 and θ_3 is artificial, intervals for both sets of parameters could be used (see, for example, Canova and Marrinan 1996; Maffezzoli 2000). An example may clarify the approach.

Example 7.5. In exercise 7.4 one of the free parameters is the coefficient of constant relative risk aversion φ. Typically, one sets φ to 1 or 2 (resulting in a mild curvature of the utility function) and, occasionally, tries a few larger values to construct upper bound measures. As an alternative, one could limit the range of values using economic arguments to, say, [0, 20] and construct a histogram over this interval by using existing estimates. Since most estimates are in the range $[1, 2]$ and since in some asset pricing models researchers have tried values up to 10, the empirical distribution of φ could be approximated with a $\chi^2(4)$, which has the mode at 2 and about 5% probability in the region above 10. When no empirical information exists, a uniform distribution or a distribution capturing subjective beliefs about the likelihood of the parameter (see chapter 9) can be employed.

Exercise 7.5. Suppose a representative agent maximizes $E_0 \sum_t \beta^t (c_t^{1-\varphi}/(1-\varphi) + \vartheta_M (M_{t+1}/p_t)^{1-\varphi_\mathrm{m}}/(1-\varphi_\mathrm{m}))$ subject to $c_t + K_{t+1} + M_{t+1}/p_t = \zeta_t K_t^{1-\eta} N_t^{1-\eta} + (1-\delta)K_t + M_t/p_t + T_t/p_t$, where T_t are money transfers, $\ln M_{t+1} = \bar{M} + \rho_M \ln M_t + \epsilon_{3t+1}$, $\ln \zeta_{t+1} = \bar{\zeta} + \rho_\zeta \ln \zeta_t + \epsilon_{1t+1}$, and $\epsilon_{1t+1}, \epsilon_{3t+1}$ are i.i.d. with standard errors equal to σ_ζ, σ_M. What distributions would you choose for the parameters $(\eta, \varphi, \delta, \vartheta_M, \varphi_M, \rho_\zeta, \rho_\mathrm{G}, \sigma_\zeta, \sigma_M)$? What would be a reasonable *a priori* range for them?

Standard statistical estimation of the free parameters has three main advantages: it avoids arbitrary choices; it provides a coherent framework for choosing *all* the parameters; and it produces measures of uncertainty which can be used to evaluate the quality of the approximation of the model to the data. The disadvantages are of various kinds. First, it requires the selection of the moments/statistics to be matched, and that may lead to inconsistencies across studies. The method employed in example 7.3 can indeed be thought of as a method of moments estimation where parameters are chosen to match the first moments of the data (i.e., the long-run averages). Christiano and Eichenbaum (1992), Fève and Langot (1994), and others use first and second moments of actual and simulated data to obtain GMM estimates of the parameters while Smith (1993) uses VAR coefficients. While the selection of moments depends on the question asked, efficient estimation requires all moments containing information on the parameters to be used (see chapter 5). Second, GMM estimates are biased in small (or nonstationary) samples (see chapter 5). Therefore, simulations conducted with these estimates may lead to spurious answers to the questions asked. Third, SMM approaches may produce estimates of parameters even though they are not identifiable (see chapter 5). Finally, one should note that the type of uncertainty present in the outcomes of the model when parameters are estimated is different from the uncertainty existing when a calibrator is ignorant about the magnitude of a parameter. In fact, once the data and moments are selected, sample uncertainty is typically small so that uncertainty in measurement is also small. However, the uncertainty present in, for example, choosing a risk-aversion parameter is typically large.

As we have seen in chapter 5, ML estimation can be thought of as a GMM procedure where the moments are the scores of the likelihood function. Therefore, discrepancies between these two types of estimate indicate either that the orthogonality conditions span a different informational space (GMM may use only parts of the model while ML uses all of it) or that the sample strongly deviates from normality. Asymptotically, when the moment restrictions and the scores span the same space, the two procedures must give identical results. Hence, all the arguments we have given for GMM or SMM also apply to ML.

It is useful to compare the parameter selection process used by a calibrator with the one used in a traditional econometric approach. In the latter approach parameters are chosen to minimize some statistical criteria, e.g., the MSE. Such a loss function does not have any economic justification; its conventional use reflects mathematical convenience and imposes stringent requirements on the structure of v_t. The loss function used by calibrators does have an economic interpretation: parameters are chosen so that the steady state of the model matches the long-run averages of the data. However, since not all parameters are pinned down by these conditions, a calibrator may look like an econometrician who uses different loss functions in different parts of the model. Furthermore, since choosing parameters to match long-run averages is equivalent to using GMM on first moments, a calibrator may also look like an inefficient GMM econometrician.

Finally, note that when intervals are chosen for the free parameters and empirical distributions are used, calibration becomes a special case of the Bayesian procedures, which we will discuss in detail in chapters 9–11.

7.4 Model Evaluation

Before the measurement of interest is undertaken, it is necessary to assess the quality of the model's approximation to the data. The most active branch of the literature is concerned with the development of methods to evaluate the fit of calibrated models. Earlier works, such as Kydland and Prescott (1982), are silent on this issue. But this is not entirely surprising: since there are no free parameters and no uncertainty is allowed in either the selected parameters or the moments used for comparison, the model deterministically links the endogenous variables to the parameters and exogenous stochastic processes. Hence, unless the sampling variability of the exogenous processes is used, measures of distance between the model and the data cannot be defined. The lack of formal model validation does not seem to bother some researchers. Kydland and Prescott (1991, 1996), for example, emphasize that the trust a researcher puts in an answer given by the model does not depend on a statistical measure of discrepancy, but on how much she believes in the economic theory used and in the measurement undertaken — in other words, trust could be an act of faith.

Nowadays, most calibrators informally compare the properties of simulated data with a set of stylized facts of the actual data. Such an approach is also in fashion with econometric skeptics: simple sample statistics are believed to be sufficient to do the job since "either you see it with the naked eye or no fancy econometrics will find it." The choice of stylized facts obviously depends on the question asked but one should be aware that there are many ways to summarize the outcome of a calibration exercise and some may be more informative than others for comparison purposes.

In a business cycle context one typically selects a subset of auto- and cross-covariances of the data, but there is no reason for focusing on unconditional second moments, except that their measurement does not require the estimation of time series models. One could also use the distributions of actual and simulated data — which also do not need parametric time series models to be estimated — or their VAR representation and examine some of their statistical features (e.g., the number of unit roots or exclusion restrictions as in Canova et al. (1994), the magnitude of VAR coefficients as in Smith (1993) or DeJong et al. (1996), or the pattern of semi-structural impulse responses as in Cogley and Nason (1994)). Alternatively, one could reduce the model to one or two equations and compare the time series representations of the variables in the model and in the actual data (as in Canova et al. (1994) or Cogley and Nason (1995a)). Finally, business cycle turning points (as in King and Plosser (1994) or Simkins (1994)), variance bounds (as in Hansen and Jagannathan (1991)), business cycle durations and amplitudes of the cycle (as in Pagan and Harding (2002)), or historical episodes (as in Ohanian (1997) or Beaudry and Portier (2002)) could also be used for evaluation purposes.

Example 7.6 (magnitude of the VAR coefficients/exclusion restrictions). The RBC model of example 7.3 has a (log-linear) solution for the controls of the form $\mathcal{A}_0^1(\theta)y_{1t} = \mathcal{A}_1^1(\theta)y_{2t-1} + \mathcal{A}_2^1(\theta)y_{3t}$, where the matrices $\mathcal{A}_i^1(\theta)$, $i = 0, 1, 2$, are functions of the "deep" parameters θ of the model. Hence, once the θ are selected, $\mathcal{A}_i^1(\theta)$ are matrices of real numbers. A simple RBC model then poses two types of restriction on the VAR of say, output, consumption, investment, and hours. First, lagged values of these four variables should not help us to predict current values once lagged values of the states are included. Second, in a regression of y_{1t} on y_{2t-1}, the matrix of coefficients must be equal to $(\mathcal{A}_0^1(\theta))^{-1}\mathcal{A}_1^1(\theta)$.

Table 7.2. Dynamics of hours (standard errors in parentheses).

	Standard deviation	$\text{corr}(N_t, N_{t-1})$	$\text{corr}(N_t, N_{t-2})$	$\text{corr}(N_t, N_{t-3})$
Actual data	0.517 (0.10)	0.958 (0.09)	0.923 (0.09)	0.896 (0.09)
Simulated data	0.473	0.848	0.704	0.570
		Estimated ARMA(2, 2) for actual hours		
	AR(1)	AR(2)	MA(1)	MA(2)
Actual data	1.05 (0.24)	−0.07 (0.21)	−0.12 (0.21)	−0.05 (0.09)

Example 7.7 (final-form comparison). The RBC model described in example 7.3 can also be reduced to a bivariate VARMA(1, 1) for $(\hat{N}_t, \hat{c}_t)$. Furthermore, $\hat{N}_t$ has a univariate representation of the type $A(\theta)(\ell)\hat{N}_{t+1} = D(\theta)(\ell)e_{t+1}$, where the reduced-form parameters $A(\theta)(\ell)$, $D(\theta)(\ell)$ are functions of the "deep" parameters θ, $\hat{e}_t = (\hat{\zeta}_t, \hat{g}_t)$, and $A(\theta)(\ell)$, $D(\theta)(\ell)$ are of infinite length. Given this representation there are at least two ways of comparing the data and the model. First, one can compare the autocorrelation function of hours produced by the model (conditional on some θ) with the autocorrelation function of hours found in the data. Second, one can estimate an ARMA model and verify whether the estimated coefficients are exactly equal to those implied by the model.

Table 7.2 reports a few terms of the ACRF of a version of the model where $u(c_t, N_t) = \ln(c_t) + \vartheta_N(1 - N_t)$, there is no government, and $\beta = 0.99$, $\eta = 0.64$, $\vartheta_N = 2.6$, $\delta = 0.025$, $\rho_\zeta = 0.95$, $\sigma_\zeta^2 = 0.007$; the same ACRF terms obtained from linearly detrended U.S. data (using seasonally adjusted average weekly hours of private nonagricultural establishments for the sample 1964:1–2003:1) and estimates of the best ARMA specification obtained in the data. It is clear that while standard deviations are similar, the model's ACRF function is less persistent than the data's. In fact, the 12th-order correlation in the data is still 0.786, while it is roughly zero in the model. Moreover, the estimated parameters of an ARMA(2, 2) are significantly different from those implied by the model. For example, the AR(1) and AR(2) coefficients of the model are, respectively, 1.57 and −0.53. While it is obvious that the model fails to capture the dynamics of actual hours, it is hard to see how to reduce the discrepancy. Lack of persistence could be due to many reasons (lack of investment propagation, lack of intertemporal substitutability, etc.) and the reduced-form approach used here does not allow us to disentangle them.

Exercise 7.6. Suppose the representative agent maximizes $E_0 \sum_t \beta^t c_t^{1-\varphi}/(1-\varphi)$ subject to $p_t c_t \leqslant M_t + T_t$ and $c_t + K_{t+1} + M_{t+1}/p_t \leqslant r_t K_t + (1-\delta)K_t + (M_t + T_t)/p_t$, where $T_t = M_{t+1} - M_t$, $\ln M_{t+1} = \bar{M} + \rho_M \ln M_t + \epsilon_{3t}$, $\epsilon_{3t} \sim$ i.i.d. $(0, \sigma_M^2)$. Assume that $\text{GDP}_t = \zeta_t K_t^{1-\eta}$, where $\ln \zeta_t$ is an AR(1) with persistence ρ_ζ and variance σ_ζ^2.

(i) Derive a trivariate log-linear (final-form) representation for (c_t, M_t, p_t).

(ii) Using U.S. data on consumption, M1, and CPI, estimate a trivariate VAR and compare the magnitude of VAR coefficients and of the auto- and cross-correlation function of M1 growth and of consumption growth in the model and in the data. (Hint: careful — the model is a VAR(∞).)

Exercise 7.7. Consider the RBC model described in example 7.3 but now assume that preferences are $u(c_t, c_{t-1}, N_t) = (c_t^{\gamma} c_{t-1}^{1-\gamma})^{1-\varphi}/(1-\varphi) + \vartheta_N(1-N_t)$, where γ is a constant. Log-linearize, select $(\beta, \varphi, \gamma, \eta, \delta, \vartheta_N)$, the parameters governing the stochastic process for ζ_t, G_t and steady-state ratios, and simulate data. Define an upturn at t as the situation where $\text{GDP}_{t-2} < \text{GDP}_{t-1} < \text{GDP}_t > \text{GDP}_{t+1} > \text{GDP}_{t+2}$ and a downturn at t as a situation where $\text{GDP}_{t-2} > \text{GDP}_{t-1} > \text{GDP}_t < \text{GDP}_{t+1} < \text{GDP}_{t+2}$. Examine whether the model matches the turning points of U.S. output by using Solow residuals to proxy for technology disturbances and actual government expenditure for G_t.

Exercise 7.8. Using the model of exercise 7.1 and the selected parameters, examine whether the model reproduces the persistence of U.S. inflation where persistence is measured by $\mathcal{S}(\omega = 0) = \sum_{\tau-\infty}^{\infty} \text{ACF}_{\pi}(\tau)$, and $\text{ACF}_{\pi}(\tau)$ is the autocovariance of inflation at lag τ.

At times, it may be more relevant to know how good a model is, not in absolute terms, but relative to other competitors. Such a "horse race" is important, for example, when two models "poorly" approximate the data or when one model is a restricted version of the other. Canova et al. (1994), for example, take the capacity utilization model of Burnside et al. (1993), reduce it to two equations involving output and investment, and compare its performance to a simple investment accelerator model. More recently, by using the techniques described in chapters 9–11, Schorfheide (2000), DeJong et al. (2000), or Smets and Wouters (2003) have undertaken similar comparisons.

Exercise 7.9. Consider two variants of the model of example 7.3. In variant (i) assume that there are production externalities, i.e., $\text{GDP}_{it} = \zeta_t \bar{K}_t^{\aleph} K_{it}^{1-\eta} N_{it}^{\eta}$, where $\bar{K}_t = \int_0^1 K_{it}\,\mathrm{d}i$ is the aggregate capital stock. In variant (ii) assume one-period labor contracts and $w_t = E_{t-1}\text{GDP}_t/N_t$. Suggest ways to compare the relative performance of the two models with the data.

Comparisons based on stylized facts are important for two reasons. First, they shift the emphasis away from statistical quantities (such as the autocovariance function of the residuals) toward more interesting economic objects (such as functions of conditional and unconditional moments). Second, they allow the construction of a larger set of diagnostics and therefore a better understanding of the properties of different models. Within this generic comparison methodology, several variants are available. To describe them we need some notation.

Let $\mathfrak{S}_y$ be a set of interesting economic statistics of the actual data and let $\mathfrak{S}_x(\{\epsilon_t\}, \theta)$ be the corresponding statistics obtained from simulated data, given a vector of parameters θ and a vector of driving forces $\{\epsilon_t\}$. Model evaluation consists in selecting a loss function $\mathfrak{L}$ measuring the distance between $\mathfrak{S}_y$ and $\mathfrak{S}_x$ and assessing its magnitude. At the risk of oversimplifying, we divide existing procedures into four groups:

(i) Approaches based on R^2-type measure, such as Watson (1993).

(ii) Approaches which measure distance by using the sampling variability of the actual data. Among these are the GMM based approach of Christiano and Eichenbaum (1992) or Fève and Langot (1994), the indirect approach of Cecchetti et al. (1993), and the frequency domain approach of Diebold et al. (1998).

(iii) Approaches which measure distance by using the sampling variability of the simulated data. Among these procedures we distinguish those which take the driving forces as stochastic and the parameters as given, such as Gregory and Smith (1991), Soderlin (1994), or Cogley and Nason (1994), and those who take both as random, such as Canova (1994, 1995a) or Maffezzoli (2000).

(iv) Approaches which measure distance by using the sampling variability of both actual and simulated data. Again, we distinguish approaches which allow for variability in the parameters but not in the exogenous processes, such as DeJong et al. (1996, 2000), Geweke (1999), and Schorfheide (2000), or allow both to vary.

7.4.1 *Watson's* R^2

Statistical measures of fit use the size of the sampling errors to judge the coherence of a model to the data. That is, disregarding the approximation error, if ACF_y is the autocovariance function of the actual data and ACF_x is the autocovariance function of simulated data, standard measures examine whether $\text{ACF}_x = \text{ACF}_y$, given that differences between ACF_x and its estimated counterpart arise from sampling errors. While this is a sensible procedure when the model represents the data under the null, it is much less sensible when the model is false even under the null.

Rather than relying on the properties of the sampling error, Watson asks how much error should be added to x_t so that its autocovariance function equals the autocovariance function of y_t. The autocovariance function of this error is $\text{ACF}_v = \text{ACF}_y + \text{ACF}_x - \text{ACF}_{xy} - \text{ACF}_{yx}$, where ACF_{yx} is the cross-covariance function of x and y. Hence, to study the properties of ACF_v we need a sample from the joint distribution of (x_t, y_t), which is unavailable. Typically, one of two assumptions is made (see, for example, Sargent 1989): (i) $\text{ACF}_{xy} = \text{ACF}_x$, so that x_t and v_t are uncorrelated at all leads and lags (this yields a classical error-in-variables problem); (ii) $\text{ACF}_{xy} = \text{ACF}_y$, so that v_t is a signal extraction noise and y_t is the observable counterpart of x_t.

Example 7.8. Let $y_t = x_t + v_t$, where $E(v_t v_{t-\tau}) = 0$, for $\tau \neq 0$ and $E(v_t v_t) = \sigma_v^2$. If x_t is predetermined, $E(y_t x_{t-\tau}) = E(x_t x_{t-\tau})$ for all $\tau \neq 0$ (this is case (i)).

If x_t is orthogonal to v_t at all t and $x_t = \alpha y_t$, $E(y_t x_{t-\tau}) = \alpha E(y_t y_{t-\tau})$ for all τ (this is case (ii)).

Clearly, which assumption is adopted depends on the way data are collected and expectations are formed. Here, neither is very appealing since v_t is neither a proxy nor a forecast error. Because any restriction used to identify ACF_{xy} is arbitrary, Watson chooses ACF_{xy} to minimize the variance of v_t, requiring ACF_x and ACF_y to be positive semi-definite. In other words, one selects ACF_{xy} so as to give the model the best chance to fit the data. The exact form of ACF_{xy} depends on properties of the data and the dimensions of x_t and y_t.

Example 7.9. When x_t, y_t are serially uncorrelated scalars, the problem becomes $\min_{\sigma_{xy}} \sigma_v^2 = \sigma_x^2 + \sigma_y^2 - 2\sigma_{xy}$ subject to $\sigma_v^2 \geqslant 0$ whose solution is $\sigma_{xy} = \sigma_x \sigma_y$. That is, selecting a minimum approximation error makes x_t and y_t perfectly correlated, so that $x_t = (\sigma_x/\sigma_y) y_t$.

When x_t and y_t are serially uncorrelated, $m \times 1$ vectors, the situation is analogous. The problem is now

$$\min_{\Sigma_{xy}} \operatorname{tr} |\Sigma_v| = \operatorname{tr} |\Sigma_x + \Sigma_y - \Sigma_{xy} - \Sigma_{yx}|, \tag{7.13}$$

subject to $|\Sigma_v| \geqslant 0$, where $\operatorname{tr} |\Sigma_v| = \sum_{i=1}^m \Sigma_{v_{ii}}$ is the trace of Σ_v. The solution is $\Sigma_{xy} = \mathcal{P}_x' V' \mathcal{P}_y$, where $\mathcal{P}_x$ and $\mathcal{P}_y$ are square roots of Σ_x and Σ_y, $V = \Omega \Lambda^{-1/2} \Omega' \mathcal{P}'$, Ω is a matrix of orthonormal eigenvectors, and Λ is a diagonal matrix of eigenvalues of $\mathcal{P}'\mathcal{P}$, where $\mathcal{P} = \mathcal{P}_x \mathcal{P}_y$.

Exercise 7.10. Describe how to compute the predicted values of x_t when x_t and y_t are $m \times 1$ vectors. Argue that the covariance matrix of (x_t, y_t) is singular. Show how to modify (7.13) to minimize a weighted average of the diagonal elements of Σ_v.

In DSGE models, Σ_x is typically singular since the number of shocks is smaller than the number of endogenous variables. Let x_t, y_t be serially uncorrelated and let the m variables in x_t be driven by $m_1 \leqslant m$ shocks so that the rank of Σ_x is $m_1 \leqslant m$. Then, the above analysis applies to an $m_1 \times 1$ subvector of elements of x_t and y_t. Let $\mathbb{S}$ be an $m_1 \times m$ selection matrix such that $\mathbb{S}\Sigma_x\mathbb{S}'$ has rank m_1. Define $\tilde{x}_t = \mathbb{S}x_t$, $\tilde{y}_t = \mathbb{S}y_t$, $\tilde{\Sigma}_x = \mathbb{S}\Sigma_x\mathbb{S}'$, $\tilde{\Sigma}_y = \mathbb{S}\Sigma_y\mathbb{S}'$. Then $\tilde{v}_t = \tilde{x}_t - \tilde{y}_t$ is the error we wish to minimize. The solution to the problem is $\tilde{x}_t = \tilde{\mathcal{P}}_x' \tilde{V}' \tilde{\mathcal{P}}_y^{-1} \tilde{y}_t$, where $\tilde{\mathcal{P}}_x$, $\tilde{V}$, $\tilde{\mathcal{P}}_y^{-1}$ are the reduced rank analogs of $\mathcal{P}_x$, V, $\mathcal{P}_y^{-1}$.

Since both Σ_x and $\mathbb{S}\Sigma_x\mathbb{S}'$ have rank m_1, it must be the case that x_t can be written as a linear combination of $\tilde{x}_t$, e.g., $x_t = \mathcal{Q}\tilde{x}_t$, where $\mathcal{Q}$ is an $m \times m_1$ matrix. Hence, $x_t = \mathcal{Q}\tilde{\mathcal{P}}_x' \tilde{V}' \tilde{\mathcal{P}}_y^{-1} \mathbb{S} y_t$.

Example 7.10. Suppose $m = 2$ (say, output and consumption) and $m_1 = 1$. Then we have three possibilities: we could minimize the variance of output, $\mathbb{S} = [1, 0]$, the variance of consumption, $\mathbb{S} = [0, 1]$, or a linear combination of the two, $\mathbb{S} = [\varrho, 1 - \varrho]$, $0 < \varrho < 1$. The solution for $\tilde{x}_t$ clearly depends on which $\mathbb{S}$ is used.

When (x_t, y_t) are serially correlated vectors and $\text{rank}(\Sigma_x) = m_1 \leqslant m$, the same intuition applies. However, because of serial correlation, one wants to minimize the trace (weighted or unweighted) of the spectral density matrix. That is, we want to minimize $\text{tr}\,|W(\omega)\mathcal{S}_{\tilde{v}}(\omega)|$, where $W(\omega)$ is a matrix of weights for each frequency ω and $\mathcal{S}_{\tilde{v}}(\omega)$ is the spectral density matrix of $\tilde{v}_t$. When ω are Fourier frequencies, $\mathcal{S}_{\tilde{v}}(\omega)$ is uncorrelated with $\mathcal{S}_{\tilde{v}}(\omega')$, $\forall \omega \neq \omega'$. Hence, the minimization problem can be performed frequency by frequency and the solution is $\text{ACF}_{\tilde{x}\tilde{y}}(\omega) \equiv \sum_\tau \text{ACF}_{\tilde{x}\tilde{y}}(\tau)\text{e}^{-i\omega\tau} = \mathfrak{P}(\omega)\,\text{ACF}_{\tilde{y}}(\omega)$, where $\mathfrak{P}(\omega)$ is the Fourier transform of $\tilde{\mathcal{P}}_x' \tilde{V}' \tilde{\mathcal{P}}_y^{-1}$. Hence, $\tilde{x}_t$ is a function of leads and lags of $\tilde{y}_t$.

Exercise 7.11. Suppose that $x_t = \mathcal{Q}_1 v_t$, where x_t is a 2×1 vector, $\mathcal{Q}_1' = [1.0, 0.5]$, and $v_t \sim (0, 1)$, and let $y_t = \mathcal{Q}_2 e_t$, $\mathcal{Q}_2 = \left[\begin{smallmatrix} 1.0 & 0.3 \\ 0.2 & 1.0 \end{smallmatrix}\right]$ and $e_t \sim (0, \left[\begin{smallmatrix} 1.0 & 0.0 \\ 0.0 & 4.0 \end{smallmatrix}\right])$. Show how to compute $\text{ACF}_{xy}(\omega)$ and the predicted value of x_t. Show both theoretical and numerical answers (the latter based on the estimation/simulation of the relevant quantities).

Once an expression for ACF_{xy} is obtained, it is easy to design R^2-type measures of fit, e.g., $\mathfrak{S}_{1i}(\omega) = \text{ACF}_v(\omega)_{ii}/\text{ACF}_y(\omega)_{ii}$ or $\mathfrak{S}_{2i}(\omega) = \int_{[\omega_1,\omega_2]} \text{ACF}_v(\omega)_{ii}\,\text{d}\omega / \int_{[\omega_1,\omega_2]} \text{ACF}_y(\omega)_{ii}\,\text{d}\omega$. $\mathfrak{S}_{1i}$ measures the variance of the ith component of the error relative to the variance of the ith component of the data at frequency ω. Since this is analogous to $1-R^2$ in a regression, a plot of $\mathfrak{S}_{1i}$ against ω visually provides a lower bound for the "distance" between the model and the data, frequency by frequency. $\mathfrak{S}_{2i}$ may be useful for evaluating the model over a band of frequencies. Note that, since v_t and x_t are serially correlated, both $\mathfrak{S}_{1i}$ and $\mathfrak{S}_{2i}$ could be greater than 1.

Exercise 7.12. Show that linearly filtering x_t and y_t leaves $\mathfrak{S}_{1i}$ unchanged but alters $\mathfrak{S}_{2i}$. (Hint: the weights depend on the frequency.)

Example 7.11. We illustrate Watson's approach by using simulated data from a version of the model described in example 7.3, where there are only technology shocks, the utility function is $U(c_t, N_t) = \ln c_t + \vartheta_N(1 - N_t)$, and $\eta = 0.64$, $\delta = 0.025$, $\beta = 0.99$, $(c/\text{GDP})^{\text{ss}} = 0.7$, $(K/\text{GDP})^{\text{ss}} = 2.5$, $\vartheta_N = 2.6$, $\bar{\zeta} = 0$, $\rho_\zeta = 0.95$, $\sigma_\zeta = 0.007$. Figure 7.1 presents $\mathfrak{S}_{1i}$, frequency by frequency, when we minimize the variance of linearly detrended U.S. output (first column) or the variance of linearly detrended U.S. consumption (second column). Shaded areas indicate business cycle frequencies. We need to choose to minimize the variance of one of the two variables because there is only one shock in the model. Suppose we care about the variability of output, the variability of consumption and their correlation. The model does not fit the data well. In both columns, $1 - R^2$ is high for the variable whose variance is not minimized (roughly of the order of 0.9999) at business cycle frequencies. For the minimization variable, misspecification is noticeable at medium to high frequencies. Finally, the correlation of two variables is poorly matched at low frequencies; misspecification declines with the frequency but at business cycle frequencies is still substantial.

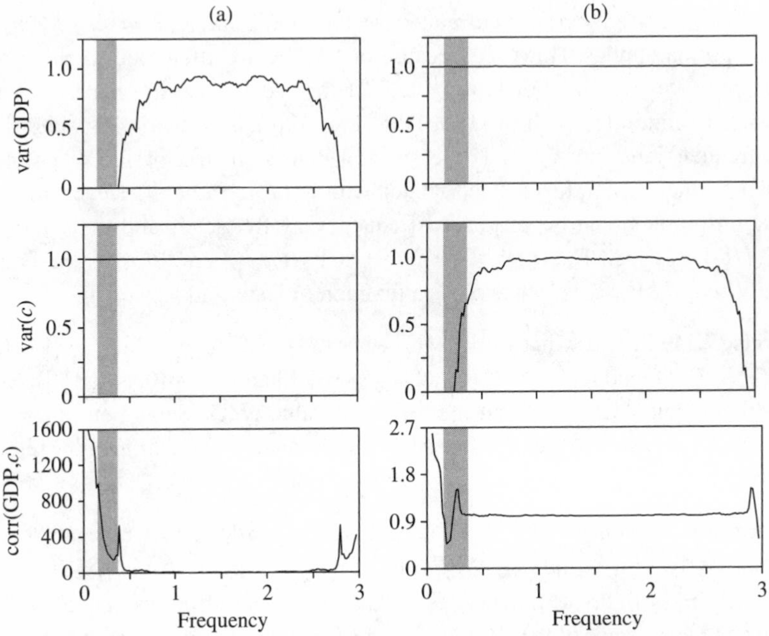

Figure 7.1. Watson's measure of fit. Minimizing (a) var(GDP) and (b) var(c).

Exercise 7.13 (Wei). Consider two versions of an RBC model, one with habit persistence in leisure, and one with production externalities. In the first case the social planner maximizes $E_0 \sum_t \beta^t [\ln(c_t) + \vartheta_N \ln(\gamma(\ell)(1-N_t))]$ subject to $c_t + K_{t+1} = K_t^{1-\eta} N_t^{\eta} \zeta_t$. In the second case she maximizes $E_0 \sum_t \beta^t [\ln(c_t) + \vartheta_N \ln(1 - N_t)]$ subject to $c_t + K_{t+1} = \bar{N}_t^{\aleph} K_t^{1-\eta} N_t^{\eta} \zeta_t$, where $\bar{N}_t$ is the average number of hours worked in the economy and $\aleph > 0$. In both cases we assume that $\ln \zeta_t = \bar{\zeta} + \rho_\zeta \ln \zeta_{t-1} + \epsilon_{1t}$. Suppose $\beta = 0.99$, $\eta = 0.64$, $\delta = 0.025$, $\sigma_\zeta = 0.007$, $\rho_\zeta = 0.9$, ϑ_N is chosen so that $N^{\text{ss}} = 0.20$, and $(c/\text{GDP})^{\text{ss}} = 0.7$, $(K/\text{GDP})^{\text{ss}} = 2.5$. Let $\gamma(\ell) = 1 + 0.85\ell - 0.3\ell^2$ and let $\aleph = 0.45$. Compare the spectral densities of the two models for consumption, investment, output, and hours to the spectra of U.S. data and to the spectra of the model of example 7.11, linearly detrending the actual data and minimizing the variance of output. Which model improves over the basic one? In which dimensions?

Exercise 7.14. Consider a one-sector monetary growth model with complete capital depreciation, inelastic labor supply, where the representative agent solves $\max_{\{c_t, K_{t+1}\}} E_0 \sum_{t=1}^{\infty} \beta^t \ln c_t$ subject to $c_t + K_{t+1} \leqslant \zeta_t K_t^{1-\eta} N_t^{\eta}$ and $\ln \zeta_t = \bar{\zeta} + \rho_\zeta \ln \zeta_{t-1} + \epsilon_{1t}$, $\epsilon_{1t} \sim$ i.i.d. $\mathbb{N}(0, \sigma_\zeta^2)$. Assume a cash-in-advance constraint $M_t \leqslant p_t c_t$ and let $\ln M_t = \bar{M} + \rho_M \ln M_{t-1} + \epsilon_{3t}$, $\epsilon_{3t} \sim$ i.i.d. $\mathbb{N}(0, \sigma_M^2)$.

(i) Assume that the uncertainty is realized before decisions are taken at each t. Solve for the optimal path for $(c_t, K_{t+1}, \text{GDP}_t, p_t)$ as a function of (K_t, ζ_t, M_t).

(ii) Assume that $\eta = 0.64$, $\beta = 0.998$, $\rho_\zeta = 0.90$, $\rho_M = 0.8$, $\sigma_\zeta = 0.007$, $\sigma_M = 0.01$. Apply Watson's approach to quarterly detrended U.S. M1 and prices. Calculate $\mathfrak{S}_{2i}(\omega)$ for $\omega \in [\pi/16, \pi/4]$.

Two shortcomings of Watson's procedure should be mentioned. First, while there is some intuitive appeal in creating lower bounds statistics, it is not clear why one should concentrate only on the best possible outcome. Canova et al. (1994) suggest using both the best and the worst fits: if the range is narrow and $1 - R^2$ of the worst outcome small, one can conclude that the model is satisfactory—a conclusion one cannot reach by using only the best fit. Second, the method does not provide information on what may cause poor fit. R^2 could be low for a variety of reasons (the variance of the shocks in the data may be high; the dynamics of the model and of the data are different; the process for the states has a large AR coefficient). Clearly, it makes a lot of difference whether it is the first or the last of these causes that makes R^2 low.

7.4.2 *Measure of Fit Based on Simulation Variability*

A class of measures of fit can be obtained if a researcher is willing to randomize on the realization of the stochastic processes of the model. This approach was popularized by, for example, Gregory and Smith (1991, 1993). When the $\{\epsilon_t\}$ are randomized, the distance between relevant functions of the model and of actual data can be evaluated by using either asymptotic or probabilistic (Monte Carlo) criteria. Measures of fit of this type give a sense of the "economic" distance between the model and the data. Standard functions used for comparison include unconditional moments, spectral densities (see Soderlin 1994), or semi-structural impulse responses (see Cogley and Nason 1994). Note that spectra-based comparisons do not require a parametric representation for the actual data, but large simulated samples are needed to ensure that the bias of the spectral estimates is small.

We illustrate how to validate a model with such a technique in the next example.

Example 7.12 (Dunlop–Tarshis puzzle). Suppose we are concerned with the correlation between hours and real wages and suppose we are willing to draw replications for the time series of the random disturbances of the model. Then there are three ways to check whether the correlations produced by the model look like the actual ones. The first is as follows.

Algorithm 7.2.

(1) Draw $(\{\epsilon_t\}_{t=1}^{T})^l$. Calculate $\text{ACRF}_{N,w}(\tau)^l$, $l = 1, \dots, L$, $\tau = 0, 1, 2, \dots$.

(2) Order simulations and construct percentiles.

(3) Calculate the number of replications for which $\text{ACRF}_{N,w}(\tau)^l$ is less than the autocorrelation found in the actual data (separately for each τ or jointly); the decile of the simulated distribution where the actual value lies or check whether the actual autocorrelation is inside a prespecified range of the simulated distribution (say, a 68% or a 95% interval).

Table 7.3. Model correlations.

	$\text{corr}(N_t, w_{t-1})$	$\text{corr}(N_t, w_t)$	$\text{corr}(N_t, w_{t+1})$
Size (% below actual)	0.40	0.27	0.32
Normality (% rejection)	0.59	0.72	0.66
Bands	[0.39, 0.65]	[0.45, 0.70]	[0.38, 0.64]
Actual correlations	0.517	0.522	0.488

The output of algorithm 7.2 is what Gregory and Smith (1993) call the "size" of calibration tests. If a model is a poor approximation to the data, the simulated distribution of correlations will be far away from the distribution in the data and extreme statistics will be obtained (e.g., actual correlations are in the tails of the simulated distribution or the number of times $\text{ACRF}_{N,w}(\tau)^l$ is less than the actual value is zero or one).

A second approach is obtained by using an asymptotic normal approximation for the distribution of correlations. For example, Anderson (1971) shows that $\widehat{\text{ACRF}}_{N,w}(\tau) \xrightarrow{D} \mathbb{N}(\text{ACRF}_{N,w}(\tau), \Sigma_{\text{ACRF}}(\tau))$, where $\Sigma_{\text{ACRF}}(\tau) = (1/2T) \times (1 - |\text{ACRF}_{N,w}(\tau)|)^2$. Therefore, given one draw for $\{\epsilon_t\}_{t=1}^T$, as long as $T \to \infty$, $\sqrt{T}(\text{ACRF}_{N,w}(\tau) - \widehat{\text{ACRF}}_{N,w}(\tau))/\sqrt{\Sigma_{\text{ACRF}}(\tau)} \xrightarrow{D} \mathbb{N}(0, 1)$, each τ. Since little is known about the properties of correlation estimates when T is moderate or small, one may prefer an approach which uses a small-sample version of this test, in which case the next algorithm could be of use.

Algorithm 7.3.

(1) Draw $(\{\epsilon_t\}_{t=1}^T)^l$ and calculate $\text{ACRF}_{N,w}(\tau)^l$, $l = 1, \dots, L$, $\tau = 0, 1, 2, \dots$.

(2) For each l, compare $\sqrt{T}(\text{ACRF}_{N,w}(\tau) - \widehat{\text{ACRF}}_{N,w}(\tau))/\sqrt{\Sigma_{\text{ACRF}}(\tau)}$ to a $\mathbb{N}(0, 1)$. Record either the p-value or construct an indicator function which is 1 if the simulated distribution is statistically different from a $\mathbb{N}(0, 1)$ at some confidence level and 0 otherwise.

(3) Construct the distribution of p-values or the percentage of times the model is rejected.

We have examined whether the RBC model of example 7.3 driven by government expenditure and technology shocks can account for the correlation found in detrended U.S. data for the sample 1964:1–2003:1. We use a version of the model with separable utility (a power specification for consumption and a linear specification for leisure). The parameters are $\beta = 0.99$, $\delta = 0.025$, $\vartheta = 0.5$, $\varphi = 2$, $N^{\text{ss}} = 0.2$, $\rho_\zeta = 0.9$, $\rho_{\text{G}} = 0.8$, $\sigma_\zeta = 0.007$, $\sigma_{\text{G}} = 0.01$.

Table 7.3 reports the percentages of times the simulated correlation is below the actual one (row labeled "Size"), the number of times the normality assumption is rejected (row labeled "Normality"), and the 68% band for simulated correlations together with the actual ones, for $\tau = -1, 0, 1$. It is remarkable that actual correlations are inside the bands generated by the model at all three horizons. Also, while the model has a tendency to produce correlations which exceed those found in the actual data, the results are reasonably good. This is not completely surprising. As suggested in exercise 2.15, the presence of demand shifters can substantially reduce the almost perfect correlation between hours and real wages produced by technology shocks.

Exercise 7.15 (Adelmann test). Consider two versions of an RBC model, one with habit persistence in consumption and one with one-period labor contracts. Assume that there are only productivity shocks, that the solutions are obtained by log-linearizing the optimality conditions, and that the productivity process is parametrized so that it reproduces the first two moments of actual Solow residuals for the U.S. economy.

(i) Appropriately select the remaining parameters of both models.

(ii) Construct probabilities of turning points in output, defining a recession at t if $\mathrm{GDP}_{t-2} > \mathrm{GDP}_{t-1} > \mathrm{GDP}_t < \mathrm{GDP}_{t+1} < \mathrm{GDP}_{t+2}$ and an expansion at t if $\mathrm{GDP}_{t-2} < \mathrm{GDP}_{t-1} < \mathrm{GDP}_t > \mathrm{GDP}_{t+1} > \mathrm{GDP}_{t+2}$. (Hint: draw sequences for the exogenous disturbances and count the number of times that at each date recession and expansion events are encountered.) Which model fits the NBER chronology better?

Exercise 7.16 (money–inflation relationship). Consider a working capital economy (like the one in exercise 2.14) and a sticky price economy (like the one in example 2.9). Suppose we want to find out which model fits the actual cross-correlation function of M1 growth and inflation found in euro area data better. Assume that there are two shocks in each model (a technology and a monetary shock), both of which are AR(1), that in both models output requires capital and labor, that there is no habit persistence in consumption, and that there are quadratic costs to adjusting capital of the form $\frac{1}{2}b((K_{t+1}/K_t) - 1)^2 K_t$, where $b \geqslant 0$ and that monetary policy is conducted according to a rule of the form $i_t = i_{t-1}^{\alpha_0}\mathrm{GDP}_t^{\alpha_1}\pi_t^{\alpha_2}\epsilon_{3t}$, where ϵ_{3t} is a monetary policy shock and i_t is the nominal interest rate. Log-linearize both models around the steady state, appropriately select the parameters, and construct probabilistic measures of fit, randomizing on the stochastic processes for monetary and technology shocks.

Instead of measuring the distance between moments, one could measure the distance between impulse responses, where meaningful economic shocks are obtained with one of the approaches described in chapter 4. A statistic to compare impulse responses is

$$\mathfrak{S}(\tau) = [\mathrm{IRF}(\tau) - \mathrm{IRF}^{\mathrm{A}}(\tau)]\Sigma(\tau)^{-1}[\mathrm{IRF}(\tau) - \mathrm{IRF}^{\mathrm{A}}(\tau)]', \qquad (7.14)$$

where $\tau = 1, 2, \dots$ refers to the horizon, $\mathrm{IRF}(\tau)$ is the mean response of the model (across replications) at horizon τ, $\mathrm{IRF}^{\mathrm{A}}(\tau)$ is the actual response at horizon τ, and $\Sigma(\tau) = (1/L)\sum_{l=1}^{L}[\mathrm{IRF}(\tau, l) - \mathrm{IRF}(\tau)^{\mathrm{A}}][\mathrm{IRF}(\tau, l) - \mathrm{IRF}(\tau)^{\mathrm{A}}]'$. Asymptotically, $T \times \mathfrak{S}(\tau) \sim \chi^2(1)$. For the sample sizes used in macroeconomics, a small-sample version of this statistic is probably more useful. Hence,

$$\mathfrak{S}(\tau, l) = [\mathrm{IRF}(\tau, l) - \mathrm{IRF}^{\mathrm{A}}(\tau)]\Sigma(\tau)^{-1}[\mathrm{IRF}(\tau, l) - \mathrm{IRF}^{\mathrm{A}}(\tau)]' \tag{7.15}$$

could be used where $\mathrm{IRF}(\tau, l)$ is the response of the model at horizon τ for replication l. As suggested in algorithm 7.3, $\mathfrak{S}(\tau, l)$ can be computed at each l by using the simulated realization of impulse responses. The empirical distribution of $\mathfrak{S}(\tau, l)$ can be constructed and the rejection frequency computed. Since $\Sigma(\tau)$ is correlated across τ, it is necessary to eliminate the correlation if comparison at more than one τ is made (see chapter 4).

Exercise 7.17 (output and prices). Continuing with the model economy described in exercise 7.14, run a VAR on simulated price and output data, and identify shocks by using the (wrong) assumption that, on impact, one of the shocks has no effect on prices. Repeat the identification exercise for actual data. Calculate $\mathfrak{S}(\tau, l)$, $\tau = 1, 4, 8$. Tabulate the rejection frequencies and interpret the results.

The setup of this subsection can be easily modified to account for parameter uncertainty. To do this we need only change the first step of algorithms 7.2 and 7.3, randomizing both ϵ_t and θ. The empirical distribution of relevant statistics can then be constructed and from there one can compute size tests or percentile rejection rates. When parameter uncertainty is "objective," as in Canova (1994, 1995a), the extension is straightforward: we simply draw from the joint empirical distribution for the parameters. When parameter uncertainty reflects sampling variabilities, the techniques described in the next subsection could be used.

7.4.3 Measures of Fit Based on Sampling Variability

If one allows estimation variability in the parameters, or if one is willing to accept the idea that stylized facts are measured with error, model evaluation can be conducted by using a metric which exploits sampling, as opposed to simulation, variability.

When parameters are random the procedure typically used resembles a J-test (see chapter 5). However, here simulated moments are random—because of parameter uncertainty—while moments of the actual data are assumed to be measured without error. Hence, data moments play the role of g_∞ and simulated moments the role of g_T in the GMM setup.

Suppose θ_T solves $(1/T)\sum_t g_1(\epsilon_t, \theta)$. Let $g_2(y_t)$ be a vector of moments of the actual data, $g_2(\epsilon_t, \theta_T)$ the same vector of moments obtained from simulated data and $\Sigma_{g_2} = (\partial g_2/\partial\theta)\Sigma_\theta(\partial g_2/\partial\theta)'$, the covariance matrix of $g_2(\epsilon_t, \theta_T)$, where Σ_θ is the covariance matrix of θ_T. Then, as $T \to \infty$, $T \times [g_2(y_t) - g_2(\epsilon_t, \theta_T)]'\Sigma_{g_2}^{-1} \times [g_2(y_t) - g_2(\epsilon_t, \theta_T)] \sim \chi^2(\dim(g_2))$.

Exercise 7.18. Assume that $g_2(y_t)$ is measured with error. Show how to modify the distance statistic and its asymptotic distribution to take this into account.

Two points need to be stressed. First, the method is closely related to those discussed in chapter 5. Therefore, standard conditions on y_t and on the g functions are required for the statistics to have asymptotic validity. Note also that here estimation and testing are conducted sequentially, as opposed to simultaneously, and that θ_T is obtained from just identified conditions. Second, a J-test is valid under the null that the model is the true DGP in the dimensions represented by g_2. That is, the model needs to be correct at least in the g_2 dimensions for the validation results to have meaningful interpretations.

An alternative approach, not requiring the assumption that the model is true, was suggested by Diebold, Ohanian, and Berkowitz (DOB) (Diebold et al. 1998). The method is close in spirit to Watson's but uses the sampling variability of the actual data to construct a finite-sample diagnostic of fit.

Let $\mathcal{S}_y(\omega)$ be the spectrum of the actual data and $\hat{\mathcal{S}}_y(\omega)$ an estimate of $\mathcal{S}_y(\omega)$. When y_t is univariate and T large, $2\hat{\mathcal{S}}_y(\omega)/\mathcal{S}_y(\omega) \sim \chi^2(2)$ for $\omega \neq 0, \pi$. For the sample sizes typically used in macroeconomics, asymptotic approximations are probably inappropriate and DOB suggest two bootstrap methods to construct small-sample confidence intervals for the spectrum of y_t. The methods differ in the way replications are constructed: in the first, the asymptotic distribution of the prediction error is the resampling distribution; in the second, it is its empirical distribution. Let $\tilde{\mathcal{P}}'\tilde{\mathcal{P}} = \mathrm{ACF}_y(\tau)$ and let $\bar{y}$ be the sample mean of y_t. The approach is summarized in the following algorithm.

Algorithm 7.4.

(1) Draw υ_t^l from a $\mathbb{N}(0, I_T)$ or from the empirical distribution of $\upsilon_t = \tilde{\mathcal{P}}^{-1}(y_t - \bar{y})$.

(2) Construct $y_t^l = \bar{y} + \tilde{\mathcal{P}}\upsilon_t^l$ and $\mathrm{ACF}_y(\tau)^l$, $l = 1, \dots, L$.

(3) Compute $\hat{\mathcal{S}}_y^l(\omega) = \sum_\tau \mathcal{K}(\tau)\,\mathrm{ACF}_y(\tau)^l \mathrm{e}^{-\mathrm{i}\omega\tau}$, where $\mathcal{K}(\tau)$ is a kernel.

(4) Order $\hat{\mathcal{S}}_y^l(\omega)$ each ω; construct percentiles and extract confidence intervals.

Recall that bootstrap procedures are valid under homoskedasticity of υ_t. Hence, if heteroskedasticity is suspected, data need to be transformed before algorithm 7.4 is used.

The multivariate analogs of these estimators are straightforward.

Exercise 7.19. Describe how to implement the parametric bootstrap algorithm 7.4 in a multivariate setting.

Bootstrap distributions are valid frequency by frequency. However, evaluation is often performed over a band of frequencies. The results obtained by connecting the p-values, frequency by frequency, are incorrect since a set of n $(1-\varrho)\%$ confidence intervals constructed for each frequency will not achieve a $(1-\varrho)\%$ joint coverage. Rather, the actual confidence level will be closer to $(1-\varrho)^n\%$ if the pointwise intervals are independent. Hence, when interest centers on a band of n frequencies, a more appropriate approximation is obtained by choosing a $(1-\varrho/n)\%$ coverage for each spectral ordinate since the resulting tunnel has coverage of, at least, $(1-\varrho)\%$.

When the parameters and the stochastic processes of a model are fixed at some $\hat{\theta}$ and $\hat{\epsilon}_t$, the spectrum of simulated data can be constructed to any degree of accuracy either by simulating a very long time series or by replicating many times a short time series using the distribution of $\hat{\epsilon}_t$ and invoking ergodicity. Let $\mathcal{S}_x(\omega, \hat{\theta}, \hat{\epsilon}_t)$ be the spectrum of the model. A measure of fit is

$$\mathfrak{L}(\hat{\theta}, \hat{\epsilon}_t) = \int_{\omega_1}^{\omega_2} \mathfrak{L}^*(\mathcal{S}_y(\omega), \mathcal{S}_x(\omega, \hat{\theta}, \hat{\epsilon}_t)) W(\omega) \, d\omega, \tag{7.16}$$

where $W(\omega)$ is a set of weights and $\mathfrak{L}^*$ is a function measuring the distance between the spectrum of actual and simulated data at frequency ω.

It easy to include parameter uncertainty in the evaluation criteria. In fact, one advantage of evaluating the fit by using (7.16) is that $\mathfrak{L}(\hat{\theta}, \hat{\epsilon}_t)$ can also be used for estimation purposes. For example, $\tilde{\theta} = \operatorname{argmin}_\theta \mathfrak{L}(\theta, \hat{\epsilon}_t)$ is a minimum distance type estimator of θ. If this route is taken, the assumption that the model is correct, at least in some dimensions, is necessary for the estimation–evaluation process to make sense.

It is also easy to combine algorithm 7.4 with estimation: the first three steps of the procedure are identical and we only need to estimate $\tilde{\theta}^l$ for each draw, $l = 1, \ldots, L$. From the distribution of $\tilde{\theta}^l$ we can construct point estimates, confidence intervals, etc.

Exercise 7.20. Show the form of $\mathfrak{L}(\hat{\theta}, \hat{\epsilon}_t)$ when $\mathfrak{L}^*$ in (7.16) is quadratic and when we are interested in comparing model and data at business cycle frequencies only. Show how the variability of θ and of $\mathcal{S}_x(\omega)$ affect estimates of $\mathfrak{L}(\theta, \hat{\epsilon}_t)$. Show that, if $\mathfrak{L}^* = \mathcal{S}_x(\omega, \hat{\theta}, \hat{\epsilon}_t)/\mathcal{S}_y(\omega)$, detrending is irrelevant in judging the closeness of the model to the data.

Example 7.13 (band spectrum regression). Suppose ω_j are Fourier frequencies and concentrate attention at business cycle frequencies (i.e., $[\pi/16, \pi/4]$). Suppose that $\mathfrak{L}^*$ is quadratic, $W(\omega) = 1, \forall\omega$, and $\mathfrak{L}(\theta, \hat{\epsilon}_t) = \sum_j (\mathcal{S}_y(\omega_j) - \mathcal{S}_x(\omega_j, \theta, \hat{\epsilon}_t))^2$. If $\mathcal{S}_x(\omega, \theta, \hat{\epsilon}_t)$ is orthogonal to $\mathcal{S}_y(\omega_j) - \mathcal{S}_x(\omega_j, \theta, \hat{\epsilon}_t)$, minimization of $\mathfrak{L}(\theta, \hat{\epsilon}_t)$ produces band spectrum regression estimates (see Engle 1974).

Exercise 7.21. For the economy of exercise 7.14 calculate the spectrum of prices and output, appropriately selecting the parameters. Calculate the spectrum of prices and output by using U.S. data and measure the distance between the model and the data by using a parametric bootstrap algorithm.

(i) Calculate $\mathfrak{L}(\hat{\theta}, \hat{\epsilon}_t)$ assuming that $\mathfrak{L}^*$ is quadratic, equally weighting deviations of prices and output from their actual counterparts at business cycle frequencies.

(ii) Repeat the calculation when $\mathfrak{L}(\theta, \hat{\epsilon}_t) = \mathcal{I}_{[\mathcal{S}_y(\omega) \geqslant \mathcal{S}_x(\omega)]}$ and $\mathcal{I}$ is an indicator function. Find the $\tilde{\theta}$ which minimizes this loss function.

Example 7.14. Continuing with the economy of example 7.11, we compute joint 68% tunnels for the spectra of consumption and output and for the coherence between the two variables by using a parametric bootstrap approach. Figure 7.2 shows the

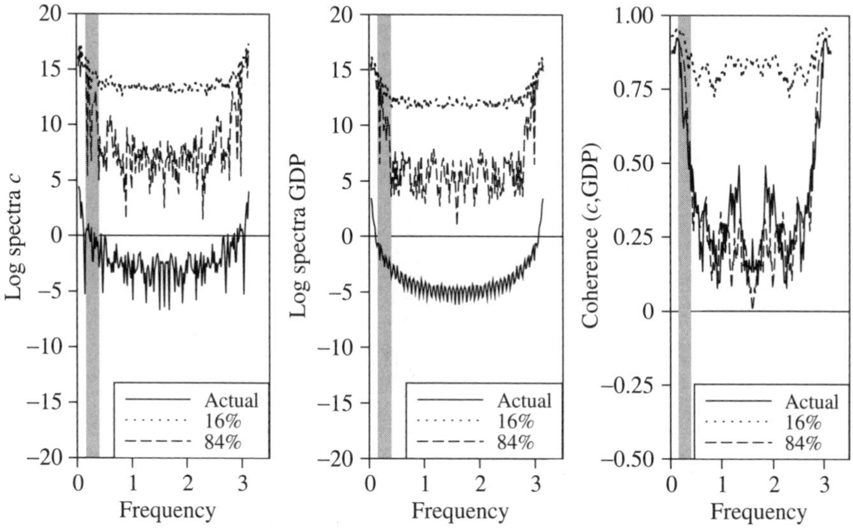

Figure 7.2. Spectra and coherences.

tunnels together with the log spectra and coherence produced by the model (business cycle frequencies are shaded). Clearly, consumption and output variabilities in the model at business cycle frequencies are lower than in the data, while the coherence is, roughly, of the same magnitude.

7.4.4 Measures of Fit Based on Sampling and Simulation Variability

There is no reason to confine our attention to either sampling or simulation uncertainty. The outcomes of models are uncertain because parameters (and forcing variables) are unknown; statistics of the data are uncertain because of sampling variability. Therefore, it makes sense to design a metric which takes both types of uncertainty into account.

For example, one could construct bootstrap distributions for statistics of the actual data and simulated distributions for the statistics produced by the model (allowing for uncertainty in both the parameters and in the stochastic processes) and measure the quality of the approximation by examining the degree of overlap between the two distributions — a large overlap for different contour probabilities should be considered a good sign. With such an approach, actual and simulated data are treated symmetrically: one can either ask if the actual data could have been generated by the model or, conversely, if the simulated data are consistent with the empirical distribution of the actual data — much in the same spirit as switching the null and the alternative in hypothesis testing.

Example 7.15. Continuing with example 7.12, we ask how much overlap there is between the distributions of the contemporaneous correlation of hours and real

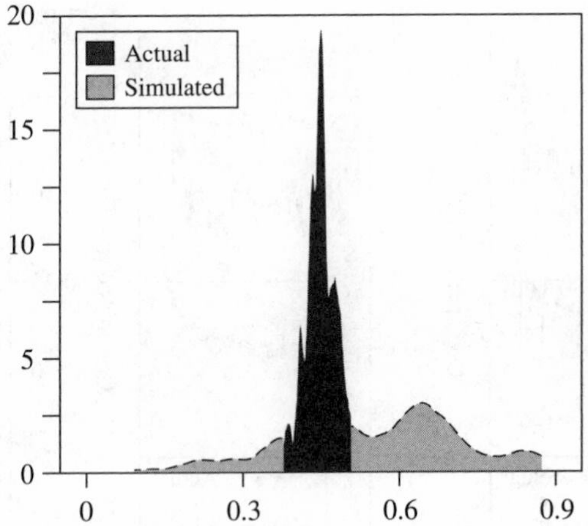

Figure 7.3. Distributions of hours and real wage correlation.

wages in the data and in the model when uncertainty in both parameters and stochastic processes is taken into account. Figure 7.3 reports the two distributions: there appears to be some overlap but the simulated distribution is much more spread out than the actual one. In fact, the small-sample 95% interval of actual correlation $(0.44, 0.52)$ is inside the 68% interval for the model correlation $(0.35, 0.75)$. Conversely, only the central 25% of the mass of the simulated distribution of the model correlation is inside the 68% interval of the small-sample distribution of the actual one.

DeJong et al. (1996) also take the view that uncertainty characterizes both models and data. However, the distributions characterizing the uncertainty present in the parameters of the model and in the coefficients of the parametric representation of the data are "subjective." Suppose the $m \times 1$ vector of actual data is represented as

$$y_t = A(\ell)y_{t-1} + e_t, \quad e_t \sim \text{i.i.d. } \mathbb{N}(0, \Sigma_e). \tag{7.17}$$

Let $\alpha = \{\text{vec}(A_1), \text{vec}(A_2), \dots, \text{vech}(\Sigma_y)\}$, where $\text{vec}(\cdot)$ $(\text{vech}(\cdot))$ are the columnwise vectorizations of rectangular (symmetric) matrices and let $\Sigma_y = (I - A(\ell)\ell)^{-1}\Sigma_e((I - A(\ell)\ell)^{-1})'$. When y_t is stationary, and given α, the second moments of y_t can be obtained as $\Sigma_Y = \mathbb{A}\Sigma_Y\mathbb{A}' + \Sigma_E$, where $\mathbb{A}$ is the companion matrix of $A(\ell)$ and $\text{ACF}_Y(\tau) = \mathbb{A}^\tau\Sigma_Y$. Let $g(\alpha)$ be a prior density for α. One possible choice is $g(\alpha) \propto |\Sigma_E|^{(m+1)/2} \times \mathcal{I}_{[\text{stationary}]}$, where $\mathcal{I}_{[\text{stationary}]}$ is an indicator function. That is, no information on α is available except that the density for α must imply stationarity of y_t.

As discussed in chapter 10, a noninformative prior for α and Σ_e and a normal likelihood for y_t generate a normal-Wishart posterior for α and Σ_e. Then, the posterior distribution for Σ_Y, ACF_Y, can be obtained by simulation, drawing α and Σ_e from such distributions, computing Σ_Y and ACF_Y for each draw and collecting relevant percentiles.

Let θ be the vector of parameters of the model. The outcomes of the model can be described by a density $f(x_t \mid \theta)$. Let $g(\theta)$ be a prior density for θ. Then $f(x_t) = \int f(x_t \mid \theta)g(\theta)\,\mathrm{d}\theta$ characterizes the realizations of the model, once parameter uncertainty is averaged out. Using draws from $g(\theta)$ and the solution to the model $f(x_t \mid \theta)$, a simulation-based distribution of Σ_x and ACF_x, accounting for prior parameter uncertainty, can be produced.

Then, given a functional form for $g(\theta)$, one can vary its dispersion to see if the degree of overlap between the distributions of Σ_x and Σ_y (or ACF_x and ACF_y) increases. Since there is disagreement in the profession on the spread of $g(\theta)$, such an exercise may help us to understand whether uncertainty in the selection of the parameters θ can mitigate differences between the model and the data.

Let $g(\mathfrak{S}_{y,i})$ be the data-based distribution of the component i of $\mathfrak{S}_y$ and let $g_j(\mathfrak{S}_{x,i})$ be the model-based distribution for $\mathfrak{S}_{x,i}$ using specification j for the prior. One way to measure the degree of overlap between $g(\mathfrak{S}_{y,i})$ and $g_j(\mathfrak{S}_{x,i})$ is, for $0 < \varrho < 1$, the following confidence interval criterion (CIC):

$$\mathrm{CIC}_{ij} = \frac{1}{1-\varrho}\int_{\varrho/2}^{1-\varrho/2} g_j(\mathfrak{S}_{x,i})\,\mathrm{d}\mathfrak{S}_{x,i}, \tag{7.18}$$

where $1-\varrho = \int_{\varrho/2}^{1-\varrho/2} g(\mathfrak{S}_{y,i})\,\mathrm{d}\mathfrak{S}_{y,i}$. Note that $0 \leqslant \mathrm{CIC}_{ij} \leqslant 1/(1-\varrho)$. When CIC_{ij} is low, the fit is poor, i.e., either the overlap is small or $g_j(\mathfrak{S}_{x,i})$ is very diffuse; values close to $1/(1-\varrho)$ indicate that the two distributions overlap substantially and values greater than 1 that $g(\mathfrak{S}_{y,i})$ is diffused relative to $g_j(\mathfrak{S}_{x,i})$. To distinguish between the two interpretations when CIC_{ij} is low, one can supplement (7.18) with another measure, analogous to a t-statistic for the mean of $g_j(\mathfrak{S}_{x,i})$ in the $g(\mathfrak{S}_{y,i})$ distribution, i.e., $[Eg_j(\mathfrak{S}_{x,i}) - Eg(\mathfrak{S}_{y,i})]/\sqrt{\mathrm{var}(g(\mathfrak{S}_{y,i}))}$. Large values of this statistic relative to a $\mathbb{N}(0,1)$ indicate differences in the locations of $g_j(\mathfrak{S}_{x,i})$ and $g(\mathfrak{S}_{y,i})$.

While we have kept ϱ fixed in the comparison, it is probably a good idea to vary it, given j, since large differences produced by different values of ϱ provide information on how and where the two distributions overlap.

Exercise 7.22. Consider the economy analyzed in exercise 7.4, where both stocks and risk-free bonds are available.

(i) Using U.S. data on equity returns (R_t^{e}) and the risk-free rate (R_t^{f}), calculate the equity premium, $\mathrm{EP}_t = (R_t^{\mathrm{e}} - R_t^{\mathrm{f}})$, the mean, and the autocovariance of (R_t^{f}, EP_t) at lags $-1, 0, 1$.

(ii) Set $n = 2$, $\mathrm{gy}_1 = 0.9873$, $\mathrm{gy}_2 = 1.0177$, $p_1 = 0.2$, $p_2 = 0.8$, $\beta = 0.99$, $\rho_y = 0.8$, $\varphi = 2$. Simulate asset price data from the model and compute $\mathfrak{S}_x = [E(R_t^{\mathrm{f}}), E(R_t^{\mathrm{e}}), \mathrm{var}(R_t^{\mathrm{f}}), \mathrm{var}(R_t^{\mathrm{e}})]$.

(iii) Consider the second moments of the two variables and assume that, as in Watson's approach, you want to minimize the variance of the risk-free rate. Provide individual and joint measures of fit for the risk-free rate and the equity premium at all frequencies.

(iv) Examine the fit of the model for the mean of the equity premium and of the risk-free rate by using a metric based on the sampling variability of simulated data.

(v) Describe a bootstrap algorithm to compute the small-sample distribution of the variance of the two variables. Using a quadratic loss function, find the φ which produces the best fit of the model to the data using the DOB approach.

(vi) Assume $\varphi \sim \mathbb{N}(2.0, 0.1)$, $\beta \sim \mathbb{N}(0.96, 0.01)$, $\rho_y \sim \mathbb{N}(0.8, 0.05)$ and still let $\text{gy}_1 = 0.9873$, $\text{gy}_2 = 1.0177$, $p_1 = 0.2$, $p_2 = 0.8$. Draw 100 values for these parameters, compute $\mathfrak{S}_x$ for each draw and calculate (plot) the joint empirical distribution. Repeat the exercise assuming $\varphi \sim \mathbb{N}(2.0, 0.2)$ and still assuming $\text{gy}_1 = 0.9873$, $\text{gy}_2 = 1.0177$, $p_1 = 0.2$, $p_2 = 0.8$, $\beta \sim \mathbb{N}(0.96, 0.02)$, $\rho_y \sim \mathbb{N}(0.8, 0.05)$.

(vii) Run a bivariate VAR using a measure of real risk-free rate of interest and of the equity premium. Draw 100 parameters from a normal-Wishart distribution for the VAR coefficients, compute $\mathfrak{S}_y$ from each draw and plot the joint distribution.

(viii) Show the degree of overlap between the distributions you have computed in (vi) and in (vii) letting $\varrho = 0.01, 0.10$. Calculate CIC in the two cases.

(ix) In what percentile of the distribution of $\mathfrak{S}_y$ lies the value of $\mathfrak{S}_x$ computed in (ii)?

One can note that there are still asymmetries in the procedure we have described. In fact, we compare the predictive density of the model $f(x_t)$ and the posterior distribution of the data. In principle, one would like to use the posterior distribution of both the model and the data. However, to do so, we need Markov chain Monte Carlo methods. We defer the discussion of such approaches to chapter 9.

Hansen and Heckman (1996) criticize users of computational experiments on the grounds that they rarely perform out-of-sample forecasting comparisons between the model and simple time series specifications. Such a comparison is useful in two senses. First, since DSGE models are restricted VARs, a comparison with unrestricted VARs helps us to gauge the validity of the restrictions. Second, if a DSGE is not too bad in forecasting relative to unrestricted time series models, policy makers may have an incentive to take the reported measurement more seriously.

Example 7.16. Once again we take the specification used in example 7.3 and use it to forecast output. Conditional on the parameters, the model produces forecasts for $\text{GDP}_t(\tau)$, $\tau = 1, 2, \dots$, at every t via the recursive formula $\mathbb{S}y_{t+\tau} = A_0^{\text{G}} A_1 \mathbb{S}y_{t+\tau-1}$, where $\mathbb{S}$ is a selection matrix which extracts GDP_t from the vector y_t and A_0^{G} is the generalized inverse of A_0. We compare the forecasts of the model to those produced by a naive random walk model, i.e., $\text{GDP}_{t+\tau} = \text{GDP}_t, \forall\tau$, by computing the ratio of the MSEs of the two models. For the sample 1990:1–2001:3 such a statistic at the one-step horizon is 1.13. At four steps its value drops to 0.97, so that the restrictions imposed by the model help at somewhat longer horizons. If we randomize on the parameters of the model, we can construct small-sample distributions for the forecasts and for the ratio of MSEs. In this case, the ratio of the two MSEs is greater than 1 in more than 70% of the cases at the one-step horizon, but less than 1 in 58% of the cases at the four-step horizon.

The setup we have discussed in this chapter also allows for other types of forecasting comparison, as explained next.

Example 7.17. Consider a bivariate VAR model with money and output and assume a flat prior on α. From the posterior distribution of α one can draw realizations α^l and use (7.17) to forecast recursively out-of-sample. Once a prior for the deep parameters θ of the model is available, a representation like (7.12) allows us to compute forecasts $\mathbb{S}y^l_{t+\tau}$, $\tau = 1, 2, \dots$, for every draw θ^l. Then to compare forecasts at each τ, one can compute the number of times the MSE of the model is lower than the MSE of the VAR or relate $T \times [\text{MSE}(\theta, l) - \text{MSE}(\alpha, l)]\Sigma^{-1}[\text{MSE}(\theta, l) - \text{MSE}(\alpha, l)]'$ to a $\chi^2(1)$ distribution, where Σ measures the dispersions of $\text{MSE}(\theta, l)$ and $\text{MSE}(\alpha, l)$ from their means, each l.

When one compares a DSGE model to the data by using out-of-sample forecasts, one does not necessarily subscribe to the idea the model is the correct DGP for the data. Comparisons based on MSEs do not require such an assumption: forecasts could be acceptable even when estimates are biased if the variance of the forecasts is small. Similarly, neither graphical analysis nor the examination of historical events requires such an assumption.

We have repeatedly emphasized that calibrators and standard econometricians take a different point of view regarding the nature of an economic model. For a standard econometrician, the distribution of outcomes of the model is the probability density function of the data, which can be used as a likelihood function to conduct inference. Calibrators which choose parameters by using GMM or similar techniques implicitly assume that the model describes only selected features (moments) of the real data. Call these features $\mathfrak{S}_y$. Since the relationship between $\mathfrak{S}_y$ and the outcomes of the model is analogous to the one assumed by traditional econometricians, the same evaluation techniques can be used. However, in constructing the mapping between $\mathfrak{S}_x$ and $\mathfrak{S}_y$, it is easy to fall into logical inconsistencies. An example can clarify why this is the case.

Example 7.18. Suppose one is interested in constructing a model to explain the average returns from holding financial assets. Let y_{it} be the return of asset i produced by the model, let $\bar{y}_i$ be its first moment and assume that returns are i.i.d. with constant variance. Then, the sampling distribution of the $\bar{y}_i$ depends on the population variance of returns since $\text{var}(\bar{y}_i) = \text{var}(y_{it})/T$. Hence, features of the data that the model wants to explain (first moment of returns) may depend on features that the model is not intended to explain (second moment of returns).

To avoid inconsistencies, Geweke (1999) suggests that we view a DSGE model as a representation of the *population moments of observable functions* of the data, not of their *sample* counterparts. This setup is advantageous because comparisons across models do not require the likelihood function of the data. However, since DSGE models have no interpretation for the observables, it is necessary to bridge population and sample statistics.

Let $\mathfrak{S}_y$ be a vector of functions of a subset of the data and $\mathcal{M}_1$ and $\mathcal{M}_2$ two different model specifications with parameters θ_1 and θ_2 respectively; let $\mathfrak{S}_{\infty,1} = E[\mathfrak{S}_y \mid \theta_1, \mathcal{M}_1]$ and $\mathfrak{S}_{\infty,2} = E[\mathfrak{S}_y \mid \theta_2, \mathcal{M}_2]$ be the population functions the models produce and $f(\mathfrak{S}_{\infty,1} \mid \mathcal{M}_1)$ and $f(\mathfrak{S}_{\infty,2} \mid \mathcal{M}_2)$ the densities for $\mathfrak{S}_\infty$ induced by the two models. Let the priors on the parameters be $g(\theta_1)$ and $g(\theta_2)$ and let $\mathcal{M}_3$ be a time series model which allows us to compute the posterior distribution of $\mathfrak{S}_\infty$, denoted by $g(\mathfrak{S}_{\infty,3} \mid y_t, \mathcal{M}_3)$, given the observables y_t.

Let $f(y_t \mid \mathfrak{S}_{\infty,3}, \mathcal{M}_1, \mathcal{M}_3) = f(y_t \mid \mathfrak{S}_{\infty,3}, \mathcal{M}_2, \mathcal{M}_3) = f(y_t \mid \mathfrak{S}_{\infty,3}, \mathcal{M}_3)$ and assume that $g(\mathfrak{S}_{\infty,1} \mid \mathcal{M}_1, \mathcal{M}_3) = f(\mathfrak{S}_{\infty,1} \mid \mathcal{M}_1)$ and $g(\mathfrak{S}_{\infty,2} \mid \mathcal{M}_2, \mathcal{M}_3) = f(\mathfrak{S}_{\infty,2} \mid \mathcal{M}_2)$. Intuitively, we require that knowledge of the two models carries no information for y_t (they are assumed to describe $\mathfrak{S}_\infty$) and that $\mathcal{M}_3$ has no information for $\mathfrak{S}_\infty$, either absolutely or relative to $\mathcal{M}_1$ and $\mathcal{M}_2$.

Exercise 7.23. Show that, if $g(\mathfrak{S}_{\infty,3} \mid \mathcal{M}_3)$ is constant and $g(\mathfrak{S}_{\infty,1} \mid \mathcal{M}_1, \mathcal{M}_3) = f(\mathfrak{S}_{\infty,1} \mid \mathcal{M}_1)$, the posterior of model $\mathcal{M}_1$, given y_t and the empirical model $\mathcal{M}_3$, is

$$g(\mathcal{M}_1 \mid y_t, \mathcal{M}_3) \propto g(\mathcal{M}_1 \mid \mathcal{M}_3) \int f(\mathfrak{S}_{\infty,1} \mid \mathcal{M}_1) g(\mathfrak{S}_{\infty,1} \mid y_t, \mathcal{M}_3)\, d\mathfrak{S}_{\infty,1}. \tag{7.19}$$

Equation (7.19) implies that a posterior odds ratio (see chapter 9) for the two models is

$$\frac{g(\mathcal{M}_1 \mid y_t, \mathcal{M}_3)}{g(\mathcal{M}_2 \mid y_t, \mathcal{M}_3)} = \frac{g(\mathcal{M}_1 \mid \mathcal{M}_3) \int f(\mathfrak{S}_{\infty,1} \mid \mathcal{M}_1) g(\mathfrak{S}_{\infty,1} \mid y_t, \mathcal{M}_3)\, d\mathfrak{S}_{\infty,1}}{g(\mathcal{M}_2 \mid \mathcal{M}_3) \int f(\mathfrak{S}_{\infty,2} \mid \mathcal{M}_2) g(\mathfrak{S}_{\infty,2} \mid y_t, \mathcal{M}_3)\, d\mathfrak{S}_{\infty,2}}. \tag{7.20}$$

Equations (7.19), (7.20) show two important facts. First, the posterior distribution of a model is proportional to the product of the density of the model for $\mathfrak{S}_\infty$, and its posterior obtained by using the empirical model $\mathcal{M}_3$ and the data y_t, with a factor of proportionality depending on the prior of the model. Second, the posterior odds of model $\mathcal{M}_1$ relative to model $\mathcal{M}_2$ depend on the degree of overlap of $f(\mathfrak{S}_\infty \mid \cdot)$ with the posterior distribution of $\mathfrak{S}_\infty$, given $\mathcal{M}_3$. Hence, $\mathcal{M}_1$ is preferable to $\mathcal{M}_2$ if the overlap of the distribution of $\mathfrak{S}_\infty$ produced by $\mathcal{M}_1$ with its posterior distribution computed by using $\mathcal{M}_3$ is higher than the overlap of the distribution of $\mathfrak{S}_\infty$ produced by $\mathcal{M}_2$ with its posterior computed by using $\mathcal{M}_3$. The term $g(\mathcal{M}_1 \mid \mathcal{M}_3)/g(\mathcal{M}_2 \mid \mathcal{M}_3)$ represents the prior odds of the two models, given $\mathcal{M}_3$. Since y_t could be a vector, (7.20) extends the univariate criteria of DeJong et al. (1996) and provides the statistical foundations of the approach described in example 7.15.

The computation of (7.20) is straightforward. $f(\mathfrak{S}_\infty)$ can be obtained for each $\mathcal{M}_i$, $i = 1, 2$, by averaging $\mathfrak{S}_\infty$ over draws of θ_i, given a draw of ϵ_t, while $g(\mathfrak{S}_{\infty,1} \mid y_{1t}, \mathcal{M}_3)$ can be obtained with the techniques described in chapter 9.

Exercise 7.24. Continuing with the economy studied in exercise 7.22, consider two versions of the model: one where dividends follow a two-state Markov chain and one where dividends follow a three-state Markov chain.

(i) Estimate a bivariate VAR for the U.S. equity premium and the U.S. real risk-free rate. Produce 100 draws from a normal-Wishart posterior distribution for the VAR coefficients (i.e., draw from a Wishart for Σ^{-1} and, conditional on this draw, draw VAR coefficients from a normal with mean equal to the OLS estimates and variance given by the draw of Σ).

(ii) Assume $\mathrm{gy}_1 = 0.9873, \mathrm{gy}_2 = 1.0177, p_1 = 0.2, p_2 = 0.8, \rho_y = 0.8$, and let $\ln(\beta/(1-\beta)) \sim \mathbb{N}(3.476, 1.418^2), \varphi \sim \mathbb{N}(0.4055, 1.3077^2)$. Also, assume that the growth rate of dividends in the third state is $\ln(\mathrm{gy}_3/(1-\mathrm{gy}_3)) \sim \mathbb{N}(0.036, 1.185^2)$. Draw 100 values for the parameters from these distributions and compute the equity premium and the risk-free rate generated by the two models for each draw.

(iii) Graphically examine the degree of overlap between the cloud of points generated by the two models and the cloud of points generated by the VAR.

(iv) Compute the posterior odds ratio (7.20) for the two models assuming that $g(\mathcal{M}_1 \mid \mathcal{M}_3)/g(\mathcal{M}_2 \mid \mathcal{M}_3) = 1$.

(v) Construct 68% posterior contour probabilities for $\mathfrak{S} = (E(\mathrm{EP}_t), E(R_t))$ given the data. Provide a probabilistic assessment of the validity of the two models by counting the number of replications generating equity premium and the risk-free rate within this contour.

It is important to note that the procedure we have described is conditional on $\mathcal{M}_3$, the empirical model bridging population moments and the data. Since under regularity conditions VARs can accurately represent economic data, they can be used to create this link. The procedure, however, is general: one could use more structural or more time series oriented specifications and could even employ "poor" models (as far as fit to the data is concerned), as long as the posterior of $\mathfrak{S}_\infty$ is easy to compute.

7.5 The Sensitivity of the Measurement

Once the quality of a model is assessed and some confidence has been placed in its approximation to the data, the measurement or the policy exercises one wants to perform can then be undertaken. In the simplest setup, the outcome of an experiment is a number (see, for example, Cooley and Hansen 1989), and, if one is interested in examining the sensitivity of the results to small variations in the neighborhood of calibrated values, local sensitivity analysis can be undertaken either informally, replicating the experiments for various parameter values, or formally, calculating the elasticity of measurement with respect to variations in some of the components of θ (as in Pagan and Shannon 1985).

When some uncertainty is allowed for in the simulations, the outcome of the experiment is the realization of a random variable. Hence, one may be interested in assessing where the realization lies relative to the range of possible outcomes of the model. Some of the techniques outlined in section 7.4 can be used for this purpose. For example, one could construct simulated standard errors or confidence intervals, drawing vectors of parameters (and/or the stochastic processes for the exogenous variables) from some distribution (*a priori*, empirical, or sampling based). In this case, the analysis is global in the sense that we analyze the sensitivity of the measurement to perturbations of the parameters over the entire range. Note that, in the approaches of Canova (1994), DeJong et al. (1996, 2000), and Geweke (1999), the evaluation procedure automatically and efficiently provides sensitivity analysis to global perturbations for the parameters within a reasonable economic range.

Besides simulation techniques, there are two alternative ways to assess the sensitivity of the measurement to parameter choices. These approaches, initially suggested by Abdelkhalek and Dufour (1998) for CGE economies, can be easily adapted to DSGE models. The first method is based on asymptotic expansions and formalizes Pagan and Shannon's (1985) local derivative approach.

Exercise 7.25. Suppose $\sqrt{T}(\theta_T - \theta) \xrightarrow{\text{D}} \mathbb{N}(0, \Sigma_\theta)$, where $\det(\Sigma_\theta) \neq 0$.

(i) Show that, if $h(\theta)$ is an $m \times 1$ vector of continuous and differentiable functions of θ, $\sqrt{T}(h(\theta_T) - h(\theta)) \xrightarrow{\text{D}} \mathbb{N}(0, \Sigma_h)$. Show the form of Σ_h.

(ii) Show that, if $\text{rank}(H(\theta)) = m$, $T[h(\theta_T) - h(\theta)]'\Sigma_h^{-1}[h(\theta_T) - h(\theta)] \xrightarrow{\text{D}} \chi^2(m)$. Conclude that an asymptotic confidence set for $h(\theta)$ at the level of $(1-\varrho)$ is $\text{CI}_h(\theta) = \{h(\theta) : T[h(\theta_T) - h(\theta)]'\Sigma_h^{-1}[h(\theta_T) - h(\theta)] \leqslant \chi^2_\varrho(m)\}$ and that $P[h(\theta) \in \text{CI}_h(\theta)] = 1 - \varrho$.

Exercise 7.25 uses the asymptotic distribution of the parameters to construct confidence intervals for $h(\theta)$. Two drawbacks of this procedure are clear: first, we need to have an asymptotic distribution for the θ and, second, we need a model where the number of endogenous variables is equal to the dimension of θ. The second problem can be remedied by constructing rectangular (as opposed to ellipsoid) confidence sets for any $i = 1, \dots, m$. That is, whenever $\dim[h(\theta)] < m$, $\text{CI}_i(\theta) = \{h_i(\theta) : T[h_i(\theta_T) - h_i(\theta)]^2/\sigma_{ii} \leqslant \chi^2(1)\}$, where $\sigma_{ii} = \text{diag}(\Sigma_{h_{ii}})$ and $P[h_i(\theta) \in \text{CI}_i(\theta)] = 1 - \varrho_i$ and a simultaneous confidence set not smaller than $1 - \varrho$ is obtained by choosing $\sum_i \varrho_i = \varrho$ (e.g., $\varrho_i = \varrho/m$).

The second method does not employ asymptotic properties and only assumes that a set Θ with $P(\theta \in \Theta) \geqslant 1 - \varrho$ is available. This could be a prior or a posterior estimate if θ is random or a classical small-sample confidence interval if Θ is random. Let $h(\Theta) = \{h(\theta_0) \in R^m$ for at least some $\theta_0 \in \Theta\}$. Then $\theta \in \Theta$ implies that $h(\theta) \in h(\Theta)$ and $P[h(\theta) \in h(\Theta)] \geqslant P(\theta \in \Theta) = 1 - \varrho$. When h is nonlinear, direct computation of $P[h(\theta)]$ is difficult. If we let $h_i(\Theta) = \{h_i(\theta_0) \in R^m$ for at least some $\theta_0 \in \Theta\}$, we can alternatively construct $P[h_i(\theta) \in h_i(\Theta),\ i = 1, \dots, m] \geqslant 1 - \varrho$ and $P[h_i(\theta) \in h_i(\Theta)] \geqslant 1 - \varrho$, $i = 1, \dots, m$. The first is a simultaneous rectangular confidence set, the second a marginal rectangular confidence set. The next result establishes that these sets are intervals under general conditions.

Result 7.1. If h is continuous and Θ compact and connected, then each $h_i(\Theta)$ is compact and connected and $h_i(\Theta) = [h_i^{\text{lo}}(\Theta), h_i^{\text{up}}(\Theta)]$, $i = 1, 2, \dots,$ where $h_i^{\text{lo}} > -\infty$, $h_i^{\text{up}} < \infty$. (A set is connected if it is impossible to find two subsets $O_1, O_2 \in R^m$ meeting O_3 such that $O_3 \subseteq O_1 \cup O_2$ and $O_3 \cap O_1 \cap O_2 = \emptyset$.)

To find the upper and lower limits of the interval, one can use the following algorithm.

Algorithm 7.5.

(1) Construct $\Theta = \{\theta_0 \in R^m : (\theta - \theta_0)'\Sigma_\theta^{-1}(\theta - \theta_0) \leqslant \mathfrak{C}(\theta)\}$, where $\Sigma_\theta = \text{var}(\theta)$ and $\mathfrak{C}$ is a function of θ.

(2) Set $\mathfrak{S}(\theta) = h_i(\theta_0) + \frac{1}{2}\lambda[(\theta - \theta_0)'\Sigma_\theta(\theta - \theta_0) - \mathfrak{C}(\theta)]$. Find the minimum and the maximum of this expression.

(3) Set $\theta^{\text{up}} = \operatorname{argmax} \mathfrak{S}(\theta)$ and $\theta^{\text{lo}} = \operatorname{argmin} \mathfrak{S}(\theta)$.

Note that the algorithm can be applied one dimension at a time, using rectangular intervals instead of an ellipsoid.

It is easy to verify that the first-order conditions in (2) are $\partial h_i/\partial\theta_0 - \lambda\Sigma_\theta(\theta - \theta_0) = 0$ and $(\theta - \theta_0)'\Sigma_\theta(\theta - \theta_0) - \mathfrak{C}(\theta) = 0$. When Σ_θ is nonsingular, the θ_i producing $h_i^{\text{lo}}(\Theta)$ and $h_i^{\text{up}}(\Theta)$ are $\theta_i = \theta \pm [(\partial h_i/\partial\theta_0)'\Sigma_\theta^{-1}(\partial h_i/\partial\theta_0)/\mathfrak{C}(\theta)]^{-0.5}\Sigma_\theta^{-1} \times \partial h_i/\partial\theta_0$. Then $\text{CI}(\theta) = \{\theta \in R^m; (\theta - \theta_0)'\Sigma_\theta^{-1}(\theta - \theta_0)/m \leqslant F_\varrho\}$ is a confidence set for θ which contains 95% of the values. Note that we can knock out values which are inconsistent with theory or do not give solutions since $P(\theta \in \Theta) = P(\theta \in \Theta \cap \Theta_0) \geqslant 1 - \theta$, where Θ_0 is the set of admissible values of θ. Finally, $\partial h(\theta)/\partial\theta$ can be computed as $(h(\theta + \iota) - h(\theta - \iota))/2\iota$, $\iota > 0$ and small.

Example 7.19. Consider the economy described in example 2.8, where all goods are cash goods and suppose we want to calculate the welfare costs of inflation. Cooley and Hansen (1989) showed that, depending on the average growth rate of money $\bar{M}$, the compensating variation in consumption needed to bring back consumers to the optimum varies between 0.107 and 7.59 percentage points of GDP if the cash-in-advance binds for one quarter. Suppose that $\bar{M}$ is a random variable with mean 1.04 and standard deviation 0.01 (approximately the growth rate of M1 for the United States over the 1970–2000 period). If money growth is normally distributed, then, approximately, $h(\theta) \sim \mathbb{N}(0.21, 0.025)$. Hence, a 68% confidence interval for the percentage of consumption in terms of steady-state output needed to bring consumers back to their optimum is $(0.185, 0.235)$.

Exercise 7.26 (Gourinchas and Jeanne). Consider a number of small open RBC economies. Population is growing at the rate $\text{Pop}_t = \text{gp}\,\text{Pop}_{t-1}$, where $\text{gp} \geqslant 1$ is country specific. The utility for country i is $\sum_\tau \beta^\tau \text{Pop}_{t+\tau} c_{t+\tau}^{1-\varphi}/(1 - \varphi)$. Assume that $\text{GDP}_{it} = (\zeta_{it}N_{it})^\eta K_{it}^{1-\eta}$, where ζ_{it} is a technological disturbance such that $g_{\zeta_{it}} = \zeta_{it}/\zeta_{it-1}$ could be different across i in the short run but $\lim_{t\to\infty} g_{\zeta_{it}} = g_\zeta$ and $N_{it} = \text{Pop}_{it}$. Consider two situations: financial autarky and complete financial integration. In the former capital accumulation occurs domestically; in the latter countries can borrow at the world gross interest rate $R_t = c_t^\varphi/c_{t-1}^\varphi\beta$. Evaluate whether there are gains from financial integration assuming $g_\zeta = 1.012$, $\text{gp} = 1.0074$, $\beta = 0.96$, $\varphi = 2.0$, $\delta = 0.10$, $1 - \eta = 0.3$. Repeat the calculation assuming $1-\eta \sim \mathbb{U}[0.2, 0.4]$ (Hint: if $x \sim \mathbb{U}(a_1, a_2)$, $E(x) = 0.5(a_1 + a_2)$, $\mathrm{var}(x) = \frac{1}{12}(a_2 - a_1)^2$.)

7.6 Savings, Investments, and Tax Cuts: An Example

In this section we are interested in evaluating the effects of cuts in the income tax rate on investments and consumption in open economies. To study this issue we employ a two-country RBC economy with complete markets. Baxter and Crucini (1993) claim that such a model can account for several features of the data, including the high correlation of domestic savings and domestic investments in open economies, without imposing restrictions on capital flows, but use informal methods to reach this conclusion. For this reason, before undertaking the measurement of interest, we evaluate the quality of the model's approximation to the data by using the techniques presented in this chapter. We assume that there is a single consumption good and labor is immobile. For each country $i = 1, 2$ preferences are given by $E_0 \sum_{t=0}^{\infty}(\beta^t/(1-\varphi))[C_{it}^{\vartheta}(1-N_{it})^{(1-\vartheta)}]^{1-\varphi}$, where C_{it} is private consumption, $1 - N_{it}$ is leisure, β is the discount factor, $1 - \vartheta(1-\varphi)$ is the coefficient of relative risk aversion, and ϑ is the share of consumption in utility. Goods are produced according to $\mathrm{GDP}_{it} = \zeta_{it}(K_{it})^{1-\eta}(X_{it}N_{it})^{\eta}$, $i = 1, 2$, where K_t is the capital, η is the share of labor in GDP, and $X_{it} = gnX_{it-1}, \forall i$ and $gn \geqslant 1$, captures the deterministic labor-augmenting technological progress. We let

$$\begin{bmatrix} \ln \zeta_{1t} \\ \ln \zeta_{2t} \end{bmatrix} = \begin{bmatrix} \bar{\zeta}_1 \\ \bar{\zeta}_2 \end{bmatrix} + \begin{bmatrix} \rho_1 & \rho_2 \\ \rho_2 & \rho_1 \end{bmatrix} \begin{bmatrix} \ln \zeta_{1t-1} \\ \ln \zeta_{2t-1} \end{bmatrix} + \begin{bmatrix} \epsilon_{1t} \\ \epsilon_{2t} \end{bmatrix},$$

where

$$\epsilon_t = [\epsilon_{1t}\ \epsilon_{2t}]' \sim \mathbb{N}\left(0, \begin{bmatrix} \sigma_\epsilon^2 & \sigma_{12} \\ \sigma_{12} & \sigma_\epsilon^2 \end{bmatrix}\right)$$

and $[\bar{\zeta}_1, \bar{\zeta}_2]'$ is a vector of constants. Here σ_{12} controls the contemporaneous and ρ_2 the lagged spillovers of the shocks. Capital goods are accumulated according to $K_{it+1} = (1-\delta_i)K_{it} + \frac{1}{2}b(K_{it+1}/K_{it} - 1)^2 K_{it}$, $i = 1, 2$, where b is a parameter. Government expenditure is deterministic and financed with income taxes T_i^y and lump sum transfers T_{it}, $G_i = T_{it} + T_i^y \mathrm{GDP}_{it}$. Finally, the resource constraint is

$$\begin{aligned} &\Psi(\mathrm{GDP}_{1t} - G_{1t} - C_{1t} - K_{1t+1} + K_{it}) \\ &\qquad + (1-\Psi)(\mathrm{GDP}_{2t} - G_{2t} - C_{2t} - K_{2t+1} + K_{it}) \geqslant 0, \qquad (7.21) \end{aligned}$$

where Ψ is the fraction of world population living in country 1. We first scale all variables by the labor-augmenting technological progress, e.g., $\mathrm{gdp}_{it} = \mathrm{GDP}_{it}/X_{it}$, $c_{it} = C_{it}/X_{it}$, etc., and solve the model by log-linearizing the optimality conditions around the steady state. The weights in the social planner problem are proportional to the number of individuals in each of the countries. Actual savings are computed as $\mathrm{Sa}_t = \mathrm{GDP}_t - C_t - G_t$. Data refer to the period 1970:1–1993:3 for the United States and for Europe; it is seasonally adjusted in real terms and from OECD Main

Table 7.4. Parameter selection.

Parameter	Basic	Empirical density	Subjective density
Share of consumption (ϑ)	0.5	$\mathbb{U}[0.3, 0.7]$	$\mathbb{N}(0.5, 0.02)$
Steady-state hours (N^{ss})	0.20	$\mathbb{U}[0.2, 0.35]$	$\mathbb{N}(0.2, 0.02)$
Discount factor (β)	0.9875	$\mathbb{N}[0.9855, 1.002]$[a]	$\mathbb{N}(0.9875, 0.01)$
Utility power (φ)	2.00	$\chi^2(2)[0, 10]$[a]	$\mathbb{N}(2, 1)$
Share of labor in output (η)	0.58	$\mathbb{U}[0.50, 0.75]$	$\mathbb{N}(0.58, 0.05)$
Growth rate (gn)	1.004	$\mathbb{N}(1.004, 0.001)$	1.004
Depreciation rate of capital (δ)	0.025	$\mathbb{U}[0.02, 0.03]$	$\mathbb{N}(0.025, 0.01)$
Persistence of disturbances (ρ_1)	0.93	$\mathbb{N}(0.93, 0.02)$	$\mathbb{N}(0.93, 0.025)$
Lagged spillover (ρ_2)	0.05	$\mathbb{N}(0.05, 0.03)$	$\mathbb{N}(0.05, 0.02)$
Standard deviation of technology innovations (σ_ϵ)	0.008 52	$\chi^2(1)[0, 0.0202]$[a]	$\mathbb{N}(0.008\,52, 0.004)$
Contemporaneous spillover (σ_{12})	0.40	$\mathbb{N}(0.35, 0.03)$	$\mathbb{N}(0.4, 0.02)$
Country size (Ψ)	0.50	$\mathbb{U}[0.10, 0.50]$	0.5
Adjustment cost to capital (b)	1.0	1.0	1.0
Tax rate (T^y)	0.0	0.0	0.0

[a]Truncated with the range in brackets.

Economic Indicators. The properties of actual savings and investments are computed by eliminating from the raw time series a linear time trend. The parameters of the model are $\theta = [\beta, \varphi, \vartheta, gn, \delta, \rho_1, \rho_2, \sigma_\epsilon, \sigma_{12}, \Psi, b, T^y]$ plus steady-state hours.

The exogenous processes are the two productivity disturbances $[\ln \zeta_{1t}, \ln \zeta_{2t}]'$. We generate samples of 95 observations to match the actual data and the number of replications is 500. We evaluate the quality of the model by using the diagonal elements of the 4×4 spectral density matrix of the data (savings and investments for the two countries) and the coherence between savings and investments in the two countries. Spectral density estimates are computed by smoothing periodogram ordinates with a flat window. In the benchmark parametrization the θ vector is the same as in Baxter and Crucini (1993) (see the first column of table 7.4) except for σ_ϵ, which we take from Backus et al. (1995), and ϑ, which does not appear in their specification. We also allow for parameter uncertainty by using the approaches of Canova (1994) and of DeJong et al. (1996). In the first case empirical-based distributions are constructed by using existing estimates or, when there are none, choosing *a priori* an interval and assuming a uniform distribution. In the second case distributions are normal, with means equal to the calibrated parameters and dispersions *a priori* chosen. The distributions are displayed in the second and third columns of table 7.4. A comparison of the model and the data at business cycle frequencies (3–8 years) is in table 7.5. The first two rows report the average spectral densities and coherences at business cycle frequencies for actual and simulated data when parameters are fixed. The next two rows report Watson's average measure of fit at business cycle frequencies. The first is obtained by minimizing the variance of

Table 7.5. The fit of the model.

	U.S. spectra		European spectra		U.S. coherence	European coherence
	Sa	Inv	Sa	Inv	Sa–Inv	Sa–Inv
Actual data	0.75	0.88	0.68	0.49	85.41	93.14
Simulated data	0.36	0.18	0.35	0.18	94.04	93.00
			Watson			
Identification 1	0.02	0.05	0.20	0.23	0.04	0.13
Identification 2	0.24	0.21	0.05	0.04	0.20	0.15
			Covering			
Fixed parameters	46.46	8.63	55.71	43.57	98.99	92.91
Subjective density	35.30	23.40	32.89	37.00	98.17	90.34
Empirical density	19.63	18.60	21.11	20.20	94.71	95.69
			Critical value			
Fixed parameters	90.80	99.89	82.16	93.91	15.60	49.04
Subjective density	71.80	89.90	66.00	76.60	19.80	51.89
Empirical density	62.50	79.70	73.30	74.60	33.46	29.60
			Error			
Fixed parameters	0.25	0.55	0.30	0.28	−9.17	0.37
Subjective density	0.19	0.56	0.29	0.28	−9.01	0.81
Normal density	0.13	0.58	0.42	0.35	−6.07	−2.86

saving and investment in country 1 and the second by minimizing the variance of saving and investment in country 2.

National saving is highly correlated with domestic investment in both areas and the average coherence at business cycle frequencies is higher for Europe than for the United States. The variability of both U.S. series is higher and U.S. investment is almost twice as volatile as European investment. Because the model is symmetric, the variability of simulated data is similar in the two countries, but low relative to the data. However, consistent with the data the variability of national savings is higher than that for domestic investment. Consistent with Baxter and Crucini's claim, the model produces high national saving and investment correlations at business cycle frequencies for the United States. The model coherences are even higher than those in the actual data. Watson's measures suggest that, on average, the size of the error at business cycle frequencies is between 2% and 5% of the spectral density of those variables whose variance is minimized and between 20% and 25% of the spectral density of other variables. Changes in the coherences across identifications are somewhat relevant and the model fits them better when we minimize the variance of U.S. variables.

The next three rows ("Covering") report how many times on average, at business cycle frequencies, the diagonal elements of the spectral density matrix and the coherences of model-generated data lie within a 95% confidence band for the corresponding statistics of actual data. Clearly, a number close to 95% indicates a "good" model performance. We compute 95% confidence bands for the actual data in two ways: using asymptotic theory and using a version of the parametric bootstrap procedure of Diebold et al. (1998). In this latter case, we run a four-variable VAR with six lags and a constant, construct replications for saving and investment for the two countries, bootstrapping the residuals of the VAR model, estimate the spectral density matrix of the data for each replication, and extract 95% confidence bands, frequency by frequency. Replications for the time series generated by the model are constructed by using Monte Carlo techniques in three different ways: keeping the parameters fixed at the values displayed in the first column of table 7.4 or randomizing them by using draws from the distributions listed in the second and third columns of table 7.4. Since results are similar we only report probability coverings using an asymptotic 95% band. This third set of statistics confirms that the model matches coherences better than volatilities at business cycle frequencies and that the covering properties of the model do not improve when parameter uncertainty is allowed.

Under the heading "Critical value" we report the percentile of the simulated distribution of the spectral density matrix of saving and investment in the two countries where the value of the spectral density matrix of the actual data (taken here to be estimated without an error) lies, on average, at business cycle frequencies. Values close to 0% (100%) show poor fit — the actual spectral density matrix is in the tail of the distribution of the spectral density matrix of simulated data — while values close to 50% should be considered good. We also report here a case with fixed parameters and two with random parameters.

With fixed parameters the model generates average coherences which are much higher than in U.S. data but close to the median for Europe (actual values are in the 15th and 50th percentiles). With random parameters (and empirical-based priors), the situation improves for the United States but not for Europe. Also, with fixed parameters the model generates a distribution for variability which is skewed to the left and only partly overlaps a normal asymptotic range of variabilities for the data. Parameter uncertainty, by tilting and stretching the shape of the simulated distribution, ameliorates the situation.

Finally, we compute the distribution of the error needed to match the spectral density matrix of the actual data, given the model's simulated spectral density matrix. To do this, at each replication we draw parameters and innovations from the posterior distribution of the VAR representation of the actual data, construct time series of interest, and estimate the spectral density matrix of the four series. At each replication, we also draw parameters and innovations from the distributions presented

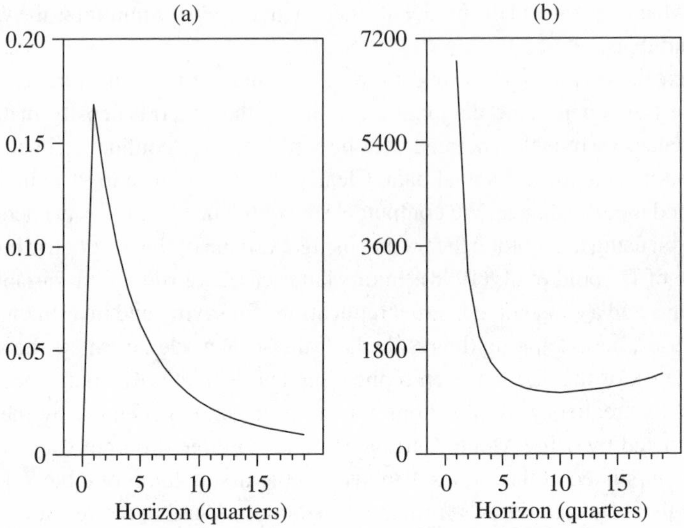

Figure 7.4. Effects of tax cuts: (a) investment differences; (b) utility differences.

in table 7.4, construct the spectral density matrix of simulated data, and compute $\mathcal{S}_v^l(\omega) = \mathcal{S}_y^l(\omega) - \mathcal{S}_x^l(\omega)$ at each $l = 1, \dots, L$. If the model replicates the DGP, the distribution for this error would be degenerate at each frequency. Otherwise, features of this distribution (median value, skewness, kurtosis, etc.) may help us to pinpoint what is missing from the model. The last three rows in table 7.5 ("Error") present the median (across replications) of the average error at business cycle frequencies for the six statistics. The first row reports results when parameters are fixed and the next two when parameters are random. The results are similar in the three cases: the model fails to generate enough variability at business cycle frequencies for U.S. investments while for the other three variables the error is smaller. The results for coherences depend on the country. For the United States, the model generates systematically higher coherences (negative spectral errors) while for Europe the opposite is true.

In conclusion, in agreement with Baxter and Crucini (1993), the model generates high coherence between national saving and investment at business cycle frequencies. Its magnitude is similar to the one observed in European data, but uniformly higher than the one observed in U.S. data, regardless of whether parameters are fixed or random. However, the model has a hard time accounting for the variability of saving and investment in both countries at business cycle frequencies.

To measure the effects of tax cuts we perform two simulations: one with a tax rate of 0.20 and one with a tax rate of 0.0, using the parameters listed in the first column of table 7.4, and ask how large the difference in investment responses along the adjustment path is when a positive productivity shock hits the domestic economy. Figure 7.4 graphically reports this difference in percentage terms: investment response is significantly larger without taxes in the first few periods but the gains dissipate reasonably fast. The utility differences induced by these two paths are also significant, but level off after about five periods. In fact, the compensating variation in consumption needed to restore the utility level obtained with no taxes is 0.11 in each period, about 14% of steady-state consumption. The magnitude of this number is robust. For example, the lower bound to the level of compensating variations obtained for $\vartheta \in [0.3, 0.7]$ and $\varphi \in [1, 4]$ is 0.09 in each period.

8
Dynamic Macro Panels

Panels of macroeconomic time series are used in many fields. For example, in studying the transmission of shocks, one may want to have a cross-country point of view. Similarly, when examining convergence of income per capita of nations or regions, one would like to account for both cross-sectional and time series interactions.

The models we consider in this chapter borrow from the microeconomic literature in the sense that the specifications employed do not allow for lagged interdependencies across units. This is an important shortcoming: since interdependencies are the results of world market integration they can hardly be neglected in applied macroeconomic analysis. In chapter 10 we study how to introduce them using a Bayesian point of view. The setup we describe is different from the standard treatments of panel data since models are explicitly dynamic, either because of the presence of lagged dependent variables or exogenous variables. For a comprehensive account of existing approaches with static models, see Hsiao (1989), Baltagi (1995), or Hayashi (2002). For most of this chapter, we consider models which are stationary or display time-invariant structures. Again, we alter this setup in chapter 10, where panel VAR models with time-varying coefficients are considered.

The econometric theory developed in the context of micro panels is somewhat inappropriate for macro applications. Estimators are typically constructed for data featuring a small time series (T) and large cross section (n). Therefore, the properties of estimators are derived by exploiting asymptotics in the cross section. In macro panels, typically, neither n nor T is large and, often, $T > n$. This should be kept in mind when deciding which estimator to use and the inference one is allowed to make. Another crucial problem in macro data is dynamic heterogeneity. In micro panels, even when the model is dynamic, no slope heterogeneity is allowed for and unit-specific characteristics are mostly captured with a time-invariant fixed or random effect. In macro panels this restriction is, in general, inappropriate: heterogeneous dynamics reflect policies or regulations and one wants to be able to evaluate differences, if they emerge.

We start in section 8.1 with an example to motivate our interest in dynamic panel analysis. In section 8.2 we consider panel (VAR) models with no slope heterogeneities and unit-specific intercepts; we describe how to estimate them by using instrumental variables; we illustrate the problems that traditional fixed and random-effect estimators encounter in this specification; we examine how to construct estimates of the unit-specific (time-invariant) effect; and, finally, we study how to test interesting hypotheses. In section 8.3 we introduce slope heterogeneities, describe a series of estimators for this type of model, study their properties, and propose a test to detect slope heterogeneities. In section 8.4 we describe approaches to pooling cross-sectional information and examine the pros and cons of such approaches. In many situations, in fact, single unit (time series) estimates can be improved upon by pooling cross-sectional information, even when no interdependencies are allowed for. Finally, in section 8.5 we use the methods presented in this chapter to examine whether or not money is superneutral in the cross section of G7 countries.

8.1 From Economic Theory to Dynamic Panels

To motivate our interest in dynamic panels for macroeconomic analysis we consider the problem of modeling growth in open economies. Barro et al. (1995) presented an extension of the standard Solow model which has interesting insights from a theoretical point of view and important empirical implications.

We have a set of countries, indexed by i, which are small, in the sense that they take the world interest rate as given, and accumulate two types of capital: human and physical. The representative agent in country i maximizes $\sum_t \beta^t c_{it}^{1-\varphi}/(1-\varphi)$ subject to the constraint

$$\begin{aligned} &c_{it} + K_{it+1} + \mathrm{hk}_{it+1} + \mathrm{sa}_{it+1} \\ &\qquad \leqslant \zeta_t^{\eta_i} K_{it}^{\eta_k} \mathrm{hk}_{it}^{\eta_{\mathrm{hk}}} + (1-\delta_k)K_{it} + (1-\delta_{\mathrm{hk}})\mathrm{hk}_{it} + (1+r_t)\mathrm{sa}_{it}, \end{aligned} \tag{8.1}$$

where K_{it} is physical capital, hk_{it} is human capital, sa_{it} is lending to (borrowing from) the rest of the world, and $1+r_t$ is the gross world real rate; ζ_t represents total factor productivity and its efficiency, measured by η_i, may differ across i. We assume that each country i has limited borrowing capacity. In particular, $-\mathrm{sa}_{it} \leqslant K_{it}$, while hk_{it} cannot be used as collateral in international borrowing. When the constraint is binding, capital and borrowing are perfect substitutes in the portfolio of agents and $1 + r_t = (1-\delta_k) + \eta_k \mathrm{GDP}_{it}/K_{it}$, which implies that

$$K_{it} = [(1+r_t) - (1-\delta_k)]^{-1}\eta_k \mathrm{GDP}_{it}. \tag{8.2}$$

Using (8.2) in the production function we have $\mathrm{GDP}_{it} = \zeta_{it}^{\dagger}\mathrm{hk}_{it}^{\eta_1}$, where $\eta_1 = \eta_{\mathrm{hk}}/(1-\eta_k)$ and $\zeta_{it}^{\dagger} = \{\zeta_t^{\eta_i}\eta_k^{\eta_k}/[(1+r_t)-(1-\delta_k)]^{\eta_k}\}^{1/(1-\eta_k)}$. Maximizing utility with respect to $(c_{it}, \mathrm{hk}_{it})$ and using (8.2) in the resource constraint yields the following two equilibrium conditions:

$$\mathrm{hk}_{it+1} = (1-\eta_k)\zeta_{it}^{\dagger}\mathrm{hk}_{it}^{\eta_1} + (1-\delta_{\mathrm{hk}})\mathrm{hk}_{it} - c_{it}, \tag{8.3}$$

$$c_{it}^{-\varphi} = \beta E_t\{c_{it+1}^{-\varphi}[\eta_{\mathrm{hk}}\zeta_{it+1}^{\dagger}\mathrm{hk}_{it+1}^{\eta_1-1} + (1-\delta_{\mathrm{hk}})]\}. \tag{8.4}$$

Exercise 8.1. Verify that, in the steady states, $c_i^{\mathrm{ss}} = (1-\eta_k)\zeta_i^{\dagger}(\mathrm{hk}_i^{\mathrm{ss}})^{\eta_1} - \delta_{kh}\mathrm{hk}_i^{\mathrm{ss}}$ and $\mathrm{hk}_i^{\mathrm{ss}} = [(1-\beta(1-\delta_{kh}))/\beta\eta_{\mathrm{hk}}\zeta_i^{\dagger}]^{(1-\eta_{\mathrm{hk}})/(\eta_{\mathrm{hk}}-1+\eta_k)}$. Show that steady states are different if $\eta_i \neq \eta_{i'}, i \neq i'$.

Verify that, by setting $\psi_{i1} = (1-\eta_k)\eta_1\zeta_i^\dagger(\mathrm{GDP}_i/\mathrm{hk}_i)^{\mathrm{ss}} + (1-\delta_{\mathrm{hk}})$, $\psi_{i2} = \eta_{\mathrm{hk}}(\eta_1-1)\zeta_i^\dagger(\mathrm{hk}_i^{\mathrm{ss}})^{\eta_1-1}/[\eta_{\mathrm{hk}}\zeta_i^\dagger(\mathrm{hk}_i^{\mathrm{ss}})^{\eta_1-1} + (1-\delta_{\mathrm{hk}})]$, $\psi_{i3} = \eta_{\mathrm{hk}}\zeta_i^\dagger(\mathrm{hk}_i^{\mathrm{ss}})^{\eta_1-1}/[\eta_{\mathrm{hk}}\zeta_i^\dagger(\mathrm{hk}_i^{\mathrm{ss}})^{\eta_1-1} + (1-\delta_{\mathrm{hk}})]$, and log-linearizing (8.3) and (8.4), we have (in percentage deviations from the steady states)

$$\widehat{\mathrm{hk}}_{it+1} = \psi_{i1}\widehat{\mathrm{hk}}_{it} + (1-\eta_k)\frac{\mathrm{GDP}_i^{\mathrm{ss}}}{\mathrm{hk}_i^{\mathrm{ss}}}\hat{\zeta}_{it}^\dagger - \frac{c_i^{\mathrm{ss}}}{\mathrm{hk}_i^{\mathrm{ss}}}\hat{c}_{it}, \tag{8.5}$$

$$-\varphi\hat{c}_{it} = -\varphi E_t\hat{c}_{it+1} + \psi_{i2}E_t\widehat{\mathrm{hk}}_{it+1} + \psi_{i3}E_t\hat{\zeta}_{it+1}^\dagger. \tag{8.6}$$

Letting $\hat{y}_{1t} = [\hat{c}_{it}, \hat{hk}_{it}]$ and adding an expectational error to equation (8.6) to capture differences between actual and expected values of $\hat{c}_{it+1}$, $\hat{\zeta}_{it+1}^\dagger$, and $\widehat{\mathrm{hk}}_{it+1}$, we can rewrite (8.5), (8.6) as a vector of first-order difference equations for each i of the form $\mathcal{A}_{i0}\hat{y}_{it+1} = \mathcal{A}_{i1}\hat{y}_{it} + \mathcal{A}_{i2}\hat{e}_{it}$, where $\hat{e}_{it}$ is a function of $\hat{\zeta}_{it}^\dagger$ and of the expectational error $\hat{v}_{it}$. Letting $\bar{y}_i, \bar{e}_i$ be the steady-state values of y_i and e_i, we have

$$\mathcal{A}_{i0}y_{it+1} = \mathcal{A}_{i1}y_{it} + \varrho_i + \epsilon_{it}, \tag{8.7}$$

where $\varrho_i = (\mathcal{A}_{i0} - \mathcal{A}_{i1} - \mathcal{A}_{i2})\bar{y}_i$, $\epsilon_{it} = (\mathcal{A}_{i2}\bar{y}_i/\bar{e}_i)e_i$.

Equation (8.7) is a bivariate VAR(1) model for each i, with unit-specific fixed effects and heterogeneous dynamics. Note that, by construction, there is no interaction across units. This is entirely due to the small open economy assumption. For example, if a world budget constraint is added to the problem, important interactions across units would emerge. Hence, the panel VAR models with interdependencies considered in chapter 10 can be originated, for example, from a two-country model with an international market for borrowing and lending.

The model implies that, in general, whenever the steady states are different across units, the dynamics leading to the steady state will also be different. Therefore, models of this type deliver the framework examined in section 8.3. There are two special cases of equation (8.7) which are of interest. The first obtains when dynamics are homogeneous and there are unit-specific fixed effects. In the model we have used, this is possible if and only if β is different across units (it is the only parameter which appears in the steady state but not in the dynamics) and if $\eta_i = \eta_i'$, i.e., if the total factor productivity (TFP) has the same efficiency across units. Such a framework will be dealt with in section 8.2. A second special case emerges when fixed effects are absent and the dynamics are heterogeneous. This occurs only when expectations are different, i.e., when $E_t\zeta_{it+1}^\dagger$ differs across i.

Exercise 8.2. Consider a basic RBC model and suppose that government expenditure provides utility to the agents and that private and public consumption are substitutes in the utility function. Assume that the instantaneous utility function of the representative agent of country i is $u(c_{it}, G_{it}, N_{it}) = (c_{it} + \vartheta_g G_{it})^{\vartheta}(1-N_{it})^{1-\vartheta}$, that the budget constraint is $c_{it} + K_{it+1} + G_{it} = \zeta_t^{\eta_i}K_{it}^{1-\eta}N_{it}^{\eta} + (1-\delta_k)K_{it}$, that $G_{it} = G_t + a_{ig}\zeta_t$, and that expenditure is financed by lump sum taxation on a period-by-period basis, where G_t is an i.i.d. process and a_{ig} a parameter which regulates the response of country i's expenditure to the state of the technology.

(i) Derive the Euler equation for the problem for each i and log-linearize it.

(ii) Under what conditions would the vector of log-linearized Euler equations produce a panel with homogeneous dynamics and a country-specific intercept or a panel with heterogeneous dynamics and no fixed effects?

8.2 Panels with Homogeneous Dynamics

The model we consider in this section has the form

$$y_{it} = A_{0t} + \sum_{j=1}^{q_1} A_{1jt} y_{it-j} + \sum_{j=1}^{q_2} A_{2jt} x_{it-j} + A_{3t} \varrho_i + e_{it}, \qquad (8.8)$$

where e_{it} is a martingale difference with covariance matrix Σ_i, y_{it} is an $m_1 \times 1$ vector, $i = 1, \dots, n$, $t = 1, \dots, T$, x_{it} is an $m_2 \times 1$ vector of exogenous variables, ϱ_i is the (unobservable) unit-specific effect, and, for each j, A_{1jt} is an $m_1 \times m_1$ matrix, A_{2jt} an $m_1 \times m_2$ matrix, and A_{3t} an $m_1 \times m_3$ matrix.

In equation (8.8) lagged dependent and exogenous variables appear on the right-hand side and, in principle, time-varying coefficients are allowed for. Furthermore, heterogeneities are possible both in the level and in the variance. One important restriction, which will be relaxed later on, is that the dynamics are identical across units. Such a restriction allows us to construct estimators of the parameters by using cross-sectional information at each t and permits the use of standard asymptotic theory when testing hypotheses, even when y_{it} is nonstationary. We also assume that x_{it} includes, or may be composed entirely of, variables which are common across units. Note that we treat ϱ_i as a fixed effect. While in micro panels one has the choice between fixed and random effects, in macro data a fixed-effect specification is preferable for two reasons. First, if ϱ_i captures omitted variables, it is likely to be correlated with the regressors (a possibility typically excluded by a random-effect specification). Second, a macro panel in general contains all the units of interest and thus is less likely to be a random sample from a larger population (e.g., an OECD panel typically includes all the OECD countries). Since e_t is a martingale difference, $E(x_{it-\tau} e_{it}) = E(y_{it-\tau} e_{it}) = 0, \forall \tau < 0$, and $E(\varrho_i e_{it}) = 0, \forall i$.

Equation (8.8) is not estimable since ϱ_i is unobservable. In a static model, one eliminates this fixed effect by subtracting time averages from (8.8) and estimate the model in deviations from the average with OLS. In the next exercise we ask the reader to verify that estimates obtained from the transformed model are consistent in a static setup where ϱ_i are unobservable and could be correlated with other regressors.

Exercise 8.3. Consider the model $y_{it} = x_{it} A_2 + \varrho_i + e_{it}$, where $i = 1, \dots, n$, $t = 1, \dots, T$, $E(e_{it} \mid x_{it}) = 0$, $E(e_{it}^2 \mid x_t) = \sigma_e^2$, $E(e_{it}, e_{i'\tau}) = 0, \forall i \neq i'$, $\tau \neq t$; $E(\varrho_i \mid x_{it}) \neq 0$ and $E(e_{it} \mid \varrho_i) = 0$.

(i) Show that OLS estimates of the parameters are inconsistent.

(ii) Show that consistent estimates can be obtained by running the OLS regression $y_{it} - \bar{y}_i = (x_{it} - \bar{x}_i) A_2 + (e_{it} - \bar{e}_i)$, $\bar{y}_i = (1/T) \sum_t y_{it}$; $\bar{x}_i = (1/T) \sum_t x_{it}$;

$\bar{e}_i = (1/T)\sum_t e_{it}$. Show that coefficients which are constant for each i in every t cannot be estimated.

(iii) Assume that $E(e_{i,t} \mid x_{i,t}) \neq 0$. Derive a 2SLS estimator for the specifications in (i) and (ii) assuming that $E(e_{i,t} \mid z_{i,t}) = 0$, $E(x_{i,t} \mid z_{i,t}) \neq 0$, where $z_{i,t}$ is a set of instruments. Show that a 2SLS estimator is consistent in the original model but not necessarily so in the transformed one. (Hint: $E(\bar{e}_i \mid z_{it}) \neq 0$ even if $E(e_{it} \mid z_{i,t}) = 0$.)

Exercise 8.3 shows a peculiar result: OLS in the transformed model is consistent but 2SLS, in general, is not. To ensure consistency of a 2SLS estimator we need to strengthen the orthogonality condition to $E((e_{i,\tau} - \bar{e}_i) \mid z_{i,t}) = 0, \forall t, \tau$.

The case of ϱ_i correlated with regressors is common in macroeconomics. For example, suppose one is interested in studying the effects of money on inflation across countries. Clearly, the path of money supply may be related to country-specific characteristics (like the stance of fiscal policy), therefore making potential regressors correlated with ϱ_i.

Example 8.1 (growth and volatility). Theoretically, it is unclear what the sign of the relationship between growth and volatility should be: volatility could be a manifestation of the adoption of new technologies that induce cost restructuring and this could provide a positive link between the two. The relationship could also be negative as volatility can result in wasted human capital or deter investment. Letting the growth rate of value added be ΔGDP_{it}, the volatility of the growth rate of value added be x_{1it} and the growth rate of other regressors be x_{2it}, a typical model studied in the empirical literature is $\Delta\text{GDP}_{it} = A_0 + x_{1it}A_1 + x_{2it}A_2 + \varrho_i + e_{it}$. Since ϱ_i are unobservable, they are typically pooled together with e_{it} into an error term. Note that OLS cannot be used to estimate A_1 and A_2 if, for example, ϱ_i captures political factors, since, in units where instability is strong, volatility may be high and growth low so the residuals are negatively correlated with the regressors. Alternatively, if i refers to sectors and ϱ_i captures industry-specific technological breakthroughs, the residuals will be positively correlated with the regressors. Imbs (2002) presents estimates of the parameters obtained by using deviations from time means and the UNIDO database; x_{2it} measures competitiveness and is excluded from the first specification. The data refer to 15 OECD countries, covers the sample 1970–92 and has a maximum of 28 sectors for each country. Estimates are obtained when i represents a sector–country combination and shown in table 8.1.

The relationship between volatility and growth is statistically positive and economically significant. For example, in the first regression a 1% increase in volatility increases the average yearly sectorial output growth by 0.5%. Note also that competitiveness for the sector–country pairs is insignificant, once fixed effects are taken into account. Finally, the explanatory power of both regressions is small: volatility has only a marginal explanatory power for value-added growth.

Exercise 8.4. Consider the model $y_{it} = \bar{y} + \varrho_i + T_t + \alpha x_{it} + e_{it}$, $i = 1, \dots, n$, where T_t is a time effect and suppose $\sum_i \varrho_i = 0$, $\sum_t T_t = 0$. Suppose that you

Table 8.1. Growth and volatility.

Specification	A_1	A_2	A_0	R^2
1	4.893		0.121	0.02
	(2.63)		(3.68)	
2	5.007	−0.059	0.133	0.02
	(2.66)	(−0.39)	(2.94)	

estimate this model by using a dummy variable for each i and a time trend. Show that OLS estimates of (ϱ_i, α) are consistent if T is large. Show that estimates of ϱ_i are inconsistent for large n. Show that, for large n, it is better to assume that ϱ_i is a random variable with mean ϱ and variance σ_ϱ^2.

8.2.1 *Pitfalls of Standard Methods*

When lagged dependent variables are present and the time series dimension of the panel is small or fixed, taking deviations from the mean does not produce consistent estimates.

Example 8.2. We illustrate the problem existing in this case by using a version of equation (8.8) where $m_1 = 1$, $A_{0t} = x_{it} = 0, \forall t$, $A_{1jt} = A_{1j} < 1$, and $A_{1j} = 0$, $j \geqslant 2$, and $A_{3t} = 1, \forall t$. Hence, (8.8) reduces to an AR(1) model with unit-specific fixed effects. We assume y_{i0} fixed and $\text{var}(e_{it}) = \sigma^2$. A pooled estimator for A_1 is

$$A_{1\text{p}} = \frac{\sum_{i=1}^{n}\sum_{t=1}^{T}(y_{it} - \bar{y}_i)(y_{it-1} - \bar{y}_{i,-1})}{\sum_{i=1}^{n}\sum_{t=1}^{T}(y_{it-1} - \bar{y}_{i,-1})^2}$$
$$= A_1 + \frac{\sum_{i=1}^{n}\sum_{t=1}^{T}(e_{it} - \bar{e}_i)(y_{it-1} - \bar{y}_{i,-1})/nT}{\sum_{i=1}^{n}\sum_{t=1}^{T}(y_{it-1} - \bar{y}_{i,-1})^2/nT}, \qquad (8.9)$$

where $\bar{y}_{i,-1}$ is the mean of y_{it-1}. Repeatedly substituting into the model and summing over t, we have

$$\sum_t y_{it-1} = \frac{1 - A_1^T}{1 - A_1} y_{i0} + \frac{(T-1) - TA_1 + A_1^T}{(1 - A_1)^2}\varrho_i + \sum_{j=0}^{T-2} \frac{1 - A_1^{T-1-j}}{1 - A_1} e_{i,1+j}.$$

Since $E(\varrho_i e_{it}) = 0$,

$$p \lim_{n\to\infty} \frac{1}{nT}\sum_i\sum_t (e_{it} - \bar{e}_i)(y_{it-1} - \bar{y}_{i,-1}) = -p \lim_{n\to\infty} \frac{1}{n}\sum_i \bar{y}_{i,-1}\bar{e}_i$$
$$= -\frac{\sigma_e^2}{T^2}\frac{(T-1) - TA_1 + A_1^T}{(1 - A_1)^2}, \qquad (8.10)$$

Table 8.2. Bias in the AR(1) coefficient.

T	$A_1 = 0.2$	$A_1 = 0.5$	$A_1 = 0.8$	$A_1 = 0.95$
10	−0.1226	−0.1622	−0.2181	−0.2574
20	−0.0607	−0.0785	−0.1044	−0.1300
30	−0.0403	−0.0516	−0.0672	−0.0853
40	−0.0302	−0.0384	−0.0492	−0.0629

$$p \lim_{n\to\infty} \sum_i \sum_t (y_{it-1} - \bar{y}_{i,-1})^2 = \frac{\sigma_e^2}{1-A_1^2}\left(1 - \frac{1}{T} - \frac{2A_1}{(1-A_1)^2}\frac{(T-1) - TA_1 + A_1^T}{T^2}\right). \quad (8.11)$$

For consistency we need (8.10) to converge to zero and (8.11) to converge to a fixed number. As $T \to \infty$, (8.10) does indeed go to zero and (8.11) goes to $\sigma_e^2/(1-A_1^2)$. However, if T is fixed, (8.10) does not go to zero, even when $n \to \infty$.

Exercise 8.5. Show that the asymptotic bias of $A_{1\text{p}}$ in the model of example 8.2 is

$$p \lim_{n\to\infty} (A_{1\text{p}} - A_1) = -\frac{1+A_1}{T-1}\left(1 - \frac{1}{T}\frac{1-A_1^T}{1-A_1}\right)\left[1 - \frac{2A_1}{(1-A_1)(T-1)}\left(1 - \frac{1-A_1^T}{T(1-A_1)}\right)\right]^{-1}.$$

Show that for T large, $p \lim_{n\to\infty}(A_{1\text{p}} - A_1) \approx -(1 + A_1)/(T-1)$.

Intuitively, the bias appears because, to eliminate ϱ_i, we have introduced a correlation of order $1/T$ between the explanatory variable and the residual of the model $(y_{it} - \bar{y}) = A_1(y_{it-1} - \bar{y}_{i,-1}) + (e_{it} - \bar{e}_i)$. In fact, $\bar{y}_{i,-1}$ is correlated with $(e_{it} - \bar{e}_i)$ even if e_{it} are serially uncorrelated since $\bar{e}_i$ contains e_{it-1}, which is correlated with y_{it-1}. When T is large, the right-hand side variables are uncorrelated with the errors, but, for T small, estimates of the mean effect are biased and this bias is transmitted to the estimates of A_1.

Table 8.2 shows that, if $A_1 > 0$, the bias in A_1 is generally negative and not negligible. For highly persistent processes, like those typically observed in macroeconomic time series, the bias is about 13% when $T = 20$ and still 6% when $T = 40$.

Example 8.3 (production function estimation). One typical case where problems with lagged dependent variables occur is in estimating production functions across sectors. Let $\text{GDP}_{it} = N_{it}^{\eta_N} K_{it}^{\eta_k} \zeta_{it}$, where, in principle, $\eta_N + \eta_k \neq 1$ and where the technological progress ζ_{it} is parametrized as $\ln \zeta_{it} = \bar{\zeta}_i + A_1 \ln \zeta_{it-1} + e_{it}$. Taking logs and quasi-differencing the production function, we have $\ln \text{GDP}_{it} = A_1 \ln \text{GDP}_{it-1} + \eta_N(\ln N_{it} - A_1 \ln N_{it-1}) + \eta_k(\ln K_{it} - A_1 \ln K_{it-1}) + \bar{\zeta}_i + e_{it}$. Unless ζ_t is i.i.d., estimation of η_k, η_N using production functions in deviation from the mean will produce biased estimates, even when n is large.

The problem described in example 8.2 is generic and is present even when cross-sectional techniques (as opposed to pooled techniques) are used to estimate the parameters.

Exercise 8.6 (Nickell). Consider the OLS estimator A_{1t} obtained by using the tth cross section, $A_{1t} = \sum_{i=1}^{n}(y_{it-1} - \bar{y}_{i,-1})(y_{it} - \bar{y}_i)/\sum_{i=1}^{n}(y_{it-1} - \bar{y}_{i,-1})^2$, where $\bar{y}_{i,-1}$ is the mean of y_{it-1}.

(i) Show that

$$p\lim_{n\to\infty}(A_{1t} - A_1) = -\frac{1 + A_1}{T-1}\left[1 - A_1^{t-1} - A_1^{T-t} + \frac{(1 - A_1^T)}{T(1 - A_1)}\right] \times \left[1 - \frac{2A_1}{(T-1)(1-A_1)}\left(1 - A_1^{t-1} - A_1^{T-t} + \frac{(1 - A_1^T)}{T(1 - A_1)}\right)\right]^{-1}$$

(this is the same as the bias obtained in exercise 8.5).

(ii) Argue that the inconsistency of A_{1t} is of order $(1/T)$, that its bias depends on which cross section is used, and that it is smaller at the end of the sample.

The standard alternative to de-meaning the variables is to use a random-effect estimator. Although we have argued that such an approach is conceptually problematic for macroeconomic data, we show that treating ϱ_i as random does not solve inconsistency problems in models with lagged dependent variables.

Example 8.4. Suppose we move ϱ_i into the error term and construct a pooled estimator

$$\tilde{A}_{1\text{p}} = A_1 + \frac{\sum_{i=1}^{n}\sum_{t=1}^{T}(e_{it} + \varrho_i)y_{it-1}/nT}{\sum_{i=1}^{n}\sum_{t=1}^{T}(y_{it-1})^2/nT}. \tag{8.12}$$

The numerator of this expression can be written as $(1/T)[(1 - A_1^T)/(1 - A_1)] \times \text{cov}(y_{i0}, \varrho_i) + (1/T)[\sigma_\varrho^2/(1 - A_1)^2][(T-1) - TA_1 + A_1^T]$ and the denominator is

$$\frac{1 - A_1^{2T}}{T(1 - A_1)^2}\frac{\sum y_{i0}^2}{n} + \frac{\sigma_\varrho^2}{(1 - A_1)^2}\frac{1}{T}\left(T - 2\frac{1 - A_1^T}{1 - A_1} + \frac{1 - A_1^{2T}}{1 - A_1^2}\right) + \frac{2}{T(1 - A_1)}\left(\frac{1 - A_1^T}{1 - A_1} - \frac{1 - A_1^{2T}}{1 - A_1^2}\right)\text{cov}(\varrho_i, y_{i0}) + \frac{1}{T}\frac{\sigma_e^2}{(1 - A_1^2)^2}[(T-1) - TA_1^2 - A_1^{2T}].$$

If y_{i0} is fixed, the covariance term drops out of the expression (otherwise, it would be positive—you might be able to guess why), but the numerator is different from zero even when $T \to \infty$ and is larger the larger the variance of the unit-specific effects σ_ϱ^2.

Exercise 8.7. Consider the model $y_{it} = A_1 y_{it-1} + A_2 x_{it} + \varrho_i + e_{it}$ and let $\tilde{y}_{it} = y_{it} - \bar{y}_i$, $\tilde{y}_{it-1} = y_{it-1} - \bar{y}_{i,-1}$, $\tilde{x}_{it} = x_{it} - \bar{x}_i$, $\tilde{e}_{it} = e_{it} - \bar{e}_i$.

(i) Show that, by using a pooled OLS estimator on the de-meaned model, we obtain

$$A_{1p} = A_1 + (\tilde{y}'_{-1}(I - \tilde{x}(\tilde{x}'\tilde{x})^{-1}\tilde{x}')\tilde{y}_{-1})^{-1}\tilde{y}'_{-1}(I - \tilde{x}(\tilde{x}'\tilde{x})^{-1}\tilde{x}')\tilde{e},$$
$$A_{2p} = A_2 - (\tilde{x}'\tilde{x})^{-1}\tilde{x}'\tilde{y}_{-1}(A_{1p} - A_1) + (\tilde{x}'\tilde{x})^{-1}\tilde{x}'\tilde{e}.$$

(ii) Show that

$$p \lim_{n\to\infty}(A_{1p} - A_1) = \left(p \lim_{n\to\infty}\frac{1}{nT}\tilde{y}'_{-1}[I - \tilde{x}(\tilde{x}'\tilde{x})^{-1}\tilde{x}']\tilde{y}_{-1}\right)^{-1} \times \left(p \lim_{n\to\infty}\frac{1}{nT}\tilde{y}'_{-1}\tilde{e}\right),$$
$$p \lim_{n\to\infty}(A_{2p} - A_2) = -\left(p \lim_{n\to\infty}(\tilde{x}'\tilde{x})^{-1}\tilde{x}'\tilde{y}_{-1}\right)p \lim_{n\to\infty}(A_{1p} - A_1).$$

Exercise 8.7 shows that the bias in A_{2p} depends on the bias in A_{1p} and the relationship between the exogenous variables x and the lagged endogenous variables y_{-1}, in deviations from their mean. If $E(\tilde{x}\tilde{y}_{-1}) > 0$, the bias in A_{2p} is positive (recall that the bias in A_{1p} is negative).

It is important to stress that disregarding dynamic effects does not help. In fact, if the true model has lagged dynamics and a static model is estimated, the error term will be correlated with the regressors and this correlation remains even after de-meaning the variables.

Exercise 8.8. Suppose $y_{it} = \rho_i + A_1 y_{it-1} + A_2 x_t + e_{it}$ and one estimates $y_{it} = \rho_i + A_2 x_{it} + v_{it}$, where $v_{it} = e_{it} + A_1 y_{it-1}$. Show that v_{it} is correlated with the regressor if x_{it} is serially correlated. Show that de-meaning the estimated model does not eliminate this correlation.

One implication of exercise 8.8 is the following: running a static de-meaned regression and correcting for serial correlation is unlikely to produce consistent estimates of the parameters when the true model for each unit is dynamic, which we take to be the standard case with macroeconomic time series.

8.2.2 The Correct Approach

To deal with unobservable variables when lagged dependent variables are present, define $\xi_t = A_{3t}/A_{3t-1}$ and quasi-difference (8.8) to get

$$y_{it} = A^{+}_{0t} + \sum_{j=1}^{q_1+1} A^{+}_{1jt} y_{it-j} + \sum_{j=1}^{q_2+1} A^{+}_{2jt} x_{t-j} + e^{+}_{it}, \tag{8.13}$$

where $A^{+}_{0t} = A_{0t} - \xi_t A_{0t-1}$, $A^{+}_{11t} = \xi_t + A_{11t}$, $A^{+}_{1jt} = A_{1jt} - \xi_t A_{1,j-1,t-1}$, $A^{+}_{1q_1+1t} = -\xi_t A_{q_1,t-1}$, $A^{+}_{21t} = A_{21t}$, $A^{+}_{2jt} = A_{2jt} - \xi_t A_{2j-1,t-1}$, $A^{+}_{2q_2+1t} = -\xi_t A_{2q_2t-1}$, $e^{+}_{it} = e_{it} - \xi_t e_{it-1}$. If $A_{3t} = A_3$, $\forall t$, (8.13) is simply the differenced version of (8.8) and the approach to eliminate the unobserved fixed effect corresponds to the one suggested by Anderson and Hsiao (1982). Note that in (8.13) the orthogonality conditions are $E(x_{t-\tau}e^{+}_{it}) = E(y_{it-\tau}e^{+}_{it}) = 0$ for all $i, \tau > 0$. The Anderson–Hsiao estimator, which was designed for the AR(1) version of this model with no x_{it}, uses y_{it-2} or $(y_{it-2} - y_{it-3})$ as instruments to estimate A^{+}_{j1}. Because of differencing, y_{it-1} is correlated with the error term. Therefore, it is not a valid instrument.

Exercise 8.9. Suppose in (8.13) that $q_1 = 1$, $q_2 = 0$, $A_{0t} = A_0$, $A_{1t} = A_1$, $A_{2t} = 0, \forall t$, $A_{3t} = A_3 = 1$. Write down an IV estimator for the parameters and describe the instruments you would use. Give conditions that ensure consistency, when $n \to \infty$, when $T \to \infty$, or both.

Since the orthogonality conditions are valid for any $\tau > 0$, there are many instruments one could use; the Anderson–Hsiao estimator selects one particular set of instruments but, as we saw in chapter 5, we can improve efficiency by appropriately combining all available information. In the case of constant coefficients the derivation of a GMM-style estimator is a straightforward application of the ideas described in chapter 5.

Example 8.5 (Arellano and Bond). Let y_{it} and x_{it} be scalars. The model in this case is $\Delta y_{it} = \sum_j A_{1j}\Delta y_{it-j} + \sum_j A_{2j}\Delta x_{it-j} + \Delta e_{it}$ or $\Delta y_{it} = \Delta X^{*}_{it}\alpha + \Delta e_{it}$, where $\alpha = [A_{11}, \dots, A_{1q_1}, A_{21}, \dots, A_{2q_2}]'$ is a $k = q_1 + q_2 \times 1$ vector and ΔX^{*}_{it} includes the right-hand side regressors. Stacking for each i the $(T - q + 1)$ observations where $q = \max(q_1, q_2)$ and then stacking the i vectors we have $\Delta y = \Delta X^{*}\alpha + \Delta e$, where Δy and Δe are $N(T - q + 1) \times 1$ vectors and ΔX^{*} is an $N(T - q + 1) \times k$ matrix. Let $Z_i = \text{diag}[y_{1i}, \dots, y_{si}, x_{1i}, \dots, x_{Ti}]$, $s = 1, \dots, T-2$. This is appropriate since the x_{it} is exogenous. Stack the Z_i elements into the matrix Z. Then $\alpha_{\text{GMM}} = (\Delta x^{*\prime}Z'WZ\Delta x^{*})^{-1}(\Delta x^{*\prime}Z'WZ\Delta y)$, where W is a weighting matrix. As in chapter 5, the optimal W depends on the covariance of the instruments. An estimator for W is $W = [(1/T)\sum_i Z_i'\Omega Z_i]^{-1}$, where Ω is a $(T-2) \times (T-2)$ matrix with 2 on the main diagonal, -1 on the first subdiagonals, and 0 elsewhere.

Time series comprising a macro panel are typically of uneven quality due to differences in recorded practices or statistical procedures. Therefore, it is important to understand what happens when (y_{it}, x_t) are measured with error. Suppose that $x^{\text{c}}_t = x_t + \epsilon^{x}_t$, $y^{\text{c}}_{it} = y_{it} + \epsilon^{y}_{it}$, where $E(e_{it}\epsilon^{y}_{it}) = E(e_{it}\epsilon^{x}_t) = 0$, and that measurement errors are i.i.d. and uncorrelated with the true value of the series.

Exercise 8.10. Consider the version of (8.8) where $A_{1jt} = A_{1j}$, $A_{2jt} = A_{2j}$, $A_{0t} = 0, \forall t$, but where both y_{it} and x_t are measured with error. Show that the system has the form $\Delta y_{it} = \sum_j A_{1j}\Delta y_{it-j} + \sum_j A_{2j}\Delta x_{t-j} + v_{it}$, where Δ is the differencing operator and $v_{it} = \Delta e_{it} + \Delta\epsilon^{y}_{it} + \sum_j A_{1j}\Delta\epsilon^{y}_{it-j} + \sum_j A_{2j}\Delta\epsilon^{x}_{t-j}$. Let $z_{it} = [1, y^{\text{c}}_{it-q-2}, \dots, y^{\text{c}}_{i1}, x^{\text{c}}_{it-q-2}, \dots, x^{\text{c}}_{i1}]$, where $q = \max(q_1, q_2)$. Show that z_{it} is uncorrelated with v_{it}.

Since the presence of (classical) measurement error introduces an MA structure in the error term, efficiency can be improved if this structure is taken into account in the estimation process. Consistency is not affected by the presence of measurement error.

When the coefficients are time varying, a little more work is needed to derive a GMM estimator. The next two results give the conditions for identification in the original and the transformed models (see Holtz Eakin et al. 1988).

Result 8.1. The order condition for identification of the parameters of the transformed model (8.13) is $T > \max(q_1, q_2) + 3$. The order condition for identification of the parameters of the original model (8.8) is $T > 3\max(q_1, q_2) + 2$.

Result 8.2. If $\xi_t = 1$, the order condition for identification of the original parameters is $T > 2\max(q_1, q_2) + 2$. If the original parameters are time invariant, the order condition for the identification is $T > \max(q_1, q_2) + 2$.

Example 8.6. Suppose $y_{it} = A_1 y_{it-1} + \varrho_i + e_{it} - \phi e_{it-1}$ and suppose $T = 4$. Then the model in first differences is $\Delta y_{i4} = A_1 \Delta y_{i3} + e_4 - \phi e_3$, $\Delta y_{i3} = A_1 \Delta y_{i2} + e_3 - \phi e_2$, $\Delta y_{i2} = A_1 \Delta y_{i1} + e_2 - \phi e_1$. Since $q = 1$, $T = 4 \geqslant q + 3$ and since there are $(T - q - 2)(T - q - 1)/2 = 1$ restrictions, to estimate the AR coefficient we have to use y_{i1} as an instrument for y_{i3}, when $T = 4$ is considered. The equations for $T = 3$ and $T = 2$ are not estimable.

To estimate time-varying parameters let $y_t = [y_{it}, \dots, y_{nt}]'$, $E_t = [e_{it}, \dots, e_{nt}]'$, $X_t = [\mathbf{1}, y_{t-1}, \dots, y_{t-q_1-1}, x_{t-1}, \dots, x_{t-q_2-1}]$, $\alpha_t = [A_{0t}^+, A_{11t}^+, \dots, A_{2,q_1+1,t}^+, A_{21t}^+, \dots, A_{2,q_2+1,t}^+]'$. Then (8.8) can be written in simultaneous equation format as $y_t = X_t \alpha_t + E_t$ and stacking the $T - q - 2$ observations we have

$$y = X\alpha + E. \tag{8.14}$$

Let $z_t = [\mathbf{1}, y_{t-2}, \dots, y_1, x_{t-2}, \dots, x_1]$ and $Z = \text{diag}[z_{q+3}, \dots, z_t]$. For the instruments to be valid we need $p\lim_{n\to\infty} Z'E/n = 0$ (this is a $(T - q - 2)n \times 1$ vector of conditions). Then, by using the logic of GMM, α can be estimated with a standard two-step approach.

Exercise 8.11. Describe a two-step approach to estimate α. Show that a 2SLS estimator is $\alpha_{\text{2SLS}} = [X'Z'W^{-1}Z'X]^{-1}X'Z'W^{-1}Z'y$, where $W_{\tau t} = \sum_{i=1}^{n} e_{it}' e_{it} \times Z_{it}' Z_{i\tau}$ and e_{it} is the (i, t) element of E. Is α_{2SLS} efficient?

As usual, consistent estimates of e_{it}, e.g., $e_{it,(\text{SLS})} = y - X\alpha_{\text{2SLS}}$, can be used in the formula for $W_{\tau t}$.

It is worthwhile examining in detail GMM estimation when there are no exogenous variables and the dynamics are restricted to be AR(1) since several empirical applications (convergence exercises, production function estimation, growth accounting) fit into this framework if the left-hand side variables are appropriately scaled.

Example 8.7. Consider the model $y_{it} = A_1 y_{it-1} + \varrho_i + e_{it}$, where $|A_1| < 1$ and $E(e_{it}) = E(e_{it}e_{i\tau}) = 0, \forall t \neq \tau$, T fixed and n large. Suppose we wish to estimate A_1 in the absence of any distributional assumptions on ϱ_i and e_{it}. With the assumptions on ϱ_i and e_{it} with the assumptions made, y_{it-2} is a valid instrument for the estimation of A_1 in the model in first differences. For $T \geqslant 3$, there are $(T-2) \times (T-1)/2$ linear moment restrictions of the type $E[(e_{it} - e_{it-1})y_{it-\tau}] = 0$, where $t = 3, \dots, T, \tau = 2, \dots, t-1$. For example, if $T = 4$, there are three orthogonality restrictions $E[(e_{i4}-e_{i3})y_{i2}] = 0$, $E[(e_{i4}-e_{i3})y_{i1}] = 0$, and $E[(e_{i3}-e_{i2})y_{i1}] = 0$. Rewrite the restriction as $E[z_i' \Delta e_{it}] = 0$, where z_i is a $(T-2) \times (T-2)(T-1)/2$ block diagonal matrix $z_i = \text{diag}\{y_{i1}, \dots, y_{i\tau}\}$, $\tau = 1, \dots, T-2$.

A GMM estimator of A_1 is based on the sample counterpart of $0 = E(z_i' \Delta e_{it})$, i.e., $(1/n) \sum_{i=1}^n z_i'(e_i - e_{i,-1}) = n^{-1} Z' \Delta e = 0$, where $\Delta e = e - e_{-1} = [(e-e_{-1})_1, \dots, (e-e_{-1})_n]'$ is an $n(T-2) \times 1$ vector and $Z = (Z_1, \dots, Z_n)$ is an $n(T-2) \times (T-2)(T-1)/2$ matrix. Then

$$A_{1,\text{GMM}} = \underset{A_1}{\text{argmin}} (\Delta E' Z) W_n (Z' \Delta E) = \frac{\Delta y_{-1}' Z W_n Z' \Delta y}{\Delta y_{-1}' Z W_n Z' \Delta y_{-1}}, \qquad (8.15)$$

where y_{-1} indicates lagged variables, $\Delta y = y - y_{-1}$, and W_n is a weighting matrix.

Under appropriate regularity conditions we have that $(Z' \Delta E)/(\sqrt{n \Sigma}) \xrightarrow{\text{D}} \mathbb{N}(0, 1)$, where Σ_n is the average (over the cross section) covariance matrix of $z_i' \Delta e_i$. With the assumptions made, Σ_n can be replaced by $\hat{\Sigma}_n = n^{-1} \sum_{i=1}^n (z_i' \widehat{\Delta e}_i \widehat{\Delta e}_i z_i)$, where $\widehat{\Delta e}_i = \Delta y_i - \hat{A}_1 \Delta y_{i,-1}$ and $\hat{A}_1$ is a preliminary consistent estimate and a consistent estimate of the asymptotic covariance matrix of $A_{1,\text{GMM}}$ is $\widehat{\text{avar}}(A_{1,\text{GMM}}) = (n \Delta y_{-1}' Z W_n \hat{\Sigma}_n W_n \hat{\Sigma}_n Z' \Delta y_{-1})/(\Delta y_{-1} Z W_n Z' \Delta y_{-1})$.

As in chapter 5 we can derive the optimal choice for W_n by minimizing $\widehat{\text{avar}}(A_{1,\text{GMM}})$.

Exercise 8.12. (i) Show that a one-step estimator is obtained by setting $W_n = (n^{-1} \sum_i z_i' \Omega z_i)^{-1}$, where Ω is a $(T-2) \times (T-2)$ matrix with $+2$ on the main diagonal, -1 on the first subdiagonals, and 0 otherwise.

(ii) Show that $W_n = \hat{\Sigma}_n^{-1}$ is optimal (it produces an estimator we denote by $A_{1,\text{2step}}$).

(iii) Show that $A_{1,\text{GMM}}$ and $A_{1,\text{2step}}$ are asymptotically equivalent if e_{it} are independent and homoskedastic across n and T.

Clearly, since IV estimation is inefficient relative to GMM estimation, the Anderson–Hsiao estimator of A_1, obtained by regressing Δy_{it} on Δy_{it-1} using either Δy_{it-2} or y_{it-2} as instruments, is inefficient relative to the GMM estimators derived in example 8.7 and exercise 8.12.

8.2.3 Restricted Models

At times in the estimation process, one would like to consider (linear) restrictions of the form $\alpha_t = R\theta_t + r$, where $\dim(\theta_t) < \dim(\alpha_t)$. Restrictions of this type may be theory based or they may come from stationarity constraints. It is relatively easy to estimate restricted models and test the validity of these restrictions. Before describing the machinery necessary to do this, we present an example where such restrictions may occur.

Example 8.8. Consider the case of a group of small open economies which take the world interest rate as given. Suppose that we are interested in examining the effect of a capital tax rebate on investments by using a model like (8.8), where the world interest rate is included in x_{it}. Suppose that some of these economies are dollarized and some of them are not. In this case, it may make sense to model interdependencies within each group but not across groups. Hence, there are restrictions on the A_{1jt} matrices one should take into account in the estimation process.

Following the steps we used in chapter 4, define $Y_t^\dagger \equiv Y_t - X_t r = X_t R\theta_t + E_t \equiv X_t^\dagger \theta_t + E_t$ and assume that $E(Z'E) = 0$ and $E(Z'X^\dagger) \neq 0$. Then a GMM estimator for $\theta = (\theta_1, \dots, \theta_t)$ is $\theta_{\text{GMM}} = [(X^\dagger)' Z W^{-1} Z' X^\dagger]^{-1}((X^\dagger)' Z W^{-1} Z' Y^\dagger)$.

To test the validity of the restrictions one could use any of the tests described in chapter 5. For example, let

$$n \times \mathfrak{S}_{\text{un},t} = (Y_t - X_t \alpha_{t,\text{GMM}})' Z_t W_{n(\alpha)}^{-1} Z_t' (Y_t - X_t \alpha_{t,\text{GMM}})$$

and

$$n \times \mathfrak{S}_{\text{re},t} = (Y_t^\dagger - X_t^\dagger \theta_{t,\text{GMM}})' Z_t W_{n(\theta)}^{-1} Z_t' (Y_t^\dagger - X_t^\dagger \theta_{t,\text{GMM}}).$$

Let $\alpha = (\alpha_1, \dots, \alpha_t)$ and $\theta = (\theta_1, \dots, \theta_t)$. Using standard asymptotic arguments, it follows that, for $n \to \infty$,

$$\mathfrak{S}_{\text{un},t} \xrightarrow{\text{D}} \chi^2(\dim(Z_t) - \dim(\alpha)) \quad \text{and} \quad \mathfrak{S}_{\text{re},t} \xrightarrow{\text{D}} \chi^2(\dim(\alpha) - \dim(\theta)), \quad \forall t.$$

Hence, as $n \to \infty$, the statistics $\mathfrak{S}_{\text{re},t} - \mathfrak{S}_{\text{un},t} \xrightarrow{\text{D}} \chi^2(\dim(Z_t) - \dim(\theta))$, $t = 1, \dots, T$.

Exercise 8.13. Assume $\alpha_t = \alpha$, $\forall t$. Describe how to implement a Wald test for the hypothesis $\alpha = R\theta + r$.

As in VAR models, one may be interested in testing a series of hypotheses and proceed at each stage conditional on the results obtained at the previous stage. For example, one would like to test how many lags should be included in the model and, conditional on the results, test some economic restriction, such as long-run neutrality or steady-state convergence. As in chapter 4, the significance level needs to be appropriately adjusted to take into account the sequential testing approach.

Example 8.9. Let the first restriction be $\alpha_t = R\theta_t + r$ and the second $\theta_t = \bar{R}\phi_t + \bar{r}$. Let $n \times \mathfrak{S}_{\text{un},t} = (Y_t - X_t \alpha_{t,\text{GMM}})' Z_t W_{n(\alpha)}^{-1} Z_t' (Y_t - X_t \alpha_{t,\text{GMM}})$, $n \times \mathfrak{S}_{\text{re}_1,t} = (Y_t^\dagger - X_t^\dagger \theta_{t,\text{GMM}})' Z_t W_{n(\theta)}^{-1} Z_t' (Y_t^\dagger - X_t^\dagger \theta_{t,\text{GMM}})$, $n \times \mathfrak{S}_{\text{re}_2,t} = (Y_t^\ddagger - X_t^\ddagger \phi_{t,\text{GMM}})' \times Z_t W_{n(\phi)}^{-1} Z_t' (Y_t^\ddagger - X_t^\ddagger \phi_{t,\text{GMM}})$, where $Y_t^\ddagger \equiv Y_t^\dagger - X_t \bar{r} = X_t \bar{R}_1 \phi_t + E_t \equiv X_t^\ddagger \phi_t + E_t$. Define $\text{LR}_{1,t} = \mathfrak{S}_{\text{re}_1,t} - \mathfrak{S}_{\text{un},t}$, $\text{LR}_{2,t} = \mathfrak{S}_{\text{re}_2,t} - \mathfrak{S}_{\text{re}_1,t}$, where the latter is a test of the second set of restrictions, conditional on the first set being true. If a_j is the significance of test $j = 1, 2$, a test of the second hypothesis has general significance $a_1 + a_2 - a_1 a_2$. Hence, for $a_1 = a_2 = 0.10$, the significance level of the second restrictions, conditional on the first being correct, is 0.19.

These testing ideas can be used to examine whether there is heterogeneity in levels among units. From a practical point of view this is important since, if $\varrho_i = \varrho, \forall i$, and the parameters are time invariant, cross-sectional/pooled OLS estimates of the parameters of interest are consistent. However, if $\varrho_i \neq \varrho_{i'}$, first differencing and instrumental variables are needed. This distinction allows us to design a GMM-type test for the hypothesis of interest.

Example 8.10. Consider the univariate model $y_{it} = \varrho_i + A_1 y_{it-1} + e_{it} = A_1 y_{it-1} + \epsilon_{it}$. $A_{1\mathrm{p}}$, obtained by pooling the cross sections, is inconsistent since ϵ_{it} is correlated with $y_{it-\tau}$ for all τ. First differencing the specification we have $\Delta y_{it} = A_1 \Delta y_{it-1} + \Delta\epsilon_{it}$. Since $E(y_{it-\tau}, \Delta\epsilon_{it}) = 0$, $\tau \geqslant 2$, y_{it-2} is a valid instrument. Suppose $T = 3$. If $\varrho_i = \varrho, \forall i$, there are three orthogonality conditions $E(y_{i2}\epsilon_{i3}) = E(y_{i1}\epsilon_{i3}) = E(y_{i1}\epsilon_{i2}) = 0, \forall i$, which can be used to estimate one (common) AR parameter. The last two conditions imply $E[y_{i1}(\epsilon_{i3} - \epsilon_{i2})] = 0$. Since this condition holds both under the null and the alternative, it can be employed to estimate A_1. The other two conditions, $E(y_{i2}\epsilon_{i3}) = E(y_{i1}\epsilon_{i2}) = 0, \forall i$, are valid only under the null. Therefore, given an estimate of A_1, they can be used to test whether an individual effect is present or not.

A general formulation of the testing idea contained in example 8.10 is the following. Let $y_{it} = \sum_{j=1}^{q_1} A_{1j} y_{it-j} + \varrho_i + e_{it} = \sum_{j=1}^{q_1} A_{1j} y_{it-j} + \epsilon_{it}$. Under the null, $E(y_{it-j}\epsilon_{it}) = 0$ for $j = 1, \dots, T$, $t = q_1 + 1, \dots, T$. Under the alternative, $E(y_{it-j}\Delta\epsilon_{it}) = 0$ for $j = 1, \dots, T$, $t = q_1 + 2, \dots, T$, but $E(y_{it-j}\epsilon_{it}) \neq 0$. Given q_1 lags and T observations, there are $[T(T-1) - q_1(q_1 - 1)]$ orthogonality conditions. Since there are q_1 parameters to be estimated under the null, there are $\nu = [T(T-1) - q_1(q_1 - 1) - q_1]/2$ overidentifying restrictions. Therefore, $\mathfrak{S} = (Y - \sum_j A_{1j} Y_{-j}) Z W^{-1} Z'(Y - \sum_j A_{1j} Y_{-j})/n \to \chi^2(\nu)$.

Exercise 8.14. Suppose $y_{it} = \sum_{j=1}^{q_1} A_{1j} y_{it-j} + \sum_{j=1}^{q_2} A_{2j} x_{t-j} + \varrho_i + e_{it}$, where $E(x_{t-\tau} e_{it}) = 0$, for $\tau = 1, \dots, T$, $t = q + 1, \dots, T$, and $q = \max(q_1, q_2)$. How many orthogonality conditions are there? How many degrees of freedom has the test for homogeneity in this case?

In time-invariant models, typically only a subset of the orthogonality conditions are used, since the information contained in, for example, $E(z_{t-\tau}, e_{it})$, τ large, may be negligible. In this case, let j be the number of covariances of interest and let $jT - 0.5[j(j+1) + q_1(q_1 + 1)]$ be the number of orthogonality conditions. If $j > q_1$, the orthogonality conditions in an AR(q_1) model under the null are

$$E(y_{it-\tau}\Delta e_{it}) = 0, \quad \tau = 2, \dots, t-1, \quad t = (q_1 + 2), \dots, j, \tag{8.16}$$

$$E(y_{it-\tau}\Delta e_{it}) = 0, \quad \tau = 2, \dots, j, \quad t = (j + 1), \dots, T, \tag{8.17}$$

$$E(y_{iq_1+1-\tau}e_{iq_1+1}) = 0, \quad \tau = 1, \dots, q_1, \tag{8.18}$$

$$E(y_{it-1}e_{it}) = 0, \quad t = (q_1 + 2), \dots, T. \tag{8.19}$$

Here (8.16), (8.17) hold under the null and the alternative; (8.18), (8.19) hold only under the null. As usual, employing a limited number of instruments produces a less efficient test.

Exercise 8.15. Consider the model $y_{it} = A_1 y_{it-1} + \varrho_i + e_{it}$; let $T = 4$ and $j = 2$.

(i) Write down the orthogonality conditions implied by the model, distinguishing between those valid under both hypotheses and those valid only under the null.

(ii) Stack the equations for all time periods and write the model as $Y = A_1 Y_{-1} + e$. Using $Z = \text{diag}(z_1, \dots, z_n)$, construct IV and GMM estimators for A_1.

(iii) Write down a J-style test for the validity of the overidentifying restrictions.

Note that a GMM-style test for heterogeneity is inappropriate if some time series have a unit root. In that case one should use likelihood ratio tests, which have good properties, even when unit roots are present (see, for example, Smith and Fuertes 2003).

8.2.4 *Recovering the Individual Effect*

In macroeconomic applications it is important to obtain estimates of ϱ_i and have a feeling of their cross-sectional distribution, since these parameters may capture differences in national policies and/or other cross-unit characteristics. When first differences are taken, ϱ_i is nonidentifiable from the estimated specification. Nevertheless, it is easy to obtain an estimate of it. Let $\hat{\alpha}$ be an estimator of α obtained from the model in first difference. Let $\hat{\epsilon}_{it} = y_{it} - x_{it}\hat{\alpha}$. Taking time series averages $\bar{\hat{\epsilon}}_i = (1/T)\sum_{t=1}^{T} \hat{\epsilon}_{it} = \bar{y}_i - \hat{\alpha}\bar{x}_i$, where $\bar{y}_i = (1/T)\sum_t y_{it}$ and $\bar{x}_i = (1/T)\sum_t x_{it}$. Since $(1/T)\sum_{t=1}^{T} \hat{e}_{it} \to E(e_i) = 0$ as $T \to \infty$, $\bar{\hat{\epsilon}}_i = \hat{\varrho}_i$.

Example 8.11. We have estimated a panel AR(1) model with country-specific intercepts by using quarterly real GDP data for eleven European nations for the sample 1988:1–2003:3. We have taken first differences to estimate the common AR parameter, pooling the data, using eleven lags as instruments, and averaging over T the residuals for each i. Figure 8.1 shows that the distribution of country-specific effects is clearly skewed and somewhat leptokurtic. We have tested for homogeneity of the individual effects, assuming they are all equal to the mean. The test has a p-value of 0.07, indicating that heterogeneities are somewhat important. However, if we exclude Austria and Finland, homogeneity is not rejected.

8.2.5 *Some Practical Issues*

There are at least three issues of practical interest worth discussing when estimating models with homogeneous dynamics and unit-specific fixed effects. First, we have seen that OLS estimates of the (common) AR parameters are biased when the model is dynamic. Does the magnitude of the bias change as T increases? Second, we know

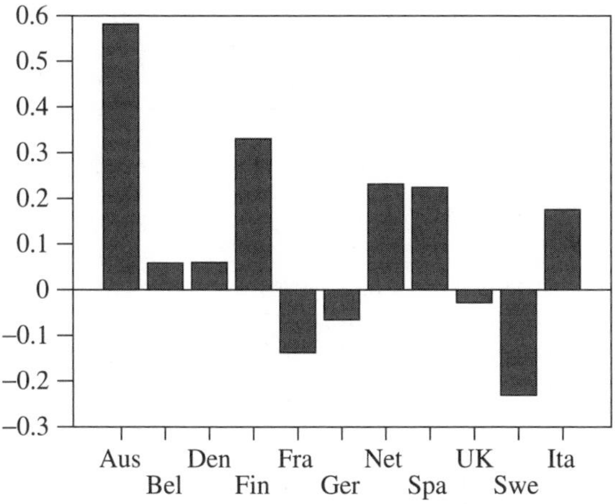

Figure 8.1. Individual effects, GDP.

Table 8.3. Monte Carlo evidence I.

T	A_1	Bias in A_1	Bias in A_2
10	0.2	−0.059 (0.025)	0.017 (0.026)
	0.8	−0.232 (0.033)	0.004 (0.043)
20	0.2	−0.027 (0.015)	0.010 (0.018)
	0.8	−0.104 (0.018)	0.006 (0.026)
40	0.2	−0.017 (0.011)	0.007 (0.014)
	0.8	−0.056 (0.013)	0.006 (0.023)

that GMM is more efficient than IV, but also that estimates of the weighting matrix converge very slowly, therefore introducing important small-sample biases. What can we say about the trade-off between bias and efficiency in GMM estimators? Finally, how large are the relative biases of OLS and IV for panels of the typical size found in macroeconomics? To answer these questions we have simulated data by using

$$\left.\begin{aligned} y_{it} &= A_1 y_{it-1} + A_2 x_{it} + \varrho_i + e^y_{it}, \\ x_{it} &= A_3 x_{it-1} + e^x_{it}, \end{aligned}\right\} \tag{8.20}$$

where $e^y_{it} \sim$ i.i.d. $\mathbb{N}(0, \sigma^2_y)$, $e^x_{it} \sim$ i.i.d. $\mathbb{N}(0, \sigma^2_x)$. We set $A_2 = 1 - A_1$, so that changes in A_1 affect short-run dynamics but not the long-run relationship between x and y. The parameters controlling the experiments are A_1, A_3, σ^2_y, σ^2_x. In the first experiment, we set $\sigma_x = 1$, $A_3 = 0.5$, $\sigma_y = 2$, and we let A_1 vary with T. We also set $y_{i0} = x_{i0} = 0$ and discard the first 100 observations. We perform 500 replications for each combination of the parameters using $n = 100$. Table 8.3 reports the results. Numerical standard errors are in parentheses.

Table 8.4. Monte Carlo evidence II.

			GMM one-step		GMM two-step	
T	n	A_1	Two instruments	Five instruments	Two instruments	Five instruments
10	20	0.2	−0.041 (0.066)	−0.050 (0.056)	−0.043 (0.081)	−0.077 (0.102)
		0.8	−0.222 (0.124)	−0.241 (0.115)	−0.249 (0.168)	−0.336 (0.198)
10	100	0.2	−0.011 (0.035)	−0.012 (0.022)	−0.009 (0.036)	−0.011 (0.032)
		0.8	−0.056 (0.071)	−0.079 (0.059)	−0.056 (0.072)	−0.081 (0.066)
20	20	0.2	−0.032 (0.044)	−0.038 (0.038)	−0.084 (0.118)	−0.263 (0.199)
		0.8	−0.137 (0.081)	−0.144 (0.066)	−0.441 (0.281)	−0.880 (0.498)
20	100	0.2	−0.005 (0.022)	−0.007 (0.019)	−0.005 (0.025)	−0.008 (0.027)
		0.8	−0.028 (0.040)	−0.039 (0.039)	−0.030 (0.039)	−0.048 (0.040)
40	20	0.2	−0.022 (0.034)	−0.026 (0.032)	−0.188 (0.148)	−0.423 (0.363)
		0.8	−0.108 (0.059)	−0.111 (0.044)	−0.837 (0.294)	−1.154 (0.509)
40	100	0.2	−0.003 (0.018)	−0.005 (0.013)	−0.004 (0.017)	−0.017 (0.028)
		0.8	−0.024 (0.030)	−0.030 (0.025)	−0.031 (0.036)	−0.089 (0.049)

The bias in A_1 is typically more severe than the bias in A_2: it increases with the value of A_1 and decreases with T. Note that the bias is about 10% when $A_1 = 0.8$ and 20 data points are available but it increases to about 30% when $T = 10$. When time series are persistent, the bias is significant even when $T = 40$.

In the second experiment we let n vary with T and A_1. We focus on GMM estimators, obtained with two and five instruments, using both one-step and two-step approaches.

Two important conclusions can be drawn from table 8.4. First, the bias induced by estimating the optimal weighting matrix is significant and the one-step estimator is always best. Note that the bias in the two-step estimator increases, surprisingly, with T and, as expected, is larger the larger is the AR coefficient. Second, using two instruments typically produces smaller biases. However, it is also the case that with five instruments, the bias is more precisely estimated.

Comparing tables 8.3 and 8.4, one can see that GMM estimators are better when n is large but, for a fixed n, their performance is far from appealing. Also, estimators become less biased when T increases, except when n is small. Overall, GMM and OLS biases are similar, when using a one-step estimator and $T = 40$.

8.3 Dynamic Heterogeneity

So far we have examined panels where the dynamics are homogeneous across units. However, there are many situations when the homogeneity assumption is not particularly attractive and dynamic heterogeneities should be allowed for. For example, in growth theory it has become common to empirically study issues of convergence and polarization of income distributions (see Barro and Sala-i-Martin 1992; Quah

1996; Boldrin and Canova 2001) and policy circles are often interested in predicting the (long-run) effects of certain policy choices across units. Alternatively, it is often emphasized that political economy issues may shape the dynamics of government debt (see, for example, Alesina and Perotti 1995). Finally, in many situations researchers care if market forces or policies induce similarities in the transitional dynamics of units with different characteristics.

When both n and T are large, there are at least four approaches one can use to estimate the parameters of the model and continuous functions of them with interesting economic and/or policy interpretations.

(i) Estimate the parameters for each unit $i = 1, \dots, n$ separately by using the time series dimension of the panel (call the estimator $\alpha_{i\mathrm{A}}$), construct the required continuous function (steady-state, long-run effect, etc.) $h(\alpha_{i\mathrm{A}})$, and average over the cross section to obtain a "typical" effect, i.e., $h_{\mathrm{A}}(\alpha) = (1/n)\sum_i h(\alpha_{i\mathrm{A}})$.

(ii) Pool cross sections and time series, estimate one average parameter vector (call the estimator α_{p}), and construct one average function $h(\alpha_{\mathrm{p}})$.

(iii) Average over n for each $t = 1, \dots, T$; estimate the parameter vector (call the estimator α_{TS}) and the relevant function $h(\alpha_{\mathrm{TS}})$ by using the constructed average time series.

(iv) Average over T and estimate the parameter vector (call the estimator α_{CS}) and the relevant function $h(\alpha_{\mathrm{CS}})$ by using the constructed average cross-sectional data.

Example 8.12. The magnitude of the savings and investment correlation in open economies (the so-called Feldstein and Horioka puzzle) has attracted the attention of many researchers. Here a large cross section of data for national savings and domestic investment is typically available, so all four estimators are feasible. Nevertheless, the literature has concentrated on the average cross-sectional estimator and regressions of the type $(\mathrm{Sa/GDP})_i = \varrho_i + A(\mathrm{Inv/GDP})_i + e_i$ are run, where $(\mathrm{Sa/GDP})_i$ is the average saving rate and $(\mathrm{Inv/GDP})_i$ is the average investment rate for unit i over the sample. Since both saving and investment rates are correlated over time, and since the sample typically includes both OECD and LDC countries, one may guess that a reasonable empirical specification could be $(\mathrm{Sa/GDP})_{it} = \varrho_i + \alpha_{1i}(\mathrm{Sa/GDP})_{it-1} + \alpha_{2i}(\mathrm{Inv/GDP})_{it} + \alpha_{3i}(\mathrm{Inv/GDP})_{it-1} + e_{it}$. Hence, one may be interested in knowing how A_{CS} relates to α_{ji}, $j = 1, 2, 3$, and whether systematic biases are present.

The task of this section is to analyze the properties of the four estimators when dynamic heterogeneity is suspected to exist and highlight the problems one is likely to encounter in practical situations. To anticipate the results the first estimator is consistent and a modified version of the fourth one can also yield consistent estimates of $h(\alpha)$ (but not necessarily of α) when $T \to \infty$. However, since α_{p} and α_{TS} are inconsistent for $T \to \infty$, $h(\alpha_{\mathrm{p}})$ and $h(\alpha_{\mathrm{TS}})$ are also inconsistent.

The model we consider has the form

$$y_{it} = A_{1i}(\ell)y_{it-1} + A_{2i}(\ell)x_{it} + \varrho_i + e_{it}, \tag{8.21}$$

$$\alpha_{ji} = \alpha_j + v_{ji}, \quad j = 1, 2, \tag{8.22}$$

where $\alpha_{ji} = \text{vec}(A_{ji}(\ell))'$. Given (8.21), (8.22), possible functions of interest are $h_1(\alpha_i) = E(1 - A_{1i}(1))^{-1}A_{2i}(1)$, the long-run effect of a permanent change in x_{it} on y_{it}, $h_2(\alpha_i) = E(1 - A_{1i}(1))^{-1}A_{1i}(1)$, the mean-lag effect, and $h_3(\alpha_i) = (1 - A_{1i}(1))^{-1}$, the convergence rate, where $\alpha_i = \text{vec}(A_{1i}(\ell), A_{2i}(\ell))'$.

Note that, while we have specified how $A_{ji}(\ell)$ are distributed across i, we could have also specified how $h(\alpha_i)$ are distributed across i; for example, we could have assumed that

$$h(\alpha_i) = h(\alpha) + v_i^h. \tag{8.23}$$

Most of the arguments given below go through with both specifications. To ensure that the problem is well-defined we make four assumptions:

(i) x_{it} and $e_{i\tau}$ are mutually independent for all t, τ, and independent of $v_i = [v_{1i}, v_{2i}]$ (or of v_i^h) with $e_{it} \sim$ i.i.d. $(0, \sigma_{e_i}^2)$ and $v_{ji} \sim$ i.i.d. $(0, \sigma_{v_j}^2)$, $j = 1, 2$.

(ii) The $m_2 \times 1$ vector x_{it} satisfies $x_{it} = \bar{x}_i + \rho x_{it-1} + e_{it}^x$, where $\bar{x}_i$ is the mean; the eigenvalues of ρ are all less than 1 in absolute value; $e_{it}^x \sim$ i.i.d. $(0, \sigma_{e_i^x}^2)$ and $\lim_{T\to\infty}(1/T)\sum_{\tau=1}^{T} \text{ACF}_x(\tau) = 0$, that is, x_t is mean square ergodic.

(iii) $|(1/n)\sum_{i=1}^{n} \bar{x}_i\bar{x}_i'| \neq 0$ for a finite n and $\lim_{n\to\infty}(1/n)\sum_{i=1}^{n} \bar{x}_i\bar{x}_i' = \Sigma_{xx}$.

(iv) $|A_{1i}(1)| < 1$ and the cross-sectional moments of $A_{ji}(\ell)$ and of $h(\alpha_i)$ exist and are finite for each i.

These assumptions imply, among other things, that e_{it} are innovations in y_{it}, that x_{it} are strictly exogenous, that y_{it} is stationary, and that $h(\alpha_i)$ is computable.

8.3.1 *Average Time Series Estimator*

When T is sufficiently large, one can run separate regressions for each i, compute $h(\alpha_{i\text{A}})$ and average the results over n to obtain a "typical" effect. When both n and $T \to \infty$, $\alpha_{i\text{A}}$, $h(\alpha_{i\text{A}})$, and $h_{\text{A}}(\alpha)$ are consistent estimators of α_i, $h(\alpha_i)$, and $h(\alpha)$. Clearly, if T is short, estimates of $A_{1i}(\ell)$ are biased and, unless cointegration is present, estimates of $A_{2i}(\ell)$ will also be biased. These biases, in turn, induce biases in $h_{\text{A}}(\alpha)$ and inconsistencies, even when n is large. Intuitively, averaging biased estimates will not, in general, eliminate the bias.

To show consistency of $\bar{\alpha}_{\text{A}} = (1/n)\sum_i \alpha_{i\text{A}}$, for T large, rewrite the model as

$$y_{it} = \varrho_i + X_{it}\alpha_i + e_{it}, \tag{8.24}$$

where $X_{it} = [y_{it-1}, \dots, y_{it-q_1}, x_{it}, \dots, x_{it-q_2}]$. Then $\alpha_{i\text{A}} = (X_i'\Omega_T X_i)^{-1} \times (X_i'\Omega_T y_i)$, where X_i is a $T \times (q_1 - 1 + q_2)$ matrix, y_i a $T \times 1$ vector, $\Omega_T = I_T - \mathbf{1}_T(\mathbf{1}_T'\mathbf{1}_T)^{-1}\mathbf{1}_T'$, and $\mathbf{1}_T$ a $T \times 1$ unit vector. Let $\bar{\alpha} = (1/n)\sum_i \alpha_i$.

Exercise 8.16. Give conditions that guarantee $p\lim_{T\to\infty} \bar{\alpha}_{\mathrm{A}} = \bar{\alpha}$. (Hint: note that $\bar{\alpha} + (1/n)\sum_i p\lim_{T\to\infty}(X_i'\Omega_T X_i/T)^{-1} p\lim_{T\to\infty}(X_i'\Omega_T e_i/T) = p\lim_{T\to\infty}\bar{\alpha}_{\mathrm{A}}$.)

If also $n \to \infty$, $\bar{\alpha} \to E(\alpha)$, since α_i are i.i.d. across i, so that $\bar{\alpha}_{\mathrm{A}}$ asymptotically approaches the population average.

Exercise 8.17. An estimate of the covariance matrix of $\bar{\alpha}_{\mathrm{A}}$ is $\Sigma_\alpha = (1/(n^2-n)) \times \sum_i(\alpha_{i\mathrm{A}} - \bar{\alpha}_{\mathrm{A}})(\alpha_{i\mathrm{A}} - \bar{\alpha}_{\mathrm{A}})'$. Show that $E(\Sigma_\alpha) = (1-(1/n))\sum_i \Sigma_{\alpha_i} + \sum_i E(\alpha_{i\mathrm{A}}) \times E(\alpha_{i\mathrm{A}}') - (1/n)\sum_i\sum_{i'} E(\alpha_{i\mathrm{A}})E(\alpha_{i'A}')$, where the last two terms measure small-sample biases. Argue that, for n fixed, if T is large, the bias disappears and Σ_α is consistent. (You will need a lot of algebra to show this!)

We can immediately show that any of the $h(\alpha)$ we consider is also consistent. For example, $h_{2\mathrm{A}}$ converges to $E\{A_{2i}(1)/[1 - A_{1i}(1)]\}$ if n is large, provided that the expression in the denominator is nonzero. Its variance is then $\Sigma_{h_2(\alpha)} = (1/(n^2-n))\sum_i[h_2(\alpha_{i\mathrm{A}}) - h_{2\mathrm{A}}(\alpha)][h_2(\alpha_{i\mathrm{A}}) - h_{2\mathrm{A}}(\alpha)]'$.

Example 8.13. Suppose we are interested in estimating inflation persistence in G7 countries, where persistence is measured either by the spectral density at frequency zero or by the sum of the coefficients of a regression of inflation on its own lags. Data run from 1970:1 to 2000:12. In the first case, we compute the ACFs for inflation in each country and the spectral density at frequency zero is obtained by summing 40 covariances and averaging over the seven countries. In the second case, regressions are performed with 10 lags for each country, the sum of coefficients is computed and an average is taken. We find that the range of $\mathcal{S}_i(\omega = 0)$ across i is large, that the average persistence is 7.03, and that its cross-sectional variance is 3.57. The sum of coefficients is also somewhat dispersed: on average, it equals 1.32 and its variance is 0.42. In general, both statistics suggest that inflation is indeed persistent.

Exercise 8.18. Suppose heterogeneity is of binary form, i.e., there are two groups in the data and their composition is known. Describe how to implement an average estimator for inflation persistence in this case. What kind of properties will the estimator have? Under what conditions will it be consistent?

Example 8.14. It is relatively easy to design a test for the hypothesis $\sigma_i = \sigma, \forall i$, assuming that both ϱ_i and α_i are heterogeneous. In fact, the estimated residuals of the model are $e_{it} = y_{it} - \varrho_{i\mathrm{A}} + X_{it}\alpha_{i\mathrm{A}}$. Under the null, $\sigma_{\mathrm{A}}^2 = (1/nT)\sum_{i=1}^n\sum_{t=1}^T e_{it}^2$. Under the alternative, $\sigma_{i\mathrm{A}}^2 = (1/T)\sum_{t=1}^T e_{it}^2$. Then the concentrated likelihood functions under the null and the alternative are $\mathcal{L}_{\mathrm{re}} \propto -\frac{1}{2}nT\ln\sigma_{\mathrm{A}}^2$ and $\mathcal{L}_{\mathrm{un}} \propto -\frac{1}{2}T\sum_{i=1}^n \ln\sigma_{i\mathrm{A}}^2$ and $2(\ln\mathcal{L}_{\mathrm{un}} - \ln\mathcal{L}_{\mathrm{re}}) \sim \chi^2(n-1)$ as $T \to \infty$.

Exercise 8.19. Propose an LR test for the hypothesis: $\alpha_i = \alpha$ and $\sigma_i = \sigma, \forall i$.

Averaging time series estimates is feasible when T is large enough, for example, in convergence regressions at U.S. state level, in studies focusing on the cross-state effect of local fiscal policy, or in cross-sectional analyses of unemployment rates and labor accidents. However, it is relatively unusual to see researchers estimating n separate regressions and averaging the results. A typical choice is to pool cross sections and time series and directly estimate one average α.

8.3.2 Pooled Estimator

Substituting (8.22) into (8.21) we have

$$y_{it} = A_1(\ell)y_{it-1} + A_2(\ell)x_{it} + \varrho_i + e^{\mathrm{p}}_{it}, \tag{8.25}$$

$$e^{\mathrm{p}}_{it} = e_{it} + v'_{1i}y_{it-1} + v'_{2i}x_{it}. \tag{8.26}$$

Since, e^{p}_{it} is correlated with both y_{it-1} and x_{it}, OLS estimates of $A_1(\ell)$ and $A_2(\ell)$ in (8.25) are inconsistent. Formal evidence of this outcome is provided in the next exercise.

Exercise 8.20. Suppose $A_{1i}(\ell) = A_{1i}$, $A_{2i}(\ell) = A_{2i}$, and $\varrho_i = 0$.

(i) Show that $E(x_{it}, e^{\mathrm{p}}_{it}) = \sum_{\tau=0}^{\infty} E(v_{1i}A_{2i}A^{\tau}_{1i})\,\mathrm{ACF}_i(|\tau+1|)$, where $\mathrm{ACF}_i(\tau)$ is the autocovariance of x_{it} at lag τ. Note that this expectation goes to zero if x_{it} is serially uncorrelated.

(ii) Show that $E(y_{it-1}, e^{\mathrm{p}}_{it}) = \sum_{\tau=0}^{\infty}\sum_{\tau'=0}^{\infty} E(v_{1i}A^2_{2i}A^{\tau+\tau'}_{i})\,\mathrm{ACF}_i(|\tau-\tau'|) + \sigma_i^2\sum_{\tau=1}^{\infty} E(v_{1i}A^{2\tau}_{1i}) + \sum_{\tau=0}^{\infty} E(v_{2i}A_{2i}A^{\tau}_{i})\,\mathrm{ACF}_i(|\tau+1|)$. Argue that this term does not vanish even when x_{it} is i.i.d.

When dynamics are heterogeneous and the data are pooled, an IV approach is also unlikely to work. In fact, given the structure of e^{p}_{it}, it is difficult to find instruments that are correlated with the regressors and uncorrelated with the errors.

Example 8.15. Let $z_{it} = [x_{it-1}, \dots, x_{it-\tau}]$ be a vector of instruments and consider an AR(1) version of the model. z_{it} is a potential candidate since it is uncorrelated with the e_{it} and it is correlated with the regressors of (8.25). However, from (8.25) we have that

$$E(v_{it}z_{it}) = E\left(\frac{\varrho_i v_{1i}}{1-A_{1i}}\right)E(z_{it}) + \sum_{\tau=0}^{\infty} E(v_{1i}A^{j}_{1i}A'_{2i})E(x_{it-j-1}z_{it}), \tag{8.27}$$

$$E(y_{it-1}z_{it}) = E\left(\frac{\varrho_i}{1-A_{1i}}\right)E(z_{it}) + \sum_{\tau=0}^{\infty} E(A^{j}_{1i}A'_{2i})E(x_{it-j-1}z_{it}). \tag{8.28}$$

For z_{it} to be valid it must be the case that $E(v_{it}z_{it}) = 0$ and $E(y_{it-1}z_{it}) \neq 0$. Looking at (8.27) and (8.28) it is clear that the two conditions cannot be simultaneously satisfied since, in general, $E(\varrho_i v_{1i}/(1-A_{1i})) \neq 0$ or $E(v_{1i}A^{j}_{1i}A'_{2i}) \neq 0$.

Exercise 8.21. In example 8.15, show that z_{it} is a valid instrument if $A_{1i} = A_1, \forall i$.

Since pooled estimators are widely used, it is worthwhile investigating the type of biases and inconsistencies they produce when dynamic heterogeneity is present. In what follows we focus on the simplest version of the model (8.21), (8.22), where there is one lag of y_{it} and one exogenous variable.

Exercise 8.22. Let $x_{it} = \bar{x}_i + \rho_x x_{it-1} + e^x_{it}$, where $\rho_x < 1$ and $e^x_{it} \sim$ i.i.d. $(0, \sigma^2_{x_i})$; let $\sigma^2 = (1/n)\sum_i \sigma^2_i$ and $\sigma^2_x = (1/n)\sum_i \sigma^2_{x_i}$. Assume that $A_{1i} = A_1, \forall i$, but that A_{2i} differs across i.

(i) Show that $p\lim_{n,T\to\infty} A_{1\mathrm{p}} = A_1 + [\rho_x(1 - A_1\rho_x)(1 - A_1^2)\sigma^2_{A_2}]/\psi_1$ and that $p\lim_{n,T\to\infty} A_{2\mathrm{p}} = A_2 - (A_2\rho^2_x(1 - A_1^2)\sigma^2_{A_2})/\psi_1$, where $\psi_1 = (\sigma^2/\sigma^2_x) \times (1 - \rho^2_x)(1 - A_1\rho_x)^2 + (1 - A_1^2\rho^2_x)\sigma^2_{A_2} + (1 - \rho^2_x)A_2$ and $\sigma^2_{A_2} = \mathrm{var}(A_2)$.

(ii) Show that the large sample bias of $A_{1\mathrm{p}}$ is positive when $\rho_x > 0$, while $p\lim \hat{A}_2 < A_2$ for all parameter values. Argue that the larger the degree of heterogeneity (i.e., the larger $\sigma^2_{A_2}$ is), the greater is the bias. Show that the bias disappears if and only if $\rho_x = 0$.

(iii) Show that $p\lim_{n,T\to\infty} A_{2\mathrm{p}}/(1 - A_{1\mathrm{p}}) = A_2/[(1 - A_1)(1 - \rho_x)\psi_2]$ with $\psi_2 = (1 + A_1)\sigma^2_{A_2}/[(\sigma^2/\sigma^2_x)(1 + \rho_x)(1 - A_1\rho_x)^2 + (1 + \rho_x)(A_2^2 + \sigma^2_{A_2})] > 0$.

Exercise 8.22 shows that OLS in the pooled model overestimates both A_1 and $A_2/(1 - A_1)$ when $\rho_x > 0$ and that the bias washes out if either $\rho_x = 0$ or $\sigma^2_{A_2} = 0$. Furthermore, it is easy to see that $p\lim A_{1\mathrm{p}} = 1$ and $p\lim A_{2\mathrm{p}} = 0$ if $\rho_x \to 1$, irrespective of the true A_1, while $p\lim A_{1\mathrm{p}} = A_1$ and $p\lim A_{2\mathrm{p}} = A_2$ if $A_1 \to 1$.

The results of exercise 8.22 appear to depend on the presence of serial correlation in the exogenous variables. However, $\rho_x \neq 0$ is inessential and a similar result obtains when x_{it} are i.i.d. but current and lagged values of the x_t enter the model, as shown next.

Example 8.16. Suppose that the true model is $y_{it} = \varrho_i + A_{i2}x_{it} + A_{i3}x_{it-1} + e_{it}$ and that $A_i = [A_{i2}, A_{i3}]' = A + v_i$, $v_i \sim$ i.i.d. $(0, \Sigma_v)$. Suppose that x_{it} are i.i.d. and suppose an investigator estimates $y_{it} = a_{i1}y_{it-1} + a_{i2}x_{it} + a_{i3}x_{it-1} + \varrho_i + \epsilon_{it}$. Using OLS on the pooled model we have that $a_{2\mathrm{p}} = A_2$ and $a_{3\mathrm{p}} = A_3 - a_1^* A_2$, where $a_1^* = p\lim a_{1\mathrm{p}} = \sigma_{12}/[\sigma_{11} + \sigma_{22} + (A_3^2 + \sigma^2/\sigma^2_x)]$ and σ_{ij} are the elements of Σ_v, for $T, n \to \infty$. Therefore, no matter how large T and n are, $a_1^* = 0$ if and only if $\sigma_{12} = 0$. Consequently, estimates of the long-run effect of x on y, $(a_{2\mathrm{p}} + a_{3\mathrm{p}})/(1 - a_{1\mathrm{p}})$ will converge to $A_2 + A_3 + a_1^* A_3/(1 - a_1^*) \neq A_2 + A_3$ as $T \to \infty$.

The biases and inconsistencies of example 8.16 occur because the heterogeneity in the coefficients of the x is ignored and serial correlation in the x makes the problem worse. Clearly, the size of the bias depends on the sign and the magnitude of σ_{12} and ρ_x. When these are positive, $a_1^* > 0$, and there will be a tendency to underestimate the impact of x_{it-j} on y_{it} and overestimate its long-run effect.

When T is short, a pooled estimator is inconsistent even without dynamic heterogeneity. In this situation, either an Anderson–Hsiao (AH) or a GMM estimator after differencing is typically used. But while both approaches produce consistent estimates of the parameters with homogeneous dynamics, this is not the case with heterogenous dynamics.

Example 8.17. First differencing (8.25) and (8.26), we have

$$\Delta y_{it} = A_1(\ell)\Delta y_{it-1} + A_2(\ell)\Delta x_{it} + \Delta e^{\mathrm{p}}_{it}, \tag{8.29}$$

$$\Delta e^{\mathrm{p}}_{it} = \Delta e_{it} + v'_{1i}\Delta y_{it-1} + v'_{2i}\Delta x_{it}. \tag{8.30}$$

Clearly, any instrument uncorrelated with the errors will also be uncorrelated with the regressors. For example, lagged values of y_{it} are not valid instruments since they depend on v_{ji} which, in turn, are correlated with Δe^{p}_t. Similarly, current and lagged values of x_{it} are invalid even when they are uncorrelated with e_{it}.

There is one special case when differencing solves the problem. In fact, when $v_{i1} = 0, \forall i$, simple algebra shows that $E(\Delta e^{\mathrm{p}}_{it} z_{it}) = 0$ but $E(\Delta y_{it-1} z_{it}) = \sum_{\tau=0}^{\infty} E(A^{\tau}_{1i} A'_{2i}) E(\Delta x_{it-\tau-1} z_{it}) \neq 0$. Therefore, IV estimation after differencing yields consistent estimators of the means of A_{1i} and A_{2i} if lags of x_{it} are used (lags of y_{it} are invalid instruments).

Exercise 8.23. Show that, if A_{1i} is independent of A_{2i}, differencing and using appropriate lags of Δx_{it} as instruments yield consistent estimates of the mean value A_1 and A_2.

Example 8.18 (Sorensen, Wu, and Yosha). Suppose we wish to examine the cyclicality of the share of government expenditure in output over a sample of countries and run the regression $(G/\mathrm{GDP})_{it} = \varrho_i + \alpha_{1i}\Delta\mathrm{GDP}_{it} + \alpha_{2i}\Delta\mathrm{GDP}_{it-1} + e_{it}$. If $\alpha_{ji} = \alpha_j, \forall i$, a pooled regression after differencing produces consistent estimates of the responses of $(G/\mathrm{GDP})_{it}$ to a shock in $\Delta\mathrm{GDP}_{it}$ for each i, if proper instruments are used. Consistent estimates could also be obtained even if dynamic heterogeneity is neglected as long as $\mathrm{cov}(\alpha_{1i}, \alpha_{2i}) = 0$. Furthermore, consistent estimates could be obtained even when $(G/\mathrm{GDP})_{it-1}$ enters the regression as long as its coefficient is homogeneous across i.

8.3.3 Aggregate Time Series Estimator

Let $\bar{y}_t = (1/n)\sum_i y_{it}$, $\bar{x}_t = (1/n)\sum_i x_{it}$, $\bar{e}_t = (1/n)\sum_i e_{it}$, and $\bar{\varrho} = (1/n) \times \sum_i \varrho_i$. The model we consider is

$$\bar{y}_t = A_1(\ell)\bar{y}_{t-1} + A_2(\ell)\bar{x}_t + \bar{\varrho} + \bar{e}^{\mathrm{TS}}_t, \tag{8.31}$$

$$\bar{e}^{\mathrm{TS}}_t = \bar{e}_t + \frac{1}{n}\sum_{i=1}^{n}(v'_{1i} y_{it-1} + v'_{2i} x_{it}). \tag{8.32}$$

Serial correlation in x_{it} clearly produces a complex serial correlation pattern in $\bar{e}^{\mathrm{TS}}_t$. What is perhaps less easy to see at first is that $\bar{e}^{\mathrm{TS}}_t$ is correlated with the regressors of (8.31), so that OLS will yield inconsistent estimates even when $T \to \infty$ or $T, n \to \infty$.

Example 8.19. We demonstrate this problem when there is only one lag of y_{it}, when $\dim(x_{it}) = 1$ and $A_2(\ell) = 0, \forall \ell \geqslant 1$. The OLS estimator of A_2 in (8.31) is

$$A_{2,\mathrm{TS}} - A_2 = \frac{(\sum_t \bar{y}^2_{t-1})(\sum_t \bar{x}_t \bar{e}^{\mathrm{TS}}_t) - (\sum_t \bar{x}_t \bar{y}_{t-1})(\sum_t \bar{y}_{t-1}\bar{e}^{\mathrm{TS}}_t)}{(\sum_t \bar{y}^2_{t-1})(\sum_t \bar{x}^2_t) - (\sum_t \bar{x}_t \bar{y}_{t-1})^2}.$$

Then, as $T \to \infty$,

$$p \lim A_{2,\mathrm{TS}} - A_2 = \frac{(E\bar{y}_{t-1}^2)(E\bar{x}_t\bar{e}_t^{\mathrm{TS}}) - (E\bar{x}_t\bar{y}_{t-1})(E\bar{y}_{t-1}\bar{e}_t^{\mathrm{TS}})}{(E\bar{y}_{t-1}^2)(E\bar{x}_t^2) - (E\bar{x}_t\bar{y}_{t-1})^2}. \tag{8.33}$$

For consistency we need $\sum_t \bar{x}_t\bar{e}_t^{\mathrm{TS}} \to 0$ and $\sum_t \bar{y}_{t-1}\bar{e}_t^{\mathrm{TS}} \to 0$. But, for example,

$$E(\bar{x}_{t-\tau}\bar{e}_t^{\mathrm{TS}}) = \frac{1}{n}\sum_{i=1}^{n}\sum_{\tau'=1}^{\infty} E(v_{2i}A_{2i}A_{1i}^{\tau'})E(\bar{x}_{t-\tau}, x_{i,t-\tau'-1}) \neq 0 \tag{8.34}$$

unless either x_t is serially uncorrelated (the second term vanishes) or there is no parameter heterogeneity (the first term vanishes). Hence, the expression in the numerator (8.33) will not, in general, be equal to zero.

Exercise 8.24. Show that, in general, $\sum_t \bar{y}_{t-1}\bar{e}_t^{\mathrm{TS}}$ does not converge to zero as $T \to \infty$. Show the conditions under which this may occur.

Since the terms in (8.34) are of order n^{-1} and since $E(\bar{x}_t\bar{e}_t^{\mathrm{TS}})$ and $E(\bar{y}_{t-1}\bar{e}_t^{\mathrm{TS}})$ converge to a finite limit, increasing n will not eliminate the inconsistency of the aggregate time series estimator. Also, since the serial correlation properties of $\bar{e}^{\mathrm{TS}}$ are sufficiently complex, an IV approach is unlikely to work. For example, looking at (8.34), one can see that lags of $\bar{x}_t$ are invalid instruments. The problem is similar to the one encountered with the pooled estimator: variables which are uncorrelated with $\bar{e}_t^{\mathrm{TS}}$ will also be uncorrelated with the regressors. Therefore, proper instruments are hard to find.

One reason why the aggregate time series estimator is inconsistent is that averaging over n aggregates cross-sectional information optimally. Pesaran (1995) showed that in a heterogeneous dynamic model the optimal cross-sectional aggregator has the form $\bar{y}_t = \sum_{\tau=0}^{\infty} a_\tau'\bar{x}_{t-\tau} + \bar{\epsilon}_t$, where $a_\tau = E(A_{2i}A_{1i}^{\tau})$, $\tau = 0, 1, \ldots$, and $\bar{\epsilon}_t$ are independent of x_t. Equation (8.31) misspecifies this expression because important regressors, correlated with included ones, are omitted from the specification. Therefore, inconsistencies are produced.

Exercise 8.25. Consider the case where $h(\alpha_i)$ is distributed as in (8.23). Show that the aggregate time series estimator of $h(\alpha)$ is inconsistent.

Example 8.20. Continuing with example 8.13 we compute the spectral density at frequency zero of inflation by using pooled and aggregate time series estimators. The point estimate for the pooled data is 9.84, which is within one standard error of the estimate obtained with the average estimator. With aggregated data the point estimate is 13.00, a value which is in the 99th percentile of the distribution of the average estimator. The point estimate of the sum of coefficients of the regression is 0.91 in the pooled case and 0.97 in the aggregate case, both of which are substantially smaller than the point estimate obtained with the average estimator, but not statistically different from it.

8.3.4 Average Cross-Sectional Estimator

The average cross-sectional estimator is also popular in applied work and believed to unbiasedly measure the size of the parameters and of continuous functions of them. But while in static models such a presumption is correct, this is not necessarily the case when heterogeneous dynamic models are considered.

Example 8.21 (Fatas and Mihov). There has been some interest in examining whether macroeconomic volatility, typically measured by the standard deviation of output growth, is systematically related to government size, typically measured by the log of the share of government expenditure in GDP, since simple Keynesian models predict a negative relationship between the two. To check this hypothesis, the literature has estimated one volatility for each unit, averaged the expenditure share over time, and run a cross-sectional regression, with or without additional controls. Typically, a negative coefficient is found but there may be doubts about the reliability of these estimates since, as we will see, neglecting dynamic heterogeneity induces large negative biases.

Let $\bar{y}_i = (1/T)\sum_t y_{it}$, $\bar{x}_i = (1/T)\sum_t x_{it}$, and $\bar{e}_i = (1/T)\sum_t e_{it}$. Then the model we are estimating is

$$\bar{y}_i = A_1(\ell)\bar{y}_{i,-1} + A_2(\ell)\bar{x}_i + \varrho_i + \bar{e}_i^{\text{CS}}, \tag{8.35}$$

$$\bar{e}_i^{\text{CS}} = \bar{e}_i + v'_{1i}\bar{y}_{i,-1} + v'_{2i}\bar{x}_i. \tag{8.36}$$

The regression defined by (8.35) is the so-called "between" regression of the dynamic model. Such a model, when estimated with OLS, yields inconsistent estimates of $A_j(\ell)$ when $n \to \infty$ or $n, T \to \infty$, since $\bar{e}^{\text{CS}}$ is correlated with the regressors, even when n is large. Consequently, functions of a "between" regression estimator obtained from a heterogenous panel will also be inconsistent.

One way to produce consistent estimates is to replace (8.35) with

$$\bar{y}_i = A_{2i}(\ell)\bar{x}_i + A_{1i}(\ell)(\bar{y}_i - \Delta_T y_i) + \bar{e}_i, \tag{8.37}$$

where $\Delta_T y_i = (y_{iT} - y_{i0})/T$. Note that equation (8.37) is equivalent to $\bar{y}_i = [1 - A_{1i}(\ell)]^{-1}A_{2i}\bar{x}_i - [1 - A_{1i}(\ell)]^{-1}A_{1i}(\ell)\Delta_T y_i + [1 - A_{1i}(\ell)]^{-1}\bar{e}_i \equiv a_{1i}\bar{x}_i + a_{2i}\Delta_T y_i + \bar{\epsilon}_i$. If a_{ji}, $j = 1, 2$, are randomly distributed around the mean, then

$$\bar{y}_i = a_1\bar{x}_i - a_2\Delta_T y_i + \bar{\epsilon}_i^{\text{CS}}, \tag{8.38}$$

$$\bar{\epsilon}_i^{\text{CS}} = (1 - A_{1i}(\ell))^{-1}\bar{e}_i + v'_{2i}\bar{x}_i - v'_{1i}\Delta_T y_i. \tag{8.39}$$

In the next exercise we ask the reader to verify that consistent estimates of a_1 and a_2 in (8.38), (8.39) can be obtained with OLS if T is large enough.

Exercise 8.26. Let the cross-sectional estimator of a'_1 be $a'_{1,\text{CS}} = (\sum_i \bar{x}_i\bar{x}'_i)^{-1} \times (\sum_i \bar{x}_i\bar{y}'_i)$.

(i) Show that $E(a'_{1,\text{CS}} - a'_1) = (\sum_i \bar{x}_i\bar{x}'_i)^{-1}(\sum_i \bar{x}_i\bar{x}'_i)v_{2i} + (\sum_i \bar{x}_i\bar{x}'_i)^{-1} \times \sum_i(1 + a_{2i})\bar{x}_i\bar{\bar{e}}_i^{\text{CS}} - (\sum_i \bar{x}_i\bar{x}'_i)^{-1}$ or, by using the assumptions made, that

$E(a'_{1,\mathrm{CS}} - a'_1) = -\sum_{\tau=0}^{\infty}(\sum_i \bar{x}_i \bar{x}'_i)^{-1} \sum_{i=1}^{n} \bar{x}_i (\bar{x}_{i,-\tau} - \bar{x}_{i,-\tau-1})' E(a_{2i} A_{2i} A^{\tau}_{1i})$. Hence, for finite T, $E(a'_{1,\mathrm{CS}})$ is biased even if $n \to \infty$.

(ii) Show that, for $T \to \infty$, $\bar{x}_i (\bar{x}_{i,-\tau} - \bar{x}_{i,-\tau-1})' = O_p(T^{-1})$. Conclude that, since $E(a_{2i} A_{2i} A^{\tau}_{1i})$ is finite, $E(a'_{1,\mathrm{CS}} - a'_1) \to 0$ in probability.

It is important to stress that the estimator in (8.35) is inconsistent not because the model is misspecified. The omitted term, $\Delta_T y_i$, is asymptotically uncorrelated with the level variables so it will not affect estimates of long-run effects. The inconsistency is instead produced by the presence of a correlation between the error and the regressors.

In sum, if dynamic heterogeneity is present, cross-sectional regressions where variables are time series averages for each unit are problematic since, for fixed T, OLS estimates of the parameters will be inconsistent, even when n is large.

In certain applied situations one may want to use cointegration ideas to get estimates of the parameters of a dynamic model. If x_{it} were integrated variables and each i had its own cointegrating relationship, then unit-specific regressions yield superconsistent estimates of $A_2(1)$ and $h(\alpha_i)$ and the average estimator of $h_{\mathrm{A}}(\alpha)$ will also be consistent. Note that since parameter estimates converge at the rate T and since the average converges at the rate $\sqrt{n}$, the estimator of $h(\alpha)$ converges at the rate $T\sqrt{n}$. Note also that a pooled regression will not yield a consistent estimate of α, even in the presence of cointegration. This is because the error term has an $I(0)$ component, the residuals of the cointegrating relationship for unit i, and an $I(1)$ component, the product of the difference between the coefficient of each i from the imposed common coefficient and the $I(1)$ regressor. Therefore, the composite error is $I(1)$ and the regression does not define a cointegrating relationship.

The next exercise examines what happens to the other two estimators when the variables of the model are integrated.

Exercise 8.27. (i) Consider the model $\bar{y}_t = A_2 \bar{x}_t + \bar{e}^{\mathrm{TS}}_t$, where $\bar{e}^{\mathrm{TS}}_t = \bar{e}_t + (1/n) \times \sum_i v_i x_{it}$, $A_{2i} = \bar{A}_2 + v_i$, and x_{it} strictly exogenous. Show that, if $x_{i,t} = x_{i,t-1} + e^x_{i,t}$, $e^x_{i,t} \sim$ i.i.d. $(0, \sigma^2_{x_i})$, $A_{2,\mathrm{TS}}$ is inconsistent.

(ii) Let $A_{2,\mathrm{CS}} = A_2 + \sum_i (v_{2i}\bar{x}_i^2 - \bar{e}_i \bar{x}_i)/\sum_i \bar{x}_i^2$. Show that, if $x_{it} = x_{it-1} + \bar{x}_i + e^x_{it}$, $e^x_{it} \sim$ i.i.d. $(0, \sigma^2_{x_i})$, $A_{2,\mathrm{CS}}$ is consistent for T fixed and $n \to \infty$.

8.3.5 *Testing for Dynamic Heterogeneity*

Since the presence of heterogeneous dynamics causes problems for standard estimators even when first differencing and instrumental variables are used, it is crucial to have a method for assessing whether homogeneity holds in the sample under consideration. One way of testing for dynamic heterogeneities is to use a Hausman-type test, which we described in chapter 5. The idea of the test is very similar to the one presented in section 8.2: we wish to find one estimator which is consistent under the two hypotheses and another which is consistent (and efficient) under the null and inconsistent under the alternative.

Given these requirements we can, for example, compare the pooled estimator and the average time series estimator. Under the null of homogeneity, both are consistent and the pooled estimator is more efficient. Under the alternative of heterogeneity, only the average time series estimator is consistent.

The asymptotic variances of the two estimators (for fixed n and large T) are $\sigma^2 \times (\sum_i p\lim_{T\to\infty}(X_i'\Omega_T X_i/T))^{-1}$ and $(\sigma^2/n^2)\sum_i[p\lim_{T\to\infty}(X_i'\Omega_T X_i/T)^{-1}]$. Hence, the covariance matrix of the difference between the estimators is positive definite except when $p\lim_{T\to\infty}(X_i'\Omega_T X_i/T) = p\lim_{T\to\infty}(X_{i'}'\Omega_T X_{i'}/T)$, $i' \neq i$. Then a test for heterogeneity can be conducted by using $\mathfrak{S}_1 = \sigma_{\rm A}^2(\alpha_{\rm A} - \alpha_{\rm P})' \times \Sigma^{-1}(\alpha_{\rm A} - \alpha_{\rm P})$, where $\Sigma = (1/n^2)\sum_i(X_i'\Omega_T X_i)^{-1} - (\sum_i X_i'\Omega_T X_i)^{-1}$, $\sigma_{\rm A}^2 = (1/n)\sum_i \sigma_i^2$, and $\alpha = \operatorname{vec}(A_{1i}(\ell), A_{2i}(\ell))$. Under the null that $A_{1i}(\ell) = A_1(\ell)$, $A_{2i}(\ell) = A_2(\ell)$, $\sigma_i^2 = \sigma^2$, $\forall i$, $\mathfrak{S}_1 \sim \chi^2(\dim(x_t) + \dim(y_t))$. Note that using $\sigma_{\rm P}^2$ in place of $\sigma_{\rm A}^2$ does not change the asymptotic distribution of the test.

Example 8.22. A Hausman-type test can also be used to verify hypotheses concerning relevant functions of the parameters. Consider estimating $h_2(\alpha) = E[1 - A_{1i}(1)]^{-1}A_{2i}(1)$. The pooled estimator is

$$h_{2\rm P} = [1 - A_{1\rm P}(1)]^{-1}A_{2\rm P}(1) = E[1 - A_{1i}(1)]^{-1}A_{2i}(1) + \frac{(A_{1\rm P}(1) - A_1)E(1 - A_{i1}(1))^{-1}A_{2i}(1) + (A_{2\rm P}(1) - A_2)}{1 - A_{1\rm P}(1)}$$

and the average time series estimator is

$$h_{2\rm A} = \frac{1}{n}\sum_i h_2(\alpha_i).$$

The asymptotic variance of the former is $D(\sum_i p\lim(X_i'\Omega_T X_i/T))^{-1}D' \times [\sigma^2/(1 - A_1(1))^2]$ and that of the latter is $D(\sum_i[p\lim(X_i'\Omega_T X_i/T)^{-1}])D' \times [\sigma^2/n^2(1 - A_1(1))^2]$, where $D = (a_2, G_{m_2})$ and G_{m_2} is an $m_2 \times (m_2 + 1)$ matrix.

Then, $\mathfrak{S}_2 = (\hat\sigma^2/[1 - \hat A_1(1)]^2)(h_{2\rm A} - h_{2\rm P})'(\hat D\hat\Sigma\hat D')^{-1}(h_{2\rm A} - h_{2\rm P})$ can be used to test for heterogeneity, where the "hat" variables can be obtained from either the pooled or the average time series estimator and

$$\hat\Sigma = \frac{\hat\sigma^2}{n^2(1 - \widehat{A_1(1)})^2}\hat D\Big(\sum_i[p\lim(X_i'\Omega_T X_i/n)^{-1}]\Big)\hat D' - \frac{\hat\sigma^2}{(1 - \widehat{A_1(1)})^2}\hat D\Big(\sum_i p\lim(X_i'\Omega_T X_i/nT)\Big)^{-1}\hat D'.$$

Under the null, $\mathfrak{S}_2 \sim \chi^2(m_2)$. Note that $\hat\Sigma$ may be nonpositive definite in small samples.

These tests are appropriate when T is large; for small T the average time series estimator is biased. When T is small it is still possible to conduct homogeneity tests for $h(\alpha)$ by using the modified cross-sectional estimator, which is consistent under the alternative. However, since the Hausman test is asymptotically justified only when T is large, care must be exercised when comparing pooled and cross-sectional estimators. It is also worth mentioning that the Hausman test has poor power properties when outliers are present since the variance of the estimators tends to be large. Similarly, if the cross-sectional data are of uneven quality, the null of homogeneity could be difficult to reject.

Exercise 8.28. Suppose T is short. Provide a statistic to test heterogeneities in $h_1(\alpha) = (1 - A_1(\ell))^{-1} A_1$.

Example 8.23. It is usually difficult to interpret rejections of the homogeneity hypothesis since heterogeneity may result from a misspecified but homogeneous model. When homogeneity is rejected, one typically finds a very large dispersion of estimates, with several economically implausible individual estimates, but the average of the estimates may turn out to be quite sensible. Can this pattern provide information for the likely causes of heterogeneity? Suppose that the estimated model is $y_{it} = \alpha_i x_{1it} + \epsilon_{it}$, $\epsilon_{it} = x_{2it} + e_{it}$, and $x_{2it} = \theta_{it} x_{1it} + v_{it}$, where x_{2it} are omitted variables linked in a time-varying fashion to the regressors x_{1it}. It is easy to see that $E(\hat{\alpha}_{it}) = \alpha_i + \theta_{it}$. Consequently, the specification error in $\hat{\alpha}_{it}$ is large and significant if x_{2it} are important for y_{it} and θ_{it} nonnegligible. If x_{2it} are common to all i for all t, $\hat{\alpha}_T = (1/n) \sum_i \hat{\alpha}_{iT}$ will have a systematic bias. However, if x_{2it} are random over the cross section, it is possible that $E(\theta_{iT}) = 0$, so that average estimates are more reliable than individual ones. The same result would occur if x_{2it} are randomly correlated for each i across T. Note, finally, that the structure considered in this example may not only cause heterogeneities but also instabilities since the correlation structure between y_{1t} and x_{2t} evolves over time for each i.

8.4 To Pool or Not to Pool?

In many applied exercises, a researcher is interested in examining estimates of, say, long-run coefficients, elasticities, or impulse responses across countries or regions hoping to infer whether certain individual characteristics (say, labor market regulations or government policies) are responsible for the differences. When T is short comparisons are difficult and, at times, uninformative since estimates are biased and estimation uncertainty is large. Hence, one question of interest is whether it is possible to improve upon single-unit estimation of the parameters by using cross-sectional information. We have already seen that complete pooling is efficient under dynamic homogeneity but produces biases and inconsistencies if dynamic heterogeneities are present. Here we are concerned with the question of whether some form of pooling is advisable, even under heterogeneity, and on how partial pooling could be made operative in a tractable way.

The simplest procedure one can use to check whether pooling is appropriate is a preliminary test of equality of the coefficients over the cross section. Suppose

$$y_{it} = X_{it}\alpha_i + e_{it}, \quad e_{it} \sim \text{i.i.d. } (0, \sigma^2 I), \tag{8.40}$$

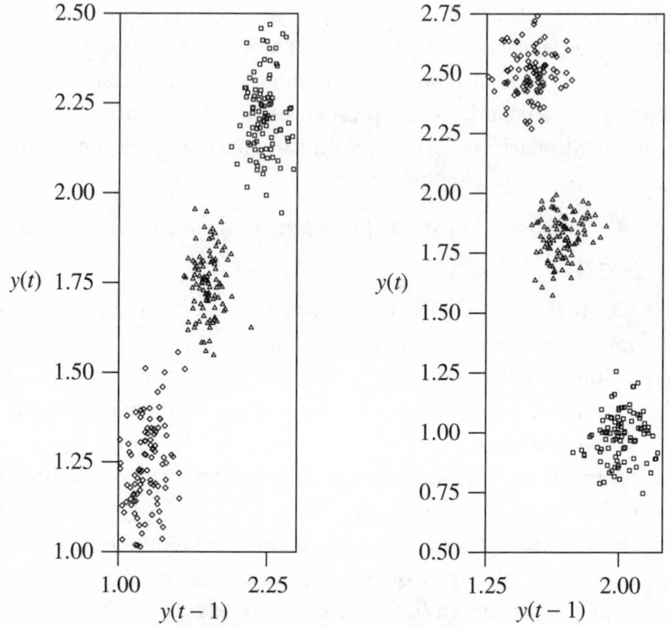

Figure 8.2. Cross-sectional distributions.

where X_t includes a vector of 1s, exogenous and lagged dependent variables, and α_i are the regression parameters of unit i. If the null hypothesis is $\alpha_1 = \alpha_2 = \cdots = \alpha_{n_1} = \alpha, n_1 \leqslant n$, a pooled model for n_1 units is just the unpooled model with some (exact) linear restrictions on the α. Hence, to verify the null hypothesis one could compare the R^2 of two regressions, one with and one without the restrictions. Given that $F = [(R^2_{\text{un}} - R^2_{\text{re}})/(n-1)]/[(1 - R^2_{\text{un}})/(nT - n - 1)]$, where R^2_{re} (R^2_{un}) is the R^2 of the restricted (unrestricted) model, choosing the unpooled specification is equivalent to choosing the alternative hypothesis when the F-ratio exceeds 1, which implies a classical significance level of 50%. Hence, one should be aware that the significance level used in pretesting is different from the one used in other standard hypothesis testing. Also, the pretest estimator of α_i is discontinuous (it is $\alpha_{i,\text{OLS}}$ if the F-ratio is greater than 1 and α_{OLS} otherwise), so that its asymptotic distribution is complicated. Finally, a pretest estimator is dominated under a quadratic loss function by other estimators (see Judge et al. 1985, pp. 72–80).

Apart from these theoretical considerations, it is common in applied work to encounter situations where, without exact knowledge of the distribution of the observations across units, surprising results may appear when pooling is performed if pretesting is used.

Example 8.24. Suppose $n = 3$ and consider a simple AR(1) regression with unit-specific parameters. Figure 8.2 plots a cloud of points for two distributions of i. Here the regression slopes are identical for each i so one may end up pooling observations if the standard error of the intercept is large enough. However, while pooling in the first case will maintain the positive slope (biasing upwards the estimate of the AR coefficient), in the second it will produce a negative estimate of the common slope parameter. Since there is no reason to *a priori* exclude the second distribution, one may find that y_{it} and y_{it-1} are positively correlated with individual data and negatively correlated when pooled data are used.

Given these problems, pretesting does not seem to be the way to go to reduce biases and improve the quality of the standard errors of the estimates.

A Stein-type shrinkage estimator also produces improved estimates of the parameters by using cross-sectional information. Such an estimator is given by

$$\alpha_{i\mathrm{S}} = \alpha_{\mathrm{p}} + \left(1 - \frac{\kappa}{F}\right)(\alpha_{i,\mathrm{OLS}} - \alpha_{\mathrm{p}}), \quad i = 1, \dots, n, \tag{8.41}$$

where $\alpha_{i,\mathrm{OLS}}$ is the OLS estimator obtained with data from unit i, α_{p} is the pooled estimator, F is the F-statistic for the null hypothesis $\alpha_i = \alpha, \forall i$ (i.e., $F = (\alpha_i - \alpha)'(\alpha_i - \alpha)/n\sigma^2$), and $\kappa = [(n-1)\dim(\alpha) - 2]/[n(T - \dim(\alpha)) + 2]$, which, for large n, reduces to $\kappa \approx \dim(\alpha)/(T - \dim(\alpha))$.

Note that a Stein-type estimator combines individual and pooled estimates by using a weight which, for large n, depends on the dimension of α relative to the size of the time series. The larger $\dim(\alpha)$ is relative to T, the smaller will be the shrinkage factor κ/F.

Another way to partly pool heterogenous cross-sectional information is to use a random coefficient approach. Random coefficient models also lead to shrinkage-style estimators but, contrary to Stein estimators, they combine individual estimators with a weighted average of individual estimators. Suppose the model is

$$y_{it} = x_{it}\alpha_i + e_{it}, \tag{8.42}$$

$$\alpha_i = \bar{\alpha} + v_i, \tag{8.43}$$

where $e_i \sim$ i.i.d. $(0, \sigma_i^2 I)$ and $v_i \sim$ i.i.d. $(0, \Sigma_v)$. There are four ways to construct improved estimates of α_i in this model which correspond, roughly speaking, to classical, Bayesian, prior likelihood, and empirical Bayes approaches.

In a classical approach α and Σ_v are estimable but individual α_i are not. In this case, one substitutes (8.43) into (8.42) so that $y_{it} \sim (x_{it}\alpha, \Sigma_{it})$, where $\Sigma_{it} = \sigma_i^2 I + x_{it}'\Sigma_v x_{it}$. This is what the literature typically calls an error-component model. The GLS estimator for α, obtained by stacking the T observations for each unit is $\alpha_{\mathrm{GLS}} = (\sum_i x_i \Sigma_i^{-1} x_i)^{-1}(\sum_i x_i \Sigma_i^{-1} y_i)$, which collapses to the OLS estimator $\alpha_{i,\mathrm{OLS}} = (\sigma_i^{-2} x_i' x_i)^{-1}(\sigma_i^{-2} x_i' y_i)$ if $\Sigma_v = 0$.

Exercise 8.29. Show that $\alpha_{\mathrm{GLS}} = \sum_i (\sum_{j=1}^n \Omega_j^{-1})^{-1} \Omega_i^{-1} \alpha_{i,\mathrm{OLS}}$, where $\Omega_i = \sigma_i^2 (x_i' x_i)^{-1} + \Sigma_v$.

Exercise 8.29 shows that the GLS estimator of α is a weighted average of the OLS estimators for each α_i (constructed by treating σ_i^2 and Σ_v as fixed), with weights given by a function of Σ_v and the data matrix $x_i'x_i$. α_{GLS} is unfeasible. Therefore, one would use $\Sigma_{v,\text{OLS}} = (1/(n-1))\sum_{i=1}^{n}(\alpha_{i,\text{OLS}} - (1/n)\sum_{i=1}^{n}\alpha_{i,\text{OLS}})(\alpha_{i,\text{OLS}} - (1/n)\sum_{i=1}^{n}\alpha_{i,\text{OLS}})' - (1/n)\sum_i \sigma_{i,\text{OLS}}^2(x_i x_i')^{-1}$ and $\sigma_{i,\text{OLS}}^2 = \{1/[T - \dim(\alpha_i)]\} \times (y_i'y_i - y_i x_i \alpha_{i,\text{OLS}})^2$ into the GLS formula. Since $\Sigma_{v,\text{OLS}}$ is not necessarily positive definite, the last term of the expression is usually neglected: the resulting estimator is biased but nonnegative definite and consistent as $T \to \infty$.

In the other three approaches, equation (8.43) is treated as a prior and α and Σ_v represent a second layer of parameters (the hyperparameters) describing the features of the prior. If e_i and v_i are normal, and α and Σ_v known, the posterior of α_i is normal with mean $\tilde{\alpha}_i = [(1/\sigma_i^2)x_i'x_i + \Sigma_v^{-1}]^{-1}[(1/\sigma_i^2)x_i'x_i\alpha_{i,\text{OLS}} + \Sigma_v^{-1}\bar{\alpha}]$, where $\alpha_{i,\text{OLS}}$ is the OLS estimator of α_i. It is easy to see that, if Σ_v is large, $\tilde{\alpha}_i \approx \alpha_{i,\text{OLS}}$, that is, there is no information in the prior which can be used to improve estimates of α_i. α_{GLS} is related to $\tilde{\alpha}_i$ via $\alpha_{\text{GLS}} = (1/n)\sum_{i=1}^{n}\tilde{\alpha}_i$, that is, the GLS estimator equals the cross-sectional average of Bayesian estimators $\tilde{\alpha}_i$.

When $\bar{\alpha}$, σ_i^2, Σ_v are unknown, one should specify a prior distribution for these parameters (see, for example, chapter 9). If this is done, no analytical solution for the posterior mean of α_i exists. If normality is likely to hold, one could approximate posterior means with posterior modes (see Smith 1973), i.e., use

$$\bar{\alpha}^* = \frac{1}{n}\sum_{i=1}^{n}\alpha_i^*, \tag{8.44}$$

$$(\sigma_i^*)^2 = \frac{1}{T+2}[(y_i - x_i\alpha_i^*)'(y_i - x_i\alpha_i^*)], \tag{8.45}$$

$$\Sigma_v^* = \frac{1}{n - \dim(\alpha) - 1}\left[\sum_i(\alpha_i^* - \bar{\alpha}^*)(\alpha_i^* - \bar{\alpha}^*)' + \kappa\right], \tag{8.46}$$

where an asterisk indicates modal estimates and, typically, $\kappa = \text{diag}[0.001]$.

As an alternative, one can use the so-called prior likelihood approach. Here, one jointly selects $(\alpha_i, \sigma_i^2, \bar{\alpha}, \Sigma_v)$ to maximize $-\frac{1}{2}\{T\sum_{i=1}^{n}\ln\sigma_i^2 - \sum_{i=1}^{n}(y_i - x_i\alpha_i)' \times (y_i - x_i\alpha_i)/\sigma_i^2 - n\ln|\Sigma_v| - \sum_{i=1}^{n}(\alpha_i - \bar{\alpha})^{-1}\Sigma_v^{-1}(\alpha_i - \bar{\alpha})\}$. The solution is

$$\alpha_{i,\text{PL}} = \left(\frac{1}{\sigma_{i,\text{PL}}^2}x_i'x_i + \Sigma_{v,\text{PL}}^{-1}\right)^{-1}\left(\frac{1}{\sigma_{i,\text{PL}}^2}x_i'x_i\alpha_{i,\text{OLS}} + \Sigma_{v,\text{PL}}^{-1}\bar{\alpha}_{\text{PL}}\right), \tag{8.47}$$

$$\bar{\alpha}_{\text{PL}} = \frac{1}{n}\sum_{i=1}^{n}\alpha_{i,\text{PL}}, \tag{8.48}$$

$$\sigma_{i,\text{PL}}^2 = \frac{1}{T}(y_i - x_i\alpha_{i,\text{PL}})'(y_i - x_i\alpha_{i,\text{PL}}), \tag{8.49}$$

$$\Sigma_{v,\text{PL}} = \frac{1}{n}\sum_{i=1}^{n}(\alpha_{i,\text{PL}} - \bar{\alpha}_{\text{PL}})(\alpha_{i,\text{PL}} - \bar{\alpha}_{\text{PL}})'. \tag{8.50}$$

Note the similarities between (8.44)–(8.46) and (8.48)–(8.50) and between (8.47) and the formula for $\tilde{\alpha}_i$.

Exercise 8.30. Suggest an iterative procedure to obtain $\alpha_{i,\mathrm{PL}}$, $\bar{\alpha}_{\mathrm{PL}}$, $\sigma^2_{i,\mathrm{PL}}$, $\Sigma_{v,\mathrm{PL}}$.

Finally, one could use empirical Bayes (EB) methods. As we will see in more detail in chapter 9, this approach treats Σ_v, σ_i^2, and $\bar{\alpha}$ as unknown and estimates them by using the marginal likelihood of y in a training sample. An EB estimator is (see, for example, Rao 1975)

$$\bar{\alpha}_{\mathrm{EB}} = \frac{1}{n}\sum_{i=1}^{n}\alpha_{i,\mathrm{OLS}}, \tag{8.51}$$

$$\sigma^2_{i,\mathrm{EB}} = \frac{1}{T-\dim(\alpha)}(y_i'y_i - y_i'x_i\alpha_{i,\mathrm{OLS}}), \tag{8.52}$$

$$\hat{\Sigma}_{v,\mathrm{EB}} = \frac{1}{n-1}\sum_{i=1}^{n}(\alpha_{i,\mathrm{OLS}} - \bar{\alpha}_{\mathrm{EB}})(\alpha_i - \bar{\alpha}_{\mathrm{EB}})' - \frac{1}{n}\sum_{i=1}^{n}(x_i'x_i)^{-1}\sigma^2_{i,\mathrm{OLS}}. \tag{8.53}$$

Clearly, the Bayes and the empirical Bayes estimators of α are similar but while the former is an average of $\tilde{\alpha}_i$, the latter is an average of OLS estimates. Note that both estimators can be computed in two steps and do not require iterative solutions. Alternative empirical Bayes estimators for dynamic heterogeneous panels are presented in chapter 10.

Pooling subsets of the cross-sectional units is straightforward, as the next example shows.

Example 8.25. Suppose that it is known that

$$\alpha_i = \begin{cases} \bar{\alpha}_1 + v_{i1}, & v_{i1} \sim \text{i.i.d. } \mathbb{N}(0, \Sigma_1) \quad \text{if } i \leqslant n_1, \\ \bar{\alpha}_2 + v_{i2}, & v_{i2} \sim \text{i.i.d. } \mathbb{N}(0, \Sigma_2) \quad \text{if } n_1 > i > n. \end{cases} \tag{8.54}$$

Then the four procedures described in this subsection can be used to estimate $\bar{\alpha}_1$, $\bar{\alpha}_2$, Σ_1, Σ_2, and α_i separately for each group.

Clearly, in many applications, the assumption that n_1 is known is unrealistic. Furthermore, standard tests for break points developed in the time series literature are inappropriate for panel data since the ordering of the n units is arbitrary. In chapter 10 we describe how to choose the break point optimally when the ordering of the cross section is unknown.

Exercise 8.31. Consider a VAR model for unit i of the form $y_{it} = A_i(\ell)y_{it-1} + e_{it}$, where $\alpha_i \equiv \mathrm{vec}(A_i(\ell)) = \bar{\alpha} + v_i$. Provide classical and Bayesian estimators of the parameters of the model which combine unit-specific and cross-sectional information. How would you check for dynamic heterogeneities?

8.4.1 What Goes Wrong with Two-Step Regressions?

There are situations, both in macroeconomics and in finance, where the parameters of a relationship are assumed to be related to some observable (unit-specific) characteristics and researchers employ two-step methods to uncover this relationship.

Example 8.26. In estimating the cyclicality of government expenditure one may, for example, be interested in knowing if balanced-budget restrictions matter or not. Using coefficients estimated from a time series regression as if they were the true ones, a second-stage regression on a dummy variable, describing whether a state has a balanced-budget restriction or not, is typically run. Alternatively, in estimating the speed of adjustment of employment to macroeconomic disturbances, one may want to know if labor market institutions account for the empirical differences found. In this case, a regression of the estimated speed of adjustments on cross-country indicators of labor market flexibility is usually run.

Are the two-step approaches of example 8.26 reasonable? What sort of biases should one expect to find in the second-stage estimates? Intuitively, an estimation error is artificially introduced in the second regression and this has important consequences. To illustrate why estimates and standard errors computed from these two-step regressions are incorrect, consider

$$y_{it} = x_{0it}\varrho_i + x_{1it}\alpha_i + e_{it}, \tag{8.55}$$

$$\alpha_i = x_{2i}\theta + v_i, \tag{8.56}$$

where $i = 1, 2, \ldots, n$ and x_{1it} is a $1\times m_2$ vector of exogenous and lagged dependent variables, x_{2i} is an $m_2\times m_3$ vector of time-invariant unit-specific characteristics, and x_{0it} is a $1 \times m_1$ vector of unit-specific intercepts (possibly depending on t). Finally, θ is an $m_3 \times 1$ vector of parameters. We assume that $E(x_{1it}e_{it}) = E(x_{2i}v_i) = 0$, that $e_{it} \sim$ i.i.d. $\mathbb{N}(0, \sigma_i^2)$, that $E(e_{it}, e_{i'\tau}) = 0, \forall t \neq \tau$ and $i \neq i'$, and $v_i \sim$ i.i.d. $\mathbb{N}(0, \Sigma_v)$. Stacking the observations for each i and substituting (8.56) into (8.55) we have $y_i = x_{0i}\varrho_i + X_i\theta + \epsilon_i$, where $X_i = x_{1i}x_{2i}$ is a $T \times m_3$ matrix, and $\epsilon_i = x_{1i}v_i + e_i$ so that $\text{var}(\epsilon_i) = x_{1i}\Sigma_v x_{1i}' + \sigma_i^2 I \equiv \Sigma_{\epsilon_i}$.

Exercise 8.32. Show that, given Σ_{ϵ_i} and θ, the ML estimator of ϱ_i is $\varrho_{i,\text{ML}} = (x_{0i}'\Sigma_v^{-1}x_{0i})^{-1}x_{0i}'\Sigma_v^{-1}(y_i - x_i\theta)$ and that $\theta_{\text{ML}} = (\sum_i X_i\Omega_i X_i)^{-1}(\sum_i X_i\Omega_i y_i)$, given Σ_{ϵ_i}, where $\Omega_i = \Sigma_{\epsilon_i}^{-1} - \Sigma_{\epsilon_i}^{-1}x_{0i}(x_{0i}'\Sigma_{\epsilon_i}^{-1}x_{0i})^{-1}x_{0i}'\Sigma_{\epsilon_i}^{-1}$.

Using the logic of exercise 8.29, we can write $\theta_{\text{ML}} = (\sum_i x_{2i}'\tilde{\Omega}_i^{-1}x_{2i})^{-1} \times (\sum_i x_{2i}'\tilde{\Omega}_i^{-1}\alpha_{i,\text{OLS}})$, where $\tilde{\Omega} = (x_{1i}'x_{1i})^{-1}\Omega_i$. Therefore, the ML estimator of θ, which corresponds to the GLS estimator of the transformed model, is a weighted average of the first-stage estimators $\alpha_{i,\text{OLS}}$ with weights which depend on $\tilde{\Omega}$.

Second-stage estimates are $\theta_{\text{2step}} = (\sum_i x_{2i}'\Sigma_v^{-1}x_{2i})^{-1}(\sum_i x_{2i}'\Sigma_v^{-1}\alpha_{i,\text{OLS}})$. Therefore, θ_{2step} incorrectly measures the effect of x_{2i} on α_i for two reasons. First, suppose that $x_{i0t} = 0, \forall t$. Then θ_{2step} neglects the fact that α_i are estimated (i.e., it neglects the term $\sigma^2(x_{1i}'x_{1i})^{-1}$). Moreover, the weights used in θ_{2step} are homoskedastic while those in θ_{ML} depend on unit-specific regressors x_{1i}. Second, if $x_{i0t} \neq 0$, there are additional terms in Ω_i which θ_{2step} neglects. It is difficult to predict what the combined effect of these two errors would be. In general, treating estimates as if they were the true ones will make θ_{2step} artificially significant and may, in some cases, bias the sign of the relationship.

Given that ML estimates are easy to compute and are feasible once estimates of σ_i^2 and Σ_v are plugged into the formulas, there is no reason to prefer two-step estimators. The mismeasurement caused by a two-step approach can be important, as shown next.

Example 8.27. We use U.S. state data to estimate whether the cyclicality of the share of government expenditure in local output in states with strict (*ex post*) balanced-budget restrictions is different from that of states with weak (*ex ante*) balanced-budget restrictions. We use annual data for 48 states (and 13 have only weak restrictions) from 1969 to 1995 and compute two regressions: one with a two-step model, i.e., $\ln G_{it}/\text{GDP}_{it} = \varrho_i + \alpha_{1i} \ln G_{it-1}/\text{GDP}_{it-1} + \alpha_{2i} \Delta \ln \text{GDP}_{it} + e_{it}$ and $\alpha_{2i,\text{OLS}} = \text{BB}\theta_1 + (1-\text{BB})\theta_2 + v_i$, where BB_i is a dummy variable taking the value of 1 if strict restrictions are present and 0 otherwise; and one with a one-step model, i.e., $(1 - \alpha_{1i}\ell) \ln G_{it}/\text{GDP}_{it} = \varrho_i + \theta_1 \text{BB}(\Delta \ln \text{GDP}_{it}) + \theta_2(1 - \text{BB}) \times (\Delta \ln \text{GDP}_{it}) + \epsilon_{it}$. Estimates of the coefficients in the two regressions are the same, $\theta_1 = 0.54$, $\theta_2 = 0.81$, suggesting that states with weak balanced-budget constraints have government expenditure which is more cyclical. However, while with the two-step procedure the standard error of the estimates are 0.11 and 0.06, they turn out to be 1.58 and 1.87 in the one-step regression. Hence, a t-test for equality of θ_1 and θ_2 has a p-value of 0.04 in the two-step regression and of 0.88 in the one-step regression.

8.5 Is Money Superneutral?

To illustrate some of the methods discussed in this chapter we study the effects of money on output in the long run using the cross section of G7 countries. The majority of monetary dynamic general equilibrium models have built in some form of money neutrality so that, in the long run, real variables are insulated from nominal ones. However, in some cash-in-advance models, variations of the growth rate of money may have real effects, even in the long run, because they alter the marginal rate of substitution between consumption and leisure and induce agents to work less in the steady state.

Example 8.28. Consider the cash-in-advance model described in example 2.8. Suppose the utility function is $u(c_{1t}, c_{2t}, N_t) = \vartheta_c \ln c_{1t} + (1 - \vartheta_c) \ln c_{2t} - \vartheta_N N_t$, where c_{1t} are cash goods and c_{2t} are credit goods. Letting the growth rate of money ΔM follow an AR(1) process with mean $\bar{M}$, persistence ρ_M, and standard deviation σ_M, log-linearizing the conditions around the steady state and setting $\beta = 0.989$, $\delta = 0.019$, $\eta = 0.6$, $\vartheta_N = 2.53$, $\vartheta_c = 0.4$, $\bar{M} = 0.015$, $\rho_\zeta = 0.95$, $\rho_M = 0.45$, $\sigma_\zeta^2 = 0.07$, $\sigma_M^2 = 0.0089$, the decision rule for hours is $\ln N = 0.25 + 1.51\zeta_t - 0.05\Delta M_t - 0.45 \ln K_t$. Hence, ceteris paribus, increases in the growth rate of money have depressing short-run effects on hours worked and therefore, via the production function, real activity. However, the level of money growth affects the steady state. In fact, the compensating variations in consumption needed to bring agents back to the optimum are 0.520 when steady-state inflation is 10% and 0.972 when steady-state inflation is 20%.

The literature has thoroughly discussed the problems one may encounter when using variations in the growth rate of money to proxy for monetary policy actions (see, for example, Gordon and Leeper 1994). First, there are variations which may represent responses to the state of the economy. Second, even when innovations in growth rates are considered, they may capture demand variations, as opposed to supply changes. With these caveats in mind we examine whether innovations in money growth have long-run effects on output growth in the G7 by using three different estimators. In one case we average the responses of output growth to money growth shocks across countries; in the second, we compute one average response by pooling the data across countries; in the third, we aggregate cross-sectional data for each t and compute the response of aggregate output growth to aggregate money growth shocks. Our interest here is multiple. First, we would like to see if different estimators tell us different stories about the superneutrality of money. Second, we want to relate differences, if they exist, to the properties of estimators. Third, we want to examine whether the evidence is consistent with the prediction of the model of example 8.28.

The data cover the sample 1980:1–2004:4. For each specification we run a bivariate VAR(5) on de-meaned data. We made the somewhat heroic assumption that no variable, other than output or money, is helpful in understanding the relationship between these two variables. Given the approximate diagonality of the covariance matrix of reduced-form shocks for all countries, different identifying restrictions imposed to separate money growth shocks from output growth shocks give very similar results.

Figure 8.3 shows that different estimators produce very different responses. When the pooled and the aggregate estimators are used (both of which are inconsistent when dynamic heterogeneity is present) we observe negative short-run output growth responses and a jagged pattern in the medium term. With the average estimator (which is consistent under dynamic heterogeneity) point estimates of the responses are consistently positive, albeit insignificant after about a year. We checked whether dynamic heterogeneity is important by using the pooled and the average estimators of the responses for steps from 1 to 35. The smallest statistic (across steps) is 27.55, so that the null of homogeneity is soundly rejected when compared with a $\chi^2(10)$. This is not surprising: it is well-known that the money growth paths of Italy and the United Kingdom had very different properties than the paths of, say, Germany or Japan in the 1980s. What is remarkable is that with the pooled or the aggregate estimators one may be led to accept some of the predictions of the simple cash-in-advance model of example 8.28, while the opposite would occur when the average estimator is used.

We examine long-run superneutrality in two ways. First, we check if output growth responses at the ten-year horizon are statistically significant. Second, we examine

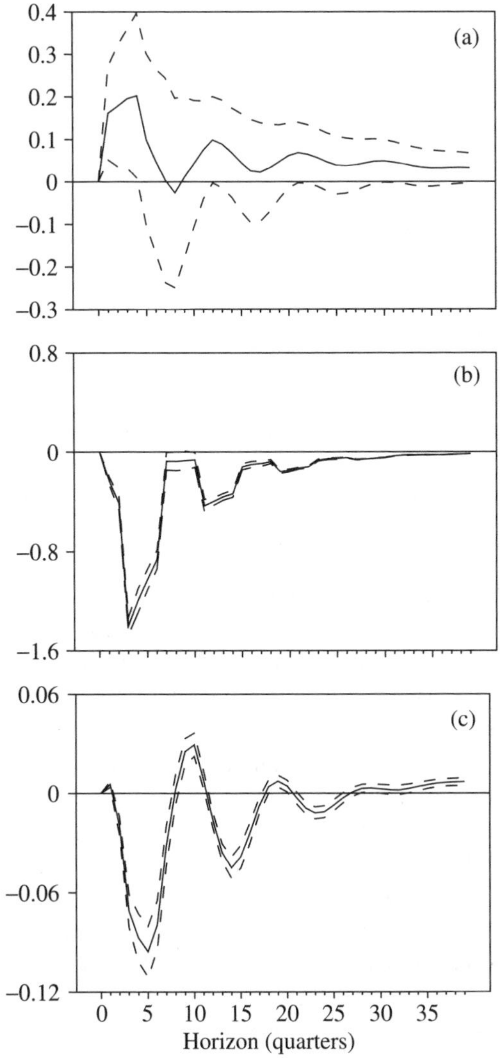

Figure 8.3. Output growth responses: (a) average; (b) pooled; (c) aggregate.

whether the contribution of money growth shocks to the variance of output growth at the same horizon is economically significant. Differences across estimators also emerge with these statistics. The average and the pooled estimators produce insignificant responses while responses obtained with the aggregate estimator are statistically significant. The economic differences are, however, small. In fact, in the latter case, a 68% band for the contribution of money growth shocks to output growth variability at the ten-year horizon is $[0.02, 0.14]$, which covers almost entirely the band obtained with the other two estimators.

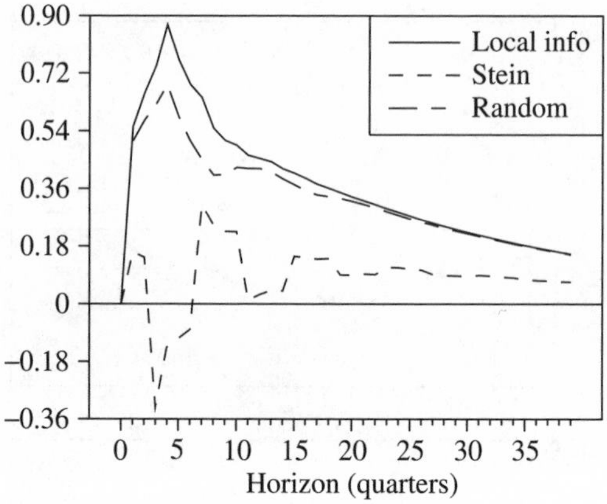

Figure 8.4. Alternative estimators of output responses in Japan.

Next, we examine the contribution of cross-sectional information when measuring the responses of output growth to money growth shocks in Japan. Figure 8.4 presents point estimates of the responses obtained by using (a) only local information, (b) a Stein estimator, (c) a random coefficient estimator, where *a priori* the mean of all the responses is zero and the prior variance is 0.05. Responses obtained by using local information are hump shaped and positive throughout the range, converging to zero rather slowly. The pattern is maintained with the random coefficient estimator but the peak response is reduced and the response is smoother. Responses obtained with the Stein estimator are oscillatory, reflecting the jagged pattern of the pooled estimator (see figure 8.3). Also, while with the first two estimators responses are significant up to the ten-year horizon, with the latter they are statistically significant only at the third- and seventh-quarter horizons.

To conclude, money appears to be superneutral in the long run and economic deviations from the null are small. The short- and the medium-run responses of output growth to money growth shocks depend on the estimation technique. Since with dynamic heterogeneity two of the three estimators we consider are inconsistent, we conclude that, on average in the G7, money growth has a positive short-run effect on output growth, lasting about one year.

9

Introduction to Bayesian Methods

Bayesian analysis of statistical and economic models differs substantially from classical (frequentist) analysis. In classical analysis the probability of an event is the limit of its relative frequency. Furthermore, the parameters of a model are treated as fixed, unknown quantities. In this framework, unbiased estimators are useful because the average value of the sample estimator converges to the true value via some law of large numbers. Also, minimum variance estimators are preferable because they yield values closer to the true parameter. Finally, estimators and tests are evaluated in repeated samples since this ensures that they give correct results with high probability.

Bayesian analysis takes a different point of view on all these issues. Probabilities, in general, capture the beliefs that a researcher has in an event. Parameters are random variables with a probability distribution. Properties of estimators and tests in repeated samples are uninteresting since beliefs are not necessarily related to the relative frequency of an event in a large number of hypothetical experiments. Finally, estimators are chosen to minimize the expected loss function (with expectations taken with respect to the posterior distribution), conditional on the data. Despite philosophical and semantic differences, the two approaches are equivalent in large samples. That is, under regularity conditions, the posterior mode converges to some "true" parameter value as $T \to \infty$; furthermore, the posterior distribution converges to a normal with mean equal to the "true" parameter and variance which is proportional to Fisher's information matrix.

This chapter describes the basics of Bayesian analysis. These tools are fundamental for the study of interesting macroeconomic problems encountered in the next two chapters. The building block of the analysis is the Bayes theorem. Section 9.1 presents examples of how the Bayes theorem can be used to construct and to recursively update posterior information. Crucial for the analysis is the specification of a prior distribution for the parameters. We describe ways of selecting such a prior, distinguishing between subjective and objective approaches, compare informative and noninformative priors, and present conjugate priors, which play an important role in many applied problems.

Section 9.2 deals with decision theory and section 9.3 with inference. We describe how to obtain point and interval estimates and discuss asymptotic properties of Bayesian estimators; we then describe how to compare hypotheses and models and how to construct distributions of forecasts. Section 9.4 deals with hierarchical models. Such models feature either a two-stage prior or a latent variable structure, which naturally lends itself to a prior interpretation. Since models of this type are common in applied work and make posterior analysis less sensitive to prior specifications, we describe in detail the steps needed to construct posterior distributions in these setups. We also discuss empirical Bayes methods here. These methods use plug-in estimates of the parameters of the second-stage hierarchy to construct posterior estimates of the first-stage parameters; they are useful for complex problems where the construction of the joint posterior of first- and second-stage parameters is demanding, and have a number of applications, in particular to VARs. Section 9.5 deals with posterior simulators. When the form of the posterior distribution is unknown, one can conduct posterior analysis drawing sequences from a distribution which approximates it. We discuss normal approximations, more sophisticated acceptance/importance sampling approximations, and recent Markov chain Monte Carlo methods, which are powerful and will be used extensively in the multiparameter, hierarchical, nonlinear, state space and latent variable models considered in chapters 10 and 11.

Section 9.6 briefly deals with robustness. Whenever samples are short, the prior is important in determining the shape of the posterior. We describe an approach to assess how important a prior specification is and to rebalance posterior information in case a different prior is preferred. Section 9.7 applies some of the tools described in the chapter to the problem of measuring returns to scale in the Spanish production function.

9.1 Preliminaries

Throughout this chapter, we assume that the vector of parameters of interest α lies in a compact set A. Prior information is summarized by a density $g(\alpha)$. Sample information is represented by a density $f(y \mid \alpha) \equiv \mathcal{L}(\alpha \mid y)$, interpreted as the likelihood of α once the data y are observed. $\tilde{\alpha}$ represents a posterior estimator and α_{OLS} the sample estimator of α.

9.1.1 *Bayes Theorem*

The Bayes theorem allows us to compute the posterior of α from the prior and the likelihood:

$$g(\alpha \mid y) = \frac{f(y \mid \alpha)g(\alpha)}{f(y)} \propto f(y \mid \alpha)g(\alpha) = \mathcal{L}(\alpha \mid y)g(\alpha) \equiv \breve{g}(\alpha \mid y),$$

where $f(y) = \int f(y \mid \alpha)g(\alpha)\,\mathrm{d}\alpha$ is the marginal likelihood of y, $g(\alpha \mid y)$ is the posterior density of α, and $\breve{g}(\alpha \mid y)$ is the posterior kernel. By construction, $g(\alpha \mid y) = \breve{g}(\alpha \mid y)/\int \breve{g}(\alpha \mid y)\,\mathrm{d}\alpha$.

Example 9.1. Suppose a central bank observes whether a recession occurs or not and decides on an interest rate policy—it can choose to increase the rate, to decrease it, or leave it unchanged; and it observes whether a recession occurs or not. Let i_1

indicate an interest rate increase, i_2 an unchanged interest rate, and i_3 an interest rate decrease. Let Re be a recession event and NRe a nonrecession event. Suppose that $f(\text{Re} \mid i_1) = 0.5$, $f(\text{Re} \mid i_2) = 0.4$, $f(\text{Re} \mid i_3) = 0.3$, and that all interest rate policies are equally probable *a priori*. Then, the probability that the interest rate will decrease, given that a recession is observed, is $g(i_3 \mid \text{Re}) = (0.3 * 0.33)/(0.5 * 0.33 + 0.4 * 0.33 + 0.3 * 0.33) = 0.25$ and the probability that the interest rate will increase, given that no recession is observed, is $g(i_1 \mid \text{NRe}) = (0.5 * 0.33)/(0.5 * 0.33 + 0.6 * 0.33 + 0.7 * 0.33) = 0.27$.

The next example uses the Bayes theorem to recursively update prior information.

Example 9.2. Suppose you are betting on the winner of the soccer World Cup. Your team is Brazil. Let α_1 (α_2) represent the event that your team will win (lose) the championship. Suppose Brazil meets Spain in the group stages. Your prior is $g(\alpha_1) = 0.6$, $g(\alpha_2) = 0.4$. Let $y_1 = 1$ if Brazil wins the game and $y_1 = 0$ otherwise. Suppose that $f(y_1 = 1 \mid \alpha_1) = 0.8$, $f(y_1 = 1 \mid \alpha_2) = 0.3$. Then $f(y_1 = 1) = 0.8 * 0.6 + 0.3 * 0.4 = 0.6$ and

$$g(\alpha_1 \mid y_1 = 1) = \frac{f(y_1 = 1 \mid \alpha_1)g(\alpha_1)}{f(y_1 = 1)} = \frac{0.8 * 0.6}{0.6} = 0.8, \tag{9.1}$$

$$g(\alpha_2 \mid y_1 = 1) = \frac{f(y_1 = 1 \mid \alpha_2)g(\alpha_2)}{f(y_1 = 1)} = \frac{0.3 * 0.4}{0.6} = 0.2. \tag{9.2}$$

Hence, having beaten Spain, the probability that Brazil will win the championship increases from 0.6 to 0.8. Suppose that the next opponent is Cameroon. Let $y_2 = 1$ if Brazil wins this game and $y_2 = 0$ otherwise. Let $g(\alpha_1) = g(\alpha_1 \mid y_1 = 1) = 0.8$ and $g(\alpha_2) = g(\alpha_2 \mid y_1 = 1) = 0.2$, that is, the prior at this stage is the posterior of the previous stage. Let again $f(y_2 = 1 \mid \alpha_1) = 0.8$, $f(y_2 = 1 \mid \alpha_2) = 0.3$. Then $f(y_2 = 1 \mid y_1 = 1) = 0.8 * 0.8 + 0.3 * 0.2 = 0.7$ and

$$\begin{aligned} g(\alpha_1 \mid y_1 = 1,\ y_2 = 1) &= \frac{f(y_2 = 1 \mid \alpha_1, y_1 = 1)g(\alpha_1 \mid y_1 = 1)}{f(y_2 = 1 \mid y_1 = 1)} \\ &= \frac{0.64}{0.7} = 0.91, \end{aligned} \tag{9.3}$$

$$\begin{aligned} g(\alpha_2 \mid y_1 = 1,\ y_2 = 1) &= \frac{f(y_2 = 1 \mid \alpha_2, y_1 = 1)g(\alpha_2 \mid y_1 = 1)}{f(y_2 = 1 \mid y_1 = 1)} \\ &= \frac{0.06}{0.7} = 0.09. \end{aligned} \tag{9.4}$$

Having beaten Cameroon, Brazil now has a probability of 0.91 of winning the championship.

Exercise 9.1. Consider a computer chip: it can either be working or faulty. In each of the two cases, the computer may or may not work. Let α_1 be the event that the chip is working, α_2 the event that is faulty, and let y be the event that the computer is working. Suppose it is known that $f(y \mid \alpha_1) = 0.995$ (that is, the probability that a computer works when the chip is working) and $f(y \mid \alpha_2) = 0.005$. Previous records show that $g(\alpha_1) = 0.997$ and $g(\alpha_2) = 0.003$. Calculate $g(\alpha_1 \mid y)$, the probability that the chip is working, given that the computer works.

Exercise 9.2. Consider n independent draws of a two-point event, e.g., high versus low inflation. Let α be the probability that high inflation occurs. If n_1 episodes of high inflation are observed, the likelihood function is $f(n_1 \mid \alpha, n) = [n!/(n_1!\,(n-n_1)!)]\,\alpha^{n_1}(1-\alpha)^{n-n_1}$. Suppose that $g(\alpha) = (\alpha(1-\alpha))^{-1}$ for $0 \leqslant \alpha \leqslant 1$. Show the form of the posterior density for α. Calculate the mean and the mode of the posterior distribution and $g(\alpha \mid n_1 = 5,\ n = 20)$.

Exercise 9.3. Consider two types of worker, high skilled (Hs) and low skilled (Ls), and let their employment status be denoted by Em (employed) or Un (unemployed). Suppose that, historically, $P(\text{Em} \mid \text{Hs}, \text{Em}) = 0.85$, $P(\text{Em} \mid \text{Ls}, \text{Em}) = 0.6$, $P(\text{Un} \mid \text{Hs}, \text{Un}) = 0.3$, $P(\text{Un} \mid \text{Ls}, \text{Un}) = 0.7$, so that, for example, the probability that a low-skilled (high-skilled) unemployed person will find a job this period is 0.3 (0.7). Suppose that *a priori* it is known that job flows are such that $P(\text{Un}) = 0.4$ and $P(\text{Em}) = 0.6$. Calculate the posterior probability that a low-skilled unemployed worker will still be unemployed two periods from now. How would this probability change if a training program alters $P(\text{Un} \mid \text{Ls}, \text{Un})$ from 0.7 to 0.6?

There are many situations when α contains parameters which are of little importance for the goal of the investigation. Posterior distributions for the objects of interest when nuisance parameters are present, can be easily computed. Suppose that $\alpha = [\alpha_1, \alpha_2]$ and that we are interested in α_1. The joint posterior is $g(\alpha_1, \alpha_2 \mid y) \propto f(y \mid \alpha_1, \alpha_2) g(\alpha_1, \alpha_2)$ and $g(\alpha_1 \mid y) = \int g(\alpha_1, \alpha_2 \mid y)\,\mathrm{d}\alpha_2 = \int g(\alpha_1 \mid \alpha_2, y) g(\alpha_2 \mid y)\,\mathrm{d}\alpha_2$, that is, the marginal posterior of α_1 weighs the conditional posterior of α_1 with the marginal posterior of α_2. When the dimension of α_2 is large, integrating α_2 out of the joint posterior is difficult and one could use Monte Carlo methods to obtain an i.i.d. sequence from $g(\alpha_1 \mid y)$. Suppose that $g(\alpha_2 \mid y)$ and $g(\alpha_1 \mid y, \alpha_2)$ are available. Then the following can be used.

Algorithm 9.1.

(1) Draw α_2^l from $g(\alpha_2 \mid y)$. For each α_2^l, draw $\alpha_1^{l'}$ from $g(\alpha_1 \mid y, \alpha_2^l)$, $l' = 1, \dots, L'$.

(2) Average $\alpha_1^{l'}$ over draws, i.e., compute $\alpha_1 = (1/L') \sum_{l'} \alpha_i^{l'}$.

(3) Repeat (1) and (2) L times.

The sample $(\alpha_1^1, \dots, \alpha_1^L)$ is then a sequence from the marginal posterior $g(\alpha_1 \mid y)$.

In many applied situations one has available two (short) samples over which to conduct inference, for example, data from two different countries or a sample which can be split into two because a structural break has occurred. If the two samples are independent, then $\breve{g} = f(y_1, y_2 \mid \alpha) g(\alpha) = f_2(y_2 \mid \alpha) f_1(y_1 \mid \alpha) g(\alpha) \propto f_2(y_2 \mid \alpha) g(\alpha \mid y_1)$.

Example 9.3. In underdeveloped countries y is typically short. Therefore, it is difficult to estimate α and to forecast future y with reasonable precision. If data from other underdeveloped countries are available, the above result instructs us to construct the posterior for α by using foreign data and to use it as a prior in the analysis of domestic data.

9.1.2 *Prior Selection*

Bayes theorem requires the specification of a prior density $g(\alpha)$. At one extreme, $g(\alpha)$ may represent the subjective beliefs a researcher has in the occurrence of an event (e.g., the probability that there is a defective CD in a batch). At the other, it may represent an objective evaluation: it may reflect recorded information (e.g., how many times has a lightning storm occurred in Rome on August 15 in the last 100 years), or the outcomes of previous experiments. Halfway between are priors displaying subjective general features (e.g., the form of the distributions) and objective details (e.g., the moments). Priors can also be distinguished on the basis of their informational content. In this case, we classify a prior as informative or noninformative.

9.1.2.1 *Subjective Priors*

Subjective informative priors can be constructed in a number of ways. For example, one can split the support of α into intervals, attribute a probability to each interval, and connect piecewise the intervals (histogram approach). Alternatively, one subjectively computes the "likelihood" of various $\alpha \in A$ and connects the likelihood points (likelihood approach). Finally, one can choose a generic parametric representation for $g(\alpha) = g(\alpha \mid \theta)$ and choose the vector θ that matches the beliefs of the researcher as well as possible (functional form approach).

Noninformative priors are typically selected when information is scarce or when a researcher wants to minimize the influence of the prior on the posterior. Historically, considerable effort has been expended to obtain noninformative priors, but the task has proved elusive for several reasons. First, noninformative (flat) priors may create problems in the computation of posterior distributions if A is unbounded. In this case, noninformative priors are improper, in the sense that $g(\alpha) = \kappa \geqslant 0$, $\forall \alpha \in A$, and $\int g(\alpha)\,\mathrm{d}\alpha$ is divergent, so that $f(y)$ may not be finite. Second, flat priors are, in general, not invariant to reparametrization.

Example 9.4. Suppose α is scalar, A the real line, and $g(\alpha) = 1, \forall \alpha \in A$. This prior is noninformative. Consider the reparametrization $\alpha_1 = \mathrm{e}^{\alpha}/(1 + \mathrm{e}^{\alpha})$. Then $\alpha_1 \in (0, 1)$ and $g(\alpha_1) \propto (\alpha_1)^{-1}(1 - \alpha_1)^{-1}$, which is informative (it is heavily concentrated around 0 and 1).

Exercise 9.4. Suppose $g(\alpha) = 1$, $\alpha > 0$. Consider the reparametrization $\alpha_1 = \ln(\alpha)$. Show that the prior for α_1 is $g(\alpha_1) = \mathrm{e}^{\alpha_1}$, $-\infty < \alpha_1 < \infty$.

To avoid these problems the literature has developed *reference noninformative priors*, i.e., priors which are invariant to the parametrization of either their location, their scale, or both. The next example describes how to obtain a location-invariant prior.

Example 9.5. Suppose that $\mathbb{R}_1$ and $\mathbb{R}_2$ are subsets of $\mathbb{R}^m$, that the density of y is of the form $f(y-\alpha)$, where $\alpha \in \mathbb{R}_2$ is a location parameter, and $y \in \mathbb{R}_1$. For example, a normal distribution with mean α and known variance σ^2 is a location distribution. To derive a reference noninformative prior for α suppose that, instead of observing y, we observe $y_1 = y + \varrho$, $\varrho \in \mathbb{R}^m$. Letting $\alpha_1 = \alpha + \varrho$, the density of y_1 is of the form $f(y_1 - \alpha_1)$. Since the densities of (y, α) and (y_1, α_1) are identical in structure, α and α_1 must have the same noninformative prior; that is, we want

$$g(\alpha \in \mathbb{R}_2) = g(\alpha_1 \in \mathbb{R}_2) \tag{9.5}$$

for all $\mathbb{R}_2 \in \mathbb{R}^m$. Since $g(\alpha_1 \in \mathbb{R}_2) = g(\alpha + \varrho \in \mathbb{R}_2) = g(\alpha \in \mathbb{R}_2 - \varrho)$, where $\mathbb{R}_2 - \varrho = \{z - \varrho : z \in \mathbb{R}_2\}$, we have that $g(\alpha \in \mathbb{R}_2) = g(\alpha \in \mathbb{R}_2 - \varrho)$. Since ϱ is arbitrary, a prior satisfying this equality is a location-invariant prior. Integrating the above expression we have

$$\int_{\mathbb{R}_2} g(\alpha)\, d\alpha = \int_{\mathbb{R}_2 - \varrho} g(\alpha)\, d\alpha = \int_{\mathbb{R}_2} g(\alpha - \varrho)\, d\alpha, \tag{9.6}$$

which is true if and only if $g(\alpha) = g(\alpha - \varrho)$, $\forall \alpha$. Setting $\alpha = \varrho$ we have $g(\alpha) = g(0)$, $\forall \varrho$, i.e., g must be a constant. For convenience, we typically choose $g(\alpha) = 1$.

Exercise 9.5. Consider a scale density of the form $\sigma^{-1} f(y/\sigma)$, where $\sigma > 0$. For example, $y \sim \mathbb{N}(0, \sigma^2)$ is a scale density. Show that a reference noninformative prior for σ is $g(\sigma) = \sigma^{-1}$. (Hint: repeat the steps of example 9.5, assuming you observe $y_1 = \varrho y$, $\varrho \in \mathbb{R}^m$.)

A general method of constructing reference noninformative priors based on the Fisher information matrix, i.e., the matrix of expected second-order derivatives of the density of the data with respect to the parameters, was developed by Jeffreys (1966). The idea of the approach is simple: let $g(\alpha)$ be given and let $h(\alpha)$ be a continuous and differentiable function of α. Then, the prior for $h(\alpha)$ can be calculated in two ways: by using the Jacobian of h, i.e., $g(h(\alpha)) = g(\alpha)|\partial h(\alpha)/\partial \alpha|$, or by using Bayes theorem $g(h(\alpha)) = g(h(\alpha), y)/f(y \mid h(\alpha))$. When $g(\alpha) \propto [I(\alpha)]^{0.5}$, where $I(\alpha) = -E\{[\partial^2 \ln f(y \mid \alpha)/\partial \alpha^2] \mid \alpha\}$, the two approaches produce the same prior for $h(\alpha)$.

Example 9.6. Let α represent the probability that the output growth is above average and $1-\alpha$ the probability that it is below average at each t and let y be the proportion of cases above the average in the sample. Then $f(y \mid \alpha) = \alpha^y (1-\alpha)^{1-y}$ and $-E[\partial^2 \ln f(y \mid \alpha)/\partial \alpha \partial \alpha'] \approx E\{[\partial \ln f(y \mid \alpha)/\partial \alpha]^2\} = E\{[\alpha^{-1} y + (1-\alpha)^{-1} \times (y-1)]^2\} = \alpha^{-1}(1-\alpha)^{-1}$. Hence, Jeffreys's prior for α is $g(\alpha) = \alpha^{-0.5}(1-\alpha)^{-0.5}$, $0 \leqslant \alpha \leqslant 1$.

Example 9.7. Consider the model $y = x\alpha + e$, where α is a scalar and $e \sim$ i.i.d. $\mathbb{N}(0, 1)$. Then $f(y \mid \alpha, x) = \mathrm{e}^{-0.5(y - x\alpha)^2}/\sqrt{2\pi}$ and $\partial^2 \ln f(y \mid \alpha)/\partial \alpha^2 = -x^2$ so $g(\alpha) \propto \sqrt{E(x^2)}$ is an invariant prior for α. Note that this prior is data based.

It is easy to extend Jeffreys's formulation when α is a vector. In this case $g(\alpha) = \{\det[I(\alpha)]\}^{0.5}$, where $I_{i,j}(\alpha) = -E_\alpha\{[\partial^2 \ln f(y \mid \alpha)/\partial\alpha_i\alpha_j] \mid \alpha\}$. While this formula is theoretically straightforward, it is computationally cumbersome. A more common approach, justified by the fact that ignorance is consistent with independence, is to obtain a noninformative prior for α_j and then form $g(\alpha) = \prod_j g(\alpha_j)$.

Exercise 9.6. Consider a location-scale density of the form $\sigma^{-1} f((y-\alpha)/\sigma)$, where (α, σ) are unknown and assume that $f((y-\alpha)/\sigma) \propto \mathrm{e}^{-(y-\alpha)/2\sigma^2}$. Show that the Fisher information is $I(\alpha, \sigma) = \mathrm{diag}(1/\sigma^2, 3/\sigma^2)$, so that a noninformative prior for (α, σ) is $g(\alpha, \sigma) \propto \sigma^{-2}$.

9.1.2.2 Objective Priors

In formulating objective priors or subjective priors with objective details, the marginal likelihood of the data plays a crucial role. Such a density measures the likelihood of y and is the normalizing constant in Bayes theorem, i.e.,

$$f(y) = \int f(y \mid \alpha) g(\alpha)\,\mathrm{d}\alpha \equiv \mathcal{L}(y \mid g). \tag{9.7}$$

Example 9.8. Suppose that y represents the number of papers a researcher publishes in the *American Economic Review* (AER) in a lifetime and let y be normally distributed around an unobservable ability variable α. Suppose that abilities in the population vary according to a normal distribution with mean $\bar{\alpha}$ and variance σ_{a}^2. Then $f(y)$ represents the actual distribution of AER articles of a researcher. Any idea what the median of this distribution in the cross section of economists is? Zero!

Important insights can be gained with a closer look at (9.7). Since $f(y \mid \alpha)$ is fixed, $\mathcal{L}(y \mid g)$ reflects the plausibility of g in the data. Therefore, if g_1 and g_2 are two prior distributions, $\mathcal{L}(y \mid g_1) > \mathcal{L}(y \mid g_2)$ implies that the support for g_1 in the data is larger than the one for g_2. Taken one step further this idea implies that we can estimate the "best" g by using $\mathcal{L}(y \mid g)$. Suppose $g(\alpha) \equiv g(\alpha \mid \theta)$, where θ is a vector of hyperparameters. Then $\mathcal{L}(y \mid g) \equiv \mathcal{L}(y \mid \theta)$, and θ_{ML}, typically called the maximum likelihood type II (ML-II) estimator, is the θ that maximizes $\mathcal{L}(y \mid \theta)$, and $g(\alpha \mid \theta_{\mathrm{ML}})$ is an ML-II-based prior.

Example 9.9. Let $y \mid \alpha \sim \mathbb{N}(\alpha, \sigma_y^2)$, $\alpha \sim \mathbb{N}(\bar{\alpha}, \bar{\sigma}_{\mathrm{a}}^2)$, σ_y^2 known. Then $\mathcal{L}(y \mid g) \sim \mathbb{N}(\bar{\alpha}, \sigma^2 = \sigma_y^2 + \bar{\sigma}_{\mathrm{a}}^2)$. If T observations are available, $\mathcal{L}(y_1, \dots, y_T \mid g)$ can be written as

$$\mathcal{L}(y_1, \dots, y_T \mid g) = [2\pi(\sigma^2)]^{-0.5T} \mathrm{e}^{-0.5Ts^2/\sigma^2} \mathrm{e}^{-0.5T(\bar{y}-\bar{\alpha})^2/\sigma^2}, \tag{9.8}$$

where $\bar{y} = (1/T)\sum_t y_t$, $s^2 = (1/T)\sum_t (y_t - \bar{y})^2$. Maximizing (9.8) with respect to $\bar{\alpha}$ yields $\bar{\alpha}_{\mathrm{ML}} = \bar{y}$. Substituting this into (9.8) we obtain

$$\mathcal{L}(y_1, \dots, y_T \mid \bar{\alpha}_{\mathrm{ML}}, g) = [2\pi(\sigma_y^2 + \bar{\sigma}_{\mathrm{a}}^2)]^{-0.5T} \mathrm{e}^{-0.5Ts^2/(\sigma_y^2 + \bar{\sigma}_{\mathrm{a}}^2)}. \tag{9.9}$$

Maximizing (9.9) with respect to $\bar{\sigma}_{\mathrm{a}}^2$ we have $\bar{\sigma}_{\mathrm{a,ML}}^2 = s^2 - \sigma_y^2$ when $s^2 \geqslant \sigma_y^2$ and $\bar{\sigma}_{\mathrm{a,ML}}^2 = 0$ otherwise. Hence, an ML-II prior for α is normal with mean $\bar{\alpha}_{\mathrm{ML}}$ and variance $\bar{\sigma}_{\mathrm{a,ML}}^2$.

9.1.2.3 Conjugate Priors

Conjugate priors are convenient because they allow the analytical computation of the posterior distribution of the unknowns in linear models.

Definition 9.1. Let $\mathfrak{F}$ be a class of sampling distributions and $\mathfrak{G}$ a class of prior distributions. $\mathfrak{G}$ is conjugate for $\mathfrak{F}$ if $g(\alpha \mid y) \in \mathfrak{G}$ for all $f(y \mid \alpha) \in \mathfrak{F}$ and $g(\alpha) \in \mathfrak{G}$.

Definition 9.1 states that a prior is conjugate to the likelihood if the beliefs it represents are such that it leads to a posterior which has the same form as the prior.

Example 9.10. Let $y \sim \mathbb{N}(\alpha, \sigma^2)$, where σ^2 is known. Since $f(y \mid \alpha) = (1/\sigma\sqrt{2\pi})\mathrm{e}^{-(y-\alpha)^2/2\sigma^2}$, a conjugate prior for α must be quadratic in the exponent, i.e., $g(\alpha) \propto \mathrm{e}^{-A_0\alpha^2+A_1\alpha-A_2}$, where A_0, A_1, A_2 are constants. Set, for example, $g(\alpha) = (1/\bar{\sigma}_\alpha\sqrt{2\pi})\mathrm{e}^{-(\alpha-\bar{\alpha})^2/2\bar{\sigma}_\alpha^2}$, $\bar{\alpha}, \bar{\sigma}_\alpha$ known. Then $f(y, \alpha) = (1/2\pi\sigma\bar{\sigma}_\alpha) \times \mathrm{e}^{[(\alpha-\bar{\alpha})^2/2\bar{\sigma}_\alpha^2+(y-\alpha)^2/2\sigma^2]}$. Note that

$$\frac{(\alpha-\bar{\alpha})^2}{\bar{\sigma}_\alpha^2} + \frac{(y-\alpha)^2}{\sigma^2} = \alpha^2\left(\frac{1}{\bar{\sigma}_\alpha^2} + \frac{1}{\sigma^2}\right) - 2\alpha\left(\frac{y}{\sigma^2} + \frac{\bar{\alpha}}{\bar{\sigma}_\alpha^2}\right) + \left(\frac{y^2}{\sigma^2} + \frac{\bar{\alpha}^2}{\bar{\sigma}_\alpha^2}\right)$$
$$= (\bar{\sigma}_\alpha^{-2} + \sigma^{-2})\left[\alpha^2 - \frac{2\alpha}{\bar{\sigma}_\alpha^{-2} + \sigma^{-2}}\left(\frac{y}{\sigma^2} + \frac{\bar{\alpha}}{\bar{\sigma}_\alpha^2}\right)\right] + \left(\frac{y^2}{\sigma^2} + \frac{\bar{\alpha}^2}{\bar{\sigma}_\alpha^2}\right).$$

Since

$$\left[\alpha^2 - \frac{2\alpha}{\bar{\sigma}_\alpha^{-2} + \sigma^{-2}}\left(\frac{y}{\sigma^2} + \frac{\bar{\alpha}}{\bar{\sigma}_\alpha^2}\right)\right]$$
$$= \left[\alpha - \frac{1}{\bar{\sigma}_\alpha^{-2} + \sigma^{-2}}\left(\frac{y}{\sigma^2} + \frac{\bar{\alpha}}{\bar{\sigma}_\alpha^2}\right)\right]^2 - \frac{1}{\bar{\sigma}_\alpha^{-2} + \sigma^{-2}}\left(\frac{y^2}{\sigma^2} + \frac{\bar{\alpha}^2}{\bar{\sigma}_\alpha^2}\right)^2,$$

we have

$$\frac{(\alpha-\bar{\alpha})^2}{\bar{\sigma}_\alpha^2} + \frac{(y-\alpha)^2}{\sigma^2}$$
$$= (\bar{\sigma}_\alpha^{-2} + \sigma^{-2})\left(\alpha - \frac{1}{\bar{\sigma}_\alpha^{-2} + \sigma^{-2}}\left(\frac{y}{\sigma^2} + \frac{\bar{\alpha}}{\bar{\sigma}_\alpha^2}\right)\right)^2 + \frac{(y-\bar{\alpha})^2}{\sigma^2 + \bar{\sigma}_\alpha^2}, \quad (9.10)$$

so that

$$f(y, \alpha) = \frac{1}{2\pi\sigma\bar{\sigma}_\alpha}\exp\left\{-0.5(\bar{\sigma}_\alpha^{-2} + \sigma^{-2})\left[\alpha - \frac{1}{\bar{\sigma}_\alpha^{-2} + \sigma^{-2}}\left(\frac{y}{\sigma^2} + \frac{\bar{\alpha}}{\bar{\sigma}_\alpha^2}\right)\right]^2\right\}$$
$$\times \exp\left\{-\frac{(y-\bar{\alpha})^2}{2(\sigma^2 + \bar{\sigma}_\alpha^2)}\right\}.$$

Integrating α out we have

$$f(y) = \int f(y, \alpha)\,\mathrm{d}\alpha = \frac{1}{\sqrt{2\pi(\bar{\sigma}_\alpha^{-2} + \sigma^{-2})}}\frac{1}{\sigma\bar{\sigma}_\alpha}\exp\left\{-\frac{(\bar{\alpha}-y)^2}{2(\sigma^2 + \bar{\sigma}_\alpha^2)}\right\} \quad (9.11)$$

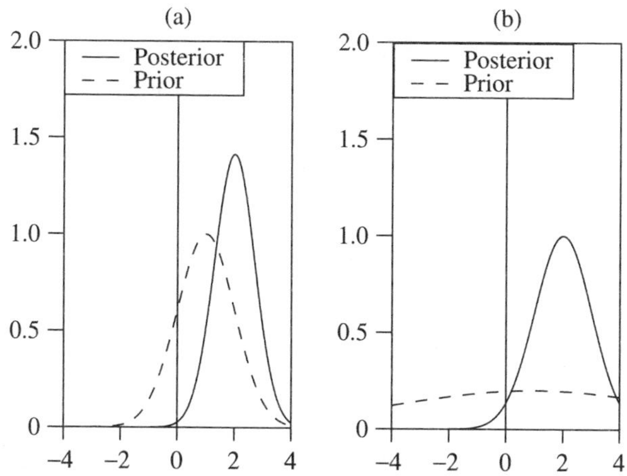

Figure 9.1. Prior and posterior densities: (a) tight prior; (b) loose prior.

and

$$g(\alpha \mid y) = \frac{f(y,\alpha)}{f(y)}$$
$$= \sqrt{\frac{\bar{\sigma}_\alpha^{-2} + \sigma^{-2}}{2\pi}} \exp\left\{-\tfrac{1}{2}(\bar{\sigma}_\alpha^{-2} + \sigma^{-2})\left[\alpha - \frac{1}{\bar{\sigma}_\alpha^{-2} + \sigma^{-2}}\left(\frac{\bar{\alpha}}{\bar{\sigma}_\alpha^2} + \frac{y}{\sigma^2}\right)\right]^2\right\}. \tag{9.12}$$

Hence, $(\alpha \mid y) \sim \mathbb{N}(\tilde{\alpha}, (\bar{\sigma}_\alpha^{-2} + \sigma^{-2})^{-1})$, where $\tilde{\alpha}(y) = [1/(\bar{\sigma}_\alpha^{-2} + \sigma^{-2})] \times (\bar{\alpha}/\bar{\sigma}_\alpha^2 + y/\sigma^2) = y - [\sigma^2/(\bar{\sigma}_\alpha^2 + \sigma^2)](y - \bar{\alpha})$.

In example 9.10 the posterior mean $\tilde{\alpha}$ is a weighted average of the prior mean $\bar{\alpha}$ and of the observed y, with weights given by $\sigma^2/(\bar{\sigma}_\alpha^2 + \sigma^2)$ and $\bar{\sigma}_\alpha^2/(\bar{\sigma}_\alpha^2 + \sigma^2)$. Hence, if $\bar{\sigma}_\alpha^2 \to 0$, sample information has no influence on the posterior while, if $\bar{\sigma}_\alpha^2 \to \infty$, the posterior of α only reflects sample information (see figure 9.1).

Exercise 9.7. Let $y_t \sim$ i.i.d. $\mathbb{N}(0, \sigma_y^2)$, where σ_y^2 is unknown. A conjugate prior for σ_y^2 is obtained from the inverse-gamma family $g(\sigma_y^2) \propto (\sigma_y^2)^{-a_1-1}\mathrm{e}^{-a_2/\sigma_y^2}$, where a_1, a_2 are parameters. Note that, when $a_1 = 0.5\bar{\nu}$ and $a_2 = 0.5\bar{s}^2$, $\bar{s}^2\sigma_y^{-2} \sim \chi^2(\bar{\nu})$, where $\bar{\nu}$ are degrees of freedom and $\bar{s}^2$ is a scale parameter. Assume T observations are available. Show that $g(\sigma_y^{-2} \mid y)$ is χ^2 with $(\bar{\nu} + T)$ degrees of freedom and scale equal to $(\bar{\nu}\bar{s}^2 + \sum_{t=1}^T y_t^2)$.

Exercise 9.8. Continuing with exercise 9.2, consider n independent draws of a two-point event; let α be the probability that a high event occurs and n_1 the number of high event episodes observed. Assume that a Beta(a_1, a_2) prior for α, i.e., $g(\alpha) = [\Gamma(a_1 + a_2)/\Gamma(a_1)\Gamma(a_2)]\alpha^{a_1-1}(1-\alpha)^{a_2-1}$, where $a_1, a_2 > 0$, and $\Gamma(\cdot)$ is the gamma function. Show that the posterior distribution for α is Beta$(a_1 + n_1, a_2 + n - n_1)$. Suppose $a_1 = a_2 = 2, n = 20, n_1 = 9$. Using the fact that, if $\alpha \sim$ Beta(a_1, a_2), then $a_2\alpha/a_1(1-\alpha)$ has an F-distribution with $(2a_1, 2a_2)$ degrees of freedom, provide an estimate of the posterior mean and of the posterior standard error of the odds ratio $\alpha/(1-\alpha)$. What happens if a_1 and a_2 approach zero?

Next, we describe how conjugate priors can be employed in regression models. We do this in detail as many problems can be cast into a (restricted) linear regression format.

Example 9.11. Let $y_t = x_t\alpha + e_t$, where $e_t \mid x_t \sim$ i.i.d. $\mathbb{N}(0, \sigma_e^2)$; assume $\text{rank}(x) = k$, and let $x = (x_1, \ldots, x_T)'$, $y = (y_1, \ldots, y_T)'$. The likelihood of y is $f(y \mid x,\ \alpha,\ \sigma_e^2) = (2\pi)^{-0.5T}\sigma_e^{-T}\mathrm{e}^{-0.5\sigma_e^{-2}(y-x\alpha)'(y-x\alpha)}$. Assume $g(\alpha, \sigma_e^2) = g(\alpha)g(\sigma_e^2)$; let $g(\alpha) \sim \mathbb{N}(\bar{\alpha}, \bar{\Sigma}_\alpha)$ and $\bar{s}^2\sigma_e^{-2} \sim \chi^2(\bar{\nu})$. The posterior kernel is

$$\begin{aligned}\breve{g}(\alpha, \sigma_e^2 \mid y, x) &= (2\pi)^{-0.5(T+k)}[2^{0.5\bar{\nu}}\Gamma(0.5\bar{\nu})]^{-1} \\ &\quad\times |\bar{\Sigma}_\alpha|^{-0.5}(\bar{s}^2)^{0.5\nu}\sigma_e^{-0.5(T+\bar{\nu}+2)}\exp(-0.5\bar{\nu}\bar{s}^2\sigma_e^{-2}) \\ &\quad\times \exp\{-0.5[\sigma_e^{-2}(y-x\alpha)'(y-x\alpha) + (\alpha-\bar{\alpha})\bar{\Sigma}_\alpha^{-1}(\alpha-\bar{\alpha})]\}.\end{aligned} \tag{9.13}$$

The exponent in (9.13) can be written as $(\alpha-\tilde{\alpha})'\tilde{\Sigma}_\alpha^{-1}(\alpha-\tilde{\alpha}) + \mathcal{Q}$, where

$$\tilde{\Sigma}_\alpha = (\bar{\Sigma}_\alpha^{-1} + \sigma_e^{-2}x'x)^{-1}, \tag{9.14}$$

$$\tilde{\alpha} = \tilde{\Sigma}_\alpha(\bar{\Sigma}_\alpha^{-1}\bar{\alpha} + \sigma_e^{-2}x'y) = \tilde{\Sigma}_\alpha(\bar{\Sigma}_\alpha^{-1}\bar{\alpha} + \sigma_e^{-2}x'x\alpha_{\text{OLS}}), \tag{9.15}$$

$$\mathcal{Q} = \sigma_e^{-2}y'y + \bar{\alpha}'\bar{\Sigma}_\alpha^{-1}\bar{\alpha} - \tilde{\alpha}'\tilde{\Sigma}_\alpha^{-1}\tilde{\alpha}, \tag{9.16}$$

and $\alpha_{\text{OLS}} = (x'x)^{-1}(x'y)$. Given σ_e^2, $g(\alpha \mid \sigma_e^{-2}, y, x) \propto \exp\{-0.5(\alpha-\tilde{\alpha}) \times \tilde{\Sigma}_\alpha^{-1}(\alpha-\tilde{\alpha})\}$ so that $(\alpha \mid \sigma_e^{-2}, y, x) \sim \mathbb{N}(\tilde{\alpha}, \tilde{\Sigma}_\alpha)$. Given α, $g(\sigma_e^{-2} \mid \alpha, y, x) \propto \sigma_e^{-(T+\bar{\nu}+2)}\exp\{-0.5\sigma_e^{-2}[\bar{\nu}\bar{s}^2 + (y-x\alpha)'(y-x\alpha)]\}$. Hence, $[\bar{\nu}\bar{s}^2 + (y-x\alpha)' \times (y-x\alpha)]\sigma_e^{-2} \mid (\alpha, y, x) \sim \chi^2(T+\bar{\nu})$.

Note that, if a gamma density was used as a prior for σ_e^{-2}, the conditional posterior for α would have been unchanged and the conditional posterior for σ_e^{-2} would be of gamma type. It is also important to stress that in example 9.11 we calculate *conditional* posteriors. The *marginal* posterior of α is proportional to $[\bar{s}^2 + (\alpha-\tilde{\alpha})' \times \tilde{\Sigma}_\alpha^{-1}(\alpha-\tilde{\alpha}) + \mathcal{Q}]^{-0.5(T+k+\bar{\nu})}$. One can recognize (see, for example, the appendix) that this is the kernel of a t-distribution with parameters $(\tilde{\alpha}, (\bar{s}^2+\mathcal{Q})\tilde{\Sigma}_\alpha/(T+\bar{\nu}), (T+\bar{\nu}))$.

We consider two useful variants of the linear regression model in the next exercises.

Exercise 9.9. Consider the model of example 9.11 where σ_e^2 is held fixed and $\alpha \sim \mathbb{N}(\bar{\alpha}, \bar{\Sigma}_\alpha)$. Show the form of $g(\alpha \mid \sigma_e^2, y, x)$ in this case. (Hint: it is still normal.)

Exercise 9.10. Suppose that the joint prior for α and σ_e^2 is $g(\alpha, \sigma_e^2) \propto \sigma_e^{-2}$. Show the form of the conditional posterior distribution for α. Is it still true that the $g(\alpha \mid y, x)$ is t-distributed? What are the parameters of this distribution? Show that $g(\sigma_e^2 \mid y, x)$ is proportional to $\sigma_e^{-T-2}\exp((T-2)s^2/2\sigma_e^2)$. Conclude that the marginal posterior for σ_e^2 is of gamma type. Find the parameters of this distribution.

Exercise 9.10 shows that the posterior can be proper even when the prior is not. This typically occurs when the information content of the likelihood dominates that of the prior.

9.2 Decision Theory

Bayesian decision theory is voluminous and too vast to be discussed here. Since some inferential decisions are based on such a theory and since Bayesian decision theory differs from classical theory, we sketch the basic ideas needed to understand what will come next.

Suppose a policymaker has data on y and she needs to either (i) forecast y, potentially conditioning on policy intervention (say, interest rate decision), or (ii) choose an interest rate policy which maximizes consumer welfare. With each decision $d(y)$ there is an associated loss function $\mathfrak{L}(\alpha, d)$, where α describes how the economy reacts to $d(y)$.

How would a frequentist and a Bayesian approach the problem of selecting d? We show this in the context of an example.

Example 9.12. Consider the following three-equation model:

(i) Phillips curve: $\text{GDP}_t = \alpha\pi_t + e_{s,t}$, $e_{s,t} \sim$ i.i.d. (0, 1).

(ii) Demand: $\pi_t = \Delta m_t + e_{d,t}$, $e_{d,t} \sim$ i.i.d. (0, 1).

(iii) Policy: $\Delta m_t = de_{s,t}$,
where variables are in deviation from steady states and suppose that the welfare function is $\mathfrak{W}_t = \pi_t^2 + \text{GDP}_t^2$.

Substituting the three equations into the welfare function and taking expected values with respect to the shocks, we have that the risk is $\mathfrak{R}(\alpha, d) \equiv E(\mathfrak{W}_t(\alpha, d)) = \int \mathfrak{W}_t f(e_{d,t}, e_{s,t})\, \mathrm{d}e_{d,t}\, \mathrm{d}e_{s,t} = 1+d^2+(1+\alpha d)^2+\alpha^2$. How would an optimizing policymaker choose d? Suppose data for $y_t = (\pi_t, \text{GDP}_t, m_t)$ are available and that a policymaker observes $y = (y_1, \dots, y_T)$.

A frequentist would estimate α from the data and minimize $E\mathfrak{W}(\hat{\alpha}, d) = 1+\hat{\alpha}^2+(1+\hat{\alpha})E(d(y))^2 + E(d(y))^2$, given $\hat{\alpha}$. This amounts to averaging the outcomes over all possible past trajectories that could have been generated by d. We can immediately see that the solution to the problem is $d_{\text{ML}}(y) = -\hat{\alpha}_{\text{ML}}/(1 - \hat{\alpha}_{\text{ML}}^2)$. A Bayesian would, instead, treat α as a random variable and minimize $E\mathfrak{W}(\alpha, d) = 1+d^2+(1+dE(\alpha \mid y))^2+E(\alpha \mid y)^2$, that is, she would average the outcomes over α, given the observed y. The solution to the problem is $d_{\text{Bayes}}(y) = -E(\alpha \mid y)/(1 - E(\alpha^2 \mid y))$. In some cases the ranking of decisions is not uniform across α. In these situations a robust approach could be preferable; that is, a Bayesian would want to minimize the loss obtained with the worst possible outcome, i.e., $\inf_{d\in D} \sup_{\alpha\in A} \mathfrak{W}(\alpha, d \mid y)$.

One advantage of a Bayesian approach to decision making is that the optimal choice automatically takes into account parameter (model) uncertainty. In fact, in example 9.12 the expectation is taken with respect to the posterior $g(\alpha \mid y) \propto \mathcal{L}(\alpha \mid y)g(\alpha)$.

In general, decisions in a Bayesian framework are based on the so-called likelihood principle. This principle states that all information about the unknown α is contained in the likelihood, given the data. Hence, two likelihoods for α (from the same or different experiments) contain the same information about α if and only if they are proportional to each other. Note that the likelihood principle underlies the selection of ML-II priors.

9.3 Inference

Bayesian inference is easy since $g(\alpha \mid y)$ contains all the information one may need. Bayesian inference amounts to computing $E(h(\alpha)) = \int h(\alpha)\,\mathrm{d}g(\alpha \mid y)$, where h is a continuous function of α. Examples that fit this characterization are numerous. For instance, $h(\alpha)$ could represent moments or quantiles of α; the difference in the loss function corresponding to two actions, e.g., $h(\alpha) = \mathfrak{L}(\alpha, d_1) - \mathfrak{L}(\alpha, d_2)$, or restrictions on α, i.e., $h(\alpha) = \mathcal{I}_{A_1}(\alpha)$, where A_1 is a set and $\mathcal{I}$ an indicator function. Alternatively, $h(\alpha)$ could represent future values of the endogenous variables, i.e., $h(\alpha) = h(y^{\tau})$, where $y^{\tau} = (y_{t+1}, \dots, y_{t+\tau})$ and h captures turning points, prediction intervals, etc. Finally, it could represent impulse responses, variance decompositions, or other statistics which are deterministic functions of α.

Sometimes, and primarily for comparison with non-Bayesian methods, one needs to summarize the posterior of $h(\alpha)$ with a point estimate and an associated measure of uncertainty. These measures are justified from a Bayesian point of view either as crude approximations to the peak and the curvature of the posterior or as a summary of posterior information as $T \to \infty$.

Let $\mathfrak{L}(\hat{h}, h)$ be a loss function $H \times H \to \mathbb{R}$, where $h \equiv h(\alpha)$ and $\hat{h}$ is an estimator of h. A Bayes point estimate $\tilde{h}$ is obtained as

$$\tilde{h} = \operatorname*{argmin}_{\hat{h}} E(\mathfrak{L}(\hat{h}, h) \mid y) = \operatorname*{argmin}_{\hat{h}} \int \mathfrak{L}(\hat{h}, h) g(h \mid y)\,\mathrm{d}h. \tag{9.17}$$

There are several loss functions one could use in (9.17). Here is a brief list of candidates.

(i) Quadratic loss: $\mathfrak{L}(\hat{h}, h) = (\hat{h} - h)'W(\hat{h} - h)$, where W is a positive definite weighting matrix. Then $\tilde{h} = E(h \mid y) = \int h\,\mathrm{d}g(h \mid y)$.

(ii) Quantile loss: $\mathfrak{L}(\hat{h}, h) = \mathfrak{L}_1(\hat{h} - h)\mathcal{I}_{[-\infty, \hat{h}]}(h) + \mathfrak{L}_2(h - \hat{h})\mathcal{I}_{[\hat{h}, \infty]}(h)$, $\mathfrak{L}_1$, $\mathfrak{L}_2 > 0$. Then $\tilde{h} = P(h \leqslant \hat{h} \mid y) = \mathfrak{L}_2/(\mathfrak{L}_1 + \mathfrak{L}_2)$. When $\mathfrak{L}_1 = \mathfrak{L}_2$, $\tilde{h}$ is the median.

(iii) 0–1 loss: $\mathfrak{L}(\hat{h}, h, \epsilon) = 1 - \mathcal{I}_{\epsilon(\hat{h})}(h)$, where $\epsilon(\hat{h})$ is an open ϵ-neighborhood of $\hat{h}$ and $\mathcal{I}$ is an indicator function. Since $\lim_{\epsilon \to 0} \operatorname{argmin} \mathfrak{L}(\hat{h}, h) = \operatorname{argmax} g(h \mid y)$, then $\tilde{h} = \operatorname{argmax} g(h \in \epsilon(\hat{h}) \mid y)$.

For proofs of the above statements, see, for example, Berger (1985, pp. 161–62). Clearly, if the posterior is normal, the choice of loss function is irrelevant: posterior mean, median, and mode coincide. Note that, if the loss is quadratic and $W = I$,

$$\begin{aligned} E[(\hat{h} - h)(\hat{h} - h)' \mid y] &= [\hat{h} - E(h \mid y)][\hat{h} - E(h \mid y)]' \\ &\quad + E[E(h \mid y) - h][E(h \mid y) - h]' \\ &= \text{Bias} + \text{Variance} = \text{MSE}. \end{aligned} \tag{9.18}$$

Hence, $\tilde{h} = E(h \mid y)$ minimizes the mean square error (MSE) of h.

It is useful to digress for a moment and compare classical and Bayesian point estimation procedures. In classical analysis an estimator is obtained conditional on a "true" parameter value, i.e., $\tilde{h} = \text{argmin}_{\hat{h}} E[\mathfrak{L}(\hat{h}, h) \mid \alpha] = \text{argmin}_{\hat{h}} \int \mathfrak{L}(\hat{h}, h) \times f(y \mid \alpha)\,dy$, where $f(y \mid \alpha)$ is a proper pdf for y. Since this expression depends on α, the solution is a function of α. Suppose $h(\alpha) = \alpha$ and we choose an estimator as follows: $\tilde{h} = \text{argmin}_{\hat{\alpha}} E_\alpha E_y[\mathfrak{L}(\hat{\alpha}, \alpha) \mid \alpha]$. Then

$$\begin{aligned} \tilde{h} &= \underset{\hat{\alpha}}{\text{argmin}} \int\int \mathcal{W}(\alpha)\mathfrak{L}(\hat{\alpha}, \alpha) f(y \mid \alpha)\,dy\,d\alpha \\ &= \underset{\hat{\alpha}}{\text{argmin}} \int \left[\int \mathfrak{L}(\hat{\alpha}, \alpha) f(\alpha \mid y)\,d\alpha\right] \mathcal{W}(y)\,dy, \end{aligned} \tag{9.19}$$

where $\mathcal{W}(\alpha)$ is a weighting function and $f(\alpha \mid y)\mathcal{W}(y) = f(y \mid \alpha)\mathcal{W}(\alpha)$. The minimizer of (9.19) is the one which minimizes the expression in brackets, and this is a Bayes estimator. Hence, a specification which sets up a loss function and weights parameter values by $\mathcal{W}(\alpha)$ implies that the Bayes estimator is also best from a frequentist point of view.

In classical analysis, one construct confidence intervals to give a sense of the uncertainty around point estimates. In Bayesian analysis one uses credible sets.

Definition 9.2 (credible set). A set H such that $P(h \in H \mid y) \equiv \int_H g(h \mid y)\,dh = 1 - \varrho$ is the $100(1 - \varrho)\%$ credible set for h with respect to $g(h \mid y)$.

A credible set measures *a posteriori* the beliefs that $h \in H$. A confidence interval $\text{CI}(y)$ satisfies $P(h \in \text{CI}(y) \mid \alpha) \equiv \int_y [\int_{\text{CI}(y)} g(h \mid y, \alpha)\,dh] \times f(y \mid \alpha)\,dy = 1 - \varrho$. Also, $\text{CI}(y)$ depends on α. Therefore, a classical confidence interval is a random variable chosen so that it covers the true parameter value with probability $1 - \varrho$.

Example 9.13. Suppose a potential manager has scored 115 points in an aptitude test, and suppose that the test score $y \sim \mathbb{N}(\alpha, 100)$, where α is the "true" ability of the manager. If *a priori* $\alpha \sim \mathbb{N}(100, 225)$, the marginal likelihood $f(y)$ is normal with mean 100 and variance 325. Using the logic of example 9.10, we can immediately show that $g(\alpha \mid y)$ is normal with mean $(100 * 100 + 115 * 225)/(100 + 225) = 110.39$ and variance $100 * 225/(100 + 225) = 69.23$. Hence, a 95% credible set for α is $[110.39 \pm (1.96)(\sqrt{69.23})] = [94.08, 126.7]$. A classical 95% confidence interval for α is $[115 \pm (1.96)10] = [95.4, 134.6]$, which is larger than the Bayesian credible set.

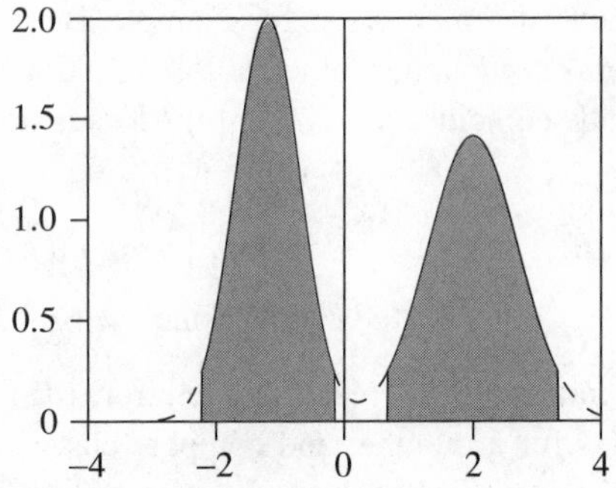

Figure 9.2. Highest credible set.

Exercise 9.11. Suppose that the number of firms which go bankrupt every week in a region has a Pareto distribution with parameters (a_0, a_1), i.e., $f(y \mid a_0, a_1) = (a_1/a_0)(a_0/y)^{a_1+1}\mathcal{I}_{(a_0,\infty)}(a)$ for $0 < a_0 < \infty$, $a_1 > 1$. Suppose a_0 is known and that nothing is known about a_1 so that $g(a_1) = a_1^{-1}\mathcal{I}_{(0,\infty)}(a_1)$. Suppose that the numbers of bankruptcies observed in 10 weeks are $[0, 2, 5, 1, 0, 1, 3, 4, 0, 5]$. Find a 68% credible set for a_1.

Since credible sets may not be unique, one chooses the highest $100(1 - \varrho)\%$ credible set, i.e., a set such that $g(h \mid y) \geqslant \kappa(\varrho)$, $\forall h \in H$, where $\kappa(\varrho)$ is the largest constant such that $P(h \in H \mid y) = 1 - \varrho$.

Example 9.14. Problems in computing credible sets may occur when the posterior has multiple modes. In that case a credible set may be disjoint. For example, in figure 9.2, such a set includes the area between −2.2 and −0.2 and between 0.8 and 3.5. Highest credible sets can also differ from centered credible sets if, for example, the posterior distribution is asymmetric.

In classical analysis, examining model adequacy typically involves checking the properties of the residuals and making sure that the assumptions of, for example, linearity, normality, variance homogeneity, etc., are satisfied. A similar analysis can be conducted in a Bayesian framework by using out-of-sample observations. Suppose that we can split $y_t = [y_{1t}, y_{2t}]$, where y_{1t} is the estimation sample and y_{2t} the validation sample. If y_{1t} and y_{2t} are independent, one can compute $y_{2t} - E[y_{2t} \mid y_{1t}]$ and check if the assumptions of linearity, variance homogeneity, etc., are correct with graphical techniques. On the other hand, scaling the predictive residuals by their variance may help to detect deviations from normality. Note that, if it is impossible to have two independent samples, one can still undertake model validation by randomly leaving out elements of y_t and predicting them by using cross-validation methods (see Gelfand and Dey 1994).

9.3.1 Inference with Multiple Models

In many situations one is faced with the dilemma of choosing a model for the analysis among a variety of alternatives. In a classical framework, one uses various types of test to decide which specification to employ (e.g., the length of a VAR, the variables to be used, etc.). In a Bayesian framework it is optimal not to discard any model but instead appropriately weight their outcomes by using their posterior probability.

Let $f(y \mid \alpha_j, \mathcal{M}_j)$ be the likelihood for model j; let $g(\alpha_j \mid \mathcal{M}_j)$ be the prior for α_j and $g(\mathcal{M}_j)$ the prior for model j, $j = 1, \dots, J$, where $\sum_j g(\mathcal{M}_j) = 1$. Suppose we are interested in $h(\alpha)$. Then

$$E[h(\alpha)] = \sum_j E[h(\alpha) \mid y, \mathcal{M}_j] g(\mathcal{M}_j \mid y). \tag{9.20}$$

The first element of (9.20) was previously calculated. Conditional on $\mathcal{M}_j$,

$$E[h(\alpha) \mid y, \mathcal{M}_j] = \frac{\int_{A_j} h(\alpha_j) f(y \mid \alpha_j, \mathcal{M}_j) g(\alpha_j \mid \mathcal{M}_j)\, \mathrm{d}\alpha_j}{\int_{A_j} f(y \mid \alpha_j, \mathcal{M}_j) g(\alpha_j \mid \mathcal{M}_j)\, \mathrm{d}\alpha_j}, \tag{9.21}$$

where A_j is the space where the α_j belong. The posterior for model j is

$$\begin{aligned} g(\mathcal{M}_j \mid y) &= \frac{f(y \mid \mathcal{M}_j) g(\mathcal{M}_j)}{f(y)} = \frac{g(\mathcal{M}_j) \int f(y \mid \alpha_j, \mathcal{M}_j) g(\alpha_j \mid \mathcal{M}_j)\, \mathrm{d}\alpha_j}{f(y)} \\ &\propto g(\mathcal{M}_j) \int f(y \mid \alpha_j, \mathcal{M}_j) g(\alpha_j \mid \mathcal{M}_j)\, \mathrm{d}\alpha_j = g(\mathcal{M}_j) f(y \mid \mathcal{M}_j). \end{aligned} \tag{9.22}$$

Hence, $g(\mathcal{M}_j \mid y)$ is proportional to the product of the prior probability of model j and its marginal likelihood.

To calculate $E[h(\alpha)]$ we therefore need three steps: (i) compute the posterior expectation of $h(\alpha)$ for each model $\mathcal{M}_j$ by using (9.21); (ii) obtain the marginal likelihood and combine it with the prior $g(\mathcal{M}_j)$ as suggested in (9.22) for each $\mathcal{M}_j$; (iii) average $E[h(\alpha \mid y, \mathcal{M}_j)]$ across models as suggested in (9.20).

When is it appropriate to choose only one of the J available models? It is easy to check that such a choice is appropriate when $g(\mathcal{M}_j \mid y)$ is independent of j and $E[h(\alpha \mid y, \mathcal{M}_j)]$ is roughly constant across j or when $g(\mathcal{M}_j \mid y)$ is close to 1 for some j. In general, averaging across models is preferable to using any single model individually, since $E\{\ln[\sum_j g(\alpha \mid \mathcal{M}_j, y) g(\mathcal{M}_j \mid y)]\} \geqslant E\{\ln[g(\alpha \mid \mathcal{M}_j, y)]\}$.

Example 9.15. Suppose two forecasters are producing forecasts of GDP growth one quarter ahead. Suppose that $(y_{t+1} \mid \mathcal{M}_1) = 2.5$ and that $(y_{t+1} \mid \mathcal{M}_2) = 1.5$, and that both forecasters have been equally successful in the past, so that $g(\mathcal{M}_1) = g(\mathcal{M}_2) = 0.5$. Suppose that $f(y \mid \mathcal{M}_1) = 0.8$ and $f(y \mid \mathcal{M}_2) = 1.2$. Optimal model combination implies that the Bayes forecast of GDP growth is $2.5 * (0.5 * 0.8) + 1.5 * (0.5 * 1.2) = 1.0 + 0.9 = 1.9$.

9.3.2 Normal Approximations

In classical analysis one uses asymptotic approximations to derive the properties of estimators and to test hypotheses. One could also take similar approximations in a Bayesian framework. For example, when $g(\alpha \mid y)$ is unimodal and roughly symmetric, and the mode α^* is in the interior of A, a normal distribution centered at α^* could be used. That is,

$$\ln g(\alpha \mid y) \approx \ln g(\alpha^* \mid y) + 0.5(\alpha-\alpha^*)' \left[\frac{\partial^2 \ln g(\alpha \mid y)}{\partial\alpha\,\partial\alpha'} \bigg|_{\alpha=\alpha^*} \right] (\alpha-\alpha^*). \quad (9.23)$$

Since $\ln g(\alpha^* \mid y)$ is a constant from the point of view of α, letting $\Sigma(\alpha^*) = -[(\partial^2 \ln g(\alpha \mid y)/\partial\alpha^2)|_{\alpha=\alpha^*}]$, we have that $g(\alpha \mid y) \approx \mathbb{N}(\alpha^*, \Sigma(\alpha^*)^{-1})$ and an approximate $100(1-\varrho)\%$ highest credible set is $\alpha^* \pm \mathbb{SN}(\varrho/2)(\Sigma(\alpha^*)^{-0.5})$, where $\mathbb{SN}(\varrho/2)$ is the standard normal evaluated at $(\varrho/2)$.

This approximation is valid under regularity conditions when $T \to \infty$ (see below) or when the posterior kernel is roughly normal. It is highly inappropriate when

(i) the likelihood function is flat in some dimension ($\Sigma(\alpha^*)$ is poorly measured);

(ii) the likelihood function has multiple peaks (a single-peak approximation is incorrect);

(iii) the likelihood function is unbounded (no posterior mode exists);

(iv) the mode is on the boundary of A (there is a natural truncation);

(v) $g(\alpha \mid y) = 0$ in the neighborhood of α^*.

Example 9.16. Let y_t be i.i.d. $\mathbb{N}(\alpha, \sigma^2)$ and assume a noninformative prior for $(\alpha, \ln\sigma)$. The joint posterior density is $g(\alpha, \ln\sigma \mid y) \propto -T\ln\sigma - (0.5/\sigma^2) \times [(T-1)s^2 - T(\bar{y}-\alpha)^2]$, where $\bar{y}$ is the sample mean and s^2 is the sample variance of y. Then $\partial g(\alpha, \ln\sigma \mid y)/\partial\alpha = T(\bar{y}-\alpha)/\sigma^2$, $\partial g(\alpha, \ln\sigma \mid y)/\partial\ln\sigma = -T + ((T-1)s^2 + T(\bar{y}-\alpha)^2)/\sigma^2$, and the mode is $\alpha^* = \bar{y}$, $\ln\sigma^* = 0.5\ln((T-1)s^2/T)$. The matrix of second derivatives with respect to $(\alpha, \ln\sigma)$ evaluated at the mode is diagonal with elements equal to $-T/\sigma^2$ and $-2T$. Hence

$$g(\alpha, \ln\sigma \mid y) \approx \mathbb{N}\left(\begin{bmatrix} \bar{y} \\ 0.5\ln(T-1)s^2/T \end{bmatrix}, \begin{bmatrix} \sigma^2/T & 0 \\ 0 & 1/2T \end{bmatrix} \right).$$

Exercise 9.12. Suppose you want to study the effects of fiscal policy in a stagflation. You have data (x_i, n_i, y_i) across countries (or across experiments by using DSGE models), where x_i represents the magnitude of the fiscal impulse in country i given in the n_ith experiment and y_i is the proportion of cases the economy has recovered (n_i is the number of instances in which a fiscal policy shock of a particular size has occurred). Suppose $f(y_i \mid \alpha_1, \alpha_2, n_i, x_i) \propto (e^{\alpha_1+\alpha_2 x_i})^{y_i}(1-e^{\alpha_1+\alpha_2 x_i})^{n_i-y_i}$. Suppose the prior for (α_1, α_2) is noninformative, i.e., $g(\alpha_1, \alpha_2) \propto 1$. Compute a normal approximation to the posterior of (α_1, α_2) and obtain approximate 68% and 95% credible sets.

Because of the focus of this book, we only briefly describe what happens to Bayes estimators when $T \to \infty$. In classical analysis one would provide conditions for consistency and asymptotic normality of the estimators. Here there is no true parameter value toward which the estimator would converge asymptotically and which could be used as a pivot for constructing the asymptotic (normal) distribution. However, the following holds.

Result 9.1 (consistency). Suppose data come from a parametric distribution function $f(y \mid \alpha)$ and a prior $g(\alpha)$ is assumed. Suppose that true data density belongs to $f(y \mid \alpha)$, i.e., $f^+ = f(y \mid \alpha_0)$, for some α_0. Then, as $T \to \infty$, $\alpha^* \xrightarrow{\text{P}} \alpha_0$.

Example 9.17. Suppose that $y_t = x_t\alpha + e_t$, $e_t \sim$ i.i.d. $\mathbb{N}(0, 1)$. Assume that $(1/T)\sum_t x_t'x_t \xrightarrow{\text{P}} \Sigma_{xx}$, $(1/T)\sum_t x_t'e_t \xrightarrow{\text{P}} 0$, and $\alpha \sim \mathbb{N}(0, \sigma_\alpha^2 I)$. The posterior mode of α is $\alpha^* = (x'x + \sigma_\text{a}^{-2}I)^{-1}x'y$, where $x = (x_1, \dots, x_T)$ and $y = (y_1, \dots, y_T)$. Note that, as $T \to \infty$, $\alpha^* = \alpha_0 + (x'x + \sigma_\text{a}^{-2}I)^{-1}x'e = \alpha_0 + [(1/T)\sum_{t=1}^T x_t'x_t + (1/(T\sigma_\text{a}^2))I]^{-1}(1/T)\sum_{t=1}^T x_t'e_t \to \alpha_0$ as $T \to \infty$, for some α_0.

When the true data density is not included in the parametric family there is no longer a true α_0. To have something which resembles consistency in this case we need the following concept of information.

Definition 9.3. Let the density of the model be $f(y \mid \alpha)$ and let the true density be $f^+(y)$. Let $t = 1, \dots, T$. The Kullback–Leibler (KL) information is defined at any value α by

$$\text{KL}(\alpha) = E\left[\ln \frac{f^+(y_t)}{f(y_t \mid \alpha)}\right] = \int \ln \frac{f^+(y_t)}{f(y_t \mid \alpha)} f^+(y_t)\,\text{d}y_t. \tag{9.24}$$

In words, the KL(α) measures the discrepancy between the model distribution and the true distribution of the data. If α_0 is the minimizer of KL(α), consistency can still be proved (see, for example, Bauwens et al. 1999). Furthermore, we have the following result.

Result 9.2 (asymptotic normality). Suppose α_0 is not on the boundary of the parameter space. If $\alpha^* \xrightarrow{\text{P}} \alpha_0$ as $T \to \infty$, $g(\alpha \mid y) \xrightarrow{\text{D}} \mathbb{N}(\alpha_0, [T\Sigma(\alpha_0)]^{-1})$, where $\Sigma(\alpha_0) = -E[(\partial^2 \ln g(\alpha \mid y)/\partial\alpha\partial\alpha')|_{\alpha=\alpha_0}]$. Here $\Sigma(\alpha_0)$ can be estimated by using $\Sigma(\alpha^*)$ and α_0 either satisfies $f^+ = f(y \mid \alpha_0)$ or is the minimizer of (9.24).

9.3.3 Testing Hypotheses/Relative Fit of Different Models

Testing hypotheses or contrasting models in a Bayesian framework means calculating their relative posterior support. One simple way of evaluating alternatives is the posterior odds (PO) ratio

$$\text{PO} = \frac{g(\mathcal{M}_j \mid y)}{g(\mathcal{M}_{j'} \mid y)} = \frac{g(\mathcal{M}_j)}{g(\mathcal{M}_{j'})} \times \frac{f(y \mid \mathcal{M}_j)}{f(y \mid \mathcal{M}_{j'})}. \tag{9.25}$$

In (9.25) the first term is the prior odds and the second is the Bayes factor.

Example 9.18. Suppose you are asked to evaluate the stability of a fixed exchange rate regime. Suppose that under the null hypothesis (say, normal conditions) there is a 50–50 chance that the regime will be maintained. Under the alternative hypothesis (say, increasing oil prices) the probability that the fixed exchange rate regime will be maintained is 0.25. Suppose that *a priori* both hypotheses are equally probable and that the fixed exchange rate regime has been maintained in 90 of the 100 months for which you have data. Then

$$\mathrm{PO} = \frac{0.5}{0.5} \times \frac{(0.5)^{0.1}(0.5)^{0.9}}{(0.75)^{0.1}(0.25)^{0.9}} = \frac{0.5}{0.2790} = 1.79. \tag{9.26}$$

Hence, 90 months of fixed exchange rates have changed the odds of the null from 1 to 1.79.

Exercise 9.13. Continuing with example 9.13 suppose you are interested in classifying managers as being below or above average. Let $\mathcal{M}_0 : \alpha \leqslant 100$ and $\mathcal{M}_1 : \alpha > 100$. Find the posterior odds ratio for $\mathcal{M}_0$ versus $\mathcal{M}_1$.

As is clear from example 9.18, the Bayes factor is the ratio of the marginal likelihood of the two models, where $f(y \mid \mathcal{M}_j) = \int f(y \mid \mathcal{M}_j, \alpha_j) g(\alpha_j)\, \mathrm{d}\alpha_j$. Marginal likelihoods, like likelihood functions, can be decomposed into the product of the densities of one-step-ahead prediction errors (see later on). Hence, they inform us on the relative fit of the two models to the data.

As we have done with Bayes estimators, it is possible to derive the asymptotic properties of the Bayes factor. The interested reader may consult Kass and Raftery (1995). Roughly speaking, the Bayes factor provides a consistent model selection criterion when (a) the posterior distribution asymptotically concentrates around the pseudo-ML estimator, (b) the pseudo-ML converges in probability to the pseudo-true value, and (c) the Bayes factor chooses the model which is closest to the pseudo-true model in a KL sense.

A Bayes factor differs from a likelihood ratio statistic: in fact, the relative agreement of prior and likelihood and the least squares fit of the models matter for the selection.

Example 9.19. Let $y_j = x_j \alpha_j + e_j$, $e_j \sim$ i.i.d. $\mathbb{N}(0, \sigma_j^2)$, $j = 1, 2$. Suppose $g(\alpha_j) \sim \mathbb{N}(\bar{\alpha}_j, (\sigma_j^2 \bar{\Sigma}_{\alpha_j})^{-1})$ and $\bar{s}_j^2 \sigma_j^{-2} \sim \chi^2(\bar{v}_j)$. If $\bar{v}_1 = \bar{v}_2 = \bar{v}$ and $\bar{s}_1^2 = \bar{s}_2^2$, the Bayes factor of model 1 relative to model 2 is proportional to

$$\left(\frac{v_1 s_1^2 + (\alpha_{1,\mathrm{OLS}} - \tilde{\alpha}_1)' X_1 X_1 (\alpha_{1,\mathrm{OLS}} - \tilde{\alpha}_1) + (\bar{\alpha}_1 - \tilde{\alpha}_1)' \bar{\Sigma}_{\alpha_1} (\bar{\alpha}_1 - \tilde{\alpha}_1)}{v_2 s_2^2 + (\alpha_{2,\mathrm{OLS}} - \tilde{\alpha}_2)' X_2 X_2 (\alpha_{2,\mathrm{OLS}} - \tilde{\alpha}_2) + (\bar{\alpha}_2 - \tilde{\alpha}_2)' \bar{\Sigma}_{\alpha_2} (\bar{\alpha}_2 - \tilde{\alpha}_2)}\right)^{-0.5(T+v)},$$

where the factor of proportionality is

$$\left(\frac{|\bar{\Sigma}_{\alpha_1}||\tilde{\Sigma}_{\alpha_2}|}{|\bar{\Sigma}_{\alpha_2}||\tilde{\Sigma}_{\alpha_1}|}\right)^{0.5},$$

$\alpha_{j,\mathrm{OLS}} = (x_j' x_j)^{-1}(x_j' y_j)$, and $s_j^2 = (y_j - x_j \alpha_{j,\mathrm{OLS}})^2$. The likelihood ratio statistics is $(v_1 s_1^2 / v_2 s_2^2)^{-0.5T}$.

Marginal likelihoods are typically hard to compute analytically since they require multidimensional integration. Two approximations are available in the literature.

9.3.3.1 Laplace Approximation

When the likelihood is highly peaked around the mode and close to symmetric, the posterior density can be quadratically approximated around the mode. Let $e^{g^{\ddagger}(\alpha_j)} \equiv f(y \mid \mathcal{M}_j, \alpha_j) g(\alpha_j \mid \mathcal{M}_j)$, and let $g^{\ddagger}(\alpha_j) \approx g^{\ddagger}(\alpha_j^*) + 0.5(\alpha_j - \alpha_j^*)' \Sigma_j(\alpha_j^*) \times (\alpha_j - \alpha_j^*)$, where the remainder is $o(\|\alpha_j - \alpha_j^*\|^2)$ and $\Sigma(\alpha_j) = \partial^2 g^{\ddagger}(\alpha)/\partial\alpha\partial\alpha'$. Integrating with respect to α we have $f^*(y \mid \mathcal{M}_j) = (2\pi)^{0.5k_j} |-\Sigma(\alpha_j^*)|^{-0.5} \times e^{g^{\ddagger}(\alpha_j^*)}$, where k_j is the dimension of α_j. Then the approximate Bayes factor is

$$\frac{f^*(y \mid \mathcal{M}_j)}{f^*(y \mid \mathcal{M}_{j'})} = \frac{e^{g^{\ddagger}(\alpha_j^*)}(2\pi)^{0.5k_j} |-\Sigma(\alpha_j^*)|^{-0.5}}{e^{g^{\ddagger}(\alpha_{j'}^*)}(2\pi)^{0.5k_{j'}} |-\Sigma(\alpha_{j'}^*)|^{-0.5}}. \tag{9.27}$$

Exercise 9.14. Show that $2 \ln \mathrm{PO} \approx 2[\ln f(\alpha_j^* \mid y) - \ln f(\alpha_{j'}^* \mid y)] - (k_j - k_{j'}) \times \ln T + (k_j - k_{j'}) \ln(2\pi) + 2(\ln[g(\alpha_j \mid \mathcal{M}_j)] - \ln[g(\alpha_{j'} \mid \mathcal{M}_{j'})]) + 2(\ln[g(\mathcal{M}_j) - \ln g(\mathcal{M}_{j'})]) + [\ln(|-T^{-1}\Sigma(\alpha_j^*)|) - \ln(|-T^{-1}\Sigma(\alpha_{j'}^*)|)]$.

Exercise 9.15. Show the form of $2 \ln \mathrm{PO}$ when $\mathcal{M}_j$ and $\mathcal{M}_{j'}$ are nested (i.e., $\alpha_j = (\alpha_{j'}, a)$).

Exercise 9.14 shows that a Laplace approximation to the PO ratio is composed of several parts: the first term is the likelihood ratio statistics (evaluated at the mode) with $k_j - k_{j'}$ degrees of freedom; the second and third measures are the relative dimensions of the two models. This makes the Laplace approximation consistent under both the null and the alternative. The next two involve the priors of the parameters and the priors of the models. The last term represents a small-sample correction due to the estimated curvature at the mode in the two models. For $T \to \infty$, this term disappears.

9.3.3.2 Schwarz Approximation

The Laplace approximation to the PO ratio requires the specification of $g(\alpha \mid \mathcal{M}_j)$ and of $g(\mathcal{M}_j)$. The Schwarz approximation (SCA) does not need either. However, while the error in the Laplace approximation is $O(T^{-1})$, in the Schwarz approximation it is $O(1)$; that is, it is independent of the sample size (see Kass and Vaidyanathan 1992). The Schwarz approximation is $\ln[f(y \mid \mathcal{M}_j, \alpha_{j,\mathrm{ML}})] - \ln[f(y \mid \mathcal{M}_{j'}, \alpha_{j',\mathrm{ML}})] - 0.5(k_j - k_{j'}) \ln(T)$, where $\alpha_{j,\mathrm{ML}}$ is the maximum likelihood estimator of α in model j. It is easy to see that this approximation uses the first two terms of the Laplace approximation to $2 \ln \mathrm{PO}$ but evaluates them at α_{ML} instead of at α^*. Note also that, as $T \to \infty$, $(\mathrm{SCA} - \ln \mathrm{PO})/\ln \mathrm{PO} \to 0$.

Testing a point null is difficult in a Bayesian framework since a continuous prior on A implies that $g(\alpha_0) = 0$. There are two routes one can take. First, since a point null is a restriction on an interval around α_0, we could consider a prior on $\alpha_0 \pm \epsilon$, where ϵ is small relative to the posterior standard deviation of α. This would be the case, for example, when the likelihood is flat over $\alpha_0 \pm \epsilon$. In this situation, the PO ratio is well-defined.

Alternatively, a prior mixing discrete and continuous distributions could be specified, i.e., $g(\alpha_0) = g_0$ and $g(\alpha \neq \alpha_0) = (1 - g_0)g_1(\alpha)$, where $g_1(\alpha)$ is a proper prior. Examples of this specification appear, for example, in Bayesian testing of unit roots (see Sims 1988). There, a discrete prior is given to the unit root and a mixed discrete–continuous prior to the stationary region.

A question that often arises in practice is what to do when we need to compare several models, not just two. In that case one could select the $\mathcal{M}_j$ with the highest $g(\mathcal{M}_j \mid y)$ or use Leamer's measure of posterior probability, which is given by

$$\text{LEA}(\mathcal{M}_j \mid y) = \frac{g(\mathcal{M}_j \mid y)\,\text{PO}_{j1}}{\sum_{j'} g(\mathcal{M}_{j'} \mid y)\,\text{PO}_{j'1}}, \tag{9.28}$$

where model 1 is taken as the benchmark model.

When the set of possible models is large, one should be careful in assuming equal *a priori* probability on each of them since such a choice may counterintuitively assign a large weight on models which are large in size.

Example 9.20 (Sala-i-Martin, Doppelhofer, and Miller). Suppose you have a large number of possible determinants of growth and you are interested in examining what is the posterior probability that a variable is important for growth, where models here are characterized by combinations of the potential explanatory variables. It is easy to verify that if there are k possible regressors, the number of possible models is 2^k. If an equal prior probability of $1/2^k$ is used on each model, the expected model size is $k/2$. This means that, if $k = 20$, the *a priori* expected number of regressors is 10.

In such a situation it is better to select the prior mean for the model size and let each regressor have prior probability equal to $1/k$ times this prior mean.

Exercise 9.16. Consider the problem of forecasting quarterly exchange rate changes and suppose you have five possible candidate variables: a constant, the price differential, the interest rate differential, the output differential, and the money differential (there are therefore 32 possible model specifications). Using the dollar–yen exchange rate and data on prices, output, interest rates, and money for the United States and Japan, compute the posterior mean and the posterior standard deviation for each regressor and the posterior probability that each regressor is zero (i.e., compute one minus the sum of posterior probabilities of the models where that variable appears). What is the posterior probability that the best model for the dollar–yen exchange rate is a random walk with drift?

9.3.4 Forecasting

Forecasting is straightforward in a Bayesian framework since, as we have seen, the problem fits well into the calculation of $E(h(\alpha))$. The predictive density for future

y in model j is

$$f(y_{t+1}, \dots, y_{t+\tau} \mid y_t, \dots, y_1, \mathcal{M}_j) = \int g(\alpha_j \mid y_t, \mathcal{M}_j) \prod_{i=t+1}^{t+\tau} f(y_i \mid y_{i-1}, \alpha_j, \mathcal{M}_j)\, d\alpha_j. \quad (9.29)$$

The first term in (9.29) is the posterior of α, conditional on model j, and the second term is the recursive one-step-ahead predictive density constructed from the model.

Example 9.21. Let $y_t = x_t\alpha + e_t$, $e_t \sim$ i.i.d. $\mathbb{N}(0, \sigma_e^2)$. Suppose that σ_e^2 is fixed, let $g(\alpha) \sim \mathbb{N}(\bar{\alpha}, \bar{\Sigma}_\alpha)$, and let $x_t^\tau = [x_{t+1}, \dots, x_{t+\tau}]$ be known. Since $g(\alpha \mid y) \sim \mathbb{N}(\tilde{\alpha}, \tilde{\Sigma}_\alpha)$ and since $(y_t^\tau \mid \alpha, y_t, x_t, x_t^\tau) \sim \mathbb{N}(x_t^\tau\alpha, \sigma_e^2 I)$, we have that $(y_t^\tau \mid y_t, x_t, x_t^\tau, \tilde{\alpha}, \sigma_e^2) \sim \mathbb{N}(x_t^\tau\tilde{\alpha}, (x_t^\tau)'\tilde{\Sigma}_\alpha x_t^\tau + \sigma_e^2 I)$ and $(y_t^\tau \mid y_t, x_t, x_t^\tau) = \int (y_t^\tau \mid y_t, x_t, x_t^\tau, \bar{\alpha}, \sigma_e^2)\, d\alpha\, d\sigma_e^2$.

Exercise 9.17. Using the same setup of example 9.21 show that, if *a priori* $\bar{s}^2\sigma_e^{-2} \sim \chi^2(\bar{v})$, $(y_t^\tau \mid y_t, x_t, x_t^\tau)$ has a t-distribution. Show the parameters of this distribution.

If one is interested in choosing the best forecasting model (the model which has the highest posterior support), and two alternatives are available, one can use the predictive odds ratio which is given by

$$\text{PRO} = \frac{g(\mathcal{M}_j)}{g(\mathcal{M}_{j'})} \frac{f(y_{t+1}, \dots, y_{t+\tau} \mid y_t, \dots, y_1, \mathcal{M}_j)}{f(y_{t+1}, \dots, y_{t+\tau} \mid y_t, \dots, y_1, \mathcal{M}_{j'})}. \quad (9.30)$$

Note that, for each i, $f(y_i, \mid y_{i-1}, \alpha_j, \mathcal{M}_j)$ in (9.29) is a measure of the density of the out-of-sample one-step-ahead error made in predicting y_i, given y_{i-1}. Therefore, examining model adequacy is the same as checking its one-step-ahead out-of-sample forecasting performance.

9.4 Hierarchical and Empirical Bayes Models

Hierarchical structures are useful to model situations where repeated observations on the same phenomena are available or when either the prior or the likelihood can be broken down into stages. For example, one may guess that parameter estimates obtained in different experiments may be connected (e.g., learning about rationality in experiments with different groups of individuals). Alternatively, parameters may come in two layers and at one level there is some information while, at the other, little is known (e.g., there is some knowledge about the time evolution of the parameters of a Phillips curve but little is known about the distribution of the parameters regulating its evolution). Finally, there could be latent variables and a parametric model that describes how latent variables are generated is available (e.g., in arbitrage pricing theory (APT) models).

Consider first the case of a prior density with two stages, that is, $g(\alpha, \theta) = g(\alpha \mid \theta)g(\theta)$, where θ is a vector of *hyperparameters*. The joint posterior is $g(\alpha, \theta \mid y) \propto f(y \mid \alpha, \theta)g(\alpha \mid \theta)g(\theta)$ and the marginal posteriors are $g(\alpha \mid y) = \int g(\alpha, \theta \mid y)\, d\theta$ and $g(\theta \mid y) = \int g(\alpha, \theta \mid y)\, d\alpha$.

When the likelihood has two stages, let $f(y \mid z, \alpha, \theta) = f(y \mid z, \alpha) f(z \mid \theta)$. If $g(\alpha, \theta)$ is the prior, $g(z, \alpha, \theta) = f(z \mid \theta) g(\alpha, \theta)$ is the joint prior and the joint posterior is $g(\alpha, \theta, z \mid y) \propto f(y \mid z, \alpha) g(z, \alpha, \theta)$. Then, the marginal posterior for the latent variable is $g(z \mid y) = \int g(\alpha, \theta, z \mid y)\, d\alpha d\theta$ and the marginal posterior for α or θ can be similarly computed. Hence, a latent variable model is just a hierarchical model with a two-stage hierarchy.

This result is important: missing data and signal extraction problems involving unobservable variables can be handled with the same latent variable setup.

Example 9.22 (experimental data). Suppose you have experimental data for different groups of individuals at different points in time. Suppose each experiment is characterized by the vector (α_j, y_{ij}, n_j), where α_j represents some interesting parameter (e.g., the proportion of individuals who are rational), y_{ij} is the data generated for individual i participating in experiment j, and n_j is the number of individuals in experiment j. Under some conditions, it may be reasonable to assume that α_j are drawn from the same distribution. Hence, a hierarchical model for the data is $\prod_j f(y_j \mid \alpha_j) g(\alpha_j \mid \theta) g(\theta)$, where θ is a set of hyperparameters.

Example 9.23 (probit model). Suppose we have T independent observations on y_t, each being Bernoulli distributed with $P(y_t = 1) = \mathbb{N}(x_t\alpha)$, where $\mathbb{N}$ is the normal distribution. For example, we have collected recession dates and $P(y_t = 1)$ is the probability of a recession at t. The model can be rewritten as $z_t = x_t\alpha + e_t$, $e_t \sim$ i.i.d. $\mathbb{N}(0, \sigma_e^2)$ and $y_t = \mathcal{I}_{[z_t > 0]}$, where $\mathcal{I}_.$ is an indicator function. Here z_t is a latent variable and the likelihood of y_t has two stages.

At times it is hard to distinguish the prior from the model as the next example shows.

Example 9.24 (panel data). Let $y_{it} = \alpha_i + e_{it}$, $e_{it} \sim$ i.i.d. $\mathbb{N}(0, \sigma_e^2)$. Assume $\alpha_i \sim \mathbb{N}(\bar{\alpha}, \bar{\sigma}_\alpha^2)$ and $\bar{\alpha} \sim \mathbb{N}(\bar{\alpha}_0, \bar{\sigma}_0^2)$, and let $\bar{\sigma}_\alpha^2$, $\bar{\sigma}_0^2$ be fixed. These assumptions imply

$$\alpha_i = \bar{\alpha} + v_{1i}, \quad v_{1i} \sim \mathbb{N}(0, \bar{\sigma}_\alpha^2), \tag{9.31}$$

$$\bar{\alpha} = \bar{\alpha}_0 + v_2, \quad v_2 \sim \mathbb{N}(0, \sigma_0^2). \tag{9.32}$$

So $\alpha_i = \bar{\alpha}_0 + v_2 + v_{1i}$ and $y_{it} = \bar{\alpha}_0 + v_2 + v_{1i} + e_{it}$. Here α_i could be a latent variable and (9.32) a prior. Alternatively, (9.31), (9.32) are two stages of a hierarchical prior for α_i.

A natural way to model the dependence of parameters in experimental data or in panels is the notion of exchangeability.

Definition 9.4. Consider $j = 1, \ldots, J$ experiments (observations on different individuals or units) for which $f(y_j \mid \alpha_j)$ is available. If only y_j is available to distinguish the α_j and no ordering or grouping can be made, α_j must be *a priori* similar. Then $(\alpha_1, \ldots, \alpha_J)$ are exchangeable if $g(\alpha_1, \ldots, \alpha_J)$ is invariant to permutations of the order of the α_j.

An exchangeable prior for α is obtained by setting $g(\alpha \mid \theta) = \prod_j g(\alpha_j \mid \theta)$, i.e., α_j are independent draws from a distribution with parameter θ. Then, the marginal prior of α is a mixture of i.i.d. distributions with weights given by $g(\theta)$, i.e., $g(\alpha) = \int \prod_j g(\alpha \mid \theta) g(\theta)\, d\theta$.

The next example describes when the exchangeability assumption is appropriate.

Example 9.25. Suppose you have a sample of five inflation rates from countries in the euro area ($y_1 = 1.7$, $y_2 = 1.0$, $y_3 = 0.9$, $y_4 = 3.0$, $y_5 = 1.8$) and suppose you are interested in predicting the inflation rate in another country (call this y_6). What kind of prior can we specify for $(y_1, \dots, y_5)$?

(i) If there is no information to distinguish one country from the others, the prior on y_i, $i = 1, \dots, 5$, should be exchangeable and, lacking information about the time series pattern of inflation rates, $g(y_1, \dots, y_5)$ should be noninformative.

(ii) Suppose you know that the five states are Ireland, Germany, the Netherlands, France, and Belgium, but that their order is random (so you cannot say which country corresponds to which number). In this case, $g(y_1, \dots, y_5)$ should still be exchangeable.

(iii) Suppose now that you know that the data you have sampled come from Germany, the Netherlands, France, Ireland, and Belgium in that order. Now exchangeability is inappropriate since you have information that distinguishes one country from another.

Note that for experiments conducted at different times, with different agents and in different laboratories, it may still be reasonable to use exchangeability since these differences imply different outcomes and not necessarily different *a priori* distributions.

Posterior analysis with hierarchical models is simple and exploits the version of Bayes theorem with nuisance parameters described in section 9.1. For example, $g(\alpha, \theta \mid y)$ is proportional to $f(y \mid \alpha, \theta) g(\alpha \mid \theta) g(\theta) = f(y \mid \alpha) g(\alpha \mid \theta) g(\theta)$. Similarly, predictive distributions can be easily computed. In hierarchical models we distinguish between two types of predictive distribution for (future) y^{τ}: those conditional on $\tilde{\alpha}$, a posterior estimate of α; and those conditional on α^l, a draw from $g(\alpha \mid \tilde{\theta}, y)$, where $\tilde{\theta}$ is a posterior estimate of θ.

To simulate samples for the unknowns from the posterior distribution one would set up the likelihood function $f(y \mid \alpha)$, the priors $g(\alpha \mid \theta)$, $g(\theta)$, and proceed as follows.

Algorithm 9.2.

(1) Compute the posterior kernel $\breve{g}(\alpha, \theta \mid y)$.

(2) Compute $g(\alpha \mid \theta, y)$ (for fixed y, this is a function of θ only).

(3) Compute $g(\theta \mid y)$ either as $g(\theta \mid y) = \int g(\alpha, \theta \mid y)\, d\alpha$ or as $g(\theta \mid y) = g(\alpha, \theta \mid y) / g(\alpha \mid \theta, y)$.

(4) Draw θ^l from $g(\theta \mid y)$ and α^l from $g(\alpha \mid \theta^l, y)$. If α_j is exchangeable, draw α_j, $g(\alpha_j \mid \theta^l, y)$ for each j. Compute $h(\alpha^l)$. In the case of prediction, draw y_τ^l from $f(y_\tau \mid \tilde{\alpha})$ or from $f(y_\tau \mid \alpha^l)$.

(5) Repeat step (4) L times and compute $h(\alpha^l)$ each time. If draws are i.i.d., estimate $E[h(\alpha \mid y)]$ via $E[h(\alpha \mid y)] = \lim_{L\to\infty}(1/L)\sum_l h(\alpha^l)$.

Note that step (3) is easy if $g(\alpha \mid \theta)$ is conditionally conjugate. $h(\alpha)$ could include, as usual, functions of economic interest (impulse responses, welfare costs, forecasts, etc.).

Example 9.26 (estimating the individual productivity (random effect) and the average productivity in a plant (fixed effect)). Let y_{jt} be the number of pieces completed by worker j at hour t of the day. Suppose $(y_{jt} \mid \alpha_j) \sim \mathbb{N}(\alpha_j, \sigma^2)$, $j = 1, \dots, J$, σ^2 fixed, where α_j is the average productivity of the worker. Let $\bar{y}_j = (1/t_j)\sum_{t=1}^{t_j} y_{jt}$ and $\sigma_j^2 = \sigma^2/t_j$. Then $\bar{y}_j \mid \alpha_j \sim \mathbb{N}(\alpha_j, \sigma_j^2)$. There are three possible estimators for α_j: (i) the individual mean, $\bar{y}_j$, (ii) the pooled mean, $y_p = \sum_j(\bar{y}_j/\sigma_j^2)/\sum_j(1/\sigma_j^2)$, and (iii) the weighted mean $\bar{y}_{wj} = \varrho_j\bar{y}_j + (1-\varrho_j)y_p$, $\varrho_j \in [0, 1]$.

Exercise 9.18. Show how to use between and within variations in y_{jt} to choose the estimator in (i) or the estimator in (ii).

What kind of exchangeable prior would induce a researcher to choose as posterior estimator (i), (ii), or (iii)? Estimator (i) will be chosen if the prior for each α_j is independent and uniform over $(-\infty, +\infty)$; estimator (ii) will be chosen if $\alpha_j = \alpha, \forall j$, and α is uniform over $(-\infty, +\infty)$; finally, estimator (iii) will be selected if the prior for α_j is i.i.d. normal. Note that (i) and (ii) are special cases of (iii): (i) obtains if $\text{var}(\alpha_j) = \infty$; (ii) obtains if $\text{var}(\alpha_j) = 0$.

Assume that σ^2 is known and let $g(\alpha_1, \dots, \alpha_J \mid \bar{\alpha}, \bar{\sigma}_\alpha^2) = \prod_j \mathbb{N}(\alpha_j \mid \bar{\alpha}, \bar{\sigma}_\alpha^2)$, where $\bar{\alpha}$ is the average productivity and $\bar{\sigma}_\alpha^2$ its dispersion across workers. Let $g(\bar{\alpha}, \bar{\sigma}_\alpha^2) = g(\bar{\alpha} \mid \bar{\sigma}_\alpha^2)g(\bar{\sigma}_\alpha^2) \propto g(\bar{\sigma}_\alpha^2)$ (i.e., no information about $\bar{\alpha}$ is available). Then, the joint posterior of $(\alpha_j, \bar{\alpha}, \bar{\sigma}_\alpha^2)$ is

$$g(\alpha, \bar{\sigma}_\alpha^2, \bar{\alpha} \mid y) \propto \prod_{j=1}^{J} \mathbb{N}(\bar{y}_j \mid \alpha_j, \sigma_j^2) \prod_j \mathbb{N}(\alpha_j \mid \bar{\alpha}, \bar{\sigma}_\alpha^2) g(\bar{\sigma}_\alpha^2, \bar{\alpha}). \qquad (9.33)$$

Using the logic of example 9.10, the marginal for α_j is $g(\alpha_j \mid \bar{\alpha}, \bar{\sigma}_\alpha^2, y) \sim \mathbb{N}(\tilde{\alpha}_j, \tilde{\Sigma}_j)$, where $\tilde{\alpha}_j = \tilde{\Sigma}_j(\bar{y}_j/\sigma_j^2 + \bar{\alpha}/\bar{\sigma}_\alpha^2)$, $\tilde{\Sigma}_j = (1/\sigma_j^2 + 1/\bar{\sigma}_\alpha^2)^{-1}$ while the marginal posterior for $\bar{\alpha}$ and $\bar{\sigma}_\alpha^2$ is

$$\begin{aligned} g(\bar{\alpha}, \bar{\sigma}_\alpha^2 \mid y) &= \int g(\alpha, \bar{\alpha}, \bar{\sigma}_\alpha^2 \mid y, x)\, \mathrm{d}\alpha \propto g(\bar{\sigma}_\alpha^2) f(y \mid \bar{\alpha}, \bar{\sigma}_\alpha^2) \\ &= g(\bar{\sigma}_\alpha^2) \prod_j \mathbb{N}(\bar{y}_j \mid \bar{\alpha}, \bar{\sigma}_\alpha^2 + \sigma_j^2), \end{aligned} \qquad (9.34)$$

which can be obtained by substituting the prior into the model, i.e., $y_{ij} = \bar{\alpha} + e_{ij}$, $e_{ij} \sim \mathbb{N}(0, \sigma_j^2 + \bar{\sigma}_\alpha^2)$ and by using the sufficient statistic $\bar{y}_j$ to rewrite the likelihood of y_{ij}. From (9.34) it is easy to see that the marginal of $\bar{\alpha}$, conditional on $\bar{\sigma}_\alpha^2$, is normal with mean $\tilde{\bar{\alpha}} = \tilde{\Sigma}_{\bar{\alpha}} \sum_j \bar{y}_j/(\bar{\sigma}_\alpha^2 + \sigma_j^2)$ and variance $\tilde{\Sigma}_{\bar{\alpha}} = [\sum_j 1/(\bar{\sigma}_\alpha^2 + \sigma_j^2)]^{-1}$. The marginal posterior for $\bar{\sigma}_\alpha^2$ is

$$g(\bar{\sigma}_\alpha^2 \mid y) = \frac{g(\bar{\alpha}, \bar{\sigma}_\alpha^2 \mid y)}{g(\bar{\alpha} \mid \bar{\sigma}_\alpha^2 y)} \propto \frac{g(\bar{\sigma}_\alpha^2) \prod_j \mathbb{N}(\bar{y}_j \mid \bar{\alpha}, \sigma_j^2 + \bar{\sigma}_\alpha^2)}{\mathbb{N}(\bar{\alpha} \mid \tilde{\bar{\alpha}}, \tilde{\Sigma}_{\bar{\alpha}})}$$
$$\propto \tilde{\Sigma}_{\bar{\alpha}}^{0.5} \Big[\prod_j (\sigma_j^2 + \bar{\sigma}_\alpha^2) \Big]^{-0.5} \exp\left\{ -\frac{(\bar{y}_j - \tilde{\bar{\alpha}})^2}{2(\sigma_j^2 + \bar{\sigma}_\alpha^2)} \right\}, \quad (9.35)$$

where the second line is obtained by evaluating the likelihood function at $\tilde{\bar{\alpha}}$, when $g(\bar{\sigma}_\alpha^2)$ is noninformative. Then, a posterior 68% credible set for the average productivity is $\tilde{\bar{\alpha}} \pm \sqrt{\tilde{\Sigma}_{\bar{\alpha}}}$ and a posterior 68% credible set for the individual productivity is $\tilde{\alpha}_j \pm \sqrt{\tilde{\Sigma}_j}$.

Suppose now you want to predict the productivity of a new worker j', $j' \neq 1, \dots, J$, whose ability is similar to that of existing workers. To construct prediction $y_{j',t}$ one could use the following.

Algorithm 9.3.

(1) Draw $(\bar{\alpha}^l, (\bar{\sigma}_\alpha^2)^l)$ from $g(\bar{\alpha}, \bar{\sigma}_\alpha^2 \mid y)$ and α_j^l from $g(\alpha_j \mid \bar{\alpha}^l, (\bar{\sigma}_\alpha^2)^l, y)$.

(2) Draw $y_{j',t}$ from $\mathbb{N}(\alpha_{\bar{j}}^l, \sigma_j^2)$.

(3) Repeat steps (1) and (2) L times and average $y_{j',t}$ over l.

Exercise 9.19. In example 9.26, what would you do if the new worker is different from all those currently employed? What if she is similar only to a subset of current workers?

Example 9.27. Consider the problem of predicting financial crises and suppose that they occur when a vector of z variables passes a threshold z^*. Suppose z_t are unobservable but related to some observable x_t (e.g., liquidity of the banking system, trade balance, or the state of government finances) and that we observe $y_t = 1$ if $z_t \geqslant z^*$ and $y_t = 0$ otherwise. Then the model is $z_t = \alpha x_t + e_t$, $e_t \mid x_T \sim \mathbb{N}(0, \sigma_e^2)$, $y_T = \mathcal{I}_{[z^*,\infty)} z_T$, where σ_e^2 is known. Let $y = [y_1, \dots, y_T]'$, $z = [z_1, \dots, z_T]'$, $x = [x_1, \dots, x_T]'$, and $f(y, z \mid x, \alpha) = f(z \mid x, \alpha) f(y \mid z)$. Then

$$f(y, z \mid x, \alpha) = (2\pi)^{0.5T} \exp\Big\{ -0.5(z - x\alpha)'(z - x\alpha) \times \prod_{t=1}^{T} [y_t \mathcal{I}_{[z^*,\infty)} + (1 - y_t) \mathcal{I}_{(-\infty, z^*]}] \Big\}, \quad (9.36)$$

$$f(y \mid x, \alpha) = \int f(y, z \mid x, \alpha) \, \mathrm{d}z = \prod_{t=1}^{T} [y_t \mathbb{N}(\alpha x) + (1 - y_t)(1 - \mathbb{N}(\alpha x))], \quad (9.37)$$

where $\mathbb{N}(x\alpha)$ is the normal distribution evaluated at $x\alpha$. Since $g(\alpha, y \mid z, x) \propto f(y, z \mid x, \alpha)g(\alpha)$ and the marginal posterior for α is normal with variance $\tilde{\Sigma}_\alpha = (\bar{\Sigma}_\alpha^{-1} + \sigma_e^{-2}x'x)^{-1}$ and mean $\tilde{\alpha} = \tilde{\Sigma}_\alpha(\bar{\Sigma}_\alpha^{-1}\bar{\alpha} + \sigma_e^{-2}x'y)$, where $\bar{\alpha}$ and $\bar{\Sigma}_\alpha$ are the prior mean and the prior variance of α. Furthermore, conditional on (α, y, x), the posterior for z_t is normal with mean αx_t and variance σ_e^2 and $z_t > z^*$ if $y_t = 1$ and $z_t \leqslant z^*$ if $y_t = 0$.

9.4.1 Empirical Bayes Methods

Empirical Bayes (EB) methods attempt to reduce the costs of computing marginal posteriors in hierarchical models. They do so by estimating features of the prior from the data.

In example 9.26, the posterior distribution of the individual effect α_j is obtained by integrating $\bar{\alpha}$ and $\bar{\sigma}_\alpha^2$ out of the joint posterior. Alternatively, one could estimate $\bar{\alpha}$ and $\bar{\sigma}_\alpha^2$ by, for example, $\hat{\bar{\alpha}} = (1/J_1)\sum_j^{J_1} \bar{y}_j$ and $\hat{\bar{\sigma}}_\alpha^2 = T^{-1}(\sum_j(\bar{y}_j - \hat{\bar{\alpha}})^2/(J_1 - 1) - \sum_t\sum_j(y_{tj} - \bar{y}_j)^2/T(J_1 - 1))$, $J_1 \ll J$, and substitute these estimates in the formulas for the moments of the posterior distribution. That is, instead of computing $g(\alpha \mid y) = \int g(\alpha, \bar{\alpha}, \bar{\sigma}_\alpha^2, \theta \mid y)\,\mathrm{d}\bar{\alpha}\,\mathrm{d}\bar{\sigma}_\alpha^2$, we calculate $g(\alpha \mid y, \hat{\bar{\alpha}}, \hat{\bar{\sigma}}_\alpha^2)$.

We discussed data-driven priors in section 9.1.2. As in that framework, the marginal likelihood can be used to estimate features of the prior distribution.

Example 9.28. Let the model for unit i of a panel be $y_{it} = \alpha_i y_{it-1} + e_t$, $t = -1, 0, 1, \dots, T$, where $\alpha_i \sim (\bar{\alpha}, \bar{\sigma}_\alpha^2)$, $\bar{\alpha} \sim (\bar{\alpha}_0, \sigma_0^2)$, and $e_t \sim$ i.i.d. $(0, \sigma_e^2)$. If σ_0^2 and σ_{a}^2 are known (or estimable from the data), an estimator of $\bar{\alpha}_0$ is $\bar{\bar{\alpha}}_0 = (y_{-1}'\Sigma^{-1}y_{-1})^{-1}(y_{-1}'\Sigma^{-1}y)$, where $\Sigma = (\sigma_e^2 + \bar{\sigma}_\alpha^2 y_{-1}'y_{-1} + \bar{\sigma}_0^2 y_{-1}'y_{-1})$, $y_{-1} = [y_{1-1}, \dots, y_{n-1}]'$, and $y = [y_1, \dots, y_n]'$.

There are advantages and disadvantages in using EB methods. On the one hand, computations are simpler; furthermore, priors are data driven which makes them more appealing to non-Bayesian audiences; finally, despite the fact that some parameters are estimated, the form of the posterior for α is unchanged. On the other hand, posterior estimates obtained with EB methods disregard the uncertainty present in $(\bar{\alpha}, \bar{\sigma}_\alpha^2)$. This problem can be fixed (see, for example, Morris 1983). Another problem is that estimates of $\bar{\sigma}_\alpha^2$ may be negative; finally, while there is no problem in selecting some observations to estimate the prior in time series (use a training sample), it is unclear how to do this in cross-sectional environments (which units should be used?). Hence, validation techniques need to be employed to examine the robustness of the conclusions one reaches.

Exercise 9.20. Why could estimates of $\bar{\sigma}_\alpha^2$ be negative? How would you fix this problem?

As we will see in chapter 10, BVARs with a Minnesota prior can be handled with EB methods. There, $(\bar{\alpha}, \bar{\sigma}_\alpha^2)$ could be estimated in a training sample by using EB ideas.

9.4.2 Meta-Analysis

Despite the mysterious name, meta-analysis is relatively straightforward; it tries to efficiently summarize the findings produced in different studies. Questions which fit into such a framework are quite common in economics. Here is a brief list.

- Is the bank lending channel an important mechanism in transmitting monetary policy shocks? (The evidence is across countries (see, for example, Angeloni et al. 2003).)
- Does trade increase in monetary unions? (The evidence is across studies with different samples or estimators (see, for example, Rose 2004).)
- Can financial variables predict inflation in the medium term? (The evidence may be across regimes (high/low inflation), time periods, countries, etc.)
- Do agents behave in a risk averse fashion when faced with fair bets? (The evidence may come from individuals of different age, social, cultural background, etc.)
- Does local fiscal policy affect local to union-wide prices? (The evidence comes from different countries, regimes, time periods (see, for example, Canova and Pappa 2003).)

The best way to understand how to use meta-analysis is through an example.

Example 9.29. Consider the question of whether monetary policy can shield economies from recessions. Suppose we have $j = 1, \dots, J$ studies coming from different regimes or countries. For each j we have two sets of data: (i) an action is undertaken in T_{0j} episodes and y_{0j} recessions are observed; (ii) no action is undertaken in T_{1j} episodes and y_{1j} recessions are observed, $T_j = T_{0j} + T_{1j}$. Let the probabilities of a recession in the two cases be p_{0j} and p_{1j}. Consider $\alpha_j = \ln(p_{1j}/(1-p_{1j}))/(p_{0j}/(1-p_{0j}))$, that is, the relative probability of a recession in the two scenarios, suppose we care about $\alpha_j, \forall j$ (single-study effect), and $\bar{\alpha}$ (average effect) and suppose no information other than (T_{ij}, y_{ij}), $i = 0, 1$, is available. A crude estimate of $(\alpha_j, \bar{\alpha})$ can be obtained by taking a normal approximation to the outcome of each experiment j, i.e., assume $\alpha_j \sim \mathbb{N}(\hat{\alpha}_j, \hat{\sigma}_j^2)$, where $\hat{\alpha}_j = \ln(y_{1j}/(T_{1j}-y_{1j})) - \ln(y_{0j}/(T_{0j}-y_{0j}))$ and $\hat{\sigma}_j^2 = 1/y_{1j} + 1/(T_{1j}-y_{1j}) + 1/y_{0j} + 1/(T_{0j} - y_{0j})$, in which case $\hat{\bar{\alpha}} = (1/j)\sum_j \hat{\alpha}_j$. Can we improve upon these estimates?

Suppose that the J studies are compatible in some sense. Here there is some latitude regarding what compatible means. It could be that the outcomes are all drawn from the same distribution, that study j carries no information about study j', or that no study has more information than others. In all these cases information is exchangeable.

Let $\hat{\alpha}_j$ be an estimate of α_j obtained from experiment j and consider a hierarchical structure where the likelihood of $(\hat{\alpha}_j \mid \alpha_j, \sigma_j^2)$ is $\mathbb{N}(\alpha_j, \sigma_j^2)$, σ_j^2 known; the conditional prior for α_j is exchangeable and $(\alpha_j \mid \bar{\alpha}, \bar{\sigma}_\alpha^2) \sim \mathbb{N}(\bar{\alpha}, \bar{\sigma}_\alpha^2)$; and the marginal

Table 9.1. Length of recessions.

	Before			After		
	Min	Mean	Max	Min	Mean	Max
1	25	38	62	18	24	38
2	26	29	37	19	21	25
3	22	25	34	24	25	32
4	27	32	40	21	33	37

Table 9.2. Effect of CAP funds.

	Region							
	1	2	3	4	5	6	7	8
Estimate	28.39	7.94	−2.75	6.82	−0.64	0.63	18.01	12.16
Standard error	14.9	10.2	16.3	11.0	9.4	11.4	10.4	17.6

for $(\bar{\alpha}, \bar{\sigma}_\alpha^2)$ is noninformative. This setup fits the one described in example 9.26. Hence, improved (meta-)estimates can be obtained by calculating the posteriors of α_j and $\bar{\alpha}$ using this hierarchical setup.

Exercise 9.21. Consider four studies measuring the length (in months) of recession in four countries before and after the government started using Keynesian policies. The data are assumed to be of the same quality across time periods and are as in table 9.1.

Using a hierarchical model where the length of a recession is assumed to be exponential with parameter α and a suitable prior for α (e.g., uniform on the positive side of the real line), provide an estimate of the difference in the mean across regimes in each study and on average. Construct a posterior 95% credible set for this difference. Is there any evidence that Keynesian policies had any effect on the length of recessions?

Exercise 9.22. Suppose you are interested in evaluating the effects of EU agricultural funds (the so-called CAP funds) on regional growth. Suppose you have run a time series regression in each region, obtaining agricultural funds with output growth on the left-hand side and a number of variables controlling for the individual characteristics of the regions on the right-hand side and found the coefficients on the amount of structural funds received to be as in table 9.2.

(i) Argue about the advisability of continuing to provide structural funds to these regions.

(ii) Using a hierarchical model, where the estimates in the table play the role of $\bar{y}_j$ and the standard errors the role of σ_j, assume σ_j are known, and that $g(\alpha, \ln(\sigma_\alpha))$ is uniform. Calculate meta-estimates of the effect of structural funds in each region

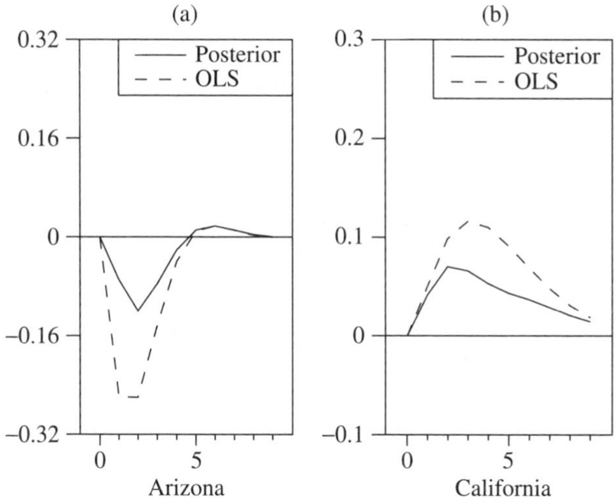

Figure 9.3. Price differential responses, U.S. states.

and on average. What is the value of σ_α you would condition on? That is, what is the posterior estimate of the dispersion parameter of the effects of structural funds across regions?

(iii) Simulate the posterior for $(\alpha_j, \sigma_\alpha, \alpha)$ by using the hierarchical structure in (ii). Calculate $E(\alpha_j \mid y, \sigma_\alpha)$ for a grid of values of σ_α between 0 and 10. Calculate $E(\alpha \mid y, \sigma_\alpha)$ and the (simulated) interquartile range for each α_j. Is it fair to say that CAP funds do not boost growth? (Hint: to make the point stronger, compute the posterior of $\max(\alpha_j)$.)

Example 9.30 (Canova and Pappa). Suppose you want to estimate the effect of local government expenditure shocks on local to union-wide prices in monetary unions and you are interested in getting posterior estimates of relative price responses in each state or country. Suppose that $y_{it} \equiv P_{it}/P_t = D_i(\ell)e_t$, where e_t are structural shocks and $D(\ell)$ are structural impulse responses. Suppose also that $D_i \equiv \text{vec}(D_{1i}(\ell)) = D + \epsilon_i$, where $\epsilon_i \sim N(0, \sigma_\epsilon^2)$ measures deviations of the $k \times 1$ vector of responses for each unit i from the vector of mean responses D. Assume further that $g(D)$ is constant and σ_ϵ^2 is fixed. We need to compute $g(D_i \mid y_{jt},\ j = 1, \dots, N)$. In general, $g(D_i \mid y_{jt},\ j = 1, \dots, N) \neq g(D_i \mid y_{it})$, as figure 9.3 shows for two randomly chosen U.S. states (the dashed line represents the point estimate obtained with local information, the solid one the point estimate using information from all states). Overall, cross-sectional information makes relative price responses smoother and better behaved.

9.5 Posterior Simulators

As we will see in more detail in the next two chapters, there is a large number of problems for which the posterior distribution of α cannot be computed analytically.

In others, only the kernel of the posterior is available but $f(y)$ is unknown. In the most favorable situation one can take a normal approximation to the posterior to conduct inference. In others, posterior simulators are needed. This section describes both approaches in detail.

9.5.1 Normal Posterior Analysis

When the number of data points is large, the likelihood will be quite peaked so that small changes in the prior will have little effect on the posterior. In this case, the likelihood will be concentrated in a small region where $g(\alpha)$ is constant and the posterior distribution will be approximately normal. Since the Bayesian central limit theorem, described in section 9.3.2, holds, one can undertake posterior inference simulating sequences for the unknowns from an approximate normal distribution. To do so we need the following four steps.

Algorithm 9.4.

(1) Find a measure of location (typically, the mode) of the posterior distribution. Several mode-finding algorithms exist in the literature. Here are two.

- *Conditional maximization algorithm*. Partition $\alpha = (\alpha_1, \alpha_2)$ and choose $\alpha_0 = (\alpha_1^0, \alpha_2^0)$ as initial conditions.
  (i) Maximize $g(\alpha_1, \alpha_2 = \alpha_2^0 \mid y)$ with respect to α_1. Let α_1^1 the maximizer.
  (ii) Maximize $g(\alpha_1^1, \alpha_2 \mid y)$ with respect to α_2. Let α_2^1 the maximizer.
  (iii) Set $\alpha_2^0 = \alpha_2^1$. Iterate on (i) and (ii) until convergence is achieved.
  (iv) Start from any other α_2^0 and check if the maximum is global.
- *Newton-type algorithm*. Choose α^0, and let $\text{LG} = \ln g(\alpha \mid y)$ or $\text{LG} = \ln \breve{g}(\alpha \mid y)$.
  (i) Compute $\text{LG}' = (\partial \text{LG}/\partial\alpha)|_{\alpha^0}$ and $\text{LG}'' = (\partial^2 \text{LG}/\partial\alpha\partial\alpha')|_{\alpha^0}$; approximate LG quadratically.
  (ii) Set $\alpha^l = \alpha^{l-1} - \varrho[\text{LG}''(\alpha^{l-1} \mid y)]^{-1}[\text{LG}'(\alpha^{l-1} \mid y)]$, $\varrho \in (0, 1)$, $l = 1, 2, \ldots$.
  (iii) Iterate on (i) and (ii) until convergence is achieved.

  Whenever analytic derivatives are difficult to calculate, one could use $\text{LG}' = [\text{LG}(\alpha + \delta_i e_i \mid y) - \text{LG}(\alpha - \delta_i e_i \mid y)]/2\delta_i$ and $\text{LG}'' = [\text{LG}(\alpha + \delta_i e_i + \delta_j e_j \mid y) - \text{LG}(\alpha + \delta_i e_i - \delta_j e_j \mid y)]/4\delta_i\delta_j + [\text{LG}(\alpha - \delta_i e_i - \delta_j e_j \mid y) - \text{LG}(\alpha - \delta_i e_i + \delta_j e_j \mid y)]/4\delta_i\delta_j$. This algorithm is fast if α^0 is "good" and LG close to quadratic. It does not work if LG'' is not positive definite.

In both algorithms, crude estimates, obtained by discarding parts of the model and/or the data, can be used as initial conditions. For example, in hierarchical models, one could fix $(\bar{\alpha}, \bar{\sigma}^2_\alpha)$, and use $g(\alpha \mid \bar{\sigma}^2_\alpha, \bar{\alpha}, y)$ as a conjugate prior in the calculations.

The mode α^* does not have a special role here; it is simply the point around which we map the shape of the posterior distribution.

(2) Find an analytic approximation to posterior density, centered at the mode.

The most typical approximation is a normal one, that is, $g(\alpha \mid y) \approx \mathbb{N}(\alpha^*, \Sigma_{\alpha^*})$, where $\Sigma_{\alpha^*} = [-\mathrm{LG}''(\alpha^*)]^{-1}$. When multiple modes are present, one constructs an approximation to each mode, and sets $g(\alpha \mid y) \approx \sum_i \varrho_i \mathbb{N}(\alpha_i^*, \Sigma_{\alpha_i^*})$, where $0 \leqslant \varrho_i \leqslant 1$. If the modes are clearly separated and a normal approximation is chosen for each of them, one typically selects $\varrho_i = \breve{g}(\alpha_i^* \mid y)|\Sigma_{\alpha_i^*}|^{0.5}$. If the sample is small and/or the normal approximation inappropriate, one could use a t-distribution with a small number of degrees of freedom ν, i.e., $g(\alpha \mid y) \approx \sum_i \breve{g}(\alpha \mid y)[\nu + (\alpha - \alpha_i^*)' \Sigma^{-1}_{\alpha_i^*} \times (\alpha - \alpha_i^*)]^{-0.5(k+\upsilon)}$, where k is the dimension of α. When $\nu = 1$, $g(\alpha \mid y)$ is approximated with a Cauchy, a distribution with large overdispersion (no moment exists). In typical macroeconomic applications, $\nu = 4$ or 5 is appropriate.

(3) Draw samples from the approximate posterior distribution. If draws are i.i.d., the law of large numbers permits us to approximate $E(h(\alpha))$ or the posterior probability contours of $h(\alpha)$ with $(1/L) \sum_l h(\alpha^l)$ or the ordered values of $h(\alpha^l)$. Note that, if a Laplace approximation to $g(\alpha \mid y)$ is used, $E(h(\alpha \mid y)) \approx h(\alpha^*)\breve{g}(\alpha^* \mid y)| - \partial^2 \ln[h(\alpha)\breve{g}(\alpha \mid y)]/\partial\alpha\partial\alpha'|_{\alpha=\alpha^*}|^{0.5}$.

(4) Check the accuracy of the approximation by computing the *importance ratio* $\mathrm{IR}^l = \breve{g}(\alpha^l \mid y)/g^{\mathrm{A}}(\alpha^l \mid y)$, where g^{A} is the approximating distribution. If IR^l is roughly constant across l, the approximation is good. If it is not, other simulation methods are needed.

Note that the normal approximation provides a first-order approximation to $h(\alpha)$, in the sense that the error is $O(T^{-1})$ while the Laplace approximation provides a second-order approximation; the error here is $O(T^{-2})$.

Exercise 9.23. Consider estimating a reduced-form Phillips curve $\pi_{t+1} = \alpha_\pi \pi_t + \alpha_{\text{gap}} \text{gdpgap}_t + e_t$, where gdpgap_t is the difference between actual and potential output and $e_t \sim$ i.i.d. $(0, \sigma_e^2)$. Assume that $\alpha = (\alpha_\pi, \alpha_{\text{gap}}) \sim \mathbb{N}(\bar{\alpha}, \bar{\Sigma}_\alpha)$ and that $g(\sigma_e^2)$ is noninformative. Derive the marginal posterior for α. Using U.S. data on CPI inflation and linearly detrended GDP as a proxy for the gdpgap, construct a posterior normal approximation and report a 68% credible set for α_{gap}.

9.5.2 Basic Posterior Simulators

When normal or t-distributions are inappropriate for approximating $g(\alpha \mid y)$, other posterior simulators can be used. The next two employ noniterative methods and work well when IR^l is approximately constant across l.

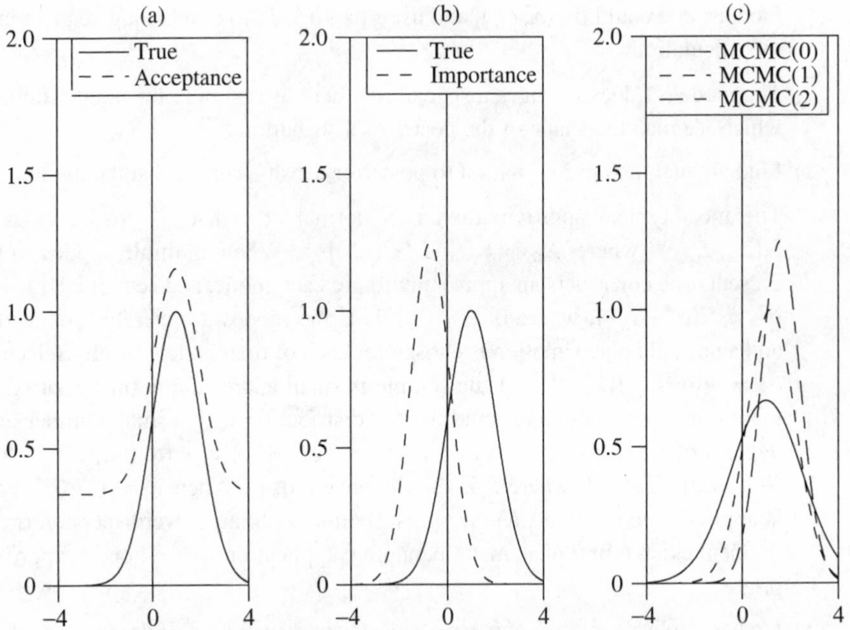

Figure 9.4. Posterior simulators: (a) acceptance sampling; (b) importance sampling; (c) Markov chain sampling.

9.5.2.1 Acceptance Sampling

Let $g^{\mathrm{AS}}(\alpha)$ be any function from which it is easy to simulate, defined for all $\alpha \in A$ for which $\breve{g}(\alpha \mid y) > 0$. Assume $\int g^{\mathrm{AS}}(\alpha)\,\mathrm{d}\alpha < \infty$ (not necessarily equal to 1) and that $\mathrm{IR} = \breve{g}(\alpha \mid y)/g^{\mathrm{AS}}(\alpha) \leqslant \varrho < \infty, \forall \alpha \in A$. Figure 9.4(a) illustrates these assumptions. We want $\varrho g^{\mathrm{AS}}(\alpha)$ uniformly above and approximately at the same distance from $g(\alpha \mid y)$ for every $\alpha \in A$. To generate an i.i.d. sequence from $g(\alpha \mid y)$, choose a $\varrho > 0$ and use the following.

Algorithm 9.5.

(1) Draw $\alpha^{\dagger}$ from $g^{\mathrm{AS}}(\alpha)$ and $\mathfrak{U}$ from a $\mathbb{U}(0, 1)$.

(2) If $\mathfrak{U} > \breve{g}(\alpha^l \mid y)/\varrho g^{\mathrm{AS}}(\alpha^l)$, reject $\alpha^{\dagger}$ and repeat (1); else set $\alpha^l = \alpha^{\dagger}$.

(3) Repeat (1) and (2) L times.

The intuition behind the algorithm is as follows. Once appropriately scaled the draws produce a density like $\varrho g^{\mathrm{AS}}(\alpha)$. For each α the second (rejection) step of the algorithm has the effect of slicing the area between $\varrho g^{\mathrm{AS}}(\alpha)$ and $\breve{g}(\alpha)$, since only points such that $\mathfrak{U}\varrho g^{\mathrm{AS}}(\alpha^l) < \breve{g}(\alpha^l \mid y)$ are retained. Since this occurs at every α in the range, a histogram of accepted draws should closely mimic $\breve{g}(\alpha^l \mid y)$, which we know is proportional to $g(\alpha^l \mid y)$.

To make algorithm 9.5 operative we need to select ϱ. There are two requirements one should consider. First, ϱ should be chosen as small as possible to avoid wasting draws. Second, since $g^{\text{AS}}(\alpha) \propto \breve{g}(\alpha \mid y)$, $\forall\alpha$, ϱ should be constants. Since ϱ will be varying across draws, hopefully not too much; it can be selected as follows. Let K be the number of draws required to get one accepted candidate. Then K is geometrically distributed with $P(K = i) = (1 - p)^{i-1}p$ and $E(K) = 1/p = \varrho/\kappa$, where κ is the normalizing constant in the posterior. Hence, while ideally $\varrho = \kappa$, in which case the acceptance rate is 1, one fiddles with ϱ until a 40–50% acceptance rate is achieved. Note that algorithm 9.5 is self-monitoring: if ϱ is too large, it will reject frequently; if it is too small, it will accept all draws. Typical choices of $g^{\text{AS}}(\alpha)$ are t-distributions for problems with normal errors and exponential or beta distributions for problems with binomial or multinomial errors.

Example 9.31 (consumption function). Let $c_t = \text{GDP}_t\alpha + e_t, e_t \sim \text{i.i.d. } \mathbb{N}(0, \sigma_e^2)$, σ_e^2 fixed and let $g(\alpha) \propto \exp[-0.5(\alpha - \bar{\alpha})'\bar{\Sigma}_\alpha^{-1}(\alpha - \bar{\alpha})]$ if $0 < \alpha < 1$ and $g(\alpha) = 0$ otherwise. The posterior kernel is $\exp[-0.5(\alpha - \tilde{\alpha})'\tilde{\Sigma}_\alpha^{-1}(\alpha - \tilde{\alpha})]\mathcal{I}_{(0<\alpha<1)}$, where $\mathcal{I}(\cdot)$ is an indicator function, $\tilde{\Sigma}_\alpha = (\bar{\Sigma}_\alpha^{-1} + \sigma_e^{-2}\,\text{GDP}'\,\text{GDP})^{-1}$, $\tilde{\alpha} = \tilde{\Sigma}_\alpha(\bar{\Sigma}_\alpha^{-1}\bar{\alpha} + \sigma^{-2}\,\text{GDP}'\,\text{GDP}\,\alpha_{\text{OLS}})$, and α_{OLS} is the OLS estimator of α. Suppose $g^{\text{AS}}(\alpha)$ is $\mathbb{N}(\tilde{\alpha}, \tilde{\Sigma}_\alpha)$. Then a draw $\alpha^\dagger$ is accepted if $0 < \alpha^\dagger < 1$ and rejected otherwise.

Exercise 9.24. Consider studying the duration dependence of recessions. Negative duration dependence occurs if the longer you have been in a particular state the higher is the probability of switching away from that state. Suppose we model the duration of recessions as Weibull with shape parameter a_1 and scale parameter a_2 and assume an appropriate prior for a_1 and a_2 (e.g., a beta or a uniform). Using U.S. post-WWII GDP data, draw samples from the posteriors of a_1 and a_2, keeping only draws which produce negative duration. What is the mean of a_2? What is a 68% credible posterior interval? How would you verify the hypothesis that $a_2 = 0$ (i.e., no duration dependence)?

If $g^{\text{AS}}(\alpha)$ is far away from $g(\alpha \mid y)$, sampling is time-consuming since many draws will be discarded. The alternative is to keep all the draws but weight them appropriately.

9.5.2.2 *Importance Sampling*

Let $g^{\text{IS}}(\alpha)$ be an importance sampling density and suppose that $g^{\text{IS}}(\alpha)$ roughly approximates $\varrho\breve{g}(\alpha)$. Let $\text{IR}(\alpha) = \breve{g}(\alpha \mid y)/g^{\text{IS}}(\alpha)$ be a weighting function with finite expected value. If $E(h(\alpha) \mid y)$ and $\text{var}(h(\alpha) \mid y)$ exist for a continuous $h(\alpha)$ and the support of $g^{\text{IS}}(\alpha)$ includes the support of $g(\alpha \mid y)$, then

$$h_L \equiv \frac{\sum_{l=1}^{L} h(\alpha^l)\text{IR}(\alpha^l)}{\sum_l \text{IR}(\alpha^l)} \xrightarrow{\text{P}} E(h(\alpha) \mid y), \tag{9.38}$$

$$\sqrt{L}(h_L - E[h(\alpha) \mid y]) \xrightarrow{\text{D}} \mathbb{N}(0, \sigma^2), \tag{9.39}$$

$$\sigma_L^2 = \frac{L^{-1}\sum_{l=1}^{L}[h(\alpha^l) - E(h(\alpha) \mid y)]^2 \mathrm{IR}(\alpha^l)^2}{[\sum_l \mathrm{IR}(\alpha^l)]^2} \xrightarrow{\mathrm{P}} \sigma^2. \qquad (9.40)$$

An importance sampling density is pictured in figure 9.4(b). Equation (9.38) implies that the acceptance sampling algorithm 9.5 can be simplified as follows.

Algorithm 9.6.

(1) Draw $\alpha^\dagger$ from $g^{\mathrm{IS}}(\alpha)$; weight $h(\alpha^\dagger)$ with $\breve{g}(\alpha^\dagger \mid y)/g^{\mathrm{IS}}(\alpha^\dagger) = \mathrm{IR}(\alpha^\dagger)$.

(2) Repeat step (1) L times and compute (9.38).

Acceptance and importance sampling have similarities and differences. $g^{\mathrm{IS}}(\alpha)$ must integrate to 1 but, if $\int g^{\mathrm{AS}}(\alpha)\,\mathrm{d}\alpha = 1$ and $g^{\mathrm{AS}}(\alpha)$ satisfies $\breve{g}(\alpha \mid y)/g^{\mathrm{AS}}(\alpha) \leqslant \varrho < \infty, \forall \alpha \in A$, it can be used as importance sampling. Importance sampling can be used to compute draws from the marginal posterior of α_1, $g(\alpha_1 \mid y) = \int g(\alpha_1, \alpha_2 \mid y)\,\mathrm{d}\alpha_2$, where $\alpha = (\alpha_1, \alpha_2)$, while this cannot be easily done with acceptance sampling. In fact, one could use

$$g(\alpha_1 \mid y) = \left[\int \frac{g(\alpha_1, \alpha_2 \mid y)}{\mathrm{IR}(\alpha_1 \mid \alpha_2, y)}\right] \mathrm{IR}(\alpha_1 \mid \alpha_2, y)\,\mathrm{d}\alpha_2 \equiv E_{\mathrm{IR}} \int \frac{g(\alpha_1, \alpha_2 \mid y)}{\mathrm{IR}(\alpha_1 \mid \alpha_2 y)}.$$

For the computations to be successful it is necessary to choose $\mathrm{IR}(\alpha)$ so that $g(\alpha \mid y)/\mathrm{IR}(\alpha)g^{\mathrm{IS}}(\alpha)$ is constant. While a good importance density for interesting macroeconomic problems can sometimes be found (see example 10.2), there are situations where $\mathrm{IR}(\alpha)$ varies wildly, making this posterior simulator unusable. Since the properties of $\mathrm{IR}(\alpha)$ are application dependent, careful experimentation is needed before the results obtained with importance sampling are to be trusted.

Example 9.32. Consider the regression $y_t = x_t\alpha + e_t$, $e_t \sim \mathbb{N}(0, \sigma^2)$, σ^2 fixed, and let $g(\alpha)$ be defined for all $\alpha \in (-\infty, \infty)$. Then one could use a t-density with $T - \dim(\alpha)$ degrees of freedom as importance sampling. Since $\mathrm{IR}(\alpha)$ is now the ratio of a normal to a t-density, it is bounded for all α. Hence, a t-density is a good importance density for drawing α.

Exercise 9.25. A simple model of returns states that $R_{it} = R_{Mt}\alpha_i + e_{it}$, where $i = 1, \dots, I, t = 1, \dots, T$, and R_{Mt} is a market portfolio (say, the return on the S&P500 index). Suppose that, because of risk considerations, the prior for α_i is normal truncated outside the range $(-2, 2)$, i.e., $g(\alpha_i) = \mathbb{N}(\bar{\alpha}, \bar{\sigma}_\alpha^2) * \mathcal{I}_{[-2,2]}$. Describe how to implement an importance sampling algorithm to construct $g(\alpha \mid R_i, R_M)$.

Exercise 9.26. Suppose $y_t = a_0 + \sum_{j=1}^{q} a_j y_{t-j} + e_t$ and suppose you are interested in $h(\alpha) = \sum_{j=1}^{q} \alpha_j$, a measure of the persistence of the process. Assume that $g(\sum_j \alpha_j) \sim \mathbb{U}(0, 1)$. Using euro area data on CPI inflation from 1970 to 2004, draw a posterior sample for $h(\alpha)$ by using both acceptance and importance sampling. What is the interquartile range for $h(\alpha)$ in the two cases? (Hint: make appropriate assumptions about e_t and its variance σ_e^2.)

Finally, note that, regardless of the variations in $\mathrm{IR}(\alpha)$, both acceptance and importance sampling are difficult to use in hierarchical models or in structures where the dimension of α is large (e.g., in VARs). The methods described next can be used in both of these situations.

9.5.3 Markov Chain Monte Carlo Methods

Markov chain Monte Carlo (MCMC) methods are simulation techniques that generate a sample from some target distribution. The idea is to specify a transition kernel for a Markov chain such that starting from some initial value and iterating a number of times, we produce a limiting distribution which is the target distribution we need to sample from. The two most popular MCMC methods are the Gibbs sampling and the Metropolis–Hastings (MH) algorithms.

The generated sample can be used to summarize the target density by using graphical methods and expectations of integrable functions can be estimated by using appropriate averages of the functions. Under general conditions, the ergodicity of the Markov chain guarantees that this estimate is consistent and has a normal distribution as the length of the simulations increases. Note that, while with acceptance and importance sampling draws are i.i.d., here the draws are correlated because of the Markov nature of the process. Therefore, averages should be computed from approximately independent elements of the sequences or the asymptotic covariance matrix appropriately modified.

MCMC methods can be applied directly to the kernel of the target density (that is, no knowledge of $f(y)$ is needed) and this makes them particularly useful for Bayesian analysis. However, MCMC methods can also be used as classical devices to explore intractable likelihoods or to find the maximum of nasty functions with a "data-augmentation" technique.

To see how MCMC methods work take $\mu(\alpha) \equiv \breve{g}(\alpha \mid y)$ as the limiting distribution. Then we need a transition $P(A_s, \alpha)$, where $A_s \subseteq A$, which converges as the number of iterations goes to infinity to $\mu(\alpha)$, starting from any α_0. Suppose $P(A_s, \alpha) = p(\alpha', \alpha)\,\mathrm{d}\alpha' + p_1(\alpha)p_2(\mathrm{d}\alpha')$ for some p, where $\alpha' \in A_s$, $p(\alpha, \alpha) = 0$, $p_2(\mathrm{d}\alpha')$ has a point mass at α (i.e., it equals 1 if $\alpha \in \mathrm{d}\alpha'$) and $p_1(\alpha) = 1 - \int p(\alpha, \alpha')\,\mathrm{d}\alpha'$ is the probability that the chain remains at α. Suppose $\mu(\alpha)p(\alpha, \alpha') = \mu(\alpha')p(\alpha', \alpha)$ (this condition is called reversibility). Then

$$\int P(A_s, \alpha)\mu(\alpha)\,\mathrm{d}\alpha = \int_{A_s} \mu(\alpha')\,\mathrm{d}\alpha'. \tag{9.41}$$

Exercise 9.27. Show that (9.41) holds. (Hint: use the reversibility condition and the fact that $\int p(\alpha', \alpha)\mu(\alpha')\,\mathrm{d}\alpha = [1 - p_1(\alpha')]\mu(\alpha')$.)

Example 9.33. Consider a chain with $n < \infty$ states and transition matrix $P_{j,j'}$. Then condition (9.41) is satisfied if $P\mu = \mu$. If $P_{j,j'}$ is reversible, then $\mu_j P_{j,j'} = \mu_{j'} P_{j',j}$ and $(P\mu)_j = \sum_{j'} \mu_{j'} P_{j',j} = \sum_{j'} \mu_j P_{j,j'} = \mu_j \sum_{j'} P_{j,j'} = \mu_j$.

Condition (9.41) defines an invariant distribution $\mu(\alpha)$ for $P(A_s, \alpha)$. Therefore, if $\mu(\alpha)$ is unique, $P(A_s, \alpha)$ is chosen as above and iterated L times, the result will be the target distribution (see figure 9.4(c) for the first two steps in the iterations). To show the details of this argument we first need a few definitions.

Definition 9.5. A Markov chain is a collection of random variables. The transition matrix of a Markov chain is $P(A, \alpha^\ddagger) = \text{pr}(\alpha' \in A \mid \alpha = \alpha^\ddagger) = \int_A \mathcal{K}(\text{d}\alpha', \alpha^\ddagger)$, where $\mathcal{K}$ is the kernel of the chain, $\mathcal{K}(\cdot\,, \alpha^\ddagger)$ is a probability measure for all $\alpha^\ddagger$, and $\mathcal{K}(A, \cdot)$ is measurable for all A. The L-step transition matrix is $P^L(A, \alpha^\ddagger) = \text{pr}(\alpha^L \in A \mid \alpha = \alpha^\ddagger) = \int \mathcal{K}(\text{d}\alpha', \alpha^\ddagger)\mathcal{K}^{L-1}(A^{L-1}, \alpha')$ with $\mathcal{K}^1(\text{d}\alpha', \alpha^\ddagger) = \mathcal{K}(\text{d}\alpha', \alpha^\ddagger)$.

Definition 9.6. A function $\mu(\alpha)$ is an invariant density for the kernel of the Markov chain if $\mu(A_1) \equiv \int_{A_1} \mu(\alpha)\,\text{d}\alpha = \int \mathcal{K}(A_1, \alpha^\ddagger)\mu(\text{d}\alpha^\ddagger)$ for all measurable $A_1 \subseteq A$.

Definition 9.7. Let $A_2 = \{\alpha \in A,\ \text{pr}(\alpha) > 0\}$. The kernel of a Markov chain is irreducible if there exists an $L \geqslant 1$ such that $\mathcal{K}^L(A_2, \alpha^\ddagger) > 0$ for all $\alpha^\ddagger \in A$.

Definition 9.8. The period of a state j is the greater common divisor of the sets of integers n such that $\mathcal{K}_{j,j} > 0$. An irreducible chain is aperiodic if all the states have period 1.

Definition 9.9. A Markov chain is Harris recurrent if there exists a measure P such that the kernel of the chain is irreducible and, for every A_3 with $p(A_3) > 0$, $P(\eta_{A_3} = \infty) = 1$, where η_∞ is the number of passages of the chain in A_3.

Example 9.34. Consider the transition $P(A, \alpha^\ddagger) = P(\alpha^\ddagger) > 0$ for all $\alpha^\ddagger \in A$. Then a chain with this transition is independent, irreducible, and aperiodic.

Exercise 9.28. Show that a two-state Markov chain with transition matrix P such that $P_{1,2} = 0$ is reducible. Show that a two-state Markov chain with transition matrix P such that $P_{j,j'} = 1$, $j \neq j'$, is periodic.

The meaning of the irreducibility condition is shown in figure 9.5. The sequences in the first box stay within a particular region. Therefore, there is a part of the space which has zero probability of being visited starting either from A or B. This does not happen in the second box. The aperiodicity condition implies that all states can be visited with positive probability from any initial state. That is, we do not want the chain to cycle through a finite number of sets. Aperiodicity and irreducibility are sufficient to ensure that the limiting distribution will exist and will have positive entries. Finally, the Harris recurrent condition is needed when A is not denumerable. It implies that the expected number of times the chain will visit the set A_3 is infinite.

With these definitions we can present the two main results which justify the use of MCMC methods to draw sequences from unknown posterior distributions.

Result 9.3 (Tierney). If a Markov chain is Harris recurrent and has a proper ergodic $\mu(\alpha)$, then $\mu(\alpha)$ is the unique invariant distribution of the Markov chain.

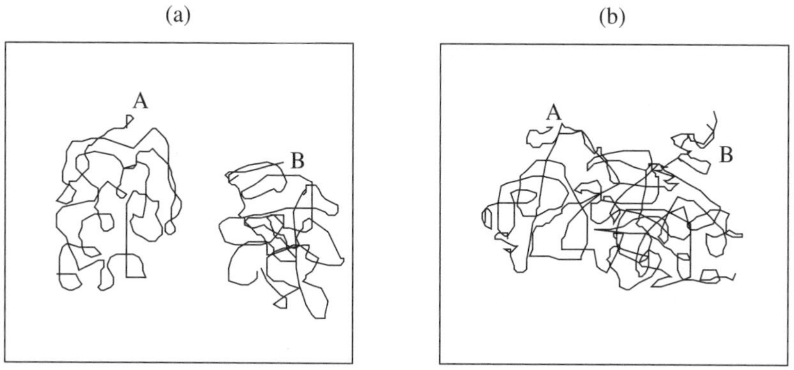

Figure 9.5. MCMC draws: (a) reducible chain; (b) irreducible chain.

Result 9.4 (Tierney). If a Markov chain with invariant distribution $\mu(\alpha)$ is Harris recurrent and aperiodic, then, for all $\alpha_0 \in A$ and all A_0,

(i) $\|P^L(A_0, \alpha_0) - \mu(\alpha)\| \to 0$ as $L \to \infty$, where $\|\cdot\|$ is the total variation distance;

(ii) for all functions $h(\alpha)$ which are absolutely integrable with respect to $\mu(\alpha)$,

$$\lim_{L\to\infty} \frac{1}{L} \sum_{l=1}^{L} h(\alpha^l) \xrightarrow{\text{a.s.}} \int h(\alpha)\mu(\alpha)\,\mathrm{d}\alpha.$$

Result 9.4(i) tells us that, for L large, draws from $P^L(A_0, \alpha_0)$ are draws from the invariant distribution, regardless of the initial value α_0. Result 9.4(ii) indicates that the averages of functions evaluated at the sample values converge to their expected values calculated by using the invariant distribution. Sufficient conditions which ensure that the chain is Harris recurrent and aperiodic are given below for each posterior simulator.

9.5.3.1 Gibbs Sampler

Given that the object is to find a transition density that has the joint posterior as its invariant distribution, the Gibbs sampler partitions the vector of unknowns into blocks and the transition density is defined by the product of conditional densities. The next item in the chain is obtained by successively sampling from the densities of each block, given the most recent values of the conditioning parameters. The main value of the algorithm lies in the fact that conditional densities are usually easy to compute and cheap to sample from.

To see exactly what the algorithm involves, partition α as $\alpha = (\alpha_1, \alpha_2, \dots, \alpha_k)$. Suppose $g(\alpha_i \mid \alpha_{i'}, y,\ i' \neq i)$ are available (e.g., choose the partition so this is the case). Then we have the following.

Algorithm 9.7.

(1) Choose initial values $(\alpha_1^{(0)}, \alpha_2^{(0)}, \ldots, \alpha_k^{(0)})$ from an approximate $g(\alpha \mid y)$, for example, a normal approximation or the output of another (simpler) simulator.

(2) For $l = 1, 2, \ldots,$ draw α_1^l from $g(\alpha_1 \mid \alpha_2^{l-1}, \ldots, \alpha_k^{l-1}, y)$, α_2^l from $g(\alpha_2 \mid \alpha_1^l, \ldots, \alpha_k^{l-1}, y)$, $\ldots$, α_k^l from $g(\alpha_k \mid \alpha_1^l, \ldots, \alpha_{k-1}^l, y)$.

(3) Repeat step (2) L times.

The process of drawing in step (2) defines a transition from α^{l-1} to α^l. The algorithm therefore produces a sequence which is the realization of a Markov chain with transition:

$$P(\alpha^l, \alpha^{l-1}) = \prod_{i=1}^{k} g(\alpha_i^l \mid \alpha_{i'}^{l-1}\ (i' > i),\ \alpha_{i'}^l\ (i' < i), y). \tag{9.42}$$

By result 9.4, the sample $\alpha^L = (\alpha_1^L, \alpha_2^L, \ldots, \alpha_k^L)$, L large, is a draw from the joint posterior $g(\alpha \mid y)$. Furthermore, α_i^L, $i = 1, \ldots, k$, is a draw from the marginal $g(\alpha_i \mid y)$.

What kinds of condition ensure that the transition kernel (9.42) is Harris recurrent and aperiodic? A sufficient condition is the following: if for every $\alpha_0 \in A$ and every $A_1 \subset A$ with $\mathrm{pr}(\alpha \in A_1 \mid y) > 0$, $P(\alpha^l \in A_1 \mid \alpha^{l-1}, y) > 0$, where P is the transition induced by (9.42), then the Gibbs transition kernel is ergodic and its unique invariant distribution is $g(\alpha \mid y)$.

For finite state problems, the condition $P(\alpha^l \in A_1 \mid \alpha^{l-1}, y) > 0$ is simple and easy to verify. In fact, it requires that all the cells of the chain can be visited with positive probability starting from any α^{l-1}. All the applications we discuss in the remaining chapters satisfy this mild condition.

The Gibbs sampler works well when the components are independent. Therefore, highly correlated components (e.g., the parameters of an AR process) should be grouped together in blocks. Tractable conditional structures from intractable likelihood functions can be derived at times by using a data-augmentation technique. An example of this technique is given below while applications to factor and Markov switching models are in chapter 11.

There are a few implementation issues worth discussing. The first is how to draw uncorrelated samples for α from $g(\alpha \mid y)$. There are two alternatives. The first one produces one sample (of dimension $J * L$) after an initial sequence of $\bar{L}$ observations is discarded. Then one uses only elements $(L, 2L, \ldots, J * L)$ to eliminate the correlation among the draws. The second produces J samples each of length $L + \bar{L}$ and the last observation in each sample is used for inference. If $\bar{L}$ is chosen appropriately, the two approaches are equivalent. The second important issue has to do with the magnitude of $\bar{L}$, the length of the burnout period. There are many ways to check how long $\bar{L}$ should be to ensure that the algorithm has converged. Here we describe three: the first two are appropriate when draws are made from one large sample; the last is applicable when J samples of $L + \bar{L}$ observations are used.

One way to check for convergence is to choose two points, say $\bar{L}_1 < \bar{L}_2$, and compute distributions/moments of α after these points. If the distributions/moments are stable, then the algorithm has converged at $\bar{L}_1$. Taking this approach one step further, one can compute recursive moments of α^l over l and graphically check if they settle after an initial period (CUMSUM statistic). Alternatively, one could fix $\bar{L}$ and compute distributions/moments by using J_1 and J_2 sampled values, $J_2 > J_1$. If convergence is achieved, the distributions/moments computed with J_1 observations should be similar to those computed by using J_2 observations. A variant of this approach is the following. Let $h(\alpha)$ be a continuous function of α. Then, given $\bar{L}$, one could also split the simulation sample into two pieces $(J_1 * L)$ and $(J_2 * L)$, $J = J_1 + J_2$, and compute $h_1 = (1/J_1)\sum_l h(\alpha^l)$, $h_2 = (1/J_2)\sum_l h(\alpha^l)$, $\sigma_1^2 = (1/J_1)\sum_l (h(\alpha^l) - h_1)^2$, $\sigma_2^2 = (1/J_2)\sum_l (h(\alpha^l) - h_2)^2$. Convergence obtains if observations in the two samples have the same distribution, that is, $(h_1 - h_2)/(\sigma_1^2 + \sigma_2^2)^{0.5} \xrightarrow{\text{D}} \mathbb{N}(0, 1)$ as $J \to \infty$. Both $\bar{L}$ and J are application dependent. For simple problems $\bar{L} \approx 50$ and $J \approx 200$ suffice. For more complicated ones (for example, VARs or panel VARs), $\bar{L} \approx 100$ and $J \approx 300$–500 should be selected.

The third approach examines whether the variance within an iteration is approximately the same as the variance across iterations. Failure to converge is indicated by the former being significantly smaller than the latter. That is, compute $\Sigma_{\text{B}} = [L/(J-1)]\sum_j (\bar{h}_{.j} - \bar{h}_{..})^2$, where $\bar{h}_{.j} = (1/L)\sum_i h(\alpha_{ij})$, $\bar{h}_{..} = (1/J)\sum_j \bar{h}_{.j}$, and $\Sigma_{\text{W}} = (1/J)\sum_j [(1/(L-1))\sum_i (h(\alpha_{ij}) - \bar{h}_{.j})]^2$. Then $\sqrt{\{[(L-1)/L]\Sigma_{\text{W}} + (1/L)\Sigma_{\text{B}}\}/\Sigma_{\text{W}}} \to 1$ as $L \to \infty$. Hence, if $\Sigma_{\text{B}} \approx \Sigma_{\text{W}}$, convergence is achieved.

Example 9.35. We examine convergence of Gibbs sampler estimates in a linear regression model where the log of output is regressed on a number of lags of the log of money. This could be of some interest, for example, in studying money neutrality in the short or the long run. Data for the United States from 1973:1 to 1993:12 are used in the exercise. We ran 50 replications of the Gibbs sampler using 150, 300, 500 draws for a model with one intercept and two lags of the log of money. The adjusted ratio of Σ_{W} to Σ_{B} was respectively 1.01, 1.003, 1.001 indicating that convergence was achieved after 150 draws. For each of the replications with 500 draws, we split the sample in two with 300 observations in the first part and 200 in the second part and computed the normal test. Out of 500 replications, we rejected the null of convergence in just one case.

Inference with the output of the Gibbs sampler presents no difficulty. As suggested by result 9.4, $E(h(\alpha \mid y)) = (1/J)\sum_j h(\alpha^{j\bar{L}})$, where the notation $\alpha^{j\bar{L}}$ indicates the jLth draw after $\bar{L}$ iterations are performed. The variance of $h(\alpha)$ can be computed by using the spectral density at frequency zero, i.e., $E[h(\alpha \mid y)h(\alpha \mid y)'] = \sum_{-J(\tau)}^{J(\tau)} \mathcal{K}(\tau)\,\text{ACF}_h(\tau)$, where $\text{ACF}_h(\tau)$ is the autocovariance of $h(\alpha)$ for draws separated by τ periods and $J(\tau)$ is the maximum number of covariances considered. Note that this measure takes into account the possibility that the selected draws are

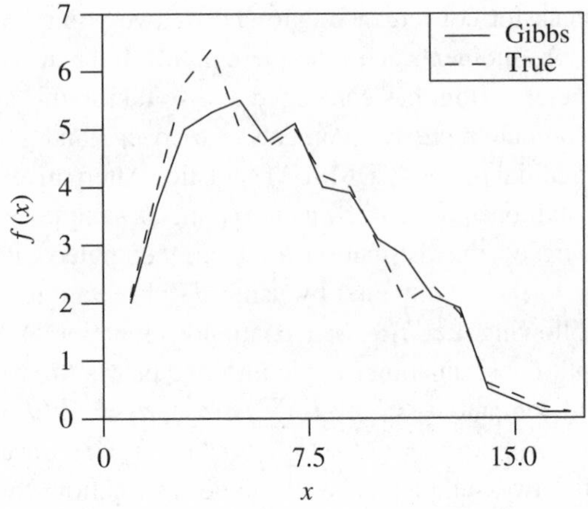

Figure 9.6. True and Gibbs sampling distributions.

not spaced enough to make them independent of each other. The marginal density for α_i can be estimated by using kernel methods directly from the sequence $(\alpha_i^1, \ldots, \alpha_i^J)$ or by using the fact that $g(\alpha_i \mid y) = (1/J)\sum_{j=1}^{J} g(\alpha_i \mid y, \alpha_{i'}^j, i' \neq i)$.

Predictive inference is also straightforward. The predictive density $f(y_{t+\tau} \mid y_t) = \int f(y_{t+\tau} \mid y_t, \alpha) g(\alpha \mid y_t)\, \mathrm{d}\alpha$ can be easily simulated by using Gibbs sampler draws for α and the model specification $f(y_{t+\tau} \mid y_t, \alpha)$, averaging simulated values of $y_{t+\tau}$ over α draws. Finally, tests of model adequacy can also be implemented by using the output of the Gibbs sampler. Recall that the Bayes factor is the ratio of the marginal likelihood of two models. Hence, it can be numerically calculated by drawing α from $g(\alpha)$, constructing $f(y \mid \alpha)$ for each draw, and averaging over α for each of the two models. Gelfand and Dey (1994) and Chib (1995) provide practical ways to compute $f(y)$.

We illustrate the properties of the Gibbs sampler in a simple example next.

Example 9.36. Suppose that $f(x, y) \propto [n!/(x!(n-x)!)] y^{x+\alpha_0-1}(1-y)^{n-x+\alpha_1-1}$, $x = 0, 1, \ldots, n, 0 \leqslant y \leqslant 1$, and suppose that we are interested in the marginal $f(x)$. Direct integration produces $f(x) \propto [n!/(x!(n-x)!)][\Gamma(\alpha_0+\alpha_1)/\Gamma(\alpha_0)\Gamma(\alpha_1)] \times [\Gamma(x+\alpha_0)\Gamma(n-x+\alpha_1)/\Gamma(\alpha_0+\alpha_1+n)]$, which is the beta–binomial distribution. It is also easy to calculate the conditional distributions $f(x \mid y)$ and $f(y \mid x)$. The first one is binomial with parameters (n, y), the second is beta with parameters $(x+\alpha_0, n-x+\alpha_1)$. Figure 9.6 presents the histogram generated from the true $f(x)$ when $\alpha_0 = 2, \alpha_1 = 4$, and from the marginal computed via the Gibbs sampler with $J = 500$, $L = 100$, and $\bar{L} = 20$. It is remarkable how close the two distributions are, even for such a small $\bar{L}$.

In the next example we use the Gibbs sampler to obtain the posterior distribution of the parameters of a seemingly unrelated regression (SUR) model; it is a good idea to store these derivations as we will use them extensively in chapter 10.

Example 9.37 (seemingly unrelated regression). Let $y_{it} = x'_{it}\alpha_i + e_{it}$ and $e_t = (e'_{1t}, \ldots, e'_{mt})' \sim$ i.i.d. $\mathbb{N}(0, \Sigma_e)$, where $i = 1, \ldots, m$, $t = 1, \ldots, T$, and α_i is a $k \times 1$ vector. Stacking the observations for each i we have $y_t = x_t\alpha + e_t$, where $y_t = (y'_{it}, \ldots, y'_{mt})'$, $x_t = \operatorname{diag}(x'_{it}, \ldots, x'_{mt})$, $\alpha = (\alpha'_1, \ldots, \alpha'_m)'$ is an $mk \times 1$ vector. Suppose that $g(\alpha, \Sigma_e^{-1}) = g(\alpha)g(\Sigma_e^{-1})$. Then

$$\breve{g}(\alpha, \Sigma_e^{-1} \mid y) \propto g(\alpha)g(\Sigma_e^{-1})|\Sigma_e^{-1}|^{0.5T} \exp\left\{-0.5\sum_t (y_t - x_t\alpha)'\Sigma_e^{-1}(y_t - x_t\alpha)\right\}. \quad (9.43)$$

The target density to be simulated is $\breve{g}(\alpha, \Sigma_e^{-1} \mid y)/\int \breve{g}(\alpha, \Sigma_e^{-1} \mid y)\, d\alpha\, d\Sigma_e$. Assume a conjugate prior for α and Σ_e^{-1} of normal-Wishart form. Then the conditions posteriors are $g(\alpha \mid Y, \Sigma_e^{-1}) \sim \mathbb{N}(\tilde{\alpha}, \tilde{\Sigma}_\alpha)$ and $g(\Sigma_e^{-1} \mid \alpha, Y) \sim \mathbb{W}(T+\bar{\nu}, \tilde{\Sigma})$, where $\tilde{\alpha} = \tilde{\Sigma}_\alpha(\bar{\Sigma}_\alpha^{-1}\bar{\alpha} + \sum_t x'_t\Sigma_e^{-1}y_t)$, $\tilde{\Sigma}_\alpha = (\bar{\Sigma}_\alpha^{-1} + \sum_t x'_t\Sigma_e^{-1}x_t)^{-1}$, and $\tilde{\Sigma} = (\bar{\Sigma}^{-1} + \sum_t(y_t - x_t\alpha_{\text{OLS}})(y - x_t\alpha_{\text{OLS}})')^{-1}$, where $(\bar{\alpha}, \bar{\Sigma}_\alpha)$ are the prior mean and variance of α, $\bar{\Sigma}$ is the prior scale matrix, $\bar{\nu}$ the prior degrees of freedom, and α_{OLS} is the OLS estimator of α. If we treat α and Σ_e as two Gibbs sampler blocks, simulations of the two conditional posteriors asymptotically yield a sample such that $\alpha^{j\bar{L}} \sim g(\alpha \mid y)$, $\Sigma_e^{-1(j\bar{L})} \sim g(\Sigma_e^{-1} \mid y)$, and $(\alpha^{j\bar{L}}, \Sigma_e^{-1(j\bar{L})}) \sim g(\alpha, \Sigma_e^{-1} \mid y)$.

Exercise 9.29. Suppose in example 9.37 that $m = 1$, i.e., $y_t = x_t\alpha + e_t$, $e_t \sim$ i.i.d. $\mathbb{N}(0, \sigma_e^2)$.

(i) Assume a noninformative prior for σ_e^{-2} and that $\alpha \sim \mathbb{N}(\bar{\alpha}, \bar{\Sigma}_\alpha)$. Calculate the conditional posterior for α and σ_e^{-2}. Describe how to employ the Gibbs sampler in this situation.

(ii) Suppose that $e_t \sim$ i.i.d. $\mathbb{N}(0, \sigma_e^2 * x'_t x_t)$ and assume that the priors are $\bar{s}^2\sigma_e^{-2} \sim \chi^2(\bar{\nu})$ and $\alpha \sim \mathbb{N}(\bar{\alpha}, \bar{\Sigma}_\alpha)$. Find the conditional posterior for α and σ_e^2 and show how to implement the Gibbs sampler in this case. (Hint: transform the model to get rid of heteroskedasticity.)

Example 9.38 (hierarchical models). Consider the model $y_{it} = \alpha_i + e_{it}$, $i = 1, \ldots, n$, $t = 1, \ldots, T$, where $\alpha_i \sim \mathbb{N}(\bar{\alpha}, \bar{\sigma}_\alpha^2)$, $e_{it} \sim$ i.i.d. $\mathbb{N}(0, \sigma_e^2)$. Assume that $\bar{\alpha} \sim \mathbb{N}(\bar{\alpha}_0, \sigma_0^2)$, $\bar{\sigma}_\alpha^{-2} \sim \mathbb{G}(a_1^\alpha, a_2^\alpha)$, $\sigma_e^{-2} \sim \mathbb{G}(a_1^e, a_2^e)$, where $(\sigma_0^2, \bar{\alpha}_0, a_1^\alpha, a_2^\alpha, a_1^e, a_2^e)$ are known, and let $\alpha = [\alpha_1, \ldots, \alpha_n]'$, $y = [y_{11}, \ldots, y_{nT}]'$. The conditional posteriors are $(\bar{\sigma}_\alpha^{-2} \mid y, \bar{\alpha}, \alpha, \sigma_e^{-2}) \sim \mathbb{G}(a_1^\alpha + 0.5n, a_2^\alpha + 0.5\sum_i(\alpha_i - \bar{\alpha})^2)$, $(\sigma_e^{-2} \mid y, \bar{\alpha}, \alpha, \bar{\sigma}_\alpha^{-2}) \sim \mathbb{G}(a_1^e + 0.5nT, a_2^e + 0.5\sum_i\sum_t(y_{it} - \alpha_i)^2)$, $(\bar{\alpha} \mid \bar{\sigma}_\alpha^2, y, \alpha, \sigma_e^2) \sim \mathbb{N}((\bar{\sigma}_\alpha^2\bar{\alpha}_0 + \sigma_0^2\sum_i\alpha_i)/(\bar{\sigma}_\alpha^2 + n\sigma_0^2), \bar{\sigma}_\alpha^2\sigma_0^2/(\bar{\sigma}_\alpha^2 + n\sigma_0^2))$, and $(\alpha \mid \bar{\sigma}_\alpha^2, y, \bar{\alpha}, \sigma_e^2) \sim \mathbb{N}((T\sigma_\alpha^2/(T\bar{\sigma}_\alpha^2 + \sigma_e^2))\bar{y} + [\sigma_e^2/(T\bar{\sigma}_\alpha^2 + \sigma_e^2)]\bar{\alpha}\mathbf{1}, [\bar{\sigma}_\alpha^2\sigma_e^2/(T\bar{\sigma}_\alpha^2 + \sigma_e^2)]I)$, where $\bar{y} = (\bar{y}_1, \ldots, \bar{y}_n)'$, $\bar{y}_i = (1/T)\sum_t y_{it}$, $\mathbf{1}$ is an $n \times 1$ vector of 1s, and I is the identity matrix. The Gibbs sampler can then be implemented on these four blocks and will produce the posterior for $(\bar{\sigma}_a^2, \sigma_e^{-2}, \bar{\alpha}, \alpha)$.

Exercise 9.30. Let $y_{it} \sim \mathbb{N}(\alpha_i, \sigma_i^2)$, $i = 1, \ldots, n$, $t = 1, \ldots, T_i$, where $\alpha_i \sim \mathbb{N}(\bar{\alpha}, \bar{\sigma}_\alpha^2)$, $\sigma_i^{-2} \sim \mathbb{G}(a_1^i, a_2^i)$, $\bar{\sigma}_\alpha^{-2} \sim \mathbb{G}(a_1^\alpha, a_2^\alpha)$, $\bar{\alpha} \sim \mathbb{N}(\bar{\alpha}_0, \sigma_0^2)$, and $(a_1^i, a_2^i, a_1^\alpha,$

$a_2^{\alpha}, \bar{\alpha}_0, \sigma_0^2$) are known. Let $\bar{y}_i = (1/T_i)\sum_t y_{it}$, $s_i^2 = [1/(T_i - 1)]\sum_t (y_{it} - \bar{y}_i)^2$, $\alpha = (\alpha_1, \ldots, \alpha_n)'$, $Y = (\bar{y}_1, \ldots, \bar{y}_n, s_1^2, \ldots, s_n^2)'$, $\sigma^2 = (\sigma_1^2, \ldots, \sigma_n^2)'$.

(i) Derive $(\alpha_i \mid Y, \sigma_i^2, \bar{\alpha}, \bar{\sigma}_\alpha^2)$, $(\sigma_i^{-2} \mid Y, \alpha, \bar{\alpha}, \sigma_\alpha^2)$, and $(\bar{\sigma}_\alpha^{-2} \mid Y, \alpha, \bar{\alpha}, \sigma_i^2)$.

(ii) Assume $\bar{\alpha}_0 = 0$, $\sigma_0^2 = 1000$, $a_1^i = 0.5$, $a_2^i = 1$, $\forall i$, $a_1^\alpha = a_2^\alpha = 0$, $n = 3$, and suppose you have the following data: $T_i = (6, 8, 5)$, $\bar{y}_i = (0.31, 2.03, 6.39)$, $s_i^2 = (0.23, 2.47, 8.78)$. Draw posterior samples for α. Produce the posterior of $\alpha_2 - \alpha_1$ and of $\alpha_3 - \alpha_1$.

(iii) Suppose a fourth unit is added to the sample with $T_4 = 2$, $\bar{y}_4 = 5.67$, $s_4^2 = 4.65$. Construct a time series of five observations for this new unit.

The Gibbs sampler is very useful for evaluating likelihoods with latent variables.

Example 9.39 (latent variables). Consider the problem of modeling monthly purchases of certain nondurable goods. We have a sample with many consumers but only a fraction of them acquired the good under consideration (say, tomatoes). We assume that agents purchase tomatoes on the basis of individual characteristics. Suppose to explain purchases we write the following censored regression model: $z_i = x_i'\alpha + e_i$, $e_i \sim$ i.i.d. $\mathbb{N}(0, \sigma_e^2)$, and $y_i = \max(0, z_i)$. Here z_i is a latent variable. Given n consumers, n_1 of which buy tomatoes, the likelihood for (α, σ^2) is

$$\mathcal{L}(\alpha, \sigma_e^2 \mid y) = \prod_{i \in (n-n_1)} \left(1 - \mathbb{SN}\left(\frac{x_i'\alpha}{\sigma_e}\right)\right) \prod_{i \in n_1} \sigma_e^{-2} \exp\left\{-\frac{(y_i - x_i'\alpha)^2}{2\sigma_e^2}\right\}, \tag{9.44}$$

where $\mathbb{SN}$ is a standard normal distribution. This function is difficult to manipulate and maximize. However, if we treat z_i as a latent variable and use the model for z_i to artificially augment the parameter space (we have called this approach a data-augmentation technique), then the posterior distribution can be easily sampled from the conditionals of (α, σ_e^2, z). If $g(\alpha) \sim \mathbb{N}(\bar{\alpha}, \bar{\Sigma}_\alpha)$ and $\sigma_e^{-2} \sim \mathbb{G}(a_1, a_2)$, then $(\alpha \mid \sigma_e^2, z, y) \sim \mathbb{N}(\tilde{\alpha}, \tilde{\Sigma}_\alpha)$ and $(\sigma_e^{-2} \mid \alpha, z, y) \sim \mathbb{G}(a_1 + 0.5n, a_2 + 0.5(y - x'\alpha_{\text{OLS}})'(y - x'\alpha_{\text{OLS}}))$. Furthermore, since e_i are i.i.d., $g(z \mid y, \alpha, \sigma_e^2) = \prod_{i \in (n-n_1)} g(z_i \mid y, \alpha, \sigma_e^2) = \prod_{i \in (n-n_1)} \mathcal{I}_{(-\infty, 0]} \mathbb{N}(x_i'\alpha, \sigma_e^2)$, where $\mathcal{I}_{(-\infty,0]}$ truncates the normal distribution outside the support $(-\infty, 0]$. This simplification is possible because (α, σ_e^2) depend on z_i only through y_i (see Tanner and Wong 1987).

In applied work missing data cause headaches. However, if we treat missing data as latent variables, the Gibbs sampler can be used to reconstruct them.

Exercise 9.31 (missing data). Suppose we have missing data from a time series y_t. Let y_t^{M} be the missing data and y_t^{A} the available data and let $y_t = [y_t^{\text{M}}, y_t^{\text{A}}]' = x_t\alpha + e_t$, where $e_t \sim$ i.i.d. $\mathbb{N}(0, \Sigma_e)$, x_t is a vector of observable variables, and

$$\Sigma_e = \begin{bmatrix} \sigma_1^2 + \sigma_2^2 & \sigma_2^2 \\ \sigma_2^2 & \sigma_1^2 + \sigma_2^2 \end{bmatrix}.$$

Assume a normal prior for α and a noninformative prior for (σ_1^2, σ_2^2). Show that $(y_t^{\text{M}} \mid y_t^{\text{A}}, \alpha, \sigma_1^2, \sigma_2^2)$ is normal. Show the moments of the distribution. Describe how to use the Gibbs sampler to draw missing data. Explain why treating y_t^{M} as a vector of unknown parameters makes the posterior tractable.

9.5.3.2 Metropolis–Hastings Algorithm

The Metropolis–Hastings (MH) algorithm is a general simulation procedure which allows us to sample from intractable distributions. There are two typical applications of this algorithm: to sample blocks within a Gibbs sampler which have truncated distributions or distributions where only a part of the kernel is tractable; and to sample in problems where the block structure of the Gibbs sampler is not available.

The MH algorithm works as follows: given that the latest value of α is α^{l-1}, the next value of the sequence is generated by drawing from a candidate density $\mathfrak{P}(\alpha^{\dagger}, \alpha^{l-1})$. The draw is accepted with a probability which depends on the ratio of values of $\breve{g}(\alpha^{\dagger} \mid y)\mathfrak{P}(\alpha^{\dagger}, \alpha^{l-1})$ to $\breve{g}(\alpha^{l-1} \mid y)\mathfrak{P}(\alpha^{l-1}, \alpha^{\dagger})$. If a candidate is rejected, $\alpha^{l} = \alpha^{l-1}$. Hence, starting from some $\alpha^{0} \in A$ and an arbitrary transition $\mathfrak{P}(\alpha^{\dagger}, \alpha^{l-1})$, where $\alpha^{\dagger} \in A$, one proceeds as follows.

Algorithm 9.8. For $l = 1, 2, \dots, L$,

(1) draw $\alpha^{\dagger}$ from $\mathfrak{P}(\alpha^{\dagger}, \alpha^{l-1})$ and $\mathfrak{U}$ from $\mathbb{U}(0, 1)$;

(2) if $\mathfrak{U} < \mathfrak{E}(\alpha^{l-1}, \alpha^{\dagger}) = [\breve{g}(\alpha^{\dagger} \mid y)/g(\alpha^{l-1} \mid y)] \times [\mathfrak{P}(\alpha^{\dagger}, \alpha^{l-1})/\mathfrak{P}(\alpha^{l-1}, \alpha^{\dagger})]$ set $\alpha^{\ell} = \alpha^{\dagger}$, otherwise set $\alpha^{\ell} = \alpha^{\ell-1}$.

The recursions produced by algorithm 9.8 define a Markov chain with a mixture of continuous and discrete transitions:

$$P(\alpha^{l-1}, \alpha^{l}) = \begin{cases} \mathfrak{P}(\alpha^{l}, \alpha^{l-1})\mathfrak{E}(\alpha^{l-1}, \alpha^{l}) & \text{if } \alpha^{l} \neq \alpha^{l-1}, \\ 1 - \displaystyle\int_{A} \mathfrak{P}(\alpha, \alpha^{l-1})\mathfrak{E}(\alpha^{l-1}, \alpha)\, \mathrm{d}\alpha & \text{if } \alpha^{l} = \alpha^{l-1}. \end{cases} \tag{9.45}$$

Note that, if $\mathfrak{P}(\alpha^{l-1}, \alpha^{\dagger}) = \mathfrak{P}(\alpha^{\dagger}, \alpha^{l-1})$, the acceptance rate is independent of $\mathfrak{P}$ and we have the Metropolis version of the algorithm.

The logic of algorithm 9.8 is simple. Suppose $\mathfrak{P}(\alpha^{l-1}, \alpha^{\dagger}) = \mathfrak{P}(\alpha^{\dagger}, \alpha^{l-1})$ so that $\mathfrak{E}(\alpha^{l-1}, \alpha^{\dagger}) = \breve{g}(\alpha^{\dagger} \mid y)/\breve{g}(\alpha^{l-1} \mid y)$. Here, if $\mathfrak{E}(\alpha^{l-1}, \alpha^{\dagger}) > 1$, the chain moves to $\alpha^{\dagger}$ unconditionally, otherwise it moves with probability $\breve{g}(\alpha^{\dagger} \mid y)/\breve{g}(\alpha^{l-1} \mid y)$. That is, we always accept the draw if we move uphill in the distribution since we want to visit areas where the density is higher. If the draw makes us move downhill, we stay at the same point with probability equal to $1 - \mathfrak{E}(\alpha^{l-1}, \alpha^{\dagger})$ and explore new areas with probability equal to $\mathfrak{E}(\alpha^{l-1}, \alpha^{\dagger})$. Note that, if we are already in an area with high probability, $\mathfrak{E}(\alpha^{l-1}, \alpha^{\dagger})$ will be small.

As with the Gibbs sampler, a sufficient condition which ensures that the MH algorithm converges only requires some restrictions on (9.45). In fact, if, for every $\alpha_0 \in A$ and every $A_1 \in A$ with $\mathrm{pr}(\alpha \in A_1 \mid y) > 0$, $P(\alpha^{l} \in A_1 \mid \alpha^{l-1}, y) > 0$, where P is the transition induced by (9.45), then the MH transition kernel is ergodic and its unique invariant distribution is $g(\alpha \mid y)$.

For the MH algorithm to work, one has to choose the transition density appropriately. One possibility is to set $\mathfrak{P}(\alpha^{\dagger}, \alpha^{l-1}) = \mathfrak{P}(\alpha^{\dagger} - \alpha^{l-1})$, so that the candidate draw is taken from, for example, a multivariate distribution centered at α^{l-1}. This is what we call the random walk version of the MH algorithm: $\alpha^{\dagger} = \alpha^{l-1} + v$. To get "reasonable" acceptance rates we need to carefully adjust Σ_v and the choice is application dependent. Alternatively, one could use the independent chain version of the algorithm where $\mathfrak{P}(\alpha^{\dagger}, \alpha^{l-1}) = \mathfrak{P}(\alpha^{\dagger})$, in which case $\mathfrak{E}(\alpha^{l-1}, \alpha^{\dagger}) = \min\{[\breve{g}(\alpha^{\dagger} \mid y)/\breve{g}(\alpha^{l-1} \mid y)][\mathfrak{P}(\alpha^{\dagger})/\mathfrak{P}(\alpha^{l-1})], 1\}$. If this alternative is chosen, both the location and the shape of $\mathfrak{P}(\alpha^{\dagger})$ need to be monitored to ensure reasonable acceptance rates.

The independent chain version of the MH algorithm shares features with both acceptance and importance sampling. However, while the last two approaches place a low probability of acceptance (or a low weight) on a draw far away from the posterior, the independent chain assigns a low probability of accepting the candidate draw if the weighted ratio of the kernels at the previous and current draws is low.

In practice, one needs to make sure that the algorithm avoids excessively high or excessively low acceptance rates since, in the first case, the exploration of the posterior is slow and, in the second, a large region of the posterior is left undersampled. An acceptance rate of 35–40% should typically be considered as good.

Example 9.40. In example 9.31 we drew $\alpha^{\dagger} \sim \mathbb{N}(\tilde{\alpha}, \tilde{\Sigma}_{\alpha})$ and accepted the draw if $0 < \alpha^{\dagger} < 1$, so that the probability of acceptance is $(2\pi)^{-0.5}|\Sigma_{\alpha}|^{-0.5} \times \int_{0<\alpha<1} \exp\{-0.5(\alpha - \tilde{\alpha})' \tilde{\Sigma}_{\alpha}^{-1}(\alpha - \tilde{\alpha})\}\, d\alpha$. If this probability is too small, the algorithm is impractical. Suppose instead we draw from $\mathfrak{P}(\alpha^{\dagger}, \alpha^{l-1}) = (2\pi)^{-0.5k} \times |\Sigma^{\dagger}|^{-0.5} \exp\{-0.5(\alpha^{\dagger} - \alpha^{l-1})'(\Sigma^{\dagger})^{-1}(\alpha^{\dagger} - \alpha^{l-1})\}$, where $\Sigma^{\dagger}$ is the variance of the shocks. If $\Sigma^{\dagger}$ is too small, a large number of draws is needed to cover the set $0 < \alpha < 1$. If it is too large, $\alpha^{\dagger}$ will be outside the bounds in a large number of cases. Hence, to ensure an appropriate coverage of the posterior, $\Sigma^{\dagger}$ has to be carefully selected.

Example 9.41. Consider a bivariate normal distribution for $z = (x, y)$ with mean $(1, 2)$, variances equal to 1, and covariance equal to 0.8. A scatter plot (using 4000 draws) obtained by simulating (x, y) from this distribution is in the first box of the left-hand side column of figure 9.7. It is easy to see that the ellipsoids are very thin and positively inclined. To approximate this distribution we use an MH algorithm with a reflecting random walk transition $(z^{\dagger} - \bar{z}) = (z^{l-1} - \bar{z}) + v$, where the incremental variable v is uniform in the interval $[-0.5, 0.5]$ for both coordinates. Here, the probability of accepting the draw is equal to $\min\{\exp[-0.5(z^{\dagger} - \bar{z})\Sigma^{-1}(z^{\dagger} - \bar{z})]/\exp[-0.5(z^{l-1} - \bar{z})\Sigma^{-1}(z^{l-1} - \bar{z})], 1\}$. We also consider a Gibbs sampler, which uses $(x \mid y) \sim \mathbb{N}(1 + \rho(y-2), 1-\rho^2)$, $(y \mid x) \sim \mathbb{N}(2 + \rho(x-1), 1-\rho^2)$, where ρ is the correlation coefficient, to produce a sample from the posterior. The second and third rows of figure 9.7 present a sample of 4000 draws from the posteriors obtained with these two simulators. Both approaches approximate the target reasonably well. The Gibbs sampler is slightly superior but the acceptance rate of the MH algorithm is

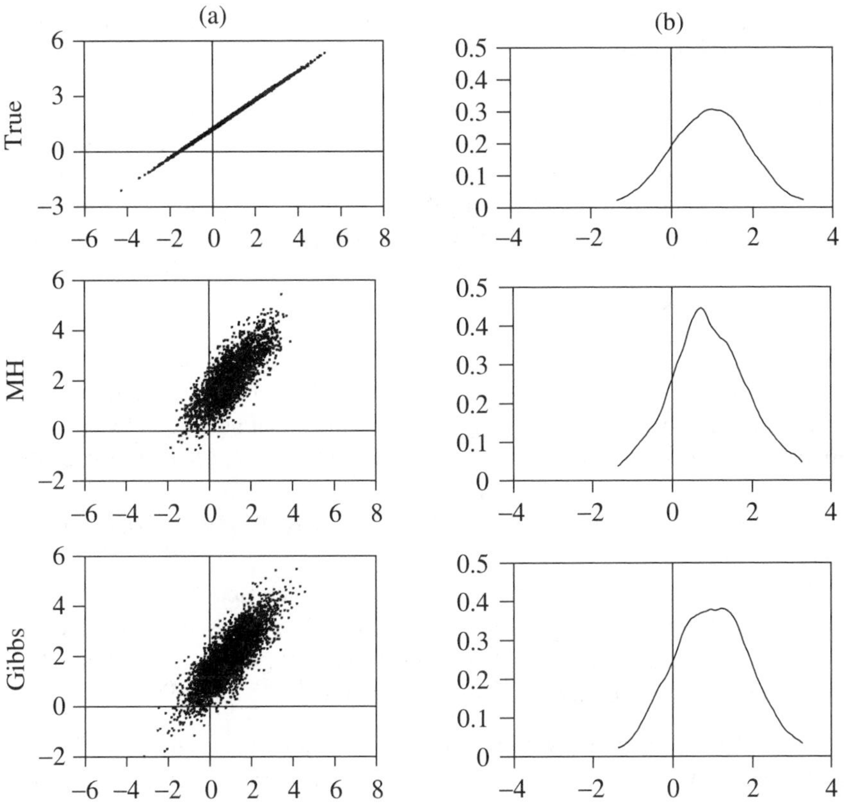

Figure 9.7. MCMC simulations: (a) joint (x, y); (b) marginal of x.

high (55%) and the tails of the distribution are not fully explored. Better acceptance rates would probably lead to a better covering of the target distribution. Note also the similarities in the estimates of the marginal of x (see the second column of figure 9.7).

Before we close this section we would like to emphasize a few important features of MCMC methods. First, Markov chain methods work better than importance or acceptance sampling because the distribution from which draws are taken changes at each iteration (see figure 9.4). Therefore, the transition kernel is time dependent. Second, although these methods are based on Markov chains, the Markov property can be dispensed with. For example, the chain may depend on the whole history of draws. Still, if the sufficiency conditions for convergence are satisfied, both the Gibbs and the MH samplers will generate a sequence from the posterior.

Exercise 9.32. Using the setup of example 9.41, vary $\text{cov}(x, y)$ from 0.1 to 0.9 in increments of 0.2. Show the values of Σ_B and Σ_W, when you start from $\alpha_1 = \pm 2.5$, $\alpha_2 = \pm 2.5$, and the interquartile range of the simulated distribution for samples of

100, 500, 1000 elements. Show the scatter plots obtained with the Gibbs sampler and the MH algorithm.

Exercise 9.33. Suppose $y_t = \alpha y_{t-1} + e_t$, $e_t \sim$ i.i.d. $\mathbb{N}(0, \sigma_e^2)$. The density of $(y_1, \dots, y_t)$ is $f(y \mid \alpha, \sigma_e^2) \propto (\sigma_e^2)^{0.5(T-1)} \exp\{-0.5\sigma_e^{-2} \sum_{t=2}^{T} (y_t - \alpha y_{t-1})^2\} \times \exp\{-0.5\sigma_e^{-2} y_1^2 (1-\alpha^2)\}[\sigma_e^{-2}(1-\alpha^2)]^{-0.5}$, where the last term is the density of y_1. Suppose the only available prior information is $\alpha < 1$. Show the form of the posterior for (α, σ_e^2) and describe how to use an MH algorithm to sample from it.

9.6 Robustness

Whenever the prior distribution has subjective features and/or the sample is small, it is important to know how sensitive are posterior outcomes to the choice of prior distributions. Robustness is crucial, for example, in evaluating the quality of a DSGE model. Since prior distributions are conveniently chosen so as to make calculations simple, and are typically centered around calibrated values, it is imperative to verify that posterior inference does not depend on the form of the prior distributions or on their spreads.

A way to assess the robustness of the posterior conclusions is to select an alternative prior density $g_1(\alpha)$, with support included in $g(\alpha)$, and use it to reweigh posterior draws. Let $w(\alpha) = g_1(\alpha)/g(\alpha)$. Then $E_1[h(\alpha)] = \int h(\alpha) g_1(\alpha)\, d\alpha = \int h(\alpha) w(\alpha) g(\alpha)\, d\alpha$ so that $h_1(\alpha) \approx [\sum_l w(\alpha^l) h(\alpha^l)] / \sum_l w(\alpha^l)$.

Example 9.42. Continuing with exercise 9.29, suppose $g(\alpha)$ is normal with mean 1 and variance 10. Then $g(\alpha \mid y)$ is normal with mean $\tilde{\alpha} = \tilde{\Sigma}_\alpha(0.1 + \sigma_e^{-2} x'x\alpha_{\mathrm{OLS}})$ and variance $\tilde{\Sigma}_\alpha = (0.1 + \sigma_e^{-2} x'x)^{-1}$. If one wishes to examine how forecasts produced by the model change if the prior variance is reduced (for example, to 5), two alternatives are possible: (i) draw a sequence α_1^l from a normal posterior with mean $\Sigma_\alpha^{-1}(0.2 + \sigma^{-2} x'x\alpha_{\mathrm{OLS}})$ and variance $\Sigma_\alpha^{-1} = (0.2 + \sigma^{-2} x'x)^{-1}$, compute forecasts for each α_1^l and compare results; (ii) weight each original posterior draw with $w(\alpha)$, i.e., calculate $\alpha_1^l = [g_1(\alpha^l)/g(\alpha^l)]\alpha^l$; compute forecasts and compare results, $l = 1, 2, \dots, L$.

Exercise 9.34. Suppose you are interested in comparing the welfare costs of a certain policy in a model like the one considered in example 9.12 when you use a noninformative prior for α and a sequence of informative priors, which are characterized by smaller and smaller prior variances. How would you check robustness here? What ingredients do you need to report to allow the reader to reweigh your results according to her prior preferences?

9.7 Estimating Returns to Scale in Spain

In this section we use Bayesian methods to measure the magnitude of the returns-to-scale parameter in the aggregate Spanish production function. The literature dealing with production function estimation is vast and cannot be summarized here. The exercise we conduct lies in the growth-accounting branch where output changes are explained by input changes and all unexplained variations are lumped together under the total factor productivity (TFP) label. We assume that output is produced with capital and labor by using a Cobb-Douglas specification $Y_t = (\alpha_0 t^{\alpha_1} \zeta_t e_t) K_t^{\alpha_2} N_t^{\alpha_3}$, where K_t and N_t are measured capital and labor inputs, ζ_t captures efficiency improvements, e_t is a multiplicative measurement error, α_0 a constant, and t a time trend. Taking logarithms and linearly detrending leads to

$$y_t = \alpha_2 \ln K_t + \alpha_3 \ln N_t + \ln \zeta_t + \ln e_t, \tag{9.46}$$

where $y_t = \ln Y_t - \alpha_1 \ln t - \ln \alpha_0$. If we set $v_t = \ln \zeta_t + \ln e_t$, (9.46) is a standard regression model with two explanatory variables. The composite error term v_t is likely to be serially correlated but, as a first step, we neglect this possibility and assume $v_t \sim \mathbb{N}(0, \sigma_v^2)$. Let $x_t = (\ln K_t, \ln N_t)$ and $\alpha = (\alpha_2, \alpha_3)$.

Consider first a normal approximation. Using the results of example 9.10 we know that the marginal posterior for α has a multivariate t-format. We take a normal approximation to each of the two components separately, centered at the mode α^* with curvature equal to $\Sigma(\alpha^*)$. The first row of table 9.1 gives the quartiles of the posterior of the returns-to-scale parameter obtained in this case: the interquartile range is small and the median of the posterior is only 0.39, suggesting the presence of strong decreasing returns to scale. Posterior estimates of $(\alpha_2, \alpha_3, \sigma_v^2)$ can also be obtained with the Gibbs sampler. Suppose that $\alpha \sim \mathbb{N}(\bar{\alpha}, \bar{\Sigma}_\alpha)$ and that $\sigma_v^{-2} \sim \mathbb{G}(a_1, a_2)$, where $\bar{\alpha} = (0.4, 0.6)$, $\bar{\Sigma}_\alpha = \text{diag}(0.05, 0.05)$, and we let $a_1 = a_2 = 10^{-5}$, to make the prior on σ_v^{-2} noninformative. The two conditional distributions are $(\alpha \mid \sigma_v^2, y, x) \sim \mathbb{N}(\tilde{\alpha}, \tilde{\Sigma})$, where $\tilde{\alpha} = \tilde{\Sigma}_\alpha(\bar{\Sigma}_\alpha^{-1}\bar{\alpha} + \sigma_v^{-2} x'x\alpha_{\text{OLS}})$, $\tilde{\Sigma}_\alpha = (\bar{\Sigma}_\alpha^{-1} + \sigma_v^{-2} x'x)^{-1}$, a_{OLS} is the OLS estimator of α, and $(\sigma_v^{-2} \mid \alpha, y, x) \sim \mathbb{G}(a_1 + 0.5T, a_2 + 0.5(y - x\alpha_{\text{OLS}})'(y - x\alpha_{\text{OLS}}))$. Posterior distributions are obtained by discarding the initial 500 draws and keeping one in every 50 of the next 5000 draws. The second row of the table shows that the interquartile range of the returns-to-scale parameter is smaller than with a normal approximation and the median is slightly higher. However, decreasing returns are strong also in this case.

Next, we allow for serial correlation in v_t. We assume $\rho(\ell)v_t = \epsilon_t$, so that model (9.46) is transformed into $y_t^0 \equiv \rho(\ell)y_t = \rho(\ell)x_t\alpha + \epsilon_t = x_t^0\alpha + \epsilon_t$. The situation is now identical to the previous one, except that a new vector of parameters $\rho(\ell)$ needs to be estimated. Let $\rho(\ell) = 1 - \rho\ell$ and take the first observation to be fixed. The likelihood function is $\mathcal{L}(\alpha, \rho \mid y, x) \propto (\sigma_e^2)^{-(T-1)/2} \exp\{\sum_{t=2}^T (y_t^0 - x_t^0\alpha)^2 / 2\sigma_e^2\}$. Assume the same prior for α, let the prior for σ_ϵ^{-2} to be $\mathbb{G}(0.5, 0.5)$, and let $g(\rho)$ be normal, centered at 0.8, with variance 0.1, truncated outside the range $(-1, 1)$, i.e., $\rho \sim \mathbb{N}(0.8, 0.1) \times \mathcal{I}_{(-1,1)}$. The conditional posterior for α is identical to the one previously derived and the one for σ_ϵ^{-2} has the same format as the one for σ_v^{-2}. The conditional distribution for ρ is normal with mean $\tilde{\rho} = \tilde{\Sigma}_\rho(8 + \sigma_\epsilon^{-2} V'v)$ and variance $\tilde{\Sigma}_\rho = (10 + \sigma^{-2} V'V)^{-1}$, truncated outside the range $(-1, 1)$, where $v = (v_2, \dots, v_T)' = y - \alpha_2 \ln K - \alpha_3 \ln N$, and V is a $(T-1) \times 1$ vector with jth element given by v_{t-j-1}. Drawing from this distribution is easy since we

Table 9.3. Posterior distribution of returns to scale.

Method	Percentiles		
	25th	50th	75th
Normal approximation	0.35	0.39	0.47
Basic Gibbs	0.36	0.41	0.44
Gibbs with AR(1) errors	0.35	0.41	0.48
Gibbs with latent variable	0.33	0.41	0.45

have taken the first observation as given. Had we not done that, the computation of the conditional posterior for ρ would have required an intermediate MH step. Serial correlation is important: the median value of the posterior of ρ is 0.86 and the interquartile range is $(0.84, 0.90)$. However, the distribution of returns-to-scale estimates is unchanged; only the estimate of the upper 75th percentile is slightly larger (see the third row of table 9.3).

It is clear that ζ_t, apart from technological progress, includes everything which is excluded from the production function; for example, public capital or human capital. One way of thinking about these influences is to treat ζ_t as a latent variable and let $\zeta_t = \delta z_t + \epsilon_t^{\zeta}$, where z_t are observables (in our case z_t measures public capital) and ϵ_t^{ζ} represents the true technological progress. With this specification, the model has a hierarchical latent variable structure: conditional on (x_t, ζ_t), y_t is normal with mean $x_t\alpha + \delta z_t$ and variance $\sigma_e^2 + \sigma_\zeta^2$; conditional on (y_t, x_t), ζ_t is normal with mean δz_t and variance σ_ζ^2. The specification has two new parameters σ_ζ^2 and δ. We let $\delta \sim \mathrm{N}(\bar{\delta}, \bar{\Sigma}_\delta)$ and set $\bar{\delta} = 0$ and $\bar{\Sigma}_\delta = 0.5$. Since the available sample is short and it is difficult to separately identify σ_ζ^2 and σ_e^2, we set $\sigma_\zeta^2 = \sigma_e^2$. The conditional posterior for δ is normal with mean $\tilde{\delta} = \tilde{\Sigma}_\delta(\bar{\Sigma}_\delta^{-1}\bar{\delta} + 0.5\sigma_e^{-2}z'\zeta_t)$ and variance $\tilde{\Sigma}_\delta = (\bar{\Sigma}_\delta^{-1} + 0.5\sigma_e^{-2}z'z)^{-1}$. Since the posterior distribution for δ is centered around zero (median -0.0004, interquartile range $(-0.003, 0.004)$), there is little evidence that ζ_t is influenced by public capital. Hence, the shape of the posterior distribution of the returns-to-scale parameter is roughly unchanged (see the fourth row of table 9.3).

There are many extensions one could consider to refine these estimates. For example, we could think that measured inputs are different from effective ones and let, for example, $N_t = \mathrm{e}^{a_N z_{Nt}} N_{1t}$, where z_{Nt} are factors which affect the efficiency of measured input, such as education, unionization, etc. In cross-sectional comparisons, this refinement could be important. N_t now becomes a latent variable and a_N is an additional set of parameters which can be estimated once z_{Nt} are specified. Note that, in this case, the model has a bilinear form, but the posterior distribution of the parameters can still be obtained with the Gibbs sampler, as shown by Koop et al. (2000).

10
Bayesian VARs

We saw in chapter 4 that VAR models can be used to characterize any vector of time series under a minimal set of conditions. We have also seen that, since VARs are reduced-form models, identification restrictions, motivated by economic theory, are needed to conduct meaningful policy analyses. Reduced-form VARs are also typically unsuitable for out-of-sample forecasting. To reasonably approximate the Wold representation, it is in fact necessary to have a VAR with long lags. A generous parametrization means that unrestricted VARs are not operational alternatives to either standard macroeconometric models, where insignificant coefficients are purged out of the specification, or parsimonious time series models since, with a limited number of degrees of freedom, estimates of VAR coefficients are imprecise and forecasts have large standard errors.

The construction of an empirical model requires historical and *a priori* information, both of a statistical and an economic nature. Alternative modeling techniques use different *a priori* information or attribute different relative weights to sample and prior information. Unrestricted VARs employ *a priori* information very sparsely: in choosing the variables of the VAR; in selecting the maximum lag length of the model; in imposing identification restrictions. Because of this choice, overfitting may result when the data set is short, sample information is weak, or the number of parameters is large. In-sample overfitting typically translates into poor forecasting performance, both in the unconditional and conditional senses. Bayesian methods can solve these problems: they can make in-sample overfitting less dramatic and improve out-of-sample performance. While Bayesian VARs (BVARs) were originally devised to improve macroeconomic forecasts, they are now used for a variety of purposes.

This chapter describes Bayesian methods for a variety of VAR models. First, we present a useful decomposition of the likelihood function of a VAR and the construction of the posterior distribution for a number of prior specifications. We also show the link between posterior mean estimates and classical estimates obtained when the coefficients of the VAR model are subject to stochastic linear constraints. The third section describes Bayesian structural VARs and block recursive structures which arise, for example, in models with some exogenous variables or in two-country models with (overidentifying) linear restrictions on the contemporaneous impact of the shocks. The fourth section presents time-varying-coefficient BVAR

(TVC-BVAR) models and discusses both empirical Bayes and fully hierarchical posterior estimates of the VAR coefficients and of the covariance matrix. TVC-BVAR models generate a variety of distributional patterns and can be used to model series with thick tails, with smoothly evolving patterns, or that display switches over a finite number of states.

The fifth section deals with multiple BVAR models: these structures are becoming popular in empirical practice, for example, when comparing the effects of monetary policy shocks in different countries or the growth behavior in different regions, and present interesting complications relative to single-unit BVAR models. We show how to obtain posterior estimates of the coefficients for each unit and for the mean effect across units, which often is the center of interest for applied investigators. We also describe a procedure to endogenously group units with similar characteristics. This is useful when one wants to distinguish the impact of certain shocks on, for example, small or large firms, or when policy advice requires some particular endogenous classifications (e.g., income per capita, education level, indebtedness, etc.). The last part of the section studies Bayesian panel VAR models with cross-unit interdependencies. These models are suited to the study of, for example, the transmission of shocks across countries or the effects of increased interdependencies in various world economies. Because of the large number of parameters, it is impossible to estimate them with classical methods and suitable (prior) restrictions need to be imposed for estimation. With such a respecification, these models are easily estimable with Markov chain Monte Carlo methods.

Since this chapter deals with models of increasing complexity, increasingly complex methods will be used to compute posteriors. The techniques described in chapter 9 are handy: conjugate priors allow the derivation of analytic forms for the conditional posteriors; Markov chain Monte Carlo methods are used to draw sequences from the posterior distributions.

10.1 The Likelihood Function of an m-Variable VAR(q)

Throughout this chapter we assume that the VAR has the form $y_t = A(L)y_{t-1} + C\bar{y}_t + e_t$, $e_t \sim$ i.i.d. $(0, \Sigma_e)$, where y_t includes m variables, each with q lags, while the constant and other deterministic variables (trends, seasonal dummies) are collected into the $m_c \times 1$ vector $\bar{y}_t$. Hence, each equation has $k = mq + m_c$ regressors and the VAR has mk coefficients.

Following the steps described in chapter 4, we can rewrite the VAR in two alternative formats, both of which will be used in this chapter:

$$Y = XA + E, \tag{10.1}$$

$$y = (I_m \otimes X)\alpha + e, \tag{10.2}$$

where Y and E are $T \times m$ matrices and X is a $T \times k$ matrix, $X_t = [y'_{t-1}, \dots, y'_{t-q}, \bar{y}'_t]$, y and e are $mT \times 1$ vectors, I_m is the identify matrix of dimension m, and $\alpha = \text{vec}(\boldsymbol{A})$ is an $mk \times 1$ vector. Using (10.2) and assuming that e is normally distributed with covariance $\Sigma_e \otimes I_T$, the likelihood function is

$$\mathcal{L}(\alpha, \Sigma_e) \propto |\Sigma_e \otimes I_T|^{-0.5} \exp\{-0.5[y-(I_m \otimes \boldsymbol{X})\alpha]'(\Sigma_e^{-1} \otimes I_T)[y-(I_m \otimes \boldsymbol{X})\alpha]\}. \tag{10.3}$$

To derive a useful decomposition of (10.3), note that

$$\begin{aligned}
&[y - (I_m \otimes \boldsymbol{X})\alpha]'(\Sigma_e^{-1} \otimes I_T)[y - (I_m \otimes \boldsymbol{X})\alpha] \\
&\quad = (\Sigma_e^{-0.5} \otimes I_T)[y - (I_m \otimes \boldsymbol{X})\alpha]'(\Sigma_e^{-0.5} \otimes I_T)[y - (I_m \otimes \boldsymbol{X})\alpha] \\
&\quad = [(\Sigma_e^{-0.5} \otimes I_T)y - (\Sigma_e^{-0.5} \otimes \boldsymbol{X})\alpha]'[(\Sigma_e^{-0.5} \otimes I_T)y - (\Sigma_e^{-0.5} \otimes \boldsymbol{X})\alpha].
\end{aligned}$$

Also $(\Sigma_e^{-0.5} \otimes I_T)y - (\Sigma_e^{-0.5} \otimes \boldsymbol{X})\alpha = (\Sigma_e^{-0.5} \otimes I_T)y - (\Sigma_e^{-0.5} \otimes \boldsymbol{X})\alpha_{\text{OLS}} + (\Sigma_e^{-0.5} \otimes \boldsymbol{X})(\alpha_{\text{OLS}} - \alpha)$, where $\alpha_{\text{OLS}} = (\Sigma_e^{-1} \otimes \boldsymbol{X}'\boldsymbol{X})^{-1}(\Sigma_e^{-1} \otimes \boldsymbol{X})'y$. Therefore,

$$\begin{aligned}
&[y - (I_m \otimes \boldsymbol{X})\alpha]'(\Sigma_e^{-1} \otimes I_T)[y - (I_m \otimes \boldsymbol{X})\alpha] \\
&\qquad = [(\Sigma_e^{-0.5} \otimes I_T)y - (\Sigma_e^{-0.5} \otimes \boldsymbol{X})\alpha_{\text{OLS}}]' \\
&\qquad\qquad \times [(\Sigma_e^{-0.5} \otimes I_T)y - (\Sigma_e^{-0.5} \otimes \boldsymbol{X})\alpha_{\text{OLS}}] \qquad (10.4) \\
&\qquad\quad + (\alpha_{\text{OLS}} - \alpha)'(\Sigma_e^{-1} \otimes \boldsymbol{X}'\boldsymbol{X})(\alpha_{\text{OLS}} - \alpha). \qquad (10.5)
\end{aligned}$$

The term in (10.4) is independent of α and looks like a sum of squared residuals. The one in (10.5) looks like the scaled square error of α_{OLS}. Putting the pieces together:

$$\begin{aligned}
\mathcal{L}(\alpha, \Sigma_e) \propto |\Sigma_e \otimes I_T|^{-0.5} &\exp\{-0.5(\alpha - \alpha_{\text{OLS}})'(\Sigma_e^{-1} \otimes \boldsymbol{X}'\boldsymbol{X})(\alpha - \alpha_{\text{OLS}}) \\
&\qquad -0.5[(\Sigma_e^{-0.5} \otimes I_T)y - (\Sigma_e^{-0.5} \otimes \boldsymbol{X})\alpha_{\text{OLS}}]' \\
&\qquad \times [(\Sigma_e^{-0.5} \otimes I_T)y - (\Sigma_e^{-0.5} \otimes \boldsymbol{X})\alpha_{\text{OLS}}]\} \\
= |\Sigma_e|^{-0.5k} &\exp\{-0.5(\alpha - \alpha_{\text{OLS}})'(\Sigma_e^{-1} \otimes \boldsymbol{X}'\boldsymbol{X})(\alpha - \alpha_{\text{OLS}})\} \\
\times |\Sigma_e|^{-0.5(T-k)} &\exp\{-0.5\,\text{tr}[(\Sigma_e^{-0.5} \otimes I_T)y - (\Sigma_e^{-0.5} \otimes \boldsymbol{X})\alpha_{\text{OLS}}]' \\
&\qquad \times [(\Sigma_e^{-0.5} \otimes I_T)y - (\Sigma_e^{-0.5} \otimes \boldsymbol{X})\alpha_{\text{OLS}}]\} \\
\propto \mathbb{N}(\alpha \mid \alpha_{\text{OLS}}, \Sigma_e, &\boldsymbol{X}, y) \times \mathbb{W}(\Sigma_e^{-1} | y, \boldsymbol{X}, \alpha_{\text{OLS}}, T - k - m - 1),
\end{aligned} \tag{10.6}$$

where "tr" denotes the trace of a matrix. The likelihood function of a VAR(q) is therefore the product of a normal density for α, conditional on α_{OLS} and Σ_e, and a Wishart density for Σ_e^{-1}, conditional on α_{OLS}, with $(T - k - m - 1)$ degrees of freedom and scale matrix $[(y - (I_m \otimes \boldsymbol{X})\alpha_{\text{OLS}})'(y - (I_m \otimes \boldsymbol{X})\alpha_{\text{OLS}})]^{-1}$ (see the appendix for the forms of the various distributions).

Hence, under appropriate conjugate prior restrictions, we can analytically derive the conditional posterior distribution for the VAR coefficients and the covariance matrix of the reduced-form shocks. As we have seen in chapter 9, a normal-Wishart prior conjugates the two blocks of the likelihood. Therefore, with this prior, the conditional posterior for α will be normal and the conditional posterior of Σ_e^{-1} will be Wishart. Other prior assumptions also allow analytical computation of conditional posteriors. We examine them next.

10.2 Priors for VARs

In this section we consider four alternative types of prior specification.

1. A normal prior for α, with Σ_e^{-1} fixed.
2. A noninformative prior for both α and Σ_e^{-1}.
3. A normal prior for α and a noninformative prior for Σ_e^{-1}.
4. A normal prior for α and a Wishart prior for Σ_e^{-1}.

We examine in detail the derivation of the posterior distribution for the VAR coefficients for case 1. Let the prior be $\alpha = \bar{\alpha} + v_a$, $v_a \sim$ i.i.d. $\mathbb{N}(0, \bar{\Sigma}_a)$, with $\bar{\alpha}$, $\bar{\Sigma}_a$ fixed. Then

$$\begin{aligned} g(\alpha) &\propto |\bar{\Sigma}_a|^{-0.5} \exp\{-0.5(\alpha - \bar{\alpha})'\bar{\Sigma}_a^{-1}(\alpha - \bar{\alpha})\} \\ &\propto |\bar{\Sigma}_a|^{-0.5} \exp\{-0.5[\bar{\Sigma}_a^{-0.5}(\alpha - \bar{\alpha})]'[\bar{\Sigma}_a^{-0.5}(\alpha - \bar{\alpha})]\}. \end{aligned} \tag{10.7}$$

Let $\mathcal{Y} = [\bar{\Sigma}_a^{-0.5}\bar{\alpha}, (\Sigma_e^{-0.5} \otimes I_T)y]'$ and $\mathcal{X} = [\bar{\Sigma}_a^{-0.5}, (\Sigma_e^{-0.5} \otimes \boldsymbol{X})]'$. Then

$$\begin{aligned} g(\alpha \mid y) &\propto |\bar{\Sigma}_a|^{-0.5} \exp\{-0.5[\bar{\Sigma}_a^{-0.5}(\alpha - \bar{\alpha})]'[\bar{\Sigma}_a^{-0.5}(\alpha - \bar{\alpha})]\} \\ &\quad \times |\Sigma_e \otimes I_T|^{-0.5} \exp\{[(\Sigma_e^{-0.5} \otimes I_T)y - (\Sigma_e^{-0.5} \otimes \boldsymbol{X})\alpha]' \\ &\quad\quad \times [(\Sigma_e^{-0.5} \otimes I_T)y - (\Sigma_e^{-0.5} \otimes \boldsymbol{X})\alpha]\} \\ &\propto \exp\{-0.5(\mathcal{Y} - \mathcal{X}\alpha)'(\mathcal{Y} - \mathcal{X}\alpha)\} \\ &\propto \exp\{-0.5(\alpha - \tilde{\alpha})'\mathcal{X}'\mathcal{X}(\alpha - \tilde{\alpha}) + (\mathcal{Y} - \mathcal{X}\tilde{\alpha})'(\mathcal{Y} - \mathcal{X}\tilde{\alpha})\}, \end{aligned} \tag{10.8}$$

where

$$\tilde{\alpha} = (\mathcal{X}'\mathcal{X})^{-1}(\mathcal{X}'\mathcal{Y}) = [\bar{\Sigma}_a^{-1} + (\Sigma_e^{-1} \otimes \boldsymbol{X}'\boldsymbol{X})]^{-1}[\bar{\Sigma}_a^{-1}\bar{\alpha} + (\Sigma_e^{-1} \otimes \boldsymbol{X})'y]. \tag{10.9}$$

Since Σ_e and $\bar{\Sigma}_a$ are fixed, the second term in (10.8) is independent of α and

$$\begin{aligned} g(\alpha \mid y) &\propto \exp\{-0.5(\alpha - \tilde{\alpha})'\mathcal{X}'\mathcal{X}(\alpha - \tilde{\alpha})\} \\ &\propto \exp\{-0.5(\alpha - \tilde{\alpha})'\tilde{\Sigma}_a^{-1}(\alpha - \tilde{\alpha})\}. \end{aligned} \tag{10.10}$$

Hence, the posterior density of α is normal with mean $\tilde{\alpha}$ and variance $\tilde{\Sigma}_a = [\bar{\Sigma}_a^{-1} + (\Sigma_e^{-1} \otimes \boldsymbol{X}'\boldsymbol{X})]^{-1}$. For (10.10) to be operational we need $\bar{\alpha}$, $\bar{\Sigma}_a$ and Σ_e. Typically, $\bar{\Sigma}_a$ is chosen to have a loose prior, in which case the choice of $\bar{\alpha}$ is irrelevant, and one uses $\Sigma_{e,\mathrm{OLS}} = [1/(T-1)] \sum_{t=1}^{T} e'_{t,\mathrm{OLS}} e_{t,\mathrm{OLS}}$, $e_{t,\mathrm{OLS}} = y_t - (I_m \otimes \boldsymbol{X})\alpha_{\mathrm{OLS}}$, in the formulas.

10.2.1 Least Squares under Uncertain Restrictions

The posterior mean for α displayed in (10.9) has the same format as a classical estimator obtained with Theil's mixed-type approach when coefficients are stochastically restricted. To illustrate this point consider a univariate AR(q) with no constant:

$$\left.\begin{aligned} \boldsymbol{Y}_t &= \boldsymbol{X}_t A + \boldsymbol{E}_t, & \boldsymbol{E}_t &\sim \text{i.i.d. } (0, \Sigma_e), \\ A &= \bar{A} + v_a, & v_a &\sim \text{i.i.d. } (0, \bar{\Sigma}_a), \end{aligned}\right\} \tag{10.11}$$

where $A = [A_1, \ldots, A_q]'$ and $X_t = [y_{t-1}, \ldots, y_{t-q}]$. Set $\mathcal{Y}_t = [Y_t, \bar{A}']'$, $\mathcal{X}_t = [X_t, I]'$, and $E_t = [E_t, v_a']'$. Then $\mathcal{Y}_t = \mathcal{X}_t A + E_t$, where $E_t \sim (0, \Sigma_E)$, and $\bar{A}$ and Σ_E are assumed to be known. The (generalized) least squares estimator is $A_{\text{GLS}} = (\mathcal{X}'\Sigma_E^{-1}\mathcal{X})^{-1}(\mathcal{X}'\Sigma_E^{-1}\mathcal{Y})$, which is identical to $\tilde{A}$, the mean of the posterior of A obtained with fixed Σ_e, $\bar{A}$, $\bar{\Sigma}_a$ and a normal prior for A. There is a simple but useful interpretation of this result. Prior restrictions can be treated as dummy observations which are added to the system of VAR equations. The posterior estimator will efficiently combine sample and prior information by using their precisions as weights. Additional restrictions can be tacked on to the system in exactly the same fashion and posterior estimates can be obtained by combining the vector of prior restrictions with the data. We will exploit this feature later on, when we design restrictions intended to capture the existence of trends, seasonal fluctuations, etc.

Exercise 10.1 (Hoerl and Kennard). Suppose that $\bar{A} = 0$ in (10.11). Show that the posterior mean of A is $\tilde{A} = (\bar{\Sigma}_a^{-1} + X'\Sigma_e^{-1}X)^{-1}(X'\Sigma_e^{-1}Y)$. Show that, if $\Sigma_e = \sigma_e^2 \times I_T$, $\bar{\Sigma}_a = \sigma_v^2 \times I_q$, $\tilde{A} = (I_q + (\sigma_e^2/\sigma_v^2)(X'X)^{-1})^{-1} A_{\text{OLS}}$, where A_{OLS} is the OLS estimator of A.

Two features of exercise 10.1 are worth discussing. First, since the restriction $\bar{A} = 0$ imposes the belief that all the coefficients are small, it is appropriate if y_t is the growth rate of financial variables like exchange rates or stock prices. Second, under the assumptions made, the posterior estimator increases the smallest eigenvalues of the data matrix by the factor σ_e^2/σ_v^2. Hence, the specification is particularly useful when the $(X'X)$ matrix is ill-conditioned, for example, when near multi-collinearity is present.

Exercise 10.2. Treating $\tilde{\alpha}$ in (10.9) as a classical estimator, show what conditions ensure its consistency and its asymptotic normality.

There is an alternative representation of the prior for case 1. Set $R\alpha = r + v_a$, $v_a \sim$ i.i.d. $\mathbb{N}(0, I)$, where R is a square matrix. Then $g(\alpha)$ is $\mathbb{N}(R^{-1}r, R^{-1}(R^{-1})')$ and $\tilde{\alpha} = [R'R + (\Sigma_e^{-1} \otimes X'X)]^{-1}[R'r + (\Sigma_e^{-1} \otimes X)'y]$. This last expression has two advantages over (10.9). First, it does not require the inversion of the $mk \times mk$ matrix $\bar{\Sigma}_a$, which could be complicated in large-scale VARs. Second, zero restrictions on some coefficients are easy to impose; in (10.9) this must be done by setting some diagonal elements of $\bar{\Sigma}_a$ to infinity.

Exercise 10.3. Using $R\alpha = r + v_a$, $v_a \sim$ i.i.d. $\mathbb{N}(0, I)$, show that $\sqrt{T}(\tilde{\alpha} - \alpha_{\text{OLS}}) \xrightarrow{\text{P}} 0$ as $T \to \infty$.

The intuition for the result of exercise 10.3 is clear: since, as T grows, the importance of the data increases relative to the prior, $\tilde{\alpha}$ coincides with the unrestricted OLS estimator.

10.2.2 The Minnesota Prior

The so-called Minnesota (Litterman) prior is obtained from case 1 prior when $\bar{\alpha}$ and Σ_α are functions of a small number of hyperparameters. In particular (see, for example, the RATS manual 2005) this prior assumes that $\bar{\alpha} = 0$ except for $\bar{\alpha}_{i1} = 1$, $i = 1, \dots, m$, that Σ_a is diagonal, and that the $\sigma_{ij,\ell}$ element, corresponding to lag ℓ of variable j in equation i, has the form

$$\sigma_{ij,\ell} = \begin{cases} \dfrac{\phi_0}{h(\ell)} & \text{if } i = j,\ \forall \ell, \\ \phi_0 \times \dfrac{\phi_1}{h(\ell)} \times \left(\dfrac{\sigma_j}{\sigma_i}\right)^2 & \text{if } i \neq j,\ j \text{ endogenous},\ \forall \ell, \\ \phi_0 \times \phi_2 & \text{if } i \neq j,\ j \text{ exogenous}. \end{cases} \tag{10.12}$$

Here $\phi_i, i = 0, 1, 2$, are hyperparameters, $(\sigma_j/\sigma_i)^2$ is a scaling factor, and $h(\ell)$ is a deterministic function of ℓ. The parametrization in (10.12) is intended to capture features of interest to the investigator: ϕ_0 represents the tightness on the variance of the first lag, ϕ_1 the relative tightness of other variables, ϕ_2 the relative tightness of the exogenous variables, and $h(\ell)$ the relative tightness of the variance of lags other than the first one. Typically, one assumes a harmonic decay $h(\ell) = \ell^{\phi_3}$ (a special case of which is $h(\ell) = \ell$, a linear decay) or a geometric decay $h(\ell) = \phi_3^{-\ell+1}$, $\phi_3 > 0$. Since $\sigma_i, i = 1, \dots, m$, are unknown, consistent estimates of the standard errors of the variables i, j are typically used in (10.12).

To understand the logic of this prior, note that the m time series are *a priori* represented as random walks. This specification is selected because univariate random walk models are typically good at forecasting macroeconomic time series. Note also that the random walk hypothesis is imposed *a priori*: *a posteriori*, each time series may follow a more complicated process if there is sufficient information in the data to require it.

The variance–covariance matrix is *a priori* selected to be diagonal. Hence, there is no relationship among the coefficients of various VAR equations. Moreover, the most recent lags of a variable are *a priori* expected to contain more information about the variable's current value than earlier lags. Hence, the variance of lag ℓ_2 is smaller than the variance of lag ℓ_1 if $\ell_2 > \ell_1$ for every endogenous variable of the model. Furthermore, since lags of the other variables typically have less information than own lags, $\phi_1 \leqslant 1$. Note that, if $\phi_1 = 0$, the VAR is *a priori* collapsed into a vector of univariate models. Finally, ϕ_2 regulates the relative importance of the information contained in the exogenous variables and ϕ_0 controls the relative importance of sample and prior information. From (10.9), if ϕ_0 is large, prior information becomes diffuse so the posterior essentially contains sample information. If ϕ_0 is small, prior information is tight and the posterior primarily reflects prior information.

A graphical representation of this prior is shown in figure 10.1: all coefficients have zero prior mean (except the first own lag) and the priors become more concentrated for coefficients on longer lags. Moreover, the distributions of the lags of the variables

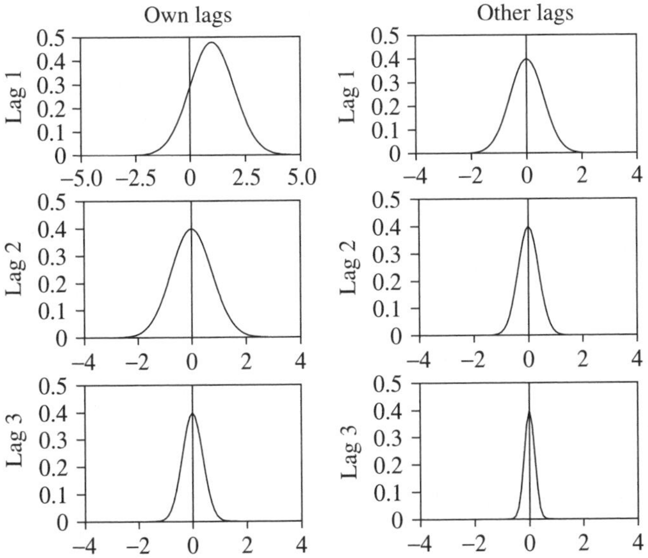

Figure 10.1. Minnesota prior.

not appearing on the left-hand side of an equation are more concentrated than those of their own lags.

Example 10.1. To see what the Minnesota prior implies, consider a VAR(2) with $q = 2$, $\bar{y} = 0$, $h(\ell) = \ell$. Here $\bar{\alpha} = [1, 0, 0, 0 \mid 0, 1, 0, 0]$ and, if $\kappa = \sigma_2/\sigma_1$,

$$\bar{\Sigma}_a = \begin{bmatrix} \phi_0 & 0 & 0 & 0 & 0 & 0 & 0 & 0 \\ 0 & \phi_0\phi_1\kappa^2 & 0 & 0 & 0 & 0 & 0 & 0 \\ 0 & 0 & \frac{1}{2}\phi_0 & 0 & 0 & 0 & 0 & 0 \\ 0 & 0 & 0 & \frac{1}{2}\phi_0\phi_1\kappa^2 & 0 & 0 & 0 & 0 \\ 0 & 0 & 0 & 0 & \phi_0\phi_1\kappa^{-2} & 0 & 0 & 0 \\ 0 & 0 & 0 & 0 & 0 & \phi_0 & 0 & 0 \\ 0 & 0 & 0 & 0 & 0 & 0 & \frac{1}{2}\phi_0\phi_1\kappa^{-2} & 0 \\ 0 & 0 & 0 & 0 & 0 & 0 & 0 & \frac{1}{2}\phi_0 \end{bmatrix}.$$

There are advantages in specifying $\bar{\Sigma}_a$ to be diagonal. Since the same variables appear on the right-hand side of each equation, if $\phi_1 = 1$, a diagonal $\bar{\Sigma}_a$ implies a diagonal $\tilde{\Sigma}_a$ so that $\tilde{\alpha}$ is the same as the vector of $\tilde{\alpha}_i$ computed equation by equation. This property is lost with other prior specifications, regardless of the assumptions made on $\bar{\Sigma}_a$ and ϕ_1.

Exercise 10.4. Using the logic of seemingly unrelated regressions, show that, when $g(\alpha)$ is of Minnesota type and $\phi_1 = 1$, estimating the VAR jointly gives the same posterior estimator for the coefficients of equation i as estimating the ith VAR equation separately.

The dimension of α for moderate VARs is typically large: for example, if there are five endogenous variables, five lags, and a constant, $k = 26$ and $mk = 130$. With standard macro data, say, 40 years of quarterly data ($T = 160$), maximum likelihood estimates are unlikely to have reasonable properties. The Minnesota-type prior makes this large number of coefficients depend on a smaller vector of hyperparameters. If these are the objects estimated from the data, a better precision is to be expected because of the sheer dimensionality reduction (the noise-to-signal ratio is smaller), and out-of-sample forecasts can be improved. Note that, even when the prior is false, in the sense that it does not reflect sample information well, this approach may reduce the MSE of the estimates. A number of authors have shown that VARs with a Minnesota prior produce forecasts that are superior to those of univariate ARIMA models and of traditional multivariate simultaneous equations systems (see, for example, Robertson and Tallman (1999) for a recent assessment). Therefore, it is not surprising that BVARs are routinely used for short-term forecasting in central banks and international institutions.

It is useful to contrast the Minnesota approach with other methods used to deal with the "curse of dimensionality." In classical approaches, "unimportant" lags are purged from the specification by using a t-test or similar procedures (see, for example, Favero 2001). This approach therefore imposes strong *a priori* restrictions on what variables and which lags should be in the VAR. However, dogmatic restrictions are unpalatable because they are hard to justify on both economic and statistical grounds. The Minnesota prior introduces restrictions in a flexible way: by imposing probability distributions on the coefficients of the VAR, it reduces the dimensionality of the problem and, at the same time, gives a reasonable account of the uncertainty faced by an investigator.

The choice of $\phi = (\phi_0, \phi_1, \phi_2, \phi_3)$ is important since if the prior is too loose, overfitting is hard to avoid; while if it is too tight, the data are not allowed to speak. There are three approaches one can use. In the first two, one obtains estimates of ϕ and substitutes these estimates into the expression for $\bar{\alpha}$ and $\bar{\Sigma}_a$. Then the posterior distribution of α can be obtained from (10.9) in an empirical Bayes fashion, conditional on the ϕ estimates. In the third approach, one treats ϕ as random, assumes a prior distribution, and computes fully hierarchical posterior estimates of α. To do this we need MCMC methods. In this section we focus on the first two methods.

One way to choose ϕ is to use simple rules of thumb or experience. The RATS manual (2005), for example, suggests as default values $\phi_0 = 0.2$, $\phi_1 = 0.5$, $\phi_2 = 10^5$, a harmonic specification for $h(\ell)$ with $\phi_3 = 1$ or 2, implying a relatively loose prior on the VAR coefficients and an uninformative prior for the exogenous variables. These values work reasonably well in forecasting a number of macroeconomic and financial variables and should be used as a benchmark or as a starting point for further investigations.

The alternative is to estimate ϕ by using the information contained in the data. In this case, the marginal likelihood $f(\phi \mid y) = \int \mathcal{L}(\alpha \mid y, \phi) g(\alpha \mid \phi) \, d\alpha$, constructed on a training sample $(-\tau, \ldots, 0)$, could be used. The next example shows how to do this in a simple model.

Example 10.2. Suppose $y_t = Ax_t + e_t$, where A is a random scalar and $e_t \sim$ i.i.d. $\mathbb{N}(0, \sigma_e^2)$, σ_e^2 known, and let $A = \bar{A} + v_a$, $v_a \sim$ i.i.d. $\mathbb{N}(0, \bar{\sigma}_a^2)$, $\bar{A}$ is fixed and $\bar{\sigma}_a^2 = h(\phi)^2$, where ϕ is a vector of hyperparameters. Then $y_t = \bar{A}x_t + \epsilon_t$, where $\epsilon_t = e_t + v_a x_t$, and the posterior kernel is

$$\breve{g}(\alpha, \phi \mid y) = \frac{1}{\sqrt{2\pi}\sigma_e h(\phi)} \exp\left\{-0.5\frac{(y - Ax)^2}{\sigma_e^2} - 0.5\frac{(A - \bar{A})^2}{h(\phi)^2}\right\}, \quad (10.13)$$

where $y = [y_1, \ldots, y_t]'$, $x = [x_1, \ldots, x_t]'$. Integrating (10.13) with respect to A we obtain

$$f(\phi \mid y) = \frac{1}{\sqrt{2\pi h(\phi)^2 \operatorname{tr}|x'x| + \sigma_e^2}} \exp\left\{-0.5\frac{(y - \bar{A}x)^2}{\sigma_e^2 + h(\phi)^2 \operatorname{tr}|x'x|}\right\}, \quad (10.14)$$

which can be constructed and maximized by using the prediction error decomposition of $f(\phi \mid y)$ generated by the Kalman filter.

While A is a scalar in example 10.2, the same logic applies when α is a vector.

Exercise 10.5. Let $y_t = A(\ell)y_{t-1} + e_t$, $e_t \sim$ i.i.d. $\mathbb{N}(0, \Sigma_e)$, Σ_e known, let $\alpha = \operatorname{vec}(A_1, \ldots, A_q)' = \bar{\alpha} + v_a$, $\bar{\alpha}$ known, and $\bar{\Sigma}_a = h(\phi)^2$. Show $f(\phi \mid y)$ and its prediction error decomposition.

Exercise 10.6. Suppose in example 10.2 that $\bar{A} = h_1(\phi)$ and $\bar{\Sigma}_a = h_2(\phi)$. Derive the first-order conditions for the optimal ϕ. Describe how to numerically find ML-II estimates of ϕ.

We summarize the features of the posterior distribution of α and Σ_e obtained with the other prior specifications in the next three exercises (see Kadiyala and Karlsson (1997) for details).

Exercise 10.7. Suppose that $g(\alpha, \Sigma_e^{-1}) \propto |\Sigma_e^{-1}|^{0.5(m+1)}$. Show that $g(\alpha \mid \Sigma_e, y) \sim \mathbb{N}(\alpha_{\text{OLS}}, (\Sigma_e^{-1} \otimes X'X)^{-1})$, $g(\Sigma_e^{-1} \mid y) \sim \mathbb{W}([(y - (I \otimes X)\alpha_{\text{OLS}})' \times (y - (I \otimes X)\alpha_{\text{OLS}})]^{-1}, T - k)$, and that $(\alpha \mid y)$ has a t-distribution with parameters $((I \otimes X)'(I \otimes X), (y - (I \otimes X)\alpha_{\text{OLS}})'(y - (I \otimes X)\alpha_{\text{OLS}}), \alpha_{\text{OLS}}, T - k)$, where α_{OLS} is the OLS estimator of α. Conclude that, *a posteriori*, the elements of α are dependent. (Hint: look at the variance of α.)

Exercise 10.8. Suppose that the joint prior for (α, Σ_e^{-1}) is normal-diffuse, i.e., $g(\alpha) \sim \mathbb{N}(\bar{\alpha}, \bar{\Sigma}_a)$, where both $\bar{\alpha}$ and $\bar{\Sigma}_a$ are known and $g(\Sigma_e) \propto |\Sigma_e^{-1}|^{0.5(m+1)}$. Show the form of $g(\alpha \mid y)$. Argue that there is posterior dependence among equations, even when $\bar{\Sigma}_a$ is diagonal.

Exercise 10.9. Let $g(\alpha \mid \Sigma_e) \sim \mathbb{N}(\bar{\alpha}, \Sigma_e \otimes \bar{\Omega})$ and $g(\Sigma_e^{-1}) \sim \mathbb{W}(\bar{\Sigma}_e, \bar{\nu})$. Show that $g(\alpha \mid \Sigma_e, y) \sim \mathbb{N}(\tilde{\alpha}, \Sigma_e \otimes \tilde{\Omega})$, $g(\Sigma_e^{-1} \mid y) \sim \mathbb{W}(\tilde{\Sigma}_e, T + \bar{\nu})$. Give the form of $\tilde{\alpha}$, $\tilde{\Omega}$, and $\tilde{\Sigma}_e$. Show that $(\alpha \mid y)$ has a t-distribution with parameters $(\tilde{\Omega}^{-1}, \tilde{\Sigma}_e, \tilde{\alpha}, T + \bar{\nu})$. Show that there is posterior dependence among the equations.

10.2.3 Adding Other Prior Restrictions

We can add a number of other statistical restrictions to the standard Minnesota prior without altering the form of the posterior moments. For example, an investigator may be interested in studying the dynamics at seasonal frequencies and therefore want to use seasonal information to set up prior restrictions. The simplest way to deal with seasonality is to include a set of dummies in the VAR and treat their coefficients in the same way as the coefficients of the exogenous variables.

Example 10.3. In quarterly data, a prior for a bivariate VAR(2) with four seasonal dummies has mean equal to $\bar{\alpha} = [1, 0, 0, 0, 0, 0, 0, 0 \mid 0, 1, 0, 0, 0, 0, 0, 0]$ and the block of Σ_a corresponding to the seasonal dummies has diagonal elements, $\sigma_{\text{dd}} = \phi_0 \phi_{\text{s}}$. Here ϕ_{s} represents the tightness of the seasonal information (and a large ϕ_{s} implies little prior information).

Seasonality, however, is hardly deterministic (if it were, it would be easy to eliminate if we did not want it) and seasonal dummies only roughly account for seasonal variations. As an alternative, note that a series is seasonal if it displays a peak (or a wide mass) in the spectrum at some or all seasonal frequencies. For a peak at frequency ω_0 to exist, it must be the case that, in the model $y_t = D(\ell)e_t$, $|D(\omega_0)|^2$ is large. A large $|D(\omega_0)|^2$ implies that $|A(\omega_0)|^2$ should be small, where $A(\ell) = D(\ell)^{-1}$, which in turns implies $\sum_{j=1}^{\infty} A_j \cos(\omega_0 j) \approx -1$.

Example 10.4. In quarterly data, $\omega_0 = \frac{1}{2}\pi, \pi$ (the frequencies corresponding to cycles of four and two quarters) and a peak at, say, $\frac{1}{2}\pi$ implies that $-A_2 + A_4 - A_6 + A_8 + \cdots$ must be close to -1.

The same idea applies to multivariate models. Omitting constants, the MA representation for y_t is $y_t = D(\ell)e_t$ and its spectral density is $\mathcal{S}_y(\omega) = |D(\omega)|^2 \Sigma_e / 2\pi$. Since $D(\omega) = \sum_j D_j(\cos(\omega j) + \mathrm{i}\sin(\omega j))$, a peak in $\mathcal{S}_y(\omega)$ at $\omega = \omega_0$ implies that $\sum_j D_j \cos(\omega_0 j)$ is large and $\sum_{j=1}^{\infty} A_j \cos(\omega_0 j) \approx -1$.

We can cast these restrictions in the form $R\alpha = r + v_a$, where $r = [-1, \dots, -1]'$, R is an $m_1 \times mk$ matrix, and m_1 is the number of seasonal frequencies. In quarterly data, if the first variable of the VAR displays seasonality at both $\frac{1}{2}\pi, \pi$, then

$$R = \begin{bmatrix} 0 & -1 & 0 & 1 & 0 & -1 & \cdots & 0 \\ -1 & 1 & -1 & 1 & -1 & 1 & \cdots & 0 \end{bmatrix}.$$

These restrictions can be added to those of the original (Minnesota) prior and combined with the data following the logic of Theil's mixed-type estimation, once Σ_{v_a} is selected. The same approach can also be used to account for the presence of peaks in other parts of the spectrum, as shown in the next exercise.

Exercise 10.10 (Canova). (i) Show that a peak in the spectral density at frequency zero in variable i implies $\sum_{j=1}^{\infty} A_{ji} \approx -1$.

(ii) Show that, if variable i displays a large mass over the band $[\omega_1, \omega_2]$, then $\sum_{j=1}^{\infty} A_{ji} \cos(\omega_0 j) \approx -1$, for all ω_0 in the band.

(iii) Show that a high coherence at $\omega_0 = \frac{1}{2}\pi$ in series i and i' of a VAR implies that $\sum_{j=1}^{\infty}(-1)^j A_{i'i'(2j)} + \sum_{j=1}^{\infty}(-1)^j A_{ii(2j)} \approx -2$.

Cast the constraints in (i), (ii), and (iii) in the form of an uncertain linear restriction.

Other types of probabilistic constraints can be imposed in a similar way. As long as r, R, and $\text{var}(v_a)$ are fixed, combining prior and sample information presents no conceptual difficulty: the dimensionalities of R and r change, but the form of the posterior moments of α is unchanged.

10.2.4 Some Applied Tips

There are few practical issues a researcher faces in setting up a Minnesota prior for a VAR. First, in simple applications one typically uses default values for the hyperparameters ϕ. While this is a good starting point, it is not clear that this choice is appropriate in all forecasting situations or when structural inference is required. Hence, sensitivity analysis is needed to provide information about interesting local derivatives, for example, how much the MSE of the forecasts changes when ϕ varies. If differences are large, should hyperparameters be chosen to get the best out-of-sample performance? Since hyperparameters describe features of the prior, they should be chosen by using the marginal likelihood. Using *ex post* MSE statistics poses few operational problems. Which forecasting horizon should be chosen to select the hyperparameters? If different horizons require different hyperparameters, how should one proceed? The use of the marginal likelihood provides a natural answer to these questions. Since marginal likelihoods can be decomposed into the product of one-step-ahead prediction errors, hyperparameters chosen by optimizing the marginal likelihood in the training sample minimize the one-step-ahead prediction error in that sample.

Second, in certain applications the default values of the Minnesota prior are clearly inappropriate: for example, a mean of 1 for the first lag of a variable in growth rates is unlikely to be useful. In others, one may want to have additional parameters controlling the relative importance of certain variables in one equation or across equations. For example, one would expect lags of other variables to be less important when there is a financial variable on the left-hand side of an equation, but very important when there is a macroeconomic variable. These alterations of the Minnesota prior do not change the form of the posterior so long as $\bar{\Sigma}_a$ is diagonal and Σ_e is fixed.

Although the emphasis of this section has been on case 1 priors, all the arguments made remain valid when a general normal-Wishart prior is used. Conditional on Σ_e, the posterior for α is still normal. However, in this case, equation-by-equation computations are inefficient. For VARs with five or six variables and four or five lags, system-wide calculations are not computationally demanding, given existing computer technology. For larger-scale models such as the one of Leeper et al. (1996), careful choices for the prior may dramatically simplify the computations.

How does one select the variables to be included in a BVAR? Using the same logic described in chapter 9, specifications with different variables can be treated as

Table 10.1. One-year-ahead Theil-U statistics.

Sample	ARIMA	VAR	BVAR1	BVAR2
1996:1–2000:4	1.04	1.47	1.09 (0.03)	0.97 (0.02)
1990:1–1995:4	0.99	1.24	1.04 (0.04)	0.94 (0.03)

different models. Therefore, a posterior odds ratio or the Leamer's version of it can be used to select the specification that best fits the data in a training sample. Such calculations can be performed both for nested and nonnested models.

Example 10.5 (forecasting inflation). We use a BVAR with a Minnesota prior to forecast inflation rates in Italy. The features of inflation rates have changed dramatically in the 1990s all over the world and in Italy in particular. In fact, while the autocovariance function displays remarkable persistence in the 1980s (AR(1) coefficient equals 0.85), it decays pretty quickly in the 1990s (AR(1) coefficient equals 0.48). In this situation, using data from the 1980s to choose a model or its hyperparameters may severely impair its ability to forecast in the 1990s. As a benchmark for comparison we use a univariate ARIMA model, chosen by using standard Box–Jenkins methods, and a three-variable unrestricted VAR, including the annualized three-month inflation, the unemployment rate, and the annualized three-month rent inflation, each with four lags. These variables were chosen from among a set of ten candidates by using Leamer's posterior odds ratio approach. We present results for two alternative specifications: a BVAR with fixed hyperparameters and one with hyperparameters chosen to maximize the marginal likelihood for the sample 1980:1–1995:4. The prior variance is characterized by a general tightness parameter, a decay parameter, and a parameter for lags of other variables. In the first case they are set to 0.2, 1, 0.5, respectively. In the second, their point estimates are 0.14, 2.06, 1.03. The prior variance on the constant is diffuse. Table 10.1 reports one-year-ahead Theil-U statistics (the ratio of the MSE of the model to the MSE of a random walk) for the four specifications. Posterior standard error for the two BVAR are in parentheses.

Three features deserve comment. First, forecasting Italian inflation one year ahead is difficult: all models have a hard time beating a random walk and three of them do worse. Second, an unrestricted VAR performs poorly. Third, a BVAR with default choices is superior to an unrestricted VAR but hardly better than an ARIMA model. Finally, a BVAR with optimally chosen parameters outperforms both random walk and ARIMA models at the one-year horizon but the gains are small. The results are robust: repeating the exercise by using data from 1980:1 to 1989:4 to choose the variables and the hyperparameters and estimate the models with data from 1991:1 to 1995:4 to forecast produces qualitatively similar Theil-Us.

10.2.5 Priors Derived from DSGE Models

The priors considered so far are either statistically motivated or are based on rules-of-thumb useful for forecasting macroeconomic time series. In both cases, economic theory plays no role, except perhaps in establishing the range of values for the prior. To be able to use BVARs for purposes other than forecasting, one may want to consider priors based on economic theory. In addition, one may be interested in knowing if theory-based priors are as good as statistically based priors in forecasting, unconditionally, out-of-sample.

Here we consider priors which are derived from DSGE models. The nature of the model and the prior for the structural parameters imply a prior for the reduced-form VAR coefficients. One can dogmatically take these restrictions or simply consider their qualitative content in constructing posterior distributions. In this setup prior information measures the confidence a researcher has that the DSGE structure has generated the observed data.

An alternative representation for the log-linearized solution of a DSGE model is

$$y_{2t+1} = \mathcal{A}_{22}(\theta) y_{2t} + \mathcal{A}_{23}(\theta) y_{3t+1}, \tag{10.15}$$

$$y_{1t} = \mathcal{A}_{12}(\theta) y_{2t}, \tag{10.16}$$

where y_{2t} is an $m_2 \times 1$ vector including the states and the driving forces, y_{1t} is an $m_1 \times 1$ vector including all the endogenous variables, and y_{3t+1} are the shocks. Here $\mathcal{A}_{jj'}(\theta)$ are time-invariant functions of θ, the vector of preferences, technologies, and policy parameters of the model. It is easy to transform (10.15), (10.16) into a (restricted) VAR(1) for $y_t = [y_{1t}, y_{2t}]'$ of the form

$$\begin{bmatrix} 0 & 0 \\ 0 & I_{m_2} \end{bmatrix} y_{t+1} = \begin{bmatrix} -I_{m_1} & \mathcal{A}_{12}(\theta) \\ 0 & \mathcal{A}_{22}(\theta) \end{bmatrix} y_t + \begin{bmatrix} 0 \\ \mathcal{A}_{23}(\theta) \end{bmatrix} y_{3t+1}, \tag{10.17}$$

or $\mathcal{A}_0 y_{t+1} = \mathcal{A}_1(\theta) y_t + \epsilon_{t+1}(\theta)$. Hence, given a prior for θ, the model implies a prior for $\mathcal{A}_{12}(\theta)$, $\mathcal{A}_{22}(\theta)$, $\mathcal{A}_{23}(\theta)$. In turn, these priors imply restrictions for the reduced-form parameters $A(\ell) = \mathcal{A}_0^{-1}\mathcal{A}_1(\ell)$ and $\Sigma_e = \mathcal{A}_0^{-1}\Sigma_\epsilon \mathcal{A}_0^{-1}$. Expressions for the priors for $\mathcal{A}_{12}(\theta)$, $\mathcal{A}_{22}(\theta)$, $\mathcal{A}_{23}(\theta)$ can be obtained by using δ-approximations, i.e., if $\theta \sim \mathbb{N}(\bar{\theta}, \bar{\Sigma}_\theta)$, $\text{vec}(\mathcal{A}_{12}(\theta)) \sim \mathbb{N}(\text{vec}(\mathcal{A}_{12}(\bar{\theta}))$, $[\partial \text{vec}(A_{12}(\theta))/\partial\theta']\bar{\Sigma}_\theta[\partial \text{vec}(A_{12}(\theta))/\partial\theta']')$, etc.

Example 10.6. Consider the VAR(q): $y_{t+1} = A(\ell)y_t + e_t$. From (10.17) the prior for A_1 is normal with mean $\mathcal{A}_0^{\text{G}}\mathcal{A}_1(\bar{\theta})$, where $\mathcal{A}_0^{\text{G}}$ is the generalized inverse of $\mathcal{A}_0$, and variance $\Sigma_a = (A_0^{\text{G}} \otimes I_{m_1+m_2})\Sigma_{a_1}(A_0^{\text{G}} \otimes I_{m_1+m_2})'$, where Σ_{a_1} is the variance of $\text{vec}(\mathcal{A}_1(\theta))$. A DSGE prior for $A_2, A_3, \dots, A_q$ has a dogmatic form: mean zero and zero variance.

Since the states of a DSGE model typically include unobservable variables (e.g., the Lagrangian multiplier or the driving forces of the model) or variables typically reconstructed by researchers (e.g., the capital stock), it may be more convenient to set up prior restrictions for VARs which include only observable variables, as the next example shows.

Example 10.7 (Ingram and Whiteman). An RBC model with utility function $u(c_t, c_{t-1}, N_t, N_{t-1}) = \ln(c_t) + \ln(1 - N_t)$ implies a log-linearized law of motion for the states of the form

$$\begin{bmatrix} K_{t+1} \\ \zeta_{t+1} \end{bmatrix} = \begin{bmatrix} \mathcal{A}_{kk}(\theta) & \mathcal{A}_{k\zeta}(\theta) \\ 0 & \rho_\zeta \end{bmatrix} \begin{bmatrix} K_t \\ \zeta_t \end{bmatrix} + \begin{bmatrix} 0 \\ \epsilon_{1t+1} \end{bmatrix} \equiv \mathcal{A}_{22}(\theta) \begin{bmatrix} K_t \\ \zeta_t \end{bmatrix} + \epsilon_{t+1}, \tag{10.18}$$

where K_t is the capital stock and ζ_t is a technological disturbance. The equilibrium mapping between the endogenous variables and the states is

$$\begin{bmatrix} c_t \\ N_t \\ \text{gdp}_t \\ \text{inv}_t \end{bmatrix} = \mathcal{A}_{12}(\theta) \begin{bmatrix} K_t \\ \zeta_t \end{bmatrix}, \tag{10.19}$$

where c_t is consumption, N_t hours, gdp_t output, and inv_t investments. Here $\mathcal{A}_{12}(\theta)$ and $\mathcal{A}_{22}(\theta)$ are functions of η, the share of labor in production, β the discount factor, δ the depreciation rate, and ρ_ζ the AR parameter of the technology shock. Let $y_{1t} = [c_t, N_t, \text{gdp}_t, \text{inv}_t]'$, $y_{2t} = [K_t, \zeta_t]'$, $\theta = (\eta, \beta, \delta, \rho_\zeta)$. Then $y_{1t} = A(\theta) y_{1t-1} + e_{1t}$, where $A(\theta) = \mathcal{A}_{12}(\theta)\mathcal{A}_{22}(\theta)[\mathcal{A}_{12}(\theta)'\mathcal{A}_{12}(\theta)]^{-1}\mathcal{A}_{12}(\theta)$, $e_{1t} = \mathcal{A}_{12}(\theta)\epsilon_t$, and $[\mathcal{A}_{12}(\theta)'\mathcal{A}_{12}(\theta)]^{-1}\mathcal{A}_{12}(\theta)$ is the generalized inverse of $\mathcal{A}_{12}(\theta)$. If *a priori*

$$\theta \sim \mathbb{N}\left(\begin{bmatrix} 0.58 \\ 0.988 \\ 0.025 \\ 0.95 \end{bmatrix}, \begin{bmatrix} 0.0006 & & & \\ & 0.0005 & & \\ & & 0.0004 & \\ & & & 0.00015 \end{bmatrix} \right),$$

the prior mean of $A(\theta)$ is

$$A(\bar{\theta}) = \begin{bmatrix} 0.19 & 0.33 & 0.13 & -0.02 \\ 0.45 & 0.67 & 0.29 & -0.10 \\ 0.49 & 1.32 & 0.40 & 0.17 \\ 1.35 & 4.00 & 1.18 & 0.64 \end{bmatrix},$$

which implies, for example, substantial feedbacks from consumption, output, and hours to investment (see the last row). The prior variance for $A(\theta)$ is $\Sigma_A = (\partial A(\theta)/\partial\theta')\bar{\Sigma}_\theta(\partial A(\theta)/\partial\theta')'$, where $\partial A(\theta)/\partial\theta'$ is a 16×4 vector. Hence, an RBC prior for y_{1t} implies a normal prior on the first VAR lag with mean $A(\bar{\theta})$ and variance proportional to Σ_A. To relax the dogmatic prior on higher lags, we could assume a normal prior with zero mean and variance proportional to $\Sigma_A/h(\ell)$, where $h(\ell)$ is an increasing function of ℓ.

Exercise 10.11 (RBC cointegrating prior). In example 10.7 suppose that ζ_t has a unit root. Then all variables except hours are nonstationary and the stochastic trend is a common one.

(i) Argue that $(I - \mathcal{A}_{kk}(\theta), -\mathcal{A}_{k\zeta}(\theta))$ must be a cointegrating vector for K_t.

(ii) Argue that $(I_4, -\mathcal{A}_{12}(\theta))$ must be a cointegrating vector for y_{1t}.

(iii) Given a normal prior on θ, derive a cointegrating prior for the $\mathcal{A}$'s.

Exercise 10.12. Suppose a representative agent maximizes $u(c_t, c_{t-1}, N_t) = \ln c_t - \epsilon_{2t} \ln N_t$ subject to the constraint $c_t + B_{t+1} \leqslant \text{GDP}_t + (1 + r_t^{\text{B}})B_t - T_t$, where $\text{GDP}_t = N_t \epsilon_{1t}$, ϵ_{1t} is a technology shock with mean $\bar{\epsilon}_1$ and variance $\sigma^2_{\epsilon_1}$, ϵ_{2t} is a labor supply shock with mean $\bar{\epsilon}_2$ and variance $\sigma^2_{\epsilon_2}$. Here T_t are lump sum taxes, B_t are real bonds, and the government finances a random stream of expenditure by using lump sum taxes and real bonds according to the budget constraint $G_t - T_t = B_{t+1} - (1 + r_t^{\text{B}})B_t$. In this model there are three shocks: two supply-type shocks $(\epsilon_{1t}, \epsilon_{2t})$ and one demand-type shock (G_t).

(i) Find a log-linearized solution for N_t, GDP_t, c_t, and labor productivity (np_t).

(ii) Use the results in (i) to construct a prior for a bivariate VAR in hours and output. Derive the posterior distribution for the VAR parameters and the covariance matrix of the shocks. Be precise about the assumptions and the choices you make (careful: there are three shocks and two variables). Would it have made a difference if you had used a trivariate model with consumption or labor productivity?

(iii) Describe how to construct impulse responses to G_t shocks by using posterior estimates.

(iv) Suppose that, for identification purposes, an investigator makes the assumption that demand shocks have zero contemporaneous effect on hours. Is this assumption reasonable in the logic of the model? Under what conditions do the estimated demand shocks you recover from posterior analysis correctly represent G_t shocks?

Del Negro and Schorfheide (2004) have suggested an alternative way to append theory-based priors onto a VAR. The advantage of their approach is that the posterior distributions for both VAR and DSGE parameters can be simultaneously obtained. Their basic specification differs from the one so far described in an important way. Until now DSGE models have provided only the "form" of the prior restrictions (zero mean on lags greater than one, etc.). Here the prior is tightly based on the data produced by the DSGE model.

The logic of the approach is simple. Since the prior can be thought of as an additional observation tacked on to the VAR, one way to add DSGE information is to augment the VAR for the actual data with a prior based on the data simulated from the model. The proportion of actual and simulated data points will then reflect the relative importance that a researcher gives to the two types of information.

Let the data be represented by a VAR with parameters (α, Σ_e). Assume that $g(\alpha, \Sigma_e)$ is of the form $\alpha \sim \mathbb{N}(\bar{\alpha}(\theta), \bar{\Sigma}(\theta))$, $\Sigma_e \sim \mathbb{IW}(T_{\text{s}}\bar{\Sigma}_e(\theta), T_{\text{s}} - k)$, where

$$\left.\begin{aligned} \bar{\alpha}(\theta) &= [(X^{\text{s}})'X^{\text{s}}]^{-1}[(X^{\text{s}})'y^{\text{s}}], \\ \bar{\Sigma}(\theta) &= \Sigma_e(\theta) \otimes [(X^{\text{s}})'X^{\text{s}}]^{-1}, \\ \bar{\Sigma}_e(\theta) &= [y^{\text{s}} - X^{\text{s}}\bar{\alpha}(\theta)][y^{\text{s}} - X^{\text{s}}\bar{\alpha}(\theta)]'. \end{aligned}\right\} \tag{10.20}$$

Here y^{s} is data simulated from the DSGE model, $X^{\text{s}} = (I_m \otimes X^{\text{s}})$ is a matrix of lags in the VAR representation of simulated data, and θ are the structural parameters. In (10.20), the moments of $g(\alpha, \Sigma_e)$ depend on θ through the simulated data $(y^{\text{s}}, X^{\text{s}})$.

If T_s is the length of simulated data, $\kappa = T_s/T$ controls the relative informational content of actual and simulated data.

The model has a hierarchical structure $f(\alpha, \Sigma_e \mid y)g(\alpha \mid \theta)g(\Sigma_e \mid \theta)g(\theta)$. Conditional on θ, the posteriors for α, Σ_e are easily derived. In fact, since the likelihood and the prior are conjugate, $(\alpha \mid \theta, y, \Sigma_e) \sim \mathbb{N}(\tilde{\alpha}(\theta), \tilde{\Sigma}(\theta))$, and $(\Sigma_e \mid \theta, y) \sim \mathbb{IW}((\kappa + T)\tilde{\Sigma}_e(\theta), T + \kappa - k)$, where

$$\left.\begin{aligned}
\tilde{\alpha}(\theta) &= \left(\kappa\frac{(X^s)'X^s}{T^s} + \frac{X'X}{T}\right)^{-1}\left(\kappa\frac{(X^s)'y^s}{T^s} + \frac{X'y}{T}\right),\\
\tilde{\Sigma}(\theta) &= \Sigma_e(\theta) \otimes [(X^s)'X^s + X'X]^{-1},\\
\tilde{\Sigma}_e(\theta) &= \frac{1}{(1+\kappa)T}\{[(y^s)'y^s + y'y]\\
&\qquad - [(y^s)'X^s + y'X][(X^s)'X^s + X'X]^{-1}[(X^s)'y^s + X'y]\},
\end{aligned}\right\} \tag{10.21}$$

and $X = (I \otimes X)$. The posterior for θ can be computed by using the hierarchical structure of the model. In fact, $g(\theta \mid y) \propto f(\alpha, \Sigma_e, y \mid \theta)g(\theta)$, where $f(\alpha, \Sigma_e, y \mid \theta) \propto |\Sigma_e|^{-0.5(T-m-1)} \exp\{-0.5\,\mathrm{tr}[\Sigma_e^{-1}(y - X\alpha)'(y - X\alpha)]\} \times |\tilde{\Sigma}_e(\theta)|^{-0.5(T_s-m-1)} \exp\{-0.5\,\mathrm{tr}[\Sigma_e^{-1}(y^s - X^s\tilde{\alpha}(\theta))'(y^s - X^s\tilde{\alpha}(\theta))]\}$. We will discuss how to draw from this posterior in chapter 11.

Exercise 10.13. Use the fact that $g(\alpha, \Sigma_e, \theta \mid y) = g(\alpha, \Sigma_e \mid y, \theta)g(\theta \mid y)$ to suggest an algorithm to draw posterior sequences for (α, Σ_e). How would you compute impulse responses?

Exercise 10.14. Suppose $g(\Sigma_e)$ is noninformative. Show the form of $(\tilde{\alpha}(\theta), \tilde{\Sigma}_e(\theta))$ in this case.

All posterior moments in (10.21) are conditional on κ. Since this parameter regulates the relative importance of sample and prior information, it is important to appropriately select it. As in standard BVARs, there are two ways to proceed. First, we can arbitrarily set it, e.g., $\kappa = 1$, meaning that T simulated data are added to the actual data. Second, we can choose it to maximize the marginal likelihood of the model.

Exercise 10.15. Show the form of $f(y \mid \kappa)$. Describe how to find its maximum numerically.

Note that the optimal κ can be implicitly used to test the quality of the model. In fact, if κ is small, the data produced by the model has little use in the posterior, while, if κ is large, the opposite is true. This is, for example, the approach used by Del Negro et al. (2005) to verify the quality of current state-of-the-art models.

Example 10.8. We simulate data from the sticky price, sticky wage economy described in example 2.19. We set $\eta = 0.66$, $\pi^{ss} = 1.005$, $N^{ss} = 0.33$, $\beta = 0.99$, $c^{ss}/\mathrm{GDP}^{ss} = 0.8$, $\zeta_p = \zeta_w = 0.75$, $a_0 = 0$, $a_1 = 0.5$, $a_2 = -1.0$, $a_3 = 0.1$, where η is the share of labor in production, π^{ss} is the steady-state inflation, N^{ss} the

Table 10.2. Marginal likelihood, sticky price, sticky wage model.

$\kappa = 0$	$\kappa = 0.1$	$\kappa = 0.25$	$\kappa = 0.5$	$\kappa = 1$	$\kappa = 2$
−1228.08	−828.51	−693.49	−709.13	−913.51	−1424.61

steady-state share of time devoted to market activities, β the discount factor, ζ_{p} and ζ_{w} the degrees of price and wage stickiness, and a_0, a_1, a_2, a_3 the parameters of the monetary policy rule. We run a VAR with output, interest rates, and inflation by using actual quarterly data from 1973:1 to 1993:4 and use the model to construct quantities like $(X^{\mathrm{s}})'X^{\mathrm{s}}$ and $(X^{\mathrm{s}})'y^{\mathrm{s}}$. Table 10.2 reports the value of the resulting marginal likelihood when different values of κ are used. Overall, it appears that the model is far from the process generating the data and only a modest amount of simulated data (roughly 20 data points) should be used to set up a prior.

Exercise 10.16. Simulate data from the working-capital model described in exercise 2.14 when there are shocks to technology, government expenditure, and the monetary policy rule. Choose appropriate priors for the parameters (for example, a beta density for parameters that lie in an interval). Simulate data for output, inflation, and the nominal interest rate. Explore the marginal likelihood of inflation numerically for different values of κ, integrating out the parameters of the model. How would you compare such a model against a sticky price, sticky wage model of example 10.8?

10.2.6 Probability Distributions for Forecasts: Fan Charts

BVAR models can be used to construct probability distributions for future events and therefore are well-suited to produce, for example, fan charts or probabilities of turning points. To see how this can be done, set $\bar{y} = 0$ and rewrite the VAR model in a companion form,

$$\mathbb{Y}_t = \mathbb{A}\mathbb{Y}_{t-1} + \mathbb{E}_t, \tag{10.22}$$

where $\mathbb{Y}_t$ and $\mathbb{E}_t$ are $mq \times 1$ vectors, and $\mathbb{A}$ is an $mq \times mq$ matrix.

Repeatedly substituting, we have $\mathbb{Y}_t = \mathbb{A}^{\tau}\mathbb{Y}_{t-\tau} + \sum_{j=0}^{\tau-1} \mathbb{A}^j \mathbb{E}_{t-j}$. This can also be written as $y_t = \mathbb{S}\mathbb{A}^{\tau}\mathbb{Y}_{t-\tau} + \sum_{j=0}^{\tau-1} \mathbb{A}^j e_{t-j}$, where $\mathbb{S}$ is such that $\mathbb{S}\mathbb{Y}_t = y_t$, $\mathbb{S}\mathbb{E}_t = e_t$, and $\mathbb{S}'\mathbb{S}E_t = E_t$. A "point" forecast for $y_{t+\tau}$ is obtained by substituting some location measures of the posterior of $\mathbb{A}$ into $y_t(\tau) = \mathbb{S}\mathbb{A}^{\tau}\mathbb{Y}_t$. Call this point forecast $\hat{y}_t(\tau)$. The forecast error is $y_{t+\tau} - \hat{y}_t(\tau) = \sum_{j=0}^{\tau-1} \mathbb{A}^j e_{t+\tau-j} + [y_t(\tau) - \hat{y}_t(\tau)]$ and the MSE of the forecasts can be computed once a posterior estimate of $\mathbb{A}$ is available. This is easy when $\tau = 1$. For $\tau \geqslant 2$ only approximate expressions for the MSE are available (see, for example, Lutkepohl 1991, p. 88).

Exercise 10.17. Show the MSE of the forecasts when $\tau = 1$.

When a distribution of forecasts is actually needed we can exploit the fact that we can draw from $g(\alpha \mid y)$. We describe how "fan charts" can be obtained for the case 1 prior. Let $\tilde{\mathcal{P}}\tilde{\mathcal{P}}'$ be any orthogonal factorization of Σ_e^{-1}. Then, at a given t, we have the following.

Algorithm 10.1.

(1) Draw v_a^l from a $\mathbb{N}(0,1)$ and set $\alpha^l = \tilde{\alpha} + \tilde{\mathcal{P}}^{-1}v_a^l$, $l = 1, \dots, L$.

(2) Construct point forecasts $y_t^l(\tau)$, $\tau = 1, 2, \dots$, by using the α^l produced in (1).

(3) Construct distributions at each τ by using kernel methods; extract percentiles.

Exercise 10.18. Consider the case 4 prior (i.e., a normal prior for α and a Wishart prior for Σ_e^{-1}). Modify algorithm 10.1 to fit this prior specification.

Algorithm 10.1 can also be used recursively. The only difference is that $\tilde{\alpha}$ and $\tilde{\mathcal{P}}$ now depend on t and are updated through the sample.

Example 10.9. Suppose one wants to compute an "average" forecast at step τ, i.e., to compute the predictive density $f(y_{t+\tau} \mid y_t) = \int f(y_{t+\tau} \mid y_t, \alpha) g(\alpha \mid y_t)\,\mathrm{d}\alpha$, where $f(y_{t+\tau} \mid y_t, \alpha)$ is the conditional density of $y_{t+\tau}$, given α and the model, and $g(\alpha \mid y_t)$ is the posterior of α at t. Given draws from algorithm 10.1, an estimate of this average is $\hat{y}_t(\tau) = L^{-1}\sum_{l=1}^{L} y_t^l(\tau)$ and its numerical variance is $L^{-1}\sum_{l=1}^{L}\sum_{j=-J(L)}^{J(L)} \mathcal{K}(j)\,\mathrm{ACF}_\tau^l(j)$, where $\mathcal{K}(j)$ is a kernel and $\mathrm{ACF}_\tau(j)$ is the autocovariance of $\hat{y}_t(\tau)$ at lag j.

Turning-point probabilities can also be computed from the numerically constructed predictive density of future observations. For example, given $y_t^l(\tau)$, $l = 1, \dots, L$, we only need to check whether, for example, a two-quarters rule is satisfied for each draw α^l. The fraction of draws for which the condition is satisfied is an estimate of the probability of the event at $t + \tau$.

Example 10.10. Continuing with example 10.5, figure 10.2(a) presents BVAR-based 68 and 95% bands for inflation forecasts one year ahead, when we recursively update posterior estimates. The forecasting sample is 1996:1–1998:2. The bands are relatively tight, reflecting very precise estimates. This precision can also be seen from part (b), which reports the density of the forecasts one year ahead obtained with data up to 1995:4. We calculate the distribution of the number of downturns that the annualized inflation rate is expected to experience over the sample 1996:1–2002:4. Downturns are identified with a two-quarters rule. In the actual data there are four downturns. The median number of forecasted downturns is three. Moreover, in 90% of the cases the model underpredicts the actual number of downturns and never produces more than four downturns.

10.3 Structural BVARs

The priors we specified in section 10.2 are designed for reduced-form VAR models. What kinds of prior are reasonable for structural VARs?

There are two approaches in the literature. A naive one, employed by Canova (1991) and Gordon and Leeper (1994), is to use a normal-Wishart structure for

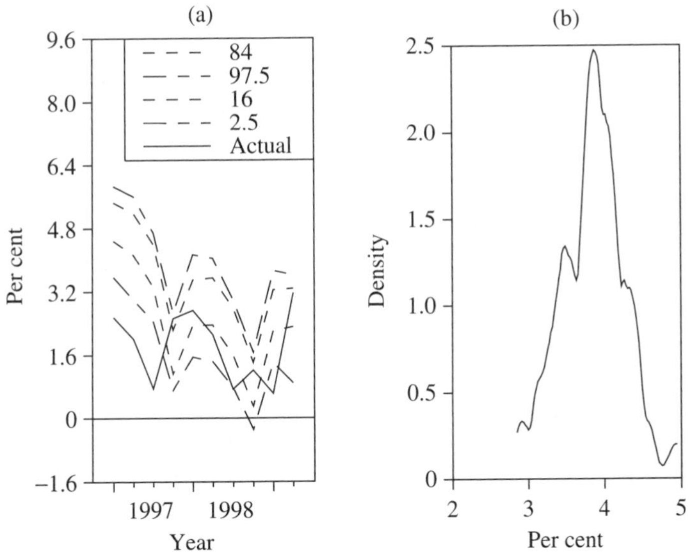

Figure 10.2. Forecasts of Italian inflation: (a) recursive forecasts; (b) data up to 1995:4.

reduced-form parameters (α, Σ_e). Then, draws for the structural parameters are made conditional on the identification restrictions. Hence, using the notation of chapter 4, if $(\Sigma_e^{-1})^l = (\mathcal{A}_0^{-1})^l D^{-1} (\mathcal{A}_0^{-1})^l$ is a draw for Σ_e^{-1}, then $(\mathcal{A}_0^{-1})^l A_j^l = (\mathcal{A}_j)^l$ are the draws for the structural parameters, where A_j^l is a draw for the VAR coefficients. This approach is appropriate if $\mathcal{A}_0$ is just identified since there is a unique mapping between draws of Σ_e and draws of $\mathcal{A}_0$. When $\mathcal{A}_0$ is overidentified this method neglects the (overidentifying) restrictions. In this case, it is better to work with the structural model and the prior suggested by Sims and Zha (1998). Consider the following structural model:

$$\mathcal{A}_0 y_t - \mathcal{A}(\ell) y_{t-1} - \mathcal{C}\bar{y}_t = \epsilon_t, \quad \epsilon_t \sim \text{i.i.d. } \mathbb{N}(0, I), \tag{10.23}$$

where $\mathcal{A}(\ell) = \mathcal{A}_1 + \cdots + \mathcal{A}_q \ell^{q-1}$, $|\mathcal{A}_0| \neq 0$, and $\bar{y}$ only includes deterministic variables.

Staking the t observations we have

$$\boldsymbol{Y}\mathcal{A}_0 - \boldsymbol{X}\mathcal{A}_- = \varepsilon, \tag{10.24}$$

where $\boldsymbol{Y}$ is a $T \times m$ matrix, $\boldsymbol{X}$ is a $T \times k$ matrix of lagged and exogenous variables, $k = mq + m_c$, and ε is a $T \times m$ matrix. Let $\boldsymbol{Z} = [\boldsymbol{Y}, -\boldsymbol{X}]$ and $\mathcal{A} = [\mathcal{A}_0, \mathcal{A}_-]'$. The likelihood function is

$$\begin{aligned} L(\mathcal{A} \mid y) &\propto |\mathcal{A}_0|^T \exp\{-0.5 \operatorname{tr}(\boldsymbol{Z}\mathcal{A})'(\boldsymbol{Z}\mathcal{A})\} \\ &= |\mathcal{A}_0|^T \exp\{-0.5 b'(I_{mk} \otimes \boldsymbol{Z}'\boldsymbol{Z})b\}, \end{aligned} \tag{10.25}$$

where $b = \operatorname{vec}(\mathcal{A})$ is an $m(k+m) \times 1$ vector, $b_0 = \operatorname{vec}(\mathcal{A}_0)$ is an $m^2 \times 1$ vector, $b_- = \operatorname{vec}(\mathcal{A}_-)$ is an $mk \times 1$ vector, and I_{mk} is an $(mk \times mk)$ identity matrix.

Suppose $g(b) = g(b_0)g(b_- \mid b_0)$, where $g(b_0)$ may have singularities (due to zero identification restrictions) and let $g(b_- \mid b_0) \sim \mathbb{N}(\bar{h}(b_0), \bar{\Sigma}(b_0))$. Then

$$g(b \mid y) \propto |\mathcal{A}_0|^T \exp\{-0.5b'(I_{mk} \otimes \boldsymbol{Z}'\boldsymbol{Z})b\}|\Sigma(b_0)|^{-0.5} \times \exp\{-0.5[b_- - \bar{h}(b_0)]'\bar{\Sigma}(b_0)^{-1}[b_- - \bar{h}(b_0)]\}g(b_0). \quad (10.26)$$

Since $b'(I_{mk} \otimes \boldsymbol{Z}'\boldsymbol{Z})b = b_0'(I_{mk} \otimes \boldsymbol{Y}'\boldsymbol{Y})b_0 + b_-'(I_{nk} \otimes \boldsymbol{X}'\boldsymbol{X})b_- - 2b_-'(I_{mk} \otimes \boldsymbol{X}'\boldsymbol{Y})b_0$, conditional on b_0, the quantity in the exponent in (10.26) is quadratic in b_- so that $g(b_- \mid b_0, y) \sim \mathbb{N}(\tilde{h}(b_0), \tilde{\Sigma}(b_0))$, where the posterior mean is $\tilde{h}(b_0) = \tilde{\Sigma}(b_0)[(I_{mk} \otimes \boldsymbol{X}'\boldsymbol{Y})\hat{h}(b_0) + \bar{\Sigma}(b_0)^{-1}\bar{h}(b_0)]$ and the posterior variance is $\tilde{\Sigma}(b_0) = [(I \otimes \boldsymbol{X}'\boldsymbol{X}) + \bar{\Sigma}(b_0)^{-1}]^{-1}$. Furthermore,

$$g(b_0 \mid y) \propto g(b_0)|\mathcal{A}_0|^T |(I_{mk} \otimes \boldsymbol{X}'\boldsymbol{X})\bar{\Sigma}(b_0) + I|^{-0.5} \times \exp\{-0.5[b_0'(I_{mk} \otimes \boldsymbol{Y}'\boldsymbol{Y})b_0 + h(b_0)'\bar{\Sigma}(b_0)^{-1}h(b_0) - \tilde{h}(b_0)\tilde{\Sigma}(b_0)\tilde{h}(b_0)]\}. \quad (10.27)$$

Since $\dim(b_-) = mk$, the calculation of $g(b_- \mid b_0, y)$ may be time-consuming. Equation-by-equation computations are possible if the structural model is in SUR format, i.e., if we can run m separate least squares regressions with k parameters each. To do this we need to choose $\bar{\Sigma}(b_0)$ appropriately. For example, if $\bar{\Sigma}(b_0) = \bar{\Sigma}_1 \otimes \bar{\Sigma}_2$ and $\bar{\Sigma}_1 \propto I$, then, even if $\bar{\Sigma}_{2i} \neq \bar{\Sigma}_{2j}$, independence across equations is guaranteed since $(I_{mk} \otimes \boldsymbol{X}'\boldsymbol{X}) + \bar{\Sigma}(b_0)^{-1} \propto (I_{mk} \otimes \boldsymbol{X}'\boldsymbol{X}) + \text{diag}\{\bar{\Sigma}_{21}, \dots, \bar{\Sigma}_{2m}\} = \text{diag}\{\bar{\Sigma}_{21} + \boldsymbol{X}'\boldsymbol{X}, \dots, \bar{\Sigma}_{2m} + \boldsymbol{X}'\boldsymbol{X}\}$.

Note that, if we had started from a reduced-form VAR (as in exercise 10.9), the structure of $\tilde{\Sigma}(b_0)$ would have been $\tilde{\Sigma}(b_0) = [(\Sigma_e \otimes \boldsymbol{X}'\boldsymbol{X}) + \bar{\Sigma}(b_0)^{-1}]^{-1}$, where Σ_e is the covariance matrix of the disturbances. This means that, to keep the computations simple, $\bar{\Sigma}(b_0)$ must allow correlation across equations (contrary, for example, to what the Minnesota prior assumes).

It is interesting to map structural priors into Minnesota priors. Let $\mathcal{A}_0$ be given and let the VAR be $y_t = A(\ell)y_{t-1} + C\bar{y}_t + e_t$. Let $\alpha = \text{vec}[A_1, \dots, A_q, C]$. Since $A(\ell) = \mathcal{A}_0^{-1}\mathcal{A}_-$, $E(\alpha) = [I_m, 0, \dots, 0]$ and $\text{var}(\alpha) = \bar{\Sigma}_\alpha$, where $\bar{\Sigma}_\alpha$ was defined in (10.12), imply

$$E(\mathcal{A}_- \mid \mathcal{A}_0) = [\mathcal{A}_0, 0, \dots, 0], \quad (10.28)$$

$$\text{var}(\mathcal{A}_- \mid \mathcal{A}_0) = \text{diag}(b_{-(ijl)}) = \frac{\phi_0\phi_1}{h(\ell)\sigma_j^2}, \quad i, j = 1, \dots, m, \ \ell = 1, \dots, q, \quad (10.29)$$

$$= \phi_0\phi_2, \quad \text{otherwise}, \quad (10.30)$$

where i stands for equation, j for variable, ℓ for lag, ϕ_0 (ϕ_1) controls the tightness of the prior variance of $\mathcal{A}_0$, ($\mathcal{A}_-$) and ϕ_2 the tightness of the prior variance of $\mathcal{C}$.

Three features of (10.28)–(10.30) are worth mentioning: first, there is no distinction between own lags and lags of other variables coefficients since, in simultaneous equation models, no normalization with one right-hand side variable is available; second, the scale factors differ from those of reduced-form BVARs since $\text{var}(\epsilon_t) = I$; third, since $\alpha = \text{vec}(\mathcal{A}_0^{-1}\mathcal{A}_-)$, beliefs about α may be correlated across equations (if beliefs about $\mathcal{A}_0$ are).

As in a reduced-form BVARs, stochastic linear restrictions can be added to the specification and combined with the data using the logic of Theil's mixed estimation.

Exercise 10.19 (controlling for trends: sum-of-coefficients restriction). Suppose the average value of lagged y_i (say, $\bar{\bar{y}}_i$) is a good predictor of y_{it} for equation i. Write this information as $\boldsymbol{Y}^{\dagger}\mathcal{A}_0 - \boldsymbol{X}^{\dagger}\mathcal{A}_- = V$, where $y^{\dagger} = \{y_{ij}^{\dagger}\} = \phi_3\bar{\bar{y}}_i$ if $i = j$ and zero otherwise, $i, j = 1, \dots, m$; $x^{\dagger} = \{x_{i\tau}^{\dagger}\} = \phi_3\bar{\bar{y}}_i$ if $i = j$, for $\tau < k$ and zero otherwise, $i = 1, \dots, m$, $\tau = 1, \dots, k$. Construct the posterior for b_- under this restriction.

Adding the sum-of-coefficients restriction introduces correlation among the coefficients of a variable in an equation. When $\phi_3 \to \infty$, the restriction implies a model in first difference, i.e., the VAR has m unit roots and no cointegration.

Exercise 10.20 (controlling for seasonality: seasonal sum-of-coefficients restriction). Suppose the average value of y_{t-j} is a good predictor of y_t for each equation. Set up this restriction as a dummy observation and construct the posterior for b_-.

To calculate (10.27) we need to specify $g(b_0)$. Since for identification purposes, some elements of b_0 may be forced to be zero, we need to distinguish between hard restrictions (those imposing identification, possibly of blocks of equations) and soft restrictions (those involving a prior on nonzero coefficients). Since little is typically known about b_0, a noninformative prior should be preferred, i.e., $g(b_0^0) \propto 1$, where b_0^0 are the nonzero elements of b_0. In some occasions, a normal prior may also be appropriate.

Example 10.11. Suppose we have $m(m-1)/2$ restrictions so that $\mathcal{A}_0$ is just identified. Assume, for example, that $\mathcal{A}_0$ is lower triangular and let b_0^0 be the nonzero elements of $\mathcal{A}_0$. Suppose $g(b_0^0) = \prod_i g(b_{0i}^0)$, where each $g(b_{0i}^0)$ is $\mathbb{N}(0, \sigma^2(b_0^0))$ so that the coefficients of, say, GDP and unemployment in equation i may be related to each other but are unrelated to the coefficients of GDP and unemployment in equation i'. Set $\sigma^2(b_{0ij}^0) = (\phi_5/\sigma_i)^2$ so that all the elements of equation i have the same variance. Since the system is just identified one can also use a Wishart prior for Σ_e^{-1}, with $\bar{\nu}$ degrees of freedom and scale matrix $\bar{\Sigma}$ to derive a prior for b_0^0. In fact, a lower triangular $\mathcal{A}_0$ is just the Choleski factor of Σ_e^{-1}. If $\bar{\nu} = m + 1$, $\bar{\Sigma} = \text{diag}(\phi_5/\sigma_i)^2$, the prior for b_0^0 is proportional to a $\mathbb{N}(0, \sigma^2(b_0^0))$, where the factor of proportionality is the Jacobian of the transformation, i.e., $|\partial\Sigma_e^{-1}/\partial\mathcal{A}_0| = 2^m \prod_{j=1}^m b_{jj}^j$. Since the likelihood contains a term $|\mathcal{A}_0|^T = \prod_{j=1}^T b_{jj}^T$, ignoring the Jacobian is irrelevant if $T \gg m$.

The posterior $g(b_0 \mid y)$ cannot be computed analytically. To simulate a sequence we can use one of the algorithms we described in chapter 9. For example:

Algorithm 10.2.

(1) Calculate the posterior mode b_0^* of $g(b_0 \mid y)$ and the Hessian at b_0^*.

(2) Draw b_0 from a normal centered at b_0^* with covariance equal to the Hessian at b_0^* or from a t-distribution with the same mean and the same covariance and $\nu = m + 1$ degrees of freedom.

(3) Use importance sampling to weight the draws, checking the magnitude of $\mathrm{IR}^l = \tilde{g}(b_0^l)/\tilde{g}^{\mathrm{IS}}(b_0^l)$, where $\tilde{g}^{\mathrm{IS}}(b_0)$ is the kernel of the selected importance density, $\tilde{g}(b_0)$ is the kernel of the true distribution, and $l = 1, \dots, L$.

As an alternative one could use a Metropolis–Hastings (MH) algorithm with a normal or a t-distribution as the target, or the restricted Gibbs sampler of Waggoner and Zha (2003).

Exercise 10.21. Describe how to use an MH algorithm to draw a sequence from $g(b_0 \mid y)$.

We can immediately extend the framework to the case where noncontemporaneous restrictions are used to identify the VAR.

Exercise 10.22. Suppose $\mathcal{A}_0$ is just identified by using long-run restrictions. How would you modify the prior for $\mathcal{A}_0$ to account for this?

Exercise 10.23. Suppose $\mathcal{A}_0$ is overidentified. How should the prior for $\mathcal{A}_0$ in exercise 10.22 be changed?

Exercise 10.24. Suppose $\mathcal{A}_0$ is identified by using sign restrictions. Let $\Sigma_e = \tilde{\mathcal{P}}(\omega)\tilde{\mathcal{P}}'(\omega)$, where ω is an angle. How would you modify the prior for $\mathcal{A}_0$ to take this into account? How would you modify the algorithm to draw from the posterior distribution of $\mathcal{A}_0$? (Hint: treat ω as a random variable and select an appropriate prior distribution.)

There are a number of extensions one can consider. Here we analyze two.

(i) Structural VAR models with exogenous stochastic variables, for example, oil prices in a structural VAR for domestic variables.

(ii) Structural VAR models with block exogenous variables and overidentifying restrictions in some block, for example, a two-country structural model where one is block exogenous.

We assume that y_t is de-meaned so that $\bar{y}_t$ is omitted from the model. For the case of structural models with exogenous variables, let

$$\mathcal{A}_{i0} y_t - \mathcal{A}_i(\ell) y_{t-1} = \epsilon_{it}, \quad \epsilon_{it} \sim \text{i.i.d. } \mathbb{N}(0, I), \tag{10.31}$$

where $i = 1, \dots, n$ refers to the number of blocks, $m = \sum_{i=1}^{n} m_i$ with m_i equations in each block, ϵ_{it} is $m_i \times 1$ for each i, $\mathcal{A}_i(\ell) = (\mathcal{A}_{i1}(\ell), \dots, \mathcal{A}_{in}(\ell))$, and each $\mathcal{A}_{ij}(\ell)$ is an $m_i \times m_j$ matrix for each ℓ. Equation (10.31) is just the block representation of (10.23). Rewrite (10.31) as

$$y_{it} = A_i(\ell) y_{it-1} + e_{it}, \tag{10.32}$$

where $A_i(\ell) = (0_{i-}, I_i, 0_{i+}) - \mathcal{A}_{i0}^{-1} \mathcal{A}_i(\ell)$, 0_{i-} is a matrix of zeros of dimension $m_i \times m_{i\_}$, 0_{i+} is a matrix of zeros of dimension $m_i \times m_{i_+}$, where $m_{i\_} = 0$ for $i = 1$ and $m_{i\_} = \sum_j^{i-1} m_j$ for $i = 2, \dots, n$, $m_{i_+} = 0$ for $i = n$, $m_{i_+} = \sum_{j=i+1}^{n} m_j$ for $i = 1, \dots, n-1$, and where $E(e_t e_t') = \operatorname{diag}\{\Sigma_{ii}\} = \operatorname{diag}\{\mathcal{A}_{i0}^{-1}(\mathcal{A}_{i0}^{-1})'\}$. Stacking the T observations we have

$$\boldsymbol{Y}_i = \boldsymbol{X}_i \boldsymbol{A}_i + \boldsymbol{E}_i, \tag{10.33}$$

where $\boldsymbol{Y}_i$ and $\boldsymbol{E}_i$ are $T \times m_i$ matrices, $\boldsymbol{X}_i$ is a $T \times k_i$ matrix, and k_i is the number of coefficients in each block. The likelihood function is

$$\begin{aligned}
&f(A_i, \Sigma_{ii} \mid y_T, \dots, y_0, \dots) \\
&\quad \propto \prod_{i=1}^{n} |\mathcal{A}_{i0}|^T \exp\{-0.5 \operatorname{tr}[(\boldsymbol{Y}_i - \boldsymbol{X}_i \boldsymbol{A}_i)'(\boldsymbol{Y}_i - \boldsymbol{X}_i \boldsymbol{A}_i)\mathcal{A}_{i0}'\mathcal{A}_{i0}]\} \\
&\quad \propto \prod_{i=1}^{n} |\mathcal{A}_{i0}|^T \exp\{-0.5 \operatorname{tr}[(\boldsymbol{Y}_i - \boldsymbol{X}_i \boldsymbol{A}_{i,\text{OLS}})'(\boldsymbol{Y}_i - \boldsymbol{X}_i \boldsymbol{A}_{i,\text{OLS}})\mathcal{A}_{i0}'\mathcal{A}_{i0} \\
&\qquad\qquad + (\boldsymbol{A}_i - \boldsymbol{A}_{i,\text{OLS}})'\boldsymbol{X}_i'\boldsymbol{X}_i(\boldsymbol{A}_i - \boldsymbol{A}_{i,\text{OLS}})\mathcal{A}_{i0}'\mathcal{A}_{i0}]\},
\end{aligned} \tag{10.34}$$

where $\boldsymbol{A}_{i,\text{OLS}} = (\boldsymbol{X}_i'\boldsymbol{X}_i)^{-1}(\boldsymbol{X}_i'\boldsymbol{Y}_i)$ and "tr" denotes the trace of a matrix. Suppose $g(\mathcal{A}_{i0}, \mathcal{A}_i) \propto |\mathcal{A}_{i0}|^{k_i}$. Then the posterior for $\mathcal{A}_{i0}$ and $\alpha_i = \operatorname{vec}(\mathcal{A}_i)$ has the same form as the likelihood and

$$\left.\begin{aligned}
g(\mathcal{A}_{i0} \mid y) &\propto |\mathcal{A}_{i0}|^T \exp\{-0.5 \operatorname{tr}[(\boldsymbol{Y}_i - \boldsymbol{X}_i \boldsymbol{A}_{i,\text{OLS}})'(\boldsymbol{Y}_i - \boldsymbol{X}_i \boldsymbol{A}_{i,\text{OLS}})\mathcal{A}_{i0}'\mathcal{A}_{i0}]\}, \\
g(\alpha_i \mid \mathcal{A}_{i0}, y) &\sim \mathbb{N}(\alpha_{i,\text{OLS}}, (\mathcal{A}_{i0}'\mathcal{A}_{i0})^{-1} \otimes (\boldsymbol{X}_i'\boldsymbol{X}_i)^{-1}),
\end{aligned}\right\} \tag{10.35}$$

where $\alpha_{i,\text{OLS}} = \operatorname{vec}(\boldsymbol{A}_{i,\text{OLS}})$. As before, if $\mathcal{A}_{i0}$ is the Choleski factor of Σ_{ii}^{-1} and $g(\Sigma_{ii}^{-1}) \propto |\Sigma_{ii}^{-1}|^{0.5k_i}$, the posterior for Σ_{ii}^{-1} has Wishart form with parameters $([(\boldsymbol{Y}_i - \boldsymbol{X}_i \boldsymbol{A}_{i,\text{OLS}})'(\boldsymbol{Y}_i - \boldsymbol{X}_i \boldsymbol{A}_{i,\text{OLS}})]^{-1}, T - m_i - 1)$. Hence, one could draw from the posterior of Σ_{ii}^{-1} and use the Choleski restrictions to draw $\mathcal{A}_{i0}$. When $\mathcal{A}_{i0}$ is overidentified, we need to draw $\mathcal{A}_{i0}$ from the marginal posterior (10.35), which is of unknown form. To do so one could use, for example, a version of the importance sampling algorithm 10.2.

Exercise 10.25. Extend algorithm 10.2 to the case where the VAR has different lags in different blocks.

Exercise 10.26. Suppose $g(\mathcal{A}_i)$ is $\mathbb{N}(\bar{\mathcal{A}}_i, \bar{\Sigma}_{\mathcal{A}})$. Show the form of $g(\alpha_i \mid \mathcal{A}_{i0}, y)$ in this case.

For the case of block exogenous variables with overidentifying restrictions, suppose there are linear restrictions on $\mathcal{A}_{ij0}$, $j > i$. This case is different from the previous one since overidentifying restrictions were placed on $\mathcal{A}_{ii0}$. Define $\mathcal{A}_i^*(\ell) = \mathcal{A}_{i0} - \mathcal{A}_i(\ell)$, $i = 1, \dots, n$, and rewrite the system as $\mathcal{A}_{i0} y_t = \mathcal{A}_i^*(\ell) y_t + \epsilon_{it}$. Stacking the observations we have

$$Y \mathcal{A}_{i0}' = X_i \mathbb{A}_i^* + \epsilon_i, \tag{10.36}$$

where X_i is a $T \times k_i^*$ matrix including all right-hand side variables, $k_i^* = k_i - m_{i+1} - \dots - m_n$, $\mathbb{A}_i^*$ is the $k_i^* \times m_i$ companion matrix of $\mathcal{A}_i^*(\ell)$, ϵ_i is a $T \times m_i$ matrix, $Y = [Y_1, \dots, Y_n]$ is a $T \times m$ matrix, and $\mathcal{A}_{i0} = \{\mathcal{A}_{i10}, \dots, \mathcal{A}_{in0}, \ \mathcal{A}_{ij0} = 0, \ j < i\}$ is an $m \times m_i$ matrix. Let $A_{i,\text{OLS}}^* = (X_i' X_i)^{-1} X_i' Y$ and let $g(\mathcal{A}_i(0), A_i^*) \propto |\mathcal{A}_{i0}|^{-0.5 m_i}$. If $\alpha_i^* = \text{vec}(A_i^*)$, the posteriors are

$$\left.\begin{aligned} g(\mathcal{A}_{i0} \mid y) &\propto |\mathcal{A}_{i0}|^T \exp\{-0.5 \operatorname{tr}[(Y_i - X_i A_{i,\text{OLS}}^*)'(Y_i - X_i A_{i,\text{OLS}}^*) \mathcal{A}_{i0}' \mathcal{A}_{i0}]\}, \\ g(\alpha_i^* \mid \mathcal{A}_{i0}, y) &\sim \mathbb{N}(\alpha_{i,\text{OLS}}^*, (I_i \otimes (X_i' X_i)^{-1})). \end{aligned}\right\} \tag{10.37}$$

Exercise 10.27. Describe how to draw posterior sequences for $(\alpha_i^*, \mathcal{A}_{i0})$ from (10.37).

We conclude with an example illustrating the techniques described in this section.

Example 10.12. We take monthly U.S. data from 1959:1 to 2003:1 for the log of GDP, the log of CPI, the log of M2, the Federal funds rate, and the log of commodity prices. We are interested in the dynamic responses of the first four variables to an identified monetary policy shock and in knowing how much of the variance of output and prices is explained by monetary policy shocks. We use contemporaneous restrictions and overidentify the system by assuming that the monetary authority only looks at M2 when manipulating the Federal funds rate. Hence, the system has a Choleski form (in the order in which the variables are listed) except for the (3, 1) and (3, 2) entries, which are zero. We assume $b_0^0 \sim \mathbb{N}(0, I)$ and use as importance sampling a normal centered at the mode and with dispersion equal to the Hessian at the mode. We monitor the draws by using the importance ratio and find that in only 11 out of 1000 draws the weight given to the draw exceeds 0.01.

The median response and the 68% band for each variable are in figure 10.3. Both output and money persistently decline in response to an interest rate increase. The response of prices is initially zero but turns positive and significant after a few quarters — reminiscent of what is typically called the "price puzzle." Monetary shocks explain 4–18% of the variance of output at the twentieth-quarter horizon and only 10–17% of the variance of prices. One may wonder what moves prices then: it turns out that output shocks explain 45–60% of the variability of prices in the sample.

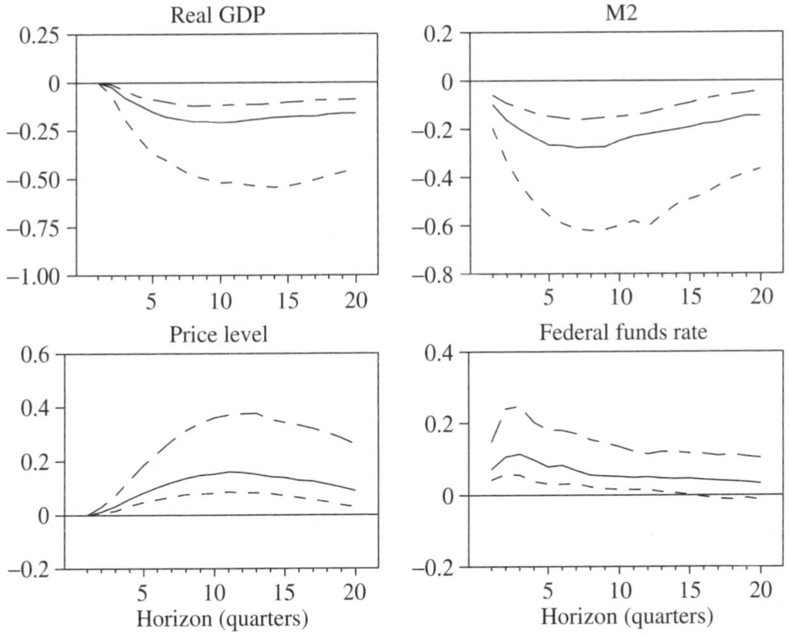

Figure 10.3. Median and 68% band for the responses to a U.S. monetary policy shock.

10.4 Time-Varying-Coefficient BVARs

Economic time series tend to show evolving features. One could think of these changes as abrupt and model the switch as a structural break (either in the intercept, in the slope coefficients, or in both). Alternatively, one may suspect that changes are related to some unobservable state, for example, the business cycle, in which case the coefficients or the covariance matrix or both could be made a function of a finite-order Markov chain (as we will do in chapter 11). Since structural changes are rare but coefficients tend to evolve continuously, one may finally prefer a model with smoothly changing coefficients. Time-varying-coefficient models have a long history in applied work going back, at least, to Cooley and Prescott (1973), and classical estimation methods, ranging from generalized least squares (Swamy 1970) to Kalman filtering, are available. Here we treat the law of motion of the coefficients as the first layer of a hierarchical prior and specify, in a second layer, the distributions for the parameters of this law of motion.

The model we consider is of the form

$$y_t = A_t(\ell)y_{t-1} + C_t\bar{y}_t + e_t, \quad e_t \sim \text{i.i.d. } \mathbb{N}(0, \Sigma_e), \tag{10.38}$$

$$\alpha_t = \mathbb{D}_1\alpha_{t-1} + \mathbb{D}_0\bar{\alpha} + v_t, \quad v_t \sim \text{i.i.d. } \mathbb{N}(0, \Sigma_t), \tag{10.39}$$

where $\alpha_t = \text{vec}[A_t(\ell), C_t]$ and $\mathbb{D}_0$, $\mathbb{D}_1$ are $mk \times mk$ matrices. Equation (10.39) allows for stationary and nonstationary behavior in α_t. For example, the law of motion of the coefficients displays reversion toward the mean $\bar{\alpha}$ if the roots of $\mathbb{D}_1$

are all less than 1 in absolute value. In principle, Σ_t depends on time, therefore imparting conditional heteroskedastic movements to both the coefficients and the variables of the VAR.

The specification in (10.38), (10.39) is flexible and can generate a variety of nonlinearities in the conditional moment structure. In fact, substituting (10.39) into (10.38) we have

$$y_t = (I_m \otimes X_t)(\mathbb{D}_1\alpha_{t-1} + \mathbb{D}_0\bar{\alpha}) + (I_m \otimes X_t)v_t + e_t \equiv X_t\alpha_t^\dagger + e_t^\dagger, \quad (10.40)$$

where $(I_m \otimes X_t)$ is the matrix of regressors. Depending on the nature of the X_t and the relationship between X_t and v_t, (10.40) encompasses several specifications used in the literature. We consider three such cases in the next example.

Example 10.13. Suppose that $m = 1$, that X_t and v_t are conditionally independent, and that $\text{var}(v_t) = \Sigma_v$. Then, y_t is conditionally heteroskedastic with mean $X_t\alpha_t^\dagger$ and variance $\Sigma_e + X_t'\Sigma_v X_t$. In addition, if X_t includes lagged dependent variables and a constant and $(v_t \mid X_t) \sim \mathbb{N}(0, \Sigma_v)$, then (10.40) generates a conditionally normal ARMA-ARCH structure. Finally, if X_t includes latent variables or variables which are imperfectly predictable at t, then y_t is non-Gaussian and heteroskedastic (as in Clark's (1973) mixture model).

Exercise 10.28. Suppose $m = 1$, $X_t = (X_{1t}, X_{2t})$, and assume X_{1t} is correlated with v_t. Show that (10.40) produces a version of the bilinear model of Granger and Anderson (1978). Suppose now that $v_t = v_{1t} + v_{2t}$, where v_{1t} is independent of X_t and v_{2t} and has covariance matrix Σ_1, and v_{2t} is perfectly correlated with X_t. Show that (10.38), (10.39) can generate a model with features similar to an ARCH-M model (see Engle et al. 1987).

Equations (10.38), (10.39) also include, as a special case, Hamilton's (1989) two-state shift model, if we allow the errors in (10.39) to be nonnormal.

Exercise 10.29. Suppose $\Delta y_t = a_0 + a_1\varkappa_t + \Delta y_t^c$, where $\varkappa_t = (1 - p_2) + (p_1 + p_2 - 1)\varkappa_{t-1} + e_t^x$, e_t^x is a binomial random variable and $\Delta y_t^c = A(\ell)\Delta y_{t-1}^c + e_t^c$. Cast such a model into a TVC framework. (Hint: find its state space format and match coefficients with (10.38), (10.39).)

Despite the normal errors, a model like (10.38), (10.39) can produce nonnormalities in y_t. Typically, nonnormalities are produced when X_t is a latent variable. Here they occur, even when X_t includes only observable variables, e_t and v_t are independently distributed and v_t and X_t conditionally independent. To see this, set $m = 1$ and define $\hat{e}_{t+\tau} = (\mathbb{D}_1^{\tau+1}\alpha_{t-1} + \mathbb{D}_0\bar{\alpha}\sum_{j=0}^{\tau}\mathbb{D}_1^j)'(X_{t+\tau} - E_{t-1}X_{t+\tau}) + (\sum_{j=0}^{\tau-1}\mathbb{D}_1^{\tau-j}v_{t+j})'X_{t+\tau} - E_{t-1}(\sum_{j=0}^{\tau-1}\mathbb{D}_1^{\tau-j}v_{t+j})'X_{t+\tau} + v_{t+\tau}'X_{t+\tau} + e_{t+\tau}$.

Exercise 10.30. Show that, for fixed t and all τ, $E_{t-1}y_{t+\tau} = (\mathbb{D}_1^{\tau+1}\alpha_{t-1} + \mathbb{D}_0 \times \bar{\alpha}\sum_{j=0}^{\tau}\mathbb{D}_1^j)'E_{t-1}X_{t+\tau} + E_{t-1}(\sum_{j=0}^{\tau-1}\mathbb{D}_1^{\tau-j}v_{t+j})'X_{t+\tau}$, $\text{var}_{t-1}\,y_{t+\tau} = E_{t-1} \times \hat{e}_{t+\tau}^2$, $\text{sk}_{t-1}(y_{t+\tau}) = E_{t-1}\hat{e}_{t+\tau}^3/(\text{var}_{t-1}\,y_{t+\tau})^{3/2}$, $\text{kt}_{t-1}(y_{t+\tau}) = E_{t-1}\hat{e}_{t+\tau}^4/(\text{var}_{t-1}\,y_{t+\tau})^2$, where sk_{t-1} and kt_{t-1} are the conditional skewness and kurtosis coefficients. Show that, for $\tau = 0$, $\mathrm{sk}_{t-1}(y_t) = 0$, $\mathrm{kt}_{t-1}(y_t) = 3$, i.e., y_t is conditionally normal.

For $\tau = 1$ the conditional mean of y_{t+1} is $E_{t-1}(\alpha'_{t+1}X_{t+1}) = [\mathbb{D}_1^2\alpha_{t-1} + \mathbb{D}_0 \times (I + \mathbb{D}_1)\bar{\alpha}]' E_{t-1}X_{t+1} + E_{t-1}v'_t\mathbb{D}_1 X_{t+1}$, where $E_{t-1}X_{t+1} = [E_{t-1}y_t, y_{t-1}, \dots, y_{t-\ell+1}]$, while its conditional variance is $E_{t-1}[(\mathbb{D}_1^2\alpha_{t-1} + \mathbb{D}_0\bar{\alpha}(1 + \mathbb{D}_1))' \times (X_{t+1} - E_{t-1}X_{t+1}) + (v'_t\mathbb{D}'_1 X_{t+1} - E_{t-1}v'_t\mathbb{D}'_1 X_{t+1}) + v'_{t+1}X_{t+1} + e_{t+1}]^2$. Note that $(X_{t+1} - E_{t-1}X_{t+1})' = [e_t^{\dagger}, 0, \dots, 0]$ and that $(v'_t\mathbb{D}'_1 X_{t+1}) - E_{t-1}(v'_t\mathbb{D}'_1 X_{t+1})$ involves, among other things, terms of the form $v'_t\mathbb{D}'_1 e_t$. Hence, even when v_t and e_t are normal and independent, y_{t+1} is conditionally nonnormal because the prediction errors involve the product of normal random variables. The above argument also holds for any $\tau > 1$.

10.4.1 Minnesota Style Prior

If (10.38) is the model for the data and (10.39) the first layer for the prior, we need to specify $\bar{\alpha}$, the evolution of Σ_t, and the form of $\mathbb{D}_1$ and $\mathbb{D}_0$. For example, we could use

$$\mathbb{D}_1 = \phi_0 I, \qquad \mathbb{D}_0 = I - \mathbb{D}_1, \tag{10.41}$$

$$\bar{\alpha}_{ij\ell} = 1 \quad \text{if } i = j,\ \ell = 1, \tag{10.42}$$

$$\bar{\alpha}_{ij\ell} = 0 \quad \text{otherwise}, \tag{10.43}$$

$$\Sigma_t = \sigma_t \Sigma_0, \quad \Sigma_0 = \mathrm{diag}\{\sigma_{0,ij\ell}\}, \tag{10.44}$$

$$\sigma_{0,ij\ell} = \begin{cases} \phi_1 \dfrac{h_1(i,j)}{h_2(\ell)} \times \left(\dfrac{\sigma_j}{\sigma_i}\right)^2, & h_1(i,i) = 1, \\ \phi_1 \times \phi_4 & \text{if exogenous}, \end{cases} \tag{10.45}$$

where $\sigma_t = \phi_3^t + \phi_2(1 - \phi_3^{t-1})/(1 - \phi_3)$. As in the basic Minnesota prior we assume that Σ_e is fixed, but there is no conceptual difficulty in assuming a Wishart prior for Σ_e^{-1}.

With (10.41) the law of motion of the coefficients has a first-order autoregressive structure with decay toward the mean. ϕ_0 controls the speed of the decay: for $\phi_0 = 0$ the coefficients are random around $\bar{\alpha}$ and for $\phi_0 = 1$ they are random walks. Higher-order processes can be obtained by substituting the identity matrix in (10.41) with an appropriate matrix. The prior mean and the prior variance for the time-zero coefficients are identical to those of the basic Minnesota prior except that we allow a general pattern of weights for different variables in different equations via the function $h_1(i, j)$. The variance of the innovation in the coefficients evolves linearly. The nature of time variations can be clearly understood by noting that (10.44) can also be written as $\Sigma_t = V_0\Sigma_0 + V_1\Sigma_{t-1}$, where $V_0 = \phi_2 * I$, $V_1 = \phi_3 * I$, which has the same structure as the law of motion of the coefficients. For $\phi_3 = 0$ the coefficients are time varying but no heteroskedasticity is allowed, while for $\phi_2 = 0$ the variance of the coefficients is geometrically related to Σ_0. Finally, if $\phi_2 = \phi_3 = 0$, time variations and heteroskedasticity are absent.

Empirical Bayes methods can be employed to estimate the hyperparameters ϕ on a training sample of data going from $(-\tau, 0)$. If this sample does not exist, they could be estimated by using a fixed-coefficient version of (10.38) on the full sample. As usual, the likelihood can be constructed and evaluated numerically by using the Kalman filter.

Exercise 10.31. Write down the likelihood function for the TVC-VAR model (10.38), (10.39). Specify exactly how to use the Kalman filter to numerically maximize it.

Posterior inference can be conducted conditional on the estimates of ϕ, i.e., we use $g(\alpha \mid y, \hat{\phi}_{\text{ML-II}}) \propto f(y \mid \alpha)g(\alpha \mid \hat{\phi}_{\text{ML-II}})$ in place of $g(\alpha \mid y)$. Note that, while the full posterior averages over all possible values of ϕ, the empirical-Bayes posterior uses ML-II estimates. Clearly, if $f(y \mid \phi)$ is flat in the hyperparameter space, differences will be minor.

Example 10.14. Continuing with example 10.5, we add time variations to the coefficients of the BVAR and forecast Italian inflation by using the same style of Minnesota prior outlined above, but set $\phi_3 = 0$. We use a simplex algorithm to maximize $f(y \mid \phi)$ with respect to the ϕ. The optimal values are $\phi_0 = 0.98$, $\phi_1 = 0.11$, $\phi_2 = 0.1 \times 10^{-8}$, $\phi_4 = 1000$, while $h_1(i, j) = 0.4, \forall i, j$, $h_2(\ell) = \ell^{0.4}$. The Theil-U statistics one year ahead are 0.93 for the sample 1996:1–2000:4 and 0.89 for the sample 1991:1–1995:4 (the posterior standard error is 0.03 in both cases). Therefore, time variations in the coefficients appear to be important. However, time variations in the variance hardly matter. In fact, setting $\phi_2 = 0$, the Theil-U statistics are 0.95 and 0.90, respectively.

Exercise 10.32 (Ciccarelli and Rebucci). Let $y_{1t} = A_{11}(\ell)y_{1t-1} + y_{2t}A_{12}$ and $y_{2t} = A_{22}(\ell)y_{1t-1} + v_t$ and suppose a researcher estimates $y_{1t} = A(\ell)y_{1t-1} + e_t$.

(i) Show that $A(\ell)_{\text{OLS}}$ is biased unless $A_{22}(\ell) = 0$.

(ii) Consider the approximating model $y_{1t} = A(\ell)y_{1t-1} + A^{\text{c}}(\ell)y_{1t-1} + e_t$, where $A^{\text{c}}(\ell) = A_{22}(\ell)A_{12}$ and $e_t = v_t A_{12}$. Clearly, the estimated model sets $A^{\text{c}}(\ell) = 0$, otherwise perfect collinearity would result. Suppose $\alpha = \text{vec}(A^{\text{c}}(\ell), A(\ell)) \sim \mathbb{N}(\bar{\alpha}, \bar{\Sigma}_\alpha)$, where $\bar{\alpha} = (0, \bar{\alpha}_2)$ and $\bar{\Sigma}_\alpha = \text{diag}[\bar{\Sigma}_{\alpha_1}, \bar{\Sigma}_{\alpha_2}]$. Show that $g(\alpha \mid y) \sim \mathbb{N}(\tilde{\alpha}, \tilde{\Sigma}_\alpha)$. Show the form of $\tilde{\alpha}$, $\tilde{\Sigma}_\alpha$. In particular, show that, in the formula for the posterior mean, the OLS estimator receives less weight than in standard problems. Show that the posterior for $A^{\text{c}}(\ell)$ is centered away from zero to correct for the skewness produced by omitting a set of regressors. How would your answer change if coefficients were functions of time?

10.4.2 Hierarchical Prior

A BVAR with time-varying coefficients is a state space model where the coefficients are the unobservable states. Full hierarchical estimation of such models does not present difficulties once it is understood that time-varying and time-invariant features can be jointly estimated. The Gibbs sampler is particularly useful for this purpose.

Here we consider a simple version of the model (10.38), (10.39) and leave the discussion of a more complicated setup to a later section. The specification we employ has the form

$$\left.\begin{aligned} y_t &= X_t\alpha_t + e_t, & e_t &\sim \text{i.i.d. } \mathbb{N}(0, \Sigma_e), \\ \alpha_t &= \mathbb{D}_1\alpha_{t-1} + v_t, & v_t &\sim \text{i.i.d. } \mathbb{N}(0, \Sigma_a), \end{aligned}\right\} \tag{10.46}$$

where $X_t = (I_m \otimes \boldsymbol{X}_t)$. We assume that $\mathbb{D}_1$ is known and discuss in an exercise how to estimate it if it is unknown. Posterior draws for (Σ_e, Σ_a) and of the unobserved state $\{\alpha_t\}_{t=1}^T$ can be obtained with the Gibbs sampler. Let $\alpha^t = (\alpha_0, \dots, \alpha_t)$, $y^t = (y_0, \dots, y_t)$. To use the Gibbs sampler we need the conditional posteriors $g(\Sigma_a \mid y^t, \alpha^t, \Sigma_e)$, $g(\Sigma_e \mid y^t, \alpha^t, \Sigma_a)$, and $g(\alpha^t \mid y^t, \Sigma_e, \Sigma_a)$.

Suppose that $g(\Sigma_e^{-1}, \Sigma_a^{-1}) = g(\Sigma_e^{-1})g(\Sigma_a^{-1})$ and that each is Wishart with $\bar{\nu}_0$ and $\bar{\nu}_1$ degrees of freedom and scale matrices $\bar{\Sigma}_e$, $\bar{\Sigma}_a$, respectively. Then, since e_t, v_t are normal,

$$(\Sigma_e^{-1} \mid y^t, \alpha^t, \Sigma_a^{-1}) \sim \mathbb{W}\left(\bar{\nu}_0 + T, \left(\bar{\Sigma}_e^{-1} + \sum_t (y_t - X_t\alpha_t)(y_t - X_t\alpha_t)'\right)^{-1}\right),$$

$$(\Sigma_a^{-1} \mid y^t, \alpha^t, \Sigma_e^{-1})$$
$$\sim \mathbb{W}\left(\bar{\nu}_1 + T, \left(\bar{\Sigma}_a^{-1} + \sum_t (\alpha_t - \mathbb{D}_1\alpha_{t-1})(\alpha_t - \mathbb{D}_1\alpha_{t-1})'\right)^{-1}\right).$$

To obtain the conditional posterior for α^t, note that $g(\alpha^t \mid y^t, \Sigma_e, \Sigma_a) = g(\alpha_t \mid y^t, \Sigma_e, \Sigma_a)g(\alpha_{t-1} \mid y^t, \alpha_t, \Sigma_e, \Sigma_a) \cdots g(\alpha_0 \mid y^t, \alpha_1, \Sigma_e, \Sigma_a)$. Therefore, a sequence α^t can be obtained by drawing each element from the corresponding conditional posterior while α_t is drawn from the marginal $g(\alpha_t \mid y^t, \Sigma_e, \Sigma_a)$. Let $y_\tau^t = (y_\tau, \dots, y_t)$. Note that

$$\begin{aligned} g(\alpha_\tau \mid y^t, \alpha_{\tau+1}, \Sigma_e, \Sigma_a) &= \frac{g(\alpha_\tau, y^t, \alpha_{\tau+1} \mid \Sigma_e, \Sigma_a)}{f(y^t, \alpha_{\tau+1})} \\ &\propto g(\alpha_\tau \mid y^\tau, \Sigma_e, \Sigma_a)g(\alpha_{\tau+1} \mid y^\tau, \alpha_\tau, \Sigma_e, \Sigma_a) \\ &\qquad \times f(y_{\tau+1}^t \mid y^\tau, \alpha_\tau, \alpha_{\tau+1}, \Sigma_e, \Sigma_a) \qquad (10.47) \\ &= g(\alpha_\tau \mid y^\tau, \Sigma_e, \Sigma_a)g(\alpha_{\tau+1} \mid \alpha_\tau, \Sigma_e, \Sigma_a). \qquad (10.48) \end{aligned}$$

The first two terms in (10.47) involve posterior distributions obtained with data up to τ and the last term the distribution of the data from $\tau + 1$ until t. Equation (10.48) follows from the fact that α_τ is independent of $y_{\tau+1}^t$, conditional on $(y^\tau, \Sigma_e, \Sigma_a)$. We can immediately recognize that the two densities in (10.48) are both normal and their mean and variances can be computed from the output of the Kalman filter (see chapter 6). Let $\alpha_{t|t} \equiv E(\alpha_t \mid y^t, \Sigma_e, \Sigma_a) = \alpha_{t|t-1} + \mathfrak{K}_t(y_t - X_t\alpha_{t|t-1})$, $\Sigma_{t|t} \equiv \text{var}(\alpha_t \mid y^t, \Sigma_a, \Sigma_e) = (I - \mathfrak{K}_t X_t)\Sigma_{t|t-1}$, where $\alpha_{t|t-1} = \mathbb{D}_1\alpha_{t-1|t-1}$, $\mathfrak{K}_t = \Sigma_{t|t-1}X_t'(X_t\Sigma_{t|t-1}X_t' + \Sigma_e)^{-1}$, and $\Sigma_{t|t-1} \equiv \text{var}(\alpha_t|y^{t-1}, \Sigma_e, \Sigma_a) = \mathbb{D}_1\Sigma_{t-1|t-1}\mathbb{D}_1' + \Sigma_a$. Then, given a prior for α_0, $g(\alpha_\tau \mid y^\tau, \Sigma_e, \Sigma_a)$ is normal with mean $\alpha_{\tau|\tau}$ and variance $\Sigma_{\tau|\tau}$, while $g(\alpha_{\tau+1} \mid y^{\tau}, \alpha_{\tau}, \Sigma_e, \Sigma_a)$ is normal with mean $\mathbb{D}_1\alpha_{\tau}$ and variance Σ_a. Hence, to draw samples from $g(\alpha^t \mid y^t, \Sigma, \Sigma_a)$ we use the following algorithm.

Algorithm 10.3.

(1) Run the Kalman filter, save $\alpha_{t|t}$, $\Sigma_t = \Sigma_{t|t} - \mathbb{M}_t \Sigma_{t+1|t} \mathbb{M}_t'$, and $\mathbb{M}_t = \Sigma_{t|t}\Sigma_{t+1|t}^{-1}$.

(2) Draw $\alpha_t^l \sim \mathbb{N}(\alpha_{t|t}, \Sigma_{t|t})$, $\alpha_{t-j}^l \sim \mathbb{N}(\alpha_{t-j|t-j} + \mathbb{M}_{t-j}(\alpha_{t-j+1}^l - \alpha_{t-j|t-j}), \Sigma_{t-j})$, $j \geqslant 1$.

(3) Repeat $l = 1, \dots, L$ times

As usual, if a training sample does not exist, the prior at time zero could be calibrated by using a fixed-coefficient version of the model. It is straightforward to allow for an unknown $\mathbb{D}_1$ and a time-varying Σ_a.

Exercise 10.33. Assume that $\mathbb{D}_1$ is unknown and assume a normal prior on its nonzero elements, i.e., $\mathbb{D}_1^0 \sim \mathbb{N}(\bar{\mathbb{D}}_1, \bar{\sigma}_{D_1}^2)$. Show that $g(\mathbb{D}_1^0 \mid \alpha^t, y^t, \Sigma_e, \Sigma_a) \sim \mathbb{N}((\alpha_{t-1}'\Sigma_a^{-1}\alpha_{t-1} + \sigma_{D_1}^{-2})^{-1}(\alpha_{t-1}'\Sigma_a^{-1}\alpha_t + \sigma_{D_1}^{-2}\bar{\mathbb{D}}_1), (\alpha_{t-1}'\Sigma_a^{-1}\alpha_{t-1} + \sigma_{D_1}^{-2})^{-1})$.

Exercise 10.34. Let $\Sigma_{at} = \sigma_t \Sigma_a$. How would you construct the conditional posterior distribution for Σ_{at}? (Hint: treat σ_t parametrically and assume a conjugate prior.)

The next extension is useful to compute the conditional posterior of DSGE models which are not linearized around the steady state.

Exercise 10.35 (nonlinear state space models). Consider the state space model,

$$\left.\begin{aligned} y_t &= f_{1t}(\alpha_t) + e_t, \qquad & e_t &\sim \text{i.i.d. } \mathbb{N}(0, \Sigma_e), \\ \alpha_t &= f_{2t}(\alpha_{t-1}) + v_t, \qquad & v_t &\sim \text{i.i.d. } \mathbb{N}(0, \Sigma_a), \end{aligned}\right\} \tag{10.49}$$

where f_{1t} and f_{2t} are given but perhaps depend on unknown parameters. Show that $(\alpha_t \mid \alpha_{j\neq t}, \Sigma_e, \Sigma_a, y^t) \propto \mathfrak{h}_1(\alpha_t)\mathfrak{h}_2(\alpha_t)\mathbb{N}(f_{2t}(\alpha_{t-1}), \Sigma_a)$, where $\mathfrak{h}_1(\alpha_t)$ and $\mathfrak{h}_2(\alpha_t)$ are given by $\mathfrak{h}_1(\alpha_t) = \exp\{-0.5[\alpha_{t+1} - f_{2t}(\alpha_t)]'\Sigma_a^{-1}[\alpha_{t+1} - f_{2t}(\alpha_t)]\}$ and $\mathfrak{h}_2(\alpha_t) = \exp\{-0.5[y_t - f_{1t}(\alpha_t)]'\Sigma_e^{-1}[y_t - f_{1t}(\alpha_t)]\}$. Describe how to draw sequences for α from this posterior distribution.

Finally, we consider the case of nonnormal errors. While for macroeconomic data the assumption of normality is, by and large, appropriate, for robustness purposes it may be useful to allow for general errors. As noted, (10.46) produces nonnormal $y_{t+\tau}$ when $\tau \geqslant 1$. To generate nonnormalities, when $\tau = 0$, it is sufficient to add a nuisance parameter ϕ_5 to the variance of the error term, i.e., $(\alpha_t \mid \alpha_{t-1}, \phi_5, \Sigma_a) \sim \mathbb{N}(\mathbb{D}_1\alpha_{t-1}, \phi_5\Sigma_a)$, where $g(\phi_5)$ is chosen to mimic a distribution of interest. For example, suppose that ϕ_5 is exponentially distributed with mean equal to 2. Since $g(\alpha_t \mid \alpha_{t-1}, \Sigma_a, \phi_5)$ is normal with mean $\mathbb{D}_1\alpha_{t-1}$ and variance $\phi_5\Sigma_a$, $g(\phi_5 \mid y^t, \alpha^t, \Sigma_a) \propto \sqrt{(1/\phi_5)}\exp\{-0.5[\phi_5 + (\alpha_t - \mathbb{D}_1\alpha_{t-1})'\phi_5^{-1}\Sigma_a^{-1}(\alpha_t - \mathbb{D}_1\alpha_{t-1})]\}$, which is the kernel of the generalized inverse Gaussian distribution. A similar approach can be used to model a general error structure in the measurement equation.

Exercise 10.36. Suppose $(y_t \mid \alpha_t, x_t, \phi_6, \Sigma_e) \sim \mathbb{N}(x_t\alpha_t, \phi_6\Sigma_e)$ and that $g(\phi_6)$ is $\mathrm{Exp}(2)$. Show the form of the conditional posterior for ϕ_6. Describe how to draw sequences for ϕ_6.

Exercise 10.37. Let $y_t = x_t\alpha_t$, $t = 1, \dots, T$, where, conditional on x_t, $\alpha_t' = (\alpha_{1t}, \dots, \alpha_{kt})$ is i.i.d. with mean $\bar{\alpha}$ and variance $\bar{\Sigma}_\alpha$, $|\bar{\Sigma}_\alpha| \neq 0$. Let $\bar{\alpha}$ and $\bar{\Sigma}_\alpha$ be known and let $\alpha = (\alpha_1, \dots, \alpha_t)$.

(i) Show that the minimum MSE estimator of α is $\tilde{\alpha} = (I_T \otimes \bar{\Sigma}_\alpha)x'\Omega^{-1}y + [I_{Tk} - (I_T \otimes \bar{\Sigma}_\alpha)x'\Omega^{-1}x](\mathbf{1} \otimes \bar{\alpha})$, where $\Omega = x(I_T \otimes \Sigma_\alpha)x'$, $x = \mathrm{diag}(x_1', \dots, x_t')$ and $\mathbf{1} = [1, \dots, 1]'$.

(ii) Show that, if $\bar{\alpha} = \alpha_0 + v_a$, $v_a \sim$ i.i.d. $(0, \Sigma_{\bar{a}})$ and $\Sigma_{\bar{a}}$ is known, the best minimum MSE estimator of $\bar{\alpha}$ equals $(x'\Omega^{-1}x + \Sigma_{\bar{a}}^{-1})^{-1}(x'\Omega^{-1}y + \Sigma_{\bar{a}}^{-1}\alpha_0)$. Show that, as $\Sigma_{\bar{a}} \to \infty$, the optimal MSE estimator is the GLS estimator.

Exercise 10.38 (Cooley and Prescott). Let $y_t = x_t\alpha_t$, where x_t is a $1 \times k$ vector, $\alpha_t = \alpha_t^{\mathrm{P}} + e_t$, $\alpha_t^{\mathrm{P}} = \alpha_{t-1}^{\mathrm{P}} + v_t$, where $e_t \sim$ i.i.d. $(0, (1-\varrho)\sigma^2\Sigma_e)$, $v_t \sim$ i.i.d. $(0, \varrho\sigma^2\Sigma_v)$, and assume Σ_e, Σ_v known. Here ϱ measures the speed of adjustment of α_t to structural changes (for $\varrho \to 1$ permanent changes are large relative to transitory ones). Let $y = [y_1, \dots, y_T]'$, $x = [x_1, \dots, x_T]'$, and $\alpha^p = (\alpha_{1t}^p, \dots, \alpha_{kt}^p)'$.

(i) Show that the model is equivalent to $y_t = x_t'\alpha_t^{\mathrm{P}} + \epsilon_t$, where $\epsilon_t \sim$ i.i.d. $(0, \sigma^2\Omega(\varrho))$. Show the form of $\Omega(\varrho)$.

(ii) Show that, conditional on ϱ, the minimum MSE estimators for (α^p, σ^2) are $\alpha_{\mathrm{ML}}^p(\varrho) = (x'\Omega(\varrho)^{-1}x)^{-1}(x'\Omega(\varrho)^{-1}y)$ and $\sigma_{\mathrm{ML}}^2(\varrho) = (1/T)(y - x\alpha_{\mathrm{ML}}^p(\varrho))' \times \Omega(\varrho)^{-1}(y - x\alpha_{\mathrm{ML}}^p(\varrho))$. Describe a way to maximize the concentrated likelihood as a function of ϱ.

(iii) Obtain posterior estimators for $(\alpha, \varrho, \sigma^2)$ when $g(\alpha, \varrho, \sigma^2)$ is noninformative. Set up a Gibbs sampler algorithm to compute the joint posterior of the three parameters.

Example 10.15. We use a TVC-VAR model with output, inflation, nominal M1, and interest rates for the United States and estimate a structure like (10.46). We recursively produce responses to monetary shocks consistent with the information at each t. Monetary shocks are identified by imposing a liquidity effect (interest rate increases require money to decline for two quarters). We draw 10 000 vectors for α^t and keep 1 out of every 5 of the last 5000. Figure 10.4 presents the median responses of detrended GDP, obtained by using information up to the date reported on the horizontal axis. The first sample period is 1960:1–1978:4, the last 1960:1–2003:4. Remarkably, the posterior median responses are similar across time despite the commonly held view that the structure of the U.S. economy has changed over this sample period.

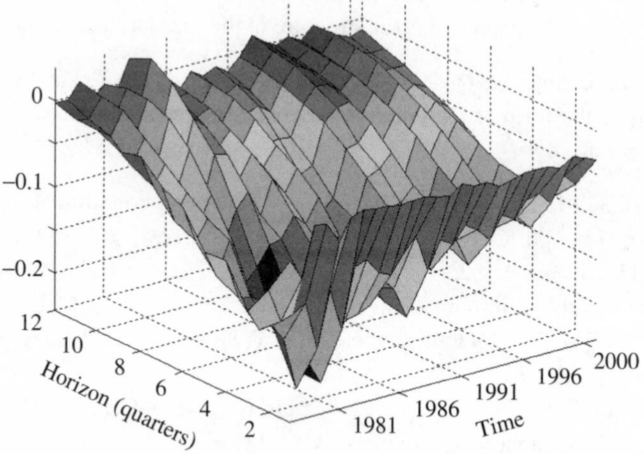

Figure 10.4. Median GDP responses to U.S. monetary policy shock.

10.5 Panel VAR Models

We extensively discussed macro panels in chapter 8. Therefore, the focus of this section is narrow. Our attention centers on three problems. First, how to specify Bayesian univariate dynamic panels. Second, how to dynamically group units in the cross section. Third, how to set up panel VAR models with cross-sectional interdependencies. Univariate dynamic panels emerge, for example, when estimating steady-state income per capita, or when examining the short- and long-run effects of oil shocks on output across countries. Grouping is particularly useful, for example, if one is interested in knowing if there are countries which react differently than others after, for example, financial crises. Finally, models with interdependencies are useful for the study of a variety of transmission issues across countries or sectors which cannot be dealt with by using the models of chapter 8.

10.5.1 Univariate Dynamic Panels

For $i = 1, \dots, n$, the model we consider is

$$y_{it} = A_{1i}(\ell)y_{it-1} + \bar{y}_i + A_{2i}(\ell)Y_t + e_{it}, \quad e_{it} \sim \text{i.i.d. } (0, \sigma_i^2), \qquad (10.50)$$

where $A_{ji}(\ell) = A_{ji1}\ell + \cdots + A_{jiq_j}\ell^{q_j}$, $j = 1, 2$, and $\bar{y}_i$ is the unit specific fixed effect. Here Y_t includes variables which account for cross-sectional interdependencies. For example, if y_{it} are regional sales, one element of Y_t could be a national business cycle indicator. Because variables like Y_t are included, $E(e_{it}e_{j\tau}) = 0$, $\forall i \neq j$, all t, τ. We can calculate a number of statistics from (10.50). For example, long-run multipliers to shocks are $(1 - A_{1i}(1))^{-1}$ and long-run multipliers to changes in Y_t are $(1 - A_{1i}(1))^{-1}A_{2i}(1)$.

Example 10.16. Let y_{it} be the output in the ith Latin American country and let $Y_t = (x_{1t}, i_t)$, where i_t is the U.S. interest rate. Suppose $i_t = A_3(\ell)\epsilon_t$. Then

$(1-A_{1i}(\ell))^{-1}A_{2i}(\ell)A_3(\ell)$ traces out the effect of a unitary U.S. interest rate shock at t on the output of country i from t on.

Stacking the T observations for (y_{it}, Y_t, e_{it}) and the coefficients on the fixed effect into the vectors $(y_i, Y, e_i, \mathbf{1})$, letting $\boldsymbol{X}_i = (y_i, Y, \mathbf{1})$, $\Sigma_i = \sigma_i^2 I_T$, $\alpha = [A_1, \dots, A_n]'$, $A_i = (A_{1i1}, \dots, A_{iq_1}, \bar{y}_i, A_{2i1}, \dots, A_{2iq_2})$, and setting $y = (y_1, \dots, y_n)'$, $e = (e_1, \dots, e_n)'$ we have

$$y = \boldsymbol{X}\alpha + e, \quad e \sim (0, \Sigma), \tag{10.51}$$

where $\boldsymbol{X} = \operatorname{diag}\{\boldsymbol{X}_i\}$ and $\Sigma = \operatorname{diag}\{\Sigma_i\}$. Clearly, (10.51) has the same format as a VAR, except that $\boldsymbol{X}_i$ are unit specific and the covariance matrix of the shocks has a diagonal heteroskedastic structure. The first feature is due to the fact that we do not allow for interdependencies across units. The latter is easy to deal with once (10.51) is transformed so that the innovations have spherical disturbances.

If e is normal, the likelihood function of a univariate dynamic panel is therefore the product of a normal for α, conditional on Σ, and n gamma densities for Σ_i^{-1}. Since the variance of e is diagonal, α_{ML} can be obtained equation by equation.

Exercise 10.39. Show that α_{ML} obtained from (10.51) is the same as the estimator obtained by stacking weighted least squares estimators obtained from (10.50) for each i.

Conjugate priors for dynamic panels are similar to those described in section 10.2. Since $\operatorname{var}(e)$ is diagonal, we can choose $\sigma_i^{-2} \sim \mathbb{G}(a_1, a_2)$, each i. Given the panel framework we can use the exchangeability assumption if, *a priori*, we expect the A_i to be similar across units. An exchangeable prior on A_i takes the form $A_i \sim \mathbb{N}(\bar{A}, \bar{\sigma}_A^2)$, where $\bar{\sigma}_A^2$ measures the degree of heterogeneity an investigator expects to find in the cross section.

Exercise 10.40 (Lindlay and Smith). Suppose the model (10.50) has k coefficients in each equation and that $A_i = \bar{A} + v_i$, $i = 1, \dots, n$, $v_i \sim$ i.i.d. $\mathbb{N}(0, \bar{\sigma}_A^2)$, where $\bar{A}$, $\bar{\sigma}_A^2$ are known. Show the form of the posterior mean for A_i. Show the form of the posterior variance for A_i, assuming that σ_i^2 is fixed.

Exercise 10.40 highlights the importance of exchangeable priors in a model like (10.51). Exchangeability, in fact, preserves independence across equations and the posterior mean of the coefficients of a dynamic panel can be computed equation by equation.

Exercise 10.41 (Canova and Marcet). Suppose you want to set up an exchangeable prior on the difference of the coefficients across equations, i.e., $A_i - A_{i'} \sim$ i.i.d. $\mathbb{N}(0, \Sigma_a)$. This is advantageous since there is no need to specify the prior mean $\bar{A}$. Show the structure of Σ_a which ensures that the ordering of the units in the cross section does not matter.

We have already mentioned the pooling dilemma in section 8.4. We return to this problem in the next exercise, which gives conditions under which the posterior distribution for A_i reflects prior, pooled, and/or single-unit sample information.

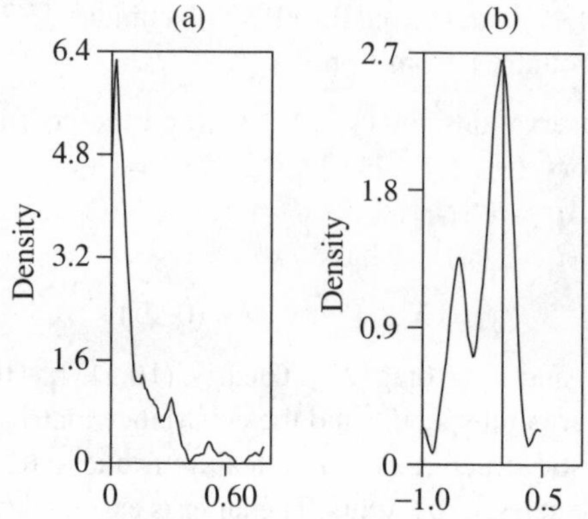

Figure 10.5. Cross-sectional densities: (a) convergence rate; (b) steady state.

Exercise 10.42 (Zellner and Hong). Let $y_i = x_i\alpha_i + e_i$, $i = 1,\dots,n$, where x_i may include lags of y_i and for each i, y_i is a $T \times 1$ vector, x_i a $T \times k$ vector, α_i a $k \times 1$ vector, and $e_i \sim$ i.i.d. $\mathbb{N}(0, \sigma_e^2)$. Assume that $\alpha_i = \bar{\alpha} + v_i$, where $v_i \sim$ i.i.d. $\mathbb{N}(0, \kappa^{-1}\sigma_v^2 I_k)$ with $0 < \kappa \leqslant \infty$.

(i) Show that a conditional point estimate for $\alpha = (\alpha_1', \dots, \alpha_N')'$ is the $Nk \times 1$ vector $\tilde{\alpha} = (x'x + \kappa I_{nk})^{-1}(x'x\alpha_{\text{OLS}} + \kappa \mathbb{I}\alpha_{\text{p}})$, where $x = \text{blockdiag}\{x_i\}$, $\alpha_{\text{OLS}} = (x'x)^{-1}(x'y)$, $y = (y_1', \dots, y_N')'$, $\alpha_{\text{OLS}} = (\alpha_{1,\text{OLS}}', \dots, \alpha_{N,\text{OLS}}')'$, $\alpha_{i,\text{OLS}} = (x_i'x_i)^{-1}(x_i'y_i)$, $\mathbb{I} = (I_k, \dots, I_k)$, $\alpha_{\text{p}} = (\sum_i x_i'x_i)^{-1}(\sum_i x_i'x_i\alpha_{i,\text{OLS}})$. Conclude that $\tilde{\alpha}$ is a weighted average of individual OLS estimates and of the pooled estimate α_{p}. Show that, as $\kappa \to \infty$, $\tilde{\alpha} = \alpha_{\text{p}}$.

(ii) (g-prior) Show that $\tilde{\alpha}_i = [\alpha_{i,\text{OLS}} + (\sigma_e^2/\sigma_v^2)\bar{\alpha}]/(1 + \sigma_e^2/\sigma_v^2)$ if $v_i \sim$ i.i.d. $\mathbb{N}(0, (x_i'x_i)^{-1}\sigma_v^2)$. Conclude that $\tilde{\alpha}_i$ is a weighted average of the OLS estimate and the prior mean $\bar{\alpha}$.

(iii) Show that $\tilde{\alpha}_i = [\alpha_{i,\text{OLS}} + (\sigma_e^2/\sigma_v^2)\alpha_{\text{p}}]/(1 + \sigma_e^2/\sigma_v^2)$ if $g(\bar{\alpha})$ is noninformative. Conclude that, as $\sigma_e^2/\sigma_v^2 \to \infty$, $\tilde{\alpha}_i = \alpha_{\text{p}}$, and, as $\sigma_e^2/\sigma_v^2 \to 0$, $\tilde{\alpha}_i = \alpha_{i,\text{OLS}}$.

Next we describe how dynamic univariate panels can be used to estimate the steady-state distribution of income per capita and of the convergence rates in a panel of EU regions.

Example 10.17. Here $A_{1i}(\ell)$ has only one nonzero element (the first one), Y_t is the average EU GDP per capita, and $A_{2ij} = 1$ if $j = 0$ and zero otherwise. Hence (10.50) is

$$\ln\left(\frac{y_{it}}{Y_t}\right) = \bar{y}_i + A_i \ln\left(\frac{y_{it-1}}{Y_{t-1}}\right) + e_{it}, \quad e_{it} \sim \text{i.i.d. } \mathbb{N}(0, \sigma_i^2). \tag{10.52}$$

We let $\alpha_i = (\bar{y}_i, A_i)$ and assume $\alpha_i = \bar{\alpha} + v_i$, where $v_i \sim$ i.i.d. $\mathbb{N}(0, \Sigma_a)$, and $\Sigma_a = \text{diag}\{\sigma_{a_j}^2\}$.

We treat σ_i^2 as known (and estimate it from individual OLS regressions), assume $\bar{\alpha}$ known (estimated by averaging individual OLS estimates), and treat $\sigma_{a_j}^2$ as fixed. Let

$\sigma_i^2/\sigma_{a_j}^2$, $j = 1, 2$, measure the relative importance of prior and sample information: if this ratio goes to infinity, sample information does not matter; conversely, if it is close to zero, prior information is irrelevant. We choose a relatively loose prior ($\sigma_i^2/\sigma_{a_j}^2 = 0.5$, $j = 1, 2$). Using income per capita for 144 EU regions from 1980 to 1996, we calculate the relative steady state for unit i by using $\widetilde{\mathrm{SS}}_i = \tilde{\bar{y}}_i(1 - \tilde{A}_i^T)/(1 - \tilde{A}_i) + \tilde{A}_i^{T+1} y_{i0}/Y_0$, where $\tilde{\bar{y}}_i$, $\tilde{A}_i$ are posterior mean estimates. The rate of convergence to the steady state is $\widetilde{\mathrm{CV}}_i = 1 - \tilde{A}_i$. (If $\tilde{A} > 1$, we set $\widetilde{\mathrm{CV}} = 0$.) We plot the cross-sectional densities of $\widetilde{\mathrm{CV}}$ and $\widetilde{\mathrm{SS}}$ in figure 10.5. The mode of the convergence rate is 0.09, implying much faster catch up than the literature has found (see, for example, Barro and Sala-i-Martin 2003). The highest 95% credible set is, however, large (it goes from 0.03 to 0.55). The cross-sectional distribution of relative steady states has at least two modes: one at low relative levels of income and one just below the EU average.

At times, when the panel is short, one wishes to use cross-sectional information to get better estimates of the parameters of each unit. In other cases, one is interested in estimating the average cross-sectional effect. In both situations, the tools of meta-analysis come in handy.

Example 10.18. In example 10.17, suppose that $g(\mathrm{SS}_i) \sim \mathbb{N}(\overline{\mathrm{SS}}, \sigma_{\mathrm{SS}}^2)$, where $\sigma_{\mathrm{SS}} = 0.4$ and assume that $g(\overline{\mathrm{SS}}) \propto 1$. Using the logic of hierarchical models, $g(\overline{\mathrm{SS}} \mid y)$ combines prior and data information and $g(\mathrm{SS}_i \mid y)$ combines unit specific and pooled information. The posterior mean for $\overline{\mathrm{SS}}$ is -0.14 indicating that the distribution is highly skewed to the left, the variance is 0.083 and a credible 95% interval is $(-0.30, 0.02)$. Since a credible 95% interval for SS_i is $(-0.51, 0.19)$, this posterior distribution largely overlaps with the one produced in figure 10.5.

10.5.2 Endogenous Grouping

There are many situations when one would like to know whether there are groups in the cross section of a dynamic panel. For example, one type of growth theory predicts the existence of convergence clubs, where clubs are defined by similarities in the features of the various economies or government policies. In monetary economics, one is typically interested in knowing whether regional economies respond differently to union-wide monetary policy disturbances or whether the behavioral responses of certain groups of agents (credit-constrained versus credit-unconstrained consumers, large versus small firms, etc.) can be identified. In general, these classifications are exogenously chosen (see, for example, Gertler and Gilchrist 1994) and somewhat arbitrary.

This subsection describes a procedure which simultaneously allows for endogenous grouping of cross-sectional units and for Bayesian estimation of the parameters of the model. The basic idea is simple: if units i and i' belong to a group, the vector of coefficients will have the same mean and the same dispersion, but if they do not, the vector of coefficients of the two units will have different moments.

Let n be the size of the cross section, T the size of the time series, and $\mathcal{O} = 1, 2, \ldots, n!$ the ordering of the units of the cross section (the ordering producing a group is unknown). We assume there could be $\psi = 1, 2, \ldots, \bar{\psi}$ break points, $\bar{\psi}$ given. For each group $j = 1, \ldots, \psi + 1$ and each unit $i = 1, \ldots, n^j(\mathcal{O})$ we have

$$y_{it} = \bar{y}_i + A_{1i}(\ell)y_{it-1} + A_{2i}(\ell)Y_{t-1} + e_{it}, \quad e_{it} \sim \text{i.i.d. } (0, \sigma_i^2), \tag{10.53}$$

$$\alpha_i^j = \bar{\alpha}^j + v_i^j, \quad v_i^j \sim \text{i.i.d. } (0, \bar{\Sigma}_j), \tag{10.54}$$

where $\alpha_i = [\bar{y}_i, A_{1i1}, \ldots, A_{1iq_1}, A_{2i1}, \ldots, A_{2iq_2}]'$ is the $k_i \times 1$ vector of coefficients of unit i, $k_i = q_1 + q_2 + 1$, $n^j(\mathcal{O})$ is the number of units in group j, given the $\mathcal{O}$th ordering, $\sum_j n^j(\mathcal{O}) = n$, for each $\mathcal{O}$. In (10.54), α_i is random but the coefficients of the $n^j(\mathcal{O})$ units belonging to group j have the same mean and same covariance matrix. Since the exchangeable structure may differ across groups, (10.53), (10.54) capture the idea that there may be clustering of units within groups but that groups may drift apart.

The alternative to (10.53), (10.54) is a model with homogeneous dynamics in the cross section, that is, $\bar{\psi} = 0$, and an exchangeable structure for all units of the cross section, i.e.,

$$\alpha_i = \bar{\alpha} + v_i, \quad i = 1, \ldots, n, \ v_i \sim \text{i.i.d. } (0, \bar{\Sigma}). \tag{10.55}$$

Let Y be the $(nTm) \times 1$ vector of left-hand side variables in (10.53) ordered to have the n cross sections for each $t = 1, \ldots, T$, m times, X an $(nTm) \times (nk)$ matrix of the regressors, α an $(nk) \times 1$ vector of coefficients, E an $(nTm) \times 1$ vector of disturbances, $\bar{\alpha}$ a $(\psi + 1)k \times 1$ vector of means of α, A an $(nk) \times (\psi + 1)k$ matrix, $A = \text{diag}\{A_j\}$, where A_j has the form $\mathbf{1} \otimes I_k$, where I_k is a $k \times k$ identity matrix, and $\mathbf{1}$ is an $n^j(\mathcal{O}) \times 1$ vector of 1s. Given an ordering $\mathcal{O}$, the number of groups ψ, and the location of the break point $h^j(\mathcal{O})$, we can rewrite (10.53), (10.54) as

$$Y = X\alpha + E, \quad E \sim (0, \Sigma_E), \tag{10.56}$$

$$\alpha = \Xi\bar{\alpha} + V, \quad V \sim (0, \Sigma_V), \tag{10.57}$$

where Σ_E is $(nTm) \times (nTm)$, $\Sigma_V = \text{diag}\{\bar{\Sigma}_j\}$ is an $(nk) \times (nk)$ matrix, and Ξ is a matrix of 0s and 1s. To complete the specification we need priors for $(\bar{\alpha}, \Sigma_E, \Sigma_V)$ and for the submodel characteristics $\mathcal{M}$, indexed by $(\mathcal{O}, \psi, h^j(\mathcal{O}))$. Since the calculation of the posterior distribution is complicated, we take an empirical Bayes approach.

The method to group units proceeds in three steps. Given $(\bar{\alpha}, \Sigma_E, \Sigma_V, \mathcal{O})$, we examine how many groups are present. Given $\mathcal{O}$ and $\hat{\psi}$, we check for the location of the break points. Finally, we iterate on the first two steps, altering $\mathcal{O}$. The selected submodel is the one that maximizes the marginal likelihood over orderings $\mathcal{O}$, groups ψ, and break points $h^j(\mathcal{O})$.

Let $f(Y \mid H_0)$ be the marginal likelihood of the data under cross-sectional homogeneity. Furthermore, let I^{ψ} be the set of possible break points when there are ψ groups. Let $f(Y^j \mid H_{\psi}, h^j(\mathcal{O}), \mathcal{O})$ be the marginal likelihood for group j, under the assumption that there are ψ break points with location $h^j(\mathcal{O})$, using ordering $\mathcal{O}$, and let $f(Y \mid H_\psi, h^j(\mathcal{O}), \mathcal{O}) = \prod_{j=1}^{\psi+1} f(Y^j \mid H_\psi, h^j(\mathcal{O}), \mathcal{O})$. Define the quantities

$$f^-(Y \mid H_\psi, \mathcal{O}) \equiv \sup_{h^j(\mathcal{O}) \in I^\psi} f(Y \mid H_\psi, h^j(\mathcal{O}), \mathcal{O}),$$

$$f^\dagger(Y \mid H_\psi) \equiv \sup_{\mathcal{O}} f^-(Y \mid H_\psi, \mathcal{O}),$$

$$f^0(Y \mid H_\psi, \mathcal{O}) \equiv \sum_{h^j(\mathcal{O}) \in I^\psi} g_i^j(\mathcal{O}) f(Y \mid H_\psi, h^j(\mathcal{O}), \mathcal{O}),$$

where $g_i^j(\mathcal{O})$ is the prior probability that there is a break at location $h^j(\mathcal{O})$ for group j of ordering $\mathcal{O}$. f^- gives the maximized marginal likelihood with respect to the location of break points, for each ψ and $\mathcal{O}$; $f^\dagger$ the maximized marginal likelihood, for each ψ, once the location of the break point and the ordering of the data are chosen optimally. f^0 gives the average marginal likelihood with ψ breaks where the average is calculated over all possible locations of the break points, using the prior probability that there is a break point in each location as weight. We choose $g_i^j(\mathcal{O})$ to be uniform over each $(j, \mathcal{O})$ and set $\bar{\psi} \ll \sqrt{N/2}$.

Examining the hypothesis that the dynamics of the cross section are group-based, given $\mathcal{O}$, is equivalent to verifying the hypothesis that there are ψ breaks against the null of no breaks. Such a hypothesis can be examined with a posterior odds ratio,

$$\text{PO}(\mathcal{O}) = \frac{g_0 f(Y \mid H_0)}{\sum_\psi g_\psi f^0(Y \mid H_\psi, \mathcal{O}) \mathbb{J}_1(n)}, \tag{10.58}$$

where g_0 (g_ψ) is the prior probability that there are 0 (ψ) breaks. Verification of the hypothesis that there are $\psi - 1$ versus ψ breaks in the cross section can be done by using

$$\text{PO}(\mathcal{O}, \psi - 1) = \frac{g_{\psi-1} f^{0(\psi-1)}(Y \mid H_{\psi-1}, \mathcal{O})}{g_\psi f^{0(\psi)}(Y \mid H_\psi, \mathcal{O}) \mathbb{J}_2(n)}. \tag{10.59}$$

Here $\mathbb{J}_i(n)$, $i = 1, 2$, are penalty functions which account for the fact that a model with ψ breaks is more densely parametrized than a model with a smaller number of breaks. Once the number of break points has been found (say, equal to $\hat{\psi}$), we assign units to groups so as to provide the highest total predictive density, i.e., compute $f^-(Y \mid H_{\hat{\psi}}, \mathcal{O})$. Since there are $\mathcal{O}$ possible permutations of the cross section over which to search for groups, the optimal permutation rule of units in the cross section is the one which achieves $f^\dagger(Y \mid H_{\hat{\psi}})$.

Two interesting questions which emerge are the following. First, can we proceed sequentially to test for breaks? Bai (1997) shows that such a procedure produces consistent estimates of the number and the locations of the breaks. However, when there are multiple groups, the estimated break point is consistent for *any* of the existing break points and its location depends on the "strength" of the break. Second, how can we maximize the marginal likelihood over $\mathcal{O}$ when n is large? When no information on the ordering of the units is available and n is moderately large, the approach is computationally demanding. Geographical, economic, or sociopolitical factors may help to provide a restricted set of ordering worth examining. But even when economic theory is silent, the maximization does not require $n!$ evaluations, since many orderings give the same marginal likelihood.

Example 10.19. Suppose $n = 4$, so there are $n! = 24$ possible orderings to examine. Suppose the initial ordering is 1234 and two groups are found: 1 and 234. Then all permutations of 234 with unit 1 coming first, i.e., 1243, 1342, etc., give the same marginal likelihood. Similarly, permutations which leave unit 1 last need not be examined, i.e., 2341, 2431, etc. This reduces the number of orderings to be examined to 13. By trying another ordering, say 4213, and finding, for example, two groups, 42 and 13, we can further eliminate all the orderings which rotate the elements of each group, i.e., 4132, 2341, etc. It is easy to verify that, once four carefully selected ordering have been tried and, say, two groups found in each trial, we have exhausted all possible combinations.

Once the submodel characteristics have been determined, we can estimate $[\bar{\alpha}', \text{vech}(\Sigma_E)', \text{vech}(\Sigma_V)']'$ by using $f^\dagger(Y \mid H_\psi)$. For example, if e_{it} and v_i are normally distributed,

$$\left.\begin{aligned}
\hat{\bar{\alpha}}^j &= \frac{1}{n^j(\mathcal{O})} \sum_{i=1}^{n^j(\mathcal{O})} \alpha^j_{i,\text{OLS}}, \\
\hat{\Sigma}_j &= \frac{1}{n^j(\mathcal{O}) - 1} \sum_{i=1}^{n^j(\mathcal{O})} (\alpha^j_{i,\text{OLS}} - \hat{\bar{\alpha}}^j)(\alpha^j_{i,\text{OLS}} - \hat{\bar{\alpha}}^j)' - \frac{1}{n^j(\mathcal{O})} \sum_{i=1}^{n^j(\mathcal{O})} (x_i x_i')^{-1} \hat{\sigma}_i^2, \\
\hat{\sigma}_i^2 &= \frac{1}{T-k}(y_i' y_i - y_i' x_i \alpha_{i,\text{OLS}}),
\end{aligned}\right\} \tag{10.60}$$

where x_i is the matrix of regressors, y_i is the vector of dependent variables for unit i, and $\alpha^j_{i,\text{OLS}}$ is the OLS estimator of α^j obtained by using the information for unit i (in group $j = 1, \dots, \psi + 1$). Then an empirical Bayes estimate for the α vector is $\tilde{\alpha} = (X'\hat{\Sigma}_E^{-1} X + \hat{\Sigma}_V^{-1})^{-1}(X'\hat{\Sigma}_E^{-1} Y + \hat{\Sigma}_V^{-1} A\hat{\bar{\alpha}})$. Alternatively, if the e_{it} and the v_i are normal and $g(a_0, \Sigma_E, \Sigma_V)$ is diffuse, we can jointly estimate $(\bar{\alpha}^j, \Sigma_j, \sigma_i^2)$ and the posterior of α as follows:

$$\left.\begin{aligned}
\hat{\bar{\alpha}}^j &= \frac{1}{n^j(\mathcal{O})} \sum_{i=1}^{n^j(\mathcal{O})} (\alpha_i^*)^j, \\
\hat{\Sigma}_j &= \frac{1}{n^j(\mathcal{O}) - k - 1}\left[\delta I + \sum_{i=1}^{n^j(\mathcal{O})} [(\alpha_i^*)^j - \hat{\bar{\alpha}}^j][(\alpha_i^*)^j - \hat{\bar{\alpha}}^j]'\right], \\
\hat{\sigma}_i^2 &= \frac{1}{T+2}(y_i - x_i\alpha_i^*)'(y_i - x_i\alpha_i^*), \\
(\alpha_i^*)^j &= \left(\frac{1}{\hat{\sigma}_i^2} x_i' x_i + \hat{\Sigma}_j^{-1}\right)^{-1} \left(\frac{1}{\hat{\sigma}_i^2} x_i' x_i \alpha_{i,\text{OLS}} + \hat{\Sigma}_j^{-1} \hat{\bar{\alpha}}^j\right),
\end{aligned}\right\} \tag{10.61}$$

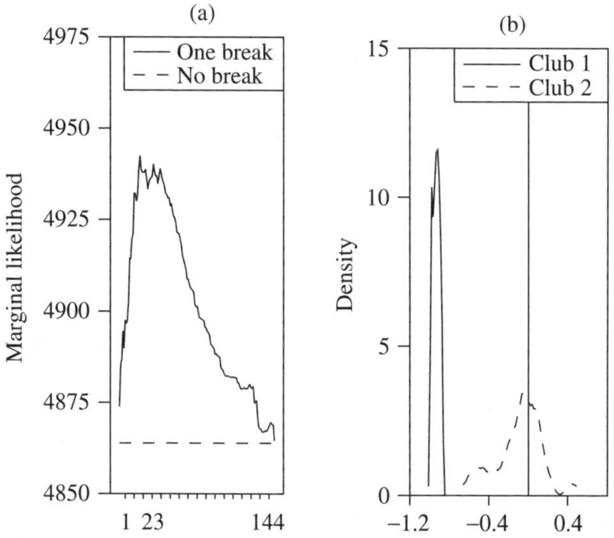

Figure 10.6. Convergence clubs: (a) break point test; (b) steady-state densities.

where $j = 1, \dots, \psi + 1$ and $i = 1, \dots, n^j(\Theta)$, and $\delta > 0$ but small ensures that $\hat{\hat{\Sigma}}_j$ is positive definite.

Exercise 10.43. Derive (10.60) and (10.61).

Example 10.20 (convergence clubs). The cross-sectional posterior density of steady states in example 10.17 shows a multimodal shape. One may therefore be interested in knowing whether there are convergence clubs in the data and where the break point is.

We examined several orderings of cross-sectional units based on initial income conditions, growth patterns, or geographical characteristics. The one which is optimal orders units by using the initial conditions of relative income per capita. With this ordering, we set $\bar{\psi} = 4$ and sequentially examine ψ against $\psi + 1$ breaks starting from $\psi = 0$. There are up to three breaks in the data with PO ratios of 0.06, 0.52, 0.66, respectively. Conditioning on one break ($\psi = 1$) we plot in figure 10.6(a) the marginal likelihood as a function of the break point, together with the marginal likelihood for $\psi = 0$. Visual inspection indicates that the former is always above the latter and that units up to 23 belong to the first group and from 24 to 144 to the second. The average convergence rates of the two groups are 0.78 and 0.20, suggesting faster convergence to below-average steady states in the first group. Figure 10.6(b) suggests that the densities of posterior steady states for the two groups are distinct. Unsurprisingly, the first 23 units are all poor, Mediterranean, and peripheral regions of the EU.

10.5.3 Panel VARs with Interdependencies

Neither the panel VAR model studied in chapter 8 nor the specifications we have considered so far allow for cross-unit lagged feedbacks. This features may be important, for example, when one is interested in the transmission of shocks across countries. A panel VAR model with interdependencies has the form,

$$y_{it} = A_{1it}(\ell)y_t + A_{2it}(\ell)Y_t + e_{it}, \tag{10.62}$$

where $i = 1, \dots, n$, $t = 1, \dots, T$, y_{it} is an $m_1 \times 1$ vector for each i, $y_t = (y'_{1t}, y'_{2t}, \dots, y'_{nt})'$, A^j_{1it} are $m_1 \times (nm_1)$ matrices, and A^j_{2it} are $m_1 \times m_2$ matrices for each j, Y_t is an $m_2 \times 1$ vector of exogenous variables, common to all i, e_{it} is an $m_1 \times 1$ vector of disturbances, and, for convenience, we have omitted constants and other deterministic components. In (10.62) cross-unit lagged interdependencies appear whenever $A^j_{1it,i'} \neq 0$, for $i' \neq i$ at some lag j, that is, when the matrix of lagged coefficients is not block diagonal at all lags. The presence of lagged cross-unit interdependencies adds flexibility to the specification but is costly: the number of coefficients is greatly increased (there are $k = nm_1q_1 + m_2q_2$ coefficients in each equation). In (10.62) we allow coefficients to vary over time.

To construct posterior distributions for the unknowns, rewrite (10.62) as

$$Y_t = X_t\alpha_t + E_t, \quad E_t \sim \mathbb{N}(0, \Sigma_E), \tag{10.63}$$

where $X_t = (I_{nm_1} \otimes \boldsymbol{X}_t)$, $\boldsymbol{X}_t = (y'_{t-1}, y'_{t-2}, \dots, y'_{t-q_1}, Y'_t, \dots, Y'_{t-q_2})$, $\alpha_t = (\alpha'_{1t}, \dots, \alpha'_{nt})'$, and $\alpha_{it} = (\alpha^{1\prime}_{it}, \dots, \alpha^{m_1\prime}_{it})'$. Here α^j_{it} are $k \times 1$ vectors containing the coefficients for equation j of unit i, while Y_t and E_t are $nm_1 \times 1$ vectors.

Since α_t varies with cross-sectional units in different time periods, it is impossible to employ classical methods to estimate it. Three shortcuts are typically used: it is assumed that the coefficient vector does not depend on the unit (apart from a time-invariant fixed effect), that there are no interdependencies (see, for example, Holtz Eakin et al. 1988; Binder et al. 2005), or that lagged interdependencies can be captured with a single indicator (see Pesaran et al. 2003). Neither of these assumptions is appealing in our context. Instead, we assume that α_t can be decomposed as

$$\alpha_t = \Xi_1\theta^1_t + \Xi_2\theta^2_t + \sum_{f=3}^{F} \Xi_f\theta^f_t, \tag{10.64}$$

where Ξ_1 is a vector of 1s of dimensions $nm_1k \times 1$, Ξ_2 is a matrix of 1s and 0s of dimensions $nm_1k \times n$, and Ξ_f are conformable matrices. Here θ^1_t is the common factor, θ^2_t is an $n \times 1$ vector of unit-specific factors, and θ^f_t is a set of factors which is indexed by the unit i, the variable j, the lag, or combinations of all of the above.

Example 10.21. In a two-variable, two-lag, two-country model with $Y_t = 0$, (10.64) implies, for example,

$$\alpha_t = \theta^1_t + \theta^{2i}_t + \theta^{3j}_t + \theta^{4s}_t + \theta^{5\ell}_t, \tag{10.65}$$

where θ_t^1 is a common factor, $\theta_t^2 = (\theta_t^{21}, \theta_t^{22})'$ is a 2×1 vector of country-specific factors, $\theta_t^3 = (\theta_t^{31}, \theta_t^{32})'$ is a 2×1 vector of equation-specific factors, $\theta_t^{4s} = (\theta_t^{41}, \theta_t^{42})'$ is a 2×1 vector of variable-specific factors, and $\theta_t^{5\ell} = (\theta_t^{51}, \theta_t^{52})'$ is a 2×1 vector of lag-specific factors.

All factors in (10.64) are allowed to be time varying; time-invariant structures can be obtained via restrictions on the law of motion of the θ_t. Also, while the factorization in (10.64) is exact, in practice only a few θ will be specified: in that case all the omitted factors will be aggregated into an error term v_{1t}. Note also that with (10.64) the over-parametrization of the original model is dramatically reduced because the $nm_1k \times 1$ vector α_t depends on a much lower-dimensional vector of factors.

Let $\theta_t = [\theta_t^1, (\theta_t^2)', (\theta_t^3)', \dots, (\theta_t^{f_1})',\ f_1 < F]$ and write (10.64) as

$$\alpha_t = \Xi\theta_t + v_{1t}, \quad v_{1t} \sim \mathbb{N}(0, \Sigma_E \otimes \Sigma_V), \tag{10.66}$$

where $\Xi = [\Xi_1, \Xi_2, \dots, \Xi_{f_1}]$ and Σ_V is a $k \times k$ matrix. We assume a hierarchical structure for θ_t which allows for time variations and exchangeability:

$$\theta_t = (I - \mathbb{D}_1)\bar{\theta} + \mathbb{D}_1\theta_{t-1} + v_{2t}, \quad v_{2t} \sim \mathbb{N}(0, \Sigma_{v_{2t}}), \tag{10.67}$$

$$\bar{\theta} = \mathbb{D}_0\theta_0 + v_3, \quad v_3 \sim \mathbb{N}(0, \Sigma_{v_3}). \tag{10.68}$$

We set $\Sigma_V = \sigma_v^2 I_k$, where $\sigma_v^2 = \sigma^2/(1 - \rho^2)$ and, as in section 10.4, we let $\Sigma_{v_{2t}} = \phi_3 * \Sigma_{v_{2t-1}} + \phi_2 * \Sigma_0$, where $\Sigma_0 = \operatorname{diag}(\Sigma_{01}, \Sigma_{02}, \dots, \Sigma_{0,f_1})$. We assume that v_{it}, $i = 1, 2, 3$, and E_t are mutually independent and that $(\rho, \phi_3, \phi_2, \mathbb{D}_1, \mathbb{D}_0)$ are known. Here $\mathbb{D}_0$ is a matrix which restricts (part of the) means of the factors of the coefficients via an exchangeable prior.

To sum up, the prior for α_t has a hierarchical structure: with (10.66) we make a large number of VAR coefficients depend on a smaller number of factors. The factors are then allowed to have a general evolving structure (equation (10.67)) and the prior mean of, for example, unit-specific factors is potentially linked across units (equation (10.68)). The variance of the innovations in θ_t is allowed to be time varying to account for heteroskedasticity and other generic volatility clustering that are unit specific or common across units. To complete the specification we need prior densities for $(\Sigma_E^{-1}, \theta_0, \sigma^{-2}, \Sigma_0^{-1}, \Sigma_{v_3}^{-1})$. Canova and Ciccarelli (2003) study both informative and uninformative priors. Here we consider a special case of the noninformative framework they use.

Since α_t is an $nm_1k \times 1$ vector, the derivation of its posterior distribution is numerically demanding when m_1 or n is large. To avoid this problem, rewrite the model as

$$\left.\begin{aligned} y_t &= X_t\Xi\theta_t + e_t, \\ \theta_t &= (I - \mathbb{D}_1)\bar{\theta} + \mathbb{D}_1\theta_{t-1} + v_{2t}, \\ \bar{\theta} &= \mathbb{D}_0\theta_0 + v_{3t}, \end{aligned}\right\} \tag{10.69}$$

where $e_t = E_t + X_t v_{1t}$ has covariance matrix $\sigma_t \Sigma_E = (1 + \sigma_v^2 X_t' X_t) \Sigma_E$. In (10.69) we have integrated α_t out of the model so that θ_t becomes the vector of parameters of interest.

We assume that $\Sigma_{01} = \phi_{11}$ and $\Sigma_{0i} = \phi_{1i} I$, $i = 2, \ldots, f_1$, where ϕ_{1i} controls the tightness of factor i of the coefficient vector. Furthermore, we assume that $g(\Sigma_E^{-1}, \sigma^{-2}, \theta_0, \Sigma_{v_3}, \phi_1) = g(\Sigma_E^{-1}) g(\sigma^{-2}) g(\theta_0, \Sigma_{v_3}) \prod_i g(\phi_{1i})$, where $g(\Sigma_E^{-1})$ is $\mathbb{W}(\bar{\nu}_1, \bar{\Sigma}_1)$, $g(\sigma^{-2}) \propto \sigma^{-2}$, $g(\theta_0, \Sigma_{v_3}) \propto \Sigma_{v_3}^{-(\bar{\nu}_2+1)/2}$, $\bar{\nu}_2 = 1 + N + \sum_{j=1}^{m_1} \dim(\theta_{j,t}^f)$, $f > 1$, and $g(\phi_{1i}) \propto (\phi_{1i})^{-1}$, and the hyperparameters $\bar{\Sigma}_1$, $\bar{\nu}_1$ are assumed to be known or estimable from the data. The assumptions made imply that the prior for e_t has the form $(e_t \mid \sigma_t) \sim \mathbb{N}(0, \sigma_t \Sigma_E)$, and that σ_t^{-2} is gamma distributed so that e_t is distributed as a multivariate t centered at 0, with scale matrix which depends on Σ_E and degrees of freedom equal to $\dim(X_t)$. Since the likelihood function is proportional to $(\prod_{t=1}^{T} \sigma_t)^{-0.5Nm_1} |\Sigma_E|^{-0.5T} \times \exp[-0.5 \sum_t (y_t - X_t \Xi \theta_t)' (\sigma_t \Sigma_E)^{-1} (y_t - X_t \Xi \theta_t)]$, it is easy to derive the conditional posteriors of the unknowns. In fact, conditional on the other parameters, Σ_E^{-1} is Wishart, σ_t^{-2} is gamma, θ_0 is normal, $\Sigma_{v_3}^{-1}$ is Wishart, and ϕ_{1i}^{-1} is gamma distributed.

Exercise 10.44. Derive the parameters of the posterior of Σ_E^{-1}, σ_t^{-2}, $\Sigma_{v_3}^{-1}$, ϕ_i^{-1}, and θ_0.

Finally, the conditional posterior distribution of $(\theta_1, \ldots, \theta_T \mid y^T, \psi_{-\theta_t})$ is obtained as in section 10.4. With these conditional, the Gibbs sampler can be used to draw a sequence for the parameters of interest.

10.5.4 Indicators

The panel VAR (10.63) with the hierarchical prior (10.66)–(10.68) provides a framework to recursively construct coincident/leading indicators. In fact, the first equation in (10.69) is

$$y_t = \sum_{f=1}^{f_1} X_{f,t} \theta_t^f + e_t, \tag{10.70}$$

where $X_{ft} = X_t \Xi_f$. In (10.70) y_t depends on a common time index X_{1t}, on an $n \times 1$ vector of unit-specific indices X_{2t}, and on a set of indices which depend on variables, lags, units, etc. These indices are particular combinations of lags of the VAR variables, while θ_t^j measure the impact that different linear combinations of the lags of the right-hand side variables have on the current endogenous variables. Hence, it is possible to construct leading indicators directly from the VAR, without any preliminary distinction between leading, coincident, and lagging variables. Also, because the model is recursive, multi-step leading indicators can be easily obtained from the posterior for θ_t. Finally, fan charts can be constructed by using the predictive density of future observations and the output of the Gibbs sampler.

Example 10.22. Suppose we are interested in a model featuring a common, a unit-specific, and a variable-specific indicators. Given (10.70), a leading indicator for y_t

based on the common information available at time $t-1$ is $\mathrm{CLI}_t = X_{1t}\theta^1_{t|t-1}$; a vector of leading indicators based on the common and unit-specific information is $\mathrm{CULI}_t = X_{1t}\theta^1_{t|t-1} + X_{2t}\theta^2_{t|t-1}$; a vector of indicators based on the common and variable-specific information is $\mathrm{CVLI}_t = X_{1t}\theta^1_{t|t-1} + X_{3t}\theta^3_{t|t-1}$; and a vector of indicators based on the common, unit-specific, and variable-specific information is $\mathrm{CUVLI}_t = X_{1t}\theta^1_{t|t-1} + X_{2t}\theta^2_{t|t-1} + X_{3t}\theta^3_{t|t-1}$.

While we have derived (10.70) from a hierarchical prior on the panel VAR, one may want to start the investigation directly from (10.70). In this case, a researcher may be interested in assessing how many indices are necessary to capture the heterogeneities in the coefficients across time, units, and variables. We can use predictive Bayes factors to make this choice. A model with i indices is preferable to a model with $i+1$ indices, $i = 1, 2, \dots, f_1 - 1$, if $f(y^{t+\tau} \mid \mathcal{M}_i)/f(y^{t+\tau} \mid \mathcal{M}_{i+1}) > 1$, where $f(y^{t+\tau} \mid \mathcal{M}_i) = \int f(y^{t+\tau} \mid \theta_{t,i}, \mathcal{M}_i, y_t) g(\theta_{t,i} \mid \mathcal{M}_i, y_t)\, \mathrm{d}\theta_{t,i}$ is the predictive density of a model with i indices for $y^{t+\tau} = [y_{t+1}, \dots, y_{t+\tau}]$, $g(\theta_{t,i} \mid \mathcal{M}_i, y_t)$ is the posterior for θ in model i, and $f(Y^{t+\tau} \mid \theta_{t,i}, \mathcal{M}_i, y_t)$ is the density of future data, given $\theta_{t,i}$ and $\mathcal{M}_i$. Predictive Bayes factors can be computed with the output of the Gibbs sampler. In fact, with a draw θ^l_t from the posterior, we can construct forecast $y^l_{t+\tau}$, obtain the prediction errors for each τ and average across draws for each specification.

10.5.5 Impulse Responses

Impulse responses in TVC models can be computed as posterior revisions of the forecast errors. Since the model is nonlinear, forecasts for the vector of endogenous variables may change because the innovations in the model or the innovations in the coefficients are different from zero. Furthermore, because of time variations, revisions depend on the history and the point in time where they are computed.

To see this set $Y_t = 0$, rewrite (10.63) as $\mathbb{Y}_t = \mathbb{A}_t\mathbb{Y}_{t-1} + \mathbb{E}_t$, and let $\alpha_t = \mathrm{vec}(\mathbb{A}_{1t})$, where $\mathbb{A}_{1t}$ are the first m_1 rows of $\mathbb{A}_t$. Iterating τ times we have

$$y_{t+\tau} = \mathbb{S}\left(\prod_{s=0}^{\tau-1} \mathbb{A}_{t+\tau-s}\right)\mathbb{Y}_t + \sum_{i=0}^{\tau-1} \mathbb{A}^*_{i,t+\tau} e_{t+\tau-i}, \tag{10.71}$$

where $\mathbb{S} = [I, 0, \dots, 0]$ and $\mathbb{A}^*_{i,t+\tau} = \mathbb{S}(\prod_{s=0}^{i-1} \mathbb{A}_{t+\tau-s})\mathbb{S}'$, $\mathbb{A}^*_{0,t+\tau} = I$. Substituting (10.67) into (10.66) and iterating gives

$$\begin{aligned}\alpha_{t+\tau} &= \Xi\theta_{t+\tau} + v_{1t+\tau}\\ &= \Xi\mathbb{D}_1^{\tau+1}\theta_{t-1} + \Xi\sum_{i=1}^{\tau}\mathbb{D}_1^i(I-\mathbb{D}_1)\bar{\theta} + \Xi\sum_{i=1}^{\tau}\mathbb{D}_1^i v_{2t+\tau-i} + v_{1t+\tau}.\end{aligned} \tag{10.72}$$

Define responses at step j as $\mathrm{Rev}_{t,j}(\tau) = E_{t+j}\mathbb{Y}_{t+\tau} - E_t\mathbb{Y}_{t+\tau}$, $\forall\tau \geqslant j+1$, given information at t and terminal horizon τ. Using $E_t y_{t+\tau} = \mathbb{S}E_t(\prod_{s=0}^{\tau-1} A_{t+\tau-s})\mathbb{Y}_t$, we have that

$$\begin{aligned}\mathrm{Rev}_{t,j}(\tau) &= \sum_{s=0}^{j-1}(E_{t+j}\mathbb{A}^{*}_{\tau-j+s,t+\tau})e_{t+j-s} \\ &\quad + \mathbb{S}\left[E_{t+j}\left(\prod_{s=0}^{\tau-j-1}\mathbb{A}_{t+\tau-s}\right)\prod_{s=\tau-j}^{\tau-1}\mathbb{A}_{t+\tau-s} - E_t\left(\prod_{s=0}^{\tau-1}\mathbb{A}_{t+\tau-s}\right)\right]\mathbb{Y}_t.\end{aligned} \tag{10.73}$$

From (10.73) it is clear that forecast revisions can occur because new information present in the innovations of the model, e_t, or in the coefficients, v_{2t}, alters previous forecasts of $\mathbb{Y}_{t+\tau}$.

Example 10.23. In (10.73) take $j = 1$ and $\tau = 2$. Then $\mathrm{Rev}_{t,1}(2) = E_{t+1}\mathbb{Y}_{t+2} - E_t\mathbb{Y}_{t+2} = E_{t+1}(\mathbb{S}\mathbb{A}_{1,t+2}\mathbb{S}')e_{t+1} + \mathbb{S}[E_{t+1}(\mathbb{A}_{t+2})\mathbb{A}_{t+1} - E_t(\mathbb{A}_{t+2}\mathbb{A}_{t+1})]\mathbb{Y}_t$. Similarly, taking $j = 2$ and $\tau = 3$ implies $\mathrm{Rev}_{t,2}(3) = E_{t+2}\mathbb{Y}_{t+3} - E_t\mathbb{Y}_{t+3} = \mathbb{S}[E_{t+2}(\mathbb{A}_{t+3})\mathbb{A}_{t+2}\mathbb{A}_{t+1} - E_t(\mathbb{A}_{t+3}\mathbb{A}_{t+2}\mathbb{A}_{t+1})]\mathbb{Y}_t + \mathbb{S}E_{t+2}(\mathbb{A}_{t+3})\mathbb{S}'e_{t+2} + \mathbb{S}E_{t+2}(\mathbb{A}_{t+3})\mathbb{A}_{t+2}\mathbb{S}'e_{t+1}$. Hence, changes in $\mathbb{Y}_{t+3}$ due to the innovations of the model are $\mathbb{S}E_{t+2}(\mathbb{A}_{t+3})\mathbb{S}'e_{t+2} + \mathbb{S}E_{t+2}(\mathbb{A}_{t+3})\mathbb{A}_{t+2}\mathbb{S}'e_{t+1}$ and changes in $\mathbb{Y}_{t+3}$ due to the innovations in the coefficients are $\mathbb{S}[E_{t+2}(\mathbb{A}_{t+3})\mathbb{A}_{t+2}\mathbb{A}_{t+1} - E_t(\mathbb{A}_{t+3}\mathbb{A}_{t+2}\mathbb{A}_{t+1})]\mathbb{Y}_t$. Clearly, responses depend on the time when they are generated (e.g., t versus $t+1$), the history of y_t, and the estimate of $\mathbb{A}_t$.

The output of the Gibbs sampler can be used to compute the expressions appearing in (10.73). Conditioning on $\mathbb{A}_t$, assuming that $e_t \neq 0$, and that all future innovations in both coefficients and variables are integrated out, $\mathrm{Rev}_{t,j}(\tau)$ can be computed as follows.

Algorithm 10.4.

(1) Draw $(\mathbb{A}^l_{t+1}, \dots, \mathbb{A}^l_{t+\tau})$ from their posterior distribution, $l = 1, \dots, L$.

(2) For each l, compute $\mathbb{S}\prod_{s=0}^{i-1}\mathbb{A}^l_{t+\tau-s}\mathbb{S}'$ and $\prod_{s=0}^{\tau-j-1}\mathbb{A}^l_{t+\tau-s}$, $\tau = 1, 2, \dots$. Average over l.

(3) Draw $(e^l_{t+1}, \dots, e^l_{t+j})$ from their posterior $l = 1, \dots, L$. Average over l.

(4) Given $\mathbb{Y}_t$, the averages in (2), and the average draw for $e_{t+1}, \dots, e_{t+j}$ in (3), compute $\mathrm{Rev}_{t,j}(\tau)^{l_1}$, each τ.

(5) Repeat (1)–(4) L_1 times. Order $\mathrm{Rev}_{t,j}(\tau)^{l_1}$ for each τ and report percentiles.

Example 10.24. We use a VAR model for G7 countries with GDP growth, inflation, employment growth, and the real exchange rate for each country and three indices: a 2×1 vector of common factors (one for EU and one for non-EU countries), a 7×1 vector of country-specific factors, and a 4×1 vector of variable-specific factors.

We assume time variations in the factors, use noninformative priors on the hyperparameters but do not impose exchangeability. Figure 10.7 presents a centered 68%

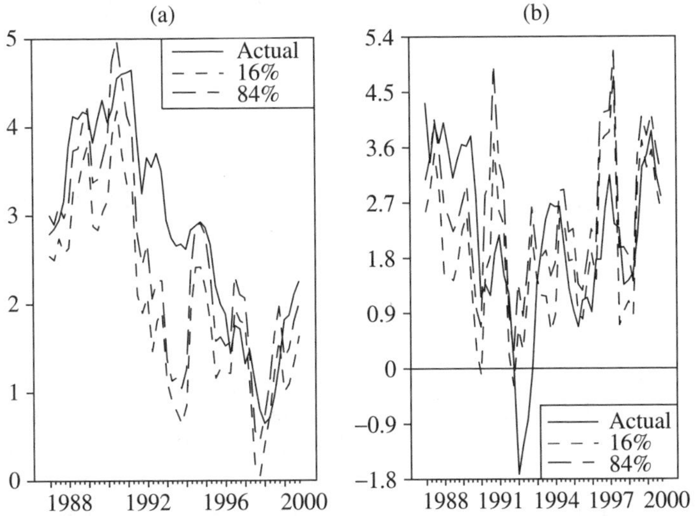

Figure 10.7. One-year-ahead 68% prediction bands: (a) EU inflation; (b) EU GDP growth.

posterior band for the CUVLI indicator for EU GDP growth and inflation, constructed recursively by using information available one year in advance. Actual values of EU GDP growth and inflation are superimposed. The model predicts the ups and downs of both series reasonably well. However, the probability that a dip in GDP as large as the one observed in the data in 1992 will occur is essentially zero.

11

Bayesian Time Series and DSGE Models

This chapter covers Bayesian estimation of three popular time series models and returns to the main goal of this book: estimation and inference in DSGE models, this time from a Bayesian perspective. All three types of time series model have a latent variable structure: the data y_t depend on a latent variable x_t and on a vector of parameters α, and the latent variable x_t is a function of another set of parameters θ. In factor models, x_t is a common factor or a common trend; in stochastic volatility models, x_t is a vector of volatilities; and in Markov switching models, x_t is an unobservable finite-state process. While, for the first and the third types of model, classical methods to evaluate the likelihood function are available (see, for example, Sims and Sargent 1977; Hamilton 1989), for the second type, approximations based on either a method of moments or quasi-ML are typically used. Approximations are needed because the density of the observables $f(y \mid \alpha, \theta)$ is a mixture of distributions, that is, $f(y \mid \alpha, \theta) = \int f(y \mid x, \alpha) f(x \mid \theta)\, \mathrm{d}x$. Since the computation of the likelihood function requires a T-dimensional integral, no analytical solution is generally available.

As mentioned in chapter 9, the model for x_t can be interpreted either as a prior or as a description of how the latent variable evolves. This means that all three models have a hierarchical structure which can be handled with the "data-augmentation" technique of Tanner and Wong (1987). Such a technique treats $x = (x_1, \dots, x_T)$ as a vector of parameters for which we have to compute the conditional posterior — as we have done with the time-varying parameters of a TVC model in chapter 10. Cyclical sampling across the conditional distributions provides, in the limit, posterior draws for the parameters and the unobservable x. The Markov property for x_t is useful to simplify the calculations since we can break the problem of simulating the x vector into the problem of simulating its components in a conditional recursive fashion. For the models we examine, the likelihood is bounded. Therefore, if the priors are proper, the transition kernel induced by the Gibbs sampler (or by the mixed Gibbs–MH sampler) is irreducible, aperiodic, and has an invariant distribution. Hence, sufficient conditions for convergence hold in these setups.

The kernel of (x, α, θ) is the product of the conditional distribution of $(y \mid x, \alpha)$, the conditional distribution of $(x \mid \theta)$, and the prior for (α, θ). Hence, $g(\alpha, \theta \mid y) = \int g(x, \alpha, \theta \mid y)\, \mathrm{d}x$ can be used for inference, while $g(x \mid y)$ provides a solution to the problem of estimating x. The main difference between the setup of this chapter and a traditional signal extraction problem is that here we produce the distribution of x at each t, not just its conditional mean. It is also important to emphasize that, contrary to classical methods, the tools we describe allow the computation of the exact posterior distribution of x. Therefore, we are able to describe posterior uncertainty surrounding the latent variable and the parameters.

Forecasting $y_{t+\tau}$ and the latent variable $x_{t+\tau}$ is straightforward and can be handled with the tools described in chapter 9. Since many inferential exercises have to do with the problem of obtaining a future measure of the unobserved state (the business cycle in policy circles, the volatility process in business and finance circles, etc.), it is important to have ways to estimate it. Draws for future $x_{t+\tau}$ can be obtained from the marginal posterior of x and the structure of its conditional.

Although this chapter primarily focuses on models with normal errors, more heavy-tailed distributions could also be used, particularly, in finance applications. As in the case of state space models, such an extension presents few complications.

The last section of the chapter studies how to obtain posterior estimates of the structural parameters of DSGE models, how to conduct posterior inference and model comparisons, and reexamines the link between DSGE models and VARs. There is very little new material in this section: we bring together the models discussed in chapter 2 and the ideas contained in chapters 5–7 with the simulation techniques presented in chapter 9 to develop a framework where structural inference can be conducted in false models, taking both parameter and model uncertainty into consideration.

11.1 Factor Models

Factor models are used in many fields of economics and finance. They exploit the insight that there may be a common source of fluctuations in a vector of economic time series. Factor models are therefore alternatives to the (panel) VAR models analyzed in chapter 10. In the latter, detailed cross-variable interdependencies are modeled but no common factor is explicitly considered. Here, most of interdependencies are eschewed and a low-dimensional vector of unobservable variables is assumed to drive the comovements across variables. Clearly, combinations of the two approaches are possible (see, for example, Bernanke et al. 2005; Giannone et al. 2003). The factor structure we consider is

$$\left.\begin{aligned} y_{it} &= \bar{y}_i + \mathbb{Q}_i y_{0t} + e_{it}, \\ A_i^e(\ell)e_{it} &= v_{it}, \\ A^y(\ell)y_{0t} &= v_{0t}, \end{aligned}\right\} \tag{11.1}$$

where $E(v_{it}, v_{i't-\tau}) = 0, \forall i \neq i', i = 1, \dots, m$, $E(v_{it}, v_{it-\tau}) = \sigma_i^2$ if $\tau = 0$ and zero otherwise, $E(v_{0t}, v_{0t-\tau}) = \sigma_0^2$ if $\tau = 0$ and zero otherwise, and y_{0t} is unobservable. Two features of (11.1) need to be noted. First, the unobservable factor can have arbitrary serial correlation. Second, since the relationship between observables and unobservables is static, e_{it} is allowed to be serially correlated. y_{0t}

could be a scalar or a vector, as long as its dimension is smaller than the dimension of y_t. An interesting case emerges when $e_t = (e_{1t}, \dots, e_{mt})'$ follows a VAR, i.e., $A^e(\ell)e_t = v_t$, and $A^e(\ell)$ is of order q_e, $\forall i$.

Example 11.1. There are several specifications which fit into this framework. For example, y_{0t} could be a coincident business cycle indicator which moves a vector of macroeconomic time series y_{it}. In this case, e_{it} captures idiosyncratic movements in y_{it}. Alternatively, y_{0t} could be a common stochastic trend while e_{it} is stationary for all i. In this latter case, (11.1) resembles the common trend-UC decomposition studied in chapter 3. Furthermore, many of the models used in finance have a structure similar to (11.1). For example, in a capital asset pricing model (CAPM), y_{0t} is an unobservable market portfolio.

We need restrictions to identify the parameters of (11.1). Since $\mathbb{Q}_i$ and y_{0t} are nonobservable, neither the scale nor the sign of the factor and its loading can be separately identified. For normalization, we choose $\mathbb{Q}_1 > 0$ and assume that σ_0^2 is a fixed constant.

Let $\alpha_{1i} = (\bar{y}_i, \mathbb{Q}_i)$. Let $\alpha = (\alpha_{1i}, \sigma_0^2, \sigma_i^2, A_i^e, A^y,\ i = 1, \dots, m)$, where $A_i^e = (A_{i,1}^e, \dots, A_{i,q_i}^e)$ and $A^y = (A_1^y, \dots, A_{q_0}^y)$, be the vector of parameters of the model. Let $y_i = (y_{i1}, \dots, y_{it})'$ and $y = (y_1', \dots, y_m')'$. Given $g(\alpha)$, $g(\alpha \mid y, y_0) \propto f(y \mid \alpha, y_0)g(\alpha)$ and $g(y_0 \mid \alpha, y) \propto f(y \mid \alpha, y_0) f(y_0 \mid \alpha)$. To compute these conditional distributions, we need $f(y \mid \alpha, y_0)$ and $f(y_0 \mid \alpha) = \int f(y, y_0 \mid \alpha)\, dy$.

Consider first $f(y \mid \alpha, y_0)$. Let $y_i^1 = (y_{i,1}, \dots, y_{i,q_i})'$ be random and let $y_0^1 = (y_{0,1}, \dots, y_{0,q_0})'$ be the vector of initial observations on the factors, y_0^1 given, $x_i^1 = [\mathbf{1}, y_0^1]$, where $\mathbf{1} = [1, 1, \dots, 1]'$, and let $\mathbb{A}_i$ be a $(q_i \times q_i)$ companion matrix representation of $A_i^e(\ell)$. If the errors are normal, $(y_i^1 \mid \bar{y}_i, \mathbb{Q}_i, \sigma_i^2, y_0^1) \sim \mathbb{N}(\bar{y}_i + \mathbb{Q}_i y_0^1, \sigma_i^2 \Sigma_i)$, where Σ_i solves $\Sigma_i = \mathbb{A}_i \Sigma_i \mathbb{A}_i + (1, 0, \dots, 0)'(1, 0, \dots, 0)$.

Exercise 11.1. Provide a closed-form solution for Σ_i.

Define $y_i^{1*} = \Sigma_i^{-0.5} y_i^1$ and $x_i^{1*} = \Sigma_i^{-0.5} x_i^1$. To build the rest of the likelihood, let $e_i = [e_{i,q_i+1}, \dots, e_{i,T}]'$ (this is $(T - q_i) \times 1$ vector); $e_{it} = y_{it} - \bar{y}_i - \mathbb{Q}_i y_{0t}$ and $E = [e_1, \dots, e_{q_i}]$ (this is a $(T - q_i) \times q_i$ matrix). Similarly, let $y_0 = (y_{01}, \dots, y_{0t})'$ and $Y_0 = (y_{0,-1}, \dots, y_{0,-q_0})$. Let y_i^{2*} be a $(T - q_i) \times 1$ vector with the t-row equal to $A_i^e(\ell) y_{it}$ and let x_i^{2*} be a $(T - q_i) \times 2$ matrix with the t-row equal to $(A_i^e(1), A_i^e(\ell) y_{0t})$. Let $x_i^* = [x_i^{1*}, x_i^{2*}]'$ and $y_i^* = [y_i^{1*}, y_i^{2*}]$.

Exercise 11.2. Derive the likelihood of $(y_i^* \mid x_i^*, \alpha)$, when e_t are normally distributed.

To obtain $g(\alpha \mid y, y_0)$, assume that $g(\alpha) = \prod_j g(\alpha_j)$, let σ_0^2 be fixed, and assume that $a_{1i} \sim \mathbb{N}(\bar{\alpha}_{1i}, \bar{\Sigma}_{\alpha_{1i}})$, $A_i^e \sim \mathbb{N}(\bar{A}_i^e, \bar{\Sigma}_{A_i^e})\mathcal{I}_{(-1,1)}$, $A^y \sim \mathbb{N}(\bar{A}^y, \bar{\Sigma}_{A^y})\mathcal{I}_{(-1,1)}$, $\sigma_i^{-2} \sim \mathbb{G}(a_{1i}, a_{2i})$, where $\mathcal{I}_{(-1,1)}$ is an indicator function for stationarity; that is, the prior for $A_i^e(A^y)$ is normal, truncated outside the range $(-1, 1)$. Then, the conditional posteriors are

$$\left.\begin{aligned}
(\alpha_{1i} \mid y_i, \alpha_{-\alpha_{1i}}) &\sim \mathbb{N}(\tilde{\Sigma}_{\alpha_{1i}}(\bar{\Sigma}_{\alpha_{1i}}^{-1}\bar{\alpha}_{1i} + \sigma_i^{-2}(x_i^*)'y_i^*), \tilde{\Sigma}_{\alpha_{1i}}),\\
(A_i^e \mid y_i, y_0, \alpha_{-A_i^e}) &\sim \mathbb{N}(\tilde{\Sigma}_{A_i^e}(\bar{\Sigma}_{A_i^e}^{-1}\bar{A}_i^e + \sigma_i^{-2}E_i'e_i), \tilde{\Sigma}_{A_i^e})\mathcal{I}_{(-1,1)} \times \mathcal{N}(A_i^e),\\
(A^y \mid y_i, y_0, \alpha_{-A^y}) &\sim \mathbb{N}(\tilde{\Sigma}_{A^y}(\bar{\Sigma}_{A^y}^{-1}\bar{A}^y + \sigma_0^{-2}Y_0'y_0), \tilde{\Sigma}_{A^y})\mathcal{I}_{(-1,1)} \times \mathcal{N}(A^y),\\
(\sigma_i^{-2} \mid y_i, y_0, \alpha_{-\sigma_i}) &\sim \mathbb{G}((a_{1i} + T), a_{2i} + (y_i^* - x_i^*\alpha_{1i,\mathrm{OLS}})^2),
\end{aligned}\right\} \tag{11.2}$$

where $\tilde{\Sigma}_{a_i} = (\bar{\Sigma}_{a_i}^{-1} + \sigma_i^{-2}x_i^{*\prime}x_i^*)^{-1}$, $\tilde{\Sigma}_{A_i^e} = (\bar{\Sigma}_{A_i^e}^{-1} + \sigma_i^{-2}E_i'E_i)^{-1}$, $\tilde{\Sigma}_{A^y} = (\bar{\Sigma}_{A^y}^{-1} + \sigma_0^{-2}Y_0'Y_0)^{-1}$, while

$$\mathcal{N}(A_i^e) = |\Sigma_{A_i^e}|^{-0.5}\exp\{-(1/2\sigma_i^2)(y_i^1 - \bar{y}_i - \mathbb{Q}_i y_0^1)'\Sigma_{A_i^e}^{-1}(y_i^1 - \bar{y}_i - \mathbb{Q}_i y_0^1)\}$$

and

$$\mathcal{N}(A^y) = |\Sigma_{A^y}|^{-0.5}\exp\{-(1/2\sigma_0)(y_0^1 - A^y(\ell)y_{0,-1}^1)'\Sigma_{A^y}^{-1}(y_0^1 - A^y(\ell)y_{0,-1}^1)\}.$$

Sampling $(\bar{y}_i, \mathbb{Q}_i, \sigma_i^2)$ from (11.2) is straightforward. To impose the sign restriction necessary for identification, discard the draws producing $\mathbb{Q}_1 \leqslant 0$. The conditional posterior for $A_i^e(A^y)$ is complicated by the presence of the indicator for stationarity and the conditional distribution of the first $q_i\,(q_0)$ observations (without these two, drawing these parameters would also be straightforward). Since these distributions are of unknown form, one could use the following variation of the MH algorithm to draw, for example, A_i^e.

Algorithm 11.1.

(1) Draw $(A_i^e)^\dagger$ from $\mathbb{N}(\tilde{\Sigma}_{A_i^e}(\bar{\Sigma}_{A_i^e}^{-1}\bar{A}_i^e + \sigma_i^{-2}E_i'e_i), \tilde{\Sigma}_{A_i^e})$. If $\sum_{j=1}^{q_i}(A_{i,j}^e)^\dagger \geqslant 1$, discard the draw.

(2) Otherwise, draw $\mathfrak{U} \sim \mathbb{U}(0, 1)$. If $\mathfrak{U} < \mathcal{N}((A_i^e)^\dagger)/\mathcal{N}((A_i^e)^{l-1})$, set $(A_i^e)^l = (A_i^e)^\dagger$. Else set $(A_i^e)^l = (A_i^e)^{l-1}$.

(3) Repeat (1) and (2) L times.

The derivation of $g(y_0 \mid \alpha, y)$ is straightforward. Define the $T \times T$ matrix

$$\mathcal{Q}_i^{-1} = \begin{bmatrix} \mathcal{Q}_{i1} \\ \mathcal{Q}_{i2} \end{bmatrix},$$

where $\mathcal{Q}_{i1} = \begin{bmatrix} \Sigma_i^{-0.5} & 0 \end{bmatrix}$ and

$$\mathcal{Q}_{i2} = \begin{bmatrix} -A_{i,q_i}^e & \cdots & -A_{i,1}^e & 1 & 0 & \cdots & 0 \\ 0 & -A_{i,q_i}^e & \cdots & -A_{i,1}^e & 1 & \cdots & 0 \\ \cdots & \cdots & \cdots & \cdots & \cdots & \cdots & \cdots \\ 0 & 0 & \cdots & -A_{i,q_i}^e & \cdots & \cdots & 1 \end{bmatrix},$$

Σ_i is a $q_i \times q_i$ matrix, and 0 is a $q_i \times (T - q_i)$ matrix. Similarly, define $\mathcal{Q}_0^{-1}$.

Let $x_i^\dagger = \mathcal{Q}_i^{-1} x_i$ and $y_i^\dagger = \mathcal{Q}_i^{-1}(y_i - \mathbf{1}\bar{y}_i)$. Then the likelihood function is $\prod_{i=1}^m f(y_i^\dagger \mid \mathbb{Q}_i, \sigma_i^2, A_i^e, y_0)$, where $f(y_i^\dagger \mid \mathbb{Q}_i, \sigma_i^2, A_i^e, y_0) = (2\pi\sigma_i^2)^{-0.5T} \times \exp\{-(y_i^\dagger - \mathbb{Q}_i \mathcal{Q}_i^{-1} y_0)'(y_i^\dagger - \mathbb{Q}_i \mathcal{Q}_i^{-1} y_0)/2\sigma_i^2\}$. Since the marginal of the factor is $f(y_0 \mid A^y) = (2\pi\sigma_0^2)^{-0.5T} \exp\{-(\mathcal{Q}_0^{-1} y_0)'(\mathcal{Q}_0^{-1} y_0)/2\sigma_0^2\}$, the joint likelihood is $f(y^\dagger, y_0 \mid \alpha) = \prod_{i=1}^m f(y_i^\dagger \mid \mathbb{Q}_i, \sigma_i^2, A_i^e, y_0) f(y_0 \mid A^y)$. Completing the squares we have

$$g(y_0 \mid y_i^\dagger, \alpha) \sim \mathbb{N}(\tilde{y}_0, \tilde{\Sigma}_{y0}), \tag{11.3}$$

where $\tilde{y}_0 = \tilde{\Sigma}_{y0}[\sum_{i=1}^m \mathbb{Q}_i \sigma_i^{-2} (\mathcal{Q}_i^{-1})' \mathcal{Q}_i^{-1}(y_i - \mathbf{1}\bar{y}_i)]$, $\tilde{\Sigma}_{y0} = [\sum_{i=0}^m \mathbb{Q}_i^2 \sigma_i^{-2} \times (\mathcal{Q}_i^{-1})'(\mathcal{Q}_i^{-1})]^{-1}$ with $\mathbb{Q}_0 = 1$. Note that $\tilde{\Sigma}_{y0}$ is a $T \times T$ matrix. Given (11.2) and (11.3), the Gibbs sampler can be used to compute the joint conditional posterior of α and of y_0, and their marginals.

To make the Gibbs sampler operative we need to select σ_0^2 and the parameters of the prior distributions. For example, σ_0^2 could be set to the average variance of the innovations in an AR(1) regression for each y_{it}. Since little information is typically available on the loadings and the autoregressive parameters, one could set $\bar{a}_{i1} = \bar{A}_i^e = \bar{A}^y = 0$ and assume a large prior variance. Finally, a relatively diffuse prior for σ_i^{-2} could be chosen, for example, $\mathbb{G}(4, 0.001)$, a distribution without the third and fourth moments.

The calculation of the predictive density of y_{0t} is straightforward and it is left as an exercise for the reader. Note that when the factor is a common business cycle indicator, the construction of this quantity produces the density of a leading indicator.

Exercise 11.3. Describe how to construct the predictive density of $y_{0t+\tau}$, $\tau = 1, 2, \ldots$.

Exercise 11.4. Suppose that $i = 4$ and let $A_i^e(\ell)$ be of first order. In addition, suppose that $\bar{y} = [0.5, 0.8, 0.4, 0.9]'$ and $\mathbb{Q}_1 = [1, 2, 0.4, 0.6, 0.5]'$. Let $A^e = \text{diag}[0.8, 0.7, 0.6, 0.9]$, $A^y = [0.7, -0.3]$, $v_0 \sim$ i.i.d. $\mathbb{N}(0, 5)$, and

$$v \sim \text{i.i.d. } \mathbb{N}\left(0, \begin{bmatrix} 3 & 0 & 0 & 0 \\ 0 & 4 & 0 & 0 \\ 0 & 0 & 9 & 0 \\ 0 & 0 & 0 & 6 \end{bmatrix}\right).$$

Let the priors be $(\bar{y}_i, \mathbb{Q}_i) \sim \mathbb{N}(0, 10 * I_2)$, $i = 1, 2, 3, 4$, $A^e \sim \mathbb{N}(0, I_4)\mathcal{I}_{(-1,1)}$, $A^y \sim \mathbb{N}(0, I_2)\mathcal{I}_{(-1,1)}$, and $\sigma_i^{-2} \sim \mathbb{G}(4, 0.001)$, where $\mathcal{I}_{(-1,1)}$ instructs us to drop values such that $\sum_j A_{ij}^e \geqslant 1$ or $\sum_j A_j^y \geqslant 1$. Draw sequences from the posterior of α and construct an estimate of the posterior distribution of y_0.

Exercise 11.5. Let the prior for $(\bar{y}_i, \mathbb{Q}_i, A_i^e, A^y, \sigma_i^{-2})$ be noninformative. Show that the posterior mean of y_0 is the same as the one obtained by running the Kalman filter/smoother on model (11.1).

Example 11.2. We construct a coincident indicator for the euro area business cycle by using quarterly data on real government consumption, real private investment,

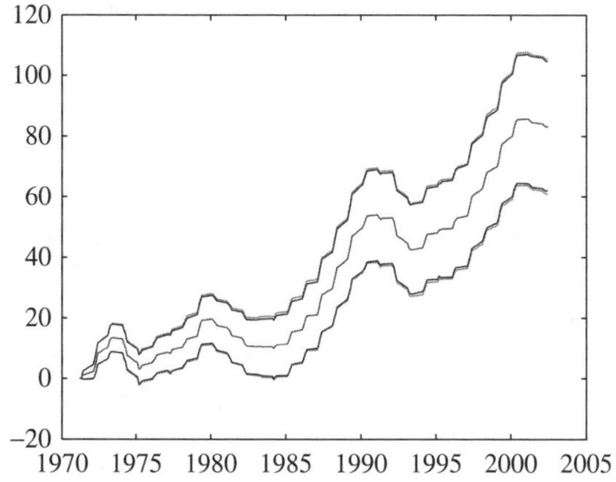

Figure 11.1. Coincident indicator, euro area.

real employment, and real GDP from 1970:1 to 2002:4. We allow an AR(2) structure on the indicator and an AR(1) on the errors of the model. Posterior estimates are obtained by using 10 000 draws from the conditional posterior: 5000 are used as burnout; of the remaining, 1 out of every 5 is used to construct the indicator. The mean value of the indicator together with a 68% confidence band are shown in figure 11.1. The posterior means of the two AR coefficients are 0.711 and 0.025, and the posterior standard errors are 0.177 and 0.134. The coincident indicator we construct shows (classical) recessions, roughly, at the same dates the CEPR selected as recession dates. Furthermore, it displays a considerable slowdown after 2001.

11.1.1 Arbitrage Pricing Theory (APT) Models

Apart from the construction of business cycle or trend indicators, factor models are extensively used in finance (see, for example, Campbell et al. (1997) for references). Here the unobservable factor is a vector of portfolio excess returns, a vector of macroeconomic variables, or a vector of portfolio of real returns, typically restricted to span the mean–variance frontier. APT models are useful since economic theory imposes restrictions on nonlinear combinations of their parameters.

For illustrative purposes, consider a version of an APT model where a vector of m asset returns y_t is related to a vector of k factors y_{0t} according to the linear relationship

$$y_t = \bar{y} + \mathbb{Q}_1 y_{0t} + e_t, \tag{11.4}$$

where $y_0 \sim \mathbb{N}(0, I)$, $e \mid y_0 \sim$ i.i.d. $\mathbb{N}(0, \Sigma_e)$, $\bar{y}$ is a vector of conditional mean returns, $\mathbb{Q}_1$ is an $m \times k$ matrix of loadings, and both $\mathbb{Q}_1$ and y_{0t} are unknown. Traditionally, a model like (11.4) is estimated in two steps: in the first step either the factor loadings or the factors themselves are estimated (with a cross-sectional regression). Then, taking the first-step estimates as if they were the true ones, a second-pass regression (typically, in time series) is used to estimate the other parameters (see, for example, Roll and Ross 1980). Clearly, this approach suffers from error-in-variables problems and leads to incorrect inference.

A number of authors, starting from Ross (1976), have shown that, as $m \to \infty$, absence of arbitrage opportunities implies that $\bar{y}_i \approx \phi_0 + \sum_{j=1}^{k} \mathbb{Q}_{1ij}\phi_j$, where ϕ_0 is the intercept of the pricing relationship (the so-called zero-beta rate) and ϕ_j is the risk premium on factor $\mathbb{Q}_{1ij}$, $j = 1, 2, \dots, k$. With the two-step procedure we have described, and treating the estimates of $\mathbb{Q}_{1ij}$ and of $\bar{y}_i$ as given, the restrictions imposed become linear and tests can be easily developed by using restricted and unrestricted estimates of ϕ_j (see Campbell et al. 1997).

One way to test (11.4) is to measure the pricing errors and check their sizes relative to the average returns (with large relative errors indicating an inappropriate specification). This measure is given by $\mathfrak{S} = (1/m)\bar{y}'[I - \mathbb{Q}(\mathbb{Q}'\mathbb{Q})^{-1}\mathbb{Q}']\bar{y}$, where $\mathbb{Q} = (\mathbf{1}, \mathbb{Q}_1)$ and $\mathbf{1}$ is a vector of 1s of dimension m. For fixed m, $\mathfrak{S} \neq 0$, while as $m \to \infty$, $\mathfrak{S} \to 0$. While it is hard to compute the sampling distribution of $\mathfrak{S}$, its exact posterior distribution can be easily obtained with MCMC methods.

For identification we require that $k < \frac{1}{2}m$. Letting $\mathbb{Q}_1^k$ be a lower triangular matrix containing the Choleski transformation of the first k independent rows of $\mathbb{Q}_1$, we also want $\mathbb{Q}_{1ii}^k > 0$, $i = 1, \dots, k$.

Exercise 11.6. Show that $k < \frac{1}{2}m$ and $\mathbb{Q}_{1ii}^k > 0$, $i = 1, \dots, k$, are necessary for identification.

Let $\alpha_{i1} = (\bar{y}_i, \mathbb{Q}_i)$. Since the factors capture common components, $\Sigma_e = \operatorname{diag}\{\sigma_i^2\}$. Then $f(\alpha_{i1} \mid y_0, \sigma_i) \propto \exp\{-(\alpha_{i1} - \alpha_{i1,\mathrm{OLS}})'x'x(\alpha_{i1} - \alpha_{i1,\mathrm{OLS}})/2\sigma_i^2\}$, where $x = (\mathbf{1}, y_0)$ is a $T \times (k+1)$ matrix and $\alpha_{i1,\mathrm{OLS}}$ are the OLS estimators of the coefficients in a regression of y_{it} on $(1, y_0)$. We want to compute $g(\alpha \mid y_{0t}, y_t)$ and $g(y_{0t} \mid \alpha, y_t)$, where $\alpha = (\alpha_{1i}, \sigma_i^2,\ i = 1, 2, \dots)$. We assume independence across i and the following priors: $\mathbb{Q}_{1i} \sim \mathbb{N}(\bar{\mathbb{Q}}_{1i}, \bar{\sigma}^2_{Q_1})$, $\mathbb{Q}_{1ii} > 0$, $i = 1, \dots, k$, $\mathbb{Q}_{1i} \sim \mathbb{N}(\bar{\mathbb{Q}}_{1i}, \bar{\omega}^2_{Q_1})$, $i = k+1, \dots, m$, $\bar{s}_i^2\sigma_i^{-2} \sim \chi^2(\bar{\nu}_i)$, $\bar{y}_i \sim \mathbb{N}(\bar{y}_{i0}, \bar{\sigma}^2_{\bar{y}_i})$, where $\bar{y}_{i0} = \phi_0 + \sum_j \mathbb{Q}_{1ij}\phi_j$ and ϕ_i are constant. The hyperparameters of all prior distributions are assumed to be known. Note that we impose the theoretical restrictions directly — the prior distribution of $\bar{y}_i$ is conditional on the value of $\mathbb{Q}_1$ — and that by varying $\bar{\sigma}^2_{y_i}$ we can account for different degrees of credence in the ATP restrictions. The conditional posterior distributions for the parameters are easily obtained.

Exercise 11.7. (i) Show that $g(\bar{y}_i \mid y_t, y_{0t}, \mathbb{Q}_1, \sigma_i^2) \sim \mathbb{N}(\tilde{\bar{y}}_i, \tilde{\sigma}^2_{\bar{y}_i})$, where $\tilde{\bar{y}}_i = [\bar{\sigma}^2_{\bar{y}_i}\bar{y}_{i,\mathrm{OLS}} + (\sigma_i^2/T)\bar{y}_{i0}]/[\sigma_i^2/T + \bar{\sigma}^2_{\bar{y}_i}]$, $\tilde{\sigma}^2_{\bar{y}_i} = [(\sigma_i^2\bar{\sigma}^2_{\bar{y}_i})/T]/[\sigma_i^2/T + \bar{\sigma}^2_{\bar{y}_i}]$, $\bar{y}_{i,\mathrm{OLS}} = (1/T)\sum_{t=1}^{T}(y_{it} - \sum_{j=1}^{k}\mathbb{Q}_{1j}y_{0tj})$.

(ii) Show that $g(\mathbb{Q}_{1i} \mid y_t, y_{0t}, \bar{y}_i, \sigma_i^2) \sim \mathbb{N}(\tilde{\mathbb{Q}}_{1i}, \tilde{\Sigma}_{Q_{1i}})$, with $\tilde{\mathbb{Q}}_{1i} = \Sigma_{Q_{1i}} \times (\bar{\mathbb{Q}}_{1i}\bar{\sigma}^{-2}_{\mathbb{Q}_1} + x_i^{\dagger\prime}x_i^{\dagger}\mathbb{Q}_{1i,\mathrm{OLS}}\sigma_i^{-2})$, $\tilde{\Sigma}_{Q_{1i}} = (\bar{\sigma}^{-2}_{\mathbb{Q}_{1i}} + \sigma_i^{-2}x_i^{\dagger\prime}x_i^{\dagger})^{-1}$, $i = 1, \dots, k$, and $\tilde{\mathbb{Q}}_{1i} = \Sigma_{Q_{1i}}(\bar{\mathbb{Q}}_{1i}\bar{\omega}^{-2}_{\mathbb{Q}_1} + x_i^{\dagger\prime}x_i^{\dagger}\mathbb{Q}_{1i,\mathrm{OLS}}\sigma_i^{-2})$, $\tilde{\Sigma}_{Q_{1i}} = (\bar{\omega}^{-2}_{\mathbb{Q}_1} + \sigma_i^{-2}x_i^{\dagger\prime}x_i^{\dagger})^{-1}$, $i = k+1, \dots, m$, where $\mathbb{Q}_{1i,\mathrm{OLS}}$ is the OLS estimator of a regression of $(y_{it} - \bar{y}_0)$ on $y_{01}, \dots, y_{0i-1}$ and $x_i^{\dagger}$ is the matrix x_i without the first row.

(iii) Show that $(\tilde{s}^2\sigma_i^{-2} \mid y_t, y_{0t}, \mathbb{Q}_1, \bar{y}_i) \sim \chi^2(\tilde{\nu})$, where $\tilde{\nu} = \bar{\nu} + T$ and $\tilde{s}_i^2 = \bar{\nu}\bar{s}_i^2 + (T - k - 1)\sum_t(y_{it} - \bar{y}_i - \sum_j \mathbb{Q}_{1j}y_{0tj})^2$.

The joint density of the data and the factor is

$$\begin{bmatrix} y_{0t} \\ y_t \end{bmatrix} \sim \mathbb{N}\left[\begin{pmatrix} 0 \\ \bar{y} \end{pmatrix}, \begin{pmatrix} I & \mathbb{Q}_1' \\ \mathbb{Q}_1 & \mathbb{Q}_1\mathbb{Q}_1' + \Sigma_e \end{pmatrix}\right].$$

Using the properties of conditional normal distributions we have $g(y_{0t} \mid y_t, \alpha) \sim \mathbb{N}(\mathbb{Q}_1'(\mathbb{Q}_1'\mathbb{Q}_1 + \Sigma_e)^{-1}(y_t - \bar{y}), I - \mathbb{Q}_1'(\mathbb{Q}_1'\mathbb{Q}_1 + \Sigma_e)^{-1}\mathbb{Q}_1)$, with $(\mathbb{Q}_1'\mathbb{Q}_1 + \Sigma_e)^{-1} = \Sigma_e^{-1} - \Sigma_e^{-1}\mathbb{Q}_1(I + \mathbb{Q}_1'\Sigma_e^{-1}\mathbb{Q}_1)^{-1}\mathbb{Q}_1'\Sigma_e^{-1}$, where $(I + \mathbb{Q}_1'\Sigma_e^{-1}\mathbb{Q}_1)$ is a $k \times k$ matrix.

Exercise 11.8. Suppose the prior for α is noninformative, that is, $g(\alpha) \propto \prod_j \sigma_{\alpha_j}^{-2}$. Derive the conditional posteriors for $\bar{y}$, $\mathbb{Q}_1$, Σ_e, and y_{0t} in this case.

Exercise 11.9. Using monthly returns data on the stocks listed in Eurostoxx 50 for the last five years, construct five portfolios with the quintiles of the returns. Using informative priors compute the posterior distribution of the pricing error in an APT model using one and two factors (averaging over portfolios). You may want to try two values for σ_0^2, one large and one small. Report a posterior 68% credible set for $\mathfrak{S}$. Do you reject the theory? What can you say about the posterior mean of the proportion of idiosyncratic to total risk?

11.1.2 Conditional Capital Asset Pricing Models

A conditional CAPM combines data-based and model-based approaches to portfolio selection into a specification of the form

$$\left.\begin{aligned} y_{it+1} &= \bar{y}_{it} + \mathbb{Q}_{it}y_{0t+1} + e_{it+1}, \\ \mathbb{Q}_{it} &= x_{1t}\phi_{1i} + v_{1it}, \\ \bar{y}_{it} &= x_{1t}\phi_{2i} + v_{2it}, \\ y_{0t+1} &= x_{2t}\phi_0 + v_{0t+1}, \end{aligned}\right\} \tag{11.5}$$

where $x_t = (x_{1t}, x_{2t})$ is a set of observable variables, $e_{it+1} \sim$ i.i.d. $\mathbb{N}(0, \sigma_e^2)$, $v_{0t+1} \sim$ i.i.d. $\mathbb{N}(0, \sigma_0^2)$, and both v_{1it} and v_{2it} are assumed to be serially correlated, to take into account the possible misspecification of the conditioning variables x_{1t}. Here y_{it+1} is the return on asset i and y_{0t+1} is the return on an unobservable market portfolio. Equations (11.5) fit the factor model structure we have so far considered when $v_{2it} = v_{1it} = 0, \forall t$, x_{2t} are the lags of y_{0t} and $x_{1t} = I$ for all t. Various versions of (11.5) have been considered in the literature.

Example 11.3. Consider the model

$$\left.\begin{aligned} y_{it+1} &= \mathbb{Q}_{it} + e_{it+1}, \\ \mathbb{Q}_{it} &= x_t\phi_i + v_{it}. \end{aligned}\right\} \tag{11.6}$$

Here the return on asset i depends on an unobservable risk premium $\mathbb{Q}_{it}$ and on an idiosyncratic error term, and the risk premium is a function of observable variables.

If we relax the assumption that the cost of risk is constant and allow time variations in the conditional variance of asset i, we have

$$y_{it+1} = x_t \mathbb{Q}_t + e_{it+1}, \quad e_{it} \sim \text{i.i.d. } \mathbb{N}(0, \sigma^2_{e_i}), \tag{11.7}$$

$$\mathbb{Q}_t = \mathbb{Q} + v_t, \quad v_t \sim \text{i.i.d. } \mathbb{N}(0, \sigma^2_v). \tag{11.8}$$

Here the return on asset i depends on observable variables. The loadings on the observables, assumed to be the same across assets, are allowed to vary over time. Note that by substituting the second expression into the first we have that the model's prediction error is heteroskedastic (the variance is $x'_t x_t \sigma^2_v + \sigma^2_{e_i}$).

Exercise 11.10. Suppose that $v_{2it} = v_{1it} = 0$, $\forall t$, and assume that y_{0t+1} is known. Let $\alpha = [\phi_{21}, \dots, \phi_{2m}, \phi_{11}, \dots, \phi_{1m}]$. Assume *a priori* that $\alpha \sim \mathbb{N}(\bar{\alpha}, \bar{\Sigma}_\alpha)$. Let the covariance matrix of $e_t = [e_{1t}, \dots, e_{MT}]$ be Σ_e and assume that, *a priori*, $\Sigma_e^{-1} \sim \mathbb{W}(\bar{\Sigma}, \bar{\nu})$. Show that, conditional on $(y_{it}, y_{0t}, \Sigma_e, x_t)$, the posterior of α is normal with mean $\tilde{\alpha}$ and variance $\tilde{\Sigma}_\alpha$ and that the marginal posterior of Σ_e^{-1} is Wishart with scale matrix $(\bar{\Sigma}^{-1} + \Sigma_{\text{OLS}})^{-1}$ and $\bar{\nu} + T$ degrees of freedom. Show the exact form of $\tilde{\alpha}$, $\tilde{\Sigma}_\alpha$, and Σ_{OLS}.

Exercise 11.11. Assume $v_{2it} = v_{1it} = 0$, $\forall t$, but allow y_{0t+1} to be unobservable. Postulate a law of motion for y_{0t} of the form $y_{0t+1} = x_{2t}\phi_0 + v_{0t+1}$, where x_{2t} are observables. Describe the steps needed to find the conditional posterior of y_{0t}.

The specification in (11.5) is more complicated than the one in exercises 11.10 and 11.11 because of time variations in the coefficients. To highlight the steps involved in this case, we describe a version of (11.5) where $v_{2it} = 0$, $\forall t, m = 1, x_t = x_{1t} = x_{2t}$, and we allow for AR(1) errors in the law of motion of $\mathbb{Q}_t$, that is,

$$\left.\begin{aligned} y_{t+1} &= x_t\phi_2 + \mathbb{Q}_t y_{0t+1} + e_{t+1}, \\ \mathbb{Q}_t &= (x_t - \rho x_{t-1})\phi_1 + \rho\mathbb{Q}_{t-1} + v_t, \\ y_{0t} &= x_t\phi_0 + v_{0t}, \end{aligned}\right\} \tag{11.9}$$

where ρ measures the persistence of the shock driving $\mathbb{Q}_t$.

Let $\alpha = [\phi_0, \phi_1, \phi_2, \rho, \sigma^2_e, \sigma^2_v, \sigma^2_{v0}]$ and let $g(\alpha) = \prod_j g(\alpha_j)$. Assume that $g(\phi_i) \sim \mathbb{N}(\bar{\phi}_i, \bar{\Sigma}_{\phi_i})$, $i = 0, 1, 2$, $g(\rho) \sim \mathbb{N}(0, \bar{\Sigma}_\rho)\mathcal{I}_{(-1,1)}$, $g(\sigma_v^{-2}) \sim \chi(\bar{s}^2_v, \bar{\nu}_v)$, $g(\sigma_e^{-2}, \sigma_{v0}^{-2}) \propto \sigma_e^{-2}\sigma_{v0}^{-2}$, and that all hyperparameters are known.

To construct the conditional posterior of $\mathbb{Q}_t$ note that, if ρ is known, $\mathbb{Q}_t$ can be easily simulated as in state space models. Therefore, partition $\alpha = (\alpha_1, \rho)$. Conditional on ρ, the law of motion of $\mathbb{Q}_t$ is $y \equiv \mathbb{Q} - \rho\mathbb{Q}_{-1} = x^+\phi_1 + v$, where $\mathbb{Q} = [\mathbb{Q}_1, \dots, \mathbb{Q}_t]'$, $x = [x_1, \dots, x_t]'$, $x^+ = x - \rho x_{-1}$, and $v \sim \text{i.i.d. } \mathbb{N}(0, \sigma^2_v I_T)$. Setting $\mathbb{Q}_{t=-1} = 0$, we have two sets of equations, one for the first observation and one for the others, $y_0 \equiv \mathbb{Q}_0 = x_0^+\phi_1 + v_0$ and $y_t \equiv \mathbb{Q}_t - \rho\mathbb{Q}_{t-1} = x_t^+\phi_1 + v_t$. When the errors are normal, the likelihood function $f(y \mid x, \phi_1, \rho)$ is proportional to $(\sigma^2_v)^{-0.5T} \exp\{-0.5[(y_0 - x_0^+\phi_1)\sigma_v^{-2}(y_0 - x_0^+\phi_1)' - \sum_{t=1}^T (y_t - x_t^+\phi_1)\sigma_v^{-2} \times (y_t - x_t^+\phi_1)']\}$.

Let $\phi^0_{1,\text{OLS}}$ be the OLS estimator obtained from the first observation and $\phi^1_{1,\text{OLS}}$ the OLS estimator obtained from the other observations. Combining the prior and the likelihood, the posterior kernel of ϕ is proportional to $\exp\{-0.5(\phi^0_1 - \phi^0_{1,\text{OLS}})' \times (x^+_0)'\sigma_v^{-2}x^+_0(\phi^1_0 - \phi^1_{0,\text{OLS}}) - 0.5\sum_t(\phi^1_1 - \phi^1_{1,\text{OLS}})'(x^+_t)'\sigma_v^{-2}x^+_t(\phi^1_1 - \phi^1_{1,\text{OLS}}) - 0.5(\phi_1 - \bar{\phi}_1)'\bar{\Sigma}^{-1}_{\phi_1}(\phi_1 - \bar{\phi}_1)\}$. Therefore, the conditional posterior for ϕ_1 is normal. The mean is a weighted average of prior mean and two OLS estimators, i.e., $\tilde{\phi}_1 = \tilde{\Sigma}_{\phi_1}(\bar{\Sigma}^{-1}_{\phi_1}\bar{\phi}_1 + (x^+_0)'\sigma_v^{-2}y_0 + \sum_t(x^+_t)'\sigma_v^{-2}y_t)$ and $\tilde{\Sigma}_{\phi_1} = (\bar{\Sigma}^{-1}_{\phi_1} + (x^+_0)'\sigma_v^{-2}x^+_0 + \sum_t(x^+_t)'\sigma_v^{-2}x^+_t)^{-1}$. The conditional posterior for σ^2_v can be found by using the same logic.

Exercise 11.12. Show that the posterior kernel for σ^2_v has the form $(\sigma^2_v)^{-0.5(T-1)} \times \exp\{-0.5\sum_t\sigma_v^{-2}(y_t - x^+_t\phi_1)'(y_t - x^+_t\phi_1)\}[(\sigma^2_v/(1-\phi^2_1))^{0.5}]^{-0.5(\bar{\nu}_v+1+2)} \times \exp\{-0.5[\sigma^2_v/(1-\phi^2_1)]^{-1}[(y_0 - x^+_0\phi_1)'(y_0 - x^+_0\phi_1) + \bar{\nu}_v]\}$. Suggest an algorithm to draw from this (unknown) distribution.

Once the distribution for the components of α_1 is found, we can use the Kalman filter/smoother to construct $\mathbb{Q}_t$ and the posterior of y_{0t}, conditional on ρ. To find the posterior distribution of ρ requires little more work. Conditional on ϕ_1, rewrite the law of motion for $\mathbb{Q}_t$ as $y^\dagger_t \equiv \mathbb{Q}_t - x_t\phi_1 = x^\dagger_{t-1}\rho + v_t$, where $x^\dagger_{t-1} = \mathbb{Q}_{t-1} - x_{t-1}\phi_1$. Once again, split the data in two: initial observations $(y^\dagger_1, x^\dagger_0)$ and the rest $(y^\dagger_t, x^\dagger_{t-1})$. The likelihood function is

$$f(y^\dagger \mid x^\dagger, \phi_1, \rho) \propto \sigma_v^{-T}\exp\{-0.5(y^\dagger_1 - x^\dagger_0\phi_1)'\sigma_v^{-2}(y^\dagger_1 - x^\dagger_0\phi_1)\} + \exp\left\{-0.5\sum_t(y^\dagger_t - x^\dagger_{t-1}\phi_1)'\sigma_v^{-2}(y^\dagger_t - x^\dagger_{t-1}\phi_1)\right\}. \quad (11.10)$$

Let ρ_{OLS} be the OLS estimator of ρ obtained with T data points. Combining the likelihood with the prior produces a kernel of the form $\exp\{-0.5\sum_t(\rho - \rho_{\text{OLS}})' \times (x^\dagger_t)'\sigma_v^{-2}x^\dagger_t(\rho - \rho_{\text{OLS}}) + (\rho - \bar{\rho}')\bar{\Sigma}^{-1}_\rho(\rho - \bar{\rho})\}[(\sigma^2_v/(1-\phi^2_1))^{0.5}]^{-0.5(\bar{\nu}_v+1+2)} \times \exp\{-0.5[\sigma^2_v/(1-\phi^2_1)]^{-1}\bar{\nu}_v + (y^\dagger_1)'[\sigma^2_v/(1-\phi^2_1)]^{-1}y^\dagger_1\}$. Hence, the conditional posterior for ρ is normal, truncated outside the range $(-1, 1)$, with mean $\tilde{\rho} = \tilde{\Sigma}_\rho(\bar{\Sigma}^{-1}_\rho\bar{\rho} + \sum_t(x^\dagger_t)'\sigma_v^{-2}y^\dagger_t)$, variance $\tilde{\Sigma}_\rho = (\bar{\Sigma}^{-1}_\rho + \sum_t(x^\dagger_t)'\sigma_v^{-2}x^\dagger_t)^{-1}$.

Exercise 11.13. Provide an MH algorithm to draw from the conditional posterior of ρ.

Once $g(\alpha_1 \mid \rho, y_{0t}, y_t)$, $g(\rho \mid \alpha_1, y_{0t}, y_t)$, $g(y_{0t} \mid \alpha_1, \rho, y_t)$ are available, the Gibbs sampler can be used to find the joint posterior of the quantities of interest.

11.2 Stochastic Volatility Models

Stochastic volatility models are alternatives to GARCH or TVC models. In fact, they can account for time-varying volatility and leptokurtosis as GARCH or TVC models but produce excess kurtosis without heteroskedasticity. Since the logarithm of σ^2_t is assumed to follow an AR process, changes in y_t are driven by shocks in the model for the observables or shocks in the model for the logarithm of σ^2_t. Such a feature adds flexibility to the specification and produces richer dynamics for the observables as compared with, for example, GARCH-type models, where the same random variable drives both observables and volatilities.

The most basic stochastic volatility specification is

$$\left.\begin{aligned} y_t &= \sigma_t e_t, & e_t &\sim \mathbb{N}(0,1), \\ \ln(\sigma_t^2) &= \rho_0 + \rho_1 \ln(\sigma_{t-1}^2) + \sigma_v v_t, & v_t &\sim \text{i.i.d. } \mathbb{N}(0,1), \end{aligned}\right\} \tag{11.11}$$

where v_t and e_t are independent. In (11.11) we have implicitly assumed that y_t is de-meaned. Hence, this specification could be used to model, for example, asset returns or changes in exchange rates. Also, for simplicity, only one lag of $\ln \sigma_t^2$ is considered.

Let $y = (y_1, \dots, y_t)$, $\sigma^2 = (\sigma_1^2, \dots, \sigma_t^2)$, and let $f(\sigma^2 \mid \rho, \sigma_v)$ be the probability mechanism generating σ^2, where $\rho = (\rho_0, \rho_1)$. The density of the data is $f(y \mid \rho, \sigma_v) = \int f(y \mid \sigma^2) f(\sigma^2 \mid \rho, \sigma_v)\,\mathrm{d}\sigma^2$. As in factor models, we treat σ^2 as an unknown vector of parameters, whose conditional distribution needs to be found.

We postpone the derivation of the conditional distribution of (ρ, σ_v) to a later (more complicated) application and concentrate on the problem of drawing a sample from the conditional posterior of σ_t^2. First, note that, because of the Markov structure, we can break the joint posterior of σ^2 into the product of conditional posteriors of the form $g(\sigma_t^2 \mid \sigma_{t-1}^2, \sigma_{t+1}^2, \rho, \sigma_v, y_t)$, $t = 1, \dots, T$. Second, these univariate densities have an unusual form: they are the product of a conditional normal for y_t and a lognormal for σ_t^2,

$$\begin{aligned} g(\sigma_t^2 &\mid \sigma_{t-1}^2, \sigma_{t+1}^2, \rho, \sigma_v, y_t) \\ &\propto f(y_t \mid \sigma_t^2) f(\sigma_t^2 \mid \sigma_{t-1}^2, \rho, \sigma_v) f(\sigma_{t+1}^2 \mid \sigma_t^2, \rho, \sigma_v) \\ &\propto \frac{1}{\sigma_t} \exp\left\{-\frac{y_t^2}{2\sigma_t^2}\right\} \times \frac{1}{\sigma_t^2} \exp\left\{-\frac{(\ln \sigma_t^2 - E_t(\ln \sigma_t^2))^2}{2\operatorname{var}(\ln \sigma_t^2)}\right\}, \end{aligned} \tag{11.12}$$

where $E_t(\ln \sigma_t^2) = [\rho_0(1-\rho_1) + \rho_1(\ln \sigma_{t+1}^2 + \ln \sigma_{t-1}^2)]/(1+\rho_1^2)$, $\operatorname{var}(\ln \sigma_t^2) = \sigma_v^2/(1+\rho_1^2)$. Because $g(\sigma_t^2 \mid \sigma_{t-1}^2, \sigma_{t+1}^2, \rho, \sigma_v, y_t)$ is nonstandard, we need either a candidate density to be used as importance sampling or an appropriate transition function to be used in an MH algorithm. There is an array of densities one could use as importance sampling densities. For example, Jacquier et al. (1994) noticed that the first term in (11.12) is the density of an inverse of gamma distributed random variable, that is, $x^{-1} \sim \mathbb{G}(a_1, a_2)$, while the second term can be approximated by an inverse of a gamma distribution (matching first and second moments). The inverse of a gamma is a good "blanketing" density for the lognormal because it dominates the latter on the right tail. Furthermore, the two densities can be combined into one inverse gamma with parameters $\tilde{a}_1 = [1 - 2\exp(\operatorname{var}(\ln \sigma_t^2))]/[1 - \exp(\operatorname{var}(\ln \sigma_t^2))] + 0.5$ and $\tilde{a}_2 = [(\tilde{a}_1 - 1)[\exp(E_t(\ln \sigma_t^2) + 0.5 \operatorname{var}(\ln \sigma_t^2))] + 0.5 y_t^2]$ and draws made from this target density. As an alternative, since the kernel of $\ln(\sigma_t^2)$ is known, we could draw $\ln(\sigma_t^2)$ from $\mathbb{N}(E(\ln \sigma_t^2) - 0.5 \operatorname{var}(\ln \sigma_t^2), \operatorname{var}(\ln \sigma_t^2))$ and accept the draw with probability $\exp\{-y_t^2/2\sigma_t^2\}$ (see Geweke 1994).

Table 11.1. Percentiles of the approximating distributions.

	Percentiles				
	5th	25th	50th	75th	95th
Gamma	0.11	0.70	1.55	3.27	5.05
Normal	0.12	0.73	1.60	3.33	5.13

Example 11.4. We have run a small Monte Carlo experiment to check the quality of these two approximations. Table 11.1 reports the percentiles using 5000 draws from the posterior when $\rho_0 = 0.0$, $\rho_1 = 0.8$, and $\sigma_v = 1.0$. Both approximations appear to produce similar results.

It is worthwhile stressing that (11.11) is a particular nonlinear Gaussian model which can be transformed into a linear but non-Gaussian state space model without loss of information. In fact, letting $x_t = \ln \sigma_t$, $\epsilon_t = \ln e_t^2 + 1.27$, the model (11.11) could be written as

$$\left.\begin{aligned} \ln y_t^2 &= -1.27 + x_t + \epsilon_t, \\ x_{t+1} &= \rho x_t + \sigma_v v_t, \end{aligned}\right\} \tag{11.13}$$

where ϵ_t has zero mean but is nonnormal. A framework like this was encountered in chapter 10 and techniques designed to deal with such models were outlined there. Here it is sufficient to point out that a nonnormal density for ϵ_t can be approximated with a mixture of J normals, that is, $f(\epsilon_t) \approx \sum_j \varrho_j f(\epsilon_t \mid \mathcal{M}_j)$, where each $f(\epsilon_t \mid \mathcal{M}_j) \sim \mathbb{N}(\bar{\epsilon}_j, \sigma^2_{\epsilon_j})$ and $0 \leqslant \varrho_j \leqslant 1$. Chib (1996) provides details on how this can be done.

Cogley and Sargent (2005) have recently applied the mechanics of stochastic volatility models to a BVAR with time-varying coefficients. Since the setup they use could be employed as an alternative to the linear time-varying conditional structures we studied in chapter 10, we will examine in detail how to obtain conditional posterior estimates for the parameters of such a model.

A VAR model with stochastic volatility has the form

$$\left.\begin{aligned} y_t &= (I_m \otimes X_t)\alpha_t + e_t, \qquad & e_t &\sim \mathbb{N}(0, \Sigma_t^\dagger), \\ \Sigma_t^\dagger &= \mathcal{P}^{-1}\Sigma_t(\mathcal{P}^{-1})', & & \\ \alpha_t &= \mathbb{D}_1\alpha_{t-1} + v_{1t}, & v_{1t} &\sim \mathbb{N}(0, \Sigma_{v_1}), \end{aligned}\right\} \tag{11.14}$$

where $\mathcal{P}$ is a lower triangular matrix with 1s on the main diagonal, $\Sigma_t = \mathrm{diag}\{\sigma_{it}^2\}$,

$$\ln \sigma_{it}^2 = \ln \sigma_{it-1}^2 + \sigma_{v_{2i}} v_{2it}, \tag{11.15}$$

where $\mathbb{D}_1$ is such that α_t is a stationary process. In (11.14) the process for y_t has time-varying coefficients and time-varying variances. To compute conditional posteriors note that it is convenient to block together the α_t and the σ_t^2 and draw a whole sequence for these two vectors of random variables.

We make standard prior assumptions, i.e., $\alpha_0 \sim \mathbb{N}(\bar{\alpha}, \bar{\Sigma}_a)$, $\Sigma_{v1}^{-1} \sim \mathbb{W}(\bar{\Sigma}_{v1}, \bar{\nu}_{v1})$, where $\bar{\Sigma}_{v1} \propto \bar{\Sigma}_a$, $\bar{\nu}_{v1} = \dim(\alpha_0) + 1$, $\sigma_{v2i}^{-2} \sim \mathbb{G}(a_1, a_2)$, $\ln \sigma_{i0} \sim \mathbb{N}(\ln \bar{\sigma}_i, \bar{\Sigma}_\sigma)$, and letting ϕ represent the nonzero elements of $\mathcal{P}$, $\phi \sim \mathbb{N}(\bar{\phi}, \bar{\Sigma}_\phi)$.

Given these priors, the calculation of the conditional posterior for $(\alpha_t, \Sigma_{v1}, \sigma_{v2i})$ is straightforward. The conditional posterior for α_t can be obtained with a run of the Kalman filter as detailed in chapter 10; the conditional posterior for Σ_{v1}^{-1} is $\mathbb{W}((\bar{\Sigma}_{v1}^{-1} + \sum_t v_{1t} v_{1t}')^{-1}, \bar{\nu}_{v1} + T)$, and that for σ_{v2i}^{-2} is $\mathbb{G}(a_1 + T, a_2 + \sum_t (\ln \sigma_{it}^2 - \ln \sigma_{it-1}^2)^2)$.

Example 11.5. Suppose $y_t = \alpha_t y_{t-1} + e_t$, $e_t \sim$ i.i.d. $\mathbb{N}(0, \sigma_t^2)$, $\alpha_t = \rho \alpha_{t-1} + v_{1t}$, $v_{1t} \sim$ i.i.d. $\mathbb{N}(0, \sigma_{v_1}^2)$, $\ln \sigma_t^2 = \ln \sigma_{t-1}^2 + \sigma_{v_2} v_{2t}$, $v_{2t} \sim$ i.i.d. $\mathbb{N}(0, 1)$. If $\sigma_{v_2}^{-2} \sim \mathbb{G}(a_{v_2}, b_{v_2})$ and $\sigma_{v_1}^{-2} \sim \mathbb{G}(a_{v_1}, b_{v_1})$, then, given ρ, the conditional posteriors of $(\sigma_{v_1}^{-2}, \sigma_{v_2}^{-2})$ are gamma with parameters $(a_{v_1} + T, b_{v_1} + \sum_t v_{1t}^2)$ and $(a_{v_2} + T, \bar{b}_{v_2} + \sum_t (\ln \sigma_t^2 - \ln \sigma_{t-1}^2)^2)$, respectively.

Exercise 11.14. Derive the conditional posteriors of $(\rho, \sigma_{v_1}^{-2}, \sigma_{v_2}^{-2})$ in example 11.5 when ρ is unknown and has prior $\mathbb{N}(\bar{\rho}, \bar{\sigma}_\rho^2)\mathcal{I}_{(-1,1)}$, where $\mathcal{I}_{(-1,1)}$ is an indicator for stationarity.

To construct the conditional of ϕ, note that, if $\epsilon_t \sim (0, \Sigma_t)$, then $e_t = \mathcal{P}\epsilon_t \sim (0, \mathcal{P}\Sigma_t\mathcal{P}')$. Hence, if e_t is known, and given (y_t, x_t, α_t), the free elements of $\mathcal{P}$ can be estimated as follows. Since $\mathcal{P}$ is lower triangular, the mth equation is

$$\sigma_{mt}^{-1} e_{mt} = \phi_{m1}(-\sigma_{mt}^{-1} e_{1t}) + \cdots + \phi_{m,m-1}(-\sigma_{mt}^{-1} e_{m-1t}) + (\sigma_{mt}^{-1} \epsilon_{mt}). \quad (11.16)$$

Hence, letting $E_{mt} = (-\sigma_{mt}^{-1} e_{1t}, \dots, -\sigma_{mt-1}^{-1} e_{mt})$, $\varepsilon_{mt} = -\sigma_{mt}^{-1} \epsilon_{mt}$, it is easy to see that the conditional posterior for ϕ_i is normal with mean $\tilde{\phi}_i$ and variance $\tilde{\Sigma}_{\phi_i}$.

Exercise 11.15. Show the form of $\tilde{\phi}_i$ and $\tilde{\Sigma}_{\phi_i}$.

To draw σ_{it}^2 from its conditional distribution, let $\sigma_{(-i)t}^2$ be the sequence of σ_t^2 excluding its ith element and let $e = (e_1, \dots, e_t)$. Then $g(\sigma_{it}^2 \mid \sigma_{(-i)t}^2, \sigma_{\epsilon_i}, e) = g(\sigma_{it}^2 \mid \sigma_{it-1}^2, \sigma_{it+1}^2, \sigma_{\epsilon_i}, e)$, which is given in (11.12). To draw from this distribution for each i we could choose as candidate distribution $\sigma_{it}^{-2} \exp\{-(\ln \sigma_{it}^2 - E_t(\ln \sigma_{it}^2))^2 / 2\operatorname{var}(\ln \sigma_t^2)\}$ and accept or reject the draw with probability $(\sigma_{it}^{\dagger})^{-1} \times \exp\{-e_{it}^2/2(\sigma_{it}^2)^{\dagger}\}/(\sigma_{it}^{\ell-1})^{-1} \exp\{-e_{it}^2/2(\sigma_{it}^2)^{l-1}\}$, where $(\sigma_{it}^2)^{l-1}$ is the last draw and $(\sigma_{it}^2)^{\dagger}$ is the candidate draw.

Exercise 11.16. Suppose you are interested in predicting future values of y_t. Let $y^{t+\tau} = (y_{t+1}, \dots, y_{t+\tau})$, $\alpha = (\alpha_1, \dots, \alpha_t)$, and $y = (y_1, \dots, y_t)$. Show that, conditional on time t information,

$$\begin{aligned} g(y^{t+\tau} \mid \alpha, \Sigma_t^{\dagger}, \Sigma_{v_1}, \phi, \sigma_{v_{2i}}, y) &= \iint g(\alpha^{t+\tau} \mid \alpha, \Sigma_t^{\dagger}, \Sigma_{v_1}, \phi, \sigma_{v_{2i}}, y) \\ &\quad \times g(\Sigma^{\dagger,t+\tau} \mid \alpha^{t+\tau}, \Sigma_t^{\dagger}, \Sigma_{v_1}, \phi, \sigma_{v_{2i}}, y) \\ &\quad \times f(y^{t+\tau} \mid \alpha^{t+\tau}, \Sigma^{\dagger,t+\tau}, \Sigma_{v_1}, \phi, \sigma_{v_{2i}}, y)\, d\alpha^{t+\tau}\, d\Sigma^{\dagger,t+\tau}. \end{aligned}$$

Describe how to sample (y_{t+1}, y_{t+2}) from this distribution. How would you construct a 68% prediction band?

Stochastic volatility models are typically used to infer values for the unobservable conditional volatilities, both in-sample (smoothing) and out-of-sample (prediction). For example, option pricing formulas require estimates of conditional volatilities and event studies often relate specific occurrences to changes in volatility. Here we concentrate on the smoothing problem, that is, on the computation of $g(\sigma_t^2 \mid y)$, where $y = (y_1, \dots, y_T)$. An analytic expression for this posterior density is not available but since $g(\sigma_t^2 \mid y) = \int g(\sigma_t^2, \mid \alpha_t, y) g(\alpha_t \mid y)\, d\alpha_t$ it can be numerically obtained by using the draws of σ_t^2 and α_t. The mean of this distribution can be used as an estimate of the smoothed volatility.

Exercise 11.17. Suppose the volatility model is $\ln \sigma_t^2 = \rho_0 + \rho(\ell) \ln \sigma_{t-1}^2 + \sigma_v v_t$, where $\rho(\ell)$ is unknown of order q. Show how to extend the Gibbs sampler to this case. Assume now that the model is of the form $\ln \sigma_t^2 = \rho_0 + \rho_1 \ln \sigma_{t-1}^2 + \sigma_{v_t} v_t$, where $\sigma_{v_t} = f(x_t)$, x_t are observable variables, and f is linear. Show how to extend the Gibbs sampler to this case.

As with factor models, cycling through the conditionals of $(\Sigma_t^\dagger, \alpha_t, \sigma_{v_{2i}}, \Sigma_{v_1}, \phi)$ with the Gibbs sampler produces, in the limit, a sample from the joint posterior.

Uhlig (1994) proposed an alternative specification for a stochastic volatility model which, together with a particular distribution of the innovations of the stochastic volatility term, produces closed-form solutions for the posterior distribution of the parameters and of the unknown vector of volatilities. The approach treats some parameters in the stochastic volatility equation as fixed but has the advantage of producing recursive estimates of the quantities of interest.

Consider an m-variable VAR(q) with stochastic volatility of the form

$$\left.\begin{aligned} Y_t &= AX_t + \mathcal{P}_t^{-1} e_t, & e_t &\sim \mathbb{N}(0, I), \\ \Sigma_{t+1} &= \frac{\mathcal{P}_t' v_t \mathcal{P}_t}{\rho}, & v_t &\sim \text{Beta}((\nu + k)/2, 1/2), \end{aligned}\right\} \tag{11.17}$$

where X_t contains the lags of the endogenous and the exogenous variables, $\mathcal{P}_t$ is the upper Choleski factor of Σ_{t+1}, ν and ρ are (known) parameters, Beta denotes the m-variate beta distribution, and k is the number of parameters in each equation.

To construct the posterior of the parameters of (11.17) we need a prior for (A, Σ_1). We assume $g_1(A, \Sigma_1) \propto g_0(A) g(A, \Sigma_1 \mid \bar{A}_0, \rho\bar{\Sigma}_A, \bar{\Sigma}_0, \bar{\nu})$, where $g_0(A)$ is a function restricting the prior for A (e.g., to be stationary) and $g(\alpha, \Sigma_1 \mid \bar{A}_0, \rho\bar{\Sigma}_A, \bar{\Sigma}_0, \bar{\nu})$ is of normal-Wishart form, i.e., $g(A \mid \Sigma_1) \sim \mathbb{N}(\bar{A}_0, \rho\bar{\Sigma}_A)$, $g(\Sigma_1^{-1}) \sim \mathbb{W}(\bar{\Sigma}_0, \bar{\nu})$, $\bar{A}_0$, $\bar{\Sigma}_0$, $\bar{\Sigma}_A$, $\bar{\nu}$, ρ known.

Combining the likelihood of (11.17) with these priors and exploiting the fact that the beta distribution conjugates with the gamma distribution, we have that the posterior kernel for (A, Σ_{t+1}) is $\grave{g}_t(A, \Sigma_{t+1}) = \grave{g}_t(A) \grave{g}(A, \Sigma_{t+1} \mid \tilde{A}_t, \rho\tilde{\Sigma}_{At}, \tilde{\Sigma}_t, \nu)$, where $\grave{g}$ is of normal-Wishart type, $\tilde{\Sigma}_{At} = \rho\tilde{\Sigma}_{At-1} + X_t X_t'$, $\tilde{A}_t = (\rho\tilde{A}_{t-1}\tilde{\Sigma}_{At-1} + Y_t X_t')\tilde{\Sigma}_{At}^{-1}$, $\tilde{\Sigma}_t = \rho\tilde{\Sigma}_{t-1} + (\rho/\nu)e_t(1 - X_t'\tilde{\Sigma}_{At}^{-1}X_t)\tilde{e}_t'$, $\tilde{e}_t = Y_t - \tilde{A}_{t-1}X_t$, and $\grave{g}_t(A) = \grave{g}_{t-1}(A)|(A - \tilde{A}_t)\tilde{\Sigma}_{At}(A - \tilde{A}_t)' + (\nu/\rho)\tilde{\Sigma}_t|^{-0.5}$.

Example 11.6. Consider a univariate AR(1) version of (11.17) of the form

$$y_t = \alpha y_{t-1} + \sigma_t^{-1}e_t, \quad e_t \sim \mathbb{N}(0, 1), \tag{11.18}$$

$$\rho\sigma_{t+1}^2 = \sigma_t^2 v_t, \quad v_t \sim \text{Beta}((\nu + 1)/2, 1/2). \tag{11.19}$$

Let $g(\alpha, \sigma_1^2) \propto g_0(\alpha)g(\alpha, \sigma_1^2 \mid \bar{\alpha}_0, \rho\bar{\sigma}_{\alpha_0}^2, \bar{\sigma}_0^2, \bar{\nu})$, where $(\bar{\alpha}_0, \sigma_{\alpha_0}, \bar{\sigma}_0, \bar{\nu})$ are hyperparameters and assume that $g(\alpha, \sigma_1^2 \mid \bar{\alpha}_0, \rho\bar{\sigma}_{\alpha_0}^2, \bar{\sigma}_0^2, \bar{\nu})$ is of normal-inverted gamma type. Recursive posterior estimates of the parameters of $g_t(\alpha)$ are $\tilde{\sigma}_{\alpha,t}^2 = \rho\tilde{\sigma}_{\alpha,t-1}^2 + y_{t-1}^2$, $\tilde{\alpha}_t = (\rho\tilde{\alpha}_{t-1}\sigma_{\alpha,t-1}^2 + y_t y_{t-1})/\sigma_{\alpha,t}^2$, $\tilde{\sigma}_t^2 = \rho\tilde{\sigma}_{t-1}^2 + (\rho/\nu)\tilde{e}_t^2(1 - y_{t-1}^2/\sigma_{\alpha,t}^2)$, $\tilde{e}_t = y_t - \tilde{\alpha}_{t-1}y_{t-1}$, $g_t(\alpha) = g_{t-1}(\alpha)[(\alpha - \tilde{\alpha}_t)^2\sigma_{\alpha,t}^2 + (\nu/\rho)\sigma_t^2]^{-0.5}$. Hence both $\tilde{\sigma}_{\alpha_t}^2$ and $\tilde{\alpha}$ are weighted averages, with ρ measuring the memory of the process. Note that past values of $\tilde{\alpha}$ are weighted by the relative change in $\tilde{\sigma}_{\alpha,t}^2$. When $\sigma_{\alpha,t}^2$ is constant, $\tilde{\alpha}_t = \rho\tilde{\alpha}_{t-1} + y_t y_{t-1}/\rho\sigma_{\alpha}^2$.

When $\rho = \nu/(\nu + 1)$, $\nu/\rho = 1 - \rho$. In this case, $\tilde{\sigma}_t^2$ is a weighted average of $\tilde{\sigma}_{t-1}^2$ and the information contained in the square of the recursive residuals, adjusted for the relative size of y_t^2, to the weighted sum of y_{t-1}^2 up to $t - 1$. Note also that $E_{t-1}\sigma_t^2 = \sigma_{t-1}^2(\nu + 1)/\rho(\nu + 2)$. Hence, when $\rho = (\nu + 1)/(\nu + 2)$, σ_t^2 is a random walk.

For comparison, it may be useful to map the general prior of (11.17) into a Minnesota-type prior. For example, we could set $\bar{\Sigma}_0 = \text{diag}\{\bar{\sigma}_{0i}\}$ and compute $\bar{\sigma}_{0i}$ from the average square residuals of an AR(1) regression for each i in a training sample. Also, one could set $\bar{\Sigma}_A = \text{blockdiag}[\bar{\Sigma}_{A1}, \bar{\Sigma}_{A2}]$, where the split reflects the distinction between endogenous and exogenous variables. For example, if the second block contains a constant and linear trend, then

$$\bar{\Sigma}_{A2} = \begin{bmatrix} \phi_2 & -\phi_2^2/2 \\ \phi_2^2/2 & -\phi_2^3/3 \end{bmatrix},$$

where ϕ_2 is a hyperparameter, while we could set the diagonal elements of Σ_{A1} equal to $\theta_0^2\theta_1^2/\ell$, where ℓ refers to the lag, and ϕ_1 for the lags of the variables in an equation, and the off-diagonal elements to zero. Unless required by the problem, set $g_0(A) = 1$. Finally, set $\nu \approx 20$ for quarterly data and $\rho = \nu/(\nu + 1)$.

Given the generic structure for the posterior of (A_t, Σ_{t+1}) (a time-varying density multiplied by a normal-Wishart density), we need numerical methods to draw posterior sequences. Any of the approaches described in chapter 9 will do it.

Example 11.7. To draw from the posterior we could use the following importance sampling algorithm.

(1) Find the marginal for A_T. Integrating Σ_{T+1} out of $\breve{g}(A_T, \Sigma_{t+1} \mid y)$ we have $\breve{g}(A_T \mid y) = 0.5\sum_t \ln|(A - \tilde{A}_T)\tilde{\Sigma}_{AT}(A - \tilde{A}_T)' + (\nu/\rho)\Sigma_T| - 0.5(k + \nu)| \times (A - \tilde{A}_T)\tilde{\Sigma}_{AT}(A - \tilde{A}_T)' + (\nu/\rho)\Sigma_T|$.

(2) Find the mode of $\breve{g}(A_T \mid y)$ (call it A_T^*) and compute the Hessian at the mode.

(3) Conditional on A_T, $g(\Sigma_{T+1}^{-1} \mid y)$ is $\mathbb{W}([\rho(A - \tilde{A}_T)\tilde{\Sigma}_{AT}(A - \tilde{A}_T)' + \nu\tilde{\Sigma}_T]^{-1}, \nu + k)$.

(4) Draw A_T^l from a multivariate t-distribution centered at A_T^* and with variance equal to the Hessian at the mode and degrees of freedom $\nu \ll T - k(M+1)$. Draw $(\Sigma_{T+1}^{-1})^l$ from the Wishart distribution derived in step (3).

(5) Calculate the importance ratio: $\ln \mathrm{IR}(A_T^l, \Sigma_{T+1}^l) = \text{const.} + \ln(\breve{g}(A_T^l)) - \ln(\breve{g}^{\mathrm{IS}}(A_T^l))$, where $g^{\mathrm{IS}}(A^l)$ is the value of the importance sampling density at A^l.

(6) Use $\bar{h}_L = \sum_{l=1}^{L} h(A_T^l, \Sigma_{T+1}^l)\mathrm{IR}(A_T^l, \Sigma_{T+1}^l) / \sum_{l=1}^{L} \mathrm{IR}(A_T^l, \Sigma_{T+1}^l)$ to approximate any function $h(A_T, \Sigma_{T+1})$.

Exercise 11.18. Describe an MH algorithm to draw posterior sequences for (A_T, Σ_{T+1}).

Exercise 11.19 (Cogley). Consider a bivariate model with consumption and income growth of the form $y_t = \bar{y} + A_t(\ell)y_{t-1} + e_t$, $\alpha_t \equiv \mathrm{vec}(A_t(\ell)) = \alpha_{t-1} + v_{1t}$, $\Sigma_t = \mathrm{diag}\{\sigma_{it}^2\}$, $\ln \sigma_t^2 = \ln \sigma_{t-1}^2 + \sigma_{v_2} v_{2t}$, where $\bar{y}$ is a constant. In a constant-coefficient version of the model the trend growth rate of the two variables is $(I - A(\ell))^{-1}\bar{y}$. Using a Gibbs sampler, describe how to construct a time-varying estimate of the trend growth rate, $(I - A_t(\ell))^{-1}\bar{y}$.

We conclude this section applying Bayesian methods to the estimation of the parameters of a GARCH model.

Example 11.8. Consider the model $y_t = x_t'A + \sigma_t e_t$, $e_t \sim$ i.i.d. $\mathbb{N}(0, 1)$, and $\sigma_t^2 = \rho_0 + \rho_1\sigma_{t-1}^2 + \rho_2 e_{t-1}^2$. Assume that $A \sim \mathbb{N}(\bar{A}, \bar{\sigma}_A^2)$, $\rho_0 \sim \mathbb{N}(\bar{\rho}_0, \bar{\sigma}_{\rho_0}^2)$, and that $g(\rho_1, \rho_2)$ is uniform over [0, 1] and restricted so that $\rho_1 + \rho_2 \leqslant 1$. The posterior kernel can be easily constructed from these densities. Let $\alpha = (A, \rho_i, i = 0, 1, 2)$; let the mode of the posterior be α^*, and let $\breve{t}(\cdot)$ be the kernel of a t-distribution with location α^*, scale proportional to the Hessian at the mode, and $\bar{\nu}$ degrees of freedom. Posterior draws for the parameters can be obtained by using, for example, an independence Metropolis algorithm, that is, generate $\alpha^\dagger$ from $\breve{t}(\cdot)$ and accept the draw with probability equal to $\min\{[\breve{g}(\alpha^\dagger \mid y_t)/\breve{t}(\alpha^\dagger)]/[\breve{g}(\alpha^{l-1} \mid y_t)/\breve{t}(\alpha^{l-1})], 1\}$. A t-distribution is appropriate in this case because $\breve{g}(\alpha \mid y_t)/\breve{t}(\alpha)$ is typically bounded from above.

11.3 Markov Switching Models

Markov switching models are extensively used in macroeconomics, in particular, when important relationships are suspected to be functions of an unobservable variable (e.g., the state of a business cycle). Hamilton (1994) provides a classical nonlinear filtering method which can be used to obtain estimates of the parameters and of the unobservable state. Here we consider a Bayesian approach to the problem.

As with factor and stochastic volatility models, the unobservable state is treated as "missing" data and sampled together with other parameters in the Gibbs sampler.

To set up ideas we start from a static model where the slope varies with the state:

$$y_t = x_{1t}A_1 + x_{2t}A_2(\varkappa_t - 1) + e_t, \quad e_t \sim \text{i.i.d. } \mathbb{N}(0, \sigma_e^2). \tag{11.20}$$

Here $\varkappa_t$ is a two-state Markov switching indicator. We take $\varkappa_t = 1$ to be the normal state so that $y_t = x_{1t}A_1 + e_t$. In the extraordinary state, $\varkappa_t = 0$ and $y_t = x_{1t}A_1 - x_{2t}A_2 + e_t$.

We let $p_1 = P(\varkappa_t = 1 \mid \varkappa_{t-1} = 1)$, $p_2 = p(\varkappa_t = 0 \mid \varkappa_{t-1} = 0)$, both of which are unknown; also we let $y^{t-1} = (y_1, \dots, y_{t-1}, x_{11}, \dots, x_{1t-1}, x_{21}, \dots, x_{2t-1})$, $\varkappa^t = (\varkappa_1, \dots, \varkappa_t)$, $\alpha = (A_1, A_2, \sigma_e^2, \varkappa^t, p_1, p_2)$. We want to obtain the posterior for α. We assume $g(\alpha) = g(A_1, A_2, \sigma_e^2) g(\varkappa^t \mid p_1, p_2) g(p_1, p_2)$. We let $g(p_1, p_2) = p_1^{\bar{d}_{11}}(1 - p_1)^{\bar{d}_{12}} p_2^{\bar{d}_{22}}(1 - p_2)^{\bar{d}_{21}}$, where $\bar{d}_{ij}$ are the *a priori* proportions of the (i, j) elements in the sample. As usual, we assume $g(A_1, A_2, \sigma_e^{-2}) \propto \mathbb{N}(\bar{A}_1, \bar{\Sigma}_1) \times \mathbb{N}(\bar{A}_2, \bar{\Sigma}_2) \times \mathbb{G}(a_1, a_2)$.

The posterior kernel is $\breve{g}(\alpha \mid y) = \sum_{t=1}^{T} f(y_t \mid \alpha, y^{t-1}) g(\alpha)$, where each $f(y_t \mid \alpha, y^{t-1}) \sim \mathbb{N}(Ax_t, \sigma_e^2)$, $x_t = (x_{1t}, x_{2t})$, and $A = (A_1, A_2)$. To sample from this kernel we need starting values for α and $\varkappa_t$ and the following algorithm.

Algorithm 11.2.

(1) Sample (p_1, p_2) from $g(p_1, p_2 \mid y) = p_1^{\bar{d}_{11}+d_{11}}(1 - p_1)^{\bar{d}_{12}+d_{12}} p_2^{\bar{d}_{22}+d_{22}} \times (1 - p_2)^{\bar{d}_{21}+d_{21}}$, where d_{ij} is the actual number of shifts between state i and state j.

(2) Sample A_i from $\breve{g}(A_i \mid \sigma_e^2, \varkappa^T, y)$. This is the kernel of a normal with mean $\tilde{A} = \tilde{\Sigma}_A(\sum_t x_t y_t / \sigma^2 + \bar{\Sigma}_A^{-1}\bar{A})$ and variance $\tilde{\Sigma}_A = (\sum_t x_t' x_t / \sigma^2 + \bar{\Sigma}^{-1})^{-1}$, where $\bar{A} = (\bar{A}_1, \bar{A}_2)$ and $\bar{\Sigma} = \text{diag}(\bar{\Sigma}_1, \bar{\Sigma}_2)$.

(3) Sample σ_e^{-2} from $\breve{g}(\sigma_e^{-2} \mid \varkappa^T, y, A)$. This is the kernel of a gamma with parameters $a_1 + 0.5(T-1)$ and $a_2 + 0.5\sum_t (y_t - A_1 x_{1t} + A_2 x_{2t}(\varkappa_t - 1))^2$.

(4) Sample $\varkappa^T$ from $\breve{g}(\varkappa^T \mid y, A, \sigma_e^2, p_1, p_2)$. As usual we do this in two steps. Given $g(\varkappa_0)$ we run forward into the sample by using $g(\varkappa_t \mid A, \sigma_e^2, y^t, p_1, p_2) \propto f(y_t \mid y^{t-1}, A, \sigma_e^2, \varkappa_t)\, g(\varkappa_t \mid A, \sigma_e^2, y^{t-1}, p_1, p_2)$, where $f(y_t \mid y^{t-1}, A, \sigma_e^2, \varkappa_t) \sim N(Ax_t, \sigma_e^2)$ and $g(\varkappa_t \mid A, \sigma_e^2, y^{t-1}, p_1, p_2) = \sum_{\varkappa_{t-1}=0}^{1} g(\varkappa_{t-1} \mid A, \sigma_e^2, y^{t-1}, p_1, p_2) P(\varkappa_t = i \mid \varkappa_{t-1} = j)$. Then, starting from $\varkappa_T$, we run backward in the sample to smooth estimates, that is, given $g(\varkappa_T \mid y^T, A, \sigma_e^2, p_1, p_2)$, we compute $g(\varkappa_\tau \mid \varkappa_{\tau+1}, y^\tau, A, \sigma_e^2, p_1, p_2) \propto g(\varkappa_\tau \mid A, \sigma_e^2, y^\tau, p_1, p_2) P(\varkappa_\tau = i \mid \varkappa_{\tau+1} = j)^{-1}$, $\tau = T-1, T-2, \dots$. Note that we have used the Markov properties of $\varkappa_t$ to split the forward and backward problems of drawing T joint values into the problem of drawing T conditional values.

We can immediately see that step (4) of algorithm 11.2 is the same as the one we used to extract the unobservable state in state space models. In fact, the first

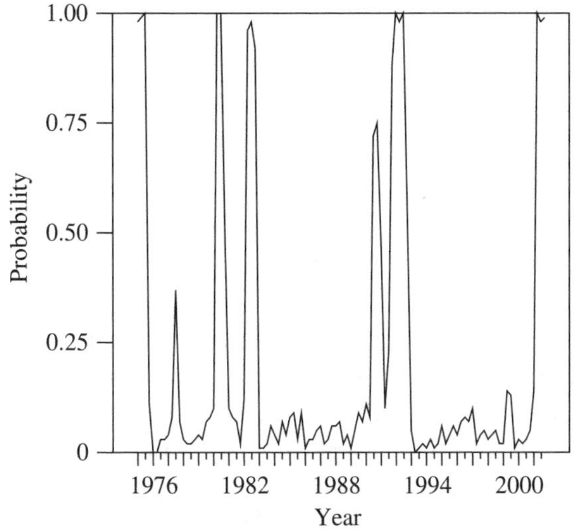

Figure 11.2. Recession probabilities.

part is similar to drawing the AR parameters in a factor model and the second to the estimation of the factor at each stage of the simulation. This is not surprising: a two-state Markov chain model can always be written as a first-order AR process with AR coefficient equal to $p_2 + p_1 - 1$. The difference, as already mentioned, is that the AR process here has binary innovations.

Exercise 11.20. Suppose that $g(p_1, p_2)$ is noninformative. Show the form of the conditional posterior of $(A_1, A_2, \sigma_e^{-2})$. Alter algorithm 11.2 to take into account this change.

Example 11.9. We use equation (11.20) to study fluctuations in EU industrial production. To construct an EU measure we aggregate IP data for Germany, France, and Italy by using GDP weights and let y_t be the yearly changes in industrial production. Data run from 1974:1 to 2001:4. The posterior means are $\tilde{A}_2 = 0.46$ and $\tilde{A}_1 = 0.96$ and the standard deviations are 0.09 for both coefficients. Hence, the annual growth rate in expansions is about two percentage points higher and the difference is statistically significant. Estimates of the probability of being in the extraordinary state (a "recession") are in figure 11.2: the algorithm picks up standard recessions and indicates the presence of a new contractionary phase starting in 2001:1.

11.3.1 A More Complicated Structure

The model we consider here is

$$A^y(\ell)(y_t - \bar{y}(\varkappa_t, x_t)) = \sigma(\varkappa_t)e_t, \tag{11.21}$$

where $A^y(\ell)$ is a polynomial in the lag operator, $\bar{y}(\varkappa_t, x_t)$ is the mean of y_t, which depends on observable regressors x_t and on the unobservable state $\varkappa_t$, $\text{var}(e_t) = 1$,

$\sigma(\varkappa_t)$ also depends on the unobservable state, and $\varkappa_t$ is a two-state Markov chain with transition matrix P. We set $\bar{y}(\varkappa_t, x_t) = x_t' A_0 + A_1 \varkappa_t, \sigma^2(\varkappa_t) = \sigma^2 + A_2 \varkappa_t$ and assume $A_2 > 0$, $A_1 > 0$ for identification purposes. Moreover, we restrict the roots of $A^y(\ell)$ to be less than 1.

Let $y^t = (y_1, \dots, y_t)$, $\varkappa^t = (\varkappa_1, \dots, \varkappa_t)$; let $\mathbb{A}$ be the companion matrix of $A^y(\ell)$ and $\mathbb{A}_1$ its first m rows. Define $\kappa = A_2/\sigma^2$ and let $\alpha = (A_0, A_1, \mathbb{A}_1, \sigma^2, \kappa, p_{ij})$. The likelihood function is $f(y^t \mid \varkappa^t, \alpha) = f(y^q \mid \varkappa^q, \alpha) \times \prod_{\tau=q+1}^{t} f(y_\tau \mid y^{\tau-1}, \varkappa^{t-1}, \alpha)$, where the first term is the density of the first q observations and the second term is the one-step-ahead conditional density of y_τ.

The density of the first q observations (see derivation in the factor model case) is normal with mean $x^q A_0 + \varkappa^q A_1$ and variance $\sigma^2 \Omega_q$, where $\Omega_q = W_q \Sigma_q W_q$, $\Sigma_q = \mathbb{A}\Sigma_q \mathbb{A}' + (1, 0, 0, \dots, 0)'(1, 0, 0, \dots, 0)$, $W_q = \operatorname{diag}\{(1 + \kappa\varkappa_j)^{0.5},\ j = 1, \dots, q\}$. Using the prediction error decomposition we have that $f(y_\tau \mid y^{\tau-1}, \varkappa^{\tau-1}, \alpha) \propto \exp\{-(y_\tau - y_{\tau|\tau-1})^2/2\sigma^2(\varkappa_\tau)\}$, where $y_{\tau|\tau-1} = (1 - A^y(\ell))y_t + A^y(\ell)(x_\tau' A_0 + A_1 \varkappa_\tau)$. Therefore, y_t is conditionally normal with mean $y_{t|t-1}$ and variance $\sigma^2(\varkappa_t)$. Finally, the joint density of $(y^t, \varkappa^t)$ is $f(y^t \mid \varkappa^t, \alpha) \prod_{\tau=2}^{t} f(\varkappa_\tau \mid \varkappa_{\tau-1}) f(\varkappa_1)$ and the likelihood of the data is $\int f(y^t, \varkappa^t \mid \alpha)\, d\varkappa^t$. In chapter 3 we produced estimates of $(\alpha, \varkappa^t)$ by using a two-step approach: in the first step α_{ML} is obtained by maximizing the likelihood function; in the second step, inference about $\varkappa^t$ is obtained conditional on α_{ML}. That is,

$$\begin{aligned} f(\varkappa_t, \dots, \varkappa_{t-\tau+1} \mid y^t, \alpha_{\mathrm{ML}}) \\ &= \sum_{\varkappa_{t-\tau}=0}^{1} f(\varkappa_t, \dots, \varkappa_{t-\tau} \mid y^{t-1}, \alpha_{\mathrm{ML}}) \\ &\propto f(\varkappa_t \mid \varkappa_{t-1}) f(\varkappa_{t-1}, \dots, \varkappa_{t-\tau} \mid y^{t-1}, \alpha_{\mathrm{ML}}) f(y_t \mid y^{t-1}, \varkappa^t, \alpha_{\mathrm{ML}}), \end{aligned} \tag{11.22}$$

where the factor of proportionality is given by $f(y_t \mid y^{t-1}, \alpha_{\mathrm{ML}}) = \sum_{\varkappa_t} \cdots \sum_{\varkappa_{t-\tau}} f(y_t, \varkappa_t, \dots, \varkappa_{t-\tau} \mid y^{t-1}, \alpha_{\mathrm{ML}})$. Since the log likelihood of the sample is $\ln f(y_{q+1}, \dots, y_t \mid y^q, \alpha) = \sum_\tau \ln f(y_\tau \mid y^{\tau-1}, \alpha)$, once α_{ML} is obtained, transition probabilities can be computed by using $f(\varkappa_t \mid y^t, \alpha_{\mathrm{ML}}) = \int \cdots \int f(\varkappa_t, \dots, \varkappa_{t-\tau+1} \mid y^t, \alpha_{\mathrm{ML}})\, d\varkappa_{t-1} \cdots d\varkappa_{t-\tau+1}$. Note that in this case uncertainty in α_{ML} is not incorporated in the calculations.

To construct the conditional posteriors of the parameters and of the unobservable state, assume that $g(A_0, A_1, \sigma^{-2}) \propto \mathbb{N}(\bar{A}_0, \bar{\Sigma}_{A_0})\mathbb{N}(\bar{A}_1, \bar{\Sigma}_{A_1})\mathcal{I}_{(A_1>0)}\mathbb{G}(a_1^\sigma, a_2^\sigma)$, where $\mathcal{I}_{(A_1>0)}$ is an indicator function. Further assume that $g((1+\kappa)^{-1}) \sim \mathbb{G}(a_1^\kappa, a_2^\kappa)\mathcal{I}_{(\kappa>0)}$ and $g(\mathbb{A}_1) \sim \mathbb{N}(\bar{\mathbb{A}}_1, \bar{\Sigma}_{\mathbb{A}_1})\mathcal{I}_{(-1,1)}$, where $\mathcal{I}_{(-1,1)}$ is an indicator for stationarity. Finally, we let $p_{12} = 1 - p_{11} = 1 - p_1$ and $p_{21} = 1 - p_{22} = 1 - p_2$ and $g(p_i) \propto \mathrm{Beta}(\bar{d}_{i1}, \bar{d}_{i2})$, $i = 1, 2$, and assume that all hyperparameters are known.

Exercise 11.21. Let $\alpha_{-\psi}$ be the vector α except for ψ and let $A = (A_0, A_1)$.

(i) Assuming that the first q observations come from the low state, show that the conditional posteriors for the parameters and the unobserved state are

$$\left.\begin{aligned}
g(A \mid y^t, \varkappa^t, \alpha_{-A}) &\sim \mathbb{N}(\tilde{A}, \tilde{\Sigma}_A)\mathcal{I}_{A_1>0},\\
g(\sigma^{-2} \mid y^t, \varkappa^t, \alpha_{-\sigma^2}) &\sim \mathbb{G}(a_1^\sigma + T, a_2^\sigma\\
&\quad + (\Sigma_q^{-0.5}y - \Sigma_q^{-0.5}xA_0 + \Sigma_q^{-0.5}\varkappa A_1)^2),\\
g((1+\kappa)^{-1} \mid y^t, \varkappa^t, \alpha_{-\kappa}) &\sim \mathbb{G}(a_1^\kappa + T_1, a_2^\kappa + \text{rss})\mathcal{I}_{(\kappa>0)},\\
g(\mathbb{A}_1 \mid y^t, \varkappa^t, \alpha_{-\mathbb{A}_1}) &\sim \mathbb{N}(\tilde{\mathbb{A}}_1, \tilde{\Sigma}_{\mathbb{A}_1})\mathcal{I}_{(-1,1)}|\Omega_q|^{-0.5}\\
&\quad \times \exp\{-(y^q - x^q A)'\Omega_q^{-1}(y^q - x^q A)/2\sigma^2\},\\
g(p_i \mid y^t, \varkappa^t, \alpha_{-p_i}) &\sim \text{Beta}(\bar{d}_{i1} + d_{i1}, \bar{d}_{i2} + d_{i2}), \quad i = 1, 2,\\
g(\varkappa_t \mid y^t, \alpha_{-\varkappa_{-t}}) &\propto f(\varkappa_t \mid \varkappa_{t-1}) f(\varkappa_{t+1} \mid \varkappa_t) \prod_\tau f(y_\tau \mid y^{\tau-1}, \varkappa^\tau),
\end{aligned}\right\} \tag{11.23}$$

where T_1 is the number of elements in T for which $\varkappa_t = 1$, d_{ij} is the number of actual transitions from state i to state j, and $\text{rss} = \sum_{t=1}^{T_1}\{[(1-\kappa x_t^{0.5})(y - x_t' A_0 - \varkappa_t A_1)]/2\}$.

(ii) Show the exact form of $\tilde{\mathbb{A}}_1$, $\tilde{\Sigma}_{\mathbb{A}_1}$, $\tilde{A}$, and $\tilde{\Sigma}_A$.

(iii) Describe how to draw $\mathbb{A}_1$ and A restricted to the correct domain.

Recently, Sims (2001) and Sims and Zha (2004) have used a similar specification to estimate a Markov switching VAR model, where the switch may occur in the lagged dynamics, in the contemporaneous effects, or in both. To illustrate their approach consider the equation

$$A_1(\ell)i_t = \bar{i}(\varkappa_t) + b(\varkappa_t)A_2(\ell)\pi_t + \sigma(\varkappa_t)e_t, \tag{11.24}$$

where $e_t \sim$ i.i.d. $\mathbb{N}(0,1)$, i_t is the nominal interest rate, π_t is inflation, and $\varkappa_t$ has three states with transition

$$P = \begin{bmatrix} p_1 & 1-p_1 & 0 \\ (1-p_2)/2 & p_2 & (1-p_2)/2 \\ 0 & 1-p_3 & p_3 \end{bmatrix}.$$

The model (11.24) imposes restrictions on the data: the dynamics of interest rates do not depend on the state; the form of the lag distribution on π_t is the same across states, except for a scale factor $b(\varkappa)$; there is no possibility of jumping from state 1 to state 3 (or vice versa) without passing through state 2; finally, the nine elements of P depend only on three parameters.

Let $\alpha = [\text{vec}(A_1(\ell)), \text{vec}(A_2(\ell)), \bar{i}(\varkappa_t), b(\varkappa_t), \sigma(\varkappa_t), p_1, p_2, p_3]$. The marginal likelihood of the data, conditional on the parameters (but integrating out the unobservable state) can be computed numerically and recursively. Let $\mathcal{F}_t$ be the information set at t.

Exercise 11.22. Show that $f(i_t, \varkappa_t \mid \mathcal{F}_{t-1})$ is a mixture of continuous and discrete densities. Show the form of $f(i_t \mid \mathcal{F}_{t-1})$, the marginal of the data, and of $f(\varkappa_t \mid \mathcal{F}_t)$, the updating density.

Once $f(\varkappa_t \mid \mathcal{F}_t)$ is obtained we can compute

$$f(\varkappa_{t+1} \mid \mathcal{F}_t) = \begin{bmatrix} f(\varkappa_t = 1 \mid \mathcal{F}_t) \\ f(\varkappa_t = 2 \mid \mathcal{F}_t) \\ f(\varkappa_t = 3 \mid \mathcal{F}_t) \end{bmatrix}' P$$

and from there we can calculate $f(i_{t+1}, \varkappa_{t+1} \mid i_t, \pi_t, \dots)$, which makes the recursion complete. Given a flat prior on α, the posterior will be proportional to $f(\alpha \mid i_t, \pi_t)$ and posterior estimates of the parameters and of the states can immediately be obtained.

Exercise 11.23. Provide formulas to obtain smoothed estimates of $\varkappa_t$.

More complicated VAR specifications are possible. For example, let $y_t \mathcal{A}_0(\varkappa_t) = x_t' \mathcal{A}_+(\varkappa_t) + e_t$, where x_t includes all lags of y_t and $e_t \sim$ i.i.d. $\mathbb{N}(0, I)$. Assume $\mathcal{A}_+(\varkappa_t) = \mathcal{A}(\varkappa_t) + [I, 0]' \mathcal{A}_0(\varkappa_t)$. Given this specification there are two possibilities: either $\mathcal{A}_0(\varkappa_t) = \bar{A}_0 \Lambda(\varkappa_t)$ and $\mathcal{A}(\varkappa_t) = \bar{\mathcal{A}} \Lambda(\varkappa_t)$ or $\mathcal{A}_0(\varkappa_t)$ free and $\mathcal{A}(\varkappa_t) = \bar{\mathcal{A}}$. In the first specification changes in the contemporaneous and lagged coefficients are proportional; in the second the state affects the contemporaneous relationship but not lagged ones.

Equation (11.24) is an equation of a bivariate VAR. Hence, so long as we are able to keep the posterior of the system in a SUR format (as we have done in chapter 10), the above ideas can be applied to each of the VAR equations.

11.3.2 A General Markov Switching Specification

Finally, we consider a general Markov switching specification which embeds as a special case the two previous ones. So far we have allowed the mean and the variance of y_t to change with the state but we have forced the dynamics to be independent of the state, apart from a scale effect. This is a strong restriction: in fact, it is conceivable that the autocovariance function of the data is different in expansions and in recessions.

The general two-state Markov switching model we consider is

$$y_t = \begin{cases} x_t' A_{01} + Y_t' A_{02} + e_{0t} & \text{if } \varkappa_t = 0, \\ x_t' A_{02} + Y_t' A_{12} + e_{1t} & \text{if } \varkappa_t = 1, \end{cases} \tag{11.25}$$

where x_t is a $1 \times q_2$ vector of exogenous variables for each t, $Y_t' = (y_{t-1}, \dots, y_{t-q_1})$ is a vector of lagged dependent variables and e_{jt}, $j = 0, 1$, are i.i.d. random variables, normally distributed with mean zero and variance σ_j^2. Once again the transition probability for $\varkappa_t$ has diagonal elements p_i. In principle, some of the elements of A_{ji} may be equal to zero for some i, so the model may have different dynamics in different states.

For identification, we choose the first state to be a "recession", so that $A_{02} < A_{12}$ is imposed. We let α_c be the parameters which are common across states, α_i the parameters which are unique to the state, and $\alpha_{i\mathrm{r}}$ the parameters which are restricted to achieve identification. Then (11.25) can be written as

$$y_t = \begin{cases} X'_{\mathrm{c}t}\alpha_{\mathrm{c}} + X'_{0t}\alpha_0 + X'_{\mathrm{r}t}\alpha_{0r} + e_{0t} & \text{if } \varkappa_t = 0, \\ X'_{\mathrm{c}t}\alpha_{\mathrm{c}} + X'_{1t}\alpha_1 + X'_{\mathrm{r}t}\alpha_{1r} + e_{1t} & \text{if } \varkappa_t = 1, \end{cases} \tag{11.26}$$

where $(X'_{\mathrm{c}t}, X'_{it}, X'_{\mathrm{r}t}) = (x'_t, Y'_t)$ and $(\alpha'_{\mathrm{c}}, \alpha'_i, \alpha'_{i\mathrm{r}}) = (A'_{01}, A'_{02}, A'_{11}, A'_{12})$.

To construct conditional posteriors for the unknowns we assume conjugate priors: $\alpha_{\mathrm{c}} \sim \mathbb{N}(\bar{\alpha}_{\mathrm{c}}, \bar{\Sigma}_{\mathrm{c}})$; $\alpha_i \sim \mathbb{N}(\bar{\alpha}_i, \bar{\Sigma}_i)$; $\alpha_{i\mathrm{r}} \sim \mathbb{N}(\bar{\alpha}_{\mathrm{r}}, \bar{\Sigma}_{\mathrm{r}})\mathcal{I}_{\mathrm{rest}}$; $\bar{s}_i^2\sigma_i^{-2} \sim \chi^2(\bar{\nu}_i)$; $p_i \sim \mathrm{Beta}(d_{i1}, d_{i2})$, $i = 1, 2$, where $\mathcal{I}_{\mathrm{rest}}$ is a function indicating whether the identification restrictions are satisfied. As usual we assume that the hyperparameters $(\bar{\alpha}_{\mathrm{c}}, \bar{\Sigma}_{\mathrm{c}}, \bar{\alpha}_i, \bar{\Sigma}_i, \bar{\alpha}_{\mathrm{r}}, \bar{\Sigma}_{\mathrm{r}}, \bar{\nu}_i, \bar{s}_i^2, \bar{d}_{ij})$ are known or can be estimated from the data. We take the first $\max[q_1, q_0]$ observations as given in constructing the posterior distribution of the parameters and of the latent variable.

Given these priors, it is straightforward to compute conditional posteriors. For example, $g(\alpha_{\mathrm{c}} \mid x_t, y_t)$ has mean $\tilde{\alpha}_{\mathrm{c}} = \tilde{\Sigma}_{\mathrm{c}}(\sum_{t=\min[q_1,q_0]}^{T} X_{\mathrm{c}t}y'_{\mathrm{c}t}/\sigma_t^2 + \bar{\Sigma}_{\mathrm{c}}^{-1}\bar{\alpha}_{\mathrm{c}})$, variance $\tilde{\Sigma}_{\mathrm{c}} = (\sum_{t=\min[q_1,q_0]}^{T} X_{\mathrm{c}t}X'_{\mathrm{c}t}/\sigma_t^2 + \bar{\Sigma}_{\mathrm{c}}^{-1})^{-1}$, where $y_{\mathrm{c}t} = y_t - X_{it}\alpha_i - X_{\mathrm{r}t}\alpha_{i\mathrm{r}}$ and it is normal.

Exercise 11.24. Let T_i be the number of observations in state i.

(i) Show that the conditional posterior of α_i is $\mathbb{N}(\tilde{\alpha}_i, \tilde{\Sigma}_i)$, where $\alpha_i = \tilde{\Sigma}_i \times (\sum_{t=1}^{T_i} X_{it}y'_{it}/\sigma_t^2 + \bar{\Sigma}_i^{-1}\bar{\alpha}_i)$, $\tilde{\Sigma}_i = (\sum_{t=1}^{T_i} X_{it}X'_{it}/\sigma_t^2 + \bar{\Sigma}_i^{-1})^{-1}$, and $y_{it} = y_t - X_{\mathrm{c}t}\alpha_{\mathrm{c}} - X_{\mathrm{r}t}\alpha_{i\mathrm{r}}$.

(ii) Show that the conditional posterior of α_{r} is $\mathbb{N}(\tilde{\alpha}_{\mathrm{r}}, \tilde{\Sigma}_{\mathrm{r}})$. What are $\tilde{\alpha}_{\mathrm{r}}$ and $\tilde{\Sigma}_{\mathrm{r}}$?

(iii) Show that the conditional posterior of σ_i^{-2} is such that $(\bar{s}_i^2 + \mathrm{rss}_i^2)/\sigma_i^2 \sim \chi^2(\nu_i + T_i - \max[q_1, q_2])$. Write down the expression for rss_i^2.

(iv) Show that the conditional posterior for p_i is $\mathrm{Beta}(\bar{d}_{i1} + d_{i1}, \bar{d}_{i2} + d_{i2})$.

Finally, the conditional posterior for the latent variable $\varkappa_t$ can be computed as usual. Given the Markov properties of the model, we restrict attention to the subsequence $\varkappa_{t,\tau} = (\varkappa_t, \dots, \varkappa_{t+\tau-1})$. Define $\varkappa_{t(-\tau)}$ as the sequence $\varkappa_t$ with the τth subsequence removed. Then $g(\varkappa_{t,\tau} \mid y, \varkappa_{t(-\tau)}) \propto f(y \mid \varkappa_t, \alpha, \sigma^2) \times g(\varkappa_{t,\tau} \mid \varkappa_{t(-\tau)}, p_i)$, which is a discrete distribution with 2^τ outcomes. Using the Markov property, $g(\varkappa_{t,\tau} \mid \varkappa_{t(-\tau)}, p_i) = g(\varkappa_{t,\tau} \mid \varkappa_{t-1}, \varkappa_{t+\tau}, p_i)$ while $f(y^T \mid \varkappa_t, \alpha) \propto \prod_{j=t}^{t+\tau-1}(1/\sigma_j)\exp\{-e_j^2/2\sigma_j^2\}$. Note that, since the $\varkappa_t$ are correlated, it is a good idea to choose $\tau > 1$.

Exercise 11.25. Write down the components of the conditional posterior for $\varkappa_t$ when $\tau = 1$.

In all Markov switching specifications, it is important to wisely select the initial conditions. One way to do so is to assign all the observations in the training sample to one state, obtain initial estimates for the parameters, and arbitrarily set the parameters of the other state to be equal to the estimates plus or minus a small number (say, 0.1). Alternatively, one can split the points arbitrarily but equally across the two states.

Exercise 11.26. Suppose $\Delta y_t = \alpha_0 + \alpha_1 \Delta y_{t-1} + e_t$, $e_t \sim$ i.i.d. $\mathbb{N}(0, \sigma_e^2)$ if $\varkappa_t = 0$ and $\Delta y_t = (\alpha_0 + A_0) + (\alpha_1 + A_1)\Delta y_{t-1} + e_t$, $e_t \sim$ i.i.d. $\mathbb{N}(0, (1 + A_2)\sigma_e^2)$ if $\varkappa_t = 1$. Using quarterly GDP growth data for the euro area, construct posterior estimates for A_0, A_1, A_2. Separately test if there is evidence of switching in the intercept, the dynamics, or the variance of Δy_t.

11.4 Bayesian DSGE Models

The use of Bayesian methods to estimate and evaluate Dynamic Stochastic General Equilibrium (DSGE) models does not present new theoretical aspects. We have repeatedly mentioned that DSGE models are false in at least two senses.

- They only provide an approximate representation to the DGP of the actual data. In particular, since the vector of structural parameters is typically of low dimension, strong restrictions are implied both in the short and in the long run.
- The number of driving forces is smaller than the number of endogenous variables so that the covariance matrix of a vector of variables generated by the model is singular.

These features make the estimation and testing of DSGE models with GMM or ML tricky. In fact, with these methods inference is (asymptotically) justified only when the model is the DGP of the data up to a set of unknown parameters, while stochastic singularity prevents numerical routines based on the Hessian from working properly in the search for the maximum of the objective function. In chapter 4 we described a minimalist approach, which only uses qualitative restrictions to identify shocks in the data, and can be employed to examine the match between the theory and the data, when the model is false in the two above senses.

Bayesian methods are also well-suited to dealing with false models. Posterior inference, in fact, does not hinge on the model being the correct DGP and it is feasible even when the covariance matrix of the vector of endogenous variables is singular — we do not need the Hessian to explore the shape of the posterior. Bayesian methods have another advantage over alternatives, which makes them appealing to macroeconomists. Posterior distributions in fact incorporate uncertainty about the parameters and the model specification.

Since log-linearized DSGE models are state space models with nonlinear restrictions on the mapping between reduced-form and structural parameters, posterior estimates of the structural parameters can be obtained, for appropriately designed prior distributions, by using the posterior simulators described in chapter 9. Given the nonlinearity of the mapping, Metropolis, or MH algorithms are generally employed. Numerical methods can also be used to compute marginal likelihoods and Bayes factors; to obtain any posterior function of the structural parameters (for example, impulse responses, variance decompositions, ACFs, turning-point predictions, and forecasts) and to examine the sensitivity of the results to variations in the prior specification. Once the posterior distribution of the structural parameters is obtained, any interesting inferential exercise becomes trivial.

To estimate the posterior for the structural parameters and for the statistics of interest, and to evaluate the quality of a DSGE model, the following steps are typically used.

Algorithm 11.3.

(1) Construct a log-linear approximation to the DSGE economy and transform it into a state space model. Add measurement errors if the dimension of the vector of endogenous variables used in estimation/evaluation exceeds the dimension of the vector of driving forces of the model.

(2) Specify prior distributions for the structural parameters θ.

(3) Perform prior analysis to study the range of potential outcomes of the model.

(4) Draw sequences from the joint posterior of θ by using Metropolis or MH algorithms. Check convergence.

(5) Compute marginal likelihood numerically by using draws from the prior distribution and the Kalman filter. Compute the marginal likelihood for any alternative or reference model. Calculate Bayes factors or other measures of (relative) forecasting fit.

(6) Construct statistics of economic interest by using the draws in (4) (after an initial set has been discarded). Use loss-based measures to evaluate the discrepancy between the theory and the data.

(7) Examine the sensitivity of the results to the choice of priors.

Step (1) is unnecessary. We will see later on what to do if a nonlinear specification is used. Adding measurement errors helps computationally to reduce the singularity of the covariance matrix of the endogenous variables but it is not needed for the approach to work.

In step (2) prior distributions are generally centered around standard values of the parameters, while standard errors typically reflect subjective prior uncertainty. One could also specify objective prior standard errors, so as to “cover” the range of existing estimates, as we have done in chapter 7. For convenience, the prior distribution for the vector of parameters is assumed to be the product of univariate distributions of each of the parameters. In some applications, it may be convenient to select diffuse priors over a fixed range to avoid imposing too much structure on the data. In general, the form of the prior reflects computational convenience. Conjugate priors are typically preferred. For parameters which must lie in an interval, truncated normal or beta distributions are often chosen.

Step (3) logically precedes posterior analysis and can be used to evaluate whether models have any chance of producing the interesting features we observe in the actual data. This is precisely the analysis we performed in chapter 7, where we compare statistics of the data with the range of statistics produced by models. While this step is often skipped, it may provide very useful information about the potential outcomes of the models.

Step (4) requires choosing an updating rule and a transition function $\mathfrak{P}(\theta^\dagger, \theta^{l-1})$ satisfying the regularity conditions described in chapter 9, estimating joint and marginal distributions by using kernel methods and the draws from the posterior, and checking convergence. In particular, the following steps are needed.

Algorithm 11.4.

(i) Given a θ^0, draw $\theta^\dagger$ from $\mathfrak{P}(\theta^\dagger, \theta^0)$, and compute the prediction error decomposition of the likelihood, i.e., estimate $f(y \mid \theta^0)$ and $f(y \mid \theta^\dagger)$.

(ii) Evaluate the posterior kernel at $\theta^\dagger$ and θ^0, i.e., calculate $\breve{g}(\theta^\dagger) = f(y \mid \theta^\dagger) \times g(\theta^\dagger)$ and $\breve{g}(\theta^0) = f(y \mid \theta^0)g(\theta^0)$.

(iii) Draw $\mathfrak{U} \sim \mathbb{U}(0,1)$. If $\mathfrak{U} < \min\{[(\breve{g}(\theta^\dagger)/\breve{g}(\theta^0))][\mathfrak{P}(\theta^0, \theta^\dagger)/\mathfrak{P}(\theta^\dagger, \theta^0)], 1\}$, set $\theta^1 = \theta^\dagger$, otherwise set $\theta^1 = \theta^0$.

(iv) Repeat steps (i)–(iii) $\bar{L} + JL$ times. Discard the first $\bar{L}$ draws, keep one draw every L for inference. Alternatively, repeat steps (i)–(iii) J times by using $\bar{L} + 1$ different θ^0, and keep the last draw from each run. Check convergence by using the methods described in chapter 9.

(v) Estimate marginal/joint posteriors with kernel methods. Compute location estimates and credible sets. Compare them with those computed from the prior.

Step (5) requires drawing parameters from the prior, calculating the sequence of prediction errors for each draw, and averaging over draws. To do so, one could use the modified harmonic mean, $\{(1/L)\sum_l [g^{\mathrm{IS}}(\theta^*)/f(y \mid \theta^*)g(\theta^*)]\}^{-1}$, suggested by Gelfand and Dey (1994), where θ^* is a point with high posterior probability and g^{IS} is a density with tail thinner than $f(y \mid \theta)g(\theta)$, or could use the Bayes theorem directly, as suggested by Chib (1995). Similar calculations can be undertaken for any alternative model and Bayes factors can then be numerically computed. When the dimensionality of the parameter space is large, Laplace approximations can reduce the computational burden and give a more accurate picture of the properties of various models. The competitors could be a structural model, which nests the one under consideration (e.g., a model with flexible prices can be obtained by restricting one parameter of a model with sticky prices), a nonnested structural specification (e.g., a model with sticky wages), or a more densely parametrized reduced-form model (e.g., a VAR or a BVAR).

In step (6) loss functions are needed to compare statistics of interest because DSGE models typically have low posterior probability. As we will see later on, posterior odds ratios may not be very informative in such a case.

In step (7), to check the robustness of the results to the choice of prior, one can reweigh the posterior draws by using the techniques described in section 9.5.

11.4.1 Identification

Since log-linearized DSGE models feature a nonlinear mapping between the parameters of the theory and those of the state space representation, and since there is no condition that can be easily employed to check the informational content of the data, any method which is concerned with the estimation of DSGE parameters must deal with potential identification problems. We have already seen aspects of such phenomena in chapters 5 and 6, when dealing with (classical) impulse response matching and maximum likelihood estimation. Since Bayesian inference is based on the likelihood principle, and since the model structure determines, to a large extent, whether parameters are identified or not, all the arguments previously made also apply to a Bayesian context. However, Bayesian methods have two important advantages over classical ones in the presence of identification problems: they can employ information from other data sets to reduce parameter underidentification; they can generate coherent inference even in the presence of identification problems.

Suppose that $\theta = [\theta_1, \theta_2]$, assume that $\Theta = \Theta_1 \times \Theta_2$, and suppose that the likelihood function has no information for θ_2, i.e., $f(y \mid \theta) = f^*(y \mid \theta_1)$. Straightforward application of the Bayes theorem implies that $g(\theta \mid y) = g(\theta_1 \mid y) \times g(\theta_2 \mid \theta_1) \propto f^*(y \mid \theta_1) g(\theta_1, \theta_2)$. Hence, a proper prior for θ can add curvature to a flat likelihood function. This facilitates both the maximization of the posterior, if needed, and its calculations with MCMC methods, and makes the posterior well-behaved. Nevertheless, there is no updating of the prior of $\theta_2 \mid \theta_1$. Hence, a comparison of the prior and the posterior of θ can indicate how informative the data are (priors and posteriors of identified parameters will be different, priors and posteriors of unidentified parameters will not). Furthermore, a sequence of prior distributions with different spreads can be used to assess the extent of identification problems. In fact, the posterior of parameters with dubious identification features will become more and more diffuse, while the posterior of identified parameters will hardly change.

When the space of parameters Θ is not variation free, i.e., $\Theta \neq \Theta_1 \times \Theta_2$, because of stability constraints or restrictions required for the solution to the model to generate nonimaginary time series, the prior of θ_2 could be marginally updated even when the likelihood has no information, since changes in the distribution of θ_2 imply that the domain of θ_1 changes (see, for example, Poirier 1998). In this situation, a comparison of priors and posteriors will not be informative about potential identification problems, unless the parameters constrained by economic requirements are known. This is unlikely to be true in DSGE setups since, for example, the eigenvalues which regulate stability are complicated functions of all the parameters of the model.

Complete lack of identification is typically limited to textbook examples. However, partial or weak identification problems are extremely common. Partial identification occurs when the likelihood displays a ridge in some dimension (see example 6.21), while weak identification implies that the likelihood function is flat in some or all dimensions. Both these phenomena are difficult to detect in practice

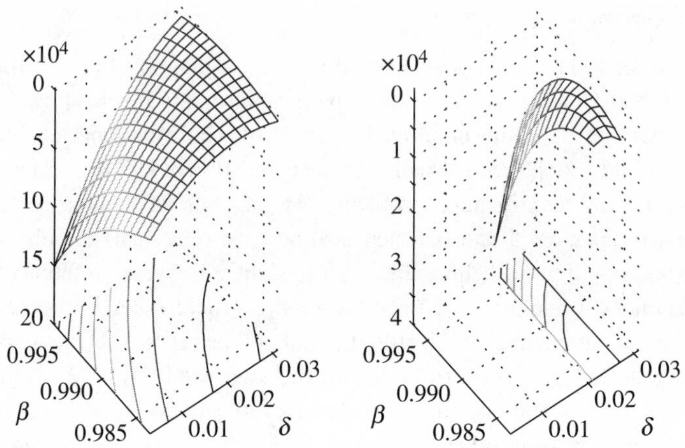

Figure 11.3. Likelihood and posterior, RBC model.

since, in the first case, it is the joint posterior which is indistinguishable from the joint prior (univariate posteriors may move away from univariate priors), while, in the second case, the size of the differences between the priors and the posteriors may depend on the details of MCMC routine employed.

As mentioned, well-behaved priors can induce well-behaved posteriors, even when the data have no information about the parameters. Therefore, it is very important that the priors of potentially nonidentifiable parameters truly contain information external to the data used to estimate the model and effectively reflect the objective uncertainty a researcher faces in specifying it. When these two general principles are not followed, Bayesian inference can mask rather than highlight identification problems. In fact, a sufficiently tight prior may give the illusion that parameter estimation is successful, that the model fits the data well, therefore creating the preconditions for its use for policy purposes. We show how this can occur with the model of example 6.21, which has a likelihood function with both flat sections and ridges.

Example 11.10. Figure 11.3 reproduces the likelihood function presented in the second panel of figure 6.1, which we have seen displays a ridge in β, δ running from $(\delta = 0.005, \beta = 0.975)$ up to $(\delta = 0.03, \beta = 0.99)$, and presents the joint posterior for these two parameters, when a sufficiently tight prior on δ is used. Clearly, while the likelihood has a diagonal ridge, the posterior appears to be much better behaved, since there is very low prior probability that δ lies outside the range $(0.018, 0.025)$.

While there may be reasonable economic arguments for *a priori* limiting the support of δ, they should be clearly spelled out. Furthermore, when bounds are imposed, the prior should be made reasonably uninformative to avoid misleading conclusions. Note that centering estimates at standard calibrated values is not the best strategy to follow since such values are likely to have been obtained with the same data that is employed for estimation, making the prior too data based.

11.4.2 Examples

Next, we present a few examples, highlighting the practical details of the implementation of Bayesian methods for inference in DSGE models.

Example 11.11. The first example is simple. We simulate data from a basic RBC model where the solution is contaminated by measurement errors. Armed with reasonable prior specifications for the structural parameters and a Metropolis algorithm, we examine where the posterior distribution of some crucial parameters lies relative to the "true" parameters we used in the simulations, when samples typical in macroeconomic data are available. We also compare true and estimated moments to give an economic measure of the fit we obtain.

The solution to an RBC model driven by i.i.d. technological disturbances when capital depreciates instantaneously, leisure does not enter the utility function, and the latter is logarithmic in consumption is

$$K_{t+1} = (1-\eta)\beta K_t^{1-\eta}\zeta_t + v_{1t}, \tag{11.27}$$

$$\mathrm{GDP}_t = K_t^{1-\eta}\zeta_t + v_{2t}, \tag{11.28}$$

$$c_t = \eta\beta\,\mathrm{GDP}_t + v_{3t}, \tag{11.29}$$

$$r_t = (1-\eta)\frac{\mathrm{GDP}_t}{K_t} + v_{4t}. \tag{11.30}$$

We have added four measurement errors v_{jt}, $j = 1, 2, 3, 4$, to the equations to reduce the singularity of the system and to mimic the typical situation an investigator is likely to face. Here β is the discount factor, $1-\eta$ the share of capital in production. We simulate 1000 data points by using $k_0 = 100.0$, $(1-\eta) = 0.36$, $\beta = 0.99$, $\ln\zeta_t \sim \mathbb{N}(0, \sigma_\zeta^2 = 0.1)$, $v_{1t} \sim \mathbb{N}(0, 0.06)$, $v_{2t} \sim \mathbb{N}(0, 0.02)$, $v_{3t} \sim \mathbb{N}(0, 0.08)$, $v_{4t} \sim \mathbb{U}(0, 0.1)$, and keep only the last 160 data points to reduce the dependence on the initial conditions and match a typical sample size.

We treat σ_ζ^2 as fixed and focus attention on the two economic parameters. We assume that the priors are $(1-\eta) \sim \mathrm{Beta}(4, 9)$ and $\beta \sim \mathrm{Beta}(99, 2)$. Beta distributions are convenient because they are easy to draw from. In fact, if $x \sim \chi^2(2a)$ and $y \sim \chi^2(2b)$, then $z = x/(x+y) \sim \mathrm{Beta}(a, b)$. Since the mean of a $\mathrm{Beta}(a, b)$ is $(a/a+b)$ and the variance is $ab/[(a+b)^2(a+b+1)]$, the prior mean of $1-\eta$ is about 0.31, and the prior mean of β about 0.99. The variances, approximately equal to 0.011 and 0.0002, imply sufficiently loose prior distributions.

We draw 10 000 replications. Given $1-\eta^0 = 0.55$, $\beta^0 = 0.97$, we produce candidates $\theta^\dagger = [(1-\eta)^\dagger, \beta^\dagger]$ by using a reflecting random walk process, i.e., $\theta^\dagger = \bar{\theta} + (\theta^{l-1} - \bar{\theta}) + v_\theta^l$, where θ^{l-1} is the previous draw, $\bar{\theta}$ is the mean of the process and v_θ^l is a vector of errors. The first component of v_θ (corresponding to $1-\eta$) is drawn from a $\mathbb{U}(-0.03, 0.03)$ and the second (corresponding to β) from a $\mathbb{U}(-0.01, 0.01)$ and $\bar{\theta} = [0.01, 0.001]'$. These ranges produce an acceptance rate of about 75%.

Since we are interested in $(1-\eta)$ and β, we are free to select which equations to use to estimate them. We arbitrarily choose those determining consumption and the real

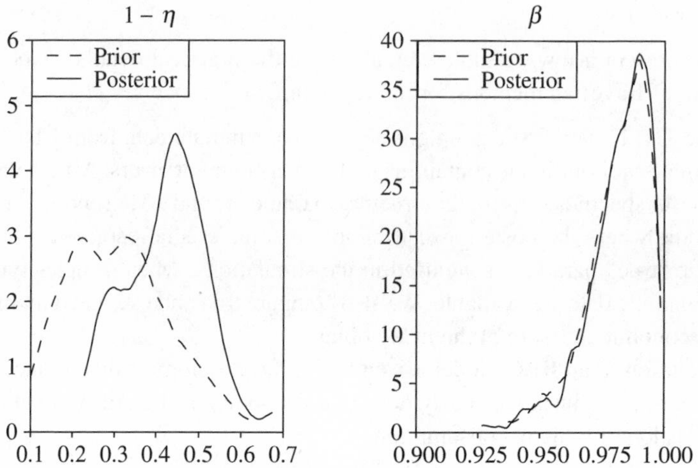

Figure 11.4. Priors and posteriors, basic RBC.

Table 11.2. Variances and covariances.

	True	Posterior 68% range
var(c)	40.16	$[3.65, 5.10 \times 10^{10}]$
var(r)	1.29×10^{-5}	$[2.55 \times 10^{-4}, 136.11]$
cov(c, r)	−0.0092	$[-0.15 \times 10^{-5}, -0.011]$

interest rate. We assume a normal likelihood and since $g(1-\eta, \beta) = g(1-\eta)g(\beta)$, we calculate the prior at the draw for each of the two parameters separately. Since the transition matrix $\mathfrak{P}(\theta^{\dagger}, \theta^{0})$ is symmetric, the ratio of the kernels at $\theta^{\dagger}$ and θ^{l-1} is all that is needed to accept or reject the candidates.

We discard the first 5000 draws. Out of the last 5000 we keep 1 out of every 5 to reduce the serial correlation present in the draws. We check that the Metropolis algorithm has converged in two ways: splitting the sequences of draws in two and computing a normal test; calculating recursive means for the estimates of each parameter. In both cases, the sequence converged after about 2000 draws.

Figure 11.4 presents the marginal densities of $1-\eta$ and β, estimated with the 1000 saved draws from the prior and the posterior. Two features are worth mentioning. First, the data are more informative about $1-\eta$ than they are about β. Second, both posteriors are unimodal and roughly centered around the true parameter values.

Using the 1000 posterior draws we have calculated three statistics, the variances of consumption and of the real interest rate and the covariance between the two, and compared the posterior 68% credible range with the statistics computed by using the "true" parameters. Table 11.2 shows that the posterior 68% range includes the actual value of the consumption variance but not the one for the real rate or for the

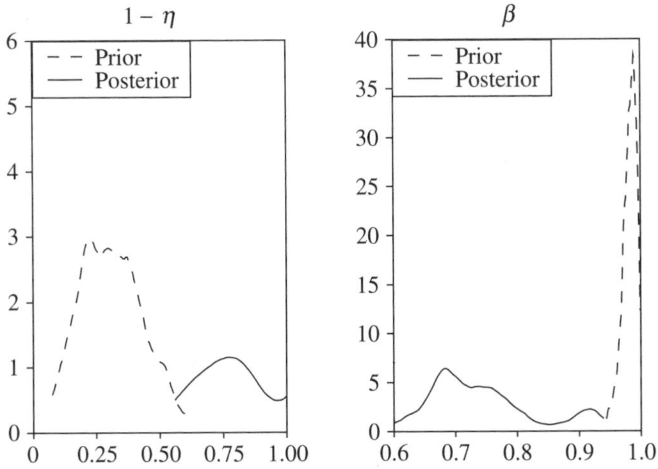

Figure 11.5. Priors and posteriors, RBC with habit persistence.

covariance. Also, there are posterior combinations of parameters which make the two variances very large.

Exercise 11.27. Using the same setup as example 11.11, modify the transition matrix $\mathfrak{P}(\theta^{\dagger}, \theta^{0})$ or the range for σ_v^2 in order to reduce the acceptance rate to about 50%. What would be the consequences of drawing candidates from normals rather than from uniform distributions?

Exercise 11.28. Vary the parameters of the prior for β and $1 - \eta$ so as to make them more diffuse. Do the posteriors change? In what way?

Example 11.12. In this example we simulate data from an RBC model with habit in consumption, still assuming that capital depreciates in one period and that leisure does not enter the utility function. We assume $u(c_t, c_{t-1}) = \ln(c_t - \gamma c_{t-1})$, set $\gamma = 0.8$, and add to the solution the same measurement errors used in equations (11.27)–(11.30). We are interested in the shape of the posteriors of β and $1 - \eta$ when we mistakenly assume that there is no habit (i.e., we condition on $\gamma = 0$). This experiment is interesting since it can give some indications of the consequences of using a dogmatic (and wrong) prior on some of the parameters of the model.

Perhaps unsurprisingly, the posterior distributions presented in figure 11.5 are very different from those in figure 11.4. What is somewhat unexpected is that the misspecification is so large that the posterior probability for the "true" parameters is roughly zero.

Exercise 11.29. Simulate data from an RBC model with production function $f(K_t, \mathrm{ku}_t, \zeta_t) = (K_t \mathrm{ku}_t)^{1-\eta}\zeta_t$, where ku_t is capital utilization and assume that the depreciation rate depends on the utilization of capital, i.e., $\delta(\mathrm{ku}_t) = \delta_0 + \delta_1 \mathrm{ku}_t^{\delta_2}$, where $\delta_0 = 0.01$, $\delta_1 = 0.005$, $\delta_2 = 2$. Suppose you mistakenly neglect utilization and estimate a model like the one in equations (11.27)–(11.30). Evaluate the distortions induced by this misspecification.

Example 11.13. The next example considers a standard New Keynesian model with sticky prices and monopolistic competition. Our task here is twofold. First, we want to know how good this model is relative to, say, an unrestricted VAR in capturing the dynamics of the nominal interest rate, the output gap, and inflation. Second, we are interested in knowing the location of the posterior distribution of some important structural parameters. For example, we would like to know how much price stickiness is needed to match actual dynamics, whether policy inertia is an important ingredient to characterize the data, and whether the model has some internal propagation mechanism or if, instead, it relies entirely on the dynamics of the exogenous variables to match the dynamics of the data.

The model economy we use is a simplified version of the structure considered in chapter 2 and comprises a log-linearized (around the steady-state) Euler equation, a New Keynesian Phillips curve, and a Taylor rule. We assume that, in equilibrium, consumption is equal to output and use output in deviation from steady states in the Euler equation directly. Each equation has a shock attached to it: there is an i.i.d. policy shock, ϵ_{3t}, a cost push shock in the Phillips curve, ϵ_{2t}, and an arbitrary demand shock in the Euler equation, ϵ_{4t}. While the latter shock is unnecessary for the estimation, it is clearly needed to match the complexities of the output, inflation, and interest rate processes observed in the real world. The equations are

$$\text{gdpgap}_t = E_t\,\text{gdpgap}_{t+1} - \frac{1}{\varphi}(i_t - E_t\pi_{t+1}) + \epsilon_{4t}, \tag{11.31}$$

$$\pi_t = \beta E_t \pi_{t+1} + \kappa\,\text{gdpgap}_t + \epsilon_{2t}, \tag{11.32}$$

$$i_t = \phi_r i_{t-1} + (1-\phi_r)(\phi_\pi \pi_{t-1} + \phi_{\text{gap}}\,\text{gdpgap}_{t-1}) + \epsilon_{3t}, \tag{11.33}$$

where i_t is the nominal interest rate, π_t is the inflation rate, gdpgap_t is the output gap, $\kappa = (1-\zeta_{\text{p}})(1-\beta\zeta_{\text{p}})(\varphi+\vartheta_N)/\zeta_{\text{p}}$, ζ_{p} is the degree of stickiness in the Calvo setting, β is the discount factor, φ is the risk aversion parameter, ϑ_N is the inverse elasticity of labor supply, ϕ_r is the persistence of the nominal rate, while ϕ_π and ϕ_{gap} measure the responses of interest rates to lagged inflation and lagged output gap movements. We assume that ϵ_{4t} and ϵ_{2t} are AR(1) processes with persistence ρ_4, ρ_2 and variances σ_4^2, σ_2^2, while ϵ_{3t} is i.i.d. $(0, \sigma_3^2)$.

The model has 12 parameters, $\theta = (\beta, \varphi, \vartheta, \zeta_{\text{p}}, \phi_\pi, \phi_{\text{gap}}, \phi_r, \rho_2, \rho_4, \sigma_2^2, \sigma_3^2, \sigma_4^2)$, seven structural, and five auxiliary ones, whose posterior distributions need to be found. Our interest centers in the posterior distributions of $(\zeta_{\text{p}}, \phi_r, \rho_2, \rho_4)$. It is easy to check that ζ_{p} and ϑ_N are not separately identifiable so that inference about ζ_{p} will be meaningful only to the extent that the priors of these two parameters are carefully specified. We use U.S. quarterly detrended data from 1948:1 to 2002:1. We assume that $g(\theta) = \prod_{j=1}^{12} g(\theta_j)$ and use the following priors: $\beta \sim \text{Beta}(98, 3)$, $\varphi \sim \mathbb{N}(1, (0.375)^2)$, $\vartheta_N \sim \mathbb{N}(2, (0.75)^2)$, $\zeta_{\text{p}} \sim \text{Beta}(9, 3)$, $\phi_r \sim$

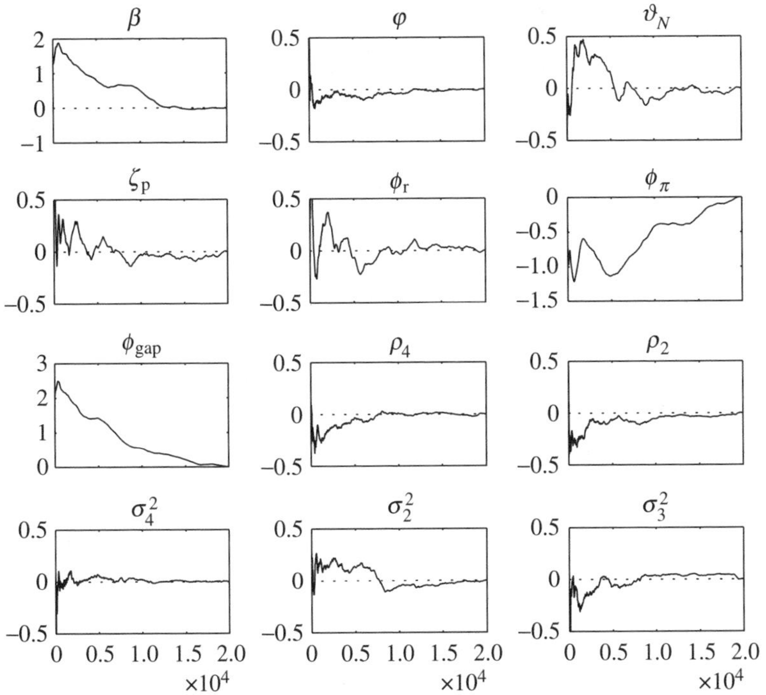

Figure 11.6. CUMSUM statistic.

Beta(6, 2), $\phi_\pi \sim \mathbb{N}(1.7, (0.1)^2)$, $\phi_{\text{gap}} \sim \mathbb{N}(0.5, (0.05)^2)$, $\rho_4 \sim$ Beta(17, 3), $\rho_2 \sim$ Beta(17, 3), $\sigma_i^{-2} \sim \mathbb{G}(4, 0.1)$, $i = 2, 3, 4$.

To generate a candidate vector $\theta^\dagger$, we use a random walk Metropolis algorithm with small uniform errors (the range is tuned up for each parameter so as to achieve a 40% acceptance rate) and check convergence by using a CUMSUM statistic: $(1/J)\sum_j(\theta_j^i - E(\theta_j^i))/\sqrt{\text{var}\,\theta_j^i}$, where $j = 1, 2, \dots, JL + \bar{L}$ and $i = 1, 2, \dots, 12$. Figure 11.6, which presents this statistic, indicates that the chain has converged, roughly, after 15 000 draws. Convergence is hard to achieve for ϕ_π and ϕ_{gap}, while it is quickly reached (at times in less than 10 000 iterations) for the other parameters. As shown later the difficulties encountered with ϕ_π and ϕ_{gap} are not necessarily due to subsample instability. Instead, they appear to be related to the near nonidentifiability of these parameters from the data. Figure 11.7 presents prior and posterior distributions (estimated with kernel methods) using 1 out of every 5 of the last 5000 draws. The data appear to be informative in at least two senses. First, posterior distributions often have smaller dispersions than prior ones. Second, in some cases, the whole posterior distribution is shifted relative to the prior. Table 11.3, which presents some statistics of the prior and the posterior, confirms these visual impressions. Note also that, except for isolated cases, posterior distributions are roughly symmetric.

Table 11.3. Prior and posterior statistics.

	Prior		Posterior 1948–2002				
	Mean	Std	Median	Mean	Std	Min	Max
β	0.98	0.01	0.978	0.976	0.007	0.952	0.991
φ	0.99	0.37	0.836	0.841	0.118	0.475	1.214
ϑ_N	2.02	0.75	1.813	2.024	0.865	0.385	4.838
$\zeta_{\rm p}$	0.75	0.12	0.502	0.536	0.247	0.030	0.993
ϕ_r	0.77	0.14	0.704	0.666	0.181	0.123	0.992
ϕ_π	1.69	0.10	1.920	1.945	0.167	1.568	2.361
$\phi_{\rm gap}$	0.49	0.05	0.297	0.305	0.047	0.215	0.410
ρ_4	0.86	0.07	0.858	0.857	0.038	0.760	0.942
ρ_2	0.86	0.07	0.842	0.844	0.036	0.753	0.952
σ_4^2	0.017	0.01	0.017	0.017	0.007	0.001	0.035
σ_2^2	0.016	0.01	0.011	0.012	0.008	0.0002	0.036
σ_3^2	0.017	0.01	0.015	0.016	0.007	0.001	0.035

	Posterior 1948–1981		Posterior 1982–2002	
	Mean	Std	Mean	Std
β	0.986	0.008	0.983	0.008
φ	1.484	0.378	1.454	0.551
ϑ_N	2.587	0.849	2.372	0.704
$\zeta_{\rm p}$	0.566	0.200	0.657	0.234
ϕ_r	0.582	0.169	0.695	0.171
ϕ_π	2.134	0.221	1.925	0.336
$\phi_{\rm gap}$	0.972	0.119	0.758	0.068
ρ_4	0.835	0.036	0.833	0.036
ρ_2	0.831	0.036	0.832	0.036
σ_4^2	0.017	0.006	0.016	0.007
σ_2^2	0.016	0.006	0.016	0.007
σ_3^2	0.013	0.007	0.014	0.007

As far as the posterior of the four parameters of interest is concerned, note that the shocks are persistent (the posterior mean is 0.85) but there is no pileup of the posterior distribution for the AR parameters around 1. This means that, although the model does not have sufficient internal propagation to replicate the dynamics of the data, no exogenous unit-root-like processes are needed.

The posterior distribution of economic parameters is reasonably centered. The posterior mean of $\zeta_{\rm p}$, the parameter regulating the stickiness in prices, is only 0.5,

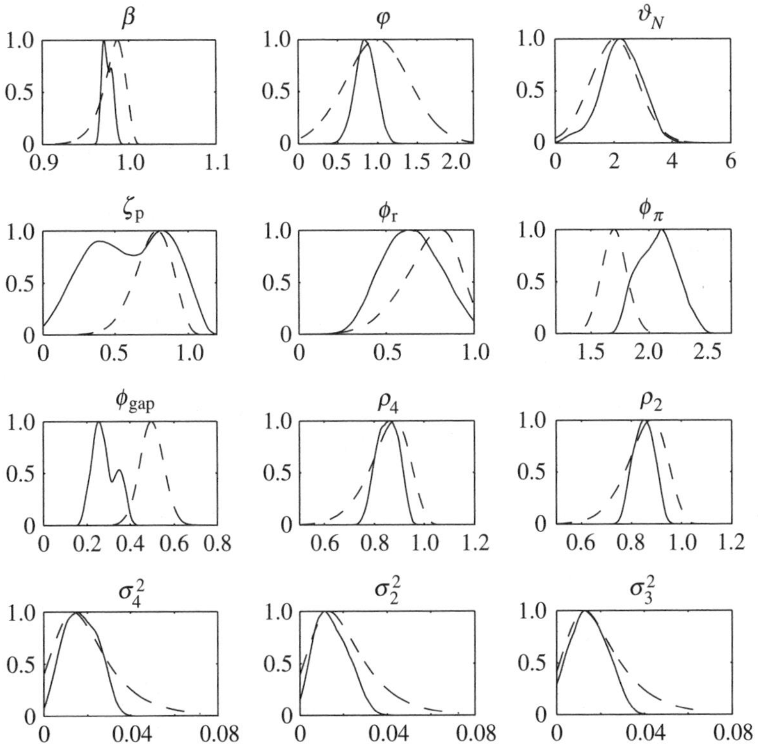

Figure 11.7. Priors (dashed) and posteriors (solid), sticky price model.

implying an average time of about two quarters between price changes — the prior was centered at an average of three quarters. However, since the posterior of ζ_p is bimodal, care must be exercised in using the posterior mean as a location measure. ϕ_r, the parameter measuring policy persistence, has a posterior mean of 0.7, implying some degree of policy smoothness, but not an excessive one.

Note that the posterior mean of κ is about 0.5, implying a moderate reaction of inflation to output gap movements. In comparison with the estimates obtained in chapter 5, the mean effect is slightly stronger, even though lower values have nonnegligible posterior probabilities.

The majority of these conclusions remain after splitting the sample in two. For example, ζ_p has a posterior mean of 0.566 in the 1948–81 sample and a posterior mean of 0.657 in the 1982–2002 sample. However, since the posterior standard error is around 0.22, differences in the two samples are statistically small. The other parameters also have stable posteriors. In particular, splitting the sample does not change the fact that the coefficients in the policy rule imply a strong reaction of interest rates to inflation.

The location and the shape of the posterior distributions are largely independent of the priors we have selected since priors are broadly noninformative. For example, reweighing the posterior draws with a prior whose range is 90% of the range of the original prior in all 12 dimensions produces posterior distributions which are qualitatively very similar to those of figure 11.7.

Finally, we examine the forecasting performance of the model by comparing its marginal likelihood to that of a VAR(3) and that of a BVAR(3) with Minnesota prior and standard parameters (tightness equal to 0.1, linear lag decay and weight on other variables equal to 0.5), both with a constant. Bayes factors are small (of the order of 0.19) in both cases, indicating that the model can be improved upon in a forecasting sense. Note that, while both alternatives are more densely parametrized than our DSGE model (30 versus 12 parameters), Bayes factors take model size into account and no adjustment for the number of parameters is needed.

Exercise 11.30. Repeat the estimation of the model of example 11.13 by substituting (11.33) with the rule $i_t = \phi_r i_{t-1} + (1-\phi_r)(\phi_\pi \pi_t + \phi_{\text{gap}} \text{gdpgap}_t) + \epsilon_{3t}$. Compare the results. In particular, describe how the posterior distributions of ϕ_r, ρ_2, and ρ_4 are altered. Evaluate the probability that the data have been generated by a model with indeterminacies (i.e., evaluate what is the posterior probability that $\phi_\pi < 1$). (Hint: set the location of the prior for ϕ_π to 1.0.)

Exercise 11.31. Consider the model of example 11.13, but replace the Phillips curve by the following: $\pi_t = [\omega/(1+\omega\beta)]\pi_{t-1} + [\beta/(1+\omega\beta)]E_t\pi_{t+1} + [\kappa/(1+\omega\beta)] \times \text{gdpgap}_t + \epsilon_{2t}$, where ω is the degree of indexation of prices. Estimate this model and test whether indexation is necessary to match the data. (Hint: be careful about the identification of this parameter.)

Exercise 11.32. Add to the model of example 11.13 the following wage equation: $\Delta w_t = \beta E_t \Delta w_{t+1} + [(1-\zeta_{\text{w}})(1-\zeta_{\text{w}}\beta)/\zeta_{\text{w}}(1+\varsigma_{\text{w}}\vartheta_N)][\text{mrs}_t - (w_t - p_t)] + \epsilon_{2t}$, where ζ_{w} is the probability of not changing the wage, ς_{w} is the elasticity of substitution between types of labor in production, and mrs_t is the marginal rate of substitution. Estimate this model and test whether wage stickiness adds to the fit of the basic sticky price model.

11.4.3 A Few Applied Tips

Although the models we have considered so far are of small scale, it has become standard in central banks and international institutions to estimate large-scale DSGE models with Bayesian methods. Care should be exercised when estimating large-scale models for several reasons.

First, large-scale models, while more articulate and potentially less misspecified, are more prone to identification problems. Furthermore, the variables used in estimation need not carry information about the parameters researchers care about. For example, it is quite common to try to get estimates of import and export price stickiness by using CPI inflation of different countries. Obviously, the informational content of CPI inflation for these parameters may be very small.

Second, as we have seen in chapter 6, the likelihood function of a small-scale DSGE model may have large flat sections or very rocky appearance. The likelihood function of a large-scale DSGE model typically contains both features and, at times, multiple peaks may be present. Calculation of posterior distributions in such a situation is difficult and the prior plays a crucial role in making inference possible. Hence, the choice of prior distributions should be carefully documented, the sensitivity of the results to variations in the spread presented, and the temptation to use reverse engineering (i.e., set a prior so that the posterior is well-behaved and confirms one's "gut" feeling) avoided. Note that multiple peaks in the likelihood may indicate the presence of breaks or multiple regimes and may give important information about features one is interested in examining. Once again, robustness analysis may inform the investigator on the likely presence of these problems.

Third, while it is common to start from a model with a large number of frictions and shocks, Bayesian methods can be used even with models which are misspecified in their dynamics or their probabilistic nature. This means that the type of sequential exercise performed in early calibration exercises (e.g., start from a competitive structure with only technology shocks, add government shocks, introduce noncompetitive markets, etc.) can also be fruitfully employed here. Frictions and shocks which add little to the ability of the model to reproduce interesting features of the data should be discarded. Such an analysis could also help to give some of the black-box shocks estimated in the factor literature an interesting economic content.

Finally, models are hardly built to explain the macroeconomic series that one finds in standard databanks. Therefore, data transformations, such as detrending or outlier elimination, and massaging techniques, such as the selection of appropriately stable sample periods or the elimination of structural breaks, are necessary before the model is taken to the data. When one is interested in the estimation of a model designed to capture only the cyclical properties of the data and dogmatically selects one trend specification, Bayesian and standard classical methods face the same arbitrariness problems and everything we said in chapter 3 applies without change. If more than one alternative trend specification is contemplated, one could put a prior on the various alternatives, compute the posterior probability of each specification, and use the techniques described in the next subsection to undertake inference.

11.4.4 Comparing the Quality of Models to the Data

While Bayesian estimation of structural parameters is simple, it is less straightforward to compare the model outcomes to the actual data and to assess the superiority of a model among alternative candidate specifications. Two methods are available. The first, preferred by macroeconomists, is based on informal analysis of some interesting economic statistics.

Example 11.14. Continuing with example 11.13, we present 68% impulse response bands to interest rate shocks in figure 11.8. While responses are economically reasonable there are three features of the figure which stand out. First, shocks which

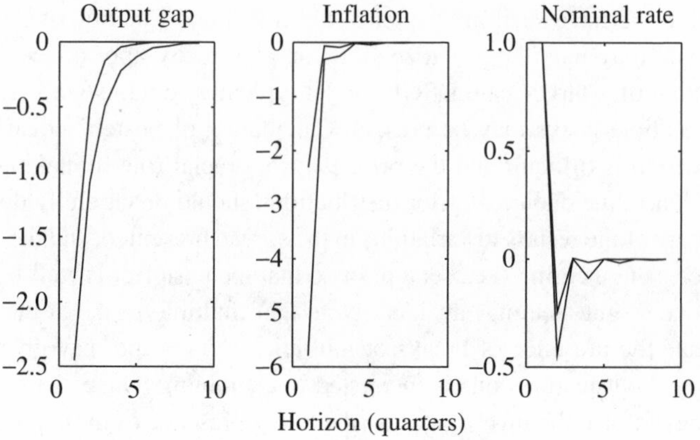

Figure 11.8. Responses to monetary shocks, 1948–2002.

increase interest rates make inflation and the output gap fall with very high probability. Second, responses die out after a few periods. Third, despite the assumed price stickiness, the largest inflation effect is instantaneous.

Figure 11.9 reports response bands obtained by estimating the model over different windows of data, keeping a constant number of observations in each sample. It is remarkable that the sign, the shape, and the magnitude of the posterior 68% credible bands are unchanged as we move from the late 1970s to the early 2000s. Hence, the transmission properties of monetary shocks have hardly changed over the last 30 years.

As an alternative to the presentation of economic statistics of various nested or nonnested models, one could compute measures of forecasting performance of various specifications. As we have seen in chapter 9, the marginal likelihood is the product of one-step-ahead forecast errors. Hence, selecting a model by using Bayes factors, as we did in example 11.13, is equivalent to choosing the specification with smallest one-step (in-sample) MSE. Clearly, out-of-sample forecasting races are also possible, in which case predictive Bayes factors can be computed (see, for example, DeJong et al. 2000). This is easy to do: we leave it to the reader to work out the details.

Exercise 11.33. Show how to construct the predictive density of future $y_{t+\tau}$, $\tau = 1, 2, \dots$, given the model of example 11.13. (Hint: use the restricted VAR representation of the model.)

Despite their popularity, Bayes factors may not be very informative about the quality of the approximation of the model to the data, in particular, when the models one wishes to compare are grossly misspecified.

Example 11.15. Suppose there are three models, two structural ones ($\mathcal{M}_1$, $\mathcal{M}_2$) and a densely parametrized (e.g., a VAR) reference one ($\mathcal{M}_3$). The Bayes factor between the two structural models is $[f(y, \mathcal{M}_1)/f(y)] \times [f(y)/f(y, \mathcal{M}_2)]$, where

$f(y) = \int f(y, \mathcal{M}_i)\, \mathrm{d}\mathcal{M}_i$. If we use a 0–1 loss function, and assume that the prior probability of each model is 0.5, the posterior risk is minimized by selecting $\mathcal{M}_1$ if the Bayes factor exceeds 1. The presence of a third model does not affect the choice since it only enters in the calculation of $f(y)$, which cancels out of the Bayes factor. If the prior odds do not depend on this third model, the posterior odds ratio will also be independent of it. When $\mathcal{M}_1$ and $\mathcal{M}_2$ are misspecified, they will have low posterior probability relative to $\mathcal{M}_3$, but this has no influence on the inference one makes. Hence, comparing misspecified models with a Bayes factor may be uninteresting: one model may be preferable to another but it may have close to zero posterior probability.

Schorfheide (2000) provided a simple procedure to choose among misspecified models (in his case a cash-in-advance and a working-capital model). The actual data are assumed to be generated by a mixture of the competing structural models and a reference one, which has two characteristics: (i) it is more densely parametrized than the DSGE models; (ii) it can be used to compute a vector of population statistics $h(\theta)$. One such model could be a VAR or a BVAR. Given this setup, loss functions can be used to compare models. In particular, when several alternatives are available, the following algorithm could be used.

Algorithm 11.5.

(1) Compute the posterior distribution for the parameters of each model by using tractable priors and one of the available posterior simulators.

(2) Obtain the marginal likelihood, for each $\mathcal{M}_i$, that is, compute $f(y \mid \mathcal{M}_i) = \int f(y \mid \theta_i, \mathcal{M}_i) g(\theta_i \mid \mathcal{M}_i)\, \mathrm{d}\theta_i$.

(3) Compute posterior probabilities $\tilde{P}_i = \bar{P}_i f(y \mid \mathcal{M}_i) / \sum_i \bar{P}_i f(y \mid \mathcal{M}_i)$, where $\bar{P}_i$ is the prior probability of model i. Note that, if the distribution of y is degenerated under $\mathcal{M}_i$ (e.g., if the number of shocks is smaller than the number of endogenous variables), $\tilde{P}_i = 0$.

(4) Calculate the posterior distribution of any continuous function $h(\theta)$ of the parameters for each model and average by using posterior probabilities, i.e., obtain $g(h(\theta) \mid y, \mathcal{M}_i)$ and $g(h(\theta) \mid y) = \sum_i \tilde{P}_i g(h(\theta) \mid y, \mathcal{M}_i)$. Note that $g(h(\theta) \mid y) = g(h(\theta) \mid y, \mathcal{M}_{i'})$ if all but model i' produce degenerate distributions.

(5) Set up a loss function $\mathfrak{L}(h_T, h_i(\theta))$ measuring the discrepancy between model i's predictions of $h(\theta)$ and data h_T. Since the optimal predictor in model $\mathcal{M}_i$ is $\hat{h}_i(\theta) = \operatorname{argmin}_{h_i(\theta)} \int \mathfrak{L}(h_T, h_i(\theta)) g(h_i(\theta) \mid y, \mathcal{M}_i)\, \mathrm{d}h_T$, one can compare models by using the risk of $\hat{h}_i(\theta)$ under the overall posterior distribution $g(h(\theta) \mid y)$, i.e., $\min \mathfrak{R}(\hat{h}_i(\theta) \mid y) = \min \int \mathfrak{L}(h_T, \hat{h}_i(\theta)) g(h(\theta) \mid y)\, \mathrm{d}h_T$.

Since $\mathfrak{R}(\hat{h}_i(\theta) \mid y)$ measures how well model $\mathcal{M}_i$ predicts h_T, a model is preferable to another if it has a lower risk. Note also that, while model comparison is relative, $g(h(\theta) \mid y)$ takes into account information from all models. Taking

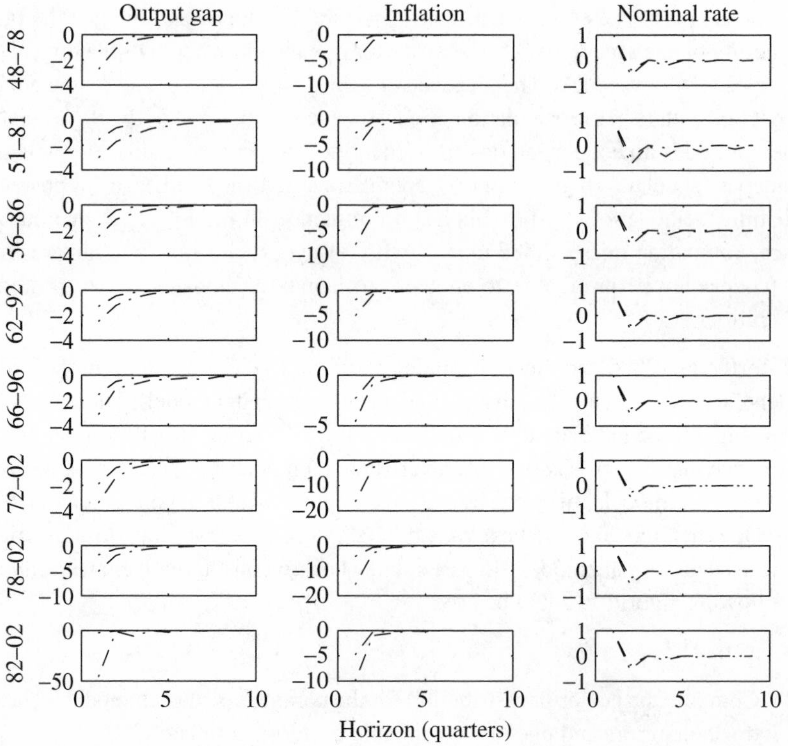

Figure 11.9. Responses to a monetary shock, various samples.

step (5) further, one should note that, for each i, θ can be selected so as to minimize $\mathfrak{R}(\hat{h}_i(\theta) \mid y)$. Such an estimate provides a lower bound to the posterior risk obtained by the "best" candidate model in the dimensions represented by h_T.

To make algorithm 11.5 operative a loss function must be selected. We have presented a few options in chapter 9. For DSGE models, the most useful are as follows.

(a) Quadratic loss: $\mathfrak{L}_2(h_T, h(\theta)) = [h_T - h(\theta)]' W [h_T - h(\theta)]$, where W is an arbitrary positive definite weighting matrix.

(b) Penalized loss: $\mathfrak{L}_p(h_T, h(\theta)) = \mathcal{I}_{[g(h(\theta)|y) < g(h_T|y)]}$, where $\mathcal{I}_{[x_1 < x_2]} = 1$ if $x_1 < x_2$.

(c) χ^2 loss: $\mathfrak{L}_{\chi^2}(h(\theta), h_T) = \mathcal{I}_{[\mathcal{Q}_{\chi^2}(h(\theta)|y) > \mathcal{Q}_{\chi^2}(h_T|y)]}$, where $\mathcal{Q}_{\chi^2}(h(\theta) \mid y) = [h(\theta) - E(h(\theta) \mid y)]' \Sigma_{h(\theta)}^{-1} [h(\theta) - E(h(\theta) \mid y)]$, $\Sigma_{h(\theta)}$ is the covariance of $h(\theta)$, and $\mathcal{I}_{[x_1 > x_2]} = 1$ if $x_1 > x_2$.

(d) 0–1 loss: $\mathfrak{L}(h_T, h(\theta), \epsilon) = 1 - \mathcal{I}_{\epsilon(h(\theta))}(h_T)$, where $\epsilon(h(\theta))$ is an ϵ-neighborhood of $h(\theta)$.

Three features of these loss functions should be mentioned. First, with penalized and χ^2 loss functions, two DSGE models are compared on the basis of the height of the posterior distribution at $h_i(\theta)$. Second, with a quadratic loss function, comparison is based on the weighted distance between $h_i(\theta)$ and the posterior mean. Third, as already mentioned, a 0–1 loss implies that $\mathcal{M}_1$ is preferred if the posterior odds exceed 1.

Exercise 11.34. (i) Show that $\mathfrak{R}_2 = [h_T - E(h(\theta)) \mid y]' W [h_T - E(h(\theta)) \mid y] + \varrho_0$, where ϱ_0 does not depend on $Eh(\theta)$. How would you choose W optimally?

(ii) Show that, if $g(\theta \mid y)$ is normal, $\mathfrak{L}_2 = \mathfrak{L}_{\chi^2}$ and the optimal predictor is $E(h(\theta) \mid y, \mathcal{M}_i)$.

(iii) Show that the optimal predictor for the $\mathfrak{L}_p$ loss is the mode of $g(h(\theta) \mid y, \mathcal{M}_i)$.

Two interesting special cases obtain when the $\mathfrak{L}_2$ loss is used.

Exercise 11.35 (Schorfheide). Suppose there are three models. Suppose that $\tilde{P}_1 \xrightarrow{\text{P}} 1$, $E(h_i(\theta) \mid y_T, \mathcal{M}_i) \xrightarrow{\text{P}} \bar{h}_i(\theta)$, and $\bar{h}_1(\theta) - \bar{h}_2(\theta) = \delta_\theta$, where $|\delta_\theta| > 0$. Show that, as $T \to \infty$, $\mathfrak{R}(\hat{h}_1(\theta)) \xrightarrow{\text{P}} 0$ and $\mathfrak{R}(\hat{h}_2(\theta)) \xrightarrow{\text{P}} \delta_\theta' W \delta_\theta$. Suppose now that, as $T \to \infty$, $\tilde{P}_{3,T} \to 1$ and $E(h_i(\theta) \mid y, \mathcal{M}_i) \xrightarrow{\text{P}} \bar{h}_i(\theta)$. Show that $E(h(\theta) \mid y) - E(h(\theta) \mid y, \mathcal{M}_3) \xrightarrow{\text{P}} 0$.

Exercise 11.35 reaches a couple of interesting conclusions. First, if for any positive definite W model $\mathcal{M}_1$ is better than $\mathcal{M}_2$ with probability 1, model selection using $\mathfrak{L}_2$ is consistent and gives the same result as a posterior odds ratio in large samples. To restate this concept differently, under these conditions, $\mathfrak{L}_2$-model comparison is based on the relative one-step-ahead predictive ability. Second, if the two models are so misspecified that their posterior probability goes to zero as $T \to \infty$, the ranking of these models only depends on the discrepancy between $E(h(\theta) \mid y, \mathcal{M}_3) \approx E(h(\theta) \mid y)$ and $\hat{h}_i(\theta)$, $i = 1, 2$. If $\mathcal{M}_3$ is any empirical model, then using an $\mathfrak{L}_2$ loss is equivalent to comparing sample and population moments obtained from different models. This means that, when one makes decisions based on the $\mathfrak{L}_2$ loss function and the models are highly misspecified, an informal comparison between the predictions of the model and the data, as is done in the simplest calibration exercises, is optimal from a Bayesian point of view. Intuitively, this surprising outcome obtains because the posterior variance of $h(\theta)$ does not affect the ranking of models—this conclusion does not hold with the $\mathfrak{L}_p$ or the $\mathfrak{L}_{\chi^2}$ loss functions.

Example 11.16. Continuing with example 11.13, we calculate the risk associated with the model when $h(\theta)$ represents the persistence of inflation and persistence is measured by the height of the spectrum at zero frequency. This number is large (227.09), reflecting the inability of the model to generate persistence in inflation. In comparison, for example, the risk generated by a univariate AR(1) is 38.09.

11.4.5 DSGEs and VARs, Once Again

As mentioned in chapter 10, it is possible to use a DSGE model to construct a prior for reduced-form VAR coefficients. Such an approach is advantageous since it jointly allows posterior estimation of both reduced-form and structural parameters. We have already derived the posterior for VAR parameters in section 10.2.5. Here we describe how to obtain posterior distributions for the structural ones. Let $f(y \mid \alpha, \Sigma_e)$ be the likelihood function of the data, conditional on the VAR parameters, let $g(\alpha, \Sigma_e \mid \theta)$ be the prior for the VAR parameters, conditional on the DSGE model parameters, and $g(\theta)$ the prior distribution for the DSGE parameters. Here $g(\alpha, \Sigma_e \mid \theta)$ is the prior for the reduced-form parameters induced by the prior on the structural parameters and the details of the model. The joint posterior of VAR and structural parameters is $g(\alpha, \Sigma_e, \theta \mid y) = g(\alpha, \Sigma_e, \mid \theta, y) g(\theta \mid y)$.

We have seen that $g(\alpha, \Sigma_e, \mid \theta, y)$ has a normal-inverted Wishart form so that it can be easily computed analytically or by simulation. The computation of $g(\theta \mid y)$ is more complicated since its form is unknown. The kernel of this distribution is $\breve{g}(\theta \mid y) = f(y \mid \theta) g(\theta)$, where

$$\begin{aligned} f(y \mid \theta) &= \int f(y \mid \alpha, \Sigma_e) g(\alpha, \Sigma_e, \theta) \, \mathrm{d}\alpha \, \mathrm{d}\Sigma_e \\ &= \frac{f(y \mid \alpha, \Sigma_e) g(\alpha, \Sigma_e \mid \theta)}{g(\alpha, \Sigma_e \mid y, \theta)}. \end{aligned} \tag{11.34}$$

Since the posteriors of (α, Σ_e) depend on θ only through y, $g(\alpha, \Sigma_e \mid y, \theta) = g(\alpha, \Sigma_e \mid y)$ and we can use the fact that both the numerator and the denominator of (11.34) have normal-inverted Wishart format to obtain

$$\begin{aligned} f(y \mid \theta) = {} & \frac{|(X^{\mathrm{s}})'(\theta) X^{\mathrm{s}}(\theta) + X'X|^{-0.5m} |(T_{\mathrm{s}} + T) \tilde{\Sigma}_e(\theta)|^{-0.5(T_{\mathrm{s}}+T-k)}}{|(X^{\mathrm{s}})'(\theta) X^{\mathrm{s}}(\theta)|^{-0.5m} |T_{\mathrm{s}} \bar{\Sigma}_e^s(\theta)|^{-0.5(T_{\mathrm{s}}-k)}} \\ & \times \frac{(2\pi)^{-0.5mT} 2^{0.5m(T_{\mathrm{s}}+T-k)} \prod_{i=1}^m \Gamma((T_{\mathrm{s}} + T - k + 1 - i)/2)}{2^{0.5m(T_1-k)} \prod_{i=1}^m \Gamma((T_{\mathrm{s}} - k + 1 - i)/2)}, \end{aligned} \tag{11.35}$$

where $\tilde{\Sigma}_e(\theta) = (1/(1+\kappa)T)\{(y^{\mathrm{s}})'y^{\mathrm{s}} + y'y - [(y^{\mathrm{s}})'X^{\mathrm{s}} + y'X][(X^{\mathrm{s}})'X^{\mathrm{s}} + X'X]^{-1} \times [(X^{\mathrm{s}})'y^{\mathrm{s}} + X'y]\}$ and $\bar{\Sigma}_e^{\mathrm{s}} = (1/T_{\mathrm{s}})\{(y^{\mathrm{s}})'y^{\mathrm{s}} - (y^{\mathrm{s}})'x^{\mathrm{s}}[(x^{\mathrm{s}})'x^{\mathrm{s}}]^{-1}(x^{\mathrm{s}})'y^{\mathrm{s}}\}$, T_{s} is the number of observations from the DSGE model added to the actual data, Γ is the gamma function, $X = (I \otimes X)$ includes all the lags of y, the superscript "s" indicates simulated data, and k is the number of coefficients in each VAR equation.

Exercise 11.36. Suggest an algorithm to draw sequences from $g(\theta \mid y)$.

11.4.6 Nonlinear Specifications

So far we have focused attention on DSGE models that are (log-)linearized around some pivotal point. As seen in chapter 2, there are applications for which (log-) linearizations are unappealing; for example, when economic experiments involve changes of regime or large perturbations of the relationships. In these cases one may want to work directly with the nonlinear version of the model and some steps of the algorithms of this chapter need to be modified to take this into account. Consider the model

$$y_{2t+1} = h_1(y_{2t}, \epsilon_{1t}, \theta), \quad (11.36)$$

$$y_{1t} = h_2(y_{2t}, \epsilon_{2t}, \theta), \quad (11.37)$$

where ϵ_{2t} are measurement errors, ϵ_{1t} are structural shocks, θ is a vector of structural parameters, y_{2t} is the vector of states, and y_{1t} is the vector of controls. Let $y_t = (y_{1t}, y_{2t})$, $\epsilon_t = (\epsilon_{1t}, \epsilon_{2t})$, $y^{t-1} = (y_0, \dots, y_{t-1})$, and $\epsilon^t = (\epsilon_1, \dots, \epsilon_t)$. Integrating the initial conditions and the shocks out, the likelihood of the model can be written as (see Fernandez-Villaverde and Rubio-Ramirez 2003a,b)

$$\mathcal{L}(y^T, \theta) = \int \left[\prod_{t=1}^{T} \int f(y_t \mid \epsilon^t, y^{t-1}, y_{20}, \theta) f(\epsilon^t \mid y^{t-1}, y_{20}, \theta) \, d\epsilon^t \right] f(y_{20}, \theta) \, dy_{20}, \quad (11.38)$$

where y_{20} is the initial state. Clearly, (11.38) is intractable. However, if we have L draws for y_{20} from $f(y_{20}, \theta)$ and L draws for $\epsilon^{t|t-1}$ from $f(\epsilon^t \mid y^{t-1}, y_{20}, \theta)$, $t = 1, \dots, T$, we can approximate (11.38) with

$$\mathcal{L}(y^T, \theta) = \frac{1}{L} \left[\prod_{t=1}^{T} \frac{1}{L} \sum_{l} f(y_t \mid \epsilon^{t|t-1,l}, y^{t-1}, y_{20}^l, \theta) \right]. \quad (11.39)$$

Drawing from $f(y_{20}, \theta)$ is simple, but drawing from $f(\epsilon^t \mid y^{t-1}, y_{20}, \theta)$ is, in general, complicated. Fernandez-Villaverde and Rubio-Ramirez suggest using $f(\epsilon^{t-1} \mid y^{t-1}, y_{20}, \theta)$ as importance sampling for $f(\epsilon^t \mid y^{t-1}, y_{20}, \theta)$. We summarize their approach in the next algorithm.

Algorithm 11.6.

(1) Draw y_{20}^l from $f(y_{20}, \theta)$. Draw $\epsilon^{t|t-1,l}$ L times from $f(\epsilon^t \mid y^{t-1}, y_{20}^l, \theta) = f(\epsilon^{t-1} \mid y^{t-1}, y_{20}^l, \theta) f(\epsilon_t \mid \theta)$.

(2) Set $\text{IR}_t^l = f(y_t \mid \epsilon^{t|t-1,l}, y^{t-1}, y_{20}^l, \theta) / \sum_{l=1}^{L} f(y_t \mid \epsilon^{t|t-1,l}, y^{t-1}, y_{20}^l, \theta)$ and assign it as a weight to each draw $\epsilon^{t|t-1,l}$.

(3) Resample from $\{\epsilon^{t|t-1,l}\}_{l=1}^{L}$ with probabilities equal to IR_t^l. Call this draw $\epsilon^{t,l}$.

(4) Repeat steps (1)–(3) for every $t = 1, 2, \dots, T$.

Step (3) is crucial to making the algorithm work. If omitted, only one particle will asymptotically remain and the integral in (11.38) will diverge as $T \to \infty$. The resampling step prevents this from happening. Note that such a step is similar to the one employed in genetic algorithms: you resample from candidates which have high probability and create new branches at each step.

Clearly, algorithm 11.6 is computationally demanding: in fact, at each iteration, the model needs to be solved to find an expression for $f(y^t \mid \epsilon^t, y^{t-1}, y_{20}, \theta)$. At this point only the most basic RBC model has been estimated by nonlinear likelihood methods and some gains have been reported by Fernandez-Villaverde and Rubio-Ramirez (2004). When Bayesian analysis is performed, algorithm 11.6 must be inserted between steps (3) and (4) of algorithm 11.3. This makes such an approach very demanding on currently available computers.

11.4.7 Which Approach to Use?

There is surprisingly little work comparing estimation/evaluation approaches in models which are misspecified, tightly parametrized, and feature fewer driving forces than endogenous variables. Ruge-Murcia (2002) is one recent example. Despite the lack of formal evidence, there are a few general ideas which may be useful to the applied investigator.

First, there are economic and statistical advantages in jointly estimating a system of structural equations. From an economic point of view, this is appealing since parameter estimates are obtained by employing all the model's restrictions. On the other hand, statistical efficiency is enhanced when all available information is used. Joint estimation may be problematic when a researcher is not necessarily willing to subscribe to all the details of a model. After all, tight parameter estimates which are economically unreasonable are hard to justify and interpret.

Misspecification, a theme we have repeatedly touched upon in several chapters of this book, creates problems for full-information estimation techniques in at least two ways. When the number of shocks is smaller than the number of endogenous variables, parameter estimates can be obtained only from a restricted number of series — essentially transforming full-information methods into limited-information ones. Furthermore, since not all variables have the same informational content about the parameters of interest, one is forced to experiment, with little guidance from economic or statistical theory. Second, if the model cannot be considered the DGP of the data (because of the assumptions made or because of the purely qualitative nature of the behavioral relationships it describes), both full-information estimation and testing are problematic. Maximum likelihood, in fact, attempts to minimize the largest discrepancy between the model's equations and the data. That is to say, it will choose parameter estimates that are best in the dimensions where misspecification is the largest. Therefore, it is likely to produce estimates which are either unreasonable from an economic point of view or on the boundary of the parameter space.

There are a few solutions to these problems. Adding measurement errors may eliminate the singularity of the system but it cannot remedy dynamic misspecification problems. Adding serially correlated measurement errors, on the other hand, may solve both problems, but such an approach lacks economic foundations. Roughly speaking, it amounts to giving up the idea that the model is a good representation of the data, both in an economic and in a statistical sense. The methods we have described in the last three chapters can elegantly deal with these problems. The prior plays the role of a penalty function and if appropriately specified, it may make a full-information approach look for a local, but economically interesting, maximum of the problem. In addition, it may reduce both biases and skewness in ML estimates. However, it is still to be proved that computer-intensive MCMC methods have good size and power properties in the types of model we have studied in this book. The simple examples we have presented suggest that a lot more work needs to be done.

The alternative is to use less information and therefore be theoretically less demanding about the quality of the approximation of the model to the data. Still, the singularity of the system imposes restrictions on the vector of moments (functions) used to estimate the structural parameters — the functions must be linearly independent, otherwise the asymptotic covariance matrix of the estimates will not be well-defined. Nevertheless, there are situations when the model is extremely singular (for example, there is one source of shocks and ten endogenous variables) and limited-information procedures like GMM, SMM, or indirect inference may paradoxically use more information than ML. We have also mentioned that limited-information approaches may fall into logical inconsistencies whenever they claim to approximate only parts of the DGP. To avoid these inconsistencies, what an investigator wants to explain and what she does not should naturally have a block recursive structure, which is hardly a feature of currently available DSGE models.

Despite the remarkable progress in the specification of DSGE models, one may still prefer to take the point of view that models are still too stylized to credibly represent the data and choose an estimation approach where only the qualitative implications (as opposed to the quantitative ones) are entertained. Such an approach sidesteps both the singularity and the misspecification issues, since qualitative implications can be embedded, as seen in chapter 4, as identification devices for structural VAR models. Combining DSGE and VAR models either informally or more formally, as in Del Negro and Schorfheide (2004), seems to be the most promising way to compare stylized models and the data.

In terms of computations, a VAR-based approach has clear advantages. Bayesian and ML estimation are time-consuming especially when the objective function is not well-behaved (a typical case with DSGE models), while SMM and indirect inference may require substantial computer capabilities and may be subject to important identification problems. GMM is a close competitor, but its severe small-sample problems may well wipe out the gains from simplicity. This makes GMM (and simulation estimators) unsuitable for macroeconomic problems where samples are typically short and breaks or regime changes make the time series of data heterogeneous.

It is also important to stress that different small-sample distributions for the structural parameters do not necessarily translate into statistically and economically large differences in the interesting functions a researcher wants to compute. For example, Ruge-Murcia (2002) documents that ML, GMM, SMM, and indirect inference have somewhat different small-sample biases and markedly different efficiency properties. Yet, small-sample impulse response bands computed with estimates obtained with the four approaches are similar in size and shape.

Appendix A

Statistical Distributions

There are a number of statistical distributions which play a central role in Monte Carlo and Bayesian analysis. Generating random sequences from these distributions typically involves generating random variables from some basic distributions (uniform, normal, or gamma) and taking appropriate functions of these random variables. While many statistical and mathematical packages have functions which draw random variables from most of the distributions, it is, at times, necessary to have portable random number generators which are flexible and can easily be inserted into optimization or complex Monte Carlo routines. Here we give the mathematical form of the density $f(x)$, provide the mean $E(x)$, the variance $\mathrm{var}(x)$, and the mode x^* of the distribution, specify how to choose the parameters so as to obtain noninformative distributions, and describe one or more ways to draw random variables. Additional information can be found in Hastings and Peacock (1982), Ripley (1987), or Robert and Casella (1999).

Uniform distribution: $x \sim \mathbb{U}(a_1, a_2)$.
$f(x) = 1/(a_2 - a_1)$, $x \in [a_1, a_2]$, $a_2 > a_1$.
$E(x) = \frac{1}{2}(a_1 + a_2)$, $\mathrm{var}(x) = \frac{1}{12}(a_2 - a_1)^2$; no mode exists.
Random number generator: $y = a_1 + (a_2 - a_1)z$, where $z \sim \mathbb{U}(0, 1)$.
Noninformative distribution: $a_1 \to -\infty$, $a_2 \to \infty$.

Normal distribution (multivariate): $x \sim \mathbb{N}(\mu, \Sigma)$, $x = (x_1, \dots, x_m)'$, Σ symmetric and positive definite.
$f(x) = (\sqrt{2\pi})^{-0.5M} |\Sigma|^{-0.5} \exp\{-0.5(x - \mu)'\Sigma^{-1}(x - \mu)\}$.
$E(x) = \mu$, $\mathrm{var}(x) = \Sigma$, $x^* = \mu$.
Random number generator: $y = \mu + Pz$, $P'P = \Sigma$, where $z \sim \mathbb{N}(0, I_m)$ or $z_i = \sum_{j=1}^{12} v_j - 6$, where $v_j \sim \mathbb{U}(0, 1)$, $i = 1, \dots, m$.
Noninformative distribution: $\Sigma^{-1} \to 0$.

Lognormal distribution (univariate): $\ln x \sim \mathbb{N}(\mu, \sigma^2)$.
$f(x) = (\sqrt{2\pi}\sigma x)^{-1} \exp\{-0.5(\ln x - \mu)^2/\sigma^2\}$.
$E(x) = \exp\{\mu + 0.5\sigma^2\}$, $\mathrm{var}(x) = \mathrm{e}^{2\mu\sigma^2}(\mathrm{e}^{\sigma^2} - 1)$, $x^* = \mathrm{e}^{\mu - \sigma^2}$.

Random number generator: $y = \exp(\mu + \sigma z)$, where $z \sim \mathbb{N}(0,1)$, or $y = \mathrm{e}^{\mu} \exp[\sigma(\sum_{i=1}^{12} z_i - 6)]$, where $z_i \sim \mathbb{U}(0,1)$.
Noninformative distribution: $\sigma^{-2} \to 0$.

Gamma: $x \sim \mathbb{G}(a_1, a_2)$.
$f(x) = [a_2^{a_1}/\Gamma(a_1)]x^{a_1-1}\exp\{-a_2 x\}$, $x > 0$, $a_1, a_2 > 0$; a_1 controls the shape, a_2^{-1} the scale; $\Gamma(a_1)$ is the gamma function with parameter a_1.
$E(x) = a_1/a_2$, $\operatorname{var}(x) = a_1/a_2^2$, $x^* = (a_1 - 1)/a_2$, $a_1 \geqslant 1$.
Random number generator: $y = -(1/a_2)\ln(\prod_{i=1}^{a_1} z_i)$, where $z_i \sim \mathbb{U}(0,1)$.
Noninformative distribution: $a_1, a_2 \to 0$.
Special cases: $\mathbb{G}(0.5\nu, 0.5) \equiv \chi^2(\nu)$; $\mathbb{G}(1, a_2) \equiv \operatorname{Exp}(a_2)$.

Exponential: $x \sim \operatorname{Exp}(a)$, $a > 0$.
$f(x) = a\mathrm{e}^{-ax}$, $x \geqslant 0$, a^{-1} controls the scale.
$E(x) = a^{-1}$, $\operatorname{var}(x) = a^{-2}$, $x^* = 0$.
Random number generator: $y = -\ln(z)/a$, where $z \sim \mathbb{U}(0,1)$.
Noninformative distribution: $a \to 0$.

Chi-squared: $x \sim \chi^2(\nu)$, ν degrees of freedom.
$f(x) = [2^{-0.5\nu}/\Gamma(0.5\nu)]x^{0.5\nu-1}\mathrm{e}^{-0.5x}$, $x \geqslant 0$; $\Gamma(0.5\nu)$ is the gamma function with parameter 0.5ν.
$E(x) = \nu$, $\operatorname{var}(x) = 2\nu$, $x^* = \nu - 2$, $\nu \geqslant 2$.
Random number generator: $y = \sum_{i=1}^{\nu} z_i^2$, where $z_i \sim \mathbb{N}(0,1)$.
Noninformative distribution: $\nu \to 0$.

F-distribution: $x \sim \mathbb{F}(\nu_1, \nu_2)$.

$$f(x) = \frac{\Gamma(0.5(\nu_1+\nu_2))\nu_1^{0.5\nu_2}\nu_2^{0.5\nu_1}}{\Gamma(0.5\nu_1)\Gamma(0.5\nu_2)} \frac{x^{0.5\nu_1-1}}{(\nu_1+\nu_2 x)^{0.5(\nu_1+\nu_2)}}, \quad x > 0;$$

$\nu_1, \nu_2 > 0$ are degrees of freedom.
$E(x) = \nu_2/(\nu_2 - 2)$ for $\nu_2 > 2$; $\operatorname{var}(x) = 2\nu_2^2(\nu_1 + \nu_2 - 2)/[\nu_1(\nu_2 - 4)(\nu_2 - 2)^2]$ for $\nu_2 > 4$ and $x^* = \nu_2(\nu_1 - 2)/\nu_1(\nu_2 + 2)$ for $\nu_1 \geqslant 2$.
Random number generator: $y = \nu_2 x_1/\nu_1 x_2$, where $x_1 \sim \chi^2(\nu_1)$ and $x_2 \sim \chi^2(\nu_2)$.
Noninformative: $\nu_1, \nu_2 \to 0$.
Special case: if $x \sim \mathbb{F}(\nu_1, \nu_2)$, $\nu_1 x/(\nu_2 + \nu_1 x) \sim \operatorname{Beta}(0.5\nu_1, 0.5\nu_2)$.

Inverse gamma: $x \sim \mathbb{IG}(a_1, a_2)$.
$f(x) = [a_2^{a_1}/\Gamma(a_1)]x^{-a_1-1}\mathrm{e}^{-a_2/x}$, $x \geqslant 0$, $a_1, a_2 > 0$.
$E(x) = a_2/(a_1 - 1)$ for $a_1 > 1$, $\operatorname{var}(x) = a_2^2/(a_1-1)^2(a_1 - 2)$ for $a_1 > 2$, $x^* = a_2/(a_1 + 1)$.

Random number generator: $y = 1/z$, where $z \sim \mathbb{G}(a_1, a_2)$.

Noninformative distribution: $a_1, a_2 \to 0$.

Special cases: if $x^{-1} \sim \mathbb{G}(a_1, a_2)$, $x \sim \mathbb{IG}(a_1, a_2)$; $\mathbb{IG}(0.5\nu, 0.5) \equiv I\chi^2(\nu)$; $x_1^{-1} \sim \mathbb{G}(a_1, a_{21})$, $x_2^{-1} \sim \mathbb{G}(a_1, a_{22})$, $x_1^{-1}/(x_1^{-1} + x_2^{-1}) \sim \text{Beta}(a_{21}, a_{22})$.

Inverse scaled chi-squared: $x \sim I\chi^2(\nu, \bar{s}^2)$.

$f(x) = [(0.5\nu)^{0.5\nu}/\Gamma(0.5\nu)]\bar{s}^{\nu} x^{-0.5\nu-1} \exp\{-\nu\bar{s}^2/2x\}$, $x \geqslant 0$.

$E(x) = [\nu/(\nu-2)]\bar{s}^2$ for $\nu > 2$, $\text{var}(x) = 2\nu^2\bar{s}^4/(\nu-2)^2(\nu-4)$ for $\nu > 4$, $x^* = \nu s^2/(\nu+2)$.

Random number generator: $y = \nu\bar{s}^2/z$, where $z \sim \mathbb{G}(0.5\nu, 0.5)$.

Noninformative distribution: $\nu \to 0$.

Wishart: $\Sigma \sim \mathbb{W}(\bar{\Sigma}, \nu)$, $\text{rank}(\Sigma) = q$, $\bar{\Sigma}$ is an $m \times m$ positive definite scale matrix; $\nu > q + 1$ are degrees of freedom.

$f(\Sigma) = [2^{0.5\nu m}\pi^{0.25m(m-1)} \prod_{i=1}^{m} \Gamma(0.5(\nu+1-i))]^{-1} |\bar{\Sigma}|^{-0.5\nu} |\Sigma|^{-0.5(\nu+m-1)} \times \exp\{-0.5\,\text{tr}(\Sigma^{-1}\bar{\Sigma})\}$, where "tr" denotes the trace of the matrix; $E(\Sigma) = \nu\bar{\Sigma}$.

Random number generator: $y = z'z$, where z is an $m \times 1 \sim \mathbb{N}(0, \bar{\Sigma})$.

Noninformative distribution: $\nu \to 0$.

Special case: if $\Sigma^{-1} \sim \mathbb{W}(\nu, \bar{\Sigma})$, then $\Sigma \sim \mathbb{IW}(\nu, \bar{\Sigma}^{-1})$.

t-distribution (univariate): $x \sim t(\nu, \mu, \sigma^2)$, ν = degrees of freedom, μ = location, σ = scale.

$f(x) = [\Gamma(0.5(\nu+1))]/[\sigma\sqrt{\nu\pi}\,\Gamma(0.5\nu)]\{1 + (1/\nu)[(x-\mu)^2/\sigma]^2\}^{-0.5(\nu+1)}$.

$E(x) = \mu$ for $\nu > 1$, $\text{var}(x) = \nu\sigma^2/(\nu-2)$ for $\nu > 2$, $x^* = \mu$.

Random number generator: $y = \mu + \sigma z_1\sqrt{\nu/z_2}$, where $z_1 \sim \mathbb{N}(0,1)$ and $z_2 \sim \chi^2(\nu)$.

Noninformative distribution: $\sigma^{-2} \to 0$.

Special cases: $t(\infty, \mu, \sigma^2) \equiv \mathbb{N}(\mu, \sigma^2)$, $t(1, \mu, \sigma^2) \equiv \mathbb{C}(\mu, \sigma^2)$; if $x \sim t(\nu_1, \mu, \Sigma)$, $(x-\mu)\Sigma^{-1}(x-\mu)/\nu_2 \sim \mathbb{F}(\nu_1, \nu_2)$, where Σ is a $\nu_2 \times \nu_2$ matrix.

Beta distribution: $x \sim \text{Beta}(a_1, a_2)$, $a_1 > 0$, $a_2 > 0$ are prior sizes.

$f(x) = [\Gamma(a_1+a_2)/\Gamma(a_1)\Gamma(a_2)]x^{a_1-1}(1-x)^{a_2-1}$, $0 \leqslant x \leqslant 1$.

$E(x) = a_1/(a_1+a_2)$, $\text{var}(x) = a_1a_2/(a_1+a_2)^2(a_1+a_2+1)$, $x^* = (a_1-1)/(a_1+a_2-2)$, $a_1 > 1$, $a_2 > 1$.

Random number generator: $y = z_1/(z_1+z_2)$, where $z_1 \sim \chi^2(2a_1)$ and $z_2 \sim \chi^2(2a_2)$ or $z_1 = -\ln\prod_{i=1}^{a_1} v_i$; $z_2 = -\ln\prod_{i=1}^{a_2} v_i$, where $v_i \sim \mathbb{U}(0,1)$.

Noninformative distribution: $a_1, a_2 \to 0$.

Special case: $\text{Beta}(1,1) \equiv \mathbb{U}(0,1)$.

Weibull: $x \sim \mathbb{WE}(a_1, a_2)$, $a_1, a_2 > 0$, a_1 controls the shape, a_2 the scale.

$f(x) = (a_1/a_2^{a_1})x^{a_1-1}\exp\{-(x/a_2)^{a_1}\}$.
$E(x) = a_2\Gamma(1+a_1^{-1})$, $\text{var}(x) = a_2^2(\Gamma(1+2/a_1) - \Gamma(1+a_1^{-1})^2)$; $x^* = a_2(1-a_1^{-1})^{a_1^{-1}}$ for $a_1 \geqslant 1$ and $x^* = 0$ otherwise.
Random number generator: $y = a_2(-\ln z)^{1/a_1}$, where $z \sim \mathbb{U}(0,1)$.
Noninformative distribution: $a_1, a_2 \to 0$.
Special case: if $x \sim \mathbb{WE}(1, a_2)$, then $x \sim \text{Exp}(a_2)$.

Dirichlet: $x \sim \text{Dir}(a_1, \dots, a_m)$, $a_j > 0$, $\sum_{j=1}^m a_j = a_0$, $a_1, \dots, a_m$ are prior sizes.
$f(x) = [\Gamma(a_0)/\prod_j \Gamma(a_j)]\prod_j x_j^{a_j-1}$.
$E(x_j) = a_j/a_0$; $\text{var}(x_j) = a_j(a_0 - a_j)/a_0^2(a_0 - 1)$; $x_j^* = (a_j - 1)/(a_0 - m)$.
Random number generator: $y_j = z_j/\sum_{i=1}^m z_i$, where $z_j \sim \mathbb{G}(a_j, 1)$.
Noninformative distribution: $a_j \to 0$.
Special case: if $x \sim \text{Dir}(a_i, \dots, a_m)$, $x_j \sim \text{Beta}(a_j, a_0 - a_j)$.

Pareto: $x \sim \text{Pa}(a_0, a_1)$, $a_1, a_0 > 0$.
$f(x) = a_1 a_0^{a_1}/(x^{a_1+1})$, $x \geqslant a_0$.
$E(x) = a_1 a_0/(a_1 - 1)$ for $a_1 > 1$; $\text{var}(x) = a_1 a_0^2/(a_1 - 1)^2(a_1 - 2)$ for $a_1 > 2$; $x^* = a_0$.
Random number generator: $x \sim \text{Exp}(z)$, where $z \sim \mathbb{G}(a_1, a_0)$.
Noninformative distribution: $a \to 0$.

Cauchy: $x \sim \mathbb{C}(\mu, \sigma^2)$; $f(x) = (1/\pi\sigma)[(x-\mu)^2/\sigma^2 + 1]$; no moments; $x^* = \mu$.
Random number generator: $y = \mu + \sigma z_1/z_2$, where $z_1 \sim \mathbb{N}(0,1)$ and $z_2 \sim \mathbb{N}(0,1)$.

Interpolation

In applied work it is often the case that series with different frequencies need to be used. For example, when studying the transmission of monetary policy shocks, interest data are available at the daily frequency while GDP data are available only at the quarterly or the annual frequency. The dilemma concerning the frequency of the data is well understood: more series are typically available at low frequencies, but the number of observations at these frequencies is typically small. On the other hand, from a pure economic theory perspective, one would like to have as high frequency data as possible since agents are assumed to make decisions in almost continuous time. Furthermore, when trying to examine the effect of a shock, it is not unusual to find insignificant responses in annual data, but significant reactions with higher frequency data.

Data for many series do not exist at high frequencies and they are interpolated by statistical agencies using low frequency data and some proxy indicator at the required frequency. Wilcox (1992), for example, forcefully argued that consumption data at the quarterly frequency may be subject to large measurement errors since consumption is really measured every five years and smoothly interpolated using monthly sales as a proxy indicator. Given that the data are constructed in this way, it is perhaps not surprising to find that consumption data are too smooth relative to what one would expect based on standard permanent income theory.

As we mentioned in chapter 9, missing data can be reconstructed with the Gibbs sampler and all available information. The disadvantage of this approach is that recursivity of information flow is lost. This means that, for example, a generated value at time t may contain more information than an actual value of the series at time $t + \tau$, $\tau > 0$. In this case, innovation analysis may be problematic. To solve this problem one could generate data with a recursive algorithm that uses only information available up to the point of interest.

The most common approach to the interpolation of data from low to high frequencies is the Chow–Lin method. Suppose we want to create T monthly observations for y_t, e.g., GDP, and assume that y_t is related to a vector of observable monthly indicators x_t (e.g., interest rates, sales, or exports) via the linear regression $y_{t\mathrm{m}} = x_{t\mathrm{m}}\alpha + e_{t\mathrm{m}}$, where the subscript "m" refers to the monthly frequency. Stacking the T observations we have $y_{\mathrm{m}} = x_{\mathrm{m}}\alpha + e_{\mathrm{m}}$, where we assume that $e_{\mathrm{m}} = \rho_{\mathrm{m}} e_{\mathrm{m}-1} + v_{\mathrm{m}}$ with $v_{\mathrm{m}} \sim$ i.i.d. $(0, \sigma^2 I)$. Hence, e_{m} has a zero mean and covariance equal to $\Sigma_e = (\sigma^2/(1-\rho_{\mathrm{m}}^2))\Omega_{\mathrm{m}}$, where

$$\Omega_{\mathrm{m}} = \begin{bmatrix} 1 & \rho_{\mathrm{m}} & \cdots & \rho_{\mathrm{m}}^{T-1} \\ \rho_{\mathrm{m}} & 1 & \cdots & \rho_{\mathrm{m}}^{T-2} \\ \cdots & \cdots & \cdots & \cdots \\ \rho_{\mathrm{m}}^{T-1} & \cdots & \cdots & 1 \end{bmatrix}.$$

Suppose that the $T/3$ quarterly observations of y_t are related to the T monthly observations via the averaging matrix $\mathcal{Q}$ with the form

$$\mathcal{Q} = \frac{1}{3}\begin{bmatrix} 1 & 1 & 1 & 0 & \cdots & \cdots & \cdots & \cdots & \cdots & 0 \\ 0 & 0 & 0 & 1 & 1 & 1 & \cdots & \cdots & \cdots & 0 \\ \cdots & \cdots & \cdots & \cdots & \cdots & \cdots & \cdots & \cdots & \cdots & \cdots \\ 0 & 0 & 0 & \cdots & \cdots & \cdots & \cdots & 1 & 1 & 1 \end{bmatrix}.$$

Then observable quarterly values of y_t are linked to observable quarterly values of x_t via the equation $y_{\mathrm{q}} = \mathcal{Q} y_{\mathrm{m}} = x_{\mathrm{q}}\alpha + e_{\mathrm{q}}$, where $E(e_{\mathrm{q}} e_{\mathrm{q}}') = \mathcal{Q}\Sigma_e\mathcal{Q}'$. Therefore, a linear unbiased estimator for y_{m} which has the smallest possible variance can be obtained via

$$\hat{y}_{\mathrm{m}} = X_{\mathrm{m}}\alpha_{\mathrm{q,GLS}} + \hat{\Omega}_{\mathrm{m}}\mathcal{Q}'(\mathcal{Q}\hat{\Omega}_{\mathrm{m}}\mathcal{Q}')^{-1} e_{\mathrm{q,GLS}}, \tag{A.1}$$

where $\alpha_{\mathrm{q,GLS}}$ is the generalized least squares estimate of α obtained by using quarterly data, $e_{\mathrm{q,GLS}} = \mathcal{Q} y_{\mathrm{m}} - x_{\mathrm{q}}\alpha_{\mathrm{q,GLS}}$, and $\hat{\Omega}_{\mathrm{m}}$ is an estimate of Ω_{m}. To maintain the information flow, a recursive version of equation (A.1) could be used.

References

Aadland, D. 2005. Detrending time aggregated data. *Economic Letters* 89:287–93.

Abdelkhalek, T., and J. M. Dufour. 1998. Statistical inference for CGE models with application to a model of the Moroccan economy. *Review of Economics and Statistics* 80:520–34.

Ahmed, S., B. Ickes, P. Wang, and B. Yoo. 1993. International business cycles. *American Economic Review* 83:335–59.

Albert, J., and S. Chib. 1993. Bayes inference via Gibbs sampling of autoregressive time series subject to Markov mean and variance shifts. *Journal of Business and Economic Statistics* 11:1–16.

Alesina, A., and R. Perotti. 1995. Fiscal expansions and adjustments in OECD countries. *Economic Policy* 21:207–48.

Altug, S. 1989. Time to build and aggregate fluctuations: some new evidence. *International Economic Review* 30:883–920.

Amemiya, T. 1985. *Advanced Econometrics*. Cambridge, MA: Harvard University Press.

Angeloni, I., A. Kashyap, B. Mojon, and D. Terlizzese. 2003. Monetary Transmission in the euro area: where do we stand. In *Monetary Transmission in the Euro Area* (ed. I. Angeloni, A. Kashyap, B. Mojon, and D. Terlizzese). Cambridge University Press.

Anderson, B., and J. Moore. 1979. *Optimal Filtering*. Engelwood Cliffs, NJ: Prentice Hall.

Anderson, T. W. 1971. *The Statistical Analysis of Time Series*. Wiley.

Anderson, T. W., and C. Hsiao. 1982. Formulation and estimation of dynamic models using panel data. *Journal of Econometrics* 18:47–82.

Anderson, T., and B. Sörenson. 1996. GMM estimation of stochastic volatility models: a Monte Carlo study. *Journal of Business and Economic Statistics* 14:328–52.

Andrews, D. 1991. Heteroskedasticity and autocorrelation consistent covariance matrix estimation. *Econometrica* 59:817–58.

Andrews, D., and C. Mohanan. 1992. An improved heteroskedasticity and autocorrelation consistent covariance matrix estimator. *Econometrica* 60:953–66.

Arellano, M., and S. Bond. 1991. Some tests of specification for panel data: Monte Carlo evidence and an application to employment equations. *Review of Economic Studies* 58:277–97.

Backus, D., P. Kehoe, and F. Kydland. 1994. Dynamics of the trade balance and the terms of trade: the *J*-curve? *American Economic Review* 84:84–103.

——. 1995. International business cycles: theory and evidence. In *Frontiers of Business Cycle Analysis* (ed. T. Cooley), pp. 331–56. Princeton University Press.

Bai, J. 1997. Estimation of multiple breaks one at a time. *Econometric Theory* 13:315–52.

Ballabriga, F. 1997. Bayesian vector autoregressions. ESADE.

Baltagi, B. 1995. *Econometric Analysis of Panel Data*. Wiley.

Barro, R., and X. Sala-i-Martin. 1992. Convergence. *Journal of Political Economy* 100:223–51.

——. 2003. *Economic Growth*, 2nd edn. Cambridge, MA: MIT Press.

Barro, R., N. Mankiw, and X. Sala-i-Martin. 1995. Capital mobility in neoclassical models of growth. *American Economic Review* 85:103–15.

Basu, S., and J. Fernand. 1997. Returns to scale in U.S. production: estimates and implications. *Journal of Political Economy* 105:249–83.

Bauwens, L., M. Lubrano, and J. F. Richard. 1999. *Bayesian Inference in Dynamics Econometric Models*. Oxford University Press.

Baxter, M., and M. Crucini. 1993. Explaining saving–investment correlations. *American Economic Review* 83:416–36.

Baxter, M., and R. King. 1999. Measuring business cycles: approximate band-pass filters for economic time series. *Review of Economics and Statistics* 81:575–93.

Bayraktar, N., P. Sakellaris, and P. Vermeulen. 2003. Real vs. financial frictions to capital investment. AUEB Athens.

Beaudry, P., and F. Portier. 2002. The French Depression in the 1930's. *Review of Economic Dynamics* 5:73–99.

Bell, W. 1984. Signal extraction for nonstationary time series. *Annals of Statistics* 12:644–64.

Benassy, J. P. 1995. Money and wage contracts in an optimizing model of the business cycle. *Journal of Monetary Economics* 35:303–15.

Benhabib, J., and R. Farmer. 2000. The monetary transmission mechanism. *Review of Economic Dynamics* 3:523–50.

Berger, J. 1985. *Statistical Decision Theory and Bayesian Analysis*. Springer.

Berger, J., and R. Wolpert. 1998. *The Likelihood Principle*, 2nd edn. Hayward, CA: Institute of Mathematical Statistics.

Bernanke, B., J. Boivin, and P. Eliasz. 2005. Measuring the effects of monetary policy: a factor augmented VAR approach. *Quarterly Journal of Economics* 120:387–422.

Beveridge, S., and C. Nelson. 1981. A new approach to decomposition of economic time series into permanent and transitory components with particular attention to the measurement of the business cycle. *Journal of Monetary Economics* 7:151–74.

Binder, M., C. Hsiao, and H. Pesaran. 2005. Estimation and inference in short panel VAR with unit roots and cointegration. *Econometric Theory* 21:795–837.

Blanchard, O., and C. Kahn. 1980. The solution of difference equations under rational expectations. *Econometrica* 48:1305–11.

Blanchard, O., and D. Quah. 1989. The dynamic effect of aggregate demand and supply disturbances. *American Economic Review* 79:655–73.

Boldrin, M., and F. Canova. 2001. Inequality and convergence: reconsidering European regional policies. *Economic Policy* 32:205–53.

Boldrin, M., L. Christiano, and J. Fisher. 2001. Asset pricing lessons for modeling business cycles. *American Economic Review* 91:146–66.

Box, G., and G. Tiao. 1973. *Bayesian Inference in Statistical Analysis*. Wiley.

Braun, P., and S. Mittnik. 1993. Misspecifications in VAR and their effects on impulse responses and variance decompositions. *Journal of Econometrics* 59:319–41.

Brockwell, P., and R. Davis. 1991. *Time Series: Theory and Methods*, 2nd edn. Springer.

Bry, G., and C. Boschen. 1971. *Cyclical Analysis of Time Series: Selected Procedures and Computer Programs*. New York: NBER.

Burns, A., and W. Mitchell. 1946. *Measuring Business Cycles*. New York: NBER.

Burnside, C., and M. Eichenbaum. 1996. Small sample properties of GMM-based Wald tests. *Journal of Business and Economic Statistics* 14:294–308.

Burnside, C., M. Eichenbaum, and C. Evans. 1993. Labor hoarding and the business cycle. *Journal of Political Economy* 101:245–73.

Campbell, J. 1994. Inspecting the mechanism: an analytic approach to the stochastic growth model. *Journal of Monetary Economics* 33:463–506.

Campbell, J., A. Lo, and C. McKinley. 1997. *The Econometrics of Financial Markets*. Princeton University Press.

Canova, F. 1991. Source of financial crisis: pre and post-Fed evidence. *International Economic Review* 32:689–713.

——. 1992. An alternative approach to modelling and forecasting seasonal time series. *Journal of Business and Economic Statistics* 10:97–108.

——. 1993. Forecasting time series with common seasonal patterns. *Journal of Econometrics* 55:173–200.

——. 1993. Forecasting exchange rates with a Bayesian time-varying coefficient model. *Journal of Economic Dynamics and Control* 17:233–61.

——. 1994. Statistical inference in calibrated models. *Journal of Applied Econometrics* 9:S123–S144.

——. 1995a. Sensitivity analysis and model evaluation in simulated dynamic general equilibrium economies. *International Economic Review* 36:477–501.

——. 1995b. VAR models: specification, estimation, inference and forecasting. In *Handbook of Applied Econometrics* (ed. H. Pesaran and M. Wickens), chapter 2. Oxford: Blackwell.

——. 1995c. The economics of VAR models. In *Macroeconometrics: Tensions and Prospects* (ed. K. Hoover), pp. 30–69. New York: Kluwer.

——. 1998. Detrending and business cycle facts. *Journal of Monetary Economics* 41:475–540.

——. 1999. Reference cycle and turning points: a sensitivity analysis to detrending and dating rules. *Economic Journal* 109:126–50.

——. 2002a. Validating two DSGE monetary models with VARs. CEPR Working Paper 3442.

——. 2002b. G-7 inflation forecasts. *Macroeconomic Dynamics* (in press).

——. 2004. Testing for convergence club: a predictive density approach. *International Economic Review* 45:49–77.

Canova, F., and M. Ciccarelli. 2003. Bayesian panel VARs: specification, estimation, testing and leading indicators. CEPR Working Paper 4033.

——. 2004. Forecasting and turning point prediction in a Bayesian panel VAR model. *Journal of Econometrics* 120:327–59.

Canova, F., and G. De Nicolò. 2002. Money matters for business cycle fluctuations in the G7. *Journal of Monetary Economics* 49:1131–59.

Canova, F., and J. Marrinan. 1993. Profits, risk and uncertainty in exchange rates. *Journal of Monetary Economics* 32:259–86.

——. 1996. Reconciling the term structure of interest rates with a consumption based I-CAP model. *Journal of Economic Dynamics and Control* 32:259–86.

Canova, F., and E. Ortega. 2000. Testing calibrated general equilibrium models. In *Inference Using Simulation Techniques* (ed. R. Mariano, R. Schuermann, and M. Weeks), pp. 400–36. Cambridge University Press.

Canova, F., and E. Pappa. 2003. Price differential in monetary unions: the role of fiscal shocks. CEPR Working Paper 3746. *Economic Journal* (in press).

Canova, F., and J. Pina. 2005. What VARs tell us about DSGE models? In *New Trends in Macroeconomics* (ed. C. Diebolt and C. Kyrtsou). Springer.

Canova, F., and L. Sala. 2005. Back to square one: identification in DSGE models. ECB Working Paper.

Canova, F., M. Finn, and A. Pagan. 1994. Evaluating a real business cycle model. In *Nonstationary Time Series Analysis and Cointegration* (ed. C. Hargreaves), pp. 225–55. Oxford University Press.

Carlin, B. P., A. E. Gelfand, and A. F. M. Smith. 1992. Hierarchical Bayesian analysis of change point problem. *Applied Statistics* 41:389–405.

Carlin, B., N. Polsom, and D. Stoffer. 1992. A Monte Carlo approach to nonnormal and nonlinear state-space modeling. *Journal of the American Statistical Association* 87:493–500.

Carter, C., and P. Kohn. 1994. On the Gibbs sampling for state space models. *Biometrika* 81:541–53.

Casella, G., and E. George. 1992. Explaining the Gibbs sampler. *American Statistician* 46:167–74.

Cecchetti, S. G., P. Lam, and N. Mark. 1993. The equity premium and the risk free rate: matching moments. *Journal of Monetary Economics* 31:21–45.

Chari, V., P. Kehoe, and E. McGrattan. 2000. Sticky price models of the business cycle: can the contract multiplier solve the persistence problem? *Econometrica* 68:1151–79.

——. 2005. Are structural VARs useful guides for developing business cycle theories. Federal Reserve Bank of Minneapolis, Working Paper 631.

Chib, S. 1995. Marginal likelihood from the Gibbs output. *Journal of the American Statistical Association* 90:1313–21.

——. 1996. Calculating posterior distributions and model estimates in Markov mixture models. *Journal of Econometrics* 75:79–98.

Chib, S., and E. Greenberg. 1995. Understanding the Hastings–Metropolis algorithm. *The American Statistician* 49:327–35.

——. 1996. Markov chain Monte Carlo simulation methods in econometrics. *Econometric Theory* 12:409–31.

Cho, J., and T. Cooley. 1995. The business cycle with nominal contracts. *Economic Theory* 6:13–33.

Christiano, L., and W. den Haan. 1996. Small sample properties of GMM for business cycle analysis. *Journal of Business and Economic Statistics* 14:309–27.

Christiano, L., and M. Eichenbaum. 1992. Current real business cycle theories and aggregate labor market fluctuations. *American Economic Review* 82:430–50.

Christiano, L., and T. Fitzgerald. 2003. The band pass filter. *International Economic Review* 44:435–65.

Christiano, L., M. Eichenbaum, and C. Evans. 1999. Monetary policy shocks: what have we learned and to what end. In *Handbook of Macroeconomics* (ed. J. Taylor and M. Woodford). Elsevier.

——. 2005. Nominal rigidities and the dynamic effects of a shock to monetary policy. *Journal of Political Economy* 113:1–45.

Christiano, L., C. Gust, and J. Roldos. 2003. Monetary policy in a financial crisis. *Journal of Economic Theory* 119:64–103.

Ciccarelli, M., and A. Rebucci. 2002. Has the transmission mechanism of monetary policy changed over time? *European Economic Review* (in press).

——. 2003. Measuring contagion with a Bayesian TVC model. ECB Working Paper 263.

Clark, P. 1973. Subordinated stochastic process model with finite variance for speculative prices. *Econometrica* 41:136–56.

Coddington, J., and A. L. Winters. 1987. The Beveridge–Nelson decomposition of time series: a quick computation method. *Journal of Monetary Economics* 19:125–27.

Cogley, T., and J. M. Nason. 1994. Testing the implications of long-run neutrality for monetary business cycle models. *Journal of Applied Econometrics* 9:S37–S70.

——. 1995a. The effects of the Hodrick and Prescott filter on integrated time series. *Journal of Economic Dynamics and Control* 19:253–78.

Cogley, T., and J. M. Nason. 1995b. Output dynamics in real business cycle models. *American Economic Review* 85:492–511.

Cogley, T., and T. Sargent. 2005. Bayesian prediction intervals in evolving monetary systems. NYU University.

Cooley, T. (ed.). 1995. *Frontiers of Business Cycle Research*. Princeton University Press.

Cooley, T., and M. Dwyer. 1998. Business cycle analysis without much theory: a look at structural VARs. *Journal of Econometrics* 83:57–88.

Cooley, T., and G. Hansen. 1989. The inflation tax in a real business cycle model. *American Economic Review* 79:733–48.

Cooley, T., and LeRoy, S. 1985. A theoretical macroeconomics: a critique. *Journal of Monetary Economics* 16:283–308.

Cooley, T., and E. Prescott. 1973. Estimation in the presence of stochastic parameter variation. *Econometrica* 44:167–84.

Corbae, D., and S. Ouliaris. 2001. Extracting cycles from nonstationary data. IMF.

Corbae, D., S. Ouliaris, and P. Phillips. 2002. Band spectral regression with trending data. *Econometrica* 70:1067–109.

Cumby, R., M. Obstfeld, and J. Huizinga. 1982. Two step, two stage least square estimation in models with rational expectations. *Journal of Econometrics* 21:333–53.

Danthine, J. P., and J. Donaldson. 1992. Non-Walrasian economies. Cahiers de Recherche Economique, Université de Lausanne, no. 9301.

Davidson, J. 1994. *Stochastic Limit Theory*. Oxford University Press.

Dedola, L., and S. Neri. 2004. What does a technology shock do? A VAR analysis with model-based sign restrictions. CEPR Working Paper 4537. *Journal of Monetary Economics* (in press).

DeJong, D., B. Ingram, and C. Whiteman. 1996. Beyond calibration. *Journal of Business and Economic Statistics* 14:1–10.

——. 2000. A Bayesian approach to dynamic macroeconomics. *Journal of Econometrics* 98:203–23.

Del Negro, M., and F. Schorfheide. 2004. Priors from general equilibrium models for VARs. *International Economic Review* 95:643–73.

Del Negro, M., F. Schorfeide, F. Smets, and R. Wouters. 2005. On the fit of New-Keynesian models. *Journal of Business and Economic Statistics* (in press).

Den Haan, W., and A. Levin. 1996. Inference from parametric and nonparametric covariance matrix estimation procedures. UCSD.

Diebold, F., and R. Mariano. 1995. Predictive accuracy. *Journal of Business and Economic Statistics* 13:253–65.

Diebold, F., L. Ohanian, and J. Berkowitz. 1998. Dynamics general equilibrium economies: a framework for comparing models and data. *Review of Economic Studies* 68:433–51.

Doan, T. 2005. *Rats 6.1 Manual*. Estima, Il.

Doan, T., R. Litterman, and Sims, C. 1984. Forecasting and conditional projection using realistic prior distributions. *Econometric Reviews* 3:1–100.

Dotsey, M., R. King, and A. Wolman. 1999. State dependent pricing and the general equilibrium dynamics of money and output. *Quarterly Journal of Economics* 114:655–90.

Dridi, R., and E. Renault. 1998. Semiparametric indirect inference. University of Toulouse.

Dridi, R., A. Guay, and E. Renault. 2003. Indirect inference and calibration of dynamic stochastic general equilibrium models. University of Montreal.

Duffie, D., and K. Singleton. 1993. Simulated moments estimation of Markov models of asset prices. *Econometrica* 61:929–50.

Edge, R. 2002. The equivalence of wage and price staggering in monetary business cycle models. *Review of Economic Dynamics* 5:559–85.

Eichenbaum, M., and J. Fisher. 2003. Evaluating the Calvo model of sticky prices. Federal Reserve of Chicago Working Paper 02-23.

Eichenbaum, M., L. Hansen, and K. Singleton. 1988. A time series analysis of the representative agent models of consumption and leisure choice under uncertainty. *Quarterly Journal of Economics* 103:51–78.

Engle, R. 1974. Band spectrum regression. *International Economic Review* 15:1–11.

——. 1983. Wald, likelihood ratio and Lagrange multiplier tests in econometrics. In *Handbook of Econometrics* (ed. Z. Griliches and M. Intrilligator), volume II, pp. 775–826. Amsterdam: North-Holland.

Engle, R., D. Lilien, and R. Robins. 1987. Estimating time varying risk premia in term structures: the ARCH-M model. *Econometrica* 55:391–408.

Erceg, C., D. Henderson, and A. Levin. 2000. Optimal monetary policy with staggered wage and price contracts. *Journal of Monetary Economics* 46:281–313.

Evans, G., and L. Reichlin. 1994. Information, forecasts and the measurement of the business cycles. *Journal of Monetary Economics* 33:233–54.

Farmer, R. 1997. Money in a RBC model. *Journal of Money Banking and Credit* 29:568–611.

Fatas, A., and I. Mihov. 2001. Government size and the automatic stabilizers: international and intranational evidence. *Journal of International Economics* 55:2–38.

Faust, J. 1998. On the robustness of identified VAR conclusions about money. *Carnegie-Rochester Conference Series on Public Policy* 49:207–44.

Faust, J., and E. Leeper. 1997. Do long run restrictions really identify anything? *Journal of Business and Economic Statistics* 15:345–53.

Favero, C. 2001. *Applied Macroeconometrics*. Oxford University Press.

Fernandez-Villaverde, J., and J. Rubio-Ramirez. 2003a. Estimating dynamic equilibrium economies: a likelihood approach. Federal Reserve of Atlanta.

——. 2003b. Estimating dynamic equilibrium economies: linear vs. nonlinear likelihood. Federal Reserve of Atlanta.

——. 2004. Comparing dynamic equilibrium models to the data. *Journal of Econometrics* 123:153–87.

Fernandez-Villaverde, J., J. Rubio-Ramirez, and T. Sargent. 2005. A, B, C (and D's) for understanding VARs. NBER Technical Working Paper 308.

Ferson, W., and S. Foerster. 1994. Finite sample properties of GMM in tests of conditional asset pricing models. *Journal of Financial Economics* 36:29–55.

Fève, P., and F. Langot. 1994. The RBC models through statistical inference: an application with French data. *Journal of Applied Econometrics* 9:S11–S37.

Finn, M. 1998. Cyclical effects of government's employment and goods purchases. *International Economic Review* 39:635–57.

Fisher, S. 1977. Long term contracts, rational expectations and the optimal money supply rule. *Journal of Political Economy* 85:191–205.

Fruhwirth-Schnatter, S. 2001. MCMC estimation of classical and dynamic switching and mixture models. *Journal of the American Statistical Association* 96:194–209.

Fry, R., and A. Pagan. 2005. Some issues in using VARs for macroeconomic research. Australian National University.

Furher, J., J. Moore, and S. Schuh. 1995. Estimating the linear quadratic inventory model, ML vs GMM. *Journal of Monetary Economics* 35:115–57.

Gali, J. 1992. How well does the ISLM model fit postwar U.S. data? *Quarterly Journal of Economics* 107:709–38.

Gali, J. 1999. Technology, employment and business cycle: do technology shocks explain aggregate fluctuations? *American Economic Review* 89:249–71.

Gali, J., and M. Gertler. 1999. Inflation dynamics: a structural econometric analysis. *Journal of Monetary Economics* 44:195–222.

Gallant, R. 1987. *Nonlinear Statistical Models*. Wiley.

Gallant, R., and G. Tauchen. 1996. Which moments to match? *Econometric Theory* 12:657–81.

Gallant, A. R., P. Rossi, and G. Tauchen. 1993. Nonlinear dynamic structures. *Econometrica* 61:871–908.

Gelfand, A. E., and D. K. Dey. 1994. Bayesian model choice: asymptotics and exact calculations. *Journal of the Royal Statistical Society* B 56:501–14.

Gelfand, A. E., and A. F. M. Smith. 1990. Sampling-based approaches to calculating marginal densities. *Journal of the American Statistical Association* 85:398–409.

Gelman, A., J. B. Carlin, H. S. Stern, and D. B. Rubin. 1995. *Bayesian Data Analysis*. London: Chapman & Hall.

Gertler, M., and S. Gilchrist. 1994. Monetary policy, business cycles and the behavior of small manufacturing firms. *Quarterly Journal of Economics* 109:309–40.

Geweke, J. 1989. Bayesian inference in econometric models using Monte Carlo integration. *Econometrica* 57:1317–39.

——. 1994. Comment to Jacquier, Polson and Rossi. *Journal of Business and Economic Statistics* 12:397–98.

——. 1995. Monte Carlo simulation and numerical integration. In *Handbook of Computational Economics* (ed. H. Amman, D. Kendrick, and J. Rust), pp. 731–800. Elsevier.

——. 1999. Computational experiment and reality. University of Iowa.

Geweke, J., and G. Zhou. 1996. Measuring the pricing error of the arbitrage pricing theory. *Review of Financial Studies* 9:557–87.

Giannone, D., L. Reichlin, and L. Sala. 2003. Tracking Greenspan: systematic and unsystematic monetary policy revisited. CEPR Working Paper 3550.

Giordani, P. 2004. An alternative explanation of the price puzzle. *Journal of Monetary Economics*. 51:1271–96.

Gomez, V. 1997. Three equivalent methods for filtering nonstationary time series. *Journal of Business and Economic Statistics* 17:109–66.

Gordin, M. 1969. The central limit theorem for stationary processes. *Soviet Math. Doklady* 1174–76.

Gordon, D., and E. Leeper. 1994. The dynamic impact of monetary policy: an exercise in tentative identification. *Journal of Political Economy* 102:1228–47.

Gourieroux, C., and A. Monfort. 1995. Testing, encompassing and simulating dynamic econometric models. *Econometric Theory* 11:195–228.

Gourieroux, C., A. Monfort, and E. Renault. 1993. Indirect inference. *Journal of Applied Econometrics* 8:S85–S118.

Gourinchas, J., and O. Jeanne. 2003. The elusive gains from international financial integration. *Review of Economic Studies* (in press).

Granger, C., and A. Anderson. 1978. *An Introduction to Bilinear Time Series Models*. Göttingen, Sweden: Vandenhoeck and Ruprecht.

Gregory, A., and G. Smith. 1989. Calibration as estimation. *Econometric Reviews* 9(1):57–89.

——. 1991. Calibration as testing: inference in simulated macro models. *Journal of Business and Economic Statistics* 9(3):293–303.

——. 1993. Calibration in macroeconomics. In *Handbook of Statistics* (ed. G. S. Maddala), volume 11, pp. 703–19. Elsevier.

Hall, A. 1992. Some aspects of generalized method of moment estimators. In *Handbook of Statistics* (ed. G. S. Maddala, C. R. Rao, and H. D. Vinod), volume 11, pp. 653–85. Elsevier.

Hamilton, J. 1989. A new approach to the economic analysis of nonstationary time series and the business cycle. *Econometrica* 57:357–84.

——. 1994. *Time Series Analysis*. Princeton University Press.

Hansen, L. P. 1982. Large sample properties of GMM estimators. *Econometrica* 50:1029–54.

——. 1985. A method for calculating bounds on the asymptotic covariance matrix of GMM estimators. *Journal of Econometrics* 30:203–31.

Hansen, L., and J. Heckman. 1996. The empirical foundations of calibration. *Journal of Economic Perspective* 10:87–104.

Hansen, L., and R. Hodrick. 1980. Forward exchange rates as optimal predictors of future spot rates: an econometric analysis. *Journal of Political Economy* 88:829–53.

Hansen, L., and R. Jagannathan. 1991. Implications of security market data for models of dynamic economies. *Journal of Political Economy* 99:225–62.

Hansen, L., and T. Sargent. 1979. Formulating and estimating dynamic linear rational expectations models. *Journal of Economic Dynamic and Control* 2:7–46.

——. 1982. Instrumental variables procedures for linear rational expectations models. *Journal of Monetary Economics* 9:263–96.

——. 1991. Two difficulties in interpreting vector autoregressions. In *Rational Expectations Econometrics* (ed. L. Hansen and T. Sargent). Boulder, CO: Westview Press.

——. 2005. *Recursive Linear Models of Dynamic Economies*. Princeton University Press.

Hansen, L., and K. Singleton. 1982. Generalized instrumental variables estimation of nonlinear rational expectations models. *Econometrica* 50:1269–86 (corrigenda, 1984).

——. 1988. Efficient estimation of linear asset pricing models with moving averages errors. University of Chicago.

Hansen, L., J. Heaton, and A. Yaron. 1996. Finite sample properties of alternative GMM estimators. *Journal of Business and Economic Statistics* 14:262–81.

Hansen, L., T. Sargent, and E. McGrattan. 1996. Mechanics of forming and estimating dynamic linear economies. In *Handbook of Computational Economics* (ed. H. Amman, D. Kendrick, and J. Rust). Elsevier.

Harvey, A. C. 1985. Trends and cycles in macroeconomic time series. *Journal of Business and Economic Statistics* 3:216–27.

——. 1991. *Time Series Models*. Deddington, U.K.: Philip Allan.

Harvey, A. C., and A. Jeager. 1993. Detrending, stylized facts and the business cycles. *Journal of Applied Econometrics* 8:231–47.

Hastings, N. A. J., and J. B. Peacock. 1982. *Statistical Distributions*. Wiley.

Hausman, J. 1978. Specification tests in econometrics. *Econometrica* 46:1251–71.

Hayashi, F. 2002. *Econometrics*. Princeton University Press.

Hayashi, F., and C. Sims. 1983. Nearly efficient estimation in time series models with predetermined, but not exogenous instruments. *Econometrica* 51:783–98.

Hess, G., and S. Iwata. 1997. Measuring and comparing business cycle features. *Journal of Business and Economic Statistics* 15:432–44.

Hodrick, R., and E. Prescott. 1997. Post-war U.S. business cycles: an empirical investigation. *Journal of Money Banking and Credit* 29:1–16.

Holtz Eakin, D. 1988. Testing for individual effects in autoregressive models. *Journal of Econometrics* 39:297–307.

Holtz Eakin, D., W. Newey, and H. Rosen. 1988. Estimating vector autoregression with panel data. *Econometrica* 56:1371–95.

Hsiao, C. 1989. *Analysis of Panel Data*. Cambridge University Press.

Imbs, J. 2002. Why the link between volatility and growth is both positive and negative. LBS.

Ingram, B., and B. S. Lee. 1989. Estimation by simulation of time series models. *Journal of Econometrics* 47:197–207.

Ingram, B., and C. Whiteman. 1994. Supplanting the Minnesota prior. Forecasting macroeconomic time series using real business cycle priors. *Journal of Monetary Economics* 34:497–510.

Ireland, P. 2000. Sticky price models and the business cycle: specification and stability. *Journal of Monetary Economics* 47:3–18.

——. 2004. A method for taking models to the data. *Journal of Economic Dynamics and Control* 28:1205–26.

Jacquier, E., N. Polson, and P. Rossi. 1994. Bayesian analysis of stochastic volatility models. *Journal of Business and Economic Statistics* 12:371–417.

Jeffreys, H. 1966. *Theory of Probability*, 3rd edn. Oxford: Clarendon.

Judd, K. 1998. *Numerical Methods in Economics*. Cambridge, MA: MIT Press.

Judge, G., R. Carter Hill, W. Griffiths, H. Lutkepohl, and T. Lee. 1985. *Theory and Practice of Econometrics*, 2nd edn. Wiley.

Judson, R., and A. Owen. 1999. Estimating dynamic panel data models: a practical guide for macroeconomists. *Economic Letters* 65:145–50.

Kadiyala, R., and S. Karlsson. 1997. Numerical methods for estimation and inference in Bayesian VAR models. *Journal of Applied Econometrics* 12:99–132.

Kass, R., and A. Raftery. 1995. Empirical Bayes factors. *Journal of the American Statistical Association* 90:773–95.

Kass, R., and V. Vaidyanathan. 1992. Approximate Bayes factor and orthogonal parameters, with an application to testing equality of two binomial proportions. *Journal of the Royal Statistical Society* B 54:129–44.

Kauffman, S. 2003. Business cycle of European countries. Bayesian clustering of country-individual IP growth series. Oesterreichische Nationalbank.

Keane, M., and D. Runkle. 1992. On the estimation of panel data models with serial correlation when instruments are not strictly exogenous. *Journal of Business and Economic Statistics* 10:1–9.

Kilian, L. 1998. Small sample confidence intervals for impulse response functions. *Review of Economics and Statistics* 80:218–30.

Kilian, L., and V. Ivanov. 2005. A practitioner's guide to lag order selection for VAR impulse response analysis. *Studies in Nonlinear Dynamics and Econometrics* 9:1219–29.

Kim, C., and C. Nelson. 1998. Business cycle turning points: a new coincident index and tests of duration dependence based on a dynamic factor model with regime switching. *Review of Economic Studies* 80:188–201.

——. 1999. *State Space Models with Regime Switching*. Cambridge, MA: MIT Press.

Kim, J. 2000. Constructing and estimating a realistic optimizing model of monetary policy. *Journal of Monetary Economics* 45:329–59

Kim, J., S. Kim, E. Schaumburg, and C. Sims. 2004. Calculating and using second order accurate solutions of discrete time dynamic equilibrium models. (Available at www.princeton.edu/~sims/.)

Kim, K., and A. Pagan. 1994. The econometric analysis of calibrated macroeconomic models. In *Handbook of Applied Econometrics* (ed. H. Pesaran and M. Wickens), volume I, pp. 356–90. Oxford: Blackwell.

King, R., and C. Plosser. 1994. Real business cycles and the test of the Adelmans. *Journal of Monetary Economics* 33:405–38.

King, R., and S. Rebelo. 1993. Low frequency filtering and real business cycles. *Journal of Economic Dynamics and Control* 17:207–31.

King, R., and M. Watson. 1998. The solution of singular linear difference systems under rational expectations. *International Economic Review* 39:1015–26.

King, R., C. Plosser, and S. Rebelo. 1988a. Production, growth and business cycles. I and II. *Journal of Monetary Economics* 21:195–232 and 309–42.

——. 1988b. Appendix to "Production, growth and business cycle. I. The basic neoclassical models." University of Rochester, Working Paper.

King, R., C. Plosser, J. Stock, and M. Watson. 1991. Stochastic trends and economic fluctuations. *American Economic Review* 81:819–40.

Kiviet, J. 1995. On bias, inconsistency and efficiency of various estimators in dynamic panel data models. *Journal of Econometrics* 68:53–78.

Kiyotaki, N., and J. Moore. 1997. Credit cycles. *Journal of Political Economy* 105:211–48.

Klein, P. 2000. Using the generalized Schur form to solve a multivariate linear rational expectations model. *Journal of Economic Dynamics and Control* 24:1405–23.

Kocherlakota, N. 1990. On tests of representative consumer asset pricing models. *Journal of Monetary Economics* 26:285–304.

Koop, G. 1996. Bayesian impulse responses. *Journal of Econometrics* 74:119–47.

Koop, G., H. Pesaran, and S. Potter. 1996. Impulse response analysis in nonlinear multivariate models. *Journal of Econometrics* 74:119–47.

Koop, G., J. Osiewalski, and M. Steel. 2000. Modelling the sources of output growth in a panel of countries. *Journal of Business and Economic Statistics* 18:284–99.

Koopman, S. J. 1997. Exact initial Kalman filter and smoothing for nonstationary time series models. *Journal of the American Statistical Association* 92:1630–38.

Kuhn, T. 1970. *The Structure of Scientific Revolutions*. Chicago University Press.

Kurmann, A. 2003. ML estimation of dynamic stochastic theories with an application to New Keynesian pricing. University of Quebec at Montreal.

Kydland, F., and E. Prescott. 1977. Rules rather than discretion: the inconsistency of optimal plans. *Journal of Political Economy* 85:473–91.

——. 1982. Time to build and aggregate fluctuations. *Econometrica* 50:1345–70.

——. 1991. The econometrics of the general equilibrium approach to business cycles. *Scandinavian Journal of Economics* 93(2):161–78.

——. 1996. The computational experiment: an econometric tool. *Journal of Economic Perspective* 10:69–85.

Lahiri, K., and G. Moore. 1991. *Leading Indicators: New Approaches and Forecasting Record*. University of Chicago Press.

Lam, P. 1990. The Hamilton model with general autoregressive component. *Journal of Monetary Economics* 26:409–32.

Leeper, E. 1991. Equilibria under active and passive monetary and fiscal policies. *Journal of Monetary Economics* 27:129–47.

Leeper, E., and C. Sims. 1994. Towards a modern macroeconomic model usable for policy analysis. In *NBER Macroeconomic Annual* (ed. J. Rotemberg and S. Fisher), volume 9, pp. 81–118.

Leeper, E., C. Sims, and T. Zha. 1996. What does monetary policy do? *Brookings Papers of Economic Activity* 2:1–78.

Lindé, J. 2005. Estimating New Keynesian Phillips curve: a full information maximum likelihood. *Journal of Monetary Economics* 52:1135–49.

Lindlay, D. V., and A. F. M. Smith. 1972. Bayes estimates of the linear model. *Journal of the Royal Statistical Association* B 34:1–18.

Lippi, M., and L. Reichlin. 1993. The dynamic effect of aggregate demand and supply disturbances: a comment. *American Economic Review* 83:644–52.

——. 1994. VAR analysis, non-fundamental representation, Blaschke matrices. *Journal of Econometrics* 63:307–25.

Ljung, L., and T. Söderström. 1983. *Theory and Practice of Recursive Identification*. Cambridge, MA: MIT Press.

Loeve, M. 1977. *Probability Theory*. Springer.

Long, J., and C. Plosser. 1983. Real business cycles. *Journal of Political Economy* 91:39–65.

Lucas, R. 1977. Understanding business cycles. *Carnegie Rochester Series on Public Policy* 5:7–29.

——. 1980. Two illustrations in the quantity theory of money. *American Economics Review* 70:1345–70.

——. 1985. *Models of Business Cycles*. Oxford: Blackwell.

Lukacs, E. 1975. *Stochastic Convergence*. Academic.

Lutkepohl, H. 1991. *Introduction to Multiple Time Series Analysis*, 2nd edn. Springer.

MacKinley, C., and M. Richardson. 1991. Using GMM to test mean–variance efficiency. *Journal of Finance* 44:511–27.

Maddala, G. S., and W. Hu. 1996. The pooling problem. In *Econometrics of Panel Data* (ed. L. Matyas and P. Sevestre). New York: Kluwer.

Maffezzoli, M. 2000. Human capital and international business cycles. *Review of Economic Dynamics* 3:137–65.

Malinvaud, E. 1980. *Statistical Methods in Econometrics*, 3rd edn. Amsterdam: North-Holland.

Mao, C. S. 1990. Hypothesis testing and finite sample properties of GMM estimators: a Monte Carlo study. Federal Reserve Bank of Richmond.

Maravall, A., and A. Del Rio. 2001. Time aggregation and the Hodrick–Prescott filter. Bank of Spain.

Marcet, A. 1991. Time aggregation of econometric time series. In *Rational Expectations Econometrics* (ed. L. Hansen and T. Sargent). Boulder, CO: Westview Press.

——. 1992. Solving nonlinear stochastic models by parametrizing expectations: an application to asset pricing with production. Universitat Pompeu Fabra, Working Paper 5.

Marcet, A., and W. Den Haan. 1994. Accuracy in simulation. *Review of Economic Studies* 61:3–17.

Marcet, A., and G. Lorenzoni. 1999. The parametrized expectations approach: some practical issues. In *Computational Methods for the Study of Dynamic Economies* (ed. R. Marimon and A. Scott). Oxford University Press.

Marcet, A., and M. Ravn. 2001. The HP filter in cross country comparisons. LBS.

Marimon, R., and A. Scott (eds). 1999. *Computational Methods for the Study of Dynamic Economies*. Oxford University Press.

Martin, V., and A. Pagan. 2001. Simulation based estimation of some factor models in econometrics. In *Inference Using Simulation Techniques* (ed. R. Mariano, R. Schuermann, and M. Weeks). Cambridge University Press.

McCulloch, R., and R. Tsay. 1994. Statistical analysis of economic time series via Markov switching models. *Journal of Time Series Analysis* 15:521–39.

McGrattan, E. 1994. The macroeconomic effects of distortionary taxation. *Journal of Monetary Economics* 33:573–601.

McGrattan, E., R. Rogerson, and R. Wright. 1997. An equilibrium model of the business cycle with household production and fiscal policy. *International Economic Review* 38:267–90.

McLeish, R. 1974. Dependent central limit theorem and invariance principle. *Annals of Probability* 2:620–28.

Merha, R., and E. Prescott. 1985. The equity premium: a puzzle. *Journal of Monetary Economics* 15:145–61.

Merz, M. 1995. Search in labor markets and real business cycles. *Journal of Monetary Economics* 36:269–300.

Miller, M. 1976. *Elements of Graduation*. New York: Actuarial Society of America and American Institute of Actuaries.

Miranda, M., and P. Fackler. 2002. *Applied Computational Economics and Finance*, 2nd edn. Cambridge, MA: MIT Press.

Mittnik, S., and P. Zadrozky. 1993. Asymptotic distributions of impulse responses, step responses and variance decompositions of estimated linear models. *Econometrica* 61:857–71.

Morley, J., C. Nelson, and E. Zivot. 2003. Why are Beveridge–Nelson and unobservable component decompositions of GDP so different? *Review of Economics and Statistics* 86:235–43.

Morris, C. 1983. Parametric empirical Bayes inference: theory and applications. *Journal of the American Statistical Association* 78:47–59.

Murray, C. 2002. Cyclical properties of Baxter and King filtered time series. *Review of Economics and Statistics* 85:472–76.

Neiss, K., and P. Pappa. 2005. Persistence without too much stickiness: the role of factor utilization. *Review of Economic Dynamics* 8:231–55.

Nelson, C., and H. Kang. 1981. Spurious periodicity in appropriately detrended time series. *Econometrica* 49:741–51.

Nelson, C., and R. Starz. 1990. The distribution of the instrumental variable estimator and its t-ratio when the instrument is a poor one. *Journal of Business* 63:125–64.

Newey, W. 1990. Efficient instrumental variable estimation of nonlinear models. *Econometrica* 58:809–37.

Newey, W., and D. McFadden. 1994. Large sample estimation and hypothesis testing. In *Handbook of Econometrics* (ed. R. Engle and D. McFadden), volume IV, pp. 2111–245. Elsevier.

Newey, W., and K. West. 1987. A simple, positive semi-definite, heteroskedasticity and autocorrelation consistent covariance matrix. *Econometrica* 55:703–08.

——. 1994. Automatic lag selection in covariance matrix estimation. *Review of Economic Studies* 61:631–53.

Nickell, S. 1981. Biases in dynamic models with fixed effects. *Econometrica* 49:1417–26.

Obstfeld, M., and K. Rogoff. 1996. *Foundation of International Macroeconomics*. Cambridge, MA: MIT Press.

Ogaki, M. 1993. GMM: econometric applications. In *Handbook of Statistics* (ed. G. S. Maddala, C. R. Rao, and H. D. Vinod), volume 11, pp. 455–88. Elsevier.

Ohanian, L. 1997. The macroeconomic effects of war finance in the U.S.: World War II and the Korean War. *American Economic Review* 87:23–40.

Ohanian, L., A. Stockman, and L. Kilian. 1995. The effects of real and monetary shocks in a business cycle model with some sticky prices. *Journal of Money Banking and Credit* 27:1210–40.

Osborn, D. R. 1995. Moving average detrending and the analysis of business cycles. *Oxford Bulletin of Economics and Statistics* 57:547–58.

Otrok, C. 2001. On measuring the welfare costs of business cycles. *Journal of Monetary Economics* 47:61–92.

Otrok, C., and C. Whiteman. 1998. Bayesian leading indicators: measuring and predicting economic conditions in Iowa. *International Economic Review* 39:997–1114.

Pagan, A. 1981. LIML and related estimators of single equations with moving averages. *International Economic Review* 22:719–30.

Pagan, A. 1994. Calibration and econometric research: an overview. *Journal of Applied Econometrics* 9:S1–S10.

Pagan, A., and D. Harding. 2002. Dissecting the cycle: a methodological investigation. *Journal of Monetary Economics* 49:365–81.

——. 2005. A suggested framework for classifying the modes of cycle research. *Journal of Applied Econometrics* 20:151–59.

Pagan, A., and J. Shannon. 1985. Sensitivity analysis for linearized computable general equilibrium models. In *New Developments in Applied General Equilibrium Analysis* (ed. J. Piggott and J. Whalley). Cambridge University Press.

Pagan, A., and Y. Yoon. 1993. Understanding some failures of instrumental variable estimators. University of Rochester.

Pappa, P. 2003. New Keynesian or RBC transmission? The effects of fiscal shocks in labor markets. IGIER Working Paper 293.

Paulsen, C., and H. Tjostheim. 1985. On estimating the residual variance and the order in autoregressive time series. *Journal of the Royal Statistical Association* B 47:216–28.

Pesaran, H. 1995. Cross sectional aggregation of linear dynamic models: some new results. University of Cambridge.

Pesaran, H., and R. Smith. 1992. The interaction between theory and observation in economics. University of Cambridge.

——. 1995. Estimating long run relationships from dynamic heterogeneous panels. *Journal of Econometrics* 68:79–113.

Pesaran, H., R. Smith, and K. Im. 1996. Dynamic linear models for heterogeneous panels. In *Econometrics of Panel Data* (ed. L. Matyas and P. Sevestre). New York: Kluwer.

Pesaran, H., Y. Shin, and R. Smith. 1999. Pooled mean group estimation of dynamic heterogeneous panels. *Journal of the American Statistical Association* 94:621–34.

Pesaran, H., T. Schuermann, and S. Wiener. 2003. Modeling regional interdependences using a global error correction macroeconomic model. *Journal of Business and Economic Statistics* (in press).

Poirier, D. 1998. *Intermediate Statistics and Econometrics*. Cambridge, MA: MIT Press.

Press, W., B. Flannery, S. Teukolsky, and W. Vetterling. 1986. *Numerical Recipes*. Cambridge University Press.

Priestley, I. 1981. *Spectral Analysis and Time Series*. Academic.

Proietti, T., and A. Harvey. 2000. The Beveridge smoother. *Economic Letters* 67:139–46.

Quah, D. 1990. Permanent and transitory movements in labor income: an explanation for excess smoothness in consumption. *Journal of Political Economy* 98:449–75.

——. 1996. Regional convergence cluster across Europe. *European Economic Review* 40:951–58.

Rao, C. R. 1973. *Linear Statistical Inference and Its Applications*. Wiley.

——. 1975. Simultaneous estimation of parameters in different linear models and applications to biometric problems. *Biometrics* 31:545–54.

Ravn, M., and H. Uhlig. 2002. On adjusting the HP filter for the frequency of observations. *Review of Economics and Statistics* 84:371–75.

Ripley, B. 1987. *Stochastic Simulations*. Wiley.

Robert, C., and G. Casella. 1999. *Monte Carlo Statistical Methods*. Springer.

Robertson, J., and E. Tallman. 1999. Vector autoregressions: forecasting and reality. *Federal Reserve Bank of Atlanta, Economic Review* First quarter, pp. 4–18.

Roll, R., and S. Ross. 1980. An empirical investigation of the arbitrage pricing theory. *Journal of Finance* 35:1073–103.

Rose, A. 2004. A meta-analysis of the effects of common currencies on international trade. NBER Working Paper 10373.

Rosenblatt, M. (ed.). 1978. Dependence and asymptotic dependence for random processes. *Studies in Probability Theory*. Washington, DC: Mathematical Association of America.

Ross, S. 1976. The arbitrage theory of the capital asset pricing. *Journal of Economic Theory* 13:341–60.

Rotemberg, J. 1984. Monetary equilibrium model with transaction costs. *Journal of Political Economy* 92:40–58.

——. 2003. Stochastic technical progress, smooth trends and nearly distinct business cycles. *American Economic Review* 93:1543–59.

Rotemberg, J., and M. Woodford. 1997. An optimization based econometric framework for the evaluation of monetary policy. *NBER Macroeconomic Annual* 12:297–346.

Rozanov, Y. 1967. *Stationary Random Processes*. San Francisco, CA: Holden Day.

Ruge-Murcia, F. 2002. Methods to estimate dynamic stochastic general equilibrium models. UCSD Working Paper 2002-46.

Runkle, D. 1987. Vector autoregression and reality. *Journal of Business and Economic Statistics* 5:437–42.

Sala-i-Martin, X., G. Doppelhofer, and R. Miller. 2004. Determinants of long term growth: a Bayesian averaging of classical estimates (BACE) approach. *American Economic Review* 94:567–88.

Sargent, T. 1979. A note on maximum likelihood estimation of rational expectations model of the term structure. *Journal of Monetary Economics* 5:133–43.

——. 1986. *Dynamic Macroeconomic Theory*. Cambridge, MA: Harvard University Press.

——. 1989. Two models of measurement and the investment accelerator. *Journal of Political Economy* 97:251–83.

Sargent, T., and L. Liungqvist. 2004. *Recursive Macroeconomic Theory*, 2nd edn. Cambridge, MA: MIT Press.

Schmitt-Grohe, S., and M. Uribe. 2004. Solving dynamic general equilibrium models using a second order approximation to the policy function. *Journal of Economic Dynamics and Control* 28:755–75.

Schorfheide, F. 2000. Loss function based evaluation of DSGE models. *Journal of Applied Econometrics* 15:645–70.

Serfling, R. 1980. *Approximation Theorems of Mathematical Statistics*. Wiley.

Shapiro, M., and M. Watson. 1988. Sources of business cycle fluctuations. *NBER Macroeconomic Annual* 3:111–48.

Shoven, J., and J. Whalley. 1984. Applied general equilibrium models of taxation and international trade: an introduction and survey. *Journal of Economic Literature* 22:1007–51.

——. 1992. *Applying General Equilibrium*. Cambridge University Press.

Simkins, S. P. 1994. Do real business cycle models really exhibit business cycle behavior? *Journal of Monetary Economics* 33:381–404.

Sims, C. 1971. Discrete approximations to continuous time distributed lags in econometrics. *Econometrica* 71:545–63.

——. 1980. Macroeconomics and reality. *Econometrica* 48:1–48.

——. 1988. Bayesian skepticism on unit root econometrics. *Journal of Economic Dynamics and Control* 12:463–74.

Sims, C. 1996. Macroeconomics and methodology. *Journal of Economic Perspectives* 10: 105–20.

——. 2000. Drift and breaks in monetary policy. Princeton University.

——. 2001. Solving linear rational expectations models. *Computational Economics* 20:1–20.

——. 2002. Random Lagrange multipliers and transversality. (Available at www.princeton.edu/~sims/.)

Sims, C., and T. Sargent. 1977. Business cycle modeling without pretending to have too much *a priori* economic theory. In *New Methods in Business Cycle Research*, pp. 45–109. Federal Reserve Bank of Minneapolis.

Sims, C., and T. Zha. 1998. Bayesian methods for dynamic multivariate models. *International Economic Review* 39:949–68.

——. 1999. Error bands for impulse responses. *Econometrica* 67:1113–55.

——. 2004. Macroeconomic switching. Federal Reserve of Atlanta, Working Paper 2004-12.

Sims, C., J. Stock, and M. Watson. 1990. Inference in linear time series models with some unit roots. *Econometrica* 58:113–44.

Smets, F., and R. Wouters. 2003. An estimated stochastic DGE model of the euro area. *Journal of the European Economic Association* 1:1123–75.

Smith, A. F. M. 1973. A general Bayesian linear model. *Journal of the Royal Statistical Society* B 35:67–75.

——. 1993. Estimating nonlinear time series models using simulated vector autoregressions. *Journal of Applied Econometrics* 8:63–84.

Smith, A. F. M., and G. O. Roberts. 1993. Bayesian computation via the Gibbs sampler and related Markov chain Monte Carlo methods. *Journal of the Royal Statistical Society* B 55:3–24.

Smith, R., and A. Fuertes. 2003. Panel time series. Birkbeck College.

Soderlin, P. 1994. Cyclical properties of a real business cycle model. *Journal of Applied Econometrics* 9:S113–S122.

Sorensen, B., L. Wu, and O. Yosha. 2001. Output fluctuations and fiscal policy: US state and local governments, 1978–1994. *European Economic Review* 45:1271–310.

Stock, J., and M. Watson. 1987. Testing for common trends. *Journal of the American Statistical Association* 83:1996–107.

——. 1989. New index of coincident and leading indicators. *NBER Macroeconomics Annual* 4:351–96.

——. 1991. A probability model of the coincident economic indicators. In *Leading Economic Indicators: New Approaches and Forecasting Records* (ed. K. Lahiri and G. Moore). Cambridge University Press.

——. 2002. *Econometrics*. Addison-Wesley.

Stock, J., and J. Wright. 2000. GMM with weak identification. *Econometrica* 68:1055–96.

Stock, J., and M. Yogo. 2001. Testing for weak instruments in linear IV regression. NBER Technical Working Paper 0284.

Stock, J., J. Wright, and M. Yogo. 2002. A survey of weak instruments and weak identification in generalized methods of moments. *Journal of Business and Economics Statistics* 20:518–29.

Stokey, N. and R. Lucas. 1989. *Recursive Methods in Economic Dynamics*. Cambridge, MA: Harvard University Press.

Stout, W. 1974. *a.s. Convergence*. Academic.

Swamy, P. 1970. Efficient inference in a random coefficients regression model. *Econometrica* 38:311–23.

Tamayo, A. 2001. Stock return predictability, conditional asset pricing models and portfolio selection. University of Rochester.

Tanner, M., and W. H. Wong. 1987. The calculation of posterior distributions by data augmentation (with discussion). *Journal of the American Statistical Association* 82:528–50.

Tauchen, G. 1986. Statistical properties of GMM estimators of structural parameters obtained from financial market data. *Journal of Business and Economic Statistics* 4:397–425.

Tierney, L. 1994. Markov chains for exploring posterior distributions (with discussion). *Annals of Statistics* 22:1701–62.

Uhlig, H. 1994. Bayesian vector autoregression with stochastic volatility. *Econometrica* 65: 59–73.

——. 1999. A methods for analyzing nonlinear dynamic stochastic models easily. In *Computational Methods for the Study of Dynamic Economies* (ed. R. Marimon and A. Scott), pp. 114–42. Oxford University Press.

——. 2005. What are the effects of monetary policy? Results from an agnostic identification procedure. *Journal of Monetary Economics* 52:381–419.

Wabha, G. 1980. Improper prior, spline smoothing and the problem of guarding against models errors in regression. *Journal of the Royal Statistical Association* B 40:364–72.

Waggoner, D., and T. Zha. 1999. Conditional forecasts in dynamic multivariate models. *Review of Economics and Statistics* 81:1–14.

Waggoner, D., and T. Zha. 2003. A Gibbs simulator for restricted VAR models. *Journal of Economic Dynamics and Control* 26:349–66.

Watson, M. 1986. Univariate detrending methods with stochastic trends. *Journal of Monetary Economics* 18:49–75.

——. 1989. Recursive solution methods for dynamic linear rational expectations models. *Journal of Econometrics* 41:65–89.

——. 1993. Measures of fit for calibrated models. *Journal of Political Economy* 101:1011–41.

——. 1994. Business cycle duration and postwar stabilization of the U.S. economy. *American Economic Review* 84:24–46.

——. 1995. VAR and cointegration. In *Handbook of Econometrics* (ed. R. Engle), volume IV. Elsevier.

Wei, Y. 1998. Can an RBC model pass the Watson test? *Journal of Monetary Economics* 42:185–203.

West, K. 1995. Another heteroskedastic and autocorrelation consistent covariance matrix estimator. NBER Technical Working Paper 183.

West, K., and D. Wilcox. 1996. A comparison of alternative instrumental variables estimators of a dynamic linear model. *Journal of Business and Economic Statistics* 14:282–94.

White, H. 1982. Maximum likelihood estimation of misspecified models. *Econometrica* 50:1–25.

——. 1984. *Asymptotic Theory for Econometricians*. Academic.

White, H., and I. Domowitz. 1984. Nonlinear regression with dependent observations. *Econometrica* 52:143–61.

Whittle, P. 1980. *Prediction and Regulation*. University of Minnesota Press.

Wilcox, D. 1992. The construction of U.S. consumption data: some facts and their implications for empirical work. *American Economic Review* 82:922–841.

Wolman, A. 2001. A primer on optimal monetary policy with staggered price setting. *Federal Reserve Bank of Richmond, Economic Review*, Fall, 87/4, pp. 27–52.

Woodford, M. 2003. *Interest and Prices: Foundation of a Theory of Monetary Policy*. Princeton University Press.

Wright, J. 2003. Detecting lack of identification in GMM. *Econometric Theory* 19:322–30.

Zellner, A. 1971. *Introduction to Bayesian Inference in Econometrics*. Wiley.

Zellner, A., and C. Hong. 1989. Forecasting international growth rates using Bayesian shrinkage and other procedures. *Journal of Econometrics* 40:183–202.

Zha, T. 1999. Block recursion and structural vector autoregressions. *Journal of Econometrics* 90:291–316.

Index

aggregate time series estimator, 311
aggregation, 152
Akaike information criteria, 120
almost sure convergence, 3, 4, 6
Anderson–Hsiao estimator, 297, 309
approximation
  discretizing, 50, 68
  global, 252
  local, 252
  log-linear, 53–55, 58, 59, 62, 68
  method of undetermined coefficients, 48, 56, 57, 68
  parametrized expectations, 65–68
  quadratic, 45, 46, 50, 53, 55, 68
  Vaughan's method, 56, 60, 68
APT model, 167
AR representation, 87
arbitrage pricing theory, 423–425
ARCH-M model, 398
ARIMA model, 73, 75, 77, 78, 80, 83, 138, 380, 384
ARMA model, 77, 214, 218, 220, 221, 224, 398
asymptotic uncorrelatedness, 12, 15
autocovariance
  function, 8, 9, 87, 96, 98, 105, 107, 113, 153, 390
  generating function, 9, 19, 22
average cross-sectional estimator, 312
average time series estimator, 306

Bartlett kernel, 180
Bayes
  factor, 341, 342, 441, 452, 454
  theorem, 81, 326, 329, 331, 347
Bayesian
  analysis, 125
  estimation, 407
  methods, 161, 318, 440, 452, 461
  VAR, 383–385, 388, 389, 393, 400, 442
Bellman equation, 28, 31–33, 35, 36, 38, 42, 45–48, 50
beta distribution, 334, 357, 364, 465
binomial distribution, 364
box-car kernel, 180
Bry and Boschen algorithm, 108
BVAR model, 452

calibration, 249
capital asset pricing model (CAPM), 420, 425
  consumption-based, 167
cash-in-advance model, 38, 40, 58, 62, 157, 266, 281, 321
  taxes, 67
Cauchy distribution, 355, 466
central limit theorem, 16–18
  for serially correlated processes, 179
certainty equivalence, 46, 231
chi-squared distribution, 464
Choleski factor, 224, 393, 395, 396
Chow test, 126
Chow–Lin method, 467
coherence, 21, 24
computable general equilibrium model, 253, 280
conditional heteroskedasticity, 173, 180
convergence
  in distribution, 7
  in probability, 4, 6, 7
  in the norm, 6
covariance
  stationarity, 80
  generating function, 114
  stationarity, 8–10, 76, 85, 113, 121, 123, 125
credible set, 337, 338
cross-sectional estimator, 295
CUMSUM statistic, 449
cumulative multipliers, 131

decision theory, 335
delta method, 385
Dirichlet distribution, 466
distance test, 188, 191
DSGE model, *see* dynamic stochastic general equilibrium (DSGE) model
dynamic heterogeneity, 290, 305, 309, 313, 315, 319, 322
dynamic stochastic general equilibrium prior, 384

dynamic stochastic general equilibrium (DSGE) model, 79, 110, 141, 147, 148, 153, 156, 160, 174, 177, 180, 191, 200, 221, 228, 230, 232, 251, 253, 264, 276, 385, 402, 440, 441, 452, 454, 457–459, 461

empirical Bayes
  methods, 319, 350, 380, 400, 410
  models, 345
endogenous grouping, 407
ergodicity, 10–15, 17, 80, 177, 185, 186, 197, 198
estimation
  Theil's mixed-type, 376
estimator
  ridge, 377
exponential distribution, 357, 464
extreme estimator, 166

factor models, 419, 424, 425, 428
false models, 249
fan charts, 389
F-distribution, 464
filter, 22
  aggregation, 104
  approximate
    Baxter and King, 95–98
    Christiano and Fitzgerald, 96–98
  band pass, 22, 94–96, 98, 99, 106, 108
  Butterworth, 92
  cyclical, 85, 94, 105
  exponential smoothing, 91, 92, 94
  Henderson, 94
  high pass, 22, 94
  Hodrick and Prescott, 83, 84, 86, 87, 89–92, 94, 95, 106, 108
  low pass, 22, 94, 95
  moving average, 92, 94, 95
Fisher information, 330
fixed effects, 290, 293, 302
folding operator, 104
forecast errors, 215, 216, 221
forward bias, 204, 225
F-test, 125, 157, 316

gain function, 22, 85, 86, 92, 95, 96
gamma distribution, 366, 464
GARCH model, 173, 398, 427, 433
generalized least squares, 174, 185, 317, 318, 377, 467
generalized method of moments, 166, 169, 176, 184–186, 194, 195, 197, 199, 234, 237, 251, 253, 259, 263, 270, 277, 297–299, 301–304, 309, 440, 453, 461
  two-step, 186, 196
geometric ergodicity, 200
Gibbs sampler, 365
GMM
  optimal weighting matrix, 171

HAC covariance
  estimates, 197
  matrix, 181, 182, 195, 199
Hannan and Quinn information criteria, 120
Hausman test, 189, 313
heteroskedasticity, 134
hierarchical model, 345, 350, 352, 365, 372, 388, 407, 413
Hilbert space, 112
historical decomposition, 132
HP filter, 197, 206

identifiability, 241
identification
  order condition, 142, 298
  rank condition, 143
  sign restrictions, 147, 148
importance ratio, 355, 358
impulse response matching, 207
impulse responses, 211, 239, 244, 267, 336, 415
  δ-method, 132, 133, 137
  bootstrap method, 134
  forecast revision, 131
  generalized, 137, 139, 140
  Monte Carlo method, 136
  nonrecursive calculation, 131
  orthogonalization, 137
  recursive calculation, 130
  sign restrictions, 142
  zero restrictions, 142
indirect
  inference, 204, 205, 263, 461
  least squares, 142
instrumental variables, 14, 168–170, 196, 297, 303, 310, 311, 313
inverse
  chi-squared distribution, 465
  gamma distribution, 464

Jensen's inequality, 7
J-test, 175, 193, 270

Kalman
  filter, 78, 79, 214, 217, 220, 223, 224, 227, 231, 242, 381, 397, 400, 401, 422, 427, 430, 441, 446
  gain, 216, 218, 219
  smoother, 217, 223
kernel, 23
  Bartlett, 24, 93
  box-car, 24, 93
  Parzen, 24
  quadratic spectral, 24, 93
Kullback–Leibler information, 341, 342

labor contracts, 33, 39, 41, 43, 100, 262
lag operator, 8
Lagrange multiplier test, 188
Laplace approximation, 355
latent
  factors, 190
  variables, 366, 372, 439
law of large numbers, 5, 14, 16, 184, 201, 202
leading indicators, 414, 416, 422
likelihood
  function, 82, 118, 127, 128, 136, 144, 204, 221, 237, 242, 307, 326, 332, 335, 336, 339, 340, 342, 343, 346, 347, 352, 366, 370, 375, 395, 402, 405, 420, 422, 426, 427, 436, 437, 442, 443, 446, 459
  principle, 336, 443
  ratio test, 118, 120, 188, 191, 237, 241, 307, 342, 343
linear
  regulator problem, 32, 47
  restrictions, 299, 377, 382, 413
  trend, 22
linearly
  predictable process, 112, 113
  regular process, 16, 112, 113
Lipschitz condition, 201
lognormal distribution, 463
loss function, 263, 272, 336, 455

MA representation, 87, 123, 130, 149, 152, 153
  fundamental, 114, 115, 159
  nonfundamental, 116, 158
marginal likelihood, 319, 326, 342, 381, 388, 400, 415, 441
  Laplace approximation, 342, 343, 442
  Schwarz approximation, 342, 343
Markov
  process, 79, 82
  switching model, 433, 436, 437, 439
Markov chain Monte Carlo (MCMC) methods, 276, 359, 360, 380, 443, 461
  Gibbs sampler, 359, 361, 362, 364, 369, 371, 394, 401, 403, 415, 416, 422, 427, 431, 433, 467
  Metropolis–Hastings (MH)
    algorithm, 394, 421, 427, 433, 440–442, 445, 449
    sampler, 359, 367–369
martingale, 13
  difference, 13, 16, 18, 44, 46, 177, 180, 183, 185, 186
maximum likelihood, 79, 127, 129, 161, 169, 179, 184, 188, 191, 194, 223, 225, 227, 230, 232, 234, 239, 246, 251, 253, 259, 403, 405, 440, 453, 461
  estimator, 320
  type II, 331, 381
mean square error, 120, 131, 180, 222, 337
measurement errors, 233, 245, 270, 297
meta-analysis, 351, 352, 407
method of moments, 168
minimum distance estimator, 166, 190
mixing, 11, 12, 15, 17
  conditions, 201
model validation, 260
moments, 126, 128, 134, 194, 198, 201, 336
money neutrality, 324
Monte Carlo
  methods, 140, 151
  techniques, 285, 328
Monte Carlo Markov chain methods, *see* Markov chain Monte Carlo (MCMC) methods

nonlinear
  instrumental variables, 169, 184
  least squares, 165, 169, 179, 184
  restrictions, 186
normal density, 128, 136

normal distribution, 432, 463
numerical methods
  gradient methods, 228
  grid search, 228
  simplex, 228

ordinary least squares, 14, 17, 72, 127, 130, 136, 141, 168, 178, 187, 223, 224, 226, 291, 292, 295, 303, 304, 308–310, 313, 319, 357, 365, 375, 400, 406, 407, 410, 424, 426, 427

panel VAR, 290, 414
Pareto distribution, 338, 466
Parzen kernel, 181
periodogram, 23
phase shift, 22, 93
Phillips curve, 33, 42, 175, 191, 195, 202, 205, 231, 238, 448, 452
pooled estimator, 293, 295, 301, 308, 406, 407
posterior
  approximation
    acceptance sampling, 356, 358
    importance sampling, 357, 358, 394, 395
    normal, 340, 354, 371
  density, 326, 328, 336–340, 345, 348, 350, 354, 376, 421, 424, 426, 429, 436, 439, 458
    importance sampling, 432, 459
  distribution, 136, 278, 285
  estimate, 280
  kernel, 326, 334, 365, 390, 427, 446
  odds ratio, 341, 409, 457
  simulators, 354
prediction error decomposition, 79, 204, 221, 223, 224, 381, 436, 442
predictive
  density, 345, 347, 390
  odds ratio, 345
prior, 136, 403
  conjugate, 405
  cyclical, 383
  density, 326, 329, 332, 335, 339, 340, 345, 347, 349, 352, 376, 446
  distribution, 278
  estimate, 280
  exchangeable, 346, 347, 405, 408, 413
  hierarchical, 400
  hyperparameters, 345
  likelihood estimator, 318
  Minnesota, 378, 383, 384, 392, 399, 400, 452
  odds, 341
  restrictions, 382
  seasonality, 383
  seasonals, 393
  trend, 383, 393
prior density
  conjugate, 332, 334, 348, 365, 375, 439, 441
  exchangeable, 348
  improper, 329
  informative, 329
  Minnesota, 350, 432
  ML type II, 336
  noninformative, 329, 330, 371, 422, 425, 435
  objective, 329, 331
  reference noninformative, 330
  subjective, 329

quadratic spectral kernel, 181
quasi-maximum likelihood, 226, 234

R^2, 263, 265, 316
random coefficient estimator, 324
random-effect estimator, 295
RBC model, 148
  asset pricing, 167, 200, 257, 276
  basic, 27, 28, 30, 31, 33, 34, 37, 46, 60, 65, 88, 164, 166, 189, 197, 202, 204, 235, 261, 276, 385, 387, 445
  capacity utilization, 33, 153, 256, 448
  cointegrating prior, 386
  distorting taxes, 50
  equity premium, 205
  externalities, 54
  generalized, 220
  government capital, 34
  government expenditure, 191, 245, 254, 268
  habit, 55, 153, 163, 167, 189, 240, 262, 266
  habit persistence, 66, 447
  labor hoarding, 194, 202, 231
  monopolistic competition, 57
  noncompetitive labor markets, 33
  preference shocks, 198
  prior, 387
  production externalities, 34, 262, 266
  rule-of-thumb consumers, 37, 54
  small open economy, 231

term structure, 173, 189, 205
two-country, 103
unit roots, 102, 103, 146, 160, 215
utility producing government expenditure, 33
RC model
capacity utilization, 237
Riccati equation, 47, 48, 60, 218
risk function, 456
robust estimator, 169
robustness, 370

Schwarz information criteria, 120
seemingly unrelated regression, 172, 364, 392
simulated method of moments, 201, 204, 253, 259, 461
simulated quasi-maximum likelihood, 203, 204
simulation estimator, 198, 200
small open economy model, 66, 281, 289
Solow residuals, 34
spectral density, 9, 19, 21, 22, 25, 77, 85, 87, 96, 127, 198, 267, 271, 285
state-space model, 79, 214, 221, 238, 426, 429, 435, 440
measurement equation, 214
nonlinear, 215, 219, 402
transition equation, 214
stationarity, 5, 8–15, 17, 20, 23, 79, 92, 177, 185, 186, 197, 198
Stein estimator, 317, 324
sticky
price model, 38, 42, 55, 59, 155, 161, 164, 208, 211, 233, 235, 240, 256, 262, 269, 448
capacity utilization, 62
sticky information, 195
prices, 41
wage model, 38, 42, 59, 167, 452
stochastic
Lagrange multiplier, 31, 32, 35, 45, 46
volatility models, 427
stylized facts, 249

t-distribution, 334, 355, 357, 358, 465
Theil's mixed estimation, 393
three-stage least squares, 172
time-varying-coefficient model, 218, 427
total factor productivity, 290
transfer function, 22
trend
Beveridge and Nelson, 72, 74, 76, 78, 84, 102, 103, 106
Blanchard and Quah, 100, 102, 103, 145, 239
common stochastic, 420
growth, 72
King, Plosser, Stock, and Watson, 102, 103, 106
linear, 72, 87, 90, 91, 197, 216
Markov, 83
Markov switching, 219, 398
permanent component, 74
quadratic, 87, 91, 94
segmented, 72
unobservable components, 75, 76, 78, 84
t-test, 227, 237
two-country model, 35, 37, 44, 47, 190, 256, 282
two-stage least squares, 157, 171, 178, 292, 298
two-step
estimators, 8
generalized method of moments, 176
regressions, 319, 321

uniform
distribution, 463
law of large numbers, 177
univariate panel, 404

value function, 28, 30, 31, 39, 46–48, 50
VAR models, 74, 100, 110, 117, 118, 123, 130, 134, 141, 143, 144, 148, 151, 153, 155–157, 159, 160, 162, 164, 169, 172, 203, 204, 214, 217, 221, 228, 234, 238, 242, 244, 246, 260, 277, 279, 285, 300, 374, 380, 384, 387, 394, 395, 405, 429, 431, 437, 438, 442, 452, 454, 458, 461
Portmanteau test, 122
Bayesian, 374
breaks, 125
Choleski factor, 116, 132, 145, 147, 148, 151
companion form, 126, 127, 274, 389, 436
dimensionality, 154
eigenvalue factor, 116
Granger causality, 117, 154
identification, 141

VAR models (*continued*)
  lag length, 118, 121, 122
  nonnormalities, 123
  nonstationary, 124, 144
  panel, 404
  Q-test, 122
  restrictions, 118, 129
  Sims exogeneity, 117
  simultaneous equations, 128
  stability, 117
  time-varying-coefficient, 397, 400
variance
  and historical decomposition, 239
  decomposition, 131
VARMA model, 155, 156
vector error correction model, 124

Wald test, 187, 193, 196
weak consistency, 5
Weibull distribution, 357, 465
welfare costs, 281, 287
Wishart
  density, 128, 136
  distribution, 365, 432, 465
Wold theorem, 112, 113, 123
working-capital model, 39, 157, 161, 230, 269, 389

Yule–Walker equations, 129